THE PURITANS

A Sourcebook of Their Writings

Two Volumes Bound as One

Edited by
Perry Miller
and
Thomas H. Johnson

DOVER PUBLICATIONS, INC.
Mineola, New York

Published in Canada by General Publishing Company, Ltd., 30 Lesmill Road, Don Mills, Toronto, Ontario.

Bibliographical Note

This Dover edition, first published in 2001, is an unabridged reprint of the work, originally published by Harper & Row, Publishers, Inc., in a two-volume Harper Torchbook edition, in 1963. That edition was a reprint of the work first published by American Book Company in 1938. The bibliographies were revised for the Torchbook edition by George McClandish. Selections from the poetry of Edward Taylor (ca. 1645–1729) in Vol. II are from *The Poetical Works of Edward Taylor,* published by the Princeton University Press in 1939. This Dover edition is published in one volume, with a single table of contents and index covering both volumes. As noted in the Table of Contents, the Notes and Bibliography for Vol. I are on pp. xix–lix, placed in position following page 377. The Notes and Bibliography for Vol. II are on pages 765–818.

Library of Congress Cataloging-in-Publication Data

The Puritans : a sourcebook of their writings / edited by Perry Miller and Thomas H. Johnson.
p. cm.
"An unabridged reprint of the work, originally published by Harper & Row, Publishers, Inc., in a two-volume Harper Torchbook edition, in 1963"–T.p. verso.
Includes index.
ISBN 0-486-41601-1 (pbk.)
1. American literature–Puritan authors. 2. American literature–Colonial period, ca. 1600–1775. 3. Puritans–New England–History–Sources. 4. New England–Literary collections. 5. American literature–New England. 6. Puritans–Literary collections. I. Miller, Perry, 1905–1963. II. Johnson, Thomas Herbert.

PS508.P87 P87 2001
810.8'001–dc21

2001017194

Manufactured in the United States of America
Dover Publications, Inc., 31 East 2nd Street, Mineola, N.Y. 11501

FOREWORD

Jonathan Edwards cautioned himself in his Notes on Natural Science: "What is prefatorial, not to write in a distinct preface, or introduction, but in the body of the work; then I shall be sure to have it read by every one." The editors of the following selections have been mindful of his warning, and they here need merely to say that the volume portrays the Puritans who settled New England and those of the next two generations who lived there. The focus of the work has been Puritanism in the seventeenth century, when the word had a comparatively definite meaning, and in only one respect has any effort been made to trace the modifications of it in the eighteenth century. The selections from the writings of Jonathan Mayhew have been included for the purpose of giving a continuous view of political theory. Otherwise the consistent aim has been restriction to what might be called "pure" Puritanism, leaving later ramifications to be traced out elsewhere. It has for that reason been thought wise to leave the greatest of all Puritan intellectuals, Jonathan Edwards, to be studied in the context of his different intellectual environment.

To the end that the elusive terms Puritan and Puritanism should be clearly defined, at least in so far as they apply to the colonizers of America and their spiritual descendants, the selections have been grouped into chapters;—divisions which most naturally provide opportunity for discussion of all phases of Puritan ways and ideas, with such emphasis, selectivity, and proportion as seem representative and true. The General Introduction attempts to view Puritanism as a whole: to mete its boundaries, fix its location, supply guides to its monuments, and establish that unity which so clearly runs in Puritan thought, expression, and manners.

It has seemed best to let the Puritans speak for themselves as much as possible, for they were not a reticent people, nor were they wanting in ideas. As Ælfric remarked in the foreword to his *Lives of the Saints:* "We say nothing new in this work, for it all stood written long ago, albeit laymen did not know it." Much that the Puritans wrote has been deservedly forgotten, but the dust has gathered as well upon the works of some who, when brought into the light of the present, appear to have been powerful instruments in working out the social and political, as well as the religious and cultural, destiny of America. It therefore seemed wiser to give in general ample passages from a few pivotal documents, rather than to go wide afield in an effort merely to extend the list of Puritan writers. The editors are aware that no American today can read a Puritan work without having a definite opinion of the author, and they in their turn have not been reticent in the introductory portions about speaking their minds; yet the larger purpose has been to supply enough of the Puritan literature itself to let each reader judge for himself.

The texts throughout follow the earliest edition, or the most accurately printed when the first seems inadvisable. Spelling and punctuation are reproduced exactly, except that the modern "s" has been uniformly adopted, and obvious printers' errors corrected. It should be stated that the map of New England which forms the end-papers of the volume, while based mainly upon the accurate surveys of more recent times, has been constructed to show certain features of the coast-lines and harbors as indicated by a study of many old maps, some of them published near the close of the Puritan period.

The editors have collaborated closely, and each has contributed something to almost every section; but the major task of preparation and annotation was divided, and final responsibility for expression of opinion must rest as follows: "The Puritan Way of Life" in the General Introduction, and Chapters I, II, III, and V are the work of Perry Miller; "The Puritans as Literary Artists" in the General Introduction, and Chapters IV, VI, VII, VIII, and IX are the work of Thomas H. Johnson.

First of all the editors wish to express their gratitude to Professor Harry Hayden Clark, the general editor of the series of which this volume is a part. It was he who first proposed the idea of the undertaking, and his assistance and encouragement have been constant and generous. They also wish to thank the Librarians and the staffs of Harvard College Library, Boston Public Library, the Massachusetts Historical Society, Princeton University Library, and New York Public Library for innumerable courtesies, always graciously extended. The demands on Mr. Gerald D. McDonald, Head of the Reserve Room of the last named institution, have been especially importunate, and always met with unfailing skill. Dr. Erdman Harris and Mr. Hugh King Wright have been good enough to read through and offer helpful suggestions about the chapters of the text prepared by Thomas H. Johnson. Perry Miller is indebted to Professor F. O. Matthiessen for his generous assistance in reading the introductory material and advising in the whole construction of the volume; he has also profited largely from the help of Professor David Prall, Dr. Richard B. Schlatter, and Mr. Edmund S. Morgan. To Catherine Rice Johnson and Elizabeth Williams Miller the debt is truly immense, for without their help the book could hardly have reached completion.

The editors' reliance upon the work of Professor Samuel Eliot Morison is testified by the frequent citation of his name in the Introduction and the notes; but the debt goes even further, and is acknowledged elsewhere.

P. M.
T. H. J.

FOR

SAMUEL ELIOT MORISON

Liberali liberaliter instituendi

CONTENTS

Volume I

GENERAL INTRODUCTION

Chapter III

Volume II

Chapter IV

Chapter V

Chapter VI

Chapter VII

Chapter VIII

Chapter IX

Illustrations

Volume I

Volume II

The Map of New England has been prepared especially for this volume. The page of Taylor's manuscript is reproduced through the courtesy of Yale University Library. All the other reproductions are by courtesy of the Massachusetts Historical Society.

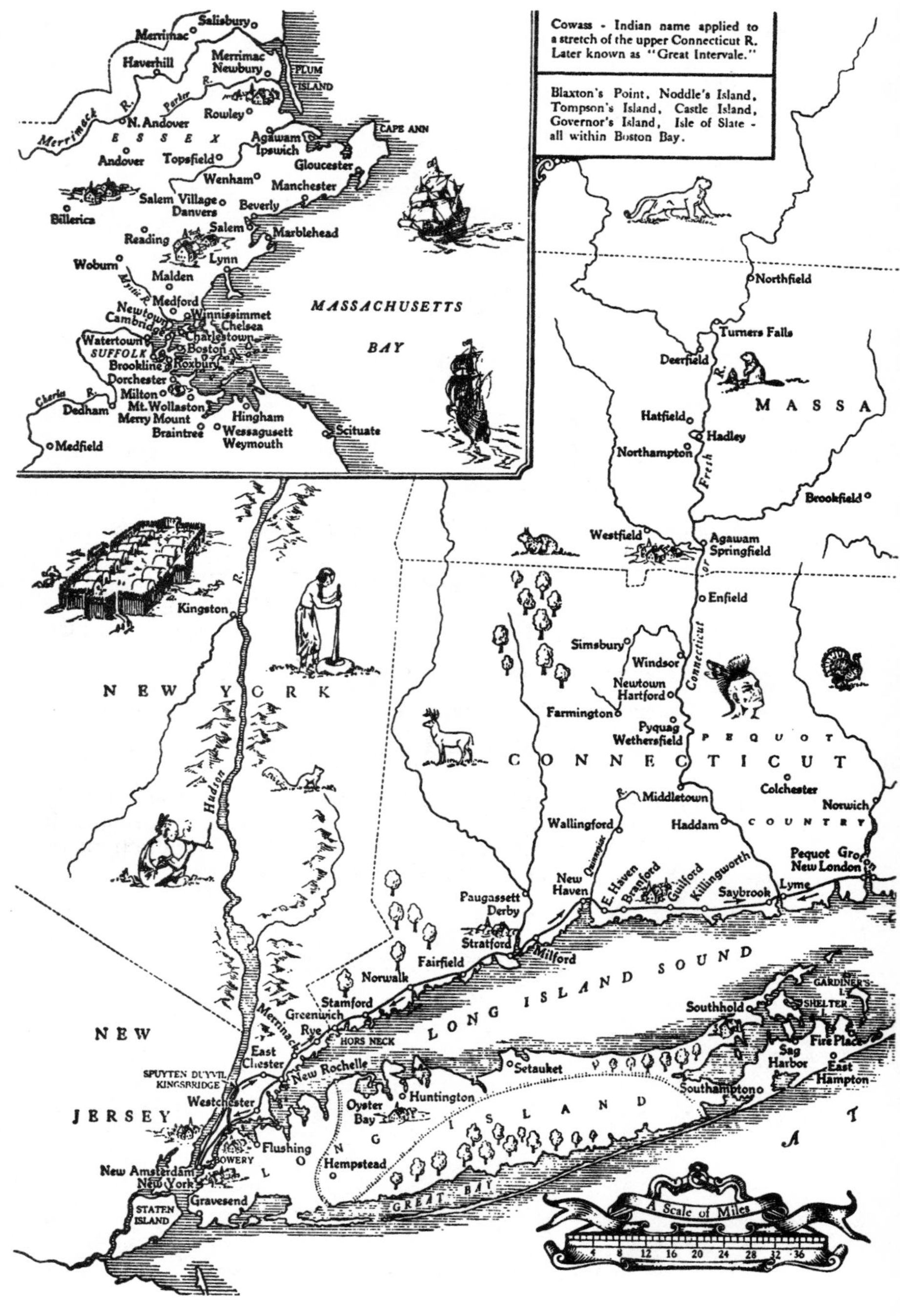

Cowass - Indian name applied to a stretch of the upper Connecticut R. Later known as "Great Intervale."
Blaxton's Point, Noddle's Island, Tompson's Island, Castle Island, Governor's Island, Isle of Slate - all within Boston Bay.
Salisbury
Merrimac
Haverhill
Merrimac
Newbury
PLUM ISLAND
Parker R.
Merrimack R.
N. Andover
Rowley
ESSEX
CAPE ANN
Agawam
Ipswich
Andover
Topsfield
Gloucester
Wenham
Manchester
Salem Village
Danvers
Beverly
Billerica
Salem
Marblehead
Reading
Woburn
Lynn
Malden
Mystic R.
Medford
MASSACHUSETTS
Newtown
Cambridge
Winnissimmet
Chelsea
Charlestown
BAY
Watertown
Boston
SUFFOLK
Brookline
Roxbury
Dorchester
Charles R.
Milton
Mt. Wollaston
Dedham
Merry Mount
Hingham
Braintree
Wessagusett
Weymouth
Scituate
Medfield
Northfield
Turners Falls
Deerfield
MASSA
Hatfield
Hadley
Northampton
Fresh R.
Brookfield
Westfield
Agawam
Springfield
Enfield
Kingston
Hudson R.
Simsbury
Windsor
Newtown
Hartford
Connecticut
NEW YORK
Farmington
Pyquag
Wethersfield
PEQUOT
CONNECTICUT
Colchester
Middletown
Norwich
Wallingford
Haddam
COUNTRY
Pequot Gro
New London
New Haven
Quinnipiac
E. Haven
Branford
Guilford
Killingworth
Paugassett
Derby
Saybrook
Lyme
Stratford
Milford
Fairfield
Norwalk
LONG ISLAND SOUND
GARDINER'S I.
Stamford
SHELTER I.
Southhold
Greenwich
Merrimack
Rye
HORS NECK
Fire Place
NEW
East Chester
Sag Harbor
East Hampton
New Rochelle
Setauket
SPUYTEN DUYVIL
KINGSBRIDGE
Huntington
Southampton
Westchester
Oyster Bay
JERSEY
LONG ISLAND
Flushing
BOWERY
Hempstead
New Amsterdam
New York
GREAT BAY
Gravesend
STATEN ISLAND
A Scale of Miles
4 8 12 16 20 24 28 32 36

A MAP OF
NEW ENGLAND
"... done in the best Pattern that could be had, which being in some places defective, it made the others less exact: yet doth it sufficiently shew the Scituation of the Countrey, and conveniently well the distance of Places."
from map published in 1677 by Wm. Hubbard.
The Journey of Madam Knight
Portion of Long Island under Connecticut jurisdiction until 1664
Present-day state boundaries
NEW HAMPSHIRE
Dover
Durham
Piscataqua
Portsmouth
Kittery
York
Rye
ISLES OF SHOALS
Excester
Exeter
Hampton
NORFOLK
Salisbury
Merrimack R.
Parker R.
PLUM ISLAND
Agawam
Ipswich
CAPE ANN
Andover
ESSEX
Gloucester
Dunstable
Groton
Chelmsford
Salem Village
Danvers
Naumkeag
Salem
Marblehead
Harvard
Concord
MIDDLESEX
Lancaster
Malden
MASSACHUSETTS BAY
CHUSETTS
Newtown
Cambridge
Sudbury
SUFFOLK
Boston
Marlborough
Dorchester
Natick
Charles R.
Worcester
Dedham
Wessagusett
Weymouth
Mendon
Oxford
Marshfield
CAPE COD
Cape Harbor
Duxbury
Kingston
Bridgewater
Plymouth
CAPE COD BAY
NARRAGANSETT
Taunton
Middleborough
Seekonk
Rehoboth
Providence
NEW PLYMOUTH
RHODE ISLAND
Eastham
Sowams
Sandwich
Pawtuxet
Swansea
Natick
Yarmouth
Shawomet
Warwick
Barnstable
CAPE MALABAR
TUCKERS TERROUR
POINTE CARE
Canterbury
Dartmouth
COUNTRY
Pocasset
Portsmouth
Wickford
NARRAGANSETT BAY
MONIMENT BAY
AQUEDNEY
AQUIDNECK
SOUTH SEA
Kingston
ELIZABETH IS.
MIDDLE GROUND
Pawcatuck R.
Newport
MARTHA'S VINEYARD
Edgartown
ISLE OF PROVIDENCE
PRUDENCE ISLE
Westerly
Great Swamp
Mystic
Stonington
NANTUCKET
BLOCK ISLAND
ATLANTIC OCEAN
Drawn by HAGSTROM COMPANY, N. Y.

THE PURITANS

VOLUME I

Mr. Richard Mather.

Reproduced from Increase Mather's *The Life and Death of . . . Richard Mather*.

☙ INTRODUCTION

I. The Puritan Way of Life

1. The Puritan in His Age

Puritanism may perhaps best be described as that point of view, that philosophy of life, that code of values, which was carried to New England by the first settlers in the early seventeenth century. Beginning thus, it has become one of the continuous factors in American life and American thought. Any inventory of the elements that have gone into the making of the "American mind" would have to commence with Puritanism. It is, indeed, only one among many: if we should attempt to enumerate these traditions, we should certainly have to mention such philosophies, such "isms," as the rational liberalism of Jeffersonian democracy, the Hamiltonian conception of conservatism and government, the Southern theory of racial aristocracy, the Transcendentalism of nineteenth-century New England, and what is generally spoken of as frontier individualism. Among these factors Puritanism has been perhaps the most conspicuous, the most sustained, and the most fecund. Its role in American thought has been almost the dominant one, for the descendants of Puritans have carried at least some habits of the Puritan mind into a variety of pursuits, have spread across the country, and in many fields of activity have played a leading part. The force of Puritanism, furthermore, has been accentuated because it was the first of these traditions to be fully articulated, and because it has inspired certain traits which have persisted long after the vanishing of the original creed. Without some understanding of Puritanism, it may safely be said, there is no understanding of America.

Yet important as Puritanism has undoubtedly been in shaping the nation, it is more easily described than defined. It figures frequently in controversy of the last decade, very seldom twice with exactly the same connotation. Particularly of recent years has it become a hazardous feat to run down its meaning. In the mood of revolt against the ideals of previous generations which has swept over our period, Puritanism has become a shining target for many sorts of marksmen. Confusion becomes worse confounded if we attempt to correlate modern usages with anything that can be proved pertinent to the original Puritans themselves. To seek no further, it was the habit of proponents for the repeal of the Eighteenth Amendment during the 1920's to dub Prohibitionists "Puritans," and cartoonists made the nation familiar with an image of the Puritan: a gaunt, lank-haired killjoy, wearing a black steeple hat and compounding for sins he was inclined to by damning those to which he had no mind. Yet any acquaintance with the Puritans of the seventeenth century will reveal at once, not only that they did not wear such hats, but also that they attired themselves in all the hues of the rainbow, and furthermore that in their daily life they imbibed what seem to us prodigious quantities of alcoholic beverages, with never the slightest inkling that they were doing anything sinful. True, they opposed drinking to excess, and ministers preached lengthy sermons condemning intoxication, but at such pious ceremonies as the ordination of new ministers the bill for rum, wine, and beer consumed by the congregation was often staggering. Increase Mather himself—who in popular imagination is apt to figure along with his son Cotton as the arch-embodiment of the Puritan—said in one of his sermons:

> Drink is in it self a good creature of God, and to be received with thankfulness, but the abuse of drink is from Satan; the wine is from God, but the Drunkard is from the Devil.[1]

Or again, the Puritan has acquired the reputation of having been blind to all aesthetic enjoyment and starved of beauty; yet the architecture of the Puritan age grows in the esteem of critics and the household objects of Puritan manufacture, pewter and furniture, achieve prohibitive prices by their appeal to discriminating collectors. Examples of such discrepancies between the modern usage of the word and the historical fact could be multiplied indefinitely.[2] It is not the purpose of this volume to engage in controversy, nor does it intend particularly to defend the Puritan against the bewildering variety of critics who on every side today find him an object of scorn or pity. In his life he neither asked nor gave mercy to his foes; he demanded only that conflicts be joined on real and explicit issues. By examining

[1] *Wo to Drunkards* (Cambridge, 1673), p. 4.

[2] Cf. Kenneth B. Murdock, "The Puritan Tradition in American Literature," *The Reinterpretation of American Literature* (New York, 1928), chap. V.

his own words it may become possible to establish, for better or for worse, the meaning of Puritanism as the Puritan himself believed and practiced it.

Just as soon as we endeavor to free ourselves from prevailing conceptions or misconceptions, and to ascertain the historical facts about seventeenth-century New Englanders, we become aware that we face still another difficulty: not only must we extricate ourselves from interpretations that have been read into Puritanism by the twentieth century, but still more from those that have been attached to it by the eighteenth and nineteenth. The Puritan philosophy, brought to New England highly elaborated and codified, remained a fairly rigid orthodoxy during the seventeenth century. In the next age, however, it proved to be anything but static; by the middle of the eighteenth century there had proceeded from it two distinct schools of thought, almost unalterably opposed to each other. Certain elements were carried into the creeds and practices of the evangelical religious revivals, but others were perpetuated by the rationalists and the forerunners of Unitarianism. Consequently our conception of Puritanism is all too apt to be colored by subsequent happenings; we read ideas into the seventeenth century which belong to the eighteenth, and the real nature of Puritanism can hardly be discovered at all, because Puritanism itself became two distinct and contending things to two sorts of men. The most prevalent error arising from this fact has been the identification of Puritanism with evangelicalism in many accounts, though in histories written by Unitarian scholars the original doctrine has been almost as much distorted in the opposite direction.

Among the evangelicals the original doctrines were transformed or twisted into the new versions of Protestantism that spawned in the Great Awakening of the 1740's, in the succeeding revivals along the frontier and through the back country, in the centrifugal speculations of enraptured prophets and rabid sects in the nineteenth century. All these movements retained something of the theology or revived something of the intensity of spirit, but at the same time they threw aside so much of authentic Puritanism that there can be no doubt the founding fathers would vigorously have repudiated such progeny. They would have had no use, for instance, for the camp meeting and the revivalist orgy; "hitting the sawdust trail" would have been an action exceedingly distasteful to the most ardent among them.

What we know as "fundamentalism" would have been completely antipathetic to them, for they never for one moment dreamed that the truth of scripture was to be maintained in spite of or against the evidences of reason, science, and learning. The sects that have arisen out of Puritanism have most strikingly betrayed their rebellion against the true spirit of their source by their attack upon the ideal of a learned ministry; Puritans considered religion a very complex, subtle, and highly intellectualized affair, and they trained their experts in theology with all the care we would lavish upon preparing men to be engineers or chemists. For the same reasons, Puritans would object strenuously to almost all recent attempts to "humanize" religion, to smooth over hard doctrines, to introduce sweetness and light at the cost of hardheaded realism and invincible logic. From their point of view, to bring Christ down to earth in such a fashion as is implied in statements we sometimes encounter—that He was the "first humanitarian" or that He would certainly endorse this or that political party—would seem to them frightful blasphemy. Puritanism was not only a religious creed, it was a philosophy and a metaphysic; it was an organization of man's whole life, emotional and intellectual, to a degree which has not been sustained by any denomination stemming from it. Yet because such creeds have sprung from Puritanism, the Puritans are frequently praised or blamed for qualities which never belonged to them or for ideas which originated only among their successors and which they themselves would have disowned.

On the other hand, if the line of development from Puritanism tends in one direction to frontier revivalism and evangelicalism, another line leads as directly to a more philosophical, critical, and even skeptical point of view. Unitarianism is as much the child of Puritanism as Methodism. And if the one accretion has colored or distorted our conception of the original doctrine, the other has done so no less. Descendants of the Puritans who revolted against what they considered the tyranny and cruelty of Puritan theology, who substituted taste and reason for dogma and authority and found the emotional fervor of the evangelicals so much sound and fury, have been prone to idealize their ancestors into their own image. A few decades ago it had become very much the mode to praise the Puritans for virtues which they did not possess and which they would not have considered virtues at all. In the pages of liberal historians, and above all in the speeches of Fourth of July orators, the Puritans have been hymned as the pioneers of religious liberty, though nothing was ever farther from their designs; they have been hailed as the forerunners of democracy, though if they were, it was quite beside their intention; they have been invoked in justification for an economic philosophy of free competition and laissez-faire, though they themselves believed in government regulation of business, the fixing of just prices, and the curtailing of individual profits in the interests of the welfare of the whole.[1]

The moral of these reflections may very well be that it is dangerous to read history backwards, to interpret something that was by what it ultimately became, particularly when it became several things. In order that the texts presented in this volume may be read for their proper meaning, it is necessary that the student divest himself as far as possible of those preconceptions which have been established only in later times, and approach the Puritans in terms of their own background. Only thus can we hope to understand what Puritanism was, or what it became and why. The Puritan had his defects, certainly, and he had his virtues, but the defects of one century may become the virtues of another, and what is considered commendable at one time may be viewed with horror by later generations. It is not easy to restrain one's own prejudices and to exercise the sort of historical imagination that is required for the understanding of a portion of the past according to its own intentions before we allow ourselves to judge it by our own standards. The Puritans were not a bashful race, they could speak out and did; in their own words they have painted their own portraits, their majestic strength and their dignity, their humanity and solidity, more accurately than any admirer has been able to do; and also they have betrayed the motes and beams in their own eyes more clearly than any enemy has been able to point them out.

2. *The Spirit of the Age*

Puritanism began as an agitation within the Church of England in the latter half of the sixteenth century. It was a movement for reform of that institution, and at the time no more

[1] See below p. 384. In 1639, John Cotton condemned as a "false principle" the assertion "that a man might sell as dear as he can, and buy as cheap as he can," and Mr. Robert Keayne was fined £200 by the General Court and admonished by the church of Boston for making a profit of sixpence or more in the shilling (*Winthrop's Journal*, ed. J. K. Hosmer [New York, 1908], I, 315–318).

constituted a distinct sect or denomination than the advocates of an amendment to the Constitution of the United States constitute a separate nation. In the 1530's the Church of England broke with the Pope of Rome. By the beginning of Elizabeth's reign it had proceeded a certain distance in this revolt, had become Protestant, had disestablished the monasteries and corrected many abuses. Puritanism was the belief that the reform should be continued, that more abuses remained to be corrected, that practices still survived from the days of Popery which should be renounced, that the Church of England should be restored to the "purity" of the first-century Church as established by Christ Himself. In the 1560's, when the advocates of purification first acquired the name of Puritans, no one, not even the most radical, knew exactly how far the process was to go or just what the ultimate goal would be; down to the days of Cromwell there was never any agreement on this point, and in the end this failure of unanimity proved the undoing of English Puritanism. Many Puritans desired only that certain ceremonies be abolished or changed. Others wanted ministers to preach more sermons, make up their own prayers on the inspiration of the moment rather than read set forms out of a book. Others went further and proposed a revision of the whole form of ecclesiastical government. But whatever the shade or complexion of their Puritanism, Puritans were those who wanted to continue a movement which was already under way. Their opponents, whom we shall speak of as the Anglicans—though only for the sake of convenience, because there was at that time not the remotest thought on either side of an ultimate separation into distinct churches, and Puritans insisted they were as stoutly loyal to the established institution as any men in England—the Anglicans were those who felt that with the enthronement of Elizabeth and with the "Elizabethan Settlement" of the Church, things had gone far enough. They wanted to call a halt, just where they were, and stabilize at that point.

Thus the issue between the two views, though large enough, still involved only a limited number of questions. On everything except matters upon which the Puritans wanted further reformation, there was essential agreement. The Puritans who settled New England were among the more radical—though by no means the most radical that the movement produced—and even before their migration in 1630 had gone to the lengths of formulating a concrete platform of church organization which they wished to see instituted in England in place of the episcopal system. Joining battle on this front gave a sufficiently extended line and provided a vast number of salients to fight over; the gulf between the belief of these Puritans and the majority in the Church of England grew so wide that at last there was no bridging it at all. But notwithstanding the depth of this divergence, the fact still remains that only certain specific questions were raised. If we take a comprehensive survey of the whole body of Puritan thought and belief as it existed in 1630 or 1640, if we make an exhaustive enumeration of ideas held by New England Puritans, we shall find that the vast majority of them were precisely those of their opponents. In other words, Puritanism was a movement toward certain ends within the culture and state of England in the late sixteenth and early seventeenth centuries; it centered about a number of concrete problems and advocated a particular program. Outside of that, it was part and parcel of the times, and its culture was simply the culture of England at that moment. It is necessary to belabor the point, because most accounts of Puritanism, emphasizing the controversial tenets, attribute everything that Puritans said or did to the fact that they were Puritans; their attitudes toward all sorts of things are pounced upon and exhibited as peculiarities of their sect, when as a matter of fact they were normal attitudes for the time. Of course, the Puritans acquired their special quality and their essential individuality from their stand on the points actually at issue, and our final conception of Puritanism must give these concerns all due importance. Yet if first of all we wish to take Puritan culture as a whole, we shall find, let us say, that about ninety per cent of the intellectual life, scientific knowledge, morality, manners and customs, notions and prejudices, was that of all Englishmen. The other ten per cent, the relatively small number of ideas upon which there was dispute, made all the difference between the Puritan and his fellow-Englishmen, made for him so much difference that he pulled up stakes in England, which he loved, and migrated to a wilderness rather than submit them to apparent defeat. Nevertheless, when we come to trace developments and influences on subsequent American history and thought, we shall find that the starting point of many ideas and practices is as apt to be found among the ninety per cent as among the ten. The task of defining Puritanism and giving an account of its culture resolves itself, therefore, into isolating first of all the larger features which were not particularly or necessarily Puritan at all, the elements in the life and society which were products of the time and place, of the background of English life and society rather than of the individual belief or peculiar creed of Puritanism.

Many of the major interests and preoccupations of the New England Puritans belong to this list. They were just as patriotic as Englishmen who remained at home. They hated Spain like poison, and France only a little less. In their eyes, as in those of Anglicans, the most important issue in the Western world was the struggle between Catholicism and Protestantism. They were not unique or extreme in thinking that religion was the primary and all-engrossing business of man, or that all human thought and action should tend to the glory of God. John Donne, Dean of St. Paul's, preached in London, "all knowledge that begins not, and ends not with his glory, is but a giddy, but a vertiginous circle, but an elaborate and exquisite ignorance"; [1] the content, though not the style, of the passage might just as well come from any Puritan preacher. Both the Anglican and the Puritan were at one in conceiving of man as sinful, they both beheld him chained and enslaved by evil until liberated by the redeeming grace of Christ. They both believed that the visible universe was under God's direct and continuous guidance, and that though effects seemed to be produced by natural causes—what at that time were called "secondary causes"—the actual government of the minutest event, the rise of the sun, the fall of a stone, the beat of the heart, was under the direct and immediate supervision of God. This conception, a fundamental one in the Puritan view of the world, was no more limited to them than their habits of eating and drinking. John Donne said:

> The very calamities are from him; the deliverance from those calamities much more. All comes from God's hand; and from his hand, by way of hand-writing, by way of letter, and instruction to us. And therefore to ascribe things wholly to nature, to fortune, to power, to second causes, this is to mistake the hand, not to know God's hand; but to acknowledge it to be God's hand, and not to read it, to say that it is God's doing, and not to consider, what God intends in it, is as much a slighting of God, as the other. [2]

[1] Donne, *Works*, ed. Henry Alford (London, 1839), I, 278.

[2] *Ibid.*, p. 120.

A New England parson later in the century would preach in exactly the same vein:

> His hand has made and framed the whole Fabrick of Heaven & Earth. He hath hung out the Globe of this World; hung the Earth upon nothing; drawn over the Canopy of the Heavens; laid the foundation of the earth in its place; Created that Fountain and Center of Light, Heat, & Influence in this lower World, the *Sun*. . . . The whole Administration of Providence in the Upholding and Government of all created Beings, in a way of highest Wisdom and exact Order, it is *all* His work. . . . Those notable changes in the World in the promoting or suppressing, exalting or bringing down of Kingdoms, Nations, Provinces or Persons, they are all wrought by Him. . . . The Yearly seasons, also Seed-time and Harvest, Summer and Winter, binding up and covering the earth with Frost, Ice and Snow, and the releasing and renewing of the face of the Earth again, it's His work.[1]

The great Anglican preacher said, "Even in natural things all the reason of all that is done is the power and the will of him who infused that virtue into that creature,"[2] and the president of Harvard College preached a sermon on God's governing through the natural causes that might well have taken Donne's utterance for its text (cf. pp. 350–367).

In its major aspects the religious creed of Puritanism was neither peculiar to the Puritans nor different from that of the Anglicans. Both were essentially Protestant; both asserted that men were saved by their faith, not by their deeds. The two sides could agree on the general statement that Christians are bound to believe nothing but what the Gospel teaches, that all traditions of men "contrary to the Word of God" are to be renounced and abhorred. They both believed that the marks of a true church were profession of the creed, use of Christ's sacraments, preaching of the word—Anglican sermons being as long and often as dull as the Puritan—and the union of men in profession and practice under regularly constituted pastors. The Puritans always said that they could subscribe the doctrinal articles of the Church of England; even at the height of the controversy, even after they had left England rather than put up with what they considered its abominations, they always took care to insist that the Church of England was a "true" church, not Anti-Christ as was the Church

[1] William Adams, *God's Eye on the Contrite* (Boston, 1685), pp. 6–7.
[2] Donne, *Works*, I, 33.

of Rome, that it contained many saints, and that men might find salvation within it. Throughout the seventeenth century they read Anglican authors, quoted them in their sermons, and even reprinted some of them in Boston.

The vast substratum of agreement which actually underlay the disagreement between Puritans and Anglicans is explained by the fact that they were both the heirs of the Middle Ages. They still believed that all knowledge was one, that life was unified, that science, economics, political theory, aesthetic standards, rhetoric and art, all were organized in a hierarchical scale of values that tended upward to the end-all and be-all of creation, the glory of God. They both insisted that all human activity be regulated by that purpose. Consequently, even while fighting bitterly against each other, the Puritans and Anglicans stood shoulder to shoulder against what they called "enthusiasm." The leaders of the Puritan movement were trained at the universities, they were men of learning and scholars; no less than the Anglicans did they demand that religion be interpreted by study and logical exposition; they were both resolute against all pretences to immediate revelation, against all ignorant men who claimed to receive personal instructions from God. They agreed on the essential Christian contention that though God may govern the world, He is not the world itself, and that though He instills His grace into men, He does not deify them or unite them to Himself in one personality. He converses with men only through His revealed word, the Bible. His will is to be studied in the operation of His providence as exhibited in the workings of the natural world, but He delivers no new commands or special revelations to the inward consciousness of men. The larger unanimity of the Puritans and the Anglicans reveals itself whenever either of them was called upon to confront enthusiasm. The selections given in this volume include Governor John Winthrop's account of the so-called Antinomian affair, the crisis produced in the little colony by the teachings of Mistress Anne Hutchinson in 1636 and 1637 (pp. 129–136). Beneath the theological jargon in which the opinions of this lady appear we can see the substance of her contention, which was that she was in direct communication with the Godhead, and that she therefore was prepared to follow the promptings of the voice within against all the precepts of the Bible, the churches, reason, or the government of Massachusetts Bay. Winthrop relates how the magistrates and the ministers defended the community against this perversion of the doctrine of regeneration, but the tenor of his condemnation would have been duplicated practically word for word had Anne Hutchinson broached her theories in an Anglican community. The Anglicans fell in completely with the Puritans when both of them were confronted in the 1650's by the Quakers. All New England leaders saw in the Quaker doctrine of an inner light, accessible to all men and giving a perfect communication from God to their inmost spirits, just another form of Anne Hutchinson's blasphemy. John Norton declared that the "light of nature" itself taught us that "madmen acting according to their frantick passions are to be restrained with chaines, when they can not be restrained otherwise." [1] About the same time George Hickes, Dean of Worcester, was advocating that Quakers be treated likewise in England, and he ended a sermon upon them by calling them "Imposters, or enthusiasts, and Blasphemers of the Holy Ghoast." [2] Enthusiasts, whether Antinomian or Quaker, were proposing doctrines that threatened the unity of life by subduing the reason and the intellect to the passions and the emotions. Whatever their differences, Puritans and Anglicans were struggling to maintain a complete harmony of reason and faith, science and religion, earthly dominion and the government of God. When we immerse ourselves in the actual struggle, the difference between the Puritan and the Anglican may seem to us immense; but when we take the vantage point of subsequent history, and survey religious thought as a whole over the last three centuries, the two come very close together on essentials. Against all forms of chaotic emotionalism, against all over-simplifications of theology, learning, philosophy, and science, against all materialism, positivism or mechanism, both were endeavoring to uphold a symmetrical union of heart and head without impairment of either. By the beginning or middle of the next century their successors, both in England and America, found themselves no longer capable of sustaining this unity, and it has yet to be re-achieved today, if achieved again it ever can be. The greatness of the Puritans is not so much that they conquered a wilderness, or that they carried a religion into it, but that they carried a religion which, narrow and starved though it may have been in some respects, deficient

[1] *The Heart of N-England Rent at the Blasphemies of the Present Generation* (Cambridge, 1659), p. 39.

[2] Paul Elmer More and Frank Leslie Cross, *Anglicanism* (1935), pp. 68, 84.

in sensuous richness or brilliant color, was nevertheless indissolubly bound up with an ideal of culture and learning. In contrast to all other pioneers, they made no concessions to the forest, but in the midst of frontier conditions, in the very throes of clearing the land and erecting shelters, they maintained schools and a college, a standard of scholarship and of competent writing, a class of men devoted entirely to the life of the mind and of the soul.

Because the conflict between the Puritans and the Churchmen was as much an intellectual and scholarly issue as it was emotional, it was in great part a debate among pundits. This is not to say that passions were not involved; certainly men took sides because of prejudice, interest, irrational conviction, or for any of the motives that may incite the human race to conflict. The disagreement finally was carried from the field of learned controversy to the field of battle. There can be no doubt that many of the people in England, or even in New England, became rabid partisans and yet never acquired the erudition necessary to understand the intricate and subtle arguments of their leaders. A great number, perhaps even a majority, in both camps were probably not intelligent or learned enough to see clearly the reasons for the cause they supported. Thomas Hooker, the clerical leader of the settlement of Connecticut—and therefore the dominant figure in that community—said frankly, "I can speak it by experience, that the meaner ordinary sort of people, it is incredible and unconceiveable, what Ignorance is among them." [1] This being the case, we who are today being made all too familiar with the horrors of the art of "popularization," can only marvel at how little allowance the divines made for the ignorance or the simplicity of the average man in the addresses and sermons they delivered to him. It is true, several Anglicans began to feel, after the dispute became acrimonious, that the wind of doctrine ought perhaps to be tempered to the uneducated lamb; the authorities ordered parish priests not to discuss the more difficult points of specula-

[1] *The Soules Preparation for Christ* (London, 1632), p. 70; the sermons in this volume were delivered in England, so that Hooker was here speaking of the level of knowledge among the English people, which was of course much lower than among the select group that settled New England; New England Puritans were undoubtedly much more skilled in following the logic of theology, and they received a thorough and lifelong course of instruction in Sunday sermons and Thursday lectures. Even so, as Winthrop points out in describing the Antinomian agitation, the debate on the theology soon got over the heads of the many (p. 131).

tion before all the people.[1] The Puritans would not show their people any such mercy. They endeavored to assist the feebler understandings of their congregations by using the simplest and most comprehensible style, by employing a schematic organization for their sermons, with heads and subheads so clearly marked that earnest listeners could take notes and study the points during the week, and by eschewing Latin quotations or glittering phrases that might distract attention from content to form. But these were the only sort of crutches that Puritan ministers would allow to the rank and file for helping them over the hard parts of divinity. Of course many texts from scripture permitted sermons that were relatively simple and ethical, but others raised perplexing enigmas, discussion of which the Medieval Church had restricted to the schools; Puritans took each kind as it came and did not flinch from struggling in the pulpit with the difficult ones any more than from expounding the more obvious. Thomas Hooker told his people that they were responsible for acquiring a certain amount of knowledge if they expected to be saved:

> Its with an ignorant sinner in the midst of all means as with a sick man remaining in an Apothecaries shop, ful of choycest Medicines in the darkest night: though there be the choycest of all receipts at hand, and he may take what he needs, yet because he cannot see what he takes, and how to use them, he may kill himself or encrease his distempers, but never cure any disease.[2]

The wonder is that by and large the populace did yield their judgments to those who were supposed to know, respected learning and supported it, sat patiently during two- and three-hour sermons while ministers expounded the knottiest and most recon-

[1] The Anglican disposition to refrain from discussing the unfathomable mysteries of the creed before the laity was reinforced by a strategic consideration; the people enjoyed listening to highly technical discussions of subtle points and flocked to Puritan sermons for that reason. The English officials believed that Puritan sermons simply inflamed popular passions without elevating the public intelligence, and therefore endeavored to restrict the discussion of unanswerable questions. As the controversy widened the leading Anglicans turned against the theology of rigorous predestination and reprobation—which had been generally accepted by the first bishops of Elizabeth's reign—and identified Puritan theology with the Puritan program in church and state; the effect on the Puritans was to make them all the more determined that no subject, no matter how involved, should be kept out of the pulpits, and that the people should be lifted by main force to the highest possible pitch of understanding. Particularly were they resolved that predestination should be thoroughly thrashed out for the benefit of the populace.

[2] *The Application of Redemption* (London, 1659), pp. 89–90; these sermons were delivered in Connecticut.

dite of metaphysical texts. The testimony of visitors, travelers, and memoirs agrees that during the Puritan age in New England the common man, the farmer and merchant, was amazingly versed in systematic divinity. A gathering of yeomen and "hired help" around the kitchen fire of an evening produced long and unbelievably technical discussions of predestination, infant damnation, and the distinctions between faith and works. In the first half of the seventeenth century the people had not yet questioned the conception of religion as a difficult art in which the authority of the skilled dialectician should prevail over the inclinations of the merely devout. This ideal of subjection to qualified leadership was social as well as intellectual. Very few Englishmen had yet broached the notion that a lackey was as good as a lord, or that any Tom, Dick, or Harry, simply because he was a good, honest man, could understand the Sermon on the Mount as well as a Master of Arts from Oxford, Cambridge, or Harvard. Professor Morison has shown that the life of the college in New England was saved by the sacrifice of the yeomen farmers, who contributed their pecks of wheat, wrung from a stony soil, taken from their none too opulent stores, to support teaching fellows and to assist poor scholars at Harvard College, in order that they and their children might still sit under a literate ministry "when our present Ministers shall lie in the Dust." [1]

When we say that the majority of the people in the early seventeenth century still acceded to the dictation of the learned in religion and the superior in society, we must also remark that the Puritan leaders were in grave danger of arousing a revolt against themselves by their very own doctrines. Puritans were attacking the sacerdotal and institutional bias which had survived in the Church of England; they were maintaining a theology that brought every man to a direct experience of the spirit and removed intermediaries between himself and the deity. Yet the authority of the infallible church and the power of the bishops had for centuries served to keep the people docile. Consequently when the Puritan leaders endeavored to remove the bishops and to deny that the Church should stand between God and man, they ran the hazard of starting something among the people that might get out of hand. Just as the Puritan doctrine that men were saved by the infusion of God's grace could lead to the An-

[1] Morison, *The Founding of Harvard College* (1935), p. 318; *Harvard College in the Seventeenth Century*, p. 28.

tinomianism of Mrs. Hutchinson, and often did warrant the simple in concluding that if they had God's grace in them they needed to pay no heed to what a minister told them, so the Puritan contention that regenerate men were illuminated with divine truth might lead to the belief that true religion did not need the assistance of learning, books, arguments, logical demonstrations, or classical languages. There was always a possibility that Puritanism would raise up a fanatical anti-intellectualism, and against such a threat the Puritan ministers constantly braced themselves. It was no accident that the followers of Mrs. Hutchinson, who believed that men could receive all the necessary instructions from within, also attacked learning and education, and came near to wrecking not only the colony but the college as well.[1] Edward Johnson, stout militia captain of the town of Woburn, and no intellectual, set forth the anguish of soul through which he passed while the citizens of Boston were under the spell of "Jezebel" (p. 158); he was particularly shocked to hear one of the heretics say flatly, "I had rather hear such a one that speakes from the meere motion of the spirit, without any study at all, then any of your learned Scollers, although they may be fuller of Scripture." [2] Puritanism was forever giving rise to such rebellions against its own ideal of learned religion; the experience of Massachusetts with the Hutchinsonians in the 1630's was only a premonition of what England was to encounter in the 1650's, when the Civil Wars generated not one form of Antinomianism but a thousand. Anabaptists and Fifth Monarchy men then began to vaunt that an ignorant man inspired with the spirit made a better preacher than one who had attended the "cob-webbed Universities," and in the disturbed state of society found an opportunity to spread their dangerous opinions among the people. The true Puritans were forced to resort to repressive measures to save Puritanism itself. Oliver Cromwell was the most liberal of seventeenth-century Puritan leaders; it is his eternal glory that he did not confront with the sword all the zealots who ran riot over the land, but strove to work out a scheme of toleration for as many of them as would behave with civil decency. But even Cromwell had to draw the line somewhere, and he drew it when the upsurge of popular religious frenzies turned against the universities and the learned ministry. His assumption of the dic-

[1] Morison, *The Founding of Harvard College*, chap. XIII.

[2] *The Wonder-working Providence*, ed. J. F. Jameson (New York, 1910), p. 128.

tatorship in 1653, unlike later seizures of arbitrary power, was prompted in great part by his determination to protect a sober and instructed clergy and the universities from an assault by the lunatic fringe in his own party.[1] Cromwell's New England brethren thoroughly sympathized with his efforts, but they thought he had invited the trouble by allowing ignorant men to preach at all; they looked upon his policy of toleration as the sole stain upon the otherwise flawless record of the pre-eminent warrior saint of the age. They were determined to run no such risks in their communities. They would have the rabble entirely submissive to the intellectual aristocracy, even though many or all of the mass were supposedly saints of God.

Both Cromwell and the New England leaders were face to face with a problem as old as the history of the Christian Church. Throughout the Middle Ages there had been such stirrings among the people as those to which Mrs. Hutchinson or the Fifth Monarchy Men gave voice. The great scholastic synthesis always remained incomprehensible to the vulgar, who demanded to be fed again and again with the sort of religious sustenance they craved. The Reformation drew upon these suppressed desires. Common men turned Protestant primarily because Protestantism offered them a religion which more effectively satisfied their spiritual hunger. Yet in Europe theologians and metaphysicians retained the leadership and kept Protestantism from becoming merely an emotional outburst. They supplied it with a theology which, though not so sophisticated as scholastic dogma, was still equipped with a logic and organon of rational demonstration. Though Protestantism can be viewed as a "liberation" of the common man, it was far from being a complete emancipation of the individual. It freed him from many intellectual restraints that had been imposed by the Church, but it did not give him full liberty to think anything he pleased; socially it freed him from many exactions, but it did not permit him to abandon his traditional subjection to his social and ecclesiastical superiors. The original settlers of New England carried this Protestantism intact from Europe to America. Except for the small band that was driven into exile with Anne Hutchinson, and one or two other groups of visionaries who also were hustled across the borders into Rhode Island, the rank and file did follow their leaders, meekly and reverently. Captain Johnson probably represents the average lay-

[1] David Masson, *The Life of John Milton* (London, 1877), IV, 566 ff.

man's loyalty to the clergy. The New England "theocracy" was simply a Protestant version of the European social ideal, and except for its Protestantism was thoroughly medieval in character.

It was only as the seventeenth century came to a close that the imported structure began to show the strain. In Europe social tradition had conspired with the ministers to check enthusiasts in religion and "levellers" in society; in England the authorities, whether Anglican or Puritan, royal or Cromwellian, were able to suppress the assault upon the scholarly and aristocratic ideal. In America the character of the people underwent a change; they moved further into the frontier, they became more absorbed in business and profits than in religion and salvation, their memories of English social stratification grew dim. A preacher before the General Court in 1705 bewailed the effects of the frontier in terms that have been echoed by "Easterners" for two hundred years and more; men were no longer living together, he said, in compact communities, under the tutelage of educated clergymen and under the discipline of an ordered society, but were taking themselves into remote corners "for worldly conveniences." "By that means [they] have seemed to bid defiance, not only to Religion, but to Civility it self: and such places thereby have become Nurseries of Ignorance, Prophaneness and Atheism." [1] In America the frontier conspired with the popular disposition to lessen the prestige of the cultured classes and to enhance the social power of those who wanted their religion in a more simple, downright and "democratic" form, who cared nothing for the refinements and subtleties of historic theology. Not until the decade of the Great Awakening did the popular tendency receive distinct articulation through leaders who openly renounced the older conception, but for half a century or more before 1740 its obstinate persistence can be traced in the condemnations of the ministers.

The Puritan leaders could withstand this rising tide of democracy only by such support as the government would give them—which became increasingly less after the new charter of 1692 took away from the saints all power to select their own governors and divorced the state and church—or else by the

[1] Joseph Easterbrooks, *Abraham the Passenger* (Boston, 1705), p. 3; cf. Increase Mather as early as 1677: "People are ready to run wild into the woods again and to be as Heathenish as ever, if you do not prevent it" (*A Discourse Concerning the Danger of Apostacy* [Boston, 1679], 2d ed., 1685, p. 104).

sheer force of their personalities. As early as the 1660's and 70's we can see them beginning to shift their attentions from mere exposition of the creed to greater and greater insistence upon committing power only to men of wisdom and knowledge. William Hubbard in an election sermon of 1676 told the citizens that piety alone in a ruler was not enough; magistrates should be such "as by the benefit of natural parts Experience, Education, and study, have advantage above others to be acquainted with the affairs of the world abroad, as well as with the Laws and Customes of their own people at home." [1] By the beginning of the eighteenth century the task of buttressing the classified society, maintaining the rule of the well-trained and the culturally superior both in church and society seems to have become the predominant concern of the clergy. Sermon after sermon reveals that in their eyes the cause of learning and the cause of a hierarchical, differentiated social order were one and the same. For example, Ebenezer Pemberton, who was a tutor at Harvard College and then colleague minister with Samuel Willard at the Old South Church, delivered a funeral sermon upon the death of the Honourable John Walley, member of the council and judge, in 1711. Judge Walley, said Pemberton, rendered his country great service; there are various ways in which the country can be served. One of them is by the promotion of "good literature":

> This is necessary for the true prosperity and happiness of a people. *Greece* and *Rome* are more renowned for the flourishing state of learning in them, than for their arms. This has for ever been in highest esteem among civilized nations. . . . The more of good literature civil rulers are furnished with, the more capable they are to discharge their trust to the honour and safety of their people. And learning is no less necessary, as an ordinary medium to secure the glory of Christ's visible kingdom. Without a good measure of this the truth can't be explained, asserted and demonstrated; nor errors detected and the heretick baffled . . . When ignorance and barbarity invade a generation, their glory is laid in the dust; and the ruin of all that is great and good among them will soon follow.[2]

A second way in which the welfare of the nation is served is by each and every person's keeping to his proper station:

[1] *The Happiness of a People* (Boston, 1676), p. 28.
[2] *Sermons and Discourses on Several Occasions* (London, 1727), pp. 212–213.

> This intends that we keep within the *line* and *place*, that providence has set us . . . We must not without God's call quit our post, thrust our selves into *anothers province*, with a conceit that *there* we may best serve, and promote the good of the world. But herein observe the will of God by keeping to the service that belongs to our station, which providence has made our peculiar business. Thus every man is to serve his generation by moving in his own orb; and discharging those offices that belong to that order that the government of heaven has assigned him to.[1]

Leadership by the learned and dutiful subordination of the unlearned—as long as the original religious creed retained its hold upon the people these exhortations were heeded; in the eighteenth century, as it ceased to arouse their loyalties, they went seeking after gods that were utterly strange to Puritanism. They demanded fervent rather than learned ministers and asserted the equality of all men.

Thus Puritanism appears, from the social and economic point of view, to have been a philosophy of social stratification, placing the command in the hands of the properly qualified and demanding implicit obedience from the uneducated; from the religious point of view it was the dogged assertion of the unity of intellect and spirit in the face of a rising tide of democratic sentiment suspicious of the intellect and intoxicated with the spirit. It was autocratic, hierarchical, and authoritarian. It held that in the intellectual realm holy writ was to be expounded by right reason, that in the social realm the expounders of holy writ were to be the mentors of farmers and merchants. Yet in so far as Puritanism involved such ideals it was simply adapting to its own purposes the ideals of the age. Catholics in Spain and in Spanish America pursued the same objectives, and the Puritans were no more rigorous in their application of an autocratic standard than King Charles himself endeavored to be—and would have been had he not been balked in the attempt.

3. *Puritan Humanism*

There is another body of assumptions, besides those underlying the Puritan philosophy of religion and of religious learning, which Puritans shared in common with Anglicans and even with Catholics. They were the heirs not only of medieval Christianity and of the Reformation, but also of the Renaissance—they were

[1] *Ibid.*, pp. 220–221.

humanists. They were students of the recently revived and rediscovered classical literature, and they shared in the reinvigoration of mind and spirit which that literature inspired in Western Europe. Their theology undoubtedly stood in the way of unrestricted appreciation, yet in the amount of Greek and Roman writing they could enjoy and utilize, they fell very little short of the most liberal of Anglican scholars. That a Puritan writer could be no less devoted to classical literature than his opponent, in spite of his theology, is demonstrated most conspicuously by John Milton. The miraculous fusion of Puritanism and Hellenism which he achieved is unique only in his grandeur of expression; the same combination of religious dogma with the classics, of Protestant theology and ancient morality, was the aim of the curriculum at Harvard College, and it was sustained, though on a rudimentary or pedestrian level, in the sermons of Yankee parsons throughout the seventeenth century.

The humanist learning had already become a regular part of the studies in the English Universities when the men who were to be ministers and magistrates in New England matriculated there. Those institutions were no longer training students solely for the ministry; they were also training men to be scholars in the classics, or even to be simply "gentlemen." [1] The same trinity of intentions was continued at Harvard. Tutor William Brattle declared in a college oration in 1689, "Liberali liberaliter instituendi"—that is, "Gentlemen must be educated like gentlemen." [2] Just how extensive a role the classics played in Puritan education can best be seen by a reading of the chapters on the subject in Professor Morison's history of Harvard College.[3] It is enough to say here that study of the arts and sciences and of good literature was among the purposes of education in New England as well as the learning of theology. The General Court itself went on record, in the name of all the citizens and presumably without dissent from the other inhabitants of Massachusetts, that though learning, "namely, skill in the tongues & liberall artes," might not be absolutely necessary "for the beinge of a common wealth & churches, yet we conceive that the judgment of the godly wise, it is beyond all question, not only laudable, but necessary for the beinge of the same." [4] In a sermon of 1677, Increase

[1] Morison, *The Founding of Harvard College*, pp. 50 ff.
[2] Morison, *Harvard College in the Seventeenth Century*, p. 165.
[3] *Ibid.*, chaps. VII–XIV.
[4] *Massachusetts Records*, ed. N. B. Shurtleff (Boston, 1853–1854), III, 279.

Mather told the legislature that they must take care of the schools and the college, "that so there might be able instruments raised up for the propagating of Truth in succeeding Generations. And some have well & truly observed, that the Interest of Religion and good Literature, hath risen and fallen together." [1] Mather's conception of what constitutes "good literature" might not coincide with what we mean by the phrase, but it would include a knowledge of the poetry, drama, and history of the ancient world, and an ability to write sentences which would not appear utterly contemptible when compared with those of classical authors.

Thanks to the labors of Professor Morison, we may now rest assured that the Puritans of New England were the disciples of Erasmus and Colet. The question with which we are concerned in the present context is what part of the Puritan mentality must be put down to their participation in the humanist tradition. How much of what Puritans said and did, how much of their belief and their judgment, is to be attributed not so much to their Puritanism as to their education? Latin and Greek contributed more to the Puritan mind than a method of pedagogy or an exercise in grammar. When these tongues were the foundation of the training for an A.B., and when there existed no alternative S.B. by which, as Dean Briggs remarked, the college could graduate a man with a sealed certification that he was totally ignorant of them, then it was inevitable that Puritan thought would appropriate some ideas from Hesiod or Horace, some wisdom from Plato, or even some wit from Plautus.

From the evidence afforded by Puritan sermons and polemics it seems clear that the tendency of the humanist culture was to accentuate the element of rationalism, to enlarge the sphere of competence of the natural reason even when not inspired with God's special grace. Neither the Puritans nor the most anti-Puritanical bishops in the early seventeenth century would have entertained for a moment the idea that merely natural training, civilized morality, and gentlemanly culture could get a man to heaven; both would have admitted that many souls can be and are saved without such embellishments. But they both would have agreed that, by and large, men who are called by God will heed the summons all the better if they know Latin, Greek, and Hebrew. John Cotton said that if knowledge is but an empty speculation or a mere collection of facts it will bring forth no

[1] *A Discourse Concerning the Danger of Apostacy*, pp. 100–101.

"heat"; but though "knowledge is no knowledge without zeal," on the other hand it is equally true that "zeale is but a wilde-fire without knowledge." [1] The great heathen moralists, particularly the Stoics, above all Seneca and Plutarch,[2] inculcated a system of ethics that was in effect so close to the precepts of Puritanism that the divines could never find it in their hearts to envisage these noble heathens languishing in the same Hell to which they consigned the minions of Anti-Christ and the deluded followers of Mistress Hutchinson, any more than Dante could confine Vergil to the Inferno. Increase Mather reveals significantly the alacrity with which a Puritan theologian made room on his shelves for the books of pagan Greece and Rome:

> Some among the Heathen have been notable *Moralists*, such as *Cato*, *Seneca*, Aristides, *&c*. And although we must not say that their Morality saved them, yet it was not altogether unprofitable to them, for God did therefore reward them with many outward blessings, and they did thereby escape many temporal Judgements, which otherwise would have befallen them: And they had more quietness in their own spirits, then otherwise would have been, being freed from those stinging Accusations of Conscience, which more profane sinners, that usually have an Hell in their Consciences, are daily tormented with. Moreover, their punishment in another world will not be so great, as of those that have been of a vicious Conversation.[3]

Hence in the sermons of Puritan ministers, side by side with passages of scripture, appear examples of the wisdom of Greece, episodes from the lives of Plutarch, tart sayings from Aristophanes,

[1] *Christ the Fountaine of Life* (London, 1651), p. 145.

[2] For the estimation in which Plutarch in particular was held, see the commendations of Cotton Mather (p. 169) and the citations made by John Wise (pp. 260–261). There is no better way of perceiving how the lamb of classical culture could lie down with the lion of Puritan theology than by reading Plutarch's *Lives*, then available to all literate men in the great translation of Sir Thomas North. Compare, for example, the Puritan theory of nature with the attitude expressed in Plutarch's remarks in the life of Pericles on the two approaches to natural phenomena of Lampon the diviner and Anaxagoras the philosopher; Lampon interprets the discovery of a ram with one horn as a portent, while Anaxagoras splits open the skull to demonstrate a natural cause for the monstrosity; Plutarch comments that the wise man will say both were right, one finding the cause by which it was produced, the other the end for which it was designed. There could be no better statement of the Puritan theory of the concurrence of God's determination and the secondary cause, or no better exposition of the Puritan attitude toward "divine providences." Seneca was so congenial to the Puritan temper that scholars strained to the limit the tradition that he had been in correspondence with St. Paul and was secretly a Christian.

[3] *Wo to Drunkards*, p. 15.

hard realism from Thucydides. Plato serves as an authority for the principles of society, subordinated of course to the Word of God, but agreeing with it nevertheless; and when a minister, painting the splendors of future bliss, wants to make clear to his auditors that the sorrows and tribulations of this life will then seem sweet in retrospect, he can find no better words to project into the Christian heaven than those of the Roman Vergil, "Haec olim meminisse Juvabit." [1] Some of the clergy carried their veneration of classical precedents to lengths that seemed dangerous to less venturesome Puritans. When Nathaniel Ward was invited by the deputies to deliver the election sermon in 1641, he grounded "his propositions much upon the old Roman and Grecian governments" (cf. p. 205). John Winthrop, the governor, thought this a little unnecessary, and protested that Christians ought to stick to the Bible and not go hunting for lessons in "those heathen commonwealths." The ministers apparently hastened to reassure him that such a mode of reasoning was perfectly orthodox; the Reverend Thomas Shepard, minister at Cambridge, wrote to him, "Your apprehensions agaynst reading & learning heathen authors, I perswade myselfe were suddenly suggested," and told him that if he would impart his objections to Brother Dunster, the president of Harvard College, they would readily be answered.[2]

The remarkable fact concerning the mental life of these Puritans is that more of them did not share Winthrop's apprehensions. Every appeal to classical models, every invocation of wisdom which men had achieved without the assistance of grace, was in effect a confession that they did not believe man was hopelessly corrupt or too abysmally sinful. Every such passage was by implication an acknowledgment that natural reason had its place in the scheme of things, and a respectable place, that natural man, employing reason, was not quite a contemptible worm. Elnathan Chauncy, when a student at Harvard in the late 1650's, copied into his commonplace book a passage from van Helmont's *Ternary of Paradoxes* which ran thus:

Truth and the rational soule are twins. For so uncessant a magnetisme or congenerous love doth the soule hold unto the truth, that she can Know no reall or permanent satisfaction, in the fruition of any other object.[3]

[1] Jonathan Mitchell, *A Discourse of the Glory To which God hath called Believers* (London, 1677), pp. 128–129.

[2] *Collections of the Massachusetts Historical Society*, Ser. 4, VII, 272.

[3] Morison, *Harvard College in the Seventeenth Century*, p. 130.

Truly, if the Puritans had been as they are often pictured, merely dogmatic Calvinists, holding a brutal and ironclad theory of innate depravity and original sin, the young student would have been playing with fire even to have let his eyes rest upon such a passage. But his jotting down this aphorism was nothing startling in the life of a Puritan. That man was, however much deformed by sin and passion, essentially a rational and responsible being was just as much an axiom of their thought as that he needed to wait upon God for the special grace that would bring him to salvation. How they reconciled the two beliefs is a complicated story, but for the moment it is necessary to make clear that the conception of man as competent to judge on the basis of his innate reason was perfectly acceptable in Puritan thought, and that it was confirmed and sustained by the influence of classical literature. [1] John Cotton said that reason flows from the soul of man and is an inherent part of it; we learn much by experience and education, he said, "yet there is also an essentiall wisdome in us, namely, our Reason which is natural." [2] William Hubbard spoke to the General Court of "Reason, our most faithful and best Councellour." [3] The first body of College Laws at Harvard required the student to be able not merely to read Scripture, but "to Resolve them Logically." [4] It was not enough for the Puritan minister to read his text and apply it as the mood or the spirit

[1] Among the theses defended at Harvard commencements there appear frequently "Voluntas est libera" (The will is free, e.g. 1653 Theses Physicae No. 15) and other enhancements of human ability, such as "An discrimen boni & mali à lege Naturae cognoscatur" (Whether discrimination of good and evil may be known by the light of nature, 1663 Quaestiones No. 3), "An Homo sit Causa libera suarum Actionum" (May man be the free cause of his own actions, 1669 Quaestiones No. 2) affirmed by John Richardson, "Anima Rationalis Creatur" (The soul is created rational, 1670 Theses Physicae No. 8), "An notitia Dei sit homini naturalis" (Whether the conception of God may be natural to man, 1679 Quaestiones No. 2) affirmed by Thomas Brattle, and again by Samuel Russell (1684 Quaestiones No. 6), "An Cognitio Dei sit Homini Naturalis" (Whether cognition of God may be natural to man, 1693 Quaestiones No. 5) affirmed by Joseph Whiting, "An Detur Actio humana involuntaria" (Whether there exists involuntary human action, 1704 Quaestiones No. 16) denied by Ephraim Woodbridge. (See Morison, *Harvard College in the Seventeenth Century*, Appendix B.) These are picked at random, but they demonstrate that, along with the theological conception of man as bound in sin and dependent upon divine grace, there flourished also the conception of man as responsible, free to choose between good and evil, naturally imbued with at least the glimmerings of some good principles.

[2] *A Practical Commentary . . . upon The First Epistle Generall of John* (London, 1656), p. 8.

[3] *The Happiness of a People*, p. 32.

[4] Morison, *The Founding of Harvard College*, p. 337.

dictated; interpretation of scripture was an abstruse art, to be learned with diligence, to be employed with caution, and to be regulated by the immutable laws of right reason and infallible logic. There is a vast difference between this point of view and the evangelical Protestantism which so largely replaced it in subsequent centuries. To define that difference—the actual antagonism of the two—is not easy, because the evangelicals arrayed their thought in theological terms which to our undiscriminating eyes seem almost identical; yet the difference can be dramatized at once if we compare the use made of scripture in the ordinary revival sermon with the manner in which the Puritan minister declared that scripture was to be interpreted:

> Sapience or Wisdome properly belongs to Syllogistical Judgement, and is a virtue of the Understanding, whereby a man discerns the dependance of things, and how one follows upon another. [It] imports in it a laying of things together in a Syllogistical way. Hence when men reason amiss, and conclude that which is not virtually contained in the Premises, or make wrong inferences, they are said to Paralogize themselves. . . . Wisdome lyes in the *Rational Application* of general Rules of Scripture to our selves and our own conditions, and in the *induction of particulars*, and due Reasoning from it.[1]

The "enthusiast" who rushes from his helter-skelter reading into some crack-brained interpretation, or the exuberant fanatic who, without the training of the scholar, the critic, the logician, and the linguist, jumps to the conclusion that he as well as any man can read and understand the word of God—these men "paralogize themselves." There was hardly a greater sin in the Puritan decalogue.

The remark of John Cotton which we have just quoted, that an essential wisdom dwells within us which is natural reason, if read hastily may seem a dull platitude, but Cotton's putting it in precisely these terms made it a very vital sentence. For to define human reason in this manner was to take sides in a great intellectual revolution that had been fought all over Europe during the previous century. The combined force of the Protestant revolt against the Papacy and of the humanistic protest against the barbarities of the Dark Ages had inspired a widespread rejection of the authority and method of scholasticism. Protestant and humanist altered their allegiance to that magnificent structure

[1] Urian Oakes, *New-England Pleaded with* (Cambridge, 1673), pp. 11–12.

which the medieval schoolmen had erected as a monument to the marriage of reason and faith, the Protestant because the system was identified in his mind with Catholicism, the humanist because it had become decayed, lopsided, and fantastic. The humanist criticism was the more pertinent. The beautiful symmetry of the scholastic philosophy, as it exists in the work of Thomas Aquinas, had been destroyed and perverted by the lesser lights of the fifteenth century; in the eyes of intelligent men, scholasticism by 1500 had become a pointless game of farfetched logic-chopping, the deductive process gone mad, a construction of syllogisms for the sake of syllogisms, and an elaborate trick of speaking nonsense through a series of intellectual handsprings. Puritan and Anglican ministers were at one in their condemnation of the schoolmen. John Donne said that in order to define ignorance, "the schools have made so many divisions, and subdivisions, and re-divisions, and post-divisions of ignorance, that there goes as much learning to understand ignorance, as knowledge." [1] John Cotton fulminated against "the subtilty and sophistry of the School-men, suppressing the reading of the Scriptures, and mixing Philosophy with Divinity, that they might as well have studied a point of *Aristotle* as their divinity, and make as good use of the one as of the other." [2] In understanding Puritan thought, we must remember that much of it was conditioned, like all Protestantism, by its active hostility to a method of thinking which, having prevailed for several centuries, was now believed to be prostituted to the ambitions of the Papacy, and become the source of all the mischief and "superstition" in the Church of Rome.[3]

Yet for men in that period to purge their minds entirely of scholasticism was almost impossible, for in many fields there existed nothing else to turn to. In so far as scholasticism was a defence of the Church of Rome, the Puritans could push it aside and set up the Bible. But in so far as scholasticism was a theory of physics and of the natural constitution of the world, it was more difficult for them to scuttle it, because, though they of course did not know it, they lived during that hiatus in scientific history when the old was disappearing but the new had not yet sufficiently emerged. Puritans were cordial enough to the new science

[1] *Works*, I, 536.
[2] *An Exposition upon The Thirteenth Chapter of the Revelation* (London, 1656), p. 27.
[3] Cf. Morison, *Harvard College in the Seventeenth Century*, pp. 130–131.

for that of Descartes, and the inferences from it proved friendly to what turned out to be the new science.

Ramus seemed to men of the Renaissance to offer liberation, simplification, and clarity. To them he seemed to have been raised up, as though by divine providence, to combine in one personality the three dominant characters of the age, humanist, Protestant, and logician; not only to Puritans but to humanists like Sir Philip Sidney he promised liberation from the gloomy cave of scholastic metaphysics into the spacious meadows of classical literature. He put into the hands of Protestant divines and scholars dialectical spears with which they could pierce the metaphysical armor of the Catholic champions. One of his principal contentions was that logical processes and figures were to be illustrated from classical poets, orators, and historians rather than from works of technical disputation; [1] for example, in order to show how dissimilar qualities may be compared, Ramus does not erect a hypothetical contrast of abstractions but employs the contrast made in a famous love lyric of Catullus between suns and the lives of lovers, that suns are able to die and to rise again, but for lovers, when the brief light of life fails, there remains but perpetual night.[2] Logic taught in this manner inevitably became fresh and exhilarating; it formed new and intoxicating alliances with rhetoric and classical scholarship. Puritan writers were logicians to a man, and Puritan sermons were severely logical in structure, but all according to the logic of Ramus, which was a relatively simple, clear-cut, and commonsense system, and one which furthermore furnished good authority for the study and even for the quotation of Catullus and Vergil in order to elucidate the fine points of divinity.

Ramus was able to assert that the principles of logic were embodied in the writings of poets, because he went upon the assumption that a simple and comprehensible order permeated the universe. Great writers, speaking out of their inward being, were speaking from nature herself, and through them, he said, nature reveals herself. "Science ought, therefore, to study the lessons that are innate in select minds . . . and upon them as a model should formulate the rules for those who desire to reason well." [3] His

[1] Petrus Ramus, *Dialecticae Libri Duo* (London, 1669), p. 50.

[2] *Ibid.*, p. 22.

[3] Frank P. Graves, *Peter Ramus and the Educational Reformation of the Sixteenth Century* (New York, 1912), pp. 145–147.

logic is a typically Renaissance product in that it was intended not so much for proof and analysis as for assertion. It will not stand up under the rigorous scrutiny of a modern logician; it could not even survive once it came into competition with Locke. Yet it was ideally adapted to the times, because it cleared away the rubbish of scholasticism and yet did not challenge but rather strengthened the authoritarianism that was still as essential to a Renaissance philosophy of religion as it had been to a medieval.[1] The Ramean logic was an instrument for setting forth only received truth, simply and concisely, and Ramus himself compressed the essential outlines into sixty pages. It was a short cut to demonstration, resting squarely and firmly upon the conviction that the world is a comprehensible logical structure to which the mind of man, in spite of the fall of Adam and human corruption, almost exactly corresponds.[2]

Though the Ramean logic was actually much less of a depar-

[1] Hardin Craig, *The Enchanted Glass* (Oxford, 1936), pp. 140–146, 149–151, 156–158, 198–202.

[2] Ramus's textbook, *Dialecticae Libri Duo*, first published 1556, frequently republished in England, was used continuously in seventeenth-century New England, and was supplemented by his other works. The *Dialecticae* was published in England with a commentary by William Temple, 1584, but it was generally read by English students bound up with *Commentarii* by George Downame (first delivered as lectures in 1590), which provide the best text for study of the full implications of the system. It can also be read in brief form in Milton's *Artis Logicae, plenior institutio, at Petri Rami methodum concinnata*, published in 1672, reprinted *Works*, ed. John Mitford (London, 1851), VII, 1–185, and in other editions of Milton. At Harvard Milton's work was used, and an earlier handbook, Marcus Friedrich Wendelin, *Logicae institutiones tironum adolescentium captui accommodatae*, 1654. For versions in English the best examples are Abraham Fraunce, *The Lawiers Logike*, 1588, and Alexander Richardson, *The Logicians School-Master*, 1657, a commentary that circulated in manuscript at both Cambridges for several decades before it was printed. However, the student of New England history can best review the system in Samuel Johnson's *Technologia Sive Technometria*, a manuscript summary by Johnson when an undergraduate at Yale, and published with an excellent introduction and a translation in *Samuel Johnson*, ed. Herbert and Carol Schneider (New York, 1929), II, 57–95. Johnson completed the manuscript on November 11, 1714, and in a later note on the margin records that by November 11, 1715, "I was wholly changed to the New Learning," by which he means the logic and philosophy of John Locke. Among the more conservative New England divines the Ramean logic died a more lingering death, but by the time of Jonathan Edwards' active career it had generally expired, and with it had gone the philosophy of original Puritanism. Edwards' Calvinism is Calvinism harmonized as far as possible with Locke; the Calvinism of early New England was colored by a totally different metaphysic. Of the general accounts of Ramus the best are still the articles in Bayle's Dictionary or in Charles Waddington, *Ramus, Sa vie, ses écrits, et ses opinions* (Paris, 1855); cf. also Frank P. Graves, *Peter Ramus and the Educational Reformation of the Sixteenth Century;* for the influence of Ramus at Cambridge University, cf. J. B. Mullinger, *History of Cambridge*, II, 406–411.

ture from Aristotle than Ramists pretended, and though Ramus' own knowledge of Plato was very imperfect, the basic premise of his system was a Platonic conception: that the world is a copy or material counterpart of an ordered hierarchy of ideas existing in the mind of God.[1] All that logic need do, therefore, is to draw up an account of how things follow one another in nature, and if the account corresponds to the way things actually are, men can safely act upon it.[2] The generalized concepts of the mind, the principles of "art," are not human constructions, not mere hypotheses or useful categories, but eternal and inviolable ideas, the authentic realities upon which the world is constructed. Truth therefore becomes for the Ramist, and through him for the Puritan, clear-eyed perception of immutable essences, beauty becomes correspondence to them, virtue becomes conformity to them. The method of discovering them is inward; they exist not only in nature but in the human intelligence, and though much study and caution are necessary in deriving them from the mind, since the mind is corrupted by sin, and the rules of logic must always preside over the formulating of them, still the soul contains an intuitive knowledge of the eternal truths, which truths also govern the world.[3]

The Ramean logic therefore was not so much what we think of as logic as it was a grouping of all the ideas, sensations, causes, and perceptions in the world, laying them out in a simple and symmetrical pattern, so that a diagram of the logic with its divisions and subdivisions was practically a blueprint of the universe. It was a simple scheme, but it was also, Ramus insisted, true and useful. Indeed, his emphasis was possibly more upon its utility than upon its simplicity or truth, and there were many dialectical

[1] For the impact of Plato on Ramus, see Waddington, pp. 24–27, 35; in the sixteenth century he was called "the French Plato" (Graves, p. 92). Of course the "Platonic" conception of a world built upon ideas or exempla in the mind of God was part and parcel of the Christian tradition, and Puritans held it as much because of Augustine as because of Ramus; but since they already entertained the fundamental belief, Ramus' logic was all the more acceptable to them.

[2] Cf. "Ars igitur naturam sibi propositam semper habeat, exercitatio artem" (Art therefore always pre-supposes nature, as exercise does art), Waddington, p. 368.

[3] Ramus said that man has in himself naturally the power to know all things, and that when he sets before his eyes the art of thinking according to these innate universal concepts, it will show him as in a mirror the universal and generalized images of all things, so that he can then recognize by them the singular species and find a place for every thing in the cosmology, though Ramus adds that many examples, hard work, and long usage are necessary to polish the mirror before it will be able to supply the images of the universals (Waddington, p. 370).

Gordian knots which he endeavored to cut rather than untangle, so that the permanent value of his contribution to the science of thought is not great. But the very utility of his system assured men of the early seventeenth century that it must be true, and Puritans seized upon it avidly. Ramus believed that he derived the guiding principle of his groupings and classifications from Plato, the principle of "dichotomy," that is, that all ideas and things go in pairs, like the animals into the ark, because the world is symmetrical. Thus logic itself is divided into halves, in the first of which individual ideas or arguments are formulated, in the second put together in axioms and doctrines, just as grammar is divided into "etymology," the study of words, and "syntax," the putting of words together in sentences. Ideas in turn are divided into two sorts, those which establish themselves to our own experience and those which rest upon the authority of a witness, as do facts in history or the assertions of the Bible. The task of the logician (and the preacher must be a logician) was that of arranging everything in pairs under the proper rubrics. Thinking was not conceived as a method by which we compose our knowledge discovery by discovery, but as the unveiling of an ideal form. Knowledge was a schedule to be filled in, and this end, it seemed to Ramus and the Puritans, was best accomplished by pairing every idea and object with its counterpart, sun with moon, man with woman, cause with effect, subject with adjunct. When all existence was thus systematized, the problem of seeing the architecture of the whole, of grasping the diagram of the universe, became relatively simple. It consisted merely of arranging the pairs so that the more general came before the specific, the genus before the species, the important before the subsidiary. The final function of logic, as Ramus taught it, was "method." "That great and famous Martyr of France, *Peter Ramus*, held forth the light to others," said Increase Mather, and by that light he discovered the proper manner "wherein Scriptural Definitions and Distributions, expressing the Sum of the only true Christian Religion, are methodically disposed, according to the golden Rules of Art." [1] In defining the intellectual character of the New England Puritans, we must always exercise caution about calling them Calvinists. John Calvin's metaphysics were still Aristotelian and scholastic; New Englanders had thrown aside

[1] Preface to James Fitch, *The first Principles of the Doctrine of Christ* (Boston, 1679), Sig. A2, verso.

much of the philosophy which is implied at every point in Calvin's theology, and had taken up a system of which the implications were quite different.

The most striking example of the difference can be seen in the uses to which the Ramists put the logical procedures historically known as "disjunction" and "hypothesis." When Ramus had arrayed all things and all ideas in pairs, he found that while some pairs harmonize with each other, as do cause and effect, others set up oppositions, as do night and day, true and false, in and out. Therefore he provided a large place in his plan for serried ranks of opposites or contraries, all of which he classified according to his system of dichotomies. His principal English commentator admitted freely that the doctrine of diversities was to be found only in Ramus,[1] but in a fashion characteristic of the Ramists, asserted that if the example of reason and experience were observed, the necessity for the doctrine would become clear at once. The reason other logicians had conspired against it, he said, was that scholastic logic had been enslaved by the syllogism, and the Aristotelians had striven to confine all thinking processes to the three figures of the syllogism as defined by Aristotle. Thus one of the chief grudges of the Ramists against Aristotle was the tyranny of the syllogism; Ramus assigned it a very minor role in his "method," where it served upon occasion merely to clear up individual arguments, so that they could be placed in their proper place in the grand sequence. As he debased the syllogism, he exalted the doctrine of contraries; ideas could be immediately distinguished by setting them against their opposites; a good could be defined by placing it against the corresponding evil, and thus sounder conclusions could be reached in the twinkling of an eye than in whole centuries of fruitless disputation with the cumbersome form of the syllogism.[2]

Ramus did not limit the doctrine of opposites to single ideas. If the principle of instantaneous recognition of contraries by the human mind would serve to sort out particular ideas and words, it would serve as well for more complex alternatives, for immediate adjudication between opposing doctrines as well as between opposing words. The Renaissance logician did not distinguish be-

[1] "Diversorum doctrina ab omnibus praeter Ramum Logicis omissa est," George Downame, *Commentarii* (London, 1669), p. 129.

[2] For the scheme of opposites, disparates, and contraries, see Ramus, *Dialecticae*, pp. 10–14; Milton, *Artis Logicae*, pp. 36–54; Johnson, *Technologia*, pp. 74–76.

tween a fact, an idea, or a doctrine to the extent of treating them as different logical counters; an opposition could be set up between black and white, bad and good, salvation by works and salvation by faith. In each case the mind was simply called upon to say which of the two corresponded to the divine order. The way to test the truth of a statement was to ask oneself a question: it is either thus and so or it is not, which? Or else the way was to suppose it true and see if it would prove itself, by saying, if it is so, then such and such must follow, and if such and such is true, then the statement must be true. The methods of disjunction and hypothesis probably take their origin from Plato, whether or not Ramus derived them from him. They are certainly methods that follow obviously from a belief in the Platonic world, where all things are ranged in a hierarchy of ideas and the philosophical problem is to sort the genus into species and the species into subspecies. The Ramists proclaimed that Ramus' rehabilitation of disjunction and hypothesis was his greatest contribution to logic; Ramus himself insisted that they be elevated to the title of "syllogisms"; calling the three conventional Aristotelian syllogisms "simple" ones, he denominated disjunction and hypothesis "composite." He remarked that "composite" syllogisms were the ones men actually used most frequently, and that this fact alone justified the dignity with which he invested them.[1] His English expositor was still more aggressive; admitting that the authority of Aristotle was opposed to composite syllogisms, Downame exultantly declared that nevertheless Aristotle himself used them again and again, once in the very passage in which he denied their validity, that furthermore the practice of the best writers and above all of the Bible itself thoroughly exonerated them.[2] Therefore if the Holy Ghost thought by means of composite syllogisms, students of Ramus considered that they were free to employ them on every occasion, and New England divines believed that a conclusion established by their aid was as strong as one confirmed by Holy Writ.

If we turn to a Puritan textbook, written according to the "golden rules" of art as taught by Petrus Ramus, we can perceive what the Ramean revolution in logic meant in practice. For example, in the book for the preface of which Increase Mather wrote the praise of Ramus already quoted, the author, James

[1] Ramus, *Dialecticae*, pp. 44–46; Johnson, *Technologia*, pp. 93–95.
[2] Downame, *Commentarii*, p. 448.

Fitch, pastor at Norwich, Connecticut, discusses the question whether the world was created or is eternal. The scholastic way of settling this inquiry would have been through the syllogism; a schoolman might argue, for example, all temporal things are made, the world is a temporal thing, ergo, the world is made.[1] He would seek to rehearse Aristotle's complicated argument for the first unmoved mover of all things, and would spend much time refuting all other propositions. But the disciple of Ramus puts all this aside as superfluous and inconclusive. He says that by using demonstrations of this sort it would be equally easy to prove that there is a continuous and eternal succession of motions, with no necessity for a first unmoved mover. Instead of employing "simple" syllogisms, the Ramist invokes the "composite" and solves the disjunctive by the hypothetical. He asks himself the question, the world was either made or not made, which? Then he answers himself to his own complete satisfaction: if it was not made, then there was no cause for its being, there is no design in it, no end for which it exists, and any man in his senses knows that these are absurd conclusions. Ergo, the world was made. Then he continues his self-interrogation, it was either made by God, or it made itself. Hypothesis demonstrates at once that the second alternative is untenable, and so the Ramist triumphantly concludes that God must have made it.[2]

Undoubtedly the Ramean logic was much too facile, and when it was employed by shallow minds that were utterly unskilled in the more noble if more tortuous logic of the schoolmen, it produced a breed of disputants so fascinated by their own logic-chopping they could not see the open fallacies in their method. Yet whether the Ramean logic was a good one or a bad one does not concern us; historically speaking, the importance of such reasoning as that of James Fitch is its recurrent appeal to an innate, *a priori* knowledge. He does not attempt to establish an invincible case in the void, but to establish a case which no human being in possession of his wits can deny. The syllogism strikes

[1] It is interesting to note that the greatest of the scholastics found the assertion of this very proposition impossible to establish by rational demonstration and was constrained to rest his case with a demonstration that no arguments for the negative were any better than those for the affirmative (St. Thomas Aquinas, *Summa Contra Gentiles*, Bk. II, chaps. XXXI–XXXVIII); where the Angelic Doctor treads cautiously through many pages of his most wary reasoning, the Puritan pastor confidently rushes in to "prove" the point in a paragraph.

[2] James Fitch, *The first Principles*, p. 17.

downward vertically, so to speak, driving the mind before it, where disjunction extends horizontally for the contemplation of self-reflecting intelligence. The Ramean logic is the logic of a *Humanist*, the conclusions come from within, they are not reached by piling one brick upon another in a shaky and top-heavy sequence, but by the prompt and decisive arbitration of the natural reason between two possibilities. Puritan preachers and disputants would use the syllogism wherever they found it profitable; more often they would establish their points by the use of disjunction, by ruling out the alternative which all men, on the strength of their native intelligence, would be compelled to admit could not hold water.[1]

Thus when John Cotton spoke of an "essentiall wisdome in us, namely, our Reason which is natural," he was speaking from his Ramean training. What such an assumption might lead to in a man's philosophy can readily enough be seen, at least in broad outline. For if the way to test the truth of things is by the measure of a rationality implicit in man, then there must be an inherent rationality in things, in the mind, in the order of the universe; only if this is so can a careful examination of the in-

[1] The rule of disjunction was crystallized into a number of convenient aphorisms which practitioners of the logic repeatedly cited as the ultimate in human wisdom. Thus Milton says, improving on Ramus, "Itaque ex altero affirmato alterum negatur" (Thus by the one affirmed the other is negated), or "Ex affirmatione unius, necessario sequitur negatio alterius" (From affirmation of the one there follows necessarily negation of the other), *Artis Logicae*, pp. 40–41. Johnson has it, "Hic etiam fictum arguet alterum verum" (For this being a fiction argues the other true), *Technologia*, p. 76. Samuel Willard, giving a young scholar directions for studying for the ministry, tells him that he must learn the wrong doctrines as well as the right ones, reduce all to their proper heads and ascertain their opposites; he then quotes the Ramean commonplace, "Quibus Argumentis Veritas astruitur, iisdem Falsitas destruitur" (By the same arguments with which truth is established, falsity is destroyed), *Brief Directions to a Young Scholar Designing the Ministry* (Boston, 1735), p. 4. How disjunction was used in actual sermons can be illustrated from Willard's method of proving that the righteousness of Christ is merely "imputed" to the elect for their legal justification and not "infused" directly into them, as the Antinomians claimed: "That the individual and personal Righteousness of Christ cannot be infused into a Believer, is a truth so plain and necessary, that to assert the contrary, is to speak a contradiction, and therefore if it be any way ours, it must needs be imputed to us. Everyone that knows anything of the nature of things" knows that the acts of one man cannot be infused into another, but, Willard says, "on the other hand, this is a notion that is very well agreeing with common reason, that another did such a thing for this man, such as one paid a Debt for him," *A Brief Discourse of Justification* (Boston, 1686), p. 65. Thus, thanks to Ramus' doctrine of opposites and his glorification of "composite" syllogisms, the actual arbiter in New England theology, time and time again, was not Calvin, not even the Bible, so much as it was "plain and necessary truth," the "nature of things," or "common reason."

tellect, a checking of all propositions by the instinctive knowledge of the soul, result in finding the true propositions. Therefore the way to avoid "paralogizing" yourself is to consult, with scrupulous care and dispassionate honesty, the essential wisdom within yourself, which, being natural and true, will enable you to reason correctly.[1] The material world is transitory and deceptive, the passions of men ebb and flow, men make mistakes, accidents happen, and God can override or turn aside all natural processes; but something eternal and immutable does exist, and by that we must live. There are a number of propositions, fitting together into a harmonious whole, upon which things are built, to which they correspond, which they must follow, which they do follow even when to earthly eyes they seem to be accidental and fortuitous. The sum total of these eternal propositions, the completed system of truth, exists only in the mind of God, but that it does exist we know, because we in small part share in it; some of the divine truth does exist in our minds. In the counsel of God, so the argument runs—a clear consequence of this Ramean position —there must be this "idea or pattern of well acting"; hence God in acting follows it of his own free choice, and he therefore must create his creatures in accordance with this pattern; "and that wisdome in the creatures is imprinted, and is the impression or Image of it." Hence the "rules of art," the rules that God follows in organizing and governing the world, the rules that enable us to tell which of the disjunctive alternatives must be wrong and which is clearly right, these rules of art must be eternal, though all material objects which exemplify them are transitory and illusory. Though men are unstable and life is full of pitfalls, there is a divine wisdom that governs and controls all. "The definitions of things are eternal Truths, whatever becomes of the things themselves." [2]

There can be no doubt that this way of thinking is a species

[1] Cf. "An Dentur Ideae innatae" (Whether there exist innate ideas), affirmed by John Whiting at the Commencement of 1703 (Quaestiones No. 2), Morison, *Harvard College in the Seventeenth Century*, Appendix B.

[2] Fitch, *The first Principles*, p. 15. Cf. among the Harvard theses: "Veritas est conformitas intellectus cum re" (Truth is intellectual conformity with fact, 1643 Theses Metaphysicae No. 5); "Artium praecepta sunt aeternae veritatis" (The precepts of the arts are of eternal truth, 1653 Theses Technologicae No. 3); "Utrum Detur Idaea omnium Entium in primo Ente" (Whether there exists an idea of all beings in the primary being, 1664 Quaestiones No. 2) affirmed by Nathaniel Chauncy; "Non ab artifice Ars, sed ab arte artifex creatur" (The art is not created by the artisan, but the artisan by the art, 1678 Theses Technologicae No. 13); "Idea est res percepta, prout est in intellectu objective" (An idea is a thing perceived, as it is objectively in the

of Platonism. It is a method of establishing the pre-existence of ideas, or of a divine pattern, to which the world roughly conforms and by which all movement and contingency are to be ex-

intellect, 1687 Theses Technologicae No. 2); "Praecepta Artium non formamus, sed formata invenimus" (We do not form the precepts of the arts, but come upon them formed, 1693 Theses Technologicae No. 5). Samuel Johnson began his summary of the system with the central doctrine of the Ramean logic: "Artem suos reflectere radios in intellectum intelligentis creaturae ab antiquissimes, ideoque cum intelligente creatura reflexum suum habere ortum manifeste apparet . . ." (It is manifest that art has reflected its rays into the intellect of intelligent creatures from greatest antiquity, and therefore has its reflex origin in the intelligent creature); he distinguishes between "art," i.e., logic, as it exists in the mind of God, which he calls "archetypal" and describes as the idea of things decreed in the divine intelligence, and art as it exists in the visible world, which he calls "typal" and describes as manifesting itself on the one hand in the ideas impressed upon the creature and on the other in the rules gathered from the actions and operations of things by the senses, observations and experience (Johnson, *Technologia*, pp. 58–68). Josiah Flynt, graduating in 1664, published the almanac for 1666 and presented therein an argument similar to that already quoted from James Fitch concerning the creation of the world; here in the one publication designed for popular consumption the citizens of Massachusetts Bay were given a succinct statement of Puritan Platonism:

". . . The *Divine Idea* (If I speak in the dialect of some learned and pious) being God contemplating himself as imitable in the creatures fabrick, or as it were capable to receive the impression of the *Image* or *Vestigium* of those divine perfections which were in himself; it follows that whatever perfection was eminently in God, and the creature was Analogically capable of, was according to divine wisdome expressed (for otherwise the *Idea* or *Exemplar* would not have been consentaneous to the *τό πραττόμενον*)" (Morison, *Harvard College in the Seventeenth Century*, p. 278).

Note the decisive use of disjunction in the last sentence. The *πραττόμενον* means roughly the achieving, the realization, the passing over of the ideal into actualization. It was this Platonic conception of a realm of eternal and pure ideas passing into realization in a realm of matter which made possible the Puritan hierarchy of values—from those of sense to those of Reason, from those of Reason to those of Faith. Thus Fitch expounded it:

"Reason in a believer is a means to let in a light and good beyond Reason, that as the senses are means to present the Reason in things to the Reason of man, although Reason is above Sense, so Reason is a means to present a divine good unto Faith, though that divine good is above Reason, but as Reason can use the *Prattomenon* of the Rule of Sense, (namely) that which is effected by it, so Faith can use the Prattomenon of the Rule of Reason, that which is effected by it, and yet these are distinct arts, and have distinct Objects, and distinct lights" (*The first Principles*, p. 4). For the philosophical significance of Platonism in the thought of the early seventeenth century, see Etienne Gilson, *Études sur le Role de la pensée médiéval dans la formation du système Cartésien*, especially pp. 30–36, 48, 193–201. To characterize the Puritans as "Platonists" may create more confusion than clarification, because Platonism has come to be a battleground of interpretation; yet if we accept Platonism in the definition of Dean Inge—"the conception of an unseen world, of which the visible world is but a pale copy"—we can list the Puritans in that camp. This is, of course, to say no more than that they were in the main stream of Christian tradition; in order to determine what special species of the Platonic genus we may call New England Puritanism we must consider the actual background, the modifying influences of the environment, with the "climate of opinion" in the seventeenth century, and the climate, meteorological and mental, of the new world. But it should be noted that if Puritanism is Platonic in that plained. The Ramean logic might be said to be one of the several forms in which Platonism was revived in the Renaissance and enlisted in the humanists' and the theologians' battle with scholasticism. But without pursuing the philosophical problem too far afield, we can for the moment rest with this reflection, that the humanist strain in Puritan culture, represented by the classical authors and the logic of Petrus Ramus, made for the conception of a fundamental rationality in the universe and in the mind of man. Because the Puritans were humanists, they could not rest in a belief that God's decrees were nothing but arbitrary fiats. They held that God was indeed sovereign and absolute lord, but not entirely a capricious, ruthless, unpredictable tyrant. They held that man was indeed caught in the toils of sin, but they did not hold that he was so empty a creature that he needed to be filled with grace in any such crude fashion as a toy balloon is filled with air. In his fallen state he still can test the validity of reasons and reach a vision, if only a sort of distant perception, of the serene order that really prevails. The grace of God, which is a special and additional imparting of His spirit to man, whose reason is already endowed with some inklings of the divine nature, this grace is not some emotional cataclysm, an attack of the jerks, an agitation "with Antick and uncouth motions." [1] On the contrary it is an elevation of reason, a freshening and quickening of the understanding; it is an imparting to man of that spark of imagination and that breadth of insight whereby he can at last perceive in part, and apprehend in the rest, the essential unity of life, and the essential reasonableness of things. As a great Puritan preacher put it, John Preston, who was the Master of Emmanuel College at Cambridge, England, and who was looked upon as one of their chief intellectual progenitors by New Englanders, divine grace "elevateth reason, and makes it higher, it makes it see further than reason could, it is contrary indeed to corrupt reason, but to reason that is right reason, it is not contrary, only it raiseth it higher: And therefore faith teacheth nothing contrary to sense and reason." [2] Thomas Hooker told his congregations that conversion made "things appear as they be," that the regenerate man is the man who at last understands

it was occupied with the detemporalized hierarchy of ideas, it is not that sort of Platonism that looks upon the visible world as mere illusion, utterly unreal, or absolutely evil.

[1] Norton, *Heart of N-England Rent*, p. 6.

[2] *The Cuppe of Blessing* (London, 1633), p. 13.

what he already knows, or could have known, in his reason: "look what the truth determines, reason approves, and Conscience witnesseth . . . Such judg not by outward appearance as it is the guise of men of corrupt minds, but upon experience, that which they have found and felt in their own hearts." [1] At the end of the century a Puritan minister is still insisting, "Spiritual Light received in Conversion, strengthens the reason of men, and makes the law of nature more legible." [2] A few decades more, and there would be ministers who insisted that spiritual light was something entirely different from the reason of man and quite other than the law of nature; and consequently other ministers would reply that in that case spiritual light must be insanity, and that if they had to choose they preferred the reason of men and the law of nature. The seamless garment of Puritanism thus was rent, and the edifice erected by the founders in order to justify God's ways to man was riven in two; in the one half came to dwell those who no longer made any effort to *justify* God's ways, and in the other those who preferred to set up the ways of man for approbation and imitation by the divinity.

In this fashion, then, Puritanism attempted to appropriate the heritage of humanism and to embody it in a system of Christian belief and a theological conception of the world. It did not turn its back upon the new literary learning, as it did not turn its back upon the still newer scientific learning that burgeoned during the century. Puritanism was an outgrowth of the advanced culture of its day; its basic ideas as to the function of the human mind and the responsibilities of the human soul were common to Christendom at the time, its fundamental doctrines were common to Protestantism at the time, the texture and range of its learning were common to educated opinion of the time, its struggle to maintain homogeneity in religious thought, to unify religion and knowledge, was common to all devout and intelligent men of the time. Thinking men were all in one way or another still dominated by the medieval tradition of unity, and could break away from the scholastic formulation of that unity only by endeavoring to achieve another formulation in more satisfactory terms. The chief elements in Puritan culture, therefore, the foundations of Puritan thought, "ninety per cent" of its ideas, roughly speaking, are to be accounted for by a study of the age and background.

[1] *The Application of Redemption*, p. 557.
[2] Solomon Stoddard, *The Danger of Speedy Degeneracy* (Boston, 1705), p. 11.

But we are still left with the question: What then was the essence of Puritanism, apart from beliefs and opinions common to others in the period, what was this precious "ten per cent" that made the difference? What particular devices did the Puritans employ in formulating the unity of knowledge and religion which divided them sharply and fatally from the Anglicans? For if the war between the Puritans and the Church of England was an engagement between men who, from our point of view at least, were agreed on the larger assumptions, the concrete issue must be narrowed down to a difference of deduction from those premises. The evidence of history goes to show that the bitterest and most furious combats are generally fought between those who agree on fundamentals, for there is no greater annoyance that a man can suffer than attack from persons who accord with him in the main, but who apply his principles to conclusions utterly foreign to his liking. Puritanism started from the background and the beliefs we have been outlining; it then worked its way to certain concrete applications, and it was these specific deductions that made Puritanism Puritanical.

4. The Essential Issue

Where Puritanism and the Church of England at last parted company, after marching abreast over so immense a terrain, may conveniently be illustrated if we begin with a statement of William Laud himself, the Archbishop of Canterbury and the archfoe of the Puritans, whose head they finally chopped off. In 1622 Laud, then Bishop of London, held a conference with a Jesuit, in the course of which he drew up an excellent statement of the position of the Church of England. Inevitably the nub of this debate was the authority of scripture, and Laud set forth the grounds upon which the Protestant, believing still in the unity of reason and faith, maintaining the harmony of knowledge and belief, could nevertheless anchor his whole system to the arbitrary word of God, to the ukase of revelation handed down from on high by the absolute Tsar of the universe. The Catholic was arguing that if the authority of the Universal Church were disowned, the Bible would prove an inadequate substitute, because the Bible would become subject to interpretation, no two men would agree on what it meant, Protestantism would split into a hundred differing sects, each one twisting Biblical meanings to suit its own convenience, and thus scripture would lose all the necessary attributes of an authority. Laud answered that there was no danger of this happening in Protestant thought, because the authority of the Bible was established by a logical necessity. In every science, he said, certain principles outside its own limits must be supplied before the science can proceed; geometry must be built upon *a priori* axioms, that the whole is greater than the part, etc. The basic principles of the sciences are "given" in the natural reason—exactly as Ramus demonstrates. But in divinity, which is the science of the divine, the basic principles must come from the divine, and therefore must be given, if at all, by God. Consequently, unless Protestants abandoned theology entirely, which was not possible for Laud to imagine, they would always proceed in the science of theology upon divine axioms, laid down by God, believed exactly as all axioms are believed, because, though they cannot be demonstrated to be true, yet no thinking can go on unless they are true. The axioms enacted by God are accepted by faith. The Bible is believed, not on the authority of any Church, but because it must be believed; nothing will "prove" that the scripture is divine, it must be believed to be divine. But there are, however, some natural or rational testimonies helping to establish the fact that scripture is divinely inspired; these considerations do not prove it, but they help to convince men. These are: the tradition of the Church, the testimony of other ages, consent of many men, the harmony of the prophets, the success Biblical teachings have enjoyed in the world, the constancy and consistency of the doctrine, the inward light and excellency of the text. Hence, though the authority of scripture cannot be proved, and is basically a matter of faith, rational arguments may be used, for "grace is never planted but in a reasonable creature, and proves by the very seat which it hath taken up that the end it hath is to be spiritual eye-water, to make reason see what 'by nature only it cannot,' but never to blemish reason in that which it can, 'comprehend.' "[1]

Now taking this argument just as it stands, any Puritan would gladly have subscribed to it. He might not stress the tradition of the Church quite so emphatically as Laud did among the rational confirmations of the authority of scripture; but that scripture was to be accepted by faith, and yet no violence to be done to reason, that reason actually proved the necessity for the faith

[1] More and Cross, *Anglicanism*, pp. 97–103.

and endorsed it with almost infallibly convincing testimonies—this was the argument of the Puritan as well as of the bishop. But the Puritan then and there challenged the bishop to be as good as his word. If the bishop submitted to the Bible as God's word, received it by faith and reinforced his faith with rational convictions—very well then, let him accept it and act accordingly. Let him not, once he has established its authority, then turn about and explain away a good part of it, invent reasons to prove that only some portions are God's law, that the Bible is not binding in every point on which it speaks, but merely on some few. If the Bible declares God is three persons in one, let that be believed, said the Puritan; if the Bible says that wigs are an abomination unto the Lord, let that also be believed.

And there the Anglican protested, and the fight commenced. For to him it seemed absurd to imagine that God, the sovereign of sovereigns, would take the time, would demean himself, to tell men whether or not they should wear wigs. He could not imagine that everything in the Bible, every incidental history, every minute circumstance, was intended by God to be universally and literally binding on all men. God had inspired the book in order that the fundamental and comprehensive truths of religion might be set down; he had inspired individual men at particular times and places to write it, and they had written in their particular dialects and told a great many things that were of only temporary importance. The difference between the Anglican and the Puritan, then, was that the Puritan thought the Bible, the revealed word of God, was the word of God from one end to the other, a complete body of laws, an absolute code in everything it touched upon; the Anglican thought this a rigid, doctrinaire, and utterly unjustifiable extension of the authority of scripture. The Puritan held that the Bible was sufficiently plain and explicit so that men with the proper learning, following the proper rules of deduction and interpretation, could establish its meaning and intention on every subject, not only in theology, but in ethics, costume, diplomacy, military tactics, inheritances, profits, marriages, and judicial procedure. The Anglican position, set forth supremely in Richard Hooker's *Of the Laws of Ecclesiastical Polity*, was simply that the Bible is God's revealed word only on the broad principles of the Christian religion, that in all minor matters, God has not intended to set up ironclad rules for men, but to leave them to the discretion of their reason, to the considerations of circumstance and propriety, to the determinations of proportion and decency. In His providence, in His government of events, through the reason He has instilled in man, through the law which governs nature, God can and does teach men; in the Bible He is concerned only with those things which they could not otherwise learn from these sources.

> Let them with whom we have hitherto disputed consider well, how it can stand with reason to make the bare mandate of sacred Scripture the only rule of all good and evil in the actions of mortal men. The testimonies of God are true, the testimonies of God are perfect, the testimonies of God are all sufficient unto that end for which they were given. Therefore accordingly we do receive them, we do not think that in them God hath omitted anything needful unto his purpose, and left his intent to be accomplished by our devisings.[1]

If the Puritan contention were correct, that the Bible is the supreme and absolute law, says the Anglican Hooker, then the law of nature and the law of reason would be effectually abrogated; they would become useless, because we would need to search scripture at every juncture and would never dare trust ourselves to decide anything on any other grounds. "In every action of common life to find out some sentence clearly and infallibly setting before our eyes what we ought to do, (seem we in Scripture never so expert) would trouble us more than we are aware." [2] The Anglican was accusing the Puritan of narrow-minded literalism, pointing out that if he had the effrontery to assume that his and only his interpretation of scripture was correct, and to set himself up as dictator to all other men on a host of points upon which God intended men to follow their own discretion, custom or political expediency, then the Puritan was guilty of arrogance and pride. "This Disciplinarian humor," said one bishop, "which will admit no latitude in religion, but makes each nicety a fundamental, and every private opinion an article of Faith." [3] Another Anglican cleric said that to give men the power of saying what scripture does and does not mean makes them "to be as much lawgivers to the Church by their uncontrolable law-interpreting, as any Pope or enthusiast can or need

[1] Book II, chap. VIII, par. 5.
[2] *Ibid.*, par. 6.
[3] More and Cross, *Anglicanism*, p. 80.

pretend to be."[1] The Puritan replied, in effect, that if the Anglican said that the Bible was the word of God, and then put aside anything in the Bible which he did not like by saying this or that particular law or precedent was peculiar to the historical circumstances and was not part of the eternal law of the Christian religion, then it was certainly the Anglican who was setting himself up to be the lawgiver and the tyrant; he was perverting the law of God to his own purposes by sophistry and fine distinctions, he did not really believe in the Bible at all, he was playing fast and loose with it and was no better than a skeptic or an atheist.

If the dispute had remained a merely academic one whether the authority of the Bible extended as far as the wearing or not wearing of wigs or hoop petticoats, New England would have remained somewhat longer in the possession of the Indians. But one of the most important discoveries made by the Puritan in his study of scripture was that it contained the perfect constitution for the organization of the visible church.[2] The Anglican denied this, and Richard Hooker wrote his book on the "laws" of ecclesiastical polity to prove that there were many kinds of laws which men were to follow in different connections, and that in ecclesiastical government they were not to follow the Bible at all, because Christ had left the form of the church to be determined by political considerations, by the particular traditions of each country, and by the principles of aesthetic judgment. Thus the argument involved very important elements in the state and society; conservatives, satisfied with things as they were, saw in Puritan radicalism a serious threat to the vested interests; those dissatisfied with the *status quo* welcomed for social as well as for religious reasons the Puritan condemnation of the episcopal hierarchy, with its wealth, its monopoly of advantages, and its alliance with the Court and the aristocracy. Political passions and economic grievances increased the tension. In the 1640's both sides appealed to the sword and the God of battles, but before the actual outbreak had come, when Charles I had dismissed his parliament and was apparently launched upon an era of absolute rule by and with the aid of the bishops, a small band of particularly earnest Puritans, fearing that the divine church polity could never be established in England, secured a charter from the king giving them title to land in Massachusetts Bay. They moved

[1] *Ibid.*, p. 91.
[2] Perry Miller, *Orthodoxy in Massachusetts* (Cambridge, 1933), chap. II.

themselves and their families thither, in order that under a government of their own constituting, the form of church government ordained by Christ might be set up, and His faithful saints might worship him in the precise manner He had decreed.

At this point certain doubts might justifiably arise in the mind of the reader concerning what has just been said about the Puritan emphasis upon reason and scholarship. If after all the Puritan erected the Bible into a hard and fast body of arbitrary law, then it might seem that the function of his reason must amount to the very inferior one of deducing concrete applications from a miscellaneous collection of arbitrary dicta, and his scholarship simply consist in the administration of a number of imposed statutes. Certainly, it was to this that Richard Hooker felt the role of the intellect would be reduced if the Puritan had his way, and the fact of the matter is that in many cases, in such unimaginative and pedantic Puritans as Cotton Mather, the solemn invocation of scriptural sanctions for decisions about the minutiae of daily life became nothing short of ludicrous. But Cotton Mather was a case for a psychiatrist in any event, and is not, fortunately, very representative of Puritanism as a whole, a fact which it is hoped these selections will make clear. The Puritan's attitude toward the Bible was called fanatical by his opponents, but it was not the worship of the book in a naïve or infatuated spirit. It was an acceptance of the Bible as revealed law from an absolute sovereign, but the law of that sovereign was not therefore erected against all reason, science, and natural wisdom. Puritanism was not, as we have said, "fundamentalism"; its conflict with the Church of England was, on the purely intellectual side, a difference in definition concerning the spheres of reason and faith, and of their connection.

As we attempt to ascertain the difference, we should remember that from now on it becomes increasingly difficult to speak of the Anglican argument as though one train of thought were common to all apologists for the Church of England, at that time or at any time since. The very freedom which Richard Hooker allowed to the reason and the intelligence made possible a variety of attitudes; Churchmen differed among themselves concerning how much or how little of the Bible was to be accounted the eternal law of God, or how much weight was to be given to the other sanctions of thought and conduct, whether more to the law or to reason or to the traditions of the Church. But if we take Hooker, and some one of his successors in the moderate and well-considered vein, Jeremy Taylor for instance, and look upon them as representative, simply because they avoided the extremes either of the "high-church" party of Laud, or of the "low-church" party of Ussher, we may safely compare them with the Puritans in order to define more precisely the exact nature of the Puritan thought.

From the description we have already given of Richard Hooker's volume, it becomes clear that he is stressing the multiformity of the revelation of God's will. As though the divinity were a great light, a sun of illumination, various rays emanate in various directions, each of them a partial revelation of his character. One of these rays is the law of reason, one the law of nature, one the conception of beauty, one His daily providence; and among these rays another one, important indeed, but only one among the others, is the Bible. This is no doubt an over-simplified statement of Hooker's very subtle position, but it will serve; it is the idea which, in one way or another, underlies almost all Anglican thinking in the seventeenth century, and it is the belief above all others that the Puritans could never swallow.

In a portentous volume called *Ductor Dubitantium*,[1] a guide for troubled consciences in some 1400 pages, published by Jeremy Taylor in 1659, this liberal and eloquent clergyman, occupying the leisure forced upon him by the reign of Oliver Cromwell, deliberately devised for the Church of England a book of practical divinity, a manual for the solution of ethical puzzles, because, for one reason, the Puritans, with their direct application of Scripture to the affairs of ordinary life, had seemed far to excel the Anglican divines in casuistical writing.[2] Before entering into particular cases, Taylor endeavored to demonstrate how first of all men might ascertain the regulations to which their consciences should conform. The measure and rule should be, he says, the law of God, but the law of God is not promulgated merely and solely in the Bible; it is also to be found in the law of nature, in the articles to which all nations have consented, in

[1] Vols. IX and X of *Works*, under general editorship of Reginald Heber, edited by Alexander Taylor (London, 1851).

[2] Taylor cites as his predecessors in this sort of divinity the work of William Perkins, William Ames, and Johann Heinrich Alsted; Perkins and Ames were English Puritans, both much read in America; Ames was intimately associated with many of the founders of Massachusetts and the book to which Taylor refers, Ames's *De Conscientia*, was the Puritan manual of casuistry throughout the seventeenth century. A comparison of this volume with Taylor's will tell the whole story of the two types of minds. Alsted was a Calvinist professor at Herborn and at Weissemburg, the author of a great encyclopedia

right reason, in laws ecclesiastical and civil, in popular proverbs, and in the wisdom of great poets.[1] The larger number of the rules which men are to obey, Taylor insists, come from these sources; the number to be derived from the Bible should be kept down to the bare minimum of those essential truths which cannot be learned from the other instructors, and the validity of much of scripture, at least in morality, is actually that it expresses felicitously what the other texts already have taught. "The best portions of scripture, even the law of Jesus Christ, which in moral things is the eternal law of nature, is written in our hearts, is reason, and that wisdom to which we cannot choose but assent." [2] The fundamental discriminations of right and wrong are such that all men must acknowledge them, "so long as a man is in his wits, and hath the natural use of reason." [3] The natural man, unless he is insane or diseased, can and does grasp these fundamentals; [4] most of his mistakes come in the application, where he is misled through ignorance or by evil customs. The way to correct him is not to bring down upon him the crushing weight of a pretended Biblical condemnation, but to discover the province in which his error lies, whether in reason or nature or civil law, and to put him to rights according to the legislation of that domain. "Every thing must be derived from its own fountain." [5]

Against this method of instructing men's consciences, Taylor continues, the Puritans protest because they say it puts reason before the Bible, and they offer instead to draw up a set of rules straight from the Bible to cover almost all moral problems. They say that we must not start with what is reasonable, and then find that the law of Christ is like unto it, but with the law of Christ, and then we must abide by it, whether it seems reasonable or not. This, says Taylor, is to make a separation between what is reasonable and what is revealed. That such a discrepancy can even imaginably exist Taylor denies emphatically.[6] He will admit that human reason is below God and cannot understand all that God is, but everything that God reveals to men must be

of the arts and of a summa of cases of conscience (1628), standard works of reference in New England (Morison, *Harvard College in the Seventeenth Century*, p. 158). The *Ductor Dubitantium*, therefore, is doubly interesting for our purposes, since it was written to supply what Taylor thought were the deficiencies in works which were the received authority in New England.

[1] *Ibid.*, IX, 13.
[2] *Ibid.*, p. 69.
[3] *Ibid.*, p. 41.
[4] *Ibid.*, pp. 29, 34.
[5] *Ibid.*, p. 60.
[6] *Ibid.*, pp. 67–68.

comprehensible to the reason, for the reason of man must come from the same God who gives the revelation. "If reason cannot consent to it when it is told of it, then it is nothing, it hath no being, it hath no possibility." [1] Therefore one cannot say of any proposition, it is against scripture and therefore against reason, "because reason is before revelation, and that this is revealed by God must be proved by reason"; but if we will define carefully and accurately what is reasonable, we are then empowered to assert that what is against reason must, *ipse facto,* be against the word of God. For, says Taylor in conclusion,

> when both sides agree that these are the words of God, and the question of faith is concerning the meaning of the words, nothing is an article of faith, or a part of religion, but what can be proved by reason to be the sense and intentions of God. Reason is never to be pretended against the clear sense of scripture, because by reason it is that we came to perceive that to be the clear sense of scripture.[2]

Taylor's argument is a permutation upon the theme announced by Richard Hooker. He is asserting the primacy of an eternal reason, which finds expression in nature, in the human intellect, experience, civil law, proverbs, and poetry; it also finds expression in the Bible. In order that there may be no conflict between the Bible and other manifestations of the immutable wisdom, Biblical teachings must be held to a minimum, and those few entertained as much as possible not because the Bible says so, but because they are clearly consistent with what men learn from all the sources of knowledge available to them.

If we now turn to the Puritan side of the debate, we shall find that Taylor's opponents have one all-important consideration to advance against his seductive pleading. If men had remained as they had been created, if they had retained the pristine innocence of creation fresh from the hand of God, then everything that Taylor says would be true. But the fact of the matter is—and by "fact" the Puritan meant not only in Christian theology but in experience—something has happened to mankind. History proves, and daily events confirm, that men are not naturally noble, reasonable, honest, kind, decent, or intelligent. Taylor's whole structure of moral instruction derived by the reasonable

[1] *Ibid.*, p. 71.
[2] *Ibid.*, p. 74.

being from natural and reasonable preceptors leaves out of account what John Cotton called "mans perverse subtilty in inventing wayes of backsliding." [1] Let human beings go free amid nature, let them read the poets and memorize the proverbs, induce them to examine their hearts for an instinctive knowledge of right and wrong, teach them what the wise and good of all nations have agreed on, and what will be the result? The same old chronicle of meanness and cruelty, bloodshed and robbery, hatred and betrayal, blunder and stupidity, which passes under the name of history. From such sources some men, like Socrates or Plutarch, may learn virtue and self-control, but only on the basis of calculation; the vast majority are totally incapable of leading the life of reason if they have only reason to inspire them. No man who knows a hawk from a handsaw can doubt for a moment "the depravation of nature, in the blindnesse of our minds: who are so far from discerning spiritual things . . . that we cannot rightly judge of moral or civil things." [2] If men are to act by the laws of right reason and in harmony with the laws of nature, they need something more than a knowledge of the laws; they must be infused with a power to keep and observe them, and only the grace of God can give it to them. Thomas Shepard said that there is a sort of knowledge which some men have "from the book of creation, some by power of education, some by the light of the law . . . some by the letter of the gospel, and so men may know much and speak well. . . ." But over against this there is quite another kind of knowledge which only the elect can acquire, whereby they "see things in another manner; to tell you how, they can not; it is the beginning of light in heaven." [3] The Puritan would not doubt that Taylor's method was admirable and his book a tribute to his own nobility of character, but the facts of life being what they are, his way of dealing with sin simply will not work; make the truth as clear as he may to the mind of man, and man "will bend the Truth to his mind though hee breake it." Thomas Hooker of Connecticut directly opposed Richard Hooker of Bishopshorne by insisting that the latter's splendid galleon of stately reason will wreck itself upon the shoals of human perversity:

[1] *A Briefe Exposition with Practicall Observations upon The Whole Book of Ecclesiastes* (London, 1654), p. 160.

[2] *Ibid.*, p. 131.

[3] *Works*, ed. John A. Albro (Boston, 1853), II, 235.

Though arguments be never so plaine, and Scriptures never so pregnant; yet a carnall wretch will carry himselfe against all, and say, it is not my judgement, I am not of that mind.[1]

The morality of mere right reason and behavior regulated by judicious analysis will not hold up very far or very long; it is not enough:

There is a weakness, impotencie and insufficiencie in the understanding to reach this right discovery of sin, for however there remaynes so much glimmering in the twilight of Natural reason, and so much sensibleness in the stupid benummedness of the corrupt conscience of a carnal man, that it can both see and sensibly check for some grosser evil, or some such sins, or venom of sin, as crosseth his own peace and Comfort, or those ends which he sets up as the chiefest good at which he aymes, but to search into the entrales of sin, and discern the spiritual composition of the accursed nature thereof, he can in no wise attayn this by all the labor and light he hath.[2]

In the Puritan view, which the Puritan pointed out was undeniably corroborated by the evidence of human affairs, men needed the aid of God to achieve what the innocent Jeremy Taylor naïvely assumed was their natural capacity.

But, it should be noted, the Puritan does not deny that truth can be discovered in nature, poetry, right reason, and the consent of nations. He does not deny that these things are emanations of God's wisdom and that from them men may gain all manner of valuable instruction. He does not doubt that there is a light of nature, which, he says, "consists in common principles imprinted upon the reasonable soul, by nature," and that man naturally inclines his assent to certain fundamental truths, not only such truths as that the whole is greater than the part, but that there is a God, that parents are to be honored, and that there is a great difference between what is good and what is bad. As we have seen, the whole methodology of Puritan logic, following the example of Ramus, was built upon the inner monitor that can tell which of any two alternatives is the right one. The discoveries of the natural reason are useful to men "as a help whence they might seek after God" and "for the preservation of humane society." What the Puritan does insist on is that the

[1] Thomas Hooker, *The Soules Humiliation* (London, 1638), pp. 147–148.

[2] Thomas Hooker, *The Application of Redemption*, pp. 43–44.

natural man, if left to himself, will not read the lessons of nature and reason correctly. "The little light that there is, is much miscarried[;] whilest it is managed by the reigning influence of the power of darkness the Judgment is corrupt as well as the will, whose corruption perverts the exercise of the faculty of reason." Therefore God must draw up for man in black and white an exhaustive and authoritative code of laws, where he can find them in terms adapted to his imperfect and benighted state, in clear and unmistakable bold-faced type:

Star-light cannot make it, otherwise then night. The light of nature since the fall, compared with the light of the image of God, before the fall, hath not the proportion of Star-light, to the bright Sun-light at noon-day. This indeed is but darkness. But, if compared with the light of the Gospell, it is worse then gross darkness.[1]

The laws of the Gospel, drawn up under these considerations, cannot be limited to a few fundamentals, but must be numerous enough to cover all the essential contingencies of life. Man was once left free to learn from reason and nature, and promptly abused the privilege; he must now submit his comprehension to the instituted law before he be allowed to seek meanings once more in the natural world. "Almost all the sin and misery that hath filled the World, hath broke in at this door, hearkning to reason against Institution." [2] The Biblical institution must fill the place man made empty through his own folly, and since he has thrown away his ability to profit from natural wisdom, he must have an explicit law imposed upon him.

Thus when we pursue the difference between the attitude of the Anglican and the Puritan toward the authority of scripture, we come upon a deeper difference in their attitude toward man. The Puritan believes as much as his opponent that the will of God is exhibited in the world of nature and in the processes of right reason, but in order for man to perceive it, there must be something added to him.

True it is that the Lord fills Heaven and Earth with his presence, yea, the Heaven of Heavens is not able to contain him. His infinite Being is every where, and one and the same every where in regard of himself; because his being is most simple, and

[1] Norton, *Heart of N-England Rent*, pp. 12–13.

[2] Samuel Mather, *A Testimony from the Scripture against Idolatry & Superstition* (Cambridge, 1670), p. 16.

not subject to any shadow of change, being all one with himself. Yet he is said to take up his abode in a special manner, when he doth put forth the peculiar expression of his Work.[1]

There must be the spark, the quickening insight, the subtle and inward genius, which makes all the difference between the men who see and understand and know, and ordinary men who live from hand to mouth, never pierce below surface meanings, and never achieve self-mastery and direction. It is not merely ignorance that condemns the run of mortals to their fate; the man of unenlightened learning is in the same fix: "Let a man live the life of reason, and so as that he can discourse never so wisely and judiciously, and that he can converse with all sorts of men, and transact businesses in great dexterity, yet it is but a dead life."[2] The spark, when it does come, is not the revelation of new and undreamed-of truths, it is not the discovery of any hitherto unknown facts. It is a reinvigoration of the inner man, it is inspiration, ecstasy: "it leaves an impression upon the most inward motions of the soul, as they meet with God in the most retired and refined actions thereof."[3] It is not merely a correct teaching of the mind or judgment, it is "a renewall of the whole soule of a man, the disposition and inclination of the whole must be changed and altered."[4] All the ideas, all the doctrines, all the reasons can be known before a man becomes regenerate, but known only with the mind, not with the heart. An unregenerate man, following the dictates of nature and cultivating the virtues celebrated in the poets, may perform many separate good actions, but these will not come "from an inward soul or principle of life," just as, says Thomas Shepard in a metaphor characteristically Puritan in its middle-class homeliness:

he that had beer given him, when milk and wine and sugar were put into it to mend it, said, the wine is good, and the milk is good, but the beer is bad; so profession, affection is good, but the heart, the man, is bad.[5]

By the grace of God, the Puritan meant the insight which sees at last what has been before the eyes all along; as though one had listened many times to a piece of music which to his ears

[1] Thomas Hooker, *The Application of Redemption*, pp. 3–4.

[2] John Cotton, *The way of Life* (London, 1641), p. 301.

[3] Thomas Hooker, *A Comment upon Christ's last Prayer In the Seventeenth of John* (London, 1656), p. 88.

[4] Cotton, *Christ the Fountaine of Life*, p. 98.

[5] *Works*, II, 282–283.

was meaningless, and then suddenly its form becomes clear to him and for the first time he really hears it, not merely with his ears, but with his whole being. Regeneration is such a comprehension of the world in a flash of vision, and it therefore "exceeds, and over-flies the most Eagle-sighted Apprehensions of any Natural Man in the World." [1] Only those who have experienced it will be able to understand aright the law of nature or be able to guide the steps of reason.

If the plight of man in the world is thus desperate, how absurd to erect his reason into a yardstick for what must be true in the reason of God, how fantastic to assert that if human reason cannot conceive a thing, then the thing is nothing, "hath no possibility"! It is the most insidious form of arrogance to proclaim that what seems reasonable and just on earth, in time and space, must also be binding in infinity, outside the realm of time and space, on God, who dwells in regions undecipherable to our discourse. Undoubtedly, the Puritans would answer Taylor's ultimate point, God *is* reasonable and just, but not necessarily in *our* terms. If He accommodates Himself to *our* notions of what is equitable, it is His gracious condescension. The finite cannot legislate for infinitude; our reason, though partaking of the divine nature, partakes of it only in part, and is not sufficiently universal to warrant our saying that what is absurd to it cannot be part of faith. Reason is not before Revelation. We do not prove the authority of scripture by testing it with reasonable laws formulated beforehand; we find out first what scripture means by exegesis, etymology, comparison of texts, analysis of words, logical deductions and inferences. Our premises are not secured by approaching the Bible convinced beforehand that what is contrary to reason cannot be contained there, or that what is against the light of nature cannot possibly be intended, but the Bible itself gives us the premises of reason. The light of reason is "an effect proceeding from the word." [2] We do not test the Bible by nature, but nature by the Bible. It is in this sense that the Puritan achieved, or thought he had achieved, the unity of faith and intellect, dogma and reason. Reason is the implement for the interpretation of given principles, and grace is the implement for the direction of reason. But reason does not discover fundamental principles in itself. The regenerate intellect does not fetch up truth from

[1] Thomas Hooker, *A Comment upon Christ's last Prayer*, p. 443.

[2] Norton, *Heart of N-England Rent*, p. 13.

its own depths, like water from a well, but is filled with truth from the fountain of scripture. Thomas Hooker thus summarized the union of the three factors, scripture, reason, and grace, into the moment of supreme insight which was the goal of all Puritan aspiration and the inspiration for all Puritan theory:

> The godly doe not onely apprehend the meaning of the words in the Scripture, and are able to discourse of the reasons therein contained, but they discern also the spiritualnesse of the work of grace, that is discovered in the same. Observe it: There being, first, the Word of God set down in his book, and then reasons that goe along with it, and lastly, a spirituall work of grace, that God hath made known in those reasons; the Saints of God alone see the spiritualnesse of the work that is manifested and communicated in that reason there set down . . . Take but an Apple, there is never a man under heaven can tell what tast it is of, whether sweet or soure, untill he have tasted of it; he seeth the colour and the quantity of it, but knoweth not the tast.[1]

Therefore Jeremy Taylor speaks from a purely external and formal knowledge when he says that we are to prove by reason whether any proposition is revealed by God. Reasons are there indeed, good reasons and bad reasons; the saints of God understand the right reasons and why they are right, exactly as a man knows the taste of an apple. The certitude is neither irrational conviction nor mere rational demonstration, but both at once. Jeremy Taylor is arguing that a body of truth exists, of which the Bible is one expression. The Puritan is arguing that the source of truth is the Bible, read with the eye of grace, and therefore rationally understood. Reason does not prove the sense and intention of God, as Taylor says, but the sense and intention of God instruct the reason. For the Puritan, reason does not make clear the sense of scripture, but the clear sense of scripture creates the reason.

5. Estimations

The Puritan attitude toward the Bible, to the extent that it was a preservation of intellectual values within the dogmatism, may elicit our hearty approbation. But when we come to the content of the dogma, to what the Puritan insisted the Bible did teach, and to what he expected the regenerate man to find reasonable,

[1] "Culpable Ignorance, or the Danger of Ignorance under Meanes," pp. 189–216 in *The Saints Dignitie* (London, 1651), pp. 208–209.

in short, when we come to Puritan theology, many persons encounter an insuperable stumbling block to an unqualified approval of Puritan thinking. Not only does the conventional picture of the Puritan creed seem exceedingly unattractive to twentieth-century taste, but the idea of theology in any form is almost equally objectionable. In most secondary accounts Puritans are called Calvinists, and then and there discussion of their intellectual life ceases. Dr. Holmes's "One-Hoss Shay" is deemed a sufficient description.

It is true, the Puritans were Calvinists, if we mean that they more or less agreed with the great theologian of Geneva. They held, that is, that men had fallen into a state of sin, that in order to be saved they must receive from God a special infusion of grace, that God gives the grace to some and not to others out of His own sovereign pleasure, and that therefore from the beginning of time certain souls were "predestined" to heaven and the others sentenced to damnation. But if the New Englanders were Calvinists, it was because they happened to agree with Calvin; they approved his doctrine not because he taught it, but because it seemed inescapably indicated when they studied scripture or observed the actions of men. The sinfulness of the average man was a fact that could be empirically verified, and in itself demonstrated that he needed divine grace in order to be lifted above himself; the men who did receive what they thought was an influx of grace learned by experience that only in such an ecstasy of illumination did truth become thoroughly evident and completely understandable. Obviously the experience was given to relatively few men; therefore God, who is outside time and who is omniscient, must have known from the beginning of time who would and who would not achieve it. This is the law of life; some men are born rich and some poor, some intelligent and some stupid, some are lucky and others unfortunate, some are happy and some melancholy, some are saved and some are not. There is no reason but that God so ordained it.

> The Lord to shew the soveraign freedom of his pleasure, that he may do with his own what he wil, and yet do wrong to none, he denyes pardon and acceptance to those who seek it with some importunity and earnestness . . . and yet bestowes mercy and makes known himself unto some *who never sought him.*[1]

[1] Thomas Hooker, *The Application of Redemption*, p. 299.

Puritan theology, therefore, is simply a statement in dogmatic guise of a philosophy of life, wherein it is held on the one hand that men must act by reason and abide by justice, and strive for an inward communication with the force that controls the world, but on the other hand that they must not expect that force always to be cribbed and confined by their conceptions of what is reasonable and just. There is an eternal obligation upon men to be equitable, fair, and good, but who can say that any such morality is also binding on the universe? There are certain amenities which men must observe in their dealings with men, but who can say that they must also be respected by the tiger, by the raging storm, by the lightning, or by the cancer? It is only when the theology of "predestination" is seen in these less technical terms that its vitality as a living faith and its strength as a sustaining philosophy become comprehensible.

But the theology of New England was not simply Calvinism, it was not a mere reduplication of the dogmas of the *Institutes.* What New Englanders believed was an outgrowth, as we have seen, of their background, which was humanistic and English, and it was conditioned by their particular controversy with the Church of England. Simon-pure Calvinism is a much more dogmatic, anti-rational creed than that of the Congregational parsons in Massachusetts. The emigrants went to New England to prove that a state and a church erected on the principles for which they were agitating in England would be blessed by God and prosper. The source of the New England ideology is not Calvin, but England, or more accurately, the Bible as it was read in England, not in Geneva.

Though, of course, the controversy in England was a political, social, and economic one, it was also the intellectual dispute we have outlined. We might summarize it at this point by saying that in order to harmonize reason and scripture, the Anglican endeavored to reduce the doctrines imposed by scripture to the barest minimum; the Puritan extended scripture to cover the whole of existence and then set himself to prove the content of all scripture essentially reasonable. Only with this definition of origins and tendencies in mind can we read Puritan theology aright. In order to demonstrate that the content of scripture was comprehensible to reason, the Puritan theorists worked out a substantial addition to the theology of Calvinism which in New England was quite as important as the original doctrine. This addition or elaboration of the Calvinist doctrine is generally called the "Covenant Theology," or the "Federal Theology." There is no necessity here for examining it in detail.[1] It was a special way of reading scripture so that the books assembled in the Bible could all be seen to make sense in the same way. The doctrine held that after the fall of man, God voluntarily condescended to treat with man as with an equal and to draw up a covenant or contract with His creature in which He laid down the terms and conditions of salvation, and pledged Himself to abide by them. The covenant did not alter the fact that those only are saved upon whom God sheds His grace, but it made very clear and reasonable how and why certain men are selected, and prescribed the conditions under which they might reach a fair assurance of their own standing. Above all, in the covenant God pledged Himself not to run athwart human conceptions of right and justice; God was represented while entering the compact as agreeing to abide by certain human ideas. Not in all respects, not always, but in the main. I have said that any Puritan would have subscribed to Laud's argument concerning the authority of scripture; it is now necessary to add that if called upon to discuss the question himself, the Puritan would not go about it in the same way. He would not make a distinction between testimonies brought in from another realm of experience besides faith, between rational confirmations and the act of belief, but he would begin with scripture itself, the object of faith and the measure of reason. His principal argument for the satisfaction of the reason would be that once the Bible is believed by faith, it appears wholly and beautifully rational; it contains a consistent doctrine, that of the covenant, which makes it at once the source of belief and the fountain of reason.

To find equivalents in modern terms for the ideas we have been discussing is well-nigh impossible. To translate seventeenth-century issues into twentieth-century phrases, when they cannot possibly mean the same things, is to forego any accurate understanding of them. The results of modern historical investigation and textual criticism have made fantastic, even for those who believe the scripture to be the word of God, acceptance of it in anything like the spirit of the seventeenth century. But if we cannot find a common denominator for equating the ideas of the

[1] Cf. Perry Miller, "The Marrow of Puritan Divinity," *Publications of the Colonial Society of Massachusetts*, XXXII, 247–300.

Puritans with ideas of today, we may possibly get at them by understanding the temperament, the mood, the psychology that underlay the theories. If Puritanism as a creed has crumbled, it can be of only antiquarian significance to us, but if Puritanism is also a state of mind, it may be something closer home.

There is probably no admirer of Puritanism so blindly devoted that he will not find the Anglican apologists in some respects much more attractive. The richness of their culture, the catholicity of their taste, the calmness of their temper, the well-controlled judgment, the mellow piety, and above all the poetry of Richard Hooker and Jeremy Taylor are qualities which unhappily are not too conspicuous in the pages reprinted in this volume. There is an air about these men of breadth and wisdom, they do not labor under terrific and incessant pressure, they are not always taut under the critical scrutiny of an implacable taskmaster. Simple humanity cries at last for some relief from the interminable high seriousness of the Puritan code, the eternal strenuousness of self-analysis, and the never-ending search of conscience. Though it is a great mistake to think the Puritans could not forget their theology and enjoy themselves, and though Nathaniel Ward proves that they could possess a rollicking sense of humor, the general impression conveyed by Puritan writing is that of men who lived far too uninterruptedly upon the heights of intensity. Perhaps the most damning feature of their intensity was that it could become, over a period of time, as conventional and as stereotyped as worldliness itself. Thomas Shepard, telling the story of his conversion (pp. 471–472), has a vivid and living sense of the eternal presence of God, but Samuel Sewall, moralizing over God's grace while feeding his chickens (p. 511), is at best quaintly amusing, and when he bears down with the authority of scripture on the question of wigs he becomes tiresome, as Madam Winthrop undoubtedly felt (p. 526). There was almost always an element of narrowness, harshness, and literal-mindedness associated with Puritanism, enough to justify some of the criticisms of the bishops and some of the condemnations that have been made on the Puritan spirit in more recent times.

The strength of Puritanism was its realism. If we may borrow William James's frequently misleading division of the human race into the two types of the "tough-minded" and the "tender-minded," and apply it with caution, it may serve our purposes. Though there were undoubtedly men in the Church of England, such as John Donne, whom we would have to describe as "tough," and a number of Puritans who would fit the description of "tender," yet in the main Anglicans such as Hooker and Taylor are quite clearly on the side of the more tender-minded, while the Puritan mind was one of the toughest the world has ever had to deal with. It is impossible to conceive of a disillusioned Puritan; no matter what misfortune befell him, no matter how often or how tragically his fellowmen failed him, he would have been prepared for the worst, and would have expected no better. At the same time, there was nothing of the fatalist about him; as so often happens in the history of thought, the believers in a supreme determining power were the most energetic of soldiers and crusaders. The charge of Cromwell's Ironsides was, on that particular score, proof positive of the superiority of the Puritan over the Anglican, and the Indians of New England learned to their very great sorrow how vehement could be the onset of troops who fought for a predestined victory. There was nothing lukewarm, halfhearted, or flabby about the Puritan; whatever he did, he did with zest and gusto. In that sense we might say that though his life was full of anguish of spirit, he nevertheless enjoyed it hugely. Existence for him was completely dramatic, every minute was charged with meaning. And when we come to an end of this roll call of characteristics, the one which yet remains the most difficult to evoke was his peculiar balance of zeal and enthusiasm with control and wariness. In his inner life he was overwhelmingly preoccupied with achieving a union with the divine; in his external life he was predominantly concerned with self-restraint. Compare, for example, these two passages from Thomas Hooker: the first in the vein of subjective rapture:

So, I would have you do, loose your selves, and all ordinances, and creatures, and all that you have, and do, in the Lord Christ. How is that? Let all bee swallowed up, and let nothing be seene but a Christ . . . As it is with the Moone and Starres, when the Sunne comes, they loose all their light, though they are there in the heavens still; and as it is with rivers, they all goe into the Sea, and are all swallowed up of the Sea: and yet there is nothing seene but the Sea . . . So let it bee with thy Soule, when thou wouldest finde mercy and grace.[1]

And then this admonition:

[1] *The Soules Humiliation*, p. 77.

I know there is wilde love and joy enough in the world, as there is wilde Thyme and other herbes, but we would have garden love and garden joy, of Gods owne planting.[1]

No wonder the Puritan has been something of a puzzlement and a trial to the Gentiles. He was a visionary who never forgot that two plus two equals four; he was a soldier of Jehovah who never came out on the losing side of a bargain. He was a radical and a revolutionary, but not an anarchist; when he got into power he ruled with an iron hand, and also according to a fundamental law. He was a practical idealist with a strong dash of cynicism; he came to New England to found the perfect society and the kingdom of the elect—and never expected it to be perfect, but only the best that fallible men could make. His creed was the revealed word of God and his life was the rule of moderation; his beliefs were handed down from on high and his conduct was regulated by expediency. He was a doctrinaire and an opportunist. Truth for him had been written down once and for all in a definitive, immutable, complete volume, and the covers closed to any further additions; thereupon he devoted all the energies he could spare from more immediate tasks to scholarship and interpretation. He lived in the world according to the principles that must govern this world, with an ever-present sense that they were only for the time being and that his true home was elsewhere. "There is," said John Cotton, "another combination of vertues strangely mixed in every lively holy Christian, And that is, Diligence in worldly businesses, and yet deadnesse to the world; such a mystery as none can read, but they that know it." The Puritan ideal was the man who could take all opportunities, lose no occasions, "and bestir himselfe for profit," and at the same time "bee a man dead-hearted to the world." He might wrest New England from the Indians, trade in the seven seas, and speculate in lands; "yet his heart is not set upon these things, he can tell what to doe with his estate when he hath got it." [2]

The most serious of charges laid against the Puritans has been their supposed deficiency in aesthetic perceptions. Because they did not want men to fix their veneration upon worldly things, they had no use for sculpture, distrusted the arts when they were prized merely for their sensuous appeal, were contemptuous of

[1] *The Soules Implantation* (London, 1637), p. 158.

[2] *Christ the Fountaine of Life*, pp. 119–120.

the beautiful ritual and ornamentation of the Church of England. The poet George Herbert, defending the habiliment of his church against what he thought the trappings of the Church of Rome, found the plainness of Puritan worship going much too far in the other direction:

> She in the valley is so shie
> Of dressing that her hair doth lie
> About her eares;
> While she avoids her neighbour's pride,
> She wholly goes on th'other side,
> And nothing wears.[1]

The New Model Army has incurred infamy with posterity for hacking to pieces the furnishings of cathedrals. But the asperity of the Puritan discipline and the Puritan distrust of merely sensuous beauty did not mean that the Puritan was without an aesthetic of his own, or that he was hostile to beauty. John Preston defined beauty in characteristic Puritan fashion: "Beauty that consists in a conformity of all the parts";[2] Thomas Hooker said that sin "defaceth the beautiful frame, and that sweet correspondence and orderly usefulness the Lord first implanted in the order of things."[3] The Puritan conceived of beauty as order, the order of things as they are, not as they appear, as they are in pure and abstract conception, as they are in the mind of God. He spoke of his church polity, his bare, crude churches, without altars or choirs, foursquare and solid, as lovely; they were so to him because they incarnated the beauty of the one polity Christ had ordained. His conception of the beautiful was, like Plato's, the efficient order of things; in that sense, he held indeed that beauty is truth, and truth beauty, though he did not think that was quite all he needed to know in life.

When the historian thus attempts to consider Puritanism in all its ramifications, he finds himself at the end hesitating to deliver judgment upon it, or to be wholly satisfied that it has passed into the limbo of anthologies. Certainly we can look upon the disappearance of some features with no regrets, and only deplore some others where they still survive. We have had enough of the Puritan censoriousness, its tendency to make every man his brother's keeper. When the Puritan habit of probing into the soul

[1] *Works*, ed. George Herbert Palmer (New York, 1905), III, 103.
[2] *The New Creature* (London, 1633), p. 52.
[3] *The Application of Redemption*, p. 59.

has degenerated into the "New England conscience"—where it is apt to remain as a mere feeling that everything enjoyable is sinful—then the ridicule heaped upon Puritan inhibitions becomes a welcome antidote. Certainly many amenities of social life have increased in New England, and in America, in direct proportion as Puritanism has receded. But while we congratulate ourselves upon these ameliorations, we cannot resist a slight fear that much of what has taken the place of Puritanism in our philosophies is just so much failure of nerve. The successors of Puritanism, both the evangelicals and the rationalists, as we survey them today, seem to have been comparatively sentimental, to have lacked a stomach for reality. The optimism and cheerfulness to which the revolters against Puritanism turned now threaten to become rather a snare and a delusion than a liberation. "Science" tells us of a world of stark determinism, in which heredity and environmental conditioning usurp the function of the Puritan God in predestining men to ineluctable fates. It is, indeed, true that the sense of things being ordered by blind forces presents a different series of problems than does the conception of determination by a divine being; no matter how unintelligible the world might seem to the Puritan, he never lost confidence that ultimately it was directed by an intelligence. Yet even with this momentous difference in our imagination of the controlling power, the human problem today has more in common with the Puritan understanding of it than at any time for two centuries: how can man live by the lights of humanity in a universe that appears indifferent or even hostile to them? We are terribly aware once more, thanks to the revelation of psychologists and the events of recent political history, that men are not perfect or essentially good. The Puritan description of them, we have been reluctantly compelled to admit, is closer to what we have witnessed than the description given in Jeffersonian democracy or in transcendentalism. The Puritan accounted for these qualities by the theory of original sin; he took the story of the fall of man in the Garden of Eden for a scientific, historical explanation of these observable facts. The value of his literature today cannot lie for us in his explanation; if there is any, it must rest in the accuracy of his observations.

II. The Puritans as Literary Artists

The tenets of Puritan faith obstructed any clear formulation of general aesthetic theory. Puritans saw images of divine things in the world about them, and drew analogies between the beautiful objects and the perfect archetype which they conceived as existing in the mind of God. William Hubbard spoke thus:

> In a curious piece of Architecture, that which first offers it self to the view of the beholder, is the beauty of the structure, the proportion that one piece bears to another, wherein the skill of the Architect most shews it self. But that which is most Admirable in sensitive and rational beings, is that inward principle, seated in some one part, able to guid[e] the whole, and influence all the rest of the parts, with an apt and regular motion, for their mutual good and safety.[1]

The emphasis is theological. Hubbard has in mind the "remains of God's Image"—that is, the remnant of the regulative power which God had originally created in perfection in the human understanding by which the will is informed and directed, and the passions balanced and utilized. Beauty is the order and harmony which God established, and art is useful only so far as the exercise of it may shape man's spirit to a better understanding of the divine purpose. Reason and emotion were given man to perceive the end for which God created the world, and if properly controlled they lead to the highest virtue. In such a scheme beauty is postulated as reason and faith conjoined; therefore to single out music, statuary, painting, drama, and the dance as subjects for considered appraisal,—to assign to such purely sensuous phenomena more than a negligible rank in the teleological scheme, would have been grossly unbefitting.

Yet within the duly proportioned framework the spoken and written word deserved considered analysis, for "The Wise Man saith, Words in season are as Apples of Gold in Pictures of Silver, or fitness of words (well tuning them) is the grace of them, and puts wheels to the Chariots to carry them to the mind. . . ."[2] Nicholas Noyes gave a further clue to the Puritan approach:

[1] *The Happiness of a People*, p. 11.

[2] William Hubbard, *The Benefits Of a Well-Ordered Conversation* (Boston, 1684), beginning of preface. Samuel Willard's *A Compleat Body of Divinity* (Boston, 1726) is a compendium of orthodox Puritan theology as he had preached it in the 1680's and 1690's. On pp. 27–33 he gives attention to the service of rhetoric in preaching.

Nor thine, nor thy Books credit, would I raise,
Within the gates thine own works thee shall praise
Or suffer for 't: For good Books now adayes
Like virtue practice need, but no man's praise.[1]

Noyes's point of view is typical of Puritan critical theory in that he does not seek to glorify literature or proclaim its laws, but rather to emphasize the fitness of a "plain style" which had been the badge of Puritan writers for a century. Even before New England was founded, the Puritans had advocated a prose, simple, clear, and restrained; fit to satisfy the reason, not charm the fancy; to instruct, not rouse the passions. "Painful" Perkins, fellow of Christ College, Cambridge, was a Puritan whose evangelical fervor made him one of the most influential leaders of New England thought. He had written, in a manual of sermonizing that was the recognized authority in New England, that "the Minister may, yea and must privately use at his libertie the arts, Philosophy, and variety of reading, whilest he is in framing his sermon: but he ought in publike to conceale all these from the people. . . ." [2] Thomas Hooker warned such of his readers as might find the manner of his discourse "too *Logical, or Scholasticall,* in regard of the *terms*" he used:

That plainesse and perspicuity, both for matter and manner of expression, are the things, that I have conscientiously indeavoured in the whole debate: for I have ever thought writings that come abroad, they are not to dazle, but direct the apprehension of the meanest, and I have accounted it the chiefest part of Judicious learning, to make a hard point easy and familiar in explication.[3]

Although Puritans cultivated a studied simplicity, we would stray quite from the truth if we imagined they countenanced prose that was flat and awkward. The audience helped to prevent a minister from neglecting good form, for the Puritan listener "esteemed that preaching best wherein was most of God, least of man, when vain flourishes of wit, and words were declined . . . yet could he distinguish between studied plainness, & negligent rudeness. . . .[4] There were several motives which led the

[1] *Ibid.*, commendatory verses, sig. A 2^{v} and A 3.

[2] William Perkins, *The Art of Prophecying* (*Works*, 1631), II, 670.

[3] *A Survey of the Summe of Church-Discipline* (London, 1648), preface, sig. b.

[4] John Geree, *The Character of an old English Puritan, Or Non Conformist* (London, 1646), p. 2.

Puritans to develop an intentional style—one which, though plain, was reached by conscious purpose. Their ministers were not so dull as to think that careless oratory or illogical analysis would hold the respect of an educated laity, nor did they intend that the uneducated among their people should be allowed to respect a slipshod utterance. They wrote voluminously and with high dedication; the art of writing well therefore was assiduously cultivated that both the intellect and the emotions might be stirred to the fullest response. One of the greatest preachers in the first quarter of the century, Richard Sibbes, whose works were widely read in New England, enunciated one part of the Puritan theory of style in writing the preface for a fellow Puritan's book:

> But because the way to come to the heart is often to pass through the fancy, therefore this godly man studied by lively representations to help men's faith by the fancy. It was our Saviour Christ's manner of teaching to express heavenly things in an earthly manner; and it was the study of the wise man, Solomon, becoming a preacher, to find out pleasant words, or words of delight.[1]

Sibbes here reveals that the source for much that is actually dramatic in Puritan writing was the Bible,—the model which justified an indulgence in rhetorical flourishes even though plainness and perspicuity were being exalted at the expense of form and finish.

However, had the Puritan style derived entirely from Biblical models, it would have lacked the hard-driving logic, the analytical and reasoned exposition, the close-knit structure which are its distinguishing characteristics. William Ames's textbook of theology was the standard work used at Harvard and Yale down to the middle of the eighteenth century; Ames defended the plain style, speaking both as logician and preacher, and his example influenced every sermon delivered in New England:

> The drinesse of the style, and harshnesse of some words will be much blamed by the same persons [as those who object to the logical structure]. But I doe profer to exercise my selfe in that heresie, that when it is my purpose to Teach, I thinke I should not say that in two words which may be said in one, and that that key is to be chosen which doth open best, although it be of wood, if there be not a golden key of the same efficacy.[2]

[1] *Complete Works*, ed. Alexander B. Grosart (Edinburgh, 1862), I, ci.

[2] *The Marrow of Sacred Divinity* (London, 1643), sig. A 4^v.

But economy of words was not to mean ineffective delivery; the plain style was not intended to become a dull style. As Ames instructed his students on another page:

> Men are to be pricked to the quick, that they may feele in every one of them that the Apostle saith, namely that the Word of the Lord is a two edged sword, that peirceth into the inward thoughts and affections, and goeth through unto the joyning together of the bones and marrow. Preaching therefore ought not to be dead, but lively and effectuall, so that an unbeliever coming into the Congregation of the faithfull he ought to be affected, and as it were digged through with the very hearing of the Word, that he may give glory to God.[1]

It is not fair to judge Puritan prose on the basis of the pamphlet wars engaged in by the Marprelates, or by William Prynne or John Milton, wherein too frequently the attacks are violent, the issue trivial, and the language harsh and coarse. The Puritans left to posterity a full harvest of sermons and tracts, histories, biographies, and journals. If much appears disproportionately argued or exhaustively analyzed, we have the writers' expressed purpose to "direct the apprehension of the meanest." The Puritan ideal might be phrased roughly in this fashion: enough rhetoric to pass through the fancy to the heart, but never so much that the apprehension of the simple or the earnest should be dazzled. Thomas Hooker pointed to the evil consequences that followed upon a too ornate sermon style:

> I have sometime admired at this: why a company of Gentlemen, yeomen and poore women, that are scarcely able to know their A. B. C. yet they have a Minister to speake Latine, Greeke, and Hebrew, and to use the Fathers, when it is certain, they know nothing at all. The reason is, because all this stings not, they may sit and sleepe in their sinnes, and goe to hell hoodwinckt, never awakened.[2]

Many features of Puritan writing, which from a purely literary point of view might seem to be faults, were deliberately cultivated in order to achieve greater clarity or more certain effectiveness with the particular audience addressed. No doubt, too, occasional carelessness of structure in Puritan tracts can be charged to the insatiable demand for theological discussion, which sometimes betrayed a Puritan minister into offering his wares before

[1] *Ibid.*, p. 159.
[2] *The Soules Preparation* (London, 1632), p. 66.

he gave them adequate trimming. Certain sterile characteristics are common to Anglican literature as well: the pedantry of learned quotation, and the unrelieved syllogistic method. In manner also there are many similarities between Anglican and Puritan style. To the extent that any writer of the second quarter of the seventeenth century was heir to Elizabethan word-consciousness, to the flavor of the Geneva Bible—the most popular version for a hundred years—he inherited a love of figure and ornament which the King James version itself drew upon.

But there are well marked differences. The Anglican love of solemn ritual, of tradition and hierarchy is often reflected in a suavity of diction which the Puritans scorned. Furthermore, the Anglicans did not share the Puritans' veneration for the Bible as the sole approach to the spiritual life; therefore they drew more consciously upon their classical culture and wide reading to enrich their style and vary their rhetorical effects. Anglican sermons less often attempt to convince the reason by clear logic and coherent summary than to stir the imagination. In constructing their sentences, modeled upon Latin, they strove for the harmony of Ciceronian periods—a rhetorical effect which Puritans looked upon as "more sauce than meat." "I professe it is beyond my care to please the nicenesse of mens palates, with any quaintnesse of language," Thomas Hooker remarks, adding: "It was a cavill cast upon *Hierom* that in his writings he was *Ciceronianus non Christianus*." [1] Anglicans unlike Puritans, made use of ornament for its own sake; they elaborated metaphors and illustrations for the purpose of enriching their prose. Let these selections, taken at random from the works of three great Anglican preachers, serve to illustrate the point: [2]

And it falls out very often, that some one Father, of Strong reputation and authority in his time, doth snatch and swallow some probable interpretation of Scripture: and then digesting it into his Homilies, and applying it in dehortations, and encouragements, as the occasions and diseases of his Auditory, or his age require, and imagining thereupon delightfull and figurative insinuations, and setting it to the Musique of his style, (as every man

[1] *A Survey of the Summe*, sig. 4^{v}. Hooker refers to Erasmus's Life of St. Jerome included in the Complete Works of the church father (9 vols., Basel, 1516–1520).

[2] The first is John Donne, *Biathanatos* [*ca.* 1610] (London, 1646), p. 206; the second, Lancelot Andrewes, "Sermons of the Resurrection," delivered Easter Sunday, April 13, 1623, in *Ninety-Six Sermons* (Anglo-Catholic Library, 5 vols., Oxford, 1841–1843), III, 75, 76; the third, Jeremy Taylor, *The Golden Grove* (London, 1656), pp. 24, 25.

which is accustomed to these Meditations, shall often finde in himselfe such a spirituall wontonnesse, and devout straying into such delicacies,) that sense which was but probable, growes necessary, and those who succeed had rather enjoy his wit, then vexe their owne; as often times we are loath to change or leave off a counterfeit stone, by reason of the well setting thereof.

By this meanes, I thinke, it became so generally to be beleeved, that the fruit which *Eve* eat was an Apple; And that *Lots* wife was turned to a pillar of Salt; And that *Absalon* was hanged by the haire of the head; And that *Iephthe* killed his Daughter; And many other such, which grew currant, not from an evidence in the Text, but because such an acceptation, was most usefull, and applyable. Of this number, *Iudas* case might be.

You see how Christs garments came to be "red." Of the wine-press that made them so we have spoken, but not of the colour itself. A word of that too. It was His colour at His Passion. They put Him in purple; then it was His weed itself, and so He made it more with the dye of His own blood. And the same colour He is now in again at His rising. Not with His own now, but with the blood of the wounded Edomites, whom treading under His feet, their blood bestained Him and His apparel. So one and the same colour at both; dying and rising in red; but with difference as much as is between His own as His enemies' blood . . .

The tincture, I say, first of our sin original, dyed in the wool; and then again of our sins actual, dyed in the cloth too. Twice dyed; so was Christ twice . . . So was it meet for crimson sinners to have a crimson Saviour; a Saviour of such a colour it behoved us to have . . . Yea, He died and rose again both in our colours, that we might die and rise too in His. We fall now again upon the same point in the colours we did before in the cups. He to drink the sour vinegar of our wild grapes, that we might drink His sweet in the cup of blessing. O cup of blessing, may we say of this cup! *O stolam formosam*, of that colour! *Illi gloriosam, nobis fructuosam;* 'glorious to Him, no less fruitful to us.' He in Mount Golgotha like to us, that we in Mount Tabor like to Him. This is the substance of our rejoicing in this colour.

Jesus Christ being taken by the Rulers of the Jews, bound and derided, buffeted and spit upon, accused weakly and persecuted violently; at last, wanting matter and pretences to condemn him, they asked him of his Person and Office; and because he affirmed that great Truth, which all the world of good men long'd for, that he was the *Messias*, and designed to sit *at the right hand of the Majesty on high*, they resolved to call it *Blasphemy*, and delivered him over to *Pilate*, and by importunity and threats, forced him against his Conscience, to give him up to be scourged, and then to be Crucified. The Souldiers therefore mocking him with a robe and reed, and pressing a Crown of thorns upon his head, led him to the place of his death; compelling him to bear his Cross, to which they presently nail'd him; on which for three hours he hang'd in extreme torture, being a sad spectacle of the most afflicted, and the most innocent person of the whole warld.

Putting aside individual idiosyncrasies for the moment, we observe certain tendencies which are common to all three selections: an eloquence which is achieved by such rhythmic periods, mannered ingenuity, grammatical subtleties, and tortuous language as rob the prose of any sense of urgency while conveying through the rich, sometimes extravagant, fancy a poetic delicacy. It seems to be the authors' conscious aim to stir the reader through the wealth and variety of ornaments, through balance, antithesis, and alliteration, through word-pairs and verbal conceits. The Puritans, on the other hand, adopted plainness to give the application of their sermons more force and directness; there is ready use of figure in their sermons, but the intent is less to enrich the color of the prose than to vitalize the point at issue, to intensify the concreteness, or clarify the doctrine. Perhaps the four examples [1] here set forth will serve to point the case:

Learn wee then hereby, every one of us to judge our selves and our families, and to teach every person to judge themselves, as at other times, so more especially in the dayes of their humiliation, and when they come to renew their promises and vowes with their God. If *David* were not able to say that his house were perfect with God, what then may we say? we have not that means which he had, such Teachers to instruct us, such guides whereby we might be brought forward, neither are wee compassed about with Prophets in a land of uprightnesse; where shall we finde an house that walks with God as *David* did? that growes as the tender grasse, and is as the Sun without cloud? We are therefore to charge our selves with our follies and failings, and to humble our selves for them, whether it be towards God, or towards one another: wee should consider how wee are failing in the true feare of

[1] The first is John Cotton, *The Covenant of Gods free Grace* (London, 1645), p. 7; the second, Thomas Shepard, *The Clear Sun-shine of the Gospel* (London, 1648), p. 37; the third, Urian Oakes, *New-England Pleaded with*, p. 34; the fourth, Samuel Willard, *The Child's Portion* (Boston, 1684), pp. 226, 227 (selection from sermon entitled "All Plots against God and his People Detected and Defeated").

God, how subject we are to eye-service, and although wee can do little in reforming kingdomes and nations, yet we may take care for our own houses, wee may judge our selves and our families in our manifold failings, we may judge our selves for our high-mindednesse, drousinesse in good duties, for our evill slow heart to get hold of any spirituall thing, for our customary performances.

Thus you have a true, but somewhat rent and ragged relation of these things; it may be most sutable to the story of naked and ragged men: my desire is that no mans Spectacles may deceive him, so as to look upon these things either as bigger or lesser, better or worser then they are; which all men generally are apt to doe at things at so great distance, but that they may judge of them as indeed they are, by which truth they see here exprest in the things themselves. I knowe that some thinke that all this worke among them is done and acted thus by the *Indians* to please the *English*, and for applause from them; and it is not unlikely but 'tis in many, who doe but blaze for a time; but certainly 'tis not so in all, but that the power of the Word hath taken place in some, and that inwardly and effectually, but how far savingly time will declare, and the reader may judge of, by the story it self of these things.

Nor am I so Severe, or Morose, as to exclaim against this or that Fashion, provided it carry nothing of Immodesty in it, or Contrariety to the Rules of Moral Honesty. The civil Custome of the place where we live is that which must regulate in this case. But when persons spend more time in trimming their Bodies then their Souls, that you may say of them (as a Worthy Divine wittily speaks) that they are like the *Cinamon Tree*, nothing good but the *Bark:* When they go beyond what their State and Condition will allow, that they are necessitated to run into Debt, and neglect works of mercy and charity, or exact upon others in their dealings, that they may maintain their Port and Garb; or when they exceed their Rank and Degree (whereas one end of Apparel is to distinguish and put a difference between persons according to their Places and Conditions) and when the Sons and Daughters of *Sion* are proud and haughty in their Carriage and Attire in an humbling time, when the *Church* is brought low, *Ierusalem* and *Iudah* is in a Ruinous Condition, and the Lord calls to deep Humiliation: This is very displeasing to God, and both Scripture and Reason condemn it. These are the most gross, and fantastical, and foolish buddings of Pride.

The Web which they [the wicked] have been for a long while in weaving, God will unravel in a moment: He will shortly muster up his Forces and draw out his Armies into the Field, and call together the Fowls of Heaven to his great Supper which he shall provide for them, where he will give them to eat of *the flesh of Kings* . . . Rev. 19.17. This is the work which he hath undertaken to do, and will certainly accomplish it throughly, who hath written on his Vesture, and on his Thigh, KING OF KINGS, AND LORD OF LORDS. And since the case stands thus, what is there then remaining more for us to do, but to be the Lord's Remembrancers. Not ceasing day nor night to be earnestly and importunately putting him in mind of his Covenant, his Name, and Glory? and in Faith pray to him in the behalf of his poor, despised, and abused Church, which is as a Lilly among the Thornes, that he would remember and not forget, or grow unmindful of the Congregation which he hath purchased of old, and arise to save those that are as sheep prepared to the slaughter, and appointed to dy: And when we have thus done, and in a way of so doing, there is nothing more but to sit and wait to see the Salvation of the Lord.

Let two good Puritans frame the idea in their own words—incidentally, in words embodying the very art they recommend: [1]

It is a good saying of one, that the Reading of many diverse heads without some interlaced meditations, is like eating of Marrow without bread. But he that shall take time to Pause upon what he reads (especially where great Truths are but in a few words hinted at) with intermixed meditations and ejaculations suitable to the matter in hand, shall find such Truths concisely delivered, to be like marrow and fatness, whereof a little goes far, and does feed and nourish much.

Those who came to New England to establish a "*Plantation Religious*" were gentlemen for whom a way to "truth" lay in advancement of learning, if not encyclopædic, then discriminating. The Puritan believed that any serious, intelligent work is a transcript of life, and necessary to an understanding of that life, whether conveyed by way of history, poetry, or exegesis. "Hee resolved well that said, Books and friends would I have few and choice," said William Morton,[2] and the sense of life as an art extends to the art of literary expression. A consciousness of style

[1] John Wise and Jonathan Mitchell, preface to Samuel Whiting, *A Discourse of the Last Judgement* (Cambridge, 1664), sig. A8.

[2] Preface to John Cotton, *The way of Life*, opening sentence.

was present from the first,[1] bred into schoolboys who did little except imitate and absorb the rhetorical exellencies of classical writers. Clearly, however, the Puritans admired the direct exposition and lucid argument of their models, not the elaborate rhetorical constructions. Roger Williams apologized to Lady Vane the Younger for "the *forme* and *stile* [which] I know will seem to this refined *age*, too rude and barbarous." [2] As a group the Puritans were in revolt against the oratorical flights, the flashing rockets of Pistolese which they had doubtless observed in the writings of the late Elizabethans. Nathaniel Ward's "world of words" was out of fashion even as he coined them. They would have seemed out of place in the writings of any preacher;—that a Puritan should affect them is curious in the extreme:

> . . . when I heare a nugiperous Gentledame inquire what dresse the Queen is in this week; what the nudiustertian fashion of the Court; I mean the very newest: with egge to be in it in all haste, what-ever it be; I look at her as the very gizzard of a trifle, the product of a quarter of a cypher, the epitome of nothing. . . .[3]

Such glittering phrases lost caste among all Puritans after 1630, for they looked upon "high style," with its definite conventions, as "Exotic Words" that led to "Carnal wisdome." [4] Some who had been trained in the Anglican tradition changed their views of style as they swung over to the Puritan faith. Cotton Mather tells of the struggle which John Cotton underwent:

> And that which added unto the Reputation, thus raised for him, was an University Sermon, wherein sinning more to preach *Self* than *Christ*, he used such Florid Strains, as extremely recommended him unto *the most*, who relished the *Wisdom of Words* above the *Words of Wisdom;* Though the pompous Eloquence of that Sermon, afterwards gave such a Distast unto his own *Reverend Soul*, that with a Sacred Indignation he threw his Notes into the Fire . . .
>
> But although he had been Educated in the *Peripatetick* way, yet like the other *Puritans* of those times, he rather affected the *Ramaean* Discipline; and chose to follow the Methods of the Excel-

[1] See E. F. Bradford, "Conscious Art in Bradford's *History of Plymouth Plantation*," *New England Quarterly*, I (1928), 133–157; F. O. Matthiessen, "Michael Wigglesworth, a Puritan Artist," *ibid.*, pp. 491–504.

[2] *Experiments of Spiritual Life & Health* (London, 1652), p. iv.

[3] *The Simple Cobler* . . . (London, 1647), pp. 24, 25.

[4] Increase Mather, *The Life* . . . *of* . . . *Mr. Richard Mather* (Cambridge, 1670), p. 85. See also pp. 489–496 following.

lent *Ramus*, who like *Justin* of old vvas not only a *Philosopher*, but a *Christian*, and a *Martyr* also; rather than the more Empty, Trifling, Altercative Notions, to which the Works of the Pagan *Aristotle* derived unto us, through the Mangling Hands of the Apostate *Prophyrie*, have Disposed his Disciples . . .[1]

The turn to plainness was thus established in Puritan America from the beginning, and the controversies over style carried on in England were but slightly reflected in the colonies. On two occasions in particular ministers took opportunity to express opinions on literary art: The funeral sermon offered them a chance to pay critical tribute to the writings of the departed,[2] and the sermon preached at the ordination of a young pastor furnished occasion to theorize on oratory and literary composition:

When instead of conveying his Ideas and Sense of Things in plain and natural Words and Expressions, the minister [makes] use of the Jargon of Logic and Metaphysics, or amuses [the auditors] with Hebrew, Greek, Latin or French Names; or soars above them in Flights of Poetry, and Flourishes of Rhetorick; or goes into the other Extream of using indecent and homely Phrases, such as savour of the Mobb or the Play-house, he gives Offence.[3]

Our discussion so far has been limited to theories of style in sermon literature. The Puritan historians were as scrupulous as the ministers in preserving the amenities of a plain, lucid style. Governor Bradford opened "Of Plimmoth Plantation" by saying that he is about to narrate events "The which I shall endeuor to manefest in a plaine stile; with singuler regard unto ye simple trueth in all things." [4] The remark is characteristic of

[1] Cotton Mather, *Johannes in Eremo* (Boston, 1695), pp. 52, 53; *idem, Magnalia*, Bk. III, chap. 1, p. 15. Ramus' reform of logic was accompanied by a reform of rhetoric, in both cases in the direction of simplicity and clarity. The two studies went hand in hand, the Puritans embracing the logic of Ramus and the rhetorical principles of Ramus' disciple, Omer Talon; while the Anglican preachers in the main clung to the traditional Aristotelian logic and scholastic rhetoric. See also Samuel Eliot Morison, *Harvard College in the Seventeenth Century*, pp. 172–187.

[2] See Benjamin Colman, *The Prophet's Death Lamented* . . . (Boston, 1723), p. 32 (sermon for Increase Mather); John Barnard, *Elijah's Mantle* . . . (Boston, 1724), p. 36 (sermon for Ezekiel Cheever); Eliphalet Adams, *A Funeral Discourse* . . . (New London, 1724), sig. K 3^v (sermon for Gurdon Saltonstall).

[3] Ebenezer Turell, *Ministers should carefully avoid giving Offence in any Thing* (Boston, 1740), p. 14. For similar ideas, see Cotton Mather, *Parentator* . . . (Boston, 1724), p. 215; Samuel Mather, *The Life of . . . Cotton Mather* . . . (Boston, 1729), pp. 33, 34; Nathaniel Appleton, *Superior Skill and Wisdom* . . . (Boston, 1737), p. 26; William Cooke, *The great Duty of Ministers* . . . (Boston, 1742), p. 7.

[4] MS (*ca.* 1650) in Massachusetts State Library, Boston. From Facsimile, ed. J. A. Doyle, (London, 1896).

Renaissance critical theory in so far as it shows the author dedicating himself to the exposition of moral truth. Bradford's nephew, drawing heavily upon his uncle's work, acknowledged that he has "more solicitously followed the truth of things" than "studied quaintness in expressions." [1] When Thomas Sprat came to write the history of the Royal Society of London, he described the practice which that body had demanded of its members. We might almost say that Sprat's words give an official sanction to a manner of writing which the Puritans for many years had approved and adopted:

And, in few words, I dare say that, of all the Studies of men, nothing may be sooner obtain'd than this vicious abundance of *Phrase*, this trick of *Metaphors*, this volubility of *Tongue*, which makes so great a noise in the World. . . .

[The members of the Royal Society] have therefore been most rigorous in putting in execution the only Remedy that can be found for this *extravagance*, and that has been a constant Resolution to reject all amplifications, digressions, and swellings of style; to return back to the primitive purity and shortness, when men deliver'd so many *things* almost in an equal number of *words*. They have exacted from all their members a close, naked, natural way of speaking, positive expressions, clear senses, a native easiness, bringing all things as near the Mathematical plainness as they can, and preferring the language of Artizans, Countrymen, and Merchants, before that of Wits or Scholars.[2]

Colonial secular writers continued to advocate the method which had been most serviceable. Daniel Gookin says that his narrative is "not clothed in elegancy of words and accurate sentences," since, he concludes, "I have endeavoured all plainness that I can, that the most vulgar capacity might understand." [3] It was a point of view carried into the eighteenth century with little variation.[4]

As expressions of critical theory passed from the rationalistic

[1] William Morton, *New-Englands Memoriall* (Cambridge, 1669), preface.

[2] *The History of the Royal-Society of London* (1667), section XX, in J. E. Spingarn, *Critical Essays of the Seventeenth Century* (Oxford, 1908), II, 117, 118.

[3] *Historical Collections of the Indians in New England* (preface dated November, 1674), in *Collections of the Massachusetts Historical Society*, first series, I (1792), 141–226; see also James Allen, *New-Englands choicest Blessing* (Boston, 1679), preface.

[4] See Howard M. Jones, "American Prose Style: 1700–1770," *Huntington Library Bulletin*, No. 6 (1934), pp. 115–151. See also Benjamin Colman, preface to Samuel Penhallow, *The History of the Wars of New-England* (Boston, 1726); Cotton Mather, *Magnalia* (1702), "General Introduction."

philosophers—men like Sprat, for instance—to such appreciators of literature as Dryden and Addison, and as the magazines sprang up in the first quarter of the eighteenth century to give general access to literary expression, the changes in literary fashions are reflected by Puritans. They wished to escape the criticism, now being leveled at them, that they were a provincial stock, out of the current of public taste in England, concerned merely with abstract theology. As early as 1708 Cotton Mather discourses of classical writers in the manner of the English essayists.[1] When Jonathan Belcher, the governor's son, was an undergraduate at Harvard (1725–1730), he kept in his commonplace book many pages of extracts from *The Spectator* and *The Guardian*, from Blackwall, Rapin, and Halifax on critical and aesthetic theories. They leave no doubt of the influence upon one young Puritan of the current English literary modes. Even the pious and cantankerous governor, no author himself, voiced gracious tribute to a study of belles lettres in the educational scheme of his son in the many letters he wrote to the young man who was studying law in England soon after 1730.[2] After 1722 a change is observable in literary taste, brought about in part by the decreasing isolation of New England from current trends abroad. As the second quarter of the century approached, nearly all tastes that may be labeled Puritan were rapidly adapting themselves to the English modes. No work on style was exerting more universal influence than Fénelon's *Dialogues on Eloquence*, wherein the archbishop of Cambray averred that he thought "the whole Art of Oratory may be reduc'd to *proving*, *painting*, and *raising* the *Passions*"; it should reach the heart, not merely stir the imagination.[3] His point of view found ready adherents among the coming generation, and to the extent it was adopted indicates that the earlier Puritan feeling—that consciousness of style should be concealed—was undergoing change. Cotton Mather leaves no doubt that the public was developing a finicky sensitivity to style:

[1] *Corderius Americanus* (Boston, 1708), sig. A2; see *idem*, *Just Commemorations* (Boston, 1715), p. ii.

[2] *The Belcher Papers*, 2 vols., in *Collections of the Massachusetts Historical Society*, sixth series, VI, VII (1893, 1894); for example, I, 125–129, 180–187, 197–205.

[3] *Dialogues . . .* (London, 1722), p. 74. See Thomas Prince, preface to Thomas Hooker, *The Poor Doubting Christian* (Boston, 1743), p. 13. In England Dennis was an advocate of emotion in the pulpit as contrasted with "correctness"; so also was Thomas Blackwall. For a recent discussion of the eighteenth-century view of the "Passions," see "The Sublime and the Pathetic," in Samuel H. Monk, *The Sublime: A Study of Critical Theories in XVIII-Century England* (New York, 1935), chap. III.

> The blades that set up for critics . . . appear to me, for the most part, as contemptible as they are a supercilious generation. For indeed no two of them have the same stile; and they are as intolerably cross-grained, and severe in their censures upon one another, as they are upon the rest of mankind . . . There is much talk of a florid stile obtaining among the pens that are most in vogue; but how often would it puzzle one, even with the best glasses to find the flowers! . . . After all, every man will have his own stile.[1]

At no point does the literary thought of the Puritans reflect the trend of the times more exactly than in their views of poetry. When Milton, searching for a worthy epic theme, finally chose to write on the fall of man, he was himself but following a trail that had been already blazed. Davenant had said that poetry "is as all good Arts subservient to Religion," [2] and Abraham Cowley, greatly admired for his learning, had begun *Davideis*, a sacred epic. The famous preface to Cowley's *Poems* remarks that "he who can write a *prophane Poem well* may write a *Divine one better*." [3] Puritans were agreed that subjects other than moral and divine were unworthy of serious treatment. It was as inheritors of the Renaissance and of the metaphysicals that Puritans conceived of poetry as a learning or a moral philosophy directed toward the highest ends within the conception of man; and believing such, they viewed mere versifying as a pleasant accomplishment for leisure hours. The Puritans who compiled the Bay Psalm Book saying that "Gods Altar needs not our pollishing"; [4] the men who "attended Conscience rather then Elegance, fidelity rather then poetry," [5] were in part tacitly acknowledging their inadequacy as poets, not belittling the power of verse—into which, after all, they were fashioning their thoughts. More influential and learned men than Wigglesworth had furnished precedent for his remark that he would traffic with

> No Toyes nor Fables (Poets wonted Crimes) . . .
> For I do much abominate
> To call the Muses to mine aid:
> Which is th' Unchristian use, and trade
> Of some that Christians would be Thought. . . . [6]

[1] *Manuductio ad Ministerium* (Boston, 1726), pp. 44–46.
[2] Preface to *Gondibert* (1650), ed. Spingarn, *op. cit.*, II, 48.
[3] *Ibid.* (1656), p. 90. [4] Conclusion to preface.
[5] Prefatory poem to Wigglesworth, *Day of Doom*, sig. xx3^{v}.
[6] *Ibid.*, sig. B1, B2.

To none of the founders would Addison's conception of poetry as an indulgence of the imagination,—a relaxation by which we are "cheared and delighted with agreeable sensations," have been adequate. But as fashions changed, as the bonds between the colonies and England became closer, the Puritans inevitably were affected, for they more and more reflected the trends in England. Thoughtful Puritans essayed verses often enough, and recommended poetic composition as good training for the young; but enthusiasm for poetry as a means of expressing great truths in exalted moods gave place to urbane appreciation of verse as a social accomplishment. Such a concept indicates that strictly Puritan theories were on the wane, even though the Bible remained the fountain of inspiration for some time to come. For simon-pure Puritans David ever remained the "Divine *Poet*," for he "derived his *Inspiration* not from *Parnassus*, but from *Zion*, the Mount of God." [1]

It is as writers of prose that the Puritans' literary art finally must be judged. Prose was the vehicle for their finest thoughts; it was the one by which they assisted a whole people to a realization of the powerful idiom at hand for all men to use. They were men who valued learning highly, who talked and wrote voluminously, and of whose style it may be said, as of their colleagues in England, that "while to the Royal Society must be given the honour of definitely hallmarking the new style, to the more temperate among the Puritan preachers belongs the praise of having demonstrated to large masses of the nation, learned and unlearned, the possibilities of a simple, straightforward, unencumbered prose." [2] It is impossible, furthermore, to escape the conviction that all who wrote were conscious of the importance of style, and that most of them adhered to some model. Many left record of their theories. The ornate fashion of Samuel Lee and Samuel Chandler is as unrepresentative of Puritan theory of style as Jonathan Edwards's youthful remark that he would scant it altogether.[3] The problem of poetic composition seldom absorbed their attention, but in so far as they were gentlemen trained in the manners of their day they were alert to the changes of taste,

[1] Thomas Walter, *The Sweet Psalmist of Israel* (Boston, 1722), p. 2.

[2] W. Fraser Mitchell, *English Pulpit Oratory from Andrewes to Tillotson* (London, 1932), p. 275.

[3] S. E. Dwight, *The Life of President Edwards* (New York, 1829), p. 601. See also John Webb's funeral sermon for Peter Thacher, *The Duty of Survivers* (Boston, 1739), p. 27, for a similar opinion.

and adapted themselves, especially in the later Puritan era, to the current modes. Prose, on the other hand, was the vehicle for their ripest thoughts and their deepest emotions. A flat, awkward, cumbrous style is rarely encountered in their treatises or sermons; the color of their rhetoric was absorbed from the world they knew about them—the sea, the market place, the moods of nature. In the hands of such men as John Cotton, Thomas Hooker, Increase Mather, or John Wise the style is seldom commonplace; frequently distinguished:—they lived in an age when devotional literature and sermons were a staple diet, when current preaching fashions were shaping literary taste. It should also be remembered that the Puritans who guided the thought of their day were never merely sectarian in their reading. The Bible was the great font of Puritan inspiration and the model for their style, yet behind the Bible was the common heritage of Renaissance learning and Elizabethan enthusiasm. The Puritans more than others shaped that learning and enthusiasm to the idiom of language with a clarity, directness, grace, and freedom from eccentricity that rendered incalculable service to English prose.

the largenesse & truthe of my Love to thee makes me allwayes mindfull
of thy wellfare, & sett me on worke to begine to write, before I heare from thee:
the verye thought of thee affordes me many a kynde refreshinge, what will then
the enjoyinge of thy sweet societye, wch I prize above all worldly comforts?
yet such is the follye & miserye of man, as he is easylye brought to contemne
the true good he enjoyes, & to neglect the best things wch he holds only in
hope, & both upon an ungrounded desire of some seeminge good wch he promiseth to
himselfe: & if it be thus wth those that are Christians, who have a sure worde to directe us
by the holy faith to live by, what is the madnesse & bondage of those who are out
of Christe? O: the riches of Christe: O: the sweetnesse of the worde of Grace: it
ravisheth my soule in the thought heerof, so as when I apprehende but a glimpse
of the dignitye & felicitye of a Christian, I can hardly perswade my heart to
hope for so great happinesse: let men talke what they will of riches, honors
pleasures &c: let us have Christ crucified, & let them take all besides: for
indeed, he who hath Christ hath all things wth him, for he enjoyeth an allsufficiencie
wch makes him abundantly riche in povertye, honorable in the lowest abasemente,
full of joye & consolation in the sharpest afflictions, livinge in deathe, &
possessinge aeternitye in this vale of miserye: therefore blesse we God, for
his free & infinite mercye in bestowinge Christ upon us: let us entertaine
& love him wth or whole hearts: let us trust in him, & cleave to him,
wth denyall of or selves, & all things besides, & accounte or portion the best
in the worlde: that so beinge strengthened & comforted in his love, we may
putt forthe or selves, to improve or life & meanes, to doe him service: there are
very fewe howers lefte of this daye of or labour, then comes the night, when
we shall take or rest, in the morninge we shall awake unto glorye &
immortalitye, when we shall have no more worke to doe, no more paine or
griefe to endure, no more care, feare, want, reproache, or infirmitye; no
more sinne, corruption or temptation

I am forced to patch up my lres, heer a peece & there another: I have
now received thine, the kindly fruits of thy most sweet Affection,
blessed be the Lorde for the wellfare of thy selfe & all or familye.
I received lres from my 2: sonnes wth thee, remember my love &
blessinge to them, & to my daughter winth: for whose safetye I
give the Lord thankes: I have so many lres to write as I cannot
write to thee now: our freinds heer are in reasonable health, &
desire to be kindly remembred to you all. Comende me to all my
good freinds, my lovinge neighbrs goodm Cole & his wife, to whom we
are allwayes much beholdinge. I will remember Mr: Lee gowne
& petticoate, & the children's girdles. so wth my most affectionate
desires of thy wellfare, & my blessinge to all or children, I kisse
my sweet wife, & comende thee & all ors to the gratious pro=
tection of or heavenly father, & rest

Thy faithfull husband,
still present wth thee in his most
unkinde absence

May 8
1629

I am sorye for my neighb: Whites
horse, but he shall loose nothinge
by him. tell my sonne Hen: I will pay the
more hee write of.

Jo: winthrop

Letter of John Winthrop to His Wife. (For text, see p. 465.)

HISTORY

In the 1660's and 1670's, as the last survivors of the first generation were dying off, and the ministers felt that the religious ardor of their successors was noticeably cooling, preachers before the General Court of Massachusetts frequently called for the composition of a history of New England. They hoped that a chronicle of the deeds of the fathers would arouse the emulation of the sons, and that a recital of the favors which God had already bestowed upon the colony would incite the present inhabitants to a determination to merit still more of them. They strove to arrest the general declension from the original ideals, upon which we have already commented (pp. 17–19), by adducing the testimonies of divine approbation evident in the history of the commonwealth. Thus in 1673 Urian Oakes dwelt at length upon this theme:

> Hath God essayed to go and take him a part of a Nation from the midst of a Nation, by temptations, by signs, by wonders, by a mighty hand & by an out-stret[c]hed arm, according to all that the Lord your God hath done for you before your eyes? God hath shewn us almost unexampled unparall[el]ed mercy. And it were very well if there were a memorial of these things faithfully drawn up, and transmitted to Posterity . . . It is our great duty to be the Lords *Remembrancers* or *Recorders* . . . that the mercies of the Lord (that hath allured us into this wilderness, spoken comfortably to us and dealt bountifully with us therein) may be faithfully registred in our hearts, and remembred by us. It is a desireable thing, that all the loving kindnesses of God, and his singular favours to this poor and despised out cast might be Chronicled and communicated (in the History of them) to succeeding Ages; that the memory of them may not dy and be extinct, with the present Generation.[1]

The call for a history of Massachusetts Bay was redoubled after 1669, when Nathaniel Morton published a history of Plymouth, *New England's Memoriall.* The General Court at last paid the Reverend William Hubbard £50 for having composed a corresponding volume for Massachusetts, declaring, "it hath binn thought necessary, & a duty incumbent vpon vs to take due notice of all occurrances & passages of Gods providence towards the people of this jurisdiction since their first arrivall in these parts." [2] Hubbard pocketed the money,

[1] *New-England Pleaded with* (Cambridge, 1673), p. 23.

[2] *Massachusetts Records,* V, 279, 378, 394.

but can hardly be said to have earned it. Neither his nor Morton's work contributed anything worth much in itself; the chief value of both books came from the fact that the authors had access to unpublished manuscripts by the two great governors of the colonies at the time of the respective settlements. Morton and Hubbard did little more than plagiarize from the *History of Plymouth Plantation* of William Bradford, and from the journal of John Winthrop. In spite of the ministerial demand, two of the three masterpieces of New England historiography were not printed until the nineteenth century, and the third, Cotton Mather's *Magnalia*, was not issued until 1701.

For our purposes, however, the important point about Oakes's paragraph is not its failure to get results, but the philosophy of history that it contains, either explicitly or by implication. He puts a somewhat exaggerated emphasis upon the use of history in arousing a lethargic generation, but even so he gives an excellent statement of what the Puritan conceived to be the function of an historian and from what point of view the narrative should be arranged. History is a memorial of the mercies of God, so that posterity may know them, remember them, and hymn His praises. The history of New England is history *par excellence*, for the mercies of God have been shown in New England above all other portions of the globe. History is not only philosophy teaching by example, but theology exemplified.

During the seventeenth century there was carried on in learned circles a debate between the "ancients" and the "moderns," between scholars who believed that the ancients, being closer to the date of creation, were inevitably of a stronger and more original genius than was any longer possible, and those who believed that genius could flourish as well in modern centuries as in classical. This dispute, being largely a literary one, did not much interest the Puritans, but had they taken sides in it, they would certainly have supported the modernists' contention. They would not have been swayed by a preference for modern literature over the ancient, but would have been determined by their fundamental belief in divine providence. To them all human affairs have always been under the continuous direction of God; history is the record of His incessant supervision, and there can be no real decline or fluctuation of God's power. The past is a drama, written, directed, produced and prompted by God. It must, therefore, be as full of meaning at one time as at another. The natural world, the customs of men, the abilities of statesmen, all purely physical aspects of existence do not vary in kind from one era to another: "In Civil matters there be the like manners of men now as of old;

the like causes and successes of warre and peace &c. whence the knowledge of History of former times is so much behovefull." It is therefore wrong to prefer "elder times before the present." Nature has not decayed; great authors of the past are indeed to be read, but we are "not to approve all their sayings and doings, as best." At whatever moment we happen to live, God has called upon us to achieve "a wise consideration of our present times." [1]

Consequently for the Puritan writer of history there is always a two-fold consideration determining his attitude toward his material, and sometimes the one reflection seems almost contradictory to the other. On the one hand, everything that has happened, disaster as well as triumph, the minutest event as well as the greatest, has been under divine control. God is not a being of whims or caprices, He is not less powerful at one moment than at another; therefore in a certain sense any event is just as significant as any other. But on the other hand, God regulates the universe for distinct ends; He does not work without purpose, and history should be seen as a long revelation of divine intentions. Therefore the first function of the historian is to relate everything that has happened, to exclude nothing, to erect no standards or criteria on a purely human basis. He must not sort out his materials, suppress some facts and accentuate others, because they conform to patterns he has himself constructed, such as economic interest, national characteristics, literary forms. Yet at the same time the historian is not merely to relate what has happened, but to interpret it. He must show wherein events have fulfilled God's purposes whenever the purposes can be ascertained. He must pass judgment on men accordingly as they served the divine design. On the first score he is not to exploit personality for the sake of personality, as the modern biographer does, but on the second he is to estimate all men from the one absolute standard, as Bradford estimates his dear friend Elder Brewster, or as Cotton Mather does John Eliot. Because every minutest happening, every fortune of war, every chance coincidence, is arranged by God, the Puritan historian does not elide minor incidents or incidental stories if their meaning is clear. In the midst of telling the broad movements or major crises he can always stop, as Bradford does, to relate "a spetiall work of Gods providence," and John Winthrop, putting into his *Journal* the material he intended ultimately to use in a formal history, finds that the rescue of the wife of one Dalkin, "dwelling near Medford," by clinging to her dog's

[1] John Cotton, *A Briefe Exposition . . . upon . . . Ecclesiastes* (London, 1654), pp. 21, 129–132.

tail, is intrinsically as important as the whole episode of the Antinomian turmoil. In reading histories of Puritan authorship it is necessary that we always remember the vast difference between their intentions and those of modern writers. The Puritan would feel that the points of view assumed by a twentieth-century scholar are determined solely by the writer's place in time and space, and therefore temporary, fallacious, and partial. Yet where the modern researcher feels bound to tell all the facts, not to generalize before exhaustive investigation, the Puritan has no hesitancy in sifting his material, placing emphases, omitting facts, generalizing upon any single piece of evidence, interpreting every action by one explicit standard. The guiding principle of his art is the extent to which anything can be made to illustrate clearly the operation of God's will. The contemporary historian would stress the economic and social inducement for the migration to New England; Thomas Shepard is concerned only with showing that in 1630 God Himself was engineering the opportunity and thereby ordering men to seize upon it.

Consequently two distinct characteristics reveal themselves when we come to the study of Puritan historiography. In the first place, the art of history, as practiced by Puritans, is bound to be specific and concrete, bound to stay close to the particular happening and episode; it is apt to be anecdotal, for the design of the whole is the will of God, which always emerges of itself if each step of the procedure is adequately noted and interpreted. In the second place, it is also a didactic art; nothing is to be told for its own sake alone; if any portion of history yields no meanings, it is either to be presented as a problem yet to be solved, like some obscure passage in scripture, or else it is to be ignored entirely. Above all, no explanations which rest merely upon natural or secondary causation, on mere economic motives, political expediency, accidental circumstance, the character of this or that man—no such explanations are to be accepted as final. God's will is the ultimate reason why things fall out one way rather than another, although God does work through natural causes; His will is intelligent, and the task of the historian is to discover, as far as the evidence will permit, the conscious and deliberate direction which lies behind all events.

Puritan history was posited upon the assumption of an eternal sameness in things, their perpetual control by the same agency for the same ends. Yet there was no denial that surfaces varied from age to age, that if the essential configurations were identical, the particular manifestations could show a vast difference from one century to another. The unity within variety for which Puritan thinkers sought in all other fields of speculation and study was also the objective of the Puritan historian, and he, not less than the theologian, strove not to lose sight of the one in the many or to over-simplify the particulars in establishing the universal. Thus John Cotton explained the historical process:

> The principal cause of all passages in the world: which is not mans weaknesse, or goodnesse, but chiefly the wise and strong and good providence of God: who presenteth every age with a new stage of acts and actors . . . And if a Poet would not present his spectators but with choyce variety of matters, how much lesse God? [1]

So New England chroniclers had first to demonstrate that their narratives exemplified once more the eternal and immutable regulations of providence, and then to indicate the particular and individual character of their own age. And when they came to this latter consideration, they explained history by what they believed to be the all-engrossing concern of the sixteenth and seventeenth centuries, the Reformation. Though all ages are under God's government, and one age should teach as much about him as any other, or equally exhibit his majesty, still some ages achieve greater exhibitions of his power than less fortunate ones. Next to the period in which Christ himself had lived, the Puritans believed that the hundred years since Luther nailed his theses on the cathedral door at Wittenberg were the most fraught with meaning of all human history.

> Truth is the Daughter of time, was the saying of old, and our daily experience gives in evidence and proof hereof, to every mans ordinary observation. Only as in other births, so here, the barrennesse and fruitfullnesse of severall ages, depend meerly upon Gods good pleasure, who opens and shuts the womb of truth from bearing, as he sees fit, according to the counsell of his own will.
>
> Not that there is any change in the truth, but the alteration grows, according to mens apprehensions, to whom it is more or lesse discovered, according to Gods most just judgement, and their own deservings.[2]

Clearly the Protestant movement had come about because men's apprehensions had been enabled to discover more of the truth than at any time since the Apostles; and as the Reformation was a continuous movement away from the Church of Rome toward the pure discipline established by Christ, the pure doctrine taught by scripture, and the

[1] John Cotton, *A Briefe Exposition . . . upon . . . Ecclesiastes* (London, 1654), p. 131.
[2] Thomas Hooker, *A Survey of the Summe of Church-Discipline* (London, 1648), A2 recto.

society built, politically and socially as well as ecclesiastically, upon divine enactments, New England was the culmination of the Reformation, the climax of world history, the ultimate revelation through events of the objective toward which the whole of human activity had been tending from the beginning of time. Winthrop preached to the emigrants during the voyage that the eyes of the world would be upon them, that they would be as a city set upon a hill for all to observe (p. 199); Captain Edward Johnson imagined that Christ himself had drawn up the "commission" for the migration; Cotton Mather modestly admitted that the churches in New England were not perfect, but that they were the best the world had yet achieved. The inspiration for the writing of histories by pious New Englanders was consequently twofold: not only to exhibit the truth as shown in the course of the world under God's providence, but to establish the climax of that course in the Reformation, of which New England was the supreme and purest embodiment.

Of course, there were many persons in the world, particularly in England, who did not agree with the New Englanders' idea of their own importance. The Anglicans naturally would not believe that any form of Puritanism was the logical result of the Reformation; Puritans who believed in the Presbyterian rather than the Congregational polity said all the discreditable things they could think of concerning New England, the soil, the climate, the inhabitants, and the practices; those Puritans who turned eventually to a philosophy of toleration attacked the New England Way for its tyranny and cruelty; Puritans who stayed at home to fight the King accused their brethren in America of having run away from danger. In order to maintain their view of history, with their contention that it had come to a peak in their own experiment, New England historians had to present the story of settlement and conquest, of ecclesiastical triumph and political institution, as they saw it. And sometimes the spokesmen for New England did not have time to tell the whole story, but were forced to take up their pens in answer to specific charges and to plead special cases against the particular reproaches.

In the selections given in this chapter there are examples of both formal history and occasional polemic. Higginson's pamphlet was sent back from Salem, to which an advance guard of the Massachusetts Bay Company had gone out in 1629; it was an advertising tract defending the region from the charge of being a barren desert, made against it by enemies of the enterprise. There are some respects in which Puritans writing about their own history are amazingly impartial; since they viewed whatever had happened as God's doing, they could suppress or twist facts only by running the danger of blaspheming God's work. But in the heat of controversy, or to score a point against mortal adversaries, they were strongly tempted to exaggerate, to put the best possible face on some rather dubious matters. Those who have lived in and with the climate of New England may very justifiably feel that good parson Higginson allowed his enthusiasm to run away with his judgment on that score. Thomas Shepard and John Allin wrote their book in direct answer to an attack upon the New England churches. In the late 1630's a group of Presbyterian Puritans had sent over a list of nine embarrassing questions concerning ecclesiastical practices. John Davenport had been commissioned to answer them, which he had done in the name of the ministers and the elders; in 1643 his manuscript was published in London, and because just at that moment the furious controversy between English Independents and Presbyterians was flaring up, Davenport's work was assailed with unanimity by the Presbyterians. One of these, John Ball, was an author much read and admired in New England for his theological writings, and his attack upon the New England church polity was exceedingly distressing to the ministers; Shepard and Allin were commissioned to reply to Ball's attack upon Davenport's answers to the original nine questions—thus did religious controversy lengthen out from book to book in the seventeenth century. Ball not only assailed the form of church organization, but raised the cry that those who fled to New England were deserters, that they had been afraid to stay in England and fight the good fight. The preface to the book, probably written by Shepard alone—for it has all the marks of his very individual style—reviews in masterly fashion the history of the settlement, and is perhaps the best surviving statement in their own terms of the intentions of the Massachusetts leaders.

The works of Bradford, Johnson, and Cotton Mather were written as full-dress, comprehensive histories, and the *Journal* of John Winthrop was undoubtedly a repository of jottings out of which he intended to compose a formal narrative. Of all the writings by New England Puritans in the seventeenth century, Bradford's *History* is the pre-eminent work of art. No other document so perfectly incarnates the Puritan ideal of the simple and plain style, is so filled with the deep feeling of religious dedication, so perfectly masters the rhythms of Biblical prose, so fluently handles the imagery of the devotional life, or so reveals the solid, broad, and generous aspects of the Puritan character. But in reading these pages, the student should remember that William Bradford was not quite a Puritan in the meaning in which the term is generally used in this volume. The true Puritan was a member of the Church of England, whose whole effort while in England was to remain within the Church and secure the mastery of it; he belonged to a strong, wealthy, organized, and powerful interest, led by important politicians and learned clergymen. Bradford was a Separatist, one of a small and earnest band of simple souls, all of humble station, who were quite incapable of containing their religion within the fine distinctions by which the Puritans endeavored to stay in the Church at the same time that they were in deadly combat with the authorities. The persons who made up the "Pilgrim" company were home-spun, hard-working farmers from Nottinghamshire and Lincolnshire; their minister, John Robinson, was a university man, and Elder Brewster had spent a couple of years at Cambridge, but otherwise they were men instructed only in the Bible and in simplicity of spirit. They had openly broken with the Church of England, and proceeded to set up a completely "separate" body. No government in Europe at that epoch would have tolerated the existence of such a society, outside and independent of the established institution, and it is no wonder that the bishops and the sheriffs of England got after this congregation with vehemence. Holland alone of all Europe would offer an asylum to these people, though not so much because the Dutch believed in toleration as because the Separatists were theologically good Calvinists, as were the Dutch. Robinson's congregation, escaping to Holland, lived there for several years, until the reasons which Bradford enumerates persuaded many of them to undertake a settlement in America. Robinson did not come with the first settlers in 1620, and died before his intended removal; the community was without funds, entirely self-supporting, too small and insignificant to be noticed by the English authorities. Bradford's history is the history of simple folk, directly inspired by a religious ideal, working out the will of God by themselves, amid incredible hardship. They underwent privation because they were absolutely confident that they were obeying the direct behests of God Himself, and that through all miseries and anguish He was watching over them and testing their fidelity. The *History of Plymouth Plantation* is the story of that ordeal, told by the man who was the leader and whose simple strength and rugged integrity were the mainstays of the community. Plymouth was a minute, relatively insignificant community, completely overshadowed by Massachusetts Bay from 1630 on, and ultimately absorbed into it by the royal charter of 1692. The leaders of Massachusetts Bay were aggressive, educated, philosophical; Plymouth was pious, struggling, and desired chiefly to be let alone. But though Bradford is not, for these reasons, altogether representative of the Puritan mind in its intellectualized and metaphysical form, he might by that very fact be said to be the essence of the Puritan. The soaring passage in which he contemplates the plight of the settlers at the moment of landing, in November, 1620, and affirms the faith in the might of which they confronted the desolate shore and the murderous climate is the masterpiece of all Puritan eloquence. No other writer will lead us so directly to the core of Puritanism as Bradford, none with such charm, generosity, largeness of spirit, with such calm assurance and massive strength will so completely reveal the essential frame of mind, the type of character, the quality of life that underlay the theology.

The *Journal* of John Winthrop lacks the form and beauty of Bradford's history by the very necessities of the case. It was a day-by-day, or at any rate month-by-month, chronicle of the adventure at Massachusetts Bay, put down in rare minutes of leisure by the outstanding leader of the expedition and the man upon whose shoulders rested the larger part of the responsibility for success or failure. Had he ever found opportunity to make a coherent history he would undoubtedly have polished the style and systematized the presentation. But even as a journal his volume frequently achieves genuine literary merit, and reveals completely the character and prowess of the Puritan statesman. In sharp contrast to Bradford, Winthrop came of distinctly aristocratic stock; his grandfather had been a wealthy clothier in the reign of Henry VIII, who obtained the manor of Groton in Suffolk when the monasteries were dispossessed; his father was a university man, a famous lawyer, who added to the family fortunes. John Winthrop himself attended Trinity College, Cambridge, though he left without taking a degree. Before he migrated to New England he was a country squire, a justice of the peace, an attorney and a member of the Inner Temple. When he left England it was at the sacrifice of a career already launched, a secure social position, a background of wealth, influence, and leisure. He came to New England determined that the experiment should succeed, and it did; if he is not as eloquent in voicing the religious inspiration as Bradford, none the less the motive was in him as intensely and as powerfully.

Edward Johnson was one of the citizens, not one of the humblest, but representative of the rank and file. The title of his book, *The Wonder-working Providence of Sions Saviour in New England*, is in itself a confession of the Puritan philosophy of history; the story of New

England is to him a protracted evidence of the assistance of God, the same God who protected Israel of old, and who still works wonders for men by his providence—whenever they will coöperate with Him in the right spirit. He is a slighter figure than either Winthrop or Bradford, and writes in a much more ornate, windy, and verbose style. Even at his most inflated moments he is not without a certain charm, however, and the zest for living which so conspicuously marked the writings of Elizabethan England had not yet died out in him.

Of Cotton Mather the most remarkable fact is that one small head could carry all he knew. He writes as a member of the third generation in New England, the grandson of Richard Mather, the son of Increase, the inheriting figure in what had become the outstanding dynasty of ministerial rule in the colony. The deep passions of the founding generation had become more regular and lukewarm in his day; times were changing, and the early Puritan creed was crumbling all about him. Though he himself contributed to the change in many respects, though he himself fought the more hidebound conservatives on the question of inoculation for smallpox, his life was generally motivated by an attempt to keep the hands of the clock at the same hour they had indicated when his grandfather had preached at Dorchester. His great history, the *Magnalia Christi Americana*, "the great achievements of Christ in America," was in large part designed to revive fading piety, as demanded in the sermon of Urian Oakes. He did not succeed in this objective, but he did manage to bring together within the covers of one Gargantuan book almost the whole account of Puritan thought and action in seventeenth-century America. He spattered his pages with his amazing erudition, and earned himself the description of pedant, but he also summarized a century of experience.

WILLIAM BRADFORD, 1590–1657

[William Bradford was born in Austerfield, of Yorkshire yeoman stock; inheriting a "comfortable" sum from his father, who died in his childhood, he might well have grown into a substantial, solid farmer, had he not at the age of twelve become a serious reader of the Bible and been driven by his religious convictions, in opposition to the wishes of his family, to join the group who met at the house of William Brewster in Scrooby. With John Robinson as minister, these persons organized a Separatist church in 1606, fled to Amsterdam in 1609, and then to Leyden, where Bradford supported himself as a fustian weaver and say worker. During these years he must have read extensively in theological literature. He was a leader in the migration to New England and was elected Governor of the Plymouth colony upon the death of John Carver in April, 1621. He served in that office for thirty out of his remaining thirty-six years, without salary until 1639 and thereafter for £20 a year. He exercised almost complete discretionary power, proved himself on every occasion shrewd, firm, and generous. In his old age he undertook the study of Hebrew, in order to see "the ancient oracles of God in their native beauty." In the inventory of his estate there was a red waistcoat, a great silver "beer bowle," and a violet cloak. He commenced writing the *History* in 1630, probably finished it about 1650. This text is from the *History of Plymouth Plantation*, ed. Worthington C. Ford (Massachusetts Historical Society, Boston, 1912), 2 vols : I, 16–18, 21–22, 24–25, 28–35, 53–60, 149–158, 189–196, 239–246, 299–303, 362–367; II, 45–58, 161–164, 308–310, 342–353. For further bibliography see this edition, or the article by Samuel Eliot Morison in *The Dictionary of American Biography*.]

HISTORY OF PLIMOTH PLANTATION

WHEN as by the travell, and diligence of some godly, and zealous preachers, and Gods blessing on their labours; as in other places of the land, so in the North parts, many became inlightened by the word of God; and had their ignorance and sins discovered unto them, and begane by his grace to reforme their lives, and make conscience of their wayes. The worke of God was no sooner manifest in them; but presently they were both scoffed and scorned by the prophane multitude, and the ministers urged with the yoak of subscription, or els must be silenced; and the poore people were so vexed with apparators, and pursuants, and the comissarie courts, as truly their affliction was not smale; which, notwithstanding, they bore sundrie years with much patience, till they were occasioned (by the continuance and encrease of these troubles, and other means which the Lord raised up in those days) to see further into things by the light of the word of God. How not only these base and beggerly ceremonies were unlawfull; but also that the lordly and tiranous power of the prelates ought not to be submitted unto; which thus (contrary to the freedome of the gospell,) would load and burden mens consciences; and by their compulsive power make a prophane mixture of persons, and things in the worship of God. . . .

So many therfore (of these proffessors) as saw the evill of these things, (in thes parts,) and whose harts the Lord had touched with heavenly zeale for his trueth; they shooke of this yoake of Antichristian bondage. And as the Lords free people, joyned them selves (by a covenant of the Lord) into a church estate, in the felowship of the Gospell, to walke in all his wayes, made known, or to be made known unto them (according to their best endeavours) whatsoever it should cost them, the Lord assisting them. And that it cost them something this ensewing historie will declare. . . .

But after these things; they could not long continue in any peaceable condition; but were hunted and persecuted on every side, so as their former afflictions were but as flea-bitings in comparison of these which now came upon them. For some were taken and clapt up in prison, others had their houses besett and watcht night and day, and hardly escaped their hands; and the most were faine to flie and leave their howses and habitations, and the means of their livelehood. Yet these and many other sharper things which affterward befell them, were no other then they looked for, and therfore were the better prepared to bear them by the assistance of Gods grace and spirite; yet seeing them selves thus molested, and that ther was no hope of their continuance ther, by a joynte consente they resolved to goe into the Low-Countries, wher they heard was freedome of Religion for all men; as also how sundrie from London, and other parts of the land, had been exiled and persecuted for the same cause, and were gone thither; and lived at Amsterdam, and in other places of the land. . . .

Being thus constrained to leave their native soyle and countrie, their lands and livings, and all their freinds and famillier acquaintance, it was much, and thought marvelous by many. But to goe into a countrie they knew not (but by hearsay) wher they must learne a new language, and get their livings they knew not how, it being a dear place, and subjecte to the misseries of warr, it was by many thought an adventure almost desperate, a case intolerable, and a misserie worse then death. Espetially seeing they were not acquainted with trads nor traffique (by which that countrie doth subsiste) but had only been used to a plaine countrie life, and the inocente trade of husbandrey. But these things did not dismay them (though they did some times trouble them) for their desires were sett on the ways of god, and to injoye his ordinances; but they rested on his providence, and knew whom they had beleeved. Yet this was not all, for though they could not stay, yet were they not suffered to goe, but the ports and havens were shut against them, so as they were faine to seeke secrete means of conveance, and to bribe and fee the mariners, and give exterordinarie rates for their passages. And yet were they often times betrayed (many of them) and both they and their goods intercepted and surprised, and therby put to great trouble and charge, of which I will give an instance or tow, and omitte the rest.

Ther was a large companie of them purposed to get passage at Boston in Lincoln-shire, and for that end had hired a shipe wholy to them selves, and made agreement with the maister to be ready at a certaine day, and take them and their goods in, at a conveniente place, wher they accordingly would all attende in readines. So after long waiting, and large expences (though he kepte not day with them) yet he came at length and tooke them in, in the night. But when he had them and their goods abord, he betrayed them, haveing before hand complotted with the serchers and other officers so to doe. Who tooke them, and put them into open boats, and ther rifled and ransaked them, searching them to their shirts for money, yea even the women furder then became modestie; and then caried them back into the towne, and made them a spectackle and wonder to the multitude, which came flocking on all sids to behould them. Being thus first, by the chatch-poule officers, rifled, and stripte of their money, books, and much other goods; they were presented to the majestrates, and messengers sente to informe the lords of the Counsell of them; and so they were commited to ward. Indeed the majestrats used them courteously, and shewed them what favour they could; but could not deliver them, till order came from the Counsell-table. But the issue was that after a months imprisonmente, the greatest parte were dismiste, and sent to the places from whence they came; but 7. of the principall were still kept in prison, and bound over to the Assises.

The nexte spring after, ther was another attempte made by some of these and others, to get over at an other place. And it so fell out, that they light of a Dutchman at Hull, having a ship of his owne belonging to Zealand; they made agreemente with him, and acquainted him with their condition, hoping to find more faithfullnes in him, then in the former of their owne nation; he bad them not fear, for he would doe well enough. He was (by appointment) to take them in betweene Grimsbe and Hull, wher was a large commone a good way distante from any towne. Now aganst the prefixed time, the women and children, with the goods, were sent to the place in a small barke, which they had hired for that end; and the men were to meete them by land. But it so fell out, that they were ther a day before the shipe came, and the sea being rough, and the women very sicke, prevailed with the seamen to put into a creeke hardby, wher they lay on ground at lowwater. The nexte morning the shipe came, but they were fast, and could not stir till aboute noone; In the mean time (the shipe maister, perceiving how the matter was) sente his boate to be getting the men abord whom he saw ready, walking aboute the shore. But after the first boat full was gott abord, and she was ready to goe for more, the m[r] espied a greate company (both horse and foote) with bills, and gunes, and other weapons (for the countrie was raised to take them). The Dutch-man seeing that, swore (his countries oath), "sacremente"; and having the wind faire, waiged his Ancor, hoysed sayles, and away. But the poore-men which were gott abord, were in great distress for their wives, and children, which they saw thus to be taken, and were left destitute of their helps; and them selves also, not having a cloath to shifte them with, more then they had on their baks, and some scarce a peney aboute them, all they had being abord the barke. It drew tears from their eyes, and any thing they had they would have given to have been a shore againe; but all in vaine, ther was no remedy, they must thus sadly part. . . .

The rest of the men that were in greatest danger, made shift to escape away before the troope could surprise them; those only staying that best might, to be assistante unto the women. But pitifull it was to see the heavie case of these poore women in this distress; what weeping and crying on every side, some for their husbands, that were caried away in the ship as is before related. Others not knowing what should become of them, and their litle ones; others againe melted in teares, seeing their poore litle ones hanging aboute them, crying for feare, and quaking with could. Being thus aprehended, they were hurried from one place to another, and from one justice to another, till in the ende they knew not what to doe with them; for to imprison so many women and innocent children for no other cause (many of them) but that they must goe with their husbands; semed to be unreasonable and all would crie out of them; and to send them home againe was as difficult, for they aledged (as the trueth was) they had no homes to goe to, for they had either sould, or otherwise disposed of their houses, and livings. To be shorte, after they had been thus turmolyed a good while, and conveyed from one constable to another, they were glad to be ridd of them in the end upon any termes; for all were wearied and tired with them. Though in the mean time they (poore soules) indured miserie enough; and thus in the end necessitie forste a way for them. . . . And in the end, notwithstanding all these stormes of oppossition, they all gatt over at length, some at one time and some at an other, and some in one place, and some in an other, And mete togeather againe according to their desires, with no small rejoycing. . . .

After they had lived in this citie about some 11. or 12. years, (which is the more observable being the whole time of that famose truce between that state and the Spaniards,) and sundrie of them were taken away by death; and many others begane to be well striken in years (the grave mistris Experience haveing taught them many things) those prudent governours, with sundrie of the sagest members begane both deeply to apprehend their present dangers, and wisely to foresee the future, and thinke of timly remedy. In the agitation of their thoughts, and much discours of things hear aboute, at length they began to incline to this conclusion, of remooyall to some other place. Not out of any newfanglednes, or other such like giddie humor, by which men are oftentimes transported to their great hurt, and danger. But for sundrie weightie and solid reasons; some of the cheefe of which I will hear breefly touch. And first, they saw and found by experience the hardnes of the place and countrie to be such, as few in comparison would come to them; and fewer that would bide it out, and continew with them. For many that came to them, and many more that desired to be with them; could not endure that great labor and hard fare, with other inconveniences which they underwent and were contented with. But though they loved their persons, approved their cause, and honoured their sufferings, yet they left them as it weer weeping, as Orpah did her mother in law Naomie; or as those Romans did Cato in Utica, who desired to be excused and borne with, though they could not all be Catoes. For many, though they desired to injoye the ordinances of God in their puritie, and the libertie of the gospell with them, yet (alass) they admitted of bondage—with deanger of conscience, rather than to indure these hardships; yea, some preferred, and chose the prisons in England, rather then this libertie in Holland, with these afflictions. But it was thought that if a better, and easier place of living, could be had, it would draw many, and take away these discouragments. Yea, their pastor would often say, that many of those who both wrote, and preached now against them, if they were in a place, wher they might have libertie and live comfortably, they would then practise as they did.

2^{ly}. They saw, that though the people generally, bore all these difficulties very cherfully, and with a resolute courage, being in the best, and strength of their years, yet old age began to steale on many of them, (and their great and continuall labours, with other crosses and sorrows, hastened it before the time) so as it was not only probably thought, but apparently seen, that within a few years more, they would be in danger to scatter (by necessities pressing them) or sinke under their burdens, or both. And therfore according to the devine proverb, that a wise man seeth the plague when it cometh, and hideth him selfe, Pro. 22. 3., so they like skillfull and beaten souldiers were fearfull, either to be intrapped or surrounded by their enimies, so as they should neither be able to fight nor flie. And therfor thought it better to dislodge betimes to some place of better advantage and less danger, if any such could be found.

Thirdly; As necessitie was a taskmaster over them, so they were forced to be such, not only to their servants (but in a sorte) to their dearest children; the which as it did not a litle wound the tender harts of many a loving father, and mother; so it produced likwise sundrie sad and sorowful effects. For many of their children, that were of best dispositions, and gracious Inclinations (haveing lernde to bear the yoake in their youth) and willing to bear parte of their parents burden, were (often times) so oppressed with their hevie labours, that though their minds were free and willing, yet their bodies bowed under the weight of the same, and became decreped in their early youth; the vigor of nature being consumed in the very budd as it were. But that which was more lamentable, and of all sorowes most heavie to be borne, was that many of their children, by these occasions, and the great licentiousness of youth in that countrie, and the manifold temptations of the place, were drawne away by evill examples into extravagante and dangerous courses, getting the raines off their neks, and departing from their parents. Some became souldiers, others tooke upon them farr viages by sea, and other some worse courses, tending to dissolutnes and the danger of their soules, to the great greefe of their parents and dishonour of God. So that they saw their posteritie would be in danger to degenerate and be corrupted.

Lastly, (and which was not least), a great hope, and inward zeall they had of laying some good foundation, or (at least to make some way therunto) for the propagating, and advancing the gospell of the kingdom of Christ in those remote parts of the world; yea, though they should be but even as stepping-stones, unto others for the performing of so great a work.

These, and some other like reasons, moved them to undertake this resolution of their removall; the which they afterward prosecuted with so great difficulties, as by the sequell will appeare.

The place they had thoughts on, was some of those vast and unpeopled countries of America, which are frutfull, and fitt for habitation; being devoyd of all civill inhabitants; wher ther are only salvage, and brutish men, which range up and downe, litle otherwise then the wild beasts of the same. This proposition being made publike, and coming to the scaning of all; it raised many variable opinions amongst men, and caused many fears, and doubts amongst them selves. Some from their reasons, and hopes conceived, laboured to stirr up and incourage the rest to undertake, and prosecute the same; others againe out of their fears, objected against it, and sought to diverte from it; aledging many things, and those neither unreasonable, nor unprobable. As that it was a great designe, and subjecte to many unconceivable perills, and dangers; as, besids the casulties of the seas (which none can be freed from) the length of the vioage was such, as the weake bodys of women and other persons worne out with age and traville (as many of them were) could never be able to endure. And yet if they should, the miseries of the land, which they should be exposed unto, would be to hard to be borne; and lickly, some, or all of them togeither, to consume, and utterly to ruinate them. For ther they should be liable to famine, and nakednes, and the wante in a maner of all things. The chang of aire, diate, and drinking of water, would infecte their bodies with sore sickneses, and greevous diseases. And also those which should escape or overcome these difficulties, should yett be in continuall danger of the salvage people; who are cruell, barbarous, and most trecherous, being most furious in their rage, and merciles wher they overcome; not being contente only to kill, and take away life, but delight to tormente men in the most bloodie manner that may be; fleaing some alive with the shells of fishes, cutting of the members, and joynts of others by peesmeale, and broiling on the coles, eate the collops of their flesh in their sight whilst they live; with other cruelties horrible to be related. And surely it could not be thought but the very hearing of these things could not but move the very bowels of men to grate within them, and make the weake to quake, and tremble. It was furder objected, that it would require greater summes of money to furnish such a voiage (and to fitt them with necessaries) then their consumed estats would amounte too; and yett they must as well looke to be seconded with supplies, as presently to be transported. Also many presidents of ill success, and lamentable misseries befalne others, in the like designes, were easie to be found, and not forgotten to be aledged. Besides their owne experience, in their former troubles, and hardships in their removall into Holand; and how hard a thing it was for them to live in that strange place, though it was a neighbour countrie, and a civill and rich comone wealth.

It was answered, that all great, and honourable actions, are accompanied with great difficulties; and must be both enterprised, and overcome with answerable courages. It was granted the dangers were great, but not desperate; the difficulties were many, but not invincible. For though their were many of them likly, yet they were not cartaine; it might be sundrie of the things feared might never befale; others by providente care and the use of good means, might in a great measure be prevented; and all of them (through the help of God) by fortitude, and patience, might either be borne, or overcome. True it was, that such atempts were not to be made and undertaken without good ground, and reason; not rashly, or lightly as many have done for curiositie, or hope of gaine, etc. But their condition was not ordinarie; their ends were good and honourable; their calling lawfull, and urgente; and therfore they might expecte the blessing of God in their proceding. Yea, though they should loose their lives in this action, yet might they have comforte in the same, and their endeavors would be honourable. . . .

These troubls being blowne over, and now all being compacte togeather in one shipe, they put to sea againe with a prosperus winde, which continued diverce days togeather, which was some incouragmente unto them; yet according to the usuall maner many were afflicted with seasicknes. And I may not omite hear a spetiall worke of Gods providence. Ther was a proud and very profane yonge man, one of the sea-men, of a lustie, able body, which made him the more hauty; he would allway be contemning the poore people in their sicknes, and cursing them dayly with greevous execrations, and did not let to tell them, that he hoped to help to cast halfe of them over board before they came to their jurneys end, and to make mery with what they had; and if he were by any gently reproved, he would curse and swear most bitterly. But it plased God before they came halfe seas over, to smite this yong man with a greeveous disease, of which he dyed in a desperate maner, and so was him selfe the first that was throwne overbord. Thus his curses light on his owne head; and it was an astonishmente to all his fellows, for they noted it to be the just hand of God upon him.

After they had injoyed faire winds and weather for a season, they were incountred many times with crosse winds, and mette with many feirce stormes, with which the shipe was shroudly shaken, and her upper works made very leakie; and one of the maine beames in the midd ships was bowed and craked, which put them in some fear that the shipe could not be able to performe the vioage. So some of the cheefe of the company, perceiveing the mariners to feare the suffisiencie of the shipe, as appeared by their mutterings, they entred into serious consulltation with the m^r and other officers of the ship, to consider in time of the danger; and rather to returne then to cast them selves into a desperate and inevitable perill. And truly ther was great distraction and differance of opinion amongst the mariners them selves; faine would they doe what could be done for their wages sake, (being now halfe the seas over,) and on the other hand they were loath to hazard their lives too desperately. But in examening of all opinions, the m^r and others affirmed they knew the ship to be stronge and firme under water; and for the buckling of the maine beame, ther was a great iron scrue the passengers brought out of Holland, which would raise the beame into his place; the which being done, the carpenter and m^r affirmed that with a post put under it, set firme in the lower deck, and otherways bounde, he would make it sufficiente. And as for the decks and uper workes they would calke them as well as they could, and though with the workeing of the ship they would not longe keepe stanch, yet ther would otherwise be no great danger, if they did not overpress her with sails. So they commited them selves to the will of God, and resolved to proseede. In sundrie of these stormes the winds were so feirce, and the seas so high, as they could not beare a knote of saile, but were forced to hull, for diverce days togither. And in one of them, as they thus lay at hull, in a mighty storme, a lustie yonge man (called John Howland) coming upon some occasion above the grattings, was, with a seele of the shipe throwne into [the] sea; but it pleased God that he caught hould of the topsaile halliards, which hunge over board, and rane out at length; yet he held his hould (though he was sundrie fadomes under water) till he was hald up by the same rope to the brime of the water, and then with a boat hooke and other means got into the shipe againe, and his life saved; and though he was something ill with it, yet he lived many years after, and became a profitable member both in church and commone wealthe. In all this viage ther died but one of the passengers, which was William Butten, a youth, servant to Samuell Fuller, when they drew near the coast. But to omite other things, (that I may be breefe,) after longe beating at sea they fell with that land which is called Cape Cod; the which being made and certainly knowne to be it, they were not a litle joyfull. After some deliberation had amongst them selves and with the m^r of the ship, they tacked aboute and resolved to stande for the southward (the wind and weather being faire) to finde some place aboute Hudsons river for their habitation. But after they had sailed that course aboute halfe the day, they fell amongst deangerous shoulds and roring breakers, and they were so farr intangled ther with as they conceived them selves in great danger; and the wind shrinking upon them withall, they resolved to bear up againe for the Cape, and thought them selves hapy to gett out of those dangers before night overtooke them, as by Gods providence they did. And the next day they gott into the Cape-harbor wher they ridd in saftie. A word or too by the way of this cape; it was thus first named by Capten Gosnole and his company, An°: 1602, and after by Capten Smith was caled Cape James; but it retains the former name amongst seamen. Also that pointe which first shewed those dangerous shoulds unto them, they called Pointe Care, and Tuckers Terrour; but the French and Dutch to this day call it Malabarr, by reason of those perilous shoulds, and the losses they have suffered their.

Being thus arived in a good harbor and brought safe to land, they fell upon their knees and blessed the God of heaven, who had brought them over the vast and furious ocean, and delivered them from all the periles and miseries therof, againe to set their feete on the firme and stable earth, their proper elemente. And no marvell if they were thus joyefull, seeing wise Seneca was so affected with sailing a few miles on the coast of his owne Italy; as he affirmed, that he had rather remaine twentie years on his way by land, then pass by sea to any place in a short time; so tedious and dreadfull was the same unto him.

But hear I cannot but stay and make a pause, and stand half amased at this poore peoples presente condition; and so I thinke will the reader too, when he well considers the same. Being thus passed the vast ocean, and a sea of troubles before in their preparation (as may be remembred by that which wente before), they had now no freinds to wellcome them, nor inns to entertaine or refresh their weatherbeaten bodys, no houses or much less townes to repaire too, to seeke for succoure. It is recorded in scripture as a mercie to the apostle and his shipwraked company, that the barbarians shewed them no smale kindnes in refreshing them, but these savage barbarians, when they mette with them (as after will appeare) were readier to fill their sids full of arrows then otherwise. And for the season it was winter, and they that know the winters of that cuntrie know them to be sharp and violent, and subjecte to cruell and feirce stormes, deangerous to travill to known places, much more to serch an unknown coast. Besides, what could they see but a hidious and desolate wildernes, full of wild beasts and willd men? and what multituds ther might be of them they knew not. Nether could they, as it were, goe up to the tope of Pisgah, to vew from this willdernes a more goodly cuntrie to feed their hops; for which way soever they turnd their eys (save upward to the heavens) they could have litle solace or content in respecte of any outward objects. For summer being done, all things stand upon them with a wether-beaten face; and the whole countrie, full of woods and thickets, represented a wild and savage heiw. If they looked behind them, ther was the mighty ocean which they had passed, and was now as a maine barr and goulfe to seperate them from all the civill parts of the world. If it be said they had a ship to sucour them, it is trew; but what heard they daly from the m^r^ and company? but that with speede they should looke out a place with their shallop, wher they would be at some near distance; for the season was shuch as he would not stirr from thence till a safe harbor was discovered by them wher they would be, and he might goe without danger; and that victells consumed apace, but he must and would keepe sufficient for them selves and their returne. Yea, it was muttered by some, that if they gott not a place in time, they would turne them and their goods ashore and leave them. Let it also be considred what weake hopes of supply and succoure they left behinde them, that might bear up their minds in this sade condition and trialls they were under; and they could not but be very smale. It is true, indeed, the affections and love of their brethren at Leyden was cordiall and entire towards them, but they had litle power to help them, or them selves; and how the case stode betweene them and the marchants at their coming away, hath allready been declared. What could now sustaine them but the spirite of God and his grace? May not and ought not the children of these fathers rightly say: *Our faithers were Englishmen which came over this great ocean, and were ready to perish in this willdernes; but they cried unto the Lord, and he heard their voyce, and looked on their adversitie, etc. Let them therfore praise the Lord, because he is good, and his mercies endure for ever. Yea, let them which have been redeemed of the Lord, shew how he hath delivered them from the hand of the oppressour. When they wandered in the deserte willdernes out of the way, and found no citie to dwell in, both hungrie, and thirstie, their sowle was overwhelmed in them. Let them confess before the Lord his loving kindnes, and his wonderfull works before the sons of men. . . .*

[1620] I shall a litle returne backe and begine with a combination made by them before they came ashore, being the first foundation of their govermente in this place; occasioned partly by the discontented and mutinous speeches that some of the strangers amongst them had let fall from them in the ship; That when they came a shore they would use their owne libertie; for none had power to command them, the patente they had being for Virginia, and not for New-england, which belonged to an other Goverment, with which the Virginia Company had nothing to doe. And partly that shuch an acte by them done (this their condition considered) might be as firme as any patent, and in some respects more sure.

The forme was as followeth.

In the name of God, Amen. We whose names are under-writen, the loyall subjects of our dread soveraigne Lord, King James, by the grace of God, of Great Britaine, Franc, and Ireland king, defender of the faith, etc., haveing undertaken, for the glorie of God, and advancemente of the Christian faith, and honour of our king and countrie, a voyage to plant the first colonie in the Northerne parts of Virginia, doe by these presents solemnly and mutualy in the presence of God, and one of another, covenant and combine our selves togeather into a civill body politick, for our better ordering and preservation and furtherance of the ends aforesaid; and by vertue hearof to enacte, constitute, and frame such just and equall lawes, ordinances, acts, constitutions, and offices, from time to time, as shall be thought most meete and convenient for the generall good of the Colonie, unto which we promise all due submission and obedience. In witnes wherof we have hereunder subscribed our names at Cap-Codd the 11. of November, in the year of the raigne of our soveraigne lord, King James, of England, France, and Ireland the eighteenth, and of Scotland the fiftie fourth. An^{o}: Dom. 1620.

After this they chose, or rather confirmed, Mr. John Carver (a man godly and well approved amongst them) their Governour for that year. And after they had provided a place for their goods, or comone store, (which were long in unlading for want of boats, foulnes of winter weather, and sicknes of diverce,) and begune some small cottages for their habitation, as time would admitte, they mette and consulted of lawes and orders, both for their civill and military Govermente, as the necessitie of their condition did require, still adding therunto as urgent occasion in severall times, and as cases did require.

In these hard and difficulte beginings they found some discontents and murmurings arise amongst some, and mutinous speeches and carriags in other; but they were soone quelled and overcome by the wisdome, patience, and just and equall carrage of things by the Govr and better part, which clave faithfully togeather in the maine. But that which was most sadd and lamentable was, that in 2. or 3. moneths time halfe of their company dyed, espetialy in Jan: and February, being the depth of winter, and wanting houses and other comforts; being infected with the scurvie and other diseases, which this long vioage and their inacomodate condition had brought upon them; so as ther dyed some times 2. or 3. of a day, in the foresaid time; that of 100. and odd persons, scarce 50. remained. And of these in the time of most distres, ther was but 6. or 7. sound persons, who, to their great comendations be it spoken, spared no pains, night nor day, but with abundance of toyle and hazard of their owne health, fetched them woode, made them fires, drest them meat, made their beads, washed their lothsome cloaths, cloathed and uncloathed them; in a word, did all the homly and necessarie offices for them which dainty and quesie stomacks cannot endure to hear named; and all this willingly and cherfully, without any grudging in the least, shewing herein their true love unto their freinds and bretheren. A rare example and worthy to be remembred. Tow of these 7. were Mr. William Brewster, ther reverend Elder, and Myles Standish, ther Captein and military comander, unto whom my selfe, and many others, were much beholden in our low and sicke condition. And yet the Lord so upheld these persons, as in this generall calamity they were not at all infected either with sicknes, or lamnes. And what I have said of these, I may say of many others who dyed in this generall vissitation, and others yet living, that whilst they had health, yea, or any strength continuing, they were not wanting to any that had need of them. And I doute not but their recompence is with the Lord. . . .

[1621] After the departure of this ship, [the *Fortune*] (which stayed not above 14. days,) the Gove[r] and his assistante haveing disposed these late commers into severall families, as they best could, tooke an exacte accounte of all their provissions in store, and proportioned the same to the number of persons, and found that it would not hould out above 6. months at halfe alowance, and hardly that. And they could not well give less this winter time till fish came in againe. So they were presently put to half alowance, one as well as an other, which begane to be hard, but they bore it patiently under hope of supply.

Soone after this ships departure, the great people of the Narigansets, in a braving maner, sente a messenger unto them with a bundl of arrows tyed aboute with a great sneak-skine; which their interpretours tould them was a threatening and a chaleng. Upon which the Gov[r], with the advice of others sente them a round answere, that if they had rather have warre then peace, they might begine when they would; they had done them no wrong, neither did they fear them, or should they find them unprovided. And by another messenger sente the sneake-skine back with bulits in it; but they would not receive it, but sent it back againe. But these things I doe but mention, because they are more at large allready put forth in printe, by Mr. Winslow, at the requeste of some freinds. And it is like the reason was their owne ambition, who, (since the death of so many of the Indeans,) thought to dominire and lord it over the rest, and conceived the English would be a barr in their way, and saw that Massasoyt took sheilter allready under their wings.

But this made them the more carefully to looke to them selves, so as they agreed to inclose their dwellings with a good strong pale, and make flankers in convenient places, with gates to shute, which were every night locked, and a watch kept and when neede required ther was also warding in the day time. And the company was by the Captaine and the Govr advise, devided into 4. squadrons, and every one had ther quarter apoynted them, unto which they were to repaire upon any suddane alarme. And if ther should be any crie of fire, a company were appointed for a gard, with muskets, whilst others quenchet the same, to prevent Indean treachery. This was accomplished very cherfully, and the towne impayled round by the begining of March, in which evry family had a prety garden plote secured. And herewith I shall end this year. Only I shall remember one passage more, rather of mirth then of waight. One the day called Chrismasday, the Govr caled them out to worke, (as was used,) but the most of this new-company excused them selves and said it wente against their consciences to work on that day. So the Govr tould them that if they made it mater of conscience, he would spare them till they were better informed. So he led-away the rest and left them; but when they came home at noone from their worke, he found them in the streete at play, openly; some pitching the barr and some at stoole-ball, and shuch like sports. So he went to them, and tooke away their implements, and tould them that was against his conscience, that they should play and others worke. If they made the keeping of it mater of devotion, let them kepe their houses, but ther should be no gameing or revelling in the streets. Since which time nothing hath been atempted that way, at least openly. . . .

[1623] They begane to thinke how they might raise as much corne as they could, and obtaine a beter crope then they had done, that they might not still thus languish in miserie. At length, after much debate of things, the Govr (with the advise of the cheefest amongest them) gave way that they should set corne every man for his owne perticuler, and in that regard trust to them selves; in all other things to goe on in the generall way as before. And so assigned to every family a parcell of land, according to the proportion of their number for that end, only for present use (but made no devission for inheritance), and ranged all boys and youth under some familie. This had very good success; for it made all hands very industrious, so as much more corne was planted then other waise would have bene by any means the Gov[r] or any other could use, and saved him a great deall of trouble, and gave farr better contente. The women now wente willingly into the feild, and tooke their litle-ons with them to set corne, which before would aledg weaknes, and inabilitie; whom to have compelled would have bene thought great tiranie and oppression.

The experience that was had in this commone course and condition, tried sundrie years, and that amongst godly and sober men, may well evince the vanitie of that conceite of Platos and other ancients, applauded by some of later times;—that the taking away of propertie, and bringing in communitie into a comone wealth, would make them happy and florishing; as if they were wiser then God. For this comunitie (so farr as it was) was found to breed much confusion and discontent, and retard much imployment that would have been to their benefite and comforte. For the yong-men that were most able and fitte for labour and service did repine that they should spend their time and streingth to worke for other mens wives and children, with out any recompence. The strong, or man of parts, had no more in devission of victails and cloaths, then he that was weake and not able to doe a quarter the other could; this was thought injuestice. The aged and graver men to be ranked and equalised in labours, and victails, cloaths, etc., with the meaner and yonger sorte, thought it some indignite and disrespect unto them. And for mens wives to be commanded to doe servise for other men, as dresing their meate, washing their cloaths, etc., they deemd it a kind of slaverie, neither could many husbands well brooke it. Upon the poynte all being to have alike, and all to doe alike, they thought them selves in the like condition, and one as good as another; and so, if it did not cut of those relations that God hath set amongest men, yet it did at least much diminish and take of the mutuall respects that should be preserved amongst them. And would have bene worse if they had been men of another condition. Let none objecte this is men's corruption, and nothing to the course it selfe. I answer, seeing all men have this corruption in them, God in his wisdome saw another course fiter for them. . . .

[1624] With the former letter write by Mr. Sherley, there were sente sundrie objections concerning which he thus writeth. "These are the cheefe objections which they that are now returned make against you and the countrie. I pray you consider them, and answer them by the first conveniencie." These objections were made by some of those that came over on their perticuler and were returned home, as is before mentioned, and were of the same suite with those that this other letter mentions.

I shall here set them downe, with the answers then made unto them, and sent over at the returne of this ship; which did so confound the objecters, as some confessed their falte, and others deneyed what they had said, and eate their words, and some others of them have since come over againe and heere lived to convince them selves sufficiently, both in their owne and other mens judgments.

1. obj. was diversitie aboute Religion. Ans: We know no such matter, for here was never any controversie or opposition, either publicke or private, (to our knowledg,) since we came.

2. ob: Neglecte of familie duties, one the Lords day.

Ans. We allow no such thing, but blame it in our selves and others; and they that thus reporte it, should have shewed their Christian love the more if they had in love tould the offenders of it, rather then thus to reproach them behind their baks. But (to say no more) we wish them selves had given better example. . . .

5. ob: Many of the perticuler members of the plantation will not work for the generall.

Ans: This allso is not wholy true; for though some doe it not willingly, and other not honestly, yet all doe it; and he that doth worst gets his owne foode and something besids. But we will not excuse them, but labour to reforme them the best we cane, or else to quitte the plantation of them.

6. ob: The water is not wholsome.

Ans: If they mean, not so wholsome as the good beere and wine in London, (which they so dearly love,) we will not dispute with them; but els, for water, it is as good as any in the world, (for ought we knowe,) and it is wholsome enough to us that can be contente therwith.

7. ob: The ground is barren and doth bear no grasse.

Ans: It is hear (as in all places) some better and some worse; and if they well consider their words, in England they shall not find such grasse in them, as in their feelds and meadows. The catle find grasse, for they are as fatt as need be; we wish we had but one for every hundred that hear is grase to keep. Indeed, this objection, as some other. are ridiculous to all here which see and know the contrary.

8. ob: The fish will not take salt to keepe sweete.

Ans: This is as true as that which was written, that ther is scarce a foule to be seene or a fish to be taken. Things likly to be true in a cuntrie wher so many sayle of ships come yearly a fishing; they might as well say, there can no aile or beere in London be kept from sowering.

9. ob: Many of them are theevish and steale on from an other.

Ans: Would London had been free from that crime, then we should not have been trobled with these here; it is well knowne sundrie have smarted well for it, and so are the rest like to doe, if they be taken.

10. ob: The countrie is anoyed with foxes and woules.

Ans: So are many other good cuntries too; but poyson, traps, and other such means will help to destroy them.

11. ob: The Dutch are planted nere Hudsons Bay, and are likely to overthrow the trade.

Ans: They will come and plante in these parts, also, if we and others doe not, but goe home and leave it to them. We rather commend them, then condemne them for it.

12. ob: The people are much anoyed with muskeetoes.

Ans: They are too delicate and unfitte to begine new-plantations and collonies, that cannot enduer the biting of a muskeeto; we would wish such to keepe at home till at least they be muskeeto proofe. Yet this place is as free as any, and experience teacheth that the more the land is tild, and the woods cut downe, the fewer ther will be, and in the end scarse any at all. . . .

[1628] Aboute some 3. or 4. years before this time, ther came over one Captaine Wolastone, (a man of pretie parts,) and with him 3. or 4. more of some eminencie, who brought with them a great many servants, with provissions and other implments for to begine a plantation; and pitched them selves in a place within the Massachusets, which they called, after their Captains name, Mount-Wollaston. Amongst whom was one Mr. Morton, who, it should seeme, had some small adventure (of his owne or other mens) amongst them; but had litle respecte amongst them, and was sleghted by the meanest servants. Haveing continued ther some time, and not finding things to answer their expectations, nor profite to arise as they looked for, Captaine Wollaston takes a great part of the sarvants, and transports them to Virginia, wher he puts them of at good rates, selling their time to other men; and writs back to one Mr. Rassdall, one of his cheefe partners, and accounted their marchant, to bring another parte of them to Verginia likewise, intending to put them of ther as he had done the rest. And he, with the consente of the said Rasdall, appoynted one Fitcher to be his Livetenante, and governe the remaines of the plantation, till he or Rasdall returned to take further order therabout. But this Morton abovesaid, haveing more craft then honestie, (who had been a kind of petiefogger, of Furnefells Inne,) in the others absence, watches an oppertunitie, (commons being but hard amongst them,) and gott some strong drinck and other junkats, and made them a feast; and after they were merie, he begane to tell them, he would give them good counsell. You see (saith he) that many of your fellows are carried to Virginia; and if you stay till this Rasdall returne, you will also be carried away and sould for slaves with the rest. Therfore I would advise you to thruste out this Levetenant Fitcher; and I, having a parte in the plantation, will receive you as my partners and consociats; so may you be free from service, and we will converse, trad, plante, and live togeather as equalls, and supporte and protecte one another, or to like effecte. This counsell was easily received; so they tooke oppertunitie, and thrust Levetenante Fitcher out a dores, and would suffer him to come no more amongst them, but forct him to seeke bread to eate, and other releefe from his neigbours, till he could gett passage for England. After this they fell to great licenciousnes, and led a dissolute life, powering out them selves into all profanenes. And Morton became lord of misrule, and maintained (as it were) a schoole of Athisme. And after they had gott some good into their hands, and gott much by trading with the Indeans, they spent it as vainly, in quaffing and drinking both wine and strong waters in great exsess, and, as some reported, 10 *li.* worth in a morning. They allso set up a Maypole, drinking and dancing aboute it many days togeather, inviting the Indean women, for their consorts, dancing and frisking togither, (like so many fairies, or furies rather,) and worse practises. As if they had anew revived and celebrated the feasts of the Roman Goddes Flora, or the beasly practieses of the madd Bacchinalians. Morton likwise (to shew his poetrie) composed sundry rimes and verses, some tending to lasciviousnes, and others to the detraction and scandall of some persons, which he affixed to this idle or idol May-polle. They chainged allso the name of their place, and in stead of calling it Mounte Wollaston, they call it Meriemounte, as if this joylity would have lasted ever. But this continued not long, for after Morton was sent for England, (as follows to be declared,) shortly after came over that worthy gentlman, Mr. John Indecott, who brought over a patent under the broad seall, for the govermente of the Massachusets, who visiting those parts caused that May-polle to be cutt downe, and rebuked them for their profannes, and admonished them to looke ther should be better walking; so they now, or others, changed the name of their place againe, and called it Mounte-Dagon.

Now to maintaine this riotous prodigallitie and profuse excess, Morton, thinking him selfe lawless, and hearing what gaine the French and fishermen made by trading of peeces, powder, and shotte to the Indeans, he, as the head of this consortship, begane the practise of the same in these parts; and first he taught them how to use them, to charge, and discharg, and what proportion of powder to give the peece, according to the sise or bignes of the same; and what shotte to use for foule, and what for deare. And having thus instructed them, he imployed some of them to hunte and fowle for him, so as they became farr more active in that imploymente then any of the English, by reason of ther swiftnes of foote, and nimblnes of body, being also quick-sighted, and by continuall exercise well knowing the hants of all sorts of game. So as when they saw the execution that a peece would doe, and the benefite that might come by the same, they became madd, as it were, after them, and would not stick to give any prise they could attaine too for them; accounting their bowes and arrowes but bables in comparison of them. . . .

This Morton having thus taught them the use of peeces, he sould them all he could spare; and he and his consorts detirmined to send for many out of England, and had by some of the ships sente for above a score. The which being knowne, and his neigbours meeting the Indeans in the woods armed with guns in this sorte, it was a terrour unto them, who lived straglingly, and were of no strenght in any place. And other places (though more remote) saw this mischeefe would quictly spread over all, if not prevented. Besides, they saw they should keep no servants, for Morton would entertaine any, how vile soever, and all the scume of the countrie, or any discontents, would flock to him from all places, if this nest was not broken; and they should stand in more fear of their lives and goods (in short time) from this wicked and deboste crue, then from the salvages them selves.

So sundrie of the cheefe of the stragling plantations, meeting togither, agreed by mutuall consente to sollissite those of Plimoth (who were then of more strength then them all) to joyne with them, to prevente the further grouth of this mischeefe, and suppress Morton and his consortes before they grewe to further head and strength. Those that joyned in this acction (and after contributed to the charge of sending him for England) were from Pascataway, Namkeake, Winisimett, Weesagascusett, Natasco, and other places wher any English were seated. Those of Plimoth being thus sought too by their messengers and letters, and waying both their reasons, and the commone danger, were willing to afford them their help; though them selves had least cause of fear or hurte. So, to be short, they first resolved joyntly to write to him, and in a freindly and neigborly way to admonish him to forbear these courses, and sent a messenger with their letters to bring his answer. But he was so highe as he scorned all advise, and asked who had to doe with him; he had and would trade peeces with the Indeans in dispite of all, with many other scurillous termes full of disdaine. They sente to him a second time, and bad him be better advised, and more temperate in his termes, for the countrie could not beare the injure he did; it was against their comone saftie, and against the king's proclamation. He answerd in high terms as before, and that the kings proclaimation was no law; demanding what penaltie was upon it. It was answered, more then he could bear, his majesties displeasure. But insolently he persisted, and said the king was dead and his displeasure with him, and many the like things; and threatened withall that if any came to molest him, let them looke to them selves, for he would prepare for them. Upon which they saw ther was no way but to take him by force; and having so farr proceeded, now to give over would make him farr more hautie and insolente. So they mutually resolved to proceed, and obtained of the Govr of Plimoth to send Captaine Standish, and some other aide with him, to take Morton by force. The which accordingly was done; but they found him to stand stifly in his defence, having made fast his dors, armed his consorts, set diverse dishes of powder and bullets ready on the table; and if they had not been over armed with drinke, more hurt might have been done. They sommaned him to yeeld, but he kept his house, and they could gett nothing but scofes and scorns from him; but at length, fearing they would doe some violence to the house, he and some of his crue came out, but not to yeeld, but to shoote; but they were so steeld with drinke as their peeces were to heavie for them; him selfe with a carbine (over charged and allmost halfe fild with powder and shote, as was after found) had thought to have shot Captaine Standish; but he stept to him, and put by his peece, and tooke him. Neither was ther any hurte done to any of either side, save that one was so drunke that he rane his owne nose upon the pointe of a sword that one held before him as he entred the house; but he lost but a litle of his hott blood. Morton they brought away to Plimoth, wher he was kepte, till a ship went from the Ile of Shols for England, with which he was sente to the Counsell of New-England; and letters writen to give them information of his course and cariage; and also one was sent at their commone charge to informe their Ho[rs] more perticulerly, and to prosecute against him. But he foold of the messenger, after he was gone from hence, and though he wente for England, yet nothing was done to him, not so much as rebukte, for ought was heard; but returned the nexte year. Some of the worst of the company were disperst, and some of the more modest kepte the house till he should be heard from. But I have been too long about so unworthy a person, and bad a cause. . . .

[1633] Mr. Roger Williams (a man godly and zealous, having many precious parts, but very unsettled in judgmente) came over first to the Massachusets, but upon some discontente left that place, and came hither, (wher he was friendly entertained, according to their poore abilitie,) and exercised his gifts amongst them, and after some time was admitted a member of the church; and his teaching well approoved, for the benefite wherof I still blese God, and am thankfull to him, even for his sharpest admonitions and reproufs, so farr as they agreed with truth. He this year begane to fall into some strang oppinions, and from opinion to practise; which caused some controversie betweene the church and him, and in the end some discontente on his parte, by occasion wherof he left them some thing abruptly. Yet after wards sued for his dismission to the church of Salem, which was granted, with some caution to them concerning him, and what care they ought to have of him. But he soone fell into more things ther, both to their and the goverments troble and disturbance. I shall not need to name perticulers, they are too well knowen now to all, though for a time the church here wente under some hard censure by his occasion, from some that afterwards smarted them selves. But he is to be pitied, and prayed for, and so I shall leave the matter, and desire the Lord to shew him his errors, and reduse him into the way of truth, and give him a setled judgment and constancie in the same; for I hope he belongs to the Lord, and that he will shew him mercie. . . .

[1642] Marvilous it may be to see and consider how some kind of wickednes did grow and breake forth here, in a land wher the same was so much witnesed against, and so narrowly looked unto, and severly punished when it was knowne; as in no place more, or so much, that I have known or heard of; insomuch as they have been somewhat censured, even by moderate and good men, for their severitie in punishments. And yet all this could not suppress the breaking out of sundrie notorious sins, (as this year, besids other, gives us too many sad presidents and instances,) espetially drunkennes and unclainnes; not only incontinencie betweene persons unmaried, for which many both men and women have been punished sharply enough, but some maried persons allso. But that which is worse, even sodomie and bugerie, (things fearfull to name,) have broak forth in this land, oftener then once. I say it may justly be marveled at, and cause us to fear and tremble at the consideration of our corrupte natures, which are so hardly bridled, subdued, and mortified; nay, cannot by any other means but the powerfull worke and grace of Gods spirite. But (besids this) one reason may be, that the Divell may carrie a greater spite against the churches of Christ and the gospell hear, by how much the more they indeaour to preserve holynes and puritie amongst them, and strictly punisheth the contrary when it ariseth either in church or comone wealth; that he might cast a blemishe and staine upon them in the eyes of [the] world, who use to be rash in judgmente. I would rather thinke thus, then that Satane hath more power in these heathen lands, as som have thought, then in more Christian nations, espetially over Gods servants in them.

2. An other reason may be, that it may be in this case as it is with waters when their streames are stopped or dammed up, when they gett passage they flow with more violence, and make more noys and disturbance, then when they are suffered to rune quietly in their owne chanels. So wikednes being here more stopped by strict laws, and the same more nerly looked unto, so as it cannot rune in a comone road of liberty as it would, and is inclined, it searches every wher, and at last breaks out wher it getts vente.

3. A third reason may be, hear (as I am verily perswaded) is not more evills in this kind, nor nothing nere so many by proportion, as in other places; but they are here more discoverd and seen, and made publick by due serch, inquisition, and due punishment; for the churches looke narrowly to their members, and the magistrats over all, more strictly then in other places. Besids, here the people are but few in comparison of other places, which are full and populous, and lye hid, as it were, in a wood or thickett, and many horrible evills by that means are never seen nor knowne; wheras hear, they are, as it were, brought into the light, and set in the plaine feeld, or rather on a hill, made conspicuous to the veiw of all. . . .

[1643] I am to begine this year whith that which was a mater of great saddnes and mourning unto them all. Aboute the 18. of Aprill dyed their Reve[d] Elder, and my dear and loving friend, Mr. William Brewster; a man that had done and suffered much for the Lord Jesus and the gospells sake, and had bore his parte in well and woe with this poore persecuted church above 36. years in England, Holand, and in this wildernes, and done the Lord and them faithfull service in his place and calling. And notwithstanding the many troubls and sorrows he passed throw, the Lord upheld him to a great age. He was nere fourskore years of age (if not all out) when he dyed. He had this blesing added by the Lord to all the rest, to dye in his bed, in peace, amongst the mids of his freinds, who mourned and wepte over him, and ministered what help and comforte they could unto him, and he againe recomforted them whilst he could. His sicknes was not long, and till the last day therof he did not wholy keepe his bed. His speech continued till somewhat more then halfe a day, and then failed him; and aboute 9. or 10. a clock that evning he dyed, without any pangs at all. A few howers before, he drew his breath shorte, and some few minuts before his last, he drew his breath long, as a man falen into a sound slepe, without any pangs or gaspings, and so sweetly departed this life unto a better.

I would now demand of any, what he was the worse for any former sufferings? What doe I say, worse? Nay, sure he was the better, and they now added to his honour. *It is a manifest token* (saith the Apostle, 2. Thes: 1. 5, 6, 7.) *of the righ[t]eous judgmente of God that ye may be counted worthy of the kingdome of God, for which ye allso suffer; seing it is a righteous thing with God to recompence tribulation to them that trouble you: and to you who are troubled, rest with us, when the Lord Jesus shall be revealed from heaven, with his mighty angels.* 1. Pet. 4. 14. *If you be reproached for the name of Christ, hapy are ye, for the spirite of glory and of God resteth upon you.* What though he wanted the riches and pleasurs of the world in this life, and pompous monuments at his funurall? yet the memoriall of the just shall be blessed, when the name of the wicked shall rott (with their marble monuments). Pro: 10. 7.

I should say something of his life, if to say a litle were not worse then to be silent. But I cannot wholy forbear, though hapily more may be done hereafter. After he had attained some learning, viz. the knowledg of the Latine tongue, and some insight in the Greeke, and spent some small time at Cambridge, and then being first seasoned with the seeds of grace and vertue, he went to the Courte, and served that religious and godly gentlman, Mr. Davison, diverce years, when he was Secretary of State; who found him so discreete and faithfull as he trusted him above all other that were aboute him, and only imployed him in all matters of greatest trust and secrecie. He esteemed him rather as a sonne then a servante, and for his wisdom and godlines (in private) he would converse with him more like a freind and familier than a maister. He attended his m^r^ when he was sente in ambassage by the Queene into the Low-Countries, in the Earle of Leicesters time, as for other waighty affaires of state, so to receive possession of the cautionary townes, and in token and signe therof the keyes of Flushing being delivered to him, in her ma^tis^ name, he kepte them some time, and committed them to this his servante, who kept them under his pilow, on which he slepte the first night. And, at his returne, the States honoured him with a gould chaine, and his maister committed it to him, and commanded him to wear it when they arrived in England, as they ridd thorrow the country, till they came to the Courte. He afterwards remained with him till his troubles, that he was put from his place aboute the death of the Queene of Scots; and some good time after, doeing him manie faithfull offices of servise in the time of his troubles. Afterwards he wente and lived in the country, in good esteeme amongst his freinds and the gentle-men of those parts, espetially the godly and religious. He did much good in the countrie wher he lived, in promoting and furthering religion, not only by his practiss and example, and provocking and incouraging of others, but by procuring of good preachers to the places theraboute, and drawing on of others to assiste and help forward in such a worke; he him selfe most comonly deepest in the charge, and some times above his abillitie. And in this state he continued many years, doeing the best good he could, and walking according to the light he saw, till the Lord reveiled further unto him. And in the end, by the tirrany of the bishops against godly preachers and people, in silenceing the one and persecuting the other, he and many more of those times begane to looke further into things, and to see into the unlawfullnes of their callings, and the burthen of many anti-christian corruptions, which both he and they endeavored to cast of; as they allso did, as in the begining of this treatis is to be seene. After they were joyned togither in comunion, he was a spetiall stay and help unto them. They ordinarily mett at his house on the Lords day, (which was a manor of the bishops,) and with great love he entertained them when they came, making provission for them to his great charge. He was the cheefe of those that were taken at Boston, and suffered the greatest loss; and of the seven that were kept longst in prison, and after bound over to the assises. Affter he came into Holland he suffered much hardship, after he had spente the most of his means, haveing a great charge, and many children; and, in regard of his former breeding and course of life, not so fitt for many imployments as others were, espetially such as were toylesume and laborious. But yet he ever bore his condition with much cherfullnes and contentation. Towards the later parte of those 12. years spente in Holland, his outward condition was mended, and he lived well and plentifully; for he fell into a way (by reason he had the Latine tongue) to teach many students, who had a disire to lerne the English tongue, to teach them English; and by his method they quickly attained it with great facilitie; for he drew rules to lerne it by, after the Latine maner; and many gentlemen, both Danes and Germans, resorted to him, as they had time from other studies, some of them being great mens sonnes. He also had means to set up printing, (by the help of some freinds,) and so had imploymente inoughg, and by reason of many books which would not be alowed to be printed in England, they might have had more then they could doe. But now removeing into this countrie, all these things were laid aside againe, and a new course of living must be framed unto; in which he was no way unwilling to take his parte, and to bear his burthen with the rest, living many times without bread, or corne, many months together, having many times nothing but fish, and often wanting that also; and drunke nothing but water for many years togeather, yea, till within 5. or 6. years of his death. And yet he lived (by the blessing of God) in health till very old age. And besids that, he would labour with his hands in the feilds as long as he was able; yet when the church had no other minister, he taught twise every Saboth, and that both powerfully and profitably, to the great contentment of the hearers, and their comfortable edification; yea, many were brought to God by his ministrie. He did more in this behalfe in a year, then many that have their hundreds a year doe in all their lives. For his personall abilities, he was qualified above many; he was wise and discreete and well spoken, having a grave and deliberate utterance, of a very cherfull spirite, very sociable and pleasante amongst his freinds, of an humble and modest mind, of a peaceable disposition, under vallewing him self and his owne abilities, and some time over valewing others; inoffencive and innocente in his life and conversation, which gained him the love of those without, as well as those within; yet he would tell them plainely of their faults and evills, both publickly and privatly, but in such a maner as usually was well taken from him. He was tender harted, and compassionate of such as were in miserie, but espetialy of such as had been of good estate and ranke, and were fallen unto want and poverty, either for goodnes and religions sake, or by the injury and oppression of others; he would say, of all men these deserved to be pitied most. And none did more offend and displease him then such as would hautily and proudly carry and lift up themselves, being rise from nothing, and haveing litle els in them to comend them but a few fine cloaths, or a litle riches more then others. In teaching, he was very moving and stirring of affections, also very plaine and distincte in what he taught; by which means he became the more profitable to the hearers. He had a singuler good gift in prayer, both publick and private, in ripping up the hart and conscience before God, in the humble confession of sinne, and begging the mercies of God in Christ for the pardon of the same. He always thought it were better for ministers to pray oftener, and devide their prears, then be longe and tedious in the same (excepte upon sollemne and spetiall occations, as in days of humiliation and the like). His reason was, that the harte and spirits of all, espetialy the weake, could hardly continue and stand bente (as it were) so long towards God, as they ought to doe in that duty, without flagging and falling of. For the govermente of the church, (which was most proper to his office,) he was carfull to preserve good order in the same, and to preserve puritie, both in the doctrine and comunion of the same; and to supress any errour or contention that might begine to rise up amongst them; and accordingly God gave good success to his indeavors herein all his days, and he saw the fruite of his labours in that behalfe. But I must breake of, having only thus touched a few, as it were, heads of things.

I cannot but here take occasion, not only to mention, but greatly to admire the marvelous providence of God, that notwithstanding the many changes and hardships that these people wente throwgh, and the many enemies they had and difficulties they mette with all, that so many of them should live to very olde age! It was not only this reve[d] mans condition, (for one swallow maks no summer, as they say,) but many more of them did the like, some dying aboute and before this time, and many still living, who attained to 60. years of age, and to 65. diverse to 70. and above, and some nere 80. as he did. It must needs be more than ordinarie, and above naturall reason, that so it should be; for it is found in experience, that chaing of aeir, famine, or unholsome foode, much drinking of water, sorrows and troubls, etc., all of them are enimies to health, causes of many diseaces, consumers of naturall vigoure and the bodys of men, and shortners of life. And yet of all these things they had a large parte, and suffered deeply in the same. They wente from England to Holand, wher they found both worse air and dyet then that they came from; from thence (induring a long imprisonmente, as it were, in the ships at sea) into New-England; and how it hath been with them hear hath allready beene showne; and what crosses, troubls, fears, wants, and sorrowes they had been lyable unto, is easie to conjecture; so as in some sorte they may say with the Apostle, 2. Cor: 11. 26, 27. they were *in journeyings often, in perils of waters, in perills of robers, in perills of their owne nation, in perils among the heathen, in perills in the willdernes, in perills in the sea, in perills among false breethern; in wearines and painfullnes, in watching often, in hunger and thirst, in fasting often, in could and nakednes.* What was it then that upheld them? It was Gods vissitation that preserved their spirits. Job. 10. 12. *Thou hast given me life and grace, and thy vissitation hath preserved my spirite.* He that upheld the Apostle upheld them. *They were persecuted, but not forsaken, cast downe, but perished not.* 2. Cor: 4. 9. *As unknowen, and yet knowen; as dying, and behold we live; as chastened, and yett not kiled.* 2. Cor: 6. 9. God, it seems, would have all men to behold and observe such mercies and works of his providence as these are towards his people, that they in like cases might be incouraged to depend upon God in their trials, and also blese his name when they see his goodnes towards others. Man lives not by bread only, Deut: 8. 3. It is not by good and dainty fare, by peace, and rest, and harts ease, in injoying the contentments and good things of this world only, that preserves health and prolongs life. God in such examples would have the world see and behold that he can doe it without them; and if the world will shut ther eyes, and take no notice therof, yet he would have his people to see and consider it. Daniell could be better liking with pulse then others were with the kings dainties. Jaacob, though he wente from one nation to another people, and passed thorow famine, fears, and many afflictions, yet he lived till old age, and dyed sweetly, and rested in the Lord, as infinite others of Gods servants have done, and still shall doe, (through Gods goodnes,) notwithstanding all the malice of their enemies: *when the branch of the wicked shall be cut of before his day,* Job. 15. 32. *and the bloody and deceitfull men shall not live out halfe their days.* Psa: 55. 23.

THOMAS SHEPARD, 1605–1649

[Thomas Shepard, one of the great preachers in the first generation of New England Puritans, was born in Towcester, the son of a grocer. He entered pensioner at Emmanuel College, Cambridge, receiving his B.A. in 1624, his M.A. in 1627. He was a lecturer in Essex until silenced by Bishop Laud in 1630, then served as tutor and chaplain in the family of Sir Richard Darley in Yorkshire, where he married. He sailed for New England in 1634, was driven back by a storm and remained in hiding until the next spring, when he was successful in reaching America. Chosen minister at Cambridge, he immediately became one of the clerical leaders of the colony, being particularly energetic in suppressing the Antinomians. His first wife died in 1636, and he married a daughter of Thomas Hooker. His works enjoyed a great reputation in their day, one of them, *The Sincere Convert*, running to twenty editions between 1641 and 1812. For biography and discussion of his work, see Samuel Eliot Morison, *Builders of the Bay Colony*. This text is from *A Defence of the Answer made unto the Nine Questions or Positions sent from New-England against the reply thereto by Mr. John Ball* (London, 1648), pp. 3–9. The book was written in collaboration with John Allin, 1596–1671, minister at Dedham from 1639, though the preface is probably the work of Shepard alone.]

A DEFENCE OF THE ANSWER

LET US intreat all the Godly wise, to consider and look back upon the season of this great enterprise,[1] undertaken by us, and the manner of our proceedings in it, with the admirable workings of Gods Providence first and last about it; and we think (though we were silent) they may easily satisfie themselves, whether this was of God or men, a sinfull neglect of the Cause of Christ, or a manifest attestation to the truth, by open profession against Corruptions of Worship in use, and for the necessity of reformation of the Church; and that confirmed by no small degree of sufferings for the same. For was it not a time when humane Worship and inventions were growne to such an intolerable height, that the consciences of Gods saints and servants inlightened in the truth could no longer bear them? was not the power of the tyrannicall Prelates so great, that like a strong Current carryed all down streame before it, what ever was from the law, or otherwise set in their way? Did not the hearts of men generally faile them? Where was the people to bee found that would cleave to their godly Ministers in their sufferings, but rather thought it their descretion, to provide for their owne quiet and safety? Yea, when some freely in zeale of the Truth preached or professed against the corruptions of the times, did not some take offence at it, judge it rashnesse, and to bee against all rules of discretion, who since are ready to censure us for deserting the Cause? Many then thought, it

[1] Superior figures through individual selections refer to correspondingly numbered notes at the back of the volume.

is an evill time, the prudent shall hold their peace, and might wee not say, this is not our resting place? And what would men have us doe in such a case? Must wee study some distinctions to salve our Consciences in complying with so manifold corruptions in Gods Worship? or should wee live without Gods ordinances, because wee could not partake in the corrupt administration thereof? or content our selves to live without those ordinances of Gods Worship and Communion of Saints which hee called us unto, and our soules breathed after? or should wee forsake the publique Assemblies, and joyne together in private separated Churches? how unsufferable it would then have been, the great offence that now is taken at it, is a full evidence.[2] And if in Cities, or some such great Townes that might have been done, yet how was it possible for so many scattered Christians all over the Countrey? It is true, we might have suffered, if wee had sought it, wee might easily have found the way to have filled the Prisons, and some had their share therein. But whether wee were called thereunto, when a wide doore was set open of liberty otherwise; and our witnesse to the truth, (through the malignant policy of those times) could not bee open before the world, but rather smothered up in close prisons or some such wayes, together with our selves, wee leave to bee considered. Wee cannot see but the rule of Christ to his Apostles and Saints, and the practise of Gods Saints in all ages, may allow us this liberty as well as others, to fly into the Wildernesse from the face of the Dragon. But if it had been so, that the Godly Ministers and Christians that fled to *New-England*, were the most timorous and faint hearted of all their Brethren, that stayed behinde, and that those sufferings were nothing in comparison of their Brethrens (for why should any boast of sufferings?) yet who doth not know that the Spirit who gives various gifts, and all to profit withall, in such times doth single out every one to such worke, as hee in wisdome intends to call them unto? And whom the Lord will honour by suffering for his Cause, by imprisonment, &c. hee gives them spirits suitable thereto: whom the Lord will reserve for other service, or imploy in other places, hee inclines their hearts rather to fly, giving them an heart suitable to such a condition. It is a case of Conscience frequently put, and oft resolved by holy *Bradford*, *Peter Martyr*, *Philpot*, and others, in Queene *Maries* bloody dayes, viz. Whether it was lawfull to flee out of the Land: To which their anwer was, that if God gave a spirit of courage and willingnesse to glorifie him by sufferings, they should stay; but if they found not such a spirit they might lawfully fly, yea, they advised them thereunto. Those Servants of Christ, though full of the spirit of glory, and of Christ to outface the greatest persecuters in profession of the Truth, unto the death, yet did not complaine of the cowardize of such as fled, because they deserted them and the Cause, but rather advised divers so to doe, and rejoyced when God gave liberty to their brethren to escape with their lives to the places of liberty, to serve the Lord according to his Word. Neither were those faithfull Saints and servants of God uselesse and unprofitable in the Church of God that fled from the bloody Prelates. The infinite and onely wise God hath many workes to doe in the World, and hee doth by his singular Providence give gifts to his Servants, and disposeth them to his Worke as seemeth best to himselfe. If the Lord will have some to beare witnesse by imprisonments, dismembring, &c. wee honour them therein; if hee will have others instrumentall to promote reformation in *England*, wee honor them, and rejoyce in their holy endeavours, praying for a blessing upon themselves and labours. And what if God will have his Church and the Kingdome of Christ goe up also in these remote parts of the world, that his Name may bee known to the Heathen, or whatsoever other end hee hath, and to this end will send forth a company of weake-hearted Christians, which dare not stay at home to suffer, why should wee not let the Lord alone, and rejoyce that Christ is preached howsoever, and wheresoever? And who can say that this work was not undertaken and carryed on with sincere and right ends, and in an holy serious manner, by the chiefe and the body of such as undertooke the same? The Lord knows whether the sincere desires of worshipping himselfe according to his will, of promoting and propagating the Gospel, was not in the hearts of very many in this enterprise; and hee that seeth in secret, and rewardeth openly, knows what prayers and teares have been poured out to God by many alone, and in dayes of fasting and prayer of Gods servants together, for his counsell, direction, assistance, blessing in this worke: How many longings and pantings of heart have been in many after the Lord Jesus, to see his goings in his Sanctuary, as the one thing their soules desired and requested of God, that they might dwell in his house for ever; the fruit of which prayers and desires this liberty of *New-England* hath been taken to bee, and thankfully received from God. Yea, how many serious consultations with one another, and with the faithfull Ministers, and other eminent servants of Christ, have been taken about this worke, is not unknowne to some; which cleares us from any rash heady rushing into this place, out of discontent, as many are ready to conceive. Wee will here say nothing of the persons whose hearts the Lord stirred up in this businesse; surely all were not rash, weake-spirited, inconsiderate of what they left behinde, or of what it was to goe into a Wildernesse. But if it were well knowne and considered, or if wee were able to expresse and recount the singular workings of divine Providence, for the bringing on of this worke, to what it is come unto, it would stop the mouths of all that have not an heart to accuse and blaspheme the goodnesse of God in his glorious workes: whatever many may say or think, wee beleeve after-times will admire and adore the Lord herein, when all his holy ends, and the wayes he hath used to bring them about shall appeare. Look from one end of the heaven to another, whether the Lord hath assayed to do such a Worke as this in any Nation, so to carry out a people of his owne from so flourishing a State, to a wildernesse so far distant, for such ends, and for such a worke: Yea, and in few yeares hath done for them, as hee hath here done for his poore despised people. When wee looke back and consider what a strange poise of spirit the Lord hath laid upon many of our hearts, wee cannot but wonder at our selves, that so many, and some so weak and tender, with such cheerfulnesse and constant resolutions against so many perswasions of friends, discouragements from the ill report of this Countrey, the straits, wants, and tryalls of Gods people in it, &c. yet should leave our accommodations and comforts, should forsake our dearest relations, Parents, brethren, Sisters, Christian friends, and acquaintances, overlooke all the dangers and difficulties of the vast Seas, the thought whereof was a terrour to many, and all this to go to a wildernesse, where wee could forecast nothing but care and temptations, onely in hopes of enjoying Christ in his Ordinances, in the fellowship of his people; was this from a stupid senslesnesse or desperate carelesnesse what became of us or ours? or want of naturall affections to our deare Countrey, or nearest relations? No surely, with what bowells of compassion to our deare Countrey; with what heart-breaking affections, to our deare relations, and Christian friends many of us at least came away, the Lord is witnesse. What shall we say of the singular Providence of God bringing so many Ship-loads of his people, through so many dangers, as upon Eagles wings, with so much safety from yeare to yeare? The fatherly care of our God in feeding and cloathing so many in a Wildernesse, giving such healthfulnesse and great increase of posterity? what shall wee say of the Worke it selfe of the kingdome of Christ? and the form of a Common-wealth erected in a Wildernesse, and in so few yeares brought to that state, that scarce the like can bee seen in any of our English Colonies in the richest places of this *America*, after many more years standing? That the Lord hath carryed the spirits of so many of his people through all their toylsome Labour, wants, difficulties, losses, &c. with such a measure of chearfulnesse and contentation? But above all wee must acknowledge the singular pity and mercies of our God, that hath done all this and much more for a people so unworthy, so sinfull, that by murmurings of many, unfaithfulnesse in promises, oppressions, and other evils which are found among us, have so dishonoured his Majesty, exposed his worke here to much scandall and obloquie, for which wee have cause for ever to bee ashamed, that the Lord should yet owne us, and rather correct us in mercy, then cast us off in displeasure, and scatter us in this Wilder-nesse, which gives us cause with Mich. 7. to say, *Who is a God like our God, that pardoneth iniquities, and passeth by the transgressions of the remnant of his heritage; even because he delighteth in mercy?* Though we be a people of many weaknesses and wants, yet wee acknowledge our God to have been to us a God of many mercies, in respect of that sweet peace which he hath taken away from so many Nations, yet continuing the same to us; in respect also of that liberty wee have in Gods house, the blessed Ministery of the Word, the sweet unity and communion of Gods Churches and Ministers, increase and multiplication of Churches, Christian government in the Common-wealth, and many other mercies wee enjoy, but especially the gracious presence of Christ to many of our soules in all these. But wee will not insist much upon this subject, being perswaded it is in the consciences and hearts of many of our dear Countrey-men to thinke that we should be an object of love and tendernesse to that State and people, by whose Laws and unkind usages we were driven out into a wildernesse, rather then to bee judged as desertors of our Brethren, and the Cause of Christ in hand: with whom (excuse us if we now speak plainly) it had been far more easie unto many of us to have suffered, then to have adventured hither upon the wildernesse sorrows wee expected to have met withall; though we must confesse the Lord hath sweetned it beyond our thoughts, and utmost expectations of prudent men.

FRANCIS HIGGINSON, 1586–1630

[Francis Higginson was born in Claybrook, Leicestershire, where his father was vicar; he took his B.A. at Jesus College, Cambridge, 1610, his M.A. in 1613. He succeeded his father at Claybrook, 1615, and from 1617 to 1627 was lecturer at St. Nicholas. Under the influence of Thomas Hooker he became a Puritan and was deprived for non-conformity. When proceedings were commenced against him in the High Commission he was engaged by the Massachusetts Bay Company and sent with the first body of settlers to Salem, 1629, where he was chosen teacher of the church and where he died of a hectic fever, August 6, 1630, leaving a widow and seven children. He wrote an account of the voyage to New England, and shortly before his death despatched back the manuscript of *New-Englands Plantation*, published by the Company in London in 1630. This text is from the first edition, pp. B1 verso–B2 recto, C1 recto–C2 verso.]

NEW-ENGLANDS PLANTATION

IT BECOMMETH not a Preacher of Truth to be a Writer of Falshood in any degree: and therefore I haue beene carefull to report nothing of *New-England* but what I haue partly seene with mine owne Eyes, and partly heard and enquired from the Mouthes of verie honest and religious person, who by liuing in the Countrey a good space of time haue had experience and knowledge of the state thereof, & whose testimonies I doe beleeue as my selfe.

First therefore of the Earth of *New-England* and all the appurtenances thereof: It is a Land of diuers and sundry sorts all about *Masathulets* Bay, and at *Charles* Riuer is as fat blacke Earth as can be seene any where: and in other places you haue a clay soyle, in other grauell, in other sandy, as it is all about our Plantation at *Salem*, for so our Towne is now named, *Psal. 76. 2.*

The forme of the Earth here in the superficies of it is neither too flat in the plainnesse, nor too high in Hils, but partakes of both in a mediocritie, and fit for Pasture, or for Plow or Meddow ground, as Men please to employ it: though all the Countrey be as it were a thicke Wood for the generall, yet in diuers places there is much ground cleared by the *Indians*, and especially about the Plantation: and I am told that about three miles from vs a Man may stand on a little hilly place and see diuers thousands of acres of ground as good as need to be, and not a Tree in the same. It is thought here is good Clay to make Bricke and Tyles and Earthen-Pots as needs to be. At this instant we are setting a Bricke-Kill on worke to make Brickes and Tyles for the building of our Houses. For Stone, here is plentie of Slates at the Ile of Slate in *Masathulets* Bay, and Lime-stone, Free-stone, and Smooth-stone, and Iron-stone, and Marble-stone also in such store, that we haue great Rockes of it, and a Harbour hard by. Our Plantation is from thence called Marble-harbour. . . .

Of the Aire of New-England with the Temper and Creatures in it.

The Temper of the Aire of *New-England* is one speciall thing that commends this place. Experience doth manifest that there is hardly a more healthfull place to be found in the World that agreeth better with our English Bodyes. Many that haue beene weake and sickly in old *England*, by comming hither hane beene thoroughly healed and growne healthfull and strong. For here is an extraordinarie cleere and dry Aire that is of a most healing nature to all such as are of a Cold, Melancholy, Flegmatick, Reumaticke temper of Body. None can more truly speake hereof by their owne experience then my selfe. My Friends that knew me can well tell how verie sickly I haue been and continually in Physick, being much troubled with a tormenting paine through an extraordinarie weaknesse of my Stomacke, and aboundance of Melancholicke humors; but since I came hither on this Voyage, I thanke God I haue had perfect health, and freed from paine and vomitings, hauing a Stomacke to digest the hardest and coursest fare who before could not eat finest meat; and whereas my Stomacke could onely digest and did require such drinke as was both strong and stale, now I can and doe oftentimes drink *New-England* water verie well; and I that haue not gone without a Cap for many yeeres together, neither durst leaue off the same, haue now cast away my Cap, and doe weare none at all in the day time: and whereas beforetime I cloathed my selfe with double cloathes and thicke Wastcoats to keepe me warme, euen in the Summer time, I doe now goe as thin clad as any, onely wearing a light Stuffe Cassocke vpon my Shirt and Stuffe Breeches of one thicknesse without Linings. Besides, I haue one of my Children that was formerly most lamentably handled with sore breaking out of both his hands and feet of the Kings-Euill, but since he came hither he is verie well ouer hee was, and there is hope of perfect recouerie shortly, euen by the verie wholesomnesse of the Aire, altering, digesting and drying vp the cold and crude humors of the Body: and therefore I thinke it is a wise course for all cold complections to come to take Physicke in *New-England*: for a sup of *New-Englands* Aire is better then a whole draft of old *Englands* Ale.

In the Summer time in the midst of *July* and *August*, it is a good deale hotter then in old *England:* and in Winter, *January* and *February* are much colder as they say: but the Spring and Autumne are of a middle temper.

Fowles of the Aire are plentifull here, and of all sorts as we haue in *England* as farre as I can learne, and a great many of strange Fowles which we know not. Whilst I was writing these things, one of our Men brought home an Eagle which he had killed in the Wood: they say they are good meat. Also here are many kinds of excellent Hawkes, both Sea Hawkes and Land Hawkes: and my selfe walking in the Woods with another in company, sprung a Partridge so bigge that through the heauinesse of his Body could fly but a little way: they that haue killed them, say they are as bigge as our Hens. Here are likewise aboundance of Turkies often killed in the Woods, farre greater then our English Turkies, and exceeding fat, sweet and fleshy, for here they haue aboundance of feeding all the yeere long, as Strawberries, in Summer all places are full of them, and all manner of Berries and Fruits. In the Winter time I haue seene Flockes of Pidgeons, and haue eaten of them: they doe flye from Tree to Tree as other Birds doe, which our Pidgeons will not doe in *England:* they are of all colours as ours are, but their wings and tayles are farr longer, and therefore it is likely they fly swifter to escape the terrible Hawkes in this Countrey. In Winter time this Countrey doth abound with wild Geese, wild Duckes, and other Sea Fowle, that a great part of winter the Planters haue eaten nothing but roastmeat of diuers Fowles which they haue killed. . . .

Though it be here somthing cold in the winter, yet here we haue plentie of Fire to warme vs, and that a great deale cheaper then they sell Billets and Faggots in *London:* nay, all *Europe* is not able to afford to make so great Fires as *New-England.* A poore Seruant here that is to possesse but 50 Acres of Land, may afford to giue more wood for Timber and Fire as good as the world yeelds, then many Noble Men in *England* can afford to doe. Here is good liuing for those that loue good Fires.

JOHN WINTHROP, 1588–1649

[The Winthrop family was decidedly one of importance in Suffolk, where John Winthrop's grandfather, a wealthy clothier, acquired the manor of Groton in 1544; his father, Adam Winthrop, was a successful lawyer and was auditor for St. John's and Trinity Colleges, Cambridge, from 1594 to 1609. John Winthrop entered pensioner at Trinity College, March, 1603, but left in less than two years when he was married at the age of seventeen. As justice of the peace and lord of Groton Manor he was a man of consequence; he was attorney of the Court of Wards, 1626, and admitted of the Inner Temple, 1628. An intense Puritan from his youth, he was profoundly discouraged about the future of religion in England; losing his attorneyship, he became interested in the Massachusetts Bay Company and was one of the twelve signatories to the agreement drawn up at Cambridge, August 26, 1629, promising to migrate to New England if the charter could be transferred and the government established there. Elected governor on October 26, he superintended the departure, and sailed, March, 1630, on the *Arbella.* He first settled at Charlestown, but moved to Boston in 1631. In most of the remaining years of his life he was either governor or deputy governor of the colony, at all times its leading citizen and most influential personage. He supported the banishment of Williams, fought the Antinomians, and guided the community through several crises in the 1640's. *Life and Letters*, by Robert C. Winthrop (Boston, 1869); Samuel Eliot Morison, *Builders of the Bay Colony.* The *Journal*, sometimes called *The History of New England*, was begun at Southampton when the expedition was about to set sail, and was kept up intermittently until his death. This text is from the edition by James Savage (Boston, 1825), 2 vols.]

JOURNAL

LANDING at Salem, June 12, 1630.] About four in the morning we were near our port. We shot off two pieces of ordnance, and sent our skiff to Mr. Peirce his ship (which lay in the harbor, and had been there [*blank*] days before). About an hour after, Mr. Allerton [1] came aboard us in a shallop as he was sailing to Pemaquid. As we stood towards the harbor, we saw another shallop coming to us; so we stood in to meet her, and passed through the narrow strait between Baker's Isle and Little Isle, and came to an anchor a little within the islands.

After Mr. Peirce came aboard us, and returned to fetch Mr. Endecott,[2] who came to us about two of the clock, and with him Mr. Skelton [3] and Capt. Levett. We that were of the assistants, and some other gentlemen, and some of the women, and our captain, returned with them to Nahumkeck,[4] where we supped with a good venison pasty and good beer, and at night we returned to our ship, but some of the women stayed behind.

In the mean time most of our people went on shore upon the land of Cape Ann, which lay very near us, and gathered store of fine strawberries.

An Indian came aboard us and lay there all night. . . .

[February 10, 1631.] The frost brake up; and after that, though we had many snows and sharp frost, yet they continued not, neither were the waters frozen up as before. It hath been observed, ever since this bay was planted by Englishmen, viz., seven years, that at this day the frost hath broken up every year.

The poorer sort of people (who lay long in tents, etc.) were much afflicted with the scurvy, and many died, especially at Boston and Charlestown; but when this ship came and brought store of juice of lemons, many recovered speedily. It hath been always observed here, that such as fell into discontent, and lingered after their former conditions in England, fell into the scurvy and died. . . .

[October 11, 1631.] The governor,[5] being at his farm house at Mistick, walked out after supper, and took a piece in his hand supposing he might see a wolf, (for they came daily about the house, and killed swine and calves, etc.;) and, being about half a mile off, it grew suddenly dark, so as, in coming home, he mistook his path, and went till he came to a little house of Sagamore John, which stood empty. There he stayed, and having a piece of match in his pocket, (for he always carried about him match and a compass, and in summer time snake-weed,) he made a good fire near the house, and lay down upon some old mats, which he found there, and so spent the night, sometimes walking by the fire, sometimes singing psalms, and sometimes getting wood, but could not sleep. It was (through God's mercy) a warm night; but a little before day it began to rain, and, having no cloak, he made shift by a long pole to climb up into the house. In the morning, there came thither an Indian squaw, but perceiving her before she had opened the door, he barred her out; yet she stayed there a great while essaying to get in, and at last she went away, and he returned safe home, his servants having been much perplexed for him, and having walked about, and shot off pieces, and hallooed in the night, but he heard them not. . . .

[January 18, 1636.] Mr. Vane[6] and Mr. Peter,[7] finding some distraction in the commonwealth, arising from some difference in judgment, and withal some alienation of affection among the magistrates and some other persons of quality, and that hereby factions began to grow among the people, some adhering more to the old governor, Mr. Winthrop, and others to the late governor, Mr. Dudley,[8]—the former carrying matters with more lenity, and the latter with more severity,—they procured a meeting, at Boston, of the governor, deputy, Mr. Cotton, Mr. Hooker, Mr. Wilson,[9] and there was present Mr. Winthrop, Mr. Dudley, and themselves; where, after the Lord had been sought, Mr. Vane declared the occasion of this meeting, (as is before noted,) and the fruit aimed at, viz. a more firm and friendly uniting of minds, etc., especially of the said Mr. Dudley and Mr. Winthrop, as those upon whom the weight of the affairs did lie, etc., and therefore desired all present to take up a resolution to deal freely and openly with the parties, and they each with other, that nothing might be left in their breasts, which might break out to any jar or difference hereafter, (which they promised to do). Then Mr. Winthrop spake to this effect: that when it pleased Mr. Vane to acquaint him with what he had observed, of the dispositions of men's minds inclining to the said faction, etc., it was very strange to him, professing solemnly that he knew not of any breach between his brother Dudley and himself, since they were reconciled long since, neither did he suspect any alienation of affection in him or others from himself, save that, of late, he had observed, that some new comers had estranged themselves from him, since they went to dwell at Newtown; and so desired all the company, that, if they had seen any thing amiss in his government or otherwise, they would deal freely and faithfully with him, and for his part he promised to take it in good part, and would endeavor, by God's grace, to amend it. Then Mr. Dudley spake to this effect: that for his part he came thither a mere patient, not with any intent to charge his brother Winthrop with any thing; for though there had been formerly some differences and breaches between them, yet they had been healed, and, for his part, he was not willing to renew them again; and so left it to others to utter their own complaints. Whereupon the governor, Mr. Haynes,[10] spake to this effect: that Mr. Winthrop and himself had been always in good terms, etc.; therefore he was loath to give any offence to him, and he hoped that, considering what the end of this meeting was, he would take it in good part, if he did deal openly and freely, as his manner ever was. Then he spake of one or two passages, wherein he conceived, that [he] dealt too remissly in point of justice; to which Mr. Winthrop answered, that his speeches and carriage had been in part mistaken; but withall professed, that it was his judgment, that in the infancy of plantation, justice should be administered with more lenity than in a settled state, because people were then more apt to transgress, partly of ignorance of new laws and orders, partly through oppression of business and other straits; but, if it might be made clear to him, that it was an error, he would be ready to take up a stricter course. Then the ministers were desired to consider of the question by the next morning, and to set down a rule in the case. The next morning, they delivered their several reasons, which all sorted to this conclusion, that strict discipline, both in criminal offences and in martial affairs, was more needful in plantations than in a settled state, as tending to the honor and safety of the gospel. Wherepon Mr. Winthrop acknowledged that he was convinced, that he had failed in over much lenity and remissness, and would endeavor (by God's assistance) to take a more strict course hereafter. . . .

[Winthrop's Account of the Antinomian Crisis]

[October 21, 1636.] One Mrs. Hutchinson, a member of the church of Boston, a woman of a ready wit and bold spirit, brought over with her two dangerous errors: 1. That the person of the Holy Ghost dwells in a justified person. 2. That no sanctification can help to evidence to us our justification.—From these two grew many branches; as, 1. Our union with the Holy Ghost, so as a Christian remains dead to every spiritual action, and hath no gifts nor graces, other than such as are in hypocrites, nor any other sanctification but the Holy Ghost himself.[11]

There joined with her in these opinions a brother of hers, one Mr. Wheelwright,[12] a silenced minister sometimes in England.

[October 25.] The other ministers in the bay, hearing of these things, came to Boston at the time of a general court, and entered conference in private with them, to the end they might know the certainty of these things; that if need were, they might write to the church of Boston about them, to prevent (if it were possible) the dangers, which seemed hereby to hang over that and the rest of the churches. At this conference, Mr. Cotton was present, and gave satisfaction to them, so as he agreed with them all in the point of sanctification, and so did Mr. Wheelwright; so as they all did hold, that sanctification did help to evidence justification. The same he had delivered plainly in public, divers times; but, for the indwelling of the person of the Holy Ghost, he held that still, as some others of the ministers did, but not union with the person of the Holy Ghost, (as Mrs. Hutchinson and others did,) so as to amount to a personal union . . .

[November 17.] The governor, Mr. Vane, a wise and godly gentleman, held, with Mr. Cotton and many others, the indwelling of the person of the Holy Ghost in a believer, and went so far beyond the rest, as to maintain a personal union with the Holy Ghost; but the deputy,[13] with the pastor[14] and divers others, denied both; and the question proceeded so far by disputation, (in writing, for the peace sake of the church, which all were tender of,) as at length they could not find the person of the Holy Ghost in scripture, nor in the primitive churches three hundred years after Christ. So that, all agreeing in the chief matter of substance, viz. that the Holy Ghost is God, and that he doth dwell in the believers, (as the Father and Son both are said also to do,) but whether by his gifts and power only, or by any other manner of presence, seeing the scripture doth not declare it,—it was earnestly desired, that the word person might be forborn, being a term of human invention, and tending to doubtful disputation in this case . . .

[December 10.] At this court the elders of the churches were called, to advise with them about discovering and pacifying the differences among the churches in point of opinion. The governor having declared the occasion to them, Mr. Dudley desired, that men would be free and open, etc. Another of the magistrates spake, that it would much further the end they came for, if men would freely declare what they held different from others, as himself would freely do, in what point soever he should be opposed. The governor said, that he would be content to do the like, but that he understood the ministers were about it in a church way, etc., which he spake upon this occasion: the ministers had met, a little before, and had drawn into heads all the points, wherein they suspected Mr. Cotton did differ from them, and had propounded them to him, and pressed him to a direct answer, affirmative or negative, to every one; which he had promised, and taken time for. This meeting being spoke of in the court the day before, the governor took great offence at it, as being without his privity, etc., which this day Mr. Peter told him as plainly of, (with all due reverence,) and how it had sadded the ministers' spirits, that he should be jealous of their meetings, or seem to restrain their liberty, etc. The governor excused his speech, as sudden and upon a mistake. Mr. Peter told him also, that before he came, within less than two years since, the churches were in peace, etc. The governor answered, that the light of the gospel brings a sword, and the children of the bondwoman would persecute those of the freewoman. Mr. Peter also besought him humbly to consider his youth, and short experience in the things of God, and to beware of peremptory conclusions, which he perceived him to be very apt unto. . . .

Mr. Wilson made a very sad speech of the condition of our churches, and the inevitable danger of separation, if these differences and alienations among brethren were not speedily remedied; and laid the blame upon these new opinions risen up amongst us, which all the magistrates, except the governor and two others, did confirm, and all the ministers but two. . . .

The speech of Mr. Wilson was taken very ill by Mr. Cotton and others of the same church, so as he and divers of them went to admonish him. But Mr. Wilson and some others could see no breach of rule, seeing he was called by the court about the same matter with the rest of the elders, and exhorted to deliver their minds freely and faithfully, both for discovering the danger, and the means to help; and the things he spake of were only in general, and such as were under a common fame. And being questioned about his intent, he professed he did not mean Boston church, nor the members thereof, more than others. But this would not satisfy, but they called him to answer publicly, [December] 31; and there the governor pressed it violently against him, and all the congregation, except the deputy and one or two more, and many of them with much bitterness and reproaches; but he answered them all with words of truth and soberness, and with marvellous wisdom. It was strange to see, how the common people were led, by example, to condemn him in that, which (it was very probable) divers of them did not understand, nor the rule which he was supposed to have broken; and that such as had known him so long, and what good he had done for that church, should fall upon him with such bitterness for justifying himself in a good cause; for he was a very holy, upright man, and for faith and love inferior to none in the country, and most dear to all men. The teacher joined with the church in their judgment of him, (not without some appearance of prejudice,) yet with much wisdom and moderation. They were eager to proceed to present censure, but the teacher staid them from that, telling them he might not do it, because some opposed it, but gave him a grave exhortation. The next day Mr. Wilson preached, notwithstanding, and the Lord so assisted him, as gave great satisfaction, and the governor himself gave public witness to him. . . .

[January 20, 1637.] The differences in the said points of religion increased more and more, and the ministers of both sides (there being only Mr. Cotton of one party) did publicly declare their judgments in some of them, so as all men's mouths were full of them. And there being, 12 mo. [February] 3, a ship ready to go for England, and many passengers in it, Mr. Cotton took occasion to speak to them about the differences, etc., and willed them to tell our countrymen, that all the strife amongst us was about magnifying the grace of God; one party seeking to advance the grace of God within us, and the other to advance the grace of God towards us, (meaning by the one justification, and by the other sanctification;) and so bade them tell them, that, if there were any among them that would strive for grace, they should come hither; and so declared some particulars. Mr. Wilson spake after him, and declared, that he knew none of the elders or brethren of the churches, but did labor to advance the free grace of God in justification, so far as the word of God required; and spake also about the doctrine of sanctification, and the use and necessity, etc., of it; by occasion whereof no man could tell (except some few, who knew the bottom of the matter) where any difference was: which speech, though it offended those of Mr. Cotton's party, yet it was very seasonable to clear the rest, who otherwise should have been reputed to have opposed free grace. Thus every occasion increased the contention, and caused great alienation of minds; and the members of Boston (frequenting the lectures of other ministers) did make much disturbance by public questions, and objections to their doctrines, which did any way disagree from their opinions; and it began to be as common here to distinguish between men, by being under a covenant of grace or a covenant of works, as in other countries between Protestants and papists. . . .

[March 9.] Mr. Wheelwright, one of the members of Boston, preaching at the last fast, inveighed against all that walked in a covenant of works, as he described it to be, viz., such as maintain sanctification as an evidence of justification, etc. and called them antichrists, and stirred up the people against them with much bitterness and vehemency. For this he was called into the court, and his sermon being produced, he justified it, and confessed he did mean all that walk in such a way. Whereupon the elders of the rest of the churches were called, and asked whether they, in their ministry, did walk in such a way. They all acknowledged they did. So, after much debate, the court adjudged him guilty of sedition, and also of contempt, for that the court had appointed the fast as a means of reconciliation of the differences, etc., and he purposely set himself to kindle and increase them. The governor and some few more (who dissented) tendered a protestation, which, because it wholly justified Mr. Wheelwright, and condemned the proceedings of the court, was rejected. The church of Boston also tendered a petition in his behalf, justifying Mr. Wheelwright's sermon. The court deferred sentence till the next court, and advised with the ministers, etc., whether they might enjoin his silence, etc. They answered, that they were not clear in that point, but desired rather, that he might be commended to the church of Boston to take care of him, etc., which accordingly was done, and he enjoined to appear at the next court. Much heat of contention was this court between the opposite parties; so as it was moved, that the next court might be kept at Newtown. . . .[15]

[May 17.] Our court of elections was at Newtown. So soon as the court was set, being about one of the clock, a petition was preferred by those of Boston. The governor would have read it, but the deputy said it was out of order; it was a court for elections, and those must first be despatched, and then their petitions should be heard. Divers others also opposed that course, as an ill precedent, etc.; and the petition, being about pretence of liberty, etc., (though intended chiefly for revoking the sentence given against Mr. Wheelwright,) would have spent all the day in debate, etc.; but yet the governor and those of that party would not proceed to election, except the petition was read. Much time was already spent about this debate, and the people crying out for election, it was moved by the deputy, that the people should divide themselves, and the greater number must carry it. And so it was done, and the greater number by many were for election. But the governor and that side kept their place still, and would not proceed. Whereupon the deputy told him, that, if he would not go to election, he and the rest of that side would proceed. Upon that, he came from his company, and they went to election; and Mr. Winthrop was chosen governor, Mr. Dudley deputy and Mr. Endecott of the standing council; and Mr. Israel Stoughton and Mr. Richard Saltonstall were called in to be assistants; and Mr. Vane, Mr. Coddington, and Mr. Dummer, (being all of that faction,) were left quite out.

There was great danger of a tumult that day; for those of that side grew into fierce speeches, and some laid hands on others; but seeing themselves too weak, they grew quiet. They expected a great advantage that day, because the remote towns were allowed to come in by proxy; but it fell out, that there were enough beside. . . .

[August 30.] The synod,[16] called the assembly, began at Newtown. There were all the teaching elders through the country, and some new come out of England, not yet called to any place here, as Mr. Davenport,[17] etc.

The assembly began with prayer, made by Mr. Shepherd, the pastor of Newtown. Then the erroneous opinions, which were spread in the country, were read, (being eighty in all: [18]) next the unwholesome expressions; then the scriptures abused. Then they chose two moderators for the next day, viz., Mr. Buckly and Mr. Hooker, and these were continued in that place all the time of the assembly. There were about eighty opinions, some blasphemous, others erroneous, and all unsafe, condemned by the whole assembly; whereto near all the elders, and others sent by the churches, subscribed their names; but some few liked not subscription, though they consented to the condemning of them. . . .

[November 1.] There was great hope that the late general assembly would have had some good effect in pacifying the troubles and dissensions about matters of religion; but it fell out otherwise. For though Mr. Wheelwright and those of his party had been clearly confuted and confounded in the assembly, yet they persisted in their opinions, and were as busy in nourishing contentions (the principal of them) as before. Whereupon the general court, being assembled in the 2 of the 9th month [November], and finding, upon consultation, that two so opposite parties could not contain in the same body, without apparent hazard of ruin to the whole, agreed to send away some of the principal; . . . Then the court sent for Mr. Wheelwright, and, he persisting to justify his sermon, and his whole practice and opinions, and refusing to leave either the place or his public exercisings, he was disfranchised and banished. Upon which he appealed to the king, but neither called witnesses, nor desired any act to be made of it. The court told him, that an appeal did not lie; for by the king's grant we had power to hear and determine without any reservation,[19] etc. So he relinquished his appeal, and the court gave him leave to go to his house, upon his promise, that, if he were not gone out of our jurisdiction within fourteen days, he would render himself to one of the magistrates.

The court also sent for Mrs. Hutchinson, and charged her with divers matters, as her keeping two public lectures every week in her house, whereto sixty or eighty persons did usually resort, and for reproaching most of the ministers (viz., all except Mr. Cotton) for not preaching a covenant of free grace, and that they had not the seal of the spirit, nor were able ministers of the New Testament; which were clearly proved against her, though she sought to shift it off. And, after many speeches to and fro, at last she was so full as she could not contain, but vented her revelations;[20] amongst which this was one, that she had it revealed to her, that she should come into New England, and should here be persecuted, and that God would ruin us and our posterity, and the whole state, for the same. So the court proceeded and banished her; but, because it was winter, they committed her to a private house, where she was well provided, and her own friends and the elders permitted to go to her, but none else. . . .

After this, many of the church of Boston, being highly offended with the governor for this proceeding, were earnest with the elders to have him called to account for it; but they were not forward in it, and himself, understanding their intent, thought fit to prevent such a public disorder, and so took occasion to speak to the congregation to this effect:—

. . . He did nothing in the cases of the brethren, but by the advice and direction of our teacher and other of the elders. For in the oath, which was administered to him and the rest, etc., there was inserted, by his advice, this clause,—In all causes wherein you are to give your vote, etc., you are to give your vote as in your judgment and conscience you shall see to be most for the public good, etc.; and so for his part he was persuaded, that it would be most for the glory of God, and the public good, to pass sentence as they did.

He would give them one reason, which was a ground for his judgment, and that was, for that he saw, that those brethren, etc., were so divided from the rest of the country in their judgment and practice, as it could not stand with the public peace, that they should continue amongst us. So, by the example of Lot in Abraham's family, and after Hagar and Ishmael, he saw they must be sent away. . . .

[March 1, 1638.] While Mrs. Hutchinson continued at Roxbury, divers of the elders and others resorted to her, and finding her to persist in maintaining those gross errors beforementioned, and many others, to the number of thirty or thereabout, some of them wrote to the church at Boston, offering to make proof of the same before the church, etc., [March] 15; whereupon she was called, (the magistrates being desired to give her license to come,) and the lecture was appointed to begin at ten. . . . When she appeared, the errors were read to her. . . . These were also clearly confuted, but yet she held her own; so as the church (all but two of her sons) agreed she should be admonished, and because her sons would not agree to it, they were admonished also.

Mr. Cotton pronounced the sentence of admonition with great solemnity, and with much zeal and detestation of her errors and pride of spirit.[21] The assembly continued till eight at night, and all did acknowledge the special presence of God's spirit therein; and she was appointed to appear again the next lecture day. . . .

[March 22.] Mrs. Hutchinson appeared again; (she had been licensed by the court, in regard she had given hope of her repentance, to be at Mr. Cotton's house, that both he and Mr. Davenport might have the more opportunity to deal with her;) and the articles being again read to her, and her answer required, she delivered it in writing, wherein she made a retractation of near all, but with such explanations and circumstances as gave no satisfaction to the church; so as she was required to speak further to them. Then she declared, that it was just with God to leave her to herself, as he had done, for her slighting his ordinances, both magistracy and ministry; and confessed that what she had spoken against the magistrates at the court (by way of revelation) was rash and ungrounded; and desired the church to pray for her. This gave the church good hope of her repentance; but when she was examined about some particulars, as that she had denied inherent righteousness, etc., she affirmed that it was never her judgment; and though it was proved by many testimonies, that she had been of that judgment, and so had persisted, and maintained it by argument against divers, yet she impudently persisted in her affirmation, to the astonishment of all the assembly. So that, after much time and many arguments had been spent to bring her to see her sin, but all in vain, the church, with one consent, cast her out. Some moved to have her admonished once more; but, it being for manifest evil in matter of conversation, it was agreed otherwise; and for that reason also the sentence was denounced by the pastor, matter of manners belonging properly to his place.

After she was excommunicated, her spirits, which seemed before to be somewhat dejected, revived again, and she gloried in her sufferings, saying, that it was the greatest happiness, next to Christ, that ever befel her. Indeed, it was a happy day to the churches of Christ here, and to many poor souls, who had been seduced by her, who, by what they heard and saw that day, were (through the grace of God) brought off quite from her errors, and settled again in the truth. . . .

After two or three days, the governor sent a warrant to Mrs. Hutchinson to depart this jurisdiction before the last of this month, according to the order of court, and for that end set her at liberty from her former constraint, so as she was not to go forth of her own house till her departure; and upon the 28th she went by water to her farm at the Mount, where she was to take water, with Mr. Wheelwright's wife and family, to go to Pascataquack; but she changed her mind, and went by land to Providence, and so to the island in the Naragansett Bay, which her husband and the rest of that sect had purchased of the Indians, and prepared with all speed to remove unto. For the court had ordered, that, except they were gone with their families by such a time, they should be summoned to the general court. . . ,

[September 25, 1638.] The court, taking into consideration the great disorder general through the country in costliness of apparel, and following new fashions, sent for the elders of the churches, and conferred with them about it, and laid it upon them, as belonging to them, to redress it, by urging it upon the consciences of their people, which they promised to do. But little was done about it; for divers of the elders' wives, etc., were in some measure partners in this general disorder. . . .

[May 26, 1639.] Mr. Hooker being to preach at Cambridge, the governor and many others went to hear him, (though the governor did very seldom go from his own congregation upon the Lord's day). He preached in the afternoon, and having gone on, with much strength of voice and intention of spirit, about a quarter of an hour, he was at a stand, and told the people, that God had deprived him both of his strength and matter, etc., and so went forth, and about half an hour after returned again, and went on to very good purpose about two hours. . . .

[December 15, 1640.] About this time there fell out a thing worthy of observation. Mr. Winthrop the younger, one of the magistrates, having many books in a chamber where there was corn of divers sorts, had among them one wherein the Greek testament, the psalms and the common prayer were bound together. He found the common prayer eaten with mice, every leaf of it, and not any of the two other touched, nor any other of his books, though there were above a thousand.

[April 13, 1641.] A godly woman of the church of Boston, dwelling sometimes in London, brought with her a parcel of very fine linen of great value, which she set her heart too much upon, and had been at charge to have it all newly washed, and curiously folded and pressed, and so left it in press in her parlor over night. She had a negro maid went into the room very late, and let fall some snuff of the candle upon the linen, so as by the morning all the linen was burned to tinder, and the boards underneath, and some stools and a part of the wainscot burned, and never perceived by any in the house, though some lodged in the chamber over head, and no ceiling between. But it pleased God that the loss of this linen did her much good, both in taking off her heart from worldly comforts, and in preparing her for a far greater affliction by the untimely death of her husband, who was slain not long after at Isle of Providence.

[September 15, 1641.] A great training at Boston two days. About 1200 men were exercised in most sorts of land service; yet it was observed that there was no man drunk, though there was plenty of wine and strong beer in the town, not an oath sworn, no quarrel, nor any hurt done.[22]

[September 22, 1642.] The sudden fall of land and cattle, and the scarcity of foreign commodities, and money, etc., with the thin access of people from England, put many into an unsettled frame of spirit, so as they concluded there would be no subsisting here, and accordingly they began to hasten away, some to the West Indies, others to the Dutch, at Long Island, etc., (for the governor there invited them by fair offers,) and others back for England. . . .

. . . They fled for fear of want, and many of them fell into it, even to extremity, as if they had hastened into the misery which they feared and fled from, besides the depriving themselves of the ordinances and church fellowship, and those civil liberties which they enjoyed here; whereas, such as staid in their places, kept their peace and ease, and enjoyed still the blessing of the ordinances, and never tasted of those troubles and miseries, which they heard to have befallen those who departed. Much disputation there was about liberty of removing for outward advantages, and all ways were sought for an open door to get out at; but it is to be feared many crept out at a broken wall. For such as come together into a wilderness, where are nothing but wild beasts and beastlike men, and there confederate together in civil and church estate, whereby they do, implicitly at least, bind themselves to support each other, and all of them that society, whether civil or sacred, whereof they are members, how they can break from this without free consent, is hard to find, so as may satisfy a tender or good conscience in time of trial. Ask thy conscience, if thou wouldst have plucked up thy stakes, and brought thy family 3000 miles, if thou hadst expected that all, or most, would have forsaken thee there. Ask again, what liberty thou hast towards others, which thou likest not to allow others towards thyself; for if one may go, another may, and so the greater part, and so church and commonwealth may be left destitute in a wilderness, exposed to misery and reproach, and all for thy ease and pleasure, whereas these all, being now thy brethren, as near to thee as the Israelites were to Moses, it were much safer for thee, after his example, to choose rather to suffer affliction with thy brethren, than to enlarge thy ease and pleasure by furthering the occasion of their ruin. . . .

[July 5, 1643.] There arose a sudden gust at N. W. so violent for half an hour, as is blew down multitudes of trees. It lifted up their meeting house at Newbury, the people being in it. It darkened the air with dust, yet through God's great mercy it did no hurt, but only killed one Indian with the fall of a tree.

[January 18, 1644.] The 18th of this month two lights were seen near Boston, (as is before mentioned,) and a week after the like was seen again. A light like the moon arose about the N. E. point in Boston, and met the former at Nottles Island, and there they closed in one, and then parted, and closed and parted divers times, and so went over the hill in the island and vanished. Sometimes they shot out flames and sometimes sparkles. This was about eight of the clock in the evening, and was seen by many. About the same time a voice was heard upon the water between Boston and Dorchester, calling out in a most dreadful manner, boy, boy, come away, come away: and it suddenly shifted from one place to another a great distance, about twenty times. It was heard by divers godly persons. About 14 days after, the same voice in the same dreadful manner was heard by others on the other side of the town towards Nottles Island.

These prodigies having some reference to the place where Captain Chaddock's pinnace was blown up a little before, gave occasion of speech of that man who was the cause of it, who professed himself to have skill in necromancy, and to have done some strange things in his way from Virginia hither, and was suspected to have murdered his master there; but the magistrates here had not notice of him till after he was blown up. This is to be observed that his fellows were all found, and others who were blown up in the former ship were also found, and others also who have miscarried by drowning, etc., have usually been found, but this man was never found. . . .

[March 21, 1644.] One Dalkin and his wife dwelling near Meadford coming from Cambridge, where they had spent their Sabbath, and being to pass over the river at a ford, the tide not being fallen enough, the husband adventured over, and finding it too deep, persuaded his wife to stay a while, but it raining very sore, she would needs adventure over, and was carried away with the stream past her depth. Her husband not daring to go help her, cried out, and thereupon his dog, being at his house near by, came forth, and seeing something in the water, swam to her, and she caught hold on the dog's tail, so he drew her to the shore and saved her life.

[July 15, 1644.] A poor man of Hingham, one Painter, who had lived at New Haven and at Rowley and Charlestown, and been scandalous and burdensome by his idle and troublesome behavior to them all, was now on the sudden turned anabaptist, and having a child born, he would not suffer his wife to bring it to the ordinance of baptism, for she was a member of the church, though himself were not. Being presented for this, and enjoined to suffer the child to be baptized, he still refusing, and disturbing the church, he was again brought to the court not only for his former contempt, but also for saying that our baptism was antichristian; and in the open court he affirmed the same. Whereupon after much patience and clear conviction of his error, etc., because he was very poor, so as no other but corporal punishment could be fastened upon him, he was ordered to be whipped, not for his opinion, but for reproaching the Lord's ordinance, and for his bold and evil behavior both at home and in the court. He endured his punishment with much obstinacy, and when he was loosed, he said boastingly, that God had marvellously assisted him. Whereupon two or three honest men, his neighbors, affirmed before all the company, that he was of very loose behavior at home, and given much to lying and idleness, etc. Nor had he any great occasion to gather God's assistance from his stillness under the punishment, which was but moderate, for divers notorious malefactors had showed the like, and one the same court.

[April 13, 1645.] Mr. Hopkins, the governor of Hartford upon Connecticut, came to Boston, and brought his wife with him, (a godly young woman, and of special parts,) who was fallen into a sad infirmity, the loss of her understanding and reason, which had been growing upon her divers years, by occasion of her giving herself wholly to reading and writing, and had written many books. Her husband, being very loving and tender of her, was loath to grieve her; but he saw his error, when it was too late. For if she had attended her household affairs, and such things as belong to women, and not gone out of her way and calling to meddle in such things as are proper for men, whose minds are stronger, etc., she had kept her wits, and might have improved them usefully and honorably in the place God had set her. He brought her to Boston, and left her with her brother, one Mr. Yale, a merchant, to try what means might be had here for her. But no help could be had.

[April 13, 1645.] The wars in England kept servants from coming to us, so as those we had could not be hired, when their times were out, but upon unreasonable terms, and we found it very difficult to pay their wages to their content, (for money was very scarce). I may upon this occasion report a passage between one of Rowley and his servant. The master, being forced to sell a pair of his oxen to pay his servant his wages, told his servant he could keep him no longer, not knowing how to pay him the next year. The servant answered, he would serve him for more of his cattle. But how shall I do (saith the master) when all my cattle are gone? The servant replied, you shall then serve me, and so you may have your cattle again.[23]

[July 3, 1645.] Divers free schools were erected, as at Roxbury (for maintenance whereof every inhabitant bound some house or land for a yearly allowance forever) and at Boston (where they made an order to allow forever 50 pounds to the master and an house and 30 pounds to an usher, who should also teach to read and write and cipher, and Indians' children were to be taught freely, and the charge to be by yearly contribution, either by voluntary allowance, or by rate of such as refused, etc., and this order was confirmed by the general court . . . Other towns did the like, providing maintenance by several means.

[July, 1646.] Great harm was done in corn (especially wheat and barley) in this month by a caterpillar, like a black worm about an inch and a half long. They eat up first the blades of the stalk, then they eat up the tassels, whereupon the ear withered. It was believed by divers good observers, that they fell in a great thunder shower, for divers yards and other bare places, where not one of them was to be seen an hour before, were presently after the shower almost covered with them, besides grass places where they were not so easily discerned. They did the most harm in the southern parts, as Rhode Island, etc., and in the eastern parts in their Indian corn. In divers places the churches kept a day of humiliation, and presently after the caterpillars vanished away.

[September 20, 1646.] There fell a sad affliction upon the country this year, though it more particularly concerned New Haven and those parts. A small ship of about 100 tons set out from New Haven in the middle of the eleventh month last (the harbor there being so frozen, as they were forced to hew her through the ice near three miles). She was laden with pease and some wheat, all in bulk, with about 200 West India hides, and store of beaver, and plate, so as it was estimated in all at 5000 pounds. There were in her about seventy persons, whereof divers were of very precious account, as Mr. Grigson, one of their magistrates, the wife of Mr. Goodyear, another of their magistrates, (a right godly woman,) Captain Turner, Mr. Lamberton, master of the ship, and some seven or eight others, members of the church there. The ship never went voyage before, and was very crank-sided, so as it was conceived, she was overset in a great tempest, which happened soon after she put to sea, for she was never heard of after. . . .

[June 28, 1648.] There appeared over the harbor at New Haven, in the evening, the form of the keel of a ship with three masts, to which were suddenly added all the tackling and sails, and presently after, upon the top of the poop, a man standing with one hand akimbo under his left side, and in his right hand a sword stretched out toward the sea. Then from the side of the ship which was from the town arose a great smoke, which covered all the ship, and in that smoke she vanished away; but some saw her keel sink into the water. This was seen by many, men and women, and it continued about a quarter of an hour. . . .

[June 4, 1647.] An epidemical sickness was through the country among Indians and English, French and Dutch. It took them like a cold, and a light fever with it. Such as bled or used cooling drinks died; those who took comfortable things, for most part recovered, and that in few days. Wherein a special providence of God appeared, for not a family, nor but few persons escaping it, had it brought all so weak as it did some, and continued so long, our hay and corn had been lost for want of help; but such was the mercy of God to his people, as few died, not above forty or fifty in the Massachusetts, and near as many at Connecticut. But that which made the stroke more sensible and grievous, both to them and to all the country, was the death of that faithful servant of the Lord, Mr. Thomas Hooker, pastor of the church in Hartford, who, for piety, prudence, wisdom, zeal, learning, and what else might make him serviceable in the place and time he lived in, might be compared with men of greatest note; and he shall need no other praise: the fruits of his labors in both Englands shall preserve an honorable and happy remembrance of him forever.

[June 14.] In this sickness the governor's wife, daughter of Sir John Tindal, Knight, left this world for a better, being about fifty-six years of age: a woman of singular virtue, prudence, modesty, and piety, and specially beloved and honored of all the country.

[August 15, 1648.] The synod [24] met at Cambridge by adjournment from the (4) [June] last. Mr. Allen of Dedham preached out of Acts 15, a very godly, learned, and particular handling of near all the doctrines and applications concerning that subject with a clear discovery and refutation of such errors, objections, and scruples as had been raised about it by some young heads in the country.

It fell out, about the midst of his sermon, there came a snake into the seat, where many of the elders sate behind the preacher. It came in at the door where people stood thick upon the stairs. Divers of the elders shifted from it, but Mr. Thomson, one of the elders of Braintree, (a man of much faith,) trode upon the head of it, and so held it with his foot and staff with a small pair of grains, until it was killed. This being so remarkable, and nothing falling out but by divine providence, it is out of doubt, the Lord discovered somewhat of his mind in it. The serpent is the devil; the synod, the representative of the churches of Christ in New England. The devil had formerly and lately attempted their disturbance and dissolution; but their faith in the seed of the woman overcame him and crushed his head.

EDWARD JOHNSON, 1598–1672

[Edward Johnson, born in Canterbury, was brought up to the trade of joiner, married in 1618, and emigrated to Boston in 1630. He went back to England for his wife and seven children, and returned to New England in the midst of the Antinomian crisis. He settled at Charlestown in 1636; in 1640 he became one of the founders of Woburn, where he remained a leading citizen for the remainder of his life, serving as proprietor, clerk, selectman, militia captain, deputy to the General Court. He was Speaker of the House of Deputies in 1655, and was employed by the government as surveyor of the boundaries and inspector of arms and ammunitions. He commenced writing his history in 1650; it was published anonymously in London in 1654. This text is from *Wonder-Working Providence of Sions Saviour in New England.* ed. J. F. Jameson (New York, 1910). For discussion see this edition, or that of William Frederick Poole (Andover, 1867).]

WONDER-WORKING PROVIDENCE OF SIONS SAVIOUR

BEING A RELATION OF THE FIRST PLANTING IN NEW ENGLAND, IN THE YEARE, 1628.

BOOK I.

CHAP. I.

THE SAD CONDITION OF ENGLAND, WHEN THIS PEOPLE REMOVED.

WHEN *England* began to decline in Religion, like luke-warme *Laodicea*, and instead of purging out Popery, a farther compliance was sought not onely in vaine Idolatrous Ceremonies, but also in prophaning the Sabbath, and by Proclamation throughout their Parish churches, exasperating lewd and prophane persons to celebrate a Sabbath like the Heathen to *Venus*, *Baccus* and *Ceres;* [1]

in so much that the multitude of irreligious lascivious and popish affected persons spred the whole land like *Grashoppers*, in this very time Christ the glorious King of his Churches, raises an Army out of our *English* Nation, for freeing his people from their long servitude under usurping Prelacy; and because every corner of *England* was filled with the fury of malignant adversaries, Christ creates a New *England* to muster up the first of his Forces in; Whose low condition, little number, and remotenesse of place made these adversaries triumph, despising this day of small things, but in this hight of their pride the *Lord Christ* brought sudden, and unexpected destruction upon them. Thus have you a touch of the time when this worke began.

Christ Jesus intending to manifest his Kingly Office toward his Churches more fully than ever yet the Sons of men saw, even to the uniting of *Jew* and *Gentile* Churches in one Faith, begins with our *English* Nation (whose former reformation being vere imperfect) doth now resolve to cast down their false foundation of Prelacy, even in the hight of their domineering dignity. And therefore in the yeere 1628, he stirres up his servants as the Heralds of a King to make this proclamation for Voluntiers, as followeth.

Oh yes! oh yes! oh yes! *All you the people of Christ that are here Oppressed, Imprisoned and scurrilously derided, gather yourselves together, your Wives and little ones, and answer to your severall Names as you shall be shipped for his service, in the Westerne World, and more especially for planting the united Collonies of new* England; *Where you are to attend the service of the King of Kings, upon the divulging of this Proclamation by his Herralds at Armes.* Many (although otherwise willing for this service) began to object as followeth:

Can it possible be the mind of Christ, (who formerly inabled so many Souldiers of his to keepe their station unto the death here) that now so many brave Souldiers disciplined by Christ himselfe the Captaine of our salvation, should turne their backs to the disheartning of their Fellow-Souldiers, and losse of further opportunity in gaining a greater number of Subjects to Christs Kingdome?

Notwithstanding this Objection, It was further proclaimed as followeth: What Creature, wilt not know that Christ thy King crusheth with a rod of Iron, the Pompe and Pride of man, and must he like man cast and contrive to take his enemies at advantage? No, of purpose hee causeth such instruments to retreate as hee hath made strong for himselfe: that so his adversaries glorying in the pride of their power, insulting over the little remnant remaining, Christ causeth them to be cast downe suddenly forever, and wee find in stories reported, Earths Princes have passed their Armies at need over Seas and deepe Torrents. Could *Cæsar* so suddenly fetch over fresh forces from *Europe* to *Asia*, *Pompy* to foyle? How much more shall Christ who createth all power, call over this 900 league Ocean at his pleasure, such instruments as he thinks meete to make use of in this place, from whence you are now to depart, but further that you may not delay the Voyage intended, for your full satisfaction, know this is the place where the Lord will create a new Heaven, and a new Earth in, new Churches, and a new Common-wealth together; Wherefore,

Chap. II.

The Commission of the People of Christ shipped for New England, and first of their gathering into Churches.

Attend to your Commission, all you that are or shall hereafter be shipped for this service, yee are with all possible speed to imbarque your selves, and as for all such Worthies who are hunted after as *David* was by *Saul* and his Courtiers, you may change your habit and ship you with what secrecy you can, carrying all things most needfull for the Voyage and service you are to be imployed in after your landing. But as soone as you shall be exposed to danger of tempestious Seas, you shall forthwith shew whose servants you are by calling on the Name of your God, sometimes by extraordinary seeking his pleasing Face in times of deepe distresse, and publishing your Masters will, and pleasure to all that Voyage with you, and that is his minde to have purity in Religion preferred above all dignity in the world; your Christ hath commanded the Seas they shall not swallow you, nor Pyrates imprison your persons, or possesse your goods. At your landing see you observe the Rule of his Word, for neither larger nor stricter Commission can hee give by any, and therefore at first filling the Land whither you are sent, with diligence, search out the mind of God both in planting and continuing Church and civill Government, but be sure they be distinct, yet agreeing and helping the one to the other; Let the matter and forme of your Churches be such as were in the Primitive Times (before *Antichrists* Kingdome prevailed) plainly poynted out by Christ and his Apostles, in most of their Epistles to be neither Nationall nor Provinciall, but gathered together in Covenant of such a number as might ordinarily meete together in one place, and built of such living stones as outwardly appeare Saints by calling. You are also to ordaine Elders in every Church, make you use of such as

Christ hath indued with the best gifts for that end, their call to Office shall be mediate from you, but their authority and commission shall be immediate from Christ revealed in his word; which, if you shall slight, despise or contemne, hee will soone frustrate your call by taking the most able among you to honour with an everlasting Crown; whom you neglected to honour on Earth double as their due, or he will carry them remote from you to more infant Churches. You are not to put them upon anxious Cares for their daily Bread, for assuredly (although it may now seeme strange) you shall be fed in this Wildernesse, whither you are to goe, with the flower of Wheate and Wine shall be plentifull among you (but be sure you abuse it not) these Doctrines delivered from the Word of God imbrace, and let not Satan delude you by perswading their learned skill is unnecessary, soone then will the Word of God be slighted as translated by such, and you shall be left wildred with strange Revelations of every phantastick brain. . . .

Chap. XII.

Of the voluntary banishment, chosen by this People of Christ, and their last farewell taken of their Country and Friends.

And now behold the severall Regiments of these Souldiers of *Christ*, as they are shipped for his service in the *Western* World, part thereof being come to the Towne and Port of *Southamptan* in *England*, where they were to be shipped, that they might prosecute this designe to the full, one Ship called the *Eagle*, they wholy purchase, and many more they hire, filling them with the seede of man and beast to sow this yet untilled Wildernesse withall, making sale of such Land as they possesse, to the great admiration of their Friends and Acquaintance, who thus expostulate with them, What, will not the large income of your yearly revenue content you, which in all reason cannot chuse but be more advantagious both to you and yours, then all that Rocky Wildernesse, whither you are going, to run the hazard of your life? Have you not here your Tables filled with great variety of Foode, your Coffers filled with Coyne, your Houses beautifully built and filled with all rich Furniture? (or otherwise) have you not such a gainfull Trade as none the like in the Towne where you live? Are you not inriched daily? Are not your Children very well provided for as they come to years? (nay) may you not here as pithily practise the two chiefe Duties of a Christian (if Christ give strength) namely Mortification and Sanctification as in any place of the World? What helps can you have there that you must not carry from hence? With bold resolvednesse these stout Souldiers of Christ reply; as Death, the King of terror with all his dreadfull attendance inhumane and barbarous, tortures doubled and trebled by all the infernal furies have appeared but light and momentany to the Souldiers of *Christ Iesus*, so also the Pleasure, Profits and Honours of this World set forth in their most glorious splendor, and magnitude by the alluring Lady of Delight, proffering pleasant embraces, cannot intice with her *Syren* Songs, such Souldiers of Christ, whose aymes are elevated by him, many Millions above that brave Warrier *Vlysses*.

Now seeing all can be said will but barely set forth the immoveable Resolutions that Christ continued in these men; Passe on and attend with teares, if thou hast any, the following discourse, while these Men, Women and Children are taking their last farwell of their Native Country, Kindred, Friends and Acquaintance, while the Ships attend them; Many make choise of some solitary place to eccho out their bowell-breaking affections in bidding their Friends farwell, deare friends (sayes one) as neare as my owne soule doth thy love lodge in my brest, with thought of the heart-burning Ravishments, that thy Heavenly speeches have wrought: my melting soule is poured out at present with these words, both of them had their farther speach strangled from the depth of their inward dolor, with breast-breaking sobs, till leaning their heads each on others shoulders, they let fall the salt-dropping dews of vehement affection, striving to exceede one another, much like the departure of *David* and *Jonathan:* having a little eased their hearts with the still streames of Teares, they recovered speech againe. Ah! my much honoured friend, hath Christ given thee so great a charge as to be Leader of his People into that far remote, and vast Wildernesse, I, oh, and alas thou must die there and never shall I see thy Face in the flesh againe, wert thou called to so great a taske as to passe the pretious Ocean, and hazard thy person in Battell against thousands of Malignant Enemies there? there were hopes of thy return with triumph, but now after two three, or foure moneths spent with daily expectation of swallowing Waves, and cruell Pirates, you are to be Landed among barbarous *Indians*, famous for nothing but cruelty, where you are like to spend your days in a famishing condition for a long space; Scarce had he uttered this, but presently hee lockes his friend fast in his armes, holding each other thus for some space of time, they weepe againe, But as *Paul* to his beloved flock: the other replies what doe you weeping and breaking my heart? I am now prest for the service of our *Lord Christ*, to re-build the most glorious Edifice of Mount *Sion* in a Wildernesse, and as *John* Baptist, I must cry prepare yee the way of the Lord, make his paths strait, for behold hee is comming againe, hee is comming to destroy *Antichrist*, and give the whore double to drinke the very dregs of his wrath.

Then my deare friend unfold thy hands, for thou and I have much worke to doe, I and all Christian Souldiers the World throughout, then hand in hand they leade each other to the Sandy-banks of the brinish Ocean, when clenching their hands fast, they unloose not til inforced to wipe their watery-eyes, whose constant streames forced a watery-path upon their Cheekes, which to hide from the eyes of others they shun society for a time, but being called by occasion, whose bauld back-part none can lay hold one; They thrust in among the throng now ready to take Ship, where they beheld the like affections with their own among divers Relations, Husbands and Wives with mutuall consent are now purposed to part for a time 900 Leagues asunder, since some providence at present will not suffer them to goe together, they resolve their tender affections shall not hinder this worke of Christ, the new Married and betrothed man, exempt by the Law of God from war, now will not claime their priviledge, but being constrained by the Love of Christ, lock up their naturall affections for a time, till the Lord shall be pleased to give them a meeting in this *Westerne* World, sweetly mixing it with spirituall love, in the meane time many Fathers now take their yong *Samuells*, and give them to this service of Christ all their Lives. Brethren, Sisters, Unkles, Nephewes, Neeces, together with all Kindred of bloud that binds the bowells of affection in a true Lovers knot, can now take their last farewell, each of other, although naturall affection will still claime her right, and manifest her selfe to bee in the body by looking out at the Windowes in a mournefull manner among this company, thus disposed doth many Reverend and godly Pastors of Christ present themselves, some in a Seamans Habit,[2] and their scattered sheepe comming as a poore Convoy loftily take their leave of them as followeth, what dolefull dayes are these, when the best choise our Orthodox Ministers can make is to take up a perpetuall banishment from their native soile, together with their Wives and Children, wee their poore sheepe they may not feede, but by stoledred should they abide here. *Lord Christ*, here they are at thy command, they go, this is the doore thou hast opened upon our earnest request, and we hope it shall never be shut: for *Englands* sake they are going from *England* to pray without ceasing for *England*, O *England!* thou shalt finde *New England* prayers prevailing with their God for thee, but now woe alas, what great hardship must these our indeared Pastors indure for a long season, with these words they lift up their voyces and wept, adding many drops of salt liquor to the ebbing Ocean; Then shaking hands they bid adue with much cordiall affection to all their Brethren, and Sisters in Christ, yet now the Scorne and Derision of those times, and for this their great enterprise counted as so many crackt-braines, but Christ will make all the earth know the wisdome he hath indued them with, shall over-top all the humane policy in the World, as the sequell wee hope will shew; Thus much shall suffice in generall to speak of their peoples farewell they tooke from time to time of their Country and Friends. . . .

Chap. XVII.

Of the first leading of these People of Christ, when the Civill Government was Established.

But to goe on with the Story, the 12 of *July* or thereabout 1630. these Souldiers of *Christ* first set foote one this *Westerne* end of the World; where arriveing in safety, both Men, Women and Children. On the North side of *Charles* River, they landed neare a small Island, called *Noddells* Island, where one Mr. *Samuel Mavereck* then living, a man of a very loving and curteous behaviour, very ready to entertaine strangers, yet an enemy to the Reformation in hand, being strong for the Lordly Prelaticall power one this Island, he had built a small Fort with the helpe of one Mr. *David Tompson*, placing therein foure Murtherers to protect him from the *Indians*. About one mile distant upon the River ran a small creeke, taking its Name from Major Gen. *Edward Gibbons*, who dwelt there for some yeares after; One the South side of the River one a point of Land called *Blaxtons* point, planted Mr. *William Blaxton*, of whom we have former spoken: to the South-East of him, neare an Island called *Tompsons* Island lived some few Planters more, these persons were the first Planters of those parts, having some small Trading with the *Indians* for *Beaver*-Skins, which moved them to make their aboade in those parts, whom these first Troopes of *Christs* Army, found as fit helpes to further their worke. At their arrivall those small number of Christians gathered at *Salem*, greatly rejoycing and the more, because they saw so many that came chiefly for promoting the great Work of *Christ* in hand, the Lady *Arrabella* [3] and some other godly Women aboad at *Salem*, but their Husbands continued at *Charles* Town, both for the settling the civill Government, and gathering another Church of *Christ*. The first Court was holden aboard the *Arrabella* the 23. of *August*. When the much honoured *John Wintrope* Esq. was chosen Governour for the remainder of that yeare, 1630. Also the worthy *Thomus Dudly* Esq. was chosen Deputy Governour, and Mr. *Simon Brodestreet* Secretary, the people after their long Voyage were many of them troubled with the *Scurvy*, and some of them died: the first station they tooke up was at *Charles.* Towne, where they pitched some Tents of Cloath, other built them small Huts, in which they lodged their Wifes and Children. The first beginning of this worke seemed very dolorous; First for the death of that worthy personage *Izaac Johnson* Esq. whom the Lord had indued with many pretious gifts, insomuch that he was had in high esteeme among all the people of God, and as a chiefe Pillar to support this new erected building. He very much rejoyced at his death, that the Lord had been pleased to keepe his eyes open so long, as to see one Church of *Christ* gathered before his death, at whose departure there was not onely many weeping eyes, but some fainting hearts, fearing the fall of the present worke. For future Remembrance of him mind this *Meeter*.

Izaac Johnson Esquire, beloved of Christ and his people, and one of the Magistrates of *New England*.

What mov'd thee on the Seas upon such toyle with Lady-taking;
Christs drawing love all strength's above, when way for his hee's making.
Christ will have thee example be, honoured with's graces, yeilding
His Churches aid, foundation laid, now new one Christ a building.
Thy Faith, Hope, Love, Joy, Meeknesse prove improved for thy Lord,
As he to thee, to people be, in Government accord.
Oh! people why, doth Christ deny this worthies life to lengthen?
Christ onely trust, Johnsons *turnd dust, and yet hee's crownd and strengthend.*

The griefe of this people was further increased by the sore sicknesse which befell among them, so that almost in every Family Lamentation, Mourning, and woe was heard, and no fresh food to be had to cherish them, it would assuredly have moved the most lockt up affections to Teares no doubt, had they past from one Hut to another, and beheld the piteous case these people were in, and that which added to their present distresse was the want of fresh water, for although the place did afford plenty, yet for present they could finde but one Spring, and that not to be come at, but when the tide was downe, which caused many to passe over to the South-side of the River, where they afterward erected some other Townes, yet most admirable it was to see with what Christian courage many of these Souldiers of *Christ* carried it amidst all these calamities, and in *October*, the Governour

Deputy and Assistants, held their second Court on the South-side of the River; Where they then began to build, holding correspondency with *Charles* Towne, as one and the same.

At this Court many of the first Planters came, and were made free, yet afterward none were admitted to this fellowship, or freedome, but such as were first joyned in fellowship with some one of the Churches of *Christ*, their chiefest aime being bent to promote his worke altogether. The number of Freemen this yeare was 110. or thereabout. . . .

Chap. XXIX.

Of the Lords remarkable providence toward his indeared servants M. Norton and Mr. Shepherd.

Now my loving Reader, let mee lead thee by the hand to our Native Land, although it was not intended to speake in particulars of any of these peoples departure from thence, purposing a generall relation should serve the turne, yet come with mee and behold the wonderous worke of *Christ* in preserving two of his most valiant Souldiers, namely Mr. *John Norton*,[4] and that soule ravishing Minister Mr. *Thomas Shepheard*, who came this yeare to *Yarmouth* to ship themselves for *New England*, where the people of God resorted privately unto them to hear them Preach, during the time of their aboade the Enemies of Christs Kingdome were not wanting to use all meanes possible to intrap them, in which perilous condition they remained about two months, waiting for the Ships readinesse, in which time some persons eagerly hunting for Mr. *Thomas Shepheard*, began to plot (for apprehending of him) with a Boy of sixteene or seventeene yeares of Age, who lived in the House where hee Lodged to open the doore for them at a certaine houre in the night; But the Lord Christ, who is the Shepheard of *Israel* kept a most sure watch over his indeared servants, for thus it befell, the sweet words of grace falling from the of lips of this Reverend and godly Mr. *Thomas Shepheard* in the hearing of the Boy (the Lords working withall) hee was perswaded this was an holy man of God, and therefore with many troubled thoughts, began to relate his former practice, although hee had a great some of money promised him, onely to let them in at the houre and time appointed; but the Boy, the more neere the time came, grew more pensive and sad, insomuch that his Master taking notice thereof began to question him about the cause of his heavinesse, who being unwilling to reveale the matter, held of from confessing a long time, till by urgent and insinuating search of his godly Master, with teares hee tells that on such a night hee had agreed to let in Men to apprehend the godly Preacher. The good Man of the house forthwith gave notice thereof unto them, who with the helpe of some well-affected persons was convay'd away by boate through a back Lane, the men at the time appointed came to the house, where finding not the doore open (when they lifted up the Latch) as they expected, they thrust their staves under it to lift it from the hookes, but being followed by some persons, whom the good man of the house had appointed for that end: yet were they boulstred out in this their wicked act by those who set them one worke. Notwithstanding they were greatly ashamed when they mist of their end.

But the Lord Christ intending to make his *New England* Souldiers the very wonder of this Age, brought them into greater straites, that this *Wonder working Providence* might the more appeare in their deliverance, for comming a shipboard, and hoiseing saile to accomplish their Voyage, in little time after they were tossed and sore beaten with a contrary winde, to the losse of the Ships upper worke, with which losse and great perill they were driven back againe, the *Lord Christ* intending to confirme their Faith in shewing them, that although they were brought back, as it were into the mouth of their enemies, yet hee could hide them from the hand of the Hunter, for the space of six moneths longer or thereabout, even till the Spring of the yeare following, at which time (God willing) you shall hear of them againe, in the meane time the Master, and other Sea men made a strange construction of the sore storme they met withall, saying, their Ship was bewitched, and therefore made use of the common Charme ignorant people use, nailing two red hot horseshoos to their maine mast. But assuredly it was the *Lord Christ*, who hath command both of Winds and Seas, and now would have his poeple know he hath delivered, and will deliver from so great a death. . . .

Chap. XXXVI.

Of the laborious worke Christs people have in planting this wildernesse, set forth in the building the Towne of Concord, being the first in-land Towne.

Now because it is one of the admirable acts of Christ Providence in leading his people forth into these Westerne Fields, in his providing of Huts for them, to defend them from the bitter stormes this place is subject unto, therefore here is a short Epitome of the manner how they placed downe their dwellings in this Desart Wildernesse, the Lord being pleased to hide from the Eyes of his people the difficulties they are to encounter withall in a new Plantation, that they might not thereby be hindered from taking the worke in hand; upon some inquiry of the *Indians*, who lived to the North-west of the Bay, one Captaine *Simon Willard* being acquainted with them, by reason of his Trade, became a chiefe instrument in erecting this Town, the land they purchase of the *Indians*, and with much difficulties traveling through unknowne woods, and through watery scrampes, they discover the fitnesse of the place, sometimes passing through the Thickets, where their hands are forced to make way for their bodies passage, and their feete clambering over the crossed Trees, which when they missed they sunke into an uncertaine bottome in water, and wade up to the knees, tumbling sometimes higher and sometines lower, wearied with this toile, they at end of this meete with a scorching plaine, yet not so plaine, but that the ragged Bushes scratch their legs fouly, even to wearing their stockings to their bare skin in two or three houres; if they be not otherwise well defended with Bootes, or Buskings, their flesh will be torne: (that some being forced to passe on without further provision) have had the bloud trickle downe at every step, and in the time of Summer the Sun casts such a reflecting heate from the sweet Ferne, whose scent is very strong so that some herewith have beene very nere fainting, although very able bodies to undergoe much travell, and this not to be indured for one day, but for many, and verily did not the Lord incourage their naturall parts (with hopes of a new and strange discovery, expecting every houre to see some rare sight never seene before) they were never able to hold out, and breake through: but above all, the thirsting desires these servants of Christ have had to Plant his Churches, among whom the forenamed Mr. *Jones* shall not be forgotten.

In Desart's depth where Wolves and Beares abide,
There Jones *sits down a wary watch to keepe,*
O're Christs deare flock, who now are wandered wide;
But not from him, whose eyes ne're close with sleepe.
Surely it sutes thy melancholly minde,
Thus solitary for to spend thy dayes,
Much more thy soule in Christ content doth finde,
To worke for him, who thee to joy will raise.
Leading thy son to Land, yet more remote,
To feede his flock upon this Westerne wast:
Exhort him then Christs Kingdome to promote;
That he with thee of lasting joyes may tast.

Yet farther to tell of the hard labours this people found in Planting this Wildernesse, after some dayes spent in search, toyling in the day time as formerly is said; like true *Jacob*, its they rest them one the Rocks where the night takes them, their short repast is some small pittance of Bread, if it hold out, but as for Drinke they have plenty, the Countrey being well watered in all places that yet are found out, their farther hardship is to travell, sometimes they know not whether, bewildred indeed without sight of Sun, their compasse miscarrying in crouding through the Bushes, they sadly search up and down for a known way, the *Indians* paths being not above one foot broad, so that a man may travell many dayes and never find one. But to be sure the directing Providence of Christ hath beene better unto them than many paths, as might here be inserted, did not hast call my Pen away to more waighty matters; yet by the way a touch thus, it befell with a servant maide, who was travelling about three or foure miles from one Towne to another, loosing her selfe in the Woods, had very diligent search made after her for the space of three dayes, and could not possible be found, then being given over as quite lost, after three dayes and nights, the Lord was pleased to bring her feeble body to her own home in safety, to the great admiration of all that heard of it. This intricate worke no whit daunted these resolved servants of Christ to goe on with the worke in hand, but lying in the open aire, while the watery Clouds poure down all the night season, and sometimes the driving Snow dissolving on their backs, they keep their wet cloathes warme with a continued fire, till the renewed morning give fresh opportunity of further travell; after they have thus found out a place of aboad, they burrow themselves in the Earth for their first shelter under some Hill-side, casting the Earth aloft upon Timber; they make a smoaky fire against the Earth at the highest side, and thus these poore servants of Christ provide shelter for themselves, their Wives and little ones, keeping off the short showers from their Lodgings, but the long raines penetrate through, to their great disturbance in the night season: yet in these poore *Wigwames* (they sing Psalmes, pray and praise their God) till they can provide them houses, which ordinarily was not wont to be with many till the Earth, by the Lords blessing, brought forth Bread to feed them, their Wives and little ones, which with sore labours they attaine every one that can lift a hawe to strike it into the Earth, standing stoutly to their labours, and teare up the Rootes and Bushes, which the first yeare beares them a very thin crop, till the soard of the Earth be rotten, and therefore they have been forced to cut their bread very thin for a long season. But the Lord is pleased to provide for them great store of Fish in the spring time, and especially Alewives about the bignesse of a Herring, many thousands of these, they used to put under their *Indian* Corne, which they plant in Hills five foote asunder, and assuredly when the Lord created this Corne, hee had a speciall eye to supply these his peoples wants with it, for ordinarily five or six graines doth produce six hundred.

As for flesh they looked not for any in those times (although now they have plenty) unlesse they could barter with the *Indians* for Venison or Rockoons, whose flesh is not much inferiour unto Lambe, the toile of a new Plantation being like the labours of *Hercules* never at an end, yet are none so barbarously bent (under the *Mattacusets* especially) but with a new Plantation they ordinarily gather into Church-fellowship, so that Pastors and people suffer the inconveniences together, which is a great meanes to season the sore labours they undergoe, and verily the edge of their appetite was greater to spirituall duties at their first comming in time of wants, than afterward: many in new Plantations have been forced to go barefoot, and bareleg, till these latter dayes, and some in time of Frost and Snow: Yet were they then very healthy more then now they are: in this Wildernesse-worke men of Estates speed no better than others, and some much worse for want of being inured to such hard labour, having laid out their estate upon cattell at five and twenty pound a Cow, when they came to winter them with in-land Hay, and feed upon such wild Fother as was never cut before, they could not hold out the Winter, but ordinarily the first or second yeare after their comming up to a new Plantation, many of their Cattell died, especially if they wanted Salt-marshes: and also those, who supposed they should feed upon Swines flesh were cut short, the Wolves commonly feasting themselves before them, who never leave neither flesh nor bones, if they be not scared away before they have made an end of their meale, as for those who laid out their Estate upon Sheepe, they speed worst of any at the beginning (although some have sped the best of any now) for untill the Land be often fed with other Cattell Sheepe cannot live; And therefore they never thrived till these latter dayes; Horse had then no better successe, which made many an honest Gentleman travell a foot for a long time, and some have even perished with extreame heate in their travells: as also the want of English graine, Wheate, Barly and Rie proved a sore affliction to some stomacks, who could not live upon *Indian* Bread and water, yet were they compelled to it till Cattell increased, and the Plowes could but goe: instead of Apples and Peares, they had

Pomkins and Squashes of divers kinds, their lonesome condition was very grievous to some, which was much aggravated by continuall feare of the *Indians* approach, whose cruelties were much spoken of, and more especially during the time of the *Peqot* wars.

Thus this poore people populate this howling Desart, marching manfully on (the Lord assisting) through the greatest difficulties, and sorest labours that ever any with such weak means have done. . . .

Chap. LXII.

Of sad effects of the pitifull and erronious Doctrines broached by the Sectuaries.

The number of these infectious persons increasing now, haveing drawn a great party on their side, and some considerable persons they grow bold, and dare question the sound and wholesome truths delivered in publick by the Ministers of *Christ*. Their Church-meetings are full of Disputes in points of difference, and their love-Feasts are not free from spots, in their Courts of civill Justice some men utter their Speeches in matters of Religion very ambiguously, and among all sorts of persons a great talke of new light, but verily it proved but old darknesse, such as sometime overshadowed the City of *Munster;* [5] But blessed be the *Lord Christ*, who now declared himselfe to be a helpe at hand for his poore *New England* Churches, being now in their infancy, whose condition at present was very dolorous, and full of difficulties, insomuch that the better part of this new transported people stood still many of them gazing one upon another, like Sheepe let loose to feed on fresh pasture, being stopped and startled in their course by a Kennell of devouring Wolves. The weaker sort wavered much, and such as were more growne Christians hardly durst discover the truth they held one unto another, the fogs of errour increasing the bright beames of the glorious Gospell of our *Lord Christ* in the Mouth of his Ministers could not be discerned through this thick mist by many, and that sweete refreshing warmth that was formerly felt from the spirits influence, was now turned (in these Erronists) to a hot inflamation of their owne conceited Revelations, ulcerating and bringing little lesse then frenzy or madnesse to the patient, the Congregation of the people of God began to be forsaken, and the weaker Sex prevailed so farre, that they set up a Priest of their own Profession and Sex, who was much thronged after, abominably wresting the Scriptures to their own destruction: this Master-piece of Womens wit, drew many Disciples after her, and to that end boldly insinuated her selfe into the favour of none of the meanest, being also backed with the Sorcery of a second, who had much converse with the Devill by her own confession, and did, to the admiration of those that heard her, utter many speeches in the Latine Tongue, as it were in a trance. . . .

Oh yee *New England* Men and Women, who hath bewitched you that you should not obey the truth? And indeed Satan, to make sure worke with semblance of Preaching the Doctrine of Free-gree by his instruments, makes shew of out-bidding all the Orthodox, and godly Ministers in the Countrey, pretending their Preaching to be but a Covenant of workes, supposing by this meanes to silence them without a Bishop, and lest the civill power should stand up for their aid, they threaten them with the high displeasure of Christ for persecuting his people, which as they said these erronious persons with their new light, were the onely Men and Women that were pure Gospell Preachers. Thus the poore people of Christ, who kept close to his antient truths invironed with many straites, having expended their Estates to voyage far through the perillous Seas, that their eyes might behold their Teachers, and that they might injoy the protection of a godly civill Government, began to deeme themselves in a more dolorous condition then when they were in the Commissaries Court, and Prelates Prisons, the hideous waves in which their brittle Barques were sometimes covered, as they passed hither, were nothing so terrible in the apprehension of some as was this floud of errors violently beating against the bankes of Church and civill Government, the wants of this Wildernesse, and pinching penury in misse of Bread, put them to no such paine by gnawing on their empty stomacks, with feare of famishing, as did the misse of the Administration of Christ in his Word and Ordinances, leaving the soule in a languishing condition for want of a continuall supply of *Christ* in his Graces.

Chap. LXIII.

Of the sorrowfull condition of the people of Christ, when they were incountred with these Erronists at their first landing.

But to end this dismall yeare of sixteene hundred thirty six, take here the sorrowfull complaint of a poore Soule in misse of its expectation at landing, who being incountered with some of these Erronists at his first landing, when he saw that good old way of *Christ* rejected by them, and hee could not skill in that new light, which was the common theame of every mans Discourse, hee betooke him to a narrow

Indian path, in which his serious Meditations soone led him, where none but sencelesse Trees and eccohing Rocks make answer to his heart-easeing mone. Oh quoth he where am I become, is this the place where those Reverend Preachers are fled, that *Christ* was pleased to make use of to rouse up his rich graces in many a drooping soule; here I have met with some that tell mee, I must take a naked *Christ*. Oh, woe is mee if *Christ* be naked to mee, wherewith shall I be cloathed, but methinks I most wonder they tell me of casting of all godly sorrow for sin as unbeseeming a Soule, that is united to *Christ* by Faith, and there was a little nimbled tongued Woman among them, who said she could bring me acquainted with one of her own Sex that would shew me a way, if I could attaine it, even Revelations, full of such ravishing joy that I should never have cause to be sorry for sinne, so long as I live, and as for her part shee had attained it already: a company of legall Professors, quoth she lie poring on the Law which *Christ* hath abolished, and when you breake it then you breake your joy, and now no way will serve your turne, but a deepe sorrow. These and divers other expressions intimate unto men, that here I shall finde little increase in the Graces of *Christ*, through the hearing of his word Preached, and other of his blessed Ordinances. Oh cunning Devill, the *Lord Christ* rebuke thee, that under pretence of a free and ample Gospell shuts out the Soule from partaking with the Divine Nature of *Christ*, in that mysticall Union of his Blessed Spirit creating, and continuing his Graces in the Soule: my deare *Christ*, it was thy worke that moved me hither to come, hoping to finde thy powerfull presence in the Preaching of the Word, although administred by sorry men, subject to like infirmities with others of Gods people, and also by the glasse of the Law, to have my sinfull corrupt nature discovered daily more and more, and my utter inabillity of any thing that is good, magnifying hereby the free grace of *Christ;* who of his good will and pleasure worketh in us to will, and to doe working all our works in us, and for us.

But here they tell me of a naked *Christ*, what is the whole life of a Christian upon this Earth? But through the power of *Christ* to die to sinne, and live to holinesse and righteousnesse, and for that end to be diligent in the use of meanes: at the uttering of this word he starts up from the greene bed of his complaint with resolution to hear some one of these able Ministers Preach (whom report had so valued) before his will should make choyce of any one principle, though of crossing the broade Seas back againe, then turning his face to the Sun, he steered his course toward the next Town,[6] and after some small travell hee came to a large plaine, no sooner was hee entred thereon, but hearing the sound of a Drum he was directed toward it by a broade beaten way, following this rode he demands of the next man he met what the signall of the Drum ment, the reply was made they had as yet no Bell to call men to meeting; and therefore made use of a Drum, who is it, quoth hee, Lectures at this Towne. The other replies, I see you are a stranger, new come over, seeing you know not the man, it is one Mr. *Shepheard*, verily quoth the other you hit the right, I am new come over indeed, and have been told since I came most of your Ministers are legall Preachers, onely if I mistake not they told me this man Preached a finer covenant of workes then the other, but however, I shall make what hast I can to heare him. Fare you well, then hasting thither hee croudeth through the thickest, where having stayed while the glasse was turned up twice, the man was metamorphosed, and was faine to hang down the head often, least his watry eyes should blab abroad the secret conjunction of his affections, his heart crying loud to the Lords ecchoing answer, to his blessed spirit, that caused the Speech of a poore weake pale complectioned man to take such impression in his soule at present, by applying the word so aptly, as if hee had beene his Privy Counseller, cleering Christs worke of grace in the soule from all those false Doctrines, which the erronious party had afrighted him withall, and now he resolves (the Lord willing) to live and die with the Ministers of *New England;* whom hee now saw the Lord had not onely made zealous to stand for the truth of his Discipline, but also of the Doctrine, and not to give ground one inch. . . .

Book III.

Chap. XII.

Of the time of the fall of Antichrist, and the increase of the Gentile Churches, even to the provoking of the twelve Tribes to submit to the kingdom of Christ.

It hath been the longing expectation of many, to see that notable and wonderfull worke of the Lord Christ, in casting down that man of sin who hath held the whole world (of those that profess any Christ) under his Lordly power, while the true professors of Christ have hardly had any appearance to the eye of the world; first, take notice the Lord hath an assured set time for the accomplishment of this work, which is set down in his word, although more darkly to be understood;

wherefore the reverend Ministers of Christ, for these many yeers have studied and laboured for the finding it out, and that holy man of God Mr. *John Cotton*, among many other, hath diligently searched for the Lords mind herein, and hath declared some sudden blow to be given to this blood-thirsty monster: but the Lord Christ hath unseparably joyned the time, meanes, and manner of this work together, and therefore all men that expect the day, must attend the means: for such hath been and is the absurdity of many, that they make semblance of a very zealous affection to see the glorious work of our Lord Christ herein, and yet themselves uphold, or at least side with those that uphold some part of Antichrists kingdome: and therefore the lordly Prelacy may pray for his fall till their lungs are spent, and their throats grow dry. But while they have a seeming shew (and hardly that) to oppose his doctrines, they themselves in the mean time, make use of his power to advance themselves to honour: as also in these dayes there are divers desperate, blasphemous, and erronious persons, whose consciences and their own self-will are unseparable companions; these are very hot in their own apprehensions to prosecute the work; but in the mean time, they not only batter down the truths of Christ, and his own Ordinances and Institutions, but also set up that part of Antichrists kingdom, which hath formerly had a great blow already, even his deceiveable and damnable doctrines: for as one badg of the beast is to be full of blasphemies, so are they, and these take unto themselves seven spirits worse then the former, making the latter end worse then the beginning, as this story may testifie: and some stories in our native country much more. But to come to the time of Antichrists fall; and all that expect it may depend upon the certainty of it: yea it may be boldly said that the time is come, and all may see the dawning of the day: you that long so much for it, come forth and fight: who can expect a victory without a battel? the lordly Prelates that boasted so much of these great atcheivements in this work, are fled into holes and corners: *Familists*, *Seekers*, *Antinomians* and *Anabaptists*, they are so ill armed, that they think it best sleeping in a whole skin, fearing that if the day of battell once go on, they shall fall among Antichrists Armies: and therefore cry out like cowards, If you will let me alone, and I will let you alone; but assuredly the Lord Christ hath said, *He that is not with us, is against us:* there is no room in his Army for toleratorists.[7] But some will say, We will never believe the day is come, till our eyes behold *Babylon* begirt with Souldiers. I pray be not too hasty; hath not the Lord said, *Come out of her my people?* &c, surely there is a little space left for this, and now is the time, seeing the Lord hath set up his standerd of resort: now, *Come forth of her, and be not partakers of her sins:* now is the time, when the Lord hath assembled his Saints together; now the Lord will come and not tarry. As it was necessary that there should be a *Moses* and *Aaron*, before the Lord would deliver his people and destroy *Pharaoh* left they should be wildred indeed in the Wilderness; so now it was needfull, that the Churches of Christ should first obtain their purity, and the civill government its power to defend them, before Antichrist come to his finall ruine: and because you shall be sure the day is come indeed, behold the Lord Christ marshalling of his invincible Army to the battell: some suppose this onely to be mysticall, and not literall at all: assuredly the spirituall fight is chiefly to be attended, and the other not. neglected, having a neer dependancy one upon the other, especially at this time; the Ministers of Christ who have cast off all lording power over one another, are created field-Officers, whose Office is extravagant in this Army, chiefly to encourage the fighting Souldiers, and to lead them on upon the enemy in the most advantagious places, and bring on fresh supplies in all places of danger, to put the sword of the spirit in their Souldiers hands: but Christ (who is their general) must onely enable them to use it aright: to give every Souldier in charge that they watch over one another, to see that none meddle with the execrable things of Antichrist, and this to be performed in every Regiment throughout the Army: and not one to exercise dominion over the other by way of superiority: for Christ hath appointed a parity in all his Regiments, *&c.* let them beware that none go apart with rebellious *Korah.* And further, behold, Kings, Rulers, or Generals of Earths Armies, doth Christ make use of in this day of battell, the which he hath brought into the field already also; who are appointed to defend, uphold, and maintain the whole body of his Armies against the insolent, beastly, and bloody cruelty of their insatiable enemies, and to keep order that none do his fellow-Souldier any wrong, nor that any should raise a mutiny in the hosts. Notwithstanding all this, if any shall say, they will not believe the day is come till they see them ingage battell with Antichrist; Verily, if the Lord be pleased to open your eyes, you may see the beginning of the fight, and what success the Armies of our Lord Christ have hitherto had: the Forlorne hopes of Antichrists Army, were the proud Prelates of *England:* the Forlorne of Christs Armies, were these *N. E.* people, who are the subject of this History, which encountring each other for some space of time, ours being overpowered with multitude, were forced to retreat to a place of greater safety, where they waited for a fresh opportunity to ingage with the main battell of Antichrist, so soon as the Lord shall be pleased to give a word of Command. Immediately upon this success, the Lord Christ was pleased to command the right Wing of his Army, to advance against the left Wing of Antichrist: where in his former forlorn hopes of proud Prelates lay: these by our right Wing had their first pay (for that they had done to our forlorne before) being quite overthrown and cut in peices by the valiant of the Lord in our right Wing, and still remain fighting. Thus far of the battell of Antichrist, and the various success: what the issue will be, is assuredly known in the generall already. *Babylon* is fallen, the God of truth hath said it; then who would not be a Souldier on Christs side, where is such a certainty of victory? nay I can tell you a farther word of encouragement, every true-hearted Souldier that falls by the sword in this fight, shall not lye dead long, but stand upon his feet again, and be made partaker of the triumph of this Victory: and none can be overcome, but by turning his back in fight. And for a word of terrour to the enemy, let them know, Christ will never give over the raising of fresh Forces, till they are overthrown root and branch. And now you antient people of *Israel* look out of your Prison grates, let these Armies of the Lord Christ Jesus provoke you to acknowledge he is certainly come, I and speedily he doth come to put life into your dry bones: here is a people not onely praying but fighting for you, that the great block may be removed out of the way, (which hath hindered hitherto) that they with you may enjoy that glorious resurrection-day, the glorious nuptials of the Lamb: when not only the Bridegroom shall appear to his Churches both of *Jews* and *Gentiles*, (which are his spouse) in a more brighter aray then ever heretofore, but also his Bride shall be clothed by him in the richest garments that ever the Sons of men put on, even the glorious graces of Christ Jesus, in such a glorious splendor to the eyes of man, that they shall see and glorifie the Father of both Bridegroom and Bride.

COTTON MATHER, 1663–1728

[Cotton Mather's very name is a proclamation of his standing in seventeenth-century New England; the grandson of John Cotton, and of Richard Mather, the first minister of Dorchester, the son of Increase Mather, minister of the North Church in Boston and President of Harvard College, Cotton was born in the clerical purple. Educated at home by his very learned father, at the age of twelve he entered Harvard, where it is said he was better liked by his tutors than by his fellow students. He took his M.A. in 1681, was ordained the colleague of his father in 1685 and married his first wife in 1686; along with his father he soon became a leader of orthodox opinion in eastern Massachusetts. He was active in the Revolution of 1689, and was made Fellow of Harvard College in 1690. After 1700 the Mathers suffered many reverses; when Increase was forced out of Harvard College Cotton, not being chosen President as he had expected he would be, resigned his fellowship. Governor Dudley was his enemy; his last days were embittered by the restriction of his influence, the insanity of his third wife, the profligacy of his favourite son. He was an indefatigable worker, publishing some five hundred books, tracts, and pamphlets, corresponding with learned men all over Europe, contributing to the *Transactions* of the Royal Society, to which he was elected in 1713. In 1721 he and his father made a heroic fight for smallpox inoculation against the enraged hostility of the majority of the citizens. For biography cf. Barrett Wendell, *Cotton Mather the Puritan Priest* (New York, 1891). This text is from *Magnalia Christi Americana; or, the Ecclesiastical History of New England* (London, 1702).]

A GENERAL INTRODUCTION

§. 1. I write the *Wonders* of the CHRISTIAN RELIGION, flying from the Depravations of *Europe*, to the *American Strand:* And, assisted by the Holy Author of that *Religion*, I do, with all Conscience of *Truth*, required therein by Him, who is the *Truth* it self, Report the *Wonderful Displays* of His Infinite Power, Wisdom, Goodness, and Faithfulness, wherewith His Divine Providence hath *Irradiated* an *Indian Wilderness*.

I Relate the *Considerable Matters*, that produced and attended the First Settlement of COLONIES, which have been Renowned for the Degree of REFORMATION, Professed and Attained by *Evangelical Churches*, erected in those *Ends of the Earth:* And a *Field* being thus prepared, I proceed unto a Relation of the *Considerable Matters* which have been acted thereupon.

I first introduce the *Actors*, that have, in a more exemplary manner served those *Colonies;* and give *Remarkable Occurrences*, in the exemplary LIVES of many *Magistrates*, and of more *Ministers*, who so *Lived*, as to leave unto Posterity, *Examples* worthy of *Everlasting Remembrance*.

I add hereunto; the *Notables* of the only *Protestant University*, that ever *shone* in that Hemisphere of the *New World;* with particular Instances of *Criolians*,[1] in our *Biography*, provoking the *whole World*, with vertuous Objects of Emulation.

I introduce then, the *Actions* of a more Eminent Importance, that have signalized those *Colonies;* Whether the *Establishments*, directed by their *Synods;* with a Rich Variety of *Synodical* and *Ecclesiastical* Determinations; or, the *Disturbances*, with which they have been from all sorts of *Temptations* and *Enemies* Tempestuated; and the *Methods* by which they have still weathered out each *Horrible Tempest.*

And into the midst of these *Actions*, I interpose an entire *Book*, wherein there is, with all possible Veracity, a *Collection* made, of *Memorable Occurrences*, and amazing *Judgments* and *Mercies*, befalling many *particular Persons* among the People of *New-England.*

Let my Readers expect all that I have promised them, in this *Bill of Fair;* and it may be they will find themselves entertained with yet many other Passages, above and beyond their Expectation, deserving likewise a room in *History:* In all which, there will be nothing but the *Author's* too mean way of preparing so great Entertainments, to Reproach the Invitation.

§. 2. The Reader will doubtless desire to know, what it was that

> ——*tot Volvere casus*
> *Insignes Pietate Viros, tot adire Labores,*
> *Impulerit.*[2]

And our *History* shall, on many fit Occasions which will be therein offered, endeavour, with all *Historical* Fidelity and Simplicity, and with as little Offence as may be, to satisfie him. The Sum of the Matter is, That from the very Beginning of the REFORMATION in the *English Nation*, there hath always been a Generation of *Godly Men*, desirous to pursue the *Reformation of Religion, according to the Word of God, and the Example of the best Reformed Churches;* and answering the Character of *Good Men*, given by *Josephus*, in his Paraphrase on the words of *Samuel* to *Saul*, μηδὲν ἄλλο πραχθήσεσθαι καλῶς ὑφ' ἑαυτῶν νομίζοντες ἢ ὅτι ἂν ποιήσωσι τοῦ Θεοῦ κεκελευκότος. *They think they do nothing Right in the Service of God, but what they do according to the Command of God.* And there hath been another Generation of Men, who have still employed the *Power* which they have generally still had in their Hands, not only to stop the Progress of the Desired *Reformation*, but also, with Innumerable Vexations, to Persecute those that most Heartily wished well unto it. There were many of the *Reformers*, who joyned with the Reverend JOHN FOX,[3] in the *Complaints* which he then entred in his *Martyrology*, about the *Baits of Popery* yet left in the Church; and in his *Wishes*, *God take them away, or ease us from them, for God knows, they be the Cause of much Blindness and Strife amongst Men!* They Zealously decreed the *Policy* of complying always with the *Ignorance* and *Vanity* of the *People;* and cried out earnestly for *Purer Administrations* in the House of God, and more *Conformity* to the *Law of Christ*, and *Primitive Christianity:* While others would not hear of going any further than the *First Essay* of *Reformation.* 'Tis very certain, that the *First Reformers* never intended, that what *They* did, should be the *Absolute Boundary* of *Reformation*, so that it should be a Sin to proceed any further; as, by their own going beyond *Wicklift*,[4] and *Changing* and *Growing* in their own *Models* also, and the Confessions of *Cranmer*, with the *Scripta Anglicana* of *Bucer*, and a thousand other things, was abundantly demonstrated. But after a Fruitless Expectation, wherein the truest Friends of the *Reformation* long waited, for to have that which *Heylin* [5] himself owns to have been the Design of the *First Reformers*, followed as it should have been, a Party very unjustly arrogating to themselves, the Venerable Name of, *The Church of* England, by Numberless Oppressions, grievously *Smote those their Fellow-Servants*. Then 'twas that, as our Great OWEN [6] hath expressed it, *Multitudes of Pious, Peaceable Protestants, were driven, by their Severities, to leave their Native Country, and seek a Refuge for their Lives and Liberties, with Freedom, for the Worship of God, in a Wilderness, in the Ends of the Earth.*

§. 3. It is the History of these PROTESTANTS, that is here attempted: PROTESTANTS that highly honoured and affected *The Church of* ENGLAND, and humbly Petition to be a *Part* of it: But by the Mistake of a few powerful *Brethren*, driven to seek a place for the Exercise of the *Protestant Religion*, according to the Light of their Consciences, in the Desarts of *America*. And in this Attempt I have proposed, not only to preserve and secure the Interest of *Religion*, in the Churches of that little Country NEW-ENGLAND, so far as the Lord Jesus Christ may please to Bless it for that End, but also to offer unto the Churches of the *Reformation*, abroad in the World, some small *Memorials*, that may be serviceable unto the Designs of *Reformation*, whereto, I believe, they are quickly to be awakened. I am far from any such Boast, concerning these Churches, *That they have Need of Nothing*, I wish their *Works* were more *perfect before God*. Indeed, that which *Austin* called *The Perfection of Christians*, is like to be, until the Term for the *Antichristian Apostasie* be expired, *The Perfection of Churches* too; *Ut Agnoscant se nunquam esse perfectas.*[7] Nevertheless, I perswade my self, that *so far as they have attained*, they have given *Great Examples* of the *Methods* and *Measures*, wherein an *Evangelical Reformation* is to be prosecuted, and of the *Qualifications* requisite in the Instruments that are to prosecute it, and of the *Difficulties* which may be most likely to obstruct it, and the most likely *Directions* and *Remedies* for those Obstructions. It may be, 'tis not possible for me to do a greater Service unto the Churches on the *Best Island* of the Universe, than to give a distinct Relation of those *Great Examples* which have been occurring among Churches of *Exiles*, that were driven out of that *Island*, into an horrible *Wilderness*, meerly for their being Well-willers unto the *Reformation*. When that Blessed Martyr *Constantine* was carried, with other Martyrs, in a *Dung-Cart*, unto the place of Execution, he pleasantly said, *Well, yet we are a precious Odour to God in Christ*. Tho' the *Reformed Churches* in the *American Regions*, have, by very Injurious Representations of their Brethren (all which they desire to Forget and Forgive!) been many times thrown into a *Dung-Cart;* yet, as they have been a *precious Odour to God in Christ*, so, I hope, they will be a *precious Odour* unto *His People;* and not only *Precious*, but *Useful* also, when the *History* of them shall come to be considered. A *Reformation of the Church* is coming on, and I cannot but thereupon say, with the dying *Cyrus* to his Children in *Xenophon*, 'Εκ τῶν προγεγεννημένων μανθάνετε, ἀυτὴ γὰρ ἀρίστη διδασκαλία. *Learn from the things that have been done already, for this is the best way of Learning*. The Reader hath here an Account of *The Things that have been done already*. *Bernard* upon that Clause in the *Canticles*, [*O thou fairest among Women*] has this ingenious Gloss, *Pulchram, non omnimode quidem, sed pulchram inter mulieres eam docet, videlicet cum Distinctione, quatenus ex hoc amplius reprimatur, & sciat quid desit sibi.*[8] Thus I do not say, That the Churches of *New-England* are the most *Regular* that can be; yet I do say, and am sure, That they are very like unto those that were in the *First Ages* of Christianity. And if I assert, That in the *Reformation* of the Church, the State of it in those *First Ages*, is to be not a little considered, the Great *Peter Ramus*,[9] among others, has emboldened me. For when the Cardinal of *Lorrain*, the *Mæcenas* of that Great Man, was offended at him, for turning *Protestant*, he replied, *Inter Opes illas, quibus me ditasti, has etiam in æternum recordabor, quod Beneficio, Poessiacæ Responsionis tuæ didici, de Quindecim a Christo sæculis, primum vere esse aureum, Reliqua, quo longius abscederent esse nequiora, atque deteriora: Tum igitur cum fieret optio, Aureum sæculum delegi.*[10] In short, The *First Age* was the *Golden Age:* To return unto *That*, will make a Măn a *Protestant*, and I may add, a *Puritan*. 'Tis possible, That our Lord Jesus Christ carried some Thousands of *Reformers* into the Retirements of an *American Desart*, on purpose, that, with an opportunity granted unto many of his Faithful Servants, to enjoy the precious *Liberty* of their *Ministry*, tho' in the midst of many *Temptations* all their days, He might there, *To* them first, and then *By* them, give a *Specimen* of many Good Things, which He would have His

Churches elsewhere aspire and arise unto: And *This* being done, He knows not whether there be not *All done*, that *New-England* was planted for; and whether the Plantation may not, soon after this, *Come to Nothing*. Upon that Expression in the Sacred Scripture, *Cast the unprofitable Servant into Outer Darkness*, it hath been imagined by some, That the *Regiones Exteræ* [11] of *America*, are the *Tenebræ Exteriores*,[12] which the *Unprofitable* are there condemned unto. No doubt, the Authors of those Ecclesiastical Impositions and Severities, which drove the English Christians into the *Dark Regions* of *America*, esteemed those *Christians* to be a very *unprofitable* sort of Creatures. But behold, ye *European* Churches. There are *Golden Candlesticks* [more than *twice Seven times Seven!*] in the midst of this *Outer Darkness:* Unto the *upright* Children of *Abraham*, here hath arisen *Light in Darkness*. And let us humbly speak it, it shall be *Profitable* for you to consider the *Light*, which from the midst of this *Outer Darkness*, is now to be Darted over unto the other side of the *Atlantick Ocean*. But we must therewithal ask your Prayers, that these *Golden Candlesticks* may not *quickly* be *Removed out of their place!*

§. 4. But whether *New England* may *Live* any where else or no, it must *Live* in our *History!*

HISTORY, in general, hath had so many and mighty Commendations from the Pens of those Numberless Authors, who, from *Herodotus* to *Howel*,[13] have been the professed Writers of it, that a tenth part of them Transcribed, would be a Furniture for a *Polyanthea in Folio*.[14] We, that have neither liberty, nor occasion, to quote those Commendations of *History*, will content our selves with the Opinion of one who was not much of a *profess'd Historian*, expressed in that passage, whereto all Mankind subscribe, *Historia est Testis temporum, Nuntia vetustatis, Lux veritatis, vita memoriæ, magistra vitæ*.[15] But of all *History* it must be confessed, that the *Palm* is to be given unto *Church History;* wherein the *Dignity*, the *Suavity*, and the *Utility* of the *Subject* is transcendent. I observe, that for the Description of the *whole World* in the Book of *Genesis*, that *First-born of all Historians*, the great *Moses*, implies but *one* or *two* Chapters, whereas he [e]mpl[oyes], it may be *seven times* as many Chapters, in describing that one little *Pavilion, The Tabernacle*. And when I am thinking, what may be the Reason of this *Difference*, methinks it intimates unto us, That the *Church* wherein the Service of God is performed, is much more Precious than the *World*, which was indeed created for the Sake and Use of the *Church*. 'Tis very certain, that the greatest Entertainments must needs occur in the History of the *People*, whom the *Son* of God hath *Redeemed* and *Purified* unto himself, as a *Peculiar People*, and whom the *Spirit* of God, by *Supernatural Operations* upon their Minds, does cause to live like *Strangers* in *this World*, conforming themselves unto the *Truths* and *Rules* of his Holy Word, in Expectation of a *Kingdom*, whereto they shall be in another and a better *World* advanced. Such a *People* our Lord Jesus Christ hath procured and preserved in all Ages *visible;* and the Dispensations of his *wonderous Providence* towards this People (for, *O Lord, thou do'st lift them up, and cast them down!*) their Calamities, their Deliverances, the Dispositions which they have still discovered, and the considerable *Persons* and *Actions* found among them, cannot but afford Matters of *Admiration* and *Admonition*, above what any other Story can pretend unto: 'Tis nothing but *Atheism* in the Hearts of Men, that can perswade them otherwise. Let any Person of good Sense peruse the History of *Herodotus*, which, like a River taking Rise, where the *Sacred Records* of the *Old Testament* leave off, runs along smoothly and sweetly, with Relations that sometimes perhaps want an *Apology*, down until the *Grecians* drive the *Persians* before them. Let him then peruse *Thucydides*, who from *Acting* betook himself to *Writing*, and carries the ancient State of the *Grecians*, down to the twenty first Year of the *Peloponnesian Wars* in a manner, which *Casaubon* judges to be *Mirandum potius quam imitandum*,[16] Let him next Revolve *Xenophon*, that *Bee* of *Athens*, who continues a Narrative of the .*Greek Affairs*, from the *Peloponnesian Wars*, to the Battle of *Mantinea*, and gives us a *Cyrus* into the bargain, at such a rate, that *Lipsius* reckons the Character of a *Suavi, Fidus & Circumspectùs Scriptor*,[17] to belong unto him. Let him from hence proceed unto *Diodorus Siculus*, who, besides a rich Treasure of *Egyptian, Assyrian, Lybian* and *Grecian*, and other *Antiquities*, in a Phrase, which according to *Photius's* Judgment, is ἱστορίᾳ μάλιστὰ, πρεπούσῃ, *of all most becoming an Historian*, carries on the Thread begun by his Predecessors, until the End of the Hundred and nineteenth *Olympiad;* and where he is defective, let it be supplied from *Arianus*, from *Justin*, and from *Curtius*, who in the relish of *Colerus* is, *Quovis melle dulcior*.[18] Let him hereupon consult *Polybius*, and acquaint himself with the Birth and Growth of the *Roman Empire*, as far as 'tis described, in *Five* of the *Forty* Books composed by an Author, who with a Learned *Professor of History* is, *Prudens Scriptor, si quis alius*.[19] Let him now run over the Table of the *Roman* Affairs, compendiously given by *Lucius Florus*, and then let him consider the Transactions of above three hundred Years reported by *Dionysius Halicarnassæus*, who, if the Censure of *Bodin* may be taken, *Græcos omnes & Latinos superasse videatur*.[20] Let him from hence pass to *Livy*, of whom the famous Critick says,

Hoc solum ingenium (*de Historicis Loquor*) *populus Romanus par Imperio suo habuit,*[21] and supply those of his *Decads* that are lost, from the best Fragments of Antiquity, in others (and especially *Dion* and *Salust*) that lead us on still further in our way. Let him then proceed unto the Writers of the *Cesarean* times, and first revolve *Suetonius*, then *Tacitus*, then *Herodian*, then a whole Army more of *Historians*, which now crowd into our *Library;* and unto all the rest, let him not fail of adding the Incomparable *Plutarch*, whose Books they say, *Theodore Gaza* preferred above any in the World, next unto the Inspired Oracles of the *Bible:* But if the Number be still too little to satisfie an *Historical Appetite*, let him add *Polyhistor* unto the number, and all the *Chronicles* of the following Ages. After all, he must sensibly acknowledge, that the two short Books of *Ecclesiastical History*, written by the Evangelist *Luke*, hath given us more *glorious Entertainments*, than all these voluminous Historians if they were put all together. The *Atchievements* of one *Paul* particularly, which that Evangelist hath *Emblazon'd*, have more *True Glory* in them, than all the Acts of those Execrable *Plunderers* and *Murderers*, and irresistible *Banditti* of the World, which have been dignified with the Name of *Conquerors*. *Tacitus* counted *Ingentia bella, Expugnationes urbium, fusos captosque Reges,*[22] the Ravages of *War*, and the glorious *Violences*, whereof great Warriors make a wretched Ostentation, to be the *Noblest Matter* for an *Historian*. But there is a *Nobler*, I humbly conceive, in the planting and forming of *Evangelical Churches*, and the *Temptations*, the *Corruptions*, the *Afflictions*, which assault them, and their *Salvations* from those Assaults, and the Exemplary *Lives* of those that Heaven employs to be Patterns of *Holiness* and *Usefulness* upon Earth: And unto such it is, that I now invite my Readers; Things, in comparison whereof, the Subjects of many other Histories, are of as little weight, as the Questions about Z, the last Letter of our Alphabet, and whether H is to be pronounced with an Aspiration, where about whole Volumes have been written, and of no more Account, than the Composure of *Didymus*.[23] But for the *manner* of my treating this *Matter*, I must now give some account unto him.

§. 5. *Reader!* I have done the part of an *Impartial Historian*, albeit not without all occasion perhaps, for the Rule which a worthy Writer, in his *Historica*, gives to every Reader, *Historici Legantur cum Moderatione & venia, & cogitetur fieri non posse ut in omnibus circumstantiis sint Lymei.*[24] *Polybius* complains of those *Historians*, who always made either the *Carthagenians* brave, and the *Romans* base, or *è contra*, in all their Actions, as their Affection for their own *Party* led them. I have endeavoured, with all *good Conscience*, to decline this writing meerly for a *Party*, or doing like the Dealer in History, whom *Lucian* derides, for always calling the Captain of his own Party an *Achilles*, but of the adverse Party a *Thersites:* Nor have I added unto the just Provocations for the Complaint made by the Baron *Maurier*,[25] That the *greatest part of Histories* are but so many *Panegyricks* composed by *Interested Hands*, which *elevate Iniquity to the Heavens*, like *Paterculus*, and like *Machiavel*, who propose *Tiberius Cesar*, and *Cesar Borgia*, as Examples fit for *Imitiation*, whereas *True History* would have Exhibited them as Horrid *Monsters* as very *Devils*. 'Tis true, I am not of the Opinion, that one cannot merit the Name of an *Impartial Historian*, except he write bare *Matters of Fact*, without all *Reflection;* for I can tell where to find this given as the Definition of *History*, *Historia est rerum gestarum, cum laude aut vituperatione, Narratio:* [26] And if I am not altogether a *Tacitus*, when *Vertues* or *Vices* occur to be Matters of *Reflection*, as well as of *Relation*, I will, for my Vindication, appeal to *Tacitus* himself, whom *Lipsius* calls one of the *Prudentest* (tho' *Tertullian*, long before, counts him the *Lyingest*) of them who have Inriched the World with *History:* He says, *Præcipuum munus Annalium reor, ne virtutes sileantur, utque pravis Dictis, Factisque ex posteritate & Infamia metus sit.*[27] I have not *Commended* any Person, but when I have really judg'd, not only *That* he *Deserved* it, but also that it would be a Benefit unto Posterity to know, Wherein he deserved it: And my Judgment of *Desert*, hath not been *Biassed*, by Persons being of my own particular Judgment in matters of *Disputation*, among the Churches of God. I have been as willing to wear the Name of *Simplicius Verinus*,[28] throughout my whole undertaking, as he that, before me, hath assumed it: Nor am I like Pope *Zachary*, impatient so much as to hear of any *Antipodes*.[29] The Spirit of a *Schlusselbergius*,[30] who falls foul with Fury and Reproach on all who differ from him; The Spirit of an *Heylin*,[5] who seems to count no Obloquy too hard for a *Reformer;* and the Spirit of those (*Folio-writers* there are, some of them, in the English Nation!) whom a Noble Historian Stigmatizes, as, *Those Hot-headed, Passionate Bigots, from whom, 'tis enough, if you be of a Religion contrary unto theirs, to be defamed, condemned and pursued with a thousand Calumnies*. I thank Heaven I Hate it with all my Heart. But how can the *Lives* of the *Commendable* be written without *Commending* them? Or, is that Law of *History* given in one of the eminentest pieces of *Antiquity* we now have in our hands, wholly antiquated, *Maxime proprium est Historiæ, Laudem rerum egregie gestarum persequi?* [31] Nor have I, on the other side, forbore to mention many *Censurable* things, even in the Best of my Friends, when the things, in my opinion, were *not Good;* or so bore away for *Placentia*, in the course of our Story, as to pass by *Verona;*[32] but been mindful of the Direction which *Polybius* gives to the Historian, *It becomes him that writes an History, sometimes to extol Enemies in his Praises, when their praise-worthy Actions bespeak it, and at the same time to reprove the best Friends, when their Deeds appear worthy of a reproof; in-as much as History is good for nothing, if Truth (which is the very Eye of the Animal) be not in it.* Indeed I have thought it my duty upon all accounts, (and if it have proceeded unto the degree of a *Fault*, there is, it may be, something in my *Temper* and *Nature*, that has betray'd me therein) to be more sparing and easie, in thus mentioning of *Censurable* things, than in my *other Liberty:* A writer of *Church-History*, should, I know, be like the *builder of the Temple*, one of the *Tribe* of *Naphthali;* and for this I will also plead my *Polybius* in my Excuse; *It is not the Work of an Historian, to commemorate the Vices and Villanies of Men, so much as their just, their fair, their honest Actions: And the Readers of History get more good by the Objects of their Emulation, than of their Indignation.* Nor do I deny, that tho' I cannot approve the Conduct of *Josephus*, (whom *Jerom* not unjustly nor ineptly calls, *The Greek Livy*) when he left out of his *Antiquities*, the Story of the *Golden Calf*, and I don't wonder to find *Chamier*, and *Rivet*,[33] and others, taxing him for his *Partiality* towards his Country-men; yet I have left unmentioned some *Censurable Occurrences* in the *Story* of our *Colonies*, as things no less *Unuseful* than *Improper* to be raised out of the Grave, wherein *Oblivion* hath now buried them; lest I should have incurred the *Pasquil* bestowed upon Pope *Urban*, who employing a *Committee* to Rip up the *Old Errors* of his Predecessors, one clap'd a pair of Spurs upon the heels of the Statue of St. *Peter;* and a Label from the Statue of St. *Paul* opposite thereunto, upon the Bridge, ask'd him, *Whither he was bound?* St. *Peter* answered, *I apprehend some Danger in staying here; I fear they'll call me in Question for denying my Master.* And St. *Paul* replied, *Nay, then I had best be gone too, for they'll question me also, for Persecuting the Christians before my Conversion.*[34] Briefly, My Pen shall Reproach none, that can give a Good Word unto any Good Man that is not of their *own Faction*, and shall *Fall out* with none, but those that can *Agree* with no body else, except those of their own *Schism.* If I draw any sort of Men with *Charcoal*, it shall be, because I remember a notable passage of the *Best Queen* that ever was in the World, our late Queen *Mary.* Monsieur *Juvien*, that he might Justifie the Reformation in *Scotland*, made a very black Representation of their old Queen *Mary;* for which, a certain *Sycophant* would have incensed our Queen *Mary* against that Reverend Person, saying, *Is it not a Shame that this Man, without any Consideration for your Royal Person, should dare to throw such Infamous Calumnies upon a Queen, from whom your Royal Highness is descended?* But that Excellent Princess replied, *No, not at all; Is it not enough that by fulsome Praises great Persons be lull'd asleep all their Lives; But must Flattery accompany them to their very Graves? How should they fear the Judgment of Posterity, if Historians be not allowed to speak the Truth after their Death?* But whether I do my self *Commend*, or whether I give my Reader an opportunity to *Censure*, I am careful above all things to do it with *Truth;* and as I have considered the words of *Plato, Deum indigne & graviter ferre, cum quis ei similem hoc est, virtute præstantem, vituperet, aut laudet contrarium:* [35] So I have had the *Ninth Commandment* of a greater *Law-giver* than *Plato*, to preserve my care of *Truth* from first to last. If any Mistake have been any where committed, it will be found meerly *Circumstantial*, and wholly *Involuntary;* and let it be remembred, that tho' no *Historian* ever merited better than the Incomparable *Thuanus*,[36] yet learned Men have said of *his* Work, what they never shall truly say of *ours*, that it contains *multa falsissima & indigna.*[37] I find *Erasmus* himself mistaking *One* Man for *Two*, when writing of the Ancients. And even our own English Writers too are often mistaken, and in Matters of a very late Importance, as *Baker*, and *Heylin*, and *Fuller*, (professed Historians) tell us, that *Richard Sutton*, a single Man, founded the *Charter-House;* whereas his Name was *Thomas*, and he was a married Man. I think I can Recite such Mistakes, it may be *Sans* Number occurring in the most credible Writers; yet I hope I shall *commit* none such. But altho' I thus challenge, as my due, the Character of an *Impartial*, I doubt I may not challenge *That* of an *Elegant Historian.* I cannot say, whether the *Style*, wherein this *Church-History* is written, will please the Modern *Criticks:* But if I seem to have used ἁπλουστάτῃ συντάξει γραφῆς,[38] a Simple, Submiss, Humble *Style*, 'tis the same that *Eusebius* affirms to have been used by *Hegesippus*, who, as far as we understand, was the first Author (after *Luke*) that ever composed an entire Body of *Ecclesiastical History*, which he divided into *Five Books*, and Entitled, ὑπομνήματα των ἐκκλησιαστικῶν πραξεων.[39] Whereas *others*, it may be, will reckon the *Style* Embellished with too much of *Ornament*, by the multiplied References to other and former Concerns, closely couch'd, for the Observation of the *Attentive*, in almost every Paragraph; but I must confess, that I am of his mind who said, *Sicuti sal modice cibis aspersus Condit, & gratiam saporis addit, ita si paulum Antiquitatis admiscueris, Oratio fit venustior.*[40] And I have seldom seen that Way of Writing faulted, but by those, who, for a certain odd Reason, sometimes find fault, *That the Grapes are not ripe.* These *Embellishments* (of which yet I only—

Veniam pro laude peto [41]) are not the puerile Spoils of *Polyanthea's;* but I should have asserted them to be as choice *Flowers* as most that occur in Ancient or Modern Writings, almost unavoidably putting themselves into the Authors Hand, while about his Work, if those words of *Ambrose* had not a little frighted me, as well as they did *Baronius, Unumquemque Fallunt sua scripta.*[42] I observe that Learned Men have been so terrified by the Reproaches of *Pedantry,* which little Smatterers at Reading and Learning have, by their *Quoting Humours* brought upon themselves, that, for to avoid all Approaches towards that which those Feeble Creatures have gone to imitate, the best way of Writing has been most injuriously deserted. But what shall we say? The Best way of Writing, under Heaven, shall be the Worst, when *Erasmus* his Monosyllable Tyrant will have it so! [43] And if I should have resign'd my self wholly to the Judgment of *others,* What way of Writing to have taken, the Story of the two Statues made by *Policletus* tells me, what may have been the Issue: He contrived one of them according to the Rules that best pleased himself, and the other according to the Fancy of every one that look'd upon his Work: The former was afterwards Applauded by all, and the latter Derided by those very Persons who had given their Directions for it. As for such *Unaccuracies* as the *Critical* may discover, *Opere in longo,*[44] I appeal to the *Courteous,* for a favourable Construction of them; and certainly they will be favourably Judged of, when there is considered the *Variety* of my *other Employments,* which have kept me in continual Hurries, I had almost said, like those of the *Ninth Sphere,* for the few Months in which this Work has been *Digesting.* It was a thing well thought, by the wise Designers of *Chelsey-Colledge,* wherein able *Historians* were one sort of Persons to be maintained; That the Romanists do in one Point condemn the Protestants; for among the Romanists, they don't burden their *Professors* with any *Parochial Incumbrances;* but among the *Protestants,* the very same *Individual* Man must *Preach, Catechize,* Administer the *Sacraments,* Visit the Afflicted, and manage all the parts of *Church-Discipline;* and if any *Books* for the Service of Religion, be written, Persons thus *extreamly incumbred* must be the Writers. Now, of all the Churches under Heaven, there are none that expect so much *Variety* of Service from their Pastors, as those of *New-England;* and of all the Churches in *New-England,* there are none that require more, than those in *Boston,* the Metropolis of the English *America;* whereof *one* is, by the Lord Jesus Christ, committed unto the Care of the unworthy Hand, by which this *History* is compiled. Reader, Give me leave humbly to mention, with him in *Tully, Antequam de Re, Pauca de Me!* [45] Constant *Sermons*, usually more than once, and perhaps three or four times, in a Week, and all the other Duties of a *Pastoral Watchfulness*, a very *large Flock* has all this while demanded of me; wherein, if I had been furnished with as many *Heads* as a *Typheus*, as many *Eyes* as an *Argos*, and as many *Hands* as a *Briareus*, I might have had Work enough to have employ'd them all; nor hath my *Station* left me free from Obligations to spend very much time in the *Evangelical Service* of *others* also. It would have been a great *Sin* in me, to have *Omitted*, or *Abated*, my Just Cares, to *fulfil my Ministry in these things*, and in a manner *Give my self wholly to them.* All the time I have had for my *Church-History*, hath been perhaps only, or chiefly, that, which I might have taken else for less profitable Recreations; and it hath all been done by *Snatches*. My Reader will not find me the Person intended in his *Littany*, when he says, *Libera me ab homine unius Negotis:*[46] Nor have I spent *Thirty Years* in shaping this my *History*, as *Diodorus Siculus* did for his, (and yet both *Bodinus* and *Sigonius* complain of the Σφαλματα[47] attending it.) But I wish I could have enjoy'd entirely for this Work, one quarter of the little more than *Two Years* which have roll'd away since I began it; whereas I have been forced sometimes wholly to throw by the Work whole Months together, and then resume it, but by a stolen hour or two in a day, not without some hazard of incurring the *Title* which *Coryat* put upon his History of his Travels, *Crudities hastily gobbled up in five Months. Protogenes* being seven Years in drawing a Picture, *Apelles* upon the sight of it, said, *The Grace of the Work was much allay'd by the length of the Time.* Whatever else there may have been to take off the *Grace of the Work*, now in the Readers hands, (whereof the *Pictures* of Great and Good Men make a considerable part) I am sure there hath not been the *length of the Time* to do it. Our English Martyrologer, counted it a sufficient *Apology*, for what Meanness might be found in the first Edition of his *Acts and Monuments*, that it was *hastily rashed up in about fourteen Months:* And I may Apologize for this Collection of our *Acts and Monuments*, that I should have been glad, in the little more than *Two Years* which have ran out, since I enter'd upon it, if I could have had one half of *About fourteen Months* to have entirely devoted thereunto. But besides the *Time*, which the *Daily Services* of *my own* first, and then many *other* Churches, have necessarily call'd for, I have lost abundance of precious *Time*, thro' the feeble and broken State of my *Health*, which hath unfitted me for *Hard Study;* I can do nothing to purpose at *Lucubrations*. And yet, in this *Time* also of the two or three Years last past, I have not been excused from the further Diversion of *Publishing* (tho' not so many as they say *Mercurius Trismegistus* did, yet) more than a *Score* of other *Books*, upon a copious Variety of other Subjects, besides the composing of several more, that are not yet published. . . . My Reader sees, why I commit the Fault of a περιαυτία,[48] which appears in the mention of these Minute-passages; 'tis to excuse whatever other Fault of Inaccuracy, or Inadvertency, may be discovered in an History, which hath been a sort of Rapsody made up (like the Paper whereon 'tis written!) with many little Rags, torn from an Employment, multifarious enough to overwhelm one of my small Capacities. . . .

§. 6. I hope 'tis a right Work that I have done; but we are not yet arrived unto the *Day, wherein God will bring every Work into Judgment* (the Day of the *Kingdom* that was promised unto *David*) and a Son of *David* hath as Truly as Wisely told us, that until the arrival of that Happy Day, this is one of the *Vanities* attending Humane Affairs; *For a right VVork a Man shall be envied of his Neighbour.* It will not be so much a Surprise unto me, if I should live to see our *Church-History* vexed with *Anie-mad-versions* of Calumnious Writers, as it would have been unto *Virgil*, to read his *Bucolicks* reproached by the *Antibucolica* of a *Nameless Scribbler*, and his *Æneids* travestied by the *Æneidomastix* of *Carbilius:* Or *Herennius* taking pains to make a Collection of the *Faults*, and *Faustinus* of the *Thefts*, in his incomparable Composures: Yea, *Pliny*, and *Seneca* themselves, and our *Jerom*, reproaching him, as a Man of no Judgment, nor Skill in Sciences; while *Pædianus* affirms of him, that he was himself, *Usque adeo invidiæ Expers, ut si quid erudite dictum inspiceret alterius, non minus gauderet ac si suum-esset.*[49] How should a Book, no better laboured than this of ours, escape *Zoilian* Outrages, when in all Ages, the most exquisite Works have been as much vilified, as *Plato's* by *Scaliger*, and *Aristotle's* by *Lactantius?* In the time of our K. *Edward* VI. there was an Order to bring in all the Teeth of St. *Apollonia*, which the People of his one Kingdom carried about them for the Cure of the *Tooth ach;* and they were so many, that they almost fill'd a Tun. Truly *Envy* hath as many *Teeth* as Madam *Apollonia* would have had, if all those pretended Reliques had been really hers. And must all these *Teeth* be fastned on thee, *O my Book?* It may be so! And yet the *Book*, when ground between these *Teeth*, will prove like *Ignatius* in the *Teeth* of the furious Tygers, *The whiter Manchet for the Churches of God.* The greatest and fiercest Rage of *Envy*, is that which I expect from those IDUMÆANS,[50] whose Religion is all Ceremony, and whose Charity is more for them who deny the most Essential things in the Articles and Homilies of the Church of *England*, than for the most Conscientious Men in the World, who manifest their being so, by their Dissent in some little Ceremony: Or those Persons whose Hearts are notably expressed in those words used by one of them ('tis *Howel* in his *Familiar Letters*, Vol. 1. Sect. 6. Lett. 32.) *I rather pitty, than hate, Turk or Infidel, for they are of the same Metal, and bear the same Stamp, as I do, tho' the Inscriptions differ; If I hate any, 'tis those Schismaticks that puzzle the sweet Peace of our Church; so that I could be content to see an Anabaptist go to Hell on a Brownists Back.* The Writer whom I last quoted, hath given us a Story of a young Man in *High-Holbourn*, who being after his death Dissected, there was a Serpent with divers tails, found in the left Ventricle of his Heart. I make no question, that our Church-History will find some Reader disposed like that Writer, with an Heart as full of Serpent and Venom as ever it can hold: Nor indeed will they be able to hold, but the Tongues and Pens of those angry Folks, will scourge me as with Scorpions, and cause me to feel (if I will feel) as many Lashes as *Cornelius Agrippa* [51] expected from their Brethren, for the Book in which he exposed their Vanities. . . .

Reader, I also expect nothing but *Scourges* from that Generation, to whom the *Mass-book* is dearer than the *Bible*. But I have now likewise confessed another Expectation, that shall be my Consolation under all. They tell us, That on the highest of the *Capsian* Mountains in *Spain*, there is a Lake, whereinto if you throw a Stone, there presently ascends a Smoke, which forms a dense Cloud, from whence issues a Tempest of Rain, Hail, and horrid Thunder-claps, for a good quarter of an hour. Our Church-History will be like a Stone cast into that Lake, for the furious Tempest which it will raise among some, whose Ecclesiastical Dignities have set them, as on the top of Spanish Mountains. The Catholick Spirit of Communion wherewith 'tis written, and the Liberty which I have taken, to tax the Schismatical Impositions and Persecutions of a Party, who have always been as real Enemies to the English Nation, as to the Christian and Protestant Interest, will certainly bring upon the whole Composure, the quick Censures of that Party, at the first cast of their look upon it. In the Duke of *Alva's* Council of twelve Judges, there was one *Hessels* a *Flemming*, who slept always at the Trial of Criminals, and when they wak'd him to deliver his Opinion, he rub'd his Eyes, and cry'd, between sleeping and waking, *Ad patibulum! ad Patibulum!* To the Gallows with 'em! (And, by the way, this Blade was himself, at the last, condemned unto the Gallows, without an Hearing!) As quick Censures must this our Labour expect from those who will not bestow waking thoughts upon the Representations of Christianity here made unto the World; but have a Sentence of Death always to pass, or at least,

Wish, upon those Generous Principles, without which, 'tis impossible to maintain the Reformation: And I confess, I am very well content, that this our Labour takes the Fate of those Principles: Nor do I dissent from the words of the Excellent *VVhitaker* upon *Luther*, *Fœlix ille, quem Dominus eo Honore dignatus est, ut Homines nequissimos suos haberet inimicos.*[52] But if the old Epigrammatist, when he saw Guilty Folks raving Mad at his Lines, could say—

Hoc volo; nunc nobis carmina nostra placent: [53]

Certainly an Historian should not be displeased at it, if the Enemies of Truth discover their Madness at the true and free Communications of his History; and therefore the more Stones they throw at this Book, there will not only be the more Proofs, that it is a Tree which hath good Fruits growing upon it, but I will build my self a Monument with them, whereon shall be inscribed, that Clause in the Epitaph of the Martyr *Stephen:*

Excepit Lapides, cui petra Christus erat: [54]

Albeit perhaps the *Epitaph*, which the old *Monks* bestow'd upon *Wickliff*, will be rather endeavour'd for me, (*If I am thought worth one!*) by the Men, who will, with all possible *Monkery*, strive to stave off the approaching *Reformation*.[55]

But since an Undertaking of this Nature, must thus encounter so much Envy, from those who are under the Power of the *Spirit that works in the Children of Unperswadeableness*, methinks I might perswade my self, that it will find another sort of Entertainment from those Good Men who have a better Spirit in them: For, as the Apostle *James* hath noted, (so with Monsieur *Claude* I read it) *The Spirit that is in us, lusteth against Envy;* and yet even in *us* also, there will be the *Flesh*, among whose Works, one is *Envy*, which will be *Lusting* against the *Spirit*. All Good Men will not be satisfied with every thing that is here set before them. In my own Country, besides a considerable number of loose and vain Inhabitants risen up, to whom the Congregational Church-Discipline, which cannot Live well, where the Power of Godliness dyes, is become distastful for the Purity of it; there is also a number of eminently Godly Persons, who are for a Larger way,[56] and unto these my Church-History will give distast, by the things which it may happen to utter, in favour of that Church-Discipline on some few occasions; and the Discoveries which I may happen to make of my Apprehensions, that *Scripture*, and *Reason*, and *Antiquity* is for it; and that it is not far from a glorious Resurrection. But that, as the Famous Mr. *Baxter*, after Thirty or Forty Years hard Study, about the true Instituted Church-Discipline, at last, not only own'd, but also invincibly prov'd, That it is *The Congregational;* so, The further that the *Unprejudiced Studies* of Learned Men proceed in this Matter, the more generally the *Congregational Church-Discipline* will be pronounced for. On the other side, There are some among us, who very strictly profess the *Congregational Church-Discipline*, but at the same time they have an unhappy Narrowness of Soul, by which they confine their value and Kindness too much unto their own Party; and unto those my *Church History* will be offensive, because my Regard unto our own declared Principles, does not hinder me from giving the Right hand of Fellowship unto the valuable Servants of the Lord Jesus Christ, who find not our Church-Discipline as yet agreeable unto their present Understandings and Illuminations. If it be thus in my own Country, it cannot be otherwise in That whereto I send this account of my own. Briefly, as it hath been said, That if all *Episcopal* Men were like Archbishop *Usher*,[57] and all *Presbyterians* like *Stephen Marshal*,[58] and all *Independents* like *Jeremiah Burroughs*,[59] the Wounds of the Church would soon be healed; my Essay to carry that Spirit through this whole Church-History, will bespeak Wounds for it, from those that are of another Spirit. And there will also be in every Country those Good Men, who yet have not had the Grace of Christ so far prevailing in them, as utterly to divest them of that piece of Ill Nature which the Comedian resents, *In homine Imperito, quo nil quicquam Injustius, quia nisi quod ipse facit, nil recte factum putat.*[60]

However, All these things, and an hundred more such things which I think of, are very small Discouragements for such a Service as I have here endeavoured. I foresee a Recompence, which will abundantly swallow up all Discouragements! It may be *Strato* the Philosopher counted himself well recompensed for his Labours, when *Ptolomy* bestow'd fourscore Talents on him. It may be *Archimelus* the Poet counted himself well recompensed, when *Hiero* sent him a thousand Bushels of Wheat for one little Epigram: And *Saleius* the Poet might count himself well recompensed, when *Vespasian* sent him twelve thousand and five hundred *Philippicks;* and *Oppian* the Poet might count himself well recompensed, when *Caracalla* sent him a piece of Gold for every Line that he had inscribed unto him. As I live in a Country where such Recompences never were in fashion; it hath no Preferments for me, and I shall count that I am well Rewarded in it, if I can escape without being heavily Reproached, Censured and Condemned, for what I have done: So I thank the Lord, I should exceedingly Scorn all such mean Considerations, I seek not out for Benefactors, to whom these Labours may be Dedicated: There is ONE to whom all is due! From Him I shall have a Recompence: And what Recompence? The Recompence, whereof I do, with inexpressible Joy, assure my self, is this, *That these my poor Labours will certainly serve the Churches and Interests of the Lord Jesus Christ.* And I think I may say, That I ask to live no longer, than I count a Service unto the Lord Jesus Christ, and his Churches, to be it self a glorious Recompence for the doing of it. When *David* was contriving to build the House of God, there was that order given from Heaven concerning him, *Go tell* David, *my Servant.* The adding of *that* more than *Royal Title* unto the Name of *David*, was a sufficient Recompence for all his Contrivance about the House of God. In our whole *Church-History*, we have been at work for the House of the Lord Jesus Christ, (Even that *Man* who is the *Lord God*, and whose *Form* seems on that occasion represented unto His *David.*) And herein 'tis Recompence enough, that I have been a *Servant* unto that heavenly Lord. The greatest *Honour*, and the sweetest *Pleasure*, out of *Heaven*, is to Serve our Illustrious Lord JESUS CHRIST, who hath *loved us, and given himself for us;* and unto whom it is infinitely reasonable that we should *give our selves*, and all that we *have* and *Are:* And it may be the *Angels* in *Heaven* too, aspire not after an higher Felicity.

Unto thee, therefore, O thou Son of God, and King of Heaven, and Lord of all things, whom all the Glorious Angels of Light, unspeakably love to Glorifie; I humbly offer up a poor History of Churches, which own thee alone for their Head, and Prince, and Law-giver; Churches which thou hast purchas'd with thy own Blood, and with wonderful Dispensations of thy Providence hitherto protected and preserved; and of a People which thou didst Form for thy self, to shew forth thy Praises. I bless thy great Name, for thy inclining of me to, and carrying of me through, the Work of this History: I pray thee to sprinkle the Book of this History with thy Blood, and make it acceptable and profitable unto thy Churches, and serve thy Truths and Ways among thy People, by that which thou hast here prepared; for 'tis THOU *that hast prepar'd it for them.* Amen.

Quid sum? Nil. Quis sum? Nullus. Sed Gratia CHRISTI,
Quod sum, quod Vivo, quodque Laboro, facit.[61]

THE
SIMPLE COBLER
OF
AGGAWAM in AMERICA.

WILLING
To help 'mend his Native Country, lamentably tattered, both in the upper-Leather and sole, with all the honest stitches he can take.

And as willing never to bee paid for his work, by Old English wonted pay.

It is his Trade to patch all the year long, gratis.

Therefore I pray Gentlemen keep your purses.

By *Theodore de la Guard.*

In rebus arduis ac tenui spe, fortissima quæque consilia tutissima sunt. Cic.

In English,
When bootes and shoes are torne up to the lefts,
Coblers must thrust their awles up to the hefts.

This is no time to feare *Apelles gramm:*
Ne Sutor quidem ultra crepidam.

LONDON,
Printed by *J. D.* & *R. I.* for *Stephen Bowtell*, at the signe of the Bible in Popes Head-Alley, 1647.

Title Page of Nathaniel Ward's *The Simple Cobler.*

Chapter II

THE THEORY OF THE STATE AND OF SOCIETY

IT HAS often been said that the end of the seventeenth and the beginning of the eighteenth century mark the first real break with the Middle Ages in the history of European thought. Even though the Renaissance and Reformation transformed many aspects of the Western intellect, still it was not until the time of Newton that the modern scientific era began; only then could men commence to regard life in this world as something more than preparation for life beyond the grave. Certainly if the eighteenth century inaugurated the modern epoch in natural sciences, so also did it in the political and social sciences. For the first time since the fall of the Roman Empire religion could be separated from politics, doctrinal orthodoxy divorced from loyalty to the state, and the citizens of a nation permitted to worship in diverse churches and to believe different creeds without endangering the public peace. Various factors contributed to effecting this revolution; the triumph of scientific method and of rationalism made impossible the older belief that government was of divine origin; the rise of capitalism, of the middle class, and eventually of democracy, necessitated new conceptions of the rôle of the state. Social leadership in England and America was assumed by a group of gentlemen who were, by and large, deists or skeptics, and to them all religious issues had become supremely boring. At the same time the churches themselves, particularly the newer evangelical denominations, were swinging round to a theology that made religious belief the subjective experience of individual men, entirely unrelated to any particular political philosophy or social theory.

In order to understand Puritanism we must go behind these eighteenth-century developments to an age when the unity of religion and politics was so axiomatic that very few men would even have grasped the idea that church and state could be distinct. For the Puritan mind it was not possible to segregate a man's spiritual life from his communal life. Massachusetts was settled for religious reasons, but as John Winthrop announced, religious reasons included "a due forme of Government both ciuill and ecclesiasticall," and the civil was quite as important in his eyes as the ecclesiastical. Only in recent years has it become possible for us to view the political aspects of Puritanism with something like comprehension and justice. For two centuries our social thinking has been dominated by ideas which were generated in the course of a sweeping revolt against everything for which the Puritans stood; the political beliefs of the Puritans were forgotten, or, if remembered at all, either deplored or condemned as unfortunate remnants of medievalism. Puritanism has been viewed mainly as a religious and ethical movement. But of late years the standards of the eighteenth century have for the first time come under serious criticism and in many quarters are showing the strain. In these circumstances the social philosophy of Puritanism takes on a new interest, and quite possibly becomes for us the most instructive and valuable portion of the Puritan heritage.

The Puritan theory of the state began with the hypothesis of original sin. Had Adam transmitted undiminished to his descendants the image of God in which he had been created, no government would ever have been necessary among men; they would all then have done justice to each other without the supervision of a judge, they would have respected each other's rights without the intervention of a policeman. But the Bible said—and experience proved—that since the fall, without the policeman, the judge, the jail, the law, and the magistrate, men will rob, murder, and fight among themselves; without a coercive state to restrain evil impulses and administer punishments, no life will be safe, no property secure, no honor observed. Therefore, upon Adam's apostasy, God Himself instituted governments among men. He left the particular form to be determined by circumstance—this was one important human art on which the Puritans said the Bible was *not* an absolute and imperious lawgiver—but He enacted that all men should be under some sort of corporate rule, that they should all submit to the sway of their superiors, that no man should live apart from his fellows, that the government should have full power to enforce obedience and to inflict every punishment that the crimes of men deserved.

There was a strong element of individualism in the Puritan creed; every man had to work out his own salvation, each soul had to face his maker alone. But at the same time, the Puritan philosophy demanded that in society all men, at least all regenerate men, be marshaled into one united array. The lone horseman, the single trapper, the solitary hunter was not a figure of the Puritan frontier; Puritans moved in groups and towns, settled in whole communities, and maintained firm government over all units. Neither was the individualistic business man, the shopkeeper who seized every opportunity to enlarge his profits, the speculator who contrived to gain wealth at the expense of his fellows, neither were these typical figures of the original Puritan society. The most obvious lesson of the selections printed herein is that Puritan opinion was at the opposite pole from Jefferson's feeling that the best government governs as little as possible. The theorists of New England thought of society as a unit, bound together by inviolable ties; they thought of it not as an aggregation of individuals but as an organism, functioning for a definite purpose, with all parts subordinate to the whole, all members contributing a definite share, every person occupying a particular status. "Society in all sorts of humane affaires is better then Solitariness," said John Cotton.[1] The society of early New England was decidedly "regimented." Puritans did not think the state was merely an umpire, standing on the side lines of a contest, limited to checking egregious fouls, but otherwise allowing men free play according to their abilities and the breaks of the game. They would have expected the rule of "laissez-faire" to result in a reign of rapine and horror. The state to them was an active instrument of leadership, discipline, and, wherever necessary, of coercion; it legislated over any or all aspects of human behavior, it not merely regulated misconduct but undertook to inspire and direct all conduct. The commanders were not to trim their policies by the desires of the people, but to drive ahead upon the predetermined course; the people were all to turn out as they were ordered, and together they were to crowd sail to the full capacity of the vessel. The officers were above the common men, as the quarter-deck is above the forecastle. There was no idea of the equality of all men. There was no questioning that men who would not serve the purposes of the society should be whipped into line. The objectives were clear and unmistakable; any one's disinclination to dedicate himself to them was obviously so much recalcitrancy and depravity. The government of Massachusetts, and of Connecticut as well, was a dictatorship, and never pretended to be anything else; it was a dictatorship, not of a single tyrant, or of an economic class, or of a political faction, but of the holy and regenerate. Those who did not hold with the ideals entertained by the righteous, or who believed God had preached other principles, or who desired that in religious belief, morality, and ecclesiastical preferences all men should be left at liberty to do as they wished—such persons had every liberty, as Nathaniel Ward said, to stay away from New England. If they did come, they were expected to keep their opinions to themselves; if they discussed them in public or attempted to act upon them, they were exiled; if they persisted in re-

[1] *A Briefe Exposition . . . upon . . . Ecclesiastes* (London, 1654), p. 85.

turning, they were cast out again; if they still came back, as did four Quakers, they were hanged on Boston Common. And from the Puritan point of view, it was good riddance.

These views of the nature and function of the state were not peculiar to the Puritans of New England; they were the heritage of the past, the ideals, if not always the actuality, of the previous centuries. That government was established by God in order to save depraved men from their own depravity had been orthodox Christian teaching for centuries; that men should be arranged in serried ranks, inferiors obeying superiors, was the essence of feudalism; that men should live a social life, that profit-making should be restrained within the limits of the "just price," that the welfare of the whole took precedence over any individual advantage, was the doctrine of the medieval church, and of the Church of England in the early seventeenth century. Furthermore, in addition to these general principles, there were two or three more doctrines in the New England philosophy which also were common to the age and the background. All the world at that moment believed with them that the church was to be maintained and protected by the civil authority, and a certain part of the world was contending that government was limited by fundamental law and that it took its origin from the consent of the people.

Every respectable state in the Western world assumed that it could allow only one church to exist within its borders, that every citizen should be compelled to attend it and conform to its requirements, and that all inhabitants should pay taxes for its support. When the Puritans came to New England the idea had not yet dawned that a government could safely permit several creeds to exist side by side within the confines of a single nation. They had not been fighting in England for any milk-and-water toleration, and had they been offered such religious freedom as dissenters now enjoy in Great Britain they would have scorned to accept such terms. Only a hypocrite, a person who did not really believe what he professed, would be content to practice his religion under such conditions. The Puritans were assured that they alone knew the exact truth, as it was contained in the written word of God, and they were fighting to enthrone it in England and to extirpate utterly and mercilessly all other pretended versions of Christianity. When they could not succeed at home, they came to America, where they could establish a society in which the one and only truth should reign forever. There is nothing so idle as to praise the Puritans for being in any sense conscious or deliberate pioneers of religious liberty—unless, indeed, it is still more idle to berate them because in America they persecuted dissenters from their beliefs after they themselves had undergone persecution for differing with the bishops. To allow no dissent from the truth was exactly the reason they had come to America. They maintained here precisely what they had maintained in England, and if they exiled, fined, jailed, whipped, or hanged those who disagreed with them in New England, they would have done the same thing in England could they have secured the power. It is almost pathetic to trace the puzzlement of New England leaders at the end of the seventeenth century, when the idea of toleration was becoming more and more respectable in European thought. They could hardly understand what was happening in the world, and they could not for a long time be persuaded that they had any reason to be ashamed of their record of so many Quakers whipped, blasphemers punished by the amputation of ears, Antinomians exiled, Anabaptists fined, or witches executed. By all the lights which had prevailed in Europe at the time the Puritans had left, these were achievements to which any government could point with pride. In 1681 a congregation of Anabaptists, who led a stormy and precarious existence for several years in Charlestown, published an attack upon the government of Massachusetts Bay; they justified themselves by appealing to the example of the first settlers, claiming that like themselves the founders had been nonconformists and had fled to New England to establish a refuge for persecuted consciences. When Samuel Willard, minister of the Third Church in Boston, read this, he could hardly believe his eyes; he hastened to assure the authors that they did not know what they were talking about:

> I perceive they are mistaken in the design of our first Planters, whose business was not Toleration; but were professed Enemies of it, and could leave the World professing they *died no Libertines*. Their business was to settle, and (as much as in them lay) secure Religion to Posterity, according to that way which they believed was of God.[1]

For the pamphlet in which Willard penned these lines Increase Mather wrote an approving preface. Forty years later, he and his son Cotton participated in the ordination of a Baptist minister in Boston, and he then preached on the need for harmony between differing sects. But by that time much water had gone under the bridge, the old charter had been revoked, there was danger that the Church of England might be made the established church of the colonies, theology had

[1] *Ne Sutor ultra Crepidam* (Boston, 1681), p. 4.

come to be of less importance in men's minds than morality, the tone of the eighteenth century was beginning to influence opinion—even in Boston. Increase was old and weary. Puritanism, in the true sense of the word, was dead.

Of course, the whole Puritan philosophy of church and state rested upon the assumption that the word of God was clear and explicit, that the divines had interpreted it correctly, and that no one who was not either a knave or a fool could deny their demonstrations. Ergo, it seemed plain, those who did deny them should be punished for being obstinate. John Cotton said that offenders should not be disciplined for their wrong opinions, but for persisting in them; he said that Roger Williams was not turned out of Massachusetts for his conscience, but for sinning against his own conscience. Roger Williams and John Cotton debated the question of "persecution" through several hundred pages; after they had finished, I think it is very doubtful whether Cotton had even begun to see his adversary's point. And still today it is hard to make clear the exact grounds upon which Roger Williams became the great apostle of religious liberty. Williams was not, like Thomas Jefferson, a man to whom theology and divine grace had become stuff and nonsense; on the contrary he was pious with a fervor and passion that went beyond most of his contemporaries. So exalted was his conception of the spiritual life that he could not bear to have it polluted with earthly considerations. He did not believe that any man could determine the precise intention of scripture with such dreadful certainty as the New England clergy claimed to possess. Furthermore, it seemed to him that even if their version were true, submission to truth itself was worth nothing at all when forced upon men by the sword. Williams evolved from an orthodox Puritan into the champion of religious liberty because he came to see spiritual truth as so rare, so elevated, so supernal a loveliness that it could not be chained to a wordly establishment and a vested interest. He was a libertarian because he contemned the world, and he wanted to separate church and state so that the church would not be contaminated by the state; Thomas Jefferson loved the world and was dubious about the spirit, and he sought to separate church and state so that the state would not be contaminated by the church. But John Cotton believed the state and church were partners in furthering the cause of truth; he knew that the truth was clear, definite, reasonable, and undeniable; he expected all good men to live by it voluntarily, and he was sure that all men who did not do so were obviously bad men. Bad men were criminals, whether their offense was theft or a belief in the "inner light," and they should be punished. Moses and Aaron, the priest and the statesman, were equally the viceregents of God, and the notion that one could contaminate the other was utter insanity.

The two other ideas which we have noted as being derived from the background of the age, rule by fundamental law and social compact, were the special tenets of English Puritanism. For three decades before the settlement of Massachusetts the Puritan party in England had been working hand in glove with the Parliament against the King. The absolutist Stuarts were allied with the bishops, and the Puritan agitator and the Parliamentary leader made common cause against them both. As a result of this combination, the Puritan theorists had taken over the essentials of the Parliamentary conception of society, the contention that the power of the ruler should be exercised in accordance with established fundamental law, and that the government should owe its existence to a compact of the governed. Because these ideas were strategically invaluable in England, they became ingrained in the Puritan consciousness; they were carried to New England and were preached from every pulpit in the land.

The Puritans did not see any conflict between them and their religious intentions. In New England the fundamental law was the Bible. The magistrates were to have full power to rule men for the specific purposes to which the society was dedicated; but they as well as their subordinates were tied to the specific purposes, and could not go beyond the prescribed limits. The Bible was clear and definite on the form of the church, on the code of punishments for crimes, on the general purposes of social existence; its specifications were binding on all, magistrates, ministers, and citizens. Consequently, the Puritans did not find it difficult to conclude that in those matters upon which the Bible left men free to follow their own discretion, the society itself should establish basic rules. The New England leaders and the people frequently disagreed as to what these rules were, or as to how detailed they should be made, but neither side ever doubted that the community must abide by whatever laws had been enacted, either by God or by the state. The government of New England was, as we have said, a dictatorship, but the dictators were not absolute and irresponsible. John Cotton was the clerical spokesman for the Massachusetts rulers, but he stoutly demanded "that all power that is on earth be limited."

The belief that government originated in the consent of the governed was equally congenial to the Puritan creed. The theology is often enough described as deterministic, because it held that men were predestined to heaven or hell; but we are always in danger of forgetting that the life of the Puritan was completely voluntaristic. The natural man was indeed bound in slavery to sin and unable to make exertions toward his own salvation; but the man into whose soul grace had been infused was liberated from that bondage and made free to undertake the responsibilities and obligations of virtue and decency. The holy society was erected upon the belief that the right sort of men could of their own free will and choice carry through the creation and administration of the right sort of community. The churches of New England were made up of "saints," who came into the church because they wanted membership, not because they were born in it, or were forced into it, or joined because of policy and convention. Though every resident was obliged to attend and to pay taxes for the support of the churches, no one became an actual member who did not signify his strong desire to be one. The saints were expected to act positively because they had in them a spirit of God that made them capable of every exertion. No doubt the Puritans maintained that government originated in the consent of the people because that theory was an implement for chastening the absolutism of the Stuarts; but they maintained it also because they did not believe that any society, civil or ecclesiastical, into which men did not enter of themselves was worthy of the name.

Consequently, the social theory of Puritanism, based upon the law of God, was posited also upon the voluntary submission of the citizens. As men exist in nature, said Thomas Hooker, no one person has any power over another; "there must of necessity be a mutuall ingagement, each of the other, by their free consent, before by any rule of God they have any right or power, or can exercise either, each towards the other." This truth appears, he argues, from all relations among men, that of husband and wife, master and servant; there must be a compact drawn up and sealed between them.

From *mutuall acts* of consenting and ingaging each of other, there is an impression of *ingagement* results, as a *relative bond*, betwixt the contractours and confederatours, wherein the *formalis ratio*, or *specificall nature* of the covenant lieth, in all the former instances especially *that of* corporations. So that however it is true, the rule bindes such to the duties of their places and relations, yet it is certain, it requires that they should *first freely ingage* themselves in such covenants, and *then* be carefull to fullfill such duties. A man is allowed freely to make choice of his wife, and she of her husband, before they need or should perform the duties of husband and wife one towards another.[1]

[1] *A Su vey of the Summe of Church-Discipline* (London, 1648), Part I, p. 69.

The rules and regulations of society, the objectives and the duties, are erected by God; but in a healthy state the citizens must first agree to abide by those regulations, must first create the society by willing consent and active participation.

These ideas, of a uniform church supported by the civil authority, of rule by explicit law, of the derivation of the state from the consent of the people, were transported to New England because they were the stock ideas of the time and place. What the New England Puritans added of their own was the unique fashion in which they combined them into one coherent and rounded theory. The classic expression of this theory is the speech on liberty delivered by John Winthrop to the General Court in 1645. In that year Winthrop was serving as lieutenant governor, and as such was a justice of the peace; a squabble broke out in the town of Hingham over the election of a militia officer; Winthrop intervened, committing one faction for contempt of court when they would not give bond to appear peaceably before the legislature and let the affair be adjudicated. Some of the citizens were enraged, and the lower house of the General Court impeached Winthrop for exceeding his commission and going beyond the basic law of the land. He was tried and acquitted; thereupon he pronounced this magnificent oration, setting before the people the unified theory of the Puritan commonwealth.

As he expounds it, the political doctrine becomes part and parcel of the theological, and the cord that binds all ideas together is the covenant. The New England divines had already refashioned the original theology of Calvinism to bring it more into accord with the disposition of Englishmen, their most important addition being their statement of the relationship between the elect and God in the form of a covenant. As they saw it, when a man received the spirit of God, he availed himself of his liberty to enter a compact with the Deity, promising to abide by God's laws and to fulfill God's will to the best of his ability. In turn God guaranteed him redemption. A regenerate man was thus by definition committed by his own plighted word to God's cause, not only in his personal life and behaviour, but in church affairs and in society. Winthrop argues that individuals, in a natural state, before grace has been given them, are at absolute liberty to do anything they can, to lie, steal, murder; obviously he is certain that natural men, being what they are, will do exactly these things unless prevented. But when men become regenerate they are then at "liberty" to do only what God commands. And God commands certain things for the group as a whole as well as for each individual. Regenerate men, therefore, by the very fact of being regenerate, come together, form churches and a state upon explicit agreements, in which they all promise to live with one another according to the laws and for the purposes of God. Thus the government is brought into being by the act of the people; but the people do not create just any sort of government, but the one kind of government which God has outlined. The governors are elected by the people, but elected into an office which has been established by God. God engenders the society by acting through the people, as in nature He secures His effects by guiding secondary causes; the collective will of regenerate men, bound together by the social compact, projects and continues the will of God into the state. As John Davenport expressed it, "In regular actings of the creature, God is the first Agent; there are not two several and distinct actings, one of God, another of the People: but in one and the same action, God, by the Peoples suffrages, makes such an one Governour, or Magistrate, and not another." [1] So, when men have made a covenant with God they have thereby promised Him, in the very terms of that agreement, to compact among themselves in order to form a holy state in which His discipline will be practiced. As one of the ministers phrased it:

> Where the Lord sets himselfe over a people, he frames them unto a willing and voluntary subjection unto him, that they desire nothing more then to be under his government . . . When the Lord is in Covenant with a people, they follow him not forcedly, but as farre as they are sanctified by grace, they submit willingly to his regiment.[2]

When men have entered these covenants, first with God, then with each other in the church and again in the state, they have thrice committed themselves to the rule of law and the control of authority. Winthrop can thus insist that though the government of Massachusetts is bound by fundamental law, and though it takes its rise from the people, and though the people elect the officials, still the people's liberty in Massachusetts consists in a "liberty to that only which is good, just and honest." By entering the covenant with God, and the covenant with each other, the citizens renounce all natural liberty, surrender the right to seek for anything that they themselves might lust after, and retain only the freedom that "is maintained and exercised in a way of subjection to authority."

The theory furnishes an excellent illustration of the intellectual ideal

[1] *A Sermon Preach'd at The Election . . . May 19th 1669* ([n. p.], 1670), in *Publications of the Colonial Society of Massachusetts*, X, 6.

[2] Peter Bulkeley, *The Gospel-Covenant* (London, 1651), pp. 219–220.

toward which all Puritan thought aspired; in the realm of government as of nature, the Puritan thinker strove to harmonize the determination of God with the exertion of men, the edicts of revelation with the counsels of reason and experience. On one side, this account exhibits the creation of society as flowing from the promptings and coaction of God; on the other side it attributes the origination to the teachings of nature and necessity. The social compact may be engineered by God, but it is also an eminently reasonable method of bringing a state into being. Delimitation of the ruler's power by basic law may be a divine ordinance to restrain the innate sinfulness of men, but it is also a very natural device to avoid oppression and despotism; the constitution may be promulgated to men from on high, but it is in fact very much the sort which, had they been left to their own devices, they might have contrived in the interests of efficiency and practicality. Men might conceivably have come upon the erection of governments through explicit compacts, in which they incorporated certain inviolable regulations and a guarantee of rights, quite as much by their own intelligence as by divine instruction. As always in Puritan thought, there was no intention to discredit either source, but rather to integrate the divine and the natural, revelation and reason, into a single inspiration. "Power of Civil Rule, by men orderly chosen, is Gods Ordinance," said John Davenport, even if "It is from the Light and Law of Nature," because "the Law of Nature is God's Law." [1] The Puritan state was thus from one point of view purely and simply a "theocracy"; God was the sovereign, His fiats were law and His wishes took precedence over all other considerations; the magistrates and ministers were His viceroys. But from another point of view, the Puritan state was built upon reason and the law of nature; it was set up by the covenant of the people, the scope of its power was determined by the compact, and the magistrates and ministers were the commissioned servants of the people.

As this theory stands on paper it is, like so many edifices erected by the Puritan mind, almost perfect. When it was realized in practice, however, there were at least two difficulties that soon became apparent. For one, not all the people, even in New England, were regenerate; in fact, the provable elect were a minority, probably no more than one fifth of the total population. But this did not dismay the original theorists, for they had never thought that mere numerical majorities proved anything. Consequently, though the social compact furnished the theoretical basis of society in New England, neverthe-

[1] *A Sermon Preach'd at The Election*, p. 4.

less it was confined to the special few; the election of officers and the passing of laws was given to those only who could demonstrate their justification and sanctification. The Congregational system, with its membership limited to those who had proved before the church that they possessed the signs of grace, offered a ready machinery for winnowing the wheat from the chaff. Therefore, under the first charter the suffrage in Massachusetts was limited to the church members. In Connecticut the franchise was not officially restrained in this fashion, but other means served as well to keep the electorate pure and orthodox. The "citizens," as they were called, elected delegates to the General Court, chose judges, and passed laws. The others, the "inhabitants," had equality before the law, property rights, police protection; they were taxed no more than the citizens or submitted to no indignities, but they were allowed no voice in the government or in the choice of ministers, and only by the mere force of numbers gained any influence in town meetings.

The restriction of the franchise to church membership seemed to solve the first difficulty confronted by the Puritan theorists. But in time it only brought them face to face with the second and more serious problem: the whole structure of theory which Winthrop outlined in his speech, and which the sermons of Mitchell, Stoughton, and Hubbard reiterated, fell apart the moment the "citizens" were no longer really and ardently holy. Just as soon as the early zeal began to die down, and the distinction between the citizens and the inhabitants became difficult to discern, then the purely naturalistic, rational, practical aspect of the political theory became detached from the theological, began to stand alone and by itself. As the religious inspiration waned, there remained no reason why all the people should not be held partners to the social compact; the idea that God worked His ends through the covenant of the people grew vague and obscure, while the notion that all the people made the covenant for their own reasons and created the state for their own purposes took on more and more definite outlines. As toleration was forced upon the colonies by royal command, or became more estimable as religious passions abated, the necessity for the social bond being considered a commitment of the nation to the will of God disappeared. Instead, men perceived the charms and usefulness of claiming that the compact had been an agreement of the people, not to God's terms, but to their own terms. The divine ordinance and the spirit of God, which were supposed to have presided over the political process, vanished, leaving a government founded on the self-evident truths of the law of nature, brought into being by social compact, instituted not for the glory of God, but to secure men's "inalienable rights" of life, liberty, and the pursuit of happiness. Until Jefferson rewrote the phrase, the three interests which were to be furthered and guaranteed by the government were more candidly summarized as life, liberty—and property.

The sermon of Samuel Willard, delivered in the 1690's, betrays the merest beginnings of the change from the theological version of political principle to the purely rational and naturalistic variant, but the real revolution in the thought was first decisively proclaimed by the Reverend John Wise. He wrote his pamphlet in defence of church government only; he was aroused by a proposal that had been tentatively suggested several years previously among a group of Boston ministers, that the local autonomy of individual congregations had perhaps been carried too far and that possibly a more centralized administration would help check the degeneration of the religious spirit. Wise wrote his vindication of the Congregational system in order to demolish this ecclesiastical proposal, but in working out the philosophy of church government he had to overhaul the fundamentals of all government. The revolution he inaugurated in the thinking of New England consisted in the very organization of his book; where the early defenders of the church system discussed the Biblical and rational arguments together, or forced them to coalesce into one argument, Wise deliberately separated them into two distinct and independent chapters. He compressed into the first section of his book a recital of all the passages of scripture that had been held to substantiate the Congregational system, and then hurried on to the argument from unaided natural wisdom. The radicalism of his pamphlet is compressed into one sentence, into his suggestion that the scheme of government might be said to have originated with nature and reason, and only subsequently to have "obtained the Royal Approbation." Where the early writers had maintained that government springs from the action of God upon the reason, Wise separates divine commands and the dictates of reason into independent sources, and establishes a direct line of communication with God through the natural reason, without any real necessity for consulting scripture. Instead of the unity of early Puritan theory, this account is actually out-and-out rationalism, and the function of the Bible is reduced to supplying a secondary confirmation of the reasonable. From Wise to the philosophy of the Declaration of Independence is a clear and inevitable progress. Barnard and Mayhew mark further steps in that development, and with Mayhew the right of revolution, the right to resist the government when it oversteps the limits established by the social compact and the fundamental law, becomes the most important doctrine in the theory. With Jonathan Mayhew the separation of God's will from man's is complete; or rather, with him, the divine will has been made over into the image of the human. The purposes of society are no longer the deity's, but the subject's; the advantages to be derived from corporate existence are no longer salvation, but the well-being of the citizen. The power of the Puritan God, and of the English King, is bound by the terms of this compact and by the basic law; we are by now certain that God will respect the law we have agreed upon, but as for the King—if he impose a tax on tea to which we do not ourselves consent, and if we thereupon resist him, "even to the dethroning him," we are not criminals, but have only taken "a reasonable way" of vindicating our natural rights.

JOHN WINTHROP, 1588–1649

[For Winthrop's life see p. 124. "A Modell of Christian Charity" was delivered as a lecture or lay-sermon to the passengers aboard the *Arbella* on the voyage to New England; it follows the standard sermon form, asserting a doctrinal truth, supporting it with reasons, applying it to the case in hand. The text is from *Winthrop Papers*, Vol. II (Massachusetts Historical Society, Boston, 1931).

"A Defence of an Order of Court" was written to silence Henry Vane. During the strain of the Antinomian crisis, when the authorities had good reason to fear an insurrection of the Hutchinsonians, the General Court passed a law that no immigrant should be allowed to remain in Massachusetts Bay unless one of the magistrates gave him a permit. The immediate purpose of the law was obviously to prevent the Hutchinsonians from receiving further reinforcements. Vane, who had just been turned out of the governorship (p. 133), called this act "tyranny." Winthrop defended it with the following tract; Vane replied with a longer document, and Winthrop answered in a still longer argument. The text is from Thomas Hutchinson, *A Collection of Papers Relating to the History of Massachusetts Bay* (Boston, 1769), pp. 63–71.

The selections from the *Journal* illustrate the workings of the Puritan state. Winthrop's speech, delivered to the General Court immediately after he had been acquitted in a trial for exceeding his magisterial authority, is the classic expression of Puritan political theory. The text is from the edition of James Savage (Boston, 1825), I, 300–302, 322–323, II, 35, 228–230.]

A MODELL OF CHRISTIAN CHARITY

Written
On Boarde the Arrabella,
On the Attlantick Ocean.
By the Honorable John Winthrop Esquire.

In His passage, (with the great Company of Religious people, of which Christian Tribes he was the Brave Leader and famous Governor;) from the Island of Great Brittaine, to New-England in the North America.

Anno 1630.

Christian Charitie.

A Modell Hereof.

God almightie in his most holy and wise providence hath soe disposed of the Condicion of mankinde, as in all times some must be rich some poore, some highe and eminent in power and dignitie; others meane and in subieccion.

The Reason Hereof.

1. Reas: *First*, to hold conformity with the rest of his workes, being delighted to shewe forthe the glory of his wisdome in the variety and differance of the Creatures and the glory of his power, in ordering all these differences for the preservacion and good of the whole, and the glory of his greatnes that as it is the glory of princes to haue many officers, soe this great King will haue many Stewards counting himselfe more honoured in dispenceing his guifts to man by man, then if hee did it by his owne immediate hand.

2. Reas: *Secondly*, That he might haue the more occasion to manifest the worke of his Spirit: first, vpon the wicked in moderateing and restraineing them: soe that the riche and mighty should not eate vpp the poore, nor the poore, and dispised rise vpp against their superiours, and shake off theire yoake; 2ly in the regenerate in exerciseing his graces in them, as in the greate ones, theire loue mercy, gentlenes, temperance etc., in the poore and inferiour sorte, theire faithe patience, obedience etc:

3. Reas: Thirdly, That every man might haue need of other, and from hence they might be all knitt more nearly together in the Bond of brotherly affeccion: from hence it appeares plainely that noe man is made more honourable then another or more wealthy etc., out of

any perticuler and singuler respect to himselfe but for the glory of his Creator and the Common good of the Creature, Man; Therefore God still reserues the propperty of these guifts to himselfe as Ezek: 16. 17. he there calls wealthe his gold and his silver etc. Prov: 3. 9. he claimes theire seruice as his due honour the Lord with thy riches etc. All men being thus (by divine providence) rancked into two sortes, riche and poore; vnder the first, are comprehended all such as are able to liue comfortably by theire owne meanes duely improued; and all others are poore according to the former distribution. There are two rules whereby wee are to walke one towards another: JUSTICE and MERCY. These are allwayes distinguished in theire Act and in theire obiect, yet may they both concurre in the same Subiect in eache respect; as sometimes there may be an occasion of shewing mercy to a rich man, in some sudden danger of distresse, and allsoe doeing of meere Justice to a poor man in regard of some perticuler contract etc. There is likewise a double Lawe by which wee are regulated in our conversacion one towardes another: in both the former respects, the lawe of nature and the lawe of grace, or the morrall lawe or the lawe of the gospell, to omitt the rule of Justice as not propperly belonging to this purpose otherwise then it may fall into consideracion in some perticuler Cases: By the first of these lawes man as he was enabled soe withall [is] commaunded to loue his neighbour as himselfe vpon this ground stands all the precepts of the morrall lawe, which concernes our dealings with men. To apply this to the works of mercy this lawe requires two things first that every man afford his help to another in every want or distresse Secondly, That hee performe this out of the same affeccion, which makes him carefull of his owne good according to that of our Saviour Math: [7. 12.] Whatsoever ye would that men should doe to you. This was practised by Abraham and Lott in entertaineing the Angells and the old man of Gibea.

The Lawe of Grace or the Gospell hath some differance from the former as in these respectes first the lawe of nature was giuen to man in the estate of innocency; this of the gospell in the estate of regeneracy: 2ly, the former propounds one man to another, as the same fleshe and Image of god, this as a brother in Christ allsoe, and in the Communion of the same spirit and soe teacheth vs to put a difference betweene Christians and others. Doe good to all especially to the household of faith; vpon this ground the Israelites were to putt a difference betweene the brethren of such as were strangers though not of the Canaanites. 3ly. The Lawe of nature could giue noe rules for dealeing with enemies for all are to be considered as freinds in the estate of innocency, but the Gospell commaunds loue to an enemy. proofe[:] If thine Enemie hunger feede him; Loue your Enemies doe good to them that hate you Math: 5. 44.

This Lawe of the Gospell propoundes likewise a difference of seasons and occasions there is a time when a christian must sell all and giue to the poore as they did in the Apostles times. There is a tyme allsoe when a christian (though they giue not all yet) must giue beyond theire abillity, as they of Macedonia. Cor: 2. 6. likewise community of perills calls for extraordinary liberallity and soe doth Community in some speciall seruice for the Churche. Lastly, when there is noe other meanes whereby our Christian brother may be releiued in this distresse, wee must help him beyond our ability, rather then tempt God, in putting him vpon help by miraculous or extraordinary meanes. . . .

1. For the persons, wee are a Company professing our selues fellow members of Christ, In which respect onely though wee were absent from eache other many miles, and had our imploymentes as farre distant, yet wee ought to account our selues knitt together by this bond of loue, and liue in the exercise of it, if wee would haue comforte of our being in Christ, this was notorious in the practise of the Christians in former times, as is testified of the Waldenses[1] from the mouth of one of the adversaries Aeneas Syluius, mutuo [solent amare] penè antequam norint, they vse to loue any of theire owne religion even before they were acquainted with them.

2ly. for the worke wee haue in hand, it is by a mutuall consent through a speciall overruleing providence, and a more then an ordinary approbation of the Churches of Christ to seeke out a place of Cohabitation and Consorteshipp vnder a due forme of Government both ciuill and ecclesiasticall. In such cases as this the care of the publique must oversway all private respects, by which not onely conscience, but meare Ciuill pollicy doth binde vs; for it is a true rule that perticuler estates cannott subsist in the ruine of the publique.

3ly. The end is to improue our liues to doe more seruice to the Lord the comforte and encrease of the body of christe whereof wee are members that our selues and posterity may be the better preserued from the Common corrupcions of this euill world to serue the Lord and worke out our Salvacion vnder the power and purity of his holy Ordinances.

4ly for the meanes whereby this must bee effected, they are 2fold, a Conformity with the worke and end wee aime at, these wee see are extraordinary, therefore wee must not content our selues with vsuall ordinary meanes whatsoever wee did or ought to haue done when wee liued in England, the same must wee doe and more allsoe where wee goe: That which the most in theire Churches maineteine as a truthe in profession onely, wee must bring into familiar and constant practice,[2] as in this duty of loue wee must loue brotherly without dissimulation, wee must loue one another with a pure hearte feruently wee must beare one anothers burthens, wee must not looke onely on our owne things, but allsoe on the things of our brethren, neither must wee think that the lord will beare with such faileings at our hands as hee dothe from those among whome wee haue liued. . . .

Thus stands the cause betweene God and vs, wee are entered into Covenant with him for this worke, wee haue taken out a Commission, the Lord hath giuen vs leaue to drawe our owne Articles wee haue professed to enterprise these Accions vpon these and these ends, wee haue herevpon besought him of favour and blessing: Now if the Lord shall please to heare vs, and bring vs in peace to the place wee desire, then hath hee ratified this Covenant and sealed our Commission, [and] will expect a strickt performance of the Articles contained in it, but if wee shall neglect the observacion of these Articles which are the ends wee haue propounded, and dissembling with our God, shall fall to embrace this present world and prosecute our carnall intencions seekeing greate things for our selues and our posterity, the Lord will surely breake out in wrathe against vs be revenged of such a periured people and make vs knowe the price of the breache of such a Covenant.[3]

Now the onely way to avoyde this shipwracke and to provide for our posterity is to followe the Counsell of Micah, to doe Justly, to loue mercy, to walke humbly with our God, for this end, wee must be knitt together in this worke as one man, wee must entertaine each other in brotherly Affeccion, wee must be willing to abridge our selues of our superfluities, for the supply of others necessities, wee must vphold a familiar Commerce together in all meekenes, gentlenes, patience and liberallity, wee must delight in eache other, make others Condicions our owne reioyce together, mourne together, labour, and suffer together, allwayes haueing before our eyes our Commission and Community in the worke, our Community as members of the same body, soe shall wee keepe the vnitie of the spirit in the bond of peace, the Lord will be our God and delight to dwell among vs, as his owne people and will commaund a blessing vpon vs in all our wayes, soe that wee shall see much more of his wisdome power goodnes and truthe then formerly wee haue beene acquainted with, wee shall finde that the God of Israell is among vs, when tenn of vs shall be able to resist a thousand of our enemies, when hee shall make vs a prayse and glory, that men shall say of succeeding plantacions: the lord make it like that of New England: for wee must Consider that wee shall be as a Citty vpon a Hill, the eies of all people are vppon vs; soe that if wee shall deale falsely with our god in this worke wee haue vndertaken and soe cause him to withdrawe his present help from vs, wee shall be made a story and a by-word through the world, wee shall open the mouthes of enemies to speake euill of the wayes of god and all professours for Gods sake; wee shall shame the faces of many of gods worthy seruants, and cause theire prayers to be turned into Cursses vpon vs till wee be consumed out of the good land whether wee are goeing: And to shutt vpp this discourse with that exhortacion of Moses that faithfull seruant of the Lord in his last farewell to Irsaell Deut. 30. Beloued there is now sett before vs life, and good, deathe and euill in that wee are Commaunded this day to loue the Lord our God, and to loue one another to walke in his wayes and to keepe his Commaundements and his Ordinance, and his lawes, and the Articles of our Covenant with him that wee may liue and be multiplyed, and that the Lord our God may blesse vs in the land whether wee goe to possesse it: But if our heartes shall turne away soe that wee will not obey, but shall be seduced and worshipp . . . other Gods our pleasures, and proffitts, and serue them; it is propounded vnto vs this day, wee shall surely perishe out of the good Land whether wee passe over this vast Sea to possesse it;

Therefore lett vs choose life,
that wee, and our Seede,
may liue; by obeyeing his
voyce, and cleaueing to him,
for hee is our life, and
our prosperity.

A DEFENCE OF AN ORDER OF COURT MADE IN THE YEAR 1637.

A Declaration of the Intent and Equitye of the Order made at the last Court, to this effect, that none should be received to inhabite within this Jurisdiction but such as should be allowed by some of the Magistrates.

For clearing of such scruples as have arisen about this order, it is to be considered, first, what is the essentiall forme of a common weale or body politic such as this is, which I conceive to be this—The consent of a certaine companie of people, to cohabite together, under one government for their mutual safety and welfare. . . .

It is clearely agreed, by all, that the care of safety and wellfare was the original cause or occasion of common weales and of many familyes subjecting themselves to rulers and laws; for no man hath lawfull power over another, but by birth or consent, so likewise, by the law of proprietye, no man can have just interest in that which belongeth to another, without his consent.

From the premises will arise these conclusions.

1. No common weale can be founded but by free consent.

2. The persons so incorporating have a public and relative interest each in other, and in the place of their cohabitation and goods, and laws, &c. and in all the means of their wellfare so as none other can claime priviledge with them but by free consent.

3. The nature of such an incorporation tyes every member thereof to seeke out and entertaine all means that may conduce to the wellfare of the bodye, and to keepe off whatsoever doth appeare to tend to theire damage.

4. The wellfare of the whole is [not] to be put to apparent hazard for the advantage of any particular members.

From these conclusions I thus reason.

1. If we heere be a corporation established by free consent, if the place of our cohabitation be our owne, then no man hath right to come into us &c. without our consent.

2. If no man hath right to our lands, our government priviledges, &c. but by our consent, then it is reason we should take notice of before we conferre any such upon them.

3. If we are bound to keepe off whatsoever appears to tend to our ruine or damage, then may we lawfully refuse to receive such whose dispositions suite not with ours and whose society (we know) will be hurtfull to us, and therefore it is lawfull to take knowledge of all men before we receive them.

4. The churches take liberty (as lawfully they may) to receive or reject at their discretion; [4] yea particular towns make orders to the like effect; why then should the common weale be denied the like liberty and the whole more restrained than any parte? . . .

10. Seeing it must be granted that there may come such persons (suppose Jesuits, &c.) which by consent of all ought to be rejected, it will follow that this law (being only for notice to be taken of all that come to us, without which we cannot avoyd such as indeed are to be kept out) is no other but just and needfull, and if any should be rejected that ought to be received, that is not to be imputed to the

law, but to those who are betrusted with the execution of it. And herein is to be considered, what the intent of the law is, and by consequence, by what rule they are to walke, who are betrusted with the keeping of it. The intent of the law is to preserve the wellfare of the body; and for this ende to have none received into any fellowship with it who are likely to disturbe the same, and this intent (I am sure) is lawful and good. Now then, if such to whom the keeping of this law is committed, be persuaded in theire judgments that such a man is likely to disturbe and hinder the publick weale, but some others who are not in the same trust, judge otherwise, yet they are to follow theire owne judgments, rather then the judgments of others who are not alike interested: As in tryall of an offender by a jury; the twelve men are satisfied in their consciences, upon the evidence given, that the party deserves death: but there are 20 or 40 standers by, who conceive otherwise, yet is the jury bound to condemn him according to their owne consciences, and not to acquit him upon the different opinion of other men, except theire reasons can convince them of the errour of theire consciences, and this is according to the rule of the Apostle, Rom. 14. 5. Let every man be fully persuaded in his own mynde.

If it be objected, that some prophane persons are received and others who are religious are rejected, I answer 1st, It is not knowne that any such thinge hath as yet fallen out. 2, Such a practice may be justifiable as the case may be, for younger persons (even prophane ones) may be of lesse danger to the common weale (and to the churches also) than some older persons, though professors of religion: for our Saviour Christ when he conversed with publicans, &c. sayth that such were nearer the kingdom of heaven than the religious pharisees, and one that is of large parts and confirmed in some erronious way, is likely to doe more harme to church and common weale, and is of lesse hope to be reclaymed, then 10 prophane persons, who have not yet beene hardened, in the contempt of the meanes of grace.

Lastly, Whereas it is objected that by this law, we reject good christians and so consequently Christ himselfe: I answer 1st, It is not knowne that any christian man hath beene rejected. 2, A man that is a true christian, may be denyed residence among us, in some cases, without rejecting Christ, as admitt a true christian should come over, and should maintaine community of goods, or that magistrates ought not to punish the breakers of the first table,[5] or the members of churches for criminal offences: or that no man were bound to be subject to those lawes or magistrates to which they should not give an explicite consent, &c. I hope no man will say, that not to receive such an one, were to reject Christ; for such opinions (though being maintained in simple ignorance, they might stand with a state of grace yet) they may be so dangerous to the publick weale in many respects, as it would be our sinne and unfaithfullness to receive such among us, except it were for tryall of theire reformation, I would demand then in the case in question (for it is bootelesse curiosity to refrayne openesse in things publick) whereas it is sayd that this law was made of purpose to keepe away such as are of Mr. Wheelwright his judgment (admitt it were so which yet I cannot confesse) where is the evill of it? If we conceive and finde by sadd experience that his opinions are such, as by his own profession cannot stand with externall peace, may we not provide for our peace, by keeping of such as would strengthen him, and infect others with such dangerous tenets? and if we finde his opinions such as will cause divisions, and make people looke at their magistrates, ministers and brethren as enemies to Christ and Antichrists, &c. were it not sinne and unfaithfullness in us, to receive more of those opinions, which we allready finde the evill fruite of: Nay, why doe not those who now complayne joyne with us in keeping out of such, as well as formerly they did in expelling Mr. Williams for the like, though lesse dangerous? Where this change of theire judgments should arise I leave to themselves to examine, and I earnestly entreate them so to doe, and for this law let the equally mynded judge, what evill they finde in it, or in the practice of those who are betrusted with the execution of it.

JOURNAL

MAY 22, 1639.] The court, finding the number of deputies to be much increased by the addition of new plantations, thought fit, for the ease both of the country and the court, to reduce all towns to two deputies. This occasioned some to fear, that the magistrates intended to make themselves stronger, and the deputies weaker, and so, in time, to bring all power into the hands of the magistrates; so as the people in some towns were much displeased with their deputies for yielding to such an order. Whereupon, at the next session, it was propounded to have the number of deputies restored; and allegations were made, that it was an infringement of their liberty; so as, after much debate, and such reasons given for diminishing the number of deputies, and clearly proved that their liberty consisted not in the number, but in the thing, divers of the deputies, who came with intent to reverse the last order, were, by force of reason, brought to uphold it; so that, when it was put to the vote, the last order for two deputies only was confirmed. Yet, the next day, a petition was brought to the court from the freemen of Roxbury, to have the third deputy restored. Whereupon the reasons of the court's proceedings were set down in writing, and all objections answered, and sent to such towns as were unsatisfied with this advice, that, if any could take away those reasons, or bring us better for what they did desire, we should be ready, at the next court, to repeal the said order.

The hands of some of the elders (learned and godly men) were to this petition, though suddenly drawn in, and without due consideration, for the lawfulness of it may well be questioned: for when the people have chosen men to be their rulers, and to make their laws, and bound themselves by oath to submit thereto, now to combine together (a lesser part of them) in a public petition to have any order repealed, which is not repugnant to the law of God, savors of resisting an ordinance of God; for the people, having deputed others, have no power to make or alter laws, but are to be subject; and if any such order seem unlawful or inconvenient, they were better prefer some reasons, etc., to the court, with manifestation of their desire to move them to a review, than peremptorily to petition to have it repealed, which amounts to a plain reproof of those whom God hath set over them, and putting dishonor upon them, against the tenor of the fifth commandment.

There fell out at this court another occasion of increasing the people's jealousy of their magistrates, viz.: One of the elders, being present with those of his church, when they were to prepare their votes for the election, declared his judgment, that a governor ought to be for his life, alleging for his authority the practice of all the best commonwealths in Europe, and especially that of Israel by God's own ordinance. But this was opposed by some other of the elders with much zeal, and so notice was taken of it by the people, not as a matter of dispute, but as if there had been some plot to put it in practice, which did occasion the deputies, at the next session of this court, to deliver in an order drawn to this effect: That, whereas our sovereign lord, King Charles, etc., had, by his patent, established a governor, deputy and assistants, that therefore no person, chosen a counsellor for life, should have any authority as a magistrate, except he were chosen in the annual elections to one of the said places of magistracy established by the patent. . . . That which led those of the council to yield to this desire of the deputies was, because it concerned themselves, and they did more study to remove these jealousies out of the people's heads, than to preserve any power or dignity to themselves above others; . . . And here may be observed, how strictly the people would seem to stick to their patent, where they think it makes for their advantage, but are content to decline it, where it will not warrant such liberties as they have taken up without warrant from thence, as appears in their strife for three deputies, etc., when as the patent allows them none at all, but only by inference. . . .[6]

[September 4, 1639.] The people had long desired a body of laws, and thought their condition very unsafe, while so much power rested in the discretion of magistrates. Divers attempts had been made at former courts, and the matter referred to some of the magistrates and some of the elders; but still it came to no effect; for, being committed to the care of many, whatsoever was done by some, was still disliked or neglected by others. At last it was referred to Mr. Cotton and Mr. Nathaniel Warde, etc., and each of them framed a model, which were presented to this general court, and by them committed to the governor and deputy and some others to consider of, and so prepare it for the court in the 3d month next. Two great reasons there were, which caused most of the magistrates and some of the elders not to be very forward in this matter. One was, want of sufficient experience of the nature and disposition of the people, considered with the condition of the country and other circumstances, which made them conceive, that such laws would be fittest for us, which should arise pro re nata upon occasions, etc., and so the laws of England and other states grew, and therefore the fundamental laws of England are called customs, consuetudines. 2. For that it would professedly transgress the limits of our charter, which provide, we shall make no laws repugnant to the laws of England, and that we were assured we must do. But to raise up laws by practice and custom had been no transgression; as in our church discipline, and in matters of marriage, to make a law, that marriages should not be solemnized by ministers, is repugnant to the laws of England; but to bring it to a custom by practice for the magistrates to perform it, is no law made repugnant, etc. At length (to satisfy the people) it proceeded, and the two models were digested with divers alterations and additions, and abbreviated and sent to every town, to be considered of first by the magistrates and elders, and then to be published by the constables to all the people, that if any man should think fit, that any thing therein ought to be altered, he might acquaint some of the deputies therewith against the next court.[7]

[June 21, 1641.] Some of the freemen, without the consent of the magistrates or governor, had chosen Mr. Nathaniel Ward to preach at this court, pretending that it was a part of their liberty. The governor (whose right indeed it is, for till the court be assembled the freemen are but private persons) would not strive about it, for though it did not belong to them, yet if they would have it, there was reason to yield it to them. . . . In his sermon he delivered many useful things, but in a moral and political discourse, grounding his propositions much upon the old Roman and Grecian governments, which sure is an error, for if religion and the word of God makes men wiser than their neighbors, and these times have the advantage of all that have gone before us in experience and observation, it is probable that by all these helps, we may better frame rules of government for oursevles than to receive others upon the bare authority of the wisdom, justice, etc. of those heathen commonwealths. Among other things, he advised the people to keep all their magistrates in an equal rank, and not give more honor or power to one than to another, which is easier to advise than to prove, seeing it is against the practice of Israel (where some were rulers of thousands, and some but of tens) and of all nations known or recorded.

WINTHROP'S SPEECH TO THE GENERAL COURT, JULY 3, 1645

I suppose something may be expected from me, upon this charge that is befallen me, which moves me to speak now to you; yet I intend not to intermeddle in the proceedings of the court, or with any of the persons concerned therein. Only I bless God, that I see an issue of this troublesome business. I also acknowledge the justice of the court, and, for mine own part, I am well satisfied, I was publicly charged, and I am publicly and legally acquitted, which is all I did expect or desire. And though this be sufficient for my justification before men, yet not so before the God, who hath seen so much amiss in my dispensations (and even in this affair) as calls me to be humble. For to be publicly and criminally charged in this court, is matter of humiliation, (and I desire to make a right use of it,) notwithstanding I be thus acquitted. If her father had spit in her face, (saith the Lord concerning Miriam,) should she not have been ashamed seven days? Shame had lien upon her, whatever the occasion had been. I am unwilling to stay you from your urgent affairs, yet give me leave (upon this special occasion) to speak a little more to this assembly. It may be of some good use, to inform and rectify the judgments of some of the people, and may prevent such distempers as have arisen amongst us. The great questions that have troubled the country, are about the authority of the magistrates and the liberty of the people. It is yourselves who have called us to this office, and being called by you, we have our authority from God, in way of an ordinance, such as hath the image of God eminently stamped upon it, the contempt and violation whereof hath been vindicated with examples of divine vengeance. I entreat you to consider, that when you choose magistrates, you take them from among yourselves, men subject to like passions as you are. Therefore when you see infirmities in us, you should reflect upon your own, and that would make you bear the more with us, and not be severe censurers of the failings of your magistrates, when you have continual experience of the like infirmities in yourselves and others. We account him a good servant, who breaks not his covenant. The covenant between you and us is the oath you have taken of us, which is to this purpose, that we shall govern you and judge your causes by the rules of God's laws and our own, according to our best skill. When you agree with a workman to build you a ship or house, etc., he undertakes as well for his skill as for his faithfulness, for it is his profession, and you pay him for both. But when you call one to be a magistrate, he doth not profess nor undertake to have sufficient skill for that office, nor can you furnish him with gifts, etc., therefore you must run the hazard of his skill and ability. But if he fail in faithfulness, which by his oath he is bound unto, that he must answer for. If it fall out that the case be clear to common apprehension, and the rule clear also, if he transgress here, the error is not in the skill, but in the evil of the will: it must be required of him. But if the case be doubtful, or the rule doubtful, to men of such understanding and parts as your magistrates are, if your magistrates should err here, yourselves must bear it.

For the other point concerning liberty, I observe a great mistake in the country about that. There is a twofold liberty, natural (I mean as our nature is now corrupt) and civil or federal. The first is common to man with beasts and other creatures. By this, man, as he stands in relation to man simply, hath liberty to do what he lists; it is a liberty to evil as well as to good. This liberty is incompatible and inconsistent with authority, and cannot endure the least restraint of the most just authority. The exercise and maintaining of this liberty makes men grow more evil, and in time to be worse than brute beasts: omnes sumus licentia deteriores. This is that great enemy of truth and peace, that wild beast, which all the ordinances of God are bent against, to restrain and subdue it. The other kind of liberty I call civil or federal, it may also be termed moral, in reference to the covenant between God and man, in the moral law, and the politic covenants and constitutions, amongst men themselves. This liberty is the proper end and object of authority, and cannot subsist without it; and it is a liberty to that only which is good, just, and honest. This liberty you are to stand for, with the hazard (not only of your goods, but) of your lives, if need be. Whatsoever crosseth this, is not authority, but a distemper thereof. This liberty is maintained and exercised in a way of subjection to authority; it is of the same kind of liberty wherewith Christ hath made us free. The woman's own choice makes such a man her husband; yet being so chosen, he is her lord, and she is to be subject to him, yet in a way of liberty, not of bondage; and a true wife accounts her subjection her honor and freedom, and would not think her condition safe and free, but in her subjection to her husband's authority. Such is the liberty of the church under the authority of Christ, her king and husband; his yoke is so easy and sweet to her as a bride's ornaments; and if through frowardness or wantonness, etc., she shake it off, at any time, she is at no rest in her spirit, until she take it up again; and whether her lord smiles upon her, and embraceth her in his arms, or whether he frowns, or rebukes, or smites her, she apprehends the sweetness of his love in all, and is refreshed, supported, and instructed by every such dispensation of his authority over her. On the other side, ye know who they are that complain of this yoke and say, let us break their bands, etc., we will not have this man to rule over us. Even so, brethren, it will be between you and your magistrates. If you stand for your natural corrupt liberties, and will do what is good in your own eyes, you will not endure the least weight of authority, but will murmur, and oppose, and be always striving to shake off that yoke; but if you will be satisfied to enjoy such civil and lawful liberties, such as Christ allows you, then will you quietly and cheerfully submit unto that authority which is set over you, in all the administrations of it, for your good. Wherein, if we fail at any time, we hope we shall be willing (by God's assistance) to hearken to good advice from any of you, or in any other way of God; so shall your liberties be preserved, in upholding the honor and power of authority amongst you.

JOHN COTTON, 1584–1652

[John Cotton, the son of a well-to-do attorney, was born in Derby, Derbyshire, and entered Trinity College, Cambridge, at the age of thirteen, taking his B.A. in 1603; he later migrated to Emmanuel College, taking his M.A. in 1606. He was chosen fellow and head lecturer of the College, was ordained in 1610 and became vicar of St. Botolph's, in Boston, Lincolnshire, in 1612, receiving degree of B.D. in 1613. For twenty years he was a conspicuous figure in the Church, enjoying a great reputation as a preacher and a theologian, protected from the Laudian power by the favor of powerful persons. He preached the farewell sermon to Winthrop's fleet in 1630; in 1633 he was at last forced to resign for nonconformity. He came to New England on the same ship with Thomas Hooker, the only other minister in New England who could approach him in reputation and learning. He was immediately chosen teacher of the Boston church. Though coming close to being ruined for the countenance he seemed to give to the teachings of Anne Hutchinson, he recovered himself in time, and remained the dominating figure in the councils of the New England clergy. His many writings on church polity were looked upon both in New England and in England as the standard expositions of the Congregational system, and his more general sermons and writings set the model for New England orthodoxy. For biography, see William Walker, *Ten New England Leaders*, and Cotton Mather, *Magnalia;* bibliography by Julius H. Tuttle in *Bibliographical Essays; A Tribute to Wilberforce Eames*, 1924.

When the New England migration occurred, the Puritan party in England had not yet come to any explicit agreement concerning the form of church organization they intended to set up in place of the episcopalian; the majority of Puritans had some species of Presbyterianism in mind, and they were often very much puzzled as stories of the New England system were carried back to England. They were still more bewildered when they heard rumors of political practices in Massachusetts which were the direct results of the church polity, but which seemed to run counter to the traditions and rights of Englishmen. Lord Say and Seal was a Puritan noble who meditated abandoning England; but Massachusetts did not sound too attractive to him, for there men were admitted to citizenship, regardless of their social position, only when they had become church members, and the noble Lord feared that he or some of his friends might be excluded. Cotton's reply is deferential but firm; he defends the franchise requirement as the very foundation of the Bible Commonwealth. The text is from Thomas Hutchinson, *History of Massachusetts Bay*, Vol. I, 1764, Appendix III.

The second passage, from a volume of Cotton's sermons, illustrates the other side of Puritan political theory, the conception of limitation by fundamental law and basic right. The letter to Lord Say and Seal can be reconciled with this passage only by means of the peculiar doctrine of the covenant found in Winthrop's speech on liberty. The text is from *An exposition upon the 13th Chapter of the Revelation* (London, 1656), pp. 71–73; published after his death, the book declares that the sermons were "Taken from his mouth in Short-writing."]

COPY OF A LETTER FROM MR. COTTON TO LORD SAY AND SEAL IN THE YEAR 1636.

RIGHT honourable,

. . . I am very apt to believe, what Mr. Perkins [1] hath, in one of his prefatory pages to his golden chaine, that the word, and scriptures of God doe conteyne a short *upoluposis*, or platforme, not onely of theology, but also of other sacred sciences, (as he calleth them) attendants, and handmaids thereunto, which he maketh ethicks, eoconomicks, politicks, church-government, prophecy, academy. It is very suitable to Gods all-sufficient wisdome, and to the fulnes and perfection of Holy Scriptures, not only to prescribe perfect rules for the right ordering of a private mans soule to everlasting blessednes with himselfe, but also for the right ordering of a mans family, yea, of the commonwealth too, so farre as both of them are subordinate to spiritual ends, and yet avoide both the churches usurpation upon civill jurisdictions, *in ordine ad spiritualia*,[2] and the commonwealths invasion upon ecclesiasticall administrations, *in ordine* to civill peace, and conformity to the civill state. Gods institutions (such as the government of church and of commonwealth be) may be close and compact, and co-ordinate one to another, and yet not confounded. God hath so framed the state of church government and ordinances, that they may be compatible to any common-wealth, though never so much disordered in his frame. But yet when a commonwealth hath liberty to mould his owne frame (*scripturæ plenitudinem adoro*)[3] I conceyve the scripture hath given full direction for the right ordering of the same, and that, in such sort as may best mainteyne the *euexia* [4] of the church. Mr. Hooker doth often quote a saying out of Mr. Cartwright (though I have not read it in him) that noe man fashioneth his house to his hangings, but his hangings to his house. It is better that the commonwealth be fashioned to the setting forth of Gods house, which is his church: than to accommodate the church frame to the civill state. Democracy, I do not conceyve that ever God did ordeyne as a fitt government eyther for church or commonwealth. If the people be governors, who shall be governed? As for monarchy, and aristocracy, they are both of them clearely approoved, and directed in scripture, yet so as referreth the soveraigntie to himselfe, and setteth up Theocracy in both, as the best forme of government in the commonwealth, as well as in the church.

The law, which your Lordship instanceth in (that none shall be chosen to magistracy among us but a church member) was made and enacted before I came into the country; but I have hitherto wanted sufficient light to plead against it. 1st. The rule that directeth the choice of supreame governors, is of like æquitie and weight in all magistrates, that one of their brethren (not a stranger) should be set over them, Deut. 17. 15. and Jethroes counsell to Moses was approved of God, that the judges, and officers to be set over the people, should be men fearing God, Exod. 18. 21. and Solomon maketh it the joy of a commonwealth, when the righteous are in authority, and their mourning when the wicked rule, Prov. 29. 21. Jab 34. 30. Your Lordship's feare, that this will bring in papal excommunication, is iust, and pious: but let your Lordship be pleased againe to consider whether the consequence be necessary. *Turpius ejicitur quam non admittitur:*[5] non-membership may be a just cause of non-admission to the place of magistracy. A godly woman, being to make choice of an husband, may justly refuse a man that is eyther cast out of church fellowship, or is not yet receyved into it, but yet, when shee is once given to him, shee may not reject him then, for such defect. Mr. Humfrey was chosen for an assistant (as I heare) before the colony came over hither: and, though he be not as yet ioyned into church fellowship (by reason of the unsetlednes of the congregation where he liveth) yet the commonwealth doe still continue his magistracy to him, as knowing he waiteth for oppertunity of enioying church fellowship shortly.

When your Lordship doubteth, that this corse will draw all things under the determination of the church, *in ordine ad spiritualia*[2] (seeing the church is to determine who shall be members, and none but a member may have to doe in the government of a commonwealth) be pleased (I pray you) to conceyve, that magistrates are neyther chosen to office in the church, nor doe governe by directions from the church, but by civill lawes, and those enacted in generall corts, and executed in corts of iustice, by the governors and assistants. In all which, the church (as the church) hath nothing to doe: onely, it prepareth fitt instruments both to rule, and to choose rulers, which is no ambition in the church, nor dishonor to the commonwealth, the apostle, on the contrary, thought it a great dishonor and reproach to the church of

Christ, if it were not able to yield able judges to heare and determine all causes amongst their brethren, I Cor. 6. 1. to 5. which place alone seemeth to me fully to decide this question: for it plainely holdeth forth this argument: It is a shame to the church to want able judges of civill matters (as v. 5.) and an audacious act in any church member voluntarily to go for judgment, otherwhere than before the saints (as v. 1.) then it will be noe arrogance nor folly in church members, nor prejudice to the commonwealth, if voluntarily they never choose any civill judges, but from amongst the saints, such as church members are called to be. But the former is cleare: and how then can the latter be avoyded. If this therefore be (as your Lordship rightly conceyveth one of the maine objections if not the onely one) which hindereth this commonwealth from the entertainment of the propositions of those worthy gentlemen, wee intreate them, in the name of the Lord Jesus, to consider, in meeknes of wisdome, it is not any conceite or will of ours, but the holy counsell and will of the Lord Jesus (whom they seeke to serve as well as wee) that overruleth us in this case: and we trust will overrule them also, that the Lord onely may be exalted amongst all his servants. What pittie and griefe were it, that the observance of the will of Christ should hinder good things from us!

But your Lordship doubteth, that if such a rule were necessary, then the church estate and the best ordered commonwealth in the world were not compatible. But let not your Lordship so conceyve. For, the church submitteth itselfe to all the lawes and ordinances of men, in what commonwealth soever they come to dwell. But it is one thing, to submit unto what they have noe calling to reforme: another thing, voluntarily to ordeyne a forme of government, which to the best discerning of many of us (for I speake not of myselfe) is expressly contrary to rule. Nor neede your Lordship feare (which yet I speake with submission to your Lordships better judgment) that this corse will lay such a foundation, as nothing but a mere democracy can be built upon it. Bodine[6] confesseth, that though it be *status popularis*, where a people choose their owne governors; yet the government is not a democracy, if it be administred, not by the people, but by the governors, whether one (for then it is a monarchy, though elective) or by many, for then (as you know) it is aristocracy. In which respect it is, that church government is iustly denyed (even by Mr. Robinson[7]) to be democratical, though the people choose their owne officers and rulers.

Nor neede wee feare, that this course will, in time, cast the commonwealth into distractions, and popular confusions. For (under correction) these three things doe not undermine, but doe mutually and strongly mainteyne one another (even those three which wee principally aime at) authority in magistrates, liberty in people, purity in the church. Purity, preserved in the church, will preserve well ordered liberty in the people, and both of them establish well-ballanced authority in the magistrates. God is the author of all these three, and neyther is himselfe the God of confusion, nor are his wayes the wayes of confusion, but of peace. . . .

Now the Lord Jesus Christ (the prince of peace) keepe and bless your Lordship, and dispose of all your times and talents to his best advantage: and let the covenant of his grace and peace rest upon your honourable family and posterity throughout all generations.

Thus, humbly craving pardon for my boldnesse and length, I take leave and rest,

Your Honours to serve in Christ Jesus,

J. C.

LIMITATION OF GOVERNMENT

THIS may serve to teach us the danger of allowing to any mortall man an inordinate measure of power to speak great things, to allow to any man uncontrollableness of speech, you see the desperate danger of it: Let all the world learn to give mortall men no greater power then they are content they shall use, for use it they will: and unlesse they be better taught of God, they will use it ever and anon, it may be make it the passage of their proceeding to speake what they will: And they that have liberty to speak great things, you will finde it to be true, they will speak great blasphemies. No man would think what desperate deceit and wickednesse there is in the hearts of men: And that was the reason why the Beast did speak such great things, hee might speak, and no body might controll him: What, saith the Lord in *Jer.* 3. 5. *Thou hast spoken and done evill things as thou couldst.* If a Church or head of a Church could have done worse, he would have done it: This is one of the straines of nature, it affects boundlesse liberty, and to runne to the utmost extent: What ever power he hath received, he hath a corrupt nature that will improve it in one thing or other; if he have liberty, he will think why may he not use it. Set up the Pope as Lord Paramount over Kings and Princes, and they shall know that he hath power over them, he will take liberty to depose one, and set up another. Give him power to make Laws, and he will approve, and disprove as he list; what he approves is Canonicall, what hee disproves is rejected: Give him that power, and he will so order it at length, he will make such a State of Religion, that he that so lives and dyes shall never be saved, and all this springs from the vast power that is given to him, and from the deep depravation of nature. Hee will open his mouth, *His tongue is his owne, who is Lord over him*, Psal. 12. 3, 4. It is therefore most wholsome for Magistrates and Officers in Church and Common-wealth, never to affect more liberty and authority then will do them good, and the People good; for what ever transcendant power is given, will certainly over-run those that give it, and those that receive it: There is a straine in a mans heart that will sometime or other runne out to excesse, unlesse the Lord restraine it, but it is not good to venture it: It is necessary therefore, that all power that is on earth be limited, Church-power or other: If there be power given to speak great things, then look for great blasphemies, look for a licentious abuse of it. It is counted a matter of danger to the State to limit Prerogatives; but it is a further danger, not to have them limited: They will be like a Tempest, if they be not limited: A Prince himselfe cannot tell where hee will confine himselfe, nor can the people tell: But if he have liberty to speak great things, then he will make and unmake, say and unsay, and undertake such things as are neither for his owne honour, nor for the safety of the State. It is therefore fit for every man to be studious of the bounds which the Lord hath set: and for the People, in whom fundamentally all power lyes, to give as much power as God in his word gives to men: And it is meet that Magistrates in the Commonwealth, and so Officers in Churches should desire to know the utmost bounds of their own power, and it is safe for both: All intrenchment upon the bounds which God hath not given, they are not enlargements, but burdens and snares; They will certainly lead the spirit of a man out of his way sooner or later. It is wholsome and safe to be dealt withall as God deales with the vast Sea; *Hitherto shalt thou come, but there shalt thou stay thy proud waves:* and therefore if they be but banks of simple sand, they will be good enough to check the vast roaring Sea. And so for Imperiall Monarchies, it is safe to know how far their power extends; and then if it be but banks of sand, which is most slippery, it will serve, as well as any brazen wall. If you pinch the Sea of its liberty, though it be walls of stone or brasse, it will beate them downe: So it is with Magistrates, stint them where God hath not stinted them, and if they were walls of brasse, they would beate them downe, and it is meet they should: but give them the liberty God allows, and if it be but a wall of sand it will keep them: As this liquid Ayre in which we breath, God hath set it for the waters of the Clouds to the Earth; It is a Firmament, it is the Clouds, yet it stands firme enough, because it keeps the Climate where they are, it shall stand like walls of brasse: So let there be due bounds set, and I may apply it to Families; it is good for the Wife to acknowledg all power and authority to the Husband, and for the Husband to acknowledg honour to the Wife, but still give them that which God hath given them, and no more nor lesse: Give them the full latitude that God hath given, else you will finde you dig pits, and lay snares, and cumber their spirits, if you give them lesse: there is never peace where full liberty is not given, nor never stable peace where more then full liberty is granted: Let them be duely observed, and give men no more liberty then God doth, nor women, for they will abuse it: The Devill will draw them, and Gods providence leade them thereunto, therefore give them no more then God gives. And so for children; and servants, or any others you are to deale with, give them the liberty and authority you would have them use, and beyond that stretch not the tether, it will not tend to their good nor yours: And also from hence gather, and goe home with this meditation; That certainly here is this distemper in our natures, that we cannot tell how to use liberty, but wee shall very readily corrupt our selves: Oh the bottomlesse depth of sandy earth! of a corrupt spirit, that breaks over all bounds, and loves inordinate vastnesse; that is it we ought to be carefull of.

ROGER WILLIAMS, 1604–1683

[Roger Williams, son of a London merchant tailor, attracted the attention of Sir Edward Coke, the great jurist, through whose influence he was elected pensioner at Sutton's Hospital (Charterhouse) in 1621; admitted pensioner at Pembroke College, Cambridge, in 1623, he took his B.A. in 1627. He first landed in New England in 1631, and was chosen teacher of the church of Salem, but objecting that the church had not "separated" from the Church of England, he refused the office and went to Plymouth, where he ministered for a year or so, but was not officially ordained; in 1633 he returned to Salem, was again chosen minister, and accepted the post. Thereupon he began a two-year career of agitation and trouble-making that ended with his banishment in October, 1635. He continued to demand that the churches of New England announce their separation from the Church of England, at a time when all the ingenuity the authorities could muster was being expended in proving that they never had seceded from the true Church of England; he attacked the charter on the ground that the King of England had no title to the land and that the colonists needed only to purchase Massachusetts from the Indians; he denied that a magistrate could tender an oath to an unregenerate man, thus promising to upset the whole judicial system of the colony; finally, when he was being dealt with for these heresies, he broached the idea that the civil magistrates had no power to punish persons for their religious opinions. Sentence of banishment was pronounced upon him in October, 1635, but he was allowed to remain in Salem for the winter on condition that he keep quiet; in January the Court heard that people of Salem were resorting to his house and sent Captain Underhill to arrest him; probably John Winthrop sent him a warning, and he fled to the Narragansett country in the dead of winter (cf. p. 484). Thus he became the founder of Providence, Rhode Island, and the principal guide and statesman for that tumultuous colony. He became a Baptist in 1639, but in a few months renounced even that creed, and for the rest of his life called himself a "seeker," one who was always searching for the pure truth but did not expect to find it in this world. He went to England as agent for Rhode Island in 1643; during the voyage he wrote his *Key into the Language of America;* he was always on particularly good terms with the Indians, and rendered the colonies of Massachusetts Bay and Connecticut great service as ambassador and spy. While in England he became a friend of John Milton and published two books attacking John Cotton as the spokesman for the orthodox theory of persecution. The more important of these, *The Bloudy Tenent of Persecution,* was ordered by Parliament to be burned by the common hangman. John Cotton replied with *The Bloudy Tenent, washed, And made white in the bloud of the Lambe* (London, 1647). Williams secured a charter for the Rhode Island settlements, and in 1651 returned to England once more to defend this charter; on this occasion he published his reply to Cotton's reply, entitled *The Bloody Tenent yet More Bloody: by Mr Cottons endevour to wash it white in the Blood of the Lambe.* He served as governor of Rhode Island from 1654 to 1657, supported himself in his last years by trade with the Indians, and died in poverty as a result of King Phillip's War. Biographies by J. M. Straus, 1894, Edmund J. Carpenter, 1909, James E. Ernst, 1932. This text is from *The Bloudy Tenent,* ed. Samuel L. Caldwell, *Publications of the Narragansett Club,* Vol. III (Providence, 1867).]

THE BLOUDY TENENT OF PERSECUTION

To every Courteous Reader.

WHILE I plead the Cause of *Truth* and *Innocencie* against the bloody *Doctrine* of *Persecution* for cause of *conscience*, I judge it not unfit to give *alarme* to my selfe, and all men to prepare to be *persecuted* or hunted for cause of *conscience*.

Whether thou standest charged with 10 or but 2 *Talents*, if thou huntest any for cause of *conscience*, how canst thou say thou followest the *Lambe* of *God* who so abhorr'd that practice? . . .

Who can now but expect that after so many scores of yeares *preaching* and *professing* of more *Truth*, and amongst so many great *contentions* amongst the very best of *Protestants*, a fierie furnace should be heat, and who sees not now the *fires* kindling?

I confesse I have little hopes till those flames are over, that this Discourse against the *doctrine* of *persecution* for cause of *conscience* should passe currant (I say not amongst the *Wolves* and *Lions*, but even amongst the *Sheep* of *Christ* themselves) yet *liberavi animam meam*,[1] I have not hid within my *breast* my *souls* belief: And although sleeping on the bed either of the pleasures or profits of sinne thou thinkest thy conscience bound to smite at him that dares to waken thee? Yet in the middest of all these *civill* and *spirituall Wars* (I hope we shall agree in these particulars.)

First, how ever the proud (upon the advantage of an higher earth or ground) or'elooke the poore and cry out *Schismatickes*, *Hereticks*, &c. shall *blasphemers* and *seducers* scape unpunished? &c. Yet there is a sorer punishment in the *Gospel* for despising of *Christ* then *Moses*, even when the despiser of *Moses* was put to death without mercie, *Heb*. 10. 28, 29. He that beleeveth not shall bee damned, *Marke* 16. 16.

Secondly, what ever Worship, Ministry, Ministration, the best and purest are practised without *faith* and true perswasion that they are the true institutions of God, they are sin, sinfull worships, Ministries, &c. And however in Civill things we may be servants unto men, yet in Divine and Spirituall things the poorest *pesant* must disdaine the service of the highest *Prince:* Be ye not the servants of men, I Cor. 14.

Thirdly, without search and triall no man attaines this faith and right perswasion, I *Thes.* 5. Try all things.

In vaine have *English Parliaments* permitted *English Bibles* in the poorest *English* houses, and the simplest man or woman to search the Scriptures, if yet against their soules perswasion from the Scripture, they should be forced (as if they lived in *Spaine* or *Rome* it selfe without the sight of a *Bible*) to beleeve as the Church beleeves.

Fourthly, having tried, we must hold fast, I *Thessal.* 5. upon the losse of a Crowne, *Revel.* 13. we must not let goe for all the flea bitings of the present afflictions, &c. having bought Truth deare, we must not sell it cheape, not the least graine of it for the whole World, no not for the saving of Soules, though our owne most precious; least of all for the bitter sweetning of a little vanishing pleasure.

For a little puffe of credit and reputation from the changeable breath of uncertaine sons of men.

For the broken bagges of Riches on Eagles wings: For a dreame of these, any or all of these which on our death-bed vanish and leave tormenting stings behinde them: Oh how much better is it from the love of Truth, from the love of the Father of lights, from whence it comes, from the love of the Sonne of God, who is the way and the Truth, to say as he, *John* 18. 37. For this end was I borne, and for this end came I into the World that I might beare witnesse to the Truth.

The ANSWER Of Mr. Iohn Cotton of Boston in New-England, . . . Professedly maintеining Persecution for Cause of Conscience.[2]

The *Question* which you put, is, Whether *Persecution* for cause of *Conscience*, be not against the *Doctrine* of *Jesus Christ* the *King of Kings*.

Now by *Persecution* for Cause of *Conscience*, I conceive you meane, either for professing some point of *Doctrine* which you believe in Conscience to be the Truth, or for practising some *Worke* which in *Conscience* you believe to be a *Religious Duty*.

Now in Points of *Doctrine* some are *fundamentall*, without right beliefe whereof a Man cannot be *saved:* Others are *circumstantiall* or lesse principall, wherein Men may differ in judgement, without prejudice of *salvation* on either part.

In like sort, in Points of *Practice*, some concerne the waightier Duties of the *Law*, as, What *God* we worship, and with what kinde of *Worship;* whether such, as if it be *Right*, fellowship with *God* is held; if *Corrupt*, fellowship with Him is lost.

Againe, in Points of *Doctrine* and *Worship* lesse Principall: either they are held forth in a meeke and *peaceable* way, though the Things be *Erroneous* or unlawfull: Or they are held forth with such *Arrogance* and *Impetuousnesse*, as tendeth and reacheth (even of it selfe) to the disturbance of *Civill Peace*.

Finally, let me adde this one distinction more: When we are persecuted for *Conscience* sake, It is either for *Conscience* rightly informed, or for erronious and blind *Conscience*.

These things premised, I would lay down mine
Answer to the Question in certaine *Conclusions*.

First, it is not lawfull to persecute any for *Conscience* sake *Rightly informed;* for in *persecuting* such, *Christ* himselfe is persecuted in them, *Acts* 9. 4.

Secondly, for an *Erronious* and *blind Conscience*, (even in fundamentall and weighty Points) It is not lawfull to persecute any, till after *Admonition* once or twice: and so the Apostle directeth, *Tit.* 3. 10. and giveth the Reason, that in *fundamentall* and principall points of Doctrine or Worship, the Word of *God* in such things is so cleare, that hee cannot but bee convinced in *Conscience* of the dangerous Errour of his way, after once or twice *Admonition*, wisely and faithfully dispensed. And then if any one persist, it is not out of *Conscience*, but against *his Conscience*, as the Apostle saith, *vers.* 11. He is subverted and sinneth, being condemned of Himselfe, that is, of his owne *Conscience*. So that if such a Man after such Admonition shall still *persist* in the Errour of his way, and be therefore punished; He is not *persecuted* for Cause of *Conscience*, but for sinning *against* his Owne *Conscience*.

Reply to the Aforesaid Answer of Mr. Cotton.

In a Conference betweene *Truth and Peace*.

Truth. In what *darke corner* of the World (*sweet Peace*) are *we two* met? How hath this present evill *World* banished *Me* from all the Coasts & Quarters of it? and how hath the Righteous *God* in judgement taken *Thee* from the *Earth*, Rev. 6. 4.

Peace. 'Tis lamentably true (*blessed Truth*) the *foundations* of the *World* have long been out of course: the *Gates* of *Earth* and *Hell* have conspired together to intercept our joyfull *meeting* and our holy *kisses:* With what a wearied, *tyred Wing* have I flowne over *Nations*, *Kingdomes*, *Cities*, *Townes*, to finde out precious *Truth?*

Truth and Peace rarely and seldom meete.

Truth. The like enquiries in my flights and travells have I made for *Peace*, and still am told, she hath left the *Earth*, and fled to *Heaven*.

Peace. Deare *Truth*, What is the *Earth* but a *dungeon of darknesse*, where *Truth* is not?

Truth. And what's the *Peace* thereof but a fleeting *dreame*, thine *Ape* and *Counterfeit?*

Peace. O where's the Promise of the *God* of *Heaven*, that *Righteousnes* and *Peace* shall *kisse* each other?

Truth. Patience (sweet *Peace*) these *Heavens* and *Earth* are growing *Old*, and shall be changed like a *Garment*, Psal. 102. They shall melt away, and be burnt up with all the *Works* that are therein; and the most high *Eternall Creatour*, shall gloriously create *New Heavens* and *New Earth*, wherein dwells *Righteousnesse*, 2 Pet. 3. Our *kisses* then shall have their *endlesse* date of pure and sweetest ioyes? till then both *Thou* and *I* must hope, and wait, and beare the furie of the *Dragons* wrath, whose *monstrous Lies* and *Furies* shall with himselfe be cast into the *lake* of *Fire*, the *second death*, Revel. 20. . . .

Truth. In the Answer Mr. *Cotton* first layes downe severall *distinctions* and *conclusions* of his owne, tending to prove persecution. . . .

Peace. The first distinction is this: By persecution for cause of *Conscience*, "I conceive you meane either for professing some point of *doctrine* which you beleeve in *conscience* to be the *truth*, or for *practising* some worke which you beleeve in *conscience* to be a *religious* dutie.["]

The first distinction discussed.

Truth. I acknowledge that to molest any person, *Jew* or *Gentile*, for either professing *doctrine*, or practising *worship* meerly *religious* or spirituall, it is to persecute him, and such a person (what ever his *doctrine* or *practice* be true or *false*) suffereth persecution for *conscience*.

Definition of persecution discussed.

But withall I desire it may bee well observed, that this *distinction* is not full and complete: For beside this that a man may be persecuted because he holdeth or practiseth what he beleeves in *conscience* to be a *Truth*, (as *Daniel* did, for which he was cast into the *Lyons* den, *Dan.* 6.) and many thousands of *Christians*, because they durst not cease to *preach* and *practise* what they beleeved was by *God* commanded, as the *Apostles* answered (*Acts* 4. & 5.) I say besides this a man may also be persecuted, because hee dares not be *constrained* to yeeld obedience to such *doctrines* and *worships* as are by men invented and appointed. So the three famous *Jewes* were cast into the fiery furnace for refusing to fall downe (in a *non-conformity* to the whole conforming world) before the golden *Image*, Dan. 3. 21. So thousands of *Christs witnesses* (and of late in those bloudy *Marian* dayes) have rather chose to yeeld their *bodies* to all sorts of *torments*, then to subscribe to *doctrines*, or practise *worships*, unto which the States and Times (as *Nabuchadnezzar* to his golden *Image*) have compelled and urged them . . .

Conscience will not be restrained from its own worship, nor constrained to another.

Truth. . . . *Gods people* were and ought to be *Nonconformitants*, not daring either to be *restrained* from the *true*, or *constrained* to *false Worship*, and yet without *breach* of the Civill or *Citie-peace*, properly so called.

Gods people must be Non-conformitants to Evill.

Peace. Hence it is that so many glorious and flourishing *Cities* of the World maintaine their *Civill* peace, yea the very *Americans* & wildest *Pagans* keep the peace of their *Towns* or *Cities;* though neither in one nor the other can any man prove a true *Church* of God in those places, and consequently no spirituall and heavenly peace: The Peace *spirituall* (whether true or false) being of a higher and farre different nature from the Peace of the place or people, being meerly and essentially *civill* and *humane.*

The difference between Spirituall and Civill Peace.

Truth. O how lost are the sonnes of men in this point? To illustrate this: The *Church* or *company* of *worshippers* (whether true or false) is like unto a Body or Colledge of *Physitians* in a *Citie;* like unto a *Corporation*, *Society*, *or Company* of *East-Indie* or *Turkie-Merchants*, or any other *Societie* or *Company* in *London:* which Companies may hold their *Courts*, keep their *Records*, hold *disputations;* and in matters concerning their *Societie*, may dissent, divide, breake into *Schismes* and *Factions*, sue and implead each other at the *Law*, yea wholly breake up and dissolve into pieces and nothing, and yet the *peace* of the *Citie* not be in the least measure impaired or disturbed; because the *essence* of being of the *Citie*, and so the *well-being* and *peace* thereof is essentially distinct from those particular *Societies;* the *Citie-Courts*, *Citie-Lawes*, *Citie-*

The difference between the Spirituall and Civill State.

punishments distinct from theirs. The *Citie* was before them, and stands absolute and intire, when such a *Corporation* or *Societie* is taken down . . .

Peace. Yea but it is said that the blinde *Pharises* misguiding the subjects of a *Civill State*, greatly sinne against a *Civill State*, and therefore justly suffer *civill punishment;* for shall the *Civill Magistrate* take care of *outsides* only, to wit, of the bodies of men, and not of soules, in labouring to procure their everlasting welfare?

Soul killing the chiefest murder. No Magistrate can execute true justice in killing soule for soule, but Christ Jesus who by typicall death in the Law, typed out spirituall in the Gospel.

Truth. I answer, It is a *truth*, the mischiefe of a blinde *Pharises* blinde *guidance* is greater then if he acted Treasons, Murders, &c. and the losse of one soule by his seduction is a greater mischiefe then if he blew up Parliaments, and cuts the throats of Kings or Emperours, so pretious is that invaluable Jewell of a Soul, above all the present lives and bodies of all the men in the world! and therefore a firme Justice calling for *eye* for *eye*, *tooth* for *tooth*, *life* for *life;* calls also *soule* for *soule*, which the blind-guiding seducing *Pharisee* shall surely pay in that dreadfull Ditch, which the Lord Jesus speakes of, but this sentence against him the Lord Jesus only pronounceth in His *Church*, His *spirituall judicature*, and executes this *sentence* in part at present and hereafter to all eternity: Such a *sentence* no *Civill Judge* can passe, such a *Death* no *Civill sword* can inflict.

A great mistake in most to conceive that dead men, that is, soules dead in sin may be infected by false doctrine.

I answer secondly, *Dead men* cannot be infected, the *civill state*, the *world*, being in a naturall state dead in sin (what ever be the *State Religion* unto which *persons* are forced) it is impossible it should be infected: . . .

All naturall men being dead in sin, yet none die everlastingly but such as are thereunto ordained.

Moreover as we see in a *common plague* or *infection* the names are taken how many are to dye, and not one more shall be strucke, then the destroying *Angel* hath the names of. So here, what ever be the soule *infection* breathed out from they lying lips of a *plague-sicke Pharisee*, yet the names are taken, not one *elect* or chosen of *God* shall perish, *Gods sheep* are safe in His *eternall hand* and *counsell*, and he that knowes his *materiall*, knows also his *mysticall stars*, their *numbers*, and calls them every one by *name*, none fall into the *Ditch* on the blinde *Pharises* backe, but such as were *ordained* to that *condemnation*, both *guid* and *followers*, I *Pet.* 2. 8. *Jude* 4. The *vessells* of *wrath* shall breake and split, and only they to the praise of *Gods* eternall *justice*, *Rom.* 9. . . .

Truth. . . . I observe that he implyes that beside the *censure* of the *Lord Jesus*, in the hands of his *spirituall governours*, for any spirituall evill in *life* or *doctrine*, the *Civill Magistrate* is also to inflict *corporall punishment* upon the contrary minded: whereas

If the Civill Magistrate be a Christian, he is bound to be like Christ in saving, not destroying mens bodies.

First, if the *Civill Magistrate* be a *Christian*, a *Disciple* or follower of the meeke *Lambe* of *God*, he is bound to be far from destroying the *bodies of men*, for refusing to receive the *Lord Jesus Christ*, for otherwise hee should not know (according to this speech of the *Lord Iesus*) what *spirit* he was of, yea and to be ignorant of the sweet end of the comming of the *Son of Man*, which was not to destroy the *bodies of Men*, but to save both *bodies* and *soules*, *vers*. 55. 56.

The Civill Magistrate bound not to inflict nor to suffer any other to inflict violence, stripes, or any corporall punishment for evill against Christ.

Secondly, if the *Civill Magistrate*, being a *Christian*, gifted, *prophesie* in the *Church*, I *Corinth*. 1. 14. although the *Lord Iesus Christ*, whom they in their owne persons hold forth, shall be refused, yet they are here forbidden to call for fire from *heaven*, that is, to procure or inflict any corporall *judgement* upon such *offenders*, remembring the end of the *Lord Iesus* his comming, not to *destroy* mens lives, but to *save* them.

Lastly, this also concernes the *conscience* of the *Civill Magistrate*, as he is bound to preserve the *civill peace* and quiet of the *place* and people under him, he is bound to suffer no man to breake the *Civill Peace*, by laying hands of *violence* upon any, though as vile as the *Samaritanes* for not receiving of the *Lord Iesus Christ*.

Revel. 13 13. Fire from heaven. What the fire from heaven is which the fals prophet bringeth downe.

It is indeed the *ignorance* and blind *zeale* of the second *Beast*, the *false Prophet*, *Rev*. 13. 13. to perswade the *civill Powers* of the earth to persecute the Saints, that is, to bring fiery *judgements* upon men in a *judiciall way*, and to pronounce that such *judgements* of *imprisonment*, *banishment*, *death*, proceed from Gods righteous *vengeance* upon such *Hereticks*. So dealt divers *Bishops* in *France*, and *England* too in Queene *Maries* dayes with the Saints of God at their putting to death, declaiming against them in their Sermons to the people, and proclaiming that these persecutions even unto death were Gods *just judgements from heaven upon these Heretickes*. . . .

Spirituall weapons only effectuall in spirituall & soule causes.

Truth. . . . To batter downe *Idolatry*, *false worship*, *heresie*, *schisme*, *blindnesse*, *hardnesse*, out of the *soule* and *spirit*, it is vaine, improper, and unsutable to bring those *weapons* which are used by *persecutors*, *stocks*, *whips*, *prisons*, *swords*, *gibbets*, *stakes*, &c. (where these seem to prevaile with some Cities or Kingdomes, a stronger force sets up againe, what a weaker pull'd downe) but against these *spirituall strong holds* in the soules of men, *Spirituall Artillery* and *weapons* are proper, which are mighty through *God* to subdue and bring under the very *thought* to *obedience*, or else to binde fast the soule with *chaines* of *darknesse*, and to locke it up in the *prison* of *unbeleefe* and hardnesse to *eternity*.

Civill weapons not only improper, but unnecessary in spirituall causes.

I observe that as *civill weapons* are improper in this businesse, and never able to effect ought in the *soule:* So (although they were proper, yet) they are *unnecessary*, for if as the *Spirit* here saith (and the *Answerer* grants) *spirituall weapons* in the hand of *Church officers* are able and ready to take *vengeance* on all disobedience, that is *able* and mighty, sufficient and ready for the *Lords* worke either to *save* the soule, or to *kill* the soule of whomsoever, be the party or parties opposite, in which respect I may againe remember that speech of *Job*, How hast thou helped him that hath no power? *Job* 26. . . .

Spirituall Ammunition. Eph. 6. applied Materiall and Spirituall Artillery unfitly joyned together.

Will the *Lord Jesus* (did He ever in His owne Person practice, or did he appoint to) joyne to His *Breastplate* of *Righteousnesse*, the *breastplate* of *iron* and *steele?* to the *Helmet* of *righteousnesse* and *salvation* in *Christ*, an helmet and crest of *iron*, *brasse*, or *steel*, a target of wood to His shield of Faith? [to] His two *edged sword* comming forth of the mouth of *Jesus*, the *materiall sword*, the worke of Smiths and Cutlers? or a girdle of shooes leather to the girdle of truth, &c. Excellently fit and proper is that *alarme* and *item*, *Psal.* 2. Be *wise* therefore O ye *Kings* (especially those ten *Horns*, *Rev.* 17.) who under pretence of fighting for *Christ Jesus* give their power to the *Beast* against *Him*, and be warned ye *Judges* of the Earth: *Kisse the Son*, that is with *subjection* and *affection*, acknowledge Him only the *King* and *Judge* of *soules* (in that power bequeathed to His *Ministers* and *Churches*) lest if His wrath be kindled, yea but a little, then *blessed* are they that *trust in* Him. . . .

An alarme to civill or earthly Rulers.

The doctrine of persecution necessarily and most commonly falls heaviest upon the most godly persons.

Peace. Yea but (say they) the *godly* will not persist in *Heresie* or turbulent *Schisme*, when they are convinced in *Conscience*, *&c.*

Truth. Sweet *Truth*, if the Civill Court and *Magistracy* must judge (as before I have written) and those Civill Courts are as lawfull, consisting of *naturall men* as of *godly* persons, then what *consequences* necessarily will follow, I have before mentioned. And I adde, according to this *conclusion* it must follow, that, if the most *godly* persons yeeld not to once or twice *Admonition* (as is maintained by the *Answerer*) they must necessarily be esteemed *obstinate* persons, for if they were *godly* (saith he) they would yeeld. Must it not then be said (as it was by one, passing sentence of *Banishment* upon some, whose godlinesse was acknowledged) that he that commanded the *Judge* not to respect the poore in the cause of *judgement*, commands him not to respect the holy or the godly person?

The doctrine of persecution drives the most godly persons out of the world.

Hence I could name the place and time when a *godly* man, a most desirable person for his trade, &c. (yet something different in *conscience*) propounded his willingnesse and desire to come to dwell in a certaine *Towne* in *New England;* it was answered by the Chiefe of the place, This man differs from us, and wee desire not to be troubled. So that in conclusion (for no other reason in the world) the poore man, though godly, usefull and peaceable, could not be admitted to a Civill Being and Habitation on the Common Earth in that Wildernesse amongst them. . . .

Peace. Mr. *Cotton* concludes with a confident perswasion of having removed the grounds of that great *errour, viz.* that persons are not to be persecuted for cause of *conscience*.

The bloody Tenent.

Truth. And I beleeve (deare *Peace*) it shall appear to them that (with feare and trembling at the word of the Lord) examine these passages, that the charge of *errour* reboundeth backe[,] even such an *errour*, as may well bee called the *bloody tenent*, so directly contradicting the *spirit* and *minde* and *practice* of the *Prince* of *Peace;* so deeply guilty of the *blood* of soules compelled and forced to *Hypocrisie* in a *spirituall* and *soule rape;* so deeply guilty of the *blood* of the *Soules* under the *Altar*, persecuted in all *ages* for the *cause* of *Conscience*, and so destructive to the *civill peace* and *welfare* of all *Kingdomes*, *Countries*, and *Commonwealths*.

LETTER TO THE TOWN OF PROVIDENCE,
January, 1655

[Upon his return from England in 1654 Roger Williams found the town of Providence torn by internal dissension; he was instrumental in restoring order, but soon afterwards a paper was circulating among the citizens proclaiming that it was contrary to the Gospel to execute judgment upon transgressors against the public or private weal. Williams thereupon wrote the following letter to the town in order to explain precisely what were the limits he prescribed to the liberal views he had maintained against John Cotton and the authorities of Massachusetts Bay. This text is from *Letters, Publications of the Narragansett Club*, Vol. VI (Providence, 1874), pp. 278–279.]

That ever I should speak or write a tittle, that tends to such an infinite liberty of conscience, is a mistake, and which I have ever disclaimed and abhorred. To prevent such mistakes, I shall at present only propose this case: There goes many a ship to sea, with many hundred souls in one ship, whose weal or woe is common, and is a true picture of a commonwealth, or a human combination or society. It hath fallen out sometimes, that both papists and protestants, Jews and Turks, may be embarked in one ship; upon which supposal I affirm, that all the liberty of conscience, that ever I pleaded for, turns upon these two hinges—that none of the papists, protestants, Jews, or Turks, be forced to come to the ship's prayers or worship, nor compelled from their own particular prayers or worship, if they practice any. I further add, that I never denied, that notwithstanding this liberty, the commander of this ship ought to command the ship's course, yea, and also command that justice, peace and sobriety, be kept and practiced, both among the seamen and all the passengers. If any of the seamen refuse to perform their services, or passengers to pay their freight; if any refuse to help, in person or purse, towards the common charges or defence; if any refuse to obey the common laws and orders of the ship, concerning their common peace or preservation; if any shall mutiny and rise up against their commanders and officers; if any should preach or write that there ought to be no commanders or officers, because all are equal in Christ, therefore no masters nor officers, no laws nor orders, nor corrections nor punishments; —I say, I never denied, but in such cases, whatever is pretended, the commander or commanders may judge, resist, compel and punish such transgressors, according to their deserts and merits. This if seriously and honestly minded, may, if it so please the Father of lights, let in some light to such as willingly shut not their eyes.

I remain studious of your common peace and liberty.

Roger Williams.

NATHANIEL WARD, 1578–1652

[Nathaniel Ward was an older man than most of the first ministers in New England and had a much more varied and secular career; these facts must be remembered in accounting for his style, the peculiar quality of his writings, his wit, and his part in formulating the laws of Massachusetts Bay. He was born at Haverhill, Essex, the son of a minister; admitted sizar at Emmanuel College, 1596, he took his B.A. in 1600, his M.A. in 1603. He studied and practised law, traveled widely on the continent, and became a minister only in 1618. He served as chaplain to an English factory at Ebling; returning to England he was curate of St. James's, Picadilly, and of Stondon Massey in Essex. A participant in the formation of the Massachusetts Bay Company, he came to New England after he was silenced by Laud in 1634. For two years he served as minister at Ipswich (of which the Indian name was Aggawam), resigned in 1636, but remained in Massachusetts until 1646. He drew up the *Body of Liberties* in 1641 (cf. p. 204). Over the mantel of his house in Ipswich a former occupant is said to have carved three words representing the sum of Puritan ethics: sobriety, justice, and piety; Nathaniel Ward added the word laughter. He is reported to have said at one time, "I have two comforts to live upon: The one is, in the Perfections of Christ: the other is in the imperfections of all Christians." After his return to England he preached a sermon before the House of Commons, and in 1648 was made minister of Shenfield, Essex. He wrote his pamphlet in 1645; it was published in London in 1647. This text is from the first and third editions. The full title of the book is:

The Simple Cobler of Aggawam in America. Willing to help 'mend his Native Country, lamentably tattered, both in the upper-Leather and sole, with all the honest stiches he can take.

And as willing never to bee paid for his work, by Old English wonted pay.
It is his Trade to patch all the year long, gratis
Therefore I pray Gentlemen keep your purses.

It was announced as written by "Theodore de la Guard." Cf. S. E. Morison, *Builders of the Bay Colony;* J. W. Dean, *Nathaniel Ward,* 1868; *New England Historical & Genealogical Register,* XVI, 365; XLI, 282.]

THE SIMPLE COBLER OF AGGAWAM

SATHAN is now in his passions, hee feeles his passion approaching; he loves to fish in royled waters. Though that Dragon cannot sting the vitals of the Elect mortally, yet that Beelzebub can fly-blow their Intellectuals miserably: The finer Religion grows, the finer he spins his Cobwebs, he will hold pace with Christ so long as his wits will serve him. Hee sees himselfe beaten out of grosse Idolatries, Heresies, Ceremonies, where the Light breakes forth with power; he will therefore bestirre him to prevaricate Evangelicall Truths, and Ordinances, that if they will needs be walking, yet they shall *laborare varicibus*,[1] and not keep their path: he will put them out of time and place; Assascinating for his Engineers, men of Paracelsian [2] parts, well complexioned for honesty; for, such are fittest to Mountebanke his Chimistry into sicke Churches and weake Judgements.

Nor shall hee neede to stretch his strength overmuch in this worke: Too many men having not laid their foundation sure, nor ballasted their Spirits deep with humility and feare, are prest enough of themselves to evaporate their owne apprehensions. Those that are acquainted with Story know, it hath ever been so in new Editions of Churches: Such as are least able, are most busy to pudder in the rubbish, and to raise dust in the eyes of more steady Repayrers. Civill Commotions make room for uncivill practises: Religious mutations, for irreligious opinions: Change of aire, discovers corrupt bodies: Reformation of Religion, unsound mindes. He that hath any well-faced phancy in his Crowne, and doth not vent it now, feares, the pride of his own heart will dub him duns for ever. Such a one will trouble the whole *Israel* of God with his most untimely births, though he makes the bones of his vanity stick up, to the view and griefe of all that are godly wise. The devill desires no better sport then to see light heads handle their heeles, and fetch their carreers in a time, when the Roofe of Liberty stands open.

The next perplexed Question, with pious and ponderous men, will be: What should be done for the healing of these comfortlesse exulcerations. I am the unablest adviser of a thousand, the unworthiest of ten thousand; yet I hope I may presume to assert what follows without just offence.

First, such as have given or taken any unfriendly reports of us *New-English*, should doe well to recollect themselves. We have been reputed a Colluvies of wild Opinionists, swarmed into a remote wildernes to find elbow-roome for our phanatick Doctrines and practises: I trust our diligence past, and constant sedulity against such persons and courses, will plead better things for us. I dare take upon me, to be the Herauld of *New-England* so farre, as to proclaime to the world, in the name of our Colony, that all Familists, Antinomians, Anabaptists, and other Enthusiasts, shall have free Liberty to keep away from us, and such as will come to be gone as fast as they can, the sooner the better.

Secondly, I dare averre, that God doth no where in his word tolerate Christian States, to give Tolerations to such adversaries of his Truth, if they have power in their hands to suppresse them.

Here is lately brought us an Extract of a *Magna Charta*, so called, compiled between the Sub-planters of a *West-Indian* Island; whereof the first article of constipulation, firmely provides free stable-roome and litter for all kinde of consciences, be they never so dirty or jadish; making it actionable, yea, treasonable, to disturb any man in his Religion, or to discommend it, whatever it be. We are very sorry to see such professed profanenesse in *English* Professors, as industriously to lay their Religious foundations on the ruine of true Religion; which strictly bindes every conscience to contend earnestly for the Truth: to preserve unity of spirit, faith and Ordinances, to be all like-minded, of one accord; every man to take his brother into his Christian care: to stand fast with one spirit, with one minde, striving together for the faith of the Gospel: and by no meanes to permit Heresies or erroneous opinions: But God abhorring such loathsome beverages, hath in his righteous judgement blasted that enterprize, which might otherwise have prospered well, for ought *I* know: I presume their case is generally known ere this.

If the devill might have his free option, I beleeve he would ask nothing else, but liberty to enfranchize all other Religions, and to embondage the true; nor should he need: It is much to be feared, that laxe Tolerations upon State-pretences and planting necessities, will be the next subtle Stratagem he will spread, to distate the Truth of God and supplant the peace of the Churches. Tolerations in things tolerable, exquisitely drawn out by the lines of the Scripture, and pensill of the Spirit, are the sacred favours of Truth, the due latitudes of Love, the faire Compartiments of Christian fraternity: but irregular dispensations, dealt forth by the facilities of men, are the frontiers of errour, the redoubts of Schisme, the perillous irritaments of carnall enmity.

My heart hath naturally detested foure things: The standing of the Apocrypha in the Bible; Forrainers dwelling in my Countrey, to crowd out native Subjects into the corners of the Earth; Alchymized coines; Tolerations of divers Religions, or of one Religion in segregant shapes: He that willingly assents to the last, if he examines his heart by daylight, his conscience will tell him, he is either an Atheist, or an Heretique, or an Hypocrite, or at best a captive to some lust: polchpiety is the greatest impiety in the world. True Religion is *Ignis probationis*, which doth *congregare homogenea & segregare heterogenia.*[3]

Not to tolerate things meerly indifferent to weak consciences, argues a conscience too strong: pressed uniformity in these, causes much disunity. To tolerate more than indifferents, is not to deale indifferently with God; He that doth it, takes his Scepter out of His hand,

and bids Him stand by. The power of all Religion and Ordinances, lies in their purity: their purity in their simplicity: then are mixtures pernicious. I lived in a City, where a Papist Preached in one Church, a Lutheran in another, a Calvinist in a third; a Lutheran one part of the day, a Calvinist the other, in the same Pulpit: the Religion of that place was but motly and meagre, their affections Leopard-like.

If the whole Creature should conspire to doe the Creator a mischiefe, or offer him an insolency, it would be in nothing more, then in erecting untruths against his Truth, or by sophisticating his Truths with humane medley's: the removing of some one iota in Scripture, may draw out all the life, and traverse all the Truth of the whole Bible: but to authorise an untruth, by a Toleration of State, is to build a Sconce against the walls of Heaven, to batter God out of his Chaire: To tell a practicall lye, is a great sinne, but yet transient; but to set up a Theoricall untruth, is to warrant every lye that lyes from its root to the top of every branch it hath.

I would willingly hope that no Member of the Parliament hath skilfully ingratiated himselfe into the hearts of the House, that he might watch a time to midwife out some ungracious Toleration for his own turne, and for the sake of that, some others. I would also hope that a word of generall caution should not bee particularly misapplied. Yet good Gentlemen, looke well about you, and remember how *Tiberius* plaid the Fox with the Senate of *Rome*, and how *Fabius Maximus* cropt his eares for his cunning.

That State is wise, that will improve all paines and patience rather to compose, then tolerate differences in Religion. There is no divine Truth, but hath much Celestiall fire in it from the Spirit of Truth: nor no irreligious untruth, without its proportion of Antifire from the Spirit of Error to contradict it: the zeale of the one, the virulency of the other, must necessarily kindle Combustions. Fiery diseases seated in the spirit, embroile the whole frame of the body; others more externall and coole, are lesse dangerous. They which divide in Religion, divide in God; they who divide in him, divide beyond *Genus Generalissimum*,[4] where there is no reconciliation, without atonement; that is, without uniting in him, who is One, and in his Truth, which is also one.

Wise are those men who will be perswaded rather to live within the pale of Truth where they may bee quiet, than in the purliev's, where they are sure to bee hunted ever and anon, doe Authority what it can. Every singular Opinion, hath a singular opinion of it self; and he that holds it, a singular opinion of himselfe, and a simple opinion of all contra-sentients: he that confutes them, must confute all three at once, or else he does nothing; which will not be done without more stirre then the peace of the State or Church can indure.

And prudent are those Christians, that will rather give what may be given, then hazard all by yeelding nothing. To sell all peace of Country, to buy some peace of Conscience unseasonably, is more avarice than thrift, imprudence than patience: they deale not equally, that set any Truth of God at such a rate; but they deale wisely that will stay till the Market is fallen.

My prognosticks deceive me not a little, if once within three seven yeares, peace prove not such a penny worth at most Marts in Christendome, that he that would not lay downe his money, his lust, his opinion, his will, I had almost said the best flower of his Crowne, for it, while he might have had it; will tell his owne heart, he plaid the very ill husband.

Concerning Tolerations I may further assert.

That Persecution of true Religion, and Toleration of false, are the *Jannes* and *Jambres* to the Kingdome of Christ, whereof the last is farre the worst. *Augustines* tongue had not owed his mouth one pennyrent though it had never spake word more in it, but this, *Nullum malum pejus libertate errandi.*[5]

He that is willing to tolerate any Religion, or discrepant way of Religion, besides his owne, unlesse it be in matters meerly indifferent, either doubts of his owne, or is not sincere in it.

He that is willing to tolerate any unsound Opinion, that his owne may also be tolerated, though never so sound, will for a need hang Gods Bible at the Devills girdle.

Every Toleration of false Religions, or Opinions hath as many Errors and sinnes in it, as all the false Religions and Opinions it tolerates, and one sound one more.

That State that will give Liberty of Conscience in matters of Religion, must give Liberty of Conscience and Conversation in their Morall Lawes, or else the Fiddle will be out of tune, and some of the strings cracke.

He that will rather make an irreligious quarrell with other Religions, then try the Truth of his own by valuable Arguments, and peaceable Sufferings; either his Religion, or himselfe is irreligious.

Experience will teach Churches and Christians, that it is farre better to live in a State united, though somewhat Corrupt, then in a State, whereof some Part is Incorrupt, and all the rest divided.

I am not altogether ignorant of the eight Rules given by Orthodox Divines, about giving Tolerations, yet with their favour I dare affirme,

That there is no Rule given by God for any State to give an Affirmative Toleration to any false Religion, or Opinion whatsoever; they must connive in some Cases, but may not concede in any.

That the State of *England* (so farre as my Intelligence serves) might in time have prevented with ease, and may yet without any great difficulty deny both Toleration, and Connivances *salva Republica.*[6]

That if the State of *England* shall either willingly Tolerate, or weakly connive at such Courses, the Church of that Kingdome will sooner become the Devills Dancing-Schoole, then Gods-Temple: The Civill State a Beare-garden, then an Exchange: The whole Realme a Pais base,[7] then an *England.* And what pity it is, that that Country which hath been the Staple of Truth to all Christendome, should now become the Aviary of Errors to the whole World, let every fearing heart judge. . . .

Concerning Novelties of opinions; I shall expresse my thoughts in these briefe passages. First, that Truth is the best boone God ever gave the world: there is nothing in the world, any further then Truth makes it so; it is better than any creat' *Ens* or *Bonum,* which are but Truths twins.[8] Secondly, the least Truth of Gods Kingdome, doth in its place, uphold the whole kingdome of his Truths; Take away the least *vericulum* [9] out of the world, and it unworlds all, potentially, and may unravell the whole texture actually, if it be not conserved by an Arme of extraordinary power. Thirdly, the least Evangelicall Truth, is more worth than all the Civill Truths in the world, that are meerly so. Fourthly, that Truth is the Parent of all Liberty whether politicall or personall; so much untruth, so much thraldome, *John* 8. 32.

Hence it is, that God is so jealous of his Truths, that he hath taken order in his due Justice: First, that no practicall sin is so sinfull as some errour in judgement; no men so accursed with indelible infamy and dedolent impenitency, as Authours of Heresie. Secondly, that the least Error, if grown sturdy and pressed, shall set open the Spittle-doore of all the squint-ey'd, wry-necked, and brasen-faced Errors that are or ever were of that litter; if they be not enough to serve its turne, it will beget more, though it hath not one crust of reason to maintain them. Thirdly, that, that State which will permit Errors in Religion, shall admit Errors in Policy unavoydably. Fourthly, that that Policy which will suffer irreligious errors, shall suffer the losse of so much Liberty in one kinde or other, I will not exempt *Venice, Rhaguse,* the *Nether-lands,* or any.

An easie head may soon demonstrate, that the prementioned Planters, by Tolerating all Religions, had immazed themselves in the most intolerable confusions and inextricable thraldomes the world ever heard of. I am perswaded the Devill himselfe was never willing with their proceedings, for feare it would break his winde and wits to attend such a Province. I speak it seriously according to my meaning. How all Religions should enjoy their liberty, Justice its due regularity, Civill cohabitation morall honesty, in one and the same Jurisdiction, is beyond the Artique of my comprehension. If the whole conclave of Hell can so compromise, exadverse, and diametriall contradictions, as to compolitize such a multimonstrous maufrey of heteroclytes and quicquidlibets quietly; I trust I may say with all humble reverence, they can doe more then the Senate of Heaven. My *modus loquendi* [10] pardoned; I entirely wish much welfare and more wisdome to that Plantation. . . .

Should I not keep promise in speaking a little to Womens fashions, they would take it unkindly: I was loath to pester better matter with such stuffe; I rather thought it meete to let them stand by themselves, like the *Quæ Genus* [11] in the Grammar, being Deficients, or Redundants, not to bee brought under any Rule[.] I shall therefore make bold for this once, to borrow a little of their loose-tongue Liberty, and mispend a word or two upon their long-wasted, but short-skirted patience: a little use of my stirrup will doe no harme.

Ridentem dicere verum, quid prohibet? [12]

Gray Gravity it selfe can well beteame,
That Language be adapted to the Theme.
He that to Parrots speaks, must parrotise;
He that instructs a foole, may act th' unwise.

It is known more then enough, that I am neither Nigard, nor Cinick, to the due bravery of the true Gentry: if any man mislikes a bully mong drassock more then I, let him take her for all mee: I honour the woman that can honour her self with her attire: a good Text alwayes deserves a fair Margent: I am not much offended, if I see a trimme, far trimmer than she that wears it: in a word, whatever Christianity or Civility will allow, I can afford with *London* measure: but when I heare a nugiperous Gentledame inquire what dresse the Queen is in this week; what the nudiustertian fashion of the Court; I mean the very newest: with egge to be in it in all haste, what ever it be; I look at her as the very gizzard of a trifle, the product of a quarter of a cypher, the epitome of nothing, fitter to be kickt, if she were of a kickable substance, than either honoured or humoured.

To speak moderately, I truely confesse, it is beyond the ken of my understanding to conceive, how those women should have any true grace, or valuable vertue, that have so little wit, as to disfigure themselves with such exotick garbes, as not onely dismantles their native lovely lustre, but transclouts them into gant bar-geese, ill-shapen shotten shell-fish, Egyptian Hieroglyphicks, or at the best into French flurts of the pastery, which a proper English-woman should scorn with her heeles: it is no marvell they weare drailes on the hinder part of their heads, having nothing as it seems in the fore-part, but a few Squirrills braines, to help them frisk from one ill-favor'd fashion to another.

These whimm' Crown'd shees, these fashion-fansying wits,
Are empty thin brain'd shells, and fidling Kits,

The very troublers and impoverishers of mankind. I can hardly forbeare to commend to the world a saying of a Lady living sometime with the Queen of *Bohemiah*, I know not where she found it, but it is pitty it should be lost.

The world is full of care, much like unto a bubble;
Women and care, and care and women, and women and care and trouble.

The Verses are even enough for such odde pegma's. I can make my self sick at any time, with comparing the dazzling splender wherewith our Gentlewomen were embellished in some former habits, with the gut-foundred goosdome, wherewith they are now surcingled and debauched. We have about five or six of them in our Colony: if I see any of them accidentally, I cannot cleanse my phansie of them for a month after. I have been a solitary widdower almost twelve years, purposed lately to make a step over to my Native Country for a yoke-fellow: but when I consider how women there have tripe-wifed themselves with their cladments, I have no heart to the voyage, lest their nauseous shapes and the Sea, should work too sorely upon my stomach. I speak sadly; me thinks it should break the hearts of Englishmen, to see so many goodly English-women imprisoned in French Cages, peering out of their hood-holes for some men of mercy to help them with a little wit, and no body relieves them.

It is a more common then convenient saying, that nine Taylors make a man: it were well if nineteene could make a woman to her minde: if Taylors were men indeed, well furnished but with meere morall principles, they would disdain to be led about like Apes, by such mymick Marmosets. It is a most unworthy thing, for men that have bones in them, to spend their lives in making fidle-cases for futilous womens phansies; which are the very pettitoes of infirmity, the gyblets of perquisquilion toyes. I am so charitable to think, that most of that mystery, would work the cheerfuller while they live, if they might be well discharged of the tyring slavery of mis-tyring women: it is no little labour to be continually putting up English-women into Outlandish caskes; who if they be not shifted anew, once in a few moneths, grow too sowre for their Husbands. What this Trade will answer for themselves when God shall take measure of Taylors consciences is beyond my skill to imagine. There was a time when

The joyning of the Red-Rose with the White
Did set our State into a Damask plight.

But now our Roses are turned to *Flore de lices*, our Carnations to Tulips, our Gilliflowers to pansies, our City-Dames, to an indenominable Quaemalry of overturcas'd things. Hee that makes Coates for the Moone, had need take measure every noone; and he that makes for women, every Moone, to keep them from Lunacy.

I have often heard diverse Ladies vent loud feminine complaints of the wearisome varieties and chargable changes of fashion: I marvell themselves prefer not a Bill of redresse. I would *Essex** Ladies would lead the *Chore*, for the honour of their County and persons; or rather the thrice honourable Ladies of the Court, whom it best beseemes: who may wel presume of a *Le Roy le veult* from our sober King, a *Les Seigneurs ont Assentus* [13] from our prudent Peers, and the like Assentus from our considerate, I dare not say wife-worne Commons: who I beleeve had much rather passe one such Bill, than pay so many Taylors Bills as they are forced to doe.

Most deare and unparallel'd Ladies, be pleased to attempt it: as you have the precellency of the women of world for beauty and feature; so assume the honour to give, and not take Law from any, in matter of attire: if ye can transact so faire a motion among your selves unanimously, I dare say, they that most renite, will least repent. What greater honour can your Honors desire, then to build a Promontory president to all foraigne Ladies, to deserve so eminently at the hands of all the English Gentry, present and to come; and to confute the opinion of all the wise men in the world; who never thought it possible for women to doe so good a work.

* [*Ward's note, marginal in the original:*] All the Counties and shires of England have had wars in them since the Conquest, but Essex, which is onely free, and should be thankful.

[Added in 3[d] ed.]—If any man think I have spoken rather merrily than seriously he is much mistaken, I have written what I write with all the indignation I can, and no more then I ought. I confesse I veer'd my tongue to this kinde of Language *de industria* though unwillingly, supposing those I speak to are uncapable of grave and rationall arguments . . .

There is a quadrobulary saying, which passes current in the Westerne world, That the Emperour is King of Kings, the Spaniard, King of Men, the French, King of Asses, the King of *England*, King of Devills: By his leave that first brayed the speech, they are pretty wise Devills and pretty honest; the worst they doe, is to keep their Kings from Divelizing, and themselves from Assing: Were I a King (a simple supposall) I would not part with one good English Divell, for two of the Emperours Kings nor three of the Spaniards Men, nor foure French Asses; if I did, *I* should thinke my selfe an Asse for my labour. *I* know nothing that Englishmen want, but true Grace, and honest pride: let them be well furnisht with those two, I feare they would make more Asses, then *Spaine* can make men, or the Emperour Kings. You will say I am now beyond my latchet; but you would not say so, if you knew how high my latchet will stretch, when I heare a lye with a latchet, that reaches up to his throat that first forged it.

He is a good King that undoeth not his Subjects, by any one of his unlimited Prerogatives: and they are a good People, that undoe not their Prince, by any one of their unbounded Liberties, be they the very least: I am sure either may, and I am sure neither would be trusted, how good soever. Stories tell us in effect, though not in termes, that over-risen Kings, have been the next evills to the world, unto falne Angels; and that over-franchized people, are devills with smooth snaffles in their mouthes. A King that lives by Law, lives by love; and he that lives above Law, shall live under hatred doe what he can. Slavery and Knavery goe as seldome asunder, as Tyranny and Cruelty.

I have a long while thought it very possible, in a time of Peace, and in some Kings Reigne, for disert Statesmen, to cut an exquisite thred between and quite through Kings Prerogatives, and Subjects Liberties of all sorts, so as *Cæsar* might have his due, and People their share, without such sharpe disputes. Good Casuists would case it, and case it, part it and part it, now it, and then it, punctually. *Aquinas*, *Suarez*, or *Valentia*,[14] would have done it long ere this, and they not been Popish, I might have said knavish; for, if they be so any where, it is in their Tractates of Priviledges. Our Common Law doth well, but it must doe better before things doe as they should. There are some *Maximes* in Law, that would bee taught to speak a little more mannerly, or else well *Anti-maxim'd:* we say, the King can doe a Subject no wrong; why may we not say, the Parliament can do the King no wrong? We say, *Nullum tempus occurrit Regi*[15] in taking wrong; why may we not say, *Nullum tempus succurrit Regi*[16] in doing wrong? which I doubt will prove a better Canon, if well examined.

Authority must have power to make and keep people honest; People, honesty to obey Authority; both, a joynt-Councell to keep both safe. Morall Laws, Royall Prerogatives, Popular Liberties, are not of Mans making or giving, but Gods: Man is but to measure them out by Gods Rule: which if mans wisdome cannot reach, Mans experience must mend: And these Essentialls, must not be Ephorized or Tribuned by one or a few Mens discretion, but lineally sanctioned by Supreame Councels. In *pro-re-nascent* occurrences, which cannot be foreseen; Diats, Parliaments, Senates, or accountable Commissions, must have power to consult and execute against intersilient dangers and flagitious crimes prohibited by the light of Nature: Yet it were good if States would let People know so much before hand, by some safe woven *manifesto*, that grosse Delinquents may tell no tales of Anchors and Buoyes, nor palliate their presumptions with pretence of ignorance. I know no difference in these Essentialls, between Monarchies, Aristocracies, or Democracies; the rule and reason will bee found all one, say Schoolemen and Pretorians what they will. And in all, the best Standard to measure Prerogatives, is the Plough-staffe; to measure Liberties, the Scepter: if the tearmes were a little altered into Loyall Prerogatives and Royall Liberties, then we should be sure to have Royall Kings and Loyall Subjects.

Subjects their King, the King his Subjects greets,
Whilome the Scepter and the Plough-staffe meets.

But Progenitors have had them for four and twenty predecessions: that would be spoken in the Norman tongue or Cimbrian, not in the English or Scottish: When a Conquerour turnes Christian, Christianity turnes Conquerour: if they had had them time out of minde of man, before *Adam* was made, it is not a pin to the point in *foro rectæ rationis:*[17] Justice and Equity were before time, and will be after it: Time hath neither Politicks nor Ethicks, good nor evill in it; it is an empty thing, as empty as a *New-English* purse, and emptier it cannot be: a man may break his neck in time, and in a lesse time then he can heale it.

JONATHAN MITCHELL, 1624–1668

[Jonathan Mitchell, the intellectual leader of New England in the second generation, was born at Halifax, Yorkshire, and was brought by his parents to New England in 1635. Graduated from Harvard in 1647, he was chosen to the important post of minister at Cambridge, where he married the widow of his great predecessor, Thomas Shepard. He was the leader of the movement for the Half-Way Covenant, was the tutor and mentor of Increase Mather. This text is from *Nehemiah on the Wall in Troublesome Times* (Cambridge, 1671), an election sermon preached in 1667. Cf. life in Cotton Mather, *Magnalia*, and J. L. Sibley, *Biographical Sketches*.]

NEHEMIAH ON THE WALL

CIVIL rulers] *are especially to seek the welfare of the people of God:* or to seek the welfare of the people over whom they are Rulers, especially when as they are the Lords people. . . .

VSE I. This Point shews us what ought to be the general End and Rule of all the Motions and Actions of Rulers, *viz.* the welfare of the poeple. To that scope *Nehemiah* bends all his Actions and Endeavours; and *Finis est mensura mediorum,* the End serves to measure, regulate, direct and limit the means, and shew what should be done. That *Maxime* of the *Romans* was and is a Principle of right Reason, *Salus Populi Suprema Lex,* (The welfare of the People is the Supreme Law) and is engraven on the Forehead of the Law and Light of *Nature.* Hence it is owned and confirmed by the *Scriptures,* as we see in the Text; and it is easily deducible from the Law of God: for that that is indeed the Law of Nature, is a part of the Eternal Law of God; and the Law of God enjoyns, that in Humane Civil Affairs, things be managed according to right Reason and Equity; and that Rulers, as they are for the people, so they are to make it their main business, and the scope of all their Actions, Laws and Motions, to seek the welfare of the people. There is Sun-light for this Maxime, and it was never doubted nor denied by any that held but to Rational and Moral Principles. Hence this Law being Supreme, it limits all other Laws and Considerations. Hence it is impossible that a people or their Rulers should be bound by any other Law, or Custome, or Consideration whatsoever, to do any thing that is really and evidently contrary to this. If it be indeed contrary or destructive to the welfare of the people, (of the Community they stand charged with) it is impossible they should be bound in *Conscience* to do it.

This is the *Compass* that Rulers are to steer by, and the *Touch-stone* of Right and Wrong in all their Motions, *viz.* What is for or against the Publick good, and the Welfare of the people, *Rom.* 13. 14. That bounds and regulates his whole Ministration. What is for the *Common good*, that and that only you are to do; and all that are set in place of Rule and Government (be they of higher or of lower quality) do stand charged with the welfare of that people, whom they are Rulers over.

I know when it comes to particulars, the doubt will still be, What is for the welfare of the people. One will say, this is most for the common good, another that. But

1. It will help much if this Principle be setled and acknowledged, That in Civil Affairs, the Consideration of the welfare of the whole, is that which shews and determines what is right, and weighs down all other Considerations whatsoever. Men will say, We must do what is right, whatsoever comes of it: *Fiat Justitia ruat Cœlum.* True, but it is most certain it is not right, if it be against the welfare of the people. It is impossible that any thing should be truly right, that is destructive to the common good: for it will constantly hold, *Salus Populi Suprema Lex.*

2. Consider the things wherein the welfare of a people does consist, which are above-mentioned, (*viz.* Religion in the first place, and then their Safety, or the Preservation of their Being, both Personal and Political, and their participation in the Rules and Fruits of Righteousness, Equity, Order and Peace) and that will help to discover and discern what is for the welfare of the people, or for the common good, and what not. There is need of much prudence and wariness in particular Applications and Cases; but those general Principles will hold, That a peoples welfare lies in such things as these, and that Rulers are bound in all their Motions and Actions to seek the welfare of the people, and to do nothing contrary thereunto.

VSE II. Hence see, that difficulties and troubles do not *excuse*, nor should *discourage* Rulers from doing the work of their Places which God calls them unto, or from seeking the welfare of the people: Such things do not excuse, nor should discourage from taking and accepting the Place of Rule when called to it. As they did not *Nehemiah*, though he heard before that their condition was a condition of great affliction and reproach, *Neh.* 1. 3. yet he voluntarily left the Court of *Persia*, to embarque with the *Jews* at *Jerusalem*, when in so stormy a time as this was; and how is he honoured in the Book of God for it? It was a difficult time and task that *Moses* was sent upon, accompanied also with a deep sense of his own infirmity and unfitness, *Exod.* 3. 4. he could not but be slow and backward to such a work; but yet when he was over-backward the Lord grew angry, and chides him into a consent: but (I say) difficulties and troubles should not discourage nor hinder Rulers from doing the work of their Places when set therein, *i.e.* from faithful seeking and acting for the welfare of the people, which is (as we have said) the summary work of the Rulers Place. Consider a little the difficulties that lay upon the *Jews* and their Rulers at this time in *Jerusalem*, after their return from Captivity, and in the dayes of *Nehemiah.*[1]

1. They were a small, weak and despised people, *Nehem.* 4. 1, 2, 4. & 1. 3. & 2. 19. Contempt and reproach is a bitter and killing thing to ingenuous Spirits; yet this they were fain to bear and pass through. It was a *day of small things*, which others, yea even themselves are apt to despise, *Zech.* 4. 10.

2. They were in the midst of Enemies, and Adversaries round about them, of several sorts and Nations; *Sanballat* a *Moabite*, (from *Horonaim* a chief City of *Moab*, *Isa.* 15. 5. *Jer.* 48. 3, 5, 34. called the *Horonite*) and *Tobiah* the Servant, the *Ammonite*, on the East, *Neh.* 2. 10. (*The Servant*, he was Governour of the *Ammonites*, but of a base and servile spirit; some think that of a mean man, he was got into Place, and therefore is called *Tobiah the Servant:* such are often worst, *Prov.* 30. 21, 22.) *Geshem* the *Arabian* (Neh. 6. 1. & 4. 7.) and others on the *South;* and the *Samaritans* on the *North*, Neh. 4. 2. Ezra 4. 9, 10. Thus they were beset round with Adversaries, and Ill-willers, and many Informers and Complainers there were against them, as before in the dayes of *Zerubbabel*, *Ezra* 4. & 5.

3. Their Adversaries did labour to affright them with the Accusation of *Rebellion*, *Neh.* 2. 19. an old *Artifice*, but it was an injurious Calumny, and most groundless Accusation. The building of the Wall of *Jerusalem* for *self-preservation*, had nothing in it of *Rebellion:* but many clamours and stories they raised of that nature, *Neh.* 6. 6, 7, 8. and see their end therein, *ver.* 9. to weaken and discourage them from their work, that their hearts and hands might fail them therein, that was it they aimed at.[2]

4. There were Discontents and Divisions among themselves, *Neh.* 5. 1. Great Complaints of the *Inferiour* sort against their *Superiours;* of the Poor against the Rich; of Brethren against Brethren: yea, there were among themselves that were helpers to their Adversaries, and complied with them, even some *chief men* and others, *Neh.* 6. 17, 18. and thereby, among other evils, it came to pass that nothing could be kept within its due compass, but every thing was carried and reported to their

Adversaries, *ver.* 19. *They uttered my words* (or my matters) *unto him;* and that doubtless not in the fairest dress. Yea, there were some of the Prophets that endeavoured to weaken the hands of faithful *Nehemiah*, and to put discouragement upon him, *Neh.* 6. 10, (This *Shemaiah* is conceived to be the same that is mentioned *Ezra* 8. 16.) 11, 12, 13. (By the way, who would have said that that would have been a sin, which might seem to be a prudent retirement for safety? yea, but for *Nehemiah*, in a case so circumstanced, to act fear and discouragement to the prejudice of his Cause and Work, would have been a sin.) But *ver.* 14. there were also that raised Slanders of others of their *Prophets*, those it's like who were of another minde, *ver.* 7.

5. They were poor, and low, and weak as to outward estate, conflicting with wants and straits, and many difficulties in that respect, very unable to support themselves, and to bear the Publick Burthens that were then upon them, *Neh.* 5. 2–5. and *ver.* 18. *The bondage was heavy upon this people:* Neh. 9. 37. *We are in great distress.*

6. Hence there was *hard* Work, and *weak* Instruments, ready many times to be discouraged, *Neh.* 4. 10. the Workmen themselves, and those that should joyn hands together to labour and carry on the work, began to mutter and be discouraged, by the difficulty of the work, and their own weakness; *We are not able*, say they, *to carry it on:* At the same time when the Adversaries were high, *president* and threatning, *ver.* 11. their own workmen began to be disheartned and *diffident*, ver. 10. Here was a juncture of discouraging trial. Hence hard shifts they were fain to make to carry on the work, and to put forth themselves to the utmost, and beyond an ordinary measure, by the care and courage and conduct of good *Nehemiah*, *ver.* 16, 17. Every one had both his hands full, and they were fain to do two works at once, the work of a *Souldier*, and of a *Labourer*, ver. 18, 21, 22, 23.

7. It was a time of many *fears;* wherein they had many fears among them, and many that heightned those fears: many Reports, Threatnings and fore-speakings of this, and that, to that purpose, *Neh.* 4. 12. & 6. 9, 13, 14, 19. It is observeable, that that was the drift and endeavours of Adversaries and Ill-willers, *Fear, fear, fear;* a discouraging *Heart* and *Hand-weakning* carnal *fear*. The great word of *God* to godly Rulers is, *Be strong, and of a good courage*, fear not when in Gods way and work, *Josh.* 1. 6, 7, 9. But the word of *Satan* and his Instruments is, *Fear*, be *afraid*, look upon the danger of being faithful: But (as to man and second Causes) they had many very great causes of fear, many dangers round about them, and to be faithful in duty in a time of fear, proves a difficult task to flesh and blood.

8. Which was worst of all, Among this people of the *Jews* after Captivity, when engaged in Reforming work, there were many sins, disorders and miscarriages, which were provoking unto God, and a great exercise of discouragement to their faithful Leaders; such in *Ezra's* time as made him *blush before God*, and fear what God would do with them, *Ezra* 9. 6, 10, 14. And before that in *Haggai's* time, such neglects of carrying on Temple-work, and of finishing what was begun, as he sharply reproves, yea as God reproved from Heaven, by Drought, Blastings, *&c. Hag.* 1. 2, 5, 6, 9, 10, 11. *&* 2. 16, 17. And here in *Nehemiahs* time there were faults, evils and distempers found among them, as *Neh.* 5. 1, 6, 7, 9. *&* 13. 4, 5, 10, 15, 18, 23, 24, 26, 27. not onely matter of *Affliction*, but sinful *Corruptions* and Distempers do sprout up among a Reforming people, and those they have to wrestle with: yet neither did these take them or their Leaders off from their Work, nor utterly overturn it; nor did the Lord cast them off (though he chastened them) but helped them along, though in much infirmity. He was with them at many a dead lift, (*Hag.* 2. 4.) and after *frowns*, yet *smiled* on them again: especially while the Leaders were faithful to search out and testifie against *evil*, and to set upon *duty* when called to it; and the people were willing to hearken to them, and to be reduced and reformed by them: both which may be observed of them all along in the story, *Hag.* 1. 12, 13. *Ezra* 10. 2, 3, 4, 7, 8, 12, 14.

9. Lastly, we may remember the long time wherein this poor people were conflicting and labouring under Difficulties and Infirmities, and what a succession of Difficulties and Troubles did attend them in the Reforming, and Rebuilding work they were upon. From their first Grant by *Cyrus*, unto the beginning of *Nehemiahs* Government (in the twentieth year of *Artaxerxes*) according to the shortest Account, were 82 years (so *Usher* in his *Annals. Junius* saith 146. *Lightfoot* saith but 37, but few embrace that.) Almost all that time, & so afterward in the time of *Nehemiahs* Government, they were followed with various Troubles and Exercises (as the story at large tells us) though they had their lucid Intervals, and the Lord still helping in the issue.

Thus that word was made good, *Dan.* 9. 25. that *Jerusalem*, both City and Wall, *should be built again in troublous times*. Yet notwithstanding all this, they went on in their Work with *Courage*, and *Constancy*, and *Confidence* in God, *Neh.* 2. 20. and he did prosper them, not by preventing Difficulties, but by carrying on the Work in their hands through all Difficulties, and in the midst of all their Infirmities. And it is observeable, That every *Tragedy* they passed through, had a glad *Catastrophe;*

every stress had a comfortable issue: God still helped them in the conclusion and upshot of every business, that they came off well at last, though with much tugging and wrestling, much exercise of Faith and Patience. So in the Building of the Temple, (thus it went on heavily, and met with many obstructions, and many Adversaries; yet they got through at last, to their great joy) *Ezra* 6. 15, 16, 22. So here in the building of the Wall, *Neh.* 6. 15, 16. *&* 12. 27, 43. And so in the Reformation of Abuses, *Ezra* 10. *Neh.* 5. *&* 13. The story of the *Church* in all Ages, & especially in the Scripture, informs us, that the best and greatest works God hath delighted to carry on through many Difficulties and Oppositions, and in much felt infirmity of Instruments. The time of *Moses*, of *David*, of *Israel*, all along in the *Old Testament*, will furnish us with many Instances of it; yea and also of the *Apostles* in their Work under the *New Testament*, *Act.* 20. 19. 1 *Cor.* 16. 9. *&* 3. 3. 2 *Cor.* 11. 23–28, 29, 30. *Gal.* 4. 13, 14. the glorious Gospel must be preached & carried on *through Infirmity of the flesh*, i.e. through outward meanness and affliction of Instruments, yet not therefore to be despised. The whole Church of God, and every particular concernment thereof, is in a *Militant* conflicting condition in this world, and it must be no stumbling to us to see it so: it occasions the more exercise of *Faith*, *Patience*, *Prayer*, *&c.* in the work (as we see in the example of *Nehemiah* all along) and the more of God to appear in the issue of it, *Neh.* 6. 16.

Go on therefore in the Work of the Lord, and in the Service of your several Places, and be not taken off by trouble, difficulties, oppositions, felt infirmities in your selves, weaknesses and distempers in persons and things round about you, (which will alwayes be.) When were there work for Patience, Faith, Fortitude, Self-denial, and for the Spirit of a Souldier, Wrestler, *&c.* if it were not for such things? We must none of us say, of one Order or other, I will serve God in my place, and help build the Wall of *Jerusalem*, if I may do it with ease, and tranquility, without trouble, without hazard, without reproaches, and ill requitals from men. *&c.* Christ is little beholden to us, if that be all we will do for him; that is too low for the Spirit of a *good Souldier of Christ Jesus*, 2. Cor. 6. 4, 5, 8. Yea, now you look like the Ministers of God, when you cheerfully discharge your Places, though surrounded and loaden with Afflictions, Distresses, Labours, false Reproaches, &c. Now you are drest like a Minister, like a Servant of God, and of his people in Publick Work; and through such things as these, you must go on in your Work, as the Apostles then did.

WILLIAM STOUGHTON, 1631–1701

[William Stoughton was the second son of Israel Stoughton, who came to New England in 1630, a founder of Dorchester and a large land owner. William graduated from Harvard in 1650, went to Oxford, where he became a fellow of New College and received his M.A. in 1653. He was a curate in Sussex in 1659, was ejected from his church and from his fellowship at the Restoration, and returned to Massachusetts in 1662. He preached at Dorchester, but refused to be ordained, and turned from theology to law and politics. He was an Assistant, 1671–1686; Commissioner of the United Colonies, 1674–1676, 1680–1686; a judge, and an agent of the colony in England, 1676–1679. He was a friend of Joseph Dudley, by whom he was appointed deputy governor in 1686; he remained on Andros's council, but went over to the Revolution in 1688. Named lieutenant governor under the new charter in 1692, he became acting governor in 1694 and was the real head of the colony from then until his death, except for the few months in 1699 and 1700 when Bellomont was in Boston. He was chief justice of the special court which tried and condemned the witches at Salem in 1692, and he is said never to have repented his share in the proceedings. The text is from *New-Englands True Interest; Not to Lie* (Cambridge, 1670), an election sermon preached on April 29, 1668. Cf. Sibley, *Biographical Sketches*.]

NEW-ENGLANDS TRUE INTEREST

AND here I shall consider that the words of the Text are spoken concerning a People, even the Body of a Nation; and so my endeavour shall be to apply the Truths delivered, unto this present Assembly standing before the Lord this day as the *Body of this People:* Such in several respects is the Capacity of this solemn Congregation, and unto you *as such*, my desire is to speak in the Name of the Lord. For many a day and year, even from our first beginnings hath this word of the Lord been verified concerning us in this Wilderness; *The Lord hath said of* New-England, *Surely they are my People, Children that will not lie, so hath he been our Saviour*. Upon this Basis have all the *Saviourly Undertakings* of the Lord been founded in the midst of us, and upon this bottom do we unto this day abide.

The solemn work of this day is *Foundation-work;* not to lay a new Foundation, but to continue and strengthen, and beautifie, and build upon that which hath been laid. Give me leave therefore, Honoured and Beloved, to awaken, and call upon you, in the Name of him who sends me, with reference unto those *Foundations* that are held forth to us in the Text, for if these should be *out of course*, what could the Righteous do? If we should so frustrate and deceive the Lords Expectations, that his Covenant-interest in us, and the Workings of his Salvation be made to cease, then All were lost indeed; Ruine upon Ruine, Destruction upon Destruction would come, until one stone were not left upon another. . . .

Use 1. *Of Information;* to let *New-England* know what that gracious infinitely wise, holy and awful dispensation of divine Providence is, under which the Lord hath set us and continued us unto this day. We must look upon our selves as under a *solemn divine Probation;* It hath been and it is a Probation-time, even to this whole People. Under great hopes, and singular eminent Expectations hath the Lord our God been trying of us, and is yet trying us in the wayes of his Salvation. There is this *one* voice of all his Providences towards us; they call aloud unto us in this language of a Probation-time, *To day if this my people will hear my voice;* To day if they will come up to the Lords Expectations, and answer his promises; To day, that is, whilest it is a day of Salvation, whilest the Lord is yet so wonderfully preserving of us, displaying his Banner over us, holding underneath the Everlasting Arms, and making us to taste so much of his loving kindness and tender mercies every way. Divine Expectations frustrated will issue dreadfully, when the Lord shall make us know his *breach of promise*, Numb. 14. 34. This we must know, that the Lords promises, and expectations of great things, have singled out *New-England*, and all sorts and ranks of men amongst us, above any Nation or people in the world; and this hath been and is a time and season of eminent trial to us. If I should say that the very world, or common ordinary Professors expect great things from us at this day, there is a great deal of weight in it; If I say that the faithful precious suffering Saints of God in all other places, that have heard of the Lords Providences towards us, do expect and promise great things from us, this is farre more; But to mention the Lords own Expectations, this is most of all, these are certainly most solemn and awfull. Every Expectation of God is most just and righteous. *Are not my wayes equal?* saith God, *Ezek.* 18. 29. Yes, most equal, blessed God; Bountiful and Rich hast thou been in all thy free Bestowings; equal and just art thou in all thy greatest Expectations. If we do but run over the forementioned grounds of divine Expectation, it will be sufficient to commit the judgement of this case even to *our selves*, as *Isa.* 5. 3.

As for special Relation unto God; whom hath the Lord more signally exalted then his people in this Wilderness? The Name and Interest of God, and Covenant-relation to him, it hath been written upon us in Capital Letters from the beginning. God had his *Creatures* in this Wilderness before we came, and his *Rational Creatures* too, a multitude of them; but as to *Sons* and *Children* that are Covenant-born unto God, Are not we the *first* in such a Relation? in this respect we are surely the Lords *first-born* in this Wilderness. Of the poor Natives before we came we may say as *Isa.* 63. 19. *They were not called by the Lords Name, he bear not Rule over them:* But we have been from the beginning, and we are the *Lords.*

As for Extraction and Descent, if we be considered as a *Posterity,* O what Parents and Predecessors may we the most of us look back unto, through whose Loins the Lord hath stretched forth the line of his Covenant, measuring of us out, and taking us in to be a peculiar Portion to himself?

As for Restipulations, and Engagements back again to God; what awfull publick Transactions of this kinde have there been amongst us? Hath not the eye of the Lord beheld us laying *Covenant-Engagements* upon our selves? hath not his ear heard us solemnly *Avouching* him, and him alone, to be our God and Saviour? Hath not a great part of the world been a witness of these things, even of our explicite ownings of, and Covenantings with the Lord as our God, laying this as a foundation-stone in our Building; and of this we may say, It hath been a special Exasperation unto Adversaries and Ill-willers, that despised *New-England* hath laid claim to, and publickly avouched and challenged a special Interest in God above others.

As for our Advantages and Priviledges in a Covenant-state, here time and strength would fail to reckon up what we have enjoyed of this kinde; if any people in the world have been lifted up to heaven as to Advantages and Priviledges, we are the people. Name what you will under this Head, and we have had it. We have had *Moses* and *Aaron* to lead us; we have had Teachings and Instructions, *line upon line, and precept upon precept;* we have had Ordinances and Gospel-dispensations the choicest of them; we have had Peace and Plenty; we have had Afflictions and Chastisements in measure; we have had the Hearts, and Prayers, and Blessing of the Lords people every where; we have had the Eye and Hand of God, watching and working every way for our good; our Adversaries have had their Rebukes, we have had our Encouragements, and a wall of fire round about us. What could have been done more for us then hath been done?

And then in the last place, as to *New-Englands first wayes;* what glorious things might here be spoken, unto the praise of free-grace, and to justifie the Lords Expectations upon this ground? Surely God hath often spoke concerning His Churches here, as in *Jer.* 2. 2. *I remember the kindness of thy youth, &c.* O what were the open Professions of the Lords people that first entred this Wilderness? How did our fathers entertain the Gospel, and all the pure Institutions thereof, and those Liberties which they brought over? What was their Communion and Fellowship in the Administrations of the Kingdome of Jesus Christ? What was the pitch of their Brotherly love, of their Zeal for God and his Wayes, and against wayes destructive of Truth and Holiness? What was their Humility, their Mortification, their Exemplariness? How much of Holiness to the Lord was written upon all their wayes and transactions? God sifted a whole Nation that he might send choice Grain over into this Wilderness.

Thus it hath been with us as to grounds of Divine Expectation: And therefore let us in the fear of God learn this great truth to day, and receive the instruction thereof sealed up unto all our souls; *That the great God hath taken up great Expectations of us, and made great Promises to himself concerning us, and this hath been, and is* New-Englands *day and season of Probation.*

WILLIAM HUBBARD, 1621–1704

[William Hubbard, son of a husbandman of Tenring, Essex, came with his family to New England in 1635, and settled at Ipswich. He graduated in the first class at Harvard College, 1642, studied medicine and did not become a minister until 1656, when he was settled as the colleague of Thomas Cobbet at Ipswich. He was a ringleader along with John Wise in the protest against Andros's taxation, 1687; he kept his head during the witchcraft panic. In 1677 he published a history of the Indian wars in New England, and wrote a general history of New England which was based chiefly on Winthrop's manuscript *Journal*. He lived to be one of the oldest and most venerated ministers in the colony, but after his first wife died he shocked his parishioners by marrying his housekeeper in 1694. This text is from *The Happiness of a People In the Wisdome of their Rulers Directing And in the Obedience of their Brethren Attending* (Boston, 1676), a sermon preached on election day, May 3, of that year. Cf. Sibley, *Biographical Sketches;* Sprague, *Annals;* Samuel G. Drake, edition of *A Narrative of the Troubles with the Indians* (Roxbury, 1865).]

THE HAPPINESS OF A PEOPLE

It was Order that gave Beauty to this goodly fabrick of the world, which before was but a confused Chaos, without form and void: Therefore when Job, when he would set out the terribleness of the grave and the dismal state of death, he calls it, the Land of darkness, and the shadow of death without any Order. *Job 10. 22.* For Order is as the soul of the Universe, the life and health of things natural, the beauty and strength of things Artificial. . . . The better to understand this we may consider what Order is? The Schools tell us, it is, *Parium, impariumque; sua cuique; tribuens loca, opta disposito.* Such a disposition of things in themselves equall and unequall, as gives to every one their due and proper place. It suited the wisdom of the infinite and omnipotent Creator, to make the world of differing parts, which necessarily supposes that there must be differing places, for those differing things to be disposed into, which is Order. The like is necessary to be observed in the rational and political World, where persons of differing endowments and qualifications need differing station to be disposed into, the keeping of which, is both the beauty and strength of such a society. Naturalists tell us that beauty in the body arises from an exact symmetry or proportion of contrary humours, equally mixed one with another: so doth an orderly and artificial distribution of diverse materials, make a comely Building, while homogeneous bodyes (as the depths of waters in the Sea, and heaps of sand on the Shore) run into confused heaps, as bodyes uncapable to maintain an order in themselves. So that it appears, whoever is for a parity in any Society, will in the issue reduce things into an heap of confusion. That God who assumes to him self the title of being the God of Glory, is the God of peace, or Order and not of confusion. 1 *Cor.* 14. 33 compar'd with *ver.* 40. He is so in his Palace of the world, as well as in his temple of his Church: in both may be observed a sweet subordination of persons and things, each unto other . . . Look we into the third heavens the high and holy place, as a Royal Pavilion pitched by the Almighty for the recidence of his Glory, although it be furnished with Inhabitants suitable to the nature of that celestial throne, yet are they not all of one rank and order; there are Cherubims as well as Seraphims, Arch-Angels as well as Angels, Thrones and Dominions, as well as Principalityes and Powers. There are also, as in a middle rank, the Spirits of just men made perfect: though no unclean thing may enter in, yet have they not attained their perfection in Glory, but do yet expect an addition of Glory: but in the outward Court, as there are diversity of gifts, so there are of places, and order: some that are to rule and go before, others that are to be subject, and to follow. If we shall but descend and take notice of the firmament, the pavement of that glorious mansion place, although it be the roof of this lower world, may we not there see, one star differing from another in glory? There is placed the Sun, the lord and ruler of the day, as well as the Moon, that rules the night, together with the stars, as the common-people of that upper region, who yet doe immediately veyle their glory, and withdraw their light, when their bridegroom cometh forth of his chamber. In the firmament of the air, may we not see the lofty eagle in his flight far surmounting the little choristers of the valleys? The like disproportion who observes not amongst those creatures that take their pastime in the deep waters, or that range upon the high mountains, hunting for their prey? And hath not the same Almighty Creator and disposer of all things made some of the sons of men as far differing in height of body one from the other, as Saul from the rest of the people. . . . And are not some advanced as high above others in dignity and power, as much as the cedars of Lebanon the low shrubs of the valley? It is not then the result of time or chance, that some are mounted on horseback, while others are left to travell on foot. That some have with the Centurion power to command, while others are required to obey, *the poor and the rich meet together, the Lord is the maker of them both*, The Almighty hath appointed her that sits behind the mill, as well as him that ruleth on the throne. And herein hath he as well consulted the good of humane nature, as the glory of his own wisdome and power: Thoase of the superiour rank, but making a supply of what is wanting in the other: otherwise might not the foolish and ignorant be like to loose themselves in the Wilderness, if others were not as eyes to them [?] The fearful and the weak might be distroyed, if others more strong and valiant, did not protect and defend them. The poor and needy might starve with hunger and cold, were they not fed with the morsells, and warmed with the fleece of the wealthy. Is it not found by experience, that the greatest part of mankind, are but as tools and Instruments for others to work by, rather then any proper Agents to effect any thing of themselves: In peace how would most people destroy themselves by slothfulness and security? In war they would be destroyed by others, were it not for the wisdome and courage of the valliant. If the virtue and valour of the good did not interpose by their authority, to prevent and save, the vice of the bad would bring mischief enough upon places to ruine both, else why is it so frequently intimated in the latter end of the book of Judges, that in those dayes, when there was no king in

Israel, but every man was left to do what seemed right in his own eyes, that these and those enormityes break forth, that violated all Lawes, and offered violence even unto nature itself? . . . Thus if Order were taken away, soon would confusion follow, and every evill work, *James* 3. 16. Nothing therefore can be imagined more remote either from right reason, or true religion, then to think that because we were all once equal at our birth, and shall be again at our death, therefore we should be so in the whole course of our lives. In fine, a body would not be more monstrous and deformed without an Head, nor a ship more dangerous at Sea without a Pilot, nor a floack of sheep more ready to be devoured without a Shepheard, then would humane Society be without an Head, and Leader in time of danger. . . .

In a curious piece of Architecture, that which first offers it self to the view of the beholder, is the beauty of the structure, the proportion that one piece bears to another, wherein the skill of the Architect most shews it self. But that which is most Admirable in sensitive and rational beings, is that inward principle, seated in some one part, able to guid the whole, and influence all the rest of the parts, with an apt and regular motion, for their mutual good and safety. The wisdome of the Creatour was more seen in the breath of life, breathed into the Nostrils of Adam, whereby he became a living soul, then in the feature and beauty of the goodly frame of his body, formed out of the dust, as the Poet speaks, *Os homini sublime dedit* . . . The Architect of that curious piece hath placed the Head in the fore-front, and highest sphear, where are lodged all the senses, as in a Watch-Tower, ready to be improved upon all occasions, for the safety and preservation of the whole. There are placed those that look out at the windows, to foresee evil and danger approaching, accordingly to alarm all the other inferiour powers, to take the signal and stand upon their guard, for defence of the whole. There also is the seat of the Daughters of musick, ready to give audience to all reports and messages that come from abroad; if any thing should occurre or happen nearer home, or further off, imparting either fear of evil, or hope of good: Their work is immediately to dispatch messages through the whole province of nature, to summon all the other Members together, to come in and yield the assistance to prevent the mischief feared, or prepare for the reception of the good promised, or pretended, as the nature of the case may require. Thus are all orders wont to be dispathched and issued from the Cinque ports of the senses in, and about the head, for the benefit and advantage of the whole body. Very fitly therefore in the body politick are the rulers by way of allusion called Heads. And in case of inability to discharge those functions, such societies may not undeservedly be compared to the *Palmists* Idols, that have eyes but see not, and have ears but hear not. Suppose the hands be never so strong for action or the feet never so swift for motion, yet if there be not discretion in the head to discerne, or judgement to determine what is meet to be done for the obviating of evil and danger, or procuring of good, it will be impossible to save such a body from ruine and destruction. If the Mast be never so well strengthened, and the Tackline never so well bound together, yet if there want a skilful Pilot to Steer and Guide, especially in a rough and tempestuous Sea, the lame will soon take the prey.

SAMUEL WILLARD, 1640–1707

[Samuel Willard, born in Concord, was the son of Major Simon Willard, a founder of the town; he graduated from Harvard College in the class of 1659, and preached for a time at Groton until the church and the town were scattered by an Indian attack in 1676. He was then called to the Old South Church in Boston, where he remained until his death, second in importance only to Increase Mather in Eastern Massachusetts. John Dunton said of him, "He's a Man of Profound Notions: Can say what he will, and prove what he says." Though less dictatorial than Increase, his scholarship was probably broader and his mind more philosophical. He delivered a series of sermons over a long period of years expounding in systematic detail the outline of the orthodox theology; the sermons were published after his death in a tremendous folio volume. He was Vice-President of Harvard College from 1701 to 1707, which office was really the headship because their was no President. Cf. Samuel Eliot Morison, *Harvard College in the Seventeenth Century;* Sibley, *Biographical Sketches;* Sprague, *Annals*. This text is from *The Character of a Good Ruler* (Boston, 1694), an election sermon, preached on May 30.]

THE CHARACTER OF A GOOD RULER

WHETHER the Ordination of *Civil Government* be an *Article of the Law of Nature*, and it should accordingly have been established upon the Multiplication of Mankind, although they had retained their Primitive Integrity: Or whether it have only a *Positive right*, and was introduced upon mans *Apostacy;* is a question about which all are not agreed. The equity of it, to be sure, is founded in the Law Natural, and is to be discovered by the light of Nature, being accordingly acknowledged by such as are strangers to Scripture Revelation; and by Christians it is reducible to the first Command in the Second Table of the Decalogue; which is supposed to be a transcript of the Law given to *Adam* at the first, and written upon the Tables of his Heart. For tho', had man kept his first state, the Moral Image Concreated in him, consisting in, *Knowledg, Righteousness, and True Holiness,* would have maintained him in a perfect understanding of, and Spontaneous Obedience to the whole duty incumbent on him, without the need of civil Laws to direct him, or a civil Sword to lay compulsion on him; and it would have been the true Golden Age, which the Heathen *Mythologists* are to Fabulous about. yet even then did the All-Wise God Ordain Orders of Superiority and Inferiority among men, and required an *Honour* to be paid accordingly. But since the unhappy Fall hath Robbed man of that perfection, and filled his heart with perverse and rebellious principles, tending to the Subversion of all Order and the reducing of the World to a *Chaos;* necessity requires, and the Political happiness of a People is concerned in the establishment of Civil Government. The want of it hath ever been pernicious, and attended on with miserable Circumstances. When there was no Governour in *Israel,* but every man did what he would, what horrible outrages, were then perpetrated, though Holy and Zealous *Phinehas* was at that time the High-Priest? and we ourselves have had a Specimen of this in the short *Anarchy* accompanying our late *Revolution.* Gods Wisdom therefore, and his goodness is to be adored in that he hath laid in such a relief for the Children of men, against the mischief which would otherwise devour them; and engraven an inclination on their hearts, generally to comply with it. But this notwithstanding, mens sins may put a curse into their Blessings, & render their remedy to be not better, possibly worse than the Malady. Government is to prevent and cure the disorders that are apt to break forth among the Societies of men; and to promote the civil peace and prosperity of such a people, as well as to suppress impiety, and nourish Religion. For this end there are to be both *Rulers,* and such as are to be *Ruled* by them: and the Weal or Wo of a People mainly depends on the qualifications of those *Rulers,* by whom we are to be Governed. . . .

Doctrine

It is of highest Consequence, that Civil Rulers should be Just Men, and such as Rule in the Fear of God. . . .

Civil Rulers are all such as are in the exercise of a rightful Authority over others. These do not all of them stand in one equal Rank, nor are alike influential into Government. There are Supream and Subordinate Powers: and of these also there are some who have a *Legislative*, others an *Executive* Power in their Hands; which two, though they may sometimes meet in the same persons, yet are in themselves things of a different Nature. There are *Superiour Magistrates* in *Provinces*, and such as are of *Council* with them, and *Assembly men*, the *Representatives* of the People. There are *Judges* in Courts, *Superiour* and *Inferiour; Justices* of the *Peace* in their several Precincts: and in each of these Orders there Resides a measure of Authority.

Now, that all these may be *Just*, it is firstly required, that they have a Principle of *Moral Honesty* in them, and Swaying of them: that they *Love Righteousness, and Hate Iniquity:* that they be *Men of Truth*, Exod. 18. 21. for every man will act in his Relation, according to the Principle that Rules in him: so that an Unrighteous man will be an Unrighteous Ruler, so far as he hath an Opportunity.

They must also be acquainted with the Rules of Righteousness; they must know what is Just, and what is Unjust, be *Able Men*, Exod. 18. 21. For, though men may know and not do, yet *without Knowledge the Mind cannot be good.* Ignorance is a Foundation for Error, and will likely produce it, when the man applies himself to act: and if he do right at any time, it is but by guess, which is a very poor Commendation.

Again, he must be one that respects the Cause, and not the persons in all his Administrations, Deut. 1. 17. *Ye shall not respect Persons in Judgment*, &c. if his Affections Oversway his Judgment at any time, they will be a crooked Biais, that will turn him out of the way, and that shall be Justice in one mans case, which will not be so in another.

Farthermore, he must be one whom neither Flattery nor Bribery may be able to remove out of his way, Deut. 16. 19. *Thou shalt not wrest Judgment, thou shalt not Respect Persons, neither take a Gift;* and hence he must be one who hates both Ambition and Covetousness, Exod. 18. 21 *Hating Covetousness;* which word signifies, a *Greedy Desire*, and is applicable to both the fore cited Vices: for if these Rule him, he will never be a just Ruler.

Finally, he must be one who prefers the publick Benefit above all private and separate Interests whatsoever. Every man in his place, owes himself to the good of the whole; and if he doth not so devote himself, he is unjust: and he who either to advance himself, or to be Revenged on another, will push on Injurious Laws, or pervert the true Intention of such as are in Force, is an unjust man: and he who is under the influence of a *Narrow Spirit*, will be ready to do so, as occasion offers.

Nor is this *Justice* to be lookt upon as separate from the *Fear of God*, but as influenced and maintained by it. He therefore that *Ruleth in the Fear of God*, is one who Acknowledgeth God to be his Soveraign, and carries in his heart an Awful Fear of him: who owns his Commission to be from him, and expects ere long to be called to give in an Account of his managing of it: which maketh him to study in all things to please him, and to be afraid of doing any thing that will provoke him.

And accordingly, he is a Student in the Law of God, and *Meditates in it Day and Night;* making it the Rule into which he ultimately resolves all that he doth in his place. We find that in the Old Law, the *King* was to *write a* Copy of it with his own hand, and to make use of it at all times: *Deut.* 17. 18, 19.

If he hath any thing to do in the making of Laws, he will consult a good Conscience, and what may be pleasing to God, and will be far from *framing mischief by a Law*. And if he be to execute any Laws of men, he will not dare to give a judgment for such an one as directly Crosseth the Command of God, but counts it *ipso facto* void, and his Conscience acquitted of his Oath.

Yea the *Fear of God* will make him not to think himself Lawless; nor dare to bear witness, by Laws and Penalties, against sins in others, which he countenanceth and encourageth by living in the Practise of himself: But to use utmost endeavours that his own life may be an exemplification of Obedience, and others may learn by Him, what a Veneration he hath for the Laws that are enacted for the good of Man-kind.

In a word, he is one that will take care to promote *Piety* as well as *Honesty* among men; and do his utmost that the true Religion may be countenanced and established, and that all Ungodliness, as well as Unrighteousness, may have a due Testimony born against it at all times. So he resolves *Psal.* 75. 10. *all the horns of the wicked also will I cut off; but the horns of the righteous shall be exalted.*

It then follows that we enquire of what great moment or consequence it is that these should be such: and there is a three-fold respect in which the high importance of it is to be discovered by us.

1. In respect to the Glory of God.

Civil Rulers are Gods Vicegerents here upon earth; hence they are somtimes honoured with the title of Gods, *Psal.* 82 6. *I have said ye are Gods*. Government is Gods Ordinance; and those that are Vested with it, however *mediately* introduced into it, have their rightful authority from him, Prov. 8. 15, 16. *By me Kings Reign, and Princes Decree Justice.* By *me Princes Rule, and Nobles, even all the Judges of the Earth,* and they that are from him, should be for him, and ought to seek the Honour of him who is *King of Kings, and Lord of Lords:* which they only then do, when they manage their whole Interest and Power with a Design for his Glory; & accordingly manage themselves in all their Ministrations by the Statutes of his Kingdom; which none will ever do, but they that are *Just, Ruling in the Fear of God.* Righteousness and Religion flourishing in these, will be as a Torch on an Hill, whose Light and Influence will be vastly extensive: every one will be advantaged to see their good works, and to Glorifie God for and in them. Their very Example will have the force of a Law in it, and win many by a powerful Attraction, to the avoiding of sin, and practising of Righteousness. They will be a good Copy, that many will be ambitious to write after: and their faithful Administrations will render them a *Terror to Evil Doers, and an Encouragement to them that do well;* which will advance the very end of Government. Whereas the Evil Deportment, and Ill Management of *Rulers,* who are unjust, and void of the Fear of God, is an open scandal, and of a more pernicious tendency than the wickedness of others; inasmuch as their Example is a discouragement to them that are well disposed, and animates those that are set in their hearts for iniquity, and they are thereby emboldned to shew their heads, and to declare their sin as *Sodom:* hence that Remark of the Psalmist, *Psal.* 12. 8. *The wicked walk on every side, when the vilest men are exalted.* Those that would bear their Testimony against Impiety and Debauchery, are frowned on and neglected; and such as would Nourish them are Countenanced: and either good Laws to suppress them are not provided, or they are laid by as things Obsolete, and of no Service: and thus all Abominations come in upon a People as a Flood, and the Name of God is wofully dishonoured by this means: and hereupon the last and most excellent end of Government comes to be frustrated, and what is there that we can conceive to be of greater weight than this? if this be lost, the Glory of such a people is gone.

2. In regard to the weal of the People over whom they Rule.

A People are not made for Rulers, But Rulers for a People. It is indeed an Honour which God puts upon some above others, when he takes them from among the People, and sets them up to Rule over them, but it is for the Peoples sake, and the Civil felicity of them is the next end of Civil Policy; and the happiness of Rulers is bound up with theirs in it. Nor can any wise men in authority think themselves happy in the Misery of their Subjects, to whom they either are or should be as Children are to their Fathers: We have the Benefit of Government expressed, 1. *Tim.* 2 : 2. *a quiet Life and a peaceable, in all Godliness and honesty.* and it lies especialy with Rulers, under God, to make a People Happy or Miserable. When men can injoy their Liberties and Rights without molestation or oppression; when they can live without fear of being born down by their more Potent Neighbours; when they are secured against Violence, and may be Righted against them that offer them any injury, without fraud; and are encouraged to serve God in their own way, with freedom, and without being imposed upon contrary to the Gospel precepts; now are they an happy People. But this is to be expected from none other but men just and Pious: they that are otherwise, will themselves be oppressours, and they that are influenced by them, and dependent on them, will adde to the grievance. They that should look after them Will Do it fast enough: Yea every one will usurp a License to do so to his Neighbour upon an advantage: and such a people must needs groan under an intollerable burden. Besides, it is a great Truth, that the Mercies and Judgments of God come upon a people, according as their Rulers carry themselves in managing of the Trust which God hath committed to them. Just and Zealous Rulers, are men that *Stand in the Gap,* and keep off Judgments from a sinning people; God *sought* for *one* such, *Ezek.* 22. 30. they *turn away wrath,* when it hath made an inroad, so it is recorded of Phinehas that he did, *Ps.* 106. 30. and God is wont to Bless such a People, as He did *Israel* and *Judah* in the days of *David, Solomon, Jehoshaphat, Hezekiah,* and *Josiah:* wheras when these fall into such sins as God is Provoked at, the People are like to Smart for it. There is such an Influence with the Prevarications of these men, that, in the righteous judgment of God, those under them suffer grievously by it. This the Heathen observed in the course of Providence, and made that remark upon it, *Delirant reges, plectuntur Achivi.* Thus *David* numbers the People, and Seventy Thousand of the men of Israel die for it, 2Sa. 24. Yea such may be the influence of the Male-administration of Rulers, though done without malice, and in an heat of misguided *zeal* for the People of God; as *Sauls* act in Slaying the *Gibeonites* is recorded to have been 2 *Sam* 21 2. that the Guilt may ly long upon a Land, and break out in Terrible Judgments a great while after, and not be expiated till the sin be openly confessed, and the Atonement sought unto.

3. With Reference to *Rulers* themselves. It is, as we before Observed, a Dignity put upon them, to be preferred to Government over their Brethren; to have the oversight, not of Beasts, but of Men. But as there is a great Trust devolved on them, so there is an answerable Reckoning which they must be called unto: And however they are setled in Authority by men, yet *God*, who Rules over all, hath put them in only *Durante Bene Plecito:* they are upon their good Behaviour; they are *Stewards*, and whensoever *God* pleaseth, He will call for a Reckoning, and put them out. *God sets up, and he pulls down;* and he hath a respect to mens Carriages in his dealings with them. Godly and Zealous *Phinehas* got a Blessing for himself and his Posterity, *Numb.* 25. 11. *&c.* Whereas *Saul* procured for himself a Rejection, and the laying aside and almost Extirpation of his Family. We have this also instanced in *Shebna* and *Eliakim Isa.* 22. 15. *&c.* Yea, what did *Jeroboam*, what did *Ahab*, and many others procure for themselves, by their ill Government, but the utter rooting out of their Names, and Posterity? The *Fourth Generation* may Rue that ever they derived from such Progenitors. The only sure way for Rulers to build up their own Houses, is to be such in their places as *David* was, of whom we have that Testimony, *Psal.* 78. 71, 72. *He brought him to Feed* Jacob *his People, and* Israel *his Inheritance. So he Fed them according to the Integrity of his heart, and guided them by the Skilfulness of his hands.* And although God doth not always peculiarly put a Brand in this World upon Impious and Unjust Rulers, yet there is a Tribunal before which they must stand e're long as other men; only their Account will be so much the more Fearful, and Condemnation more Tremendous, by how much they have neglected to take their greater advantages to Glorify God, and abused their Power to His Dishonour, by which they had a fairer opportunity than other men.

JOHN WISE, 1652–1725

[John Wise, the son of an indentured servant, graduated from Harvard College in 1673, and began to preach to the people of the Chebacco district, a corner of Ipswich township, in 1680; he was ordained minister of a formally incorporated church there in 1682. He was given ten acres of land, paid £60 a year, one third of it in money and the rest in grain, along with forty cords of wood and eight loads of marsh hay. Almost nothing can be discovered about his life except on the three or four occasions upon which he emerged to take up the cudgels for some cause or other. In 1687 he led the town of Ipswich in fiery protest against taxes levied by Governor Andros without the consent of any legislature, making a speech to the town meeting in which he said, "We had a good God, and a good King, and should do well to stand to our Priviledges." He was arrested, jailed, and fined by Andros. In 1690 he was chaplain of the disastrous expedition against Quebec; he wrote an account of the fiasco with a fine scorn for the amateur militia officers. He helped check the witchcraft panic, and in 1703 was a signer of a petition to clear the names of those that had been condemned. He supported inoculation in 1721, and in his last years agitated for paper money. On every occasion when we get a glimpse of him, Wise is a vigorous, hard-hitting, racy champion of popular causes and the agrarian point of vew. The *Proposals* against which he wrote his two most important tracts were first issued by an association of Boston and Cambridge ministers in 1705; he overwhelmed these proposals with abuse in *The Churches Quarrel Espoused* in 1710, and argued the cause of the independency and autonomy of separate congregations more soberly and learnedly in the *Vindication of the Government of New-England Churches*, 1717. This text is from the first edition of the *Vindication*. Cf. Sibley, *Biographical Sketches*.]

VINDICATION

DEMONSTRATION II

CHAP I.

THE Divine Establishment in Providence of the fore-named Churches in their Order is apparently the Royal assent of the supream Monarch of the Churches, to the grave Decisions of Reason in favour of Mans Natural state of Being, and Original Freedom. For if we should make a new *Survey* of the Constitution before named under the brightest Light of Nature, there is no greater Example of natural Wisdom in any settlement on Earth; for the present and future security of Humane Beings in all that is most Valuable and Grand, then in this. That it seems to me as though Wise and Provident Nature by the Dictates of Right Reason excited by the moving Suggestions of Humanity; and awed with the just demands of Natural Libertie, Equity, Equality, and Principles of Self-Preservation, Originally drew up the Scheme, and then obtained the Royal Approbation. And certainly it is agreeable that we attribute it to God whether we receive it nextly from Reason or Revelation, for that each is equally an Emanation of his Wisdom, *Prov.* 20. 27. The Spirit of Man is the Candle of the Lord, searching all the inward parts of the Belly. There be many larger Volumes in this dark Recess called the Belly to be read by that Candle God has Light up. And I am very well assured the fore named Constitution is a Transcript out of some of their Pages, Joh. 1. 4, 9. *And the Life was the Light of Men, which Lighteth every Man which cometh into the World.* This admirable Effect of Christs Creating Power in hanging out so many Lights to guide man through a dark World, is as Applicable to the Light of Reason, as to that of Revelation. For that the Light of Reason as a Law and Rule of Right, is an Effect of Christ's Goodness, care, and creating Power, as well as of Revelation; though Revelation is Natures Law in a fairer and brighter Edition. This is granted by the *London* Ministers,[1] *P.* 8. *C.* 3. "That, that which is evident by, and consonant to the true Light of Nature, or Natural Reason, is to be accounted, *Jure Divino*, in matters of Religion. But in the further and more distinct management of this Plea; I shall,

1. Lay before the Reader several Principles [of] Natural Knowledge.
2. Apply or Improve them in Ecclesiastical affairs.
3. Inferr from the Premises, a Demonstration that these Churches, if not properly Formed; yet are fairly Established in their present Order by the Law of Nature.

Chap II.

1. I Shall disclose several Principles of Natural Knowledge; plainly discovering the Law of Nature; or the true sentiments of Natural Reason, with Respect to Mans Being and Government. And in this Essay I shall peculiarly confine the discourse to two heads, *viz*

1. Of the Natural (in distinction to the Civil) and then,
2. Of the Civil Being of Man. And I shall Principally take Baron *Puffendorff*[2] for my Chief Guide and Spokes-man.

1. I shall consider Man in a state of Natural Being, as a Free-Born Subject under the Crown of Heaven, and owing Homage to none but God himself. It is certain Civil Government in General, is a very Admirable Result of Providence, and an Incomparable Benefit to Man-kind, yet must needs be acknowledged to be the Effect of Humane Free-Compacts and not of Divine Institution; it is the Produce of Mans Reason, of Humane and Rational Combinations, and not from any direct Orders of Infinite Wisdom, in any positive Law wherein is drawn up this or that Scheme of Civil Government. Government (says the Lord *Warrington*[3]) is necessary—in that no Society of Men can subsist without it; and that Particular Form of Government is necessary which best suits the Temper and Inclination of a People.

Nothing can be Gods Ordinance, but what he has particularly Declared to be such; there is no particular Form of Civil Government described in Gods Word, neither does Nature prompt it. The Government of the *Jews* was changed five Times. Government is not formed by Nature, as other Births or Productions; If it were, it would be the same in all Countries; because Nature keeps the same Method, in the same thing, in all Climates. If a Common Wealth be changed into a Monarchy, is it Nature that forms, and brings forth the Monarch? Or if a Royal Family be wholly Extinct (as in *Noah's* Case, being not Heir Apparent from Descent from *Adam*) is it Nature that must go to work (with the King Bees, who themselves alone preserve the Royal Race in that Empire) to Breed a Monarch before the People can have a King, or a Government sent over them? And thus we must leave Kings to Resolve which is their best Title to their Crowns, whether Natural Right, or the Constitution of Government settled by Humane Compacts, under the Direction and Conduct of Reason. But to proceed under the head of a State of Natural Being, I shall more distinctly Explain the State of Humane Nature in its Original Capacity, as Man is placed on Earth by his Maker, and Cloathed with many Investitures, and Immunities which properly belong to Man separately considered. As,

1. The Prime Immunity in Mans State, is that he is most properly the Subject of the Law of Nature. He is the Favourite Animal on Earth; in that this Part of Gods Image, *viz.* Reason is Congenate with his Nature, wherein by a Law Immutable, Instampt upon his Frame, God has provided a Rule for Men in all their Actions, obliging each one to the performance of that which is Right, not only as to Justice, but likewise as to all other Moral Vertues, the which is nothing but the Dictate of Right Reason founded in the Soul of Man. . . . That which is to be drawn from Mans Reason, flowing from the true Current of that Faculty, when unperverted, may be said to be the Law of Nature; on which account, the Holy Scriptures declare it written on Mens hearts. For being indowed with a Soul, you may know from your self, how, and what you ought to act, Rom. 2. 14. *These having not a Law, are a Law to themselves.* So that the meaning is, when we acknowledge the Law of Nature to be the dictate of Right Reason, we must mean that the Understanding of Man is Endowed with such a power, as to be able, from the Comtemplation of humane Condition to discover a necessity of Living agreeably with this Law: And likewise to find out some Principle, by which the Precepts of it, may be clearly and solidly Demonstrated. The way to discover the Law

of Nature in our own state, is by a narrow Watch, and accurate Contemplation of our Natural Condition, and propensions. Others say this is the way to find out the Law of Nature. *scil.* If a Man any ways doubts, whether what he is going to do to another Man be agreeable to the Law of Nature, then let him suppose himself to be in that other Mans Room; And by this Rule effectually Executed. A Man must be a very dull Scholar to Nature not to make Proficiency in the Knowledge of her Laws. But more Particularly in pursuing our Condition for the discovery of the Law of Nature, this is very obvious to view, *viz.*

1. A Principle of Self-Love, & Self-Preservation, is very predominant in every Mans Being.

2. A Sociable Disposition.

3. An Affection or Love to Man-kind in General. And to give such Sentiments the force of a Law, we must suppose a God who takes care of all Mankind, and has thus obliged each one, as a Subject of higher Principles of Being, then meer Instincts. For that all Law properly considered, supposes a capable Subject, and a Superiour Power; And the Law of God which is Binding, is published by the Dictates of Right Reason as other ways: Therefore says *Plutarch*, *To follow God and obey Reason is the same thing.* But moreover that God has Established the Law of Nature, as the General Rule of Government, is further Illustrable from the many Sanctions in Providence, and from the Peace and Guilt of Conscience in them that either obey, or violate the Law of Nature. But moreover, the foundation of the Law of Nature with relation to Government, may be thus Discovered. *scil.* Man is a Creature extreamly desirous of his own Preservation; of himself he is plainly Exposed to many Wants, unable to secure his own safety, and Maintenance without the Assistance of his fellows; and he is also able of returning Kindness by the furtherance of mutual Good; But yet Man is often found to be Malicious, Insolent, and easily Provoked, and as powerful in Effecting mischief, as he is ready in designing it. Now that such a Creature may be Preserved, it is necessary that he be Sociable; that is, that he be capable and disposed to unite himself to those of his own species, and to Regulate himself towards them, that they may have no fair Reason to do him harm; but rather incline to promote his Interests, and secure his Rights and Concerns. This then is a Fundamental Law of Nature, that every Man as far as in him lies, do maintain a Sociableness with others, agreeable with the main end and disposition of humane Nature in general. For this is very apparent, that Reason and Society render Man the most potent of all Creatures.

And Finally, from the Principles of Sociableness it follows as a fundamental Law of Nature, that Man is not so Wedded to his own Interest, but that he can make the Common good the mark of his Aim: And hence he becomes Capacitated to enter into a Civil State by the Law of Nature; for without this property in Nature, *viz.* Sociableness, which is for Cementing of parts, every Government would soon moulder and dissolve.

2. The Second Great Immunity of Man is an Original Liberty Instampt upon his Rational Nature. He that intrudes upon this Liberty, Violates the Law of Nature. In this Discourse I shall wave the Consideration of Mans Moral Turpitude, but shall view him Physically as a Creature which God has made and furnished essentially with many Enobling Immunities, which render him the most August Animal in the World, and still, whatever has happened since his Creation, he remains at the upper-end of Nature, and as such is a Creature of a very Noble Character.[4] For as to his Dominion, the whole frame of the Lower Part of the Universe is devoted to his use, and at his Command; and his Liberty under the Conduct of Right Reason, is equal with his trust. Which Liberty may be briefly Considered, Internally as to his Mind, and Externally as to his Person.

1. The Internal Native Liberty of Mans Nature in general implies, a faculty of Doing or Omitting things according to the Direction of his Judgment. But in a more special meaning, this Liberty does not consist in a loose and ungovernable Freedom, or in an unbounded Licence of Acting. Such Licence is disagreeing with the condition and dignity of Man, and would make Man of a lower and meaner Constitution then Bruit Creatures; who in all their Liberties are kept under a better and more Rational Government, by their Instincts. Therefore as *Plutarch* says, *Those Persons only who live in Obedience to Reason, are worthy to be accounted free: They alone live as they Will, who have Learnt what they ought to Will.* So that the true Natural Liberty of Man, such as really and truely agrees to him, must be understood, as he is Guided and Restrained by the Tyes of Reason, and Laws of Nature; all the rest is Brutal, if not worse.[5]

2. Mans External Personal, Natural Liberty, Antecedent to all Humane parts, or Alliances must also be considered. And so every Man must be conceived to be perfectly in his own Power and disposal, and not to be controuled by the Authority of any other. And thus every Man, must be acknowledged equal to every Man, since all Subjection and all Command are equally banished on both sides; and considering all Men thus at Liberty, every Man has a Prerogative to Judge

for himself, *viz.* What shall be most for his Behoof, Happiness and Well-being.

3. The Third Capital Immunity belonging to Mans Nature, is an equality amongst Men; Which is not to be denyed by the Law of Nature, till Man has Resigned himself with all his Rights for the sake of a Civil State; and then his Personal Liberty and Equality is to be cherished, and preserved to the highest degree, as will consist with all just distinctions amongst Men of Honour, and shall be agreeable with the publick Good. For Man has a high valuation of himself, and the passion seems to lay its first foundation (not in Pride, but) really in the high and admirable Frame and Constitution of Humane Nature. The Word Man, says my Author, is thought to carry somewhat of Dignity in its sound; and we commonly make use of this as the most proper and prevailing Argument against a rude Insulter, *viz. I am not a Beast or a Dog, but am a Man as well as your self.* Since then Humane Nature agrees equally with all persons; and since no one can live a Sociable Life with another that does not own or Respect him as a Man; It follows as a Command of the Law of Nature, that every Man Esteem and treat another as one who is naturally his Equal, or who is a Man as well as he. There be many popular, or plausible Reasons that greatly Illustrate this Equality, *viz.* that we all Derive our Being from one stock, the same Common Father of humane Race. On this Consideration *Bœthius* checks the pride of the Insulting Nobility.

Quid Genus et Proavos Strepitis?
Si Primordia Vestra,
Auteremque Deum Spectas,
Nullus Degener Extat
Nisi vitiis Pejora fovens,
Proprium Deserat Ortum.

Fondly our first Descent we Boast;
If whence at first our Breath we Drew,
The common springs of Life we view,
The Airy Notion soon is Lost.

The Almighty made us equal all;
But he that slavishly complyes
To do the Drudgery of Vice,
Denyes his high Original.

And also that our Bodies are Composed of matter, frail, brittle, and lyable to be destroyed by thousand Accidents; we all owe our Existence to the same Method of propagation. The Noblest Mortal in his Entrance on to the Stage of Life, is not distinguished by any pomp or of passage from the lowest of Mankind; and our Life hastens to the same General Mark: Death observes no Ceremony, but Knocks as loud at the Barriers of the Court, as at the Door of the Cottage. This Equality being admitted, bears a very great force in maintaining Peace and Friendship amongst Men. For that he who would use the Assistance of others, in promoting his own Advantage, ought as freely to be at their service. when they want his help on the like Occasions. *One Good turn Requires another*, is the Common Proverb; for otherwise he must need esteem others unequal to himself, who constantly demands their Aid, and as constantly denies his own. And whoever is of this Insolent Temper, cannot but highly displease those about him, and soon give Occasion of the Breach of the Common Peace. It was a Manly Reproof which *Charactacus* gave the *Romans*. *Num Si vos Omnibus* &c. What! because you desire to be Masters of all Men, does it follow therefore that all Men should desire to be your Slaves, for that it is a Command of Natures Law, that no Man that has not obtained a particular and special Right, shall arrogate to himself a Larger share then his fellows, but shall admit others to equal Priviledges with himself. So that the Principle of Equality in a Natural State, is peculiarly transgressed by Pride, which is when a Man without sufficient reason prefers himself to others. And though as *Hensius*, Paraphrases upon *Aristotle's* Politicks to this Purpose. *viz. Nothing is more suitable to Nature, then that those who Excel in Understanding and Prudence, should Rule and Controul those who are less happy in those Advantages*, &c. Yet we must note, that there is room for an Answer, *scil.* That it would be the greatest absurdity to believe, that Nature actually Invests the Wise with a Sovereignity over the weak; or with a Right of forcing them against their Wills; for that no Sovereignty can be Established, unless some Humane Deed, or Covenant Precede: Nor does Natural fitness for Government make a Man presently Governour over another; for that as *Ulpian* says, *by a Natural Right all Men are born free;* and Nature having set all Men upon a Level and made them Equals, no Servitude or Subjection can be conceived without Inequality; and this cannot be made without Usurpation or Force in others, or Voluntary Compliance in those who Resign their freedom, and give away their degree of Natural Being And thus we come,

2. To consider Man in a Civil State of Being; wherein we shall observe the great difference betwen a Natural, and Political State; for in the Latter State many Great disproportions appear, or at least many obvious distinctions are soon made amongst Men; which Doctrine is to be laid open under a few heads.

1. Every Man considered in a Natural State, must be allowed to be Free, and at his own dispose; yet to suit Mans Inclinations to Society; And in a peculiar manner to gratify the necessity he is in of publick Rule and Order, he is Impelled to enter into a Civil Community; and Divests himself of his Natural Freedom, and puts himself under Government; which amongst other things Comprehends the Power of Life and Death over Him; together with Authority to Injoyn him some things to which he has an utter Aversation, and to prohibit him other things, for which he may have as strong an Inclination; so that he may be often under this Authority, obliged to Sacrifice his Private, for the Publick Good. So that though Man is inclined to Society, yet he is driven to a Combination by great necessity. For that the true and leading Cause of forming Governments, and yielding up Natural Liberty, and throwing Mans Equality into a Common Pile to be new Cast by the Rules of fellowship; was really and truly to guard themselves against the Injuries Men were lyable to Interchangeably; for none so Good to Man, as Man, and yet none a greater Enemy. So that,

2. The first Humane Subject and Original of Civil Power is the People. For as they have a Power every Man over himself in a Natural State, so upon a Combination they can and do bequeath this Power unto others; and settle it according as their united discretion shall Determine. For that this is very plain, that when the Subject of Sovereign Power is quite Extinct, that Power returns to the People again. And when they are free, they may set up what species of Government they please; or if they rather incline to it, they may subside into a State of Natural Being, if it be plainly for the best. In the *Eastern* Country of the *Mogul*, we have some resemblance of the Case; for upon the Death of an absolute Monarch, they live so many days without a Civil Head; but in that *Interregnum*, those who survive the Vacancy, are glad to get into a Civil State again; and usually they are in a very Bloody Condition when they return under the Covert of a new Monarch; this project is to indear the People to a Tyranny, from the Experience they have so lately had of an Anarchy.

3. The formal Reason of Government is the Will of a Community, yielded up and surrendred to some other Subject, either of one particular Person, or more, Conveyed in the following manner.

Let us conceive in our Mind a multitude of Men, all Naturally Free & Equal; going about voluntarily, to Erect themselves into a new Common-Wealth. Now their Condition being such, to bring themselves into a Politick Body, they must needs Enter into divers Covenants.

1. They must Interchangeably each Man Covenant to joyn in one

lasting Society, that they may be capable to concert the measures of their safety, by a Publick Vote.

2. A Vote or Decree must then nextly pass to set up some Particular species of Government over them. And if they are joyned in their first Compact upon absolute Terms to stand to the Decision of the first Vote concerning the Species of Government: Then all are bound by the Majority to acquiesce in that particular Form thereby settled, though their own private Opinion, incline them to some other Model.

3. After a Decree has specified the Particular form of Government, then there will be need of a New Covenant, whereby those on whom Sovereignty is conferred, engage to take care of the Common Peace, and Welfare. And the Subjects on the other hand, to yield them faithful Obedience. In which Covenant is Included that Submission and Union of Wills, by which a State may be conceived to be but one Person. So that the most proper Definition of a Civil State, is this. *viz.* A Civil State is a Compound Moral Person. whose Will (United by those Covenants before passed) is the Will of all; to the end it may Use, and Apply the strength and riches of Private Persons towards maintaining the Common Peace, Security, and Well-being of all. Which may be conceived as tho' the whole State was now become but one Man; in which the aforesaid Covenants may be supposed under Gods Providence, to be the Divine *Fiat*, Pronounced by God, let us make Man. And by way of resemblance the aforesaid Being may be thus Anatomized.

1. The Sovereign Power is the Soul infused, giving Life and Motion to the whole Body.
2. Subordinate Officers are the Joynts by which the Body moves.
3. Wealth and Riches are the Strength.
4. Equity and Laws are the Reason.
5. Councellors the Memory.
6. *Salus Populi*, or the Happiness of the People, is the End of its Being; or main Business to be attended and done.
7. Concord amongst the Members, and all Estates, is the Health.
8. Sedition is Sickness, and Civil War Death.

4. The Parts of Sovereignty may be considered: So,

1. As it Prescribes the Rule of Action: It is rightly termed *Legislative Power*.
2. As it determines the Controversies of Subjects by the Standard of those Rules. So is it justly Termed Judiciary Power.
3. As it Arms the Subjects against Foreigners, or forbids Hostility, so its called the Power of Peace and War.

4. As it takes in Ministers for the discharge of Business, so it is called the Right of Appointing Magistrates. So that all great Officers and Publick Servants, must needs owe their Original to the Creating Power of Sovereignty. So that those whose Right it is to Create, may Dissolve the being of those who are Created, unless they cast them into an Immortal Frame. And yet must needs be dissoluble if they justly forfeit their being to their Creators.

5. The Chief End of Civil Communities, is, that Men thus conjoyned, may be secured against the Injuries, they are lyable to from their own Kind. For if every Man could secure himself singly; It would be great folly for him, to Renounce his Natural Liberty, in which every Man is his own King and Protector.

6. The Sovereign Authority besides that it inheres in every State as in a Common and General Subject. So farther according as it resides in some One Person, or in a Council (consisting of some Select Persons, or of all the Members of a Community) as in a proper and particular Subject, so it produceth different Forms of Common-wealths, *viz.* Such as are either simple and regular, or mixt.

1. The Forms of a Regular State are three only, which Forms arise from the proper and particular Subject, in which the Supream Power Resides. As,

1. A Democracy, which is when the Sovereign Power is Lodged in a Council consisting of all the Members, and where every Member has the Priviledge of a Vote. This Form of Government, appears in the greatest part of the World to have been the most Ancient. For that Reason seems to shew it to be most probable, that when Men (being Originally in a condition of Natural Freedom and Equality) had thoughts of joyning in a Civil Body, would without question be inclined to Administer their common Affairs, by their common Judgment, and so must necessarily to gratifie that Inclination establish a Democracy; neither can it be rationally imagined, that Fathers of Families being yet Free and Independent, should in a moment, or little time take off their long delight in governing their own Affairs, & Devolve all upon some single Sovereign Commander; for that it seems to have been thought more Equitable, that what belonged to all, should be managed by all, when all had entered by Compact into one Community. The Original of our Government, says *Plato*, (speaking of the *Athenian* Commonwealth) *was taken from the Equality of our Race. Other States there are composed of different Blood, and of unequal Lines, the Consequence of which are disproportionable Soveraignty, Tyrannical or Oligarchycal Sway; under which men live in such a manner, as to Esteem themselves partly*

Lords, and partly Slaves to each other. But we and our Country-men, being all Born Brethren of the same Mother, do not look upon our selves, to stand under so hard a Relation, as that of Lords and Slaves; but the Parity of our Descent incline us to keep up the like Parity by our Laws, and to yield the precedency to nothing but to Superiour Vertue and Wisdom. And moreover it seems very manifest that most Civil Communities arose at first from the Union of Families, that were nearly allyed in Race and Blood. And though Ancient Story make frequent mention of Kings, yet it appears that most of them were such that had an Influence rather in perswading, then in any Power of Commanding. So *Justin* discribes that Kind of Government, as the most Primitive, which *Aristotle* stiles an Heroical Kingdom. *viz.* Such as is no ways Inconsistent with a Democratical State. *De Princip. Reru.* 1. *L.* 1. *C.*

A democracy is then Erected, when a Number of Free Persons, do Assemble together, in Order to enter into a Covenant for Uniting themselves in a Body: And such a Preparative Assembly hath some appearance already of a Democracy; it is a Democracy in *Embrio* properly in this Respect, that every Man hath the Priviledge freely to deliver his Opinion concerning the Common Affairs. Yet he who dissents from the Vote of the Majority, is not in the least obliged by what they determine, till by a second Covenant, a Popular Form be actually Established; for not before then can we call it a Democratical Government, *viz.* Till the Right of Determining all matters relating to the publick Safety, is actually placed in a General Assembly of the whole People; or by their own Compact and Mutual Agreement, Determine themselves the proper Subject for the Exercise of Sovereign Power. And to compleat this State, and render it capable to Exert its Power to answer the End of a Civil State: These Conditions are necessary.

1. That a certain Time and Place be Assigned for Assembling.

2. That when the Assembly be Orderly met, as to Time and Place, that then the Vote of the Majority must pass for the Vote of the whole Body.

3. That Magistrates be appointed to Exercise the Authority of the whole for the better dispatch of Business, of every days Occurrence; who also may with more Mature diligence, search into more Important Affairs; and if in case any thing happens of greater Consequence, may report it to the Assembly; and be peculiarly Serviceable in putting all Publick Decrees into Execution. Because a large Body of People is almost useless in Respect of the last Service, and of many others, as to the more Particular Application and Exercise of Power. Therefore

it is most agreeable with the Law of Nature, that they Institute their Officers to act in their Name, and Stead

2. The Second Species of Regular Government, is an Aristocracy; and this is said then to be Constituted when the People, or Assembly United by a first Covenant, and having thereby cast themselves into the first Rudiments of a State; do then by Common Decree, Devolve the Sovereign Power, on a Council consisting of some Select Members; and these having accepted of the Designation, are then properly invested with Sovereign Command; and then an Aristocracy is formed.

3. The Third Species of a Regular Government, is a Monarchy which is settled when the Sovereign Power is confered on some one worthy Person. It differs from the former, because a Monarch who is but one Person in Natural, as well as in Moral account, & so is furnished with an Immediate Power of Exercising Sovereign Command in all Instances of Government; but the fore named must needs have Particular Time and Place assigned; but the Power and Authority is Equal in each. . . .

An Aristocracy is a dangerous Constitution in the Church of Christ, as it possesses the Presbytery of all Church Power: What has been observed sufficiently Evinces it. And not only so but from the Nature of the Constitution, for it has no more Barrier to it, against the Ambition, Insults, and Arbitrary measures of Men, then an absolute Monarchy. But to abbreviate; it seems most agreeable with the Light of Nature, that if there be any of the Regular Government settled in the Church of God it must needs be.

3. A Democracy. This is a form of Government, which the Light of Nature does highly value, & often directs to as most agreeable to the Just and Natural Prerogatives of Humane Beings. This was of great account, in the early times of the World. And not only so, but upon the Experience of several Thousand years, after the World had been tumbled, and tost from one Species of Government to another, at a great Expence of Blood and Treasure, many of the wise Nations of the World have sheltered themselves under it again; or at least have blendished, and balanced their Governments with it.

It is certainly a great Truth, *scil.* That Mans Original Liberty after it is Resigned, (yet under due Restrictions) ought to be Cherished in all wise Governments; or otherwise a man in making himself a Subject, he alters himself from a Freeman, into a Slave, which to do is Repugnant to the Law of Nature. Also the Natural Equality of Men amongst Men must be duly favoured; in that Government was never Established by God or Nature, to give one Man a Prerogative to insult over another; therefore in a Civil, as well as in a Natural State of Being, a just Equality is to be indulged so far as that every Man is bound to Honour every Man, which is agreeable both with Nature and Religion, 1 Pet. 2. 17. *Honour all Men.*—The End of all good Government is to Cultivate Humanity, and Promote the happiness of all, and the good of every Man in all his Rights, his Life, Liberty, Estate, Honour, *&c.* without injury or abuse done to any. Then certainly it cannot easily be thought, that a company of Men, that shall enter into a voluntary Compact, to hold all Power in their own hands, thereby to use and improve their united force, wisdom, riches and strength for the Common and Particular good of every Member, as is the Nature of a Democracy; I say it cannot be that this sort of Constitution, will so readily furnish those in Government with an appetite, or disposition to prey upon each other, or imbezle the common Stock; as some Particular Persons may be apt to do when set off, and Intrusted with the same Power. And moreover this appears very Natural, that when the aforesaid Government or Power, settled in all, when they have Elected certain capable Persons to Minister in their affairs, and the said Ministers remain accountable to the Assembly; these Officers must needs be under the influence of many wise cautions from their own thoughts (as well as under confinement by their Commission) in their whole Administration: And from thence it must needs follow that they will be more apt, and inclined to steer Right for the main Point, *viz.* The peculiar good, and benefit of the whole, and every particular Member fairly and sincerely. And why may not these stand for very Rational Pleas in Church Order?

For certainly if Christ has settled any form of Power in his Church he has done it for his Churches safety, and for the Benefit of every Member: Then he must needs be presumed to have made choice of that Government as should least Expose his People to Hazard, either from the fraud, or Arbitrary measures of particular Men. And it is as plain as day light, there is no Species of Government like a Democracy to attain this End. There is but about two steps from an Aristocracy, to a Monarchy, and from thence but one to a Tyranny; an able standing force, and an Ill-Nature, *Ipso facto*, turns an absolute Monarch into a Tyrant; this is obvious among the Roman *Cæsars*, and through the World. And all these direful Transmutations are easier in Church affairs (from the different Qualities of things) then in Civil States. For what is it that cunning and learned Men can't make the World swallow as an Article of their Creed, if they are once invested with an Uncontroulable Power, and are to be the standing Oratours to Mankind in matters of Faith and Obedience?

JOHN BARNARD, 1681–1770

[John Barnard was born in Boston, the son of a housewright and selectman, educated at the Latin school under Ezekiel Cheever, and graduated from Harvard College in 1700. While an undergraduate he was much stimulated by the poetry of Cowley. He joined the North Church, assisted in the preparation of a pamphlet in defense of Increase and Cotton Mather against the accusations of Robert Calef, and took his M.A. in 1703. Though for a time regarded as a "tool of the Mathers," he nevertheless won the esteem and friendship of Benjamin Colman. He served as chaplain in the melancholy expedition against Port Royal in 1707; he indulged in a game of cards during this enterprise, was censured by the Mathers, and though he made public acknowledgment of his fault, turned his affections to the more liberal wing of the clergy. He went to London, 1709–1710; when he returned he was opposed by the Mathers, but in spite of them was finally settled over a church at Marblehead in 1716. His influence in the town was large; at the time of his settlement Marblehead was a straggling fishing village; he guided not only the spiritual but the material career of his congregation and was instrumental in transforming the town into a thriving seaport in the course of his long ministry. He was influential in getting his friend Holyoke chosen President of Harvard College in 1737. A tall, energetic figure, he was a scholar, linguist, mathematician, an expert on ships and shipbuilding, an amateur musician, an upholder of inoculation; he was active in reassembling a library for the college after the fire of 1764. All told, he was one of the finest examples of the eighteenth-century New England parson. His autobiography is printed in *Collections of the Massachusetts Historical Society*, Series 3, V, 177–243. This text is from *The Throne Established by Righteousness* (Boston, 1734), an election sermon. Cf. Sibley, *Biographical Sketches.*]

THE THRONE ESTABLISHED BY RIGHTEOUSNESS

1. The first Thing I would observe here is, the *Original* of Government, and whence it takes its Rise. And I doubt not to say, That it is from God, who is the *God of Order and not of Confusion:* That is to say, that, upon Supposition that Mankind dwell together in Societies, which the humane Nature cannot well avoid, it is not a matter of Liberty and Freedom, and left to the Option and Choice of the Will of Man, whether there shall be Government, or no, or whether there shall be any Rules for the regulating of that Society; but it has the

stamp of the Divine Authority upon it, and comes to us with a *thus saith the Lord.*

This the Voice of *Nature* plainly declares to us. Forasmuch as the Divine Sovereignty, and unerring Wisdom, has formed, and fitted, the humane Nature for Rule and Government, and necessitated it to it, this may be justly looked upon as the Voice of God to Mankind; because the Almighty's adapting his Creatures to a particular End, is one way of making known His Mind and Will concerning them; and every true dictate of right Reason, is no other than God speaking to his rational Creatures, by the inward Sentiments of their own Mind. Thus 'tis that they, who are destitute of the written Law, *are a Law unto themselves*, as the Apostle expresses it, The Law or Will of God being written upon their Hearts, and legible, in some measure, by the Candle of the Lord, which he hath lighted up within them.

'Tis very evident, the Nature of Man is formed for Government, and necessitated to it, from that Power of Reason and Understanding that is in him, his fixed Bent to Society, and the many Weaknesses and Imperfections that attend him.

Thro' the distinguishing Favour of the Almighty, He has, by His Inspiration, given us Understanding, & made us wiser than the Beasts of the Field, or the Fowls of the Air; and thus He hath formed us capable of acting by Rule, which sufficiently intimates His Will to us, that we are not left to live and range at Large, but that we keep ourselves within due Bounds, and walk by Rule; and this necessarily supposes some certain Rule for us to regulate ourselves by.

And because Society is the natural result of Reason, in a dependent Being, and he must have all in himself, and be Master of an unbounded Understanding, and unlimited Power, or be void of all true Reason and Knowledge, that can subsist by himself without having any Regards to an other; therefore it is necessary, that this rational Agent, who yet falls short of Perfection, should be under Subjection, not only to such Laws as more especially relate to his Conduct to his Maker, but such also as have a more particular Referrence to his Fellow Creature, to whom he stands related, on whom he has some dependance for the necessaries, and conveniencies, of the present Life, and all adapted to the nature of that Society of which he is a part; and this clearly infers the Superiority of Some to give Law, for the well ordering of the Society, and the subjection of all to those Laws, according as they have a special referrence to them: And what is this but Government?

Thus I doubt not but Government would have been necessary to Man, even in a state of Innocency; because Society would then have been as agreable to his rational Nature, and more delightful to his pure Mind, and as necessary to him upon many Accounts, as now; and, in the midst of all his Purity, he would still have remained but a fallible Creature; all of which would have required a Rule suited to direct his Actions, in the several Relations he would sustain, and Businesses he would have been employed in: and this infers Government; tho', probably, very different, in its kind, from what is to be found in the World, in our Day. In short, the *Fifth Commandment*, as well as others, of the moral Law, would have been in force, and obligatory upon the innocent Creature. . . .

However, since Sin has broke in upon the World, and vitiated the humane Nature, there is but so much the more Reason and Necessity for Government among Creatures that are become so very weak, and depraved; to restrain their unruly Lusts, and keep, within due Bounds, the rampant Passions of Men, which else would soon throw humane Society into the last Disorder and Confusion. For if all Men were left to live, and act, as they please, 'tis undoubted, the different Views and Interests, Humours and Passions of Mankind, and these often excited by false Principles, and strongly moved by a corrupt Bias upon the Mind, would unavoidably produce a continual Jarr and Strife, a constant Endeavour in every one to promote his own, and gratify Self, and so a perpetual Preying of the Stronger upon the Weaker; and no Man would be able to call any thing his own, nor be secure of his Life and Limbs, from the Rapine, and Violence, of his Fellow Creature; and by how much the Views, Interest, and Passions of Men, are more numerous, appropriated, and strong, by so much would they become fiercer upon one another than the Beasts of Prey. And does not this necessitate Laws to tame this fierce Creature, to bound his Appetites, & bridle his Passions, that he may not be injurious to his Neighbour! Who is the Man, that would be willing that all the Injury of ungoverned Lust and Passion should fall upon himself? And what is the Result of all this? but that there be a legislative Power, to enact such Laws, and an executive one, to put the Laws in Force, and compel to Obedience to them, lodged somewhere, as shall be best adapted to the Order, and Preservation of the Society. And this is Government. Thus the light of Nature shews us the Reason, and Necessity, of Government; and this Voice of Nature is the Voice of God. Thus 'tis that *vox populi est vox Dei*. . . .

So that we see, the Original of Government is from God, who has taught it, to Mankind, by the Light of natural Reason, † and plainly

† Hence is that of *Hesiod*, Εκ δὲ δìος βασιλῆες: and thus *Homer*, τ'μη δ'ἐκ δìες ἐsι.[1]

required it, in His holy Word. And that there are any, who walk in the Shape of Men, that do not diligently attend to the voice of Reason, nor enquire after Understanding, but sit down contented in the most abject Stupidity, scarce distinguishing themselves from the Brute, by any true Acts of Reason, is no more an Objection to Government's being a true Dictate of Nature, than one Man's shutting his Eyes would be, against the Sun's being risen, when all, who have their Eyes open, walk in the full Light of it.

2. The second thing I proposed to offer something upon, under the Head of Government, was, the *Form* of it. And here the Enquiry is, What Form of Government is chiefly to be regarded by a People? Since Government originates from God, and is of Divine appointment, is there any particular Form of Divine Ordination? Or if not, what Form shall a People put themselves under as most eligible?

To the First of these Enquiries, I think there is no great difficulty in Answering, That I know of no particular Form of Civil Government, that God Himself has, directly, and immediately, appointed, by any clear Revelation of His Mind and Will, to any People whatever. The Scripture speaks of Civil Rulers under the several Denominations that were in use, at that Day; but it no where directs to, and enjoyns, any one Scheme of Civil Government, even upon God's own peculiar favorite People; but we find, when they became a settled Nation, in the Land which God had promised to their Fathers, it was the People's own Choice to come under a *Monarchical* Form of Government, and they said, *Nay, but we will have a King over us; that we also may be like all the Nations, and that our King may Judge us, and go out before us, and fight our Battles.* And tho' there was some manifestation of the Divine Displeasure against them, for their asking a King, yet this was not for their assuming that particular Form of Civil Government, but for their throwing off the *Theocracy*, they and their Fathers, had so long experienced the Benefit of.

So that it is evident God Almighty has left it to the natural Reason of Mankind, in every Nation and Country, to set up that Form, which, upon a thorow Consideration of the Nature, Temper, Inclinations, Customs, Manners, Business, and other Circumstances of a People, may be thought best for them. And hence it is that some Nations have tho't it best for them to keep the Power of Government in the Hands of the Body of the People, while others have thought fit to lodge it in the Hands of their chief Families and Nobles; others again have devolved the Weight of the Government upon a single Person, leaving it wholly with Him to assign what Part, to what Persons, he pleases;

and another People have looked upon it most adviseable, for them. to take a middle way between these Extreams, and have laid up the Honours of Government, in a single Person, as their Supream Head, to flow from him down to all the Members; and then have divided the Weight and Burden of it, between this single Person, a Body of Nobles of his creating, and a Select Assembly of their own choosing; by which Means, Sovereignty is so happily tempered with Righteousness and Mercy, and Will and Pleasure directed and limited by Liberty and Property, as to guard against Tyranny on the one Hand, and Anarchy on the other. Tho' neither of these Schemes, nor any other that may be tho't of, are immediately and directly of Divine Appointment, yet so far as any, or all of them, are the Result of right Reason so far it may be said of them, that they are of God. Thus, the *Powers that be*, be they what they will, meaning Government, *are ordained of God.* And as every People are left to their Liberty to constitute what Form of Civil Gove.nment, all things considered, may appear best to them, as to any thing to the contrary from the Law of God, so, doubtless, it remains with any civil Society to alter, and change, the Form of their Government, when they see just Reason for it, and all Parties are consenting to it.

But if there be no particular Form of Civil Government appointed by God, and every Nation and People are left to their own Prudence to establish what Form they please, which Form and Scheme is best? If this Enquiry means, What Form is best, considered absolutely, and by it self? I answer, That Form which is best accommodated to all the Ends of Government. What That is, may be tho't an hard Question, and it is not my Business to determine it. Tho' I would observe, that, possibly, it may be a just Answer to the Enquiry, to say, that it is an improper Question; because there can be no Government without a People, or Subject of it; and the good, or ill, Qualities of it, can fall under no Consideration, but as Government stands related to its Subject; so that the Circumstances of a particular People must come into Consideration, to determine what is best. If the Question mean, what Form is relatively best? I answer, That which will suit the People best: which requires a thorow Knowledge of them, their Scituation, Produce, Genius, and the like, to resolve. If still it be insisted on, what Form is best for our selves? To this I answer, were we absolutely free to choose for ourselves, it must be left to the wisest Heads, the greatest Politicians among us, and those best acquainted with the People, and Country, to advise upon it: but as we are not at Liberty now to choose, I can readily Answer, that Form of Civil

Government is best for us, which we are under; I mean the *British Constitution.* And this I can say, not only because we are a dependant Government, but because were I at full Liberty, I should choose to be (as, blessed be God, we are,) of the Number of the happy Subjects of *Great Britain,* whom God hath blessed above all People upon the Face of the Earth, in the Felicity of their Constitution: and I look upon my self happy, that I know not of a single true *New England* Man, in the whole Province, but what readily subscribes to these Sentiments, and hopes we shall continue, to be the genuine Members of that glorious Constitution, thro'out all Ages. . . .

4. I am now to consider what are the great *Ends* of Government. And here I must observe, that the ultimate and supreme Ends of Government, are the same with the last End of all Creatures, and all their Actions; *that God in all things may be glorified:* but then the subordinate End, and that which is the main, as it respects Man, is the common Good of the Society, State or Kingdom.

It is beneath the Dignity of a rational Agent to act for no End; and it is contrary to Reason, and Religion, to propound any but a good one; and the Good aimed at cannot be appropriated to this or that Set or Party, of Men, in the State, without having a suitable Regard to others; but must necessarily extend to the whole Body, otherwise it would soon be subversive of it self. For let us consider the Ends of Government as having Respect either to the Ruler, or Ruled, seperately taken.

If, on the one Hand, we could suppose the Good, Benefit, and Advantage of the Throne, or Ruler, were the sole Ends of Government, this would introduce Tyranny, Oppression, Injustice, and, by Degrees, prove the Overthrow of the State. For while civil Rulers either thro' mistake of their End, or want of Rectitude to act up to it, appropriate all unto themselves, and seek only their own Grandure, the making of their Families, and the gratifying of their own Appetites, and Passions; while their constant Cry is, *give, give,* and they cannot content themselves without their Subjects Vineyard, and snatch his Ewe Lamb from his Bosome, and exert their Authority to suppress all that they think stands in their way; whether by placing them in the Front of the Battle, to fall by a foreign Hand, or proceeding against them with an apparent solemn Form, but real Prostitution, of Justice, or dispatching them with a Bow-string; it is evident that they will be no better than *roaring Lyons, and ranging Bears,* which gradually devour up their Subjects, and their Substance, till there is no more to give, or none to give it: or else, the continual Oppressions, *which make wise Men mad,* will produce such Ferments, and Tumults among the People, as in Time, to shake off the Yoke, and free themselves from the Tyrant. . . .

One would be ready to think it hardly possible for any, who are not destitute of the Understanding of Men, and lost to all true Reverence to the Deity, to entertain such a monstrous Conception, That God Almighty, the wisest, and the best of Beings, should make whole Nations of Men, and bring them together in Societies, for no other End, but the promoting the Honour, the increasing the Riches, and nourishing the Lusts of any single Person, or any particular Sett of Men.

On the other Hand, if the Good of the Subject, considered as distinct from that of the Ruler, were the End of Government, what would the Consequence of this be, but Anarchy, wild Disorder, and universal Confusion? Which would be as destructive to Government as the hottest Tyranny could be. For the civil Rulers of a People have not only their Interests in many Respects, twisted together with the Subjects, but some things which belong to them, in a peculiar Manner, as Rulers, which are very essential to the Support of Government; I mean, their distinguishing Honour, their Authority and Power, their more special Security, and the like; and if these Interests which are appropriated to them, should not be duely consulted, in the Administration, their Glory would soon become dim, their Authority be trampled on, and their Persons liable to the insult of every one that had more Sense than Understanding, and more of Passion than either: And any one may easily see where this would End.

So that it is the Good of the whole Community both Rulers and Ruled in Conjunction, that is the great and main End of Government; and therefore we find Dr. *Tillotson* [2] thus expressing himself, *The great End of Government is, to preserve Men in their Rights, against the Encroachments of Fraud and Violence.* To preserve *Men,* not this or that Person, or this Set of Men, only, but the whole Body of Mankind, and every individual Member of the Body Politick. Hence I suppose arose that Maxim, *Salus Populi est suprema Lex,* the Safety and Welfare of the whole, (not the Subjects only, as some are ready enough to understand it,) is to give Law to the Government, and to be preferred to the seperate Interest of any particular Person whatever. As the Rights, Liberties, Defence, Protection, and Prosperity of the Subjects are to be consulted; so the Honour, Majesty and Authority, of the Ruler are to be considered as, unitedly the Ends of Government; and tho', possibly, the first may be tho't the Primary, and the latter the Secondary Ends, yet cannot they well be separated without the Destruction of the Government.

JONATHAN MAYHEW, 1720–1766

[Jonathan Mayhew was born on Martha's Vineyard, where his father, Experience Mayhew, was a famous missionary to the Indians. Graduating from Harvard in 1744, Jonathan Mayhew was from the beginning of his career a radical, an agitator, a dominating figure. His theological opinions were so liberal that when he was ordained at the West Church in Boston, in 1747, only two other ministers would attend; he was a forerunner of Unitarian belief as early as the 1750's, asserted free will, opposed the Great Awakening, fought the growing influence of Episcopalianism, and preached the right of revolution. He was a leader of sentiment against the Stamp Act, and was regarded by Otis and the Adamses as a prophet of the Revolution. A volume of sermons published in 1749 won him a D.D. from Aberdeen. His most famous sermon, *A Discourse concerning Unlimited Submission*, was delivered on January 30, 1750, the anniversary day of the execution of Charles I; this text is from the first edition. Cf. Alden Bradford, *Memoir of the Life and Writings of Rev. Jonathan Mayhew*.]

A DISCOURSE CONCERNING UNLIMITED SUBMISSION

If we calmly consider the nature of the thing itself, nothing can well be imagined more directly contrary to common sense, than to suppose that *millions* of people should be subjected to the arbitrary, precarious pleasure of *one single man;* (who has *naturally* no superiority over them in point of authority) so that their estates, and every thing that is valuable in life, and even their lives also, shall be absolutely at his disposal, if he happens to be wanton and capricious enough to demand them. What unprejudiced man can think, that God made All to be thus subservient to the lawless pleasure and phrenzy of One, so that it shall always be a sin to resist him! Nothing but the most plain and express revelation from heaven could make a sober impartial man believe such a monstrous, unaccountable doctrine, and, indeed, the thing itself, appears so shocking—so out of all *proportion*, that it may be questioned, whether all the *miracles* that ever were wrought, could make it credible, that this doctrine *really* came from God. At present, there is not the least syllable in scripture which gives any countenance to it. The hereditary, indefeasible, divine right of kings, and the doctrine of non-resistance, which is built upon the supposition of such a right, are altogether as fabulous and chimerical, as transubstantiation; or any of the most absurd reveries of ancient or modern visionaries. These notions are fetched neither from divine revelation, nor human reason; and if they are derived from neither of those sources, it is not much matter from *whence they come, or whither they go.* Only it is a pity that such doctrines should be propagated in society, to raise factions and rebellions, as we see they have, in fact, been both in the *last,* and in the *present,* REIGN.

But then, if unlimited submission and passive obedience to the *higher powers,* in all possible cases, be not a duty, it will be asked, "How far are we obliged to submit? If we may innocently disobey and resist in some cases, why not in all? Where shall we stop? What is the measure of our duty? This doctrine tends to the total dissolution of civil government; and to introduce such scenes of wild anarchy and confusion, as are more fatal to society than the worst of tyranny."

After this manner, some men object; and, indeed, this is the most plausible thing that can be said in favor of such an absolute submission as they plead for. But the worst (or rather the best) of it, is, that there is very little strength or solidity in it. For similar difficulties may be raised with respect to almost every duty of natural and revealed religion.—To instance only in two, both of which are near akin, and indeed exactly parallel, to the case before us. It is unquestionably the duty of children to submit to their parents; and of servants, to their masters. But no one asserts, that it is their duty to obey, and submit to them, in all supposeable cases; or universally a sin to resist them. Now does this tend to subvert the just authority of parents and masters? Or to introduce confusion and anarchy into private families? No. How then does the same principle tend to unhinge the government of that larger family, the body politic? We know, in general, that children and servants are obliged to obey their parents and masters respectively. We know also, with equal certainty, that they are not obliged to submit to them in all things, without exception; but may, in some cases, reasonably, and therefore innocently, resist them. These principles are acknowledged upon all hands, whatever difficulty there may be in fixing the exact limits of submission. Now there is at least as much difficulty in stating the measure of duty in these two cases, as in the case of rulers and subjects. So that this is really no objection, at least no reasonable one, against resistance to the *higher powers:* Or, if it is one, it will hold equally against resistance in the other cases mentioned.—It is indeed true, that turbulent, vicious-minded men, may take occasion from this principle, that their rulers may, in some cases, be lawfully resisted, to raise factions and disturbances in the state; and to make resistance where resistance is needless, and therefore, sinful. But is it not equally true, that children and servants of turbulent, vicious minds, may take occasion from this principle, that parents and masters may, in some cases be lawfully resisted, to resist when resistance is unnecessary, and therefore, criminal? Is the principle in either case false in itself, merely because it may be abused; and applied to legitimate disobedience and resistance in those instances, to which it ought not to be applied? According to this way of arguing, there will be no true principles in the world; for there are none but what may be wrested and perverted to serve bad purposes, either through the weakness or wickedness of men.*

* We may very safely assert these two things in general, without undermining government: One is, That no civil rulers are to be obeyed when they enjoin things that are inconsistent with the commands of God: All such disobedience is lawful and glorious; particularly, if persons refuse to comply with any *legal establishment of religion*, because it is a gross perversion and corruption (as to doctrine, worship and discipline) of a pure and divine religion, brought from heaven to earth by the *Son of God*, (the only King and Head of the *christian* church) and propagated through the world by his inspired apostles. All commands running counter to the declared will of the supreme legislator of heaven and earth, are null and void: And therefore disobedience to them is a duty, not a crime. . . . Another thing that may be asserted with equal truth and safety, is, That no government is to be submitted to, at the *expence* of that which is the *sole end* of all government,—the common good and safety of society. Because, to submit in this case, if it should ever happen, would evidently be to set up the *means* as more valuable, and above, the *end:* than which there cannot be a greater solecism and contradiction. The only reason of the institution of civil government; and the only rational ground of submission to it, is the common safety and utility. If therefore, in any case, the common safety and utility would not be promoted by submission to government, but the contrary, there is no ground or motive for obedience and submission, but, for the contrary.

Whoever considers the nature of civil government must, indeed, be sensible that a great degree of *implicit confidence*, must unavoidably be placed in those that bear rule: this is implied in the very notion of authority's being originally a *trust*, committed by the people, to those who are vested with it, as all just and righteous authority is; all besides, is mere lawless force and usurpation; neither God nor nature, having given any man a right of dominion over any society, independently of that society's approbation, and consent to be governed by him—Now as all men are fallible, it cannot be supposed that the public affairs of any state, should be always administred in the best manner possible, even by persons of the greatest wisdom and integrity. Nor is it sufficient to legitimate disobedience to the *higher powers* that they are not so administred; or that they are, in some instances, very ill-managed; for upon this principle, it is scarcely supposeable that any government at all could be supported, or subsist. Such a principle manifestly tends to the dissolution of government; and to throw all things into confusion and anarchy.—But it is equally evident, upon the other hand, that those in authority may abuse their *trust* and power *to such a degree*, that neither the law of reason, nor of religion, requires, that any obedience or submission should be paid to them; but, on the contrary, that they should be totally *discarded;* and the authority which they were before vested with, transferred to others, who may exercise it more to those good purposes for which it is given.—Nor is this principle, that resistance to the *higher powers*, is, in some extraordinary cases, justifiable, so liable to abuse, as many persons seem to apprehend it. For although there will be always some petulant, querulous men, in every state—men of factious,

A People, really oppressed to a great degree by their sovereign, cannot well be insensible when they are so oppressed. And such a people (if I may allude to an ancient *fable*) have, like the *hesperian* fruit, a Dragon for their *protector* and *guardian:* Nor would they have any reason to mourn, if some Hercules should appear to dispatch him—For a nation thus abused to arise unanimously, and to resist their prince, even to the dethroning him, is not criminal; but a reasonable way of vindicating their liberties and just rights; it is making use of the means, and the only means, which God has put into their power, for mutual and self-defence. And it would be highly criminal in them, not to make use of this means. It would be stupid tameness, and unaccountable folly, for whole nations to suffer *one* unreasonable, ambitious and cruel man, to wanton and riot in their misery. And in such a case it would, of the two, be more rational to suppose, that they that did not *resist*, than that they who did, would *receive to themselves damnation.*

---

turbulent and carping dispositions,—glad to lay hold of any trifle to justify and legitimate their caballing against their rulers, and other seditious practices; yet there are, comparatively speaking, but few men of this *contemptible character:* It does not appear but that mankind, in general, have a disposition to be as submissive and passive and tame under government as they ought to be.—Witness a great, if not the greatest, part of the known world, who are now groaning, but not murmuring, under the heavy yoke of tyranny! While those who govern; do it with any tolerable degree of moderation and justice, and, in any good measure act up to their office and character, by being public benefactors; the people will generally be easy and peaceable; and be rather inclined to flatter and adore, than to insult and resist, them. Nor was there ever any *general* complaint against any administration, *which lasted long*, but what there was good reason for. Till people find themselves greatly abused and oppressed by their governors, they are not apt to complain; and whenever they do, in fact, find themselves thus abused and oppressed, they must be stupid not to complain. To say that subjects in general are not proper judges when their governors oppress them, and play the tyrant; and when they defend their rights, administer justice impartially, and promote the public welfare, is as great *treason* as ever man uttered;—'tis treason,—not against one *single* man, but the state—against the whole body politic;—'tis treason against mankind;—'tis treason against common sense; —'tis treason against God. And this impious principle lays the foundation for justifying all the tyranny and oppression that ever any prince was guilty of. The people know for what end they set up, and maintain, their governors; and they are the proper judges when they execute their *trust* as they ought to do it;—when their prince exercises an equitable and paternal authority over them;—when from a prince and common father, he exalts himself into a tyrant—when from subjects and children, he degrades them into the class of slaves;—plunders them, makes them his prey, and unnaturally sports himself with their lives and fortunes——

Chapter III

THIS WORLD AND THE NEXT

THE historian of the New England Puritans frequently has occasion to lament the many dry bones of metaphysics and abstruse theology which he is compelled to turn up in the effort to resurrect a semblance of that extinct species; his construction is bound all too often to resemble one of those grinning skeletons of antediluvian monsters, imperfectly wired together and stored in some museum of paleontology, making altogether too exorbitant a demand upon the imagination of the spectator to carry the conviction that the creature ever lived and breathed and moved. The vast differences between the intellect of the seventeenth century and the present necessitate so much laborious restatement of the abstractions of Puritanism that the flesh and blood realities of the Puritans themselves are lost to view. It is supremely difficult for us to imagine that the doctrine was not always present in their minds as we find it embalmed in a crabbed catechism, and still more difficult for us to understand that to them it was an all pervading sensibility, a depth of feeling, and a way of life, that it was not only of the mind but just as much of the heart and the passions.

When we come to examine the sermons, the words delivered from the pulpits by living men to living ears, we find that the ideas therein discussed were indeed those of the creed, the dogmas of original sin, irresistible grace, and predestination. But they were not developed as points in a formal lecture, or expounded as curious and technical problems; they were not preached as doctrines, or contentions, or theories, but as vivid facts. The systematized theology served primarily as a frame of reference within which the issues of human existence could be confronted immediately. The language employed was not that of the schoolroom and the textbook, but of the streets, of trades, of adventures. The sentences were not bare abstractions, but concrete dramatizations, replete with the imagery of fishing, farming, carpentering, of the city and the meadow, of the seasons and of the moods of men. The method of developing sermons from texts in the Bible strengthened this tendency to concrete and solid presentation; the ministers did not select a doctrine to preach upon, and then hunt texts to support it, but they took this or that text and deciphered its meaning. That man is naturally bound in sin and must hang upon the dispensations of grace from God—this was a dogma; but as

Thomas Hooker preaches, it takes form no longer as a colorless generalization, but as an unforgettable picture:

> You know the Dog must stay till his Master comes in, and when hee is come, hee must stay till he sit downe, and till hee cut his meate, and hee must not have the meate from his trencher neither, when he hath stayed all this while, he hath nothing but the crums. So it is with a poore sinner; you must not thinke that God will bee at your becke: No, you must bee content with the crums of mercy, and pity, and lye under the table til the Lord let the crums fall.[1]

That a regenerate man progresses from the initial stage of illumination to a fuller and deeper immersion in grace was a tenet of the creed; but as John Cotton develops it in the passage below, through the metaphor of a man wading into the waters of a shallow beach and at last reaching the cool depths, out of sight of land, the paragraph, instead of being a logical proof, becomes an ecstatic prose poem.

The most persistent misunderstanding of the Puritan mind in contemporary criticism results in the charge that it was fatalistic. To one unfamiliar with the inward power of the belief, who judges merely upon the external evidence of the doctrine, there seems no conceivable motive for positive human exertion; the logical inference from the decrees of predestination and reprobation would seem to be the attitude which Increase Mather is found herein discussing, the frame of mind in which a man says, "God does not send me grace, I can't convert myself," and gives over trying. Though the Puritan did indeed live much of his life by logic, he did not so live all of it or even the most important part of it. Dialectics and syllogisms do not account for the driving force of the Massachusetts settlers, or for the vehemence of the Ironsides' cavalry charges, whose enemies "God made as stubble to our swords." In these selections Increase Mather disposes of this question of passivity in what had become the conventional response; but by his day the zeal was already beginning to decline, and his answer is probably not the best solution of the problem. Perhaps the finest statement of the invigorating effects of a philosophy of divine determination is Oliver Cromwell's account of his thoughts before the battle of Naseby, when his ranks of "poor, ignorant men" were being drawn up to face the oncoming host of gallant and flashing cavaliers; then, says Cromwell, "I could not, riding alone about my business, but smile out to God in praises, in assurance of victory, because God would, by things that are not, bring to naught things that are. Of

[1] *The Soules Humiliation* (London, 1638), p. 127.

which I had great assurance, and God did it."[1] How men could work themselves into this frame of mind, combining trust in God's disposing power with an assurance of victory, going through fire and water in order that what was decreed might be fulfilled, what sort of thinking brought them to this conclusion, may appear by the selections in this chapter from the sermons of Thomas Hooker. His exhaustive analysis of the true sight of sin, and his stirring account of the struggle of the saint with inherent evil uncover the sources of that almost titanic energy of which the Puritans were so abundantly possessed. A true sight of sin, he says, consists in perceiving it "clearly" and "convictingly," and the imagery by which he brings home the full brilliance of the clarity and the overwhelming weight of the conviction makes clear why there was little need for him to dwell upon a remote and semi-mythological fall of Adam, or no need whatsoever to entangle his auditors in the subtleties of free will, foreordination and absolute decree. Anyone who ever saw himself as pitilessly as Hooker requires would thereafter spend his days and nights in feverish exertions to lift himself out of such a mire of depravity. When the soul saw its task, thus clearly and convictingly, as a fact, not a theory, then also the need for divine assistance in escaping the clutch of sin was no longer something to be proved by a series of geometrical corollaries but became a desperate hunger gnawing ceaselessly at a man's very vitals. The thrill, the excitement, the challenge of the conflict against Satan would entirely drive out of his mind the suggestion that he might better fold his hands and await the pleasure of God. When we consider how intense, in Puritan eyes, was the warfare of the spirit and the flesh, and how interminable a campaign the true soldier of Christ undertook when he enrolled himself in the regiment of the godly, then we can perhaps gauge the true sublimity of Puritanism as we find Hooker insisting, and his congregation no doubt agreeing, that the awakened sinner should actually be grateful to the minister who by his winged sermons had pierced the doors of his complacency, he should be overjoyed that he had been dragged against all his natural inclinations from the peace and security of a false contentment into the heat and fury of this battle.

Inspired volunteers, going forth under the banners of truth, do not make lazy or half hearted campaigners. But if the religion of the Puritan was intense, it was not foolhardy. He was ecstatic, but not insane. He employed self-analysis, meditation, and incessant soul-searching to drive out sin from one stronghold after another; in every

[1] Charles Firth, *Oliver Cromwell* (London, 1900), p. 127.

siege he had to be not only valiant, but self-controlled, patient, wary, and crafty. It was an entirely subjective struggle; the victories were gained within the soul, and the final triumph could never be won on this side of the grave. Consequently while the saints were occupied internally with the conquest of evil, they could not expect to fare externally any better than others. All men must live among men and as men; whether their souls are filled with the Holy Ghost or not, they must suffer the diseases and decays to which men are subject. The exhilaration of faith is known to the heart of the believer, but, as Samuel Willard explains, those inward supports are remote from public view. Appearances therefore are deceiving, and the saint must keep his wits about him; he must remain calm in the midst of ardor, he must burn with fervor, but always be detached and analytical, to make sure that his agitation is genuinely of the spirit, not of mere human cupidity, and to guard against suffocating the flame with false assurances and outward conformity. Puritanism would make every man an expert psychologist, to detect all makeshift "rationalizations," to shatter without pity the sweet dreams of self-enhancement in which the ego takes refuge from reality. A large quantity of Puritan sermons were devoted to exquisite analyses of the differences between "hypocrites" and saints, and between one kind of hypocrite and another, to exposing not merely the conscious duplicity of evil men, but the abysmal tricks which the subconscious can play upon the best of men. The duty of the Puritan in this world was to know himself—without sparing himself one bit, without flattering himself in the slightest, without concealing from himself a single unpleasant fact about himself.

In the course of this sustained and unmitigated meditation, he perpetually measured himself by the highest imaginable excellency. The Puritan was taught to approve of no act because it was good enough for the circumstances, to rest content with no performance because it was the best that could be done in this or that situation. He knew indeed that life is imperfect, that the purest saints do not ever entirely disentangle themselves from the meshes of corruption, but though perfection was unattainable—even more because it was so—he bent every nerve and sinew to attempting the attainment. The Puritan life might be compared to that of a poet laboring under penalty of death to produce several hundred lines a day, and yet driven by an acute critical sense to despise every passage, every phrase that did not flow from the fountain of fresh and original inspiration. Nothing was to be done by the force of habit, in the facility of mere technical proficiency, by mechanical routine; ideally every moment and every action should reveal radiations of the supernal vitality. So far as men fell short of this ideal, they were contemptible. Over against this transcendent standard, physical existence was inevitably seen as frail, transitory, and unprofitable. When two Harvard students broke through the ice while skating, and were drowned, Increase Mather drew the moral that the times of men are in the hand of God, that no one knows when the blow will fall upon himself, or what lies in wait for him tomorrow or the day after. No trust is to be put in the things of this world, no reliance placed upon material devices. Life is a chronicle of accidents and blunders, reversals and hopes defeated.

But at the same time, if life in the world is a melancholy spectacle, it is not a tale told by an idiot; there is indeed sound and fury, but behind the meaningless futility of appearances there stand the ranks of the eternal verities. The ax-head may slip, as Urian Oakes says, and the skull of an innocent and good man be split; but the Puritan is not thereupon to cry, "Out, out—." The blade was guided by the steady hand of God, and somewhere, somehow there is a reason for this casualty, there must be a justice behind the apparent injustice. Men may not readily see it; like John Winthrop telling of the lady whose linen was burned and whose husband was shortly afterwards slain (p. 137), they may be hard pressed to explain why some events turn out as they do, and be brought time and time again to confess that in this or that series of misfortunes or streaks of luck they can not discover the wisdom of God. Nevertheless, that He who orders all things does order them by the counsel of His perfect reason and that nothing in the world is really chance, accident, or blind fate—this was the constant and unshakable conviction of the Puritan. The one thing he insisted upon, however, was that in order that this conviction might be upheld, no realities should be glossed over, no horror and no agony denied. The assertion was to be made with a clear-eyed perception of things as they do fall out, for weal or for woe.

All events therefore have their reason and their logic. We must strain to the full extent of our capacities to discover the reason and comprehend the logic. But our finite minds can not grasp all things, and our corrupted intellects can not understand all the things we grasp. No matter how much we know, there will always remain a margin to the page of knowledge which we cannot explore; the limits of the universe are not searchable with the human eye. The labor demanded of the intelligent man is that he give over no exertion to account for things, that he never accept without endeavouring to explain, that he never take a conclusion on trust until he has exhausted all means to take it on reason; but all the time he must remember that explanation can only go so far, that mortal reason is not God's reason, that there is always more ignorance to be confessed than certain knowledge to be enjoyed. The Puritan was completely hospitable to the revolutionizing discoveries made by physical science during the seventeenth century, but as long as he remained true to the fundamentals of Puritanism he was not deceived into concluding that man had at last unriddled the universe.

What the admirable sagacity of future ages may compass as to thousands of problems within the circle of Sciences, or in that most noble Art of Chymistry, or the Analysis of the three kingdoms of nature: the tubes and glasses of our present inventions give us no sufficient prospect. . . . The learned of this age wonder at the denial of the motion of the Earth, tho now the truth of it appears clear to all the generality of the ingenious of *Europe* . . .

Indeed so may posterity deride at these our ages, and the more ingenious of future times, may stand amazed at our dulness and stupidity about minerals, meteors and the cure of diseases, and many thousand things besides, about the lustre of stars and precious stones, which may be as easy to them as letters to us . . . Such rare inventions may be given in of God to beautifie the glory of the latter days. All our writings in Divinity, will be like insipid water, to what shall then appear upon the Stage, . . . and the Artists that shall then be born, may discover more things in the works of God to be discust and endeavoured to be explained, then they themselves shall arrive to. The superfine Wisdom and Learned Wits of those acute times will discover vast regions of darkness and ignorance. There will be a *plus ultra* to the end of the world . . . if in millions of things we are stunted and fooled at every turn, that we may cry out with the Satyrist—*Auriculas Asini quis non habet?* What fearful sots are we in the things before us? Then what shall dull reason do in the great sublimities and solemnities of faith, and the doctrine set forth by Infinite Wisdom. [1]

It was in the eighteenth century, along with their reaction against the religious theory of society, that New Englanders abandoned the caution inculcated by this passage, and then many of them jumped as blithely as did the rest of the learned world to the comfortable conclusion that Sir Isaac Newton had explained the mind of God. Two hundred years afterwards physics has become more metaphysical than scholasticism itself, astronomers turn to writing "in Divinity," and before our superfine wisdoms loom vast regions of darkness and

[1] Samuel Lee, Χαρὰ τηs Πιsεωs, *The Joy of Faith* (Boston, 1687), pp. 212–214.

ignorance, as the visible universe has become once again relative to itself and full of exceedingly deceptive appearances.

Urian Oakes concludes his sermon on providence with an injunction which was constantly delivered from New England pulpits: "labour to be prepared and provided for Disappointments." Put beside this another instruction which was equally recurrent through the sermons of Puritan ministers: "as the things and objects are, great, or mean, that men converse withall; so they are high or low spirited." [1] Take these two rules together—on the one hand, to expect nothing but disappointment in this life, on the other, to cultivate a high-spirited frame of mind by converse with the highest objects of contemplation, and between these two poles the daily life of the Puritans oscillated. John Cotton gives instructions to artisans, farmers, and merchants for the prosecution of their callings, explaining that men should pursue their worldly vocations, but not expect too much from them, should work in them, and yet labor in faith. His requirements would seem full of inconsistencies and impossibilities to one unadjusted to the dual contention of the Puritan synthesis: the fallibility of material existence and the infallibility of the spiritual, the necessity for living in a world of time and space according to the laws of that time and that place, with never once forgetting that the world will pass, be resolved back into nothingness, that reality and permanence belong to things not as they appear to the eye but to the mind.

> It is by the Spiritual Operations and Actions of our minds that we meet with the Lord, and have a kind of intercourse with the Almighty, who is a Spirit. For al outward things are for the body, the body for the soul, the soul is nextly for God, and therefore meets as really with him in the Actions of Understanding, as the Eye meets with the Light in Seeing; which no other Creature can do, nor no action of a bodily Creature doth. Our Sences in their sinful and inordinate swervings, when they become means and in-lets of evil from their objects, they meet with the Creature firstly, and there make the jar: It's the beauty of the Object that stirs up to lust by the Eye, the daintiness of the Diet that provokes to intemperance by the tast, the harsh and unkind language that provokes to wrath and impatience by the Ear: But the Mind and Understanding toucheth the Lord directly, meets with his Rule, and with God acting in the way of his Government there, and when it goes off from the Rule as before, and attends its own vanity and folly, it justles with the Almighty, stands in open defyance and resistance against him.[2]

[1] Jonathan Mitchell, *A Discourse of the Glory To which God hath called Believers* (London, 1677), pp. 225–226.

[2] Thomas Hooker, *The Application of Redemption* (London, 1659), pp. 158–159.

The man who is misled by appearances "justles" with God, and is not merely a sinner and a reprobate; he is, still more tragically, a man to whom reality, the order of things "as they be," will never become known. Puritanism was regulated by the possibility of each man's achieving this insight, on whatever level of culture or education he dwelt, with the aid of divine grace; the assumption was that once this comprehension was gained, men would be able to live amid disappointments without being dissappointed, amid deceptions without being deceived, amid temptations without yielding to them, amid cruelties without becoming cruel.

The ideal of conduct thus held out was definitely affirmative. There is very little preaching of hell-fire in seventeenth-century sermons; Hooker's sentences are as far in that direction as any minister went before the beginning of the evangelical revival and the thunderings of Jonathan Edwards. So often are the first Puritans accused of living in fear and trembling under the threat of eternal torment that this point needs to be heavily underscored. That the ministers did not play upon their congregations' nerves by painting the horrors of the pit was because, for one thing no doubt, the sensibilities of people in the seventeenth century were inured to violence. This was still the age in which mothers took their children for a treat to public executions. In part the lack of brimstone sermons is accounted for by the Puritan disinclination to make religion emotional at the cost of judicious analysis and sound intellectual conviction. In converting sinners, said Samuel Willard, we must "imitate God"; we must "first deal with their understandings; to raise the affections, without informing the mind, is a fruitlesse unprofitable labour, and serves but to make zeal without knowledge." [1] But still more fundamentally, Puritan ministers did not bludgeon their people with the bloody club of damnation because their eyes were fixed upon the positive side of religion, upon the beauties of salvation, the glory of God, and the joy of faith. The worst they could imagine for the reprobate was not physical burnings and unslaked thirst, but the deprivation of God's spirit.

> There is a great deal goes to the eternal life of a soul, and thou hast none of it; thou wantest the love of God, which is better than life; thou wantest grace which is indeed the inward principle of life in the soul; thou wantest the promise which is the support of the soul here in this life.[2]

[1] *Mercy Magnified on a Penitent Prodigal* (Boston, 1684), p. 150.

[2] *Ibid.*, p. 106.

What were racks and tortures compared to the want of these things? The applications or "uses" of all doctrines stated in the sermons stress continually the note of hope, the possibility that anyone, no matter how immoral or depraved he has been, may yet be saved; it is only with the next century that men are bluntly told how God abhors them and holds them over the pit of Hell as one holds a spider or some loathsome insect over the fire. When the seventeenth-century preacher wanted to arouse men he would tell them not of the irreversible sentence passed upon them in the future world, but would instance afflictions already suffered, or predict those to come, in this world—plagues, fires, earthquakes, and shipwrecks—punishments that men might survive and from which they might profit. This tendency undoubtedly produced some unpleasant characteristics, and gave opportunity for such an egotist as Increase Mather, or for such an egomaniac as his son Cotton, to hurl the vengeance of God at persons or actions they themselves did not happen to like, and even forced solid minds like John Winthrop's to twist coincidences into special interpositions of the deity. The bent of the seventeenth-century Puritan was to portray God as indeed a stern disciplinarian and one not to be trifled with, but nevertheless not as a savage chief exulting in the protracted writhings of his helpless captives. The deity was first and foremost the source of that spirit of peace to which some men might attain, "and sometimes in that unspeakable measure, as that it passeth the understanding of a man to conceive." [1] Not all men would or could reach this light, but no single individual need ever give over the hope that he might discover himself one of the favored, or ever abandon the endeavor to make himself one of them.

Thus the Puritan lived in this world, and tried desperately not to be of it; he followed his calling, plowed his land, laid away his shillings, and endeavored to keep his mind on the future life. He looked upon the physical world as the handiwork of God, and the charms of the universe as His creations, and yet he told himself, "Get thy heart more and more weaned from the Creature, the Creature is empty, its not able to satisfie thee fully, nor make thee happy." [2] He came to New England to make an earthly home, but for many years he looked upon his home, as far as any conscious expression would indicate, entirely in terms of the right ecclesiastical polity and the place of true doctrine; he lived through New England summers, the splen-

[1] John Cotton, *Christ the Fountaine* (London, 1651), p. 102.

[2] Edward Reyner, *The Rule of the New Creature*, appended to Hooker, *The Danger of Desertion* (London, 1641), p. 29.

dors of the fall, he inhaled the sea airs and heard the pine boughs sway, and he believed he was thinking only of election and serving the will of God. He reminded himself again and again that "the beauty of the object stirs up to lust by the Eye."

Samuel Sewall, solid, bulky judge, literal-minded, no match for the quick wit of Madam Winthrop, would hardly in the wildest stretch of the imagination be called a poetic soul. He wrote two treatises on the fulfillment of Biblical prophecies, and worried over the bewildering texts of the Book of Revelations, until we wonder how even a person who believed that every single letter and dot of punctuation in the Scripture was directly dictated by God could still spend so much time so fruitlessly and unimaginatively as in arguing the precise years of the opening of the seven seals, or in trying to decide in just what thousand years Satan would be bound. These were indeed Puritan compositions, exhibiting the worst qualities of the Puritan mind, its slavish literalness, its deficient sense of proportion, its bearing down upon minutiae with the same emphasis brought to larger and fundamental points. And then at the end, in asserting that a certain prophecy might be fulfilled in America, Sewall finds himself justifying the land itself, as a fit scene for the enactment of God's triumph, and without quite knowing what he is doing sings a hymn of praise to the purely physical and sensuous New England. He had been a boy at Newbury, had played on the beach at Plum Island, and although his determination had been set upon the other world and his efforts devoted to rendering mystical visions into dull prose, he himself proves that all this time the beauty of the land, the loveliness of the objects, had not been entirely lost upon him. He had felt the hectoring wind on Plum Island, heard the sea-gull, smelt the marshes. The Puritans were not blind or insensitive. They saw and loved the perch and pickerel, the dove and the white oak and the rows of Indian corn; but even from a world as beautiful and lovely as this they yet hoped to be translated, "to be made partakers of the Inheritance of the Saints in Light."

THOMAS HOOKER, 1586–1647

[Thomas Hooker was probably born in Marfield, Leicestershire, of yeomen stock. Admitted sizar at Queen's College, Cambridge, he migrated to Emmanuel, taking his B.A. in 1608, his M.A. in 1611. He was a fellow of Emmanuel College, 1609–1618, acquiring the reputation of a great teacher and preacher; rector of Esher in Surrey, 1620, lecturer at St. Mary's, Chelmsford, in Essex, 1626, he was finally forced by Bishop

Laud to retire when he had become one of the most conspicuous leaders of Puritan sentiment in the land. For a year he kept a school at Little Baddow, where John Eliot was his assistant. Cited before the High Commission in 1630, he was given the amount of his bail by devoted followers and fled to Holland. For two years he was minister of an English Puritan church at Delft, then at Rotterdam, where he was associated with the great William Ames. A group of his friends from Chelmsford migrated to New England in a body, and persuaded him to come over to be their pastor. He sailed on the same ship with Stone and Cotton, after various adventures escaping the Anglican authorities, and was ordained pastor of the church at Newtown. In 1635 his congregation asked permission to move to Connecticut and the magistrates refused; in 1636 Hooker led his people to Hartford, apparently in spite of the Massachusetts authorities, who put the best face possible on the secession. For the rest of his life he was the virtual dictator of Connecticut; he returned several times to the Bay, once to be moderator of the synod at which the opinions of Anne Hutchinson were condemned. He was a powerful and dominating figure; Cotton Mather said of him that he could put a King in his pocket. He was one of the most eloquent of Puritan preachers, perhaps the most powerful pulpit orator among the ministers of New England. His manner seems to have been less scholastic and logical than that of Cotton, his style more popular and more ornamented with similes and figures. At the same time he was as great a master of dialectic and argument; his *Survey of the Summe of Church Discipline* is the supreme exposition of the Congregational church polity, couched in the terms and figures of the Ramean logic, and containing a complete expression not merely of New England ecclesiastical theory but of political doctrine and of the philosophical concepts of law, nature, and reason. He has frequently been claimed as an exponent of a more democratic social philosophy than that embraced by the Massachusetts leaders, but this opinion rests upon a misreading of two or three of his utterances; his religious and political opinions were thoroughly orthodox and he maintained them with vigor. See G. L. Walker, *Thomas Hooker*, 1891; Perry Miller, *New England Quarterly*, IV (1931), 663–712. This text is from *The Application of Redemption By the Effectual Work of the Word, and Spirit of Christ, for the bringing home of Lost Sinners to God. The Ninth and Tenth Books*, 2d. edition (London, 1659), pp. 52–66, 210–217, 234–238, 453–459. The sermons in this volume were delivered at Hartford.]

A TRUE SIGHT OF SIN

Wherein this true sight, and apprehension of sin properly discovers it self.

I ANSWER, A true sight of sin hath two Conditions attending upon it; or it appears in two things: We must see sin, 1. Cleerly. 2. Convictingly, what it is in it self, and what it is to us, not in the appearance and paint of it, but in the power of it; not to fadam it in the notion and conceit only, but to see it with Application.

We must see it cleerly in its own Nature, its Native color and proper hue: It's not every slight conceit, not every general and cursorie, confused thought or careless consideration that will serve the turn, or do the work here, we are all sinners; it is my infirmity, I cannot help it; my weakness, I cannot be rid of it; no man lives without faults and follies, the best have their failings, *In many things we offend all.* But alas all this wind shakes no Corn, it costs more to see sin aright than a few words of course; It's one thing to say sin is thus and thus, another thing to see it to be such; we must look wis[e]ly and steddily upon our distempers, look sin in the face, and discern it to the full; the want whereof is the cause of our mistaking our estates, and not redressing of our hearts and waies, *Gal.* 6. 4. *Let a man prove his own work.* Before the Goldsmith can sever and see the Dross asunder from the Gold, he must search the very bowels of the Mettal, and try it by touch, by tast, by hammer, and by fire; and then he will be able to speak by proof what it is; So here. We perceive sin in the crowd and by hearsay, when we attend some common and customary expressions taken up by persons in their common converse, and so report what others speak, and yet never knew the Truth, what either others or we say, but we do not single out our corruptions and survey the loathsomness of them, as they come naked in their own Natures; this we ought to do: There is great ods betwixt the knowledg of a Traveller, that in his own person hath taken a view of many Coasts, past through many Countries, and hath there taken up his abode some time, and by Experience hath been an Eye-witness of the extream cold, and scorching heats, hath surveyed the glory and beauty of the one, the barrenness and meanness of the other; he hath been in the Wars, and seen the ruin and desolation wrought there; and another that sits by his fire side, and happily reads the story of these in a Book, or views the proportion of these in a Map, the ods is great, and the difference of their knowledg more than a little: the one saw the Country really, the other only in the story; the one hath seen the very place, the other only in the paint of the Map drawn. The like difference is there in the right discerning of sin; the one hath surveyed the compass of his whol course, searched the frame of his own heart, and examined the windings and turnings of his own waies, he hath seen what sin is, and what it hath done, how it hath made havock of his peace and comfort, ruinated and laid wast the very Principles of Reason and Nature, and Morality, and made him a terror to himself, when he hath looked over the loathsom abominations that lie in his bosom, that he is afraid to approach the presence of the Lord to bewail his sins, and to crave pardon, lest he should be confounded for them, while he is but confessing of them; afraid and ashamed lest any man living should know but the least part of that which he knows by himself, and could count it happy that himself was not, that the remembrance of those hideous evils of his might be no more; Another happily hears the like preached or repeated, reads them writ or recorded in some Authors, and is able to remember and relate them. The ods is marvelous great. The one sees the History of sin, the other the Nature of it; the one knows the relation of sin as it is mapped out, and recorded; the other the poyson, as by experience he hath found and proved it. It's one thing to see a disease in the Book, or in a mans body, another thing to find and feel it in a mans self. There is the report of it, here the malignity and venom of it.

But how shall we see cleerly the Nature of sin in his naked hue?

This will be discovered, and may be conceived in the Particulars following. Look we at it: First, As it respects God. Secondly, As it concerns our selves. As it hath reference to God, the vileness of the nature of sin may thus appear.

It would dispossess God of that absolute Supremacy which is indeed his Prerogative Royal, and doth in a peculiar manner appertayn to him, as the Diamond of his Crown, and Diadem of his Deity, so the Apostle, *He is God over all blessed for ever*, Rom. 9. 5. All from him and all for him, he is the absolute first being, the absolute last end, and herein is the crown of his Glory. Al those attributes of Wisdom, Goodness, Holiness, Power, Justice, Mercy, the shine and Concurrency of all these meeting together is to set out the unconceivable excellency of his Glorious name, which exceeds all praise, *Thyne is the kingdom, the power and the glory*, the right of all and so the rule of all and the Glory of all belongs to him.

Now herein lyes the unconceavable hainousness of the hellish nature of sin, it would justle the Almighty out of the Throne of his Glorious Soveraignty, and indeed be above him. For the will of man being the chiefest of all his workmanship, all for his body, the body of the soul, the mind to attend upon the will, the will to attend upon God, and to make choyce of him, and his wil, that is next to him, and he onely above that: and that should have been his Throne and Temple or Chair of State, in which he would have Set his Soveraignty for ever. He did in an Especial manner intend to meet with man, and to communicate himself to man in his righteous Law, as the rule of his Holy and righteous will, by which the will of *Adam* should have been ruled and guided to him, and made happie in him; and all Creatures should have served God in man, and been happy by or through him, serving of God being happy in him; But when the will went from under the government of his rule, by sin, *it would be above God, and be happy without him*, for the rule of the law in each command of it, holds forth a three-fold expression of Soveraignty from the Lord, and therein the Soveraignty of all the rest of his Attributes.

1. The Powerful Supremacy of his just will, as that he hath right to dispose of all and authority to command all at his pleasure; *What if God will? Rom.* 9. 22 *My Counsel shall stand and I wil do all my pleasure, Isa.* 46. 10. And as its true of what shal be done upon us, so his wil hath Soveraignty of Command in what should be done by us we are to say *the will of the Lord be done; Davids* warrant was *to do all Gods wils Acts.* 13. 22. and our Saviour himself professeth, *John.* 6. 38. *that he came not to do his own will but the will of him that sent him*, and therfore his wrath and jealousie and judgment will break out in case that be disobeyed.

2. There is also a fulness of wisdom in the law of God revealed to guide & direct us in the way we should walk, *Psal.* 19. 7. *the law of God makes wise the simple*, 2. *Tim.* 3. 15. *it's able to make us wise unto Salvation.*

3. There's a Sufficiency of God to content and satisfy us. *Blessed are they who walk in his wayes, and blessed are they that keep his Testimonies. Psal.* 119. 1. 2. *Great prosperity have they that love the law, and nothing shal offend them*, ver. 16. and in truth there can be no greater reward for doing wel, than to be enabled to do well, he that hath attayned his last end he cannot go further, he cannot be better;

Now by sin we justle the law out of its place, and the Lord out of his Glorious Soveraignty, pluck the Crown from his head, and the Seepter out of his hand, and we say and profess by our practice, there is not authority and power there to govern, nor wisdom to guide, nor good to content me, but I will be swayed by mine own wil and led by mine own deluded reason and satisfied with my own lusts. This is the guise of every graceless heart in the commission of sin; so *Pharaoh who is the Lord? I know not the Lord, nor will I lett Israel go. Exod.* 5. 2. in the time of their prosperity see how the Jews turn their backs and shake off the authority of the Lord, *we are Lords* (say they) *we will come no more at thee. Jer.* 2. 31. *and our tongues are our own who shal be Lords over us? Psal.* 12. 4. So for the wisdom of the world, see how they set light by it as not worth the looking after it *Jer.* 18. 12. *we wil walk after our own devices & we wil every one do the imagination of his own evil heart, yea they sett up their own traditions,* their own Idols and delusions, and Lord it over the law, *making the command of God of none effect Math.* 15. 8. 9. So for the goodness of the word; *Job.* 22. 17. *Mat.* 3. 14. *It is in vayn to serve God and what profit is there that we have kept his ordinances, yea his Commandemnts are ever grievous,* Its a grievous thing to the loose person he cannot have his pleasures but he must have his guilt and gall with them; Its grievous to the worlding that he cannot lay hold on the world by unjust means, but Conscience layes hold upon him as breaking the law. Thou that knowest and keepest thy pride and stubbornness and thy distempers, know assuredly thou dost justle God out of the Throne of his glorious Soveraignty and thou dost profess, Not Gods wil but thine own (which is above his) shall rule thee, thy carnal reason and the folly of thy mind, is above the wisdome of the Lord and that shal guide thee; to please thine own stubborn crooked pervers spirit, is a greater good than to please God and enjoy happines, for this more Contents, thee; That when thou considerest but thy Course, dost thou not wonder that the great and Terrible God doth not pash such a poor insolent worm to pouder, and send thee packing to the pitt every moment.

2. It smites at the Essence of the Almighty and the desire of the sinner, is not only that God should not be supream but that indeed he should *not be at all,* and therefore it would destroy the being of Jehovah. *Psal.* 81. 15. sinners are called *the haters of the Lord.* John. 15. 24. *they hated both me and my Father.* Now he that hates endeavours if it be possible the annihilation of the thing hated, and its most certain were it in their power, they would pluck God out of Heaven the light of his truth out of their Consciences, and the law out of the Societies and Assemblies where they live, that they might have elbow room to live as they list. Nay what ever they hate most and intend, and plott more evil against in al the world, they hate God most of all, and intend more evil against him than against all their Enemies besides, because they hate all for his sake, therefore wicked men *are said to destroy the law Psal.* 126. 119 the Adulterer loaths that law that condemns, uncleaness; the Earthworm would destrow that law that forbids Covetousness, they are sayd to *hate the light* John 3. 21. to hate the Saints and Servants of the Lord John 15. 18. *the world hates you,* he that hates the Lanthorn for the lights sake, he hates the light much more, he that hates the faithful because

of the Image of God, and the Grace that appears there, he hates the God of all, Grace and Holiness, most of all, so God to *Zenacharib*, Isa. 37. 28. *I know thy going out and thy Comming in, and thy rage against me*, Oh it would be their content, if there was no God in the world to govern them, no law to curbe them, no justice to punish, no truth to trouble them, Learn therfore to see how far your rebellions reach, It is not arguments you gainsay, not the Counsel of a Minister you reject, the command of a Magistrate ye oppose, evidence of rule or reason ye resist; but be it known to you, you fly in the very face of the Almighty, and it is not the Gospel of Grace ye would have destroyed, but the spirit of Grace, the author of Grace the Lord Jesus, the God of all Grace that ye hate.

It crosseth the whol course of Providence, perverts the work of the Creature and defaceth the beautiful frame, and that sweet correspondence and orderly usefulness the Lord first implanted in the order of things; The Heavens deny their influence, the Earth her strength, the Corn her nourishment, thank sin for that. Weeds come instead of herbs, Cockle and Darnel instead of Wheat, thank sin for that, *Rom.* 8. 22. *The whol Creature* (or Creation) *grones under vanity*, either cannot do what it would or else misseth of that good and end it intended, breeds nothing but vanity, brings forth nothing but vexation, It crooks all things so as that none can straiten them, makes so many wants that none can supply them, *Eccles.* 1. 15. This makes crooked Servants in a family no man can rule them, crooked inhabitants in towns, crooked members in Congregations, ther's no ordering nor joynting of them in that comly accord, and mutual subjection; know they said, *the adversary sin hath done all this*. Man was the mean betwixt God and the Creature to convey all good with all the constancy of it, and therefore when Man breaks, Heaven and Earth breaks all asunder, the Conduit being cracked and displaced there can be no conveyance from the Fountain.

In regard of our selves, see we and consider nakedly the nature of sin, in Four particulars.

Its that which makes a separation between God and the soul, breaks that Union and Communion with God for which we were made, and in the enjoyment of which we should be blessed and happie, *Isai.* 59. 1. 2. *Gods ear is not heavy that it cannot hear nor his hand that it cannot help, but your iniquities have separated betwixt God and you & your sins have hid his face that he wil not hear for he professeth*, Psal. 5. 4. *that he is a God that wills not wickedness neither shal iniquity dwell with him. Into the new Jerusalem shal no unclean thing enter, but without shal be doggs Rev.* 21. 27. The Dogs to their Kennel, and Hogs to their Sty and Mire: but if an impenitent wretch should come into Heaven, the Lord would go out of Heaven; *Iniquity shall not dwell with sin.* That then that deprives me of my greatest good for which I came into the world, and for which I live and labor in the world, and without which I had better never to have been born; nay, that which deprives me of an universal good, a good that hath all good in it, that must needs be an evil, but have all evil in it: but so doth sin deprive me of God as the Object of my will, and that wills all good, and therefore it must bring in Truth all evil with it. Shame takes away my Honor, Poverty my Wealth, Persecution my Peace, Prison my Liberty, Death my Life, yet a man may still be a happy man, lose his Life, and live eternally: But sin takes away my God, and with him all good goes; Prosperity without God will be my poyson, Honor without him my bane; nay, the word without God hardens me, my endeavor without him profits nothing at all for my good. A Natural man hath no God in any thing, and therefore hath no good.

It brings an incapability in regard of my self to receive good, and an impossibility in regard of God himself to work my spiritual good, while my sin Continues, and I Continue impenitent in it. An incapability of a spiritual blessing, *Why trangress ye the Commandement of the Lord that ye cannot prosper do what* ye can, 2 Chron. 24. 20. And *He that being often reproved hardens his heart, shal be consumed suddenly and there is no remedy,* He that spils the Physick that should cure him, the meat that should nourish him, there is no remedy but he must needs dye, so that the Commission of sin makes not only a separation from God, but obstinate resistance and continuance in it, maintains an infinit and everlasting distance between God and the soul: So that so long as the sinful resistance of thy soul continues; God cannot vouchsafe the Comforting and guiding presence of his grace; because it's cross to the Covenant of Grace he hath made, which he will not deny, and his Oath which he will not alter. So that should the Lord save thee and thy Corruption, carry thee and thy proud vnbeleeving heart to heaven he must nullify the Gospel, (Heb. 5. 9. *He's the Author of Salvation to them that obey him*) and forswear himself, (Heb. 3. 18. *He hath sworn unbeleevers shall not enter into his rest*) he must cease to be just and holy, and so to be God. As *Saul* said to *Jonathan* concerning *David,* 1 Sam. 20. 30, 31. *So long as the Son of* Jesse *lives, thou shalt not be established, nor thy Kingdom:* So do thou plead against thy self, and with thy own soul; So long as these rebellious distempers continue, Grace and Peace, and the Kingdom of Christ can never be established in thy heart For this obstinate resistance differs nothing from the plagues of the state of the damned, when they come to the highest measure, but that it is not yet total and final, there being some kind of abatement of the measure of it, and stoppage of the power of it. Imagine thou sawest the Lord Jesus coming in the clouds, and heardest the last trump blow, *Arise ye dead, and come to judgment:* Imagine thou sawest the Judg of all the World sitting upon the Throne, thousands of Angels before him, and ten thousands ministring unto him, the Sheep standing on his right hand, and the Goats at the left: Suppose thou heardest that dreadful Sentence, and final Doom pass from the Lord of Life (whose Word made Heaven and Earth, and will shake both) *Depart from me ye cursed;* How would thy heart shake and sink, and die within thee in the thought thereof, wert thou really perswaded it was thy portion? Know, that by thy dayly continuance in sin, thou dost to the utmost of thy power execute that Sentence upon thy soul: It's thy life, thy labor, the desire of thy heart, and thy dayly practice to depart away from the God of all Grace and Peace, and turn the Tomb-stone of everlasting destruction upon thine own soul.

It's the Cause which brings all other evils of punishment into the World, and without this they are not evil, but so far as sin is in them. The sting of a trouble, the poyson and malignity of a punishment and affliction, the evil of the evil of any judgment, it is the sin that brings it, or attends it, *Jer.* 2. 19. *Thine own wickedness shall correct thee, and thy back slidings shall reprove thee, know therefore that it is an evil, and bitter thing that thou hast forsaken the Lord.* Jer. 4. 18. *Thy waies and doings have procured these things unto thee, therefore it is bitter, and reacheth unto the heart.* Take miseries and crosses without sin, they are like to be without a sting, the Serpent without poyson, ye may take them, and make Medicines of them. So *Paul* 1 *Cor.* 15. 55. he plaies with death it self, sports with the Grave. *Oh death, where is thy sting? Oh Grave where is thy Victory? the sting of death is sin.* All the harmful annoyance in sorrows and punishments, further than either they come from sin, or else tend to it, they are rather improvements of what we have than parting with any thing we do enjoy, we rather lay out our conveniences than seem to lose them, yea, they encrease our Crown, and do not diminish our Comfort. *Blessed are ye when men revile you, and persecute you, and speak all manner of evil of you for my sake, for great is your reward in Heaven:* Matth. 5. 11. There is a blessing in persecutions and reproaches when they be not mingled with the deserts of our sins; yea, our momentary short affliction for a good cause, and a good Conscience, works an excessive exceeding weight of Glory. If then sin brings all evils, and makes all evils indeed to us, then is it worse than all those evils.

It brings a Curse upon all our Comforts, blasts all our blessings, the best of all our endeavors, the use of all the choycest of all Gods Ordinances: it's so evil and vile, that it makes the use of all good things, and all the most glorious, both Ordinances and Improvements evil to us. *Hag.* 2. 13. 14. When the Question was made to the Priest; *If one that is unclean by a dead Body touch any of the holy things, shall it be unclean? And he answered, Yea. So is this People, and so is this Nation before me, saith the Lord; and so is every work of their hands, and that which they offer is unclean:* If any good thing a wicked man had, or any action he did, might be good, or bring good to him, in reason it was the Services and Sacrifices wherein he did approach unto God, and perform Service to him, and yet *the Sacrifice of the wicked is an abomination to the Lord,* Prov. 28. 9. and Tit. 1. 15. *To the pure all things are pure; but to the unbeleeving there is nothing pure, but their very Consciences are defiled.* It is a desperate Malignity in the temper of the Stomach, that should turn our Meat and diet into Diseases, the best Cordials and Preservatives into Poysons, so that what in reason is appointed to nourish a man should kill him. Such is the venom and malignity of sin, makes the use of the best things become evil, nay, the greatest evil to us many times; *Psal.* 109. 7. *Let his prayer be turned into sin.* That which is appointed by God to be the choycest means to prevent sin, is turned into sin out of the corrupt distemper of these carnal hearts of ours.

Hence then it follows; *That sin is the greatest evil in the world, or indeed that can be.* For, That which separates the soul from God, that which brings all evils of punishment, and makes all evils truly evil, and spoils all good things to us, that must needs be the greatest evil, but this is the nature of sin, as hath already appeared.

But that which I will mainly press, is, Sin is only opposite to God, and cross as much as can be to that infinite goodness and holiness which is in his blessed Majesty; it's not the miseries or distresses that men undergo, that the Lord distasts them for, or estrangeth himself from them, he is with *Joseph* in the Prison, with the three Children in the Furnace, with *Lazarus* when he lies among the Dogs, and gathers the Crums from the rich Mans Table, yea with *Job* upon the dung-hil, but he is not able to bear the presence of sin: yea, of this temper are his dearest servants, the more of God is in them, the more opposite they are to sin where ever they find it. It was that he commended in the Church of *Ephesus, That she could not bear those that were wicked,* Rev. 2. 3. As when the Stomach is of a pure temper and good strength, the least surfet or distemper that befals, it presently distasts and disburdens it self with speed. So *David* noted to be *a man after Gods own heart.* He professeth, 101. *Psal.* 3. 7. *I hate the work of them that turn aside, he that worketh deceit shall not dwell in my house, he that telleth lyes, shall not tarry in my sight.* But when the heart becomes like the Stomach, so weak it cannot help it self, nor be helped by Physick, desperate diseases and dissolution of the whol follows, and in reason must be expected. Hence see how God looks at the least connivance, or a faint and feeble kind of opposition against sin, as that in which he is most highly dishonored, and he follows it with most hideous plagues, as that indulgent carriage of *Ely* towards the vile behavior of his Sons for their grosser evils, 1 *Sam.* 2. 23. *Why do you such things, It's not well my Sons that I hear such things: It is not well,* and is that all? why, had they either out of ignorance not known their duty or out of some sudden surprisal of a temptation neglected it, it had not been well, but for them so purposedly to proceed on in the practice of such gross evils, and for him so faintly to reprove: The Lord looks at it as a great sin thus feebly to oppose sin, and therefore verse 29. he tells him, *That he honored his Sons above God,* and therefore he professeth, *Far be it from me to maintain thy house and comfort, for he that honors me I wil honor, and he that despiseth me shall be lightly esteemed,* verse 30. Hence it is the Lord himself is called *the holy one of Israel,* 1. Hab. 12. *Who is of purer eyes than to behold evil, and cannot look upon iniquity,* no not in such as profess themselves Saints, though most deer unto him, no, nor in his Son the Lord Jesus, not in his Saints, *Amos,* 8. 7. *The Lord hath sworn by himself, I abhor the excellency of* Jacob; what ever their excellencies, their priviledges are, if they do not abhor sin, God will abhor them, *Jer.* 22. 24. *Though* Coniah *was as the Signet of my right hand, thence would I pluck him.* Nay, he could not endure the appearance of it in the Lord Christ, for when but the reflection of sin (as I may so say) fell upon our Savior, even the imputation of our transgressions to him, though none iniquity was ever committed by him, the Father withdrew his comforting presence from him, and let loose his infinite displeasure against him, forcing him to cry out, *My God, my God, why hast thou forsaken me?*

Yea, Sin is so evil, (that though it be in Nature, which is the good Creature of God) that there is no good in it, nothing that God will own; but in the evil of punishment it is otherwise, for the torments of the Devils, and punishments of the damned in Hell, and all the plagues inflicted upon the wicked upon Earth, issue from the righteous and revenging Justice of the Lord, and he doth own such execution as his proper work, *Isa.* 45. 7. *Is there any evil in the City,* viz. of punishment, *and the Lord hath not done it? I make peace, I create evil, I the Lord do all these things:* It issues from the Justice of God that he cannot but reward every one according to his own waies and works; those are a mans own, the holy one of Israel hath no hand in them; but he is the just Executioner of the plagues that are inflicted and suffered for these; and hence our blessed Savior becoming our Surety, and standing in our room, he endured the pains of the Second death, even the fierceness of the fury of an offended God; and yet it was impossible he could commit the least sin, or be tainted with the least corrupt distemper. And it's certain it's better to suffer all plagues without any one sin, than to commit the least sin, and to be freed from all plagues. Suppose that all miseries and sorrows that ever befel all the wicked in Earth and Hell, should meet together in one soule, as all waters gathered together in one Sea: Suppose thou heardest the Devils roaring, and sawest Hell gaping, and flames of everlasting burnings flashing before thine eyes; it's certain it were better for thee to be cast into those inconceivable torments than to commit the least sin against the Lord: Thou dost not think so now, but thou wilt find it so one day.

MEDITATION

MEDITATION *is a serious intention of the mind whereby wee come to search out the truth, and settle it effectually upon the heart.*

An intention of the mind; when one puts forth the strength of their understanding about the work in hand, takes it as an especial task whereabout the heart should be taken up and that which wil require the whol man, and that to the bent of the best ability he hath, so the word is used *Jos.* 1. 8. *thou shalt not suffer the word to depart out of thy mind, but thou shalt meditate therein day and night,* when either the word would depart away or our corruptions would drive it away, meditation layes hold upon it and wil not let it go, but exerciseth the strength of the attention of his thoughts about it, makes a buisiness of it as that about which he might do his best, and yet fals short of what he should do in it. So *David* when he would discover where the stream and overflowing strength of his affections vented themselves, he points at this practice as that which employes the mind to the ful. *Psal* 119. 197. *Oh how I love thy law, it is my meditation all the day,* love is the great wheel of the soul that sets al on going, and how doth that appear? it is my meditation day and night; the word in the original signifyeth to swim, a man spreads the breadth of his understanding about that work, and layes out himself about the service wherein there is both difficulty and worth.

Serious.] Meditation is not a flourishing of a mans wit, but hath a set bout at the search of the truth, beats his brain as wee use to say, hammers out a buisiness, as the Gouldsmith with his mettal, he heats it and beats it turnes it on this side and then on that, fashions it on both that he might frame it to his mind; meditation is hammering of a truth or poynt propounded, that he may carry and conceive the frame and compass in his mind, not salute a truth as we pass by occasionally but solemnly entertain it into our thoughts; Not look upon a thing presented as a spectator or passenger that goes by: but lay other things aside, and look at this as the work and employment for the present to take up our minds. It's one thing in our diet to take a snatch and away, another thing to make a meal, and sit at it on purpose until wee have seen al set before us and we have taken our fil of al, so we must not cast an eye or glimpse at the truth by some sudden or fleighty apprehension, a snatch and away, but we must make a meal of musing. Therefore the Psalmist makes it the main trade that a Godly man drives, professedly opposite to the carriage of the wicked, whether in his outward or inward work, in his disposition or expression of himself in his common practice; whereas they walk in the corrupt counsels of their own hearts, stand in the way of sinners, not only devise what is naught, but practice and persevere in what they have devised, and sit in the seat of the scorners; A blessed man his rode in which he travels, his set trade *he meditates in the Law of God day and night:* that is the counsel in which he walks, the way in which he stands, the seat in which he sits. Look at this work as a branch of our Christian calling, not that which is left to our liberty, but which is of necessity to be attended and that in good earnest as a Christian duty, which God requires, not a little available to our spiritual welfare.

The end is doubly expressed in the other part of the description.

1. *The searching of the truth.*
2. *The effectual setling of it upon the heart.*

The search of the truth: Meditation is a coming in with the truth or any cause that comes to hand, that we may enquire the ful state of it before our thoughts part with it, so that we see more of it or more clearly and fully than formerly we did, this is one thing in that of the Prophet *Hos.* 6. 3. *Then shall yee know if you follow on to know*, when we track the footsteps of the truth, in al the passages, until we have viewed the whol progresse of it, from truth to truth from point to point. *This it is to dig for wisdom, Prov.* 2. 2. When men have found a mine or a veyn of Silver, they do not content themselves, to take that which is uppermost and next at hand within sight which offers it self upon the surface of the Earth, but they dig further as hoping to find more, because they see somewhat. So meditation rests not in what presents it self to our consideration, but digs deeper gathers in upon the truth, and gaynes more of it then did easily appear at the first, and this it doth.

1. *When it recals things formerly past, sets them in present view before our consideration and judgment* Meditation sends a mans thoughts afar off, cals over and revives the fresh apprehension of things done long before, marshals them al in rank together, brings to mind such things which were happily quite out of memory, & gone from a man, which might be of great use and special help to discover our condition according to the quality of it; may be Conscience starts the consideration but of one sin, but meditation looks abroad, and brings to hand many of the same, and of the like kind and that many dayes past and long ago committed, This distemper now sticks upon a man and brings him under the arrest of Conscience and the condemnation thereof. But saies meditation let me mind you of such and such sins at such and such times, in such and such companies, committed and multiplyed both more and worse than those that now appear so loathsom and so troublesom to you; meditation is as it were the register and remembrancer, that looks over the records of our daily corruptions, and keeps them upon file, and brings them into court and fresh consideration *Job.* 13. 26. *Thou makest me to possess the sins of my youth:* This makes a man to renew the sins of his youth, makes them fresh in our thoughts, as though new done before our eyes. This Interpreters make the meaning of that place *Job.* 14. 17. *My trangression is sealed up in a bag, and thou sewest up mine iniquity,* though God do thus, yet he doth it by this means in the way of his Providence, *i.e.* by recounting and recalling our corruptions to mind, by serious meditation we sew them all up together, we look back to the linage and pedegree of our lusts, and track the abominations of our lives, step by step, until we come to the very nest where they are hatched and bred, even of our original corruption, and body of death, where they had their first breath and being, links al our distempers together from our infancy to our youth, from youth to riper age, from thence to our declining daies. So *David,* from the vileness of his present lusts is led to the wickedness *in which he was warmed,* Psal. 51. 5. This was typed out in the old Law by *the chewing of the cud;* Meditation cals over again those things that were past long before, and not within a mans view and consideration.

Meditation *takes a special Survey of the compass of our present condition, and the Nature of those corruptions that come to be considered:* It's the traversing of a mans thoughts, the coasting of the mind and imagination into every crevis and corner, pryes into every particular, takes a special view of the borders and confines of any corruption or condition that comes to be scanned, *Psal.* 119. 59. *I considered my waies, and turned my feet unto thy testimonies;* he turned them upside down, looked through them as it were; a present apprehension peeps in as it were through the crevis or key-hole, looks in at the window as a man passeth by; but Meditation lifts up the latch and goes into each room, pries into every corner of the house, and surveyes the composition and making of it, with all the blemishes in it. Look as the Searcher at the Sea-Port, or Custom-house, or Ships, satisfies himself not to over-look carelessly in a sudden view, but unlocks every Chest, romages every corner, takes a light to discover the darkest passages. So is it with Meditation, it observes the woof and web of wickedness, the ful frame of it, the very utmost Selvage and out-side of it, takes into consideration all the secret conveyances, cunning contrivements, all bordering circumstances that attend the thing, the consequences of it, the nature of the causes that work it, the several occasions and provocations that lead to it, together with the end and issue that in reason is like to come of it, *Dan.* 12. 4. *Many shall run to and fro, and knowledg shall encrease:* Meditation goes upon discovery, toucheth at every coast, observes every creek, maps out the dayly course of a mans conversation and disposition.

The second End of Meditation is, *It settles it effectually upon the heart.* It's not the pashing of the water at a sudden push, but the standing and soaking to the root, that loosens the weeds and thorns, that they may be plucked up easily. It's not the laying of Oyl upon the benummed part, but the chafing of it in, that suppleth the Joynts, and easeth the pain. It is so in the soul; Application laies the Oyl of the Word that is searching and savory, Meditation chafeth it in, that it may soften and humble the hard and stony heart: Application is like the Conduit or Channel that brings the stream of the Truth upon the soul; but Meditation stops it as it were, and makes it soak into the heart, that so our corruptions may be plucked up kindly by the Roots.

This settling upon the heart appears in a three-fold work.

It affects the heart with the Truth attended, and leaves an Impression upon the Spirit answerable to the Nature of the thing which is taken into Meditation: 2 *Pet.* 2. 8. It's said of *Lot, in seeing and hearing, he vexed his righteous soul.* Many saw and heard the hideous abominations, and were not touched nor affected therewith. No more had he been, but that he vexed and troubled his own righteous soul, because he was driven to a dayly consideration of them which cut him to the quick. The word is observable, it signifies to try by a touch-stone, and to examine, and then upon search to bring the soul upon the rack: therefore the same word is used, *Matth.* 14. 24. *The Ship was tossed by the waves;* the consideration of the abominations of the place raised a tempest of trouble in *Lots* righteous soul. This the wise man calls *laying to the heart*, Eccles. 7. 1, 2. *It's better to go to the house of mourning than to the house of laughter; for this is the end of all men, and the living will lay it to his heart.* When the Spectacle of Misery and Mortality is laid in the grave, yet savory Meditation laies it to a mans heart, and makes it real there in the work of it. The Goldsmith observes that it is not the laying of the fire, but the blowing of it that melts the Mettal: So with Meditation, it breaths upon any Truth that is applied, and that makes it really sink and soak into the soul; and this is the reason why in an ordinary and common course of Providence, and Gods dealing with sinners, (leaving his own exceptions to his own good pleasure) that the most men in the time and work of Conversion have that scorn cast upon them, *that they grow melancholly.* And it's true thus far in the course of ordinary appearance; The Lord usually never works upon the soul by the Ministry of the Word to make it effectual, but he drives the sinner to sad thoughts of heart, and makes him keep an audit in his own soul by serious meditation, and pondering of his waies; otherwise the Word neither affects throughly, nor works kindly upon him.

It keeps the heart under the heat and authority of the Truth that it's taken up withal, by constant attendance of his thoughts. Meditation keeps the Conscience under an arrest, so that it cannot make an escape from the Evidence and Authority of the Truth, so that there is no way, but either to obey the Rule of it, or else be condemned by it. But escape it cannot, Meditation meets and stops al the evasions and sly pretences the fals-hearted person shal counterfeit. If a man should deny his fault, and himself guilty, Meditation will evidence it beyond all gainsaying, by many testimonies which Meditation wil easily cal to mind; remember ye not in such and such a place: upon such an occasion, you gave way to your wicked heart to do thus and thus; you know it, and God knows it, and I have recorded it: If the sinner would lessen his fault, Meditation aggravates it; or if he seem to slight it, and look at it as a matter of no moment, yet Meditation will make it appear, there is greater evil in it, and greater necessity to bestow his thoughts upon it than he is aware of.

Hence it is Meditation laies siege unto the soul, and cuts off al carnal pretences that a wretched self-deceiving hypocrite would relieve himself by; and stil lies at the soul, this you did, at that time, in that place, after that manner; so that the soul is held fast prisoner, and cannot make an escape; but as *David* said, *Psal.* 51. 3. *My sins are ever before me:* Consideration keeps them within view, and will not suffer them to go out of sight and thoughts; and therefore it is *Paul* joyns those two together, 1 *Tim.* 3. 15. *Meditate in these things, and be in them.*

It provokes a man (by a kind of over-bearing power) to the practice of that with which he is so affected: A settled and serious Meditation of any thing, is as the setting open of the Flood-gates, which carries the soul with a kind of force and violence, to the performance of what he so bestows his mind upon; as a mighty stream let out turns the mill. *Phil.* 4. 9. *Think of these things, and do them:* thinking men are doing men. *Psal.* 39. 3. *While I was thus musing, the fire brake out, and I spake:* the busie stirring of Meditation is like the raising of a tempest in the heart, that carries out all the actions of the man by an uncontroulable command. *I considered my waies, and turned my feet unto thy Statutes:* right Consideration, brings in a right Reformation with it.

WANDERING THOUGHTS

THE Marriner, because the Channel is narrow, and the wind somwhat scant, he toucheth in many places, tacks about, and fetcheth many points, but stil because it's to attain the Haven; therfore each man in reason concludes, that was the cause that invited him to al that variety in his course. It's so in the carriage of the soul; the cause why a man fetcheth such a compass, and tacks about in his own contrivements; now this, now that; one while one way, another while this or that presented and pursued busily; yet in the issue we land al our thoughts, and look at the last how to bring in content to such a lust: It's certain the vanity of that lust occasioned and drew the vanity of thy thoughts after it.

The cause being thus conceived, the Cure is fair and easie to comprehend; namely, *Cure these inordinate and raging lusts*, and thence wil follow a stil and quiet composure of mind; purge the stomach if it be foul, and that wil ease the pain of wind in the Head, because that is caused by the fumes that arise from thence. Take off the plummet, or lessen but the weight of it, the minutes though they hurried never so fast before, yet wil not move at all, or at least very slowly and quietly. So here, take off the poyse of the affections, purge away these noysom lusts which carry and command the head, and send up dunghil steams which distemper the mind, and disturb it, and those windy imaginations wil cease, and those thoughts of the mind like the minutes, either wil not move, or move in order and manner as may help and not hinder. Here the great skil and care ought to be to labor the clensing and sanctification of such affections which are most tainted, and where the vein and sourse of original corruption, either through custom, or constitution, or company, hath vented it self most usually, and so hath taken up the soul, and gained, and so exercised greater power over it. For as in bruised or weak parts, all the humors run thither, so commonly this corruption is the sink and drain of the soul, all distempered thoughts, and other inferior lusts, empty themselves, and become Servants unto this. If once the affections had gained such a tast and rellish of the sweetness that is in Christ, and his Truth, that al these baggage and inferior things here below seemed sapless, and that the heart were endeared to him & his Truth, and carried strongly after both: this would carry the thoughts vehemently, & keep them so strongly to both, that they would be so far from wandring away from Christ, that they would not be taken from bestowing the strength of their intentions about him, *Psal.* 119 97. *Oh how I love thy Law, it is my Meditation all the day;* verse 93. *I will never forget thy Precepts, for thereby thou hast quickened me;* ver. 23. *Princes sate and spake against me, but thy servant did meditate in thy Statutes.* In reason he would have conceived it was high time for him to bethink himself how to prevent their fury, & it would cost him sad thoughts of heart how to provide for his succor and safty; no truly, *Thy servant did meditate in thy law.*

Possess thy heart with an actual consideration, and a holy dread of the glorious presence of the Almighty, who sees and pondereth all thy paths, and therefore wil take an account, and that strictly, of all the outstrainings of thy thoughts when thou comest to give attendance upon him, and to draw neer into his presence, in some peculiar and spiritual Service: There is a kind of heedless wantonness which like a Canker breeds in our Atheistical dispositions, whereby we see not the Rule that should guide us, we lay aside also the consideration of that power that doth rule us, and wil bring us to judgment, and so missing the guide that should shew us the path, and the power that should awe us, and constrain us to keep the rode, a mans mind powrs out it self to every vanity that next offers it self unto its view. Whereas were we aware of his presence, and awed with it, it would cause us to eye him, and attend him in his way and work, wherein he commands us to walk with him. As it is with trewantly Schollers who are sporting and gaming out of their place, and from any serious attendance upon their books, when nothing wil stil them, and force them to their studies, as soon as ever there is but the least inkling of the Master, or any eye they can cast upon his approach, they are all as stil as may be, repair presently to their place, fal close, and let their minds to their work; O Master, Master, our Master is yonder; there follows stilness and attendance presently. Our trewantly and wanton minds are of this temper, we are apt to straggle out of our places, or from giving attendance to those special Services which the Lord cals for at our hands, and to lay out themselves upon things that are not pertinent, and further than we are awed with the apprehension of Gods sight and presence, who cals for the dayly attendance of our thoughts when we draw neer unto him, doth see and observe our carelessness, and wil proceed in Judgment, and execute punishment upon us for it, it's scant possible to hold the bent of our thoughts awfull, to the business we have in hand. It was the Curse which attended *Jonah* when he departed away from the presence of the Lord, and from following his Command, he followed *lying vanities*, Jonah, 2. 8. And it's the peculiar plague which is appointed in the way of Providence, and the Lords righteous proceedings to befal al who bestow not their hearts upon him, *Eph.* 4. 21. *They walk in the vanity of their minds;* and the reason is rendred, *they are strangers from the life of God.* When our thoughts start aside from under the Government of Gods Wisdom, the Rule of Truth and stability, they wander up and down in the waies of error and vanity, and find no end or measure, follow vanity, and become vain, nor can they attain any stability before they return thither. As your vagabond beggars, and vagrant persons in the Country from whence we came, there is no possibility to fasten them to any imployment, or settle them in any place before they come under the eye of Authority, and power of the Magistrate. So fares it with our vagabond and vagrant thoughts; further than they are under the eye of God, and awed with his presence, it's not possible to stop them from the pursuit of vanity, or confine them to setled consideration of that which concerns our duty and comfort. The Rule is one, like it self accompanied with stability and rest; if once we go astray from that, there is neither end nor quiet in error, but restlessness and emptiness. The Sea, while it keeps the Channel, the course is known, and the Marriners can tel how to advantage their passage; but if once it exceeds the banks, no man can tel whither it wil go, or where it will stay. Our imaginations are like the vast Sea, while we eye the

Rule, and are ordered by the Authority of it, we know our compass; but once go off, and we know not whither we shal go, or where we shal stay.

Be watchfully careful to observe the first wandrings and out-strayings of thy thoughts, how they first go off from the attendance to the work in hand, and look off from the matter, thou settest thy self to meditate in; immediately recal them back, bring them to their task again, and set them about their intended work. If often they fly out and follow fresh occasions that Satan or a mans corruptions shal suggest take them at the first turn and often again settle them upon the service, until at last by constant custom our mind and thoughts wil buckle handsomly to their business, after they be kept in by a daily care; I have heard Hunts-men say when they have young dogs, raw and that hath not been entred nor accquainted with their sport, if a fresh game come in view, or some other unexpected prey cross them in their way, they forsake the old sent and follow that which is in their eye, but their manner is to beat them off, and cal them away from that, and then to bring them to the place where they left their former pursuit, and there set them to find the sent afresh, until at last being often checked and constantly trayned up they wil take and attend the first game, so here, with our wandring minds which are not trayned up to this work of meditation, if they begin to fly off and follow a new occasion, suffer not thy thoughts to range, but bring your mind back again, and set it upon the former service, and then by thy constant care and Gods blessing thy mind wil fal in sweetly and go away with the work, or as men use to do with some kind of wand that is warped & bent somwhat much one way, they bend it a little, at the first & there hold it. Bend it & hold it, at last it comes fully to the fashion they desire it. So here often bend and hold thy mind bent to the work in hand, *Heb.* 2. 1. *let us give earnest heed to the things wee have heard;* our roving thoughts are like riven vessels, if the parts be not glewed and the breaches brought together again by strong hand, they wil leak out, so here &c.

REPENTANT SINNERS AND THEIR MINISTERS

DOCT. They whose hearts are pierced by the Ministry of the word, they are carryed with love and respect to the Ministers of it.

Men and Brethren, they be words of honor & love, & they spoke them seriously and affectionaley, they mocked them before, and they now embrace them, they cared not what tearms of reproach they cast upon their persons, they know not now what titles of love and tenderness to put upon them, they now fal at their feet as clients, who flouted them before as enemies, so it was with the jalour *Acts* 16. 30, 31, 34. how kindly doth he *Paul* and *Silas* whome erewhile he handled so currishly, beyond the bounds of reason and humanity, he entertains them in the best room of his house who before thought the worst place in the prison too good for them. He baths their wounded parts which he had whipped and stocked before, fears and trembles before them as his counsellors, whom he handled most harshly before as Prisoners; he feasts them as his guests whom he had struck as Malefactors; the wind was in another dore, the man is of another mind yea is another man than he was. God had no sooner opened the heart of *Lydia* to attend the word but her affections were exceedingly enlarged, towards the dispensers thereof. *Acts* 16. 15. so that the cords of her loving invitation led *Paul* and held him captive, he professed *she compelled them i.e.* by her loving and affectionate expressions, prevailed with them for a stay. And while *Paul* had the *Galathians* under the Pangs of the new birth and Christ was now *forming in them*, they professed they *would have plucked out their eyes* and have given them to the Apostle, *Gal*. 4. 15.

Naaman hath no sooner his leprosy healed, and his heart humbled and cut off from his corruption, but he professed himself and what he had is at the devotion of the Prophet, and that not out of complement but in truth, 2 *Kings* 5. 15. *Take a blessing from thy servant.*

Reasons are two.

They see and know more than formerly they did, when happily the crooked counsels of others deceived them, and their own carnal reason couzened and deluded their own souls that they mis-judged the men and their doctrine also. As that they did not speak the truth, or else had some crooked and self-seeking ends in what they spak; As either to gratify other mens humors whom they would please or else to set up their own persons and praise and esteem in the apprehensions of others as singular men and more than of an ordinary frame; and therefore would wind men up to such a high pitch of holiness, and force them to such a singular care to fly the very appearance of al evil, when its more than needs and more than God requires, and more than any man can do but now they find by proof and are forced out of their own sence and feeling to acknowledg the truth of what they have spoken, and what they have heard, & themselves also, to be the faithful embassadors of the Lord Jesus, and therefore worthy to be believed and attended in their dispensations and honored of al. *So*

Paul 2 *Cor.* 4. 3. *We hope we are made manifest unto your consciences* Thus the Woman of *Samaria* when our Savior came home to the quick and met with the secrets of her heart, she then fel from her taunting and slighting of our Savior to admiring of him, *Come faith she behould the man that told me al that ever I did, is not he the Christ.* John, 4. 29. Look as *Nabuchadnezzar* said, *Dan.* 4. last, now I know the God of *Daniel* is the true God, *and now I praise the living God,* so when they have been in the fire, and God hath had them upon the anvil, now I know what sin is, now I know what the danger is, now I know what necessity there is to part with sin; when the Patient hath found the relation and direction of the Physitian hath proved real it makes him prize and honor his skil and counsel, for ever; and for ever to have his custom, As the Pythonist was compelled from the power of *Pauls* administration to confess, *these are the Servants of the living God which shew unto us the way of Salvation,* so here.

As they see more and can therefore judge better of the worth of persons and things; *so their conscience now hath more scope, and the light of reason hath more liberty, and allowance to express that they know, and nothing now can withstand and hinder;* for while men are held captive under the power of their lusts and corruptions of their hearts, in which they live, and which for the while they are resolved to follow; though their reason happily do yeild it, and their own hearts and Consciences cannot but inwardly confess it, the persons are holy, the sins are vile which they condemn, and dangers dreadful which they forewarn; yet to profess so much openly to others, and to the world were to judg themselves while they would acquit others, and condemn their own courses, while they should praise and honor the carriages and persons of others, and therefore darken the evidence of the word by carnal cavils and reproaches, stifle the wittness of Conscience, and stop its mouth that it cannot speak out. Thus *Rom.* 1. 18. *they hold down the truth in unrighteousness.* When the truth that is by their judgments assented unto, and by their hearts yeilded, and therefore should break out and give in testimony to the good wayes of God: their corrupt and unrighteous and rebellious hearts hold it prisoner, wil not suffer it either to appear unto others or prevail with themselves; As it fared with the Scribes & Pharisees when the wonder was wrought by *Peter,* say they *Acts,* 4. 16. *that indeed a notable miracle hath been done by them is manifest to all that dwel in Jerusalem, and we cannot deny it* (*q. d.* they would have done it if they could) *but that it spread no further, let us charge them straitly that they speak no more in this name.* But here when the conscience of a poor sinner is convinced, and the heart wounded, and that resistance and gainsaying distemper is taken off and crushed, now Conscience is in commission and hath his scope & the coast is now clear that reason may be heard, now the broken hearted sinner wil speak plainly, these are the guides that God hath set up, their direction I wil attend, these are the dear and faithful servants of the Lord whom I must honor, and with them I would betrust my soul, not with the blind guides, and false teachers, who daub with untempered morter and are not trustie to God, nor their own souls, and therefore cannot be to me. Oh send for such though in their life time they could not endure the sight, abide the presence, nor allow them a good word, reviled their persons and proceedings and professions, (yea that they wil confess) but it was directly against their own judgment and knowledg and Conscience, myne own heart often gave my tongue the lye, when I did so speak and so disparage their conversation, otherwise I must have condemned mine own course and Conscience also, but the Lord is with them, and the truth is with them, and a Blessing wil undoubtedly follow them. Ask why these poor pierced sinners did not go to the Scribes, they would tel the truth. Oh it was they that deceived us, led and drew us to the commission of this hellish wickedness; we cannot cal them teachers but murtherers, they could never help themselves, therefore not help us.

INSTRUCTION, *Sound contrition and brokenness of heart brings a strange & a sudden alteration into the world, varies the price and valew of things and persons beyond imagination, turnes the market upside down;* makes the things appear as they be, & the persons to be honored and respected as they are in truth, that look what the truth determines, reason approves, and Conscience witnesseth, that account is current in the hearts and apprehensions of those, whose hearts have been pierced with godly sorrow for their sins. Because such judg not by outward appearance as it is the guise of men of corrupt minds, but upon experience, that which they have found and felt in their own hearts, what they have seen and judged in their own spirits, they cannot but see so and judg so of others. Those who were mocked as *men ful of new wine*, are now the precious servants of the Lord, flouted to their faces not long since, now they attend them, honor and reverence them, yea fal at their very feet. It was before men and drunkards, now men and bretheren, the world you see is wel amended but strangely altered. It was said of *John* Baptist the fore-runner of our Savior, and the scope of whose doctrine was mainly to prepare the way for the Lord, it's said of him that *Elias* is come and hath reformed al, set a new face and frame in the profession of the Gospel, *Math.* 17. 11. *Turned the disobedient to the wisdom of the just men, the hearts of children to the fathers,* that though they were so degenerate that *Abraham* would not own them had he been alive, yet when the Ministery of *John* had hammered and melted them for the work of our Savior, they bcame to be wholly altered, their judgments altered and their carriage also. For in truth the reason why men see not the loathsomness of other mens sins, or else have not courage to pass a righteous sentence upon them, It is because they were never convinced to see the Plague sore of their own corruptions, never had their hearts affected with the evil of them in their own experience but their own Conscience was misled out of authority, and stifled that it durst not outwardly condemn that which inwardly they could not but approve. They therefore who either do not see their own evil, or dare not proceed in open judgment to condemn, they wil either not see or not pass a righteous judgment upon others, so *Paul* intimates to *Agrippa*, *Acts*, 26. 8. 9. *let it not seem strange Oh King for I my self did think I should do many things against the name of Jesus, which I also did. q. d.* whiles thou so continuest thou wilt see as I did, and do as I did, but after God had entered into combate with him and spoken dreadfully to his soul see, he is another man, and of another mind; he destroyed the Churches, *now takes care of them;* he that hated the name and Gospel of Jesus *counts al things dung and dross for the excellent knowledg of Jesus*, the world is well amended but its mervailously altered, and therfore *we have found this man a Pestilent fellow Acts*, 17. 16. he hath subdued the state of the world.

TERROR, *this shewes the dreadful and miserable condition of al those who after al the light that hath been let into their minds, conviction into their Consciences, horror into their hearts touching the evils that have been committed and come now to be discovered unto them, they loath the light that hath layd open their evils, distast those persons and preachers and Christians most, that have dealt most plainly to descover the loathsomness of their distempers*, it shewes the irrecoverable corruption of the mind and heart that grows worst under the best means, and cleaves most to its sins under al the choycest means that would pluck their sins from their heart, and their heart from them, they are either fools or mad men that cannot endure the presence of the Physitian without whose help they could not be cured. This is made an evidence of the estrangment of Gods heart from a people, and an immediate fore-runner of their ruin. *Isa.* 9. 13. 14. 17. *For this people turneth not unto him that smote them, neither do they seek the Lord, therefore the Lord wil cut off from Israel head & tail, branch & rush, one day therfore the Lord shal have no pity on their young men nor mercy on their fatherless, for every one is an Hipocrite.* It takes away al pity in God, al hopes in themselves of any good. After *Pharoah* had many qualmes & recoylings of spirit by *Moses* dealing with him, & the miracles which he had wrought for his repentance, & at last sides it with the hellish stiffness of his own stubborn heart, so that he cannot endure the speech or presence of *Moses* any more, Exod. 10. 28. *get thee from me, see my face no more, for the day thou seest my face thou shalt die*, God sends *Moses* no more, but sends his plagues to destroy his first born he wil not see the face of *Moses* he shal feel the fierceness of the wrath of the Lord.

JOHN COTTON, 1584–1652

[For Cotton's life see p. 207. Cotton's sermons are perfect examples of the Puritan ideal of the plain style. Restrained and self-possessed, meticulously logical and rigorously organized, they stay close to the texts, and use hardly any metaphors or figures but those supplied by the Bible itself.

The texts of the first two selections are from *The New Covenant, or A Treatise, unfolding the order and manner of the giving and receiving of the Covenant of Grace to the Elect* (London, 1654), pp. 44–47, 64–69.

The texts of the third and fourth selections are from *The way of Life* (London, 1641), pp. 104–105, 436–451. These sermons were probably delivered in England.

The text of the fifth selection is from *Christ the Fountaine* (London, 1651), pp. 15–21, 25–30.]

SWINE AND GOATS

ALL THE men in the world are divided into two ranks, Godly or Ungodly, Righteous or Wicked; of wicked men two sorts, some are notoriously wicked, others are Hopocrites: Of Hypocrites two sorts (and you shall find them in the Church of God) some are washed Swine, others are Goats.

1. The *Swine* are those of whom our Saviour Christ saith, *That they returne unto their wallowing in the mire;* like unto these are such men who at the hearing of some Sermon have been stomach sick of their sins, and have rejected their wicked courses, but yet the swines heart remaineth in them, as a Swine when he cometh where the puddle is, will readily lye down in it: so will these men wallow in the puddle of uncleannesse when their conscience is not pricked for the present: But these are a grosser kind of Hypocrites.

2. There is another sort that goe far beyond these, and they are *Goats*, so called, *Matth.* 25. 32, 33. and these are clean Beasts such as chew the cudd, meditate upon Ordinances, and they divide the hoofe, they live both in a generall and particular calling, and will not be idle; they are also fit for sacrifice; what then is wanting? Truly they are not *sheep* all this while, they are but *Goats*, yet a Goat doth loath that which a Swine will readily break into; but where then doe they fall short of the nature of sheep? A difference there is, which standeth principally in these particulars.

1. The Goat is of a Capricious nature, and affecteth Eminency, his gate also is stately, *Prov.* 30. 30. *Agur* reckoneth the He-goat among the 4 things that are comely in going: And they are full of Ambition, they cannot abide swamps and holes, but will be climbing upon the tops of mountains; there is not that plain lowly sheepish frame that attendeth unto the voyce of the Shepheard, to be led up and downe in fresh pastures: they attend upon their ends, and will outshoot God in his own Bowe, and therefore when they have done many things for Christ, he will say unto them, *Depart from me, ye workers of iniquity.* More Eminency they did affect, then they were guided unto. Thus it was with *Jehu*, who in his zeal for God thought to promote himselfe, and herein he will not be perswaded of his sin, and therefore going into crooked wayes, he cometh at length to cleave unto the sins of *Jeroboam* the Son of *Nebat*, who made *Israel* to sin; yet notwithstanding, you may rec[e]ive a Goat into Church-fellowship for all his capricious nature, and he will be a clean creature, and of much good use. The five foolish *Mat.* 25. 2. were all of them *Virgins*, all of them abhorring Idolatry, and all go forth to meet the Bridegroome, and yet they are foolish and never shall you make them wise, to be all for Christ, onely hearing and obeying his voyce.

2. They are of a Rankish nature all of them, specially the old Goats will have an unsavory relish, far from that pleasant sweetnesse that is in a sheep; and herein Hypocrites are greatly different from the sheep of Christ, as the Prophet speaketh, *Ezek.* 34. 21. and they marre the Pastures with their feet, and will be at length mudling the faire waters of the Sanctuary also; and in your best sanctification they fall far short of a sheep-like frame of spirit, diligently to heare the voyce of the Shepheard, this will not be found in the sanctification of the best Hypocrite under Heaven, they may goe far and yet fall away, and this is no Arminianism, but if you search the Scriptures diligently, you will find these things to be true.

HYPOCRITES AND SAINTS

TRULY it is hard to perceive when men differ, and therefore it is not an easie matter to make such use of Sanctification, as by it to beare witnesse unto Justification: [1] and it will be a very hard case and much more difficult, when men cannot feele the presence of spirituall gifts, but want spirituall light: and when they doe finde faith in themselves, they doe finde it in hypocrites also, even in hypocrites also, even faith to seeke the Lord, & faith to waite upon him, and faith to apply him, saying, *My God*, and faith to stay upon the *God of Israel;* and yet these men doe vanish away in hypocrisie; this hypocrites may doe; seeing therefore what easines of errour may befall Christians, whether this or that grace be of the right stampe or no, it will behove Christians to be wary, for even Eagle-eyed Christians will have much adoe so to discerne of sanctification in themselves, before they see their justification, as to cut off all hypocrites from having the like in them, for the sanctified frame of Gods children, and that which seemeth to be like it in hypocrites, both of them spring from the holy Ghost, and both from faith: but now the Spirit of God hath further worke in his own people, beyond what he worketh upon others, though he melteth both, yet hypocrites are melted as iron, which will returne againe to his former hardnes, but his owne people are melted into flesh, which will never returne to his hardnes more, neither can they rest in any measure of softnes unto which they have attained, but still are carryed toward Jesus Christ: so that the one is a temporary faith, and the other persevereth; though both worke in the name of Christ, yet this difference will be found between them, not only when hypocrites come to be blasted, but even in the middest of their profession: As for the faith of the Gospell of Jesus Christ, it is never president of its own power, but his strength lyeth out of himselfe in Christ; whereas hypocrites and legall Christians are confident of their faith, that they can make use of it unto such and such ends, they think they need no more but look up to Christ, and their worke is at an end; and such strength they finde in themselves, as that they doe not feare, but that they shall carry an end all their worke to Gods glory and their own: whereas the strongest faith even of the *Thessalonians* (whose faith was such, as none of all the Churches went before them) if it be not supplyed and strengthened, they know, & the Apostle *Paul* knoweth that it will warpe & shrinke. This may we see by comparing, 1 *Thes.* 1. 3. with *Chap.* 3. 2, 10. And the faithfull people of God, *Isa.* 26. 12. acknowledge Him to *worke all their works for them.* And therefore as there is a reall difference in the presence of the Spirit; so also in the worke of faith in hypocrites, and the children of God, for the one putteth confidence in himselfe in the gift received, and the other in *Jehovah.* This is the first difference of Sanctification.

2. There is Difference also in the Rule whereby they are guided, though both seeke to the word of God & take delight in that, insomuch as you shall not be able to difference them there, yet a great difference there is in the apprehension of the word: the one is so confident of the comfort that he hath in the word, and he will be ready to take it ill at Gods hand, if he finde not acceptance before him: Now the other see the need they have of the Lord to maintaine their comfort for them. This manner of affection we finde in *David,* when the Lord had brought him and his people into a sweet frame and temper of spirit to offer willingly towards the building of the Temple; what saith *David* now? Doth he thinke this to be enough? No, no, but he prayeth to the Lord, 1 *Chron.* 29. 18. *O Lord God of Abraham, Isaack, and Israel our fathers keepe this for ever in the imagination of the thoughts of the heart of thy people, and prepare their heart unto thee.* Thus is he sensible that these comforts would soone faile them, & they should againe waxe barren and uncomfortable. And here is the nature of true Consolation in Christ, to looke up unto the Lord to preserve and maintaine it, and so he is still drawne neerer & neerer to Christ. But now though both attend unto the Word, as their Rule of Sanctification, if you take it in the way, in which the one and the other hold it forth, yet there is a great difference. *Psal.* 119. 6. *Then shall I not be ashamed,* &c. Here is a Rule; what, may not hypocrites walke according to this rule? Truly they professe no lesse, and they think it enough, if they have but a Rule in their eye, and therfore under a spirit of bondage they are confident and say, *What soever the Lord commandeth us, we will heare it and doe it,* Deut. 5. 27. And what saith *Balaam; Though* Balaack *would give me an house full of silver and gold, I cannot goe beyond the Commandement of the Lord, Numb.* 22. 18. and yet he loved the wages of iniquity; and indeed those that undertake so much in their owne strength, they come afterward to be weary of the Lord, and weary of his Commandements: as *Amos* 8. 5. and they say at last, *It is in vaine to serve God, and what profit is it that we have kept his ordinances?* Mal. 3. 14. These are but like washed swine, that will crop grasse for a while in a faire Pasture, but if you keepe them long there, they will not delight in such manner of feeding, but will rather choose to go into the mire; but as for goats they will delight in the Commandments of the Lord, *Isa.* 58. 2. It is not a very hard thing unto them, nor grievous for them to keep solemne fasting dayes together, they come willingly,

they delight to come, therefore the difference will be hardly discovered, and unles you be a Christian of a very cleere discerning, you will not finde the difference.

WADING IN GRACE

FOR further encouragement hereunto, consider that place, *Ezech.* 47. 3, 4, 5. It shewes you the marvailous efficacy of the spirit of Grace in the dayes of the Gospel: First a Christian wades in the rivers of God his grace up to the ankles, with some good frame of spirit; yet but weakly, for a man hath strength in his ankle bones, *Acts* 3. and yet may have but feeble knees, *Heb.* 12. 12. So farre as you walk in the waters, so far are you healed; why then in the next place, he must wade till he come to the knees, goe a thousand Cubits, a mile further, and get more strength to pray, and to walk on in your callings with more power and strength.

Secondly, but yet a man that wades but to the knees, his loynes are not drenched, for nothing is healed but what is in the water. Now the affections of a man are placed in his loynes, God tries the reines; a man may have many unruly affections, though he be padling in the wayes of grace; he may walk on in some eavennesse, and yet have many distempered passions, and may have just cause to complaine of the rottennesse of his heart in the sight of God: why then, thou hast waded but to the knees, and it is a mercy that thou art come so farre; but yet the loynes want healing, why, wade a mile further then; the grace of God yet comes too shallow in us, our passions are yet unmortified, so as we know not how to grieve in measure, our wrath is vehement and immoderate, you must therefore wade untill the *loynes bee girt with a golden girdle;* wade an-end, & think all is not well untill you be so deep, & by this you may take a scantling, what measure of grace is poured out upon you. And if thou hast gone so farre, that God hath in some measure healed thy affections, that thou canst be angry and sin not, &c. it is well, and this we must attain to. But suppose the loyns should be in a good measure healed, yet there is more goes to it then all this; and yet when a man is come thus farre, he may laugh at all temptations, and blesse God in all changes: But yet goe another thousand Cubits, and then you shall swimme; there is such a measure of grace in which a man may swimme as fish in the water, with all readinesse and dexterity, gliding an-end, as if he had water enough to swimme in; such a Christian doth not creep or walk, but he runs the wayes of Gods Commandements; what ever he is to doe or to suffer he is ready for all, so every way drenched in grace, as let God turn him any way, he is never drawn dry.

CHRISTIAN CALLING

WEE are now to speake of living by faith in our outward and temporall life: now our outward and temporall life is twofold, which wee live in the flesh. It is either a civill, or a naturall life, for both these lives we live, and they are different the one from the other: Civill life is that whereby we live, as members of this or that City, or Town, or Commonwealth, in this or that particular vocation and calling.

Naturall life I call that, by which we doe live this bodily life, I meane, by which we live a life of sense, by which we eate and drinke, by which we goe through all conditions, from our birth to our grave, by which we live, and move, and have our being. And now both these a justified person lives by faith; To begin with the former.

A true beleeving Christian, a justified person, hee lives in his vocation by his faith.

Not onely my spirituall life, but even my Civill life in this world, all the life I live, is by the faith of the Son of God: he exempts no life from the agency of his faith, whether he live as a Christian man, or as a member of this or that Church, or Commonwealth, he doth it all by the faith of the Son of God.

Now for opening this point, let me shew you what are those severall acts of faith which it puts forth about our occasions, and vocations, that so we may live in Gods sight therein.

First, Faith drawes the heart of a Christian to live in some warrantable calling; as soone as ever a man begins to looke towards God, and the wayes of his grace, he will not rest, till he find out some warrantable Calling and imployment: An instance you have in the Prodigall son, that after he had received & spent his portion in vanity, and when being pinched, he came home to himself, & comming home to his Father, the very next thing after confession and repentance of his sin, the very next petition he makes, is, *Make mee one of thy hired servants;* next after desire of pardon of sin, then put me into some calling, though it be but of an hired servant, wherein he may bring in God any service; A Christian would no sooner have his sinne pardoned, then his estate to be setled in some good calling, though not as a mercenary slave, but he would offer it up to God as a free-will Offering, he would have his condition and heart setled in Gods peace, but his life setled in a good calling, though it be but of a day-labourer, yet make me as one that may doe thee some service; *Paul* makes it a matter of great thankfulnesse to God, that he had given him ability, and put him in place where he might doe him service, 1 *Tim.* 1. 12. And in the Law, they were counted uncleane beasts that did not divide the hoofe into two, *Lev.* 11. 3. therefore the Camell, though he chewed the cud, yet because he did not divide the hoofe, hee was counted uncleane; and God by the Beasts, did signifie to us sundry sorts of men, who were cleane, who not, as you may see in *Peters* Vision, in *Acts* 10. It shewes you then, that it is onely a cleane person, that walkes with a divided hoofe, that sets one foote in his generall, and the other in his particular calling; he strikes with both, he serves both God and man, else he is an uncleane beast, if he have no calling but a generall, or if no calling but a particular, he is an uncleane creature; But now as soone as ever faith purifies the heart, it makes us cleane creatures, *Acts* 15. 9. and our callings doe not interfeire one upon another, but both goe an end evenly together, he drives both these plowes at once; *As God hath called every man, so let him walke,* 1 Cor. 7. 19, 20. This is the cleane worke of faith, hee would have some imployment to *fill the head and hand with.*

Now more particularly, faith doth warily observe the warrantablenesse of its calling.

Three things doth faith finde in a particular calling.

First, It hath a care that it be a *warrantable* calling, wherein we may not onely aime at our own, but at the publike good, that is a warrantable calling, *Seek not every man his owne things, but every man the good of his brother,* 1 *Cor.* 10. 24. *Phil.* 2. 4. Seek one anothers welfare; faith works all by love, *Gal.* 5. 6. And therefore it will not think it hath a comfortable calling, unlesse it will not onely serve his owne turne, but the turn of other men. Bees will not suffer drones among them, but if they lay up any thing, it shall be for them that cannot work; he would see that his calling should tend to publique good.

Secondly, Another thing to make a calling warrantable, is, when God gives a man *gifts* for it, that he is acquainted with the mystery of it, and hath gifts of body and minde sutable to it: *Prov.* 16. 20. *He that understands a matter shall finde good;* He that understands his businesse wisely. God leads him on to that calling, 1 *Cor.* 7. 17. To shew you that when God hath called me to a place, he hath given me some gifts fit for that place, especially, if the place be sutable and fitted to me and my best gifts; for God would not have a man to receive five Talents, and gaine but two, he would have his best gifts improved to the best advantage.

Thirdly, That which makes a calling warrantable, is, when it is attained unto by warrantable and direct *meanes,* when a man enterprises not a calling, but in the use of such meanes as he may see Gods providence leading him to it: so *Amos* manifests his calling against the High Priest, *Amos* 7. 14, 15. *The Lord tooke me, and said unto me, Goe, feed my people:* So he had a warrant for it, Gods hand led him to it in Gods Ordinance, and therein he comforted himselfe, whereas another man that hath taken up such a calling without warrant from God, he deales ingenuously, *Zach.* 13. 5. and leaves it; to shew you that a man ought to attend upon his owne warrantable calling. Now faith that hath respect unto the word of God for all its wayes, he would see his calling ayming at the publique good, he would see gifts for it, and an open doore for his entrance into it, hee would not come unto it by deceit and undermining of others, but he would see the *providence and ordinance* of God leading him unto it, the counsell of friends, and encouragement of neighbours; this is the first work of faith.

2. Another work of faith, about a mans vocation and calling, when faith hath made choyce of a warrantable calling, then he *depends* upon God for the quickning, and sharpning of his gifts in that calling, and yet depends not upon his gifts for the going through his calling, but upon God that gave him those gifts, yea hee depends on God for the use of them in his calling; faith saith not, Give me such a calling and turne me loose to it; but faith lookes up to heaven for skill and ability, though strong and able, yet it looks at all its abilities but as a dead work, as like braided wares in a shop, as such as will be lost and rust, unlesse God refresh and renue breath in them. And then if God doe breathe in his gifts, hee depends not upon them for the acting his work, but upon Gods blessing in the use of his gifts; though he have never so much skill and strength, he looks at it as a dead work, unlesse God breathe in him; and he lookes not at his gifts as breathed onely on by God, as able to doe the work, unlesse also he be followed by Gods blessing. *Blessed bee the Lord my strength, that teacheth my hands to warre, and my fingers to fight, Psal.* 44. 1. He had been trained up to skill that way, yet he rests onely in Gods teaching of him, *Psal.* 18. 32, 33, 34. *It is the Lord that girds me with strength;* he puts strength into his hands, so that a *Bow of steele is broken with my armes;* And therefore it was that when he went against *Goliah*, though he had before found good successe in his combats with the Lyon and the Beare, yet he saith not, I have made my part good enough with them, and so shall I doe with this man; no, but this is the voyce of faith; *The Lord my God that delivered me out of their hands, he will deliver me out of the hand of this Philistim;* Hee that gave me strength and skill at that time, hee is the same, *his hand is not shortned:* And then what is this Philistim more then one of them? 1 *Sam.* 17. 37. And so when hee comes in *Goliahs* presence,

and looks in his face, he tels him he comes to him *in the name of the Lord of Hosts;* and hee comes not onely in the Lords name, but he *looks up to him for skill and strength to help;* and therefore saith ver. 40. *The Lord will close thee in my hands;* so that by his owne strength shall no flesh prevaile; *It is in vaine*, saith faith, *to rise early, and goe to bed late, but it is God that gives his beloved rest*, *Psal.* 127. 1, 2, 3. *Prov.* 3. 5, 6. The strongest Christian is never more foyled, then when he goes forth in strength of gifts received, and his owne dexterity.

Thirdly, We live by faith in our vocations, in that faith, *in serving God, serves men, and in serving men, serves God:* The Apostle sweetly describes it in the calling of servants, *Eph.* 6. 5. *to* 8. *Not with eye service as men-pleasers, but as the servants of Christ, doing the will of God from the heart with good will, as unto the Lord, and not unto men;* Not so much man, or onely man, but chiefly the Lord; so that this is the work of every Christian man in his calling, even then when he serves man, he serves the Lord; he doth the work set before him, and he doth it *sincerely*, and *faithfully*, so as he may give account for it; and he doth it *heavenly* and *spiritually; He uses the world as if he used it not*, 1 *Cor.* 7. 31. This is not the thing his heart is set upon, hee lookes for greater matters then these things can reach him, he doth not so much look at the world as at heaven. And therefore that which followes upon this, he doth it all *comfortably*, though he meet with little encouragements from man, though the more faithfull service he doth, the lesse he is accepted; whereas an unbeleeving heart would be discontented, that he can finde no acceptance, but all he doth is taken in the worst part; but now if faith be working and stirring, he wil say, *I passe very litle to be judged by you, or by mans judgement*, 1 *Cor.* 4. 3. I passe little what you say, or what you do, God knows what I have done, & so his spirit is satisfied, 1 *Thess.* 2. 6. *We were tender over you, as a Nurse over her childe;* We wrought not for wages, nor for the praise of you, if so, wee had not been the servants of Christ. A man therefore that serves Christ in serving of men, he doth his work sincerely as in Gods presence, and as one that hath an heavenly businesse in hand, and therefore comfortably as knowing God approves of his way and work.

Fourthly, Another act of faith about a mans vocation is this; It *encourageth* a man in his calling to the most homeliest, and difficultest, and most dangerous things his calling can lead and expose himselfe to; if faith apprehend this or that to be the way of my calling, it encourages me to it, though it be never so *homely*, and *difficult*, and *dangerous*. Take you a carnall proud heart, and if his calling lead him to some homely businesse, he can by no meanes embrace it, such homely employments a carnall heart knowes not how to submit unto; but now faith having put us into a calling, if it require some homely employment, it encourageth us to it, he considers, It is my calling, and therefore he goes about it freely, and though never so homely, he doth it as a work of his calling, *Luke* 15. 19. *Make mee one of thy hired servants:* A man of his rank and breeding was not wonted to hired servile work, but the same faith that made him desirous to be in a calling, made him stoop to any work his calling led him to; there is no work too hard or too homely for him, for faith is conscious, that it hath done most base drudgery for Satan. No lust of pride, or what else so insolent, but our base hearts could be content to serve the Devil and nature in it, and therefore what drudgery can be too homely for me to doe for God? *Phil.* 2. 5, 7. *Let the same minde bee in you that was in Christ Iesus, hee made himselfe of no reputation;* he stood not upon it, that he was borne of God, and equall to the most High, but he made himselfe a servant, and of no reputation, and so to serve God, and save men; and when his Father called him to it, he stooped to a very low employment, rose up from Supper, and girded himselfe with a Towell, and washed his Disciples feet, *Iohn* 13. They thought it was a service too homely for him to doe, but he tells them, that even they ought thus to serve one another. So faith is ready to embrace any homely service his calling leads him to, which a carnall heart would blush to be seene in; a faithfull heart is never squeamish in this case, for repentance will make a man revenge himselfe upon himselfe, in respect of the many homely services he hath done for Satan, and so faith encourageth us to the most difficult and homely businesses. *Ezra* 10. 4. *It is a great thing* thou art now about, yet *arise and bee doing, for the matter belongs to thee:* Yea, and though sometimes the work be more dangerous, yet if a man be called to it, faith dares not shrink; It was an hard point that *Herod* was put upon, either now hee must bee prophane, or discover his hypocrisie; now therefore *Iohn* dischargeth his conscience, and though it was dangerous for him to bee so plaine, yet faith encourageth him to it; if it appeare to bee his Calling, faith doth not picke and choose, as carnall reason will doe.

Firstly, Another act of faith, by which a Christian man lives in his vocation, is, That faith *casts all the failings and burthens of his calling upon the Lord;* that is the proper work of faith, it rolls and casts all upon him.

Now there are three sorts of burthens that befall a man in his calling.

1. *Care about the successe of it;* and for this faith casts its care upon

God, 1 *Pet.* 5. 7. *Pro.* 16. 3. *Commit thy workes unto the Lord, and thy thoughts shall be established, Psal.* 55. 22. 24. *Cast thy burthen upon the Lord, and he will deliver thee;* faith will commend that wholly to God.

2. A second burthen, is *feare of danger* that may befall us therein from the hand of man. *Luke* 13. 31. 32. Some bids Christ goe out of the Country, for *Herod* will kill him; what saith Christ to that? *Goe tell that foxe I must worke to day and to morrow, &c.* He casts that upon God and his calling, God hath set me a time, and while that time lasts, my calling will beare me out, and when that time is out, then I shall be perfect.

3. Another burthen, is the burthen of *injuries*, which befalls a man in his calling. I have not hastened that evill day, Lord thou knowest; he had not wronged himselfe nor others in his calling, and therefore all the injuries that befall him in his calling, he desires the Lord to take it into his hands.

Sixtly, Faith hath another act about a mans vocation, and that is, it takes *all successes* that befall him in his calling with *moderation*, hee equally beares good and evill successes as God shall dispense them to him. Faith frames the heart to moderation, be they good or evill, it rests satisfied in Gods gracious dispensation; *I have learned in what estate soever I am, therewith to bee content, Phil.* 4. 11, 12. This he had learned to doe, if God prosper him, he had learned not to be puffed up, and if he should be exposed to want, he could do it without murmuring. It is the same act of unbeleefe, that makes a man murmure in crosses, which puffes him up in prosperity; now faith is like a poyse, it keeps the heart in an equall frame, whether matters fall out well or ill, faith takes them much what alike, faith moderates the frame of a mans spirit on both sides.

Seventhly, The last work which faith puts forth about a mans calling, is this, faith with boldnesse *resignes up* his calling into the hands of God or man; when ever God calls a man to lay downe his calling, when his work is finished, herein the sons of God farre exceed the sons of men; another man when his calling comes to bee removed from him, hee is much ashamed, and much afraid, but if a Christian man be to forgoe his calling, he layes it downe with comfort and boldnesse, in the sight of God and man.

First, *In the sight of God*, 2 Tim. 4. 7. *I have fought the fight, I have kept the faith, and finished my course*, and therefore, *henceforth is laid up for me a crowne of righteousnesse, which God according to his righteous* word and promise will give him, as a reward for his sincere and faithfull walking; he lookes up to God, and resignes up his calling into his hand; he tels *Timothy*, the day of his departure is at hand; and now, this is matter of strong consolation to him; faith beleeving, that God put him into his calling, and hath beene helpfull to him hitherto, and now growne nigh to the period of his calling, here was his comfort, that he had not throwne himself out of his work; but God cals him to leave it, and so he leaves it, in the same hand from whom he received it. A man that in his calling hath sought himselfe, and never looked farther then himselfe, he never comes to lay downe his calling, but he thinks it is to his utter undoing: a Swine that never did good office to his owner, till hee comes to lye on the hurdle, he then cryes out; but a Sheep, who hath many times before yeelded profit, though you take him and cut his throat, yet hee is as a Lamb dumb before the shearer; so a carnall man, that never served any man but himselfe, call him to distresse in it, and he murmures and cries out at it; but take you a Christian man, that is wonted to serve God in serving of men, when hee hath beene faithfull and usefull in his calling, he never layes it downe but with some measure of freedome and boldnesse of spirit; as it was with the three Princes in the furnace, they would live and dye in Gods service, and therefore God marvailously assisted them in their worst houres; the soule knows whom it hath lived upon: This is the life of faith in the upshot of a mans calling, he layes it downe in confidence of Gods acceptance: and for *man*, he hath this boldnesse in his dealings with men, he boldly challenges all the sons of men, of any injury done to them, and he freely offers them restitution and recompence, if any such there should be: It was the comfort of *Samuel* when hee was growne old, and the people were earnest for a King, 1 *Sam.* 12. 3. he saith unto them; Behold, here am I before you this day, beare witnesse against me this day, *Whose Oxe or Asse have I taken? &c.* hee makes an open challenge to them all, and they answered, *Thou hast done us no wrong*. This is the comfort of a Christian, when he comes to lay downe his calling, he cannot onely with comfort looke God in the face, but all the sons of men. There is never a Christian that lives by faith in his calling, but hee is able to challenge all the world for any wrong done to them, *We have wronged and defrauded no man*, Acts 20. 26. 2 Cor. 12. We have done most there, where we are least accepted; that is the happinesse of a Christian, those who have beene the most weary of him, have had the least cause.

Vse 1. From hence you see a just reproofe of the infidelity found in them that live without a calling, they either want faith, or the exercise of faith; if thou beest a man that lives without a calling, though thou hast two thousands to spend, yet if thou hast no calling, tending to publique good, thou art an uncleane beast; if men walke without a cloven hoofe, they are uncleane: and hast thou a Calling, and art never so diligent in it, it is but *dead worke*, if thou want faith. It likewise reproves such Christians, as consider not what gifts they have for this and that calling; he pleads for himselfe, his wife and children, further then himselfe he respects no calling; and this is want of faith in a Christians calling: or if men rest in the strength of their owne gifts, for the performing of their callings, and will serve God in some things, and themselves and theirs in other some, or if we can tell how to be eye-servants, it is but a dead worke, for want of faith; or if thou lose thy selfe, and thy heart is carnall, and not heavenly minded, thou mayest have faith, but that is but a dead worke. And if thou cast not all thy care and burthen upon God, thou wilt be very dead when ill successes fall out; but had we faith, it would support us in our worst successes; and if better successes come, if faith be wanting, our vaine heart will be lifted up; and if Christians be confounded before God and men, when they are to resigne up their callings, it is a signe that either they have no faith, or it puts not forth life and courage into them; and if it so fall out, know that the root of it springs from an unbeleeving heart.

Vse 2. It is an Use of instruction to every Christian soule that desires to walke by faith in his calling, If thou wouldst live a lively life, and have thy soule and body to prosper in thy calling, labour then to get into a good calling, and therein live to the good of others; take up no calling, but that thou hast understanding in, and never take it unlesse thou mayest have it by lawfull and just meanes, and when thou hast it, serve God in thy calling, and doe it with cheerfulnesse, and faithfulnesse, and an heavenly minde; and in difficulties and dangers, cast thy cares and feares upon God, and see if he will not beare them for thee; and frame thy heart to this heavenly moderation in all successes to sanctifie Gods name; and if the houre and power of darknesse come, that thou beest to resigne up thy calling, let it bee enough that conscience may witnesse to thee, that thou hast not sought thy selfe, nor this world, but hast wrought the Lords workes; thou mayest then have comfort in it, both before God and men.

Vse 3. It is a word of consolation to every such soule, as hath beene acquainted with this life of faith in his calling, Bee thy calling never so meane and homely, and never so hardly accepted, yet, if thou hast lived by faith in thy calling, it was a lively worke in the sight of God, and so it will be rewarded when thy change shall come; Many a Christian is apt to be discouraged and dismaid if crosses befall him in his calling, but be not afraid, let this cheare up thy spirit, that what ever thy calling was, yet thou camest into it honestly, and hast lived in it faithfully, your course was lively and spirituall, and therefore you may with courage looke up for recompence from Christ.

PURCHASING CHRIST

1 John 5. 12

He that hath the Son, hath life, and he that hath not the Son, hath not life.

BECAUSE in Scripture phrase, there are more wayes of having Christ requisite for the knowledge of every soul[,] I thought it therefore not amisse to open those other wayes by which in Scripture we are said to have Christ.

Secondly, as therefore we have him first by worshipping of him, so secondly we have him by purchase; this way of having Christ is expressed to us partly in the parable of the Merchant man, *Matth.* 13. 46, *Who when he had found a pearle of precious price, he sold all that* [*he*] *had and bought it;* that is one way of having Christ, to purchase him, to buy him: you have the like also held out in *Esa.* 55. 1, 2. *every one that is a thirst, come and buy without money or without price,* wherein the Holy Ghost calleth upon us to receive the Lord Jesus Christ as revealed in his ordinances, and he makes a solemne proclamation to all, to come to *these waters and buy without money?* or how without money? It is true, should a man offer his house full of Treasure for Christ, it would be despised *Cant.* 8. 7. and when *Simon Magus* offered to buy the gifts of the Holy Ghost for money, it was rejected with a curse. *Act.* p. 8, 9, 10, and if the gift of the Holy Ghoast cannot be bought for money, how can the Lord Jesus Christ be bought for money?

And yet thus much I say, that many times without laying out of money, he cannot be had, without parting with money we cannot get him, the case so stands that sometimes, the holding fast a mans money lets go the Lord Jesus Christ, you have a famous example in the Young man, *Matth.* 19. 21. *to* 24. Where our Saviour shewes how hard a thing it is for a rich man to enter into the Kingdome of Heaven, because it is hard for a rich man to part with all that he hath, when God calls for it at his hands, so that without mony sometimes Christ cannot be had; And yet for mony he cannot be had, it was upon the point of mony, that the Lord Jesus parted with the *Pharisees, Luke* 16. 11. 12. *If you be unfaithfull with the mammon of iniquity, who will trust you with true treasure;* if you use not outward things well, who will give you saving grace in Jesus Christ? so that sometimes for want of spending of money in a right way, many a man looses the Lord Jesus; so that though Christ cannot be had for money, yet sometimes without expence of mony he cannot be had.

For opening of this point there are three Cases in which money must be layed out, or else Christ cannot be had, and in refusing to lay out money, we refuse life in him.

First, when the Lord by some speciall command requires it, as was the case of the young man in the Gospel, there was a speciall commandement given to him, not given to every man, nor to every rich man, nor scarce any man in ordinary course now adayes, yet then given to him; and now to stick for money, and rather lose eternall life then his goods, in such a case as this, he loseth his life in Christ; and upon the same poynt, or the like, broke *Ananias* and *Saphira*, it was the common resolution of the Church of God in that Age to sell all that they had, and to give to the poore, and to live after the same rate that other men did, a like proportion to every man; and to distribute faithfully to every man as every man had need, and as the Apostles saw cause; and when they come and keep back part of the price for which their possessions was sold, you see how bitter a curse from the presence of the Lord fell upon them, they were cut off from the Congregation of Gods people, and it is much to be feared, cut off from the Lord Jesus Christ, and from all hope of eternall life, and to stand as a terrible example to the whole Church of God, to shew what a dangerous thing it is to stand upon termes with Christ, and not to part with money for him; they could not have fellowship with the people of God, unlesse they parted with all they had, and live upon the common distribution; but this case is not alwayes.

But secondly, there is another time, namely, when in case of persecution the market of Christ goes at so high a rate, that a man cannot have Christ with any comfort in his soule, or peace to his Conscience, or purity of heart or life, unlesse he hazzard all his estate, or a good part of it: In buying and selling of a precious commodity, a good Chapman will have it what ever it cost him: So Christ is sometimes at an higher, and sometimes at a lower rate, but whatever he costs him, he will have him; it is spoken in commendation of the *Hebrews*, that *they suffered joyfully the spoyling of their goods*, Heb. 10. 34. to shew you, that sometimes it comes to that passe, that unlesse a man be content to part with all his goods, he cannot have the recompence of reward, the Lord Jesus Christ to his soule; and therefore the Servants of God have been content to loose all that they had, and willing to resigne up all for the maintaining the integrity of their spirits, and the purity of their hearts and lives in the presence of God, and then let all goe, they can *suffer the spoyle of all joyfully*.

3. It is in case that by Gods providence you be cast to live in such Congregations, where you cannot have the Ordinances of God but at a great charge, as it is the case of many places, that unlesse they be at charge for the Ministery of the Gospel it cannot be had; then we must communicate freely that way, then *be not deceived, God is not mocked, for what a man sowes that shall he also reap*, Gal. 6. 6, 7, 8. Where the Apostle doth encourage men at such a time as this, when the Gospel, cannot be had but at great charge, then lay out liberally for the Gospel of Christ, and he calls it, A sowing to the Spirit; as a man that layes out his money for an earthly commodity, for a good bargaine, he reapes corruption; so he that sowes of the Spirit, shall of the Spirit reape life everlasting. When a man layes out his money unto Spirituall ends, to obtaine the free passage of the Ordinances of Christ, to enjoy the liberty of the Gospel, he thereby sowes to the Spirit, and shall of the Spirit reap life everlasting; for this is the blessing promised unto it, such as so sow, *shall of the Spirit reap life everlasting;* so that when a man out of a good and honest heart, and an hungering desire after Gods Ordinances, shall be willing to be at charge for them, he hath this promise made to him, and it shall be fulfilled, *He shall of the Spirit reap life everlasting*. But yet, when a man hath layed out his money for this end, if he then thinke his money is worthy of Christ, he gets him not; but this is the first way of having Christ by way of Purchase, a seasonable laying out our money for him as God requires it.

Secondly, Christ is to be purchased, not so much by money, as chiefly this purchase must be made by parting with all those many and strong Lusts, and Corruptions, and sinfull rebellions of heart, by which we keep off Christ from comming into our hearts; this is that which the Prophet *Esay* directs us to, *Esa.* 55. 7. *Let the wicked forsake his way, and the unrighteous man his thoughts*, &c. where he tels us what we must give for Christ, for sinne is neither money nor moneys worth; but he makes a good bargaine that parts with his sins, though he should get no Christ for his parting with them. He speakes of the first and principall part of the life of a Christian man, the life of his Justification that springs from pardon of sinne; let a man forsake those sins and lusts that he hath been most carried captive with; let a wicked man forgoe his thoughts and wayes, both his secret and open sins, and let him *then turne to God, and he will abundantly pardon;* then God will receive him graciously, to the justification of life. This is the thing that we must doe, this was the point upon which sundry of them that have been hopefull for Religion, have broken off from Christ, and Christ from them; they have forsooke him, and he left them; *Jehu* stuck upon this very point, he would goe a great way, but when it comes (as he thinkes) to hazzard his title to the Crowne, then he will set up the *golden Calves;* when he saw that all must be parted with, rather then he would forgoe that, without which he could not maintaine his Kingdome, he would rather loose Christ, then venture the losse of that, 2 *King.* 10. 29. 31. *He regarded not to walke in all the Commandements of the Lord*, and then as he cut short with God in reformation, and did not fulfill to walke after the Lord, therefore God cut *Jehu* short of all the hopes of grace that ever he might have attained, to vers. 32. so that if we cut at a scanting with God, and will part with some lusts and corruptions, but not with others, then will God cut you short of all your hopes of eternall life: and it was upon the same termes that *Herod* fell short of Christ, *Mar.* 6. 10. *Luk.* 3. 18. he had done many things according to *Johns* Ministry, but when God would cut him short of *Herodias* his darling Lust, that nothing might lye between God and him, but might now become fit for Christ, because he would not cut himselfe short of *Herodias*, and cut short his reformation there, then this was added to all his other sins, he *shut up* John *in prison*, and afterward cut off his head also; so that when there is any sinne, whether honour or pleasure, or any comfort in this life, that men will not be content to cut themselves short of, it is the way to utter ruine; God will not be abundantly ready to pardon such. And so was it with *Dæmas*, when the love of money did so prevaile with his heart, after he had been much esteemed of the Apostles, and mentioned honourably in their Writings, yet in the end it is said of him, *He hath forsaken me, and loved this present world*, 2 Tim. 4. 10. Love of the world had so prevailed with him, that he fell off from *Paul*, and from the Lord, whose Servant *Paul* was, and from fellowship in the Gospel, and so did not finde Christ; this rule is universally to be followed, and the care of it not to be neglected in any case, that our sins are to be put out of our hearts and hands, as ever we looke to finde Christ, and life in him; notable is that expression recorded in *Judg.* 10. 10. to 16. the people come and *cry to the Lord*, to deliver them out of the hands of their enemies; but they had got to themselves other gods, and now he would deliver them no more; When the people heard that, that God would not deliver them, and could finde no acceptance from him, so long as they continued in such a sinne; they thereupon goe and put away all their Idols, and leaves not one to be seen among them; and when God sees that they had put them away, the text saith, *that his soule was grieved for their misery*, and his bowels rowled within him for them, and he delivered them: So that when men are willing to fore-go their honourable sinnes, their sweet and delightfull sinnes, their profitable sinnes, and those wherewith they have been most captivated; and he knowes one may as well pull their hearts out of their bellies, as some sinnes out of them; but when he sees men are willing to fore-go their most darling delightfull sins, willing to breake off all impediments that stand between God and them, the Soule of God is grieved in such a case, and it pitties him now that such a soule should be without him; and then it will not be long ere God stirres them up meanes of deliverance, and he himselfe will reveale himselfe unto them. Notable is that speech, *Hos.* 14. 3. 8. when they *take words to themselves*, and promise to leave all their evil wayes, whereby they sinne against God, they make this request to God, That *he would take away their iniquities from them;* and least God should answer them, but be you doing something in the meane time; they professe, that for their owne parts they will set about the doing of their iniquities away, and they say; Ashur *shall not save us, and we will have no more to doe with them;* wherein he shewes you, that God lookes not that only his people shall pray him to take away their iniquities, for we may pray so long enough, and not finde it done; but when we desire God to doe it, and set our hearts and hands to it, and now with heart and hand say, *Ashur shall not save us, nor will we say any more to the workes of our hands, Ye are our gods;* then saith God in vers. 4. *I will heale their back-slidings, and will love them freely*, &c. God is then abundantly ready to pardon, when men forsake their owne wayes and thoughts, and throw away the sins that hang about them, God will say of such a people, *I will heale them, and love them freely, mine anger is turned away from them.* And you may presume, when Gods anger is turned away, it is by and through Christ, or else there is no healing; and therefore in vers. 8. *Ephraim* saith, *What have I to doe any more with Idols;* the heart of a Christian, or of a Nation, shall openly acknowledge, that they wil have no more fellowship with these abominations; and then saith God, *I have heard him, and observed him.* God heares us, and understands what we say, and observes us well, and offers to be a covert to us from the storme, when we begin solemnly to abandon such evils, then he heares us, and answers us according to the desire of our hearts; you have many a soule that cryes to God, Take away our iniquity, and many Petitions we put up to God to that purpose; and that sometimes with many bitter moanes, but God heares it not; we pour out our plaints in vaine, and he regards it not; but when we come to God, and desire him not only to take them from us, but begin to consider our owne wayes and iniquities, and to put them from us, out of our hearts and hands, and we wil no more take such bad wayes, as heretofore we have done; we *will no more ride upon horses,* nor run to forreigne Princes for succour; then God heares, and grants graciously whatever his poore people begge at his hands, and answers it according to all the desire of their hearts, then the Lord presently gives us the Lord Jesus Christ, and life and healing in him; and this is the second way of having Christ by purchase. . . .

Fourthly, there is yet something more then all this, a further price to pay, if we mean to purchase Christ; And that is, that we part with all our good parts, and all the good common gifts of grace, which are found sometimes in good nature, and sometimes in the children of the Church, we must part with them all that we may win Christ 1 *Cor.* 3. 18. *If any man among you seem to be wise in this world, let him become a foole that he may be wise:* who ever would be a wise man, (as a wise man he cannot be, if hee have not his part in Christ) he must lay aside his serious and sad deliberation, and communication with flesh and blood, and all things in the way of God, that he thinkes will be prejudiciall, if any man be so wise, as to see this and that danger in a Christian course, let him become a foole; else he shall never become a Christian: if a man will be content to forsake all for Christ, he must first be a foole, and be content to bee counted a foole, and heare every carnall man to count him a foole. And I speak not onely of carnal and civill wisdom, that, that only is to be denyed in this case, but common graces, which many times choakes all the hypocrites in the bosome of the Church; they are commonly choaked upon this point, upon these things they trust, and doe therefore verily beleeve, that this and that interest, God hath in them, and they in God; because they have received such and such gifts from him, and this is the case formerly mentioned, *Matth.* 7. 22, 23. they pleaded their spirituall gifts, though common gifts, and such as may be found in *workers of iniquity,* they *prayed to God,* a common gift; and they *prophesied in his name,* they had prophetical gifts; some measure of the spirit of ministery, and they were able *to cast out devills in Christs name;* now when as men do trust upon these, and settle themselves upon such a change, truly, hereby they loose that power in Christ which else they might have had. Its a wonder to see what a change propheticall gifts will work in a man, 1 *Sam.* 10. 10, 12. he, there *Saul* had a spirit of prophesie came upon him, and the people wondred at it, it works a strange change in a man, and so in the next chap. the 19 and 23 ver. he prophesied til he came at such a place, so that you shall see a man that is trained up in any good order, though sometimes given to loose company; when once God begins to poure into him any spirituall gift, to inlighten his mind, and to inlarge his affection, that hee begins to have some love to, and some joy in the Word, and some sorrow in hearing of the Word, and some comfort in meditation: Its wonder to see what a change this will work in the spirit; he forthwith begins to abandon his loose courses, and sets himselfe to a more strict course, then hee begins to see his acquisite learning is but a small matter to edification; hee prizes his spirituall gifts, and hee is able now to doe much; and when a mans heart is thus changed by propheticall gifts, it workes in a man such confidence in his soule, that he thinkes all the Congregation shall perish before he can perish, and if Ministers, may be thus deceived by common gifts and graces, how much more may their poor hearers bee deceived, when they by hearing the Word find such comfort, and illumination, and inlargements, that they thereby finde a great change wrought in them; and yet if ministers may bee so much deceived, in presuming vainly of their good estate, which was not so, then much more common Christians: Should any man presume at *Fœlix his trembling*, *Act.* 24. 25. *At Jehues zeale*, 2 *King.* 10. 16. *At Ahabs humiliation*, 1 *King.* 21. 28, 29. *At Herods joy* in hearing, you know what became of all these, these be graces of God, though but common graces, and if the Prophets were deceived, may not these be deceived also, that have neither Christ nor any part in him; and therefore a man that would bee sure not to goe without Christ, nor without life in him; he must not trust in any spirituall gift he hath received, though his mind be inlightened, sometimes to feare, sometimes to joy, to humiliation, to inlargement, to zealous reformation, yet rest in none of these, for these you may have and yet want Christ, and life in him; common graces may and will deceive you, a man may have all these, and yet not prize Christ, as his cheifest good; he may have all these, and yet not worship him: Notwithstanding all these, there may bee some iniquity in their hands for which cause God will not shew mercy to them: See and observe, if in the midst of all these you do not *worke some iniquity;* they were *workers of iniquity* alwayes at the best, *Matth.* 7. 23. you may be workers of iniquity, notwithstanding all these; and therefore consider if there be not some veine of pride, and hypocrisie, and covetousnesse, that cleaves fast to your hearts, which you allow your selves in, which if you doe, these very gifts will bee your ship-wracke, your anchor will breake, and your ship will bee carryed away, and you fall downe in destruction; but see that your hearts bee cleane, and see that there bee not an ill thought or way that you allow your selves in, and if so, then your heart will lay hold upon God, and you will prize Christ, and then it is a signe those gifts you have are not in hypocrisie; for in an hypocrite, they are alwayes found with some sinne, which if a man doe not willfully shut his eyes against hee may see, for our Saviour speakes of such a sinne in them, as the rest of the people of God may know them to be counterfeits, from verse 15 to 23. *You shall know them by this, doe men gather grapes of thornes, or figges of thistles?* have not they their ill haunts, but put away these from you, if you mean to have Christ.

INCREASE MATHER, 1639–1723

[Increase Mather, the most conspicuous figure in the second generation of New Englanders, was born in Dorchester, where his father, Richard, was minister. Educated at home and at the free school in Boston, he entered Harvard in 1651, though he spent most of his college years at Ipswich and Boston under the supervision of John Norton. Taking his B.A. in 1656, he went to England, studied at Trinity College, Dublin, where he received his M.A. in 1658. He became a friend of John Howe, a powerful Independent minister, whose pulpit he filled at Great Torrington, Devonshire. He served as chaplain to the garrison at Guernsey, and had just been called to an important post at Gloucester when the Restoration closed all avenues of advancement to him in England. He returned to Guernsey, then to Boston in 1661, the next year marrying Maria Cotton, daughter of John Cotton. He immediately assumed the role of a leading divine by opposing his father and Jonathan Mitchell on the Half-Way Covenant, though he was finally persuaded to change sides. Installed as teacher of the Second Church in Boston, 1664, he was thereafter strategically located to influence the policies of the colony. In 1674 he was elected fellow of Harvard College and in 1681 refused the presidency because he did not wish to leave his church; in 1685 he accepted it, though he was a nonresident administrator and still devoted much the larger share of his attentions to his church and to colonial affairs. Sent as agent for the colony to England in 1688, he remained abroad for four years, negotiating for the renewal of the charter through the shifting scenes of the Glorious Revolution. At the moment of his triumphant return in 1692, with the governor and the slate of magistrates having been nominated by himself, he was at the apex of his power. Thereafter his influence began to decline: many citizens who had no idea with what he had contended believed he had made too many concessions in securing the charter. In 1701 he was forced to resign the presidency of the College by a law requiring the president to live in Cambridge, but after his defeat Samuel Willard was put in charge under the title of vice-president and the residence requirement was not enforced. Though he gave the court at the Salem witch trials good advice—which they did not take—he and his son Cotton were attacked as though they had been responsible for the miscarriage of justice. Solomon Stoddard of Northampton dominated the Western part of the colony and inaugurated there policies that Mather abhorred. In Boston itself he was bearded by the establishment of the Brattle Street Church under Benjamin Colman in 1699, who instituted certain practices which Mather had opposed. But if his power in his last years was curtailed, he remained a commanding figure, fighting courageously for inoculation in 1721, maintaining the principles of the founders to the last ditch, and yet moving with the times on at least some important questions. In 1718 he and Cotton Mather assisted at the ordination of a Baptist minister. He was a voluminous writer, only surpassed in the number of his publications by Cotton Mather. An exponent of the plain style, he preached solid, logical, and learned sermons. For biography, see Kenneth B. Murdock, *Increase Mather.*

The text of the first selection is from *Awakening Truths Tending to Conversion,* (Boston, 1710) pp. 66–78. The second selection is from *A Discourse Concerning the Uncertainty of the Times of Men* (Boston, 1697), pp. 8–21, 34–36, a sermon delivered at Harvard College after two undergraduates, skating on Fresh Pond, broke through the ice and were drowned. The third selection is from *Practical Truths Tending to Promote the Power of Godliness* (Boston, 1682), pp. 209–212.]

PREDESTINATION AND HUMAN EXERTIONS

THERE are some Sinners so unreasonable, and so wicked. Ask them why they don't reform their Lives, why don't you Turn over a new leaf, and amend your ways and your doings, they will answer, God does not give me Grace. I can't Convert my self, and God does not Convert me. Thus do they insinuate as if God were in fault, and the blame of their Unconversion to be imputed unto him. But as Elihu speaks, *Suffer me a little, and I will shew you what I have yet to say on God's behalf.*

1. I say, God is not bound to give Sinners Grace: He is an absolute Sovereign, and may give Grace or deny Grace to whom he pleaseth. Shall the thing formed, say to him that formed it, why hast thou made me thus? has not the Potter power over the Clay, to make one vessel

unto honour, and another to dishonour? The glorious God has a greater power over his Creatures, than the Potter has over the Clay. Wherefore, *He has Mercy on whom He will have Mercy, and whom He will He hardens*, Rom. 9. 18. If He giveth Grace to any man in the World, it is from His Sovereign good pleasure. Why were such poor Fishermen as *Peter*, and *James*, and *John*, and others, as mean as they, made the Subjects of Saving Grace, when many incomparably beyond them in Learning and Wisdom, have been left to perish in their unbelief? Even so, because so it has seemed good in the sight of Him, who is the Lord of Heaven and Earth, *Math.* 11. 25, 26. Grace is a wonderful gift of God. Sinners are enemies to him, and Rebels against him: Is He bound to bestow such a gift on his Enemies, when it may be too they will not so much as humbly Pray unto him for it[?] Indeed He sometimes has done so. Sinners that never Prayed to him, that never had one thought in their hearts of returning to him, he has miraculously Prevented them with Sovereign Grace. So it was with the Converted Gentiles. Of them the Lord sayes, *I am sought of them that asked not for me, I am found of them that sought me not, I said, behold me, behold me to a Nation that was not called by my Name*, Isa. 69. 1. Nay, sometimes when Sinners have been in the height of their Resistance and Rebellion, to shew the exceeding Riches of his Grace, God has then Converted them. Thus it was with *Saul* afterwards *Paul*, when he was breathing out Slaughters against the Disciples of the Lord, then did God give him Faith in Christ, without his Praying for it. Thus also those Converts in the Second Chapter of the Acts. Not many days before their Conversion they had been Murdering the Son of God. And just before the Sermon began they were mocking of the Preacher, and yet Converted by that Sermon. Such Instances there have been known in the World, of men that have come to hear a Sermon only to deride it, and yet have been Savingly wrought upon by it. A credible Author reports, that two profane men drinking together, knowing that Mr. *Hooker* was to Preach, one of them said to the other, *Let us go hear how Hooker will baul*, yet was he Converted by that very Sermon, which he went to hear with a Scornful Spirit. And after that had such a love for Mr. *Hooker*, as to remove three thousand Miles, that so he might live under his Ministry. Such Examples are wonderful Evidences of Sovereign Grace.[1]

2. Altho' it is true, (as has been shewed) that Sinners cannot Convert themselves, their *Cannot* is a wilful *Cannot*. Math. 22. 2. *They will not come.* It is not said they *could not* (tho' they could not of themselves come to Christ) but that they *would not* come. If it were in the power

of a Sinner to Convert himself, he would not do it: For he hates Conversion. *It is abomination to fools to depart from evil*, Prov. 13. 19. Psal. 50. 17. *Thou hatest instruction.* If they hate to be Converted they will not chuse it. Prov. 1. 29. *They hated knowledge, and did not chuse the fear of the Lord.* Their hearts are in Love, and in League with their Lusts, yea they hate to be *turned* from them: They love darkness rather than light, they hate the light, neither come they to the light, *Joh.* 3. 19, 20. Sinners are haters of God: they say and think that they love him, but the Lord knows that they hate him, and therefore they will not repent of their Sins, and believe on Christ. Christ said to the Jews, *You will not come to me that you might have Life*, Joh. 5. 40. No, they would dy first. And why would they not come? The reason of their Aversion is mentioned in v. 42. *I know you, that you have not the Love of God in you.* Their carnal unregenerate Minds were full of enmity against God, and therefore they would not come to Jesus Christ the Son of God. They cannot Convert themselves, and they are not willing that God should Convert them. If Sinners were willing to have Grace and Holiness, why do they not repair to him for it, who alone can give it to them? An hungry man is willing to have bread, therefore he will seek after it, where ever it is to be had. When the Egyptians were hunger bitten, they went to Pharaoh, crying for bread, he bid them go to Joseph, and they did so. Thus if Sinners were willing to be Converted, they would cry to God to turn them: whenas there are many Sinners that did never put up one earnest Prayer to God in their Lives, that he would bestow Converting Grace on them.

3. Sinners can do more towards their own Conversion than they do or will do. They should give *diligence* to make sure of their being effectually called. They should *strive* to enter in at the strait gate. Conversion is the strait gate that leadeth unto Salvation. They should *Labour* not for the meat that perisheth, but for that which endureth to Everlasting Life: but they do not give diligence, they do not strive, they do not labour to obtain Grace and Salvation: Therefore they perish, and perish justly. Prov. 21. 25. *The desire of the slothful kills him, for his hands refuse to labour.* Men say that they desire Grace, and yet their hands refuse to Labour, they will be at no pains to obtain it: And this slothfulness kills them. It proves the death of their Souls. *The Soul of the sluggard desireth and has nothing, but the Soul of the diligent shall be made fat*, Prov. 13. 4. There are several things which Sinners have power to do in order to their own Conversion, & which they ought to do, but they will not.

(1) They have power to avoid those things which are an hindrance

of Conversion. *e.g.* They can if they will forbear the outward Acts of sin. By giving way to sin their hearts are hardned, and their Conversion becomes the more difficult. Heb. 3. 13. *Take heed lest any of you be hardned through the deceitfulness of sin.* But Sinners give way to many sins which they could abstain from, if they would. A Sabbath-breaker can forbear his profaning of the Sabbath. An ungodly Swearer can forbear his profane Oathes, if he will. A Lyar can forbear telling such Lyes. Sinners can avoid the Temptations which will endanger their falling into sin. He that knows that if he goeth to such a place, or into such a company, he will probably be drawn into sin, ought to avoid the Temptation. Prov. 4. 15. *Avoid it, turn from it, and pass away.* The Sinner can do so if he will, but he will not keep out of the way of Temptation. A drunkard will not avoid the Temptation to that his sin. Prov. 23. 31. *Look not on the Wine when it giveth his colour.* He can chuse whether he will look on the wine or no: he has power to refrain, but will not. Thus men by habituating themselves to sin, do what in them is to hinder their own Conversion. Jer. 13. 23. *Can the Ethiopian change his skin, or the Leopard his Spots? then may you also do good that are accustomed to do evil.* Again, Evil Companions hinder Conversion. *Alas! Alas! Alas!* these have been the Eternal ruin of many a Young Man, that was in an hopeful way for Conversion: He has fallen in with vain Companions, they have given him bad Counsel, so have Convictions been stifled, and the motions of Gods holy Spirit quenched in his Soul. The word of the Lord sayes, *Forsake the foolish & Live,* Prov. 9. 6. The Sinner has power to forsake them, but he will not tho' he dies for it.

(2) Sinners have power to wait on God in the use of means which has a tendency to promote Conversion. They can if they will, not only forsake evil Companions, but associate themselves with those that are good: Then are they in the way of Conversion. Prov. 13. 20. *He that walketh with wise men shall be wise, but a Companion of fools shall be destroyed.* That Learned & Holy Man Dr. *Goodwin* [2] in the account which he giveth of his Conversion, declares, That when he was a Young Schollar in the University of *Cambridge,* there were in that *College,* which he belonged unto, a *Number of holy Youth's* (that's his Expression) his associating himself with them was an happy means of furthering the work of Conversion in his Soul. This Unconverted Sinners have power to do. Their feet are as able to carry them to a godly Meeting as to an ungodly one. Reading the Scripture has sometimes been the Means of Conversion. I could tell you of several Learned Jews that were Converted from their Judaism by Reading the 53.

Chapter of Isaiah. The famous Fr. *Junius*,[3] was Converted from his *Atheism* by reading the first Chapter of John's Gospel. He that can read is able to read the Scripture, and Books which promote Godliness in the power of it, but a Sinful Creature chuseth rather to mispend his Time in reading vain Romances, or it may be worse Books. A diligent attendence to the Word of God is the way to obtain Converting Grace. Rom. 10. 17. *Faith comes by hearing, and hearing by the Word of God*. Sinners many Times do not mind what they hear. Nay, it may be they will *Set themselves to sleep when God is speaking to them* by his Minister? And shall they then complain, that they cannot Convert themselves, & that God will not Convert them? Once more, Serious thinking & Consideration on Spiritual and Eternal things is oftentimes blessed unto Conversion. This is what God has given men power to do, if they will use that power. They ought seriously to think what they have done, and what they are, and what their end is like to be. If they would do so, it may be Repentance would be the effect of it. 1 King. 8. 47. *If they shall bethink themselves, and Repent, and make Supplication.* David sayes, *I thought on my wayes, and turned my feet unto thy Testimonies*, Psal. 119. 59. If men would be perswaded *to think seriously*, it may be they would *Turn. How long shall thy vain thoughts lodge within thee?* A Sinner will suffer vain thoughts to lodge within him, but serious & holy thoughts he will give no lodging unto, he will not suffer them to abide in his heart. Serious *Consideration* is a duty incumbent on Sinners. Hag. 1. 5. *Thus sayes the Lord of hosts, Consider your wayes.* Would the Unconverted Sinner, consider sadly what his Sinful wayes have been, what numberless sins he has been guilty of, and what a fountain of sin his heart is, and whither he is going, it may be Conversion would follow upon such serious consideration. Ezek. 18. 28. *Because he considereth and turns away from all his Transgressions.* Yes, if he is set upon *Considering*, there is great hopes that he will Turn, and that he shall live, and not dye. If he will be perswaded to go alone, to think and consider sadly with himself, What is my present Condition? Am I in Christ, or am I not in Christ? If I should dy this Night, What would become of my Soul? In what World must it be to all Eternity? It may be such considerations would issue in Conversion. Sinners should consider of Death, that the thing is certain, and the Time uncertain, and that they run an infinite hazzard if they neglect making sure of an Interest in Christ one day longer. Deut. 32. 29. *O that they were wise, that they would consider their latter end!* And they should *Consider* of the *Eternity* which follows immediately upon death. If they would do that, surely it would affect their Souls. A late Writer (which I have formerly mentioned) speaks of a pious man, that One in Company with him observing a more than ordinary fixedness and concern in his Countenance, asked him, What his thoughts were upon, he then thereupon uttered that Word *For-ever*, and so continued saying nothing but repeating that Word, *For-ever! For-ever! For-ever!* a quarter of an hour together. His Thoughts and Soul was swallowed up with the consideration of ETERNITY. And truly if an Unconverted Sinner would be perswaded to go alone and think seriously of Eternity, if it were but for one quarter of an hour, it may be it would have an Everlasting Impression on his heart. This Sinners can do if they will: And if they will not do as much as this comes to, towards their own Conversion and Salvation, how inexcusable will they be? Their blood will be upon their own heads. Let them no more say, *God must do all, we can do nothing,* and so encourage themselves to Live in a careless neglect of God, and of their own Souls, and Salvation. Most certainly, altho' we cannot say, That if men improve their Natural abilities as they ought to do, that Grace will infallibly follow, yet there will not one Sinner in all the Reprobate World, stand forth at the day of Judgment, and say, Lord, Thou knowest I did all that possibly I could do, for the obtaining Grace, and for all that, Thou didst withold it from me.

MAN KNOWS NOT HIS TIME

THE DOCTRINE at present before us, is,

That for the most part the Miserable Children of Men, know not their Time.

There are three things for us here briefly to Enquire into. (1.) *What Times they are which Men know not?* (2.) *How it does appear that they are Ignorant thereof.* (3.) The Reason *Why they are kept in Ignorance of their Time.*

Quest. 1. *What Times are they which men know not?*

Ans. 1. *Time is sometimes put for the proper season for Action.* For the fittest season for a man to Effect what he is undertaking. The Seventy Greek Interpreters translate the words *KAIRON AUTOU.* There is a *Season,* a fit Time for men to go to work in. If they take hold of that nick of opportunity, they will prosper and succeed in their Endeavours. It is a great part of wisdom to know that season. Hence it is said, *A wise mans Heart discerneth both Time and Judgment.* Eccles. 8. 5. but few have that wisdom or knowledge. Therefore it is added in the next verse. *because to every purpose there is Time and Judgment, therefore the misery of man is great upon him.* The meaning is, because men discern not the proper Time for them to Effect what they purpose, their misery is great. If they would attempt such a thing just at such a Time, they would make themselves and others happy, but missing that Opportunity great misery comes upon them. So it is as to Civil Affairs very frequently: Men discern not the proper only season for them to obtain what they desire. Yea, and so it is as to Spirituals. Men are not aware of the proper season wherein they may obtain good for their Souls. There is a price put into their hands to get Wisdom, but they have no heart to know and improve it. There is a day of Grace in which if men seek to God for mercy they shall find it. Isa. 55. 6. *Seek ye the Lord while he may be found.* The most of them that have such a day know it not until their finding Time is past. Thus it was with Israel of old. Jere. 8. 7. *The Stork in the heaven knows her appointed Time, the Turtle, and the Crane, and the Swallow observe the Time of their coming, but my People know not the Judgment of the Lord.* They discerned not the *Judgments,* that is the dispensations of God. They had a Summer of prosperity but did not improve it. There was a Winter of Adversity coming on them, but they knew it not, nor did they use the proper only means to prevent it. So the Jews when Christ was amongst them, had a blessed time if they had known it: but they knew not the things of their peace, in the day of their peace; they knew not the Time of their Visitation.

2. *A man knows not what Changes shall attend him whilest in this World.* Changes of Providence are in the Scripture called *Times.* It is said that the Acts of David, and *the Times that went over him,* and over Israel, and over all the Kingdoms of the Countries, were written by *Samuel,* and *Nathan* the Prophet, and in the Book of *Gad* the *Seer,* meaning the Changes of Providence which they were subject unto. 1 *Chron.* 29. 30. A man knows not whether he shall see good or evil days for the Time to come: he knoweth what his past days have been; but does not know what they shall be for the time to come. It may be he is now in prosperity: he has Friends, Children, Relations, which he takes delight in, he has Health, an Estate, and Esteem in the World, he does not know that he shall have any of these things for the future. Indeed, men in Prosperity are apt to think (as they would have it) that they shall alwayes, or for a long time be so: but very often they find themselves greatly mistaken. The Psalmist confesseth that it was so with him. Psal. 30. 6, 7. *In my prosperity I said, I shall never be moved, Lord, by thy favour, thou hast made my Mountain to stand strong: thou didst hide thy face and I was troubled.* His Enemies were all subdued: his Mountain, that is his Kingdom, especially his Royal Palace in Mount Sion was become exceeding strong, that now he thought all dangers were over, but *Absaloms* unexpected Rebellion involved him and the

whole Land in Trouble. The good People in *Josiahs* time promised themselves great happiness for many a year under the Government of such a King as he was. Lam. 4. 20. *Of whom we said under his shadow we shall Live.* But his sudden Death made a sad Change in all the Publick Affairs. A man knows not *what* Afflictions shall come upon him whilest on the earth. This is true concerning particular Persons: they may know in general, that Afflictions shall attend them in an evil Sinful World. But what those Afflictions in particular shall be they know not. Thus the Apostle speaks, Act. 20. 22, 23. *I go bound in Spirit to Jerusalem, not knowing what things shall befall me there, save that the holy Spirit witnesseth in every City, saying, that Bonds and Afflictions abide me.* So that he knew in general that he should meet with Affliction, but not in special what the Affliction would be. So is it true concerning a People, that they know not what *Times* or *Changes* may pass over them. Little was it thought that whilest *Hoshea* (who was the best of all the Nineteen Kings that had Ruled over the Ten Tribes) was Reigning, a Powerful forreign Enemy should invade the Land and make them all Slaves. Little did the Jews think that when *Josiah* was but Thirty nine years old, he should dy before that year was out, and they never see good day more after his Death. And as men know not *What* their Changes and Afflictions must be, so neither *When* they shall come upon them. Whether it will be a long or a short time before those Changes overtake them. Mar. 13. 35. *You know not when the Master of the House comes, at even, or at mid-night, or at the Cock crowing, or in the morning.* Thus a man knoweth not whether the sharpest Afflictions which are reserved for him, shall come upon him in his Youth, or in his middle age, or in his old age; though for the most part mens greatest Afflictions overtake them in their old age. Nor can any man know whether his Afflictions will soon be over or continue for a longer time. Thus, the Lords People knew that their Captivity in *Babylon* should last for Seventy years and no longer; but that knowledge was by divine Revelation. As for some other Persecutions they knew not how long they would continue. Psal. 74. 9. *There is no more a Prophet, neither is there any that knows how long.* Those words seem to respect the Persecution under *Antiochus*, when there was no Prophet.

3. *A man knows not the Time of his Death:* Often it is so, that when Death falls upon a man, he thinks no more of it, than the Fishes think of the Net before they are Caught in it; or then the Birds think of the Snare before they are taken in it, as *Solomon* here speaks. It useth to be said, (and it is a plain, weighty known Truth) that nothing is more certain then that every man shall Dy, and nothing more un-

certain than the Time when. Old *Isaac* said, Gen. 27. 2. *Behold, I know not the day of my Death.* Though he Lived above twenty years after he spoke those words, he did not know that he should Live a day longer. A man cannot know how long himself or another shall live. It is true that *Hezekiah* was ascertained that he should not dy before fifteen years were expired. And the Prophet *Jeremy* knew that *Hananiah* should not live a year to an end. Jer. 28. 16. *This year thou shalt Dy, because thou hast Taught Rebellion against the Lord.* But those were extraordinary cases. It is not a usual thing for a man to know before hand how many months or years he shall live in this World: Nor may he desire to know it, but he ought to leave that with God. Although *David* prayed, saying, *Lord make me to know my End, and the number of my Dayes, what it is. Psal.* 39. 4. His meaning is, not that he might know just how many dayes he should live, but that he might be made duely sensible of his own frailty and mortality, and lead his life accordingly. Oftentimes Death is nearest to men when they least think of it; especially it is so with ungodly men: we have an instance of it in *Agag.* He came before *Samuel, delicately, and said, surely the bitterness of death is past.* 1 *Sam.* 15. 32. Little did he think, that within a few hours, he should be cut in pieces. When *Haman* boasted of his being the chief Favourite at Court, and that the Queen had invited no one but the King & himself to a Banquet, he little thought of the destruction which was then preparing for him. When *Belshazzar* was in the beginning of the night drinking and making merry with his profane Companions, he little thought that he should be a dead man before morning; but *that night was Belshazzar slain. Dan.* 5. 30. The Rich Fool in the Gospel dream'd of a long life and merry: He said to his Soul, Eat, Drink and be merry, thou hast Goods laid up for many years. But God said, *This night thy Soul shall be required of thee:* He must appear immediately before the dreadful Tribunal. Luk. 12. 20. Thus we see what Time it is which men know not.

The second thing to be Enquired into, is, *How it does appear that men know not their Time.*

Answ. 1. It is evident, *In that all future Contingencies are known to God only.* Hence Christ said to the Disciples, *It is not for you to know the Times and the Seasons which the Father has put in his own power. Act* 1. 7. Future Times and Contingent Events, the knowledge & disposal of them has God reserved to himself. There are future things which happen necessarily, that a man may know them long before they come to pass: *God has appointed Lights in the Heaven to be for Signs and Seasons.* Gen. 1. 14. These move regularly and unfailably according to that

Order which the Creator has established. Therefore a man may know infallibly how many hours or minutes such a day or night will be long before the Time comes; He may know when there will be an *Eclipse* of the Sun or of the Moon, twenty, or an hundred years before it comes to pass: [4] but for Contingent Things, which have no necessary dependance on the constituted Order of Nature, but upon the meer Pleasure and Providence of God, they are not known except unto God, or to them unto whom he shall reveal them. The Lord challengeth this as his Prerogative. The Idols whom the Heathen worshipped, could not make known future Contingencies. Isa. 41. 22, 23. *Let them shew us what shall happen, or declare us things for to come, shew the things that are to come heredfter, that we may know they are Gods.* To do this was past their skill. The Devil knows many future things which men are ignorant of; He could foretel *Sauls* ruin, and *Davids* coming to the Kingdom. Nevertheless, there are many future Events which he has no knowledge of. Therefore he often deludes those that Enquire of him with deceitful and uncertain Answers. But as for men they are ignorant of future things, which most nearly concern themselves, or their own Families. No man knows so much as who shall be his Heir, or Enjoy the Estate which he has laboured for. Psal. 39. 6. *Surely every man walks in a vain shew, he heapeth up riches, and knows not who shall gather them.* He knows not whether one of his Relations, or a meer stranger shall possess that Estate which he has taken so much pains, and disquieted himself so much for the obtaining of it. This meditation made *Solomon* out of Love with this World. He new as much as any man, and yet he confesseth that he did not know whether the man that should come after him, and enjoy all that he had Laboured for, would be a wise man or a fool, Eccles. 2. 18, 19. And he sayes, *A man knows not that which shall be; for who can tell him when it shall be.* Eccles. 8. 7. He knows neither what nor when it shall be. And again he saith, *A man cannot tell what shall be; and what shall be after him who can tell him!* Eccl. 10. 14. This is to be understood concerning Contingent Events. Such as the particular Afflictions which are to befall a man, or the Time, Place, or manner of his Death.

2. *The Times of men are ordered according to the Decree of God.* There is nothing comes to pass in the Earth, but what was first determined by a wise decree in Heaven. Act. 15. 18. *Known unto God are all his works from the beginning of the World.* God knows what he has to do. The Apostle speaks there concerning the Conversion of the Gentiles. This did God fore-know and decree from the beginning of the World, yea from all Eternity. The like is to be said concerning every thing which

happens in the World. Not a Sparrow falls to the Ground without his Providence, and therefore not without his decree, the one being an Infallible Effect of the other. He has decreed when and where every man that comes into the World shall be Born; and where he shall live, in what Country, and in what Town; yea, and in what House too. Act. 17. 26. *He has determined the times before appointed, & the bounds of their Habitation.* He has decreed when every man shall dy. Eccl. 3. 2. *There is a Time to be Born, and a Time to Dy.* That is to say, a Time decreed and appointed by God when every man shall be born, and when he shall dy. Nor shall any man live a day longer than the Time which the Lord has appointed for him. Job 14. 5. *His dayes are determined, the number of his months are with thee, thou hast appointed his bounds that he cannot pass.* All the Circumstances attending every mans Death, the place and the manner of it, whether he shall dy by Sickness, or by any other Accident, all is determined in Heaven before it comes to pass on the Earth. Now the decrees of God are Secret things until the Event or some divine Revelation shall discover them. Deut. 29. 29. *Secret things belong unto the Lord our God.* His divine decrees are those secret things, which Himself alone knows. Rom. 11. 34. *For who hath known the mind of the Lord? or, who has been his Counsellor?*

3. *The Conversations of men generally make it manifest, that they know not their Time.* They do many things which they would not do, and they neglect many things which they would certainly practise, if they knew what Times are near them. Math. 24. 43. *If the good man of the house had known in what watch the Theef would come, he would have watched, and would not have suffered his house to be broken up.* Thus men live in a careless neglect of God, and of their own Souls and Salvation, but if they knew that Death will come stealing suddenly upon them, they would watch and pray. Did they know that before the next week, they shall be in another World, they would live after another manner than now they do. Most commonly Persons are light and vain in their Spirits, when heavy Tidings is near to them. Did they know what sad News they shall hear shortly, they would be in a more solemn frame of Spirit. Isa. 5. 12. *The harp and the viol, the tabret, and the pipe, and wine are in their feasts, but they regard not the work of the Lord, neither consider the operation of his hands.* Had they known what work God intended to make with them speedily, they would have minded something else besides their sensual pleasures and delights.

We proceed to Enquire 3. *Whence it is that men know not their Time.*

Answ. It is from God. He will have them to be kept in ignorance and uncertainties about their Time: And this for wise & holy Ends. *e.g.*

1. That so his Children might live by Faith. That so they might live a life of holy dependance upon God continually. They must not know their Times, that so they might Trust in the Lord at all times. God would not have his Children to be anxiously solicitous about future Events, but to leave themselves and theirs with their Heavenly Father, to dispose of all their Concernments, as He in his Infinite Wisdom and Faithfulness shall see good.

2. That their Obedience may be tried. That they may follow the Lord, as it were blind-fold, whithersoever He shall lead them, though they do not see one step of their way before them, as *Abraham* did. Heb. 11. 8. *When he was called to go out into a place which he should after receive for an Inheritance, he obeyed, and went out not knowing whither he went.* We must follow God, tho' we know not what He will do with us, or how He will dispose of us, as to our Temporal Concerns, submitting our selves, yea, our lives and all entirely to the Will of God in every thing. That saying ought to be often in our mouths, *If the Lord will*, and we shall live, and do this or that. *Jam.* 4. 15.

3. Men must not know their Time, that so they may be ever watchful. Math. 25. 13. *Watch therefore, for you know neither the day nor the hour wherein the Son of Man comes.* The generality of men, if they had it revealed to them (as *Hezekiah*) that they should certainly live so many years, they would in the mean time be careless about their Souls, and the World to come. We see that notwithstanding they are uncertain how short their Time may be, they are regardless about their future eternal Estate. How much more would they be so, if they knew that Death and Judgment were not far off from them?

4. As to some they are kept in Ignorance of their Times, that so they may with the more comfort and composure of Spirit follow the work which they are called unto: That they may with diligence and chearfulness attend the duties of their general and particular Calling; which they could not do, if they knew what Evil Times and Things are appointed for them. The terror of what is coming on them, would be so dismal to them, that they could not enjoy themselves, nor take comfort in any thing they enjoy. As the Apostle speaks to the covetous Jews, Jam. 5. 1. *Go to now you rich men, weep and howl for your miseries that shall come upon you.* So there are many in the World, that would spend their days in weeping and howling, did they but know what is coming on them and theirs. When the Prophet *Elisha* had it revealed to him, that sad things were coming on the Land, by reason of a bloody Neighbour Nation, which would break in upon them, and exercise barbarous Cruelties; the holy man wept at the foreknowledge of it. 2 King. 8. 11.

The man of God wept. So there would be nothing but weeping in many Families, weeping in many Towns, and in some whole Countries, did men but know their Times. Therefore they must be kept in ignorance thereof until the things come upon them. . . .

And now as I have spoken these things to all this Assembly, so let me apply them in a special manner to you the *Scholars* of this *Colledge,* who are here present before the Lord. I am concerned in my Spirit for you. All of you are my Children: And do you think that I can see my Children Drowned, and not be troubled for it? God has come among you this last week, & lessened two of your number by a sad & awful Providence. Do you think these two were greater Sinners than any amongst you. No, no, they were both of them hopeful youths. One of them (young *Eyres*) was an only Son, and a desirable dutiful Son, of a sweet amiable Temper, beloved by every body. He was observed to read the Scriptures constantly every day with great Alacrity. A sign that there was *some good thing in him towards the God of Israel.* As for the other (*Maxwell*) the Rebuke of Heaven in taking him away is the more solemn, in that his pious Relations sent him from far: to be Educated in this Nursery, for Religion and good Literature. I took special notice of him; but could never observe any thing in him, but what was commendable, He was ingenious, and industrious, and I believe truly pious; had he lived, he was like to have been a choice Instrument of Service to the Church of God in his Time. And I am perswaded that his Soul is among the Angels of God. *But if this be done to the green Tree, what shall be done to the Dry?* This fatal blow looks ominously on the poor *Colledge.* Considering some other circumstances; there is cause to fear lest *suddenly* there will be no *Colledge* in *New England;* and this as a sign that ere long there will be no Churches there. I know there is a blessed day to the visible Church not far off; but it is the Judgment of very Learned men, that in the Glorious Times promised to the Church on Earth, *America* will be Hell. And altho there is a number of the Elect of God yet to be born here, I am verily afraid, that in process of Time, *New England* will be the wofullest place in all *America,* as some other parts of the World once famous for Religion, are now the dolefullest on the Earth, perfect Emblems and Pictures of Hell. When you see this little *Academy* fallen to the ground (as now it is shaking and most like to fall) then know it is a terrible thing which God is about to bring upon this Land. In the mean time, you the *Students* here, are concerned to bewail the Breach which the Lord has made among you. If you slight and make light of this hand of the Lord, or do not make a due improvement of it, you may fear, that God has not done with you, but that he has more arrows to shoot amongst you, that shall suddenly strike some of you ere long. But Oh that the Lord would sanctify what has hapned to awaken you unto serious thoughts about Death and Eternity. Who knows but that God may make these sudden Deaths, an occasion of promoting the Salvation, & Eternal Life of some amongst you. It is related concerning *Waldo*, (He from whom the *Waldenses* have that Name given them) [5] that the occasion of his Conversion was the *Sudden Death* of one of his Companions. The sight of that made him serious. He did not know, but that he might *dy suddenly* too, and that he was therefore concerned to be always fit to dy. So did he turn to the Lord, and became a great Instrument of Glory to God and good to his Church. Oh! that it might be so with you.

SLEEPING AT SERMONS

INSTR. 1. *We may here take notice that the nature of man is wofully corrupted and depraved*, else they would not be so apt to sleep when the precious Truths of God are dispensed in his Name, Yea, and men are more apt to sleep then, than at another time. Some woful Creatures, have been so wicked as to profess they have gone to hear Sermons on purpose, that so they might sleep, finding themselves at such times much disposed that way. This argueth as Satans malice, so the great corruption and depravation of the nature of men, whence it is that they are inclined unto evil, and indisposed to the thing that good is. Yea, some will sit and sleep under the best Preaching in the World. When *Paul* was alive, there was not a better Preacher upon the Earth then he. *Austin* [6] had three wishes: one was, that (if the Lord had seen meet) he might see Christ in the flesh: his second wish was, that he might have seen *Paul in the Pulpit;* but notwithstanding *Pauls* being so excellent a Preacher, there were some that could sit and sleep under his Ministry. When Soul-melting Sermons are Preached about Christ the Saviour, about the pardon of sin, about the glory of Heaven, there are some that will sleep under them. When soul-awakening Sermons are Preached, enough to make rocks to rend and to bleed; when the word falls down from Heaven like Thunder, the voice of the Lord therein being very powerful and full of Majesty, able to break the Cedars of *Lebanon*, and to make the wilderness to shake; yet some will sit and sleep under it: such is the woful corruption and desperate hardness of the hearts of the Children of men.

Instr. 2. *Hence see, that there is great danger in those things which men are apt to look upon as little sins, yea as no sins at all.*

As for sleeping at Sermons, some look upon it as no sin; others account it a *peccadillo*, a sin not worth taking notice of, or the troubling themselves about. But my Text sheweth that danger and death is in it. VVe have solemn Instances in the Scripture, concerning those that have lost their lives, because they have been guilty of such miscarriages, as carnal reason will say are but little sins. VVhen there was a man that gathered a few sticks upon the Sabbath day, he was put to death for it; and yet men would be apt to think his sin was not (though indeed it was) very great. Men account it a small matter to add something of their own to the worship of God: but when *Nadab* and *Abihu* did so, *there went out fire from the Lord*, and consumed them to death. VVhen *Vzzah* a good man, did with a pious intention touch the Ark, (which he being no Priest should not have done) *God smote him for his Error, that he dyed by the Ark of God*. Behold! the severity of God, and let us tremble at it. Common sins, which almost every one is guilty of, are accounted small iniquities; but there is exceeding danger in following a multitude to do evil. Sins of Omission are esteemed small, but mens Souls may be thrown into the fire and burned for ever, not only for bearing evil fruit, but because they do not bring forth good fruit, *Mat*. 3. 10. At the last day the Son of God will pronounce a Sentence of eternal death upon thousands of Millions, because they have omitted these and those duties which he required and expected from them. Sinful words are looked upon as small evils by many. How common is it for persons to say, *what shall we be made offenders for a word?* abusing that Scripture which reproveth those that make others offenders for speaking good and faithful words. But doth not the Scripture say, *by thy words thou shalt be condemned*, *Mat*. 12. 37. Corrupt communications, obscene discourses, unclean lascivious speeches, discover the persons that delight in them to be amongst the number of those that shall (without Repentance) be condemned at the day of *Judgement*, yet there are some that make light of them. Thus concerning those words which some call *Petty Oathes;* some are so profanely ignorant as to think, that they may Swear by *their Faith and Troth*, and that there is no great hurt or danger in it. But there is danger of no less than Damnation for these seemingly little sins, if men shall allow themselves therein, notwithstanding the Commandment of God to the contrary. See the word of the Lord to this purpose, *Jam*. 5. 12. *But above all things Swear not*, (i.e. vainly, or except duely called therunto) *neither by Heaven, neither by the Earth, neither by any other Oath*, therefore not by your Faith or Troth, *lest you fall into condemnation*.

Again, sinful thoughts are esteemed small evils; but I must tell you, that vain thoughts, and much more vile unclean thoughts, if indulged and delighted in, may hinder the Salvation of a mans Soul. Witness that Scripture, *Jer.* 4. 14. *O Jerusalem, wash thine heart from wickedness, that thou mayest be saved; how long shall thy vain thoughts lodge within thee?* so that there is more than a little danger, in those evils, which men account little sins.

URIAN OAKES, 1631–1681

[Urian Oakes, born in England, was brought to Cambridge by his family, his father being a solid citizen, selectman, and deputy to the General Court. He graduated from Harvard in 1649, became a teaching fellow and edited the Almanac for 1650. In 1654 he went to England, was given an important pulpit at Tichfield, Hants, from which he was ejected in 1662. He was headmaster of the Southwark Grammar school, organized a separate Congregational church at Tichfield, and was called back to the Cambridge church in 1671. For four years he was acting president of Harvard College, and in 1680 consented to be formally installed as president, but died within a year. A little man, a sharp wit, an excellent Latinist, with genuine learning and a degree of urbanity, his sermons are among the best of seventeenth-century New England productions. Cf. Cotton Mather, *Magnalia;* Sibley, *Biographical Sketches;* Morison, *Harvard College in the Seventeenth Century.* This text is from *The Soveraign Efficacy of Divine Providence; Overruling and Omnipotently Disposing and Ordering all Humane Counsels and Affairs, Demonstrated and Improved* (Boston, 1682), pp. 5–22, 32–37; this sermon, on Ecclesiastes 9 : 11, was delivered at Cambridge on September 10, 1677, on the occasion of an Artillery election; it shows the mark of careful preparation and polish and constitutes the classic exposition of the Puritan doctrine of divine concurrence in the operation of natural causes.]

THE SOVERAIGN EFFICACY OF DIVINE PROVIDENCE

DOCT. *That the Successes and Events of Vndertakings and Affairs are not determined infallibly by the greatest Sufficiency of Men, or Second Causes; but by the Counsel and Providence of God ordering and governing Time and Chance according to his own good Pleasure.*

I have endeavoured to comprize and grasp the substance of *Solomon's* Intendment, in this Doctrinal Conclusion: and shall explicate and demonstrate the Truth of it (as God shall help) in the following Propositions.

Prop. 1. *Second Causes may have a sufficiency in their Kind, to produce these and those Effects:* an hability, a congruous disposition, or an aptness, yea, a kind of sufficiency in order to the putting forth this and that Act, and the giving Existence to these and those Effects: not indeed an absolute and universal Sufficiency (which can be affirmed of none but Him that is Allsufficient and Omnipotent) but a limited sufficiency, or a sufficiency in their *Kind,* and order: The Sun, to *shine;* the Fire, to *burn* that which is combustible; the Rational Creature to act or effect this or that in a way of *counsel,* and with *freedom of will;* the Swift, to *run;* the strong and valiant, and well-instructed Souldier, to *fight well;* the wise man, to *get his bread* to gather *riches,* to gain *acceptance* among those with whom he hath to do. This is no more than to say, that created Agents and Second Causes, may have the active power and virtue of causes, all that is requisite on their parts in order to the production of their peculiar and appropriate Effects, all that sufficiency that *dependent Beings,* and *second Causes* are capable of. And indeed it belongs to the Infinite Wisdom and Goodness of God to furnish his Creatures with sufficient Ability for the operations and effects He hath made them for: and so He did at *first,* when He made every thing good in its *Kind;* and whatever Defect there is *now* in this respect, it is the fruit & punishment of Sin. Though God is *able* to give Being to things in an immediate way, yet it is his *pleasure* in the course of his Providence to use Means, and to produce many things by the mediation and Agency of second Causes, and so gives *causal virtue* and ability to these and those things in order to the producing of such and such Effects. It is a good observation, that the Lord is pleased, not through any *defect of power* in Himself but out of *the abundance of his goodness* to communicate causal power and virtue to his Creatures, & to honour them with that Dignity that they may be his Instruments, by which He will produce these and those Effects: whereby He takes them, as it were, into partnership & fellowship with Himself in the way of his providential Efficiency, that they may be *Vnder-workers* to, yea *Co-vorkers* with Himself. Hence He gives them an aptitude and sufficiency in their *kind* in order to their respective operations and effects: though some have a greater aptitude & sufficiency than others. But without some degree of such *sufficiency,* nothing can deserve the name of a *Cause;* the very essence whereof consists in its *power, virtue* & *ability* to produce an *Effect.* A *cause* cannot be a *cause* without an *active power,* or *sufficiency* to give *being* to this or that *Effect.*

Prop. 2. *The Successes, and Events of Affairs and Vndertakings do ordinarily depend in some respects upon the Sufficiency of Second Causes.*

I do not say in the *Observation;* nor is it the meaning of *Solomon,* that Successes and Events of Affairs and Undertakings do not depend at all in an ordinary course, on the sufficiency of Second Causes. For this were to deny and destroy their *causality,* and to make nothing of their *efficiency.* Second causes have their peculiar Influence into their *Effects,* and contribute something to their *Existence:* and to assert the contrary, were to say that Causes are no Causes, and to speak a flat Contradiction. This would be to suppose that the Lord hath set up an Order and course in Nature, in vain; and given to Second Causes a sufficiency *in their Kind,* for *Action,* to no purpose; and to deny the ordinary Providence of God, which is that whereby the Lord observes the Order which He hath set, and that course of Nature which is originally of his own Appointment, whereby one thing depends upon, and receives Being from another. Though the Lord is pleased sometimes upon great and important Occasions, to leave the ordinary Road of Providence, and act beyond and above the usual, stated course of Things; and not to concurre with, and shine upon the endeavours of created Agents, so as to crown them with that success which according to an ordinary course of Providence, might be rationally expected; yet it is not to be imagined that He should ordinarily dispence with the course, and methods of his ordinary Providence: For why then should it be called *ordinary?* God who is the Lord of Hosts, the great Leader Commander & Ruler of Nature, not only *permits,* but also *effectually commands* and causes his whole *Militia,* ordinarily, to *move* and *act* according to their *Natures* and *natural Properties* respectively, without *Countermanding* them, or turning them out of their way. For (as I remember One argues) He will not shew such a dislike to his own workmanship, as ordinarily to cross the Order, and alter the course He hath set in the World. Therefore the meaning of the Text is not, that *Swiftness* conduces nothing to the *winning of the Race,* or *Strength,* to the winning of the *Battel;* or *Wisdom* & *Vnderstanding,* to the getting of *Bread* and *Riches;* or *Prudence, Art,* or *Skill,* to the getting of the *Favour* and *goodwill of Princes,* or *People:* nor, that the *Race* is *never* to the *Swift,* or the *Battel never* to the *Strong;* no nor yet, that the *Race* is not *more frequently* to the *Swift,* and the *Battel usually* to the *Strong, &c.* For the Lord doth most ordinarily award *Success* unto causes of greatest *Sufficiency,* rather than *Disappointment* & *Defeatment.* Otherwise, it would be a very *heartless,* if not a *foolish* Thing (in the eye of Reason) to *use means,* or to think to get the *Race* by *Swiftness,* or *Bread* by *Labour* and *Diligence,* or *Favour* by *dexterous & prudent Behaviour;* or *Learning,* by *Study* and *Industry;* or to *win the Battel* by good *Conduct,* and *Courage,* and *numbers of men.* Yea then *Wis-*

dom would not be better than *Folly;* nor *Strength* more desirable than *Weakness;* nor *Diligence* more beneficial & available than *Idleness*, and *sitting still*. This therefore is evident, that the Issues and Events of Undertakings do *in some respect, ordinarily*, depend upon the *Sufficiency* of *Second Causes;* insomuch as the greatest probability of Success (according to an ordinary providence, and in the eye of Reason) is ordinarily on the side of Causes that are most sufficient in their kind of Efficiency.

Prop. 3. *Second Causes, though of greatest Sufficiency in their kind, have not the certain Determination of Successes & Events in their own Hands: but may be frustrated & disappointed.*

Though the Successes and Events of Undertakings ordinarily depend upon the sufficiency of Second Causes; yet they are not infallibly determined thereby. Created Agents have not Events in their own Hands, but may be disappointed: they cannot warrant the Events of their Undertakings, or Success of their Counsels and Endeavours; but may be defeated of their Hopes and Expectations. Thus no man hath the absolute command of the Issue & success of his own Undertakings. He may be sure of this or that Event, if the Lord *Promise* it to him, or *Reveal* it to be *His Pleasure* to give such Success to such Endeavours: but he cannot be secured of it from, or by any *Sufficiency* of his own. He may, as a wise man, foresee & say, what in an ordinary course of Providence is rationally to be expected; but cannot warrant the Success of his Undertakings, or carv out what Event he pleases, to himself. His Prudence, and Providence, and Diligence, and *Sufficiency for Action*, cannot assure him of the *Event*, or determin the Success on his side. And there is that Demonstration of it, that created Agents of the greatest *Sufficiency*, are sometimes disappointed. Two Things I would say here,

1. *Agents of greatest Sufficiency are subject to Disappointment, as well* (I do not say, as much, or as ordinarily and often, but as well) *as Agents of less sufficiency*. The Ablest Men in any kind may miss of the Success they expect, as well as weaker men. That Men of great Sufficiency in this or that way, may be defeated of their Ends and Hopes, *Solomon* from his own Experience, assures us, in the Text: and who is it that upon his own observation cannot set his Seal to what He asserts? He gives five Instances. 1. *The Race is not to the Swift:* not profitable, or successful to him always; but sometimes pernicious, & destructive. Many agood Runner runs Himself into mischief and Ruine. Thus *Asahel*, that is said to be as light of foot as a wild Roe, ran after *Abner* so fast, that he lost his Life in that overhasty pursuit. 2 *Sam*. 2. 18–23.

There are Times when men that are swift would run from danger, and cannot: they have neither power to run, nor success in attempting it, *Jer.* 46, 6. Sometimes the Flight perisheth from the Swift, and he that is swift of foot, or that rideth the Horse, though it be at full speed, cannot deliver himself, *Amos* 2. 14, 15. It is not absolutely in the power of the swiftest man to escape danger, or win the prize by Running. 2. *The Battel is not to the Strong.* There is *in Bello Alea, the Chance of Warre*, as they use to speak. There is, as it were, a kind of Lottery, a great Uncertainty in Warre. Great Armies are sometimes defeated by small and inconsiderable Forces; the great Host of *Midian*, by *Gideon's* three hundred men; the Garrison of the *Philistines* by *Jonathan*, and his Armour-Bearer. This hath been often observed in the World. Sometimes strong and valiant Men are overthrown by those that are in strength farre inferiour to them; *great Goliah*, by *little David.* Well might *David* say, as *Psal.* 33. 16, 17. *There is no King saved by the multitude of an host: a mighty man is not delivered by much strength. An Horse is a vain thing for safety: neither shall he deliver* any *by his great strength.* There are Times, when *the mighty Ones are beaten down*, Jer. 46. 5. & *The mighty cannot deliver himself, or the strong strengthen himself; but the couragious among the mighty is put to flight*, Amos 2. 14, 16. Sometimes the strong melt like water at approaching danger, and the stouthearted are spoiled and sleep their sleep, and the men of might cannot find their hands, to make the least Defence, or Resistance, *Psal.* 76. 5.

3. *Bread is not to the Wise.* Wise men are not able to get their Livelihood, but have much adoe to make a shift to get a bare Subsistence in the world; and, it may be, are forc'd to beg for it, or be beholding to the Charity of others. There have been strange Instances of very wise, and worthy Persons, that have been reduced to such a Condition. Some of you know the famous Story, *Date Obolum*, or (as others have it) *Panem Belisario.*[1] *David* was put to beg his Bread of *Nabal*, 1. *Sam.* 25. & *Paul* was often in Hunger and Thirst, 2 *Cor.* 11. 27.

4. *Riches are not to men of Vnderstanding.* Sometimes indeed, wise men get Estates and gather Riches; and one would think they should be best accomplish'd for it: and yet it so falls out, that some understanding Men cannot thrive in the World and grow rich, notwithstanding all their Endeavours. So it is, that many men of great Understanding and rational Forecastings and Contrivances to gather wealth, though they lay out their Parts and their Hearts this way, and would be rich, yet they cannot; but are strangely defeated. You read of the *poor* wise man, *Eccles.* 9. 15. Many men of great Understandings are too wise, and of too great Spirits to labour after wealth; or if they do,

their designs are unsuccessful. 5. *Favour is not to men of Skill.* Many very wise, and knowing, & skillful men, and experienced in Affairs, and prudent also in their Deportment, yet cannot get, or keep the *Favour* of Princes or People. Some Expositors on the Place, instance in *Joseph*, that was envied, and hated, and sold by his Brethren, & also lost the favour of *Potiphar* (though He managed the Affairs of his House prudently and prosperously, and deserved well at his Hands) and was cast into Prison by him. *David*, that was hated and persecuted by *Saul; Daniel*, that was cast into the Lions Den, though *an excellent Spirit was found in Him*, and great Prudence and Faithfulness in managing the Affairs of the Empire; and before that, though He had been in great Favour and Esteem in *Nebuchadnezzar*'s time, yet afterwards in the Reign of *Belshazzar*, He lived obscure, and as it were buried at Court, as Mr. *Cartwright* gathers from *Dan.* 5. 11, 12, 13. Many wise, and learned, and Ingenious Men cannot get the Favour of men, or keep it, when they have. The *poor* wise man delivered the City, and yet no man remembred that same poor man, *Eccl.* 9. 15. *Belisarius* (whom I mentioned before) was a most prudent, experienced, faithful General under the Emperour *Justinian*, that had won Him many Battels, reduced many Cities & Countryes to his Obedience and approved Himself for a most loyal, and worthy Subject, & yet after all his Services, even in *that* Emperour's Time, was through Envy, falsely accused, for ought appears by the Story, had his Eyes put out, and was forced to stand daily in the Temple of *Sophia*, where He held out his wooden dish, begging his Bread, and useing those words, *Give a little Bread to* Belisarius, *whom his Virtue & Valour hath raised; and Envy depressed, & cast down again.* Other Scripture Testimonies and Instances, besides those in the Text, might be produced, if it were needful. But every observing man's experience may furnish him with Demonstrations of his Truth, *That Agents of greatest Sufficiency among men are subject to Disappointments, as well as those of less Sufficiency.* Again,

2. *Agents of little, or no Sufficiency, succeed sometimes in their Undertakings; when those of greater Sufficiency, miscarry & meet with Disappointment.* There is many times one Event to both as *Solomon* speaks *Eccl.* 9. 2. when the ablest Agents are frustrated, as well as the weakest: and there is sometimes a better Event to weaker Agents, & Instruments; they prosper in their way, when abler men are disappointed. The Race is *sometimes* to the Slow, and the Swift lose the Prize. The Battel is *sometimes* to the Weak; and the Strong are put to flight: as we have many Instances both in Scripture and common History. Weak and simple people have bread enough sometimes, when wise

men are in want of their daily bread. *Nabal* had good store, when *David* was hard put to it. Men of shallow heads grow rich and get great Estates, when men of understanding can thrive at no Hand. *Solomon* tells us of the *poor* wise man; and our Saviour in that Parable, *Luk.* 12. 16, 20. tells us of a *rich Fool.* It is ordinarily seen in the World, that the thriving men in Estates, are none of the most understanding & judicious. Many a man hath this world-craft, that yet is a man of no deep or solid Understanding. So, many weak, worthless, ignorant, empty Persons find Favour with Princes and People: when men of Skill, & Learning, & great worth are neglected and despised. This is an Evil under the Sun, & an Error that proceeds from the Ruler, a great miscarriage in Government, that *Folly is set in great dignity* (Fools are favoured and advanced) *and the Rich,* i.e. men of rich Endowments for Wisdom and Piety, *sit in low places,* i.e. are depressed and discountenanced; *Servants are upon Horses,* men of poor servile Spirits and Conditions, are set up and honoured, *and Princes,* i.e. men of great worth, *walking as Servants upon the Earth.* Eccl. 10. 5, 6, 7. So that it appeares plainly, that Success doth not alwayes wait upon the Counsels and Actions of Persons of great Sufficiency; but they may suffer Disappointment, when others are prosperous: Which demonstrates that the Issues and Events of Undertakings and Affairs are not determined infallibly by the Qualifications & accomplishments of created Agents, and Second Causes.

Prop. 4. *The Defeat & Disappointment of Agents of great Sufficiency in their kind, is from the Hapning of* Time *&* Chance *unto them.*

Some read it (and the Original will bear it) *because,* or *for* Time and Chance happeneth to them all. For Explication.

1. By *Time,* understand not barely the *Duration,* or *spate* of Time, which hath no such determining Influence into humane Affairs. But Time *so & so Circumstanced.* Time is sometimes as much as a special *Season* or *Opportunity,* when there is a concurrence of Helps, means, and advantages for the furthering the Designs and undertakings of men. By *Time* sometimes, we are to understand such a *Nick,* or *Juncture* of time, wherein there is a coincidence of Difficulties, disadvantages, & hindrances to the effecting of any Business. And this seems the meaning of *Solomon* in the Text. An adverse or *evil Time,* Ec. 9. 12. Sometimes the Times favour the Enterprizes of men, Sometimes they frown upon them. At one time, wise and good men stand up for the Defence of their Country and Liberties thereof, and prosper in it; the Times favour them, there is a concurrence of all manner of Furtherances and advantages: at another time, they may endeavour it,

and the Times frown upon them, the Spirit and Humour of the People is degenerated; and they swim against the stream, & are lost in the Attempt. And we say, *Such a Man was worthy of better Times*, had been a brave man, if He had lived in better Times, his worth had been more known and prized, and He would have had better success. So when the Time of Judgment upon a People, is come, then wrath ariseth against them without remedy; and then the *strong man* may fight for the defence of such a Country; and *the wise man* endeavour to deliver the City: but all in vain; they shall miscarry in the Undertaking. *Aben Ezra* (as *Mercer* tells us) referres this to the *Conjunctions*, and *Aspects* of the Starres, by which He apprehended these inferiour Things were governed. We are sure there are certain Periods, and Revolutions of Time, respecting the Prosperity, or Adversity of Nations, Countries, Cities, Churches, Families, Persons. As Time is set to all the Successes, so to all the Defeats and disappointments of men; and when this Time comes, no Sufficiency of man can withstand Disappointments.

2. By *Chance*, Understand contingent and casual Events. Many things fall out between the *Cup*, and the *Lip;* or otherwise than expect or imagine, or can possibly foresee. Some Event chops in, and interposeth unexpectedly, to cross a man's Designs, & defeat his Hopes & rational Expectations. When *Saul* and his men were compassing *David* and his men, and ready to take them, then comes a Messenger to *Saul*, saying, *Haste & come: for the* Philistines *have Invaded the Land*. 1 Sam. 23. 27. When *Haman* had plotted the Ruine of the *Jews*, and brought his Design near to an Issue, then the King cannot sleep but calls for the Book of the Records of the Chronicles, and they read to Him of the good Service of *Mordecai*, in discovering the Treason that was plotted against his Person; and one thing falls in after another, to defeat *Haman's* cruel design, and ruine the whole fabrick of his strong built, and almost perfected Contrivance In this sence *Time* and *Chance* happens to men of greatest Sufficiency, which they cannot either foresee, (*Eccl* 9. 12.) or prevent, or help themselves against them when they come upon them: and hereby their Counsels, and Undertakings are defeated and ruined sometimes.

Prop. 5. *Time and Chance which happens to men in the way of their Vndertakings, is effectually ordered & governed by the Lord*. God is the Lord of Time, and Orderer, and Governour of all Contingences. Time and Chance that further or hinder the Designs of men, are under the Rule and Management of the Lord. His Counsel sets the *Times*, appoints the *Chances;* His Providence dispenses the *Times*, and frames the *Chances*, that befall men. The Lord hath in his own power the Dispensation of *Times*, Eph. 1. 10. *The Times and Seasons He hath put in his own power*, Act. 1. 7. He hath such a Dominion over the Times, that *He changeth Times and Seasons*, according to his own pleasure. *Dan.* 2. 31. *My Times* (saith *David*, Ps. 31. 15. *are in thy Hands*. He means the state and condition of his *Times;* his Prosperities, and Adversities; his Successes, and Disappointments; and universally, whatever should befall him in the Times that should pass over Him. Moreover, all the Chances that happen to men, as the Scripture but now mentioned shews, are in the Hand of God. *My Times* i.e. the Chances of my Times. No Contingency, or Emergency, or Accident so casual, but it is ordered & governed by the Lord. The Arrow that was shot at a venture, and smote *Ahab* throw the joints of his Harness, was directed at him by the Hand of God. So in that case of Man-slaughter, and killing a man casually, as if a man be hewing Wood, and his hand fetcheth a stroke with the Axe, to cut down a Tree, and the head slippeth from the helve, and lighteth upon his Neighbour, that he die, *Deut.* 19. 5. God is said in that case, to *deliver* that man that is slain, *into his hand*, Exod. 21. 13. God ordereth that sad event. All Casualties in the World, are guided by the steady Hand of the great God. *Thou* (saith *David*, Ps. 16. 5.) *maintainest my Lot*. The Lord makes and disposes the Lot, or Chance of every man, whatever it is. He hath appointed all Times and Chances in his *Eternal* Counsel; and in *Time* executes accordingly, in the course of his Providence.

Prop. 6. *The great God hath the absolute and infallible Determination of the Successes and Events of all the Operations & Vndertakings of created Agents & Second Causes, in his own Power*. His Counsel and soveraign Will appoints what they shall be, and his Providence (which is not determined by any Second Cause: but is the Determiner of them all) Executes accordingly. And it must needs be so, if you consider these two Particulars,

1. *God is the Absolute First Cause, and Supream Lord of all*. Of Him, and to Him, and through Him are all Things, *Rom.* 11. 36. He that understands any thing of God indeed, knows this to be a Truth. Here we might be large; as they that are acquainted with the Doctrine of *Creation* and *Providence*, in *Conservation* and *Gubernation* of all Things, will readily apprehend: for here we might shew you, 1. That God is the absolute first Cause of all the causal power and virtue that is in Creatures. He gives them power to act, furnisheth them with a Sufficiency for their Operations. He gives Swiftness to the Runner; Skill, and Strength, and Courage, to the Souldier.

2. That He supports, and continues the active power of the creature. He continues Swiftness, Wisdom, Strength, Courage, as He pleaseth. If He withdraw, all is gone. The Swift is lame, or slow-footed, the Strong is weak & timorous, the Wise is foolish and besotted, the man of Skill, is a meer Bungler at any thing. 3. That He doth by a *previous Influx* excite and stirre up, and actuate the active power of the Creature, and set all the wheels agoing. For the most operative, active created Virtue, is not a *pure Act:* but hath some *Potentiality* mixed with it; and therefore cannot put forth it self into Action, unless it be set agoing by the *first Cause*. And the creature cannot be the absolute *first Cause* of any *physical action*. In Him we live, and move, *Act.* 17. 28. Again. 4. That He determines and applyes Second Causes to the Objects of their Actions. When they stand, as it were, *in Bivio*, as it is said of *Nebuchadnezzar*, when he was marching with his Army He *stood at the parting of the way, at the head of the two wayes, to use Divination*, as doubting which way he had best to march; whether to *Jerusalem*, or some other way, *Ezek.* 21. 21, 22. Then the Lord casts the Scale and the Lot, & determines them this way, and not another. He doth not only stir up Second Causes to act at large, and set them agoing, and leave it to their own Inclination, whither they shall go, & what they shall do: but He leads them forth, and determines them to this, or that Object. 5. That He *cooperates*, and workes *jointly* with Second Causes, in producing their Effects. As He *predetermins* Second Causes, so He *concurres* with them in their Operations. And this *Prædetermination*, and *Concurse* is so necessary; that there can be no real Effect produced by the Creature without it. And it is a Truth also, that when God Improves Second Causes for the production of any Effect, He so concurres with them, that He doth withall most immediately, intimously, and without Dependence upon these Causes by which He acts, produce the *Entity*, or *Esse* of the Effect. If this be considered, it will appear that created Agents, are as it were, God's Instruments, that act as they are acted by Him; and cannot move of themselves. The busy, bustling, proud *Assyrian* was so, *Is.* 10. 15. 6. *That all the Ataxy, Disorder, Irregularity, moral Evil that is found in the Actions of Rational Agents, is by His Permission.* If it were not the Pleasure of God to permit it, no Sin should be in the World, nor in the Actions of Men. Though there is no *Legal* Permission, or allowance of it; (for the Law of God forbids it) yet there is a *Providential* Permission of it. God could have kept it out of his World. 7. *That He limits and sets Bounds to the Actions of Second Causes: what they shall do, and how farre they shall proceed in this or that way.* He set bounds to Satan, when he

had Commission to afflict *Job*. He limits, and restrains the Eruptions of the Wrath & Rage of the Churches Adversaries, *Ps*. 76. 10. He sets bounds to the sinfull Actions of Men: He regulates and governs all the Actions of Second Causes, as to time, place, degrees, and all manner of Circumstances. He is not the *Author:* but He is the *Orderer* of Sin it self. 8. *That He serves Himself, and his own Ends of all Second Causes*. He makes them all in all their Operations subservient to his own Designs: and that not only natural, but rational Agents, that act by Counsel. And not only such of them as are his professed willing Servants. Many serve God's ends beside their Intentions, and against their wills. I will do this and that saith God, by the *Assyrian, howbeit he meaneth not so*, Is. 10. 6, 7. Wicked men and Devils do God's will against their own will, and beside their Intentions. *Ye thought Evil against me* (saith *Joseph* to his Brethren) *but God meant it for good &c.* Gen. 50. 20. God elicites what good He pleases out of the actions of his Creatures. Whatever this or that Agent proposeth to himself, yet God alwayes attaineth His Ends. He serves Himself of the very Sins of his Creatures, and brings good out of them. He makes that which is not *Bonum honestum*, to be *Bonum conducibile:* [2] and though Sin is not good; yet, as God orders the matter, it is good, in order to many holy Ends, that Sin should be in the World, as *Austin observes*.

9. *That He useth means in themselves* unfit, *and improves Agents of themselves* insufficient, *to bring about his own Purposes & produce marveilous Effects*. Yea, and it is as easy with Him to do any thing by weak and insufficient, as by the ablest & most accomplished Instruments. *There is no restraint to the Lord to Save by many, or by few*. 1 Sam. 14. 6. *It is nothing with Him to help, whether with many, or with them that have no power*. 2 Chron. 14. 11. Despicable Instruments, sometimes, do great Things in His Hand. 10. *That He renders the aptest means ineffectual, and the Vndertakings of the most sufficient Agents unsuccessful, when He pleases*. He hath a *Negative Voice* upon all the Counsels and Endeavours, and Active Power of the Creature. He can stop the Sun in its course, and cause it to withdraw its shining; He can give check to the Fire, that it shall not burn; & to the hungry Lions, that they shall not devour: and He can order it so, that the men of might shall *sleep their sleep, and not find their Hands*. He can break the Ranks of the most orderly Souldiers, take away courage from the stoutest hearts, send a pannick Fear into a mighty Host, and defeat the Counsels of the wisest Leaders and Conducters. He can blow upon, and blast the likeliest Undertakings of the ablest Men. In a word: the Lord being the Absolute First Cause, and supream Governour of all his Creatures, and all their

Actions; though He hath set an Order among his Creatures, this shall be the cause of that effect, &c. yet He himself is not tied to that Order; but Interrupts the course of it, when He pleases. The Lord reserves a Liberty to Himself to interpose, and to Umpire matters of Success and Event, contrary to the Law and common Rule of Second Causes. And though He ordinarily concurreth with Second Causes according to the Law given and Order set; yet sometimes there is in his Providence a Variation and Digression. Though He hath given Creatures power to act; and Man, to act as *a Cause by Counsel*, and hath furnished him with active Abilities; yet He hath not made any Creature *Master of Events;* but reserves the Disposal of Issues, and Events to Himself. Herein the absolute Soveraignty and Dominion of God appears.

2. *Otherwise, the Lord might possibly suffer real Disappointment, and be defeated of his Ends in some Instances.* He might be cross'd in his Designs, if any of his Creatures could doe what they will, without absolute Dependence upon Him. He could not be sure of his Ends, & what He designs in the World, if He had not command of all Events that may further or hinder them. If there were any active power in Creatures that He cannot controll; or any one event that is out of his Reach, and absolutely in the Creature's power, exempted from his providential Command, it would be possible that He might be defeated of his Ends, and so far unhappy, as to his *voluntary Happiness*, which results from his having his *Pleasure done* in the World, and compassing all his Ends in the works of Creation and Providence. God hath made all Things, ruleth all Things, and manageth all Things according to the Counsel of his Will, in a way of subserviency to Himself, and his own Occasions: which He could not do universally and infrustrably, if He had not the absolute and infallible Determination of all Events in his own Hand. *But His Counsel shall stand, and He will do all his Pleasure:* Is. 46. 10. Thus much for the Explication, and Confirmation of the Doctrine.

USE I. Of Instruction, in these Particulars.

1. *We see what a poor dependent, nothing-Creature Proud Man is:* Depending absolutely upon God for his Being, Actions, and the Success of them. Men of greatest Sufficiency cannot get their own Bread, or bring any thing to effect in their own strength. Let their Abilities be what they will (*Swiftness*, for the *Race; Strength*, for the *Battel; Wisdom*, for getting their *Bread, &c.*) yet they shall stand them in no stead without the concurrence and Blessing of God. Man saith, he will do this and that: but he must ask God leave first. He saith, To day or to morrow I will go to such a place, and buy and sell, & get gain; whereas he knows

not what shall be: but it shall certainly be as the Lord will. *The way of man is not in himself; it is not in man that walketh to direct his steps*, nor perform any thing that he purposeth, without divine Concurrence, or Permission. He hath not the Success of any of his actions in his own power; nor doth he know that any thing he doth shall prosper. One would wonder poor *dependent* man should be so *proud!* Any little thing lifts him up. When the Souldier on such occasions as these, is in his Bravery, in his military Garb drest up for the purpose, with his *Buffe Coat*, his *Scarfe*, his *rich Belt*, his *Arms*, *a good Horse under him*, O what a goodly Creature is he in his own Eyes! and what wonders can he do in his own conceit! and yet he hath as absolute need of God's Assistance, if he go forth to Battel, as any naked, unarmed man. He cannot move a step, or fetch his next breath, or bring his hand to his mouth, or leap over a straw, or do any thing, without help from God, *in whose hand his breath is, and whose are all his wayes* Dan. 5. 23. It's strange to see how the hearts of men are lifted up with nothing! *O cease ye from Man: for wherein is he to be accounted of?*

2. *We see that there is, and there is not* Chance *in the World.* Chance there is, in respect of Second Causes: (so some things fall out Κατα Συγκυριαν as our Saviour speaks *Luk.* 10. 31.) but no Chance as to the first Cause. That piece of *Atheism*, and *Heathenism* ascribing things to *Fortune* and *Chance*, is hardly rooted out of the minds of men, that are or should be better instructed and informed. The *Philistines* when they were plagued, could not tell whether *God* had done it, or a meer *Chance* happened to them, 1 *Sam.* 6. 9. They understood not, that what was *a Chance to them*, was ordered by the *Providence of God.* Truth is, Chance is something that falls out beside the Scope, Intention, and foresight of *Man*, the Reason and cause whereof may be hid from him; and so it excludes the Counsel of *Men;* but it doth not exclude the Counsel and Providence of *God;* but is ordered and governed thereby. And it is so farre from being *Chance* to God, that there is as much (if not more) of the Wisdom, and Will, and Power of God appearing in matters of Chance and Contingency, as in any other Events.

3. *We see here something of the Power, and Greatness, and Glory of God appearing in his Efficiency, whereby He works all in all.* As He is himself Independent, so all Things have an absolute Dependence on Him. He gives Success, or causeth Disappointment, as he pleaseth. So that men are wholly beholden to Him for all the good they enjoy: for Victory, for Bread, for Riches, for Favour and Acceptance, for all. Nothing comes to pass without his Permission, if it be *moral Evil;* without his Concurse and cooperation, yea, Predetermination, if it be *moral* or

physical Good, or *penal Evil*. In him we live and move, and have our Being. The Counsels of the ablest Statesmen, how rational soever, shall not prosper without him: Ministers, how sufficient soever, pious, learned, industrious, zealous, shall convert no man, edify no man, comfort & establish no man, without Him. 1 *Cor*. 3. 6, 7. Though Scholars study hard, they shall make no proficiency without the Blessing of God. The Merchant may trade, and project rationally, and yet shall not grow rich upon it, unless God give him success. It is God that maketh *Zebulum rejoice in his Going out, and Issachar in his Tents:* that crowns the labours of Seamen, Merchants, and Husbandmen with Success. *Except the Lord build the House* &c Ps. 127. 1. *Training Days, Artillery Days*, tho' of great use, and very necessary; yet are all in vain, unless the Lord bless. He must instruct, and teach, and accomplish you; otherwise the help of your expert Officers, and your own endeavours to learn War, will signify nothing. And when valiant Souldiers come to fight; whatever Skill, and Strength, and Courage, and Conduct, and Advantages they have, yet they will be worsted, if the Lord do not give Success. We should learn hence to admire the Power and Greatness of God. It is a lamentable thing, that He that doth all, is thought to do nothing! He can work without Means, by insufficient Means; & blast the ablest Instruments: and yet is little minded in the World. God gives forth a Challenge to Idols, *Do good*, if you can, *or do evil*. Isai. 41. 23. It is God's Prerogative to do good or evil, i.e. not the evil of *Sin* (which argues Defect and Impotency; and comes not within the compass of Omnipotency to do it) but of *Punishment*. God only can give good, or award bad Success; and *Reward* or *Correct* and punish his Creatures that way. *Who is he that saith* (what Man or Angel?) *& it* cometh to pass, when the Lord commandeth it not? Lam. 3. 37. O see, and adore the Greatness of God in this respect! He works all in all. . . .

First, Whatever your own Sufficiencie may be, yet acknowledge God thankfully, as if you had been wholly Insufficient: for your Sufficiencie is of God, and He could have disappointed notwithstanding. The ground of our Unthankfulness for all good Issues and Events of Affairs and Undertakings, is, because we do not see the good Hand of God dispensing all to us. We make too *little* of God, and too *much* of our selves; either by thinking we deserve better than God hath done for us (Hence a proud Heart is never thankful to God or Man) or by thinking we have done all, or more than we have done, toward the getting of this or that Mercy. We put our selves too much in the place of God; as if it were in our power to make our Endeavours Successful, and to give a good Effect and Issue to them, according to *our* Desire. We get up into God's Throne, and usurp upon his Prerogative, and assume that which is peculiar to Him, when we presume we can bring any thing to pass, or do any thing successfully in our Own strength. If we make our selves the only and absolute *first Causes* of our good Success; no marvel we make our selves the *last End* also, and deny God the glorie. O do not ascribe good Success to your own Wit, and Parts, and Policy, and Industrie, and say, my Nimbleness hath won the Race; my Conduct and Courage hath won the Battel; my Wisom hath gotten me this Bread; my Understanding hath heaped up this Wealth; my Dexteritie, and Skill, and Complaisance, and agreeable Conversation hath procured me the Favour of Rulers or People; my Parts or Study hath given me this Learning. Say not with the Vapouring *Assyrian*, *By the Strength of My Hand I have done it, and by My Wisdom: for I am Prudent.* Isa. 10. 13. Let not this be so much as the secret Language of your Hearts. Say not, as *Nebuchadnezzar*, *This is great Babylon, which I have built*, and so derogate from God that works all in all; lest He turn you a grazing, as He did him, with the Beasts of the Field, and teach you better Manners by some severe Correction. Do not *Sacrifice to your own Nets, and burn Incense to your Drags; as if by them your portion were fat, and meat plenteous* (Hab. 1. 16.) but ascribe all to God. There is that deep Wickedness in the Hearts of Men, that if they get any thing by any Fraud, and crafty fetches, and overreaching of their Brethren, in a sinful way, they will be too readie to attribute *that* to the Providence and Blessing of God, and say, it was God's Providence that cast it in upon them; when they have been craftily and sinfully designing it, and bringing it about: but when they have gotten any thing honestly, by their Wisdom and Prudence, and Industrie, they are too ready to forget Providence, and ascribe all to themselves. See the Evil of this, and remember that no People in the World have greater cause of Thankfulness than we have to God, who hath governed *Time* and *Chance* on our behalf marvellously. O Bless Him for good Success, not only when you cannot but acknowledge your own *Insufficiency;* but also when you have apprehensions of the greatest *Sufficiency* of Second Causes. And *Blessed for ever be the Lord, who hath Pleasure in the Prosperity of his Servants*, Psal. 35. 27.

Secondly, *Acknowledge God also in all your Frustrations and Disappointments, so as to resent his Disposals and Dispensations towards you in a* gracious *manner*. We have met with manie Disappointments in the late Warre, and in other respects. We should see God in all. When He blasts our *Corn*, defeats our *Souldiers*, frowns upon our *Merchants*, and we are *disappointed;* now acknowledge the Hand of God, Ordering *Time*, and *Chance* according to his Good Pleasure. Justifie God in all, and bear such Frustrations patientlie. When you have done your Dutie, be quiet, though the Event doth not answer your Endeavours, and Hopes. Take heed of quarrelling at *God*'s Disappointments. Do you know VVhom you have to do with? *I was dumb, I opened not my mouth; because Thou didst it.* Psal. 89. 9. If we look at faultie Instruments, or at meer Chance onely, we shall be apt to murmur. It is the observation of One, *That the Reason why men are more apt to fly out into Cursings and Blasphemies for their bad Luck (as they call it) in those Vnlawful Games of* Cards, and Dice, *than in other Exercises, that are governed by Art and Skill, ariseth partly from the very nature of those Games: because when they have tried their Lot or Chance over and over, and their Expectation is deceived, they think that that Power that governs the Lot or Chance, is Adverse to them. They cannot blame their own Art or Skill, when no Art can infallibly determine the Event; but curse their bad Fortune.* And if we look at Disappointments, as our bad *Fortune* and *Chance* onely, looking no further, we shall be apt to fret and quarrel: but if we do indeed see God ordering our Lot for us, it may and ought to silence us. When Magistrates have done their Duty, according to the Law of God, and of the Country, and endeavoured faithfully to give check & stop to the Inundation of *Profaneness* and *Heresy;* and yet the bad Genius of the Times, and degenerous Humour of the People, and this or that Emergency happens, that frustrates the Success of their Counsels and Endeavours; truly they may sit down and mourn indeed; but yet humbly submit to the All-disposing Providence of God. When Ministers have laboured faithfully, and yet Israel is not gathered, and their Labours seem to be in vain, not successful in converting Sinners; they may weep in secret indeed; but yet patiently bear the Unsuccessfulness of their Ministry from the Hand of God. When Souldiers have shewed themselves valiant, and faithful, and done what they can; and yet are worsted: They must acknowledge God's Hand in it, and that *the Battel is the Lord*'s. 1 Sam. 17. 47. who governeth the Warre, and determins the Victory on what side He pleaseth. All men have *Briars* and *Thorns* springing up in the way of their Callings, as well as Husbandmen; and meet with Difficulties and Crosses therein. Get the Spirit *David* had 2 *Sam.* 15. 25, 26. and so acknowledge God in every thing, as to submit humbly to his Disposals, even when they are Adverse, and cross to your Desires and Expectations.

Thirdly, *Be always Prepared for Disappointments.* Do not promise your selves Success from the Sufficiency of Second Causes: God may determine otherwise. . . . Events are not in the Creatures power. The

Lord sometimes disappoints men of greatest Sufficiency, overrules and controlls their Counsels and Endeavours, and blasts them strangely. *Time* and *Chance* happens to them. If *Adam* had stood; though he would not have had the Determination of Events & Successes in his own hand; yet God would have determined them for him according to his hearts-desire: and he should never have been disappointed. But since the Fall, as no Man hath power to determine Events (which is God's Prerogative) so it is just with God that every man should meet with Crosses and Disappointments; and this is the Fruit of the Curse, under which all natural men ly: and as for the People of God; though they are delivered from the Curse of the Law, in the *Formality* of it; so that nothing befalls them *as a Curse*, how *cross* soever it be: yet they are not yet absolutely delivered from the *Matter* of the Curse, as appears by the Afflictions they meet with, and Death it self. And indeed it makes sometimes for the glory of God, to disappoint Men of greatest Abilities. When men do not see and own God; but attribute Success to the Sufficiency of Instruments, It's time for God to maintain his own Right (as Dr. *Preston* [3] speaks) and shew that He gives, or denies Success, according to His own good Pleasure. God is much seen in Controlling the ablest Agents, & blasting their Enterprizes; yea more, many times, than in backing them, & blessing their Endeavours in an ordinary Course of Providence. Herein the *Wisdom* of God is much seen. It is best, sometimes, it should be so, with respect to God's Int'rest and Glory. His *Power* also appears in giving Check to the Ablest Instruments, and turning all their Designs another way than they Intended. His *Mercy* also to his People, is seen herein; for it is best for them, in some Cases, to be defeated and disappointed. His *Justice* also appears herein, in his correcting and punishing the Self-confident, sinful Creature with unexpected Disappointments. So that it is our Wisdom, to look for Changes and Chances, some Occurrents and Emergencies that may blast our Undertakings, that Faith and Prayer may be kept agoing, and lest if such Frustrations befall us unexpectedly, we either fly out against God, or faint and sink in Discouragements. At the first going out of our Forces, in the beginning of the Warre, what great Apprehensions were there of speedy Success and ending of the Warre; that it was but going and Appearing, and the Enemy would be faced down: As if the first News from our Souldiers should be, *Venimus, Vidimus, Vicimus*.[4] And several times after, great probability of concluding that unhappy War; and yet all disappointed, contrary to Expectation.[5] VVhen there is therefore greatest Probability of Success, yet remember there may be Disappointment; and provide for it, that you may not be surprised thereby. This may be good Counsel to men of projecting Heads, that are wont to be very confident that they see their way farre before them: but they do not know what *Time* and *Chance* may happen: This may check the Confidence of Man, and teach us not to promise our selves great Things, or build upon this or that Event or Enjoyment for time to come. Labour to be prepared and provided for Disappointments.

JOSHUA MOODY, 1633–1697

[Joshua Moody was born in Ipswich, Suffolk; his father was a saddler, who migrated to Ipswich, Massachusetts, in 1634, and then to Newbury. He graduated from Harvard College in 1653, was a teaching fellow in 1655; in 1658 he began to preach in Portsmouth, New Hampshire, though he could not get a church formally organized until 1671. In 1682 he became a popular hero by stoutly resisting the attempts of Governor Cranfield to force him to administer the sacraments according to the rites of the Church of England. He was sentenced to six months in jail, served thirteen weeks, and was forbidden to preach. He came to Boston, assisted James Allen at the First Church, declined the presidency of Harvard and a call from New Haven. Still living in Boston in 1688–1689, he was a leader of the revolution against Andros. He resisted the witchcraft frenzy, actually aiding two of the accused to escape. He returned to Portsmouth in 1693. Cf. Sibley, *Biographical Sketches;* Sprague, *Annals*. This text is from *Souldiery Spiritualized, Or the Christian Souldier Orderly, and Strenuously Engaged in the Spiritual Warre* (Cambridge, 1674), an artillery election sermon preached in Boston on June 1, 1674; it is unusual among Puritan sermons for the elaborate and sustained metaphor upon which it is built. Not only does Moody portray the whole of human existence under the figure of war and battle, but he takes up in succession the technical commands of the parade ground and of formation and develops a spiritual significance for each.]

SOULDIERY SPIRITUALIZED

As for my manner of speaking in the using of many Metaphorical Expressions, and Allusions unto the Calling, Postures, and motions of Souldiers . . . though it may possibly grate upon some Critical and captious Ears, yet I hope it will be at least excusable or tolerable to your selves. . . . Had I been to handle the same Head of Divinity on another occasion and before another Auditor, I could and should have sought out other words, . . . I conceive a man should take Measure of his Theam to cut out his Language by, and make it up something according to the mode of his Auditory. . . .

The Lord takes care to make us spiritual in all our Imployments, by spiritualizing all our Imployments. Yea, all our Relations and Conditions, as well as Imployments, are so improved to our Hands by the Spirit of God in his Word as that they may be useful both as Monitors and Helpers to mind us of, and further us in those matters that are of most solemn and momentous, because of Eternal concernment . . . From the King upon the Throne to the Hewer of wood and drawer of water, the Lord is in his word teaching us by such familiar and known *Metaphors* taken from those Callings that we are versed in, in so much that all sorts of men may say concerning the voice of God in his word, as they in another Case Acts. 2. 8. 11. How is it that we hear from thence in our own Tongue wherein we have been bred, and in the proper *dialect* of those Imployments to which we have been bred, the wonderful Counsels of God declared to us: the Lords manner of speaking as it helps us to the understanding of what he saith, so his love and Care therein should quicken us to the practice of what we understand. . . .

Know, that *Death our Enemy* is upon a *swift* and *speedy march* towards us, and we are hastening toward him, and therefore must necessarily meet quickly, between this and that the Time is but short, over a few dayes (*moments* it may be) the day will discover what we have been, and done. We are now all of us *training up* under the *doctrine* and *Discipline* of the *Lords House*, and possibly (you, probably) in this Life he may put us to the Trial what we have gained, some such *plunge* we may be brought unto, as wherein we shall have occasion to use all the Skill that ever we have had an opportunity of getting. He may call us to *combate* with *Persecution*, *Poverty*, *Reproach*, Bereavements of Relations, &c. or at the utmost Death will try us all, *Death*, (I say,) which among men of all *Ages* and *Sexes* takes *promiscuously* according to the *Commission* which the *Lord of Life and Death* hath given it, though ordinarily, those that are in the Front are nextly for present Service, who *discharge*, and *Fall off*, and make way for the next to be *Front.*[1] So *one Generation passeth away, and another comes in its Room* Eccl. 1. 4. ever in motion, going off, and coming on the *stage* each hour and movement. I may not unfitly liken the *whole Race of Mankind*, or all the men in the world to a *well-Marshall'd* Army, (*well Marshall'd* I say, for notwithstanding all the *seeming*, and in themselves the real *Confusions* that there are, the Lord orders all *wisely*, and at the end will discover when all is put together, *beautifully* too) upon a *march* to meet with *Death*, where the *first Rank discharge*, (yea, and are *discharged* too) *Fall off*, yea, *Fall down*, never to return or rise more, and then the next is first, and so on: there are *Old men*, *middle-Aged*, and *Young ones*, in the *Front*, *Center*, and *Rear* of the *Army*, The *Old Fall off*, the *middle-Aged Advance*, the *Younger* are *drawing* after, now though sometimes here and there one of the *younger ones* may be pickt out of the *Reer* by a Shott out of *Deaths murthering piece*, yet we commonly say, and truly, *Young ones may* die, but Old ones must. It's a usual word of Command among you, *The First Rank make ready*, they especially should be ready; but it is a duty for us all to *watch and pray alwayes*, that we may be *accounted worthy* to stand when the Son of man shall come. Let all our *Care* and *motion* through-out our whole Life tend to the fitting us for a *safe*, *Honourable*, *and comfortable Exit* at last, that when we come to look *Death* in the *Face*, or to *look back*, (and we should often *look back*) upon our *Life past*, we may neither be *afraid*, nor *ashamed to die*.

SAMUEL WILLARD, 1640–1707

[For life of Willard see p. 250. The first selection is from *The Child's Portion* (Boston, 1684), pp. 66–70. The second selection is from *The High Esteem Which God hath of the Death of his Saints* (Boston, 1683), pp. 14–18, a funeral sermon upon John Hull, the famous mintmaster of the colony, the father-in-law of Samuel Sewall. The third selection is from *The Peril of the Times Displayed* (Boston, 1700), pp. 90–93; the passage is representative of the wails over the moral declension of New England that make up a large part of most sermons at the end of the seventeenth century.]

SAINTS NOT KNOWN BY EXTERNALS

1. The reason why the Children of God are so little regarded here in the World; it is because the World knows not who they are, nor what they are born unto: Their great Glory for the present is within; outwardly they look like other men, they eat, drink, labour, converse in earthly imployments, as others do; the communion which they have with God in all of these, is a secret thing: They are Sick, Poor, Naked, Distressed like other men; those inward supports which they have under all those exercises, are remote from publick view: They dy, and are buried under the Clods, and their bodyes putrifie and rot like other men; and none see those joyes that their souls are entred

into, nor that guard of Angels which comes as a Convoy, and carryes them into *Abraham's* bosom: Nay, they have their sins, their spots, their imperfections and weaknesses here, as well as other men; but their tears, repentance, secret mournings, and renewals of Faith, and restorings to peace and soul-comfort, are secret.

And hence,

Though the Righteous Man be indeed surpassingly more excellent than his neighbour, yet is he not thought so to be: Whereas, did the World see and understand, whose sons they are, what inheritances they are the undoubted heirs of, and what are those Gloryes they shall ere long be made to possess, it would alter their opinion, and make them afraid of them, and not dare to do them any wrong. How fearful was *Abimestech* of *Abraham*, when God did but tell him he was a Prophet? *Gen.* 20. 7, 8.

2. Here we see the reason why the People of God are often so doubtful, disquiet, discontent, and afraid to dy (I put things together) The ground of all this is because they do not as yet see clearly what they shall be: It would be a matter of just wonderment to see the Children of God so easily and often shaken, so disturbed and perplexed in hours of Temptation, were it not from the consideration, that they at present know so little of themselves or their happiness: Sometimes their sonship it self doth not appear to them, but they are in the dark, at a loss about the evidencing of it to the satisfaction of their own minds; and from hence it is that many doubtings arise, and their souls are disquieted. Sometimes their present sufferings look bigger in their thoughts, than the conceptions or apprehensions which they entertain of their future Glory, these things being near, and the other looked on at a distance, and hence they out-weigh, in their rash judgements, and now they are disquiet and discontent, and say with him, *Psal.* 73. 13. *I have cleansed my heart in vain, and washed my hands in innocency.* And usually in their good frames, they apprehend more of the sweetness of present Communion with God in his Ordinances, than of that blessed immediate communion in Glory; and this makes them, with good *Hezekiah*, to turn away their faces from the messages of death and change: All these things are arguments of the weak sight and dark thoughts which we here have of the things of another world: which yet, it is the holy pleasure of God, that it shall be so a while, for the advancing of his own ends in his Saints.

3. Learn hence a reason why the present sufferings of God's Children can neither argue against, nor yet prejudice their felicity: for the time is not yet come wherein they are to appear like themselves: *Joseph's*

prisoned condition, and prison robes set him never the further off from his preferment in *Pharaoh*'s Court; but were indeed the very harbingers of it: When the appointed time for the manifestation of the Sons of God shall come, he can fetch them out in hast, change them in the twinkling of an eye, and cloath them upon with all that excellency and splendid Glory, whereby, they who were but the other day lying among the pots, shall with their dazling lustre outshine the Sun in the Firmament. It is the Almighty's good pleasure, that their life, for the present, should be hid with Christ in God: But yet he hath his time, and will take his opportunity to reveal and make it known.

4. This teacheth us that the Glory of the sons of God must needs be wonderfully and astonishingly great: For why? Have they not already in hand, that which surpasses the knowledge of all the world, and which is in value transcendently more worth than all the Crowns and Kingdoms, and Gloryes of it? Do they not live upon, and satisfie their souls with marrow and fatness here, *Psal.* 63. 5. Are they not here replenished with the fatness of God's house? *Psal.* 36. 8. Who, but he that enjoys it, can declare what an happiness it is to enjoy peace with God, and fellowship with Christ, assurance of his love, and consolation of his spirit? Who, but he that hath felt it, can tell what it is to have the love of God shed abroad in his heart, and in his Soul to hear the sweet voice of Pardon, and promises of Glory? to ly all night in the bosom of Christ, and have his left hand underneath his head, and his right hand imbracing of him? And yet he that knows all this doth not know what he shall be: These are but the displayes of the outward Temple, or holy place; what then is to be seen in the holy of Holies? These are but drops, and rivulets which come in Pipes, and in little portions; how glorious a thing then must it needs be to dwel at the fountain, and swim for ever in those bankless, and bottomless Oceans of Glory? How happy then are the dead in Christ, who are now seeing, tasting, knowing and experiencing these things?

THE DEATH OF A SAINT

1. *When the Saints die let us mourn:* And there is no greater Argument to be found that we should excite our selves to mourn by, then the remembrance that they were *Saints:* it should more effect our hearts at the thoughts of this that they were *Saints*, then that they were our Father, or Mother, or Brethren, or nearest or dearest Friends, for this is that which makes their loss to be greater than any other Relation doth or can; others are natural, but these are pious Tears that

are shed upon this account: Another Man may be a private loss when he is gone, his Family or his Neighbours, or Consorts may miss him; but a *Saint*, though he be a private Christian, is yet, when he dies a, publick loss, and deserves the *tears of Israel;* how much more than when he hath been a Saint providentially put into a capacity of being, and by Grace helpt and enabled to be a publick benefit by the Orb he moved in? when a Saint *Dies* there is manifold ground of Mourning; there is then a Pillar pluckt out of the Building, a Foundation Stone taken out of the Wall, a Man removed out of the Gap; and now it is to be greatly feared that God is departing, and *Calamities* are coming, and are not these *things* to be lamented?

2. *When the Saints die beware of irregular Mourning:* though we are to lament their Death, yet we must beware that it be after the right manner: a dying Saint may say to his weeping Friends that stand round about, wringing their hands, after the same Language that Christ did to those weeping Women, *Luk.* 23. 27, 28, 29. *Daughters of Jerusalem, weep not for me, but for your selves, and your Children,* &c. It is we and not they that are indangered and endamaged by it: we may therefore weep for our selves, and there is good reason for it, but to mourn for them is superfluous. Is their Death precious in Gods? let it not be miserable in our esteem: and tell me you whose hearts throb, and eyes run over with sorrow, is it not a precious thing to be asleep in Jesus? to ly in the lap of his providence, and rest from the labours and sorrows of a troublesome World? to be laid out of the noise of the whistling Winds, and feel none of the impetuosity of those Storms and Tempests that are blowing abroad? to be out of the sight and hearing of the rolling and dashing waves of the roaring Sea? to sleep out the rest of the tempestuous night of this World, standing in the inner Chamber of Gods Providence, in answer to that sweet invitation? *Isai.* 26. 22. *Come my People, enter into thy Chambers, and shut thy doors about thee,* &c. . . .

3. *Is the death of the Saints precious in Gods sight? let it be so in ours too.* They are not to be accounted for contemptible things which God sets an high value upon; and it is our wisdom to think and speak of persons and things as God doth: we ought not to slight the death of the righteous, and speak meanly of it, as of a thing that is little momentous: I am sure their arrival at Heaven is there taken notice of as a thing worthy of observation; and shall not their departure be regarded? they are welcomed into the Palace of delight with *Panegyricks;* and shall then be hence dismissed with no more but a sorry saying, there is now a good Man gone, and he will be missed in the Family, or

the Church to which he once belonged? we should embalm the memory of the Saints with the sweet smelling Spices that grew in their own Gardens, and pick the chiefest Flowers out of those Beds to strew their Graves withal; we should remember and make mention of them with honourable thoughts and words: and though it be now grown a Nick-name of contempt among wicked and prophane Men, yet count it the most orient Jewel in their Crown, the most odoriferous and pleasant Flower in their Garland, that we can say of them that they lived and died Saints; all other Eschutcheons will either wear away, or be taken down, every other monument will become old, and grow over with the Moss of time, and their Titles, though cut in Brass, will be Canker-eaten and illegible: this onely will endure and be fresh and Flourishing, when Marble it self shall be turned into common dust.

Such an one it is whom we have now lost; and Oh that we knew how great a loss we have sustained in him! they are little things to be put into the account, and weigh but light in the commendations we have to give him; to say, This Government hath lost a Magistrate; this Town hath lost a good Benefactor; this Church hath lost an honourable Member; his Company hath lost a worthy Captain; his Family hath lost a loving and kind Husband, Father, Master; the Poor have lost a Liberal and Merciful Friend; that nature had furnished him with a sweet and affable Disposition, and even temper; that Providence had given him a prosperous and Flourishing Portion of this Worlds Goods; that the love and respect of the People had lifted him up to places of honour and preferment; this, this outshines them all; that he was a Saint upon Earth; that he lived like a Saint here, and died the precious Death of a Saint, and now is gone to rest with the Saints in glory: this hath raised those Relicks of his above common dust, and made them precious dust. When Conscience of duty stimulated me to perform my part of his Exequies, and put me upon it to do him honour at his Death; methoughts Justice required, and envy it self would not nibble at this Character: and if the Tree be to be known by its Fruits, his works shall praise him in the Gates: For his constant and close secret Communion with God (which none but Hypocrites are wont to do with the sound of a Trumpet) such as were most intimate with him, have known and can testifie: the care which he had to keep up constant Family Worship, in reading of the Scriptures, and praying in his Family (from which no business publick or private could divert him) was almost now unparalleld; the honourable respect he bore to God's holy Ordinances, by diligently attending upon them, and esteeming highly of God's Servants for their work sake, and care that he used to live the Truths which he heard from time to time, was very singular: the exemplariness of his Life and Converse among Men, and the endeavours which he used to shew forth the Graces of the Spirit, not being ashamed of Christ, nor being willing to be a shame unto him; let all that knew him bear witness of: his meek boldness in reproving Sin, and gentle faithfulness in endeavouring to win Sinners as he had opportunity, is known to such as lay in his way: His constancy in all these whiles times have changed, and many Professors have degenerated, when he strove to grow better as the times grew worse, will speak the sincerity of his Profession: his living above the World, and keeping his heart disentangled, and his mind in Heaven, in the midst of all outward occasions and urgency of Business, bespake him not to be of this World, but a Pilgrim on the Earth, a Citizen of Heaven: In a word, he was a true *Nathaniel.*

But God hath taken him from us, and by this stroak given us one more sad prognostick of misery a coming: when there are but a few Saints in the World, and those die apace too, what is to be thought to be at the door? I dare say his Death was precious in Gods sight, and he had some holy end in taking him away just now, who might probably have lived many years, and done much more service for God in his Generation: I shall not make it my work to Prophesie; the Lord grant we do not all know it too soon to our cost. Mean time let us have such in remembrance, and labour to be followers of them who through Faith and Patience do now inherit the promises, and that will be the best way to divert the Omen: Let us account the *Saints* precious whiles they live, and God will not begrutch them to us: but if we by contempt, obloquy, and wickedly grieving their *Righteous Souls*, make their lives a burden to them; if they cannot live in honour among Men, they shall die in favour with God, and he will make their death a precious gain to them, though it be a direful presage of a great inundation of sad Calamities coming upon those whom they leave behind them.

DEGENERATING NEW ENGLAND

I CONFESS that it must be granted, that in the best times, and in places where the power of Godliness is most flourishing, there have been, and will be those that have not the fear of God before their eyes: there were so in the times of the greatest *Reformation* that we read of in the Book of God. In this world we must expect that

Wicked men will be mixed with the Godly, and such as will dare to shew their wickedness in their Lives, and not be afraid *to Transgress in a Land of Uprightness.* But when such are not countenanced, but due testimony is born against them; when they are contemned in the places where they live, and a note of infamy and scandal is put upon them; this will not be charged on such a people for *Apostasy:* But when such sins grow frequent, and those that have taken on themselves a name of being Religious, begin to indulge themselves herein; and men that allow themselves in such things are not *Reproached* for it, but are in as good Credit as the best, it then becomes a bad symptom, and saith that the times are declining and perilous. Much more when such as these will undertake to justify, and patronize such things: and are there not sad complaints made on this account? I shall here instance only in some that are more notorious. Are not Gods *Sabbaths* wofully neglected? How little care is there used in making of due preparation for them? How wofully can such as would be esteemed Godly, encroach upon holy time, and be engaged, either in secular business, or in vain Company, and possibly in publick houses, when they should be at home, in their Closets, or with their Families, Sanctifying of Gods day, and shewing of the *Honourable esteem* they have for it? And I am well satisfyed, that *where the strict Observation of Gods Sabbath is lost, there the Power of Godliness is gone.* How much complaint is there made of woful *Dishonesty* in their dealings, practised by such as can talk high of their Religion? How many fallacious tricks they can use in their Commerce? How deceitful in their Labour? How false to their words and promises? as if dissembling and lying were no reproach to the name of Christians. How many *Intemperate Church Members* are there reported to be, who spend their precious time in frequenting Publick Houses, and keeping of loose and lewd Company? who can come to the *Lords Table* on the Sabbath, and wrong themselves by excessive Drinking on the week days? How much *Animosity, Contention,* and implacable bitterness of Spirit, breaking forth in indecent words and carriages, between such as are bound in the strongest Evangelical ties to *Love one another, and meekly to bear with each others infirmities?* How much raising, spreading, and receiving of *Slanders* and *Defamations* one of another; contrary to that Charity which ought to *Cover a Multitude of sins?* These, and a great many more of like nature, . . . so far as they spread and prevail, and begin to grow common, are an ill Omen; for, they are indisputable denials of the power of Godliness, at least in the vigour of it, in those who are Guilty of them, for *that teacheth men to Live Soberly, Righteously and Godly.*

SAMUEL SEWALL, 1652–1730

[Samuel Sewall's father first came to New England in 1634, but returned to England, where Samuel was born. The family came back to New England after the Restoration. Samuel graduated from Harvard College in 1671 and was chosen fellow shortly afterwards; for a few years he hesitated between the ministry and a more secular calling, but his mind was made up for him when he married Hannah, the daughter of John Hull, the wealthiest man in the colony; from that time Sewall was a man of substance, with an estate to administer, and with leisure to devote to learned hobbies and the public service. He was manager of the colony's printing press, 1681–84, deputy in the General Court, 1683, a member of the council, 1684–86. In England in 1688, he was of assistance to Increase Mather in the charter negotiations. A member of the council under the new charter, 1692 to 1725; he was a judge in the special court at Salem which tried and executed the supposed witches, and he was of so heroic a mold that five years later he could make public acknowledgment of his error. A justice of the superior court in 1692, he was promoted to judge of probate for Suffolk County, 1715, and from 1718 to 1728 was chief justice of the colony. Sewall's literary fame rests upon his *Diary*, but in his lifetime he published several items. Meditating upon the evil of negro slavery, he wrote and published a small pamphlet, *The Selling of Joseph*, 1700, the first antislavery tract in America. His favorite study was that of Biblical prophecies and their fulfillments; this text is from one of his pamphlets on the meaning of the Book of Revelation, *Phænomena quædam Apocalyptica ad Aspectum Novi Orbis configurata. Or, some few Lines towards a description of the New Heaven As It makes to those who stand upon the New Earth* (Boston, 1697).]

PHÆNOMENA

CAPT. *John Smith* in his History published *Anno* 1624. affirms that he found *New-England* well inhabited with a goodly, strong, and well proportioned People. And the Proverb is, *Shew me the Man, and not the Meat.* And if men can be contented with the Food and Raiment intended in 1 *Tim.* 6. 8. they need not fear subsisting where *Ash, Chesnut, Hazel, Oak* & *Walnut* do naturally and plentifully grow. But for this, let Mr. *Morden* be consulted, to whom *N. E* is beholden for the fair Character given them in his Geographie. It is remark-

able, that Mr. ***Parker*****, who was a successfull Schoolmaster** at *Newbury* in *Barkshire*, in the happy days of Dr. *Twisse;* was much about this time preaching and Proving at *Ipswich* in *Essex*, That the Passengers came over upon good Grounds, and that God would multiply them as He did the Children of *Israel*. His Text was *Exod.* 1. 7. As Mr. *Nicolas Noyes*, who was an Auditor, and is yet living, lately informed me. Mr. *Parker* was at this time; 1634. principally concerned in beginning *Newbury*, where the Learned and Ingenious Mr. *Benjamin Woodbridge*, Dr. *Twisse's* Successor, had part of his Education under his Unckle *Parker*. *Mary Brown* (now *Godfry*) the First-born of *Newbury*, is yet alive; and is become the Mother and Grandmother of many children. And so many have been born after her in the Town, that they make two Assemblies, wherein God is solemnly worshipped every Sabbath Day. And

Besides all that have issued out to begin other Plantations.

As long as *Plum Island* shall faithfully keep the commanded Post; Notwithstanding all the hectoring Words, and hard Blows of the proud and boisterous Ocean; As long as any Salmon, or Sturgeon shall swim in the streams of *Merrimack;* or any Perch, or Pickeril, in *Crane-Pond;* As long as the Sea-Fowl shall know the Time of their coming, and not neglect seasonably to visit the Places of their Acquaintance: As long as any Cattel shall be fed with the Grass growing in the Medows, which do humbly bow down themselves before *Turkie-Hill;* As long as any Sheep shall walk upon *Old Town Hills*, and shall from thence pleasantly look down upon the River *Parker*, and the fruitfull *Marishes* lying beneath; As long as any free and harmless Doves shall find a White Oak, or other Tree within the Township, to perch, or feed, or build a careless Nest upon; and shall voluntarily present themselves to perform the office of Gleaners after Barley-Harvest; As long as Nature shall not grow Old and dote; but shall constantly remember to give the rows of Indian Corn their education, by Pairs: So long shall Christians be born there; and being first made meet, shall from thence be Translated, to be made partakers of the Inheritance of the Saints in Light.

NOTES

Volume I

Chapter I—History

THOMAS SHEPARD

1. Shepard is referring to the years 1629 and 1630, when Parliament had been dissolved, the Laudians securely entrenched in power, and the outlook for Puritans apparently become hopeless; during these years "this great enterprise," the Massachusetts Bay Company, was formed and the migration undertaken. Shepard is writing eighteen years later when the Puritan and parliamentary cause seems to have triumphed, and he must remind his English critics how desperate the situation seemed in 1630.

2. These sentences summarize the intolerable dilemma which the Puritans confronted in 1630, when they were striving to reform the Church of England and yet at the same time not to separate from it or to allow themselves to be forced into the position of "schismatics." The "distinctions" by which Puritans strove to "salve" their consciences were those between the substance and accidents of a true church; they insisted that the Church of England was "true" in substantials, but corrupt in accidentals, such as the episcopal hierarchy. Since the authorities more and more insisted that the bishops and the rituals were essential to the Church of England, it became increasingly difficult for the Puritans to maintain their fine distinctions. The migration to Massachusetts was the only solution for this problem except open revolution.

JOHN WINTHROP

1. Isaac Allerton (1586–1659), an original member of the Plymouth group, the business man and financier of the colony; he later became engaged in somewhat shady trading deals and withdrew from Plymouth to New Haven.

2. John Endecott (1589–1665), governor of the outpost at Salem, continued to be one of the magistrates after Winthrop's arrival, and after Winthrop's death was several times governor; a stern Puritan of the most uncompromising variety, he cut down the Maypole at Merry Mount, caused Winthrop and the government considerable embarrassment when he cut the red cross out of the English flag because it was a Popish emblem, and as governor wrote his name in blood by his persecution of the Quakers.

3. Samuel Skelton (1584–1634), the colleague of Francis Higginson in the ministry of the church at Salem.

4. Nahumkeck was the Indian name for Salem.

5. Winthrop always speaks of himself in the third person.

6. Sir Henry Vane (1613–1662), son of a member of the Privy Council, came to Boston in 1635, and was elected governor in 1636 as a tribute rather to his high social station and influential connections than to his wisdom or experience. His conduct in New England exhibits the worst side of his erratic character; in his subsequent career he was to reveal more lofty and more courageous qualities, though he always was an incurable idealist and visionary, winning the admiration of John Milton and the scorn of Oliver Cromwell. Though not a Regicide, he was leader of the most radical republican sentiment among the Puritans, opposed the Restoration, and was executed on Tower Hill in 1662.

7. Hugh Peter (1598–1660), a vigorous and pugnacious Puritan, one of the first investors in the Massachusetts Bay Company, came to New England in 1635 and was established as minister at Salem, where he reorganized the church shattered by Roger Williams's heresies. He returned to England in 1641 and had a spectacular career as an Independent minister, army chaplain, and rabble-rouser; so conspicuous did he become that upon the Restoration he was executed, though he, like Vane, had not been an actual Regicide.

8. Thomas Dudley (1576–1653), sec-

ond in command to Winthrop, a former soldier and steward to the earl of Lincoln; he was governor in 1634, 1640, 1645, and 1650. A hard, single-minded man, he represents, as against Winthrop, the narrower and harsher features of early Puritanism.

9. See account of John Wilson (1588–1667), p. 552.

10. John Haynes (1594–1654), a man of substance from Essex, came to New England in the same ship with Hooker and Cotton; governor of Massachusetts in 1635, he was a follower of Hooker, moved to Connecticut in 1637, was chosen first governor of Connecticut and served in that office every alternate year until his death.

11. Though perhaps disguised to modern ears by the technical theological jargon, the purport of these opinions is fairly clear. The standard Protestant doctrine was that men were saved by their faith in Christ, not by their works, that Christ had fulfilled the law, satisfied the vengeance of God, and that His righteousness was "imputed" to the saints for their salvation. The legal imputation of Christ's virtue to the credit of man was called "justification"; that is, a man was justified before the tribunal of God because Christ had satisfied God's indictment against him. A justified man was expected thereafter to conduct himself in a Christian manner, or at least to strive to do so; his conduct, after his justification, was called his "sanctification." According to the orthodox view, in the moment of justification the regenerate man received an ability to pursue more or less perfectly a sanctified course of life. The evocation of such an ability was understood to be a work of the Holy Ghost. At the same time, though the impetus might come from the Divine Spirit, though a spiritual power might be thus conveyed into the soul, the individuality of the saint was deemed inviolate, and his effort toward sanctification was to proceed from his own exertions. Regeneration, so to speak, took off the chains that bound a man in sin; thereafter he was to labor as an individual, under the guidance of his own intelligence, to fulfill the law of God.

The theory of Mrs. Hutchinson, though seeming close to the orthodox version, was of a vitalistic, mystical character; by maintaining that "the Holy Ghost dwells in a justified person" she concluded that the saint in the moment of justification received an influx of energy which overwhelmed and obliterated his individuality, carrying him along on a wave of ecstasy; consequently she argued that it made no difference whether he achieved any sanctification whatsoever, that his good or bad conduct cast no light on his salvation, which was a matter entirely of inward spiritual ravishment. Whatever virtues he achieved in his life were not wrought by his own volition, but by the power of the divine spirit working in him. He was merely to surrender his will to the promptings and propulsions from within. In Winthrop's eyes, these doctrines led to the abandonment of all individual moral responsibility, to an ethical anarchy and an uncontrollable self-righteousness which might have very dangerous social consequences.

12. John Wheelwright (1592–1679), B.A., Sidney Sussex College, Cambridge, 1615; M.A., 1618. A brother-in-law of Anne Hutchinson, he emigrated to New England in 1636. After his banishment in 1637 he founded Exeter, New Hampshire; returned to England, 1656–1662; his sentence revoked by the Massachusetts government, he came back to New England and served as minister at Salisbury, 1662–1679.

13. I.e., Winthrop, in this year serving as deputy-governor.

14. I.e., John Wilson. For the distinction between "pastor" and "teacher," see p. 386.

15. Newtown was the original name for Cambridge.

16. According to the Congregational theory of church polity, a synod was not a legislative body, but merely a gathering of learned men for the purposes of discussion and clarification; their decisions were theoretically not binding upon any particular congregation unless the congregation chose to endorse them. Presbyterian Puritans, who upheld the compulsory power of synods (hence Milton's line, "New Presbyter is but Old Priest

writ large"), had criticized the Congregational polity for its lack of a central controlling power, and had predicted that in a crisis the Congregational churches would fall apart. In such works as Shepard and Allin's *Defence of the Answer,* the Congregationalists insisted that the Word of God was so clear that when the ministers would gather to formulate its teachings the results of their deliberations would win instant consent from all right-minded men. In 1637 the majority of the church of Boston were devoted to Mrs. Hutchinson, and upon the success or failure of the synod in bringing that church to the true doctrine depended the success or failure of the whole Bible Commonwealth. When the Antinomians refused to accept the conclusions of the synod the government was compelled to step in and proceed against them as persons opposing the obvious and explicit principles of the true religion. As long as the "advisory" synods of New England were thus backed by the force of the civil authority, they were able to keep the churches in line; after the charter was repealed and the government was no longer willing to enforce Congregational uniformity, the churches were left to their own devices.

17. John Davenport (1597–1670), along with Cotton and Hooker one of the most powerful of New England ministers, came to Boston in 1635, led his followers to New Haven, which colony he dominated until its unification with Connecticut; he then accepted a call from the First Church of Boston, 1668, where his coming precipitated a quarrel that split the church.

18. The formidable list of these errors is in Charles Francis Adams, *Antinomianism in the Colony of Massachusetts Bay* (Boston, 1894), pp. 95–124.

19. The contention that the charter of the Massachusetts Bay Company gave the government power to settle all cases without the possibility of an appeal to the King's courts was certainly unjustified; yet it was doggedly maintained and was the principal reason for the virtual independence enjoyed by the colony of Massachusetts Bay until the charter was revoked in 1684.

20. From the orthodox point of view, Mrs. Hutchinson's admission that she believed she had received special revelations direct from God was proof positive that she had been inspired by evil powers; the canon of revelation was believed closed with the book of Revelation, and though God might continue to betray his wishes and commands in the government of the world and the disposition of particular events, no mortal was any longer to receive commands from Him in so many words. If the possibility of continued revelation from God direct to individuals had been admitted, any man or woman might have claimed divine sanction for any conceivable notion.

21. The scene here described must have been the most dramatic and tragic in the history of New England: Mrs. Hutchinson, arraigned before the church, most of the congregation having been her followers in the beginning of the struggle but now turned against her through the masterful strategy of John Winthrop and the pressure of outside opinion, hearing the sentence pronounced against her by her beloved minister, John Cotton, upon whose words she had hung in England, whom she had followed to New England, and from whom she believed she had derived her teachings. John Cotton's role in the drama leaves much to be explained. If he did not actually proclaim what Mrs. Hutchinson thought he did, he must have used many incautious phrases, and when the storm had gathered he abandoned her entirely. His condemning her before the whole congregation must have been for her like turning the knife in a wound. His position at the moment was extremely precarious, and it was only by his opportune bending to the victorious party and his carrying out their sentence against Anne Hutchinson that he retained his influence in the community. For a moment during the crisis he meditated moving to New Haven; Roger Williams later accused him of contemplating a "separation" from the churches of Massachusetts, and Cotton endeavored to defend himself in what is one of the lamest apologies ever penned by a righteous man (*Master John Cotton's*

Answer to Master Roger Williams, ed. J. Lewis Diman, *Publications of the Narragansett Club*, II, 79–85).

22. The moderation of the militia on this occasion is a tribute to the moral power of religion among the rank and file of the first generation; it was almost unprecedented in the days of "Merrie England" for a thousand Englishmen to gather in one place without drunkenness or quarrelling. By the end of the century the ministers were unanimously complaining that training days were anything but occasions for sober drill.

23. The servant's reply is the closest approach to the humorous in the *Journal*, but to the aristocratic Winthrop the remark did not appear funny, for he wrote in the margin of his manuscript, "insolent."

24. The synod of 1648 drew up the final codification of the New England church polity in *The Cambridge Platform*.

EDWARD JOHNSON

1. Reference to manner in which it was required by law in England that Sunday should be celebrated; in 1618 James I published a declaration permitting dancing, archery, May games, and other sports on Sundays; Charles I endeavored to force the clergy to read this "Booke of Sports" from their pulpits. Many Puritan clergymen were suspended for refusing.

2. The fleeing ministers were disguised as seamen in order to escape from the Court of High Commission, before which many of them were indicted for nonconformity.

3. The "Lady Arrabella," Arbella Johnson, daughter of the earl of Lincoln; she and her husband, Isaac Johnson, sailed with the fleet in 1630, the flagship being named in her honor. They were the wealthiest of the emigrants; both died within a few months of the landing.

4. John Norton (1606–1663), B.A., Peterhouse, Cambridge, 1624; M.A., 1627; came to New England with Shepard in 1635; was ordained teacher at Ipswich; called to the First Church of Boston to succeed Cotton, 1652; along with Governor Endecott he was the leader of the persecution of the Quakers; in 1662 he went as agent for the colony to England, failed to get the expected results, and died an unpopular man.

5. Münster, a town in Germany in which there was a famous outbreak of Anabaptists in 1534; these Anabaptists, convinced that they were God's chosen people, attempted to set up a reign of the saints by putting all the unregenerate to the sword. Münster was a byword for the horrors of direct inspiration, and the possibility that Anne Hutchinson's followers might resort to the Anabaptists' tactics was always present in the minds of the Massachusetts authorities.

6. Cambridge.

7. A slur upon the English army under Cromwell, which, being recruited from many sects, was enforcing a policy of toleration in England at the time Johnson was writing.

COTTON MATHER

1. Persons born in America of European race; a word used at this time most frequently in the West Indies, so that Mather means in particular students coming to Harvard from the West Indies.

2. "Drove forth the eminent pious heroes to withstand so many misfortunes, to undertake so many labors," Vergil, *Aeneid*, I, 9, slightly altered.

3. John Foxe (1516–1587), English Protestant, author of *Acts and Monuments of these latter and perillous Dayes*, in Latin, 1559; in English, 1563; written in exile at Strasbourg during the reign of Queen Mary, the book is a chronicle of the sufferings and martyrdoms of English Protestants. It was read thoroughly by all Puritans of the seventeenth century.

4. John Wyckliffe (*c.* 1320–1384), medieval reformer, who attacked the corruption of the medieval clergy, the supremacy of the Pope, asserted the supremacy of the scriptures as a rule of faith, attacked the theory of transubstantiation; he was regarded by Protestants as a forerunner of the Reformation.

5. Peter Heylin (1600–1662), Anglican clergyman, chaplain to Charles I, violent partisan of Laud, and embittered foe of Puritanism.

6. John Owen (1616–1683), leading Independent minister, chaplain to Cromwell, Vice-Chancellor of Oxford, 1651–1659, minister of a non-conformist church in London after the Restoration. He was invited to come to New England, was a friend and correspondent of many of the New England divines, though in 1669 he wrote to New England reproving the churches for their persecution of Quakers. Reference to *Inquiry concerning Evangelical Churches*, *Works*, ed. Gold, XV, 209.

7. "That they acknowledge themselves never to be perfect."

8. "He calls her fair, not absolutely, but fair among women, that is to say with a distinction, so that she may thereby be more restrained, and may know her deficiencies."

9. For Ramus and his influence in New England see Introduction, pp. 28–39.

10. "Among the many favours with which you have enriched me, this I shall keep in remembrance, which thanks to you I learned through your reply at Poissey, that of the fifteen centuries since Christ, the first is truly golden and that the rest, the further they are removed the more they are wretched and degenerate; therefore when I had free choice, I preferred the golden age." This was the famous statement by which Ramus publicly announced his conversion to Protestantism, 1561.

11. "Remote regions."

12. "Outer darkness."

13. James Howell (*c.* 1594–1666), author of *Epistolae Ho-Elianae*.

14. "An anthology."

15. "History is the witness of time, the messenger of antiquity, the light of truth, the life of memory, the magistrate of life" (Cicero, *De Oratore*, II, 9.)

16. "Rather to be admired than imitated."

17. "A pleasant, faithful and accurate writer." Justus Lipsius (1547–1606), a humanist, scholar, and editor, who chiefly devoted himself to making available the teachings of classical Stoicism.

18. "Sweeter than honey." Photius was patriarch of Constantinople, ninth century; Colerus is Johann Coler, German theologian of the sixteenth century.

19. "A prudent writer, if ever there was one."

20. "Seems to have surpassed all Greek and Latin authors."

21. "In him alone (to speak of historians) the Roman people had a genius worthy of their empire."

22. "Great wars, the storming of cities, kings put to flight and captured."

23. Probably a grammarian of Alexandria at the end of the first century.

24. "Historians are to be read with moderation and kindness, and it is to be remembered that they can not be in all circumstances like Lynceus."

25. Louis Aubery, Seigneur du Maury, d. 1687.

26. "History is the narrative of great actions with praise or blame."

27. "I believe it is the principal function of history not to be silent respecting virtues, and to hold up before depravity, both in word and deed, the dread of infamy with posterity."

28. The name sometimes applied to himself by Claude Saumaise, or Salmasius (1588–1653), the learned scholar with whom Milton disputed.

29. Virgilius of Salzburg was condemned by Pope Zachary, 745, for a treatise on the Antipodes contending that there is another world underneath the earth.

30. Konrad Schlüsselberg (1543–1619), Lutheran theologian.

31. "It is most proper to History, to praise eminent deeds."

32. Professor Murdock interprets this obscure phrase as the equivalent of our "fail to see the woods for the trees."

33. Daniel Chaumier (*c.* 1570–1621), André Rivet (1573–1651), French Calvinist writers.

34. Howell, *Epistolae*, Bk. 1, Sect. 4, Letter xxi.

35. "It is offensive to God when anyone who is like him, excelling in virtue, is dishonoured, or praise given to the contrary."

36. Jacques Auguste de Thou (1553–1617), French historian.

37. "Much that is most false and unworthy."

38. "The simplest style of writing."

39. "Memoirs of ecclesiastical transactions."

40. "Just as salt discreetly sprinkled on food flavors it, and adds to the pleasure of the relish, so if you mingle a little of antiquity, the oration is made more lovely."

41. "I beg pardon for this self-praise."

42. "Every writer is in error about his own writings."

43. Professor Murdock indicates the explanation for this sentence in a passage from William Lambarde, *Perambulation of Kent* (1570), ed. 1826, p. 233: "Our speech at this day (for the most part) consisteth of words of one sillable. Which thing Eramus observing, merily in his Ecclesiast, compareth the English toong to a Dogs barking, that soundeth nothing els, but Baw, waw, waw, in Monosillable."

44. "In a long work."

45. "Before speaking of the thing, a little about myself."

46. "Deliver me from a man of one occupation."

47. "Mistakes."

48. "Egostistical discourse."

49. "He was so incapable of envy that if he came upon any elegant expression of another's it pleased him not less than if it had been his own."

50. I.e., members of the High-Church party in the Church of England.

51. Heinrich Cornelius Agrippa (1487–1535), attacked by the Inquisition for his *De Vanitate et Incertitude Scientiorum*, 1531.

52. "Happy he whom the Lord signalized with this honor, that he may have the most evil men for his enemies."

53. "This I wish, now my verse pleases me" (Martial, *Epig.* VI, 61. 4).

54. A play on words, roughly thus: "He received the stones, to whom Christ was a rock." An example of the bad taste of which Cotton Mather was too capable.

55. Wyckliffe's epitaph, Speed, *History*, ed. 1614, p. 610, or Fuller, *Church History*, ed. 1837, I, 494: "The Devells Instrument, Churches Enemy, Peoples Confusion, Hereticks Idoll, Hypocrites Mirrour, Schismes Broacher, Hatreds Sower, Lyes Forger, Flatteries Sinke: who at his death despaired like Cain, and stricken by the horrible judgment of God, breathed forth his wicked soule to the dark mansion of the black devell."

56. Reference to Solomon Stoddard and the ministers of the Connecticut valley under his leadership, who at the time Mather wrote were inaugurating a change in the church polity whereby all persons in a town not openly scandalous should not only be admitted to the church but also brought to both sacraments. In the next decade Stoddard and the Mathers carried on an acrimonious pamphlet controversy about this question.

57. James Ussher (1581–1656), Anglican clergyman of Calvinistic tenets, Archbishop of Armaugh, a leading moderate who strove to reconcile Anglicans and Puritans and was thoroughly respected by his Puritan opponents.

58. Stephen Marshall (1594–1655), English Puritan, advocate of the Presbyterian polity, but of a more moderate sort than the Scotch variety.

59. Jeremiah Burroughs (1594–1655), Independent divine, a spokesman along with John Owen for Cromwell's policy of toleration.

60. "No one is more oppressive than the ignorant man, because he thinks nothing done correctly unless he does it himself," Terence, *Adelphi*, ll. 98–99.

61. "What am I? Nothing. Who am I? No one. But the Grace of Christ makes what I am, what I live, what I do."

Chapter II—The State and Society

JOHN WINTHROP

1. Reference to the followers of Peter Waldo (fl. 1170) in the Piedmont, a medieval sect that resisted the authority of Rome in the thirteenth and fourteenth centuries and ultimately became merged with the Protestants; they were of great value in Protestant polemic because they could always be cited as an example of a pure and true church existing before Luther and supplying a long tradition for Protestantism.

2. Winthrop is here using one of the favorite arguments of the non-separating Congregational theorists, the contention that the Reformed Churches of the Con-

tinent and the Church of England were "true" churches, even though they maintained a Presbyterian or Episcopalian form of government; the imperfections of their government were to be regarded as unfortunate handicaps which eventually they were certain to overcome, because if they really lived up to their profession of basing their religion upon the Bible they would inevitably reorganize their churches according to the Congregational plan. Therefore, Winthrop is arguing, the settlers of New England, still members of the Church of England and maintaining fellowship with the Protestant Churches of Europe, will realize in America what the others profess but do not yet practice.

3. Note the extension of the doctrine of the covenant between God and the individual saint to include also a theoretical covenant between God and the people as a whole. The doctrine was the foundation for the Puritan theory of social cohesion, of the unified society bound together as one man by an irrevocable covenant with God Himself.

4. In the Congregational polity only those were admitted who could give evidence before the congregation that they bore the visible marks of regeneration upon them.

5. A reference to the heresy broached by Roger Williams two years before. With characteristic generosity, Winthrop is insinuating that in spite of his errors Williams might still be a genuine Christian (cf. Bradford's similar judgment, p. 111), though Winthrop is clear that Williams's errors merited banishment, however holy Williams himself might be.

6. Winthrop here witnesses the first stirrings of libertarian sentiments among the people and the emergence of the purely political attitude toward fundamental law that was ultimately to replace the more complex religious theory of the dual origin of government in the social compact and in the divine covenant.

7. The result of this action was the "Body of Liberties," drawn up by Nathaniel Ward and adopted by the General Court in 1641.

JOHN COTTON

1. William Perkins (1558–1602), one of the greatest of English Calvinists, fellow of Christ's College, Cambridge, influential preacher and pamphleteer; his works were read throughout Protestant countries and in New England.

2. "In order towards things spiritual."

3. "I speak of the plenitude of scripture."

4. "Vigour."

5. "More unseemly to be ejected than not to be admitted."

6. Jean Bodin (1530–1596), French political philosopher.

7. John Robinson, pastor of the Scrooby congregation; being a Separatist and a leader of the most extreme Congregationalists, Robinson might be expected to stress the more democratic features of the polity; hence the effectiveness of Cotton's insisting, first, that by the principles of a purely secular theorist, Bodin, Congregational theory is not democratic, and second, that even by its most radical exponent it is not made into a popular government.

ROGER WILLIAMS

1. "I have liberated my soul."

2. Cotton wrote this statement of the orthodox position in answer to questions addressed to him by a Baptist; the paper fell into Williams's hands and he used it as the text to be refuted in *The Bloudy Tenent,* by means of a dialogue between "Truth" and "Peace."

NATHANIEL WARD

1. "Labour with straddlings."

2. Paracelsus (1490–1541), the famous German physician, had the reputation for being an honest and good but misguided man; he was frequently cited in religious controversy as the supreme example of a well-meaning but dangerous person.

3. True religion is "the fire of proof" which doth "unite the homogeneous and separate the heterogeneous."

4. "The most generic genus."

5. "No evil is worse than liberty for the erring."

6. "Without violation of the state."

7. A "low country," i.e. Holland, where a certain toleration of various Protestant sects was permitted; Holland was a commercial rival of England at the time Ward was writing, and his scornful reference was an appeal to English prejudices.

8. I.e., nothing in the world exists any further than Truth gives it its existence; Truth itself is better than any entity or any good thing, because any created thing derives its being from Truth, and is therefore Truth's "twin."

9. A small javelin.

10. "Mode of speaking."

11. "In what gender."

12. "To speak truth laughing, what hinders?"

13. Traditional formulas for the assents of the King and of the House of Lords to an act of Parliament.

14. Catholic theologians.

15. "No occasion opposes the King."

16. "No occasion assists the King."

17. "In the forum of right reason"; i.e., the prerogatives of the King and the liberties of the subject are so old that they were originally formulated in the Norman or ancient British language, but their validity rests not upon even the most ancient tradition, but upon the dictates of right reason, for time, from the point of view of eternal truth, is a conception as empty of significance as a New England purse is empty of money.

JONATHAN MITCHELL

1. Mitchell's long analysis of the plight of Israel in the days of Nehemiah is clearly a discussion of the condition of New England in 1667; this sermon illustrates the fashion in which New England theorists maintained the exact analogy of the Lord's people in New England with the chosen people of the Old Testament, and therefore endeavored to apply the social and political precedents of Palestine to America.

2. A reference to the charges being levied against Puritan New England by Anglicans and Royalists after the Restoration.

JOHN WISE

1. Reference to the platform for the attempted unification of the Independent and Presbyterian churches drawn up in London, 1690. Increase Mather, then in England negotiating for the charter, had assisted in the preparation of this declaration, and he and Cotton were constantly citing it in an effort to prove to English and European Protestants that the New England way was not a peculiar or provincial system. Consequently enemies of the Mathers found it strategic to quote to the London ministers against the Mathers whenever possible; the founders of the Brattle Street Church and Solomon Stoddard had already shown Wise the advantage of this maneuver.

2. Samuel Pufendorf, 1632–1694, German theologian and philosopher, author of *De Jure Naturæ et Gentium*, one of the chief sources for eighteenth-century conceptions of natural law; it was translated into English by Basil Kennett, 1703. Wise leans heavily upon it throughout his argument.

3. Probably Archibald Johnston, Lord Warrington, Scottish judge and statesman.

4. Note that at this point Wise is simply setting aside all consideration of man as basically corrupted and inherently depraved, thus marking his departure from traditional Puritan theology.

5. Compare this statement with Winthrop's theory (p. 207), in which divine grace must assist reason before man can submit himself to the rule of justice and equity.

JOHN BARNARD

1. "From the divine King"; "Is it not from Zeus?"

2. John Tillotson (1630–1694), Archbishop of Canterbury, famous preacher of the moderate Anglican party, led the movement toward the simple, clear style in pulpit oratory and toward common-sense ethics and comprehensible teaching instead of theological complexities and intricate doctrines; that Barnard should quote Tillotson was equivalent to wearing the badge of the liberal school of thought.

Chapter III—This World and the Next

JOHN COTTON

1. See note, p. 766, for the distinction between justification and sanctification. It was probably Cotton's preaching in the vein represented by this passage that led Mrs. Hutchinson to conclude that sanctification or righteous behavior had nothing to do with whether or not one was saved, and from Cotton's strong insistence upon considering the motives from which good conduct springs rather than the goodness of the actions themselves she derived the dangerous idea that the quality of one's actions was of no consequence and that all one need be concerned about was being informed with the true spirit.

INCREASE MATHER

1. Such examples also give point to Hooker's remarks on the attitude of converted sinners toward the ministers who have wrought their repentance, pp. 309–314.

2. Dr. Thomas Goodwin (1600–1680), Independent divine, a leader of the Independent party in the Westminster Assembly, friend of Cotton and Davenport.

3. Franz Junius (1545–1602), French Huguenot divine.

4. Mather's admisson that eclipses of the sun and moon follow a regular and "unfailable" course and therefore may be predicted with certainty, with his restriction of God's unpredictable actions to the realm of "contingent things," indicates the beginning of clerical concessions to the scientific account of the universe.

5. Waldo and Waldenses, cf. note p. 770.

6. St. Augustine.

URIAN OAKES

1. "Bread for Belisarius."

2. "An honest good," i.e., intrinsically good; "an expedient good," i.e., conducible to good.

3. Dr. John Preston (1587–1628), famous Puritan divine and leader, Master of Emmanuel College, 1622; he exerted a profound influence on the first generation of New England Puritans, many of whom studied under him at Cambridge, all of whom read his works; from his sermons the New England ministers derived the particular features of their doctrine of the Covenant of Grace.

4. "We came, we saw, we conquered"—a paraphrase of Caesar's famous message.

5. Reference to King Philip's War, 1674–1676, in which the male population of New England was decimated.

JOSHUA MOODY

1. Reference to the battle tactics employed at the period, when reloading took time; troops were drawn up in three ranks, the first firing at the command "discharge," retiring to the rear to load their weapons at the command "fall off"; the second rank would then fire and retire, the third in turn, and the first rank be back in action once more.

BIBLIOGRAPHIES

Volume I

I. HISTORICAL BACKGROUND

Inevitably a bibliography in which so many divisions obtain must occasionally seem arbitrarily constructed. Additional historical items will be found in Sections IV (Manners) and V (Biography). From the earliest times New England has been more felicitously interpreted by historians than by any other single group. The number of important studies, from those of Thomas Hutchinson to those of Charles McL. Andrews, runs to a formidable length.

A. Primary Sources

Only sources of colonial history which deal with the Puritan colonies have been included.

Acts and Resolves, Public and Private, of the Province of the Massachusetts Bay, The, Boston, 1869–1922, 21 vols. (Records from 1691.)

Andrews, Charles McL., ed., *Narratives of the Insurrections, 1675–1690*, Original Narratives Series, New York, 1915; 1959.

Bartlett, John R., ed., *Records of the Colony of Rhode Island and Providence Plantations, in New England*, Providence, 1856–1865, 10 vols.

Bishop, George, *New-England Judged, Not by Man's, but the Spirit of the Lord*, London, 1661. Second part, London, 1667. Both parts, London, 1703. (Quaker attack on the Puritan regime.)

Bradford, William, "A Description and Historical Account of New England in verse; from a MS.," *Collections of the Massachusetts Historical Society*, first series, III (1794), 77–84.

—— *History of Plymouth Plantation, 1606–1646*. First printed in *Collections of the Massachusetts Historical Society*, fourth series, III (1856); the best edition is that of Worthington C. Ford, Boston, 1912; in Original Narratives Series, ed. William T. Davis, New York, 1908; 1959. Cf. *Of Plymouth Plantation*, ed., Samuel Eliot Morison with a "Modern (*not* modernized) text," notes, and an extended introduction. New York, 1952.

Calder, Isabel M., ed., *Colonial Captivities, Marches and Journeys*, New York, 1935.

Child, Major John, *New-Englands Jonas cast up at London*, London, 1647. Reprinted in *Collections of the Massachusetts Historical Society*, second series, IV (1816), 107–120.

Church, Benjamin, *Entertaining Passages Relating to Philip's War which Began in the Month of June, 1675*, Boston, 1716. Frequently reprinted; ed. Henry M. Dexter, Boston, 1865–1867, 2 vols.

Clarke, John, *Ill News from New-England; Or, A Narative of New-Englands Persecution*, London, 1652; reprinted in *Collections of the Massachusetts Historical Society*, fourth series, II (1854), 1–113. (An attack upon orthodox Puritanism by an Anabaptist.)

Donnan, Elizabeth, ed., *Documents Illustrative of the History of the Slave Trade to America*, Washington, 1930–1935, 4 vols. (Vol. I, 1441–1700; important contribution to colonial economic history.)

Dow, George F., ed., *Records and Files of the Quarterly Courts of Essex County, Massachusetts [1636–1692]*, Salem, 1911–1921, 8 vols.

Drake, Samuel G., ed., *The Old Indian Chronicle; being a Collection of Exceeding Rare Tracts*, Boston, 1836.

Dreuillettes, Father Gabriel, "Narrative of a Journey to New England, 1650," *The Jesuit Relations and Allied Documents . . . 1610–1791* (ed. Reuben G. Thwaites, Cleveland, 1896–1901, 73 vols.) XXXVI, 83–111.

Dudley, Thomas, "Letter to the Countess of Lincoln," in Joshua Scottow, *Massachusetts*, pp. 36–47; Boston, 1696; also in *Collections of the Massachusetts Historical*

Society, first series, Vol. VIII (1802); *Collections of the New Hampshire Historical Society*, Vol. IV (1834), 224–249; Force, *Tracts*, Vol. II, No. 4; Young, *Chronicles of the First Planters*. (Written in the first year of the settlement, the latter remains fresh and vivid with the very flavor of the early months.)

Force, Peter, *Tracts and Other Papers Relating Principally to the Origin, Settlement, and Progress of the Colonies in North America*, Washington, 1836–1846, 4 vols; New York, 1947.

Foxcroft, Thomas, *Observations Historical and Practical, on the Rise and Primitive State of New-England*, Boston, 1730. (Celebration of the first centennial of Massachusetts Bay.)

Gookin, Daniel, "An Historical Account of the Doings and Sufferings of The Christian Indians in New England, in the years 1675, 1676, 1677," *Transactions and Collections of the American Antiquarian Society*, II (1836), 423–534.

—— *Historical Collections of the Indians in New England* (preface dated 1674), Boston, 1792; also in *Collections of the Massachusetts Historical Society*, first series, I (1792), 141–227.

Gorton, Samuel, *Simplicities Defence against Seven-Headed Policy*, London, 1646; Force, *Tracts*, Vol. IV (1846), No. 6. (A heated but inchoate onslaught upon the Puritan regime by a religious visionary.)

Groome, Samuel, *A Glass For the People of New-England*, London, 1676; reprinted in *Magazine of History*, XXXVII (1929), No. 3, 1–44. (A Quaker tract against the Massachusetts Bay Colony.)

Haller, William, ed., *The Leveller Tracts, 1647–1653*, New York, 1944.

Hart, Albert B., ed., *American History Told by Contemporaries*, New York, 1897–1929, 5 vols. (Vols. I and II cover the Puritan period.)

Higginson, Francis, *New-England Plantation; Or, A Short and True Description of the Commodities and Discommodities of that Countrey*, London, 1630; *Collections of the Massachusetts Historical Society*, first series, I (1792), 117–124; Force, *Tracts*, Vol. I, No. 12; Young, *Chronicles*, pp. 239–267, with introduction; *Proceedings of the Massachusetts Historical Society*, LXII (1930), 301–321. (Written by the first minister at Salem, who came with the advance guard in 1629; the initial reactions of Englishmen to the new scene.)

—— *A True Relacion of the Last Voyage to New England*, MS. prepared 1629; first printed in Hutchinson, *A Collection of Papers*, Boston, 1769; also in Young, *Chronicles*, pp. 213–239; *Proceedings of the Massachusetts Historical Society*, LXII (1930), 281–299. (Journal of the voyage of the advance contingent of the Massachusetts Bay Colony in 1629.)

Hoadly, Charles J., ed., *Records of the Colony and Plantation of New Haven, from 1638 to 1649*, Hartford, 1857.

—— *Records of the Colony or Jurisdiction of New Haven, from May, 1653, to the Union*, Hartford, 1858.

Howgil, Francis, *The Popish Inquisition Newly Erected in New-England*, London, 1659. (Quaker attack on New England orthodoxy.)

Hubbard, William, *A General History of New-England, from the Discovery to MDCLXXX*. First printed from MS. in *Collections of the Massachusetts Historical Society*, second series, Vols. V–VI (1815); best edd., Boston, 1848, 1878. (Written in 1680 at the request of and by subsidy from the General Court, it is based chiefly on Bradford and Winthrop, but inserts some items not found elsewhere. It was used by Cotton Mather and Thomas Prince in compiling their histories.)

—— *A Narrative of the Troubles with the Indians In New-England*, Boston, 1677; ed. Samuel G. Drake, Roxbury, Mass., 1865, 2 vols.

Hutchinson, Thomas, comp., *A Collection of Original Papers Relative to the History of the Colony of Massachusets-Bay*, Boston, 1769; reprinted Albany, 1865, 2 vols. (An invaluable collection, containing documents of fundamental importance, the originals of which were lost at the time of the Revolution.)

Jensen, Merrill, ed., *English Historical Documents*, Vol. IX; *American Colonial Documents to 1776*, New York, 1955. (Contains basic documents and a useful bibliography of both primary and secondary works relating to American colonial history, 1607–1776.)

Johnson, Edward, *A History of New-England. From the English planting in the*

Yeere 1628, untill the Yeere 1652 . . . [better known by its running-title:] *The Wonder-working Providence of Sions Saviour in New England*, London, 1654; ed. William F. Poole, Andover, Mass., 1867; *Collections of the Massachusetts Historical Society*, second series, Vols. II, III, IV, VII, VIII (1814–1819); reprinted, 1826, 1846; ed. J. F. Jameson, Original Narratives Series, New York, 1910; 1959. (A history of the migration and first two decades of settlement, written by a layman, a militia captain, and a settler of the town of Woburn. It is valuable in that it represents the point of view of the rank and file, although in a florid style not characteristically Puritan.)

Josselyn, John, *An Account of Two Voyages to New-England*, London, 1675; reprinted in *Collections of the Massachusetts Historical Society*, third series, III (1833), 211–354. (Not a Puritan, the author is sometimes refreshingly critical of men and manners.)

—— *New-Englands Rarities Discovered: in Birds, Beasts, Fishes, Serpents, and Plants of that Country*, London, 1672; reprinted, ed. E. Tuckerman, *Transactions and Collections of the American Antiquarian Society*, IV (1860), 133–238.

Lechford, Thomas, "Note-Book Kept by Thomas Lechford, Esq., Lawyer, In Boston, Massachusetts Bay, From June 27, 1638, to July 29, 1641," ed. E. E. Hale, *Transactions and Collections of the American Antiquarian Society*, Vol. VII (1885). (Lechford, no Puritan, was a lawyer who came to Massachusetts to make a living; he could not overcome the Puritan prejudice against lawyers, and was debarred for trying to influence a jury. Leaving wife and goods, he returned to England. An invaluable firsthand record of daily life in New England.)

—— *Plain Dealing; Or, Newes from New-England*, London, 1642; reissued in 1644 with a new title; printed in *Collections of the Massachusetts Historical Society*, third series, III (1833), 55–128; also ed. J. H. Trumbull, in *Library of New England History*, No. 4, Boston, 1867. (An attack on Puritans, but surprisingly judicious.)

Lincoln, Charles H., ed., *Narratives of the Indian Wars, 1675–1699*, Original Narratives Series, New York, 1913.

MacDonald, William, ed., *Select Charters and Other Documents Illustrative of American History, 1606–1775*, New York, 1899.

Mason, John, *A Brief History of the Pequot War*, first printed in part in Increase Mather, *A Relation*, 1677; reprinted by Thomas Prince (who identified the author), Boston, 1736; ed. Charles Orr, *History*, Cleveland, 1897; *Collections of the Massachusetts Historical Society*, second series, VIII (1819), 120–153.

Masters, John, "Letter to Lady Barrington and Others, March 14, 1630/1," *New England Historical and Genealogical Register*, XCI (1937), 68–71.

Mather, Cotton, *A Brief Account of the State of the Province of the Massachusetts-Bay in New-England, Civil and Ecclesiastical*, Boston, 1717.

—— *Magnalia Christi Americana*, London, 1702; reprinted, ed. Thomas Robbins, Hartford, 1853–1855, 2 vols. (The *omnium gatherum* of seventeenth-century New England, which could appropriately be listed under every section in this bibliography. A work of monumental scholarship that is amazingly accurate and perceptive. Cf. Preface, *Selections from Cotton Mather*, ed. K. B. Murdock, New York, 1926, for best critical estimate.)

—— "Political Fables" (MS. *ca.* 1692), *Collections of the Massachusetts Historical Society*, third series, Vol. I (1825), 126–133; *The Andros Tracts*, Boston, 1868–1874, II, 325–332; reprinted in part, Murdock, *Selections*, pp. 363–371, with introduction. (In the form of beast fables Mather defends the government of New England under Phips against his detractors.)

—— *The Present State of New-England*, Boston, 1690.

Mather, Increase, *A Brief History of the Warr With the Indians in New-England*, Boston, 1676; reprinted, ed. S. G. Drake, under the title *The History of King Philip's War*, Boston and Albany, 1862.

—— *A Relation Of the Troubles which have hapned in New-England, By Reason of the Indians there*, Boston, 1677; ed. S. G. Drake, under the title *Early History of New England*, Albany, 1864.

Morton, George, comp., *Mourt's Relation*. First published as *A Relation or Journall of the beginning and proceedings of the English Plantation setled at Plimoth*, London,

1622; abbreviated in *Purchas his Pilgrims*, London, 1625, Bk. X, ch. iv; *Collections of the Massachusetts Historical Society*, first series, VIII (1802), 203–239; second series, IX (1822), 26–73; ed. Henry M. Dexter, Boston, 1865. (A minute diary of events from November, 1620, to December, 1621, and probably the joint work of Bradford and Winslow. It is continued by Winslow as *Good Newes from New-England*, London, 1624. Often reprinted.)

Morton, Nathaniel, *New-England's Memoriall*, Cambridge, 1669; facsimile ed. by Arthur Lord. Boston, Club of Odd Volumes, 1903.

Morton, Thomas, *New English Canaan*, Amsterdam, 1637; ed. Charles F. Adams, Boston, 1883. (A riotous attack on the Puritans by a gentleman of questionable antecedents who clashed with the authorities of both Plymouth and Massachusetts Bay, and was expelled for conduct which they considered both immoral and dangerous.)

Noble, John, ed., *Records of the Court of Assistants of the Colony of the Massachusetts Bay, 1630–1692*, Boston, 1901–1904, 2 vols.; Vol. III, ed. John F. Cronin, 1928.

Penhallow, Samuel, *History of the Wars of New England*, Boston, 1726; Cincinnati, 1859.

Prince, Thomas, *A Chronological History of New-England In the Form of Annals*, Boston, 1736–1755, 2 vols.; reprinted in *Collections of the Massachusetts Historical Society*, second series, VII (1818), 189–295.

Public Records of the Colony of Connecticut, The, Hartford, 1850–1890, 15 vols. Vols. 1–3, ed. J. H. Trumbull; vols. 4–15, ed. C. J. Hoadly. (Vols. 1–7 contain records from 1636 to 1735.)

Records of the Colony of New Plymouth in New England, Boston, 1855–1861, 12 vols. in 10. Vols. 1–8, ed. Nathaniel B. Shurtleff; vols. 9–12, ed. David Pulsifer.

Records of the Suffolk County Court, 1671–1680, Publications of the Colonial Society of Massachusetts, Vols. XXIX, XXX (1933). Introduction by Zechariah Chafee, Jr.

Rowlandson, Mary (White), *The Sovereignty & Goodness of God, Together, with the Faithfulness of His Promises Displayed*, 2nd ed., Cambridge, 1682; facsimile reprint, ed. H. S. Nourse and J. E. Thayer, Lancaster, Mass., 1903; ed. Frederick L. Weis, Boston, 1930. Reprinted frequently under title, *The Narrative of the Capativity . . . of Mrs. Mary Rowlandson.*

Scottow, Joshua, *Massachusetts; Or, The first Planters of New-England, The End and Manner of their coming thither, and Abode there*, Boston, 1696.

—— *A Narrative Of The Planting of the Massachusets Colony Anno 1628*, Boston, 1694; reprinted in *Collections of the Massachusetts Historical Society*, fourth series, IV (1858), 279–330.

Shurtleff, Nathaniel B., ed., *Records of the Governor and Company of the Massachusetts Bay*, Boston, 1853–1854, 5 vols. in 6. (Covering the period 1628–1686.)

Smith, John, *Advertisements For the unexperienced Planters of New-England, or any where*, London, 1631; reprinted in *Collections of the Massachusetts Historical Society*, third series, III (1833), 1–53. ("Promotion" literature designed to draw settlers to New England.)

—— *A Description of New England: or the Observations, and Discoveries, of Captain John Smith*, London, 1616; reprinted in *Collections of the Massachusetts Historical Society*, third series, VI (1837), 95–140.

Stearns, Raymond P., ed., "Correspondence of John Woodbridge, Jr., and Richard Baxter," *New England Quarterly*, X (1937), 557–583.

Ward, Ned, *A Trip to New-England*, London, 1699; reissued by the Club for Colonial Reprints, ed. G. P. Winship, Providence, 1905. (A libellous pamphlet with amusing passages on the peccadilloes of New Englanders.)

White, John, *The Planters Plea; or, The Grounds of Plantations examined*, London, 1630; facsimile, ed. Marshall H. Saville, The Sandy Bay Historical Society, Rockport, Mass., 1930; reprinted in *Proceedings of the Massachusetts Historical Society*, LXII (1929), 367–425. (A defense of the project for settling Massachusetts Bay, written by an English minister, and published while the fleet was on the water.)

Whitmore, William H., ed., *The Andros Tracts: being a Collection of Pamphlets and Official Papers*, Boston, 1868–1874, 3 vols. (A collection of original narratives concerning the Andros regime, 1686–1689, and the revolution of 1689; important sources for general history and for political theory and tradition.)

Williams, John, *The Redeemed Captive, returning to Zion*, Boston, 1707; reprinted constantly; Springfield, Mass., 1908, with bibliography. (The most popular of all narratives of captivity, a "best seller" for a century.)

Winslow, Edward, *Good Newes from New-England*, London, 1624; abbreviated in *Purchas his Pilgrims*, London, 1625, Bk. X, ch. v; reprinted in *Collections of the Massachusetts Historical Society*, first series, VIII (1802), 239–276; also second series, IX (1822), 74–104; also fourth series, I (1852), 195–218 (where it is presented in hendecasyllabic couplets as well as in prose, from the London, 1648, edition). Reprinted in Edward Arber, *The Story of the Pilgrim Fathers*, London, 1897.

—— *Hypocrisie Unmasked: by A true Relation of the Proceedings of the Governour and Company of the Massachusets against Samuel Gorton*, London, 1646; ed. H. M. Chapin, Providence, 1916.

—— *New-Englands Salamander, discovered by an irreligious and scornefull Pamphlet, called New-Englands Jonas*, London, 1647; reprinted in *Collections of the Massachusetts Historical Society*, third series, II (1830), 110–145. (A reply to Major John Child, in defense of Massachusetts.)

Winthrop, John, *Winthrop's Journal "History of New England," 1630–1649*, ed. James K. Hosmer, Original Narratives Series, New York, 1908, 2 vols.; the best edition is that of James Savage, Boston, 1825–1826. (Invaluable account from the pen of the first governor of Massachusetts Bay Colony.)

Wood, William, *New Englands Prospect*, London, 1634, 1635, 1639; ed. C. Deane, Boston, 1865; ed. H. W. Boynton, Boston, 1898.

Young, Alexander, ed., *Chronicles of the First Planters of the Colony of Massachusetts Bay, from 1623 to 1636*, Boston, 1846.

—— *Chronicles of the Pilgrim Fathers . . . from 1602 to 1625*, Boston, 1841.

B. Secondary Works

Consult also Section II B of this bibliography.

Adams, Brooks, *The Emancipation of Massachusetts*, Boston, 1887; Houghton-Mifflin paperback with introduction by Perry Miller, 1962. (A vigorous onslaught, inspired by a militant liberalism, upon what the author calls the tyranny of the Puritan priest.)

Adams, Charles Francis, *Three Episodes of Massachusetts History*, Boston, 1892, 2 vols. (The best account of the Antinomian affair.)

Adams, Elizabeth L., "The Wars of New England," *More Books*, XV (1940), 87–101. (An analysis of a manuscript version of Penhallow's history.)

Adams, James Truslow, *The Founding of New England*, Boston, 1921. (An interpretation in terms of "economic and imperial relations," confessedly hostile to the Puritan way of thought.)

—— *Revolutionary New England, 1691–1776*, Boston, 1923.

Akagi, Roy H., *The Town Proprietors of the New England Colonies . . . 1620–1770*, Philadelphia, 1924.

Andrews, Charles McL., *The Beginnings of Connecticut, 1632–1662*, New Haven, 1934.

—— *The Colonial Background of the American Revolution*, New Haven, 1924; Yale paperback, 1959.

—— *The Colonial Period*, New York, 1912. (Excellent brief summary.)

—— *The Colonial Period of American History*, IV vols., New Haven, 1934–1938. (The standard history; the culmination of a lifetime of work by the foremost authority on the field.)

—— *Colonial Self-Government, 1652–1689* (*The American Nation*, Vol. V), New York, 1904.

—— *The Fathers of New England*, New Haven, 1919. Vol. VI of *Chronicles of America*, ed. Allen Johnson. (Popular presentation.)

—— *Our Earliest Colonial Settlements*, New York, 1933.

—— *The Rise and Fall of the New Haven Colony, Publications of the Tercentenary Commission of the State of Connecticut*, New Haven, 1936.

—— *The River Towns of Connecticut*, Baltimore, 1889.

Arnold, Samuel G., *History of the State of Rhode Island and Providence Plantations*, 4th ed., New York, 1894, 2 vols.

Bailyn, Bernard, "The Apologia of Robert Keayne," *William and Mary Quarterly*, VII (1950), 568–587. (A study of the New England merchant and the Puritan ethic.)

—— "Kinship and Trade in Seventeenth-Century New England," *Explorations in Entrepreneurial History*, VI (1953–1954), no. 4.

——, and Lotte Bailyn, *Massachusetts Shipping, 1697–1714: A Statistical Study*, Cambridge, 1959. (A statistical study of the Massachusetts shipping registry.)

—— *The New England Merchants in the Seventeenth Century*, Cambridge, 1955. (Economic history in human terms.)

Banks, Charles E., *The Planters of the Commonwealth . . . 1620–1640*, Boston, 1930.

Barnes, Viola F., *The Dominion of New England*, New Haven, 1923. (The Andros regime, 1686–1689.)

—— "Richard Wharton, A Seventeenth Century New England Colonial," *Publications of the Colonial Society of Massachusetts*, XXVI (1927), 238–270.

Beard, Charles A., and Mary R., *The Rise of American Civilization*, New York, 1927, 2 vols.; revised and enlarged, 1933. (Brilliant study of American development, stressing chiefly social and economic aspects; the section on New England is regrettably brief.)

Bebb, Evelyn D., *Noncomformity and Social and Economic Life, 1660–1800*, London, 1935.

Becker, Carl L., *Beginnings of the American People*, New York, 1915; Cornell Univeristy Press paperback, 1958.

Bining, Arthur C., *British Regulation of the Colonial Iron Industry*, Philadelphia, 1933.

Boorstin, Daniel J., *The Americans: the Colonial Experience*, New York, 1958.

Bowen, Richard Le Baron, *Early Rehoboth: Documented Historical Studies of Families and Events in This Plymouth Colony Township*, 4 vols., Concord, N. H., 1945–1950. (A model of local history.)

—— *The Providence Oath of Allegiance and Its Signers, 1651–1652*, Providence, 1943.

—— *Rhode Island Colonial Money and Its Counterfeiting, 1647–1726*, Concord, N. H., 1942.

—— "The 1690 Tax Revolt of Plymouth Colony Towns," *Register, New England Historical and Genealogical Society*, CXII (1958), 4–14; reprinted in *Collected Papers: Armorial, Genealogical and Historical*, Rehoboth, 1959.

Buffinton, Arthur H., "The Isolationist Policy of Colonial Massachusetts," *New England Quarterly*, I (1928), 158–177.

—— "The Massachusetts Experiment of 1630," *Publications of the Colonial Society of Massachusetts*, XXXII (1937), 308–320.

Burrage, Champlin, *The Early English Dissenters in the Light of Recent Research*, Cambridge, Eng., 1912, 2 vols.

Burrage, Henry S., *The Beginnings of Colonial Maine 1602–1658*, Portland, 1914.

Byington, Ezra H., *The Puritan as a Colonist and Reformer*, Boston, 1899.

—— *The Puritan in England and New England*, Boston, 1896.

Calder, Isabel M., *The New Haven Colony*, New Haven, 1934. (An admirable and definitive study.)

Cambridge Modern History, The, Vol. VII, 2nd ed., New York, 1924. Chapter I, "The Colonies, 1607–1700"; Chapter II, "The Colonies, 1700–1763." ("Cheap edition," 1934, without bibliographies.)

Campbell, Mildred, "Social Origins of Some Early Americans," *Seventeenth-Century America: Essays in Colonial History*, ed., James Morton Smith, Chapel Hill, 1959, 63–89. (It was the "middling people" that provided the bulk of English migration to America in the second half of the seventeenth century.)

Carman, Harry J., *Social and Economic History of the United States*, Boston, 1930. Vol. I, *From Handicraft to Factory, 1500–1820*.

Caulkins, Frances M., *History of New London, Connecticut*, New London, 1852. (A good history of an important town.)

Channing, Edward, *History of the United States*. Vol. I (New York, 1905), *The Planting . . . 1000–1660;* Vol. II (1908), *A Century of Colonial History, 1660–1760*.

Clark, George N., *The Later Stuarts*.

1660–1714, Oxford, 1934. (The best handbook for English background; excellent bibliography.)

Clarke, Mary Patterson, *Parliamentary Privilege in the American Colonies*, New Haven, 1943.

Crouse, Nellis M., "Causes of the Great Migration," *New England Quarterly*, V (1932), 3–36.

Curti, Merle, *The Growth of American Thought*, New York and London, 1943; 1951. (A social history of American thought.)

Dexter, Henry M., *The England and Holland of the Pilgrims*, Boston, 1905.

Dorfman, Joseph, *The Economic Mind in American Civilization 1609–1865*, New York, 1946. (See Vol. I, Book 1, "Colonial America.")

Douglas, Charles H. J., *The Financial History of Massachusetts*, New York, 1892.

Dow, George F., and John H. Edmonds, *The Pirates of the New England Coast, 1630–1730*, Salem, 1923.

Dow, George F., "Shipping and Trade in Early New England," *Proceedings of the Massachusetts Historical Society*, LXIV (1932), 185–210.

—— "The Topsfield Copper Mines," *Proceedings of the Massachusetts Historical Society*, LXV (1933), 570–580.

Doyle, John A., *The English in America*. Vols. II and III, *The Puritan Colonies*, London, 1887.

Dunn, Richard S., "Seventeenth Century English Historians," *Seventeenth-Century America: Essays in Colonial History*, ed,, James Morton Smith, Chapel Hill, 1959, 195–225. (Traces the separate evolutions of the English and American historical tradition.)

Ellis, Arthur B., *History of the First Church in Boston, 1630–1880*, Boston, 1881.

Ellis, George E., *The Puritan Age and Rule in the Colony of the Massachusetts Bay, 1629–1685*, New York, 1888.

Field, Edward, ed., *State of Rhode Island and Providence Plantations*, Boston, 1902, 3 vols.

Foote, Henry W., *Annals of King's Chapel*, Boston, 1882–1896, 2 vols.

French, Allen, *Charles I and the Puritan Upheaval: A Study of the Causes of the Great Migration*, London, 1955; Boston, 1956.

Friedman, Lee M., *Early American Jews*, Cambridge, 1934.

Friis, Herman R., "A Series of Population Maps of the Colonies and the United States, 1625–1790," *Geographical Review*, XXX (1940), 463–470.

Fullerton, Kemper, "Calvinism and Capitalism," *Harvard Theological Review*, XXI (1928), 163–195.

Goodman, Abram Vossen, *American Overture: Jewish Rights in Colonial Times*, Philadelphia, 1947.

Gottfried, Marion H., "The First Depression in Massachusetts," *New England Quarterly*, IX (1936), 655–678.

Graham, Ian C. C., *Colonists from Scotland: Emigrants to North America, 1707–1783*, Ithaca, 1956.

Greene, Evarts B., *Provincial America, 1690–1740*, New York, 1905. (Vol. VI in *The American Nation: A History*, ed. A. B. Hart.)

Greene, Evarts B., and Virginia D. Harrington, *American Population before the Federal Census of 1790*, New York, 1932. (The best available data.)

Greene, Lorenzo Johnson, *The Negro in Colonial New England, 1620–1776*, New York, 1942.

Griffith, Ernest S., *History of American City Government; The Colonial Period*, New York, 1938. (Institutional and political history.)

Gutstein, Morris A., *The Story of the Jews of Newport, 1658–1908*, New York, 1936.

Hall, Albert H., "How Massachusetts Grew, 1630–1642," *Publications of the Cambridge Historical Society*, XXI (1936), 14–49.

Halsey, Abigail Fithian, *In Old Southampton*, New York, 1940. (From the founding by men from Lynn, Massachusetts [1640], through the Revolutionary War.)

Hansen, Marcus L., *The Atlantic Migration, 1607–1860*, Cambridge, 1940; Harper Torchbook edition, 1961.

Hart, Albert B., ed., *Commonwealth History of Massachusetts*, New York, 1927–1930, 5 vols.

Hartley, E. N., *Ironworks on the Saugus: The Lynn and Braintree Ventures of the Company of Undertakers of the Ironworks in New England*, Norman, 1957. (The story of iron-making in seventeenth-century America.)

Hill, Hamilton A., *History of the Old South Church*, Boston, 1890, 2 vols. (One of the most valuable of local church histories, covering the period 1669–1884.)

Holmes, Abiel, *The Annals of America*, Cambridge, 1805; 2nd ed. 1829. (Vol. I, 1492–1732.)

Hooker, Roland M., *The Colonial Trade of Connecticut, Publications of the Tercentenary Commission of the State of Connecticut*, 1936.

Howard, Leon, "The Puritans in Old and New England," *Anglo-American Cultural Relations in the Seventeenth and Eighteenth Centuries*, Leon Howard and Louis B. Wright, Los Angeles, 1959, ch. I.

Hutchinson, Thomas, *The History of the Colony of Massachusetts-Bay*, Boston, 1764–1828, 3 vols.; ed. Lawrence S. Mayo, Cambridge, 1936, 3 vols. (Both a history and a source book; indispensable; should be used in the Mayo ed.)

—— "Additions to Thomas Hutchinson's *History of Massachusetts-Bay*," ed. Catherine Barton Mayo, *Proceedings of the American Antiquarian Society*, LIX (1949), 13–74.

Jernegan, Marcus W., *The American Colonies, 1492–1750. A Study of Their Political, Economic and Social Development*, New York, 1929. (Vol. I in *Epochs of American History*. The best one-volume survey of the period, extremely compact; the bibliographies cull the best works published before 1929.)

—— *Laboring and Dependent Classes in Colonial America, 1607–1783*, Chicago, 1931; 1960.

Johnson, Edgar A. J., "Some Evidence of Mercantilism in the Massachusetts-Bay," *New England Quarterly*, I (1928), 371–396.

Jones, Howard M., "The Colonial Impulse: An Analysis of the 'Promotion' Literature of Colonization," *Proceedings of the American Philosophical Society*, XC (1946), 131–161.

—— "Origins of the Colonial Idea in England," *Proceedings of the American Philosophical Society*, LXXXV (1941–1942), 448–465.

Kennedy, William H. J., "Catholics in Massachusetts before 1750," *Catholic Historical Review*, XVII (1931), 10–28.

Kimball, Gertrude S., *Providence in Colonial Times*, Boston, 1912.

Labaree, Leonard W., "The Royal Governors of New England," *Publications of the Colonial Society of Massachusetts*, XXXII (1936), 120–131.

Leach, Douglas Edward, *Flintlock and Tomahawk: New England in King Philips' War*, New York, 1958.

Lothrop, Samuel K., *A History of the Church in Brattle Street, Boston*, Boston, 1851.

Love, William DeLoss, *The Colonial History of Hartford*, Hartford, 1914.

—— *Samson Occom, and the Christian Indians of New England*, Boston, 1900.

McCutcheon, Roger P., "Americana in English Newspapers, 1648–1660," *Publications of the Colonial Society of Massachusetts*, XX (1920), 84–96.

McElroy, John W., "Seafaring in Seventeenth-Century New England," *New England Quarterly*, VIII (1935), 331–364.

MacFarlane, Ronald O., "The Massachusetts Bay Truck-Houses in Diplomacy with the Indians," *New England Quarterly*, XI (1938), 48–65.

McKay, George L., *Early American Currency—Some Notes on the Development of Paper Money in the New England Colonies*, New York, 1944.

Marcus, Jacob Rader, ed., *American Jewry Documents: 18th Century, Primarily Hitherto Unpublished Manuscripts*, Cincinnati, 1959.

—— *Early American Jewry, 1649–1794*, Philadelphia, 1951. (Based on examination of personal and business letters.)

Maurer, Oscar Edward, *A Puritan Church and Its Relation to Community, State, and Nation. Addresses Delivered in Preparation for the Three Hundredth Anniversary of the Settlement of New Haven*, New Haven, 1938.

Mitchell, Mary H., *History of the United Church of New Haven, 1742–1792*, New Haven, 1942.

Mood, Fulmer, *The English Geographers and the Anglo-American Frontier in the Seventeenth Century, University of California Publications in Geography*, Vol. 6, No. 9, 363–396; Berkeley and Los Angeles, 1944. (A stimulating survey of the work of the geographers and its relation to the promotional literature of the seventeenth century.)

Moody, Robert Earle, "A Re-Examination of the Antecedents of the Massachusetts Bay Company's Charter of 1629," *Publications of the Massachusetts Historical Society,* LXIX (1947–1950), 1956, 56–80.

Morison, Samuel Eliot, *Builders of the Bay Colony,* Boston, 1930; Cornell paperback. (A history and interpretation of New England Puritanism in a series of brilliant biographical portraits; an essential book; counters many of the theories of J. T. Adams, and establishes and defines the essentially religious motivation of the settlement.)

—— "The Mayflower's Destination, and the Pilgrim Fathers' Patents," *Transactions of the Colonial Society of Massachusetts,* XXXVIII (1959), 387–413.

—— "New Light Wanted on the Old Colony," *William and Mary Quarterly,* XV (1958), 359–364.

—— "The Pilgrim Fathers, Their Significance in History," *Transactions of the Colonial Society of Massachusetts,* XXXVIII (1959), 364–379.

Morse, Jarvis M., "John Smith and His Critics: A Chapter in Colonial Historiography," *Journal of Southern History,* I (1935), 123–137.

Murdock, Kenneth B., "Clio in the Wilderness: History and Biography in Puritan New England," *Church History,* XXIV (1955), 221–238. (The best exposition of the Puritan view of history.)

—— "William Hubbard and the Providential Interpretation of History," *Proceedings of the American Antiquarian Society,* LII (1942), 15–37.

Neal, Daniel, *The History of New-England,* London, 1720; 2nd ed., 1747, 2 vols.

—— *The History of the Puritans,* London, 1732–1738, 4 vols.; later editions. (Superseded in factual range by subsequent works, yet still one of the best interpretations of the Puritan mind.)

Nettels, Curtis P., *The Roots of American Civilization: A History of Colonial Life,* New York, 1938. (The economic structure of colonial culture.)

Newton, Arthur P., *The Colonising Activities of the English Puritans,* New Haven, 1914.

Noe, Sydney P., "The Coinage of Massachusetts Bay Colony," *Proceedings of the American Antiquarian Society,* LX (1950), 11–20.

—— *The Pine Tree Coinage of Massachusetts,* New York, 1952. (Numismatic Notes and Monographs, No. 125.)

Notestein, Wallace, *The English People on the Eve of Colonization, 1603–1630,* New York, 1954; Harper Torchbook edition, 1962. (Social history at its best; early 17th century English society anatomized.)

O'Brien, Michael J., *Pioneer Irish in New England,* New York, 1937.

Oldmixon, John, *The British Empire in America,* London, 1708, 2 vols. Vol. I: "The History of New England," pp. 25–116.

Osgood, Herbert L., *The American Colonies in the Eighteenth Century,* New York, 1924, 3 vols. (A standard history, particularly concerned with political aspects.)

—— *The American Colonies in the Seventeenth Century,* New York, 1904–1907, 3 vols.

Palfrey, John G., *A Compendious History of New England,* Boston, 1858–1890, 5 vols. (As detailed as was possible at the time; largely superseded by later works, but still valuable as a work of reference.)

Park, Charles E., "Friendship as a Factor in the Settlement of Massachusetts," *Proceedings of the American Antiquarian Society,* N.S. XXVIII (1918), 51–62.

Perley, Sidney, *The History of Salem, Massachusetts,* Salem, 1924. (Vol. I, covering 1626–1637.)

Phillips, James Duncan, *Salem in the Eighteenth Century,* Boston, 1937.

—— *Salem in the Seventeenth Century,* Boston, 1933.

Richman, Irving B., *Rhode Island: A Study in Separatism,* Boston, 1905.

—— *Rhode Island: Its Making and Its Meaning,* New York, 1902.

Robbins, Chandler, *A History of the Second Church, or Old North, in Boston,* Boston, 1852.

Rose, John Holland, A. P. Newton, and E. A. Benians, *The Cambridge History of the British Empire,* Vol. I: *The Old Empire from the Beginnings to 1783,* Cambridge, Eng., 1929.

Rosenberry, Lois K. Mathews, *The Expansion of New England*, Boston, 1909.

Rose-Troup, Frances, *John White, the Founder of Massachusetts*, New York, 1930. (Detailed, but injudicious.)

—— *The Massachusetts Bay Company and Its Predecessors*, New York, 1930. (Neither complete nor entirely accurate.)

Rossiter, Clinton, *Seedtime of the Republic: The Origin of the American Tradition of Political Liberty*, New York, 1953. (Summary background of colonial history and conditions of life.)

Rowse, A. L., *The Elizabethans and America*, New York, 1959. (Tendentious history in the grand manner, basically unsympathetic to the Puritans and New England.)

Sachse, William L., *The Colonial American in Britain*, Madison, 1956.

Saltonstall, William G., *Ports of Piscataqua*, Cambridge, 1941.

Savelle, Max, *The Foundations of American Civilization*, New York, 1942. (Emphasis on the diplomatic aspects of early American history and on the relation of the continental colonies to the British West Indies.)

Scudder, Townsend, *Concord, American Town*, Boston, 1947.

Seybolt, Robert Francis, *The Town Officials of Colonial Boston, 1634–1775*, Cambridge, 1939. (An attempt to straighten out and correct the *Reports of the Record Commissioners of the City of Boston*.)

Shannon, Fred A., *Economic History of the People of the United States*, New York, 1934.

Shipton, Clifford K., "The New England Clergy of the 'Glacial Age,'" *Publications of the Colonial Society of Massachusetts*, XXXII (1937), 24–54.

—— "Immigration to New England, 1680–1740," *Journal of Political Economy*, LXIV (1936), 225–239.

—— "The New England Frontier," *New England Quarterly*, X (1937), 25–36.

Sly, John F., *Town Government in Massachusetts, 1620–1930*, Cambridge, 1930.

Stearns, Raymond P., "The New England Way in Holland," *New England Quarterly*, VI (1933), 747–792.

—— "The Weld-Peter Mission to England," *Publications of the Colonial Society of Massachusetts*, XXXII (1936), 188–246.

Stoughton, John, *History of Religion in England, from the Opening of the Long Parliament*, 4th ed., London, 1901, 8 vols. (The most readable and generally useful account of the English background.)

Sutherland, Stella H., *Population Distribution in Colonial America*, New York, 1936.

Sylvester, Herbert M., *Indian Wars of New England*, Boston, 1910, 3 vols.

Tillyard, E. M., *The Elizabethan World Picture*, London, 1943.

Trefz, Edward K., "The Puritans' View of History," *Boston Public Library Quarterly*, IX (1957), 115–136. (Belief in the Providence of God demanded an objective history of His workings.)

Trumbull, Benjamin, *A Complete History of Connecticut, Civil and Ecclesiastical*, New Haven, 1818, 2 vols.; new ed., New London, 1898. (Both a history and a source book; invaluable.)

Turner, Frederick J., "The First Official Frontier of the Massachusetts Bay," *Publications of the Colonial Society of Massachusetts*, XVII (1915), 250–271.

Usher, Roland G., *The Pilgrims and Their History*, New York, 1918.

Van de Wetering, John, "Thomas Prince's Chronological History," *William and Mary Quarterly*, XVIII (1961), 546–557.

Wakeman, Henry O., *The Church and the Puritans, 1570–1660*, London, 1887. (A convenient brief survey of religious background for the Puritan migration.)

Walker, George L., *History of the First Church in Hartford, 1633–1883*, Hartford, 1884.

Waters, Thomas F., *Ipswich in the Massachusetts Bay Colony*, Ipswich, 1905–1917, 2 vols. (A good history of an important town.)

Weeden, William B., *Economic and Social History of New England, 1620–1789*, Boston, 1890, 2 vols. (Still the best attempt at a complete treatment of the subject; badly organized, but a mine of information.)

Welles, Lemuel A., *The History of the Regicides in New England*, New York, 1927.

—— *The Regicides in Connecticut*, *Publications of the Tercentenary Commission of the State of Connecticut*, New Haven, 1935.

Wertenbaker, Thomas Jefferson, *The Puritan Oligarchy: The Founding of American Civilization*, New York, 1947.

Winsor, Justin, ed., *The Memorial History of Boston, 1630–1880*, Boston, 1880–1881, 4 vols.

—— *Narrative and Critical History of America*, Boston, 1884–1889, 8 vols. (Still useful; each chapter includes an essay on authorities which is often an excellent guide to source material.)

Wright, Louis B., *The Atlantic Frontier: Colonial American Civilization, 1607–1763*, New York, 1947; London ed'n., 1949, *The Colonial Civilization of North America.*

—— *Middle-Class Culture in Elizabethan England*, Chapel Hill, 1935. (Indispensable for social and cultural backgrounds.)

—— *Religion and Empire: The Alliance between Piety and Commerce in English Expansion, 1558–1625*, Chapel Hill, 1943. (Demonstrates the importance of the religious motives in exploration and settlement of America.

II. THEORIES OF THE STATE AND SOCIETY

The most important single form of publication concerned with the theory of society was the election sermon, the discourse delivered annually to the General Court on the day of the election. Political and social issues were often discussed in the annual sermons delivered on the occasion for the electing of officers to the Ancient and Honorable Artillery Company of Boston. A complete list of these sermons would swell the pages of this bibliography beyond the point of usefulness, and only those of special importance are here listed. For further guidance to the sermons, consult in Section B: Roberts, Swift, Vail, and Whitman.

A. Primary Sources

Expressions of Puritan political and social theory are to be found scattered through sermons, journals, and letters. Very few works were dedicated solely to this particular theme, so that a complete bibliography of passages of this sort would involve a repetition of almost all the titles mentioned in these lists. Consult in addition to the items here, those listed in section III A 2, for sermons devoted to ecclesiastical polity, all of which contain statements on the relation of Church and State, the basic social problem for Puritan theorists. (For convenience the following abbreviations are used in this section: AES (Artillery Election Sermon); MES (Massachusetts Election Sermon); CES (Connecticut Election Sermon).

Appleton, Nathaniel, *The Origin of War examin'd and applied*, Boston, 1733. (AES)

Barnard, John, *The Throne Established by Righteousness*, Boston, 1734. (MES)

Belcher, Joseph, *The Singular Happiness Of such Heads Or Rulers, As Are able to Choose out their Peoples Way*, Boston, 1701. (MES)

Belcher, Samuel, *An Essay Tending to Promote the Kingdom of our Lord Jesus Christ*, Boston, 1707. (MES)

Book of the General Laws For the People within the Jurisdiction of Connecticut, The, Cambridge, 1673. (Codification of the laws after the union of Connecticut and New Haven.)

Breck, Robert, *The Only Method to Promote the Happiness of a People and their Prosperity*, Boston, 1728. (MES)

Buckingham, Thomas, *Moses and Aaron. God's Favour To His Chosen People, in Leading them by the Ministry of Civil & Ecclesiastical Rulers, Well Qualified for the Offices they are Called to Execute*, New London, 1729. (CES for 1728.)

Bulkeley, Gershom, *The People's Right to Election Or Alteration of Government in Connecticott*, Philadelphia, 1689; *Collections of the Connecticut Historical Society*, I (1860), 57–75; *Andros Tracts*, II, 83–109.

—— *Will and Doom, or The Miseries of Connecticut by and under an Usurped and Arbitrary Power* [1692]; *Collections of the Connecticut Historical Society*, III (1895), 69–269. (One of the most pronounced expressions of the radical implications of Puritan theory.)

Bulkley, John, *The Necessity of Religion*

in Societies, New London, 1713. (CES. Next to pamphlets of Wise, this is the best of early eighteenth-century treatises.)

Burnham, William, *God's Providence In Placing Men In their Respective Stations & Conditions Asserted & Shewed*, New London, 1722. (CES)

Cobbet, Thomas, *The Civil Magistrates Power In matters of Religion Modestly Debated*, London, 1653. (One of the best statements of the Puritan theory of Church and State, by the first minister at Lynn.)

Colman, Benjamin, *Faith Victorious*, Boston, 1702. (AES)

Cotton, John, *An Abstract Of Laws and Government. Wherein as in a Mirrour may be seen the wisdome & perfection of the Government of Christs Kingdome*, London, 1641; 1655. Reprinted in Thomas Hutchinson, *A Collection of Original Papers*, 1769; Force, *Tracts*, III, No. 9. (This code, known as "Moses His Judicials," was never adopted by the colony of Massachusetts, but became the fundamental law for the stricter colony of New Haven. It formulates the extreme religious program in society and law, but should be compared with that actually adopted by the Massachusetts General Court from the pen of Nathaniel Ward. Cf. Worthington C. Ford, "Cotton's 'Moses His Judicials,'" *Proceedings of the Massachusetts Historical Society*, second series, XVI (1903), 274–284; Isabel Calder, "John Cotton's 'Moses His Judicials,'" *Publications of the Colonial Society of Massachusetts*, XXVIII (1935), 86–94.

—— *The Bloudy Tenent, washed, And made white in the bloud of the Lambe*, London, 1647. (Reply to Roger Williams; the classic Puritan statement on the question of toleration.)

—— *The Controversie Concerning Liberty of Conscience in Matters of Religion, Truly stated, and distinctly and plainly handled*, London, 1646.

—— "Copy of a Letter from Mr. Cotton to Lord Say and Seal in the Year 1636," in Thomas Hutchinson, *The History of the Colony*, ed. Mayo, I, 414–417.

—— *A Discourse about Civil Government in a New Plantation Whose Design is Religion*, Cambridge, 1663. (Perhaps the fundamental text for understanding the social objectives of orthodox Puritanism. Written for the guidance of the New Haven Colony, it was intended for the planters who wished to create a society still more perfect than that of Massachusetts Bay. It was published after Cotton's death, and was long attributed to John Davenport, who saw it through the press; cf. Isabel M. Calder, "The Authorship of 'A Discourse,'" *American Historical Review*, XXXVII, 267–269.)

—— *A Letter to Mr.* [*Roger*] *Williams*, London, 1643; ed. Reuben A. Guild, *Publications of the Narragansett Club*, I (1866), 285–311.

Cutler, Timothy, *The Firm Union of a People Represented*, New London, 1717. (CES)

Danforth, Samuel, *A Brief Recognition of New-Englands Errand into the Wilderness*, Cambridge, 1671. (MES for 1670.)

Davenport, John, *A Sermon Preach'd at the Election . . . 1699*, Boston, 1670; reprinted in *Publications of the Colonial Society of Massachusetts*, X (1907), 1–6. (MES for 1669.)

Davis, Andrew M., ed., *Tracts Relating to the Currency of the Massachusetts Bay, 1682–1720*, Boston, 1902.

—— *Colonial Currency Reprints, 1682–1751*, Boston, 1910–1911, 4 vols.

Dummer, Jeremiah, *A Defence of the New-England Charters*, London, 1721; Boston, 1721, and later. (Essential for an understanding of the fashion in which seventeenth-century Puritan theory merges by degrees into the Whig theory of the eighteenth century.)

Eliot, Jared, *Give Cesar his Due; Or, The Obligations that Subjects are under to their Civil Rulers*, New London, 1738. (CES. A work that marks the complete domestication of the theories of Locke and Puffendorf in eighteenth-century Puritan theory.)

Eliot, John, *The Christian Commonwealth: or, The Civil Policy of The Rising Kingdom of Jesus Christ*, London, 1659; republished in *Collections of the Massachusetts Historical Society*, third series, IX (1846), 127–164. (Published immediately after the Restoration, this book was extremely impolitic in its assertion of radical Puritan tendencies, and was therefore condemned by the General Court of Massachusetts. The action was rather a piece of strategy than a disapproval of the ideas. The book is therefore an expression of theories that reached their fullest development during the period of the English Civil Wars, that were thereafter checked and to some extent driven underground, but that remain in the background of New England thought, to reappear in the work of Wise, Mayhew, and the Revolutionary pamphleteers.)

Farrand, Max, ed., *The Book of the General Lawes and Libertyes* (1648), Cambridge, 1929. (Cf. also review by T. F. T. Plucknett, *New England Quarterly*, III (1930), 156–159.

Fitch, James, *An Holy Connexion; Or a true Agreement Between Jehovahs being a Wall of Fire to his People, and the Glory in the midst thereof*, Cambridge, 1674. (CES)

Hancock, John, *Rulers should be Benefactors*, Boston, 1722. (MES)

Higginson, John, *The Cause of God and his people in New-England*, Cambridge, 1663. (MES)

Hooke, William, *New Englands Teares, for Old Englands Feares*, London, 1641. (Expresses New England's attitude toward the Civil Wars in England. It is also valuable as an expression of the Puritan feeling concerning war.)

Hooker, Thomas, "Rev. Thomas Hooker's Letter, in Reply to Governor Winthrop," *Collections of the Connecticut Historical Society*, I (1860), 1–18. (An angry letter, the result of a dispute between Connecticut and Massachusetts, wherein Hooker roundly asserts his political philosophy.)

Mather, Cotton, *Durable Riches*, Boston, 1695.

—— *Fair Dealing*, Boston, 1716.

Mather, Eleazer, *A Serious Exhortation to the Present and Succeeding Generation in New-England*, Cambridge, 1671; Boston, 1678.

Mather, Increase, *A Discourse Concerning the Danger of Apostacy*, Boston, 1679; 1685. (A review and summary of the state of New England; MES for 1677.)

—— *The Great Blessing of Primitive Counsellours*, Boston, 1693. (MES)

—— *The Surest way to the Greatest Honour*, Boston, 1699. (MES. The third of four election sermons Mather preached.)

—— *The Excellency of a Publick Spirit*, Boston, 1702.

Mayhew, Jonathan, *A Discourse concerning Unlimited Submission and Non-Resistance to the Higher Powers*, Boston, 1750; reprinted J. W. Thornton, *The Pulpit of the American Revolution*, Boston, 1860. (The final statement of Puritan radicalism in eighteenth-century terms.)

Mitchel, Jonathan, *Nehemiah on the Wall in Troublesom[e] Times*, Cambridge, 1671. (MES for 1667.)

Moody, Joshua, *Souldiery Spiritualized, or the Christian Souldier Orderly, and Strenuously Engaged in the Spiritual Warre, And So fighting the good Fight*, Cambridge, 1674. (AES)

Moss, Joseph, *An Election Sermon . . . frequent Readings and Studying the Scriptures and the Civil Law of the Common Wealth, is Needful and Profitable for Rulers*, New London, 1715. (CES. One of the best statements of theory of social compact.)

Noyes, James, *Moses and Aaron: Or, The Rights of Church and State*, London, 1661.

Noyes, Nicholas, *New-Englands Duty and Interest, To be an Habitation of Justice*, Boston, 1698. (MES)

Oakes, Urian, *New-England Pleaded with, And pressed to consider the things which concern her Peace, at least in this her Day*, Cambridge, 1673.

Oxenbridge, John, *New-England Freemen Warned and Warmede; To be Free indeed having an Eye to God in their Elections*, Boston, 1673. (MES for 1671.)

Pemberton, Ebenezer, *The divine Original and Dignity of Government Asserted*, Boston, 1710. (MES)

Prince, Thomas, *The People of New-England Put in mind of the Righteous Acts of the Lord to Them and their Fathers, and Reasoned with concerning them*, Boston, 1730. (MES)

Richardson, John, *The Necessity of a Well Experienced Souldiery*, Cambridge, 1679. (AES for 1675.)

Shepard, Thomas, "Thomas Shepard's Election Sermon, in 1638," *New England Historical and Genealogical Register*, XXIV (1870), 361–366. (MES. One of the best statements of the original political ideal.)

Somers, John, *The Security of Englishmen's Lives; Or, The Trust, Power and Duty of the Grand Juries of England*, London, 1718; frequently reprinted.

Stoddard, Solomon, *The Way for a People to Live Long in the Land that God Hath given them*, Boston, 1703. (MES)

Stoughton, William, *New-Englands True Interest; Not to Lie*, Cambridge, 1670. (MES for 1668.)

Wadsworth, Benjamin, *Rulers Feeding & Guiding their People*, Boston, 1716. (MES)

Whitmore, William H., *A Bibliographical Sketch of the Laws of the Massachusetts Colony from 1630 to 1686*, Boston, 1890. (Contains the "Body of Liberties," the code written by Nathaniel Ward and adopted by the General Court in 1641.)

—— ed., *The Colonial Laws of Massachusetts. Reprinted from the Edition of 1672*, Boston, 1887; 1890.

Willard, Samuel, *The Character Of a Good Ruler*, Boston, 1694. (MES)

—— *The Man of War*, Boston, 1699. (AES)

—— *The Only sure way to prevent threatned Calamity*, Boston, 1684. (MES for 1682.)

Williams, Roger, *The Bloudy Tenent of Persecution, for cause of Conscience, discussed, in A Conference betweene Truth and Peace*, London, 1644; ed. Samuel L. Caldwell, *Publications of the Narragansett Club*, Vol. III, 1867.

—— *The Bloody Tenent yet More Bloody: by Mr Cottons endevour to wash it white in the Blood of the Lambe*, London, 1652; ed. S. L. Caldwell, *Publications of the Narragansett Club*, Vol. IV, 1870.

—— *The Hireling Ministry None of Christs*, London, 1652.

—— *Mr. Cottons Letter Lately Printed, Examined and Answered*, London, 1644; ed. R. A. Guild, *Publications of the Narragansett Club*, I (1866), 313–396.

Williams, William, *A Plea for God, and An Appeal to the Consciences of a People Declining in Religion*, Boston, 1719. (MES)

Winthrop, John, "A Modell of Christian Charity," *Winthrop Papers, Collections of the Massachusetts Historical Society*, third series, VII (1838), 31–48; *The Winthrop Papers*, Massachusetts Historical Society, Boston, 1931, II, 282–295. (Written on the *Arbella* during the voyage to New England in 1630.)

Wise, John, *The Churches Quarrel Espoused*, Boston, 1710.

—— *A Vindication of the Government of New England Churches*, Boston, 1767; reprinted in "Scholars' Facsimiles and Reprints," ed. Perry Miller, Gainesville, Fla., 1958. (Reissues of both titles in one volume, Boston, 1772; 1862.)

Woodward, John, *Civil Rulers are God's Ministers, for the People's Good*, Boston, 1712.

B. Secondary Works

Puritan social and economic theory was so inextricably woven into the religious doctrine that few works were ever written specifically on the subject. Many titles in Section III also contain observations on social thought.

Aldrich, Peleg E., "John Locke and the Influence of His Works on American Thought," *Proceedings of the American Antiquarian Society*, April, 1879, 22–39.

Allen, Neal W., ed., *Province and Court Records of Maine*. Vol. IV: *The Court Records of York County, Maine, 1692–1711*, Portland, 1958.

Andrews, Charles M., "On Some Early Connecticut History," *New England Quarterly*, XVII (1944), 3–24. (Connecticut's unbroken tradition of orthodoxy and responsible self-government based on a narrow franchise of free men.)

Baldwin, Alice M., *The New England Clergy and the American Revolution*, Durham, 1928. (An able history of the development of Puritan thought into the Whig philosophy of the Revolution.)

Blodgett, John T., "The Political Theory of the Mayflower Compact," *Publications of the Colonial Society of Massachusetts*, XII (1911), 204–213.

Boorstin, Daniel J., "The Puritan Tradition: Community Above Ideology," *Commentary*, XXVI (1958), 288–299.

Borgeauc, Charles, *The Rise of Modern Democracy in Old and New England*, London, 1894.

Brauer, Jerald C., "Puritan Mysticism

and the Development of Liberalism," *Church History*, XIX (1950), 151–170.

Brennan, Ellen E., "The Massachusetts Council of the Magistrates," *New England Quarterly*, IV (1931), 54–93. (An excellent analysis of early government, contending that by 1644 political leadership had ceased to be responsible to God and had been made responsible to the freeman.)

Brockunier, Samuel H., *The Irrepressible Democrat: Roger Williams*, New York, 1940.

Brown, B. Katherine, "Freemanship in Puritan Massachusetts," *American Historical Review*, LIX (1954), 865–883.

—— "A Note on the Puritan Concept of Aristocracy," *Mississippi Valley Historical Review*, XLI (1954), 105–112. (What Cotton, Winthrop and other Puritan leaders meant by aristocracy has a close relationship to what we call democracy.)

Brown, Robert E., *Middle-Class Democracy and the Revolution in Massachusetts, 1691–1780*. Ithaca, 1955.

Buck, Edward, *Massachusetts Ecclesiatical Law*, New York, 1866.

Buffinton, Arthur H., "The Puritan View of War," *Publications of the Colonial Society of Massachusetts*, XXVIII (1935), 67–86.

Burrage, Champlin, *The Church Covenant Idea*, Philadelphia, 1904.

Calder, Isabel M., "John Cotton and the New Haven Colony," *New England Quarterly*, III (1930), 82–94.

Chafee, Zechariah, Jr., "Colonial Courts and the Common Law," *Proceedings of the Massachusetts Historical Society*, LXVIII (1944–1947), 1952, 132–159.

—— "Records of the Rhode Island Court of Equity," *Publications of the Colonial Society of Massachusetts*, XXXV (1942–1946), 91–118.

Cobb, Sanford H., *The Rise of Religious Liberty in America: A History*, New York, 1902.

Cook, George Allen, *John Wise: Early American Democrat*, New York, 1952. (All and more than there is to be known about John Wise.)

Davis, Andrew M., *Currency and Banking in the Province of the Massachusetts-Bay*, New York, 1901, 2 vols.

Davis, Charles T., "Some Thoughts on Early Colonial Development," *Proceedings of the Massachusetts Historical Society*, LXIV (1932), 507–515. (Legal development in New England.)

Dexter, Henry M., *As To Roger Williams, and his "Banishment" from the Massachusetts Plantation*, Boston, 1876. (A vigorous statement of what was the orthodox view toward such a man as Williams in the seventeenth century; valuable for securing the proper perspective upon Williams' liberalism.)

Dickinson, John, "Economic Regulations and Restrictions on Personal Liberty in Massachusetts," *Proceedings of the Pocumtuck Valley Historical Association*, VII (1929), 485–525.

Dunn, Richard S., "John Winthrop, Jr., and the Narragansett Country," *William and Mary Quarterly*, XIII (1956), 68–86.

—— "John Winthrop, Jr., Connecticut Expansionist: The Failure of His Designs on Long Island, 1663–1675," *New England Quarterly*, XXIX (1956), 3–26.

Earle, Alice M., *Curious Punishments of Bygone Days*, Chicago, 1896.

East, Robert A., "Puritanism and New Settlement," *New England Quarterly*, XVII (June), 255–264.

Eisenger, Chester E., "The Puritans' Justification for Taking the Land," *Essex Institute Historical Collections*, LXXXIV (1948), 131–143.

Ernst, James E., *The Political Thought of Roger Williams*, Seattle, 1929.

Eusden, John Dykstra, *Puritan Lawyers, and Politics in Early Seventeenth-Century England*, New Haven, 1958.

Farrand, Max, "Massachusetts Laws of 1660," *Publications of the Colonial Society of Massachusetts*, XXVII (1932), 194–197.

Farrell, John T., "The Early History of Rhode Island's Court System," *Rhode Island History*, IX (1950), 65–71, 103–117; X (1951), 14–27.

Figgis, John N., *The Divine Right of Kings*, 2nd ed., London, 1914.

Ford, Worthington C., and Albert Matthews, "Bibliography of the Laws of the Massachusetts Bay, 1641–1776," *Publications of the Colonial Society of Massachusetts*, IV (1910), 291–480.

Fowler, David H., "Connecticut's Freemen: The First Forty Years," *William and Mary Quarterly*, XV (1958), 312–333.

French, Allen, "The Arms and Military Training of our Colonizing Ancestors," *Proceedings of the Massachusetts Historical Society*, LXVII, 3–21.

Frese, Joseph Raphael, "Early Parliamentary Legislation on Writs of Assistance [1660–1696]," *Transactions of the Colonial Society of Massachusetts*, XXXVIII (1959), 318–359.

Gierke, Otto von, *Natural Law and the Theory of Society, 1500–1800*, Cambridge, Eng., 1934, 2 vols.; Beacon paperback. (Introduction by Ernest Barker.)

Gooch, George P., *The History of English Democratic Ideas in the Seventeenth Century*, ed. H. J. Laski, London, 1927; Harper Torchbook edition, 1959.

Goodman, Leonard S., "Mandamus in the Colonies—The Rise of the Superintending Power of American Courts," *American Journal of Legal History*, I (1957), 308–335; II (1958), 1–34.

Goodspeed, Charles Eliot, "Extortion, Captain Turner, and the Widow Stolion," *Transactions of the Colonial Society of Massachusetts*, XXXVIII (1959), 60–79. (Magistrates dictated the wages paid to workmen, prices of commodities and percentage of profit allowed to merchants.)

Gough, J. W., *The Social Contract*, Oxford, 1937.

Gray, Stanley, "The Political Thought of John Winthrop," *New England Quarterly* III (1930), 681–705.

Greene, Evarts B., *Religion and the State: The Making and Testing of an American Tradition*, New York, 1941.

Greene, Maria L., *The Development of Religious Liberty in Connecticut*, Boston, 1905.

Grinnell, Frank W., "John Winthrop and the Constitutional Thinking of John Adams," *Proceedings of the Massachusetts Historical Society*, LXIII (1931), 91–119.

Haffenden, Philip S., "The Anglican Church in Restoration Colonial Policy," *Seventeenth-Century America: Essays in Colonial History*, ed., James Morton Smith, Chapel Hill, 1959, 166–191.

—— "The Crown and the Colonial Charters, 1675–1688," *William and Mary Quarterly*, XV (1958), 297–311, 452–466.

Haller, William, Jr., *The Puritan Frontier: Town Planting in New England Colonial Development 1630–1660. Studies in History, Economics and Public Law*, No. 568, New York, 1951.

Harper, Lawrence A., *The English Navigation Laws: A Seventeenth-Century Experiment in Social Engineering*, New York, 1939.

Harris, Marshall, *Origin of the Land Tenure System in the United States*, Ames, 1953.

Haskins, George L., "Codification of Law in Colonial Massachusetts: A Study in Comparative Law," *Indiana Law Review*, 30 (1954–1955), 1–18.

—— *Law and Authority in Early Massachusetts: A Study in Tradition and Design*, New York, 1960. (A discussion of law and order in provincial and local government 1630–1648.)

Hedges, James B., *The Browns of Providence Plantations: Colonial Years*, Cambridge, 1952. (Studies in economic history.)

Hilkey, Charles J., *Legal Development in Colonial Massachusetts, 1630–1686*, New York, 1910.

Hirsch, Elizabeth F., "John Cotton and Roger Williams: Their Controversy Concerning Religious Liberty," *Church History*, X (1941), 38–51.

Hoon, Elizabeth, *The Organization of the English Customs System 1696–1786*, New York, 1938.

Howe, Mark DeWolfe, and Louis F. Eaton, Jr., "The Supreme Judicial Power in the Colony of Massachusetts Bay," *New England Quarterly*, XX (1947), 291–316. (A brilliant study correcting traditional misconceptions of the struggle between magistrates and deputies over the negative voice in matters of judicature.)

Hudson, Winthrop S., "Puritanism and the Spirit of Capitalism," *Church History*, XVIII (1949), 3–17. (An illuminating criticism of Weber and Tawney.)

Jacobson, Jacob M., ed., *The Development of American Political Thought: A Documentary History*, New York, 1932.

Jeffrey, William, Jr., "Early New England Court Records: A Bibliography of Published Materials," *Boston Public Library Quarterly*, VI (1954), 160–184; reprinted in *American Journal of Legal History*, I (1957), 119–147.

Johnson, Edgar A. J., *American Economic*

Thought in the Seventeenth Century, London, 1932.

—— "Economic Ideas of John Winthrop," *New England Quarterly*, III (1930), 235–250.

Jordan, Wilbur K., *The Development of Religious Toleration in England*, 4 vols., Cambridge, 1932–1940.

Labaree, Leonard Woods, *Conservatism in Early American History*, New Haven, 1948.

Lauer, Paul E., *Church and State in New England*, Baltimore, 1892.

Leach, Douglas Edwards, "The Military System of Plymouth Colony," *New England Quarterly*, XXIV (1951), 342–364.

Levitan, Tina, "Hebraic Mortar," *American Hebrew*, CLVII, Feb. 27, 1948, 2, 15. (The Old Testament as a source for colonial democratic processes.)

Lokken, Roy N., "The Concept of Democracy in Colonial Political Thought," *William and Mary Quarterly*, XVI (1959), 568–580.

Lord, Arthur, "The Mayflower Compact," *Proceedings of the American Antiquarian Society*, N.S. XXX (1920), 278–294.

McElroy, Paul Simpson, "John Wise: The Father of American Independence," *Essex Institute Historical Collections*, LXXXI (1945), 201–226. (Wise's contribution to the cause of civil liberty.)

McIlwain, Charles H., "The Transfer of the Charter to New England, and its Significance in American Constitutional History," *Proceedings of the Massachusetts Historical Society*, LXIII (1931), 53–64.

Matthews, Nathan, "The Results of the Prejudice Against Lawyers in Massachusetts in the 17th Century," *Massachusetts Law Quarterly*, XIII (May, 1928), 73–94.

Mead, Sidney E., "From Coercion to Persuasion: Another Look at the Rise of Religious Liberty and the Emergence of Denominationalism," *Church History*, XXV (1950), 317–337.

Merrian, Charles E., *A History of American Political Theories*, New York, 1903; 1926.

Mesnard, Pierre, *L'Essor de la Philosophie Politique au XVIe Siècle*, Paris, 1936.

Miller, John C., "Religion, Finance, and Democracy in Massachusetts," *New England Quarterly*, VI (1933), 29–58. (Establishes a connection between emotionalism of the frontier awakening with back-country hostility to urban financial control.)

Miller, Perry, "Religion and Society in the Early Literature: The Religious Impulse in the Founding of Virginia," *William and Mary Quarterly*, 3rd series, V (1948), 492–522; VI (1949), 24–51; reprinted in *Errand into the Wilderness*, Cambridge, 1956, 99–140.

—— "Thomas Hooker and the Democracy of Early Connecticut," *New England Quarterly*, IV (1931), 663–712; reprinted in *Errand into the Wilderness*, Cambridge, 1956; (Examination of claims for democratic origins of Connecticut in the light of orthodox Puritan theory.)

Mook, H. Telfer, "Training Day in New England," *New England Quarterly*, XI (1938), 675–697.

Morgan, Edmund S., "The Case against Anne Hutchinson," *New England Quarterly*, X (1937), 635–649.

Morris, Richard B., *Government and Labor in Early America*, New York, 1946.

—— "Legalism *versus* Revolutionary Doctrine in New England," *New England Quarterly*, IV (1931), 195–215. (Data on the low estate in which most lawyers were held in Massachusetts during the early colonial period.)

—— "Massachusetts and the Common Law: The Declaration of 1646," *American Historical Review*, XXXI (1926), 443–453.

——, and Jonathan Grossman, "The Regulation of Wages in Early Massachusetts," *New England Quarterly*, XI (1938), 470–500.

—— *Studies in the History of American Law, with Special Reference to the Seventeenth and Eighteenth Centuries*, New York, 1930.

Mosse, George L., *The Holy Pretence: A Study in Christianity and Reason of State from William Perkins to John Winthrop*, Oxford, 1957. (A study of the attempt to reconcile Christian ethic and political exigencies.)

Niebuhr, Richard, "The Idea of Covenant and American Democracy," *Church History*, XXIII (1954), 126–135.

Noble, John, "Notes on the Trial and Punishment of Crimes in . . . the Time of the Colony," *Publications of the Colonial Society of Massachusetts*, III (1900), 51–66.

Page, Elwin L., *Judicial Beginnings in New Hampshire 1640–1700*, Concord, N. H., 1959. (Based on original trial court records and the printed sources.)

Park, Charles E., "Excommunication in Colonial Churches," *Publications of the Colonial Society of Massachusetts*, XII (1911), 321–332.

—— "Two Ruling Elders of the First Church in Boston," *Publications of the Colonial Society of Massachusetts*, XIII (1912), 82–95.

Parkes, Henry B., "John Cotton and Roger Williams Debate Toleration, 1644–1652," *New England Quarterly*, IV (1931), 735–756.

Pound, Roscoe, "Puritanism and the Common Law," *American Law Review*, XLV (1911), 811–829.

Reed, Susan M., *Church and State in Massachusetts, 1691–1740*, Urbana, Ill., 1914.

Reinsch, Paul S., *English Common Law in the Early American Colonies*, University of Wisconsin, Bulletin II, No. 4, in Economics, Political Science, and History, 1899.

Roberts, Oliver A., *History of the Military Company of the Massachusetts*, Boston, 1895–1901, 4 vols.

Robertson, D. B., *The Religious Foundations of Leveller Democracy*, New York, 1951. (A significant contribution to understanding the essentially religious character of left-wing Puritanism.)

Savelle, Max, *Seeds of Liberty: The Genesis of the American Mind*, New York, 1948. (Cultural patterns, 1740–1760.)

Schapiro, Jacob S., *Social Reform and the Reformation*, New York, 1909.

Schenk, W., *The Concern for Social Justice in the Puritan Revolution*, London and New York, 1948. (Religious propulsion of Puritan thought to achieve an equitable social order.)

Scott, Kenneth, *Counterfeiting in Colonial America*, New York, 1957.

Seidman, Aaron B., "Church and State in the Early Years of the Massachusetts Bay Colony," *New England Quarterly*, XVIII (1945), 211–233.

Seybolt, Robert F., "The Ministers at the Town Meetings in Colonial Boston," *Publications of the Colonial Society of Massachusetts*, XXXII (1938), 300–304.

Sharp, Morrison, "Leadership and Democracy in the Early New England System of Defense," *American Historical Review*, L (1945), 244–260.

Shipton, Clifford K., "Puritanism and Modern Democracy," *New England Historical and Genealogical Register*, CI (1947), 181–198.

Silver, Rollo G., "Financing the Publication of Early New England Sermons," *Studies in Bibliography: Papers of the Bibliographic Society of the University of Virginia*, XI (1958), 163–178.

Simpson, Alan, "How Democratic Was Roger Williams?" *William and Mary Quarterly*, XIII (1956), 56–67.

—— *Puritanism in Old and New England: A Study in the Politics of Enthusiasm*, Chicago, 1955; University of Chicago paperback.

—— 'Saints in Arms. English Puritanism as Political Utopianism," *Church History*, XXIII (1954), 119–125. (A study of Puritan fanaticism.)

Slafter, Edmund, *John Checkley: or, The Evolution of Religious Toleration in Massachusetts Bay*, Boston, 1897, 2 vols.

Smith, Abbot E., *Colonists in Bondage*, Chapel Hill, 1941.

Smith, Chard Powers, "Church and State in Wethersfield, 1696–1699," *New England Quarterly*, XXIX (1956), 82–87. (Control of church and state by the freemen.)

Smith, Joseph H., *Appeals to the Privy Council from the American Plantations*, New York, 1950. (An examination of the appellate jurisdiction of the Privy Council over the courts of the American colonies.)

Stead, George A., "Roger Williams and the Massachusetts-Bay," *New England Quarterly*, VII (1934), 235–257.

Stearns, Raymond P., "John Wise of Ipswich Was No Democrat in Politics," *Essex Institute Historical Collections*, Jan., 1961.

Story, Irving C., "John Wise: Congregational Democrat," *Pacific University Bulletin* XXXVI (1939), No. 3. (An analysis of the *Vindication of New England Churches*.)

Swift, Lindsay, "The Massachusetts Election Sermons," *Publications of the Colonial Society of Massachusetts*, I (1895), 388–451.

Tawney, Richard H., *Religion and the Rise of Capitalism*, New York, 1926; 1952; New American Library paperback. (An able and superbly written book, presenting the economic background of the Protestant movement, with a section on New England in particular.)

—— "Religious Thought on Social and Economic Questions in the Sixteenth and Seventeenth Centuries," *Journal of Political Economy*, XXXI (1923), 461–493, 637–674, 804–825.

Vail, Robert W. G., "A Check List of New England Election Sermons," *Proceedings of the American Antiquarian Society*, XLV (1935), 233–266.

Weis, Frederick L., *The Colonial Clergy and the Colonial Churches of New England*, Lancaster, Mass., 1936. (A compendium of short biographical sketches.)

Whitman, Zechariah G., *An Historical Sketch of the Ancient and Honourable Artillery Company*, Boston, 1820; 1842.

Wigmore, John H., editor-in-chief, *Select Essays in Anglo-American Legal History*, Boston, 1907–1909, 3 vols.

Winslow, Ola Elizabeth, *Meetinghouse Hill: 1630–1783*, New York, 1952. (Origins of American democracy lie in the town meetings. The town, not the church, owned the meetinghouse and paid the minister's salary.)

Wolford, Thorp L., "The Laws and Liberties of 1648: The First Code of Laws Enacted and Printed in English America," *Boston University Law Review*, XXVIII (1948), 426–463.

Woodhouse, Arthur S. P., *Puritanism and Liberty*, *University of Toronto Quarterly*, IV, No. 3, 1935; London, 1950.

Wright, Benjamin F., Jr., *American Interpretations of Natural Law*, Cambridge, 1931.

Wright, Harry A., "The Technique of Seventeenth Century Indian-Land Purchases," *Essex Institute Historical Collections*, LXXVII (1941), 185–197.

Zagorin, Perez, *A History of Political Thought in the English Revolution*, London, 1954. (A Marxian interpretation.)

—— "The Social Interpretation of the English Revolution," *Journal of Economic History*, Sept., 1959.

Ziff, Larzer, "The Social Bond of the Church Covenant," *American Quarterly*, X (1958), 454–462.

III. PURITAN RELIGIOUS THOUGHT

In this section are listed the more important works illustrating the Puritans' general view of the world and of life. Most of them are naturally sermons or theological treatises, yet in them can be found pronouncements upon the various problems of human existence, practical and philosophical.

A. Primary Sources

Since a full list of the original sources for a history of Puritan religious thought would include almost all the publications of Puritan spokesmen, only those items are mentioned that are particularly apt.

1. The General View

Adams, Charles F., ed., *Antinomianism in the Colony of Massachusetts Bay, 1636–1638*, Boston, 1894. (A collection of the materials relating to the trial and expulsion of Anne Hutchinson; indispensable for an understanding of the philosophical issues of Puritanism. Footnotes not always reliable.)

Allin, James, *Man's Self Reflection a Means to Further his Recovery from His Apostacy from God*, Cambridge, 1680. (A discussion of the rôle of introspection in Puritan life.)

Ames, William, *Conscience with the Power and Cases thereof . . . Translated out of Latine into English, for more publique benefit*, London, 1643. (This and the following were the standard handbooks on theology and ethics in seventeenth-century New England. They are compact, methodical outlines of the official creed.)

—— *The Marrow of Sacred Divinity, Drawne out of the Holy Scriptures, and the Interpreters thereof, and brought into Method,*

London, 1638[?]. (Translated from the Latin *Medulla Sacrae Theologiae*, 1623.)

Brattle, William, *Compendium Logicæ Secundum Principia D. Renati Cartesii Plerumque Efformatum, et Catechistice Propositum*, Boston, 1735. (The first American text on logic; used as a text at Harvard as late as 1765.)

Bulkeley, Peter, *The Gospel-Covenant; or the Covenant of Grace opened*, 2nd ed., London, 1651. (The most important exposition of the concept of the covenant, a fundamental idea in New England Puritan thought.)

Bulkley, John, *The Usefulness of Reveal'd Religion, to Preserve and Improve that which is Natural*, New London, 1730. (Extremely important document for the transition from seventeenth-century Puritanism to eighteenth-century rationalism.)

Chauncy, Charles, *Enthusiasm Described and Caution'd Against*, Boston, 1742.

—— *A Letter from a Gentleman in Boston to Mr. George Wishart*, Edinburgh, 1742; reprinted, *Clarendon Historical Society Reprints*, first series, No. 7, Edinburgh, 1883. (A description of the Great Awakening.)

—— *Seasonable Thoughts on the State of Religion in New-England*, Boston, 1743. (Against Whitefield and enthusiasts of the Great Awakening.)

Checkley, John, *Choice Dialogues, between a Godly Minister and an Honest Countryman, concerning Election and Predestination*, Boston, 1720.

Clarke, Samuel, *A Mirrour or Looking-Glasse both for Saints, and Sinners*, London, 1646. (A contemporary estimate of the Antinomian heresy.)

Colman, Benjamin, *God Deals with us as Rational Creatures*, Boston, 1723.

—— *A Humble Discourse of the Incomprehensibleness of God*, Boston, 1715; 1740; Northampton, 1804.

Cooper, William, *Man humbled by being compar'd to a Worm*, Boston, 1732.

Cotton, John, *A Briefe Exposition with Practicall Observations upon The Whole Book of Ecclesiastes*, London, 1654. (A skeleton outline of a series of sermons; probably Cotton's own notes. Since Ecclesiastes more than any other book of the Bible is concerned with what might be called secular issues, this work is a mine of information on Puritan attitudes that are seldom discussed in the more strictly theological writings.)

—— *An Exposition upon the Thirteenth Chapter of the Revelation*, London, 1656.

—— *Gods Mercie mixed with his Justice*, London, 1641; reprinted in "Scholars' Facsimiles and Reprints," ed. Perry Miller, Gainesville, Fla., 1958. (A succinct statement of Puritan thought on one of the central problems.)

—— *Gods Promise To His Plantation*, London, 1630; *Old South Leaflets*, No. 53; cf. E. D. Mead, *Proceedings of the Massachusetts Historical Society*, I, 101–115. (The valedictory sermon delivered as the fleet was to set sail in 1630; succinct expression of the Puritan aim in migrating to the new world.)

—— *Milk for Babes, Drawn out of the Breasts of both Testaments, chiefly for the spirituall nourishment of Boston babes in either England, but may be of like use for any Children*, London, 1646; Cambridge, 1656. (Catechism for children; the theology is expressed in simplest terms.)

—— *The New Covenant; Or, a Treatise, unfolding the order and manner of the giving and receiving of the Covenant of Grace to the Elect*, London, 1654.

—— *The way of Life*, London, 1641. (A series of readable sermons, it is the best literary statement, in the least technical terms, of the Puritan code.)

Dudley, Paul, *An Essay On The Merchandize of Slaves & Souls of Men; . . . With an Application Thereof to the Church of Rome*, Boston, 1731.

Dummer, Jeremiah, *A Discourse on the holiness of the Sabbath-day*, Boston, 1704. (Valuable for definitions of positive and natural law; for many important ideas at the turn of the century.)

Fitch, James, *The first Principles of the Doctrine of Christ*, Boston, 1679. (The best succinct summary of the creed and philosophy of the New England variety of Calvinism.)

Flynt, Josiah, "The Worlds Eternity is an Impossibility," *Almanack*, Cambridge, 1666.

Frere, W. H., and C. E. Douglas, *Puritan Manifestoes*, London, 1907; 1954.

Haller, William, ed., *Tracts on Liberty in the Puritan Revolution, 1638–1647*, New York, 1934, 3 vols.

Haller, William, and Godfrey Davies, eds., *The Leveller Tracts, 1647–1653*, New York, 1944.

Hanbury, Benjamin, ed., *Historical Memorials Relating to the Independents or Congregationalists, from their Rise to the Restoration*, London, 1839–1844, 3 vols. (A collection of copious extracts from the writings of Congregationalists, including many of the New England apologists. It provides a text for many books not easily available, and enables New England thought to be seen as part of a whole movement in English religious life.)

Hoar, Leonard, *The Sting of Death and Death Unstung*, Boston, 1680.

Hooke, William, *New-Englands Sence, of Old-England and Irelands Sorrowes*, London, 1645.

Hooker, Thomas, *The Application of Redemption By the Effectual Work of the Word and Spirit of Christ, for the bringing home of Lost Sinners to God*, London, 1657; 1659. (Sermons delivered at Hartford; the summary of Hooker's doctrine and spirit.)

—— *The Soules Exaltation*, London, 1638.

—— *The Soules Humiliation*, 2nd ed., London, 1638.

—— *The Soules Implantation*, London, 1637.

—— *The Soules Preparation for Christ*, London, 1632.

(These four works, which logically run *Preparation, Humiliation, Implantation*, and *Exaltation*, are the masterpieces of the most impassioned orator in the first generation of preachers. They were probably written before Hooker left England. They constitute the most minute and searching analysis of the soul and the process of spiritual regeneration, the most coherent and sustained expression of the essential religious experience ever achieved by the New England divines.) Sermons selected from the *Application, Preparation*, and *Implantation* reprinted in *Redemption, Three Sermons*, ed. Everett H. Emerson, Gainesville, Fla., 1956.)

Johnson, Samuel, *Samuel Johnson . . . His Career and Writings*, ed. Herbert and Carol Schneider, New York, 1929, 4 vols.

Mather, Cotton, *Fair Weather*, Boston, 1691.

—— *The Faith of the Fathers*, Boston, 1699.

—— "A Letter on the late Disputes about the Trinity," preface to Thomas Bradbury, *Necessity of Contending for Revealed Religion*, Boston, 1720.

—— *A Man of Reason*, Boston, 1718.

—— *Manuductio ad Ministerium*, Boston, 1726; New York, 1938. (Handbook for preachers.)

—— *Reason Satisfied: and Faith Established*, Boston, 1712.

—— *Reasonable Religion*, Boston, 1700.

—— "To the Reader," *The Boston Ephemeris*, 1683.

Mather, Increase, *Angelographia*, Boston, 1696.

—— *Awakening Truths Tending to Conversion*, Boston, 1710.

—— *A Call from Heaven To the Present and Succeeding Generations*, Boston, 1679.

—— *A Discourse Proving that the Christian Religion, Is the only True Religion*, Boston, 1702.

—— *The Doctrine of Divine Providence, opened and applyed*, Boston, 1684.

—— *Practical Truths Tending to Promote the Power of Godliness*, Boston, 1682.

—— *Some Important Truths About Conversion*, London, 1674; Boston, 1684.

—— *Soul-Saving Gospel Truths*, Boston, 1703; 1712.

—— *The Times of men are in the hand of God*, Boston, 1675.

Mayhew, Experience, *A Discourse shewing that God dealeth with Men As with Reasonable Creatures*, Boston, 1720.

Mitchell, Jonathan, *A Discourse of the Glory To which God hath called Believers By Jesus Christ*, London, 1677; Boston, 1721.

More, Paul Elmer, and Frank L. Cross, *Anglicanism: The Thought and Practice of the Church of England, Illustrated from the Religious Literature of the Seventeenth Century*, Milwaukee, Wis., 1935. (The most convenient source for tenets of the Puritans' opponents.)

Morgan, Joseph, *The History of the Kingdom of Basruah*, Boston, 1715; reprinted with three formerly unpublished letters, Cambridge, 1946. (An allegory of man's fall and redemption.)

Morton, Charles, *The Spirit of Man*, Boston, 1693.

Norton, John, *The Heart of N-England rent at the Blasphemies of the Present Generation*, Cambridge, 1659. (Condemnation of the Quakers.)

—— *The Orthodox Evangelist*, London, 1654. (Compact statement of the whole system of theology.)

Oakes, Urian, *The Soveraign Efficacy of Divine Providence*, Boston, 1682.

Parker, Thomas, *The Copy of a Letter Written . . . to His Sister*, London, 1650; Boston, 1925.

Pemberton, Ebenezer, *Sermons and Discourses on Several Occasions*, ed. Benjamin Colman, London, 1727. (A collection of the writings of one of the best minds in New England in the first two decades of the eighteenth century.)

Powicke, Frederick J., ed., *Some Unpublished Correspondence of the Reverend Richard Baxter and the Reverend John Eliot, 1656–1682*, Manchester, Eng., 1931.

Prince, Thomas, *Morning Health No Security Against the Sudden Arrest of Death before Night*, Boston, 1727.

Prince, Thomas, Jr., ed., *The Christian History, containing Accounts of the Revival and Propagation of Religion in Great-Britain & America*, Boston, 1744–1745, 2 vols. (America's first religious periodical; the literary repository for the revivalist wing of the New England clergy in the Great Awakening, opposed to Charles Chauncy.)

Robinson, John, *Works*, ed. Robert Ashton, Boston, 1851, 3 vols. (The writings of the pastor of the Pilgrim congregation in England and Holland, who, though he did not come to America, exerted a great influence on the thought of New England.)

Sewall, Samuel, *Phænomena quædam Apocalyptica*, Boston, 1697; 1727.

—— *Proposals Touching the Accomplishment of Prophecies*, Boston, 1713.

—— "Samuel Sewall and the New England Company," *Proceedings of the Massachusetts Historical Society*, LXVII (1941–1944), 1945, 55–110. (Sewall's account book when he was disbursing agent for a London missionary society, ed. George P. Winship.)

Shepard, Thomas, "Letter to Hugh Peter," *American Historical Review*, IV (1898), 105.

—— *New Englands Lamentation for Old Englands present errours, and divisions, and their feared future desolations if not timely prevented*, London, 1645. (New England attitude toward religious developments in England during the Civil Wars.)

—— *Works*, ed. John Albro, Boston, 1853, 3 vols. (The collected writings of one of the four major figures in the first generation of New England divines.)

Shepard, Thomas, Jr., *Eye-Salve; Or, A Watch-Word From our Lord Jesus Christ unto his Churches*, Cambridge, 1673.

Sherman, John, "A brief Essay to promote a religious improvement of this preceding Calendar," *Almanack*, Cambridge, 1677.

—— "A Monitory Advertisement," *Almanack*, Cambridge, 1676.

Stoddard, Solomon, *The Duty of Gospel-Ministers to preserve a People from Corruption*, Boston, 1718.

Thacher, Thomas, *A Fast of God's Chusing*, Boston, 1678.

"Tracts Relating to the Attempts to Convert to Christianity the Indians of New England," *Collections of the Massachusetts Historical Society*, third series, Vol. IV, 1834. (John Eliot, *The Day-Breaking*, 1647; Thomas Shepard, *The Clear Sunshine*, 1648; Edward Winslow, comp., *The Glorious Progress*, 1649; Henry Whitfield, *The Light appearing*, 1651; *Strength out of Weakness*, 1652; John Eliot and Thomas Mayhew, *Tears of Repentance*, 1653; John Eliot, *A Late and Further Manifestation*, 1655.)

Wadsworth, Benjamin, *Christ's Fan in his hand, separating the wheat & chaff*, Boston, 1722.

—— *An Essay on the Decalogue, or Ten Commandments*, Boston, 1719.

—— *True Piety the best Policy for Times of War*, Boston, 1722.

—— *The Way of life opened in the everlasting Covenant*, Boston, 1712.

Ward, Nathaniel, *The Simple Cobler of Aggawam in America*, London, 1647; ed. David Pulsifer, Boston, 1843; Ipswich Historical Society, 1906.

Wheelwright, John, *John Wheelwright. His Writings*, ed. Charles H. Bell, Boston, 1876. (The life and writings of a minister expelled from Massachusetts Bay for his friendship with the Antinomian party.)

Willard, Samuel, *The Barren Fig Trees Doom*, Boston, 1691.

—— *A Brief Discourse of Justification*, Boston, 1686.

—— *A Brief Reply to Mr. George Kieth*, Boston, 1703.

—— *The Child's Portion; Or, The Unseen Glory Of the Children of God, Asserted, and proved*, Boston, 1684.

—— *A Compleat Body of Divinity in Two Hundred and Fifty Expository Lectures*, Boston, 1726. (The *summa* of New England theology; the first folio printed in America; an immense repository, which makes dull reading, but is the authoritative reference book for the orthodox position on all points of the creed.)

—— *The Heart Garrisoned; Or, The Wisdome, and Care of the Spiritual Souldier above all things to safeguard his Heart.* Cambridge, 1676.

—— *The High Esteem Which God hath of the Death of his Saints*, Boston, 1683. (Sermon occasioned by the death of John Hull.)

—— *The Peril of the Times Displayed; Or, The Danger of Mens taking up with a Form of Godliness, But Denying the Power of it*, Boston, 1700.

Williams, Roger, *Experiments of Spiritual Life & Health, And their Preservatives*, London, 1652; Providence, 1863.

—— *George Fox Digg'd out of his Burrowes*, Boston, 1676; ed. J. L. Dimon, *Publications of the Narragansett Club*, Vol. V (1872). (Although the apostle of religious liberty, Williams attacked Quakers furiously.)

Wolfe, Don, ed., *Leveller Manifestoes of the Puritan Revolution*, New York, 1944.

2. The Way of the Churches

Barnard, John, *The Lord Jesus Christ the only, and Supream Head of the Church*, Boston, 1738. (Important sermon, marking the ultimate outcome of the ecclesiastical polity, where the Congregational system is actually claimed to give liberty of conscience.)

Cotton, John, *The Keyes of the Kingdom of Heaven, and Power thereof, according to the Word of God*, London, 1644.

—— *The Way of Congregational Churches Cleared*, London, 1648. (The best statement in historical terms of the sources, background, and development of the New England polity.)

Davenport, John, *An Answer of the Elders of the severall Churches in New-England unto Nine Positions sent over to them*, London, 1643. (Written in 1639, it is the first attempt to systematize the principles of the New England ecclesiastical order.)

The Power of Congregational Churches Asserted and Vindicated, London, 1672.

Hooker, Thomas, *A Survey of the Summe of Church-Discipline*, London, 1648. (The most profound, philosophical, and reasoned statement of the practical program of New England Puritanism. Indispensable.)

Mather, Cotton, *Ratio Discipline Fratrum Nov-Anglorum*, Boston, 1726; ed. T. C. Upham, Portland, 1829. (The best crystallization of a century of ecclesiastical development in New England.)

Mather, Increase, *The Divine Right of Infant-Baptisme Asserted and Proved from Scripture And Antiquity*, Boston, 1680.

—— *The Order of the Gospel, Professed and Practised by the Churches of Christ in New-England, Justified*, Boston, 1700.

—— *A Dissertation, wherein The Strange Doctrine Lately Published in a Sermon, The Tendency of which, is, to Encourage Unsanctified Persons (which such) to Approach the Holy Table of the Lord, is Examined and Confuted*, Boston, 1708. (Attack on Solomon Stoddard.)

Mather, Richard, *An Apologie of the Churches in New-England for Church-Covenant*, London, 1643.

—— *Church-Government and Church-Covenant Discussed*, London, 1643. (Cf. T. J. Holmes, *Proceedings of the American Antiquarian Society*, N.S. XXXIII (1923), 291–296.)

Mather, Samuel, *An Apology For the Liberties of the Churches in New England: To which is prefix'd, A Discourse concerning Congregational Churches*, Boston, 1738.

Perkins, William, *Of the Calling of the Ministrie: Two Treatises. Describing the duties and Dignities of that Calling*, London, 1606; *Works*, 1618, III, 429–463. (Perkins was regarded as one of the greatest of theologians by New Englanders, and his works were standard texts; this treatise enunciates the Puritan conception of the role and function of the minister.)

Shepard, Thomas, and John Allin, *A Defence of the Answer made unto the Nine Questions or Positions sent from New-England*, London, 1648.

Stoddard, Solomon, *An Appeal to the Learned. Being A Vindication of the Right of Visible Saints to the Lords Supper, Though they be destitute of a Saving Work of God's Spirit on their Hearts: Against the Exceptions of Mr. Increase Mather*, Boston, 1709.

—— *The Doctrine of Instituted Churches Explained and Proved from the Word of God*, London, 1700. (A reply to Increase Mather's *The Order of the Gospel*, this work initiated the so-called Stoddardean doctrine: that all who professed belief in saving grace might therefore partake of the Lord's Supper.)

—— *The Inexcusableness of Neglecting The Worship of God, under A Pretence of being in an Unconverted Condition*, Boston, 1708. (A statement of Stoddard's theories of church polity, marking a departure from the orthodox platform, and the beginning of a bitter controversy with Increase Mather.)

B. Secondary Works

There are few substantial studies of Puritan thought before the present century. Particularly within the last generation an effort has been made to examine and appraise Puritan thought as a chapter in intellectual history. This section of the bibliography should be supplemented by Section II B.

Akers, Charles, "The Making of a Religious Liberal: Jonathan Mayhew and the Great Awakening," *New England Social Studies Bulletin*, XI, No. 3 (Mar., 1954), 18–25.

Armstrong, Maurice W., "English, Scottish and Irish Backgrounds of American Presbyterianism, 1689–1729," *Journal of the Presbyterian Historical Society*, XXXIV (1956), 3–18.

Atkins, Gaius Glenn, and Frederick L. Fagley, *History of American Congregationalism*, Boston and Chicago, 1942. (A popular and not always critical account.)

Bacon, Leonard W., *A History of American Christianity*, New York, 1897.

Banks, Charles E., "Religious 'Persecution' as a Factor in the Emigration to New England," *Proceedings of the Massachusetts Historical Society*, LXVIII (1934–1935), 136–151.

Bartlett, Irving H., "The Puritans as Missionaries," *Boston Public Library Quarterly*, II (1950), 99–118.

Beardsley, Frank G., *A History of American Revivals*, New York, 1912.

Becker, Carl L., *The Heavenly City of the Eighteenth-Century Philosophers*, New Haven, 1932; Yale paperback. (A brilliant analysis of eighteenth-century rationalism, interpreting it as a new attempt to realize the Augustinian City of God on earth. This study of the religious overtones of eighteenth-century thought helps to make comprehensible the tendencies of the seventeenth century.)

Benz, Ernest, "The Pietist and Puritan Sources of Early Protestant Missions," *Church History*, XXI (1951), 28–55. (Cotton Mather's correspondence with A. H. Francke and with missionaries from Halle.)

Boardman, George N., *A History of New England Theology*, New York, 1899. (An analysis of the theological systems, but with very limited attention to the historic settings of the New England doctrine.)

Brauer, Jerald C., "Reflections on the Nature of English Puritanism," *Church History*, XXIII (1954), 99–108. (A succinct and penetrating article.)

Buranelli, Vincent, "Colonial Philosophy," *William and Mary Quarterly*, XVI (1959), 343–362.

Calamandrei, Mauro, "Neglected Aspects of Roger Williams' Thought," *Church History*, XXI (1952), 239–256. (Argues that Roger Williams was not a man of the Renaissance nor of the Enlightenment, but a Puritan, Biblicist, and Millenarian.)

Cambridge Modern History, The, Chapters valuable for intellectual background: Vol. II (1903), Chap. xi, "Calvinism and the Reformed Church"; Chap. xix, "Tendencies of European Thought in the Age of the Reformation"; Vol. III (1905), Chap. xxii, "Political Thought in the

Sixteenth Century"; Vol. IV (1906), Chap. xxvii, "Descartes and Cartesianism"; Vol. V (1907), Chap. xi, "Religious Toleration in England"; Chap. xxiii, "European Science in the Seventeenth and Early Years of the Eighteenth Century"; Chap. xxiv, "Latitudinarianism and Pietism"; Vol. VI (1909), Chap. xxiii, "English Political Philosophy in the Seventeenth and Eighteenth Centuries."

Cambridge Platform of 1648, The; Tercentenary Commemoration, ed. Henry Wilder Foote, Boston, 1949. (Articles by F. L. Fagley, H. W. Foote, P. Miller, R. Bainton, A. C. McGiffert, Jr., A. Bradford and J. B. Conant.)

Catholic Cyclopedia, The, New York, 1907–1914, 6 vols. (Extremely useful, particularly for doctrinal history.)

Choisy, Eugene, and others, *Études sur Calvin et le Calvinisme*, Paris, 1935. (A volume of studies by many European authorities, on the foliation of Calvin, presenting many parallels to New England developments.)

Clark, George N., *The Seventeenth Century*, Oxford, 1929; Galaxy paperback. (An excellent survey of general conditions and intellectual currents.)

Clark, Henry W., *History of English Nonconformity*, London, 1911–1913, 2 vols.

Cragg, G. R., *From Puritanism to the Age of Reason: A Study of Changes in Religious Thought Within the Church of England, 1660–1700*, New York, 1950.

—— *Puritanism in the Period of the Great Persecution, 1660–1688*, New York, 1957.

Cremeans, Charles Davis, *The Reception of Calvinistic Thought in England*, Urbana, 1949. (A valuable study in the transmission of ideas.)

Cross, Arthur L., *The Anglican Episcopate and the American Colonies*, New York, 1902. (Chapters 6 and 7 deal with Mayhew and the Chandler-Chauncy controversies.)

Dale, Robert W., *History of English Congregationalism*, London, 1907.

Davenport, Frederick M., *Primitive Traits in Religious Revivals*, New York, 1905.

Davies, Godfrey, "Arminian versus Puritan in England, *ca.* 1620–1640," *Huntington Library Bulletin*, No. 5 (1934), 157–179.

Davies, Horton, *The Worship of the English Puritans*, London, 1948.

De Jong, Peter Y., *The Covenant Idea in New England Theology, 1620–1847*, Grand Rapids, 1946.

Dexter, Henry M., *The Congregationalism of the Last Three Hundred Years, as Seen in its Literature*, New York, 1880. (The monumental achievement of the greatest of Congregational historians, liberal but inevitably biased in favor of Puritanism. An immense bibliography of Congregational literature, both English and American, the fruit of years of research, is of great value.)

Dickens, A. G., *Lollards and Protestants in the Diocese of York, 1509–1558*, London, 1959. (An important study in the transmission of ideas. Documents an unbroken dissenting tradition from Lollardy to Puritanism.)

Drury, Clifford M., "Presbyterian Beginnings in New England and the Middle Colonies," *Journal of the Presbyterian Historical Society*, XXXIV (1956), 19–35.

Dunning, Albert E., *Congregationalists in America. A popular history of their origin, belief, polity, growth, and work*, Boston, 1894; New York, 1902.

Eames, Wilberforce, "Early New England Catechisms," *Proceedings of the American Antiquarian Society*, N.S. XII (1897–1898), 76–182.

Emerson, Everett H., "Calvin and Covenant Theology," *Church History*, XXV (1956), 136–144.

—— "Thomas Hooker and the Reformed Theology: The Relationship of Hooker's Conversion Preaching to Its Background," *Church History*, XXIV (1955), 369–370. (Abstract of doctoral dissertation.)

Emery, Samuel H., *The Ministry of Taunton*, Boston, 1853, 2 vols. (Reprints of sermons of William Hooke, Samuel Danforth, and Ephraim Judson.)

Faust, Clarence H., "The Decline of Puritanism," *Transitions in American Literary History*, cf. Harry Hayden Clark, Durham, N.C., 1953, 1–48.

—— Clarence H., and Thomas H. Johnson, *Jonathan Edwards*, American Writers Series, New York, 1935; American Century paperback. (Selections from sermons, treatises, and letters; bibliography; discussion of intellectual and literary background.)

Felt, Joseph B., *Ecclesiastical History of New England; comprising not only Religious, but also Moral, and other Relations*, Boston, 1855–1862, 2 vols. (A sprawling, ill-digested amassing of material, valuable for the amount of first-hand material quoted and the immense if unorganized knowledge of local history.)

Fenn, William W., *The Christian Way of Life . . . in the History of Religion in New England*, London, 1924.

—— "John Robinson's Farewell Address," *Harvard Theological Review*, XIII (1920), 236–251.

—— "The Marrow of Calvin's Theology," *Harvard Theological Review*, II (1909), 323–339. (Excellent.)

—— "The Revolt against the Standing Order," *Religious History of New England*, King's Chapel Lectures, Cambridge, 1917.

Fisher, George P., *History of Christian Doctrine*, New York, 1906. (Excellent handbook for the history of theology.)

Foote, Henry Wilder, "The Significance and Influence of the Cambridge Platform of 1648," *Proceedings of the Massachusetts Historical Society*, LXIX (1947–1950), 1956, 81–101.

Ford, Worthington C., "New England Catechisms," *Proceedings of the Massachusetts Historical Society*, LXII (1930), 28–29.

Foster, Frank H., "The Eschatology of the New England Divines," *Bibliotheca Sacra*, XLIII (1886), 6–19.

—— *A Genetic History of the New England Theology*, Chicago, 1907. (The best study of theological development. Unfortunately it devotes but one chapter to the period before Jonathan Edwards.)

Foster, Herbert D., "International Calvinism through Locke and the Revolution of 1688," *American Historical Review*, XXXII (1927), 475–499. (A penetrating study, demonstrating how Calvinism, filtered through Locke, eventuates in Lockean political philosophy.)

Frere, Walter H., *The English Church in the Reigns of Elizabeth and James I*, London, 1904. (Very useful for English religious backgrounds.)

Garrett, C. H., *The Marian Exiles*, Cambridge, Eng., 1938. (Reveals the continental influences on the Elizabethan settlement.)

Gaustad, Edwin Scott, *The Great Awakening in New England*, New York, 1957.

Gohdes, Clarence, "Aspects of Idealism in Early New England," *Philosophical Review*, XXXIX (1930), 537–555. (Points out the influence of the Cambridge Platonists in New England.)

Gordon, George A., *Humanism in New England Theology*, Boston, 1920.

Grabo, Norman S., "The Poet to the Pope: Edward Taylor to Solomon Stoddard," *American Literature*, XXXII (1960), 197–201. (Taylor urges Stoddard to lay down his innovations that threatened the peaceful order of New England churches.)

Griffiths, Olive M., *Religion and Learning: A Study in English Presbyterian Thought from the Bartholomew Ejections (1662) to the Foundation of the Unitarian Movement*, Cambridge, Eng., 1935. (An excellent study, tracing the steps of development whereby Calvinism becomes Unitarian rationalism; a parallel movement to that in New England, which is much illuminated by the comparison.)

Hall, Thomas C., *The Religious Background of American Culture*, Boston, 1930. (A brilliant and often penetrating history, maintaining the questionable thesis that English Puritanism contains an element of thought inherited from Wycliff which is antagonistic to Calvinism.)

Haller, William, "John Foxe and the Puritan Revolution," *The Seventeenth Century: Studies in the History of English Thought . . .*, R. F. Jones *et al.*, Stanford, 1948. (The *Book of Martyrs*, a powerful force on shaping Puritan thought on the church in history.)

—— *Liberty and Reformation in the Puritan Reformation*, New York, 1955. (A continuation to 1649 of the earlier study on the rise of Puritanism.)

—— *The Rise of Puritanism, or the Way to the New Jerusalem as Set Forth in Pulpit and Press . . . 1570–1643*, New York, 1938; Harper Torchbook edition 1957. (This book with the succeeding volume [supra] make a brilliant contribution to our knowledge of the inner life and dynamism of the Puritan movement.)

Hallowell, Richard P., *The Quaker Invasion of Massachusetts*, Boston, 1883.

Haroutunian, Joseph, *Piety versus Moralism: The Passing of the New England Theology*, New York, 1932.

Hastings, James, ed., *Encyclopedia of Religion and Ethics*, New York, 1908–1914, 13 vols. (Very useful; bibliographies given.)

Hazard, Paul, *La Crise de la Conscience Européenne, 1680–1715*, Paris, 1935, 3 vols.

Heimert, Alan, "Puritanism, The Wilderness, and the Frontier," *New England Quarterly*, XXVI (1953), 361–382.

Henson, Herbert H., *Studies in English Religion in the Seventeenth Century*, London, 1903. (Extremely useful and stimulating.)

Hornberger, Theodore, "Benjamin Coleman and the Enlightenment," *New England Quarterly*, XII (1939), 227–240.

—— "Samuel Lee (1625–1691), A Clerical Channel for the Flow of New Ideas to Seventeenth Century New England," *Osiris*, I (1936), 341–355.

Hunt, John, *Religious Thought in England from the Reformation to the End of Last Century*, London, 1870–1873, 3 vols.

Hutton, William H., *The English Church from the Accession of Charles I to the Death of Anne, 1625–1714*, London, 1903.

Jones, Adam L., *Early American Philosophers*, New York, 1898.

Jones, Rufus M., *Mysticism and Democracy in the English Commonwealth*, Cambridge, 1932. (Chapter on "Seeker Movement" is valuable for Williams and New England mysticism.)

—— *The Quakers in the American Colonies*, London, 1911.

——*Studies in Mystical Religion*, London, 1909.

Knappen, Marshall M., *Tudor Puritanism: A Chapter in the History of Idealism*, Chicago, 1939. (An immensely valuable book for understanding the medieval and international character of the Puritan mind.)

——, ed., *Two Elizabethan Puritan Diaries*, Chicago, 1933. (The introduction contains one of the best analyses of the Puritan character yet in print; it rebuts the thesis of Weber and Tawney.)

Lecky, William E. H., *History of the Rise and Influence of the Spirit of Rationalism in Europe*, New York, 1866, 2 vols. (Although antipathetic to the religious point of view, this classic work is still essential to an understanding of the evolution of seventeenth-century New England into eighteenth.)

Lee, Umphrey, *The Historical Backgrounds of Early Methodist Enthusiasm*, New York, 1931.

Levy, Babette May, *Preaching in the First Half Century of New England History*, Hartford, 1945.

Lowenherz, Robert J., "Roger Williams and the Great Quaker Debate,". *American Quarterly*, XI (1959), 157–165.

Lydekker, John Wolfe, "The New England Company, the First Missionary Society. Some Account of Its Foundation and Early History," *Historical Magazine of the Protestant Episcopal Church*, XIV (1944), 107–127.

McClellan, B., "Two Shepherds Contending," *New England Quarterly*, XXVII (1954), 455–472. (The correspondence of J. Ashley, Minister at the Deerfield (1732–1780) with Father Jean Baptiste Sainte Pe, one of the Jesuit leaders in Canada.)

McClurkin, Paul T., "Presbyterianism in New England Congregationalism," *Journal of the Presbyterian Historical Society*, XXXI (1953), 245–254; XXXII (1954), 109–114.

McCulloch, Samuel C., "The Foundation and Early Work of the Society for the Propagation of the Gospel in Foreign Parts, *Huntington Library Quarterly*, VIII (1945), 241–258.

McGiffert, Arthur C., Sr., *Protestant Thought Before Kant*, New York, 1929; 1951; Harper Torchbook edition, 1962. (An excellent handbook; Chapter VIII on seventeenth-century Protestantism, and the section in Chapter IX on the New England theology, are especially useful.)

McGiffert, Arthur C., Jr., *Jonathan Edwards*, New York, 1932.

McGinn, Donald, *The Admonition Controversy*, New Brunswick, 1949. (A study of the beginning of the Puritan movement.)

MacKinnon, James, *Calvin and the Reformation*, London, 1936. (Probably the most convenient one volume survey of "Calvinistic" backgrounds.)

McLachlan, H. J., *Socinianism in 17th-Century England*, Oxford, 1951.

Maclear, James Fulton, "The Heart of New England Rent: The Mystical Element in Early Puritan History," *Mississippi Valley Historical Review*, XLII (1956), 621–652.

—— " 'The True American Union' of Church and State: The Reconstruction of the Theocratic Tradition," *Church History*, XXVIII (1959), 41–62.

Masson, David, *The Life of John Milton*, London, 1859–1894, 7 vols.; New York, 1946. (Still one of the most useful studies of the background of English religious history.)

Michaelsen, Robert S., "Changes in the Puritan Concept of Calling or Vocation," *New England Quarterly*, XXVI (1953), 315–336. (The changes within the Puritan concept of vocation in England helped produce Defoe's "complete tradesman"; in America they contributed to the "wisdom" of Poor Richard and *The Way to Wealth*.)

Micklem, Nathaniel, ed., *Christian Worship: Studies in its History and Meaning*, by Members of Mansfield College, Oxford, 1936.

Miller, Perry, "The End of the World," *William and Mary Quarterly*, VIII (1951), 171–191; reprinted with some modifications in *Errand into the Wilderness*, Cambridge, 1956, 217–239.

—— "From Edwards to Emerson," *New England Quarterly*, XIII (1940), 589–617; reprinted in *Errand into the Wilderness*, Cambridge, 1956, 184–203. (The Puritan effort to confront face to face the blinding image of divinity in the physical world.)

—— "The Half-Way Covenant," *New England Quarterly*, VI (1933), 676–715.

—— "The Marrow of Puritan Divinity," *Publications of the Colonial Society of Massachusetts*, XXXII (1938), 247–300; reprinted in *Errand into the Wilderness*, Cambridge, 1956, 48–98. (Analysis of the theory of the covenant in Puritan theology and society; elements of rationalism were already in Puritan thought by 1630, differentiating New England theology from Calvinism and moving in the direction of eighteenth-century points of view.)

—— *The New England Mind: From Colony to Province*, Cambridge, 1953; Beacon paperback, 1961.

—— *The New England Mind: The Seventeenth Century*, New York, 1939; reissued with "correction of the more egregious misprints," Cambridge, 1954; Beacon paperback, 1961.

—— *Orthodoxy in Massachusetts, 1630–1650: A Genetic Study*, Cambridge, 1933; Beacon paperback. (A study of the religious objectives of the New England Puritans in terms of their origins in England.)

—— "The Puritan Theory of the Sacraments in Seventeenth Century New England," *Catholic Historical Review*, XXII (1937), 409–425.

—— "Solomon Stoddard, 1643–1729," *Harvard Theological Review*, XXXIV (1941), 277–320. (His contribution to religious thought.)

Morais, Herbert M., *Deism in Eighteenth Century America*, New York, 1934. (A pioneer work, which lists the names and the writings of American deists, but does not go very deeply into the analysis of intellectual currents.)

Morgan, Edmund S., "The Puritans' Marriage with God," *South Atlantic Quarterly*, XLVIII (1949), 107–112.

Morison, Samuel E., *The Puritan Pronaos: Studies in the Intellectual Life of New England in the Seventeenth Century*, New York, 1936; a second edition with minor revisions, *The Intellectual Life of Colonial New England*, New York, 1956; Cornell paperback. (A lively and readable survey of Puritan intellectual life, valuable for discussion of education and curriculum, but untrustworthy on literature and more philosophical aspects.)

—— "Those Misunderstood Puritans," *Forum*, LXXXV (1931), 142–147.

Mosse, George L., "Puritan Radicalism and the Enlightenment," *Church History*, XXIX (1960), 424–439. (Breaks new ground in tracing the contribution of radical Puritanism—Ranters and Seekers among others—to English deism.)

Mozley, J. F., *John Foxe and His Book*, New York, 1940. (A sympathetic examination of the author of the *Book of Martyrs*, the most widely read of all Protestant histories and one which the

Puritans considered peculiarly their own.)

Murdock, Kenneth B., "The Puritan Tradition in American Literature," Chapter V in *The Reinterpretation of American Literature*, ed. Norman Foerster, New York, 1928.

New Cambridge Modern History, The, Cambridge, Eng., 1957—. (Does not supplant *The Cambridge Modern History*, but valuable interpretations for intellectual background in those volumes published, are Vol. II (1958), ed. G. R. Elton, Chapter XII, Part 2, "Intellectual Tendencies: Science," by A. R. Hall, and Chapter XIII, "Schools and Universities," by Denys Hay, 386–414; Vol. V (1961), ed. F. L. Casten, Chapter III, "The Scientific Movement," by A. R. Hall, and Chapter IV, "Philosophy," by W. Van Leyden, 47–95.)

New Schaff-Herzog Encyclopedia of Religious Knowledge, The, New York, 1908–1912, 12 vols.

Nuesse, Celestine Joseph, *The Social Thought of American Catholics, 1634–1829*, Westminster, Md., 1945.

Nuttall, Geoffrey F., *The Holy Spirit in Puritan Faith and Experience*, Oxford, 1946. (Emphasizes the mystical and "experiential" nature of the Puritan religion.)

Paradise, S. H., "Religion in Essex County," *Americana*, XXIX (1935), 181–227.

Parrington, Vernon L., *Main Currents in American Thought*, New York, 1927–1930, 3 vols.; 1955; one vol. edition, 1939; Harvest paperback. Vol. I: *The Colonial Mind.* (A noble work inspired by a militant liberalism, consequently hostile and unsympathetic to Puritanism; based upon lamentably insufficient familiarity with the sources, and therefore to be read for stimulation, not for fact or accuracy.)

Pattison, Mark, "Tendencies of Religious Thought in England, 1680–1750," in *Essays*, Oxford, 1889, 2 vols., Vol. I, 42–119.

Pickman, Edward M., "The Collapse of the Scholastic Hierarchy in Seventeenth Century France," *Proceedings of the Massachusetts Historical Society*, LXIV (1931), 212–249. (The break-up of the scholastic world; valuable for understanding the background of Puritan intellectual history.)

Platner, John W., "The Congregationalists," *Religious History of New England*, King's Chapel Lectures, Cambridge, 1917. (Excellent.)

Plooij, Daniel, *The Pilgrim Fathers from a Dutch Point of View*, New York, 1932. (New material on the sustained interest of the emigrants from Holland in those left at Leyden.)

Plum, Harry Grant, *Restoration Puritanism*, Chapel Hill, 1943.

Porter, H. C., *Reformation and Reaction in Tudor Cambridge*, Cambridge, Eng., 1958. (A literate, informal study based largely on secondary sources.)

Randall, John H., *The Making of the Modern Mind*, Boston, 1926. (Excellent handbook for the general intellectual background.)

(Ray), Sister Mary Augustina, *American Opinion of Roman Catholicism in the Eighteenth Century*, New York, 1936.

Riley, Arthur J., "Catholicism and the New England Mind," *Publications of the Colonial Society of Massachusetts*, XXXIV (1943), 389–399.

—— *Catholicism in New England to 1788*, Washington, 1936.

Riley, I. Woodbridge, *American Philosophy: The Early Schools*, New York, 1907; 1959. (Excellent as far as it goes, but not sympathetic to Puritanism in general; it sacrifices a study of the whole thought to a concentration upon individual figures. Now outdated.)

—— *American Thought from Puritanism to Pragmatism and Beyond*, New York, 1915.

Robertson, John M., *A Short History of Freethought, Ancient and Modern*, London, 2nd ed., 1906, 2 vols. (Vol. II, Chapter 17, "Early Freethought in the United States.")

Rowley, William E., "The Puritans' Tragic Vision," *New England Quarterly*, XVII (1944), 394–417.

Rupp, E. G., *Studies in the Making of the English Protestant Tradition: Mainly in the Reign of Henry VIII*, Cambridge, Eng., 1958.

Schafer, Thomas A., "Jonathan Edwards's Conception of the Church," *Church History*, XXIV (1955), 51–66.

Schirmer, Walter F., *Antike, Renaissance und Puritanismus*, 2nd ed., München, 1933.

Schneider, Herbert W., *The Puritan*

Mind, New York, 1930; Ann Arbor paperback. (A philosophical interpretation.)

Sencourt, Robert, (pseud.,) *Outflying Philosophy*, London, 1925. (Stimulating essay on seventeenth-century thought, particularly on Sir Thomas Browne, but valuable for religious background.)

Shipton, Clifford K., "The Hebraic Background of Puritanism," *Publications of the American Jewish Historical Society*, XLVII (1958), 140–153.

—— "A Plea for Puritanism," *American Historical Review*, XL (1935), 460–467.

Sisson, Rosemary A., "William Perkins, Apologist for the Elizabethan Church of England," *Modern Language Review*, XLVII (1952), 495–502.

Smith, Chard Powers, *Yankees and God*, New York, 1954. (A popular history of New England culture and Puritanism from the seventeenth to twentieth century.)

Smyth, Egbert C., "The 'New Philosophy' against which students at Yale College were warned in 1714," *Proceedings of the American Antiquarian Society*, N.S. XI (1896–1897), 251–252.

Solt, Leo F., "Anti-Intellectualism in the Puritan Revolution," *Church History*, XXV (1956), 306–316.

Stearns, Raymond Phineas, *Congregationalism in the Dutch Netherlands: The Rise and Fall of the English Congregational Classes 1621–1635*, Chicago, 1940.

—— "The New England Way in Holland," *New England Quarterly*, VI (1933), 747–792.

Stephen, Leslie, *History of English Thought in the Eighteenth Century*, London, 1876, 2 vols. (The first chapters are useful as supplying a background for intellectual developments in early eighteenth-century New England.)

Sweet, William Warren, *Religion in Colonial America*, New York, 1942. (The Americanization of Christianity through the democratic impulse of the Great Revival.)

—— *The Story of Religions in America*, New York, 1930; 1939.

Tomas, V., "The Modernity of Jonathan Edwards," *New England Quarterly*, XXV (1952), 60–84.

Townsend, Harvey G., *Philosophical Ideas in the United States*, New York, 1934. (A popular presentation, not too reliable; the bibliography is excellent.)

Tracy, Joseph, *The Great Awakening: A History of the Revival of Religion in the Time of Edwards and Whitefield*, Boston, 1841. (Useful for the extracts from diaries, letters, colonial newspapers, etc.)

Trefz, Edward K., "Satan as the Prince of Evil. The Preaching of New England Puritans," *Boston Public Library Quarterly*, VII (1955), 3–22.

—— "Satan in Puritan Preaching," *Boston Public Library Quarterly*, VIII (1956), 71–84, 148–159.

Trinterud, Leonard J., *The Forming of an American Tradition. A Re-examination of Colonial Presbyterianism*, Philadelphia, 1949. (Emphasizes the New England influence on the colonial church.)

—— "The New England Contribution to Colonial American Presbyterianism," *Church History*, XVII (1948), 32–43.

—— "The Origins of Puritanism," *Church History*, XX (1951), 37–57. (Finds the origins in a native tradition.)

Troeltsch, Ernst, *The Social Teaching of the Christian Churches* (trans. Olive Wyon), London, 1931, 2 vols.; London and Glencoe, Ill., 1949; Harper Torchbook edition 1960. (A monumental work, emphasizing the social implications of religious and ecclesiastical groups; the section on New England is unfortunately based upon very slight familiarity with American sources.)

Tufts, James H., "Edwards and Newton," *The Philosophical Review*, XLIX (1940), 609–622. (Edwards and the "new" science.)

Tulloch, John, *Rational Theology and Christian Philosophy in England in the Seventeenth Century*, London, 1872, 2 vols. (Still the best survey of the growth of rational religious thought in England.)

Turnbull, G. H., "John Drury's Correspondence with the Clergy of New England about Ecclesiastical Peace," *Publications of the Colonial Society of Massachusetts*, XXVIII (1947–1951), 1959, 18–21.

Tuttle, Julius H., "William Whiston and Cotton Mather," *Publications of the Colonial Society of Massachusetts*, XIII (1912), 197–204.

Uhden, Herman F., *The New England Theocracy: A History of the Congregationalists in New England to the Revivals of 1740*, Boston, 1858. (Translation from the German edition of 1842.)

Voegelin, Erich, *Ueber die Form des Amerikanischen Geistes*, Tübingen, 1928.

Waddington, John, *Congregational History*, London, 1869–1880, 5. vols. (The most complete study of English origins and contemporary parallels of the ecclesiastical order.)

Walker, George L., *Some Aspects of the Religious Life of New England, with Special Reference to Congregationalists*, Boston, 1897.

Walker, Williston, *A History of the Congregational Churches in the United States*, New York, 1894. (American Church History Series. The standard short history; not so extensive on some subjects as Dexter, but more even and judicious.)

Webb, Clement C. J., *Studies in the History of Natural Theology*, Oxford, 1915.

Weber, Max, *The Protestant Ethic and the Spirit of Capitalism* (translated by Talcott Parsons), New York, 1930; London, 1948; Scribner's paperback. (The classic interpretation of Protestantism from the economic point of view; it argues that Puritanism came into being as the discipline for a rising capitalist class, and is to be interpreted as a middle-class movement.)

Weis, Frederick L., "The New England Company of 1649 and Its Missionary Enterprises, *Publications of the Colonial Society of Massachusetts*, XXXVIII (1947–1951), 1959, 134–218.

White, Eugene C., "Decline of the Great Awakening in New England, 1741–1746," *New England Quarterly*, XXIV (1951), 35–52.

Whiting, Charles E., *Studies in English Puritanism from the Restoration to the Revolution*, New York, 1931. (The best work for English backgrounds after 1660.)

Willey, Basil, *The Seventeenth Century Background*, London, 1934; Anchor paperback. (A challenging interpretation of various aspects of the century's thought, that may err on the side of a somewhat too intuitive grasp, but supplies a number of stimulating ideas that promise to be fruitful if applied more particularly to Puritan history.)

Williams, George, "The Wilderness and Paradise in the History of the Church," *Church History*, XXVIII (1959), 3–24; reprinted with minor revisions in *Wilderness and Paradise in Christian Thought*, New York, 1961. (Important for understanding the concept of the wilderness in Puritan thought.)

Winslow, Ola Elizabeth, "The Religion of Roger Williams," *Bulletin of the Congregational Library*, VIII (1957), 5–13.

Wood, T., *English Casuistical Divinity during the 17th Century*, London, 1952.

Worthley, Harold Field, "The Colonial Diaconate: an Example of the Allocation and Exercise of Authority in the Particular Churches of New England," *Proceedings of the Unitarian Historical Society*, Vol. XII, Part II (1959), 27–52.

—— "The Massachusetts Convention of Congregational Ministers: an Historical Essay," *Proceedings of the Unitarian Historical Society*, Vol. XII, Part I (1958), 49–103.

Young, Edward J., "Subjects for Master's Degree in Harvard College from 1655 to 1791," *Proceedings of the Massachusetts Historical Society*, XVIII (1881), 119–151.

Ziff, Larzer, "The Salem Puritans in the 'Free Aire of a New World' ", *Huntington Library Quarterly*, XX (1956–1957), 373–384. (Reasserts the influence of Plymouth on the church polity of Salem and subsequently the other churches of the Bay.)

THE PURITANS

VOLUME II

Nov.r 2. Midweek, went again, and found Mrs. 1720.
Alden there, who quickly went out. Gave her
ab't ½ a pound of Sugar Almonds, cost 3s per £. (158.)
Carried them on Monday. She seem'd pleas'd with 317
them, ask'd what they cost. Spake of giving her a
Hundred pounds per annum if I dy'd before her. Ask'd
her what sum she would give me, if she should dy
first? Said I would give her time to Consider of
it. She said she heard as if I had given all to
my Children by Deeds of Gift. I told her 'twas
a mistake, Point-Judith was mine &c. That
in England, I own'd, my Father's desire was yt
it should go to my eldest Son; 'twas 20£ per annum;
she thought 'twas forty. I think when I seem'd to excuse pressing this, she seem'd to think 'twas best to
speak of it; a long winter was coming on. Gave
me a Glass or two of Canary. Nov.r 4th Friday. Nov.r 4.
Went again ab't 7. a-clock; found there Mr.
John Walley and his wife: sat discoursing diet bread
pleasantly. I shew'd them Isaac Moses's Writing. Madam W. serv'd Comfeits to us. After
a-while a Table was spread, and Supper was set.
I urg'd Mr. Walley to Crave a Blessing; but he
put it upon me. About 9. they went away.
I ask'd Madam what fashion'd Neck-lace
I should present her with, She said, None at
all. I ask'd her Whereabout we left off last
time; mention'd what I had offer'd to give
her; ask'd her what she would give me;
She said she could not Change her Condition:
She had said so from ye beginning; could not
be so far from her Children, the Lecture.
Quoted the Apostle Paul affirming that a
single Life was better than a Married. I
answer'd That was for the present Distress.
Said she had not pleasure in things of that
nature as formerly: I said, you are the
fitter to make me a Wife. If she held
in that mind, I must go home and bewail my
Rashness in making more haste than good
Speed. However, considering ye Supper, I
desired her to be within next Monday
night, if we liv'd so long. Assured

Page of Samuel Sewall's *Diary*. (For text, see p. 526.)

❧ Chapter IV

MANNERS, CUSTOMS, AND BEHAVIOR

WHEN John Josselyn, naturalist and traveler, returned to England in 1671, he wrote of the civil and ecclesiastical "great masters" whom he met in the Bay Colony that some of them were "damnable rich." His objurgations went even farther:

> . . . inexplicably covetous and proud, they receive your gifts but as an homage or tribute due to their transcendency, which is a fault their Clergie are also guilty of, whose living is upon the bounty of their hearers. . . . The chiefest objects of discipline, Religion, and morality they want, some are of a *Linsie-woolsie* disposition, of several professions in Religion, all like *Aethiopians* white in the Teeth, only full of ludification and injurious dealing, . . . and savagely factious amongst themselves. . . .[1]

Some forty years had elapsed since Governor Winthrop led his earnest followers to New England, and doubtless times had changed. The authority of the earlier magistrates, most of whom by Josselyn's time had been "laid asleep in their beds of rest till the day of doom," [2] was passing; even the clergy, alarmed at the defection from high seriousness which they believed was spreading among the coming generation, had cautioned them "alwayes to remember, that Originally they are a *Plantation Religious*, not a plantation of Trade." [3] But a clergyman's privilege of straight speaking and a traveler's presumption in criticizing are two different things. Perhaps Josselyn was right, even if his censure went unheeded, for though sketched in pique his outline does not seriously misrepresent the composite Yankee.

Josselyn was one of the first among many observers of American manners who have found much to bewilder them and not a little to criticize. Colonizers as a rule do not combine high ideals with shrewd clear-sightedness, self-discipline with passion. If the leaders among the second generation of New Englanders accepted Josselyn's gifts as homage, they were but receiving a tribute due the "*Plantation Religious*"; if they were proud, then Josselyn had misjudged them in expecting servility.

Factiousness was indeed an infirmity to which early New Eng-

[1] *An Account of Two Voyages to New-England* (London, 1674), pp. 180, 181. Linsey-woolsey is a coarse fabric of linen and wool; by extension, a term of depreciation.

[2] *Ibid.*, p. 183.

[3] John Norton, *The Heart of N-England rent* (1659), p. 58. The same phrase is repeated in John Higginson's Massachusetts Election Sermon for 1663, *The Cause of God* (Cambridge), p. 11.

landers were peculiarly prone. The relative isolation of each village group compelled its members to associate in vexatious yet unavoidable propinquity. The era when "Good fences make good neighbors" had not yet arrived, and the "commonage," or unfenced village land, was shared. When horses and cattle strayed, as they might do with exasperating ease, tempers flared, and only the greatest self-control prevented bitter contention, as the diary of Joseph Green vividly testifies (see p. 448). The colonists did not welcome lawyers as a class—wisely perhaps, for the issues which made the townsmen so "savagely factious amongst themselves" could be as equitably resolved by private agreement. Petty gossip and meanness, bickering and contentiousness were the "little foxes" all too often lurking in the Puritan vineyard. We encounter them in journals and diaries, and they were the texts for innumerable sermons and "lectures." The godly were as much embroiled as the unregenerate. John Pike, the minister at Dover, New Hampshire, was prevented by the town from collecting his salary in 1702 because a large part of his congregation discovered they could get Quaker preachers "who should Preach to them freely without any Cost or Charge, not like their hireling Minister, who put them to great charge to maintain him." [1] We are glad to record, however, that the town finally came to its senses when the minister was about to depart, repudiated its heresies, and paid the arrears of Master Pike's salary.

Larger centers, such as Boston and Salem, provided a greater diversity of interests; their ministers were often quicker to perceive the smoldering embers of disaffection, and wiser in blanketing them. It was the provincial town usually that let "mighty contests rise from trivial things." The "bad book" controversy in Northampton, as late as 1744, is a case in point; [2] even more incomprehensibly serio-comic was the question of "dignifying the seats" in Deerfield in 1701. Pews were allotted townspeople according to their rank. The third meeting-house in Deerfield was newly built, and the citizens, united though they were against the very present danger of Indian attacks, split into two acrimonious parties in their views of social precedence regarding the dignity of the pews. The matter was settled only by recourse to statutory fiat:

> As to estimation of Seats ye Town agreed and voted y^t ye fore seat in ye front Gallery shall be equall in dignity with ye 2^d seat in ye Body of ye meeting house:

[1] Sibley, *Biographical Sketches*, II, 451.

[2] See Thomas H. Johnson, "Jonathan Edwards and the 'Young Folks' Bible,'" *New England Quarterly*, V (1932), 37–54.

That ye fore seats in ye side Gallerys shall be equall in dignity with ye 4th seats in ye Body of ye meeting house: [1]

The town record continues to specify in detail the ranking of the seats, and implies the status of the families which could expect to occupy them!

The characteristics observed by Josselyn were undoubtedly, for better or worse, a part of the Yankee make-up. They resulted from a way of life, and determined certain qualities of behavior peculiarly Puritan. Twentieth-century philosophy, based upon principles of toleration for religious, political, social differences; equality for all in the pursuit of happiness—often conceived as the equal ability of all to achieve "the more abundant life":—such a concept is immeasurably removed from that which obtained in the Puritan era. Clearly if Puritans believed that in the Bible lay all true and proper laws for governing human conduct, if they voluntarily relinquished to magistrates and ministers the power of interpreting the code, if they had not yet conceived the doctrine of laissez faire, then in questions of behavior the governors would tend to become "covetous and proud," the governed gradually to develop "a *Linsie-woolsie* disposition," and all men come to be their brother's keeper. The germ of the failure of Puritanism lay concealed within its fruit. The ways of the Puritan are not our ways, and it is easy for us, removed in time and point of view, to see the failure. It were wiser for us, nevertheless, not to accept Josselyn's verdict until we have observed one final aspect of the reaction of highly conceived ideals on human frailty. A glance, then, at their mode of life.

Most of the families, especially those from among the twenty thousand emigrants who left England during the 1630's, were recruited from the lesser gentry and yeoman stock, with a sprinkling of artisans and indentured servants. Frequently the servants were adventurers who departed England to escape imprisonment for debt by covenanting with another emigrant or the skipper of a sailing vessel for the amount of their passage. Their debt discharged, they could be admitted "inhabitants," and then, if they became church members, they could secure complete "citizenship." The magistrates and ministers almost without exception were university trained gentlemen of good family. Though church membership was a necessary preliminary to the franchise, all men were recognized as equal before the law, all were freeholders, and

[1] Quoted from George Sheldon, *A History of Deerfield, Massachusetts* (Deerfield, 1895–1896), I, 205.

all except the indentured servants owned their farms. Indeed, whatever trade or calling a New England settler might follow, he was always of necessity a farmer.

The severities of pioneer life, to which the rigors of a New England winter and the fear of Indian attacks were added, determined the mode of communal life. It was best that the village be closely knit, with no outlying farms. Except for a few settlements established up the Connecticut River as far as Deerfield and Northfield, the population was spread along the seacoast, from which the forest stretched almost unbroken north to Canada and west to Albany. The General Court appropriated the arable land: the fresh and salt marshes, intervales, meadows, and Indian clearings, and granted it to communities—to "proprietors" who held the "commonage." [1] The grantees were apportioned their holdings not on a basis of share and share alike, but upon principles less democratic perhaps, though equitable enough. The proprietors distributed the land according to the size of families, the number of their livestock, the wealth and position of the settler. None of the holdings was large, consequently no landed gentry established itself on great estates, as in New Netherlands or in the South. In a few instances, land was granted directly to individuals—to the ministers, for example, who received much larger apportionments, together with certain rights and privileges, in part payment as salary.

Each farm, tilled by its owner, was self-sustaining. The land was planted to such staples as wheat, rye, and Indian corn; barley for beer, oats for stock; hemp and flax for clothing. In the garden plots the husbandman grew beans, white and green peas, hops, squash, "pumpions," "pasneps," and "turneps." Potatoes were not raised until the eighteenth century. Governor Bradford left the most comprehensive picture of the subsistence that New England furnished in the first decades of the settlements. Not only were there native herbs, fruits, and vegetables, but whatever was to be found in England, he says, had been brought to the colonies, where it thrived well:

All sorts of grain which our own land doth yield,
Was hither brought, and sown in every field:
As wheat and rye, barley, oats, beans, and pease
Here all thrive, and they profit from them raise,
All sorts of roots and herbs in gardens grow,
Parsnips, carrots, turnips, or what you'll sow,
Onions, melons, cucumbers, radishes,

[1] For a brief account, see especially Robert R. Walcott, "Husbandry in Colonial New England," *New England Quarterly*, IX (1936), 218–252.

Skirets,[1] beets, coleworts, and fair cabbages.
Here grows fine flowers many, and 'mongst those,
The fair white lily and sweet fragrant rose.
Many good wholesome berries here you'll find,
Fit for man's use, almost of every kind,
Pears, apples, cherries, plumbs, quinces, and peach,
Are *now* no dainties; you may have of each.
Nuts and grapes of several sorts are here,
If you will take the pains them to seek for.[2]

After 1650, horses were bred in sufficient numbers for general use,—exported, in fact, to the West Indies, where they were used in the sugar industry,—and hay was therefore grown plentifully. As summers must be devoted chiefly to raising crops, winters were free for tending the herd. Stock raising often supplied the principal income or credit with which the settler could trade. There were goats in abundance, cattle, horses, sheep, swine, poultry, and bees; hence the larder was amply stocked with native produce. In addition, a good supply of wild game depended only upon a practiced eye and a quick trigger, and such luxuries as maple sugar depended, after 1700, only upon the industry of each farmer (see p. 747). Fish were so common that along the coast, then as now, they provided fertilizer. Only spices and condiments, principally salt, sugar, and molasses, needed to be imported. Apples were abundant, and no cellar but contained enough cider—ten to forty barrels—to last out the season. Cider and beer were the universal drinks, served to all with every meal; while cider-brandy and rum, distilled at Boston and Newport, made headier beverages.

The "selling points" by which promoters for the New England Company attracted settlers had not overstated the advantages. If their literature omitted any reference to the ravages and annoyances of hostile Indians, wolves, field mice, and sparrows, it assumed that they could soon be overcome by industry and the favor of God. The customer owned his home, he could raise a large family, and he had plenty to eat. On the whole he was satisfied.

The New England emigrants brought comparatively few furnishings with them: ship space was dear, and in mid-seventeenth century pas-

[1] A skirret is a species of water-parsnip, long cultivated in Europe for its succulent root. Like the parsnip, which it resembles in flavor, it was boiled and served in butter, or half-boiled and fried. At present it is very little used.

[2] "A Descriptive and Historical Account of New England in verse," *Collections of the Massachusetts Historical Society*, III (1794), 77–84; quoted from pp. 77, 78. Bradford died in 1657.

sage alone—and very crowded quarters at that—cost four or five pounds. Besides, why go to the expense of moving freight when all trades were represented among every shipload of passengers? Carvers and joiners, masons, coopers, and blacksmiths—all knew they would find plenty of native material on which to exercise their skill. Though some metal, bog iron particularly, was founded, wood, brick, or stone was chiefly used for building needs. The indentured servant labored as he could; and there were the negro slaves, sold directly by the ship's captain at Boston or Newport, for those who could afford them; but on the whole few servants found their way to any one household. The skilled artisan, except in the smaller towns, was supremely important. Young men learned their business as apprentices; trades flourished, and some substantial incomes were acquired by owners of sawmills, breweries, and ships, by shipbuilders, and exporters of lumber, furs, and fish. The mint-master, John Hull of Boston, held the corner on silver; from 1652 until 1686 he minted the only native coin that the General Court allowed in the colonies—the famous "Pine Tree Shilling"—on which his profit was considerable. Paper money was introduced only in 1690, in the same year that the name *dollar* (Ger. *thaler*) was given to the Spanish peso or "piece of eight."

As population increased, land values rose; a speculative fever that accompanied the subsequent prosperity forced men gradually to abandon the use of "commons" under a claim of ownership by proprietors. Thus in the early years of the eighteenth century a new town ceased to be a congregation formed about a new church; it was "a planting by land speculators of persons forced out from the old settlements by economic necessity." [1] With expansion came a demand for "cheap money," but Puritans of property and standing vehemently opposed any economic theory which argued that men were naturally equal or that a democratic government was the best. The brilliant arguments of "the first great American democrat" John Wise (see pp. 257–269) do not reflect the temper of orthodox Puritan economic theory, except in so far as he advocated the dignity of labor, the sanctity of property, and the virtue of saving.[2]

[1] James T. Adams, *Revolutionary New England* (Boston, 1927), p. 89.

[2] See for example, John Blackwell, *A Discourse in Explanation of the Bank of Credit . . . to be Erected in Boston*, Boston, 1687; *idem*, *Some Additional Considerations Addressed unto the Worshipful Elisha Hutchinson*, Boston, 1691; Cotton Mather, *Some Considerations on the Bills of Credit now passing in New-England*, Boston, 1691; *idem*, *Fair Dealing between Debtor and Creditor*, Boston, 1716. See further, Edgar A. J. Johnson, *American Economic Thought in the Seventeenth Century*, London, 1932. For the Puritan, private property was deemed necessary in a world of men actuated by self-love and incapable of achieving an ideal commonwealth. Only by labor was a decent state possible. Thus idleness was

Trade with the West Indies, begun in the 1640's, was always brisk. Lumber, horses, grain, meat, and tobacco were exchanged for wines, liquor, cheeses, sugar, tropical woods, slaves, and other merchandise not native to the colonies. From the West Indies silver coins had been first introduced during the seventeenth century, though musket balls and wampum continued to have value in barter; wampum as well as farm produce was accepted in payment for college tuition. Though the Puritans were not originally a seafaring people, their new environment gave opportunity for a development of trade that by the 1650's made New England ships, commanded by the "Bible-quoting Yankee skipper," a familiar sight in Atlantic and European waters; one which by 1676 had extended to the Levant and the Far East.[1] Pay was good, and whether the enterprise involved legitimate commerce, smuggling, or privateering, owners found adventurous fellows who were glad to take up before the mast. But the "down-Easters" who manned the vessels were not always young romantics; very often they were deserters, runaway servants, and "beach combers": a sinewy, hard-working, heavy-drinking, picturesque crew that lent color to the thriving seaport towns of Marblehead, Salem, Boston, and Newport; and caused grave concern to the ministers.

Few professions were represented in any one town. Lawyers were held in contempt,[2] and for the first ten years unrestricted judicial powers were exercised by the Court of Assistants, that is, the magistrates—the Governor, Deputy-Governor, and twelve Assistants, annually elected by the freemen on the last Wednesday in Easter Term. Legal administration was brought more into line with English precedent in 1641 by a codification of the "Body of Liberties," or "Abstract of Laws," mainly adopted from the legal books of the Old Testament. Thenceforth a codified fundamental law existed to which the magis-

---

wrong both morally and socially, for it bred disrespect, fostered contention, and restricted production; the amassing of wealth was justified and desirable in that God could thereby be further glorified. (See Cotton Mather, *Durable Riches* (Boston, 1695), pp. 13, 14.)

[1] See especially John W. McElroy, "Seafaring in Seventeenth-Century New England," *New England Quarterly*, VIII (1935), 331–364.

[2] For a summary of the legal aspects of the Puritan colonies, see the introduction by Zechariah Chafee, Jr., to *Records of the Suffolk County Court, 1671–1680*, in *Publications of the Colonial Society of Massachusetts*, Vols. XXIX, XXX (1933). The theory obtained that those who drew fees for representing their fellow men in court were usurers; but more fundamentally the objection to lawyers was simply that the colonists thought every man should be able to plead his own cause. The litigious character of the colonists, noted by travelers, was encouraged by magistrates and juries who disregarded legal precedent to the extent that lawsuits were sometimes protracted for two or three generations.

trates were bound, though as compared with the judicial procedure in English courts New England judges still exercised a wide discretionary power. Law and order were the rule, though punishments in the Puritan colonies were less severe than in England. Pirates and murderers were hanged at a public execution during which the prisoner was excoriated by the minister, his felonious life reviewed, and a plea for forgiveness entertained (see p. 413). Few survivals of medieval practices are known: two cases of burning at the stake for arson and poisoning; at least one "ordeal of touch" [1] as a means of giving evidence. The witchcraft delusion of 1692 (see pp. 758–762) was brief, very local, and is not now regarded as a phenomenon particularly Puritan. Lesser offences were punished by the customary English methods: stocking, whipping, branding, and cutting off ears.

No settlement but had a well organized town government, together with its church presided over by a college-bred minister; the wealthier towns or churches often divided the ministerial function of pastor and teacher between two equally distinguished men: the "pastor" was to concern himself with the administration of the society, and the "teacher" to devote himself primarily to expounding and maintaining the purity of doctrine. Increase Mather and his son Cotton, for example, served as pastor and teacher respectively of the Old North Church in Boston.

Physicians were scarce in the colonies. It frequently fell to the lot of the minister, who might well be the only liberally educated resident, to practice medicine in what Cotton Mather described as "Angelical Conjunction" [2] with his spiritual office. Michael Wigglesworth, in fact, was both the minister and the physician of Malden during his long occupation of the pulpit. On the whole, residents were far more dependent upon their own knowledge of herbs and simples than is commonly imagined. Midwives attended the lying-in; a few herbals, based on the writings of Galen, circulated from hand to hand; some quacks, —"chemists," or followers of Paracelsus—compounded drugs; but infant mortality was high, childbirth fever claimed many young mothers, consumption took heavy toll among adolescents, the ravages of smallpox destroyed young and old indiscriminately, and now and then one encounters what appears to have been a fatal attack of appendicitis, recorded simply as "a prodigious belly-ache." Though several reputable physicians practiced in New England, the slow development of medi-

[1] The superstition which required the person suspected of murder to touch the neck of the deceased with the index finger of the left hand; if blood appeared to flow from the corpse, the suspect was deemed guilty.

[2] *Magnalia*, III, 26.

cine itself was basically responsible for much ignorant procedure. Usually doctors learned their profession as apprentices; it is significant that but one physician in the colonies in 1716, William Douglass of Boston, held the degree of Doctor of Medicine.[1]

Surprisingly little is known of the customs and practices in the ordinary routine of Puritan life, for the journals and diaries, so numerous in the period, seldom or but incidentally record what to them were the commonplaces of existence.[2] Except in the very earliest years of the emigrations, it would appear that the colonists as a whole lived in a degree of luxury. The story of the hardships and lack of decencies among the Plymouth Pilgrims during the early years is too well known to need rehearsing; we are aware also that a few of the early settlers lived for a brief time in tents, huts, or dug-outs, heated by wooden chimneys, and lighted with oil-paper windows. But as soon as thrifty pioneers had won a foothold, aided by neighbors or servants they raised clapboarded frame houses, similar in architecture to those they knew in England. No log cabins ever were erected, though logs served for garrison houses as defense against Indian attacks. Many seventeenth-century houses survive today in New England: usually two-storey frame dwellings built around an enormous brick chimney with openings for large fireplaces in several rooms. The large kitchen, with its enormous fireplace, served often as dining room in winter, when a nor'easter penetrated through to the marrow, and thin clapboards could not repel the cold. In summer a back room or "summer kitchen" could be opened up to accommodate a more expansive way of living. The "foreroom" or parlor, occasionally plastered with "painted paper," was large and pleasant; it was probably not heated in winter except for occasional social gatherings or for funerals. In winter, especially in provincial New England, the foreroom was doubtless used for "bundling" or "tarrying"—that curious custom wherein young men courted their girls in cold weather by lying with them upon bed or couch wrapped between heavy blankets sewed together on three sides and down through the middle.

A brickworks was established at Salem in 1629, and now and then as the colonists prospered, well-to-do residents abandoned frame houses—so easily destroyed by fire—for more substantial brick edifices. A glance within the house indicates that forks were unknown to most and

[1] John Clark (1667–1728) of Boston, brother-in-law of Cotton Mather, was a talented physician. He was third in a direct line of seven generations of that name who practiced medicine in Massachusetts for over one hundred and fifty years.

[2] The best gleanings are to be found in George F. Dow, *Every Day Life in the Massachusetts Bay Colony* (Boston, 1935).

seldom used by any, though Winthrop brought one from England, perhaps as a curiosity. The food was plain: fresh meat in season, boiled or roasted, and salted at other times; corn meal, stews, and such vegetables as were ripened or could be stored in winter. The diet perhaps lacked sufficient balance, for Josselyn noticed that "Men and Women keep their complexions, but lose their Teeth: the Women are pittifully Tooth-shaken; whether through the coldness of the climate, or by sweetmeats of which they have store, I am not able to affirm."[1] False teeth were not common, and the toothbrush was only introduced in 1718; but the salt and water solution used as a dentrifice was no doubt quite as adequate as any devised today. Bathing was a luxury,—at least, observers of colonial manners gave it scant notice. As for ventilation, quite possibly the bedrooms in winter received only such circulation of air as large fireplaces supply, since chilly air was thought to be poisonous. Indeed, the modern insistence upon wide-thrown windows on winter nights would have been incomprehensible to a Puritan.

Only the wealthy could afford the imported craft or fabric of silversmith, cabinetmaker, linen draper, or tailor; furniture was plain, dishes of wood or pewter, clothing homespun though plentiful.[2] In dress decorum was preserved. Workmen wore leather; their betters, both men and women, indulged a taste for latest fashions both in clothes and in jewelry and trinkets; for, said Master Oakes, "one end of Apparel is to distinguish and put a difference between persons according to their Places and Conditions, . . . provided it carry nothing of Immodesty in it, or Contrariety to the Rules of Moral Honesty. The civil Customs of the place where we live is that which must regulate in this case."[3] In the light of Oakes's sensible opinion we may better understand why the sumptuary laws to preserve a Puritan plainness were not enforced. Such advice would not support a view that Puritans of the upper classes lived drab and colorless lives. On the contrary, too many inventories bear witness to the presence of finery, and ministers other than Oakes so often addressed congregations on the subject of dress, citing scripture and verse (see p. 454), that we know there must have been color aplenty. Ministers of the first generation thought long hair was unscriptural, and thus short hair became a party badge.

[1] *Account of Two Voyages*, p. 185.

[2] The American wing of the Metropolitan Museum of Art gives a most complete and accurate idea of colonial architecture, furniture, and decorations. One must keep in mind, nevertheless, that the art of the painter, carver, and silversmith belongs rather to the eighteenth century than to the seventeenth. The Puritan period in the colonies was substantially over by the end of Queen Anne's reign.

[3] Urian Oakes, *New-England Pleaded with* (Cambridge, 1673), p. 34.

By the end of the century, when the new fashion of periwigs came into style, the more conservative pillars of state and society transferred their animus to wigs. "Mr Chievar died this last night . . .," Judge Sewall entered briefly in his *Diary* for August 20, 1708; "The Wellfare of the Province was much upon his Spirit. He abominated Perriwigs." It is doubtful whether the naive *non sequitur* of Sewall's views obtained very widely after 1710. Times were changing, the older views seemed stuffy, and such laws as had been enacted to preserve the decorum of an earlier day were forgotten. The first generations of Yankees, never "timid souls," had been as independent in action and as restive under petty restraints as their descendants now seemed. By the close of the century the patriarchs that remained were merely exercising an old man's prerogative of plain speaking. Laws that had been enacted were not always enforced. The Puritan was opinionated, and it is inevitable that he sometimes made himself ridiculous.

Puritans were married young, though by no means so young as we often suppose. Revealing data on that matter can be gleaned from the vital records—lists of births, marriages, and deaths—relating to colonial towns. The average age for first marriages in early New England strikingly parallels that of today. Girls were almost never given in marriage under eighteen, and more often not until they had passed their twentieth or twenty-first birthday. Men were usually somewhat older. The average holds true for the colonies as a whole; certain classes, ministers' children, for instance, or those whose education was longer pursued, sometimes were well along in their twenties before they assumed the responsibilities of matrimony. Isolation doubtless compelled delay: five of the six daughters of the Reverend Solomon Stoddard of Northampton were married rather late. Furthermore, properly qualified suitors were not always at hand—the four daughters of Joseph Dudley were well into their twenties before they wed. Bachelors were uncommon, for the Biblical injunction to marry and increase was literally observed; food was ample, and there was work for all. Besides, the death rate was very high, so that oversupply of labor was no serious problem. Some have concluded that Puritan families were not very large, and it is true that no very great number reached maturity. The statement regarding Judge Sewall may fairly be considered representative: "Sewall had issue by his first wife only. There were seven sons and seven daughters, of whom only six lived to maturity, and only three survived him." [1]

[1] Sibley, *Biographical Sketches*, II, 359.

The marriage ceremony was simple and regarded as a civil, not a religious rite; banns were published and after a brief but appropriate interval the intending couple appeared before a magistrate. Elopements were uncommon, and divorces, though rare, were less so among Puritans than Anglicans, for the latter group flatly refused to sanction such a step.[1] Those who raise large families do not have time to humor their caprices; besides, man was the master and woman his helpmate; death so often separated partners that men and women often married twice, thrice, and sometimes even oftener. The choice of mate was by no means exclusively a parental matter. The florid love letter which the Reverend Edward Taylor (see p. 650) addressed to the young lady of his choice in 1674, Elizabeth Fitch of Norwich, is still preserved: [2]

. . . Looke not (I entreate you) on it as one of Loves Hyperboles, if I borrow the Beams of some Sparkling Metaphors to illustrate my Respects vnto your selfe by. For you having made my breast the Cabbinet of your Affections (as I yours, mine) I know not how to vse a fitter Comparison to set out my Love by, than to Compare it vnto a Golden Ball of pure Fire rowling vp and down my Breast, from which there flies now, and then a Sparke like a Glorious Beam from the Body of the Flaming Sun . . .

The ardent lover then goes on to prove syllogistically that "Conjugall Love ought to exceed all other," with the conclusion that "it must be kept within bounds too. For it must be Subordinate to Gods Glory." The conception was surely orthodox, and perhaps the expression of it seemed a model proposal. At any rate, it is poles removed from the courtship of Mary Stoddard of Northampton by the young Wethersfield pastor, Stephen Mix. Tradition has it that Stephen first approached the daughter by way of the father. Stoddard's consent obtained, the couple met and chatted, Mary asking simply for a brief time to consider the proposal. Her reply by letter shortly after reads as follows:

Northampton, 1695

Rev. Stephen Mix:

Yes.

Mary Stoddard.[3]

[1] See Chilton L. Powell, "Marriage in Early New England," *New England Quarterly*, I (1928), 323–334.

[2] In his MS "Poetical Works," Yale University Library; printed in part in Frances M. Caulkins, *History of Norwich, Connecticut* (Hartford, 1866), p. 154.

[3] Charles Stoddard, *Anthony Stoddard of Boston, Mass., and His Descendants* (New York, 1865), p. 4.

Letters of the period exchanged between husband and wife, parents and children, or brothers and sisters, show a tender but not effusive regard: "My dear Companion," "Dear Spouse," "My service to my sisters," "Your affectionate Friend and Father," "Your most tender and affectionate Father." For all that religion and the church played an important role in Puritan affairs, the home was the center of their lives, and for most, their love towards it must have been as deep as Anne Bradstreet's, if less expressive.

The attitude of the Puritans toward death and suffering is hardest to interpret in modern terms. Though not fatalists, they seem curiously insensitive to any great bereavement. It is not merely that they looked upon translation from the flesh to the spirit as a welcome change, though such an attitude was a principle in their ethics. It is rather the curiously immobile acceptance of a *fait accompli.* Sewall's diary for May 26, 1720 points the case: "About midnight my dear wife expired to our great astonishment, especially mine." To be sure, death stalked too frequently among people of all ages to be an uncommon sight. For that reason perhaps, and because the rites were regarded in a secular light, funerals were seized upon as occasions for impressive assembly, extravagant display, and excessive drinking. The gloves, rings, and scarves provided in nearly every will for the bearers were likewise distributed to the clergy, and the number they accumulated must have been reckoned in scores. So florid and diffuse was the stream of elegies and sermons that poured forth on such occasions that the Reverend James Fitch of Norwich wrote: "The Abusive, and justly to be Condemned practice of too too many, who in Preaching Funeral Sermons, by mis-representing the Dead, have dangerously misled the living, and by flatteries corrupted many, hath occasioned not a few to question (if not conclude against) the lawfulness of Preaching at such seasons. . . ."[1] Many of the old burying grounds are still to be seen, with their simple freestone, syenite, or slate markers undisturbed. Flat marble slabs, imported from England, occasionally dot the quiet landscape, or low brick and marble tombs; vaults were a late innovation.

Whoever wishes to learn about the sports and diversions of Puritan children should turn to Miss Earle's delightful study.[2] Dolls and toys there were; as the child matured he participated in sports: football, ball and bat, stoolball, and cricket. We nowhere encounter any objec-

[1] *Peace The End of the Perfect and Vpright* (Cambridge, 1672), preface, sig. A 1v.

[2] Alice M. Earle, *Child Life in Colonial Days* (2d ed., New York, 1927).

tion to pleasant, healthful divertisement, which indeed was encouraged. So too was a sense of humor. Colman said:

A great deal of *Pleasantry* there is in the *Town*, and very graceful and charming it is so far as it is Innocent and Wise. Our *Wit* like our *Air* is clear and *Keen*, and in very Many 'tis exalted by a *Polite Education* meeting with good *Natural Parts* . . . We daily need some respite & diversion, without which we dull our Powers; a little intermission sharpens 'em again. It spoils the *Bow* to keep it always bent, and the *Viol* if always strain'd up. Mirth is some loose or relaxation to the labouring Mind or Body, it lifts up the hands that hang down in weariness, and strengthens the feeble knees that cou'd stand no longer to work: it renews our strength, and we resume our labours again with vigour. 'Tis design'd by nature to chear and revive us thro' all the toils and troubles of life, and therefore equally a benefit with the other Rests which Nature has provided for the same end. 'Tis in our present Pilgrimage and Travel of Life refreshing as the *Angels provision for Elijah* in his sore travel.[1]

Doubtless the genial pastor knew men and times, and that wit whereof he spoke. In the next century the characteristics of "Yankee humor" are seen more clearly, though even in the seventeenth century we perceive it occasionally. At its best it is seldom worldly, though it understood the way of the world; it was quiet usually and slow, sometimes solemn and resigned, often sardonic; yet at its core never without warmth—the dry, crackling wit that mulls along, seldom breaking into flame.[2]

But all merriment was not innocent, and against such sports or games as fostered gambling, rows, immorality, drunkenness, or Sabbath-breaking strong voice was raised, and penalties enacted. Mixed dancing was condemned by some (see p. 411), as were card playing, shuffle-

[1] Benjamin Colman, *The Government & Improvement of Mirth* (Boston, 1707), preface, and p. 29. Colman's book indicates that the colonial ministers, by allying themselves with such reformers as Jeremy Collier, were establishing a respectable point of contact with England. At the same time they were keeping up with an important current of public opinion at home and demonstrating that they were not merely a provincial stock concerned with abstract theology. Cotton Mather's *Essays to do Good* was written for the same reason, and likewise shows the desire of New Englanders to co-operate with moral reforms. Colman's conception of mirth and its government is that of traditional Puritanism, but the spirit informing it is of the eighteenth-century English nonconformist and Low-Church piety.

[2] See, for instance, the letter which Timothy Cutler wrote his classmate George Curwin in 1711, quoted in Sibley, *Biographical Sketches*, V, 46, 47. But for another interpretation of early "Yankee humor"—one which gives in this writer's opinion too much weight to its broad, farcical play—see George F. Horner, *A History of American Humor to 1765* (Dissertation, University of North Carolina, 1936).

board, billiards, and bowling. Yet many diversions, if moderately indulged, were willingly countenanced as long as they did not lead to "waste of time." In the privacy of one's own home much passed unnoticed—even dancing, card playing, and other such "frolicks." A public bowling green was advertised at the present Bowdoin Square in Boston in 1700. All Yankees have had an eye for good horses, and horse racing, especially after 1715, was featured in many towns. There were pig-runs as well, and bearbaiting—sports which were never wholly approved even in England; but the tolerant colonial parson may sometimes have deemed it wise to drive with slackened rein.

Holidays were times of hilarity: training-days for militia review, commencements—then as now,—and November Fifth or "Pope's Night,"—three occasions especially licenced. But such times of public festivity by no means exhaust the tally. Puritans found excuse as well for private merrymaking in baptisms, weddings, funerals, barn-raisings, cornhuskings, quilting-parties, church-raisings, house-raisings, ship launchings, and, in truth, ministers' ordinations. Thanksgiving was a peculiarly New England holiday, observed from the first with fitting solemnity. Christmas was associated in the Puritan mind with the "Lords of Misrule," with riot and drunkenness. Though commemorated outside New England, and by the Anglicans in Boston as early as 1686, it never came to be regarded generally as a day of joy and good will until the mid-nineteenth century.

The Anglo-Saxon race has never been regarded an abstemious stock. "I will tell you," Samuel Nowell remarked in the course of an Artillery Election address,

> I will tell you how we breed up Souldiers, both in old England and New, every Farmers Son, when he goes to the Market-Town, must have money in his purse; and when he meets with his Companions, they goe to the Tavern or Ale-house, and seldome away before Drunk, or well tipled. It is rare to find men that we can call Drunkards, but there are abundance of Tiplers in *New-England*. [1]

Colman spoke his mind even more eloquently: "But above all kinds of vain Mirth deliver me from the *Drunken Club*, who belch out noisy *Ribaldry* rank of the foul lees within." [2] Taverns, though maintained for travelers, were too often the gathering places for idle drinkers. Unlike their English counterparts, they were not famous for their plenty and their genial comfort. No better account survives of the poor

[1] *Abraham in Arms* (Boston, 1678), p. 15.
[2] *Government . . . of Mirth*, p. 48.

appearance and slatternly service of early New England inns than Madam Knight's *Journal* (see p. 425). It is easy to understand why travelers preferred to lodge with friends or acquaintances along the way when business compelled them to set out upon a journey. Those who could do so went by water; the rest stayed home.

A final word on the attitude of the Puritans toward the arts. Drama they banned, because they evidently gave great weight to the injunctions urged against it by the primitive church, and also because they knew it in their day as an art supported by a court which they disapproved, and as a theater which, in the words of Chesterfield on decorum, combined the useful appearance of virtue with the solid satisfaction of vice. There was still bitter with them the caricatures of Puritans in Malvolio and Zeal-of-the-Land Busy. The Restoration stage was scarcely one to attract God-centered men; but in the eighteenth century, with the return of sentimental drama, we find *The New-England Weekly Journal* printing Lillo's *George Barnwell* (1731) within a year of its appearance in London, defending the work on the grounds that it tended to promote virtue and piety.[1]

Because Puritans held to the older tradition of *a cappella* singing in their churches, while Anglicans admitted instrumentalists, an idea has passed current that they were hostile to music. The truth is otherwise. Puritans produced the first Italian opera in England, Cromwell supported an orchestra at court, and in this country music, both secular and sacred, was encouraged (see p. 451), as Sewall's Diary often indicates.[2]

Possession of fine architecture, tapestries, painting, and sculpture depends as much upon the wealth as the taste of the purchaser. As money increased, the arts followed. An inventory of Peter Sargent's property in 1714 lists a tapestry. The great house of William Clark of Boston, with its fluted pilasters, is known to have contained at his death in 1715, oil paintings, a mosaic floor of wood, and painted arabesques.[3] It may be that Puritan inventories list few works of art because the fathers had seldom been men of property; besides, taste itself needs training. Yet we cannot be far wrong if we see the typical Puri-

[1] It is well to note that even outside New England drama revived slowly. No professional actors performed in any of the colonies until the eighteenth century, when a play was given in Charleston, South Carolina, in 1703. Professionals were not established in New York until 1732.

[2] See Percy A. Scholes, *The Puritans and Music in England and New England* (London, 1934). The organ owned by Thomas Brattle, and willed by him in 1713 to the church which he founded, was rejected solely on grounds of polity.

[3] George F. Dow, *Every Day Life*, *passim*.

tan as one dedicated to the glory of God, though living in this world; accepting its fashions as long as they did not run counter to God's Word—and sometimes interpreting that Word to fit his own taste.

JOHN SMITH, 1580–1631

[No Puritan, John Smith was of that company of Elizabethan sea dogs, the story of whose lives, written both in word and deed, is treasured up in Hakluyt's famous *Voyages*. Smith's career is too well known to need rehearsing. The "sometimes Governour of Virginia, and Admirall of New-England" was a promoter whose conscious purpose was to enlarge the King's dominions. He left several vivid and picturesque accounts of his travels. *Advertisement For the unexperienced Planters of New-England, or anywhere. Or, The Path-way to experience to erect a Plantation* (London, 1631) was his last work, dedicated to the archbishops of Canterbury and York, and prefaced by the pathetic stanzas called "The Sea Marke," wherein the aging traveler pictures himself as a battered hulk and a warning to after-comers.

Smith's description of the founding of Massachusetts Bay is a memorable account and deserves to be better known. The author tells his story with dramatic force, in crisp and racy diction, pausing in the onward rush only to limn the portrait of some founder or to exclaim over the natural beauties of the newly discovered wilderness.

The text is from a copy of the original edition in the New York Public Library (pp. 18–29, with omissions indicated). See Tyler, *A History of American Literature*, I, 18–38; *Dictionary of American Biography;* and especially Samuel E. Morison, *Builders of the Bay Colony*, chap. I.]

THE SEA MARKE.

ALOOFE, aloofe, and come no neare,[1]
the dangers doe appeare;
Which if my ruine had not beene
you had not seene:
I onely lie upon this shelfe
to be a marke to all
which on the same might fall,
That none may perish but my selfe.

If in or outward you be bound,
doe not forget to sound;
Neglect of that was cause of this
to steare amisse.

The Seas were calme, the wind was faire,
that made me so secure,[2]
that now I must indure
All weathers be they foule or faire.

The Winters cold, the Summers heat,
alternatively beat
Upon my bruised sides, that rue
because too true
That no releefe can ever come.
But why should I despaire
being promised so faire
That there shall be a day of Dome.

ADVERTISEMENT FOR THE UNEXPERIENCED PLANTERS

Chap. 8.

Extremity next despaire, Gods great mercy, their estate, they make good salt, an unknowne rich myne.

1623. At *New-Plimoth*, having planted there Fields and Gardens, such an extraordinary drought insued, all things withered, that they expected no harvest; and having long expected a supply, they heard no newes, but a wracke split upon their Coast, they supposed their Ship: thus in the very labyrinth of despaire, they solemnly assembled themselves together nine houres in prayer. At their departure, the parching faire skies all overcast with blacke clouds, and the next morning, such a pleasant moderate raine continued fourteene daies, that it was hard to say, whether their withered fruits or drooping affections were most revived; not long after came two Ships to supply them, with all their Passengers well, except one, and he presently recovered; for themselves, for all their wants, there was not one sicke person amongst them: the greater Ship they returned fraught with commodities. This yeare went from *England*, onely to fish, five and forty saile, and have all made a better voyage than ever.

Five and forty saile to fish.

1624. In this Plantation there is about an hundred and fourescore persons, some Cattell, but many Swine and Poultry: their Towne containes two and thirty houses, whereof seven were burnt, with the value of five or six hundred pounds in other goods, impailed about halfe a mile, within which within a high Mount, a Fort, with a Watch-tower, well built of stone, lome, and wood, their Ordnance well mounted, and so healthfull, that of the first Planters not one hath died this three yeares: yet at the first landing at *Cape Cod*, being an hundred passengers, besides twenty they had left behind at *Plimoth* for want of good take heed, thinking to finde all things better than I advised them, spent six or seven weekes in wandring up and downe in frost and snow, wind and raine, among the woods, cricks, and swamps, forty of them died, and threescore were left in most miserable estate at *New-Plimoth*, where their Ship left them, and but nine leagues by Sea from where they landed, whose misery and variable opinions, for want of experience, occasioned much faction, till necessity agreed them. These disasters, losses, and uncertainties, made such disagreement among the Adventurers in *England*, who beganne to repent, and rather lose all, than longer continue the charge, being out of purse six or seven thousand pounds, accounting my bookes and their relations as old Almanacks. But the Planters, rather than leave the Country, concluded absolutely to supply themselves, and to all their adventurers pay them for nine yeares two hundred pounds yearely without any other account; where more than six hundred Adventurers for *Virginia*, for more than two hundred thousand pounds, had not six pence. Since they have made a salt worke, wherewith they preserve all the fish they take, and have fraughted this yeare a ship of an hundred and fourescore tun, living so well they desire nothing but more company, and what ever they take, returne commodities to the value.

They make store of good salt.

This you may plainly see, although many envying I should bring so much from thence, where many others had beene, and some the same yeare returned with nothing, reported the Fish and Bevers I brought home, I had taken from the French men of *Canada*, to discourage any from beleeving me, and excuse their owne misprisions, some onely to have concealed this good Country (as is said) to their private use; others taxed me as much of indiscretion, to make my discoveries and designes so publike for nothing, which might have beene so well managed by some concealers, to have beene all rich ere any had knowne of it. Those, and many such like wise rewards, have beene my recompences, for which I am contented, so the Country prosper, and Gods name bee there praised by my Country-men, I have my desire; and the benefit of this salt and fish, for breeding Mariners and building ships, will make so many fit men to raise a Common-wealth, if but managed, as my generall history will shew you; it might well by this have beene as profitable as the best Mine the King of *Spaine* hath in his West Indies. . . .

An incredible rich mine.

Chap. 11.

The planting Bastable or Salem and Charlton, a description of the Massachusets.

1629. *The Planting Salem.*

In all those plantations, yea, of those that have done least, yet the most will say, we were the first; and so every next supply, still the next beginner: But seeing history is the memory of time, the life of the dead, and the happinesse of the living; because I have more plainly discovered, and described, and discoursed of those Countries than any as yet I know, I am the bolder to continue the story, and doe all men right so neere as I can in those new beginnings, which hereafter perhaps may bee in better request than a forest of nine dayes pamphlets.

Their provisions for Salem.

In the yeare 1629. about March, six good ships are gone with 350. men, women, and children, people professing themselves of good ranke, zeale, meanes and quality: also 150. head of cattell, as horse, mares, and neat beasts; 41. goats, some conies, with all provision for houshold and apparell; six peeces of great Ordnance for a Fort, with Muskets, Pikes, Corslets, Drums and Colours, with all provisions necessary for the good of man. They are seated about 42. degrees and 38. minutes, at a place called by the natives *Naemkecke*, by our Royall King *Charles*, *Bastable;* but now by the planters, *Salem;* where they arrived for most part exceeding well, their cattell and all things else prospering exceedingly, farre beyond their expectation.

The planting Salem and Charlton.

At this place they found some reasonable good provision and houses built by some few of *Dorchester*, with whom they are joyned in society with two hundred men, an hundred and fifty more they have sent to the *Massachusets*, which they call *Charlton*, or *Charles* Towne: I tooke the fairest reach in this Bay for a river, whereupon I called it *Charles* river, after the name of our Royall King *Charles;* but they find that faire Channell to divide it selfe into so many faire branches as make forty or fifty pleasant Ilands within that excellent Bay, where the land is of divers and sundry sorts, in some places very blacke and fat, in others good clay, sand and gravell, the superficies neither too flat in plaines, nor too high in hils. In the Iles you may keepe your hogs, horse, cattell, conies or poultry, and secure for little or nothing, and to command when you list, onely having a care of provision for some extraordinary cold winter. In those Iles, as in the maine, you may make your nurseries for fruits and plants where you put no cattell; in the maine you may shape your Orchards, Vineyards, Pastures, Gardens, Walkes, Parkes, and Corne fields out of the whole peece as you please into such plots, one adjoyning to another, leaving every of them invironed with two, three, foure, or six, or so many rowes of well growne trees as you will, ready growne to your hands, to defend them from ill weather, which in a champion you could not in many ages; and this at first you may doe with as much facility, as carelessly or ignorantly cut downe all before you, and then after better consideration make ditches, pales, plant young trees with an excessive charge and labour, seeing you may have so many great and small growing trees for your maine posts, to fix hedges, palisados, houses, rales, or what you will; which order in *Virginia* hath not beene so well observed as it might: where all the woods for many an hundred mile for the most part grow streight, like unto the high grove or tuft of trees, upon the high hill by the house of that worthy Knight Sir *Humphrey Mildmay,*[3] so remarkable in *Essex* in the Parish of *Danbery,* where I writ this discourse, but much taller and greater, neither grow they so thicke together by the halfe, and much good ground betweene them without shrubs, and the best is ever knowne by the greatnesse of the trees and the vesture it beareth. Now in *New-England* the trees are commonly lower, but much thicker and firmer wood, and more proper for shipping, of which I will speake a little, being the chiefe engine wee are to use in this worke, and the rather for that within a square of twenty leagues, you may have all, or most of the chiefe materials belonging to them, were they wrought to their perfection as in other places. . . .

A description of the Massachusets Bay.

Chap. 13.

Their great supplies, present estate and accidents, advantage.

1630. *Their present estate.*

Who would not thinke but that all those trials had beene sufficient to lay a foundation for a plantation, but we see many men many mindes, and still new Lords, new lawes: for those 350. men with all their cattell that so well arived and promised so much, not being of one body, but severall mens servants, few could command and fewer obey, lived merrily of that they had, neither planting or building any thing to any purpose, but one faire house for the Governour, till all was spent and the winter approached; then they grew into many diseases, and as many inconveniences, depending only of a supply from *England*, which expected Houses, Gardens, and Corne fields ready planted by them for their entertainment.

It is true, that Master *Iohn Wynthrop*,[4] their now Governour, a worthy Gentleman both in estate and esteeme, went so well provided (for six or seven hundred people went with him) as could be devised, but at Sea, such an extraordinarie storme encountred his Fleet, continuing ten daies, that of two hundred Cattell which were so tossed and brused, threescore and ten died, many of their people fell sicke, and in this perplexed estate, after ten weekes, they arrived in *New-England* at severall times, where they found threescore of their people dead, the rest sicke, nothing done, but all complaining, and all things so contrary to their expectation, that now every monstrous humor began to shew it selfe. And to second this, neare as many more came after them, but so ill provided, with such multitudes of women and children, as redoubled their necessities.

The fruits of counterfeits.

This small triall of their patience, caused among them no small confusion, and put the Governour and his Councell to their utmost wits; some could not endure the name of a Bishop, others not the sight of a Crosse nor Surplesse, others by no meanes the booke of common Prayer. This absolute crue, only of the Elect, holding all (but such as themselves) reprobates and cast-awaies, now make more haste to returne to *Babel*, as they tearmed *England*, than stay to enjoy the land they called *Canaan;* somewhat they must say to excuse themselves. . . .

THOMAS LECHFORD, *fl.* 1629–1642

[Thomas Lechford was the first professional lawyer in Massachusetts Bay. Refusing preferment abroad, he emigrated to New England in 1638, but he was not in sympathy with affairs, and, never becoming a church member, could not vote or hold public office. Debarred from practice in 1641 for trying to influence a jury, he returned to England in disgust, leaving his wife and household goods behind.

Lechford's pique found expression in a volume published in London after his return: *Plain Dealing: or, Newes from New-England* (1642). It is salutary, perhaps, to see the Bay Colony through the eyes of one whose opinions were not colored by close attachments.

Plain Dealing was shortly reissued with a new title and was reprinted twice in the nineteenth century. A "Notebook" which he kept from 1638 to 1641 is also available. See *Dictionary of American Biography.*]

PLAIN DEALING

FOR THE STATE OF THE COUNTRY IN THE BAY AND THEREABOUTS.

State of the Countrey of *New-England.*

THE LAND is reasonable fruitfull, as I think; they have cattle, and goats, and swine good store, and some horses, store of fish and fowle, venison, and * corne, both *English* and *Indian*. They are indifferently well able to subsist for victuall. They are setting on the manufacture of linnen and cotton cloath, and the fishing trade, and they are building of ships, and have good store of barks, catches, lighters, shallops, and other vessels. They have builded and planted to admiration for the time. There are good masts and timber for shipping, planks, and boards, clap-board, pipe-staves, bever, and furres, and hope of some mines. There are Beares, Wolves, and Foxes, and many other wilde beasts, as the Moose, a kind of Deere, as big as some Oxen, and Lyons, as I have heard. The Wolves and Foxes are a great annoyance. There are Rattlesnakes, which sometimes doe some harme, not much; He that is stung with any of them, or bitten, he turnes of the colour of the Snake, all over his body, blew, white, and greene spotted; and swelling, dyes, unlesse he timely get some Snake-weed;[1] which if he eate, and rub on the wound, he may haply recover, but feele it a long while in his bones and body. Money is wanting, by reason of the failing of passengers these two last yeares, in a manner. They want help to goe

*Wheat and Barley are thought not to be so good as those grains in *England;* but the Rye and Pease are as good as the English: the Pease have no wormes at all. Beanes also there are very good.

forward, for their subsistance in regard of cloathing: And great pity it would be, but men of estates should help them forward. It may bee, I hope, a charitable worke. The price of their cattell, and other things being fallen, they are not at present able to make such returns to *England*, as were to be wished for them: God above direct and provide for them. There are multitudes of godly men among them, and many poore ignorant soules. Of late some thirty persons went in two small Barks for the *Lords Isle of Providence*,[2] and for the Maine thereabout, which is held to be a beter countrey and climate by some: For this being in about 46. degrees of northerne latitude, yet is very cold in winter, so that some are frozen to death, or lose their fingers or toes every yeere, sometimes by carlesnes, sometimes by accidents, and are lost in snowes, which there are very deepe sometimes, and lye long: Winter begins in October, and lasts till Aprill. Sixty leagues Northerly it is held not habitable, yet again in Summer it is exceeding hot. If shipping for conveyance were sent thither, they might spare divers hundreds of men for any good design. The jurisdiction of the *Bay* Patent reacheth from *Pascattaqua* Patent Northeast to *Plymouth* Patent Southward. And in my travailes there, I have seene the towns of *Newberry*, *Ipswich*, *Salem*, *Lynne*, *Boston*, *Charlestowne*, *Cambridge*, *Watertowne*, *Concord*, *Roxbury*, *Dorchester*, and *Braintree* in the *Bay* Patent, *New Taunton* in *Plymouth* Patent, the Island *Aquedney*, and the two townes therein, *Newport* and *Portsmouth*, and *New Providence* within the *Bay* of *Narhiggansets*. This for the satisfaction of some that have reported I was no Travailer in *New-England*. . . .

When I was to come away, one of the chiefest in the Country wished me to deliver him a note of what things I misliked in the Country, which I did, thus:

I doubt,

1. Whether so much time should be spent in the publique Ordinances, on the Sabbath day, because that thereby some necessary duties of the Sabbath must needs be hindred, as visitation of the sick, and poore, and family.

2. Whether matters of offence should be publiquely handled, either before the whole Church, or strangers.

3. Whether so much time should be spent in particular catechizing those that are admitted to the communion of the Church, either men or women; or that they should make long speeches; or when they come publiquely to be admitted, any should speak contradictorily, or in recommendation of any, unlesse before the Elders, upon just occasion.

4. Whether the censures of the Church should be ordered, in publique, before all the Church, or strangers, other then the denunciation of the censures, and pronunciation of the solutions.

5. Whether any of our *Nation* that is not extremely ignorant or scandalous, should bee kept from the Communion, or his children from *Baptisme*.

6. That many thousands in this Countrey have forgotten the very principles of Religion, which they were daily taught in *England*, by set forms and Scriptures read, as the Psalmes, first and second Lesson, the ten Commandments, the Creeds, and publique catechizings. And although conceived Prayer be good and holy, and so publike explications and applications of the Word, and also necessary both in and out of season: yet for the most part it may be feared they dull, amaze, confound, discourage the weake and ignorant, (which are the most of men) when they are in ordinary performed too tediously, or with the neglect of the Word read, and other premeditated formes inculcated, and may tend to more ignorance and inconvenience, then many good men are aware of.

7. I doubt there hath been, and is much neglect of endeavours, to teach, civilize, and convert the *Indian Nation*, that are about the Plantations.

8. Whether by the received principles, it bee *possible* to teach, civilize, or convert them, or when they are converted, to maintain Gods worship among them.

9. That electorie courses will not long be safe here, either in Church or Common-wealth.

JASPER DANCKAERTS, 1639–*ca.* 1703

[During the last quarter of the seventeenth century a sect of the Dutch Reformed Church called Labadists settled in Maryland and Delaware. With evangelical earnestness the small group, which ceased to exist by 1727, lived a communal existence, sustained principally by agriculture. In 1679 two representatives from the central church in Friesland, Jasper Danckaerts and Peter Sluyter (1645–1722), crossed the ocean to transact business with the provincial associates. Their mission accomplished, the two men traveled north through New York to Boston before returning to Holland. They remained in Boston from June 19 to July 23, 1680, and the *Journal* of their voyage, especially of their sojourn in Cambridge and vicinity, makes delightful reading.

The manuscript in Danckaerts's handwriting is in the possession of the Long Island Historical Society. It was first printed by the Society in 1867, soon after its discovery. The text, together with the notes, is from the *Journal of Jasper Danckaerts, 1679–1680*, ed. by B. B. James and J. F. Jameson (New York, 1913), pp. 254, 255, 258–269, 272–275.]

JOURNAL OF JASPER DANCKAERTS

JUNE, 1680] About three o'clock we caught sight of the main land of Cape Cod, to which we sailed northerly. We arrived inside the cape about six o'clock, with a tolerable breeze from the west, and at the same time saw vessels to the leeward of us which had an east wind, from which circumstance we supposed we were in a whirlwind. These two contrary winds striking against each other, the sky became dark, and they whirled by each other, sometimes the one, and sometimes the other being strongest, compelling us to lower the sails several times. I have never seen such a twisting and turning round in the air as at this time, the clouds being driven against each other, and close to the earth. At last it became calm and began to rain very hard, and to thunder and lighten heavily. We drifted along the whole night in a calm, advancing only twelve or sixteen miles.

23*d*, *Sunday*. A breeze blew up from the northeast. It was fortunate for us that we arrived inside of Cape Cod yesterday evening, before this unfavorable weather, as we should otherwise have been compelled to put back to Rhode Island. We could now still proceed; and we laid our course northwest to Boston. We arrived at the entrance of the harbor at noon, where we found a considerable rolling sea caused by the ebb tide and wind being against each other. There are about thirty islands here, not large ones, through which we sailed, and reached Boston at four o'clock in the afternoon, our captain running with his yacht quite up to his house in the Milk-ditch.[1]

The Lord be praised, who has continued in such a fatherly manner to conduct us, and given us so many proofs of His care over us; words are wanting to express ourselves properly, more than occasions for them, which we have had abundantly.

We permitted those most in haste to go ashore before us, and then went ourselves. The skipper received us politely at his house, and so did his wife; but as it was Sunday, which it seems is somewhat strictly observed by these people, there was not much for us to do today. Our captain, however, took us to his sister's where we were welcome, and from there to his father's, an old corpulent man, where there was a repetition of the worship, which took place in the kitchen while they were turning the spit, and busy preparing a good supper. We arrived while they were engaged in the service, but he did not once look up. When he had finished, they turned round their backs, and kneeled on chairs or benches. The prayer was said loud enough to be heard three houses off, and also long enough, if that made it good. This done, he wished us and his son welcome, and insisted on our supping with him, which we did. . . .

24*th*, *Monday*. We walked with our captain into the town, for his house stood a little one side of it, and the first house he took us to was a tavern. From there, he conducted us to the governor, who dwelt in only a common house, and that not the most costly. He is an old man, quiet and grave.[2] He was dressed in black silk, but not sumptuously. Paddechal explained the reasons of our visit. The governor inquired who we were, and where from, and where we were going. Paddechal told him we were Hollanders, and had come on with him from New York, in order to depart from here for England. He asked further our names, which we wrote down for him. He then presented us a small cup of wine, and with that we finished. We went then to the house of one John Tayller, or merchant tailor,[3] to whom William van Cleyf had recommended us; but we did not find him. We wanted to obtain a place where we could be at home, and especially to ascertain if there were any Dutchmen. They told us of a silversmith who was a Dutchman, and at whose house the Dutch usually went to lodge. We went in search of him, but he was not at home. At noon we found this merchant tailor, who appeared to be a good sort of a person. He spoke tolerably good French, and informed us there was a ship up for England immediately, and another in about three weeks. The first was too soon for us, and we therefore thought it best to wait for the other. We also found the silversmith, who bade us welcome. His name was Willem Ros, from Wesel. He had married an Englishwoman, and carried on his business here. He told us we might come and lodge with him, if we wished, which we determined to do; for to lie again in our last night's nest was not agreeable to us. We exchanged some of our money, and obtained six shillings and six-pence each for our ducatoons, and ten shillings each for the ducats. We went accordingly to lodge at the goldsmith's, whom my comrade knew well, though he did not recollect my comrade.[4] We were better off at his house, for although his wife was an Englishwoman, she was quite a good housekeeper.

25*th*, *Tuesday*. We went in search of Mr. Paddechal this morning and paid him for our passage here, twenty shillings New England currency, for each of us. We wanted to obtain our goods, but they were all too busy then, and promised they would send them to us in the city the next day. We inquired after Mr. John Pigon, to whom Mr. Robert Sanders, of Albany, promised to send Wouter the Indian, with a letter, but he had received neither the letter nor the Indian; so that we must offer up our poor Indian to the pleasure of the Lord. We also went to look after the ship, in which we were going to leave for London. We understood the name of the captain was Jan Foy. The ship was called the *Dolphin*, and mounted sixteen guns.[5] Several passengers were engaged. There was a surgeon in the service of the ship from Rotterdam, named Johan Owins, who had been to Surinam [6] and afterwards to the island of Fayal,[7] from whence he had come here, and now wished to go home. There was also a sailor on board the ship who spoke Dutch, or was a Dutchman. The carpenter was a Norwegian who lived at Flushing.

26*th*, *Wednesday*. We strove hard to get our goods home, for we were fearful, inasmuch as our trunk was on deck, and it had rained, and a sea now and then had washed over it, that it might be wet and ruined; but we did not succeed, and Paddechal in this exhibited again his inconsiderateness, and little regard for his promise. We resolved to take it out the next day, go as it would.

27*th*, *Thursday*. We went to the Exchange in order to find the merchant tailor, and also the skipper, which we did. We agreed for our passage at the usual price of six pounds sterling for each person, with the choice of paying here or in England; but as we would have less loss on our money here, we determined to pay here. After 'change was over there was preaching,[8] to which we had intended to go; but as we had got our goods home, after much trouble, and found several articles wet and liable to be spoiled, we had to stay and dry them.

28*th*, *Friday*. One of the best ministers in the place being very sick, a day of fasting and prayer was observed in a church near by our house. We went into the church, where, in the first place, a minister made a prayer in the pulpit, of full two hours in length; after which an old minister delivered a sermon an hour long, and after that a prayer was made, and some verses sung out of the Psalms. In the afternoon, three or four hours were consumed with nothing except prayers, three ministers relieving each other alternately; when one was tired, another went up into the pulpit.[9] There was no more devotion than in other churches, and even less than at New York; no respect, no reverence; in a word, nothing but the name of Independents; and that was all. . . .

7th, Sunday. We heard preaching in three churches, by persons who seemed to possess zeal, but no just knowledge of Christianity. The auditors were very worldly and inattentive. The best of the ministers whom we have yet heard is a very old man, named Mr. John Eliot,[10] who has charge of the instruction of the Indians in the Christian religion. He has translated the Bible into their language. After we had already made inquiries of the booksellers for this Bible, and there was none to be obtained in Boston, and they told us if one was to be had, it would be from Mr. Eliot, we determined to go on Monday to the village where he resided, and was the minister, called Rocsberry [Roxbury]. Our landlord had promised to take us, but was not able to do so, in consequence of his having too much business. We therefore thought we would go alone and do what we wanted.

JULY *8th, Monday.* We went accordingly, about six o'clock in the morning, to Rocxberry, which is three-quarters of an hour from the city, in order that we might get home early, inasmuch as our captain had informed us, he would come in the afternoon for our money, and in order that Mr. Eliot might not be gone from home. On arriving at his house, he was not there, and we therefore went to look around the village and the vicinity. We found it justly called Rocxberry, for it was very rocky, and had hills entirely of rocks. Returning to his house we spoke to him, and he received us politely. As he could speak neither Dutch nor French, and we spoke but little English, we were unable to converse very well; however, partly in Latin, partly in English, we managed to understand each other. He was seventy-seven years old,[11] and had been forty-eight years in these parts. He had learned very well the language of the Indians, who lived about there. We asked him for an Indian Bible. He said in the late Indian war, all the Bibles and Testaments were carried away, and burnt or destroyed, so that he had not been able to save any for himself; but a new edition was in press, which he hoped would be much better than the first one, though that was not to be despised. We inquired whether any part of the old and new edition could be obtained by purchase, and whether there was any grammar of their language in English. Thereupon he went and brought us one of the Old Testaments in the Indian language, and also almost the whole of the New Testament, made up with some sheets of the new edition of the New Testament, so that we had the Old and New Testaments complete. . . .[12]

He deplored the decline of the church in New England, and especially in Boston, so that he did not know what would be the final result. We inquired how it stood with the Indians, and whether any good fruit had followed his work. Yes, much, he said, if we meant true conversion of the heart; for they had in various countries, instances of conversion, as they called it, and had seen it amounted to nothing at all; that they must not endeavor, like scribes and Pharisees, to make Jewish proselytes, but true Christians. He could thank God, he continued, and God be praised for it, there were Indians whom he knew, who were truly converted of heart to God, and whose profession, he believed, was sincere. It seemed as if he were disposed to know us further, and we therefore said to him, if he had any desire to write to our sort of people, he could use the names which stood on the title-page of the *Declaration*, and that we hoped to come and converse with him again. He accompanied us as far as the jurisdiction of Roxbury extended, where we parted from him.

9th, Tuesday. We started out to go to Cambridge, lying to the northeast of Boston, in order to see their college and printing office. We left about six o'clock in the morning, and were set across the river at Charlestown. We followed a road which we supposed was the right one, but went full half an hour out of the way, and would have gone still further, had not a negro who met us, and of whom we inquired, disabused us of our mistake. We went back to the right road, which is a very pleasant one. We reached Cambridge about eight o'clock. It is not a large village, and the houses stand very much apart. The college building is the most conspicuous among them. We went to it, expecting to see something unusual, as it is the only college, or would-be academy of the Protestants in all America, but we found ourselves mistaken. In approaching the house we neither heard nor saw anything mentionable; but, going to the other side of the building, we heard noise enough in an upper room to lead my comrade to say, "I believe they are engaged in disputation." We entered and went up stairs, when a person met us, and requested us to walk in, which we did. We found there eight or ten young fellows, sitting around, smoking tobacco, with the smoke of which the room was so full, that you could hardly see; and the whole house smelt so strong of it that when I was going up stairs I said, "It certainly must be also a tavern." [13] We excused ourselves, that we could speak English only a little, but understood Dutch or French well, which they did not. However, we spoke as well as we could. We inquired how many professors there were, and they replied not one, that there was not enough money to support one. We asked how many students there were. They said at first, thirty, and then came down to twenty; I afterwards understood there are probably not ten. They knew hardly a word of Latin, not one of them, so that my comrade could not converse with them. They took us to the library where there was nothing particular. We looked over it a little. They presented us with a glass of wine. This is all we ascertained there. The minister of the place goes there morning and evening to make prayer, and has charge over them; besides him, the students are under tutors or masters.[14] Our visit was soon over, and we left them to go and look at the land about there. We found the place beautifully situated on a large plain, more than eight miles square, with a fine stream in the middle of it, capable of bearing heavily laden vessels. As regards the fertility of the soil, we consider the poorest in New York superior to the best here. As we were tired, we took a mouthful to eat, and left. We passed by the printing office, but there was nobody in it; the paper sash however being broken, we looked in, and saw two presses with six or eight cases of type. There is not much work done there. Our printing office is well worth two of it, and even more.[15] We went back to Charlestown, where, after waiting a little, we crossed over about three o'clock. . . .

But before going further to sea we must give a brief description of New England, and the city of Boston in particular.

When New Netherland was first discovered by the Hollanders, the evidence is that New England was not known; because the Dutch East India Company then sought a passage by the west, through which to sail to Japan and China; and if New England had been then discovered, they would not have sought a passage there, knowing it to be the main land; just as when New Netherland and New England did become known, such a passage was sought no longer through them, but farther to the north through Davis and Hudson straits. The Hollanders, when they discovered New Netherland, embraced under that name and title all the coast from Virginia or Cape Hinloopen eastwardly to Cape Cod, as it was then and there discovered by them and designated by Dutch names, as sufficiently appears by the charts. The English afterwards discovered New England and settled there.[16] They increased so in consequence of the great liberties and favorable privileges which the king granted to the Independents, that they went to live not only west of Cape Cod and Rhode Island, but also on Long Island and other places, and even took possession of the whole of the Fresh River,[17] which the Hollanders there were not able to prevent, in consequence of their small force in New Netherland, and the scanty population. The English went more readily to the west, because the land was much better there, and more accessible to vessels, and the climate was milder; and also because they could trade more conveniently with the Hollanders, and be supplied by them with provisions. New England is now described as extending from the Fresh River to Cape Cod and thence to Kennebec, comprising three provinces or colonies: Fresh River or Connecticut, Rhode Island and the other islands to Cape Cod, and Boston, which stretches from thence north. They are subject to no one, but acknowledge the king of England for their lord,[18] and therefore no ships enter unless they have English passports or commissions. They have free trade with all countries; but the return cargoes from there to Europe go to England, except those which go secretly to Holland. There is no toll or duty paid upon merchandise exported or imported, nor is there any impost or tax paid upon land. Each province chooses its own governor from the magistracy, and the magistrates are chosen from the principal inhabitants, merchants or planters. They are all Independents in matters of religion, if it can be called religion; many of them perhaps more for the purposes of enjoying the benefit of its privileges than for any regard to truth and godliness. I observed that while the English flag or color has a red ground with a small white field in the uppermost corner, where there is a red cross, they have here dispensed with this cross in their colors, and preserved the rest.[19] They baptize no children except those of the members of the congregation. All their religion consists in observing Sunday, by not working or going into the taverns on that day; but the houses are worse than the taverns. No stranger or traveller can therefore be entertained on a Sunday, which begins at sunset on Saturday, and continues until the same time on Sunday. At these two hours you see all their countenances change. Saturday evening the constable goes round into all the taverns of the city for the purpose of stopping all noise and debauchery, which frequently causes him to stop his search, before his search causes the debauchery to stop. There is a penalty for cursing and swearing, such as they please to impose, the witnesses thereof being at liberty to insist upon it. Nevertheless you discover little difference between this and other places. Drinking and fighting occur there not less than elsewhere; and as to truth and true godliness, you must not expect more of them than of others. When we were there, four ministers' sons were learning the silversmith's trade.

The soil is not as fertile as in the west. Many persons leave there to go to the Delaware and New Jersey. They manure their lands with heads of fish. They gain their living mostly or very much by fish, which they salt and dry for selling; and by raising horses, oxen, and cows, as well as hogs and sheep, which they sell alive, or slaughtered and salted, in the Caribbean Islands and other places. They are not as good farmers as the Hollanders about New York.

INCREASE MATHER

["Seasonable merriment" was a phrase the Puritans often used approvingly, but they interpreted it after their own fashion. "Dancing (yea though mixt) I would not simply condemn." John Cotton had written a friend in 1625, justifying it from the Old Testament: "Only lascivious dancing to wanton ditties" (*Collections of the Massachusetts Historical Society*, second series, X (1823), 183). The thirty-page essay which Increase Mather published in Boston in 1684: *An Arrow against Profane and Promiscuous Dancing. Drawn out of a Quiver of the Scriptures*, resulted from a ministers' discussion. It is stricter in tone than Cotton's letter, and in the eyes of twentieth-century readers seems to lay a disproportionate stress on moral inessentials. By 1716, at least, dancing was taught in Boston by Edward Euston, the organist of the Episcopal King's Chapel, who thus augmented his salary, and he met with no interference. See *Diary of Samuel Sewall*, III, 111 note.

For Mather, see p. 334. The text is from pp. 1–3, 27–30, with omissions indicated.]

AN ARROW AGAINST PROFANE AND PROMISCUOUS DANCING

CONCERNING the Controversy about *Dancing*, the Question is not, whether all *Dancing* be in it self sinful. It is granted, that *Pyrrhical* or *Polemical Saltation:* i.e. when men vault in their Armour, to shew their strength and activity, may be of use. Nor is the question, whether a sober and grave *Dancing* of Men with Men, or of Women with Women, be not allowable; we make no doubt of that, where it may be done without offence, in due season, and with moderation. The Prince of Philosophers has observed truly, that *Dancing* or *Leaping*, is a natural expression of joy: So that there is no more Sin in it, than in laughter, or any outward expression of inward Rejoycing.

But our question is concerning *Gynecandrical Dancing*, or that which is commonly called *Mixt* or *Promiscuous Dancing, viz.* of Men and Women (be they elder or younger persons) together: Now this we affirm to be utterly unlawful, and that it cannot be tollerated in such a place as *New-England,* without great Sin. And that it may appear, that we are not transported by Affection without Judgment, let the following Arguments be weighed in the Ballance of the Sanctuary.

Arg. 1. *That which the Scripture condemns is sinful.* None but Atheists will deny this *Proposition:* But the Scripture condemns *Promiscuous Dancing.* This *Assumption* is proved, 1. *From the Seventh Commandment.* It is an Eternal Truth to be observed in expounding the Commandments, that whenever any sin is forbidden, not only the highest acts of that sin, but all degrees thereof, and all occasions leading thereto are prohibited. Now we cannot find one Orthodox and Judicious Divine, that writeth on the Commandments, but mentions *Promiscuous Dancing,* as a breach of the seventh Commandment, as being an occasion, and an incentive to that which is evil in the sight of God. Yea, this is so manifest as that the *Assembly* in the *larger Catechism,* do expresly take notice of *Dancings,* as a violation of the Commandments. It is sad, that when in times of Reformation, Children have been taught in their C[a]techism, that such *Dancing* is against the Commandment of God, that now in *New-England* they should practically be learned the contrary. The unchast Touches and Gesticulations used by *Dancers,* have a palpable tendency to that which is evil. Whereas some object, that they are not sensible of any ill motions occasioned in them, by being Spectators or Actors in such *Saltations;* we are not bound to believe all which some pretend concerning their own Mortification. . . .

Now they that frequent Promiscuous Dancings, or that send their Children thereunto, walk disorderly, and contrary to the Apostles Doctrine. It has been proved that such a practice is a *Scandalous Immorality,* and therefore to be removed out of Churches by Discipline, which is the Broom of Christ, whereby he keeps his Churches clean. . . .

And shall Churches in *N*[*ew*] *E*[*ngland*] who have had a Name to be stricter and purer than other Churches, suffer such a scandalous evil amongst them? if all that are under Discipline be made sensible of this matter, we shall not be much or long infested with a *Choreutical Dæmon.* . . .

The Catechism which Wicked men teach their Children is to Dance and to Sing. Not that Dancing, or Musick, or Singing are in themselves sinful: but if the Dancing Master be wicked they are commonly abused to lasciviousness, and that makes them to become abominable. But will you that are Professors of Religion have your Children to be thus taught? the Lord expects that you should give the Children who are Baptized into his Name another kind of Education, that you should bring them up in the nurture and admonition of the Lord: And do you not hear the Lord Expostulating the case with you, and saying, you have taken my Children, the Children that were given unto me; the Children that were solemnly engaged to renounce the Pomps of Satan; but is this a light matter that you have taken these my Children, and initiated them in the Pomps and Vanities of the Wicked one, contrary to your Covenant? What will you say in the day of the Lords pleading with you? we have that charity for you as to believe that you have erred through Ignorance, and not wickedly: and we have therefore accounted it our Duty to inform you in the Truth. If you resolve not on Reformation, you will be left inexcusable. However it shall be, we have now given our Testimony and delivered our own Souls. *Consider what we say, and the Lord give you understanding in all things.*

JOHN DUNTON, 1659–1733

[John Dunton was an eccentric bookseller of London who came to Boston in 1686 to collect bad debts, dispose of excess stock, and perhaps to escape the dangers of the Monmouth rising. He remained in New England but eight months, during which time he wrote a series of entertaining but unreliable letters, published by the Prince Society of Boston in 1867 in two volumes: *John Dunton's Letters from New-England.*

The selections chosen for the text deal in part with sermons delivered by Cotton Mather, Joshua Moody, and Increase Mather in the presence of the condemned murderer James Morgan. Dunton's version of the sermons is quite accurate, in some portions *verbatim.* Of the prisoner little is known save that he lived in Boston. All three sermons, each of which required at least an hour to expound, were published within a year of their delivery, and represent a class of literature which publishers willingly undertook in anticipation of profitable sales. Such accounts supplied the public with what we might call the murder novels of their day. They presented the horrors of sin with enough lurid detail to arouse interest, and concluded with edifying advice. The custom of publicly addressing the condemned man in the presence of the gallows was brought from England; the twentieth-century mind revolts from the barbaric practice, yet the rite was universal in English-speaking communities till well into the eighteenth century.

For accounts of Moody and the Mathers, see pp. 162, 334, and 367.

Dunton's "Ramble" from Charlestown through Medford and Cambridge, and his chat with the college librarian, John Cotton, about books, offer a pleasanter side of people and customs.

The text of the *Letters* is from I, 118–137; II, 154–163, with omissions indicated. The selections are chosen from the more reliable passages. For a discussion of the general untrustworthiness of the *Letters*, see Chester N. Greenough, "John Dunton's Letters from New England," *Publications of the Colonial Society of Massachusetts*, XIV (1913), 212–257; *idem*, "John Dunton Again," *ibid.*, XXI (1920), 232–251.

LETTERS

To Mr. George Larkin, Printer, at the Two Swans, without Bishopsgate, London.

Boston, in New-England, March 25, 1686.

Another Occurrence that happened, whilst I was here, was the Execution of Morgan, which I may send you as a Piece of News, for there has not (it seems) been seen an Execution here this seven years. So that some have come 50 miles to see it: And I do confess, Considering what serious care the two Mathers and Mr. Moody took to prepare the Dying Criminal for Death, the Relation may be worth relateing in my Summer Rambles; and in this Occurrence, I shall relate nothing but what I saw my self.

And first, I went to view the Prison, in Prison-Lane;[1] and here I think it will not be amiss, if I first give you the Character of a Prison: A Prison is the Grave of the Living, where they are shut up from the World and their Friends, and the Worms that gnaw upon them are their own Thoughts and the Jayler. 'Tis a House of meagre Looks, and ill smells: for Lice, Drink, and Tobacco, are the Compound: Or, if you will, 'tis the Subburbs of Hell; and the Persons much the same as there: You may ask, as Manippas in Lucian, which is Nevius, which Thirsites; which the Beggar, and which the Knight: for they are all suited in the same kind of nasty Poverty. The only fashion here, is to be out at the Elbows; and not to be thread-bare, is a great Indecorum.

Every Man shews here like so many Wrecks upon the Sea: here the Ribs of a thousand Pound; and there, the Relicks of so many Manners is only a Doublet without Buttons; and 'tis a Spectacle of more Pity than Executions are. Men huddle up their Lives here, as a thing of no use, and wear it out like an old suit, the faster the better; and he that deceives the time best, best spends it. Men see here much sin, and much calamity; and where the last does not mortifie, the other hardens: And those that are worse here, are desperately worse, as those from whom the Horror of sin is taken off, and the Punishment familiar. This is a School, in which much Wisdom is learnt, but it is generally too late, and with danger; and it is better to be a fool, than come here to learn it.

Here it was that I saw poor Morgan; who seem'd to be very sorrowful and penitent, and confessed that he had in his rage murdered the Man whose Death and Blood has been laid to his Charge: He told me that the other gave him some ill Language whereby he was provoked, and that he said to him, If he came within the door, he wou'd run the spit into his Bowels, and he was as wicked as his Word; and so confessed himself guilty of Murder. . . .

But to return to Morgan, whose Execution being appointed on the 11th of March, there was that Care taken for his Soul that three Excellent Sermons [2] were preached before him, before his Execution; Two on the Lord's Day, and one just before his Execution. The first was preached by Mr. Cotton Mather, who preached upon that Text in *Isa.* 45 : 22, *Look unto Me and be ye saved, all the Ends of the Earth.* He declar'd that when the no less unexpected than undeniable Request of a Dying Man, who (says he) now stands in this Assembly, that he wou'd allow him this morning, a Discourse proper to his Uncomfortable Circumstances, was brought to him, he cou'd not think of a more proper Text; Telling the poor Wretch, That he was now listening to one of the three last Sermons that ever he was like to sit under before his incounter with the King of Terrors. And then said, "Poor Man! Do you hearken diligently, and I'll study to make this whole hour very particularly suitable and serviceable to you; and methinks a Man that knows himself about to take an Eternal Farewel of all Sermons, shou'd Endeavour to hear with most Earnest heed. And a little after, "The Faithful and True Witness saith unto us, *I will give you rest;* O let the poor fetter'd Prisoner recollect himself! James! Thy Name is not excepted in these Invitations."

"I am glad for the seemingly penitent Confession of your monstrous Miscarriages, which yesterday I obtain'd in writing from you, and which indeed was no more than there was need of: But it remains yet, that you give your Dying Looks to the Lord Jesus Christ; for Salvation from all your Guilt, and from all the Plagues in the flying Roll." And a little after, "My request unto you is, That you wou'd at this hour think of an Interest in Christ.—Surely when the Executioner is laying the Cold Cloth of Death over your Eyes, the Look, with the

Shriek of your Soul, will then say, "O now a Thousand Worlds for an Interest in Jesus Christ!" Surely a few minutes after that, when your naked Soul shall appear before the Judgment-Seat of the Most High, you will again say, an Interest in Jesus Christ, is worth whole Mountains of Massive Gold!

You have murder'd the Body and (no thanks to you, if not) the Soul of your Neighbour too: And O that the Rock in your Bosom might flow with Tears at such a thought! If the Court shou'd say unto you, Beg hard, and you shall live; O, how affectionate wou'd you be! Poor dying man, The Lord Jesus Christ saith the same thing to you, If thou canst heartily look and beg, thou shalt not be hang'd up among the Monuments of my Vengeance, in Chains for Evermore.

"The sharp Ax of Civil Justice will speedily cut you down; O for a little good Fruit before the Blow! Manifest your penitence for your Iniquities by a due care to excel in Tempers quite contrary to those ill habits and Customs whereby you have heretofore blasphemed the Worthy Name of Christ and Christianity: Especially employ the last minutes of your Life, in giving a Zealous Warning unto others, to take heed of those things which have been destructive unto you. Tell them what wild Gourds of Death they are, by which you have got your Bane; point out before them those Paths of the Destroyer which have led you down So near unto the Congregation of the Dead.

"When the numerous Crowd of Spectators are, three or four days hence, throng'd about the Place where you shall then breathe your last before them all, then do you with the heart-piercing-groans of a deadly wounded Man, beseech of your Fellow-sinners, That they wou'd turn now every one from the Evil of his way. Beseech them to keep clear of ill haunts and ill houses, with as much dread of them, as they cou'd have of lying down in a Nest of poysonous Snakes: Beseech them to abhor all Uncleanness, as they wou'd the Deep Ditch which the abhorred of the Lord do fall into. Beseech of them to avoid all Excess in Drinking, as they wou'd not rot themselves with more bitter Liquors than the Waters of Jealousie. Beseech them to mortifie and moderate all inordinate Passions, as they wou'd not surrender themselves into the hands of Devils, that will hurry them down into deeper Deeps than they are aware of. Beseech them to shun Idle Swearing, as a Prophanity that the God to whom vengeance belongeth will not permit to go unpunished. Beseech them to avoid Curses on themselves or others, least whilst they like Madmen so throw about Firebrands, Arrows, and Death, they bring upon their own heads, as you have done, the things which they are apt to be wishing. Beseech them to beware of Lying, as they wou'd not be put to need, and Crave, and be deny'd, a drop of Water, to cool their Tongues in the place of Torment. Beseech of them to be as averse to all stealing, as they wou'd be to carry coals of Fire into those Nests that they so feather by their dishonesty. Beseech of them to prize the means of Grace; to sleep at, or keep from sermons no more: To love the Habitation of GOD's House, and the place where his Honour dwells; lest GOD soon send their barren, froward souls to dwell in silence, where there shall never be a Gospel-Sermon heard; Never, Never, as long as the Almighty sits upon his Christal Throne.

"And when you have given these Warnings, upon the Ladder from whence you shall not come off without taking an Irrecoverable step into Eternity; O remember still, you give unto Jesus Christ the Honour of Looking to him for his salvation. Remember, that if you wou'd do a work highly for the Honour of Him, this is The Work of GOD, that you believe on Him. Even after your Eyes are so covered, as to take their leave of all sights below, still continue Looking unto Him whom you have heard saying, *Look unto me*. And now let the Everlasting Saviour look down in much mercy upon you: O that he wou'd give this Murderer and Extraordinary Sinner, a place among the Wonders of Free Grace! O that this Wretched Man might be made meet for the Inheritance among the Saints in Light; being kept from an unrepenting and deluded Heart as unquenchable Fire will find fewel in."

This was the Substance of what Mr. Cotton Mather address'd to the Prisoner, in his Sermon in the Morning. . . .

In the Evening of the same Lord's Day, Mr. Joshua Moodey preach'd before him; his Text was *Isa.* 12 : 1.—*Tho' thou wast angry with me, thine anger is turned away*.—He told the Poor condemned Prisoner, That what he had to say to him, shou'd be under these two Heads, 1. By way of Conviction and awakening: 2. By way of Encouragement and Counsel. He told him also, That he shou'd use all Plainness and Freedom, taking it for Granted that Dying Men are past all Expectation of Flatteries or Complements; and that plain Dealing, which will do the most Good, will find the best Acceptance. . . .

"You seem to bewail your Sin of Sabbath-breaking: Well, know that you shall never have another Sabbath to break.—The Lord help you to keep this as you ought.—It is a very awful thing to us to look on you, a Person in your Youth, Health, and Strength, Brests full of Milk, and Bones moistened with Marrow, and then to think that within so many Days, this Man, tho' in his full strength, must Dye: And methinks it shou'd be much more awful to you.—Consider, You have no time to get Sin pardoned, and Wrath turn'd away, (if it be not done already) but between this and Death, into the very Borders, and under the Sentence of which, you now are. In the Grave there is no Repentance, no Remission, *Eccles.* 9: 10. Before four Days more pass over your head, (and O how swiftly do they fly away!) you will be entered into an Eternal and Unchangeable state, of Weal or Wo; and of wo it will be, if speedy, thorough Repentance prevent it not.

"But yet know, That notwithstanding all that has been spoken, there is yet hope in Israel concerning this thing. There is a way found out, and revealed by God for the Turning of his Anger even from such Sinners. Paul was a Murderer, and yet Pardon'd; Manasseh made the streets of Jerusalem to swim with Innocent Blood, and yet was forgiven. . . ."

Then addressing himself to the Congregation, he said: "You may not expect to have any come from the Dead to warn you, but here is one that is just going to the Dead, who bequeaths you this Warning, lest you also be in like manner hung up as Monuments of God's Wrath. I lived near twenty years in this Countrey, before I heard an Oath or a Curse: But now as you pass along the Streets, you may hear Children curse and swear, and take the great and dreadful name of God in vain. This they have learnt from Elder Persons, but wo to them that taught them, if they repent not.—I remember what Pious Herbert saith, in his Advice to young Men, That the Swearer has neither any fair pretence for doing it, nor Excuse when done, either from Pleasure or Profit, &c., and says, That if he were an Epicure, he cou'd forbear Swearing.

"And O you Drunkards, Let trembling take hold of you, Especially you Drunkards of Ephraim, *Isa.* 28 : 1. I mean Church-Member Drunkards. I wish there were none such, that hear me this Day, who neither are Church-Members now, nor were, till Dismembred for that Sin. . . .

He then said, "I shall conclude, in a few words more to this Dying Bloody Sinner":—And then addressing himself to the Prisoner, he said, —"Poor Man! Consider, That all who live under the Gospel, are brought to Jesus, *the Mediator of the New Covenant;* to the *Blood of Sprinkling, that speaketh better things than that of Abel.—Heb.* 12 : 24. And thereupon it is presently added, *vers.* 25, *See that ye refuse not him that speaks from Heaven.* Abel's Blood cried for Vengeance upon the Murderer, but Christ's Blood cries for Pardon, and Christ himself calls on thee, to receive, and not refuse him; unto which Call, if thou yield the obedience of Faith, his Blood will speak on thy Behalf. Thy sins speak bitter things, old sins, sins of youth, a Course of Sin; and this bloody Sin cries aloud, and speaks most bitterly; but that blood of Christ can out-speak, out-cry all these. It was from hence, that David, when under the Anguish of Soul, for his Blood-guiltiness, expected Pardon, and had it, and so mayst thou. *Psal.* 51. . . ."

This was the substance of Mr. Moody's Address to the Prisoner; who was remanded to Prison, where he continued till Thursday Morning, (the Day of his Execution) and then another Sermon (the last he ever heard) was preached before him by the Reverend Mr. Increase Mather, just before his going to Execution. . . .

"I have spoken so often to you in private, since your being apprehended, that I shall not need to say much now: Only a few Words:—

"1. Consider what a Sinner you have been; The Sin which you are to dye for, is as red as Scarlet; and many other Sins has your wicked Life been filled with. You have been a stranger to me; I never saw you; I never heard of you, until you had committed the Murder, for which you must dye this Day; but I hear by others that have known you, how wicked you have been; and you have your self confessed to the World, That you have been guilty of Drunkenness, guilty of Cursing and Swearing, guilty of Sabbath-breaking, guilty of Lying, guilty of Secret Uncleanness; as Solomon said to Shimei, *Thou knowest the Wickedness which thine own heart is privy to;* so I say to you: and that which aggravates your guiltiness not a little, is, That since you have been in Prison you have done Wickedly: You have made your self drunk several Times since your Imprisonment; yea, and you have been guilty of Lying since your Condemnation.

"2. Consider what misery you have brought upon your self: on your Body, that must dye an accursed Death; you must hang between Heaven and Earth, as it were forsaking of both, and unworthy to be in either. And what misery have you brought upon your poor Children? You have brought an Everlasting Reproach upon them. How great will their shame be, when it shall be said to them that their Father was hang'd? Not for his Goodness, as many in the World have been; but for his Wickedness: Not as a Martyr, but as a Malefactor: But that which is Ten thousand thousand times worse than all this, is, That you have (without Repentance,) brought undoing Misery upon your poor, yet precious Soul: Not only Death on your Body, but a second Death on your never-dying Soul: O tremble at that! . . ."

This, Mr. Larkin, is a part of what I heard preached at Mr. Willard's Meeting in an Auditory of near 5000 People; they went first to the New Church, but the Gallery crack'd, and so they were forced to remove to Mr. Willard's.[3] They were all preach'd with so much Awfulness, and so pathetically apply'd to the Poor Condemned Man, that all the Auditory (as well as my self) were very much affected thereat: And tho' I have been pretty long in the Rehearsal, yet you being an old Dissenter, I did not think the Reading of them wou'd be unacceptable to you. And remember this, I am rambling still, tho' it be from one subject to another.—But before I leave off this subject, I must bring Morgan to his Execution, whither I rid with Mr. Cotton Mather, after the Sermon was ended. Some thousands of the People following to see the Execution. As I rid along I had several glimpses of poor Morgan, as he went.

He seem'd penitent to the last: Mr. Cotton Mather pray'd with him at the place of Execution, and conferred with him about his Soul all the way thither, which was about a mile out of Boston. After being ty'd up, standing on the Ladder, he made the following Speech:—

"I pray God that I may be a Warning to you all, and that I may be the last that ever shall suffer after this manner. In the fear of God I warn you to have a Care of the Sin of Drunkenness, for that's a Sin that leads to all manner of Sins and Wickedness: (Mind and have a Care of breaking the Sixth Commandment, where it is said, *Thou shalt do no Murder.*) For when a Man is in drink, he is ready to commit all manner of Sin, till he fill up the Cup of the Wrath of God, as I have done, by committing that Sin of Murder. I beg of God, as I am a Dying Man, and to appear before the Lord within a few Minutes, that you may take notice of what I say to you: Have a Care of Drunkenness and ill Company, and mind all good Instruction, and don't turn your back upon the Word of God, as I have done. When I have been at a Meeting, I have gone out of the Meeting-House to commit sin, and to please the Lust of my flesh: and don't make a mock at any poor Object of Pity, but bless God, that he hath not left you, as he hath justly done me, to commit that horrid Sin of Murder. . . ."

After he had been about an hour at the Gallows, and had prayed again, his Cap was pulled over his Eyes, and then having said, "O Lord, Receive my Spirit; I come unto thee, O Lord; I come, I come, I come"; he was Turned off, and the multitude by degrees dispers'd. I think, during this Mournful Scene, I never saw more serious nor greater Compassion.

But from the House of Mourning, I rambled to the House of Feasting; for Mr. York, Mr. King, with Madam Brick, Mrs. Green, Mrs. Toy, the Damsell and my self, took a Ramble to a place call'd Governour's Island, about a mile from Boston, to see a whole Hog roasted, as did several other Bostonians. We went all in a Boat; and having treated the Fair Sex, returned in the Evening. . . .

[Ramble to Medford]

This was nothing near so pleasant a Ramble as the other; and that for three Reasons; for first, the Weather wasn't so good: For tho' the Sun flatter'd me in the Morning, and made me believe it wou'd be a fair day, yet before noon he grew sullen, drew in his exhilerating Beams, and muffl'd up his Face in a Cloud, so that there was no getting sight of him all the Day after: Nor was the Clouds' obscuring of the Sun's bright face, the only mischief that they did me; but to make my Rambling more uncomfortable yet, they pour'd down such a Prodigious Shower of Rain upon me, that if I wasn't wet to th' Skin, it was because my kinder Fate provided a good Shelter near at hand. For the chief kindness I receiv'd at Medford, was to be shelter'd by it from a Swinging shower of Rain, which only wet my Upper Garment,—and no more.

But Secondly, Neither was my Company so good; for I had only with me a young Bostonian for my Guide, who when he saw that it began to rain, turn'd a Deserter, and foolishly turn'd back again, fast as his Legs cou'd carry him; by which means he was catch'd in all the Shower, whilst I was shelter'd by making haste to Medford. Nor thirdly, Did I meet with such kind Entertainment at Medford as at Charles Town: For here I had no Acquaintance, but took Sanctuary in a Publick,[4] where there was extraordinary good Cyder, and tho' I hadn't such a Noble Treat as at Captain Jenner's; yet with the Cyder and such other Entertainment as the House afforded, (together with my Landlord and my Landlady's good Company,) I made a very pretty thing on't.

I ask'd my Landlady whether if the rain continu'd, there was any Lodging to be had, and she was pleas'd to tell me I shou'dn't want for that, tho' she set up all night her self; I told her before she shou'd do so, I'd seek a Lodging out among the Indians: And ask'd my Landlord whether he thought the Indians wou'd entertain me? My Landlord told me there was no need of my going among them, for he had Lodging enough; but as to the Indians Entertaining of me, he said that he had often known them (in the Summer time Especially) lie abroad themselves, to make room for Strangers, either English or others. I ask'd him what Beds they had, and he told me either Mats, or else Straw; and that when they lay down to sleep, they generally, both in Summer and Winter, made a great Fire, which serves them instead of Bedcloaths; and he that finds himself a-cold, must turn to the Fire to warm him; and they that wake first, must repair the Fire;

For as they have abundance of Fewel, so they don't spare in laying of it on. He told me also that when they had a Bad Dream, they look'd upon it as a threatening from God, and that on such occasions they wou'd rise and fall to Prayer, at any time of the Night.

By this time, the rain was over, tho' it still remain'd Cloudy; and therefore I thought it was best taking Time by the Fore-lock, and go back to Boston while it held up, there being nothing remarkable to be seen at Medford, which is but a small Village, consisting of a few Houses; And so paying my Reckoning, I came back to Boston in good time: For I had not been long at home, before it fell a raining again very hard.

My Third Ramble was to a Town called New-Town, which is situated three Miles from Charles-Town, on the North Side of the River, a league and a half by Water: This Town was first intended for a City, and is one of the neatest and best compacted Towns in the whole Countrey: It has many stately structures, and well-contrived Streets; Which for handsomness and beauty out-does Boston it self: The Inhabitants are generally rich, and have many hundred Acres of Land paled with one common Fence,—a mile and half long, affording store of Cattel.

You will the less wonder, Cousin, at what I have said about this Town, when you shall know this Town, that at first was called New Town, is now made an University, and called Cambridge, there being a colledge Erected there by one Mr. John Harvard, who gave £700 for the Erecting of it, in the year 1638. I was invited hither by Mr. Cotton,[5] a fellow of the Colledge, by whom I was very handsomely Treated, and shewn all that was remarkable in it. He discours'd with me about my Venture of Books; and by his means I sold many of my Books to the Colledge.

Among other Discourse that we had, he ask'd me, Who I look'd upon in England to be the best Authors, and Men of greatest Name and Repute? I told him, This was a very Comprehensive Question; For there were Authors famous in their several Faculties, some for Divinity, others for Philosophy, and some for the Mathematics; and several other Arts and Sciences; and therefore without he was more particular, 'twould be an Endless Task to answer him. He then reply'd he did intend chiefly Divinity; but since 'twas necessary for a Scholar to be universal in his knowledge, so 'twou'd be necessary for him to know who were the best Authors in every several Faculty I mention'd: I then told him I wou'd Endeavour to serve him, as far as my Memory wou'd give me leave: And as to Divinity, in England I must make a Distinction between the Establish'd Church-men and the Dissenters. . . .

"Nor must I omit [I said,] amongst these great Names, to mention that of Mr. John Bunyan, who tho' a Man of but very ordinary Education, yet was a Man of great Natural Parts, and as well known for an Author thro'out England, as any I have mention'd, by the many Books he has Publish'd, of which the Pilgrim's Progress bears away the Bell.

"But as I said of the Church-men, so I must of the Dissenters, these are scarce a Tythe of the Eminent Authors among 'em. You see Sir," said I, "what a Task you have put me upon, and therefore if I have been too tedious, and worn your Patience out, you must thank your self, since 'tis the Deference I pay to your Commands that has occasion'd it. But I shall Dispatch the others quickly.

"As to Philosophy, especially Experimental Philosophy, there are the Transactions of the Royal Society, published by Dr. Grew; and the Celebrated Works of the Honourable Robert Boyle, Esq., who is also as great a Divine as a Philosopher, as his style of the Scriptures, Occasional Reflections, and his Seraphic Love will Witness.

"For Law, Fleta, Bracton, and Cook upon Littleton, are Eminent. There are also the Reports of Sir Geoffery Palmer, and divers other Learned Judges, Eminent in their times. Among which Sir Mathew Hale, late Lord Chief Justice of England, must not be forgotten, who was the Perfect Pattern of an Upright Judge, and as great a Philosopher and Divine as a Lawyer; as Divine Origination of Mankind in Folio, and his Meditations and Contemplations, in Octavo, which are Excellent things, do abundantly Evidence.

"For Physick, the Learned Dr. Willett is a Famous Author, and Dr. Salmon by his Dispensatory, and several other Books, is very well known.

"For the Mathematicks, Sir Jonas Moore and Mr. William Leybourn are both very Eminent Authors.

"And for Poetry, the Immortal Cowley, who first brought in the use of Pindarick Poetry in English. Besides whom we have Dryden, Shadwel, Tate, Settle, and several others, very Eminent Authors.

Nor must we here forget to do justice to the Fair Sex, Mrs. Katharine Philips having made herself deservedly Famous for her Excellent Poetical Pieces; Mrs. Behn also has approved her self a Devotee to the Muses; and not the least, tho' the last, is the Incomparable Philomela; than whom, none has drunk a larger Draught at the Heliconian Spring, or been a greater Favourite of the Muses."

Mr. Cotton gave me many thanks for the Account I had given him of our English Authors; many of whom he said he had before heard on, and had some of their Works; but others of them were till now altogether unknown to him; but now that he knew them, he intended to enlarge his study with some of their Writings. I told him I was very glad I had in any measure gratified his Curiosity: And added, That since I had given him an Account of some of the most Eminent of our Old English Authors, he wou'd by way of Retaliation give me some little Account of their New-England Authors, for I did not doubt but there were many that had done worthily in this Countrey.

To this Mr. Cotton reply'd: "That I cou'd not expect New-England cou'd compare with Old, either for the Number of Authors, or the Excellency of their Parts and Endowments; New-England being only a Colony; and all their Learning but as springs from those two Fountains in Old England, Oxford and Cambridge: However, we have not been without Excellent Men in this Countrey: And amongst the first Planters here, Mr. John Cotton, and Mr. Seaborn Cotton, his Son, are deservedly Famous; and Mr. Shepherd for the many Excellent Tracts written by him, has his Praise in all the Churches: The many impressions that have been made of his Sincere Convert and Sound Believer, both at London, and here at Boston, shews what acceptance they have mett with in the World; his Parable of the Ten Virgins also, tho' in Folio, has been several times printed.

"Nor must the Famous Mr. Elliot (who is still living, tho' very aged,) [6] be Omitted; whose indefatigable Zeal and Industry, both by Printing and Preaching, for the Conversion of the Indians, has given Place to none.

"And as to our Modern Authors, the Reverend Mr. Increase Mather, the Present Rector of our Colledge, holds the chief Rank, whose Universal knowledge, both in Divine and Humane Learning, is very well known both in New-England and Old too: And his Worthy Son, Mr. Cotton Mather, does not come much short of his Father; and his Works do also praise him in the Gate: And to the Honour of our Colledge do I speak it, he was brought up in it. And tho' our Colledge does not pretend to compare it self with any either in Oxford or Cambridge, yet has there been brought up in it since its Foundation, 122 Ministers; of which Ten are dead, seventy-one remain still in the Country, and Forty-one are removed to England.

"As to the other of our Boston-Ministers, I believe you have heard 'em, and know 'em to be good Preachers, and men of great Parts; There are also several eminent Ministers in several Parts of the Countrey, but of them, I can give you but a small Account, having little Acquaintance with them, and therefore shall pass them by."

I then gave Mr. Cotton many thanks for the Trouble I had put him to, and promised him a Catalogue of my Books as soon as I cou'd write it out, and so took my leave of him.

SARAH KEMBLE KNIGHT, 1666–1727

[The most sprightly and graphic picture of rustic manners in the early eighteenth century has been left in the record of a journey made by Sarah Kemble Knight from Boston to New York in 1704. The intrepid business woman, who at one time kept a writing-school which young Benjamin Franklin is said to have attended, had interests to look after in New York. On October 2 she left Boston on horseback and alone, except for the companions she hired or fell in with along the way. The route she chose led through Rhode Island and New Haven, and she followed the same roads home in March, 1705. Such a trip, hazardous for anyone, was extraordinary for a woman. The discomforts and annoyances of the journey she met with tolerant humor and a certain mocking resignation.

Madam Knight's husband was a Boston merchant about whom little is known. In later life she removed to New Haven where she died, leaving an estate valued at £1800. Her *Journal* was first published, along with that of the Reverend Mr. Thomas Buckingham of Hartford, in New York, 1825, by Theodore Dwight. It has most recently been printed with an introduction by George P. Winship (Boston, 1920; facsimile reprint, 1935). In no other published journal of the period will the student of colonial dialect find a more racy idiom recorded.

The text is here given entire from the first edition. For an account of Madam Knight, see *Dictionary of American Biography;* also Anson Titus, "Madam Sarah Knight, Her Diary and Her Times," *Bostonian Society Publications*, IX (1912), 99–126.]

THE JOURNAL OF MADAM KNIGHT.

MONDAY, Octb'r. ye second, 1704.—About three o'clock afternoon, I begun my Journey from Boston to New-Haven; being about two Hundred Mile. My Kinsman, Capt. Robert Luist, waited on me as farr as Dedham, where I was to meet ye Western post.

I vissitted the Reverd. Mr. Belcher,[1] ye Minister of ye town, and tarried there till evening, in hopes ye post would come along. But he not coming, I resolved to go to Billingses where he used to lodg, being 12 miles further. But being ignorant of the way, Mad^{m} Billings,[2] seing no persuasions of her good spouses or hers could prevail with me to Lodg there that night, Very kindly went wyth me to ye Tavern, where I hoped to get my guide, And desired the Hostess to inquire of her guests whether any of them would go with mee. But they being tyed by the Lipps to a pewter engine, scarcely allowed themselves time to say what clownish ******

[*Here half a page of the MS. is gone.*]

*** Peices of eight, I told her no, I would not be accessary to such extortion.

Then John shan't go, sais shee. No, indeed, shan't hee; And held forth at that rate a long time, that I began to fear I was got among the Quaking tribe, beleeving not a Limbertong'd sister among them could out do Madm. Hostes.

Upon this, to my no small surprise, son John arrose, and gravely demanded what I would give him to go with me? Give you, sais I, are you John? Yes, says he, for want of a Better; And behold! this John look't as old as my Host, and perhaps had bin a man in the last Century. Well, Mr. John, sais I, make your demands. Why, half a pss. of eight and a dram, sais John. I agreed, and gave him a Dram (now) in hand to bind the bargain.

My hostess catechis'd John for going so cheep, saying his poor wife would break her heart *****

[*Here another half page of the MS is gone.*]

His shade on his Hors resembled a Globe on a Gate post. His habitt, Hors and furniture, its looks and goings Incomparably answered the rest.

Thus Jogging on with an easy pace, my Guide telling mee it was dangero's to Ride hard in the Night, (whch his horse had the sence to avoid,) Hee entertained me with the Adventurs he had passed by late Rideing, and eminent Dangers he had escaped, so that, Remembring the Hero's in Parismus and the Knight of the Oracle,[3] I didn't know but I had mett wth a Prince disguis'd.

When we had Ridd about an how'r, wee come into a thick swamp, wch. by Reason of a great fogg, very much startled mee, it being now very Dark. But nothing dismay'd John: Hee had encountered a thousand and a thousand such Swamps, having a Universall Knowledge in the woods; and readily Answered all my inquiries wch. were not a few.

In about an how'r, or something more, after we left the Swamp, we come to Billinges, where I was to Lodg. My Guide dismounted and very Complasantly help't me down and shewd the door, signing to me wth his hand to Go in; wch I Gladly did—But had not gone many steps into the Room, ere I was Interogated by a young Lady I understood afterwards was the Eldest daughter of the family, with these, or words to this purpose, (viz.) Law for mee—what in the world brings You here at this time a night?—I never see a woman on the Rode so Dreadfull late, in all the days of my versall life. Who are You? Where are You going? I'me scar'd out of my witts—with much now of the same Kind. I stood aghast, Prepareing to reply, when in comes my Guide—to him Madam turn'd, Roreing out: Lawfull heart, John, is it You?—how de do! Where in the world are you going with this woman? Who is she? John made no Ansr. but sat down in the corner, fumbled out his black Junk,[4] and saluted that instead of Debb; she then turned agen to mee and fell anew into her silly questions, without asking me to sitt down.

I told her shee treated me very Rudely, and I did not think it my duty to answer her unmannerly Questions. But to get ridd of them, I told her I come there to have the post's company with me to-morrow on my Journey, &c. Miss star'd awhile, drew a chair, bid me sitt, And then run up stairs and putts on two or three Rings, (or else I had not seen them before,) and returning, sett herself just before me, showing the way to Reding, that I might see her Ornaments, perhaps to gain the more respect. But her Granam's new Rung [5] sow, had it appeared, would affected me as much. I paid honest John wth money and dram according to contract, and Dismist him, and pray'd Miss to shew me where I must Lodg. Shee conducted me to a parlour in a little back Lento,[6] wch was almost fill'd wth the bedsted, wch was so high that I was forced to climb on a chair to gitt up to ye wretched bed that lay on it; on wch having Stretcht my tired Limbs, and lay'd my head on a Sad-colourd pillow, I began to think on the transactions of ye past day.

Tuesday, October ye third, about 8 in the morning, I with the Post proceeded forward without observing any thing remarkable; And about two, afternoon, Arrived at the Post's second stage, where the western Post mett him and exchanged Letters. Here, having called for something to eat, ye woman bro't in a Twisted thing like a cable, but something whiter; and laying it on the bord, tugg'd for life to bring it into a capacity to spread; wch having wth great pains accomplished, shee serv'd in a dish of Pork and Cabage, I suppose the remains of Dinner. The sause was of a deep Purple, wch I tho't was boil'd in her dye Kettle; the bread was Indian, and every thing on the Table service Agreeable to these. I, being hungry, gott a little down; but my stomach was soon cloy'd, and what cabbage I swallowed serv'd me for a Cudd the whole day after.

Having here discharged the Ordnary for self and Guide, (as I understood was the custom,) About Three afternoon went on with my Third Guide, who Rode very hard; and having crossed Providence Ferry, we come to a River w[ch] they Generally Ride thro'. But I dare not venture; so the Post got a Ladd and Cannoo to carry me to tother side, and hee rid thro' and Led my hors. The Cannoo was very small and shallow, so that when we were in she seem'd redy to take in water, which greatly terrified mee, and caused me to be very circumspect, sitting with my hands fast on each side, my eyes stedy, not daring so much as to lodg my tongue a hair's breadth more on one side of my mouth then tother, nor so much as think on Lott's wife, for a wry thought would have oversett our wherey: But was soon put out of this pain, by feeling the Cannoo on shore, w[ch] I as soon almost saluted with my feet; and Rewarding my sculler, again mounted and made the best of our way forwards. The Rode here was very even and y[e] day pleasant, it being now near Sunsett. But the Post told mee we had neer 14 miles to Ride to the next Stage, (where we were to Lodg.) I askt him of the rest of the Rode, foreseeing wee must travail in the night. Hee told mee there was a bad River we were to Ride thro', w[ch] was so very firce a hors could sometimes hardly stem it: But it was but narrow, and wee should soon be over. I cannot express The concern of mind this relation sett me in: no thoughts but those of the dang'ros River could entertain my Imagination, and they were as formidable as varios, still Tormenting me with blackest Ideas of my Approaching fate—Sometimes seing my self drowning, otherwhiles drowned, and at the best like a holy Sister Just come out of a Spiritual Bath in dripping Garments.

Now was the Glorious Luminary, wth his swift Coursers arrived at his Stage, leaving poor me wth the rest of this part of the lower world in darkness, with which *wee* were soon Surrounded. The only Glimering we now had was from the spangled Skies, Whose Imperfect Reflections rendered every Object formidable. Each lifeless Trunk, with its shatter'd Limbs, appear'd an Armed Enymie; and every little stump like a Ravenous devourer. Nor could I so much as discern my Guide, when at any distance, which added to the terror.

Thus, absolutely lost in Thought, and dying with the very thoughts of drowning, I come up wth the post, who I did not see till even with his Hors: he told mee he stopt for mee; and wee Rode on Very deliberatly a few paces, when we entred a Thickett of Trees and Shrubbs, and I perceived by the Hors's going, we were on the descent of a Hill, w[ch], as wee come neerer the bottom, 'twas totaly dark wth the Trees that surrounded it. But I knew by the Going of the Hors wee had entred the water, w^{ea} my Guide told mee was the hazzardos River he had told me off; and hee, Riding up close to my Side, Bid me not fear—we should be over Imediatly. I now ralyed all the Courage I was mistriss of, Knowing that I must either Venture my fate of drowning, or be left like ye Children in the wood. So, as the Post bid me, I gave Reins to my Nagg; and sitting as Stedy as Just before in the Cannoo, in a few minutes got safe to the other side, which hee told mee was the Narragansett country.

Here We found great difficulty in Travailing, the way being very narrow, and on each side the Trees and bushes gave us very unpleasent welcomes wth their Branches and bow's, wch wee could not avoid, it being so exceeding dark. My Guide, as before so now, putt on harder than I, wth my weary bones, could follow; so left mee and the way beehind him. Now Returned my distressed aprehensions of the place where I was: the dolesome woods, my Company next to none, Going I knew not whither, and encompased wth Terrifying darkness; The least of which was enough to startle a more Masculine courage. Added to which the Reflections, as in the afternoon of ye day that my Call was very Questionable, wch till then I had not so Prudently as I ought considered. Now, coming to ye foot of a hill, I found great difficulty in ascending; But being got to the Top, was there amply recompenced with the friendly Appearance of the Kind Conductress of the night, Just then Advancing above the Horisontall Line. The Raptures wch the Sight of that fair Planett produced in mee, caus'd mee, for the Moment, to forgett my present wearyness and past toils; and Inspir'd me for most of the remaining way with very divirting tho'ts, some of which, with the other Occurances of the day, I reserved to note down when I should come to my Stage. My tho'ts on the sight of the moon were to this purpose:

Fair Cynthia, all the Homage that I may
Unto a Creature, unto thee I pay;
In Lonesome woods to meet so kind a guide,
To Mee's more worth than all the world beside.
Some Joy I felt just now, when safe got or'e
Yon Surly River to this Rugged shore,
Deeming Rough welcomes from these clownish Trees,
Better than Lodgings wth Nereidees.
Yet swelling fears surprise; all dark appears—
Nothing but Light can disipate those fears.
My fainting vitals can't lend strength to say,
But softly whisper, O I wish 'twere day.

The murmer hardly warm'd the Ambient air,
E're thy Bright Aspect rescues from dispair:
Makes the old Hagg her sable mantle loose,
And a Bright Joy do's through my Soul diffuse.
The Boistero's Trees now Lend a Passage Free,
And pleasent prospects thou giv'st light to see.

From hence wee kept on, with more ease y^{n} before: the way being smooth and even, the night warm and serene, and the Tall and thick Trees at a distance, especially w^{n} the moon glar'd light through the branches, fill'd my Imagination wth the pleasent delusion of a Sumpteous citty, fill'd wth famous Buildings and churches, wth their spiring steeples, Balconies, Galleries and I know not what: Granduers wch I had heard of, and wch the stories of foreign countries had given me the Idea of.

Here stood a Lofty church—there is a steeple,
And there the Grand Parade—O see the people!
That Famous Castle there, were I but nigh,
To see the mote and Bridg and walls so high—
They'r very fine! sais my deluded eye.

Being thus agreably entertain'd without a thou't of any thing but thoughts themselves, I on a suden was Rous'd from these pleasing Imaginations, by the Post's sounding his horn, which assured mee hee was arrived at the Stage, where we were to Lodg: and that musick was then most musickall and agreeable to mee.

Being come to mr. Havens', I was very civilly Received, and courteously entertained, in a clean comfortable House; and the Good woman was very active in helping off my Riding clothes, and then ask't what I would eat. I told her I had some Chocolett, if shee would prepare it; which with the help of some Milk, and a little clean brass Kettle, she soon effected to my satisfaction. I then betook me to my Apartment, wch was a little Room parted from the Kitchen by a single bord partition; where, after I had noted the Occurrances of the past day, I went to bed, which, tho' pretty hard, Yet neet and handsome. But I could get no sleep, because of the Clamor of some the of Town tope-ers in next Room, Who were entred into a strong debate concerning ye Signifycation of the name of their Country, (viz.) *Narraganset.* One said it was named so by ye Indians, because there grew a Brier there, of a prodigious Highth and bigness, the like hardly ever known, called by the Indians Narragansett; And quotes an Indian of so Barberous a name for his Author, that I could not write it. His Antagonist Replyed no—It was from a Spring it had its name, wch hee well knew where it was, which was extreem cold in summer, and as Hott as could be imagined in the winter, which was much resorted too by the natives, and by them called Narragansett, (Hott and Cold,) and that was the originall of their places name—with a thousand Impertinances not worth notice, wch He utter'd with such a Roreing voice and Thundering blows with the fist of wickedness on the Table, that it peirced my very head. I heartily fretted, and wish't 'um tongue tyed; but wth as little succes as a freind of mine once, who was (as shee said) kept a whole night awake, on a Jorny, by a country Left.[7] and a Sergent, Insigne and a Deacon, contriving how to bring a triangle into a Square. They kept calling for tother Gill, wch while they were swallowing, was some Intermission; But presently, like Oyle to fire, encreased the flame. I set my Candle on a Chest by the bed side, and setting up, fell to my old way of composing my Resentments, in the following manner:

I ask thy Aid, O Potent Rum!
To Charm these wrangling Topers Dum.
Thou hast their Giddy Brains possest—
The man confounded wth the Beast—
And I, poor I, can get no rest.
Intoxicate them with thy fumes:
O still their Tongues till morning comes!

And I know not but my wishes took effect, for the dispute soon ended wth 'tother Dram; and so Good night!

Wedensday, Octobr 4th. About four in the morning, we set out for Kingston (for so was the Town called) with a french Docter in our company. Hee and ye Post put on very furiously, so that I could not keep up with them, only as now and then they'd stop till they see mee. This Rode was poorly furnished wth accommodations for Travellers, so that we were forced to ride 22 miles by the post's account, but neerer thirty by mine, before wee could bait so much as our Horses, wch I exceedingly complained of. But the post encourag'd mee, by saying wee should be well accommodated anon at mr. Devills, a few miles further. But I questioned whether we ought to go to the Devil to be helpt out of affliction. However, like the rest of Deluded souls that post to ye Infernal denn, Wee made all posible speed to this Devil's Habitation; where alliting, in full assurance of good accommodation, wee were going in. But meeting his two daughters, as I suposed twins, they so neerly resembled each other, both in features and habit, and look't as old as the Divel himselfe, and quite as Ugly, We desired entertainm't, but could hardly get a word out of 'um, till with our

Importunity, telling them our necesity, &c. they call'd the old Sophister, who was as sparing of his words as his daughters had bin, and no, or none, was the reply's hee made us to our demands. Hee differed only in this from the old fellow in to'ther Country: hee let us depart. However, I thought it proper to warn poor Travailers to endeavour to Avoid falling into circumstances like ours, wch at our next Stage I sat down and did as followeth:

May all that dread the cruel feind of night
Keep on, and not at this curs't Mansion light.
'Tis Hell; 'tis Hell! and Devills here do dwell:
Here dwells the Devill—surely this's Hell.
Nothing but Wants: a drop to cool yo'r Tongue
Cant be procur'd these cruel Feinds among.
Plenty of horrid Grins and looks sevear,
Hunger and thirst, But pitty's bannish'd here—
The Right hand keep, if Hell on Earth you fear!

Thus leaving this habitation of cruelty, we went forward; and arriving at an Ordinary about two mile further, found tollerable accommodation. But our Hostes, being a pretty full mouth'd old creature, entertain'd our fellow travailer, ye french Docter, wth Inumirable complaints of her bodily infirmities; and whispered to him so lou'd, that all ye House had as full a hearing as hee: which was very divirting to ye company, (of which there was a great many,) as one might see by their sneering. But poor weary I slipt out to enter my mind in my Jornal, and left my Great Landly with her Talkative Guests to themselves.

From hence we proceeded (about ten forenoon) through the Narragansett country, pretty Leisurely; and about one afternoon come to Paukataug River, wch was about two hundred paces over, and now very high, and no way over to to'ther side but this. I darid not venture to Ride thro, my courage at best in such cases but small, And now at the Lowest Ebb, by reason of my weary, very weary, hungry and uneasy Circumstances. So takeing leave of my company, tho' wth no little Reluctance, that I could not proceed wth them on my Jorny, Stop at a little cottage Just by the River, to wait the Waters falling, wch the old man that lived there said would be in a little time, and he would conduct me safe over. This little Hutt was one of the wretchedest I ever saw a habitation for human creatures. It was suported with shores enclosed with Clapbords, laid on Lengthways, and so much asunder, that the Light come throu' every where; the doore tyed on wth a cord in ye place of hinges; The floor the bear earth; no windows but such as the thin covering afforded, nor any furniture but a Bedd wth a glass Bottle hanging at ye head on't; an earthan cupp, a small pewter Bason, A Bord wth sticks to stand on, instead of a table, and a block or two in ye corner instead of chairs. The family were the old man, his wife and two Children; all and every part being the picture of poverty. Notwithstanding both the Hutt and its Inhabitance were very clean and tydee: to the crossing the Old Proverb, that bare walls make giddy hows-wifes.[8]

I Blest myselfe that I was not one of this misserable crew; and the Impressions their wretchedness formed in me caused mee on ye very Spott to say:

> Tho' Ill at ease, A stranger and alone,
> All my fatigu's shall not extort a grone.
> These Indigents have hunger wth their ease;
> Their best is wors behalfe then my disease.
> Their Misirable hutt wch Heat and Cold
> Alternately without Repulse do hold;
> Their Lodgings thyn and hard, their Indian fare,
> The mean Apparel which the wretches wear,
> And their ten thousand ills wch can't be told,
> Makes nature er'e 'tis midle age'd look old.
> When I reflect, my late fatigues do seem
> Only a notion or forgotten Dreem.

I had scarce done thinking, when an Indian-like Animal come to the door, on a creature very much like himselfe, in mien and feature, as well as Ragged cloathing; and having 'litt, makes an Awkerd Scratch wth his Indian shoo, and a Nodd, sitts on ye block, fumbles out his black Junk,[9] dipps it in ye Ashes, and presents it piping hott to his muscheeto's, and fell to sucking like a calf, without speaking, for near a quarter of an hower. At length the old man said how do's Sarah do? who I understood was the wretches wife, and Daughter to ye old man: he Replyed —as well as can be expected, &c. So I remembred the old say, and suposed I knew Sarah's case. Butt hee being, as I understood, going over the River, as ugly as hee was, I was glad to ask him to show me ye way to Saxtons, at Stoningtown; wch he promising, I ventur'd over wth the old mans assistance; who having rewarded to content, with my Tattertailed guide, I Ridd on very slowly thro' Stoningtown, where the Rode was very Stony and uneven. I asked the fellow, as we went, divers questions of the place and way, &c. I being arrived at my country Saxtons, at Stonington, was very well accommodated both as to victuals and Lodging, the only Good of both I had found since my setting out. Here I heard there was an old man and his Daughter to come that way, bound to N. London; and being now destitute of a Guide, gladly waited for them, being in so good a harbour, and accordingly, Thirsday, Octob^r^ ye 5th, about 3 in the afternoon, I sat forward with neighbour Polly and Jemima, a Girl about 18 Years old, who hee said he had been to fetch out of the Narragansetts, and said they had Rode thirty miles that day, on a sory lean Jade, wth only a Bagg under her for a pillion, which the poor Girl often complain'd was very uneasy.

Wee made Good speed along, wch made poor Jemima make many a sow'r face, the mare being a very hard trotter; and after many a hearty and bitter Oh, she at length Low'd out: Lawful Heart father! this bare mare hurts mee Dingeely, I'me direfull sore I vow; with many words to that purpose: poor Child sais Gaffer—she us't to serve your mother so. I don't care how mother us't to do, quoth Jemima, in a pasionate tone. At which the old man Laught, and kik't his Jade o' the side, which made her Jolt ten times harder.

About seven that Evening, we come to New London Ferry: here, by reason of a very high wind, we mett with great difficulty in getting over—the Boat tos't exceedingly, and our Horses capper'd at a very surprizing Rate, and set us all in a fright; especially poor Jemima, who desired her father to say so jack to the Jade, to make her stand. But the careless parent, taking no notice of her repeated desires, She Rored out in a Passionate manner: Pray suth father, Are you deaf? Say so Jack to the Jade, I tell you. The Dutiful Parent obey's; saying so Jack, so Jack, as gravely as if hee'd bin to saying Catechise after Young Miss, who with her fright look't of all coullers in ye Rain Bow.

Being safely arrived at the house of Mrs. Prentices in N. London, I treated neighbour Polly and daughter for their divirting company, and bid them farewell; and between nine and ten at night waited on the Rev^d^ Mr. Gurdon Saltonstall,[10] minister of the town, who kindly Invited me to Stay that night at his house, where I was very handsomely and plentifully treated and Lodg'd; and made good the Great Character I had before heard concerning him: viz. that hee was the most affable, courteous, Genero's and best of men.

Friday, Octo^r^ 6th. I got up very early, in Order to hire somebody to go with mee to New Haven, being in Great parplexity at the thoughts of proceeding alone; which my most hospitable entertainer observing, himselfe went, and soon return'd wth a young Gentleman of the town, who he could confide in to Go with mee; and about eight this morning, wth Mr. Joshua Wheeler my new Guide, takeing leave of this worthy Gentleman, Wee advanced on towards Seabrook. The Rodes all along this way are very bad, Incumbred wth Rocks and mountainos passages, wch were very disagreeable to my tired carcass; but we went on with a moderate pace wch made ye Journy more pleasent. But after about eight miles Rideing, in going over a Bridge under wch the River Run very swift, my hors stumbled, and very narrowly 'scaped falling over into the water; wch extreemly frightened mee. But through God's Goodness I met with no harm, and mounting agen, in about half a miles Rideing, come to an ordinary, were well entertained by a woman of about seventy and vantage, but of as Sound Intellectuals as one of seventeen. Shee entertain'd Mr. Wheeler wth some passages of a Wedding awhile ago at a place hard by, the Brides-Groom being about her Age or something above, Saying his Children was dredfully against their fathers marrying, wch shee condemned them extreemly for.

From hence wee went pretty briskly forward, and arriv'd at Saybrook ferry about two of the Clock afternoon; and crossing it, wee call'd at an Inn to Bait, (foreseeing we should not have such another Opportunity till we come to Killingsworth.) Landlady come in, with her hair about her ears, and hands at full pay scratching. Shee told us shee had some mutton wch shee would broil, wch I was glad to hear; But I supose forgot to wash her scratchers; in a little time shee brot it in; but it being pickled, and my Guide said it smelt strong of head sause, we left it, and p^{d} sixpence a piece for our Dinners, wch was only smell.

So wee putt forward with all speed, and about seven at night come to Killingsworth, and were tollerably well with Travillers fare, and Lodgd there that night.

Saturday, Oct. 7th, we sett out early in the Morning, and being something unaquainted wth the way, having ask't it of some wee mett, they told us wee must Ride a mile or two and turne down a Lane on the Right hand; and by their Direction wee Rode on but not Yet comeing to ye turning, we mett a Young fellow and ask't him how farr it was to the Lane which turn'd down towards Guilford. Hee said wee must Ride a little further, and turn down by the Corner of uncle Sams Lott. My Guide vented his Spleen at the Lubber; and we soon after came into the Rhode, and keeping still on, without any thing further Remarkabell, about two a clock afternoon we arrived at New Haven, where I was received with all Posible Respects and civility. Here I discharged Mr. Wheeler with a reward to his satisfaction, and took some time to rest after so long and toilsome a Journey; And Inform'd myselfe of the manners and customs of the place, and at the same time employed myselfe in the afair I went there upon.

They are Govern'd by the same Laws as wee in Boston, (or little differing,) thr'out this whole Colony of Connecticot, And much the same way of Church Government, and many of them good, Sociable people, and I hope Religious too: but a little too much Independant in their principalls, and, as I have been told, were formerly in their Zeal very Riggid in their Administrations towards such as their Lawes made Offenders, even to a harmless Kiss or Innocent merriment among Young people. Whipping being a frequent and counted an easy Punishment, about wch as other Crimes, the Judges were absolute in their Sentances. They told mee a pleasant story about a pair of Justices in those parts, wch I may not omit the relation of.

A negro Slave belonging to a man in ye Town, stole a hogs head from his master, and gave or sold it to an Indian, native of the place. The Indian sold it in the neighbourhood, and so the theft was found out. Thereupon the Heathen was Seized, and carried to the Justices House to be Examined. But his worship (it seems) was gone into the feild, with a Brother in office, to gather in his Pompions.[11] Whither the malefactor is hurried, And Complaint made, and satisfaction in the name of Justice demanded. Their Worships cann't proceed in form without a Bench: whereupon they Order one to be Imediately erected, which, for want of fitter materials, they made with pompions—which being finished, down setts their Worships, and the Malefactor call'd, and by the Senior Justice Interrogated after the following manner. You Indian why did You steal from this man? You sho'dn't do so—it's a Grandy wicked thing to steal. Hol't Hol't, cryes Justice Junr. Brother, You speak negro to him. I'le ask him. You sirrah, why did You steal this man's Hoggshead? Hoggshead? (replys the Indian,) me no stomany. No? says his Worship; and pulling off his hatt, Patted his own head with his hand, sais, Tatapa—You, Tatapa—you; all one this. Hoggshead all one this. Hah! says Netop, now me stomany that. Whereupon the Company fell into a great fitt of Laughter, even to Roreing. Silence is comanded, but to no effect: for they continued perfectly Shouting. Nay, sais his worship, in an angry tone, if it be so, *take mee off the Bench.*

Their Diversions in this part of the Country are on Lecture days and Training days mostly: [12] on the former there is Riding from town to town.

And on training dayes The Youth divert themselves by Shooting at the Target, as they call it, (but it very much resembles a pillory,) where hee that hitts neerest the white has some yards of Red Ribbin presented him, wch being tied to his hattband, the two ends streeming down his back, he is Led away in Triumph, wth great applause, as the winners of the Olympiack Games. They generally marry very young: the males oftener as I am told under twentie than above; they generally make public wedings, and have a way something singular (as they say) in some of them, viz. Just before Joyning hands the Bridegroom quitts the place, who is soon followed by the Bridesmen, and as it were, dragg'd back to duty—being the reverse to y[e] former practice among us, to steal m[s] Pride.

There are great plenty of Oysters all along by the sea side, as farr as I Rode in the Collony, and those very good. And they Generally lived very well and comfortably in their famelies. But too Indulgent (especially y[e] farmers) to their slaves: sufering too great familiarity from them, permitting y[m] to sit at Table and eat with them, (as they say to save time,) and into the dish goes the black hoof as freely as the white hand. They told me that there was a farmer lived nere the Town where I lodgd who had some difference wth his slave, concerning something the master had promised him and did not punctualy perform; w[ch] caused some hard words between them; But at length they put the matter to Arbitration and Bound themselves to stand to the award of such as they named—w[ch] done, the Arbitrators Having heard the Allegations of both parties, Order the master to pay 40[s] to black face, and acknowledge his fault. And so the matter ended: the poor master very honestly standing to the award.

There are every where in the Towns as I passed, a Number of Indians the Natives of the Country, and are the most salvage of all the salvages of that kind that I had ever Seen: little or no care taken (as I heard upon enquiry) to make them otherwise. They have in some places Landes of their owne, and Govern'd by Law's of their own making;—they marry many wives and at pleasure put them away, and on the y[e] least dislike or fickle humour, on either side, saying *stand away* to one another is a sufficient Divorce. And indeed those uncomely *Stand aways* are too much in Vougue among the English in this (Indulgent Colony) as their Records plentifully prove, and that on very trivial matters, of which some have been told me, but are not proper to be Related by a Female pen, tho some of that foolish sex have had too large a share in the story.

If the natives committ any crime on their own precincts among themselves, y[e] English takes no Cognezens of. But if on the English ground, they are punishable by our Laws. They mourn for their Dead by blacking their faces, and cutting their hair, after an Awkerd and frightfull manner; But can't bear You should mention the names of their dead Relations to them: they trade most for Rum, for w[ch] they[d] hazzard their very lives; and the English fit them Generally as well, by seasoning it plentifully with water.

They give the title of merchant to every trader; who Rate their Goods according to the time and spetia they pay in: viz. Pay, mony, Pay as mony, and trusting. *Pay* is Grain, Pork, Beef, &c. at the prices sett by the General Court that Year; *mony* is pieces of Eight, Ryalls, or Boston or Bay shillings (as they call them,) or Good hard money, as sometimes silver coin is termed by them; also Wampom, viz$^{t.}$ Indian beads wch serves for change. *Pay as mony* is provisions, as afores^{d} one Third cheaper then as the Assembly or Gene^{l} Court sets it; and *Trust* as they and the merch^{t} agree for time.

Now, when the buyer comes to ask for a comodity, sometimes before the merchant answers that he has it, he sais, *is Your pay redy?* Perhaps the Chap Reply's Yes: what do You pay in? say's the merchant. The buyer having answered, then the price is set; as suppose he wants a sixpenny knife, in pay it is 12d—in pay as money eight pence, and hard money its own price, viz. 6d. It seems a very Intricate way of trade and what Lex Mercatoria [13] had not thought of.

Being at a merchants house, in comes a tall country fellow, wth his alfogeos [14] full of Tobacco; for they seldom Loose their Cudd, but keep Chewing and Spitting as long as they'r eyes are open,—he advanc't to the midle of the Room, makes an Awkward Nodd, and spitting a Large deal of Aromatick Tincture, he gave a scrape with his shovel like shoo, leaving a small shovel full of dirt on the floor, made a full stop, Hugging his own pretty Body with his hands under his arms, Stood staring rown'd him, like a Catt let out of a Baskett. At last, like the creature Balaam Rode on, he opened his mouth and said: have You any Ribinen for Hatbands to sell I pray? The Questions and Answers about the pay being past, the Ribin is bro't and opened. Bumpkin Simpers, cryes its confounded Gay I vow; and beckning to the door, in comes Jone Tawdry, dropping about 50 curtsees, and stands by him: hee shows her the Ribin. *Law, You,* sais shee, *its right Gent,*[15] do You, take it, *tis dreadfull pretty.* Then she enquires, *have You any hood silk I pray?* wch being brought and bought, Have You any *thred silk to sew it wth* says shee, wch being accomodated wth they Departed. They Generaly stand after they come in a great while speachless, and sometimes dont say a word till they are askt what they want, which I Impute to the Awe they stand in of the merchants, who they are constantly almost Indebted too; and must take what they bring without Liberty to choose for themselves; but they serve them as well, making the merchants stay long enough for their pay.

We may Observe here the great necessity and bennifitt both of Education and Conversation; for these people have as Large a portion of mother witt, and sometimes a Larger, than those who have bin brought up in Citties; But for want of emprovements, Render themselves almost Ridiculos, as above. I should be glad if they would leave such follies, and am sure all that Love Clean Houses (at least) would be glad on't too.

They are generaly very plain in their dress, throuout all ye Colony, as I saw, and follow one another in their modes; that You may know where they belong, especially the women, meet them where you will.

Their Cheif Red Letter day is St. Election,[16] wch is annualy Observed according to Charter, to choose their Goven^r^: a blessing they can never be thankfull enough for, as they will find, if ever it be their hard fortune to loose it. The present Govenor in Conecticott is the Hon^lbe^ John Winthrop Esq.[17] A Gentleman of an Ancient and Honourable Family, whose Father was Govenor here sometime before, and his Grand father had bin Govr of the Massachusetts. This gentleman is a very curteous and afable person, much Given to Hospitality, and has by his Good services Gain'd the affections of the people as much as any who had bin before him in that post.

Decr 6th. Being by this time well Recruited and rested after my Journy, my business lying unfinished by some concerns at New York depending thereupon, my Kinsman, Mr. Thomas Trowbridge of New Haven, must needs take a Journy there before it could be accomplished, I resolved to go there in company wth him, and a man of the town wch I engaged to wait on me there. Accordingly, Dec. 6th we set out from New Haven, and about 11 same morning came to Stratford ferry; wch crossing, about two miles on the other side Baited our horses and would have eat a morsell ourselves, But the Pumpkin and Indian mixt Bred had such an Aspect, and the Bare-legg'd Punch so awkerd or rather Awfull a sound, that we left both, and proceeded forward, and about seven at night come to Fairfield, where we met with good entertainment and Lodg'd; and early next morning set forward to Norowalk, from its halfe Indian name *North-walk*, when about 12 at noon we arrived, and Had a Dinner of Fryed Venison, very savoury. Landlady wanting some pepper in the seasoning, bid the Girl hand her the spice in the little *Gay* cupp on ye shelfe. From hence we Hasted towards Rye, walking and Leading our Horses neer a mile together, up a prodigios high Hill; and so Riding till about nine at night, and there arrived and took up our Lodgings at an ordinary, wch a French family kept. Here being very hungry, I desired a fricasee, wch the Frenchman undertakeing, mannaged so contrary to my notion of Cookery, that

I hastned to Bed superless; And being shewd the way up a pair of stairs wch had such a narrow passage that I had almost stopt by the Bulk of my Body; But arriving at my apartment found it to be a little Lento Chamber furnisht amongst other Rubbish with a High Bedd and a Low one, a Long Table, a Bench and a Bottomless chair,—Little Miss went to scratch up my Kennell wch Russelled as if shee'd bin in the Barn amongst the Husks, and supose such was the contents of the tickin—nevertheless being exceeding weary, down I laid my poor Carkes (never more tired) and found my Covering as scanty as my Bed was hard. Annon I heard another Russelling noise in Ye Room—called to know the matter—Little miss said shee was making a bed for the men; who, when they were in Bed, complained their leggs lay out of it by reason of its shortness—my poor bones complained bitterly not being used to such Lodgings, and so did the man who was with us; and poor I made but one Grone, which was from the time I went to bed to the time I Riss, which was about three in the morning, Setting up by the Fire till Light, and having discharged our ordinary[18] wch was as dear as if we had had far Better fare—wee took our leave of Monsier and about seven in the morn come to New Rochell a french town, where we had a good Breakfast. And in the strength of that about an how'r before sunsett got to York. Here I applyd myself to Mr. Burroughs, a merchant to whom I was recommended by my Kinsman Capt. Prout, and received great Civilities from him and his spouse, who were now both Deaf but very agreeable in their Conversation, Diverting me with pleasant stories of their knowledge in Brittan from whence they both come, one of which was above the rest very pleasant to me viz. my Lord Darcy had a very extravagant Brother who had mortgaged what Estate hee could not sell, and in good time dyed leaving only one son. Him his Lordship (having none of his own) took and made him Heir of his whole Estate, which he was to receive at the death of his Aunt. He and his Aunt in her widowhood held a right understanding and lived as become such Relations, shee being a discreat Gentlewoman and he an Ingenios Young man. One day Hee fell into some Company though far his inferiors, very freely told him of the Ill circumstances his fathers Estate lay under, and the many Debts he left unpaid to the wrong of poor people with whom he had dealt. The Young gentleman was put out of countenance—no way hee could think of to Redress himself—his whole dependance being on the Lady his Aunt, and how to speak to her he knew not—Hee went home, sat down to dinner and as usual sometimes with her when the Chaplain was absent, she desired him to say Grace, wch he did after this manner:

Pray God in Mercy take my Lady Darcy
Unto his Heavenly Throne,
That little John may live like a man,
And pay every man his own.

The prudent Lady took no present notice, But finishd dinner, after wch having sat and talk't awhile (as Customary) He Riss, took his Hatt and Going out she desired him to give her leave to speak to him in her Clossett, Where being come she desired to know why hee prayed for her Death in the manner aforesaid, and what part of her deportment towards him merritted such desires. Hee Reply'd, none at all, But he was under such disadvantages that nothing but that could do him service, and told her how he had been affronted as above, and what Impressions it had made upon him. The Lady made him a gentle reprimand that he had not informed her after another manner, Bid him see what his father owed and he should have money to pay it to a penny, And always to lett her know his wants and he should have a redy supply. The Young Gentleman charm'd with his Aunts Discrete management, Beggd her pardon and accepted her kind offer and retrieved his fathers Estate, &c. and said Hee hoped his Aunt would never dye, for shee had done better by him than hee could have done for himself.—Mr. Burroughs went with me to Vendue [19] where I bought about 100 Rheem of paper wch was retaken in a flyboat from Holland and sold very Reasonably here—some ten, some Eight shillings per Rheem by the Lott wch was ten Rheem in a Lott. And at the Vendue I made a great many acquaintances amongst the good women of the town, who curteosly invited me to their houses and generously entertained me.

The Cittie of New York is a pleasant, well compacted place, situated on a Commodius River wch is a fine harbour for shipping. The Buildings Brick Generaly, very stately and high, though not altogether like ours in Boston. The Bricks in some of the Houses are of divers Coullers and laid in Checkers, being glazed look very agreeable. The inside of them are neat to admiration, the wooden work, for only the walls are plasterd, and the Sumers and Gist [20] are plained and kept very white scowr'd as so is all the partitions if made of Bords. The fire places have no Jambs (as ours have) But the Backs run flush with the walls, and the Hearth is of Tyles and is as farr out into the Room at the Ends as before the fire, wch is Generally Five foot in the Low'r rooms, and the peice over where the mantle tree should be is made as ours with Joyners work, and as I supose is fasten'd to iron rodds inside. The House where the Vendue was, had Chimney Corners like ours, and they and the hearths were laid wth the finest tile that I ever see, and the stair cases laid all with white tile which is ever clean, and so are the walls of the Kitchen w[ch] had a Brick floor. They were making Great preparations to Receive their Govenor, Lord Cornbury [21] from the Jerseys, and for that End raised the militia to Gard him on shore to the fort.

They are Generaly of the Church of England and have a New England Gentleman for their minister, and a very fine church set out with all Customary requsites. There are also a Dutch and Divers Conventicles as they call them, viz. Baptist, Quakers, &c. They are not strict in keeping the Sabbath as in Boston and other places where I had bin, But seem to deal with great exactness as farr as I see or Deall with. They are sociable to one another and Curteos and Civill to strangers and fare well in their houses. The English go very fasheonable in their dress. Dut the Dutch, especially the middling sort, differ from our women, in their habitt go loose, were French muches w[ch] are like a Capp and a head band in one, leaving their ears bare, which are sett out wth Jewells of a large size and many in number. And their fingers hoop't with Rings, some with large stones in them of many Coullers as were their pendants in their ears, which You should see very old women wear as well as Young.

They have Vendues very frequently and make their Earnings very well by them, for they treat with good Liquor Liberally, and the Customers Drink as Liberally and Generally pay for't as well, by paying for that which they Bidd up Briskly for, after the sack has gone plentifully about, tho' sometimes good penny worths are got there. Their Diversions in the Winter is Riding Sleys about three or four Miles out of Town, where they have Houses of entertainment at a place called the Bowery, and some go to friends Houses who handsomely treat them. Mr. Burroughs cary'd his spouse and Daughter and myself out to one Madame Dowes, a Gentlewoman that lived at a farm House, who gave us a handsome Entertainment of five or six Dishes and choice Beer and metheglin,[22] Cyder, &c. all which she said was the produce of her farm. I believe we mett 50 or 60 slays that day—they fly with great swiftness and some are so furious that they'le turn out of the path for none except a Loaden Cart. Nor do they spare for any diversion the place affords, and sociable to a degree, they'r Tables being as free to their Naybours as to themselves.

Having here transacted the affair I went upon and some other that fell in the way, after about a fortnight's stay there I left New-York with no Little regrett, and Thursday, Dec. 21, set out for New Haven wth my Kinsman Trowbridge, and the man that waited on me about one afternoon, and about three come to half-way house about ten miles out of town, where we Baited and went forward, and about 5 come to Spiting Devil, Else Kings bridge,[23] where they pay three pence for passing over with a horse, which the man that keeps the Gate set up at the end of the Bridge receives.

We hoped to reach the french town and Lodg there that night, but unhapily lost our way about four miles short, and being overtaken by a great storm of wind and snow which set full in our faces about dark, we were very uneasy. But meeting one Gardner who lived in a Cottage thereabout, offered us his fire to set by, having but one poor Bedd, and his wife not well, &c. or he would go to a House with us, where he thought we might be better accommodated—thither we went, But a surly old shee Creature, not worthy the name of woman, who would hardly let us go into her Door, though the weather was so stormy none but shee would have turnd out a Dogg. But her son whose name was gallop, who lived Just by Invited us to his house and shewed me two pair of stairs, viz. one up the loft and tother up the Bedd, wch was as hard as it was high, and warmed it with a hott stone at the feet. I lay very uncomfortably, insomuch that I was so very cold and sick I was forced to call them up to give me something to warm me. They had nothing but milk in the house, wch they Boild, and to make it better sweetened wth molasses, which I not knowing or thinking oft till it was down and coming up agen wch it did in so plentifull a manner that my host was soon paid double for his portion, and that in specia. But I believe it did me service in Cleering my stomach. So after this sick and weary night at East Chester, (a very miserable poor place,) the weather being now fair, Friday the 22^d^ Dec. we set out for New Rochell, where being come we had good Entertainment and Recruited ourselves very well. This is a very pretty place well compact, and good handsome houses, Clean, good and passable Rodes, and situated on a Navigable River, abundance of land well fined and Cleerd all along as wee passed, which caused in me a Love to the place, wch I could have been content to live in it. Here wee Ridd over a Bridge made of one entire stone of such a Breadth that a cart might pass with safety, and to spare—it lay over a passage cutt through a Rock to convey water to a mill not farr off. Here are three fine Taverns within call of each other, very good provision for Travailers.

Thence we travailed through Merrinak, a neet, though little place, wth a navigable River before it, one of the pleasantest I ever see—Here were good Buildings, Especialy one, a very fine seat, wch they told me was Col. Hethcoats, who I had heard was a very fine Gentleman.

From hence we come to Hors Neck, where wee Baited, and they told me that one Church of England parson officiated in all these three towns once every Sunday in turns throughout the Year; and that they all could but poorly maintaine him, which they grudg'd to do, being a poor and quarelsome crew as I understand by our Host; their Quarelling about their choice of Minister, they chose to have none—But caused the Government to send this Gentleman to them. Here wee took leave of York Government, and Descending the Mountainos passage that almost broke my heart in ascending before, we come to Stamford, a well compact Town, but miserable meeting house, wch we passed, and thro' many and great difficulties, as Bridges which were exceeding high and very tottering and of vast Length, steep and Rocky Hills and precipices, (Buggbears to a fearful female travailer.) About nine at night we come to Norrwalk, having crept over a timber of a Broken Bridge about thirty foot long, and perhaps fifty to ye water. I was exceeding tired and cold when we come to our Inn, and could get nothing there but poor entertainment, and the impertinant Bable of one of the worst of men, among many others of which our Host made one, who, had he bin one degree Impudenter, would have outdone his Grandfather. And this I think is the most perplexed night I have yet had. From hence, Saturday, Dec. 23, a very cold and windy day, after an Intolerable night's Lodging, wee hasted forward only observing in our way the Town to be situated on a Navigable river wth indiferent Buildings and people more refind than in some of the Country towns wee had passed, tho' vicious enough, the Church and Tavern being next neighbours. Having Ridd thro a difficult River wee come to Fairfield where wee Baited and were much refreshed as well with the Good things wch gratified our appetites as the time took to rest our wearied Limbs, wch Latter I employed in enquiring concerning the Town and manners of the people, &c. This is a considerable town, and filled as they say with wealthy people—have a spacious meeting house and good Buildings. But the Inhabitants are Litigious, nor do they well agree with their minister, who (they say) is a very worthy Gentleman.[24]

They have aboundance of sheep, whose very Dung brings them great gain, with part of which they pay their Parsons sallery, And they Grudg that, prefering their Dung before their minister. They Lett out their sheep at so much as they agree upon for a night; the highest Bidder always caries them, And they will sufficiently Dung a Large quantity of Land before morning. But were once Bitt by a sharper who had them a night and sheared them all before morning—From hence we went to Stratford, the next Town, in which I observed but few houses, and those not very good ones. But the people that I conversed with were civill and good natured. Here we staid till late at night, being to cross a Dangerous River ferry, the River at that time full of Ice; but after about four hours waiting with great difficulty wee got over. My fears and fatigues prevented my here taking any particular observation. Being got to Milford, it being late in the night, I could go no further; my fellow travailer going forward, I was invited to Lodg at Mrs. ——, a very kind and civill Gentlewoman, by whom I was handsomely and kindly entertained till the next night. The people here go very plain in their apparel (more plain than I had observed in the towns I had passed) and seem to be very grave and serious. They told me there was a singing Quaker lived there, or at least had a strong inclination to be so, His Spouse not at all affected that way. Some of the singing Crew come there one day to visit him, who being then abroad, they sat down (to the woman's no small vexation) Humming and singing and groneing after their conjuring way—Says the woman are you singing quakers? Yea says They—Then take my squalling Brat of a child here and sing to it says she for I have almost split my throat wth singing to him and cant get the Rogue to sleep. They took this as a great Indignity, and mediately departed. Shaking the dust from their Heels left the good woman and her Child among the number of the wicked.

This is a Seaport place and accomodated with a Good Harbour, But I had not opportunity to make particular observations because it was Sabbath day—This Evening.

December 24. I set out with the Gentlewomans son who she very civilly offered to go with me when she see no parswasions would cause me to stay which she pressingly desired, and crossing a ferry having but nine miles to New Haven, in a short time arrived there and was Kindly received and well accommodated amongst my Friends and Relations.

The Government of Connecticut Collony begins westward towards York at Stanford (as I am told) and so runs Eastward towards Boston (I mean in my range, because I dont intend to extend my description beyond my own travails) and ends that way at Stonington—And has a great many Large towns lying more northerly. It is a plentiful Country for provisions of all sorts and its Generally Healthy. No one that can and will be dilligent in this place need fear poverty nor the want of food and Rayment.

January 6th. Being now well Recruited and fitt for business I discoursed the persons I was concerned with, that we might finnish in order to my return to Boston. They delay[d] as they had hitherto done hoping to tire my Patience. But I was resolute to stay and see an End of the matter let it be never so much to my disadvantage—So January 9th they come again and promise the Wednesday following to go through with the distribution of the Estate which they delayed till Thursday and then come with new amusements. But at length by the mediation of that holy good Gentleman, the Rev. Mr. James Pierpont,[25] the minister of New Haven, and with the advice and assistance of other our Good friends we come to an accommodation and distribution, which having finished though not till February, the man that waited on me to York taking the charge of me I sit out for Boston. We went from New Haven upon the ice (the ferry being not passable thereby) and the Rev. Mr. Pierpont wth Madam Prout Cuzin Trowbridge and divers others were taking leave wee went onward without any thing Remarkabl till wee come to New London and Lodged again at Mr. Saltonstalls—and here I dismist my Guide, and my Generos entertainer provided me Mr. Samuel Rogers of that place to go home with me—I stayed a day here Longer than I intended by the Commands of the Hon[ble] Govenor Winthrop to stay and take a supper with him whose wonderful civility I may not omitt. The next morning I Crossed y[e] Ferry to Groton, having had the Honor of the Company, of Madam Livingston (who is the Govenors Daughter) and Mary Christophers and divers others to the boat—And that night Lodg[d] at Stonington and had Rost Beef and pumpkin sause for supper. The next night at Haven's and had Rost fowle, and the next day wee come to a river which by Reason of Y[e] Freshetts coming down was swell'[d] so high wee fear[d] it impassable and the rapid stream was very terryfying—However we must over and that in a small Cannoo. Mr. Rogers assuring me of his good Conduct, I after a stay of near an how'r on the shore for consultation went into the Cannoo, and Mr. Rogers paddled about 100 yards up the Creek by the shore side, turned into the swift stream and dexterously steering her in a moment wee come to the other side as swiftly passing as an arrow shott out of the Bow by a strong arm. I staid on y[e] shore till Hee returned to fetch our horses, which he caused to swim over himself bringing the furniture in the Cannoo. But it is past my skill to express the Exceeding fright all their transactions formed in me. Wee were now in the colony of the Massachusetts and taking Lodgings at the first Inn we come too had a pretty difficult passage the next day which was the second of March by reason of the sloughy ways then thawed by the Sunn. Here I mett Capt. John Richards of Boston who was going home, So being very glad of his Company we Rode something harder than hitherto, and missing my way in going up a very steep Hill, my horse dropt down under me as Dead; this new surprize no little hurt me meeting it Just at the Entrance into Dedham from whence we intended to reach home that night. But was now obliged to gett another Hors there and leave my own, resolving for Boston that night if possible. But in going over the Causeway at Dedham the Bridge being overflowed by the high waters comming down I very narrowly escaped falling over into the river Hors and all w[ch] twas almost a miracle I did not—now it grew late in the afternoon and the people having very much discouraged us about the sloughy way w[ch] they said wee should find very difficult and hazardous it so wrought on mee being tired and dispirited and disapointed of my desires of going home that I agreed to Lodg there that night w[ch] wee did at the house of one Draper, and the next day being March 3d wee got safe home to Boston, where I found my aged and tender mother and my Dear and only Child in good health with open arms redy to receive me, and my Kind relations and friends flocking in to welcome mee and hear the story of my transactions and travails I having this day bin five months from home and now I cannot fully express my Joy and Satisfaction. But desire sincearly to adore my Great Benefactor for thus graciously carying forth and returning in safety his unworthy handmaid.

JOSEPH GREEN, 1675–1715

[After graduation from college in 1695, Joseph Green, the son of a Cambridge tailor, experienced a religious conversion while teaching school at Roxbury. Thereupon he returned to college, secured his Master's degree, and was settled as pastor at Salem Village (Danvers) in 1698. He did great service restoring calm after the witchcraft panic, and fostered education in the somewhat backward town. His "Diary," kept intermittently from March 4, 1700, to June 18, 1715—five months before his death—is largely a record of the domestic contentment of a country parson who loved gardening, fishing, hunting, and dispensing quiet hospitality. His account of the *aurora borealis* on December 18, 1700, is probably the earliest notice of the phenomenon in New England.

See Samuel P. Fowler, "Biographical Sketch and Diary of Rev. Joseph Green, of Salem Village," *Essex Institute Historical Collections*, VIII (1868), 91–96, 165–174, 215–224; X (1869), pt. I, 73–104; XXXVI (1900), 325–330. The text is from *idem*, X, 86–89. See Sibley, *Biographical Sketches*, IV, 228–233.]

EXTRACTS FROM GREEN'S "DIARY."

MAY 19, 1710] I went down to ye mouth of ye harbour and lay in ye boat at an anchor.

May 20. I rowed over ye Sound and got on to Mr. Gardner's Island.[1] Ye Indian's carried me over and set me on shore at Fire Place. At sunset I travelled eight miles to E. H.[2]

21. *Sab.* I preached at East Hampton in forenoon, from Luke 7, 2, and P.M., Luke 10, 41. I was very faint with my travelling.

22. I visited ye people and found them very kind.

24. I visited Mr. White [3] at Sag [Harbor] and Mr. Whiting [4] at S. Hampton.

25. I prepared to come home.

26. After 2 o'clock I came with my mother, first to Mr. Gardner's Island, and then in a whale boat; about sun one hour and one half high. I arrived safe at New London about 11 o'clock at night. We lodged at Mr. Coits.[5]

27. We travelled heavy laden to Major Fitches at Canter.

28. *Sab.* I preached, P.M., at Canterbury.

29. My horse ran away, which hindered us two hours. Mr. Easton came eight miles and brought my mother; we travelled to Providence.

30. I hired men to bring my mother. 30 inst. we came to brother Jonathan's.

31. I came home and found all well and have had much experience of God's goodness to me abroad and to mine at home.

June 8. I went with my wife to Wenham on J. Gansons horse.

18. *Sab.* Mr. Blowers [6] was ill, and sent me word he could not exchange as he expected.

July 5. Dined at Zach. Hicks and went to Boston in Calash to brother S. Green's.

6. Bought a brass kettle, 3£. 6 shil. 6 d.; and went to Cambridge and brought my mother home with me at 6 o'clock.

9. Went to Wenham; ye most plentiful rain we have had these three summers.

10. I came home; training, half ye company pricked.

28. I tried first to catch pigeons.

Aug. 2. I got two dozen of pigeons. Mr. Blowers here.

7. Rain. Nine men 'listed for Port Royal.

8. Catched pigeons.

10. Pubb. thanksgiving, especially for rain.

16. Rain. Catched eight dozen and one half pigeons.

28. Catched eight dozen pigeons.

Sept. 1. Catched six dozen pigeons.

Sept. 4. I went to Boston to visit Br. Sam. Gerrish [7] sick. He was very bad at night. Saw old Mr. Mather.[8] Visited Mr. Wadsworth.[9]

Sept. 6. I carried my mother to Salem Lecture, dined with Maj. Sewell.

18. Our fleet of 36 sail set out for Port Royall.

28. Pubb. Fast for ye fleet against P. Royall.

Oct. 3. I went to Wenham at ye ministers meeting, and then met Mr. Rogers [10] of Ipswich and Mr. Blowers. We had deacon Fitches case.

4. I went to Wenham with my wife. Mr. Noyes [11] and I wrote over ye ministers determination. Boiled Syder.

22. *Sab.* News from Port Royall; rain A.M.

Nov. 6. Preparing for winter. Ben. H [utchinson] in my orchard.

7. Storm at night. Capt. Eastes' brother here. I went to Benj. H. and prayed him to keep his horses out of my orchard. He told me if my feed was not eaten quickly ye snow would cover it, &c.

8. B. Hu. horses in every night this week.

Nov. 11. I at study. Sent for Benj. H. and prayed him to mend up his fence, which he did and kept them out this one night.

Nov. 17. Benj. H. three jades having been here in my orchard every night this week, had got such a hank [ering] that they would not easily be drove out, so that J. H. tried last night at 9 o'clock to get them out till he was cold and tired, and forced to leave them in. And as we wer trying to get them out this morning, the two jades trying to jump out at once by ye well, one pressed another so as he jumped into my well, and altho. we got him out with Mr. Hutchinson's help, yet he soon dyed. Snow.

18. Snow. I went to Mr. H. he said I might pay for one-half of his colt, and that he could by the law force me to pay all. I told him I was no ways to blame about his colt being killed; but I looked it as a Providential rebuke unto him for suffering his jades to afflict me. I told him he only was to blame, because I had spake and sent to him ten times to look to his horses. He told me no body desired him to fetter his horses in the winter, and that folks fields was mostly common.

25. I went to Mrs. Walcuts and urged her to pole her wall.

27. I told Benj. Hutch. I would give his boys 20 shil. for his colt that fell into my well, and also ye damage his horses had done me this month, which I valued 20 shil. more. And he said that would satisfy *him* and all his family. I told him I gave it to him to make him easy and

if that end was not obtained, I should account my money thrown away. For I knew no law did oblige me to pay for his colt, that came over a lawful fence into my well.

Dec. 5. I had ground ploughed. Killed four hogs, in all 350 pounds.

23. I at study; not well. Clear and cold.

28. Killed three hogs 316 pounds, so that we have this year killed 666 pounds of pork.

1711. Jan. 2. Boys cyphering at home.

22. I was called up at 4 o'clock to pray with Benj. Hutchinson's child; it died at 6 o'clock.

26. Killed a calf; sent John Hicks to Salem with 21 3-4 lbs. to Mr. Kitchen. He bought ginger, starch, molasses and wine.

Feb. 23. Cold. I wrote deeds for J. Ross. Brewed.

25. *Sab.* Snowed hard all day; a thin assembly.

March 1. Cold. Ye church kept a Fast at ye house of Dea. Benj. Putnam's, to pray for ye pouring out of ye spirit on us, &c. a g. d.; my wife ill.

4. *Sab.* 100 communicants.

14. I went to Salem, paid 24 shil. to Mr. Noyes. Bought a hat for Nedd at Mr. K's.

19. I bought 3 acres of woodland of Benj. Hutchinson for 15£. I paid him 5£. and gave him a bond for 10£., to be paid in paper or silver, April 10, 1712.

27. Meeting of ye Inhabitants about covering ye house &c. I had three men making wall.

COTTON MATHER

[It was customary for the congregations in New England churches to use metrical versions of the Psalms during the service, alternately singing and reading line by line. But the congregations knew hardly ten tunes by ear, and few could sing words to more than five. During the first quarter of the eighteenth century discontent arose over the manner of singing, some of the more fastidious claiming that without the aid of musical notations the zeal of the worshippers often betrayed them into sounds "which made a Jar in the ears" (letter of Cotton Mather, *Collection of the Massachusetts Historical Society*, seventh series, VIII, 693). Several entered into the controversy whether singing by note, that is, "Regular Singing," should not supplant the old method of singing by ear.

Cotton Mather was among the first to champion the newer way, with a tract published in Boston in 1721 called *The Accomplished Singer. Instructions . . . How the Melody of Regular Singing, and the Skill of doing it, according to the Rules of it, may be easily arrived unto.* As most ministers heartily favored "Regular Singing," doubtless the older psalmodies lacking notations were less and less used thenceforth.

See Matt B. Jones, "Some Bibliographical Notes on Cotton Mather's 'The Accomplished Singer,'" *Publications of the Colonial Society of Massachusetts*, XXVIII (1935), 186–193.]

THE ACCOMPLISHED SINGER.

§ 1. It is the Concern of every one that would enjoy *Tranquillity* in this World, or obtain *Felicity* in the World to come, to follow that Holy Direction of Heaven, *Exercise thy self in* PIETY. And there is no *Exercise* of PIETY more unexceptionable than that of *making a Joyful* Noise of SINGING in the Praises of our GOD; That of signifying our *Delight* in Divine *Truths* by SINGING of them; That of *Uttering* the Sentiments of Devotion, with the *Voice*, and such a *Modulation of the Voice*, as will naturally express the *Satisfaction* and *Elevation* of the *Mind*, which a Grave SONG shall be expressive of. 'Tis indeed a very *Ancient Way* of Glorifying the Blessed GOD; As *Ancient* as the Day *when the Foundations of the Earth were fastened*, and *the Corner-Stone thereof was laid*. The *Morning-Stars* then *Sang together*. And it is as *Extensive* an one; For it is Remarkable, That *All Nations* make SINGING to be one part of the *Worship* which they pay unto their GOD. Those Few *Untuned Souls*, who affect upon Principle to distinguish themselves from the rest of Mankind by the Character of *Non-Singers*, do seem too much to divest themselves of an *Humanity*, whereof it may be said unto them, *Doth not Nature it self teach it you?* Be sure, they sufficiently differ from the *Primitive Christians;* For, though the *Eastern* Churches were at first Superiour to the *Western*, for the *Zeal of the House of* GOD in this matter, yet both betimes Concurr'd in it. Not only *Justin* the *Martyr*, and *Clemens* of *Alexandria*, as well as *Tertullian*, and several others of the *Primitive Writers*, but also Governour *Pliny* himself will tell us, what *Singers to their* GOD, the Faithful were then known to be; and how much they *Worshipped* Him in these *Beauties of Holiness*.

§ 2. BUT this piece of *Natural Worship* is further Confirmed by a *positive Institution* of GOD our SAVIOUR for it. The *Sacred Scriptures* with which the Holy SPIRIT of GOD has Enriched us, have directed us unto this *Way* of Worshipping. In our *Old Testament* we there find it as a Command of GOD; but Calculated particularly for Times under the

New-Testament: Psal. LXVIII. 32. *Sing Praises unto* GOD, *ye Kingdoms of the Earth, O Sing Praises unto the Lord.* And Psal. C. 1, 2. *Make a Joyful Noise unto the Lord, All ye Lands; Come into his Presence with Singing.* The *Ninety-fifth Psalm* in our Psalter, does according to the Interpretation of our Apostle *Paul*, an *Interpreter, One of a Thousand*, certainly to be relied upon!——Prescribe the *Duties* of a *Sabbath* in the Days of the Gospel. But what is the *First* of those Duties? *O come, Let us sing unto the Lord, Let us with Psalms make a Joyful Noise unto Him.* In our *New-Testament* it self 'tis a Thing so positively enjoined, that it must be a wonder, if any Christian can make any Question of it. How plainly is it commanded? Jam. V. 13. *Is any cheerful among you, Let him sing Psalms.* Yea, In the *Pauline* Epistles, we have it; how frequently, how earnestly inculcated! This Exercise is none of those *Intrusions* into our *Worship*, which the *Worshippers in the Inner-Court*, wou'd see a *Quo Warranto* serv'd upon, 'Tis *Warranted* with a most Incontestible *Institution*. . . .

IT would follow from hence, that such a *Version* of the PSALMS, as keeps most *Close to the Original*, were most of all to be wished for. Of about Three Times seven Translations of the *Psalms*, which we have seen fitted for the Tunes of our *Sacred Songs* there is not one, but what for the sake of a needless *Rhyme*, does *Leave out* very much of what the Holy SPIRIT has inserted in the *Original*, and *put in* as much of what is not *there* to be met withal. Of these Translations, there are some *Nearer* to the *Original* than others, and have more of *That* in it, with least of Diversion from it, or Addition to it: And the *Nearest* are certainly the most worthy to have our Meditations employed upon them. After all, of what Consequence is (the *Similis Desimentia* of) *Rhyme*, to our *Psalmody*, when even to *Poetry* it self, it is not Essential? The *Psalms* might easily be so turned into *Blank Verse*, that there should be ALL, and ONLY, what it has pleased the Holy One to give us in the *Original*. And no doubt there will a Time come, when Myriads of Christians will chuse to Serve GOD with such a *Pure Offering*, and present unto Him what is *purely His own*, rather than have their Devotions in Danger of being palled, by the sense of *Humane Debasements*, upon what they Address unto Him. An Honourable Counsellor in the Low-Countries, Mynheer *Bruyne*, published in Dutch, the PSALMS in such *Blank Verse*. But because his Translation differed, as it must, from what was in the *Common Bible*, another who was a Master of Musick, fitted a variety of Tunes to the Psalter, without changing a word in the *Common Bible*. However the Tunes were so various, and the necessary Repetition of the same Word so frequent, that this did not much mend the matter. . . .

The Skill of *Regular Singing*, is among the *Gifts* of GOD unto the Children of Men, and by no means unthankfully to be Neglected or Despised. For the Congregations, wherein 'tis wanting, to recover a *Regular Singing,* would be really a *Reformation,* and a Recovery out of an *Apostacy,* and what we may judge that Heaven would be pleased withal. We ought certainly to Serve our GOD with our *Best,* and *Regular Singing* must needs be *Better* than the confused Noise of a Wilderness. *GOD is not for Confusion in the Churches of the Saints;* but requires, *Let all things be done decently.* 'Tis a Great Mistake of some weak People, That the *Times* regulated with the *Notes* used in the *Regular Singing* of our Churches are the same that are used in the Church of *Rome.* And what if they were? Our *Psalms* too are used there. But the *Tunes* used in the *French Psalmody,* and from Them in the *Dutch* also, were set by a famous Martyr of JESUS CHRIST; And when *Sternhold* and *Hopkins* [1] illuminated *England,* with their Version of the *Psalms,* the *Tunes* have been set by such as a Good Protestant may be willing to hold Communion withal. The *Tunes* commonly used in our Churches, are *Few;* T'were well if there were *more.* But they are also *Grave,* and such as well *become the Oracles of GOD,* and such as do Steer clear of the Two Shelves, which *Austin* was afraid of; when he did, *In cantu Sacro fluctuare, inter Periculum Voluptatis, et Experimentum Salubritatis;* in danger of too much *Delicacy* on the one side, and *Asperity* on the other.

THE *Musick* of the Ancient Hebrews, an Adjustment whereto seems to be all the *Measure* of their *Poetry,* (after all the Attempts of *Gomarus,* and other Learned Men otherwise to *Measure* it,) being utterly Lost; and as *Aben-Ezra* [2] observes, of the *Musical Instruments* in the *Hundred and Fiftieth Psalm,* wholly Irrecoverable; we have no way Left us now, but with *Tunes* composed by the *Chief Musicians* for us, to *do as well as we can.*

SOLOMON STODDARD, 1643–1729

[It was expected of ministers, to the extent they were dialecticians and arbiters of public morals, that they should decide questions of behavior as well as polity. The ministers certainly never shirked such responsibility. When custom or logic failed, there remained the firm rock of the Bible from which to cite precedent, and thus, it was hoped, end counter-argument. A tract written by Solomon Stoddard was published in 1722, on matters of morals, called *An Answer to Some Cases of Conscience Respecting the Country.* Stoddard, the grandfather of Jonathan Edwards, had been pastor of the Northampton church since 1672, and was a man held in great esteem.

The fashion of wearing long hair, attacked by the General Court and by ministers during the mid-seventeenth century, had fallen into disfavor later in the century when periwigs came into style. The General Court condemned periwigs in 1675. But as time passed, such questions of minor morals agitated the country less and less. By 1710, though the laws forbidding long hair and periwigs continued on the statutes, enforcement was negligible.

On Stoddard, see Sibley, *Biographical Sketches,* II, 111–122. The text is from *An Answer, etc.*, pp. 4–7, 12, 13.]

AN ANSWER TO SOME CASES OF CONSCIENCE

Q. IV. Is it Lawfull to wear long Hair?

Answ. It was the Custom in *England* to cut their Hair all off, in imitation of King *Henry* the Eighth, who out of an humour, as Dr. *Fuller* [1] says, cut off his Hair. This custom continued for about three-score years: but by degrees, Men took a greater liberty; tho some Men placed Religion in it: yet in length of time, they were not so scrupulous as formerly. And some wore their Hair very long. And many of those that wear Periwigs, use such as are of a very great length. And the custom doth now prevail among Pious People. But it seems utterly Unlawful to wear their Hair long; It is a great Burden and Cumber; it is Effiminacy, and a vast Expence.

One Scripture that condemns it, 1 Cor. 11. 14. *Doth not even nature it self teach you, that if a man wear long hair, it is a shame to him?* That which the light of Nature condemns, is a Moral Evil. The light of Nature is to be our Rule in ordinary cases. The reason why it is a shame to wear long Hair is, because it is a Sin: the light of Nature doth condemn it; therefore it is sinfull.

The principal Objection that is brought to evade the Authority of this Place, is, That by *Nature*, Custom is meant. So Dr. *Hammond* [2] expounds it: I judge he doth it, that he may strengthen himself in his *Arminianism*, that he may have the better pretence to expound it so, *Eph.* 2. 3. where it is said, *We are by nature children of wrath, even as others.* His Exposition there is contrary to the Rule of *Faith;* and in this Place, contrary to the Rule of *Life*. We sometimes say that Custom is a second nature: yet it is never so used in the Scripture: the Interpretation is without Precedent: and the Apostle being presently after to speak of Custom, useth another word: 1 *Cor.* 11. 16. He saith, We have no such *Custom.* The Apostles Expression is very remarkable, He saith, *even Nature it self,* as if he had foreseen that Men would put a false interpretation on his words. He doth not content himself to say, *Nature;* but that they may not suppose he meant *Custom.* He saith, *Even Nature it self.* Undoubtedly he was guided therein by the Spirit of God. Besides, it was not true, that *Custom* taught them that it was a shame for a Man to wear long Hair: for it was the *Custom* of the *Greeks* to wear their Hair *long:* The *Romans* wore their Hair *short;* but the *Greeks* wore their Hair *long. Homer* calls the Grecians *Comati Achivi.*[3] And when *Alexander* was in a rage with *Cassander* one of his Nobles; he took him by the Hair, and knocked his head against the wall. Moreover in the next verse, 1 *Cor.* 11. 13. The Apostle to shew, that Nature teaches Women to wear their Hair *long;* He saith, *If a woman have long hair, it is a glory to her; for her hair is given her for a covering.* God gave it to *Women* for a covering, but not to *Men.*

Another Scripture doth also condemn it, *viz.* Ezek. 44. 20. *Neither shall they shave their heads, nor suffer their locks to grow long, they shall only poll their heads.* Here are two Extreams forbid; *Shaving the head,* and *suffering their locks to grow long.* This must either signify some spiritual thing; but no Man can devise what; or some Gospel Institution; and if so, why is it not enjoyned unto Ministers in the New Testament, or else it is a Moral Law: and so it must be. One part of it, is surely Moral; *They shall not shave their heads;* therefore the other part is Moral also; *They shall not suffer their locks to grow long.*

The Command of God requiring the Nazarites to nourish their Hair, is no vindication of long Hair; but a forcible reason against it; which will appear, if we consider two things.

1. Such Actions, as under their *ordinary* circumstances, are Moral Evils; under *extraordinary* circumstances, be very good: So for *Brothers* and *Sisters* to joyn in Wedlock, as *Adam's* Children did: For the *Brother,* among the *Jews,* to Marry his *Brother's* Wife: So, for a Physician, to give an intoxicating Potion: to do that which ordinarily, is contrary to a Rule of Modesty. One Command, in many cases, must give way to another.

2. The Nazarites were to deny themselves many comforts, to shew us that we should be mortified to the things of this World. Upon a Religious account, they were to abstain from Wine & Raisins, *&c.* and upon that account, they were to deny themselves of that neatness and comeliness in wearing their Hair, that was a duty in other Men.

It was a part of the Calamity that came upon *Nebuchadnezzar,* that his Hairs were grown like Eagles Feathers, *and his Nailes like birds claws,* Dan. 4. 33.

[*The following Letter, written by the same learned Author many years ago, may be here inserted.*]

Sir,

In compliance with your desire, I now send you my Thoughts concerning *Periwigs*. I cannot see sufficient Reason to condemn them Universally. God does allow Man, by *Art* to supply the defects of *Nature*. Hair artificially prepared may supply as fully & innocently, the want of Hair, as any other matter artificially prepared.

But yet I judge that there is abundance of Sin, in this Country, in wearing *Periwigs*. Particularly, in these two things;

First, When Men do wear them needlessly, in compliance with the Fashion. Their own Hair is sufficient for all those Ends that God has given Hair for. One Man's Hair is comlier than another's. And so it is with their Faces, and Bodies. Some cut off their Own because of the Colour; it is *Red* or *Grey;* Some, because it is *Streight;* Some, because it is *Frizel'd;* and some, only, because it is their *Own*.

Secondly, When those that may have just occasion to wear them, doe wear them in such a Ruffianly way, as it would be utterly unlawfull to wear their own Hair in. Some of them are of an unreasonable *Length;* and generally, they are extravagant as to their *Bushyness*. . . .

The *Practice* seems, to me, to have these four *Evils* in it:

1. It is an *Uncontentedness* with that Provision that God has made for Men. God has generally given Men such Hair as is comly; and a sufficiency of it. And when it is so, Men have cause to be well satisfyed. When God has given to Men such Hair as is sutable to answer the Ends of Hair; It seems to be a *Despising* of the Goodness of God, to cut it off, in compliance with a Vain Fashion. . . .

2. It is *Wastefullness*. Abundance of Money is *needlessly* spent in maintaining this *Practice*. Some of the Men that use it, have need enough of the Money other ways; and lay themselves under Temptation by this *Extravagancy;* either to oppress Men in their Dealings; or to be more Pinching in other Cases, than they ought to be. And those Men that have more plentiful Estates, have no Liberty to use them according to their own Pleasure. That Money that may be laid out to *Advantage*, should not be spent *Unprofitably*.

3. It is *Pride:* they do it to make a great *Shew;* It is from an Affectation of *Swaggering;* it is an Affecting of *Finery* that there is no just occasion for. They count it *Brave* to be in the Fashion; crave the honour of being counted as *Gallant* as others. It is too much *Flanting*.

4. It is *contrary to Gravity*. There is a Masculine Gravity that should

appear in the Countenances of Men, discovering a Solemnity of Spirit. But this *Practice* is *Light*, and *Effeminat*. Thô it make a *Shew;* yet it takes much away from the Presence of Men. Such *Curiosity* discovers much *Vanity* in the Mind; and makes others to esteem the more lightly of them; and not to shew that Respect to them. This *Practice* makes them look, as if they were more dispos'd *to Court a Maid;* than to bear upon their Hearts the weighty Concernments of GOD's Kingdom.

But I am fearful that the Stream runs so strong this way, that no Endeavours will work a Publick Reformation; until GOD does give Men another Spirit; or lay them under other Dispensations. Yet it may not be without good Effect on some particular Persons, if a Testimony be born against the *Practice;* if not to *Reduce* any; yet to *Prevent* some that were in danger.

Thus Sir, I have endeavoured to give some Satisfaction to your Desires; which I hope you will take in good part, from your Servant.

N——*H. July*, 29. 1701.

Q. VIII. DID WE ANY WRONG TO THE *INDIANS* IN BUYING THEIR LAND AT A SMALL PRICE?

A. 1. There was some part of the Land that was not purchased, neither was there need that it should; it was *vacuum domicilium;* [4] and so might be possessed by vertue of GOD's grant to Mankind, Gen. 1. 28. *And God blessed them, and God said unto them, Be fruitful and multiply and replenish the earth, and subdue it: and have dominion over the fish of the sea, and over the fowl of the air, and over every living thing that moveth upon the earth.* The *Indians* made no use of it, but for Hunting. By GOD's first Grant Men were to subdue the Earth. When *Abraham* came into the Land of *Canaan*, he made use of vacant Land as he pleased: so did *Isaac* and *Jacob*.

2. The Indians were well contented that we should sit down by them. And it would have been for great Advantage, both for this World, and the Other; if they had been wise enough to make use of their Opportunities. It has been common with many People, in planing this World since the Flood, to admit Neighbours, to sit down by them.

3. Tho' we gave but a small Price for what we bought; we gave them their demands, we came to their Market, and gave them their price; and indeed, it was worth but little: And had it continued in their hands, it would have been of little value. It is our dwelling on it, and our Improvements, that have made it to be of Worth.

Most louinge and good Husband. I have receued your letters. the true tokens of yor loue and care of my good now in your absence as well as when you are present. it makes me thinke that sayinge false out of sight out of minde. I am sure my hart and thoughts are all wayes neere you to doe you good and not euill all the dayse of my life . . . .

I hope through gods blessinge yor paynes will not be all together lost wch you bestow vpon me in rightinge those serious thoughts of youre owne wch you sent me did make a very good supply in stead of a sarmon I shall often reade them and desyre to be of gods famyle to home so many blessinges be-longe and pray that I may not be one separated from god whose concience is allwayes accusinge them . .

I shall not neede to right to you of any newes this time my sonne and brother Gostlinge can tell you how we are. and I shall thinke longe for yor cominge home. and thus with my best loue to you I beseech the lord to send vs a comfortable meetinge in his good time I commit you to the lord.

Your louinge and obedient wife.
Margaret Winthrope.

Letter of Margaret Winthrop to Her Husband. (For text, see p. 467.)

Chapter V

BIOGRAPHIES AND LETTERS

Among the three or four scamps and scalawags who somehow strayed into the holy communities of New England, and whose disreputable figures add a welcome touch of comic relief to the high seriousness of the Puritan drama, was Captain John Underhill. He was a soldier, brought along by the Massachusetts Bay Company more for his usefulness than for his piety; he did yeoman service in drilling farm boys and apprentices into soldiers and Indian fighters, but he succumbed to the insidious influence of Mrs. Anne Hutchinson, and gave a spectacular example of the worst implications of her teachings. Being assured that he was united to Christ by an immediate joining of spirits, he became confident he could do no wrong and need no longer respect the rules and regulations of civilized society. In 1638 he was arraigned before the General Court on the charge, among others, of calling the authorities of Massachusetts Scribes and Pharisees. A witness further deposed that he had told her how he had sought five years for grace, "and could get no assurance, till at length, as he was taking a pipe of tobacco, the Spirit set home an absolute promise of free grace with such assurance and joy, as he never since doubted of his good estate, neither should he, though he should fall into sin." Thereupon he proceeded not simply to fall, but more accurately to plunge into a considerable quantity of sin, without so much as a single qualm of conscience.

Underhill was dealt with by the usual machinery of Puritan justice. The ministers explained the nature of his sins, and the magistrates passed such sentence as those sins deserved. His ethical theories were of course exposed as dangerous fallacies; John Cotton also took occasion to point out that any sense of assurance obtained while he was occupied in so trivial and worldly a practice as smoking his pipe was suspect to begin with, and further declared that except in a few special cases, as with St. Paul, the experience of regeneration does not come upon a man in a sudden flash, but slowly and by degrees. Assurance of salvation does not hit the saint like a brickbat on the head, but is gradually and industriously acquired by his diligent pursuit of religious ordinances and strenuous meditation upon God's word. Therefore Cotton seriously "advised him well to examine the revelation and joy which he had."[1] Captain Underhill made a pretense of profiting

[1] *Winthrop's Journal*, ed. J. K. Hosmer (New York, 1908), I, 275–276.

by this advice, but still went from bad to worse, and at last the government and churches breathed a long sigh of relief when he and his erroneous assurance went off to New Amsterdam to take service with the Dutch.

It is probable that the Puritans in England had been more ready to conceive of regeneration as a clap of thunderous illumination, but in New England the heresy of the Antinomians and the whole task of holding religious passion within the limits of control and orderly procedure accentuated the tendency to regard the experience not as a sudden convulsion of the soul wrought in the twinkling of an eye, but as a laborious process. Too many of these cataclysmic conversions turned out like Captain Underhill's. Consequently the standard doctrine in New England very soon was crystallized in the statement that though in rare instances the Holy Ghost might overwhelm a soul without any previous preparation, still for most persons the call of Christ would come through a long succession of sermons carefully and inwardly digested, long conferences with ministers and saints, years of self-examination and sustained endeavor to live the saintly life. Samuel Willard explained that those who "Commence Believers" (using the academic phrase, by which a student given a degree was said "to commence") without an antecedent and long-drawn out conviction and period of humiliation were apt to prove apostates, that God carries his decree of election in secret ways "under ground a great while, before it rise and break out in effectual Calling." [1] The whole process was mysterious, it was something that happened to men and women, not something they brought about of their own volition. Another minister, seeking for a metaphor to illustrate it, hit upon one of the happier figures of Puritan sermonizing:

> It fares here, as when persons by some unobserved and unforeseen emanations of spirits from the heart, and pressing through the optick nerves flow into their mutual eyes, and dart themselves into one anothers breasts, whence they become suddenly taken, and as it were inkindled by certain lineatures in their feitures; and are rapt into deep admiration of somewhat in each other, which neither themselves nor the wisest Philosopher in being can give reason sagacious enough to unfold the surprizing influence when they are constellated to conjugal union.[2]

Some couples may indeed fall in love at first sight, but the average pair of lovers advance somewhat less precipitously, what with emanations of spirits pressing through the optic nerves, and are less aware of what

[1] *Mercy Magnified on a Penitent Prodigal*, A 3 recto.

[2] Samuel Lee, Χαρὰ τηs Πιseως, *The Joy of Faith*, pp. 119–120.

is happening to them, up to the very point of proposal; so the normal saints become aware only after a time of doubt and bewilderment that the seeds of grace have been sown in their hearts.

It is necessary to keep this doctrine in mind when we come to the reading of Puritan journals, diaries, and biographies, for it explains the purpose of the Puritan's study of his own life, or of the lives of others. The ways of grace were manifold and no two men ever underwent the crisis in a perfectly similar fashion; in order that we might know the nature and manifestations of the disease, it was necessary to peruse the records of those who had undergone it, and to keep a full medical chart upon our own pulse and temperature. The art of biography as understood by the Puritans was the preparation of case histories. And every man who was concerned about his own plight should take down a daily record of his fluctuations and his symptoms, so that he could view himself with the complete objectivity demanded for accurate diagnosis of his spiritual health or sickness. A journal covering several years' experience could, when critically perused, offer the best evidence as to whether or not the secret decree of God had been operating "under ground" during that time. Accounts of individuals' own lives, or of the lives of great men and conspicuous saints, were not to be descriptions of their appearances or of the clothes they wore or of what they ate for breakfast, but of the works of grace in their hearts and the exemplifications of the spirit in their conduct. The masterpiece of autobiography in this vein is Bunyan's *Grace Abounding*, and in *The Pilgrim's Progress* is the type figure for all Puritan journeys from birth to death, the supreme exemplar of which the biography of each particular Christian is but the individual variant.

It is probable that almost every literate Puritan kept some sort of journal; the number of diaries that remain from the seventeenth and eighteenth centuries is legion, and the habit became so thoroughly ingrained in the New England character that it remained a practice with various Yankees long after they had ceased to be Puritans, to the great enrichment of our political and literary history, as witness the diaries of John Quincy Adams and Gideon Welles, or the journals of Emerson, Thoreau, and Hawthorne. Henry Adams, dissecting his career in the search for "education," is writing in the true New England tradition, and undertakes no more than countless Puritans had done when they submitted their lives to microscopic examination to discover if they had at any time found that vision of the unity and meaning of the universe which they called regeneration and for which he endeavored to substitute a dynamic theory of history.

The preoccupation with the subjective life and the essential sameness of the experiences recorded make most of these early journals monotonous and unrevealing. Very few of them tell us anything of what people did or what they said or how they occupied their time, and of what they thought there appears but one reiterated strain. Most of them are not of great interest to the historian and of less to the general reader, but there is a brilliant exception, both for its literary charm and historical value, in that of Samuel Sewall. The reasons for its pre-eminence are in part the result of the times and circumstances in which Sewall made his jottings. He lived through the transition from the religious seventeenth century to the more wordly eighteenth, and though he was a conservative in doctrinal belief and disinclined to many new customs and ideas, whether periwigs or the Copernican hypothesis, still he was bound to move with his age. Consequently, though the early pages of his journal are concerned with probings into the state of his soul and with pious meditations, and though he continues to the end of his days "improving" occasions with spiritual moralizings, yet even with him the religious preoccupation perceptibly lessened, and for the last thirty or forty years he recorded more and more of his secular employments and worldly fortunes. In his old age, after his first wife died, he went a-courting, and put down the story of his successes and rebuffs with an attention to incidentals that would hardly have been possible in a diary of the seventeenth century. The result was that he created, all unknowingly, two minor literary triumphs, the stories of his failure to acquire the hand of either the timorous widow Denison or of the supremely competent widow Winthrop.

Sewall's journal is also exceptional because of his own prominence in the political affairs of the colony, Though trained for the ministry, his bent was for business and administration; he married the daughter of John Hull, the mintmaster and one of the wealthiest men of the community; he inherited property from his father-in-law, and always had a considerable estate to manage. He served the colony in many official capacities, as magistrate, judge, and at last chief justice. Inevitably he recorded his meetings with leading men of the colony, of discussions in the council, of squabbles among the politicians, of good dinners enjoyed by the judges while riding the circuit, and of crises in the state. He was appointed by Governor Phips to serve on the special court that tried and condemned the witches at Salem; he concurred in the decisions at the time, but a few years later he realized, along with most intelligent opinion in the colony, that the community had been stampeded by panic and that innocent men and women had been slaughtered. The chief justice of that particular court, William Stoughton, in whose address before the General Court of 1668 had glowed the confidence that New England was the apple of the divine eye (pp. 243–246), never repented his share in the executions, but Sewall was of larger mold. The custom in the churches was for anyone who wanted the prayers of the congregation during affliction, or their sympathy during repentance, to post a notice of the request before the assembly; Sewall put up the sheet which he transcribes in his diary, announcing his humiliation and repentance for misjudging the innocent, and sat during this Sabbath not in the pew to which he, as a pillar of the church and the leader of the singing, was entitled, but on the mourners' bench, where convicted sinners were customarily exhibited to the admonition and censure of the godly.

This act indicates that there is still a further reason for the quality of Sewall's diary besides the times and his official prominence. He was a limited and prosaic man, but there is an honesty about him that shines through his pages, even where he himself least intended it or where it does not show him to advantage. The unconscious humor and the unwitting self-portraiture of the story of the courtships elevate those portions of the journal into the realm of classic confessionals. His meditation, in 1727, upon the death of his classmate, when he himself was seventy-five and had but three years to live, reveals the essential depth of the man, for all his crotchets and shortcomings.

Thomas Shepard, the great preacher who succeeded Hooker at Cambridge, wrote the narrative of his life for the edification of his children. John Williams, pastor at Deerfield, told of the massacre and his captivity in Canada for the edification of all the righteous; his book was bought and read not only by them, but, one suspects, by many others, for he managed to tell a good adventure story that sold to a tune which must have warmed his publishers' hearts. Shepard was much the greater man of the two, with a larger breadth of education and vision; Williams was a back-country minister, a provincial figure with a limited imagination and not much taste, but his courage was invincible and his devotion to what he believed very little short of incredible. The two narratives reveal much about the Puritan character, and a comparison of them indicates some of the features that remained constant in a hundred years of development, and some that changed.

The literary value of letters written by Puritans is naturally fugitive. Thousands of papers survive from the seventeenth century, and most of them concern immediate affairs. Those of John Winthrop to his wife, particularly at the time of the departure for New England, not only throw light upon the circumstances of that expedition, but reveal certain depths of the Puritan spirit and the nature of conjugal affection in Puritan households. Mrs. Winthrop was to remain in England until a home was prepared in America; on Mondays and Fridays at five in the afternoons they agree to drop all distractions and to think of each other; in another letter, written on St. Valentine's Day, he closes by assuring his Margaret she is his Valentine. Tenderness and love undoubtedly existed here, but side by side with it there was religious passion, so that he mingles exhortation with his affection, and she, pining in his absence, welcomes his love letters because they serve her instead of a sermon. The letters of Roger Williams are clear revelations of the spirit of the man, and proclaim his greatness and his nobility as no panegyrics could do. The correspondence with Mrs. Sadleir furnishes a commentary upon his theories of religious liberty; it also illustrates that this splendid radical had something in him of the tactless intrusiveness of the doctrinaire, who sees nothing amiss in forcing his well-meaning attentions upon those who want none of them.

The art of formal biography is here represented by the work of Increase and Cotton Mather. Increase proposed the task of writing his father's life immediately after the old gentleman died, telling himself "it would be a service not only honorable to my Father, but acceptable & honorable to the name of God." As Professor Murdock has said, the biography reaches "a simple dignity that comes close to art." [1] Cotton Mather provided in the *Magnalia* a complete list of New England leaders and supplied their biographies; the faults of his work have already been commented upon (p. 90), and are indeed all too obvious, but it is a mine of information and a storehouse of Puritan beliefs. The life of Eliot is one of his happier efforts; it is at least an excellent illustration of the values which were to be perceived according to Puritan standards in the life of a saint, and of the manner in which the moral of a holy career was to be pointed up. The chapter on Eliot's birth, early life, and marriage makes "no more than an entrance in the history," which becomes really significant with the account of his conversion; episodes are stressed not for themselves, but for their meanings, and are shamelessly taken as occasions for generalization; the death scene is draped in the phrases appropriate to the saint's certain translation from earth to heaven.

The pilgrimage of man and woman from earth to heaven is still the theme of Parson Ebenezer Turell when he relates the lives of his

[1] Kenneth B. Murdock, *Increase Mather* (Cambridge, 1925), pp. 96–97.

father-in-law and of his wife. Jane Turell evidently possessed the authentic Puritan conscience, and agonized in the approved abasement of spirit over her salvation. But in these works a new note begins to sound; the title page proclaims the life of a lady who was not only "pious" but "ingenious"; she had "digested" English poetry, and was versed in "polite pieces in prose"; her husband was first attracted to her not only by her sanctity but by her "taste," which he feared so much that even at her request he would not venture to translate a psalm lest he do violence to her sensibilities by the grossness of his masculine meters. When such criteria began to creep into the judgment of biographers, the Puritan age was on the wane.

JOHN WINTHROP, 1588–1649

[For Winthrop's life see p. 125. Margaret Winthrop was John's third wife; they were married in 1618. She died in 1647 (see Winthrop's notice, p. 142). Texts are from *Winthrop Papers*, Vol. II (Massachusetts Historical Society, Boston, 1931).]

LETTERS OF THE WINTHROPS

John Winthrop to His Wife

The largnesse and trueth of my loue to thee makes me allwayes mindfull of thy wellfare, and settes me on to worke to beginne to write, before I heare from thee: the verye thought of thee affordes me many a kynde refreshinge, what will then the enioyinge of thy sweet societye, which I prize aboue all worldly comfortes?

Yet such is the folye and miserye of man, as he is easylye brought to contemne the true good he enioyes, and to neglect the best thinges which he holdes onely in hope, and bothe vpon an vngrounded desire of some seeminge good which he promiseth to himselfe: and if it be thus with vs, that are Christians, who haue a sure worde to directe vs, and the holy Faith to liue by, what is the madnesse and bondage of those who are out of Christ? O: the riches of Christ! O: the sweetnesse of the worde of Grace! it rauisheth my soule in the thought heerof, so as when I apprehende but a glimpse of the dignitye and felicitye of a Christian, I can hardly perswade my heart, to hope for so great happynesse: let men talke what they will of riches, honors pleasures etc.; let vs haue Christ crucified, and let them take all besides: for indeed, he who hath Christ hath all thinges with him, for he enioyeth an allsufficiencie which makes him abundantly riche in pouertye, honorable in the lowest abasementes, full of ioye and consolation in the sharpest Afflictions, liuinge in death, and possessinge aeternitye in this vale of miserye: therefore blesse we God, for his free and infinite mercye, in bestowinge Christ vpon vs: let vs entertaine and loue him with our whole heartes: let vs trust in him, and cleaue to him, with denyall of our selues, and all thinges besides, and account our portion the best in the world: that so beinge strengthned and comforted in his loue, we may putt forth our selues, to improue our life and meanes, to doe him seruice: there are very fewe howers lefte of this daye of our labour, then comes the night, when we shall take our rest, in the morninge we shall awake vnto glorye and immortalitye, when we shall haue no more worke to doe, no more paines or griefe to endure, no more care, feare, want, reproach, or infirmitye; no more sinne, corruption or temptation.

I am forced to patch vp my lettres, heer a peece and there another. I haue now receiued thine, the kyndly fruites of thy most sweet Affection. Blessed be the Lorde for the wellfare of thy selfe and all our familye. I receiued lettres from my 2: sonnes with thee, remember my loue and blessinge to them, and to my daughter Winth[rop] for whose safetye I giue the Lord thankes: I haue so many lettres to write as I cannot write to them now: our freindes heer are in reasonable health, and desire to be kindly remembered to you all. Commende me to all my good freindes, my louinge neighbours goodman Cole and his wife, to whom we are allwayes much behouldinge. I will remember M[ary] her gowne and petticoate, and the childrens girdles. So with my most affectionate desires of thy wellfare, and my blessinge to all our children, I kisse my sweet wife, and comende thee and all ours to the gratious protection of our heauenly father, and rest Thy faithfull husbande still present with thee in his most vnkinde absence

Jo: Winthrop.

May 8 1629.

I am sorye for my neighbour Bluetes horse, but he shall loose nothinge by him. tell my sonne Hen: I will pay the mony he writes of.

John Winthrop to His Wife

My good wife, I prayse the Lorde for the wished newes of thy wellfare and of the rest of our Companye, and for the continuance of ours heer: it is a great favour, that we may enioye so much comfort and peace in these so euill and declininge tymes and when the increasinge of our sinnes giues vs so great cause to looke for some heauye Scquorge and Judgment to be comminge vpon us: the Lorde hath admonished, threatened, corrected, and astonished vs, yet we growe worse and worse, so as his spirit will not allwayes striue with vs, he must needs giue waye to his furye at last: he hath smitten all the other Churches before our eyes, and hath made them to drinke of the bitter cuppe of tribulation, euen vnto death; we sawe this, and humbled not ourselues, to turne from our euill wayes, but haue prouoked him more then all the nations rounde about vs: therefore he is turninge the cuppe towards vs also, and because we are the last, our portion must be, to drinke the verye dreggs which remaine: my deare wife, I am veryly perswaded, God will bringe some heauye Affliction vpon this lande, and that speedylye: but be of good Comfort, the hardest that can come shall be a meanes to mortifie this bodye of Corruption, which is a thousand tymes more dangerous to vs then any outward tribulation, and to bringe vs into neerer communion with our Lo: Jes: Christ, and more Assurance of his kingdome. If the Lord seeth it wilbe good for vs, he will prouide a shelter and a hidinge place for vs and ours as a Zoar for Lott,[1] Sarephtah for his prophet etc: if not, yet he will not forsake vs: though he correct vs with the roddes of men, yet if he take not his mercye and louinge kindnesse from vs we shalbe safe. He onely is allsufficient, if we haue him, we haue all thinges: if he seeth it not good, to cutt out our portion in these thinges belowe equall to the largnesse of our desires, yet if he please to frame our mindes to the portion he allottes vs, it wilbe as well for vs.

I thanke thee for thy kinde lettre, I am goinge to Westm[inster], and must heere breake of. I would haue my sonne H[enry] to be heere on teusdaye that I may goe out of towne on wensdaye or thursdaye next. If marye her gowne be made I will send it down by Smith this weeke, or els next, with other thinges: all our freindes heer are indifferent well, and desire to be comended to thee, so with my hearty salut[ation]s to all our freindes with thee, my loue and blessinge to my sonnes and daughteres, In very much hast, I ende and commende thee and all ours to the gratious protection and blessinge of the Lorde so I kisse my sweet wife, and thinke longe till I see thee farewell. Thine

Jo: Winthrop.

I thanke thee for our Turkye
May 15 1629

MARGARET WINTHROP TO HER HUSBAND

To my very loueinge Husband John Winthrope Esquire theese dd.

Most louinge and good Husband, I haue receued your letters. the true tokens of your loue and care of my good, now in your abcence as well as when you are present, it makes me thinke that sayinge falce out of sight out of minde. I am sure my hart and thoughts are all wayes neere you to doe you good and not euill all the dayse of my life.

I hope through gods blessinge your paynes will not be all together lost which you bestow vpon me in rightinge those serious thoughts of your owne which you sent me did make a very good supply in stead of a sarmon. I shall often reade them and desyre to be of gods famyle to home so many blessinges be-longe and pray that I may not be one separated from god whose concience is alwayes accusinge them. I shall not neede to right to you of any thing this weke my sonne and brother Goslinge can tell you how we are. and I shall thinke longe for your cominge home. and thus with my best loue to you I beseech the lord to send vs a comfortable meetinge in his good time I commit you to the Lord. Your louinge and obedient wife

Margaret Winthrope.

[*Ca.* May 18, 1629.]

Margaret Winthrop to Her Husband

To hir very louinge and deare Husban John Winthrope Esquire at mr. Downings house in fleet strete neere thee Condite these dd.

My deare Husband, I knowe thou art desyrus to heere often from vs which makes me take plesure in rightinge to thee, and in relatinge my true affections to thee and desyers of your wished welfayer. the good lord be euer with thee and prosper all thy affayres [in] this great and waytty busines which is now in hand, that it may be for the glory of his most holy name and furtherance of his gospell, but I must part with my most deare Husban, which is a uery hard tryall for me to vndergoe, if the lord doe not supporte and healpe me in it, I shalbe vnable to beare it. I haue now receiued thy kinde letter which I cannot reade without sheding a great many teares, but I will resine thee and giue thee into the hands of the almyti god who is all soficient for thee, whome I trust will keepe thee and prosper thee in the way thou art to goe, if thou walke before him in truth and vprightnesse of hart, he will neuer fayle of his promise to thee. therefore my good Husban chere vp thy hart in god and in the expectation of his fauors and blessings in this thy change, with asurance of his loue in Crist Jesus our lord for our change heare after when we shall liue with him in glory for euer. as for me his most vnworthy seruant I will cleaue to my Husban Crist as neere as I can though my infirmytyes be great he is able to heale them and wil not forsake me in the time of neede. I know I shall haue thy prayers to god for me that what is wanting in thy presence may be supplyed by the comfort of gods spirit. I am now full of passion haueinge nuly receiued thy letter and not able to right much. my sonne F[orth] will right about other busines. I begine to feare I shall see thee no more before thou goest which I should be very sory for and earnestly intreat thee that thou wilt com once more downe if it be possible. and thus with my due respect to thy selfe brother and sister D. thankes for my leamers to my sister, my loue to my sonnes, I commit thee to god and rest Your faythfull and obedient wife

Margaret Winthrope.

My good sister F. remembers hir loue.
[Groton, February 2, 1630.]

John Winthrop to His Wife

To my very louinge wife mrs. Winthrop the Elder at Groton in Suffolk dd.

My sweet wife, Thy loue is such to me, and so great is the bonde betweene vs, that I should neglect all others to hold correspondencye of lettres with thee: but I knowe thou art willinge to dispense with somewhat of thine owne right, to giue me lib[er]ty to satisfie my other occasions for the present, which call me to much writinge this eueninge, otherwise I would haue returned a larger answeare to thy sweet lettre. I prayse God we are all in health, and we goe on cheerfully in our businesse: I purpose (if God will) to be with thee vpon thursdaye come sennight, and then I must take my Farewell of thee, for a summers daye and a winters daye, the Lorde our good God will (I hope) sende vs a happye meetinge againe in his good tyme: Amen. Comende me kindly to my good sister F[ones] I would haue written to her, but I cannot, havinge 6: Lettres to write. I wrote to mr. P[aynter] tell my sister that her mother is brought in bedd and the child dead, and she in great danger. among other thinges let the brassen quart in the Larder howse be putt vp: and my grey cloake and the coate which was my brother Fones. and let this warrant inclosed be sent to Colchester to mr. Samuell Borrowes by the next tyme the carte goes. The Lord blesse thee my sweet wife with all our children: my brother and sister salute you all: my sonnes remember their loue and dutye: comend my loue to all: farewell Thy faithfull husband,

Jo: Winthrop.

[London,] Feb: 5. 1630.

remember to putt me vp some Cardam[ons] and Cardam[on] seed.

Beinge now ready to sende away my lettres; I receiued thine, the readinge of it hath dissolued my head into tears, I can write no more, if I liue I will see thee ere I goe. I shall parte from thee with sorrowe enough, be comfortable my most sweet wife, our God wilbe with thee Farewell.

John Winthrop to His Wife

To M. W. the Elder at Groton

My faithfull and deare wife, It pleaseth God that thou shouldest once againe heare from me before our departure, and I hope this shall come safe to thy hands, I knowe it wilbe a great refreshinge to thee: And blessed be his mercye, that I can write thee so good newes, that we are all in verye good health, and hauinge tryed our shipps entertainment now more then a weeke, we finde it agree very well with vs, our boyes are well and cheerfull, and haue no minde of home, they lye both with me, and sleepe as soundly in a rugge (for we vse no sheets heer) as euer they did at Groton, and so I doe my selfe (I prayse God). the winde hath been against vs this weeke and more, but this day it is come faire to the North, so as we are preparinge (by Godes assistance) to sett sayle in the morninge: we haue onely 4: shippes ready, and some 2: or 3: hollandes goe alonge with vs: the rest of our fleet (beinge 7: shippes) will not be ready this senight. we haue spent now 2: sabbaths on shipp board, very comfortably (God be praysed) and are daylye more and more incouraged to looke for the Lords presence to goe alonge with vs: Hen: Kingesburye hath a childe or 2: in the Talbott sicke of the measells, but like to doe well: one of my men had them at Hampton, but he was soone well againe. we are in all our 11: shippes, about 700: persons passengers; and 240 Cowes, and about 60: horses. the shippe which went from Plimouth carried about 140: persons, and the shippe which goes from Bristowe, carrieth about 80: persons. And now (my sweet soule) I must once againe take my last farewell of thee in old England, it goeth verye neere to my heart to leaue thee, but I know to whom I haue committed thee, euen to him, who loues the[e] much better than any husband can, who hath taken account of the haires of thy head, and putts all thy teares in his bottle, who can, and (if it be for his glorye) will bringe vs togither againe with peace and comfort. oh how it refresheth my heart to thinke that I shall yet againe see thy sweet face in the lande of the liuinge: that louely countenance, that I haue so much delighted in, and beheld with so great contente! I haue hetherto been so taken vp with businesse, as I could seldome looke backe to my former happinesse, but now when I shalbe at some leysure, I shall not auoid the remembrance of thee, nor the greife for thy absence: thou hast thy share with me, but I hope, the course we haue agreed vpon wilbe some ease to vs both, mundayes and frydayes at 5: of the clocke at night, we shall meet in spiritt till we meet in person. yet if all these hopes should faile, blessed be our God, that we are assured, we shall meet one day, if not as husband and wife, yet in a better condition, let that staye and comfort thy heart, neither can the sea drowne thy husband, nor enemyes destroye, nor any adversity depriue thee of thy husband or children. therefore I will onely take thee now and my sweet children in mine armes, and kisse and embrace you all, and so leaue you with my God. farewell farewell. I blesse you all in the name of the Lord Jesus; I salute my daughter Winth: Matt, Nan and the rest, and all my good neighbors and freindes pray all for vs. farewell.

Comende my blessinge to my sonne John. I cannot now write to him, but tell him I haue committed thee and thine to him, labour to drawe him yet nearer to God, and he wilbe the surer staffe of comfort to thee. I cannot name the rest of my good freinds, but thou canst supply it. I wrote a weeke since to thee and mr. Leigh and diuerse others. Thine wheresoever

Jo: Winthrop.

From Aboard the Arbella rydinge at the Cowes march 28. 1630.

I would haue written to my brother and sister Gostlinge, but it is neer midnight, let this excuse and commende my love to them and all theirs.

THOMAS SHEPARD, 1605–1649

[For Shepard's life see p. 117. The autobiography was written for the benefit of his son. This text is from *The Autobiography of Thomas Shepard*, edited by Allyn B. Forbes, *Publications of the Colonial Society of Massachusetts*, XXVII (1932), 321–400.]

THE AUTOBIOGRAPHY OF THOMAS SHEPARD

THE FIRST two yeares I spent in Cambridge was in studying & in my neglect of god & priuate prayer which I had sometime vsed. & I did not regard the Lord at all vnless it were at some fits; the 3^d^ yeare wherin I was Sophister I began to be foolish & proud & to shew my selfe in the publike Schooles; & there to be a disputer about things which now I see I did not know then at all but only prated about them; & toward the end of this yeare when I was most vile (after I had bin next vnto the gates of Death by the [*small*] Pox the yeare before) the Lord began to Call me home to the fellowship of his grace; which was in this manner

1. I doe remember that I had many good affections (but blind & vnconstant) oft cast into me since my fathers sicknes by the spirit of god wrastling with me, & hence I would pray in secret & hence when I was at Cambridge I heard old Doctor Chadderton [1] the master of the Colledge when I came & the first yeare I was there to heare him vpon a Sacrament day my hart was much affected but I did breake loose from the Lord agayne & halfe a yeare after I heard m^r^ Dickinson common place in the chappell vpon those woords I will not destroy it for tens sake. Gen: 19. & then agayne was much affected, but I shooke this off also & fell from god to loose & lewd company to lust & pride & gaming & bowling & drinking; & yet the Lord left me not but a godly Scholler walking with me, fell to discourse about the misery of euery man out of Christ viz: that what euer they did was sin; & this did much affect me; & at another time when I did light in godly company I heard them discourse about the wrath of god, & the terrour of it & how intollerable it was which they did present by fire how intollerable the torment of that was for a time what then would æternity be; & this did much awaken me; & I began to pray agayne; but then by loose company I came to dispute in the Schooles & there to joyne to loose schollers of other colledges & was fearfully left of god & fell to drinke with them; & I dranke so much on day that I was dead drunke & that vpon a saturday night & so was carryed from the place I had drinke at & did feast at, vnto a Schollers chamber on Basset of Christs Colledge; & knew not where I was vntill I awakened late on that sabboth & sick with my beastly carriage; & when I awakened I went from him in shame & confusion, & went out into the feelds & there spent that sabboth lying hid in the corne feelds where the Lord who might justly haue cut me off in the mids of my sin; did meet me with much sadnes of hart & troubled my soule for this & other my sins which then I had cause & laysure to thinke of: & now when I was woorst he began to be best vnto me & made me resolue to set vpon a course of dayly meditation about the euill of sin & my own wayes; yet although I was troubled for this sin I did not know my sinfull nature all this while. . . .

At this time I cannot omit the goodnes of god as to my selfe so to all the cuntry in deliuering vs from the Pekoat furies; [2] these Indians were the stoutest proudest & most successefull in there wars of all the

Indians; there cheefe Sachem was Sasakus, a proud cruell vnhapy & headstrong prince, who not willing to be guided by the perswasions of his fellow an aged Sachem Momanattuck nor fearing the reuenge of the English, hauing first suckt the blood of captaine Ston & m[r] Oldam found it so sweet & his proceedings for on whole winter so successefull that hauing beseeged & kild about 4 men that kept Seabrook fort he aduentured to fall vpon the English vp the riuer at Wethersfeed where he slew 9 or 10. men women & children at vnawares, & tooke two maids prisoners carrying them away captiue to the Pekoat cuntry herevpon those vpon the riuer first gathered about 70 men & sent them into Pekoat cuntry, to make that the seat of war, & to reuenge the death of those innocents whom they barbarously & most vnnaturally slew; these men marched two dayes & nights from the way of the Naraganset vnto Pekoat; being guided by those Indians then the ancient enemies of the Pekoats they intended to assault Sasakus Fort but falling short of it the second night the prouidence of god guided them to another nearer, full of stout men & their best souldiers being as it were coopt vp there to the number of 3 or 400 in all for the diuine slaughter by the hand of the English; these therfore being all night making merry & singing the death of the English the next day, toward breake of the day being very heauy with sleepe the English drew neare within the sight of the fort, very weary with trauayle & want of sleepe, at which time 500 Naragansets fled for feare & only 2 of the company stood to it to conduct them to the fort & the dore & entrance thereof; the English being come to it awakened the fort with a peale of muskets directed into the midst of there wigwams; & after this some vndertaking to compasse the fort without some aduentured into the fort vpon the very faces of the enemy standing ready with there arrowes ready bent to shoot who euer should aduenture; but the English casting by there peeces tooke there swoords in there hands (the Lord doubling there strength & courage) & fell vpon the Indians where a hot fight continued about the space of an houre, at last by the direction of on Captayne Mason there wigwams were set on fire which being dry & contiguous on to another was most dreadfull to the Indians, some burning some bleeding to death by the swoord some resisting till they were cut off some flying were beat down by the men without vntill the Lord had vtterly consumed the whole company except 4 or 5. girles they tooke prisoners & dealt with them at Seabrooke as they dealt with ours at Wethersfeeld, & tis verily thought scarce on man escaped vnles on or two to carry foorth tydings of the lamentable end of there fellowes; & of the English not on man was kild but on by the musket of an Englishman (as was conceiued) some were wounded much but all recouered & restored agayne. . . .

But the Lord hath not bin woont to let me liue long without some affliction or other, & yet euer mixt with some mercy, & therefore Aprill the 2d: 1646. as he gaue me another son, John. so he tooke away my most deare precious meeke & louing wife, in childbed, after 3 weekes lying in, hauing left behind her two hopefull branches my deare children, Samuell, & John: this affliction was very heauy to me, for in it the Lord seemd to withdraw his tender care for me & mine, which he graciously manifested by my deare wife; also refused to heare prayer, when I did thinke he would haue hearkned & let me see his bewty in the land of the liuing, in restroring of her to health agayne; also in taking her away in the prime time of her life when shee might haue liued to haue glorifyed the Lord long. also in threatning me to proceed in rooting out my family, & that he would not stop hauing begun here as in Ely for not being zealous enough agaynst the sins of his son; & I saw that if I had profited by former afflictions of this nature I should not haue had this scourge; but I am the Lords, & he may doe with me what he will, he did teach me to prize a little grace gained by a crosse as a sufficient recompense for all outward losses; but this losse was very great; shee was a woman of incomparable meeknes of spirit, toward my selfe especially & very louing; of great prudence to take care for & order my family affayres being neither too lauish nor sordid in any thing so that I knew not what was vnder her hands; shee had an excellency to reprooue for sin & discerned the euills of men; shee loued gods people dearly & studious to profit by there fellowship, & therefore loued there company shee loued gods woord exceedingly & hence was glad shee could read my notes which shee had to muse on euery weeke; shee had a spirit of prayer beyond ordinary of her time & experience shee was fit to dy long before shee did dy, euen after the death of her first borne which was a great affliction to her, but her woorke not being done then shee liued almost 9. yeares with me & was the comfort of my life to me & the last Sacrament before her lying in seemd to be full of Christ & thereby fitted for heauen; shee did oft say shee should not outliue this child; & when her feuer first began (by taking some cold) shee told me soe, that we should loue exceedingly together because we should not liue long together; her feuer tooke away her sleepe, want of sleepe wrought much distemper in her head, & filled it with fantasies & distractions but without raging; the night before shee dyed, shee had about 6 houres vnquiet sleepe; but that so coold & setled her head, that when shee knew none else so as to speake to them, yet shee knew Jesus Christ & could speake to him, & therefore as soone as shee awakened out of sleepe shee brake out into a most heauenly hartbreaking prayer after Christ her deare redeemer for the sparing of life; & so continued praying vntill the last houre of her death: Lord tho I vnwoorthy Lord on woord on woord &c. & so gaue vp the ghost; thus god hath visited & scourged me for my sins & sought to weane me from this woorld, but I haue euer found it a difficult thing to profit euer but a little by the sorest & sharpest afflictions.

ROGER WILLIAMS, 1604–1683

[For Williams's life see p. 214. The text of these letters is from *Publications of the Narragansett Club*, Vol. VI (Providence, R. I., 1874), edited by John Russell Bartlett.]

LETTERS OF ROGER WILLIAMS

To his much honored Governor John Winthrop.

Providence, [April 16, 1638.]

Much honored sir,—I kindly thank you for your loving inclination to receive my late protestation concerning myself, ignorant of Mr. Greene's letter. I desire unfeignedly, to rest in my appeal to the Most High in what we differ, as I dare not but hope you do: it is no small grief that I am otherwise persuaded, and that sometimes you say (and I can say no less) that we differ: the fire will try your works and mine: the Lord Jesus help us to make sure of our persons that we seek Jesus that was crucified: however it is and ever shall be (the Lord assisting) my endeavor to pacify and allay, where I meet with rigid and censorious spirits, who not only blame your actions but doom your persons . . .

Sir, there will be new Heavens and a new Earth shortly but no more Sea. (Revel. 21. 2.) the most holy God be pleased to make us willing now to bear the tossings, dangers and calamities of this sea, and to seal up to use upon his own grounds, a great lot in the glorious state approaching. So craving pardon for prolixity, with mine and my wife's due respect to Mrs. Winthrop, Mr. Deputy, Mr. Bellingham, &c., I rest

Your worship's desirous to be ever yours unfeigned

Roger Williams.

The Correspondence of Roger Williams and Mrs. Sadleir, 1652.

[Mrs. Sadleir was the daughter of the famous lawyer, Sir Edward Coke, who had been the benefactor and patron of Roger Williams before Williams came to New England. Though the father had been one of the great maintainers of Parliamentary government against the absolutism of James I, the daughter had obviously come to feel by 1652 that constitutional opposition had long since passed into overt rebellion, and no longer held with any of the programs of the Protectorate. When Williams came to England in 1652, having published opinions that were identified with the most radical wing of the revolutionary forces, he innocently attempted to pay his respects to the daughter of his old friend, and the following correspondence ensued.]

For my much honored kind friend, Mistress Sadleir, at Stondon, Puckridge, these.

From my lodgings near St. Martin's, at Mr. Davis his house, at the sign of the Swan.

[London, 1652]

My much honored friend, Mrs. Sadleir,—The never-dying honor and respect which I owe to that dear and honorable root and his branches, and, amongst the rest, to your much honored self, have emboldened me, once more, to enquire after your dear husband's and your life, and health, and welfare. This last winter I landed, once more, in my native country, being sent over from some parts of New England with some addresses to the Parliament.

My very great business, and my very great straits of time, and my very great journey homeward to my dear yoke-fellow and many children, I greatly fear will not permit me to present my ever-obliged duty and service to you, at Stondon, especially if it please God that I may despatch my affairs to depart with the ships within this fortnight. I am, therefore, humbly bold to crave your favorable consideration, and pardon, and acceptance, of these my humble respects and remembrances. It hath pleased the Most High to carry me on eagles' wings, through mighty labors, mighty hazards, mighty sufferings, and to vouchsafe to use, so base an instrument—as I humbly hope—to glorify himself, in many of my trials and sufferings, both amongst the English and barbarians.

I have been formerly, and since I landed, occasioned to take up the two-edged sword of God's Spirit, the word of God, and to appear in public in some contests against the ministers of Old and New England, as touching the true ministry of Christ and the soul freedoms of the people. Since I landed, I have published two or three things, and have a large discourse at the press, but 'tis controversial, with which I will not trouble your meditations; only I crave the boldness to send you a plain and peaceable discourse, of my own personal experiments, which, in a letter to my dear wife—upon the occasion of her great sickness near death—I sent her, being absent myself amongst the Indians.[1] And being greatly obliged to Sir Henry Vane, junior—once Governor of New England—and his lady, I was persuaded to publish it in her name, and humbly to present your honorable hands with one or two of them. I humbly pray you to cast a serious eye on the holy Scriptures, on which the examinations are grounded. I could have dressed forth the matter like some sermons which, formerly, I used to pen. But the Father of lights hath long since shown me the vanity and soul-deceit of such points and flourishes. I desire to know nothing, to profess nothing, but the Son of God. the King of souls and consciences; and I desire to be more thankful for a reproof for ought I affirm than for applause and commendation. I have been oft glad in the wilderness of America, to have been reproved for going in a wrong path, and to be directed by a naked Indian boy in my travels. How much more should we rejoice in the wounds of such as we hope love us in Christ Jesus, than in the deceitful kisses of soul-deceiving and soul-killing friends.

My much honored friend, that man of honor, and wisdom, and piety, your dear father, was often pleased to call me his son; and truly it was as bitter as death to me when Bishop Laud pursued me out of this land, and my conscience was persuaded against the national church and ceremonies, and bishops, beyond the conscience of your dear Father. I say it was as bitter as death to me, when I rode Windsor way, to take ship at Bristow, and saw Stoke House, where the blessed man was; and I then durst not acquaint him with my conscience, and my flight. But how many thousand times since have I had honorable and precious remembrance of his person, and the life, the writings, the speeches, and the examples of that glorious light. And I may truly say, that beside my natural inclination to study and activity, his example, instruction, and encouragement, have spurred me on to a more than ordinary, industrious, and patient course in my whole course hitherto.

What I have done and suffered—and I hope for the truth of God according to my conscience—in Old and New England, I should be a fool in relating, for I desire to say, not to King David—as once Mephibosheth—but to King Jesus, "What is thy servant, that thou shouldest look upon such a dead dog?" And I would not tell yourself of this, but that you may acknowledge some beams of his holy wisdom and goodness, who hath not suffered all your own and your dear father's smiles to have been lost upon so poor and despicable an object. I confess I have many adversaries, and also many friends, and divers eminent. It hath pleased the general [2] himself to send for me, and to entertain many discourses with me at several times; which, as it magnifies his christian nobleness and courtesy, so much more doth it magnify *His* infinite mercy and goodness, and wisdom, who hath helped me, poor worm, to sow that seed in doing and suffering—I hope for God—that as your honorable father was wont to say, he that shall harrow what I have sown, must rise early. And yet I am a worm and nothing, and desire only to find my all in the blood of an holy Savior, in whom I desire to be

Your honored,
Most thankful, and faithful servant,
Roger Williams.

My humble respects presented to Mr. Sadleir.

From Mrs. Sadleir to Roger Williams.

Mr. Williams,—Since it hath pleased God to make the prophet David's complaint ours (Ps. lxxix.): "O God, the heathen," &c., and that the Apostle St. Peter has so long ago foretold, in his second epistle, the second chapter, by whom these things should be occasioned, I have given over reading many books, and, therefore, with thanks, have returned yours. Those that I now read, besides the Bible, are, first, the late King's book; Hooker's Ecclesiastical Polity; Reverend Bishop Andrew's Sermons, with his other divine meditations; Dr. Jer. Taylor's works; and Dr. Tho. Jackson upon the Creed.[3] Some of these my dear father was a great admirer of, and would often call them the glorious lights of the church of England. These lights shall be my guide; I wish they may be yours: for your new lights that are so much cried up, I believe, in the conclusion, they will prove but dark lanterns: therefore I dare not meddle with them.

Your friend in the old way,
Anne Sadleir.

For his much honored, kind friend, Mrs. Anne Sadleir, at Stondon, in Hartfordshire, near Puckridge.

My much honored, kind Friend, Mrs. Sadleir,—

. . . You were pleased to direct me to divers books, for my satisfaction. I have carefully endeavoured to get them, and some I have gotten; and upon my reading, I purpose, with God's help, to render you an ingenuous and candid account of my thoughts, result, &c. At present, I am humbly bold to pray your judicious and loving eye to one of mine.

'Tis true, I cannot but expect your distaste of it; and yet my cordial desire of your soul's peace here, and eternal, and of contributing the least mite toward it, and my humble respects to that blessed root of which you spring, force me to tender my acknowledgments, which if received or rejected, my cries shall never cease that one eternal life may give us meeting, since this present minute hath such bitter partings.

For the scope of this *rejoinder*, if it please the Most High to direct your eye to a glance on it, please you to know, that at my last being in England, I wrote a discourse entitled, "*The Bloudy Tenent of Persecution for Cause of Conscience.*" I bent my charge against Mr. Cotton especially, your standard bearer of New English ministers. That discourse he since answered, and calls his book, "*The Bloody Tenent made white in the Blood of the Lamb.*" This rejoinder of mine, as I humbly hope, unwasheth his washings, and proves that in soul matters no weapons but soul weapons are reaching and effectual.

I am your most unworthy servant, yet unfeignedly respective,

Roger Williams.

Mrs. Sadleir in reply to Roger Williams.

Sir,—I thank God my blessed parents bred me up in the old and best religion, and it is my glory that I am a member of the Church of England, as it was when all the reformed churches gave her the right hand. When I cast mine eye upon the frontispiece of your book, and saw it entitled "The Bloudy Tenent," I durst not adventure to look into it, for fear it should bring into my memory the much blood that has of late been shed, and which I would fain forget; therefore I do, with thanks, return it. I cannot call to mind any blood shed for conscience:—some few that went about to make a rent in our once well-governed church were punished, but none suffered death. But this I know, that since it has been left to every man's conscience to fancy what religion he list, there has more christian blood been shed than was in the ten persecutions. And some of that blood, will, I fear, cry till the day of judgment. But you know what the Scripture says, that when there was no king in Israel, every man did that which was right in his own eyes,—but what became of that, the sacred story will tell you.

Thus entreating you to trouble me no more in this kind, and wishing you a good journey to your charge in New Providence, I rest

Your Friend in the Old and Best Way.

From Roger Williams to Mrs. Sadleir.

My honored, kind Friend, Mrs. Sadleir,—

. . . That you admire the king's book, and Bp. Andrews his sermons, and Hooker's Polity, &c., and profess them to be your lights and guides, and desire them mine, and believe the new lights will prove dark lanterns, &c. I am far from wondering at it, for all this have I done myself, until the Father of Spirits mercifully persuaded mine to swallow down no longer without chewing: to chew no longer without tasting; to taste no longer without begging the Holy Spirit of God to enlighten and enliven mine against the fear of men, tradition of fathers, or the favor or custom of any men or times. . . .

I have read those books you mention, and the king's book, which commends two of them, Bishop Andrews's and Hooker's—yea, and a third also, Bishop Laud's: and as for the king, I knew his person, vicious, a swearer from his youth, and an oppressor and persecutor of good men (to say nothing of his own father), and the blood of so many hundred thousands English, Irish, Scotch, French, lately charged upon him. Against his and his blasphemous father's cruelties, your own dear father, and many precious men, shall rise up shortly and cry for vengeance. . . .

The Turks—so many millions of them—prefer their Mahomet before Christ Jesus, even upon such carnal and worldly respects, and yet avouch themselves to be the only Muselmanni or true believers. The catholics account us heretics, diabloes, &c.; and why? but because we worship not such a golden Christ and his glorious vicar and lieutenant. The several sects of common protestants content themselves with a traditional worship, and boast they are no Jews, no Turks, (Matt. vii. 21, 22.) nor catholics, and yet forget their own formal dead faith, (2 Tim. iii. 9.) dead hope, dead joys, and yet, *nescio vos*, I know you not, depart from me, which shall be thundered out to many gallant professors and considents, who have held out a lamp and form of religion, yea, and possibly of godliness too, and yet have denied the power and life of it. . . .

God's Spirit persuadeth the hearts of his true servants: First, to be willing to be searched by him, which they exceedingly beg of him, with holy fear of self-deceit and hypocrisy.

Second. To be led by him in the way everlasting: (Ps. cxxxix.), whether it seem old in respect of institution, or new in respect of restoration. This I humbly pray for your precious soul, of the God and Father of mercies, even your eternal joy and salvation. Earnestly desirous to be in the old way, which is the narrow way, which leads to life, which few find.

Your most humble, though most unworthy servant,

Roger Williams.

My honored Friend, since you please not to read mine, let me pray leave to request your reading of one book of your own authors. I mean the "Liberty of Prophesying," penned by (so called) Dr. Jer. Taylor. In the which is excellently asserted the toleration of different religions, yea, in a respect, that of the papists themselves, which is a new way of soul freedom, and yet is the old way of Christ Jesus, as all his holy Testament declares.

I also humbly wish that you may please to read over impartially Mr. Milton's answer to the king's book.[4]

Mrs. Sadleir in reply to Roger Williams.

Mr. Williams,—I thought my first letter would have given you so much satisfaction, that, in that kind, I should never have heard of you any more; but it seems you have a face of brass, so that you cannot blush. But since you press me to it, I must let you know, as I did before (Ps. lxxix.), that the Prophet David there complains that the heathen had defiled the holy temple, and made Jerusalem a heap of stones. And our blessed Saviour, when he whipped the buyers and sellers out of the temple, told them that they had made his Father's house a den of thieves. Those were but material temples, and commanded by God to be built, and his name there to be worshipped. The living temples are those that the same prophet, in the psalm before mentioned (verse the 2nd and 3rd), "The dead bodies of thy servants have they given to the fowls of the air, and the flesh of thy saints to the beasts of the land. Their blood have they shed like water," &c. And these were the living temples whose loss the prophet so much laments; and had he lived in these times, he would have doubled these lamentations. For the foul and false aspersions you have cast upon that king, of ever-blessed memory, Charles, the martyr, I protest I trembled when I read them, and none but such a villain as yourself would have wrote them . . .

For Milton's book, that you desire I should read, if I be not mistaken, that is he that has wrote a book of the lawfulness of divorce; and, if report says true, he had, at that time, two or three wives living. This, perhaps, were good doctrine in New England; but it is most abominable in Old England. For his book that he wrote against the late king that you would have me read, you should have taken notice of God's judgment upon him, who stroke him with blindness, and, as I have heard, he was fain to have the help of one Andrew Marvell,[5] or else he could not have finished that most accursed libel. God has began his judgment upon him here—his punishment will be hereafter in hell. . . .

I cannot conclude without putting you in mind how dear a lover and great an admirer my father was of the liturgy of the church of England, and would often say, no reform church had the like. He was constant to it, both in his life and at his death. I mean to walk in his steps; and, truly, when I consider who were the composers of it, and how they sealed the truth of it with their blood, I cannot but wonder why it should now of late be thus contemned. By what I have now writ, you know how I stand affected. I will walk as directly to heaven as I can, in which place, if you will turn from being a rebel, and fear God and obey the king, there is hope I may meet you there; howsoever, trouble me no more with your letters, for they are very troublesome to her that wishes you in the place from whence you came.

Anne Sadleir.

[Near the direction, on the outside, of Williams's first letter, there is the following note by Mrs. Sadleir:]—

This Roger Williams, when he was a youth, would, in a short hand, take sermons and speeches in the Star Chamber and present them to my dear father. He, seeing so hopeful a youth, took such liking to him that he sent him in to Sutton's Hospital, and he was the second that was placed there; full little did he think that he would have proved such a rebel to God, the king, and his country. I leave his letters, that, if ever he has the face to return into his native country, Tyburn may give him welcome.

To John Winthrop, Jr.

To my honored, kind friend, Mr. John Winthrop, [*Jr.*] *Governor, at Hartford, on Connecticut.*

Providence, 6, 12, 59–60. [6th February, 1660.]

Sir,—Loving respects to yourself and Mrs. Winthrop, &c. Your loving lines in this cold, dead season, were as a cup of your Connecticut cider, which we are glad to hear abounds with you, or of that western metheglin, which you and I have drunk at Bristol together, &c. Indeed, it is the wonderful power and goodness of God, that we are preserved in our dispersions among these wild, barbarous wretches. . . .

Sir, you were, not long since, the son of two noble fathers, Mr. John

Winthrop and Mr. H. Peters.[6] It is said they are both extinguished. Surely, I did ever, from my soul, honor and love them even when their judgments led them to afflict me. Yet the Father of Spirits spares us breath, and I rejoice, Sir, that your name (amongst the New England magistrates printed, to the Parliament and army, by H. Nort. Rous, &c.,) is not blurred, but rather honored, for your prudent and moderate hand in the late Quakers' trials amongst us. And it is said, that in the late Parliament, yourself were one of the three in nomination for General Governor over New England, which however that design ripened not, yet your name keeps up a high esteem, &c. I have seen your hand to a letter to this colony, as to your late purchase of some land at Narragansett. The sight of your hand hath quieted some jealousies amongst us, that the Bay, by this purchase, designed some prejudice to the liberty of conscience amongst us. We are in consultations how to answer that letter, and my endeavor shall be, with God's help, to welcome, with both our hands and arms, your interest in these parts, though we have no hope to enjoy your personal residence amongst us. I rejoice to hear that you gain, by new plantations, upon this wilderness. I fear that many precious souls will be glad to hide their heads, shortly, in these parts. Your candle and mine draws towards its end. The Lord graciously help us to shine in light and love universally, to all that fear his name, without that monopoly of the affection to such of our own persuasion only; for the common enemy, the Romish wolf, is very high in resolution, and hope, and advantage to make a prey on all, of all sorts that desire to fear God. Divers of our neighbors thankfully re-salute you We have buried, this winter, Mr. Olney's son, whom, formerly, you heard to be afflicted with a lethargy. He lay two or three days wholly senseless, until his last groans. My youngest son, Joseph, was troubled with a spice of an epilepsy. We used some remedies, but it hath pleased God, by his taking of tobacco, perfectly, as we hope, to cure him. Good Mr. Parker, of Boston, passing from Prudence Island, at his coming on shore, on Seekonk land, trod awry upon a stone or stick, and fell down, and broke the small bone of his leg. He hath lain by of it all this winter, and the last week was carried to Boston in a horse litter. Some fears there was of a gangrene. But, Sir, I use too much boldness and prolixity. I shall now only subscribe myself

Your unworthy friend,
Roger Williams.

Sir, my loving respects to Mr. Stone, Mr. Lord, Mr. Allen, Mr. Webster, and other loving friends.

To Major Mason

[In 1670 Connecticut and Rhode Island were involved in a dispute concerning the boundary between the two colonies; committees were appointed and in May held a stormy conference that produced no agreement; Connecticut men thereupon seized control of the town of Westerly. The Rhode Island government retaliated by capturing some of the invaders and sending them to jail at Newport. At this juncture Williams wrote the following letter to Major Mason, one of the magistrates of Connecticut:]

Providence, June 22, 1670.

Major Mason,—My honored, dear and ancient friend, my due respects and earnest desires to God, for your eternal peace, &c.

I crave your leave and patience to present you with some few considerations, occasioned by the late transactions between your colony and ours. The last year you were pleased, in one of your lines to me, to tell me that you longed to see my face once more before you died. I embraced your love, though I feared my old lame bones, and yours, had arrested traveling in this world, and therefore I was and am ready to lay hold on all occasions of writing, as I do at present.

The occasion, I confess, is sorrowful, because I see yourselves, with others, embarked in a resolution to invade and despoil your poor countrymen, in a wilderness, and your ancient friends, of our temporal and soul liberties.

It is sorrowful, also, because mine eye beholds a black and doleful train of grievous, and, I fear, bloody consequences, at the heel of this business, both to you and us. The Lord is righteous in all our afflictions, that is a maxim; the Lord is gracious to all oppressed, that is another; he is most gracious to the soul that cries and waits on him; that is silver, tried in the fire seven times.

Sir, I am not out of hopes, but that while your aged eyes and mine are yet in their orbs, and not yet sunk down into their holes of rottenness, we shall leave our friends and countrymen, our children and relations, and this land, in peace, behind us. To this end, Sir, please you with a calm and steady and a Christian hand, to hold the balance and to weigh these few considerations, in much love and due respect presented:

First. When I was unkindly and unchristianly, as I believe, driven from my house and land and wife and children, (in the midst of a New England winter, now about thirty-five years past,) at Salem, that ever honored Governor, Mr. Winthrop, privately wrote to me to steer my course to Narragansett Bay and Indians, for many high and heavenly and public ends, encouraging me, from the freeness of the place from any English claims or patents. I took his prudent motion as a hint and voice from God, and waving all other thoughts and motions, I steered my course from Salem (though in winter snow, which I feel yet) unto these parts, wherein I may say Peniel, that is, I have seen the face of God.

Second, I first pitched, and began to build and plant at Seekonk, now Rehoboth, but I received a letter from my ancient friend, Mr. Winslow,[7] then Governor of Plymouth, professing his own and others love and respect to me, yet lovingly advising me, since I was fallen into the edge of their bounds, and they were loath to displease the Bay, to remove but to the other side of the water, and then, he said, I had the country free before me, and might be as free as themselves, and we should be loving neighbors together. These were the joint understandings of these two eminently wise and Christian Governors and others, in their day, together with their counsel and advice as to the freedom and vacancy of this place, which in this respect, and many other Providences of the Most Holy and Only Wise, I called *Providence.*

Third. Sometime after, the Plymouth great Sachem, (Ousamaquin,) upon occasion, affirming that Providence was his land, and therefore Plymouth's land, and some resenting it, the then prudent and godly Governor, Mr. Bradford, and others of his godly council, answered, that if, after due examination, it should be found true what the barbarian said, yet having to my loss of a harvest that year, been now (though by their gentle advice) as good as banished from Plymouth as from the Massachusetts, and I had quietly and patiently departed from them, at their motion to the place where now I was, I should not be molested and tossed up and down again, while they had breath in their bodies; and surely, between those, my friends of the Bay and Plymouth, I was sorely tossed, for one fourteen weeks, in a bitter winter season, not knowing what bread or bed did mean, beside the yearly loss of no small matter in my trading with English and natives, being debarred from Boston, the chief mart and port of New England. God knows that many thousand pounds cannot repay the very temporary losses I have sustained. It lies upon the Massachusetts and me, yea, and other colonies joining with them, to examine, with fear and trembling, before the eyes of flaming fire, the true cause of all my sorrows and sufferings. It pleased the Father of spirits to touch many hearts, dear to him, with some relentings; amongst which, that great and pious soul, Mr. Winslow, melted, and kindly visited me, at Providence, and put a piece of gold into the hands of my wife, for our supply.

Fourth. When the next year after my banishment, the Lord drew the bow of the Pequod war against the country, in which, Sir, the Lord made yourself, with others, a blessed instrument of peace to all New England, I had my share of service to the whole land in that Pequod business, inferior to very few that acted, for,

1. Upon letters received from the Governor and Council at Boston, requesting me to use my utmost and speediest endeavors to break and hinder the league labored for by the Pequods against the Mohegans, and Pequods against the English, (excusing the not sending of company and supplies, by the haste of the business,) the Lord helped me immediately to put my life into my hand, and, scarce acquainting my wife, to ship myself, all alone, in a poor canoe, and to cut through a stormy wind, with great seas, every minute in hazard of life, to the Sachem's house.

2. Three days and nights my business forced me to lodge and mix with the bloody Pequod ambassadors, whose hands and arms, methought, wreaked with the blood of my countrymen, murdered and massacred by them on Connecticut river, and from whom I could not but nightly look for their bloody knives at my own throat also. . . .

9. However you satisfy yourselves with the Pequod conquest, with the sealing of your charter some weeks before ours; with the complaints of particular men to your colony; yet upon a due and serious examination of the matter, in the sight of God, you will find the business at bottom to be,

First, a depraved appetite after the great vanities, dreams and shadows of this vanishing life, great portions of land, land in this wilderness, as if men were in as great necessity and danger for want of great portions of land, as poor, hungry, thirsty seamen have, after a sick and stormy, a long and starving passage. This is one of the gods of New England, which the living and most high Eternal will destroy and famish.

2. An unneighborly and unchristian intrusion upon us, as being the weaker, contrary to your laws, as well as ours, concerning purchasing of lands without the consent of the General Court. . . .

From these violations and intrusions arise the complaint of many privateers, not dealing as they would be dealt with, according to law of nature, the law of the prophets and Christ Jesus, complaining against others, in a design, which they themselves are delinquents and wrong doers. I could aggravate this many ways with Scripture rhetoric and similitude, but I see need of anodynes, (as physicians speak,) and not of irritations. Only this I must crave leave to say, that it looks like a prodigy or monster, that countrymen among savages in a wilderness;

that professors of God and one Mediator, of an eternal life, and that this is like a dream, should not be content with those vast and large tracts which all the other colonies have, (like platters and tables full of dainties,) but pull and snatch away their poor neighbors' bit or crust; and a crust it is, and a dry, hard one, too, because of the natives' continual troubles, trials and vexations.

10. Alas! Sir, in calm midnight thoughts, what are these leaves and flowers, and smoke and shadows, and dreams of earthly nothings, about which we poor fools and children, as David saith, disquiet ourselves in vain? Alas? what is all the scuffling of this world for, but, *come, will you smoke it?* What are all the contentions and wars of this world about, generally, but for greater dishes and bowls of porridge, of which, if we believe God's Spirit in Scripture, Esau and Jacob were types? Esau will part with the heavenly birthright for his supping, after his hunting, for god belly: and Jacob will part with porridge for an eternal inheritance. O Lord, give me to make Jacob's and Mary's choice, which shall never be taken from me.

11. How much sweeter is the counsel of the Son of God, to mind first the matters of his kingdom; to take no care for to-morrow; to pluck out, cut off and fling away right eyes, hands and feet, rather than to be cast whole into hell-fire; to consider the ravens and the lilies, whom a heavenly Father so clothes and feeds; and the counsel of his servant Paul, to roll our cares, for this life also, upon the most high Lord, steward of his people, the eternal God: to be content with food and raiment; to mind not our own, but every man the things of another; yea, and to suffer wrong, and part with what we judge is right, yea, our lives, and (as poor women martyrs have said) as many as there be hairs upon our heads, for the name of God and the son of God his sake. This is humanity, yea, this is Christianity. The rest is but formality and picture, courteous idolatry and Jewish and Popish blasphemy against the Christian religion, the Father of spirits and his Son, the Lord Jesus. Besides, Sir, the matter with us is not about these children's toys of land, meadows, cattle, government, &c. But here, all over this colony, a great number of weak and distressed souls, scattered, are flying hither from Old and New England, the Most High and Only Wise hath, in his infinite wisdom, provided this country and this corner as a shelter for the poor and persecuted, according to their several persuasions. . . .

16. Sir, I lament that such designs should be carried on at such a time, while we are stripped and whipped, and are still under (the whole country) the dreadful rods of God, in our wheat, hay, corn, cattle,

shipping, trading, bodies and lives; when on the other side of the water, all sorts of consciences (yours and ours) are frying in the Bishops' pan and furnace; when the French and Romish Jesuits, the firebrands of the world for their god belly sake, are kindling at our back, in this country, especially with the Mohawks and Mohegans, against us, of which I know and have daily information.

17. If any please to say, is there no medicine for this malady? Must the nakedness of New England, like some notorious strumpet, be prostituted to the blaspheming eyes of all nations? Must we be put to plead before his Majesty, and consequently the Lord Bishops, our common enemies, &c. I answer, the Father of mercies and God of all consolations hath graciously discovered to me, as I believe, a remedy, which, if taken, will quiet all minds, yours and ours, will keep yours and ours in quiet possession and enjoyment of their lands, which you all have so dearly bought and purchased in this barbarous country, and so long possessed amongst these wild savages; will preserve you both in the liberties and honors of your charters and governments, without the least impeachment of yielding one to another; with a strong curb also to those wild barbarians and all the barbarians of this country, without troubling of compromisers and arbitrators between you; without any delay, or long and chargeable and grievous address to our King's Majesty, whose gentle and serene soul must needs be afflicted to be troubled again with us. If you please to ask me what my prescription is, I will not put you off to Christian moderation or Christian humility, or Christian prudence, or Christian love, or Christian self-denial, or Christian contention or patience. For I design a civil, a humane and political medicine, which, if the God of Heaven please to bless, you will find it effectual to all the ends I have proposed. Only I must crave your pardon, both parties of you, if I judge it not fit to discover it at present. I know you are both of you hot; I fear myself, also. If both desire, in a loving and calm spirit, to enjoy your rights, I promise you, with God's help, to help you to them, in a fair, and sweet and easy way. My receipt will not please you all. If it should so please God to frown upon us that you should not like it, I can but humbly mourn, and say with the prophet, that which must perish must perish. And as to myself, in endeavoring after your temporal and spiritual peace, I humbly desire to say, if I perish, I perish. It is but a shadow vanished, a bubble broke, a dream finished. Eternity will pay for all.

Sir, I am your old and true friend and servant,

Roger Williams.

INCREASE MATHER, 1639–1723

[For life of Increase Mather see p. 334. This text is from *The Life and Death of that Reverend Man in God, Mr. Richard Mather* (Cambridge, 1670), pp. 8–11, 25–33.]

THE LIFE OF RICHARD MATHER

BEING as hath been related, setled in the Ministry at *Toxteth,* he resolved to change his single condition: And accordingly he became a Suitor to Mrs. *Katharine Hoult,* Daughter to *Edmund Hoult* Esq; of *Bury* in *Lancashire.* She had (and that deservedly) the repute of a very godly and prudent Maid. The Motion for several years met with Obstructions, by reason of her Fathers not being affected towards Non-conformable Puritans: But at last he gave his Consent that Mr. *Mather* should marry his Daughter; the Match therefore was Consummated *Septemb.* 29. 1624. God made her to become a rich Blessing to him, continuing them together for the space of above 30 years. By her God gave him six Sons; four whereof (*viz. Samuel, Timothy, Nathaniel* and *Joseph*) were born in *England,* and two (*viz. Eleazar* and *Increase*) in *New-England.* After his Marriage he removed his Habitation three miles from *Toxteth,* to *Much-Woolton,* having there purchased an House of his own; yet he was wont constantly Summer and Winter to Preach the Word at *Toxteth* upon the Lords-dayes. During his abode there, he was abundant in Labours in the Gospel: For every Lords-day he Preached twice at *Toxteth,* and once in a Fortnight on the Third day of the Week he kept a *Lecture* at the Town of *Prescot.* Also, faithful and powerful Preaching being then rare in those parts, he did frequently Preach upon the *Holy dayes* (as they are called) being often thereunto desired by godly Christians of other Parishes in that Country: And this he did, not as thinking that there was any Holiness in those times (or in any other day besides the Lords-day) beyond what belongs to every day; but because then there would be an opportunity of great Assemblies,[1] and it is good casting the Net where there is much Fish: for which cause it might be that the Apostles Preached mostly in Populous Towns and Cities, and also (which suiteth with what we are speaking) on the *Jewish Sabbaths* after their abrogation as to any Religious tye upon Conscience for their observation. Yea and besides all this, he often Preached at *Funerals.* It is true that *Cartwright, Sherwood, Hildersham,* and many other Renowned Non-Conformists, have scrupled Preaching *Funerall Sermons;* Also in some Reformed Churches that practice is wholly omitted, yea and Decrees of Councils have sometimes been against it; but that hath been chiefly upon account of that Custome of *Praising the dead* upon such occasions, and that many times untruly: Which *Custome* (as many Learned men have observed) is *Ethnicall*, having its rise from the Funeral Orations of the Heathen. *Publicola* made an excellent Oration in Praise of *Brutus*, which the People were so taken with, that it became a Custome that Famous men dying should be so praised, and when (as *Plutarch* saith in the Life of *Camillus*) the Women amongst the *Romans* parted with their Golden Ornaments for the Publick Good, the Senate decreed, That it should be lawful to make Funeral Orations for them also. *Hinc mortuos laudandi mos fluxit quem nos hodiè servamus.*[2] *Pol. Verg. de Rer. Invent. lib.* 3. *cap.* 10. Nor indeed was this Rite practised in the Church afore the *Apostacy* began. *Vide Magd. Cent.* 4. *Cap.* 6. wherefore this faithful Servant of the Lord avoided that practice, his speech at Funerals being taken up not with Praising the Dead, but with *Instructing the Living* concerning Death, the Resurrection, the Judgement to come, and the like seasonable Truths. Thus did he Preach the Word, being instant in season and out of season; reproving, rebuking, exhorting, with all long-suffering and doctrine. In his publick Ministry in *England* he went over 2 *Samuel*, *Chap.* 24. *Psalm* 4. and *Psalm* 16. *Proverbs*, *Chap.* 1. *Isaiah*, *Chap.* 1. and *Chap.* 6. *Luke*, 22 and 23 *Chapters*. *Romans*, *Chap.* 8. 2 *Epist.* to *Timothy;* 2. *Epist.* of *John;* and the *Epistle* of *Jude*.

After that he had thus painfully and faithfully spent fifteen years in the Work of the Ministry, He that holds the Stars in his right hand, had more work for him to do elswhere; and therefore the rage of Satan and wrath of men must be suffered to break forth, untill this choice Instrument had his mouth stopped in unrighteousness. The *Lecture* which he kept at *Prescot* caused him to be much taken notice of, and so was the more unto the Adversaries of the Truth an object of Envy. *Magnam famam & magnam quietem eodem tempore nemo potest acquirere.* Quint.[3] Wherefore Complaints being made against him for Non-Conformity to the Ceremonies, he was by the *Prelates Suspended*. This was in *August*, *Anno* 1633. Under this Suspension he continued untill *November* following: But then, by means of the Intercession of some Gentlemen in *Lancashire*, and by the Influence of *Simon Byby* (a near Alliance of the Bishops) he was restored again to his Publick Ministry. After his Restauration he more fully searched into, and also in his Ministry handled the Points of *Church-Discipline*. And God gave him in those dayes not onely to see, but also to Instruct others in the Substance of the *Congregationall-Way*, which came to pass by his much reading of the holy Scriptures, and his being very conversant in the Writings of *Cartwright*, *Parker*, *Baynes*, and *Ames*.[4] But this restored Liberty continued not long; for *Anno* 1634. Bishop *Neal* (he who was sometimes by King *James* pleasantly admonished of his Preaching Popery, because by his carriage he taught the people to pray for a blessing upon his dead Predecessor) being now become *Archbishop of York*, sent his Visitors into *Lancashire;* of whom Doctor *Cousins* (whose *Cozening Devotions* Mr. *Pryn* [5] hath made notorious to the world) was one: These Visitors being come into the Country . . . kept their Courts at *Wigan;* where, amongst many other unrighteous proceedings, & having Mr. *Mather* convened before them, they passed a Sentence of *Suspension* against him, meerly for his *Non-Conformity* to the Inventions of men in the Worship of God. It was marvellous to see how God was with him, causing a Spirit of Courage and of Glory to rest upon him, and filling him with wisdome when he stood before those Judges, who were not willing that he should speak for himself, or declare the Reasons which convinced his Conscience of the unlawfulness of that *Conformity* which they required. Concerning the Lords presence with him at that time, himself doth in a Manuscript left in his Study thus express it: *In the passages of that day, I have this to bless the Name of God for, that the terrour of their threatning words, of their Pursevants, and of the rest of their Pomp, did not so terrifie my minde, but that I could stand before them without being daunted in the least measure, but answered for my self such words of truth and soberness as the Lord put into my mouth, not being afraid of their faces at all: which supporting and comforting presence of the Lord I count not much less mercy, then if I had been altogether preserved out of their hands.*

Being thus silenced from Publick Preaching the Word, means was again used by Mr. *Mathers* friends to obtain his Liberty; but all in vain. The Visitor asked how long he had been a Minister? Answer was made, That he had been in the Ministry fifteen years. And (said he) how often hath he worn the Surpless? Answer was returned, That he had never worn it. *What* (said the *Visitor*, swearing as he spake it) *preach Fifteen years and never wear a Surpless? It had been better for him that he had gotten Seven Bastards.* This was a Visitors judgement. . . .

Wherefore the case being thus, he betook himself to a private life: and no hope being left of enjoying Liberty again in his Native Land; foreseeing also (*Sapiens Divinat*) [6] the approaching Calamities of *England*, he meditated a Removall into *New-England*. . . .

During the time of his Pilgrimage in *New-England* he under-went not so many Changes, as before that he had done; for he never removed his Habitation out of *Dorchester*, albeit he had once serious thoughts that way, by reason that his old people in *Toxteth*, after that the *Hierarchy* was deposed in *England*, sent to him, desiring his return to them: But *Dorchester* was in no wise willing to forgoe their interest in him, therefore he left them not. Nevertheless, he did in *New-England* (as in a Wilderness might be expected) experience many Trials of his Faith and Patience. That which of outward Afflictions did most agrieve him, was the Death of his dear Wife, who had been for so many years the greatest outward Comfort and Blessing which he did enjoy: Which Affliction was the more grievous, in that she being a Woman of singular Prudence for the Management of Affairs, had taken off from her Husband all Secular Cares, so that he wholly devoted himself to his Study, and to Sacred Imployments. After he had continued in the state of Widowhood a year and half, he again changed his Condition, and was Married to the pious Widow of that deservedly Famous Man of God Mr. *John Cotton;* [7] and her did God make a Blessing and a Comfort to him during the remainder of his dayes.

Old Age now being come upon him, he was sensible of the Infirmities thereof, being in his latter years something thick of Hearing: Also (as it was with great *Zanchy*) [8] the sight in one of his Eyes failed, seven years before his Death. Yet God gave him Health of Body and Vigour of Spirit in a wonderful measure, so as that in fifty years together, he was not by Sickness detained so much as one Lords-day from Publick Labours. Which continued Health (as to Natural causes) proceeded partly from his strong Constitution of Body, and partly from his accustoming himself to a plain and wholsome Diet. *Bona Diata est potior quovis Hippocrate.*[9] He never made use of any Physician, nor was he ever in all his life sick of any acute Disease. Onely the two last years of his *Life* he was sorely afflicted with that Disease which some have called *Flagellum Studiosorum*, viz.[10] *The Stone*, which at last brought him to an end of all his Labours and Sorrows.

Concerning the Time and Manner of his Sickness and Death, thus it was. There being some Differences in *Boston*,[11] Counsel from Neighbour-Churches was by some desired, to direct them in the Lord what should be done: Accordingly the Churches sent their Messengers; and *Dorchester* Church, amongst others, sent Mr. *Mather* their aged *Teacher*, who Assembled in *Boston*, *April* 13. 1669. He was, because of his Age, Gravity, Grace and Wisdome wherewith the Lord had endowed and adorned him, chosen the *Moderator* in that *Reverend Assembly*. For divers dayes after his being thus in *Consultation*, he enjoyed his Health as formerly, or rather better then for some time of late. But as *Luther* when Assembled in a *Synod* was surprized with a violent Fit of the Stone, whence he was forced to return home, his Friends having little hopes of his life; so it was with this holy man. For *April* 16. 1669. he was in the night, being then in his Sons house in *Boston*, taken exceeding ill through a totall stoppage of his Urine. The next morning he therefore returned home to *Dorchester*. Great was the favour of God towards him, that he should be *found about* such *a blessed Work* as then he was ingaged in, for the Lord found him sincerely and earnestly endeavouring to be a Peace-maker. His being thus taken when at a Synod, brings to minde that of the *German Phoenix;*

Viximus in Synodis, & jam moriemur in illis.[12]

Now as usually Providence so ordereth, that they who have been speaking all their lives long, shall not say much when they come to die: Blessed *Hooker* in his last Sickness, when Friends would have had him answered to some Enquiries which might have made for their Edification after he was gone, he referred them wholly to the things which he had taught them in his health, because then he had enough to do to grapple with his own bodily weakness, *&c.* Neither did this good man speak much in his last Sickness either to Friends or to his Children. Onely his Son who is now *Teacher* of a Church in *Boston*, coming to visit his Father, and perceiving the Symptomes of Death to be upon him, said unto him, *Sir, if there be any speciall thing which you would recommend unto me to do, in case the Lord should spare me upon the Earth, after you are in Heaven, I would intreat you to express it.* At the which, his Father making a little pause, and lifting up his eyes and hands to Heaven, replied, *A speciall thing which I would commend to you, is, Care concerning the Rising Generation in this Country, that they be brought under the Government of Christ in his Church; and that when grown up and qualified, they have Baptism for their Children. I must confess I have been defective as to practise, yet I have publickly declared my judgement, and manifested my desires to practise that which I think ought to be attended, but the Dissenting of some in our Church discouraged me. I have thought that persons might have Right to Baptism, and yet not to the Lords Supper; and I see no cause to alter my judgement as to that particular. And I still think that persons qualified according to the Fifth Proposition of the late Synod-Book, have Right to Baptism for their Children.*[13]

His bodily Pains continued upon him untill *April* 22. when in the Morning his Son aforementioned, coming to visit him, asked his Father if he knew him; to whom he Replied that he did, but was not able to speak any more to him: Whereupon his Son saying, *Now you will speedily be in the joy of your Lord;* His Father lifted up his hands, but could not speak. Not long after his Son again spoke to him, saying,

You will quickly see Jesus Christ, and that will make amends for all your pains and sorrows: At which words his Father again lifted up his hands; but after that he took notice of no person or thing, but continuing speechless untill about 10 *h. P.M.* he quietly breathed forth his last. Thus did that Light that had been shining in the Church above Fifty years, Expire.

As he was a man faithful and fearing God above many, so the Lord shewed great faithfulness unto him, both in making him serviceable unto the last, yea and continuing the vigour of his Spirit, and power of his Ministry. Few men, though young, are known to Preach with such vigour as he did but ten dayes before his death. Also the Lord was faithful and gracious to him, in respect of his Children. It was a special token of Divine favour unto some of the Ancients, that their Sons after them succeeded in the Ministry; so was it with the Fathers of *Gregory Nazianzen, Gregory Nyssen, Basil, Hilary, &c.* And the Lord cheered the heart of this his Servant in his old Age, by giving him to see most of his Sons imployed in the Ministry many years before their precious Father's decease. He left four Sons in that Work; one of whom, *viz.* Mr. *Eleazar Mather*, late Pastor of the Church at *Northampton* in *New-England*, went to his rest about three Moneths after his Father, with him to sound forth the praises of God amongst the Spirits of just men made perfect. The other three are yet surviving, *viz.* Mr. *Samuel Mather*, Teacher of a Church in *Dublin;* Mr. *Nathaniel Mather*, late Minister of *Barnstable* in *Devon*, and since in *Rotterdam* in *Holland;* and *Increase Mather* of *Boston* in *New-England*. . . .

His way of Preaching was plain, aiming to shoot his Arrows not over his peoples heads, but into their Hearts and Consciences. Whence he studiously avoided obscure phrases, Exotick words, or an unnecessary citation of Latine Sentences, which some men addict themselves to the use of. Mr. *Dod* was wont to say, That *so much Latine was so much flesh in a Sermon:* So did this humble man look upon the affectation of such things in a *Popular Auditory* to savour of Carnal wisdome. The Lord gave him an excellent faculty in making abstruse things plain, that in handling the deepest Mysteries he would accommodate himself to Vulgar Capacities, that even the meanest might learn something. He knew how to express καινὰ κοινῶς κὰι κοινὰ καινῶς.[14] He would often use that Saying, *Artis est celare Artem.*[15] And much approved that of *Austin; If* (said he) *I preach Learnedly, then onely the Learned and not the Unlearned can understand and profit by me; but if I preach plainly, then Learned and Unlearned both can understand, so I may profit all.* He was *Mighty in the Scriptures:* Whence Mr. *Hooker* would say of him, *My Brother* Mather *is a mighty man.* Also his usuall way of Delivery was very Powerful, Awakening, and Zealous; especially in his younger years, there being few men of so great strength of body as he, which together with his natural fervour of Spirit, being sanctified, made his Ministry the more powerful. And the Lord went forth with his Labours to the Conversion of many, both in *England* and in *New-England.* Yet though his way of Preaching was plain and zealous, it was moreover Substantial and very Judicious. Even in his beginning times, Mr. *Gillebrand* (a famous Minister in *Lancashire;* and the more famous, for that though he did exceedingly Stammer in his ordinary discourse, he would Pray and Preach as fluently as any man) once having heard him Preach, asked what his Name might be? And answer being made that his Name was *Mather;* Nay (said Mr. *Gillebrand*) call him *Matter*, for believe it this man hath Substance in him. Yea, such was his *Solidity of Judgement*, that some who were his Opposites, yet did therefore greatly respect and honour him. Doctor *Parr* (then Bishop in the Isle of *Man*) having heard Mr. *Mather* was Silenced, lamented it, saying, *If* Mather *be Silenced I am sorry for it, for he was a solid man, and the Church of God hath then a great loss. . . .*

It might be said of him, as was said of that blessed *Martyr*, that he was *sparing in his Diet, sparing in his Speech, most sparing of all of his Time.* He was very diligent both as to duties of general and particular Calling, which are indeed the two Pillars upon which Religion stands. As to his general Calling; He was much in Prayer, especially in his Study, where he oft-times spent whole dayes with God in suing for a Blessing upon himself and Children, and upon the people to whom he was related, and upon the whole Country where he lived. The Requests which upon such occasions he put up to God in Jesus Christ, and also how his heart was moved to believe that God heard him, he left (many of them) in writing amongst his private Papers, I suppose that so himself might have recourse unto those *Experiences* in a time of darkness and Temptation; also that his Sons after him might see by their Fathers Example, what it is to *walk before God.* Now what a loss is it to the world when such a Righteous man is taken away! Well might *Philo* and *Jerome* weep bitterly, when they heard of the death of any such men, because it portended evil to the places where they had lived, and served God. As he was much in Prayer, so he was very frequent in *Hearing the Word.* It was his manner to attend several Lectures in Neighbour-Congregations, untill his Disease made him unable to ride; yea and usually even to his old Age (as did Mr. *Hildersham*[16]) he took Notes from those whom he heard, professing that he found profit in it.

As to his particular Calling, he was even from his youth a hard Student. Yea his minde was so intent upon his Work and Studies, that the very morning before he died, he importuned those Friends that watched with him to help him into his Study: They urging that he was not able to go so farre, he desired them to help him and try; which they did: but ere he was come to the door of his Lodging-room, *I see* (saith he) *I am not able, yet I have not been in my Study several dayes, and is it not a lamentable thing that I should lose so much time?* After his entrance upon the Ministry, he was not onely in *England* (as hath been said) but in *New-England* abundant in Labours: for except when he had an Assistant with him (which was seldome) he Preached twice every Lords-day; and a Lecture once a fortnight, besides many occasionall Sermons both in Publick and in Private. Also he was much exercised in answering many practical *Cases of Conscience*, and in Polemical, especially Disciplinary Discourses. In his Publick Ministry in *Dorchester* he went over *The Book of Genesis to Chap.* 38. *Psalm* 16. *The whole Book of the Prophet Zechariah. Matthews Gospel*, to *Chap.* 15. 1. *Epist.* to *Thess. Chap.* 5. *And the whole Second Epistle of* Peter; *his Notes whereon he reviewed, and Transcribed for the Press*, not many years before his decease.

Notwithstanding those rare Gifts and Graces wherewith the Lord had adorned him, he was exceeding low and little in his own eyes. Some have thought that his greatest errour was, that he did not magnifie his Office, as he might and sometimes should have done. If a man must erre, it is good erring on that hand. *Humble enough, and good enough*, was the frequent saying of a great Divine. And another observeth, *That every man hath just as much and no more true worth in him, as he hath Humility. Austine* being asked which was the most excellent grace, answered, *Humility;* and which was the next, answered, *Humility;* and which was the third, replied again, *Humility.* That indeed is *Comprehensively All*, being of great price in the sight of God; And if so, Mr. Mather was a man of much Reall Worth.

COTTON MATHER, 1663–1728

[For Cotton Mather's life see p. 162. This text is from *Magnalia Christi Americana* (London, 1702), Book III. John Eliot was born at Widford, Herts, 1604; emigrated in 1631 and was ordained teacher of the church at Roxbury in 1632; he died May 21, 1690. As Mather's account makes clear, he was a leader of New England Puritanism, not because like Cotton and Hooker he was a profound intellect, but because he incarnated the Puritan ideal of saintly piety.]

LIFE OF JOHN ELIOT

The Birth, Age, and Family of Mr. Eliot.

THE INSPIRED *Moses*, relating the Lives of those Anti Diluvian Patriarchs, in whom the Church of God, and Line of Christ was continued, through the first Sixteen hundred Years of Time, recites little but their *Birth*, and their *Age*, and their *Death*, and their *Sons* and *Daughters*. If those Articles would satisfie the Appetites and Enquiries of such as come to read the Life of our *Eliot*, we shall soon have dispatch'd the Work now upon our Hands.

The *Age*, with the *Death* of this Worthy Man, has been already terminated, in the Ninetieth Year of the present Century, and the Eighty sixth Year of his own Pilgrimage. And for his *Birth*, it was at a Town in *England;* the Name whereof I cannot presently recover; nor is it necessary for me to look back so far as the place of his *Nativity;* any more than 'tis for me to recite the Vertues of his *Parentage*, of which he said, *Vix ea nostra voco:* [1] Tho' indeed the pious Education which they gave him, caused him in his Age, to write these Words: *I do see that it was a great Favour of God unto me, to season my first Times with the Fear of God, the Word, and Prayer.*

The *Atlantick Ocean*, like a River of *Lethe*, may easily cause us to forget many of the things that happened on the other side. Indeed the *Nativity* of such a Man, were an Honour worthy the Contention of as many *Places*, as laid their Claims unto the famous *Homer's:* But whatever *Places* may challenge a share in the Reputation of having enjoy'd the *first Breath* of our *Eliot*, it is *New-England* that with most Right can call him *Hers;* his *best Breath*, and afterwards his *last Breath* was here; and here 'twas, that God bestow'd upon him *Sons and Daughters.*

He came to *New-England* in the Month of *November*, *A.D.* 1631. among those blessed old Planters, which laid the Foundations of a remarkable Country, devoted unto the Exercise of the Protestant Religion, in its purest and highest Reformation. He left behind him in *England*, a Vertuous young Gentlewoman, whom he had pursued and purposed a *Marriage* unto; and she coming hither the Year following, that Marriage was consummated in the Month of *October*, *A.D.* 1632.

This *Wife of his Youth* lived with him until she became to him also the *Staff of his Age;* and she left him not until about three or four Years before his own Departure to those Heavenly Regions, where they now together *see Light.* She was a Woman very eminent, both for *Holiness* and *Usefulness*, and she excelled most of the *Daughters that have done vertuously*. Her Name was *Anne*, and *Gracious* was her Nature. God made her a rich Blessing, not only to her *Family*, but also to her *Neighbourhood;* and when at last she died, I heard and saw her Aged Husband, who else very rarely wept, yet now with Tears over the Coffin, before the Good People, a vast Confluence of which were come to her Funeral, say, *Here lies my dear, faithful, pious, prudent, prayerful Wife; I shall go to her, and she not return to me*. My Reader will of his own accord excuse me, from bestowing any further *Epitaphs* upon that *gracious* Woman. . . .

Mr. Eliot's Early Conversion, Sacred Employment, and Just Removal into America.

But all that I have hitherto said, is no more than an entrance into the History of our *Eliot*. Such an *Enoch* as he, must have something more than these things recorded of him; his *Walk with God*, must be more largely laid before the World, as a thing that would bespeak us all to be *Followers* no less than we shall be *Admirers* of it.

He had not passed many *Turns* in the World, before he knew the meaning of a saving *Turn* from the Vanities of an Unregenerate State, unto God in Christ, by a true Repentance; he had the singular Happiness and Privilege of an *early Conversion* from the Ways, which *Original Sin* disposes all Men unto. One of the principal Instruments which the God of Heaven used in tingeing, and filling the Mind of this *chosen Vessel*, with good Principles, was that Venerable *Thomas Hooker*, whose Name in the Churches of the Lord Jesus, is, *As an Ointment poured forth;* even that *Hooker*, who having *Angled* many Scores of Souls into the Kingdom of Heaven, at last laid his Bones in our *New England;* it was an Acquaintance with *him*, that contributed more than a little to the Accomplishment of our *Elisha*, for that Work unto which the most High designed him. His liberal *Education*, having now the Addition of *Religion* to direct it, and improve it, it gave such a *Biass* to his young Soul, as quickly discovered it self in very signal Instances. His first Appearance in the World after his Education in the *University*, was in the too *difficult* and *unthankful* but very *necessary* Employment of a *School-Master*, which Employment he discharged with a good Fidelity. And as this *first Essay* of his Improvement was no more Disgrace unto him, than it was unto the famous *Hieron*, *Whitaker*, *Vines*, and others, that they *thus* began to be serviceable; so it rather prepared him, for the further Service, which his Mind was now set upon. He was of worthy Mr. *Thomas Wilson's* [2] Mind, that the calling of a *Minister* was the only one wherein a Man might be more serviceable to the Church of God, than in that of a *School-Master:* And with *Melchior Adam*, he reckoned, the Calling of a *School-Master, Pulverulentam, ac Molestissimam quidem, sed Deo longe gratissimam Functionem.*[3] Wherefore having dedicated himself unto God betimes, he could not reconcile himself to any lesser way of serving his Creator and Redeemer, than the Sacred *Ministry* of the Gospel; but alas, where should he have Opportunities for the Exercising of it? The *Laudian, Grotian,*[4] and *Arminian* Faction in the Church of *England,* in the Prosecution of their Grand Plot, for the reducing of *England* unto a moderate sort of *Popery,* had pitched upon *this* as one of their Methods for it; namely, to *creeple* as fast as they could, all the Learned, Godly, Painful Ministers of the Nation; and invent certain *Shibboleths* for the detecting and the destroying of such Men as were cordial Friends to the Reformation. 'Twas now a time when there were every day multiplied and imposed those unwarrantable *Ceremonies* in the Worship of God, by which the Conscience of our Considerate *Eliot* counted the *second Commandment* notoriously violated; 'twas now also a time, when some Hundreds of those Good People which had the Nick-name of *Puritans* put upon them, transported themselves, with their whole Families and Interests, into the Desarts of *America,* that they might here peaceably erect *Congregational Churches,* and therein attend and maintain all the pure Institutions of the Lord Jesus Christ; having the Encouragement of *Royal Charters,* that they should never have any Interruption in the Enjoyment of those *precious and pleasant things.* Here was a Prospect which quickly determined the devout Soul of our young *Eliot,* unto a Remove into *New-England,* while it was yet a *Land not sown;* he quickly lifted himself among those valiant Souldiers of the Lord Jesus Christ, who cheerfully encountred first the Perils of the *Atlantick Ocean,* and then the Fatigues of the *New-English Wilderness,* that they might have an undisturbed Communion with him in his Appointments here. And thus did he betimes procure himself the Consolation of having afterwards and for ever a Room in that Remembrance of God, *I remember thee, the Kindness of thy Youth, and the Love of thine Espousals, when thou wentest after me into the Wilderness.*

On his first Arrival to *New-England,* he soon joined himself unto the Church at *Boston;* 'twas *Church-work* that was his Errand hither, Mr. *Wilson,* the Pastor of that Church, was gone back into *England,* that he might perfect the Settlement of his Affairs; and in his Absence, young Mr. *Eliot* was he that supplied his place. Upon the Return of Mr. *Wilson,* that Church was intending to have made Mr. *Eliot* his Collegue, and their Teacher; but it was diverted. Mr. *Eliot* had engaged unto a select Number of his Pious and Christian Friends in

England, that if they should come into these Parts before he should be in the Pastoral Care of any other People, he would give himself to *Them*, and be for *Their* Service. It happened, that these Friends transported themselves hither, the Year after him; and chose their Habitation at the Town which they called *Roxbury*. A Church being now gathered at this place, he was in a little while *Ordained* unto the Teaching and Ruling of that Holy Society. So, 'twas in the Orb of that Church that we had him as a *Star fixed* for very near Threescore Years; it only remains that we now observe what was his *Magnitude* all this while, and how he performed his *Revolution*. . . .

His Family-Government.

The Apostle *Paul*, reciting and requiring Qualifications of a *Gospel Minister*, gives Order, that he be *The Husband of one Wife, and one that ruleth well his own House, having his Children in subjection with all gravity.* It seems, that a Man's Carriage in his *own House* is a *part*, or at least a *sign*, of his due Deportment in the *House of God;* and then, I am sure, our *Eliot*'s was very Exemplary. That *one Wife* which was given to him truly *from the Lord*, he loved, prized, cherished, with a *Kindness* that notably represented the Compassion which he (thereby) taught his Church to expect from the Lord Jesus Christ; and after he had lived with her for more than half an Hundred Years, he followed her to the Grave with *Lamentations* beyond those, which the Jews from the figure of a Letter in the Text, affirm, that *Abraham* deplored his aged *Sarah* with; her Departure made a deeper Impression upon him than what any common Affliction could. His whole Conversation with her, had that *Sweetness*, and that *Gravity* and *Modesty* beautifying of it, that every one called them *Zachary* and *Elizabeth*. His Family was a little *Bethel*, for the Worship of God constantly and exactly maintained in it; and unto the daily Prayers of the Family, his manner was to prefix the *Reading* of the *Scripture;* which being done, 'twas also his manner to make his young People to chuse a certain Passage in the Chapter, and give him some *Observation* of their own upon it. By this Method he did mightily *sharpen* and *improve*, as well as *try*, their Understandings, and endeavour to make them *wise unto Salvation*. He was likewise very strict in the Education of his Children, and more careful to mend any *error* in their Hearts and Lives, than he could have been to cure a *Blemish* in their Bodies. No *Exorbitancies* or *Extravagancies* could find a Room under his Roof, nor was his House any other than a *School of Piety;* one might have there seen a perpetual mixture of a *Spartan* and a *Christian* Disciple. Whatever Decay there might be upon *Family-Religion* among us, as for our *Eliot*, we *knew him, that he would command his Children, and his Houshold after him, that they should keep the Way of the Lord.*

His Way of Preaching.

Such was he in his *lesser Family!* And in his *greater Family*, he manifested still more of his Regards to the Rule of a *Gospel-Ministry.* To his Congregation, he was a *Preacher* that made it his Care, to *give every one their Meat in due Season.* It was *Food* and not *Froth;* which in his publick Sermons, he entertained the Souls of his People with, he did not *starve* them with empty and windy Speculations, or with such things as *Animum non dant, quia non habent;* [5] much less did he *kill* them with such *Poyson* as is too commonly exposed by the *Arminian* and *Socinian* Doctors that have too often sat in *Moses*'s Chair. His way of *Preaching* was very *plain;* so that the very *Lambs* might wade, into his Discourses on those Texts and Themes, wherein *Elephants* might *swim;* and herewithal, it was very *powerful*, his Delivery was always very graceful and grateful; but when he was to use reproofs and warnings against any *Sin*, his Voice would rise into a *Warmth* which had in it very much of *Energy* as well as *Decency;* he would sound the *Trumpets* of God against all *Vice*, with a most penetrating Liveliness, and make his Pulpit another Mount *Sinai*, for the Flashes of Lightning therein display'd against the Breaches of the *Law* given upon that *Burning Mountain.* And I observed, that there was usually a special Fervour in the Rebukes which he bestow'd upon *Carnality*, a carnal Frame and Life in Professors of Religion; when he was to brand the Earthly-mindedness of *Church-Members*, and the Allowance and the Indulgence which they often gave unto themselves in sensual Delights, here he was a right *Boanerges;* he then spoke, as 'twas said one of the Ancients did, *Quot verba tot Fulmina*, as many *Thunderbolts* as *Words.*

It was another Property of his *Preaching*, that there was evermore much of Christ in it; and with *Paul*, he could say, *I determined to know nothing but Jesus Christ;* having that Blessed Name in his Discourses, with a Frequency like that, with which *Paul* mentions it in his *Epistles.* As 'twas noted of Dr. *Bodly*, that whatever Subject he were upon, in the Application still his Use of it would be, *to drive Men unto the Lord Jesus Christ;* in like manner, the Lord Jesus Christ was the Loadstone which gave a touch to all the Sermons of our *Eliot;* a Glorious, Precious, Lovely *Christ* was the Point of Heaven which they still verged unto. From this *Inclination* it was, that altho' he Printed several *English* Books before he dy'd, yet his Heart seemed not so much in any of them, as in that serious and savoury Book of his, Entituled, *The Harmony of the*

Gospels, in the Holy History of Jesus Christ.[6] From hence also 'twas, that he would give that Advice to young Preachers, *Pray let there be much of Christ in your Ministry;* and when he had heard a Sermon, which had any special Relish of a Blessed Jesus in it, he would say thereupon, *O blessed be God, that we have Christ so much and so well preached in poor* New-England!

Moreover, he lik'd no *Preaching*, but what had been *well studied* for; and he would very much commend a Sermon which he could perceive had required some good *Thinking* and *Reading* in the Author of it. I have been present, when he has unto a Preacher then just come home from the Assembly with him, thus expressed himself, *Brother, there was Oyl required for the Service of the Sanctuary; but it must be beaten Oyl; I praise God, that I saw your Oyl so well beaten to day; the Lord help us always by good Study to beat our Oyl, that there may be no knots in our Sermons left undissolved, and that there may a clear light be thereby given in the House of God!* And yet he likewise look'd for something in a Sermon beside and beyond the meer *Study* of *Man;* he was for having the *Spirit* of *God*, breathing in it and with it; and he was for speaking *those* things, from *those* Impressions and with *those* Affections, which might compel the Hearer to say, *The Spirit of God was here!* I have heard him complain, *It is a sad thing, when a Sermon shall have that one thing,* The Spirit of God *wanting in it. . . .*

ELIOT AS AN EVANGELIST.

The Titles of a *Christian* and of a *Minister*, have rendred our *Eliot* considerable; but there is one memorable Title more, by which he has been signalized unto us. An Honourable Person[7] did once in Print put the Name of an *Evangelist* upon him; whereupon in a Letter of his to that Person afterwards Printed, his Expressions were, "There is a *Redundancy*, where you put the Title of *Evangelist* upon me; I beseech you to suppress all such things; let us do and speak and carry all things with Humility; it is the Lord who hath done what is done; and it is most becoming the Spirit of Jesus Christ to lift up him, and lay our selves low; I wish that Word could be obliterated." My Reader sees what a Caution Mr. *Eliot* long since entred against our giving him the Title of an *Evangelist;* but his *Death* has now made it safe, and his *Life* had long made it just, for us to acknowledge him with such a Title. I know not whether that of an *Evangelist*, or one separated for the Employment of Preaching the Gospel in such Places whereunto Churches have hitherto been gathered, be not an *Office* that should be continued in our Days; but this I know, that our *Eliot* very notably did the *Service* and *Business* of such an Officer.

Cambden[8] could not reach the Heighth of his Conceit, who bore in his *Shield* a Salvage of *America*, with his Hand pointing to the *Sun*, and this Motto, *Mihi Accessu, Tibi Recessu.* Reader, Prepare to behold this *Device* Illustrated!

The Natives of the Country now Possessed by the *New-Englanders*, had been forlorn and wretched *Heathen* ever since their first herding here; and tho' we know not *When* or *How* those *Indians* first became Inhabitants of this mighty Continent, yet we may guess that probably the Devil decoy'd those miserable Salvages hither, in hopes that the Gospel of the Lord Jesus Christ would never come here to destroy or disturb his *Absolute Empire* over them. But our *Eliot* was in such ill Terms with the Devil, as to alarm him with sounding the *Silver Trumpets* of Heaven in his Territories, and make some Noble and Zealous Attempts towards outing him of his Ancient Possessions here. There were, I think, Twenty several *Nations* (if I may call them so) of *Indians* upon that spot of Ground, which fell under the Influence of our *Three United Colonies;* and our *Eliot* was willing to rescue as many of them as he could, from that old usurping *Landlord* of *America*, who is *by the Wrath of God, the Prince of this World.*

I cannot find that any besides the Holy Spirit of God, first moved him to the blessed Work of *Evangelizing* these perishing *Indians;* 'twas that Holy Spirit which laid before his Mind the Idea of that which was on the *Seal* of the Massachuset Colony; *A poor Indian having a Label going from his Mouth, with a,* COME OVER AND HELP US. It was the Spirit of our Lord Jesus Christ, which enkindled in him a *Pitty* for the dark Souls of these Natives, whom the *God of this World had blinded,* through all the By-past Ages. He was none of those that make, *The Salvation of the Heathen,* an Article of their *Creed;* but (setting aside the unrevealed and extraordinary Steps which the *Holy one of Israel* may take out of his *usual Paths*) he thought men to be *lost* if our *Gospel* be hidden from them; and he was of the same Opinion with one of the Ancients, who said, *Some have endeavoured to prove* Plato *a Christian, till they prove themselves little better than Heathens.* It is indeed a Principle in the Turkish *Alcoran,* That *Let a Man's Religion be what it will, he shall be saved, if he conscientiously live up to the Rules of it:* But our *Eliot* was no *Mahometan.* He could most heartily subscribe to that Passage in the Articles of the Church of *England.* "They are to be held accursed, who presume to say, that every Man shall be saved by the Law or Sect which he professeth, so that he be diligent to frame his Life according to that Law, and Light of Nature; for Holy Scripture doth set out unto us, only the Name of Jesus Christ, whereby Men must be saved."

And it astonished him to see many dissembling Subscribers of those Articles, while they have grown up to such a *Phrensy*, as to deny peremptorily all *Church-state*, and all *Salvation* to all that are not under *Diocesan Bishops*, yet at the same time to grant that the *Heathen* might be saved without the Knowledge of the Lord Jesus Christ. . . .

The exemplary *Charity* of this excellent Person in this important Affair, will not be seen in its due Lustres, unless we make some Reflections upon several Circumstances which he beheld these forlorn *Indians* in. Know then, that these doleful Creatures are the veriest *Ruines of Mankind*, which are to be found any where upon the Face of the Earth. No such *Estates* are to be expected among them, as have been the *Baits* which the pretended *Converters* in other Countries have snapped at. One might see among them, what an *hard Master* the Devil is, to the most devoted of his *Vassals!* These abject Creatures, live in a Country full of *Mines;* we have already made entrance upon our *Iron;* and in the very Surface of the Ground among us, 'tis thought there lies *Copper* enough to supply all this World; besides other Mines hereafter to be exposed; but our shiftless *Indians* were never Owners of so much as a *Knife*, till we come among them; their Name for an *English-man* was a *Knife-man;* Stone was instead of Metal for their *Tools;* and for their *Coins*, they have only little *Beads* with Holes in them to string them upon a *Bracelet*, whereof some are *white;* and of these there go six for a Penny; some are *black* or *blew;* and of these, go *three* for a Penny; this *Wampam*, as they call it, is made of the *Shell-fish*, which lies upon the Sea Coast continually.

The[y] live in a Country, where *we* now have all the Conveniencies of human Life: But as for *them*, their *housing* is nothing but a few *Mats* ty'd about *Poles* fastened in the Earth, where a good *Fire* is their *Bed Clothes* in the coldest Seasons; their *Clothing* is but a Skin of a Beast, covering their *Hind-parts*, their *Fore-parts* having but a little Apron, where Nature calls for Secrecy; their *Diet* has not a greater Dainty than their *Nokehick*, that is a spoonful of their *parch'd meal*, with a spoonful of *Water*, which will strengthen them to travel a Day together; except we should mention the Flesh of *Deers*, *Bears*, *Mose*, *Rackoons*, and the like, which they have when they can *catch* them; as also a little *Fish*, which if they would preserve, 'twas by *drying*, not by *salting;* for they had not a grain of *Salt* in the World, I think, till we bestow'd it on them. Their *Physick* is, excepting a few odd *Specificks*, which some of them Encounter certain Cases with, nothing hardly, but an *Hot-House*, or a *Powaw;* their *Hot-House* is a little *Cave* about eight foot over, where after they have terribly heated it, a Crew of them go sit and sweat and smoke for an Hour together, and then immediately run into some very cold adjacent Brook, without the least Mischief to them; 'tis this way they recover themselves from some Diseases, particularly from the *French;* but in most of their dangerous Distempers, 'tis a *Powaw* that must be sent for; that is, a *Priest*, who has more Familiarity with Satan than his Neighbours; this Conjurer comes and Roars, and Howls, and uses Magical Ceremonies over the Sick Man, and will be well paid for it, when he has done; if this don't effect the Cure, the *Man's Time is come, and there's an end.*

They live in a Country full of the best *Ship-Timber* under Heaven: But never saw a *Ship*, till some came from *Europe* hither; and then they were scar'd out of their Wits, to see the *Monster* come sailing in, and spitting Fire with a mighty noise, out of her floating side; they cross the Water in *Canoo's*, made sometimes of *Trees*, which they burn and hew, till they have hollow'd them; and sometimes of *Barks*, which they stitch into a light sort of a Vessel, to be easily carried over Land; if they over-set, it is but a little paddling like a Dog, and they are soon where they were.

Their way of living, is infinitely Barbarous: The Men are most abominably *slothful;* making their poor *Squaws*, or Wives, to plant and dress, and barn, and beat their Corn, and build their *Wigwams* for them; which perhaps may be the reason of their extraordinary Ease in Childbirth. In the mean time, their chief Employment, when they'll *condescend* unto any, is that of *Hunting;* wherein they'll go out some scores, if not Hundreds of them in a Company, driving all before them.

They continue in a Place, till they have burnt up all the *Wood* thereabouts, and then they pluck up Stakes; to follow the *Wood*, which they cannot fetch home unto themselves; hence when they enquire about the *English*, *Why come they hither!* They have themselves very Learnedly determined the Case, '*Twas because we wanted Firing.* No *Arts* are understood among them, unless just so far as to maintain their Brutish Conversation, which is little more than is to be found among the very *Bevers* upon our Streams. . . .

This was the miserable People, which our *Eliot* propounded unto himself, to teach and save! And he had a double Work incumbent on him; he was to make Men of them, e'er he could hope to see them *Saints;* they must be *civilized* e'er they could be *Christianized;* he could not, as *Gregory* once of our Nation, see any thing *Angelical* to bespeak his Labours for their Eternal Welfare, all among them was *Diabolical.* To think on raising a Number of these hideous Creatures, unto the *Elevations* of our Holy Religion, must argue more than common or little Sentiments in the Undertaker; but the Faith of an *Eliot* could encounter it! . . .

The *First Step* which he judg'd necessary now to be taken by him, was to learn the *Indian* Language; for he saw them so stupid and senseless, that they would never do so much as enquire after the Religion of the Strangers now come into their Country, much less would they so far imitate us, as to leave off their beastly way of living, that they might be Partakers of any Spiritual Advantage by us: Unless we could first address them in a *Language* of their own. Behold, new Difficulties to be surmounted by our indefatigable *Eliot!* He hires a Native to teach him this exotick Language, and with a laborious Care and Skill, reduces it into a *Grammar* which afterwards he published. There is a Letter or two of our Alphabet, which the *Indians* never had in *theirs;* tho' there were enough of the *Dog* in their *Temper*, there can scarce be found an R in their *Language;* (any more than in the Language of the *Chinese*, or of the *Greenlanders*) save that the *Indians* to the Northward, who have a peculiar *Dialect*, pronounce an R where an N is pronounced by our *Indians;* but if their *Alphabat* be *short*, I am sure the *Words* composed of it are long enough to tire the Patience of any Scholar in the World; they are *Sesquipedalia Verba*,[9] of which their *Lingua* is composed; one would think, they had been growing ever since *Babel*, unto the Dimensions to which they are now extended. For instance, if my Reader will count how many Letters there are in this one Word, *Nummatchekodtantamooonganunnonash*, when he has done, for his Reward I'll tell him, it signifies no more in *English*, than *our Lusts*, and if I were to translate, *our Loves;* it must be nothing shorter than *Noowomantammooonkanunonnash*. Or, to give my Reader a longer Word than either of these, *Kummogkodonattoottummooetiteaongannunnonash*, is in English, *Our Question:* But I pray, Sir, count the Letters! Nor do we find in all this Language the least Affinity to, or Derivation from any *European* Speech that we are acquainted with. I know not what Thoughts it will produce in my Reader, when I inform him, that once finding that the *Dæmons* in a possessed young Woman, understood the *Latin* and *Greek* and *Hebrew* Languages, my Curiosity led me to make Trial of this *Indian* Language, and the *Dæmons* did seem as if they did not understand it. This tedious Language our *Eliot* (the Anagram of whose Name was TOILE) quickly became a Master of; he employ'd a pregnant and witty *Indian*, who also spoke *English* well, for his Assistance in it; and compiling some Discourses by his Help, he would single out a *Word*, a *Noun*, a *Verb*, and pursue it through all its Variations: Having finished his Grammar, at the close he writes, *Prayers and Pains thro'*

Faith in Christ Jesus will do any thing! And being by his *Prayers* and *Pains* thus furnished, he set himself in the Year 1646. to preach the Gospel of our Lord Jesus Christ, among these Desolate Outcasts. . . .

Mr. Eliot's Way of Opening the Mysteries of the Gospel, to Our Indians.

'Twas in the Year 1646, that Mr. *Eliot*, accompany'd by three more, gave a Visit unto an Assembly of *Indians*, of whom he desired a Meeting at such a Time and Place, that he might lay before them the Things of their Eternal Peace. After a serious *Prayer*, he gave them a *Sermon* which continued about a Quarter above an Hour, and contained the principal Articles of the Christian Religion, applying all to the Condition of the *Indians* present. Having done, he asked of them, Whether *they understood?* And with a General Reply they answered, *They understood all*. He then began what was his usual Method afterwards in treating with them; that is, he caused them to propound such *Questions* as they pleas'd unto himself; and he gave wise and good *Answers* to them all. Their *Questions* would often, tho' not always, refer to what he had newly preached; and he this way not only made a *Proof* of their profiting by his Ministry, but also gave an Edge to what he delivered unto them. Some of their *Questions* would be a little *Philosophical*, and required a good Measure of Learning in the Minister concerned with them; but for this our *Eliot* wanted not. He would also put proper *Questions* unto them, and at one of his first Exercises with them, he made the Young Ones capable of regarding those three Questions,

Q. 1. *Who made you and all the World?*
Q. 2. *Who do you look should save you from Sin and Hell?*
Q. 3. *How many Commandments has the Lord given you to keep?*

It was his Wisdom that he began with them upon such Principles as they themselves had already some Notions of; such as that of an *Heaven* for good, and *Hell* for bad People, when they dy'd. It broke his gracious Heart within him to see, what Floods of Tears fell from the Eyes of several among those degenerate Salvages, at the first Addresses which he made unto them; yea, from the very worst of them all. He was very inquisitive to learn who were the *Powawes*, that is, the *Sorcerers*, and *Seducers*, that maintained the Worship of the Devil in any of their Societies; and having in one of his first Journeys to them, found out one of those Wretches, he made the *Indian* come unto him, and said, *Whether do you suppose* God, *or* Chepian (i.e. *the Devil*) *to be the Author of all Good?* The Conjurer answered, *God.* Upon this he added with a stern

Countenance, *Why do you pray to* Chepian *then?* And the poor Man was not able to stand or speak before him; but at last made Promises of Reformation. . . .

THE CONCLUSION: OR, ELIOT EXPIRING.

By this time, I have doubtless made my Readers loth to have me tell what now remains of this little History; doubtless they are wishing that this *John* might have *Tarried unto the Second Coming of our Lord.* But, alas, All-devouring *Death* at last snatch'd him from us, and slighted all those Lamentations of ours, *My Father, My Father, the Chariots of Israel, and the Horsemen thereof!*

When he was become a sort of *Miles Emeritus*,[10] and began to draw near his *End*, he grew still more Heavenly, more Savoury, more Divine, and scented more of the Spicy Country at which he was ready to put ashore. As the Historian observes of *Tiberius*, That when his *Life* and *Strength* were going from him, his *Vice* yet remained with him; on the contrary, the *Grace* of this Excellent Man rather increased than abated, when every thing else was dying with him. 'Tis too usual with *Old Men*, that when they are past *Work*, they are least sensible of their Inabilities and Incapacities, and can scarce endure to see another succeeding them in any part of their Office. But our *Eliot* was of a Temper quite contrary thereunto; for finding many Months before his Expiration, That he had not Strength enough to Edify his Congregation with Publick *Prayers*, and *Sermons*, he importun'd his People with some Impatience to call another Minister; professing himself unable to die with Comfort, until he could see a good Successor ordained, settled, fixed among them. For this Cause, he also cry'd mightily unto the Lord Jesus Christ our *Ascended Lord*, that he would give such a *Gift* unto *Roxbury*, and he sometimes call'd his whole Town together to join with him in a *Fast* for such a Blessing. As the Return of their Supplications, our Lord quickly bestow'd upon them, a Person young in Years, but old in Discretion, Gravity, and Experience; and one whom the Church of *Roxbury* hopes to find, *A Pastor after God's own Heart.*

It was Mr. *Nehemiah Walter*, who being by the Unanimous Vote and Choice of the Church there, become the *Pastor* of *Roxbury*, immediately found the Venerable *Eliot* Embracing and Cherishing of him, with the tender Affections of a Father. The good Old Man like Old *Aaron*, as it were disrobed himself, with an unspeakable Satisfaction, when he beheld his Garments put upon a Son so dear unto him. After this, he for a Year or two before his Translation, could scarce be perswaded unto any *Publick Service*, but humbly pleaded, what none but he would ever have said, *It would be a Wrong to the Souls of the People, for him to do any thing among them, when they were supply'd so much to their Advantage otherwise.* If I mistake not, the last that ever he Preached was on a Publick *Fast;* when he fed his People with a very distinct and useful *Exposition* upon the Eighty Third Psalm; and he concluded with an Apology, begging his Hearers to pardon the *Poorness*, and *Meanness*, and *Brokenness*, (as he called it) of his Meditations; but added he, *My dear Brother here, will by'nd by mend all.*

But altho' he thus dismissed himself as one so near to the Age of *Ninety*, might well have done, from his Publick Labours; yet he would not give over his Endeavours, in a more private Sphere, to *Do good unto all.* He had always been an Enemy to *Idleness;* any one that should look into the little *Diary* that he kept in his *Almanacks*, would see that there was with him, *No Day without a Line;* and he was troubled particularly, when he saw how much *Time* was devoured by that Slavery to *Tobacco*, which too many debase themselves unto; and now he grew old, he was desirous that his *Works* should hold pace with his *Life;* the less *Time* he saw *left*, the less was he willing to have *lost*. He imagined that he could now do nothing to any purpose in any Service for God; and sometimes he would say with an Air peculiar to himself, *I wonder for what the Lord Jesus Christ lets me live; he knows that now I can do nothing for him!* And yet he could not forbear Essaying to *Do something* for his Lord; he conceived, that tho' the *English* could not be benefited by any Gifts which he now fancied himself to have only the *Ruines* of, yet who can tell but the *Negro's* might! He had long lamented it with a Bleeding and a Burning Passion, that the *English* used their *Negro*'s but as their *Horses* or their *Oxen*, and that so little Care was taken about their immortal Souls; he look'd upon it as a Prodigy, that any wearing the *Name* of *Christians*, should so much have the *Heart* of *Devils* in them, as to prevent and hinder the Instruction of the poor *Blackamores*, and confine the Souls of their miserable Slaves to a *Destroying Ignorance*, meerly for fear of thereby losing the Benefit of their Vassalage; but now he made a Motion to the *English* within two or three Miles of him, that at such a time and Place they would send their *Negro's* once a Week unto him: For he would then *Catechise* them, and *Enlighten* them, to the utmost of his Power in the Things of their Everlasting Peace; however, he did not live to make much Progress in this Undertaking. . . .

He fell into some Languishments attended with a *Fever*, which in a few days brought him into the *Pangs* (may I say? or *Joys*) of Death;

and while he lay in these, Mr. *Walter* coming to him, he said unto him, *Brother, Thou art welcome to my very Soul. Pray retire to thy Study for me, and give me leave to be gone;* meaning that he should not, by Petitions to Heaven for his Life, detain him here. It was in these Languishments, that speaking about the Work of the Gospel among the *Indians,* he did after this Heavenly manner express himself, *There is a Cloud* (said he) *a dark Cloud upon the Work of the Gospel among the poor* Indians. *The Lord revive and prosper that Work, and grant it may live when I am Dead. It is a Work, which I have been doing much and long about. But what was the Word I spoke last? I recal that Word,* My Doings *Alas, they have been poor and small, and lean Doings, and I'll be the Man that shall throw the first Stone at them all.*

It has been observed, That they who have spoke many considerable things in their *Lives,* usually speak few at their *Deaths.* But it was otherwise with our *Eliot,* who after much Speech of and for God in his *Life-time,* uttered some things little short of *Oracles* on his *Death-Bed,* which, 'tis a thousand Pities, they were not more exactly regarded and recorded. Those Authors that have taken the pains to Collect, *Apophthegmata Morientum,* have not therein been unserviceable to the Living; but the *Apophthegms* of a Dying *Eliot* must have had in them a *Grace* and a *Strain* truly extraor[di]nary; and indeed the *vulgar Error* of the signal sweetness in the Song of a *Dying Swan,* was a very Truth in our Expiring *Eliot;* his last Breath smelt strong of Heaven, and was Articled into none but very gracious Notes; one of the last whereof, was, *Welcome Joy!* and at last it went away calling upon the standers-by, to *Pray, pray, pray!* Which was the thing in which so vast a Portion of it, had been before Employ'd.

This was the Peace in the End of this *Perfect and upright Man;* thus was there another *Star* fetched away to be placed among the rest that the third Heaven is now enriched with. He had once, I think, a pleasant Fear, that the Old Saints of his Acquaintance, especially those two dearest Neighbours of his, *Cotton* of *Boston,* and *Mather* of *Dorchester,* which were got safe to Heaven before him, would suspect him to be gone the wrong way, because he staid so long behind them. But they are now together with a Blessed Jesus, *beholding of his Glory,* and celebrating the High Praises of him that has *call'd them into his marvellous Light.* Whether *Heaven* was any more *Heaven* to him, because of his finding there, so many *Saints,* with whom he once had his Desireable Intimacies, yea, and so many *Saints* which had been the Seals of his own Ministry in this lower World, I cannot say; but it would be *Heaven* enough unto him, to go unto that *Jesus,* whom he had lov'd, preach'd, serv'd, and in whom he had been long assured, there does *All Fullness dwell.* In that Heaven I now leave him: Not without *Grynæus*'s Pathetical Exclamations [*O beatum illum diem!*] "Blessed will be the Day, O Blessed the Day of our Arrival to the Glorious Assembly of Spirits, which this great Saint is now rejoicing with!"

Bereaved *New-England*, where are thy Tears, at this Ill-boding Funeral? We had a Tradition among us, "That the Country could never perish, as long as *Eliot* was alive." But into whose Hands must this *Hippo* fall, now the *Austin* of it is taken away? Our *Elisha* is gone, and now who must *next Year invade the Land?* The *Jews* have a Saying, *Quando Luminaria patiuntur Eclipsin, malum signum est mundo;* [11] But I am sure, 'tis a dismal *Eclipse* that has now befallen our *New-English* World. I confess, many of the Ancients fell into the Vanity of esteeming the Reliques of the *Dead Saints*, to be the *Towers* and *Ramparts* of the Places that enjoy'd them; and the *Dead Bodies* of two Apostles in the City, made the Poet cry out,

A Facie Hostili duo propugnacula præsunt.[12]

If the Dust of *dead Saints* could give us any Protection, we are not without it; here is a Spot of *American* Soyl that will afford a rich Crop of it, at the *Resurrection of the Just.* Poor *New-England* has been as *Glastenbury* of Old was called, *A Burying-place of Saints.* But we cannot see a more terrible Prognostick, than Tombs filling apace with such *Bones*, as those of the Renowned *Eliot*'s; the whole Building of this Country trembles at the Fall of such a Pillar.

SAMUEL SEWALL, 1652–1730

[For Sewall's life see p. 376. Text from *Collections of the Massachusetts Historical Society*, Fifth Series, Vols. V–VII.]

DIARY

JAN. 13, 1677. Giving my chickens meat, it came to my mind that I gave them nothing save Indian corn and water, and yet they eat it and thrived very well, and that that food was necessary for them, how mean soever, which much affected me and convinced what need I stood in of spiritual food, and that I should not nauseat daily duties of Prayer, &c.

Nov. 6, 1692. Joseph threw a knop of Brass and hit his Sister Betty on the forhead so as to make it bleed and swell; upon which, and for his playing at Prayer-Time, and eating when Return Thanks, I whipd him pretty smartly. When I first went in (call'd by his Grandmother) he sought to shadow and hide himself from me behind the head of the Cradle: which gave me the sorrowfull remembrance of Adam's carriage.

April 29, 1695. The morning is very warm and Sunshiny; in the Afternoon there is Thunder and Lightening, and about 2. P.M. a very extraordinary Storm of Hail, so that the ground was made white with it, as with the blossoms when fallen; 'twas as bigg as pistoll and Musquet Bullets; It broke of the Glass of the new House about 480 Quarrels [Squares] of the Front; of Mr. Sergeant's about as much; Col. Shrimpton, Major General, Gov[r]. Bradstreet, New Meetinghouse, Mr. Willard, &c. Mr. Cotton Mather dined with us, and was with me in the new Kitchen when this was; He had just been mentioning that more Ministers Houses than others proportionably had been smitten with Lightening; enquiring what the meaning of God should be in it. Many Hail-Stones broke throw the Glass and flew to the middle of the Room, or farther: People afterward Gazed upon the House to see its Ruins. I got Mr. Mather to pray with us after this awfull Providence; He told God He had broken the brittle part of our house, and prayd that we might be ready for the time when our Clay-Tabernacles should be broken. Twas a sorrowfull thing to me to see the house so far undon again before twas finish'd.

Jan. 13, 1696. When I came in, past 7. at night, my wife met me in the Entry and told me Betty had surprised them. I was surprised with the abruptness of the Relation. It seems Betty Sewall had given some signs of dejection and sorrow; but a little after dinner she burst out into an amazing cry, which caus'd all the family to cry too; Her Mother ask'd the reason; she gave none; at last said she was afraid she should goe to Hell, her Sins were not pardon'd. She was first wounded by my reading a Sermon of Mr. Norton's, about the 5th of Jan. Text Jn[o] 7. 34. Ye shall seek me and shall not find me. And those words in the Sermon, Jn[o] 8. 21. Ye shall seek me and shall die in your sins, ran in her mind, and terrified her greatly. And staying at home Jan. 12. she read out of Mr. Cotton Mather—Why hath Satan filled thy heart, which increas'd her Fear. Her Mother ask'd her whether she pray'd. She answer'd, Yes; but feared her prayers were not heard because her Sins not pardon'd. Mr. Willard though sent for timelyer, yet not being told of the message, . . . He came not till after I came home. He discoursed with Betty who could not give a distinct account, but was confused as his phrase was, and as had experienced in himself. Mr. Willard pray'd excellently. The Lord bring Light and Comfort out of this dark and dreadful Cloud, and Grant that Christ's being formed in my dear child, may be the issue of these painfull pangs.

Dec. 25, 1696. We bury our little daughter. In the chamber, Joseph in course reads Ecclesiastes 3[d] a time to be born and a time to die—Elisabeth, Rev. 22. Hanah, the 38th Psalm. I speak to each, as God helped, to our mutual comfort I hope. I order'd Sam. to read the 102. Psalm. Elisha Cooke, Edw. Hutchinson, John Baily, and Josia Willard bear my little daughter to the Tomb.

Note. Twas wholly dry, and I went at noon to see in what order things were set; and there I was entertain'd with a view of, and converse with, the Coffins of my dear Father Hull, Mother Hull, Cousin Quinsey, and my Six Children: for the little posthumous was now took up and set in upon that that stands on John's: so are three, one upon another twice, on the bench at the end. My Mother ly's on a lower bench, at the end, with head to her Husband's head: and I order'd little Sarah to be set on her Grandmother's feet. 'Twas an awfull yet pleasing Treat; Having said, The Lord knows who shall be brought hether next, I came away.

Jan. 14, 1697. Copy of the Bill I put up on the Fast day; giving it to Mr. Willard as he pass'd by, and standing up at the reading of it, and bowing when finished; in the Afternoon.

Samuel Sewall, sensible of the reiterated strokes of God upon himself and family; and being sensible, that as to the Guilt contracted upon the opening of the late commission of Oyer and Terminer at Salem (to which the order for this Day relates) he is, upon many accounts, more concerned than any that he knows of, Desires to take the Blame and shame of it, Asking pardon of men, And especially desiring prayers that God, who has an Unlimited Authority, would pardon that sin and all other his sins; personal and Relative: And according to his infinite Benignity, and Sovereignty, Not Visit the sin of him, or of any other, upon himself or any of his, nor upon the Land: But that He would powerfully defend him against all Temptations to Sin, for the future; and vouchsafe him the efficacious, saving Conduct of his Word and Spirit.

Jan. 26, 1697. I lodged at Charlestown, at Mrs. Shepards, who tells me Mr. Harvard built that house. I lay in the chamber next the street. As I lay awake past midnight, In my Meditation, I was affected to consider how long agoe God had made provision for my comfortable Lodging that night; seeing that was Mr. Harvards house: And that led me to think of Heaven the House not made with hands, which God for many Thousands of years has been storing with the richest furniture (saints that are from time to time placed there), and that I had some hopes of being entertain'd in that Magnificent Convenient Palace, every way fitted and furnished. These thoughts were very refreshing to me.

Oct. 1, 1697. Jer. Balchar's sons came for us to go to the Island. My Wife, through Indisposition, could not goe: But I carried Sam. Hannah, Elisa, Joseph, Mary and Jane Tapan: I prevail'd with Mr. Willard to goe, He carried Simon, Elisabeth, William, Margaret, and Elisa Tyng: Had a very comfortable Passage thither and home again; though against Tide: Had first Butter, Honey, Curds and Cream. For Dinner, very good Rost Lamb, Turkey, Fowls, Applepy. After Dinner sung the 121 Psalm. Note. A Glass of spirits my Wife sent stood upon a Joint-Stool which, Simon W. jogging, it fell down and broke all to shivers: I said twas a lively Emblem of our Fragility and Mortality. . . .

Jan. 14, 1701. Having been certified last night about 10. oclock of the death of my dear Mother at Newbury, Sam. and I set out with John Sewall, the Messenger, for that place. Hired Horses at Charlestown: set out about 10. aclock in a great Fogg. Din'd at Lewis's with Mr. Cushing of Salisbury. Sam. and I kept on in Ipswich Rode, John went to accompany Bro^{r} from Salem. About Mr. Hubbard's in Ipswich farms, they overtook us. Sam. and I lodg'd at Cromptons in Ipswich. Bro^{r} and John stood on for Newbury by Moon-shine. Jany. 15th Sam. and I set forward. Brother Northend meets us. Visit Aunt Northend, Mr. Payson. With Bro^{r} and sister we set forward for Newbury: where we find that day appointed for the Funeral: twas a very pleasant Comfortable day.

Bearers, Jno Kent of the Island, Lt Cutting Noyes, Deacon William Noyes, Mr. Peter Tappan, Capt. Henry Somersby, Mr. Joseph Woodbridge. I follow'd the Bier single. Then Bro^{r} Sewall and sister Jane, Bro^{r} Short and his wife, Bro^{r} Moodey and his wife, Bro^{r} Northend and his wife, Bro^{r} Tappan and sister Sewall, Sam. and cous. Hannah Tappan. Mr. Payson of Rowley, Mr. Clark, Minister of Excester, were there. Col. Pierce, Major Noyes &c. Cous. John, Richard and Betty Dummer. Went ab^{t} 4. p.m. Nathan^{l} Bricket taking in hand to fill the Grave, I said, Forbear a little, and suffer me to say That amidst our bereaving sorrows We have the Comfort of beholding this Saint put into the rightfull possession of that Happiness of Living desir'd and dying Lamented. She liv'd commendably Four and Fifty years with her dear Husband, and my dear Father: And she could not well brook the being divided from him at her death; which is the cause of our taking leave of her in this place. She was a true and constant

Lover of Gods Word, Worship, and Saints: And she always, with a patient cheerfullness, submitted to the divine Decree of providing Bread for her self and others in the sweat of her Brows. And now her infinitely Gracious and Bountiful Master has promoted her to the Honor of higher Employments, fully and absolutely discharged from all manner of Toil, and Sweat. My honoured and beloved Friends and Neighbours! My dear Mother never thought much of doing the most frequent and homely offices of Love for me; and lavish'd away many Thousands of Words upon me, before I could return one word in Answer: And therefore I ask and hope that none will be offended that I have now ventured to speak one word in her behalf; when shee her self is become speechless. Made a Motion with my hand for the filling of the Grave. Note, I could hardly speak for passion and Tears.

Jan. 24, 1704. Took 24^s in my pocket, and gave my Wife the rest of my cash £4. 3–8, and tell her she shall now keep the Cash; if I want I will borrow of her. She has a better faculty than I at managing Affairs: I will assist her; and will endeavour to live upon my Salary; will see what it will doe. The Lord give his Blessing.

April 3, 1711. I dine with the Court at Pullin's. Mr. Attorney treats us at his house with excellent Pippins, Anchovas, Olives, Nuts. I said I should be able to make no Judgment on the Pippins without a Review, which made the Company Laugh. Spake much of Negroes; I mention'd the problem, whether [they] should be white after the Resurrection: Mr. Bolt took it up as absurd, because the body should be void of all Colour, spake as if it should be a Spirit. I objected what Christ said to his Disciples after the Resurrection. He said twas not so after his Ascension.

April 11, 1712. I saw Six Swallows together flying and chippering very rapturously.

May 5, 1713. Dr. Cotton Mather makes an Excellent Dedication-Prayer in the New Court-Chamber. Mr. Pain, one of the Overseers of the Work wellcom'd us, as the Judges went up Stairs. Dr. Cotton Mather having ended Prayer, The Clark went on and call'd the Grand-Jury: Giving their Charge, which was to enforce the Queen's Proclamation, and especially against Travailing on the Lord's Day; God having return'd to give us Rest. [In the margin: My speech to Grand jury in new Court House.] I said, You ought to be quickened to your Duty, in that you have so Convenient, and August a Chamber prepared for you to doe it in. And what I say to you, I would say to my self, to the Court, and to all that are concern'd. Seeing the former decay'd Building is consum'd, and a better built in the room, Let us pray, May that Proverb, Golden Chalices and Wooden Priests, never be transfer'd to the Civil order; that God would take away our filthy Garments, and cloath us with Change of Raiment; That our former Sins may be buried in the Ruins and Rubbish of the former House, and not be suffered to follow us into this; That a Lixivium may be made of the Ashes, which we may frequently use in keeping ourselves Clean: Let never any Judge debauch this Bench, by abiding on it when his own Cause comes under Trial; May the Judges always discern the Right, and dispense Justice with a most stable, permanent Impartiality; Let this large, transparent, costly Glass serve to oblige the Attornys alway to set Things in a True Light, And let the Character of none of them be *Impar sibi;* Let them Remember they are to advise the Court, as well as plead for their clients. The Oaths that prescribe our Duty run all upon Truth; God is Truth. Let Him communicat to us of His Light and Truth, in Judgment, and in Righteousness. If we thus improve this House, they that built it, shall inhabit it; the days of this people shall be as the days of a Tree, and they shall long enjoy the work of their hands. The Terrible Illumination that was made, the third of October was Twelve moneths, did plainly shew us that our GOD is a Consuming Fire: but it hath repented Him of the Evil. And since He has declar'd that He takes delight in them that hope in his Mercy, we firmly believe that He will be a Dwelling place to us throughout all Generations.

Saturday, Feb. 6, 1714 [Queen Anne's birthday]. . . . My neighbour Colson knocks at our door about 9. or past to tell of the Disorders at the Tavern at the Southend in Mr. Addington's house, kept by John Wallis. He desired me that I would accompany Mr. Bromfield and Constable Howell thither. It was 35. Minutes past Nine at Night before Mr. Bromfield came; then we went. I took Æneas Salter with me. Found much Company. They refus'd to go away. Said were there to drink the Queen's Health, and they had many other Healths to drink. Call'd for more Drink: drank to me, I took notice of the Affront to them. Said must and would stay upon that Solemn occasion. Mr. John Netmaker drank the Queen's Health to me. I told him I drank none; upon that he ceas'd. Mr. Brinley put on his Hat to affront me. I made him take it off. I threaten'd to send some of them to prison; that did not move them. They said they could but pay their Fine, and doing that they might stay. I told them if they had not a care, they would be guilty of a Riot. Mr. Bromfield spake of raising a number of Men to Quell them, and was in some heat, ready to run into Street. But I did not like that. Not having Pen and Ink, I went to take their Names with my Pensil, and not knowing how to Spell their Names, they themselves of their own accord writ them. Mr. Netmaker, reproaching the Province, said they had not made one good Law.

At last I address'd myself to Mr. Banister. I told him he had been longest an Inhabitant and Freeholder, I expected he should set a good Example in departing thence. Upon this he invited them to his own House, and away they went; and we, after them, went away. The Clock in the room struck a pretty while before they departed. I went directly home, and found it 25. Minutes past Ten at Night when I entred my own House. . . .

Monday, Feb. 8. Mr. Bromfield comes to me, and we give the Names of the Offenders at John Wallis's Tavern last Satterday night, to Henry Howell, Constable, with Direction to take the Fines of as many as would pay; and warn them that refus'd to pay, to appear before us at 3. p.m. that day. Many of them pay'd. The rest appear'd; and Andrew Simpson, Ensign, Alexander Gordon, Chirurgeon, Francis Brinley, Gent. and John Netmaker, Gent., were sentenc'd to pay a Fine of 5^{s} each of them, for their Breach of the Law Entituled, An Act for the better Observation, and Keeping the Lord's Day. They all Appeal'd, and Mr. Thomas Banister was bound with each of them in a Bond of 20^{s} upon Condition that they should prosecute their Appeal to effect.

Capt. John Bromsal, and Mr. Thomas Clark were dismiss'd without being Fined. The first was Master of a Ship just ready to sail, Mr. Clark a stranger of New York, who had carried it very civilly, Mr. Jekyl's Brother-in-Law.

Dec. 23, 1714. Dr. C. Mather preaches excellently from Ps. 37. Trust in the Lord &c. only spake of the Sun being in the centre of our System. I think it inconvenient to assert such Problems.

Oct. 15, 1717. My Wife got some Relapse by a new Cold and grew very bad; Sent for Mr. Oakes, and he sat up with me all night.

Oct. 16. The Distemper increases; yet my Wife speaks to me to goe to Bed.

Oct. 17. Thursday, I asked my wife whether twere best for me to go to Lecture: She said, I can't tell; so I staid at home. put up a Note. It being my Son's Lecture, and I absent, twas taken much notice of. Major Genl Winthrop and his Lady visit us. I thank her that she would visit my poor Wife.

Oct. 18. My wife grows worse and exceedingly Restless. Pray'd God to look upon her. Ask'd not after my going to bed. Had the advice of Mr. Williams and Dr. Cutler.

Oct. 19. Call'd Dr. C. Mather to pray, which he did excellently in the Dining Room, having Suggested good Thoughts to my wife before he went down. After, Mr. Wadsworth pray'd in the Chamber when 'twas suppos'd my wife took little notice. About a quarter of an hour past four, my dear Wife expired in the Afternoon, whereby the Chamber was fill'd with a Flood of Tears. God is teaching me a new Lesson; to live a Widower's Life. Lord help me to Learn; and be a Sun and Shield to me, now so much of my Comfort and Defense are taken away.

Oct. 20. I goe to the publick Worship forenoon and Afternoon. My Son has much adoe to read the Note I put up, being overwhelm'd with tears.

Feb. 6, 1718. This morning wandering in my mind whether to live a Single or a Married Life; I had a sweet and very affectionat Meditation Concerning the Lord Jesus; Nothing was to be objected against his Person, Parentage, Relations, Estate, House, Home! Why did I not resolutely, presently close with Him! And I cry'd mightily to God that He would help me so to doe!

March 14, 1718. Deacon Marion comes to me, sits with me a great while in the evening; after a great deal of Discourse about his Courtship—He told [me] the Olivers said they wish'd I would Court their Aunt [Mrs. Winthrop]. I said little, but said twas not five Moneths since I buried my dear Wife. Had said before 'twas hard to know whether best to marry again or no; whom to marry.

June 9, 1718. . . . Mrs. D[eniso]n came in the morning about 9 aclock, and I took her up into my Chamber and discoursed thorowly with her; She desired me to provide another and better Nurse. I gave her the two last News-Letters—told her I intended to visit her at her own house next Lecture-day. She said, 'twould be talked of. I answer'd, In such Cases, persons must run the Gantlet. Gave her Mr. Whiting's Oration for Abijah Walter, who brought her on horseback to Town. I think little or no Notice was taken of it.

June 17, 1718. Went to Roxbury Lecture, visited Mr. Walter. Mr. Webb preach'd. Visited Govr Dudley, Mrs. Denison, gave her Dr. Mather's Sermons very well bound; told her we were in it invited to a Wedding. She gave me very good Curds.

July 25, 1718. I go in the Hackny Coach to Roxbury. Call at Mr. Walter's who is not at home; nor Govr Dudley, nor his Lady. Visit Mrs. Denison: she invites me to eat. I give her two Cases with a knife and fork in each; one Turtle shell tackling; the other long, with Ivory handles, Squar'd, cost $4^s\ 6^d$; Pound of Raisins with proportionable Almonds.

Oct. 15, 1718. Visit Mrs. Denison on Horseback; present her with a pair of Shoe-buckles, cost 5^s 3^d.

Nov. 1, 1718. My Son from Brooklin being here I took his Horse, and visited Mrs. Denison. Sat in the Chamber next Maj^r Bowls. I told her 'twas time now to finish our Business: Ask'd her what I should allow her; she not speaking; I told her I was willing to give her Two [Hundred] and Fifty pounds per annum during her life, if it should please God to take me out of the world before her. She answer'd she had better keep as she was, than give a Certainty for an uncertainty; She should pay dear for dwelling at Boston. I desired her to make proposals, but she made none. I had Thoughts of Publishment next Thorsday the 6th. But I now seem to be far from it. May God, who has the pity of a Father, Direct and help me!

Nov. 28, 1718. I went this day in the Coach; had a fire made in the Chamber where I spake with her before, 9^r the first: I enquired how she had done these 3 or 4 weeks; Afterwards I told her our Conversation had been such when I was with her last, that it seem'd to be a direction in Providence, not to proceed any further; She said, It must be what I pleas'd, or to that purpose. Afterward she seem'd to blame that I had not told her so 9^r 1. . . . I repeated her words of 9^r 1. She seem'd at first to start at the words of her paying dear, as if she had not spoken them. But she said she thought twas Hard to part with *All*, and have nothing to bestow on her Kindred. I said, I did not intend any thing of the Movables, I intended all the personal Estate to be to her. She said I seem'd to be in a hurry on Satterday, 9^r 1., which was the reason she gave me no proposals. Whereas I had ask'd her long before to give me proposals in Writing; and she upbraided me, That I who had never written her a Letter, should ask her to write. She asked me if I would drink, I told her Yes. She gave me Cider, Apples and a Glass of Wine: gathered together the little things I had given her, and offer'd them to me; but I would take none of them. Told her I wish'd her well, should be glad to hear of her welfare. She seem'd to say she should not again take in hand a thing of this nature. Thank'd me for what I had given her and Desired my Prayers. I gave Abijah Weld an Angel. Mr. Stoddard and his wife came in their Coach to see their Sister which broke off my Visit. Upon their asking me, I dismiss'd my Coach, and went with them to see Mr. Danforth, and came home by Moon-shine. Got home about 9. at night. *Laus Deo.*

My bowels yern towards Mrs. Denison: but I think God directs me in his Providence to desist. . . .

Nov. 30, 1718. Lord's-day. In the evening I sung the 120. Psalm in the family. About 7 a-clock Mrs. Dorothy Denison comes in, her Cousin Weld coming first, saying she desired to speak with me in privat. I had a fire in the new Hall, and was at prayer; was very much startled that she should come so far a-foot in that exceeding Cold Season; She enter'd into discourse of what pass'd between us at Roxbury last Friday; I seem'd to be alter'd in my affection; ask'd pardon if she had affronted me. Seem'd to incline the Match should not break off, since I had kept her Company so long. Said Mr. Denison spake to her after his Signing the Will, that he would not make her put all out of her Hand and power, but reserve somwhat to bestow on his Friends that might want. I told her She might keep all. She excus'd, and said 'twas not such an all. I Commended the estate. I could not observe that she made me any offer of any part all this while. She mention'd two Glass Bottles she had. I told her they were hers, and the other small things I had given her, only now they had not the same signification as before. I was much concern'd for her being in the Cold, would fetch her in a plate of somthing warm; (for I had not sup'd), she refus'd. However I Fetched a Tankard of Cider and drank to her. She desired that no body might know of her being here. I told her they should not. Sam. Hirst went to the door, who knew not her Cousin Weld; and not so much as he might stay in the room while we talked together. She went away in the bitter Cold, no Moon being up, to my great pain. I Saluted her at parting.

April 1, 1719. In the morning I dehorted Sam. Hirst and Grindal Rawson from playing Idle Tricks because 'twas first of April; They were the greatest fools that did so. N[ew] E[ngland] Men came hither to avoid anniversary days, the keeping of them, such as the 25th of Decr. How displeasing must it be to God, the giver of our Time, to keep anniversary days to play the fool with ourselves and others. . . .

[The courtship of the widow Denison having unhappily come to naught, Sewall looked about him once more, and in August, 1719, began calling upon the widow Abigail Tilly. His overtures were more acceptable in this quarter, and on October 29 they were married by Sewall's son, the Reverend Joseph. The new Mrs. Sewall, however, was soon taken ill, and in the night of May 26, 1720, as Sewall records, "About midnight my dear wife expired to our great astonishment, especially mine."]

Sept. 5, 1720. Going to Son Sewall's I there meet with Madam Winthrop, told her I was glad to meet her there, had not seen her a great while; gave her Mr. Homes's Sermon.

Sept. 30, 1720. Mr. Colman's Lecture: Daughter Sewall acquaints

Madam Winthrop that if she pleas'd to be within at 3. p.m. I would wait on her. She answer'd she would be at home.

Oct. 1, 1720. Satterday, I dine at Mr. Stoddard's: from thence I went to Madam Winthrop's just at 3. Spake to her, saying, my loving wife died so soon and suddenly, 'twas hardly convenient for me to think of Marrying again; however I came to this Resolution, that I would not make my Court to any person without first Consulting with her. Had a pleasant discourse about 7 Single persons sitting in the Fore-seat 7r 29th, viz. Madm Rebekah Dudley, Catharine Winthrop, Bridget Usher, Deliverance Legg, Rebekah Loyd, Lydia Colman, Elizabeth Bellingham. She propounded one and another for me; but none would do, said Mrs. Loyd was about her Age.

Oct. 3, 1720. Waited on Madam Winthrop again; 'twas a little while before she came in. Her daughter Noyes being there alone with me, I said, I hoped my Waiting on her Mother would not be disagreeable to her. She answer'd she should not be against that that might be for her Comfort. I Saluted her, and told her I perceiv'd I must shortly wish her a good Time; (her mother had told me, she was with Child, and within a Moneth or two of her Time). By and by in came Mr. Airs, Chaplain of the Castle, and hang'd up his Hat, which I was a little startled at, it seeming as if he was to lodge there. At last Madam Winthrop came too. After a considerable time, I went up to her and said, if it might not be inconvenient I desired to speak with her. She assented, and spake of going into another Room; but Mr. Airs and Mrs. Noyes presently rose up, and went out, leaving us there alone. Then I usher'd in Discourse from the names in the Fore-seat; at last I pray'd that Katharine [Mrs. Winthrop] might be the person assign'd for me. She instantly took it up in the way of Denyal, as if she had catch'd at an Opportunity to do it, saying she could not do it before she was asked. Said that was her mind unless she should Change it, which she believed she should not; could not leave her Children. I express'd my Sorrow that she should do it so Speedily, pray'd her Consideration, and ask'd her when I should wait on her agen. She setting no time, I mention'd that day Sennight. Gave her Mr. Willard's Fountain open'd with the little print and verses; saying, I hop'd if we did well read that book, we should meet together hereafter, if we did not now. She took the Book, and put it in her Pocket. Took Leave.

Oct. 6, 1720. A little after 6. p.m. I went to Madam Winthrop's. She was not within. I gave Sarah Chickering the Maid 2s, Juno, who brought in wood, 1s. Afterward the Nurse came in, I gave her 18d, having no other small Bill. After awhile Dr. Noyes came in with his

Mother; and quickly after his wife came in: They sat talking, I think, till eight a-clock. I said I fear'd I might be some Interruption to their Business: Dr. Noyes reply'd pleasantly: He fear'd they might be an Interruption to me, and went away. Madam seem'd to harp upon the same string. Must take care of her Children; could not leave that House and Neighbourhood where she had dwelt so long. I told her she might doe her children as much or more good by bestowing what she laid out in Hous-keeping, upon them. Said her Son would be of Age the 7th of August. I said it might be inconvenient for her to dwell with her Daughter-in-Law, who must be Mistress of the House. I gave her a piece of Mr. Belcher's Cake and Ginger-Bread wrapped up in a clean sheet of Paper; told her of her Father's kindness to me when Treasurer, and I Constable. My Daughter Judith was gon from me and I was more lonesom—might help to forward one another in our Journey to Canaan.—Mr. Eyre came within the door; I saluted him, ask'd how Mr. Clark did, and he went away. I took leave about 9 aclock. I told [her] I came now to refresh her Memory as to Monday-night; said she had not forgot it. In discourse with her, I ask'd leave to speak with her Sister; I meant to gain Madm Mico's favour to persuade her Sister. She seem'd surpris'd and displeas'd, and said she was in the same condition!

Oct. 10, 1720. In the Evening I visited Madam Winthrop, who treated me with a great deal of Curtesy; Wine, Marmalade. I gave her a News-Letter about the Thanksgiving Proposals, for sake of the verses for David Jeffries. She tells me Dr. Increase Mather visited her this day, in Mr. Hutchinson's Coach.

Oct. 11, 1720. I writ a few Lines to Madam Winthrop to this purpose: "Madam, These wait on you with Mr. Mayhew's Sermon, and Account of the state of the Indians on Martha's Vinyard. I thank you for your Unmerited Favours of yesterday; and hope to have the Happiness of Waiting on you to-morrow before Eight a-clock after Noon. I pray God to keep you, and give you a joyfull entrance upon the Two Hundred and twenty ninth year of Christopher Columbus his Discovery; and take Leave, who am, Madam, your humble Servt. S.S.

Oct. 12, 1720. Mrs. Anne Cotton came to door (twas before 8.) said Madam Winthrop was within, directed me into the little Room, where she was full of work behind a Stand; Mrs. Cotton came in and stood. Madam Winthrop pointed to her to set me a Chair. Madam Winthrop's Countenance was much changed from what 'twas on Monday, look'd dark and lowering. At last, the work, (black stuff or Silk) was taken away, I got my Chair in place, had some Converse, but very Cold and indifferent to what 'twas before. Ask'd her to acquit me of Rudeness if I drew off her Glove. Enquiring the reason, I told her twas great odds between handling a dead Goat, and a living Lady. Got it off. I told her I had one Petition to ask of her, that was, that she would take off the Negative she laid on me the third of October; She readily answer'd she could not, and enlarg'd upon it; She told me of it so soon as she could; could not leave her house, children, neighbours, business. I told her she might do som Good to help and support me. Mentioning Mrs. Gookin, Nath, the widow Weld was spoken of; said I had visited Mrs. Denison. I told her Yes! Afterward I said, If after a first and second Vagary she would Accept of me returning, Her Victorious Kindness and Good Will would be very Obliging. She thank'd me for my Book, (Mr. Mayhew's Sermon), But said not a word of the Letter. When she insisted on the Negative, I pray'd there might be no more Thunder and Lightening, I should not sleep all night. I gave her Dr. Preston, The Church's Marriage and the Church's Carriage, which cost me 6[s] at the Sale. The door standing open, Mr. Airs came in, hung up his Hat, and sat down. After awhile, Madam Winthrop moving, he went out. Jn[o] Eyre look'd in, I said How do ye, or, your servant Mr. Eyre: but heard no word from him. Sarah fill'd a Glass of Wine, she drank to me, I to her, She sent Juno home with me with a good Lantern, I gave her 6[d] and bid her thank her Mistress. In some of our Discourse, I told her I had rather go to the Stone-House adjoining to her, than to come to her against her mind. Told her the reason why I came every other night was lest I should drink too deep draughts of Pleasure. She had talk'd of Canary, her Kisses were to me better than the best Canary. Explain'd the expression Concerning Columbus.

Oct. 13. I tell my Son and daughter Sewall, that the Weather was not so fair as I apprehended.

Oct. 17. In the Evening I visited Madam Winthrop, who Treated me Courteously, but not in Clean Linen as somtimes. She said, she did not know whether I would come again, or no. I ask'd her how she could so impute inconstancy to me. (I had not visited her since Wednesday night being unable to get over the Indisposition received by the Treatment received that night, and *I must* in it seem'd to sound like a made piece of Formality.) Gave her this day's Gazett. Heard David Jeffries say the Lord's Prayer, and some other portions of the Scriptures. He came to the door, and ask'd me to go into Chamber, where his Grandmother was tending Little Katee, to whom she had given Physick; but I chose to sit below. Dr. Noyes and his wife came in, and sat a Considerable time; had been visiting Son and dâter Cooper. Juno came home with me.

Oct. 18, 1720. Visited Madam Mico, who came to me in a splendid Dress. I said, It may be you have heard of my Visiting Madam Winthrop, her Sister. She answered, Her Sister had told her of it. I ask'd her good Will in the Affair. She answer'd, If her Sister were for it, she should not hinder it. I gave her Mr. Homes's Sermon. She gave me a Glass of Canary, entertain'd me with good Discourse, and a Respectfull Remembrance of my first Wife. I took Leave.

Oct. 19, 1720. Midweek, Visited Madam Winthrop; Sarah told me she was at Mr. Walley's, would not come home till late. I gave her Hannah 3 oranges with her Duty, not knowing whether I should find her or no. Was ready to go home: but said if I knew she was there, I would go thither. Sarah seem'd to speak with pretty good Courage, She would be there. I went and found her there, with Mr. Walley and his wife in the little Room below. At 7 a-clock I mentioned going home; at 8. I put on my Coat, and quickly waited on her home. She found occasion to speak loud to the servant, as if she had a mind to be known. Was Courteous to me; but took occasion to speak pretty earnestly about my keeping a Coach: I said 'twould cost £100. per annum: she said twould cost but £40. . . . Exit. Came away somewhat late.

Oct. 20, 1720. . . . Madam Winthrop not being at Lecture, I went thither first; found her very Serene with her dâter Noyes, Mrs. Dering, and the widow Shipreev sitting at a little Table, she in her arm'd Chair. She drank to me, and I to Mrs. Noyes. After awhile pray'd the favour to speak with her. She took one of the Candles, and went into the best Room, clos'd the shutters, sat down upon the Couch. She told me Madam Usher had been there, and said the Coach must be set on Wheels, and not by Rusting. She spake somthing of my needing a Wigg. Ask'd me what her Sister said to me. I told her, She said, If her Sister were for it, She would not hinder it. But I told her, she did not say she would be glad to have me for her Brother. Said, I shall keep you in the Cold, and asked her if she would be within to morrow night, for we had had but a running Feat. She said she could not tell whether she should, or no. I took Leave. As were drinking at the Governour's, he said: In England the Ladies minded little more than that they might have Money, and Coaches to ride in. I said, And New-England brooks its Name. At which Mr. Dudley smiled. Govr said they were not quite so bad here.

Oct. 21, 1720. Friday, My Son, the Minister, came to me p.m by appointment and we pray one for another in the Old Chamber; more especially respecting my Courtship. About 6. a-clock I go to Madam Winthrop's; Sarah told me her Mistress was gon out, but did not tell me whither she went. She presently order'd me a Fire; so I went in, having Dr. Sibb's Bowels with me to read. I read the two first Sermons, still no body came in: at last about 9. a-clock Mr. Jn° Eyre came in; I took the opportunity to say to him as I had done to Mrs. Noyes before, that I hoped my Visiting his Mother would not be disagreeable to him; He answered me with much Respect. When twas after 9. a-clock He of himself said he would go and call her, she was but at one of his Brothers: A while after I heard Madam Winthrop's voice, enquiring something about John. After a good while and Clapping the Garden door twice or thrice, she came in. I mentioned something of the lateness; she banter'd me, and said I was later. She receiv'd me Courteously. I ask'd when our proceedings should be made publick: She said They were like to be no more publick than they were already. Offer'd me no Wine that I remember. I rose up at 11 a-clock to come away, saying I would put on my Coat, She offer'd not to help me. I pray'd her that Juno might light me home, she open'd the Shutter, and said twas pretty light abroad; Juno was weary and gon to bed. So I came hôm by Star-light as well as I could. At my first coming in, I gave Sarah five Shillings. I writ Mr. Eyre his Name in his book with the date Octob^r 21. 1720. It cost me 8^s. Jehovah jireh! Madam told me she had visited M. Mico, Wendell, and Wm Clark of the South [Church].

Oct. 22, 1720. Dâter Cooper visited me before my going out of Town, staid till about Sun set. I brought her going near as far as the Orange Tree. Coming back, near Leg's Corner, Little David Jeffries saw me, and looking upon me very lovingly, ask'd me if I was going to see his Grandmother? I said, Not to-night. Gave him a peny, and bid him present my Service to his Grandmother.

Oct. 24, 1720. I went in the Hackny Coach through the Common, stop'd at Madam Winthrop's (had told her I would take my departure from thence). Sarah came to the door with Katee in her Arms: but I did not think to take notice of the Child. Call'd her Mistress. I told her, being encourag'd by David Jeffries loving eyes, and sweet Words, I was come to enquire whether she could find in her heart to leave that House and Neighbourhood, and go and dwell with me at the Southend; I think she said softly, Not yet. I told her It did not ly in my Lands to keep a Coach. If I should, I should be in danger to be brought to keep company with her Neighbour Brooker, (he was a little before sent to prison for Debt). Told her I had an Antipathy against those who would pretend to give themselves; but nothing of their Estate. I would a proportion of my Estate with my self. And I suppos'd she would do so. As to a Perriwig, My best and greatest Friend, I could not possibly have a greater, began to find me with Hair before I was born, and had continued to do so ever since; and I could not find in my heart to go to another. She commended the book I gave her, Dr. Preston, the Church Marriage; quoted him saying 'twas inconvenient keeping out of a Fashion commonly used. I said the Time and Tide did circumscribe my Visit. She gave me a Dram of Black-Cherry Brandy, and gave me a lump of the Sugar that was in it. She wish'd me a good Journy. I pray'd God to keep her, and came away. Had a very pleasant Journy to Salem.

Oct. 31, 1720. At night I visited Madam Winthrop about 6. p.m. They told me she was gon to Madam Mico's. I went thither and found she was gon; so return'd to her house, read the Epistles to the Galatians, Ephesians in Mr. Eyre's Latin Bible. After the Clock struck 8. I began to read the 103. Psalm. Mr. Wendell came in from his Warehouse. Ask'd me if I were alone? Spake very kindly to me, offer'd me to call Madam Winthrop. I told him, She would be angry, had been at Mrs. Mico's; he help'd me on with my Coat and I came home: left the Gazett in the Bible, which told Sarah of, bid her present my Service to Mrs. Winthrop, and tell her I had been to wait on her if she had been at home.

Nov. 1, 1720. I was so taken up that I could not go if I would.

Nov. 2, 1720. Midweek, went again, and found Mrs. Alden there, who quickly went out. Gave her about ½ pound of Sugar Almonds, cost 3ˢ per £. Carried them on Monday. She seem'd pleas'd with them, ask'd what they cost. Spake of giving her a Hundred pounds per anum if I dy'd before her. Ask'd her what sum she would give me, if she should dy first? Said I would give her time to Consider of it. She said she heard as if I had given all to my Children by Deeds of Gift. I told her 'twas a mistake, Point-Judith was mine &c. That in England, I own'd, my Father's desire was that it should go to my eldest Son; 'twas 20£ per anum; she thought 'twas forty. I think when I seem'd to excuse pressing this, she seem'd to think twas best to speak of it; a long winter was coming on. Gave me a Glass or two of Canary.

Nov. 4, 1720. Friday, Went again about 7. a-clock; found there Mr. John Walley and his wife: sat discoursing pleasantly. I shew'd them Isaac Moses's [an Indian] Writing. Madam W. serv'd Comfeits to us. After awhile a Table was spread, and Supper was set. I urg'd Mr. Walley to Crave a Blessing; but he put it upon me. About 9. they went away. I ask'd Madam what fashioned Neck-lace I should present her with, She said, None at all. I ask'd her Whereabout we left off last time; mention'd what I had offer'd to give her; Ask'd her what she would give me; She said she could not Change her Condition: She had said so from the beginning; could not be so far from her Children, the Lecture. Quoted the Apostle Paul affirming that a single Life was better than a Married. I answer'd That was for the present Distress. Said she had not pleasure in things of that nature as formerly: I said, you are the fitter to make me a Wife. If she hald in that mind, I must go home and bewail my Rashness in making more haste than good Speed. However, considering the Supper, I desired her to be within next Monday night, if we liv'd so long. Assented. She charg'd me with saying, that she must put away Juno, if she came to me: I utterly deny'd it, it never came in my heart; yet she insisted upon it; saying it came in upon discourse about the Indian woman that obtained her Freedom this Court. About 10. I said I would not disturb the good orders of her House, and came away. She not seeming pleas'd with my Coming away. Spake to her about David Jeffries, had not seen him.

Nov. 7, 1720. My Son pray'd in the Old Chamber. Our time had been taken up by Son and Daughter Cooper's Visit; so that I only read the 130th and 143 Psalm. Twas on the Account of my Courtship. I went to Mad. Winthrop; found her rocking her little Katee in the Cradle. I excus'd my Coming so late (near Eight). She set me an arm'd Chair and Cusheon; and so the Cradle was between her arm'd Chair and mine. Gave her the remnant of my Almonds; She did not eat of them as before; but laid them away; I said I came to enquire whether she had alter'd her mind since Friday, or remained of the same mind still. She said, Thereabouts. I told her I loved her, and was so fond as to think that she loved me: She said had a great respect for me. I told her, I had made her an offer, without asking any advice; she had so many to advise with, that twas a hindrance. The Fire was come to one short Brand besides the Block, which Brand was set up in end; at last it fell to pieces, and no Recruit was made: She gave me a Glass of Wine. I think I repeated again that I would go home and bewail my Rashness in making more haste than good Speed. I would endeavour to contain myself, and not go on to sollicit her to do that which she could not Consent to. Took leave of her. As came down the steps she bid me have a Care. Treated me Courteously. Told her she had enter'd the 4th year of her Widowhood. I had given her the News-Letter before; I did not bid her draw off her Glove as sometime I had done. Her Dress was not so clean as somtime it had been. Jehovah jireh!

Nov. 9, 1720. Dine at Bro[r] Stoddard's: were so kind as to enquire of me if they should invite M'[m] Winthrop; I answer'd No. Thank'd my Sister Stoddard for her Courtesie; . . . She sent her servant home with me with a Lantern. Madam Winthrop's Shutters were open as I pass'd by.

[The courtship of Madam Winthrop having failed still more disastrously than that of Mrs. Denison, Sewall gave over the attack in November, 1720; in January, 1722, he turned his attentions toward Mrs. Mary Gibbs, whom he married for his third wife on March 29.]

March 5, 1721. Lord's Day, Serene, and good but very cold, yet had a comfortable opportunity to celebrate the Lord's Supper. Mr. Prince, p.m. preach'd a Funeral Sermon from Psal. 90. 10. Gave Capt. Hill a good character. Just as I sat down in my Seat, one of my Fore-teeth in my under Jaw came out, and I put it in my pocket. This old servant and daughter of Musick leaving me, does thereby give me warning that I must shortly resign my Head: the Lord help me to do it cheerfully!

June 15, 1725. I accompanied my Son to Mad. Winthrop's. She was a-bed about 10. *mane*. I told her I found my Son coming to her and took the Opportunity to come with him. She thank'd me kindly, enquired how Madam Sewall did. Ask'd my Son to go to Prayer. Present Mr. John Eyre, Mrs. Noyes, Mrs. Walley and David Jeffries. At coming I said, I kiss your hand Madame (her hand felt very dry). She desired me to pray that God would lift up upon her the Light of his Countenance.

Apr. 14, 1726. Mr. Coney died more than three years ago; and now his widow Mrs. Mary Coney died somwhat suddenly on Tuesday morning April, 12. and was inter'd in one of the new Tombs of the South-burying place; Bearers, Sam. Sewall, John Clark esqr; Sam. Brown esqr, Thomas Fitch esqr; Sam. Checkley esqr. Capt. John Ballantine. Was buried from her daughter Bromfield's. His Honour the Lieut Gov[r] follow'd his Aunt as a Mourner and his Lady. Thus death, by its regardless stroke, mows down all before it, making no distinction between our most prudent and Charming Friends, and others; May we learn more entirely to delight and trust in God who is Altogether Lovely and Lives for Ever. Three Sams being Bearers together on the right side, occasion'd my binding all the Bearers up together in this band,

> Three Sams, two Johns, and one good Tom
> Bore Prudent Mary to her Tomb.

July 26, 1726. Rode in Mr. Sheriff's Calash to Cambridge. Mr. Appleton prays. Entring upon the Charge to the Grand-Jury, I said, Since men's departure from God, there was such an aversion in them to return, that every kind of Authority was necessary to reclaim them. Notwithstanding the singular advantage Cambridge had enjoy'd in their excellent Pastors, and Presidents of the College—yet it must be said, *Venimus ipsam Cantabrigiam ad stabiliendos, et corrigendos mores.*[1]—

Dec. 17, 1727. I was surprised to hear Mr. Thacher of Milton, my old Friend, pray'd for as dangerously Sick. Next day. Dec[r] 18. 1727. I am inform'd by Mr. Gerrish, that my dear friend died last night; which I doubt bodes ill to Milton and the Province, his dying at this Time, though in the 77th year of his Age. *Deus avertat Omen!*

Dec. 22, 1727. the day after the Fast, was inter'd. Bearers, Rev[d] Mr. Nehemiah Walter, Mr. Joseph Baxter; Mr. John Swift, Mr. Sam[l] Hunt; Mr. Joseph Sewall, Mr. Thomas Prince. I was inclin'd before, and having a pair of Gloves sent me, I determined to go to the Funeral, if the Weather prov'd favourable, which it did, and I hired Blake's Coach with four Horses; my Son, Mr. Cooper and Mr. Prince went with me. Refresh'd there with Meat and Drink; got thither about half an hour past one. It was sad to see [death] triumphed over my dear Friend! I rode in my Coach to the Burying place; not being able to get nearer by reason of the many Horses. From thence went directly up the Hill where the Smith's Shop, and so home very comfortably and easily, the ground being mollified. But when I came to my own Gate, going in, I fell down, a board slipping under my Left foot, my right Legg raised off the skin, and put me to a great deal of pain, especially when 'twas washed with Rum. It was good for me that I was thus Afflicted that my spirit might be brought into a frame more suitable to the Solemnity, which is apt to be too light; and by the loss of some of my Skin, and blood I might be awakened to prepare for my own Dissolution. Mr. Walter prayed before the Corps was carried out. I had a pair of Gloves sent me before I went, and a Ring given me there. . . . I have now been at the Interment of 4 of my Class-mates. . . . Now I can go to no more Funerals of my Class-mates; nor none be at mine; for the survivers, the Rev'd Mr. Samuel Mather at Windsor, and the Rev[d] Mr. Taylor at Westfield, [are] one Hundred Miles off, and are entirely enfeebled. I humbly pray that Christ may be graciously present with us all Three both in Life, and in Death, and then we shall safely and Comfortably walk through the shady valley that leads to Glory.

JOHN WILLIAMS, 1664–1729

[John Williams was born at Roxbury, his father being a deacon in John Eliot's church, a shoemaker by trade; he was helped through college by his grandfather, and graduated in 1683. He taught school at Dorchester for two years, and settled as minister at Deerfield in 1686. The massacre occurred on February 29, 1704. Williams was redeemed in October, 1706, and returned to Boston; all his children were redeemed except a daughter, Eunice, who married an Indian and lost all memory of any other way of life. The town was resettled in 1707, and Williams went back to his post, saying, "I must return and look after my sheep in the wilderness." This text is from *The Redeemed Captive Returning to Zion* (Boston, 1707), pp. 2–9, 22–25.]

THE REDEEMED CAPTIVE

On the Twenty-ninth of *February* [1704] Not long before break of day, the Enemy came in like a Flood upon us; our Watch being unfaithful: an evil, whose awful effects, in a surprizal of our Fort, should bespeak all Watchmen to avoid, as they would not bring the charge of blood upon themselves. They came to my House in the beginning of the Onset, and by their violent endeavours to break open Doors, and Windows, with *Axes*, and *Hatchets*, Awaken'd me out of Sleep; on which I leapt out of bed, and running toward the door, perceived the Enemy making their entrance into the House: I called to awaken two Souldiers, in the Chamber; and returned towards my bedside, for my Arms: the Enemy immediately brake into the Room, I judge to the number of Twenty, with *Painted Faces*, and hideous Acclamations. I reach'd up my hands to the Bed-tester, for my Pistol, uttering a short Petition to God, *For Everlasting Mercies for me & mine, on the account of the Merits of our Glorify'd Redeemer;* Expecting a present passage through the Valley of the shadow of Death: Saying in my self, as *Isaiah* 38. 10, 11. *I said, in the cutting off my days, I shall go to the gates of the grave: I am deprived of the residue of my years. I said, I shall not see the Lord, even the Lord, in the land of the Living: I shall behold man no more with the inhabitants of the World.* Taking down my Pistol, I Cockt it, and put it to the breast of the first Indian who came up; but my Pistol missing fire, I was seized by Three Indians, who disarmed me, and bound me Naked, as I was in my Shirt, and so I stood for near the space of an hour: binding me, they told me they would carry me to *Quebeck*. My Pistol missing fire, was an occasion of my Life's being preserved: Since which I have also found it profitable to be cross'd in my own Will. The judgment of God did not long slumber against one of the Three which took me, who was a Captain, for by Sun-rising he received a Mortal Shot, from my next Neighbours house; who oppossed so great a number of *French* & *Indians* as Three hundred, and yet were no more than Seven men in an Ungarison'd house.

I cannot relate the distressing care I had for my dear Wife, who had lien-In but a few Weeks before, and for my poor Children, Family, and Christian Neighbours. The Enemy fell to riffling the house, and entred in great numbers into every room of the house. I beg'd of God, to Remember Mercy in the midst of Judgment: that He would so far restain their Wrath, as to prevent their Murdering of us: that we might have *Grace to Glorify His Name, whether in Life or Death;* and as I was able committed our State to God. The Enemies who entred the House were all of them *Indians* and *Macqua's*, insulted over me a while, holding up Hatchets over my head, threatning to burn all I had, but yet God beyond expectation made us in a great measure to be Pityed: for tho' some were so cruel and barbarous as to take & carry to the door, Two of my Children and Murder them, as also a Negro Woman; yet they gave me liberty to put on my Clothes, keeping me bound with a Cord on one arm, till I put on my Cloths to the other; and then changing my Cord, they let me dress my self and then Pinioned me again. Gave liberty to my dear Wife to dress her self, & our Children. About Sun an hour high, we were all carryed out of the house, for a March, and saw many of the Houses of my Neighbours in Flames, perceiving the whole Fort, one house excepted, to be taken. Who can tell, what Sorrows pierced our Souls, when we saw our selves carryed away from Gods Sanctuary, to go into a strange Land, exposed to so many Trials? the journey being at least Three hundred Miles we were to Travel; the Snow up to the Knees, and we never inur'd to such hardships and fatigues, the place we were to be carryed to, a Popish Country. Upon my parting from the Town they fired my House & Barn. We were carryed over the river, to the foot of the *Mountain*, about a Mile from my House, where we found, a great number of our Christian Neighbours, Men, Women & Children, to the number of an hundred, Nineteen of which were afterward Murdered by the Way, and two starved to Death, near *Cowass*, in a time of great scarcity or Famine, the Salvages underwent there. When we came to the foot of our Mountain, they took away our Shoes, and gave us, in the room of them Indian-Shoes, to prepare us for our Travel. Whilst we were there the English beat out a Company, that remained in the Town, and pursued them to the River, Killing and Wounding many of them; but the body of the Army, being Alarm'd, they repulsed those few *English* that pursued them.

I am not able to give you an account of the number of the Enemy Slain, but I observed after this night, no great insulting Mirth, as I expected; and saw many Wounded Persons, and for several days together they buryed of their party, & one of chief Note among the *Macqua's*. The Governour of *Canada*, told me, his Army had that Success with the loss but of Eleven men, Three French-men, One of which was the *Lieutenant* of the Army, Five *Macqua's*, and Three *Indians:* but after my Arrival at *Quebeck*, I spake with an English man, who was taken the last War, and Married there, and of their Religion; who told me, they lost above Forty, and that many were Wounded: I replyed the Governour of *Canada* said, they lost but Eleven men: He answered, 'tis true, That there were but Eleven killed out-right at the taking of the Fort, but that many others were Wounded, among whom was the *Ensign* of the *French;* but said he, they had a fight in the Meadow, and that in both Engagements, they lost more than Forty. Some of the Souldiers, both *French* and *Indians* then present told me so (said he) adding, That the French always endeavour, to conceal the number of their Slain.

After this, we went up the Mountain, and saw the smoak of the Fires in the Town, and beheld the awful desolations of our Town: And before we marched any farther, they kill'd a Sucking Child of the English. There were slain by the Enemy of the Inhabitants of our Town to the number of Thirty-eight, besides Nine of the Neighbouring Towns. We Travel'd not far the first day; God made the Heathen, so to Pity our Children, that though they had several Wounded Persons, of their own to carry, upon their Shoulders, for Thirty Miles, before they came to the River, yet they carryed our Children, uncapable of Travelling upon their Shoulders and in their Arms. When we came to our Lodging place, the first Night, they dugg away the snow, and made some Wigwams, cut down some of the small branches of *Spruce-trees* to lye down on, and gave the Prisoners some-what to eat; but we had but little Appetite. I was Pinioned, and bound down that Night, and so I was every Night whilst I was with the Army. Some of the Enemy who brought drink with them, from the Town, fell to drinking, and in their Drunken fit, they kill'd my Negro man, the only dead Person, I either saw at the Town, or in the Way. In the Night an *English* Man made his escape: in the Morning I was call'd for, and ordered by the General to tell the English, That if any more made their escape, they would burn the rest of the Prisoners. He that took me was unwilling to let me speak with any of the Prisoners, as we March'd; but on the Morning of the Second day, he being appointed to guard the rear, I was put into the hands of my other Master, Who permitted me to speak to my Wife, when I overtook her, and to Walk with her to help her in her Journey. On the Way we discoursed of the happiness of them who had a right to *an House not made with Hands, Eternal in the Heavens;* and *God for a Father, and Friend;* as also, That it was our reasonable Duty, quietly to submit, to the Will of God, and to say, *The Will of the Lord be done.* My Wife told me her strength of body began to fail, So that I must expect to part with her; Saying, She hoped God would preserve my Life, and the Life of some, if not of all of our Children, with us; and commended to me, under God, the care of them. She never spake any discontented Word as to what had befal'n us, but with suitable expressions justified God, in what had befal'n us. We soon made a halt, in which time my chief Surviving Master came up, upon which I was put upon Marching with the foremost, and so made to take my last fare-well of my dear Wife, *the desire of my Eyes*, and companion in many Mercies and Afflictions. Upon our Separation from each other, we askt for each other Grace sufficient, for what God should call us to. After our being parted from one another, she spent the few remaining Minutes of her stay, in Reading the Holy Scriptures; which she was wont Personally every day to delight her Soul in Reading, Praying, Meditating of, and over, by her self, in her Closet, over and above what she heard out of them in our Family Worship. I was made to Wade over a small River, and so were all the English, the Water above Knee-deep, the Stream very Swift; and after that, to Travel up a small Mountain, my Strength was almost spent, before I came to the top of it: No sooner had I overcome the difficulty of that ascent but I was permitted to sit down, & be unburthened of my Pack; I sat pitying those who were behind and intreated my Master, to let me go down, and help up my Wife, but he refused, and would not let me stir from him. I ask'd each of the Prisoners (as they passed by me) after her, and heard that in passing through the abovesaid River, she fell down and was plunged over Head and Ears in the Water after which she travelled not far, for at the Foot of this Mountain, the cruel and blood thirsty Salvage who took her, slew her with his

Hatchet, at one stroak; the tidings of which were very awful: and yet such was the hard-heartedness of the Adversary, that my Tears were reckoned to me as a reproach. My loss, and the loss of my Children was great, our hearts were so filled with Sorrow, that nothing but the comfortable hopes of her being taken away in Mercy, to her self, from the evils we were to see, feel and suffer under; (and joyn'd to the Assembly of the *Spirits of just men made perfect*, to rest in Peace, and *joy unspeakable, and full of glory;* and the good Measure of God thus to exercise us,) could have kept us from sinking under, at that time. That Scripture, *Job* 1. 21.—*Naked came I out of my Mothers womb, and Naked shall I return thither: the Lord gave, and the Lord hath taken away, blessed be the Name of the Lord:* Was brought to my Mind, and from it, That an *Afflicting God was to be Glorifyed;* with some other places of Scripture, to perswade to a Patient bearing my Afflictions. . . .

[At Quebec:] The next Morning the *Bell Rang* for *Mass:* My Master *bid me go to Church:* I refused: he threatned me, and went away in a rage. At Noon the *Jesuit* sent for me, to dine with them; for I eat at their Table all the time I was at the Fort. And after Dinner, they told me, *the Indians would not allow of any of their Captives staying in their Wigwams, whilst they were at Church; and were resolved by force and violence to bring us all to Church, if we would not go without.* I told them it was highly unreasonable so to impose upon those who were of a contrary Religion; and to force us to be present at such Service, as we *Abhor'd*, was nothing becoming Christianity. They replyed, *They were Salvages, and would not hearken to reason, but would have their Wills:* Said also, *If they were in* New-England *themselves, they would go into the Churches to see their Wayes of Worship.* I answered, the case was far different, for there was nothing (them selves being judges) as to matter or manner of *Worship*, but what was according to the Word of God, in our Churches; and therefore it could not be an offence to any mans Conscience. But among those there were *Idolatrous Superstitions* in *Worship:* they said, *Come and see, and offer us Conviction, of what is superstitious in Worship.* To which I answered, *That I was not to do Evil that Good might come on it;* and that forcing in matters of Religion was hateful. They answered, *The Indians were resolved to have it so, & they could not pacify them without my coming; and they would engage they should offer no force or violence to cause any compliance with their Ceremonies.*

The next Mass, my Master bid me go to *Church:* I objected; he arose and forcibly pulled me out by head and Shoulders out of the *Wigwam* to the *Church*, that was nigh the door. So I went in and sat down behind the door, and there saw a great confusion, instead of any *Gospel*

Order. For one of the *Jesuits* was at the Altar, saying *Mass* in a Tongue *Unknown* to the Salvages, and the other, between the Altar & the door, saying and singing *Prayers* among the *Indians* at the same time; and many others were at the same time saying over their *Pater Nosters*, and *Ave Mary*, by tale from their *Chapelit*, or *Beads* on a string. At our going out we smiled at their Devotion so managed; which was offensive to them: for they said, *We made a Derision of their Worship*. When I was here, a certain Salvagess dyed; one of the *Jesuits* told me, *She was a very holy Woman, who had not committed One Sin in Twelve Years*. After a day or two the *Jesuits* ask'd me, *What I thought of their Way, how I saw it?* I told them, I thought Christ said of it, as *Mark* 7. 7, 8, 9. *Howbeit, in vain do they Worship me, teaching for doctrines the Commandments of men. For laying aside the Commandment of God, ye hold the tradition of men, as the washing of pots, and cups: and many other such like things ye do. And he said unto them, Full well ye reject the commandment of God, that ye may keep your own tradition*. They told me, *They were not the Commandments of men*, but *Apostolical Traditions*, of equal authority with the Holy Scriptures. And that after my Death, I would bewail my not Praying to the Virgin *Mary;* and that I should find the want of her Intercession for me, *with her Son;* judging me to Hell for asserting, the Scriptures to be a perfect rule of Faith: and said, I abounded in my own sense, entertaining explications contrary to the sense of the *Pope*, regularly sitting with a general Council, explaining Scripture, and making Articles of Faith. I told them, It was my Comfort that Christ was to be my *Judge*, and not they at the *Great Day:* And as for their censuring and judging of me, I was not moved with it. One day a certain Salvage, taken Prisoner in *Philips* War, who had lived at Mr. *Buckleys* at *Wethersfield*, called *Ruth*, who could speak *English* very well; who had been often at my House but was now proselyted to the *Romish Faith*, came into the *Wigwam*, and with her an *English* Maid who was taken the last War, who was dress'd up in *Indian* Apparel, could not speak one word of *English*, who said she could neither tell her own name, or the name of the place from whence she was taken. These two talked in the *Indian* Dialect with my Master a long time; after which my Master bad me *Cross my self;* I told him I would not he commanded me several times, and I as often refused. *Ruth* said, Mr. *Williams* you know the Scripture, and therefore act against your own light, for you know the Scripture saith, *Servants obey your Masters;* he is your Master, and you his Servant. I told her she was ignorant, and knew not the meaning of the Scripture, telling her, *I was not to disobey the Great God to obey any Master*, *and that I was ready to suffer for God if called thereto:* On which she talked to my

Master, I suppose she interpreted what I said. My Master took hold of my hand to force me to *Cross my self*, but I strugled with him, and would not suffer him to guide my hand; upon this he pulled off a *Crucifix* from his own neck, and bad me *Kiss* it; but I refused once and again; he told me *he would dash out my brains with his Hatchet if I refused.* I told him I should sooner chuse death then to Sin against God; then he ran and catcht up his Hatchet, and acted as tho' he would have dashed out my Brains; seeing I was not moved, he threw down his Hatchet, saying, *he would first bite off all my nails if I still refused;* I gave him my hand and told him, I was ready to suffer, he set his teeth in my thumb nails and gave a gripe with his teeth, and then said, *no good Minister, no love God, as bad as the Devil;* and so left off. I have reason to bless God who strengthened me to withstand; by this he was so discouraged as never more to meddle with me about my Religion.

EBENEZER TURELL, 1702–1778

[Ebenezer Turell was born in Boston, graduated from Harvard College in 1721, married the daughter of Benjamin Colman, and served as minister at Medford, 1724–1778. He published *The Life and Character of the Reverend Benjamin Colman, D.D.* in Boston, 1749; this text is from pp. 5–7, 26–28, 166–167, 182–184, 210–211. The biography of his wife, *Memoirs of the Life and Death of the Pious and Ingenious Mrs. Jane Turell*, was published at Boston, 1735, and in London, 1741; this text is from the edition of 1735, pp. 60–61, 78–79, 116–119.]

BENJAMIN COLMAN

IT WAS after the Twentieth Day of *July* in the year 1695 that Mr. *Colman* imbarked for *London* (by the Will of God) on board the Ship *Swan* Capt. *Thomas Gilbert* Commander—For the whole three first Days he was on Shipboard he endured the Extremity of Sea Sickness, and at times through the Voyage. On the fourth Day the Vessel sprang a Leek, and the Water was heard to pour in on the Star-board Tack, which alarmed the Sailors, and made some of them remark his Eveness and Calmness when they expected he should have been much affrighted. When the Winds blew a Storm afterward, he governed his Fears by looking on the Captain, Mate, and Sailors to discover what he saw in their Faces. When they came into the warm Seas, a *Dolphin* which they had marked with a Scar on his shining Back, kept Company with the Ship for Ten or Twelve Days together, feeding on her Bottom.

At the End of seven Weeks a *Seeker* made after them, and soon came up with them. She was a Privateer of 20 Guns and an 100 Men, a light and fleet Ship; The Swan was heavy laden, twelve Guns and 24 Men, Sailors and Passengers together. The Swan's Company bore their Broad-sides and Vollies of small Arms six or seven Times that Afternoon, defending themselves and annoying the Enemy; but were taken the next Morning, having their Boltsprit shot away, and the Mast, and Rigging so torn and cut, that the Masts fell all together an Hour after; by which means the Ship became a perfect Wreck, and the Company were much looked at by the French when they came into Port. The French had a great Number of Men killed, for they were so full that if a shot entered it must do Execution.

God graciously preserved Mr. *Colman* in the Fight, exposed all the while on the Quarter-Deck, where four out of seven were wounded, and one mortally. He was much praised for his Courage when the Fight was over; but though he charged and discharged like the rest, yet he declared he was sensible of no Courage but of a great deal of Fear; and when they had reecived two or three Broadsides he wondered when his Courage would come, as he had heard others talk. In short, he fought like a Philosopher and a Christian. He looked Death in the Face, and prayed all the while he charged and fired,——while the Boatswain and others made a Frolick and Sport of it.

There was a young *Rake*, a Passenger on board, that lisped at Atheism, and spit at Religion every Day of the Voyage, who was now in the Terrors of Death,—when he saw Mr. *Colman* take a Musket, he was ashamed to leave the Deck; but the first Volley of small Arms laid him flat on his Belly without being touched: when the great Guns roared he would have crept through the Boards to hide himself; he lay as one Dead, and let the Men tread on him or kick him as they pleased. At last he peeped up when the firing ceased for a Minute, and asked where they were? Mr. *Colman* told him they lay by to charge again; and in a Moment he flew down into the Doctor's Room, and was seen no more till the Ship was taken. Yet this Spark when safe in *France* was ridiculing Religion again, and scorning the Ministers of it as much as ever. . . .

He took Coach on *Christmas* Day, and found in it a Gentlewoman of very good Fashion and Sense, with her little Daughter, and was much delighted in the Journey with the agreeable Conversation of the Lady and Prattle of Miss.

At *Cambridge* Mr. *Colman* found a small Congregation of inferior People, the Shadow of the University, like that of all Cathedrals, stunting the Growth of the Dissenters.

They liked illiterate Preachers, and when *Davis* and others of that Sort came to Town, he was left by one half of his Hearers. They were also sadly tinged with *Antinomian* Principles, and his Texts were too legal for them.*—So he was ashamed of his Post, and wrote earnestly to *London* to be released from it.—He saw all the Colleges there after a Sort, but had none of those honorary Advantages for doing it as he had at *Oxford*.

At twelve Weeks End he returned to *London*, and some of the City Ministers resolved to take a Turn down themselves. The Reverend and zealous Mr. *Pomfret* went first for a Month, and others followed him.

But at length they got a handsom Subscription at *London* to the ingenious and learned Mr. *Pearse*, an excellent Preacher, to fix him at *Cambridge* for two or three Years. He went; and being already well entred into the Mathematicks, soon made himself known to the learned Mr. *Whiston*,[1] and became his most esteemed Friend. A fatal Friendship! for then he also drank in Mr. *Whiston's* Arrian Principles, which has since been the Spring of so much Strife and Confusion and every evil Work among the Dissenters.

Within a few Weeks after Mr. *Colman* was invited to the great Town of *Ipswich* in *Suffolk*.—In his Way thither God graciously preserved him from a very dangerous Snare, which three ill Women laid for him. He found them in the Stage-Coach, supped with them in the Evening, and was retired to his Chamber: But as he was going to Bed one of them knocked at his Door, and told him that they had mulled a Glass of Wine, chiefly because of the Cold that was upon him, and he must needs take Part of it with them. In their Chamber were two Beds, and he heard one of them gigling behind the Curtains of the furthermost Bed. He began now to suspect them, when one of them told him, that truly they were afraid to lie in the Chamber alone; that the furthest Bed would hold them three; and they begged of him to lodge in the nearest Bed. He told them he was greatly surprised at their Motion, and ashamed of it, that their Fear was groundless; no Danger would happen to them in the Inn; if there were any he should make a poor Defence; and that in short, they utterly forgot what they owed to their Reputation and Virtue, or to his. So they begged his Pardon, and he suddenly stept into his own Chamber.

* Like as at this Day in some Places of *New-England*. [*Turell's note.*]

At *Ipswich* he spent eleven Weeks very pleasantly, and with much Satisfaction; but they needed a Preacher only every other Lord's Day. The excellent Mr. *Fairfax* divided his Time with them and some neighbouring Congregations, as the Bishop of them all. Being now got to a plentiful Fish-market, and near to the Oyster-Banks, he began to think himself again in *New-England*. . . .

Reading, and close Application of Mind to Study was early, and ever his Delight—He read much, and digested well the various Authors he perused; and often collected from them what was curious and useful, as appears by many Sheets left, and numerous Quotations in his Sermons.*

In his *younger* Times he was a Night-Student, by which his Health was greatly impaired, and he experienced the Truth of that Saying in Erasmus, *Nocturnae Lucubrationes longe periculosissimæ habentur.*[2] In his latter Years he plied his Studies chiefly in the Forenoon, and ordinarily spent the whole of it in them. And he has been heard to say on the Verge of *Seventy*, "That he found himself best in Health and Spirit, at his Table with a Book or Pen in his Hand.—All must be hushed and still when he was there employed either in Reading, writing Letters or composing Sermons—He wrote many Hundred Epistles in a Year—(*Nulla Dies sine Epistolis* [3]) to all Ranks of Persons; on all Occasions and Businesses, and with greatest Ease imaginable, to the vast Pleasure and Profit of his Friends, the Benefit of his Country and the Churches in it; and the Good of Mankind.—His Letters to his Correspondents abroad being seen and admired, created him new Friends and were a happy Means of raising up new Benefactors to these Provinces . . . —I need not therefore here observe to my Readers, how good a Master he was of the Epistolary Stile—The Letters already inserted and others to be published in our Narrative shall speak for themselves.†

When he was about making a Sermon, after he had first looked up to Heaven for Assistance, he chose a Text, and consulted the best Expositors upon it (particularly the Rev. Mr. *Matthew Henry*, for whose Writings he seems to have had the greatest Value next to the sacred Scriptures) and then drew the Scheme of it on loose Papers, and noted down not only general Heads and Subdivisions, but also some of the most leading Thoughts and brightest Quotations from Authors (around

* He had a good Library, not large, but wisely collected of the best Authors ancient and modern. He retained considerable of his School-Learning to the last—I find him to have read over Horace in his Old Age, by his Collections of some of the most beautiful Lines and Sentiments from it. [*Turell's note.*]

† And yet as I observed in my Introduction, all or the most of them are printed off from the first rough Draught. [*Turell's note.*]

him) with many Passages of Scripture for Proof and Illustration.—Thus prepared he proceeded to write his Sermon on a Sheet of Paper neatly folded and stitched, which he sometimes finished with a Celerity and Exactness incredible. I have known him begin and compleat a Discourse that would last an Hour at one Sitting in a Forenoon.* Few Interlines or Emendations were afterward inserted or needed.† . . .

The *Doctor* as became a vigilant Overseer made frequent Visits to the several Families of his Charge, not only *common* and *civil* to cultivate Friendship and Good Will, but proper *Pastoral* Ones to enquire into and know their State and Circumstances in Order to treat them agreably, wisely and faithfully, and that he might the better adapt his publick Exercises, and give to every one their Portion in due Season.

He made Conscience of visiting the Poor as well as the Rich (especially in their Afflictions) instructing, advising, admonishing and comforting as he saw Occasion: And this he did Night and Day as long as his Strength lasted, and oftentimes to the no small Hazard of his Health and Life.

And when he gave Visits to any of his Congregation or received Visits from them (or other his Friends) he generally and generously bestowed Books of Piety on them, either his own Sermons, or the Publications of others.—When he was called to minister to the Souls of the Poor at their own Dwellings, he ordinarily enquired of their bodily Wants, which were soon supplyed either by himself, or charitable Friends to whom he instantly applyed on their Behalf.

His Prayers over sick and dying Ones, were not only very affectionate and fervent, but also most instructive and edifying—By a Train of excellent Thoughts he led them into the Knowledge of Sin and Duty, of God and Christ, and from Earth to Heaven.‡

When he could not conveniently visit his People or other his Friends in distant Places, he sent his Thoughts to them in Writing, suted to the various Providences he heard they were under—A few § of the Copies which are found, and which exhibit the bright Image of his Mind, the Reader shall be entertained withal after I have just added

* One of his Twenty Sacramental Sermons in Print. [*Turell's note.*]

† And yet he saw Cause to destroy many of his Sermons. On one and another of them he has wrote—The first three or five Sermons on this Text, are burnt. [*Turell's note.*]

‡ Some of the Members (I might say Ministers) of the Church of *England* have declared themselves more raised and edified by them than by all the devout and pious Forms of their own Church. [*Turell's note.*]

§ Alas, that so few are found; for he seldom kept Copies of his familiar Letters. A large and valuable Collection of them might be obtained if sought for, equally entertaining with those that follow. [*Turell's note.*]

a Word or two (for a Close to this Chapter) on his gentlemanly Carriage and Behaviour, and other *Homiletical* Virtues which adorned him, and were so conspicuous to all he conversed with.—He was a good Master of Address, and carried all the Politeness of a Court about him.—And as he treated Mankind of various Degrees and Ranks with a Civility, Courtesy, Affability, Complaisance and Candor scarce to be equalled. So all but the Base and Mean showed him an high Degree of Respect and Reverence, Love and Affection.—Particularly Men of Figure and Parts of our own Nation and Foreigners, whom he failed not to visit upon their coming among us, greatly valued and admired him.

It has been said (perhaps not without some seeming Grounds for it) that he sometimes went too far in complemental Strains both in Word and Writing—but if he did, I am perswaded such Flights took their Rise rather from an Exuberance or Excrescence (if the Phrase be allowable) of the before-mentioned homiletical Virtues, and a too high Complacency in the appearing Excellencies of others, than from faulty Insincerity and designed Flattery in the Time of it.—As he took a sincere Pleasure in the Gifts of others, and had a natural Proneness to think favourably of all Men, and construed every Thing in the most candid Sense, it is not much to be wondered at if he sometimes exceeded in his Expressions.—And it is to be lamented that some have swollen with Pride, and made an ill Use of the Doctor's high Esteem and good Opinion of them.

JANE TURELL

HER *Father* the Reverend Dr. *Benjamin Colman* (thro' the gracious Favour of *God*) is still living among us, one universally acknowleg'd to be even from his younger Times (at Home and Abroad) a bright Ornament and Honour to his Country, and an Instrument in *God*'s Hand of bringing much Good to it.

Her *Mother* Mrs. *Jane Colman* was a truly gracious Woman, Daughter of Mr. *Thomas Clark* Gentleman.

Mrs. *Turell* was their *third* Child, graciously given them after they had mourn'd the Loss of the two former; and for *seven* Years their *only* one. Her Constitution from her early Infancy was wonderful weak and tender, yet the Organs of her Body so form'd as not to obstruct the free Operations of the active and capacious Spirit within. The Buddings of Reason and Religion appear'd on her sooner than usual.—Before her *second* Year was compleated she could speak distinctly, knew her Letters, and could relate many Stories out of the Scriptures to the Satisfaction and Pleasure of the most Judicious. I have heard that Governour *Dudley*, with other Wise and Polite *Gentlemen*, have plac'd her on a Table and setting round it own'd themselves diverted with her Stories.— Before she was *four* Years old (so strong and tenacious was her Memory) she could say the greater Part of the *Assembly's Catechism*, many of the *Psalms*, some hundred Lines of the best *Poetry*, read distinctly, and make pertinent Remarks on many things she read.—

She grew in *Knowlege* (the most useful) day by day, and had the *Fear* of *God* before her Eyes.

She *pray'd* to *God* sometimes by excellent *Forms* (recommended to her by her Father and suited to her Age & Circumstances) and at other times *ex corde*, the *Spirit of God* helping her Infirmities. When her Father upon a Time enquir'd of her what Words she used in Prayer to God, she answer'd him,—"*That when she was upon her Knees God gave her Expressions*.

Even at the Age of *four*, *five*, & *six* she ask'd many astonishing *Questions* about divine Mysteries, and carefully laid up and hid the *Answers* she received to them, in her Heart. . . .

Before She had seen *Eighteen*, she had read, and (in some measure) digested all the English *Poetry*, and polite Pieces in *Prose*, printed and Manuscripts in her Father's well furnish'd Library, and much she borrow'd of her Friends and Acquaintance. She had indeed such a Thirst after Knowledge that the Leisure of the Day did not suffice, but she spent whole Nights in reading.

I find she was sometimes fir'd with a laudable Ambition of raising the honour of her *Sex*, who are therefore under Obligations to her; and all will be ready to own she had a fine *Genius*, and is to be placed among those who have excell'd.

When I was first inclin'd (by the Motions of God's Providence and Spirit) to seek her Acquaintance (which was about the Time she entred her *nineteenth* Year) I was surpriz'd and charm'd to find her so accomplish'd. I found her in a good measure Mistress of the politest *Writers* and their Works; could point out the Beauties in them, and had made many of their best Tho'ts her own: And as she went into more free Conversation, she discours'd how admirably on many Subjects!

I grew by Degrees into such an Opinion of her good *Taste*, that when she put me upon translating a *Psalm* or two, I was ready to excuse my Self, and if I had not fear'd to displease her should have deny'd her Request.

After her *Marriage* which was on *August* 11th. 1726, her Custom was once in a Month or two, to make some *new Essay* in Verse or Prose, and to read from Day to Day as much as a faithful Discharge of the Duties of her new Condition gave Leisure for: and I think I may with Truth say, that she made the writing of Poetry a *Recreation* and not a *Business.*

What greatly contributed to increase her Knowlege in *Divinity, History, Physick, Controversy,* as well as *Poetry,* was her attentive hearing most that I read upon those Heads thro' the long Evenings of the Winters as we sat together. . . .

Having related these Things, you will not wonder if I now declare my self a *Witness* of her daily close Walk with God during her married State, and of her Retirements for Reading, Self-Examination and Devotion.

It was her Practice to read the *Bible* out in Course, once in a Year, the Book of *Psalms* much oftner, besides many *Chapters* and a Multitude of *Verses* which she kept turn'd down in *a Bible,* which she had been the Owner and Reader of more than *twenty* Years. If I should only present my *Readers* with a *Catalogue* of these *Texts,* I doubt not but that they would admire the Collection, be gratified with the Entertainment; and easily conjecture many of her holy Frames and Tempers from them.—I must own, considering her tender Make and often Infirmities she *exceeded* in Devotion. And I have tho't my self oblig'd sometimes (in Compassion to her) to call her off, and put her in mind of God's *delighting in Mercy more than in Sacrifice.*

How often has she lain whole *Nights* by me mourning for Sin, calling upon God, and praising him, or discoursing of Christ and Heaven? And when under Doubts intreating me to help her (as far as I could) to a full Assurance of God's Love. Sometimes she would say, "Well, I am content if you will shew me that I have the Truth of Grace." And I often satisfy'd her with one of Mr. *Baxter*'s Marks of Love to Christ, namely, *Lamenting & panting after him;* for this kind of Love she was sure she exercis'd in the most cloudy Hours of her Life.

I may not forget to mention *the strong and constant Guard she plac'd at the Door of her Lips.* Who ever heard her call an ill Name? or *detract* from any Body? When she apprehended she receiv'd Injuries, *Silence* and *Tears* were her highest Resentments. But I have often heard her *reprove* others for rash and angry Speeches.

In every *Relation* she sustain'd she was truly *Exemplary,* sensible how much of the Life and Power of Religion consists in the conscientious Practice and Performance of *Relative Duties.*

No *Child* had a greater Love to and Reverence for her *Parents,* she even exceeded in Fear and Reverence of her *Father,* notwithstanding all his Condescentions to her, and vast Freedoms with her.

As a *Wife* she was dutiful, prudent and diligent, not only content but joyful in her Circumstances. She *submitted as is fit in the Lord, look'd well to the Ways of her Houshold, and her own Works praise her in the Gates.*

Her very Apparel discover'd Modesty and Chastity: She lov'd to appear neat and clean, but never gay and fine.

To her *Servants* she was good and kind, and took care of them, especially of the Soul of a *Slave* who dy'd (in the House) about a Month before her.

She respected all her *Friends* and *Relatives*, and spake of them with Honour, and never forgot either their Counsels or their Kindnesses.

She often spake of her Obligations to her *Aunt Staniford*, which were great living and dying.

She honour'd all Men, and lov'd every Body. *Love and Goodness was natural to her*, as her *Father* expresses it in a Letter Years ago.

Her tender Love to her only *Sister*, has been already seen; and was on all Occasions manifested, and grew exceedingly to her Death. A few Days before it, I heard her speak to her particularly of preparing for another World. "Improve (said she) the Time of Health, 'tis the *only* Time for doing the great Work in."

And in Return for her Love and amiable Carriage, *She had the Love and Esteem of all that knew her.* Those that knew her *best* lov'd her best, and praise her most.

Her *Humility* was so great, that she could well bear (without being elated) such *Praises* as are often found in her *Father's* Letters to us. viz. "*I greatly esteem as well as highly love you: The best of Children deserves all that a Child can of a Father: My Soul rejoyces in you: My Joy, my Crown. I give Thanks to God for you daily. I am honour'd in being the Father of such a Daughter.*"

Her *Husband* also, and he *praiseth* her as a *Meet Help* both in Spirituals and Temporals.

Her *Relations* and Acquaintance ever manifested the highest Value for her.

The *People*, among whom she liv'd the last *eight* Years of her Life, both *Old* and *Young* had a Love and *Veneration* for her; as a Person of the strictest Virtue and undefil'd Religion. Her *Innocence, Modesty, Ingenuity*, & *Devotion* charm'd all into an Admiration of her. And I question whether there has been *more Grief and Sorrow* shown at the Death of any private Person, by People of all Ranks, to whom her Virtues were known; *Mourning*, for the Loss sustain'd by our selves, *not for her*, nor *as others who have no Hope*. For it is beyond Doubt that she *died in the Lord*, and is *Blessed.*

Chapter VI

POETRY

It is a commonplace that the literature of any given period too often is judged by succeeding generations according to their own standards of taste. Now and then an injudicious verdict is quickly reversed, especially when no strong sentiments—sectional prejudices or violently emotional antipathies—prevent judicial appraisal. An equitable evaluation of colonial Puritan poetry has been difficult to make until recent years because, for one thing, the era as a whole in its relation to the English background has been neglected; and again, because much that seems intolerably arid today was extravagantly praised in its time; and finally, because many earlier verdicts have so long passed unchallenged that they have at last been accepted as true. For instance, the general reader has probably known colonial poetry only through a few extracts from Anne Bradstreet, Michael Wigglesworth, and the Bay Psalm Book. Beyond that triad even scholars have not easily penetrated, for modern editions of the seventeenth-century colonial poets have rarely appeared;[1] and critical estimates of Puritan verse are almost nonexistent.[2] The conjunction of two factors might be cited to explain the neglect: very little colonial verse has literary importance; that little, executed by writers who sometimes imitated only the superficialities of their models, was conceived according to standards which soon came into disfavor. The colonial Puritans, if they wrote at all, invariably tried their hand at versifying, and a really formidable amount of poetry was issued,—sometimes, as in the case of Wigglesworth, Anne Bradstreet, and Benjamin Tompson, in book form; but more often scattered informally through almanacs, histories, biographies, funeral sermons, and broadsides in the form of elegies, anagrams, epitaphs, and occasional "effusions." A few words, then, to bring the era into focus.

The cultivated Puritan was in no sense an implacable foe to the arts, for, like the Anglicans, he expected to win from life such mental and spiritual comfort as it could be made to offer. He studied in the same universities, read the same authors, discussed the same philosophies, and attempted to live, as they, "A sweet self-privacy in a right soul." [3]

[1] For recently published texts of Puritan verse, usually in limited editions, see Bibliography, p. 818, and the headings to the poetry selections.

[2] Moses C. Tyler, *A History of American Literature During the Colonial Period, 1607–1765* (New York, 1878), chapters X and XI, first essayed a judicious criticism of Puritan verse. After Tyler's *History*, no re-examination was made until Kenneth B. Murdock published his brief introduction to *Handkerchiefs from Paul* (Cambridge, 1927).

[3] Henry Vaughan, *Rules and Lessons*, *Poems* (The Muses' Library), I, 96.

His traditions were likewise Renaissance and Elizabethan, and as there was no law or reason to the contrary in the tenets of his particular faith, he was educated by way of the classics. Though the Bible was for him

> the Sacred *Grammar*, where
> The Rules of speaking well, contained are,[1]

the Puritan expected that the example set by the classical poets might guide him to achieve a higher virtue in life; therefore exercises in imitation of Vergil and Horace were part of his school training, as they were for all liberally educated English boys; and among the modern poets Spenser, Sidney, and Du Bartas (by way of Sylvester), and later Milton were his favorites. In one respect only can we detect in his attitude a view of poetry different from that held by other Englishmen. The Puritan centered his mind on God with a keener intensity, and thus more consciously withdrew his attention from "fleshly schools." The Anglican poets juxtaposed the flesh and spirit: Herrick's "Pious Pieces," *His Noble Numbers*, are no more colorful and sincere than his *Hesperides;* Donne's secular verses occupy a greater place even in his works than the *Divine Poems;* and the same can be said of the Catholic poet Crashaw, whose fame was spread as far by *The Delights of the Muses* as by *Carmen Deo Nostro*. But for the Puritans, and especially for those who came to New England, God, not the world, inspired their "noble numbers," and they many times chose verse the better to honor Him. They were still Elizabethan enough to live intensely, though their ardor took a new direction. It is clear therefore that since the Puritan did not cut himself off from the realities which a poetic art can summon, he made such use of them as seemed to him most fitting. Fundamentally Spenser, Sidney, and Milton, the real precursors of lesser Puritan bards, are ethical poets, and it is the moral import of their art which appealed to the Puritan mind; broadly speaking, those great writers conceived poetry as a philosophy—the highest philosophy, in fact; one which taught men virtue by example, not through mere didacticism, but by the embodiment of every knowledge. Above all else, poetry, they felt, should not be written merely to delight; it should be, as Du Bartas's *Divine Week* had shown, a speculum or compendium of the profoundest spiritual mysteries drawn from the most diverse learnings. Thus the subject matter of poetry was regarded as of highest consequence to men. To such a literary ideal the Puritans clung, even when they lacked the creative fire of their originals.

[1] Cotton Mather, *Corderius Americanus* (Boston, 1708), p. 29.

All this is not to say that the Puritans developed a conscious theory by which they judged poets and fashioned verses of their own. On the contrary, most of them probably gave it little consideration as an art; they thought of it simply as a means to an end, and remained curiously indifferent to the quintessential breath and finer spirit of the poetic idiom. It remains true, nevertheless, that they display an awareness of the art even though few had the talent to rise above mediocrity. It would seem wise to distinguish between the artistry they lacked, and the honor in which they held the poet's high office. The colonial Puritans seldom produced fine verse, because authentic talent among them was rare, and that which did manifest itself was perhaps neglected because of the tacit assumption—followed to extremes—that matter counted for more than manner. Learning was all, because it led past the world to God. The marvel of Milton is not that a Puritan wrote sensuously, but that a scholar could be a poet. If lesser Puritans adopted only the machinery of conceits, puns, and mythological fancies, they did so because they lacked the feeling, not the will, to achieve a higher reality.

The great poets searched for profitable doctrine which would teach great precepts when molded into spacious lines. Among Puritans, who as a class evidenced deep interest in historical and scientific matters, we find in extreme form the will to teach. Others before Puritans had written verse for the purpose designed by John Wilson, and in like manner,—the authors of *A Mirror for Magistrates*, for instance,—yet Wilson's poem, *A Song or, Story For . . . Remembrance* (see p. 552), is typical of much Puritan verse in style and content. Written to teach children the providential shaping of English history under Protestant rule, it is done into fourteeners to help them memorize it. For his matter Wilson drew upon Speed, Camden, and current tracts on the Gunpowder Plot. The doggerel ballad meter, universally familiar as that employed in the Sternhold and Hopkins version of the Psalms, hardly seems worthy of a gentleman who had shown a talent for Latin verse, and who had been nurtured at King's College, where the Fellows were encouraged to study poetry and music; but the poem is a product of the times, and its hold during the seventeenth century was unbroken, for it was republished in 1680, with a preface recalling "how excedingly pretious the remembrance of this heavenly man of God is. . . . He was another sweet singer of Israel, whose heavenly Verses passed like to the handkerchief carryed from Paul to help and uphold disconsolate ones, and to heal their wracked Souls, by the effectual prisence of Gods holy Spirit."

Probably no body of Puritan verse has seemed to modern readers more insensible to poetic feeling than that contained in the Bay Psalm Book (see p. 555). Composed as it was by ministers who labored to fashion suitable translations of the Psalms for vocal use in the churches, its angularity has often been judged either hopelessly uninspired or consciously hostile to grace and measure. Of course, such paraphrases now are out of style; and any metrical translation of the Psalms, in addition to being shaped to a familiar tune, must compete with the sustained felicity of the Bible rendering. The reader who compares the Bay Psalm Book with versions similarly adapted by Sandys, Donne, Milton, and Dryden need not single out the colonial versifiers for apology. Evidently the metric flaws troubled the authors, for their revision ten years later was undertaken with the idea of smoothing the lines. One cannot claim for either rendering more than its authors intended: an exact translation with as much grace as they knew how to give it. Their ideal, quite defensible, proved an extreme example of matter heeded at the expense of art.

No Puritan more clearly exemplifies the ideals which Puritan poets strove to reach than Anne Bradstreet (see pp. 561–579). Her ambitious discourses of Man, Monarchies, Seasons, and Elements, modeled on Du Bartas, pay homage to the poet as philosopher, even though Mistress Bradstreet's muse soars with a middle-flight. The mythological machinery and conventional praise of nature, not as she saw it, but as she had often encountered it in others' verse, were flaws which she acquired by poetic, not Puritan, tradition. It was, after all, the ingenious display of erudition in a woman which made her a "best seller" in England for a short time, and won for her the appellation of "Tenth Muse." For us she lives rather in the moments when her contemplative spirit stirs to life a theme which touched her heart. A tender wistfulness plays through the lines which she wrote "vpon the burning of our house":

> Here stood that Trunk, and there that chest;
> There lay that store I covnted best:
> My pleasant things in ashes lye,
> And them behold no more shall I.[1]

Except it be Jonathan Edwards, no Puritan has more often been cited as the embodiment of repulsive joylessness than Michael Wigglesworth; his *Day of Doom* is still reckoned a monstrous example of unrelieved horror. Yet Wigglesworth's purpose was similar to that of Wilson. When Cotton Mather preached the funeral sermon for Wigglesworth,

[1] See p. 578.

he recalled that the late Malden pastor had written "several Composures, wherein he proposed the Edification of such Readers, as are for Truth's dressed up in a *Plain Meeter*." [1] Indeed, the "Little Feeble *Shadow of a Man*," as Mather called him, whose health was so poor that he gave up his college tutorship, preached but seldom, and turned down the Harvard presidency in 1684, had written an epic that was also a "best seller." The grim intensity of its vivid descriptions must have struck terror in the hearts of many a child who was compelled to memorize its doggerel staves, and belied the character of the country parson and doctor whose nature was essentially guileless and gentle. The verses in his second published volume, *Meat out of the Eater*, rivaled in popularity *The Day of Doom*. The songs and meditations are written in the same monotonous fourteeners adopted in the earlier epic, but though rude, the stanzas are alive and occasionally touching. The merits of Wigglesworth's poetry today are more clearly felt in the tonal quality of such lines as those from *A Song of Emptiness*, fashioned on the *ubi sunt* theme:

> If *Beauty* could the beautiful defend
> From Death's dominion, than slain *Absalom*
> Had not been brought to such a shameful end:
> But fair and foul unto the Grave must come.
>
> If *Wealth* or *Scepters* could Immortal make,
> Then wealthy *Croesus*, wherefore art thou dead?
> If *Warlike force*, which makes the World to quake,
> Then why is *Julius Caesar* perished?
>
> Where are the *Scipio's* Thunder-bolts of War?
> Renowned *Pompey*, *Caesars* Enemie?
> Stout *Hannibal*, *Romes* Terror known so far?
> Great *Alexander*, what's become of thee?
>
> If *Gifts* and *Bribes* Death's favour might but win, . . .
> All these, and more, had still surviving been: . . . [2]

We must bear in mind that the doctrines of God's immutable justice, which Wigglesworth "dressed up in a *Plain Meeter*," were not in their day considered unlovely. Cotton Mather tells how John Cotton felt about the matter: "And being asked, why in his Latter Dayes, he In-

[1] *A Faithful Man, Described and Rewarded* (Boston, 1705), p. 24.

[2] With the somewhat prolix second and fourth lines removed, the resulting couplet produces, with the preceding three stanzas, a highly creditable sonnet.

dulged *Nocturnal Studies*, more than formerly, he pleasantly Replied, *Because I Love to Sweeten my mouth with a piece of* Calvin, *before I go to sleep.*" [1] Jonathan Edwards later described in his "Personal Narrative" how he found the doctrine of God's absolute sovereignty and justice with respect to salvation and damnation exceedingly pleasant, bright, and sweet.

The Puritans wrote their most ambitious poems for "edification," but some of the most appealing and sprightly lines are the commendatory pieces written, in the current fashion, sometimes to launch an author before the public (see p. 580), or perhaps, spontaneously conceived—as the stalwart lines of Edward Johnson,—to hymn God's wonder-working providence (see p. 630). Much of the beauty of Johnson's verse lies hidden in the elusive overtones of passionate conviction and half-realized felicities that are felt rather than heard. Even less purposeful than any verses yet discussed were those "composures" of the young college graduates who during the seventeenth century prepared the yearly almanacs, and were allowed to fill any blank spaces as a remuneration for the fussy task; the authors chose usually to write an essay on science, or perhaps a poem. The theme in either case was appropriate to the work in hand, and the resulting verses derived their inspiration from Vergilian themes wherein the signs of the zodiac intertwine with classic mythology:—often the ornate narrative recounts Apollo's wooing of the earth goddess Tellus. The imagery by which Thomas Shepard allegorized September in the *Almanack* for 1656 is unusually tempered and graceful:

The glorious Monarch of the Sky,
Times moderator, keep's his Court,
The Scoales of Justice hanging by
The golden Mean. And here resort
Pomona bringing mellow fruit,
And Ceres corn upon her back,
And kind Silvanus spread's this bruit;
His budget's full of nutts to crack.

The florid style sometimes gave way to allegory on contemporary events, as for instance the lines of Samuel Danforth in the *Almanack* for 1647, where the stanza for September offers the suggestion that

Four heads should meet and counsell have,
The chickens from the kite to save,

[1] *Johannes in Eremo* (Boston, 1695), p. 54.

> The idle drones away to drive,
> The little Bees to keep i' th' hive.
> How honey may be brought to these
> By making fish to dance on trees.[1]

"Thus the Cambridge Almanac became the annual poetry magazine of Harvard College." [2]

It has been queried why the Puritans so delighted in conceits and strained rhetorical figures, in anagrams and acrostics; [3] indeed, the fad at times was carried to extravagant lengths. As its worst it produced such verses as Benjamin Tompson's "Funeral Tribute" to Governor Winthrop of Connecticut, opening thus:

> Another Black Parenthesis of woe
> The *Printer* wills that all the World should know
> Sage *Winthrop* prest with publick sorrow Dies
> As the sum total of our Miseries.[4]

But the Puritan elegy at its best, as in Oakes's lament for Shepard (see p. 641), achieves a dignity and heartfelt simplicity, a tender pathos that goes far to redeem Puritan elegiac verse from the oblivion into which most of it has fallen. Tompson (see p. 635) was a poet of very local reputation, at his best in satire, whose achievements were evidently modeled on the extravagant commonplaces of Quarles; they reflect one popular literary fashion shaped to native material.

Of the colonial writers whose poetic accomplishments fall within the later Puritan era, Roger Wolcott and Mather Byles won some recognition. The verse of Wolcott (see p. 657), like that of Tompson, has small merit. The meditations of the future statesman and soldier on Biblical themes ally him with the Puritans of the seventeenth century, and his ambitious narrative of the agency of Winthrop at King Charles's court is the first colonial epic in patriotic strain. The couplets,

[1] The allegory is not very clear, but the "four heads" evidently refer to the united colonies of New England; the "hive" is Harvard College; the last two lines suggest that the college should be aided by a tax on the fishing industry. For interpretation, see K. B. Murdock, *Handkerchiefs from Paul*, pp. 101–111.

[2] Samuel E. Morison, *Harvard College in the Seventeenth Century*, p. 133.

[3] See Murdock, *op. cit.*, p. liv. A possible explanation is suggested by the Puritan's exaggerated desire to find God's shaping hand in all affairs, and by all symbolic, implicit, or elaborate means. "A Glass of spirits my Wife sent stood upon a Joint-Stool which, Simon W[illard] jogging, it fell down and broke all to shivers: I said twas a lively Emblem of our Fragility and Mortality" (*Diary of Samuel Sewall*, I, 460). It is an easy transfer, once the mind is thinking "emblematically," to heighten any figure by elaborate device.

[4] *Benjamin Tompson . . . His Poems*, ed. Howard J. Hall (Boston, 1924), p. 99; from a unique broadside.

sad rubbish though they be, seem to look forward to the more pretentious American epics of the late eighteenth century written by Humphrey, Dwight, Barlow, and Trumbull. The greater part of Byles's verses fall outside the Puritan era both in time and in spirit. "An Hymn to Christ" (see p. 663) is in some measure a link between the earlier period when men wrote to honor Christ, and the later more urbane decades when English literary fashions, set by Pope, Thomson, and Watts, were cleaving to new molds. Those who would seek representative selections of the punster's ready wit, or enjoy the light vein of his pleasant humor, must turn to such verses as he published after the Puritan years had passed.

The intrinsic value of Puritan poetry, even when the best of it is singled out for commendation, is apparent only in snatches. Two Puritans only were distinguished in their own time, Anne Bradstreet and Michael Wigglesworth; and such characteristics of their verses as were praised by their contemporaries are now more harshly judged. To modern eyes the undigested narrative summaries, the severe theology, and the edifying tone are frankly boring. Moments of inspiration they have in a phrase, a line, or a single poem. Perhaps we scrutinize too closely if we expect to discover finished poets in a country so remote from literary inspiration, among people whose purpose in writing was generally to edify. The one poet whose stature may well develop as time reveals him has been—at his own wish—forgotten; yet Edward Taylor (see p. 650) speaks perhaps with a more genuinely inspired voice than any other colonial poet. His fertility in image-making, his rapture, tenderness, delicacy, and intense devotion communicate something of the fervor which the man himself derived from his sacramental meditations. They give us one authentic indication that the indigenous Puritan muse, even when tied down to the fashions of an earlier style, soared with metaphoric brilliance.

JOHN WILSON, 1588–1667

[John Wilson, one of the two ministers who emigrated with Winthrop in 1630, is now chiefly remembered for his opposition to the Antinomian heresy and for his persecution of Anne Hutchinson. He was, in fact, a scholar eminent for his learning and attainments. Admitted to King's College, Cambridge, in 1605, he became three years later a Fellow of that royal institution. For a short time he devoted himself to the law, but through the influence of his friends Richard Rogers and William Ames—distinguished Puritans both,—he adopted the Congregational way. In trouble for nonconformity, he came to Boston as minister of the church which he served for the remaining thirty-seven years of his life.

In 1626, he published in London *A Song or, Story, For the Lasting Remembrance of diuerse famous works, which God hath done in our time*, a second edition of which appeared in Boston in 1680, entitled *A Song of Deliverance for the Lasting Remembrance of Gods Wonderful Works never to be Forgotten.* Few of his sermons were ever published. Cotton Mather wrote his Life in 1695, *Memoria Wilsoniana* (bound into his Life of the Reverend John Cotton, *Johannes in Eremo*), later incorporated in the *Magnalia* (1702). The 1680 edition of the poem is available in complete form in Kenneth B. Murdock, *Handkerchiefs from Paul* (Cambridge, 1927), together with a biographical and critical introduction. See also Savage, *Genealogical Dictionary;* and Samuel E. Morison, *The Founding of Harvard College* (Cambridge, 1935), *passim.* The text below is from a photostat copy of the first edition (pp. 37–40) in the British Museum.]

THE LONDON PLAGUE

From *A Song or, Story, For the Lasting Remembrance of diuerse famous works.*

1625

IN THE one thousand yeare of God,
  Sixe hundred twenty fiue,
Was sent the Pestilentiall rod,
  Our rockie hearts to riue.
In the chiefe Citty of the Realme,
  It had the chiefest seate:
There like a sea to ouerwhelme,
  Pride that was growne so great;
Or like a fire to purge away,
  The drosse of hatefull sinne;
Or like a trumpet thence to fray,
  The sleepe that soules were in.
The Queene of Cities wont to sit,
  In Chaire of highest state,
Now sate in dust and lowest pit,
  All sad and desolate:
The highest Court of Parlament,
  To Oxford did remooue.
The Tearmers were to Redding sent,
  Their Titles there to prooue.

Nor were the strangers strange alone,
  To the infected City;
But her best louers all were gone,
  And left her without pitty.
I meane, the rich did flocke away,
  And bad her streetes adew,
Except the poore (which needes must stay)
  There stayed but a few.
Nothing was heard but passing-bels,
  And friends their friends lamenting,
Nothing but heauy dolefull-knells.
  (Death not at all relenting)
Nothing was seene but heapes of dead,
  To feede the hungrie graue;
Or others lying sicke a bed,
  (No way their life to saue.)
Some looked pale, and some with paine,
  Were forc't to raue and roare,
Some did the deadly markes sustaine,
  And some the deadly sore:
In one yeares space, or lesse then so,
  (From time the Plague began)
To what a number did they grow,
  That death grip't in his spanne?
Sixtie two thousand at the least,
  Sixe hundred seuenty seuen,
Were made appeare by deaths arrest,
  Before the God of heauen.
Yea, do but from Iunes second looke
  Vnto Decembers last,
Scarse shall you reade in English-booke
  Of like doome euer past.
Within this three months space alone,
  As hath bin duly counted,
Fiftie three thousand ninetie one,
  By Bills report amounted.[1]
In London and the Liberties,[2]
  (Sixe moe [3] neere Parishes adde,)
All the forenamed clos'd their eies,
  And made their friends full sad.
More dyde in *this* than *former* pest,
  By th'heauy hand of God;
In thirteene weekes (to say the lest)
  Eleuen thousand fortie and odde.

Of all which summes, the greatest part
  By death departed thence,
Were pearced through with fire dart,
  Of raging Pestilence.
If within and without one Cittie Walls,
  Were found of men such lacke,
More then six myriades of soules
  Brought to so heauy wracke:
Oh then what was the wrecke and spoile,
  Of all the land beside,
In Cities and in Country soyle,
  Throughout the kingdome wide?
Trading grew dead, and mony scant,
  The rich doubting their state,
The poore were pinched sore with want,
  All fear'd the dismall fate.

THE BAY PSALM BOOK

[Only ten known copies survive of *The Whole Booke of Psalmes Faithfully Translated into English Metre* (Cambridge, 1640), from an edition that numbered seventeen hundred. The volumes were worn threadbare with use; a second printing was issued in 1647, and within the next hundred years twenty-five more printings were necessary. Generally known as the Bay Psalm Book, it was the first book issued in the American colonies—preceded only by a broadside sheet, the Freeman's Oath, and by the 1639 Alamanac—and is probably the first book in English printed in North America.

Typographically it bears marks of hasty or unskilled workmanship; its prosodic merits are few, but not quite so few as Tyler implied when he called it "a poetic phenomenon, happily unique, we may hope, in all the literatures of English speech" (*A History of American Literature*, I, 274, 275). The authors, Thomas Weld, John Eliot, and Richard Mather, were university-trained ministers who perhaps "for the meetre sake" should not have refused Francis Quarles's offer to help in the composition. But they were translating the Hebrew with what seemed to them fitting exactness. "Neither let any think," Mather explains in the preface (see p. 670), "that for the meetre sake wee have taken liberty or poeticall licence to depart from the true and proper sence of Davids words in the hebrew verses, noe; . . . Gods Altar needs not our pollishings." Indeed, its purpose was to replace the Sternhold and Hopkins version currently used, a text which, because of its departure from the original and its sacrifice of a literal rendering for poetic effect, troubled the straightforward Puritan's scholarly conscience.

But even from the beginning the rude lines of the Bay Psalms were not regarded as sacrosanct. The first two editions (1640, 1647) having run out, what was in effect a third appeared in 1651: *The Psalms Hymns And Spiritual Songs Of the Old and New Testament, faithfully translated into English metre.* President Dunster of Harvard, assisted by a Mr. Richard Lyon, took the work over, "having a special ey," as the preface explains, "both to the gravity of the phrase" and "sweetnes of the verse." The new editors added translations from other books of the Bible, principally from the Songs of Solomon. The changes they effected are occasionally an improvement.

"It was thought," Cotton Mather said a half-century later (*Magnalia*, III, 100), "that a little more of Art was to be employ'd upon the verses"; and this edition, thus "Revised and Refined," continued to be standard until the aged Reverend John Barnard of Marblehead brought forth *A New Version of the Psalms of David* at Boston in 1752. He states by way of preface that the older version "is generally very good, and few of the same Age may be compar'd with it; yet the Flux of Languages has rendered several Phrases in it obsolete . . ." His ideal, however, was still that of the first generation. "My great Care has been to keep as close to the Original as I could . . . And all in a Stile . . . adapted to the Capacity of our Christian Assemblies; neither in such Flights of Poetry as soar above them, nor yet so low, I trust, as to be contemptible." His version, in turn, was superseded by one published by Thomas Prince in 1758.

The 1640 edition was reprinted at Cambridge in 1862, and reproduced in facsimile with an introduction by Wilberforce Eames at New York in 1903. The text of the Dunster-Lyon selections below follows the unique copy in the New York Public Library. The verses are from the 1640 edition, however, unless otherwise stated.]

THE PSALMS

23 A Psalme of David.

THE LORD to mee a shepheard is, want therefore shall not I.
2 Hee in the folds of tender-grasse, doth cause mee downe to lie:
To waters calme me gently leads (3) Restore my soule doth hee:
he doth in paths of righteousnes: for his names sake leade mee.
4 Yea though in valley of deaths shade I walk, none ill I'le feare:
because thou art with mee, thy rod, and staffe my comfort are.

5 For mee a table thou hast spread, in presence of my foes:
thou dost annoynt my head with oyle, my cup it over-flowes.
6 Goodnes & mercy surely shall all my dayes follow mee:
and in the Lords house I shall dwell so long as dayes shall bee.

PSAL: XXIII. A PSALM OF DAVID.

THE LORD to me a shepheard is: want therfore shall not I.
2 Hee in the foulds of tender grass doth make me down to ly:
Hee leads me to the waters still. (3) Restore my soul doth hee;
In paths of righteousness, he will for his names sake lead mee.

4 In valley of deaths shade although I walk I'le fear none ill:
For thou with me thy rod, also thy staff me comfort will.
5 Thou hast 'fore me a table spread, in presence of my foes:
Thou dost anoint with oyle my head, my cup it ouer-flowes.

6 Goodness and mercy my dayes all shall surely follow mee:
And in the LORDS house dwell I shall so long as dayes shall bee.

[From Dunster-Lyon revision, 1651]

PSALME 107.

O GIVE yee thanks unto the Lord, because that good is hee:
because his loving kindenes lasts to perpetuitee.
2 So let the Lords redeem'd say: whom hee freed from th'enemies hands:
3 And gathred them from East, & West, from South, & Northerne lands.
4 I'th desart, in a desart way they wandred: no towne finde,
5 to dwell in. Hungry & thirsty: their soule within them pinde.
[6] Then did they to Iehovah cry when they were in distresse:
who did them set at liberty out of their anguishes.
7 In such a way that was most right he led them forth also:
that to a citty which they might inhabit they might go.
8 O that men would Iehovah prayse for his great goodnes *then:*
& for his workings wonderfull unto the sonnes of men.
9 Because that he the longing soule doth throughly satisfy:
the hungry soule he also fills with good abundantly.

(2)

10 Such as in darknes' and within the shade of death abide;
who are in sore affliction, also in yron tyde:
11 By reason that against the words of God they did rebell;
also of him that is most high contemned the counsell.
12 Therefore with molestation hee did bring downe their heart:
downe did they fall, & none their was could help to them impart.

13 Then did they to Iehovah cry when they were in distress:
who did them set at liberty out of their anguishes.
14 He did them out of darknes bring, also deaths shade from under:
as for the bands that they were in he did them break asunder.
15 O that men would Iehovah prayse for his great goodnes *then:*
and for his workings wonderfull unto the sonnes of men.
16 For he hath all to shivers broke the gates that were of brasse:
& hee asunder cut each barre that made of yron was.

(3)

17 For their transgressions & their sins, fooles doe affliction beare.
18 All kinde of meate their soule abhorres: to deaths gate they draw neare.
19 Then did they to Iehovah cry when they were in distress:
who did them set at liberty out of their anguishes.
20 He, sent his word, & therewithall healing to them he gave:
from out of their destructions he did them also save.
21 O that men would Iehovah prayse, for his great goodnes *then:*
& for his workings wonderfull unto the sons of men.
22 And sacrifices sacrifice let them of thanksgiving:
& while his works they doe declare let them for gladnes sing.

(4)

23 They that goe downe to'th sea in ships: their busines there to doo
24 in waters great. The Lords work see, i'th deep his wonders too.
25 Because that he the stormy winde commandeth to arise:
which lifteth up the waves therof, (26) They mount up to the skyes:
Downe goe they to the depths againe, their soule with ill doth quaile.
27 They reele, & stagger, drunkard like, and all their witt doth faile.
28 Then did they to Iehovah cry when they were in distress:
and therupon he bringeth them out of their anguishes.
29 Hee makes the storme a calme: so that the waves therof are still.
30 Their rest then glads them; he them brings to'th hav'n which they did will.
31 O that men would Iehovah prayse for his great goodnes *then:*
& for his workings wonderfull unto the sons of men.
32 Also within the peoples Church him let them highly rayse:
where Elders are assembled, there him also let them prayse.

(5)

33 He rivers to a desart turnes, to drought the springing well:
34 A fruitfull soyle to barrennes; for their sin there that dwell.
35 The desart to a poole he turnes; and dry ground to a spring.

36 Seates there the hungry; who prepare their towne of habiting,
37 Vineyards there also for to plant, also to sow the field;
which may unto them fruitfull things of much revenue yield.
38 Also he blesseth them, so that they greatly are increast:
and for to be diminished he suffers not their beast.
39 Againe they are diminished & they are brought downe low,
by reason of their pressing-streights, affliction & sorrow.

(6)

40 On Princes he contempt doth powre; and causeth them to stray
i'th solitary wildernes, wherin there is no way.
41 Yet hee out of affliction doth make the poore to rise:
& like as if it were a flock, doth make him families.
42 The righteous shall it behold, and he shall joyfull bee:
in silence stop her mouth also shall all iniquitee.
43 Who so is wise, & who so will these things attentive learne:
the loving kindenes of the Lord they clearely shall discerne.

Psal: CVII.

Gods goodnes to Travellers.

(1)

With thanks unto ye Lord confess, because that good is hee:
Because his loving kindnesses last to eternitie.
2 So say the Lords redeem'd, whom bought he hath from th'enemys hands.
3 And from the East, & west hath brought from South, and northern lands.
4 I'th desert stray'd in desert way, no dwelling Town they find.
5 They hungry were, and thirstie they, their souls within them pin'd.
6 Then did they to Jehovah cry, when they were in distress:
Who did them set at liberty, out of their anguishes.

7 In such a way as was most right, he led them forth also:
That to a Citty which they might inhabit, they might go.
8 O that men praise Jehovah would, for his great goodnes then!
And for his wonders manifold unto the sonns of men!

[From Dunster-Lyon revision, 1651]

Psalme 141. A Psalme of David.

O God, my Lord, on thee I call, doe thou make hast to mee:
and harken thou unto my voice, when I cry unto thee.
2 And let my pray'r directed be as incense in thy sight:
and the up-lifting of my hands as sacrifice at night.

3 Iehovah: oh that thou would'st set a watch my mouth before:
as also of my lips with care o doe [thou] keepe the dore.
4 Bow not my heart to evill things; to doe the wicked deed
with wicked workers: & let not mee of their dainties feed.
5 Let just-men smite mee, kindenes 'tis; let him reprove mee eke,
it shall be such a pretious oyle, my head it shall not breake:
For yet my prayr's ev'n in their woes. (6) When their judges are cast
on rocks, then shall they heare my words, for they are sweet to taste.
7 Like unto one who on the earth doth cutt & cleave the wood,
ev'n so our bones at the graves mouth are scattered abroad.
8 But unto thee o God, the Lord directed are mine eyes:
my soule o leave not destitute, on thee my hope relyes.
9 O doe thou keepe mee from the snare which they have layd for mee;
& also from the grins of those that work iniquitee.
10 Together into their owne nets o let the wicked fall:
untill such time that I escape may make from them withall.

Solomons Song Chap: 6.

Fairest of women, whither is thy loved gone away:
Where is thy love by-turn'd, that so seek him with thee wee may.
2 My love to's gardens down is gone: into the beds of spice,
To feed in gardens, and to get the lilly-flowrs likewise.

3 I am for my beloved one, and my belov'd for mee:
And feed among the lilly-flowers continually doth hee.
4 Thou art my love as Tirza neat, fair as Jerusalem,
Yea, terrible, as is an hoast, that doth with banners stream.

5 Turn thou from me thine eyes, because they have me overcome:
Thine hair is as a flock of goats, which look from Gilead down.
6 Thy teeth are as a flock of sheep, up from the washing gone,
Wherof each one bears twinns, of them ther's not a barren one.

7 And in such wise within thy locks, thy temples placed are:
That to a piece of Pomgranate, the same I may compare.
8 Of Queens threescore, and fourscore is of concubins the count,
There are so many Virgins as all number do surmount.

9 My dove, my undefiled one, shee is her mothers one:
Of her that did her bear alone, shee is the choicest one:
The daughters, when they her beheld, they did her blessed call,
Yea both the Queens, and concubins, they praysed her withall.

10 Who's shee y^{t} looks as morning forth, fair as the Moon so bright?
Clear as the Sun, and terrible as hoasts with banners dight?
11 To'th garden of the nuts I went down, valley fruits to see:
To see, if Vines did bud, if bloom did the Pomgranate tree.

12 My soul had placed me before I ever was aware,
Upon the charriots of them that my willing people are.
13 Turn, turn, O Shulamite, turn, turn, that wee may look on thee:
What will you see i'th Shulamite, as two camps company.

[From Dunster-Lyon revision, 1651]

ANNE BRADSTREET, 1612–1672

[*The Tenth Muse Lately sprung up in America. or Severall Poems, compiled with great variety of Wit and Learning, full of delight* (London, 1650), by Anne Bradstreet, was the first important book of poems written in America. Daughter of Thomas Dudley, who later became governor of the Bay Colony, she married at sixteen Simon Bradstreet, emigrated with him in 1630, and lived a frontier life in North Andover, Massachusetts, on a farm near the Merrimac River. Here, as devoted wife to the man who advanced to governor and royal councillor, she raised her large family, and in moments of leisure wrote a long poem in praise of the seasons, "together with an exact epitome of the four monarchies," and songs honoring Queen Elizabeth, Sidney, Spenser, and Du Bartas. These somewhat frigid manuscript verses were taken to London by her brother-in-law and published without her knowledge. They won the attention of the public to such a degree that Edward Phillips in *Theatrum Poetarum* (1675) pronounced them "not yet wholly extinct."

Her best lyrics, however, were inspired by native settings of the world about her or the homely events of her daily life, and a second edition: *Several Poems Compiled . . . By a Gentlewoman in New-England . . . Corrected by the Author* was issued posthumously at Boston in 1678. It incorporated the "Contemplations," "The Flesh and the Spirit," and the delightful verses upon her husband and children. A few poems, including the "Meditations," remained in manuscript until John H. Ellis brought out the definitive edition of her *Works* at Charlestown, Massachusetts, in 1867 (reprinted in New York, 1932). Her burial place is unknown, and no portrait of her is known to exist.

See Oscar Wegelin, *comp.*, "A List of Editions of the Poems of Anne Bradstreet, with Several Additional Books Relating to Her," *American Book Collector*, IV (1933), 15–16. See Bibliography (p. 814) for titles of biographies. Accounts also appear in Cotton Mather, *Magnalia*,

Book II, 17; Tyler, *A History of American Literature*, I, 277–292; and *Dictionary of American Biography*. See especially the sketch in Samuel E. Morison, *Builders of the Bay Colony*, chapter XI. The text of all but "Meditations," "Verses vpon the burning of our house," and "Longing for Heaven" is from the second edition; the above named are from *Works*, ed. Ellis, 1932.]

THE TENTH MUSE

The Four Seasons of the Year.

Spring.

Another four I've left yet to bring on,
Of four times four the last *Quaternion*,
The Winter, Summer, Autumn & the Spring,
In season all these Seasons I shall bring:
Sweet Spring like man in his Minority,
At present claim'd, and had priority.
With smiling face and garments somewhat green,
She trim'd her locks, which late had frosted been,
Nor hot nor cold, she spake, but with a breath,
Fit to revive, the nummed earth from death.
Three months (quoth she) are 'lotted to my share
March, *April*, *May* of all the rest most fair.
Tenth of the first, *Sol* into *Aries* enters,
And bids defiance to all tedious winters,
Crosseth the Line, and equals night and day,
(Stil adds to th' last til after pleasant *May*)
And now makes glad the darkned northern wights
Who for some months have seen but starry lights.
Now goes the Plow-man to his merry toyle,
He might unloose his winter locked soyl:
The Seeds-man too, doth lavish out his grain,
In hope the more he casts, the more to gain:
The Gardner now superfluous branches lops,
And poles erects for his young clambring hops.
Now digs then sowes his herbs, his flowers & roots
And carefully manures his trees of fruits.
The *Pleiades their influence* now give,
And all that seem'd as dead afresh doth live.
The croaking frogs, whom nipping winter kil'd
Like birds now chirp, and hop about the field,
The Nightingale, the black bird and the Thrush
Now tune their layes, on sprayes of every bush.

The wanton frisking Kid, and soft-fleec'd Lambs
Do jump and play before their feeding Dams,
The tender tops of budding grass they crop,
They joy in what they have, but more in hope:
For though the frost hath lost his binding power,
Yet many a fleece of snow and stormy shower
Doth darken *Sol*'s bright eye, makes us remember
The pinching North-west wind of cold *December*.
My second moneth is *April*, green and fair,
Of longer dayes, and a more temperate Air:
The Sun in *Taurus* keeps his residence,
And with his warmer beams glanceth from thence.
This is the month whose fruitful showrs produces
All set and sown for all delights and uses:
The Pear the Plum, and Apple tree now flourish
The grass grows long the hungry beast to nourish.
The Primrose pale, and azure violet
Among the virduous grass hath nature set,
That when the Sun on's Love (the earth) doth shine,
These might as lace set out her garment fine.
The fearfull bird his little house now builds
In trees and walls, in Cities and in fields.
The outside strong, the inside warm and neat;
A natural Artificer compleat:
The clocking hen her chirping chickins leads
With wings & beak defends them from the gleads.[1]
My next and last is fruitfull pleasant *May*,
Wherein the earth is clad in rich aray,
The Sun now enters loving *Gemini*,
And heats us with the glances of his eye,
Our thicker rayment makes us lay aside
Lest by his fervor we be torrifi'd.
All flowers the Sun now with his beams discloses,
Except the double pinks and matchless Roses.
Now swarms the busy, witty, honey-Bee,
Whose praise deserves a page from more then me
The cleanly Huswifes Dary's now in th' prime,
Her shelves and firkins [2] fill'd for winter time.
The meads with Cowslips, Honey-suckles dight,
One hangs his head, the other stands upright:
But both rejoyce at th' heavens clear smiling face,
More at her showers, which water them a space.
For fruits my Season yields the early Cherry,
The hasty Peas, and wholsome cool Strawberry.
More solid fruits require a longer time,

Each Season hath his fruit, so hath each Clime:
Each man his own peculiar excellence,
But none in all that hath preheminence.
Sweet fragrant Spring, with thy short pittance fly
Let some describe thee better then can I.
Yet above all this priviledg is thine,
Thy dayes still lengthen without least decline.

Contemplations.

Some time now past in the Autumnal Tide,
When *Phœbus* wanted but one hour to bed,
The trees all richly clad, yet void of pride,
Where gilded o're by his rich golden head.
Their leaves & fruits seem'd painted, but was true
Of green, of red, of yellow, mixed hew,
Rapt were my sences at this delectable view.

2

I wist not what to wish, yet sure thought I,
If so much excellence abide below;
How excellent is he that dwells on high?
Whose power and beauty by his works we know.
Sure he is goodness, wisdome, glory, light,
That hath this under world so richly dight:
More Heaven then Earth was here, no winter & no night.

3

Then on a stately Oak I cast mine Eye,
Whose ruffling top the Clouds seem'd to aspire;
How long since thou wast in thine Infancy?
Thy strength, and stature, more thy years admire,
Hath hundred winters past since thou wast born?
Or thousand since thou brakest thy shell of horn,
If so, all these as nought, Eternity doth scorn.

4

Then higher on the glistering Sun I gaz'd,
Whose beams was shaded by the leavie Tree,
The more I look'd, the more I grew amaz'd,
And softly said, what glory's like to thee?
Soul of this world, this Universes Eye,
No wonder, some made thee a Deity:
Had I not better known, (alas) the same had I.

5

Thou as a Bridegroom from thy Chamber rushes,
And as a strong man, joyes to run a race,
The morn doth usher thee, with smiles & blushes,
The Earth reflects her glances in thy face.
Birds, insects, Animals with Vegative,
Thy heart from death and dulness doth revive:
And in the darksome womb of fruitful nature dive.

6

Thy swift Annual, and diurnal Course,
Thy daily streight, and yearly oblique path,
Thy pleasing fervor, and thy scorching force,
All mortals here the feeling knowledg hath.
Thy presence makes it day, thy absence night,
Quaternal Seasons caused by thy might:
Hail Creature, full of sweetness, beauty & delight.

7

Art thou so full of glory, that no Eye
Hath strength, thy shining Rayes once to behold?
And is thy splendid Throne erect so high?
As to approach it, can no earthly mould.
How full of glory then must thy Creator be?
Who gave this bright light luster unto thee:
Admir'd, ador'd for ever, be that Majesty.

8

Silent alone, where none or saw, or heard,
In pathless paths I lead my wandring feet,
My humble Eyes to lofty Skyes I rear'd
To sing some Song, my mazed Muse thought meet.
My great Creator I would magnifie,
That nature had, thus decked liberally:
But Ah, and Ah, again, my imbecility!

9

I heard the merry grashopper then sing,
The black clad Cricket, bear a second part,
They kept one tune, and plaid on the same string,
Seeming to glory in their little Art.
Shall Creatures abject, thus their voices raise?
And in their kind resound their makers praise:
Whilst I as mute, can warble forth no higher layes.

10

When present times look back to Ages past,
And men in being fancy those are dead,
It makes things gone perpetually to last,
And calls back moneths and years that long since fled.
It makes a man more aged in conceit,
Then was *Methuselah*, or's grand-sire great:
While of their persons & their acts his mind doth treat.

11

Sometimes in *Eden* fair, he seems to be,
Sees glorious *Adam* there made Lord of all,
Fancyes the Apple, dangle on the Tree,
That turn'd his Sovereign to a naked thral.
Who like a miscreant's driven from that place,
To get his bread with pain, and sweat of face:
A penalty impos'd on his backsliding Race.

12

Here sits our Grandame in retired place,
And in her lap, her bloody *Cain* new born,
The weeping Imp oft looks her in the face,
Bewails his unknown hap, and fate forlorn;
His Mother sighs, to think of Paradise,
And how she lost her bliss, to be more wise,
Believing him that was, and is, Father of lyes.

13

Here *Cain* and *Abel* come to sacrifice,
Fruits of the Earth, and Fatlings each do bring,
On *Abels* gift the fire descends from Skies,
But no such sign on false *Cain's* offering;
With sullen hateful looks he goes his wayes.
Hath thousand thoughts to end his brothers dayes,
Upon whose blood his future good he hopes to raise

14

There *Abel* keeps his sheep, no ill he thinks,
His brother comes, then acts his fratricide,
The Virgin Earth, of blood her first draught drinks
But since that time she often hath been cloy'd;
The wretch with gastly face and dreadful mind,
Thinks each he sees will serve him in his kind,
Though none on Earth but kindred near then could he find.

15

Who fancyes not his looks now at the Barr,
His face like death, his heart with horror fraught,
Nor Male-factor ever felt like warr,
When deep dispair, with wish of life hath sought,
Branded with guilt, and crusht with treble woes,
A Vagabond to Land of *Nod* [3] he goes.
A City builds, that wals might him secure from foes.

16

Who thinks not oft upon the Fathers ages.
Their long descent, how nephews sons they saw,
The starry observations of those Sages,
And how their precepts to their sons were law,
How Adam sigh'd to see his Progeny,
Cloath'd all in his black sinfull Livery,
Who neither guilt, nor yet the punishment could fly.

17

Our Life compare we with their length of dayes
Who to the tenth of theirs doth now arrive?
And though thus short, we shorten many wayes,
Living so little while we are alive;
In eating, drinking, sleeping, vain delight
So unawares comes on perpetual night,
And puts all pleasures vain unto eternal flight.

18

When I behold the heavens as in their prime,
And then the earth (though old) stil clad in green,
The stones and trees, insensible of time,
Nor age nor wrinkle on their front are seen;
If winter come, and greeness then do fade,
A Spring returns, and they more youthfull made;
But Man grows old, lies down, remains where once he's laid.

20 [19]

By birth more noble then those creatures all,
Yet seems by nature and by custome curs'd,
No sooner born, but grief and care makes fall
That state obliterate he had at first:
Nor youth, nor strength, nor wisdom spring again
Nor habitations long their names retain,
But in oblivion to the final day remain.

20

Shall I then praise the heavens, the trees, the earth
Because their beauty and their strength last longer
Shall I wish there, or never to had birth,
Because they're bigger, & their bodyes stronger?
Nay, they shall darken, perish, fade and dye,
And when unmade, so ever shall they lye,
But man was made for endless immortality.

21

Under the cooling shadow of a stately Elm
Close sate I by a goodly Rivers side,
Where gliding streams the Rocks did overwhelm;
A lonely place, with pleasures dignifi'd.
I once that lov'd the shady woods so well,
Now thought the rivers did the trees excel,
And if the sun would ever shine, there would I dwell.

22

While on the stealing stream I fixt mine eye,
Which to the long'd for Ocean held its course,
I markt, nor crooks, nor rubs that there did lye
Could hinder ought, but still augment its force:
O happy Flood, quoth I, that holds thy race
Till thou arrive at thy beloved place,
Nor is it rocks or shoals that can obstruct thy pace

23

Nor is't enough, that thou alone may'st slide,
But hundred brooks in thy cleer waves do meet,
So hand in hand along with thee they glide
To *Thetis* house,[4] where all imbrace and greet:
Thou Emblem true, of what I count the best,
O could I lead my Rivolets to rest,
So may we press to that vast mansion, ever blest.

24

Ye Fish which in this liquid Region 'bide,
That for each season, have your habitation,
Now salt, now fresh where you think best to glide
To unknown coasts to give a visitation,
In Lakes and ponds, you leave your numerous fry,
So nature taught, and yet you know not why,
You watry folk that know not your felicity.

25

Look how the wantons frisk to tast the air,
Then to the colder bottome streight they dive,
Eftsoon to *Neptun*'s glassie Hall repair
To see what trade they great ones there do drive,
Who forrage o're the spacious sea-green field,
And take the trembling prey before it yield,
Whose armour is their scales, their spreading fins their shield.

26

While musing thus with contemplation fed,
And thousand fancies buzzing in my brain,
The sweet-tongu'd Philomel [5] percht ore my head,
And chanted forth a most melodious strain
Which rapt me so with wonder and delight,
I judg'd my hearing better then my sight,
And wisht me wings with her a while to take my flight.

28 [27]

O merry Bird (said I) that fears no snares,
That neither toyles nor hoards up in thy barn,
Feels no sad thoughts, nor cruciating cares
To gain more good, or shun what might thee harm
Thy cloaths ne're wear, thy meat is every where,
Thy bed a bough, thy drink the water cleer,
Reminds not what is past, nor whats to come dost fear.

28

The dawning morn with songs thou dost prevent,[6]
Sets hundred notes unto thy feathered crew,
So each one tunes his pretty instrument,
And warbling out the old, begin anew,
And thus they pass their youth in summer season,
Then follow thee into a better Region,
Where winter's never felt by that sweet airy legion.

29

Man at the best a creature frail and vain,
In knowledg ignorant, in strength but weak,
Subject to sorrows, losses, sickness, pain,
Each storm his state, his mind, his body break,
From some of these he never finds cessation,
But day or night, within, without, vexation,
Troubles from foes, from friends, from dearest, near'st Relation.

30

And yet this sinfull creature, frail and vain,
This lump of wretchedness, of sin and sorrow,
This weather-beaten vessel wrackt with pain,
Joyes not in hope of an eternal morrow;
Nor all his losses, crosses and vexation,
In weight, in frequency and long duration
Can make him deeply groan for that divine Translation.

31

The Mariner that on smooth waves doth glide,
Sings merrily, and steers his Barque with ease,
As if he had command of wind and tide,
And now become great Master of the seas;
But suddenly a storm spoiles all the sport,
And makes him long for a more quiet port,
Which 'gainst all adverse winds may serve for fort.

32

So he that saileth in this world of pleasure,
Feeding on sweets, that never bit of th' sowre,
That's full of friends, of honour and of treasure,
Fond fool, he takes this earth ev'n for heav'ns bower.
But sad affliction comes & makes him see
Here's neither honour, wealth, nor safety;
Only above is found all with security.

33

O Time the fatal wrack of mortal things,
That draws oblivions curtains over kings,
Their sumptuous monuments, men know them not,
Their names without a Record are forgot,
Their parts, their ports, their pomp's all laid in th' dust
Nor wit nor gold, nor buildings scape times rust;
But he whose name is grav'd in the white stone [7]
Shall last and shine when all of these are gone.

THE FLESH AND THE SPIRIT.[8]

IN secret place where once I stood
Close by the Banks of *Lacrim* flood
I heard two sisters reason on
Things that are past, and things to come;
One flesh was call'd, who had her eye
On worldly wealth and vanity;

The other Spirit, who did rear
Her thoughts unto a higher sphere:
Sister, quoth Flesh, what liv'st thou on
Nothing but Meditation?
Doth Contemplation feed thee so
Regardlesly to let earth goe?
Can Speculation satisfy
Notion without Reality?
Dost dream of things beyond the Moon
And dost thou hope to dwell there soon?
Hast treasures there laid up in store
That all in th' world thou count'st but poor?
Art fancy sick, or turn'd a Sot
To catch at shadowes which are not?
Come, come, Ile shew unto thy sence,
Industry hath its recompence.
What canst desire, but thou maist see
True substance in variety?
Dost honour like? acquire the same,
As some to their immortal fame:
And trophyes to thy name erect
Which wearing time shall ne're deject.
For riches dost thou long full sore?
Behold enough of precious store.
Earth hath more silver, pearls and gold,
Then eyes can see, or hands can hold.
Affect's thou pleasure? take thy fill,
Earth hath enough of what you will.
Then let not goe, what thou maist find,
For things unknown, only in mind.
Spir. Be still thou unregenerate part,
Disturb no more my setled heart,
For I have vow'd, (and so will doe)
Thee as a foe, still to pursue.
And combate with thee will and must,
Untill I see thee laid in th' dust.
Sisters we are, ye[a] twins we be,
Yet deadly feud 'twixt thee and me;
For from one father are we not,
Thou by old Adam wast begot,
But my arise is from above,
Whence my dear father I do love.
Thou speakst me fair, but hatst me sore,
Thy flatt'ring shews Ile trust no more.
How oft thy slave, hast thou me made,

when I believ'd, what thou hast said,
And never had more cause of woe
Then when I did what thou bad'st doe.
Ile stop mine ears at these thy charms,
And count them for my deadly harms.
Thy sinfull pleasures I doe hate,
Thy riches are to me no bait,
Thine honours doe, nor will I love;
For my ambition lyes above.
My greatest honour it shall be
When I am victor over thee,
And triumph shall, with laurel head,
When thou my Captive shalt be led,
How I do live, thou need'st not scoff,
For I have meat thou know'st not off;
The hidden Manna I doe eat,
The word of life it is my meat.
My thoughts do yield me more content
Then can thy hours in pleasure spent.
Nor are they shadows which I catch,
Nor fancies vain at which I snatch,
But reach at things that are so high,
Beyond thy dull Capacity;
Eternal substance I do see,
With which inriched I would be:
Mine Eye doth pierce the heavens, and see
What is Invisible to thee.
My garments are not silk nor gold,
Nor such like trash which Earth doth hold,
But Royal Robes I shall have on,
More glorious then the glistring Sun;
My Crown not Diamonds, Pearls, and gold,
But such as Angels heads infold.
The City [9] where I hope to dwell,
There's none on Earth can parallel;
The stately Walls both high and strong,
Are made of pretious *Jasper* stone;
The Gates of Pearl, both rich and clear,
And Angels are for Porters there;
The Streets thereof transparent gold,
Such as no Eye did e're behold,
A Chrystal River there doth run,
Which doth proceed from the Lambs Throne:
Of Life, there are the waters sure,
Which shall remain for ever pure,

Nor Sun, nor Moon, they have no need,
For glory doth from God proceed:
No Candle there, nor yet Torch light,
For there shall be no darksome night.
From sickness and infirmity,
For evermore they shall be free,
Nor withering age shall e're come there,
But beauty shall be bright and clear;
This City pure is not for thee,
For things unclean there shall not be:
If I of Heaven may have my fill,
Take thou the world, and all that will.

To my Dear and loving Husband.

If ever two were one, then surely we.
If ever man were lov'd by wife, then thee;
If ever wife was happy in a man,
Compare with me ye women if you can.
I prize thy love more then whole Mines of gold,
Or all the riches that the East doth hold.
My love is such that Rivers cannot quench,
Nor ought but love from thee, give recompence.
Thy love is such I can no way repay,
The heavens reward thee manifold I pray.
Then while we live, in love lets so persever,
That when we live no more, we may live ever.

A Letter to her Husband, absent upon Publick employment.

My head, my heart, mine Eyes, my life, nay more,
My joy, my Magazine of earthly store,
If two be one, as surely thou and I,
How stayest thou there, whilst I at *Ipswich* lye?
So many steps, head from the heart to sever
If but a neck, soon should we be together:
I like the earth this season, mourn in black,
My Sun is gone so far in's Zodiack,
Whom whilst I 'joy'd, nor storms, nor frosts I felt,
His warmth such frigid colds did cause to melt.
My chilled limbs now nummed lye forlorn;
Return, return sweet *Sol* from *Capricorn;*[10]
In this dead time, alas, what can I more
Then view those fruits which through thy heat I bore?

Which sweet contentment yield me for a space,
True living Pictures of their Fathers face.
O strange effect! now thou art *Southward* gone,
I weary grow, the tedious day so long;
But when thou *Northward* to me shalt return,
I wish my Sun may never set, but burn
Within the Cancer [11] of my glowing breast,
The welcome house of him my dearest guest.
Where ever, ever stay, and go not thence,
Till natures sad decree shall call thee hence;
Flesh of thy flesh, bone of thy bone,
I here, thou there, yet both but one.

Meditations when my Soul hath been refreshed with the Consolations which the world knowes not

I.

LORD, why should I doubt any more when thov hast given me such assured Pledges of thy Loue? First, thov art my Creator, I thy creature; thov my master, I thy servant. But hence arises not my comfort: Thov art my Father, I thy child. Yee shall [be] my Sons and Daughters, saith the Lord Almighty. Christ is my Brother; I ascend vnto my Father and your Father, vnto my God and your God. But least this should not bee enough, thy maker is thy husband. Nay, more, I am a member of his Body; he, my head. Such Priviledges, had not the Word of Truth made them known, who or where is the man that durst in his heart haue presumed to haue thought it? So wonderfull are these thoughts that my spirit failes in me at the consideration thereof; and I am confovnded to think that God, who hath done so much for me, should haue so little from me. But this is my comfort, when I come into Heaven, I shall vnderstand perfectly what he hath done for me, and then shall I bee able to praise him as I ovght. Lord, haueing this hope, let me purefie myself as thou art Pure, and let me bee no more affraid of Death, but even desire to bee dissolved, and bee with thee, which is best of All. . . .

IX.

Sweet words are like hony, a little may refresh, but too much gluts the stomach.

X.

Diuerse children haue their different natures; some are like flesh which nothing but salt will keep from putrefaction; some again like tender fruits that are best preserued with sugar: those parents are wise that can fit their nurture according to their Nature.

XI.

That town which thousands of enemys without hath not been able to take, hath been deliuered vp by one traytor within; and that man, which all the temptations of Sathan without could not hurt, hath been foild by one lust within.

XII.

Authority without wisedome is like a heavy axe without an edg, fitter to bruise then polish.

XIII.

The reason why christians are so loth to exchang this world for a better, is because they haue more sence then faith: they se what they injoy, they do but hope for that which is to Come.

XIV.

If we had no winter the spring would not be so pleasant: if we did not sometimes tast of adversity, prosperity would not be so welcome.

XV.

A low man can goe vpright vnder that door, wher a taller is glad to stoop; so a man of weak faith and mean abilities, may vndergo a crosse more patiently then he that excells him, both in gifts and graces.

XVI.

That house which is not often swept, makes the cleanly inhabitant soone loath it, and that heart which is not continually purifieing it self, is no fit temple for the spirit of god to dwell in.

XVII.

Few men are so humble as not to be proud of their abilitys; and nothing will abase them more then this,—What hast thou, but what thou hast receiued? come giue an account of thy stewardship. . . .

XXVII.

It is a pleasant thing to behold the light, but sore eyes are not able to look vpon it; the pure in heart shall se God, but the defiled in conscience shall rather choose to be buried vnder rocks and mountains then to behold the presence of the Lamb.

XXVIII.

Wisedome with an inheritance is good, but wisedome without an inheritance is better then an inheritance without wisedome.

XXIX.

Lightening doth vsually preceed thunder, and stormes, raine; and stroaks do not often fall till after threat'ning.

XXX.

Yellow leaues argue want of sap, and gray haires want of moisture; so dry and saplesse performances are simptoms of little spiritall vigor.

XXXI.

Iron till it be throughly heat is vncapable to be wrought; so God sees good to cast some men into the furnace of affliction, and then beats them on his anuile into what frame he pleases.

XXXII.

Ambitious men are like hops that neuer rest climbing soe long as they haue any thing to stay vpon; but take away their props and they are, of all, the most dejected.

XXXIII.

Much Labour wearys the body, and many thoughts oppresse the minde: man aimes at profit by the one, and content in the other; but often misses of both, and findes nothing but vanity and vexation of spirit.

XXXIV.

Dimne eyes are the concomitants of old age; and short sightednes, in those that are eyes of a Republique, foretels a declineing State.

XXXV.

We read in Scripture of three sorts of Arrows,—the arrow of an enemy, the arrow of pestilence, and the arrow of a slanderous tongue; the two first kill the body, the last the good name; the two former leaue a man when he is once dead, but the last mangles him in his graue. . . .

LXIII.

He that would keep a pure heart, and lead a blamlesse life, must set himself alway in the awefull presence of God, the consideration of his all-seeing eye will be a bridle to restrain from evill, and a spur to quicken on to good dutys: we certainly dream of some remotnes betwixt God and vs, or else we should not so often faile in our whole Course of life as we doe; but he, that with David, sets the Lord alway in his sight, will not sinne against him.

LXIV.

We see in orchards some trees soe fruitfull, that the waight of their Burden is the breaking of their limbes; some again are but meanly loaden; and some haue nothing to shew but leaues only; and some among them are dry stocks: so is it in the church, which is Gods orchard, there are some eminent Christians that are soe frequent in good dutys, that many times the waight therof impares both their bodys and estates; and there are some (and they sincere ones too) who haue not attained to that fruitfullnes, altho they aime at perfection: And again there are others that haue nothing to commend them but only a gay proffession, and these are but leavie christians, which are in as much danger of being cut down as the dry stock, for both cumber the ground.

LXV.

We see in the firmament there is but one Sun among a multitude of starres, and those starres also to differ much one from the other in regard of bignes and brightnes, yet all receiue their light from that one Sun: so is it in the church both militant and triumphant, there is but one Christ, who is the Sun of righteousnes, in the midest of an innumerable company of Saints and Angels; those Saintes haue their degrees euen in this life, some are Stars of the first magnitude, and some of a lesse degree; and others (and they indeed the most in number), but small and obscure, yet all receiue their luster (be it more or lesse) from that glorious sun that inlightens all in all; and, if some of them shine so bright while they moue on earth, how transcendently splendid shall they be, when they are fixt in their heauenly spheres!

Here followes some verses vpon the burning of our House, July 10th, 1666. Copyed ovt of a loose Paper.

In silent night when rest I took,
For sorrow neer I did not look,
I waken'd was with thundring nois
And Piteovs shreiks of dreadfull voice.
That fearfull sound of fire and fire,
Let no man know is my Desire.

I, starting vp, the light did spye,
And to my God my heart did cry
To strengthen me in my Distresse
And not to leaue me succourlesse.
Then coming ovt beheld a space,
The flame consvme my dwelling place.

And, when I could no longer look,
I blest his Name that gave and took,
That layd my goods now in the dvst:
Yea so it was, and so 'twas jvst.
It was his own: it was not mine;
Far be it that I should repine.

He might of All justly bereft,
But yet sufficient for us left.
When by the Ruines oft I past,
My sorrowing eyes aside did cast,
And here and there the places spye
Where oft I sate, and long did lye.

Here stood that Trunk, and there that chest;
There lay that store I covnted best:
My pleasant things in ashes lye,
And them behold no more shall I.
Vnder thy roof no gvest shall sitt,
Nor at thy Table eat a bitt.

No pleasant tale shall 'ere be told,
Nor things recovnted done of old.
No Candle 'ere shall shine in Thee,
Nor bridegroom's voice ere heard shall bee.
In silence ever shalt thou lye;
Adeiu, Adeiu; All's vanity.

Then streight I gin my heart to chide,
And did thy wealth on earth abide?
Didst fix thy hope on mouldring dvst,
The arm of flesh didst make thy trvst?
Raise vp thy thovghts above the skye
That dunghill mists away may flie.

Thou hast an house on high erect,
Fram'd by that mighty Architect,
With glory richly furnished,
Stands permanent though: this bee fled.
It's purchaséd, and paid for too
By him who hath enovgh to doe.

A Prise so vast as is vnknown,
Yet, by his Gift, is made thine own.
Ther's wealth enovgh, I need no more;
Farewell my Pelf, farewell my Store.

The world no longer let me Love,
My hope and Treasure lyes Above.

[Longing for Heaven]

As weary pilgrim, now at rest,
  Hugs with delight his silent nest
His wasted limbes, now lye full soft
  That myrie steps, haue troden oft
Blesses himself, to think vpon
  his dangers past, and travailes done
The burning sun no more shall heat
  Nor stormy raines, on him shall beat.
The bryars and thornes no more shall scratch
  nor hungry wolues at him shall catch
He erring pathes no more shall tread
  nor wild fruits eate, in stead of bread,
for waters cold he doth not long
  for thirst no more shall parch his tongue
No rugged stones his feet shall gaule
  nor stumps nor rocks cause him to fall
All cares and feares, he bids farwell
  and meanes in safity now to dwell.
A pilgrim I, on earth, perplext
  wth sinns wth cares and sorrows vext
By age and paines brought to decay
  and my Clay house mouldring away
Oh how I long to be at rest
  and soare on high among the blest.
This body shall in silence sleep
  Mine eyes no more shall ever weep
No fainting fits shall me assaile
  nor grinding paines my body fraile
W^th^ cares and fears ne'r cumbred be
  Nor losses know, nor sorrowes see
What tho my flesh shall there consume
  it is the bed Christ did perfume
And when a few yeares shall be gone
  this mortall shall be cloth'd vpon
A Corrupt Carcasse downe it lyes
  a glorious body it shall rise
In weaknes and dishonour sowne
  in power 'tis rais'd by Christ alone
Then soule and body shall vnite
  and of their maker haue the sight

NATHANIEL WARD, JOHN ROGERS, AND JOHN NORTON

[It was customary for publishers to invite poets and scholars to write commendatory verses by way of introducing an author to the public. The aged and distinguished "simple cobler," Nathaniel Ward, who returned to England in 1646, had been a neighbor of Mrs. Bradstreet, and contributed his sprightly lines to the first edition of *The Tenth Muse*. Since Ward had previously expressed contempt for women's talents, his praise may have attracted particular notice. For an account of Ward, see *ante* p. 225. The text is from the first edition.

In the Boston edition of Mrs. Bradstreet's *Several Poems* (1678), new commendatory offerings were included, among which the verses "Vpon Mrs. Anne Bradstreet Her Poems, etc." by John Rogers (1631–1684) of Ipswich, and "A Funeral Elogy" by the Rev. John Norton (1651–1716) of Hingham deserve to be remembered. Rogers's wife was a niece of Mrs. Bradstreet. He was son of the Rev. Nathaniel Rogers of Ipswich, and though he studied divinity, he was never ordained. Offered the presidency of Harvard in 1677, he declined it to devote himself to medicine, but he later reconsidered, and served in that office the two years before his death. See Tyler, *A History of American Literature*, II, 12–15; Sibley, *Biographical Sketches*, I, 166–171; and Samuel E. Morison, *Harvard College in the Seventeenth Century*, 430–445.

John Norton, ancestor of Charles Eliot Norton, was nephew of the famous Rev. John Norton of Boston and grand-nephew of Governor Winthrop. He published, besides the poem below, but one sermon, yet this "Elogy" will keep his memory alive, for as Tyler remarks (*ibid.*, p. 10), "here is something more than mechanic poetry, something other than inspiration of the thumb-nail." It has been suggested that Norton may have edited *Several Poems* (*New England Historical and Genealogical Register*, IX, 113 note). See also Sibley, *op. cit.*, II, 394–396; Tyler, *op. cit.*, II, 9–11. The text of both the Rogers and Norton selections is from *Several Poems*, 1678.]

ON MRS. BRADSTREET'S TENTH MUSE

MERCURY shew'd *Apollo*, *Bartas* Book,[1]
Minerva this, and wisht him well to look,
And tell uprightly, which, did which excell;
He view'd, and view'd, and vow'd he could not tell.
They bid him Hemisphear his mouldy nose,
With's crackt leering-glasses, for it would pose

The best brains he had in's old pudding-pan,
Sex weigh'd, which best, the Woman, or the Man?
He peer'd, and por'd, and glar'd, and said for wore,[2]
I'me even as wise now, as I was before:
They both 'gan laugh, and said, it was no mar'l [3]
The Auth'resse was a right *Du Bartas* Girle.
Good sooth quoth the old *Don*, tel ye me so,
I muse whither at length these Girls wil go;
It half revives my chil frost-bitten blood,
To see a woman, once, do ought that's good;
And chode buy [4] *Chaucers* Boots, and *Homers* Furrs,
Let men look to't, least women weare the Spurs.

N. Ward.

VPON *MRS. ANNE BRADSTREET*

Her Poems, &c.

Madam, twice through the Muses Grove I walkt,
Under your blissfull bowres, I shrowding [5] there,
It seem'd with Nymphs of *Helicon* I talkt:
For there those sweet-lip'd Sisters sporting were,
Apollo with his sacred Lute sate by,
On high they made their heavenly Sonnets flye,
Posies around they strow'd, of sweetest Poesie.

2

Twice have I drunk the Nectar of your lines,
Which high sublim'd my mean born phantasie,
Flusht with these streams of your *Maronean* wines [6]
Above my self rapt to an extasie:
Methought I was upon Mount *Hiblas* top,[7]
There where I might those fragrant flowers lop,
Whence did sweet odors flow, and honey spangles drop.

3

To *Venus* shrine no Altars raised are,
Nor venom'd shafts from painted quiver fly,
Nor wanton Doves of *Aphrodites* Carr,
Or fluttering there, nor here forlornly lie,
Lorne Paramours, not chatting birds tell news
How sage *Apollo*, *Daphne* hot pursues,
Or stately *Jove* himself is wont to haunt the stews.

4

Nor barking Satyrs breath, nor driery [8] clouds
Exhal'd from *Styx*, their dismal drops distil
Within these *Fairy*, flowry fields, nor shrouds
The screeching night Raven, with his shady quill:
But Lyrick strings here *Orpheus* nimbly hitts,
Orion on his sadled Dolphin sits,
Chanting as every humour, age & season fits.

5

Here silver swans, with Nightingales set spells,
Which sweetly charm the Traveller, and raise
Earths earthed Monarchs, from their hidden Cells,
And to appearance summons lapsed dayes,
There heav'nly air, becalms the swelling frayes,[9]
And fury fell of Elements allayes,
By paying every one due tribute of his praise.

6

This seem'd the Scite [10] of all those verdant vales,
And purled springs, whereat the Nymphs do play,
With lofty hills, where Poets rear their tales,
To heavenly vaults, which heav'nly sound repay
By ecchoes sweet rebound, here Ladyes kiss,
Circling nor songs, nor dances circle miss;
But whilst those Syrens sung, I sunk in sea of bliss.

7

Thus weltring in delight, my virgin mind
Admits a rape; truth still lyes undiscri'd,
Its singular, that plural seem'd, I find,
'Twas Fancies glass alone that multipli'd;
Nature with Art so closely did combine,
I thought I saw the Muses trebble trine,
Which prov'd your lonely Muse, superiour to the nine.

8

Your only hand those Poesies did compose,
Your head the source, whence all those springs did flow,
Your voice, whence changes sweetest notes arose,
Your feet that kept the dance alone, I trow:
Then vail your bonnets, Poetasters all,
Strike, lower amain, and at these humbly fall,
And deem your selves advanc'd to be her Pedestal.

9

Should all with lowly Congies [11] Laurels bring,
Waste *Floraes* Magazine to find a wreathe;
Or *Pineus* [12] Banks 'twere too mean offering,
Your Muse a fairer Garland doth bequeath
To guard your fairer front; here 'tis your name
Shall stand immarbled; this your little frame
Shall great *Colossus* be, to your eternal fame.

I'le please my self, though I my self disgrace,
What errors here be found, are in *Errataes* place.

J. Rogers.

A FUNERAL ELOGY,

Upon that Pattern and Patron of Virtue, the truely pious, peerless & matchless Gentlewoman

Mrs. Anne Bradstreet,

right Panaretes,[13]

Mirror of Her Age, Glory of her Sex, whose Heaven-born-Soul leaving its earthly Shrine, chose its native home, and was taken to its Rest, upon 16th. Sept. 1672.

Ask not why hearts turn Magazines of passions,
And why that grief is clad in sev'ral fashions;
Why She on progress goes, and doth not borrow
The smallest respite from th' extreams of sorrow,
Her misery is got to such an height,
As makes the earth groan to support its weight,
Such storms of woe, so strongly have beset her,
She hath no place for worse, nor hope for better;
Her comfort is, if any for her be,
That none can shew more cause of grief then she.
Ask not why some in mournfull black are clad;
The Sun is set, there needs must be a shade.
Ask not why every face a sadness shrowdes;
The setting Sun ore-cast us hath with Clouds.
Ask not why the great glory of the Skye
That gilds the starrs with heavenly Alchamy,
Which all the world doth lighten with his rayes,
The *Perslan* [14] God, the Monarch of the dayes;
Ask not the reason of his extasie,
Paleness of late, in midnoon Majesty,

Why that the palefac'd Empress of the night
Disrob'd her brother of his glorious light.
Did not the language of the starrs foretel
A mournfull Scœne when they with tears did swell?
Did not the glorious people of the Skye
Seem sensible of future misery?
Did not the lowring heavens seem to express
The worlds great lose, and their unhappiness?
Behold how tears flow from the learned hill,
How the bereaved Nine do daily fill
The bosome of the fleeting Air with groans,
And wofull Accents, which witness their moanes.
How doe the Goddesses of verse, the learned quire
Lament their rival Quill, which all admire?
Could *Maro*'s [15] Muse but hear her lively strain,
He would condemn his works to fire again.
Methinks I hear the Patron of the Spring,
The unshorn Deity abruptly sing.
Some doe for anguish weep, for anger I
That Ignorance should live, and Art should die.
Black, fatal, dismal, inauspicious day,
Unblest for ever by *Sol*'s precious Ray,
Be it the first of Miseries to all;
Or last of Life, defam'd for Funeral.
When this day yearly comes, let every one,
Cast in their urne, the black and dismal stone.
Succeeding years as they their circuit goe,
Leap o're this day, as a sad time of woe.
Farewell my Muse, since thou hast left thy shrine,
I am unblest in one, but blest in nine.
Fair *Thespian* Ladyes, light your torches all,
Attend your glory to its Funeral,
To court her ashes with a learned tear,
A briny sacrifice, let not a smile appear.
Grave Matron, whoso seeks to blazon thee,
Needs not make use of witts false Heraldry;
Whoso should give thee all thy worth would swell
So high, as 'twould turn the world infidel.
Had he great *Maro*'s Muse, or *Tully*'s [16] tongue,
Or raping numbers like the *Thracian* Song,
In crowning of her merits he would be
Sumptuously poor, low in Hyperbole.
To write is easie; but to write on thee,
Truth would be thought to forfeit modesty.
He'l seem a Poet that shall speak but true;

Hyperbole's in others, are thy due.
Like a most servile flatterer he will show
Though he write truth, and make the subject, You.[17]
Virtue ne're dies, time will a Poet raise
Born under better Starrs, shall sing thy praise.
Praise her who list, yet he shall be a debtor
For Art ne're feign'd, nor Nature fram'd a better.
Her virtues were so great, that they do raise
A work to trouble fame, astonish praise.
When as her Name doth but salute the ear,
Men think that they perfections abstract hear.
Her breast was a brave Pallace, a *Broad-street*,
Where all heroick ample thoughts did meet,
Where nature such a Tenement had tane,
That others souls, to hers, dwelt in a lane.
Beneath her feet, pale envy bites her chain,
And poison Malice, whetts her sting in vain.
Let every Laurel, every Myrtel bough
Be stript for leaves t' adorn and load her brow.
Victorious wreathes, which 'cause they never fade
Wise elder times for Kings and Poets made.
Let not her happy memory e're lack
Its worth in Fames eternal Almanack,
Which none shall read, but straight their loss deplore,
And blame their Fates they were not born before.
Do not old men rejoyce their Fates did last,
And infants too, that theirs did make such hast,
In such a welcome time to bring them forth,
That they might be a witness to her worth.
Who undertakes this subject to commend
Shall nothing find so hard as how to end.

Finis & non. John Norton.

Omnia Romanæ *sileant Miracula Gentis.*[18]

MICHAEL WIGGLESWORTH, 1631–1705

[The eighteen hundred copies of *The Day of Doom: or A Poetical Description of the Great and Last Judgement* (Cambridge, 1662), were exhausted within a year, and no copy of the first edition is known to survive. It was immediately re-issued here and in England. It was published in broadside and hawked about the country. In the next two centuries it appeared frequently, and was last printed as recently as 1929. In the same year that it was first published Michael Wigglesworth wrote "Gods Controversy with New-England. Written in the time of the great drought," wherein the backslidings of the time are indicated as the reason that New England has become "A waste and howling wilderness." The poem has been published in *Proceedings of the Massachusetts Historical Society*, XII (1873), 83–93, from which the present selection has been taken. Wigglesworth's last verses appeared in *Meat out of the Eater or Meditations Concerning The Necessity, End, and Usefulness of Affliction unto Gods Children.* The only known copy of the first edition of 1670 is in the Yale University Library.

See Matt B. Jones, "Notes for a Bibliography of Michael Wigglesworth's *Day of Doom* and *Meat out of the Eater*," *Proceedings of the American Antiquarian Society*, N.S. XXXIX (1929), 77–84; and *idem*, "Michael Wigglesworth's *Meat Out of the Eater:* The hitherto unknown First Edition," *Yale University Gazette*, V (1931), 45–47. See also Francis O. Matthiessen, "Michael Wigglesworth, A Puritan Artist," *New England Quarterly*, I (1928), 491–504; Kenneth B. Murdock, *ed.*, *The Day of Doom*, with introduction (New York, 1929); John W. Dean, *Memoir of Rev. Michael Wigglesworth*, second ed., Albany, 1871; "Letters of Michael Wigglesworth to Increase Mather," *Collections of the Massachusetts Historical Society*, fourth series, VIII, 645–647; Moses C. Tyler, *A History of American Literature*, II, 23–35; John L. Sibley, *Biographical Sketches*, I, 259–286; and especially Samuel E. Morison, *Harvard College in the Seventeenth Century, passim.* Several unpublished Wigglesworth MSS are in possession of the New England Historical Genealogical Society and of the Massachusetts Historical Society. The text of *Meat out of the Eater* here reproduced is from the fourth edition of 1689; that of *The Day of Doom* is from the fifth edition (1701), the last to appear in the author's lifetime.]

A PRAYER UNTO CHRIST THE JUDGE OF THE WORLD.

O DEAREST Dread, most glorious King,
I'le of thy justest Judgments sing:
Do thou my head and heart inspire,
To Sing aright, as I desire.
Thee, thee alone I'le invocate,
For I do much abominate
To call the *Muses* to mine aid:
Which is th' Unchristian use, and trade
Of some that Christians would be thought,

And yet they worship worse then nought.
Oh! what a deal of Blasphemy,
And Heathenish Impiety,
In Christian Poets may be found,
Where Heathen gods with praise are Crown'd,
They make *Jehovah* to stand by,
Till *Juno*, *Venus*, *Mercury*,
With frowning *Mars*, and thundering *Jove*,
Rule Earth below, and Heaven above.
But I have learnt to pray to none,
Save unto God in Christ alone.
Nor will I laud, no not in jest,
That which I know God doth detest.
I reckon it a damning evil
To give Gods Praises to the Devil.
Thou, *Christ*, art he to whom I pray,
Thy Glory fain I would display.
Oh! guide me by thy sacred Sprite
So to indite, and so to write,
That I thine holy Name may praise,
And teach the Sons of men thy wayes.

[Prefatory lines to *The Day of Doom*]

THE DAY OF DOOM.

(1)

STILL was the night, Serene and Bright, when all Men sleeping lay; *The Security of the World before Christs coming to Judgment.*
Calm was the season, and carnal reason thought so 'twould last for ay.
Soul, take thine ease, let sorrow cease, much good thou hast in store: *Luk.* 12: 19.
This was their Song, their Cups among, the Evening before.

(2)

Wallowing in all kind of sin, vile wretches lay secure:[1]
The best of men had scarcely then their Lamps kept in good ure.[2] *Mat.* 25: 5.
Virgins unwise, who through disguise amongst the best were number'd,
Had clos'd their eyes; yea, and the wise through sloth and frailty slumber'd.

(3)

Mat. 24: 37, 38. Like as of old,[3] when Men grow bold Gods' threatnings to contemn,
Who stopt their Ear, and would not hear, when Mercy warned them:
But took their course, without remorse, till God began to powre
Destruction the World upon in a tempestuous showre.

(4)

They put away the evil day, And drown'd their care and fears,
Till drown'd were they, and swept away by vengeance unawares:
1 *Thes.* 5: 3. So at the last, whilst Men sleep fast in their security,
Surpriz'd they are in such a snare as cometh suddenly.

(5)

The Suddenness, Majesty, & Terror of Christ's appearing. *Mat.* 25: 6. 2 *Pet.* 3: 10.

For at midnight brake forth a Light, which turn'd the night to day,
And speedily an hideous cry did all the world dismay.
Sinners awake, their hearts do ake, trembling their loynes surprizeth;
Amaz'd with fear, by what they hear, each one of them ariseth.

(6)

They rush[4] from Beds with giddy heads, and to their windows run,
Mat. 24: 29, 30. Viewing this light, which shines more bright then doth the Noon-day Sun.
Straightway appears (they see't with tears) the Son of God most dread;
Who with his Train comes on amain to Judge both Quick and Dead.

(7)

2 *Pet.* 3: 10. Before his face the Heav'ns gave place, and Skies are rent asunder,
With mighty voice, and hideous noise, more terrible than Thunder.
His brightness damps heav'ns glorious lamps and makes them hide their heads,
As if afraid and quite dismay'd, they quit their wonted steads.

(8)

Ye sons of men that durst contemn the Threatnings of Gods Word.
How cheer you now? your hearts, I trow, are thrill'd as with a sword.
Now Atheist blind, whose brutish mind a God could never see,
Dost thou perceive, dost now believe that Christ thy Judge shall be?

(9)

Stout Courages, (whose hardiness could Death and Hell out-face)
Are you as bold now you behold your Judge draw near apace?
They cry, no, no: Alas! and wo! our Courage all is gone:
Our hardiness (fool hardiness) hath us undone, undone.

(10)

No heart so bold, but now grows cold and almost dead with fear:
No eye so dry, but now can cry, and pour out many a tear. *Rev.* 6:16.
Earths Potentates and pow'rful States, Captains and Men of Might
Are quite abasht, their courage dasht at this most dreadful sight.

(11)

Mean men lament, great men do rent their Robes, and tear their hair:
They do not spare their flesh to tear through horrible despair. *Mat.* 24:30.
All Kindreds wail: all hearts do fail: horror the world doth fill
With weeping eyes, and loud out-cries, yet knows not how to kill.

(12)

Some hide themselves in Caves and Delves, in places under ground: *Rev.* 6:15, 16.
Some rashly leap into the Deap, to scape by being drown'd:
Some to the Rocks (O sensless blocks!) and woody Mountains run,
That there they might this fearful sight, and dreaded Presence shun.

(13)

In vain do they to Mountains say, Fall on us, and us hide
From Judges ire, more hot than fire, for who may it abide?
No hiding place can from his Face sinners at all conceal,
Whose flaming Eyes hid things doth 'spy, and darkest things reveal.

(14)

Mat. 25 : 31. The Judge draws nigh, exalted high upon a lofty Throne,
Amidst the throng of Angels strong, lo, Israel's Holy One!
The excellence of whose presence and awful Majesty,
Amazeth Nature, and every Creature, doth more than terrify.

(15)

Rev. 6 : 14. The Mountains smoak, the Hills are shook, the Earth is rent and torn,
As if she should be clean dissolv'd, or from the Center born.
The Sea doth roar, forsakes the shore, and shrinks away for fear;
The wild Beasts flee into the Sea, so soon as he draws near.

(16)

Whose Glory bright, whose wondrous might, whose Power Imperial,
So far surpass whatever was in Realms Terrestrial;
That tongues of men (nor Angels pen) cannot the same express,
And therefore I must pass it by, lest speaking should transgress.

(17)

1 *Thes.* 4 : 16. *Resurrection of the Dead.* *John* 5 : 28, 29.

Before his Throne a Trump is blown, Proclaiming th' Day of Doom:
Forthwith he cries, *Ye Dead arise, and unto Judgment come.*
No sooner said, but 'tis obey'd; Sepulchers open'd are:
Dead Bodies all rise at his call, and's mighty power declare.

(18)

Both Sea and Land, at his Command, their Dead at once surrender:
The Fire and Air constrained are also their dead to tender.
The mighty word of this great Lord links Body and Soul together
Both of the Just, and the unjust, to part no more for ever.

(19)

The same translates, from Mortal states to Immortality, *The living Changed.*
All that survive, and be alive, i' th' twinkling of an eye:
That so they may abide for ay to endless weal or woe; *Luk.* 20 : 36.
Both the Renate [5] and Reprobate are made to dy no more. 1 *Cor.* 15 : 52.

(20)

His winged Hosts flie through all Coasts, together gathering *All brought to Judgment.*
Both good and bad, both quick and dead, and all to Judgment bring. *Mat.* 24 : 31.
Out of their holes those creeping Moles, that hid themselves for fear,
By force they take, and quickly make before the Judge appear.

(21)

Thus every one before the Throne of Christ the Judge is brought, 2 *Cor.* 5 : 10.
Both righteous and impious that good or ill had wrought. *The Sheep separated from the Goats.*
A separation, and diff'ring station by Christ appointed is *Mat.* 25 : 32.
(To sinners sad) 'twixt good and bad, 'twixt Heirs of woe and bliss.

(22)

At Christ's right hand the Sheep do stand, his holy Martyrs, who *Who are Christ's Sheep.*
For his dear Name suffering shame, calamity and woe. *Mat.* 5 : 10, 11.
Like Champions stood, and with their Blood their testimony sealed;
Whose innocence without offence, to Christ their Judge appealed.

(23)

Heb. 12 : 5, 6, 7. Next unto whom there find a room all Christ's afflicted ones,
Who being chastised, neither despised nor sank amidst their groans:
Who by the Rod were turn'd to God, and loved him the more,
Not murmuring nor quarrelling when they were chast'ned sore.

(24)

Luke 7 : 41, 47. Moreover, such as loved much, that had not such a tryal,
As might constrain to so great pain, and such deep self denyal:
Yet ready were the Cross to bear, when Christ them call'd thereto,
And did rejoyce to hear his voice, they're counted Sheep also.

(25)

Joh. 21 : 15. *Mat.* 19 : 14. *Joh.* 3 : 3.

Christ's Flock of Lambs there also stands, whose Faith was weak, yet true;
All sound Believers (Gospel receivers) whose Grace was small, but grew:
And them among an Infant throng of Babes, for whom Christ dy'd;
Whom for his own, by wayes unknown to men, he sanctify'd.

(26)

Rev. 6 : 11. *Phil.* 3 : 21.

All stand before their Saviour in long white Robes yclad,
Their countenance full of pleasance, appearing wondrous glad.
O glorious sight! Behold how bright dust heaps are made to shine,
Conformed so their Lord unto, whose Glory is Divine.

(27)

The Goats described or the several sorts of Reprobates on the left hand. *Mat.* 24 : 51.

At Christ's left hand the Goats do stand, all whining hypocrites,
Who for self-ends did seem Christ's friends, but foster'd guileful sprites:
Who Sheep resembled, but they dissembled (their hearts were not sincere)
Who once did throng Christ's Lambs among, but now must not come near.

(28)

Apostates and Run-awayes, such as have Christ forsaken, *Luk.* 11 : 24, 26.
Of whom the Devil, with seven more evil, hath fresh possession taken: *Heb.* 6 : 4, 5, 6. *Heb.* 10 : 29.
Sinners in grain, reserv'd to pain and torments most severe:
Because 'gainst light they sinn'd with spight, are also placed there.

(29)

There also stand a num'rous band, that no Profession made *Luk.* 12 : 47. *Prov.* 1 : 24, 26.
Of Godliness, nor to redress their wayes at all essay'd: *Joh.* 3 : 19.
Who better knew, but (sinful Crew) Gospel and Law despised;
Who all Christ's knocks withstood like blocks and would not be advised.

(30)

Moreover, there with them appear a number, numberless
Of great and small, vile wretches all, that did Gods Law transgress: *Gal.* 3 : 10. 1 *Cor.* 6 : 9.
Idolaters, false worshippers, Prophaners of Gods Name, *Rev.* 21 : 8.
Who not at all thereon did call, or took in vain the same.

(31)

Blasphemers lewd, and Swearers shrewd, Scoffers at Purity,
That hated God, contemn'd his Rod, and lov'd Security; *Exod.* 20 :
Sabbath-polluters, Saints persecuters, Presumptuous men and Proud, 7, 8.
Who never lov'd those that reprov'd; all stand amongst this Crowd. 2 *Thes.* 1 : 6, 8, 9.

(32)

Adulterers and Whoremongers were [6] there, with all unchast: *Heb.* 13 : 4. 1 *Cor.* 6 : 10.
There Covetous, and Ravenous, that Riches got too fast:
Who us'd vile ways themselves to raise t' Estates and worldly wealth,
Oppression by, or Knavery, by force, or fraud, or stealth.

(33)

Moreover, there together were Children flagitious,
And Parents who did them undo by Nurture vicious.

Zach. 5 : 3, 4. *Gal.* 5 : 19, 20, 21.
False-witness-bearers, and self-forswearers, Murd'rers, and Men of blood,
Witches, Inchanters, & Ale house-haunters, beyond account there stood.

(34)

Their place there find all Heathen blind, that Natures light abused,
Rom. 2 : 13. Although they had no tydings glad of Gospel-grace refused.
There stands all Nations and Generations of *Adam*'s Progeny,
Whom Christ redeem'd not, who Christ esteem'd not through Infidelity.

(35)

Act. 4 : 12. Who no Peace-maker, no Undertaker, [7] to shrow'd them from Gods ire
Ever obtain'd; they must be pained with everlasting fire.
These num'rous bands wringing their hands, and weeping all stand there,
Filled with anguish, whose hearts do languish through self-tormenting fear.

(36)

Fast by them stand at Christ's left hand the Lion fierce and fell,
The Dragon bold, that Serpent old, that hurried Souls to Hell.
1 *Cor.* 6 : 3. There also stand, under command, Legions of Sprights unclean,
And hellish Fiends, that are no friends to God, nor unto Men.

(37)

With dismal chains, and strongest reins, like Prisoners of Hell,
Jude 6. They're held in place before Christ's face, till He their Doom shall tell.
These void of tears, but fill'd with fears, and dreadful expectation
Of endless pains, and scalding flames, stand waiting for Damnation.

(38)

All silence keep both Goats and Sheep before the Judge's Throne:
With mild aspect to his Elect then spake the Holy One; *The Saints cleared & justified.*
My Sheep draw near, your Sentence hear, which is to you no dread,
Who clearly now discern, and know your sins are pardoned.

(39)

'Twas meet that ye should judged be, that so the world may spy *2 Cor.* 5 : 10. *Eccles.* 3 : 17. *Joh.* 3 : 18.
No cause of grudge, when as I Judge and deal impartially.
Know therefore all, both great and small, the ground and reason why
These Men do stand at my right hand, and look so chearfully.

(40)

These Men be those my Father chose before the worlds foundation, *Joh.* 17 : 6. *Eph.* 1 : 4.
And to me gave, that I should save from Death and Condemnation.
For whose dear sake I flesh did take, was of a Woman born.
And did inure my self t' indure, unjust reproach and scorn.

(41)

For them it was that I did pass through sorrows many one:
That I drank up that bitter Cup, which made me sigh and groan. *Rev.* 1 : 5.
The Cross his pain I did sustain; yea more, my Fathers ire
I underwent, my Blood I spent to save them from Hell fire.

(42)

Thus I esteem'd, thus I redeem'd all these from every Nation,
That they may be (as now you see) a chosen Generation.
What if ere-while they were as vile, and bad as any be, *Eph.* 2 : 1, 3.
And yet from all their guilt and thrall at once I set them free?

(43)

Mat. 20: 13, 15. *Rom.* 9: 20, 21.
My grace to one is wrong to none: none can Election claim,
Amongst all those their souls that lose, none can Rejection blame.
He that may chuse, or else refuse, all men to save or spill,
May this Man chuse, and that refuse. redeeming whom he will.

(44)

Isa. 53: 4, 5, 11.
But as for those whom I have chose Salvations heirs to be,
I underwent their punishment, and therefore set them free;
I bore their grief, and their relief by suffering procur'd,
That they of bliss and happiness might firmly be assur'd.

(45)

Acts 13: 48. *Jam.* 2: 18. *Heb.* 12: 7. *Mat.* 19: 29.
And this my grace they did imbrace, believing on my Name;
Which Faith was true, the fruits do shew proceeding from the same:
Their Penitence, their Patience, their Love and Self-denial
In suffering losses, and bearing Crosses, when put upon the tryal.

(46)

1 *John* 3: 3. *Mat.* 25: 39, 40.
Their sin forsaking, their chearful taking my yoke, their Charity
Unto the Saints in all their wants, and in them unto me,
These things do clear, and make appear their Faith to be unfaigned,
And that a part in my desert and purchase they have gained.

(47)

Isa. 53: 11, 12. *Rom.* 8: 16, 17, 33, 34. *John* 3: 18.
Their debts are paid, their peace is made, their sins remitted are;
Therefore at once I do pronounce, and openly declare
That Heav'n is theirs, that they be Heirs of Life and of Salvation!
Nor ever shall they come at all to Death or to Damnation.

(48)

Come, Blessed Ones, and sit on Thrones, Judging the World with me: *Luk.* 22: 29, 30.
Come, and possess your happiness, and bought felicitie. *Mat.* 19: 28.
Henceforth no fears, no care, no tears, no sin shall you annoy,
Nor any thing that grief doth bring: Eternal Rest enjoy.

(49)

You bore the Cross, you suffered loss of all for my Names sake: *Mat.* 25: 34.
Receive the Crown that's now your own; come, and a Kingdom take.
Thus spake the Judge, the wicked grudge, and grind their teeth in vain;
They see with groans these plac't on Thrones which addeth to their pain: *They are placed on Thrones to joyn with Christ in judging the wicked.*

(50)

That those whom they did wrong and slay, must now their judgment see!
Such whom they slighted, and once despighted, must now their Judges be!
Thus 'tis decreed, such is their meed, and guerdon glorious! 1 *Cor.* 6: 2.
With Christ they sit, Judging is fit to plague the Impious.

(51)

The wicked are brought to the Bar, like guilty Malefactors, *The wicked brought to the Bar.*
That oftentimes of bloody Crimes and Treasons have been Actors. *Rom.* 2: 3, 6, 11.
Of wicked Men, none are so mean as there to be neglected:
Nor none so high in dignity, as there to be respected.

(52)

The glorious Judge will priviledge nor Emperour, nor King: *Rev.* 6: 15, 16.
But every one that hath mis-done doth into Judgment bring. *Isa.* 30: 33.
And every one that hath mis-done, the Judge impartially
Condemneth to eternal wo, and endless misery.

(53)

Thus one and all, thus great and small, the Rich as well as Poor,
And those of place as the most base, do stand the Judge before.
They are arraign'd, and there detain'd, before Christ's Judgment-seat
With trembling fear, their Doom to hear, and feel his angers heat.

(54)

Eccles. 11 : 9 & 12 : 14.

There Christ demands at all their hands a strict and strait account
Of all things done under the Sun, whose number far surmount
Man's wit and thought: yet all are brought unto this solemn Tryal;
And each offence with evidence, so that there's no denial.

(55)

There's no excuses for their abuses, since their own Consciences
More proof give in of each Man's sin, than thousand Witnesses,
Though formerly this faculty had grosly been abused,
Men could it stifle, or with it trifle, when as it them accused.

(56)

Now it comes in, and every sin unto Mens charge doth lay:
It judgeth them, and doth condemn, though all the world say nay.
It so stingeth and tortureth, it worketh such distress,
That each Man's self against himself, is forced to confess.

(57)

Secret sins and works of darkness brought to light. *Psal.* 139 : 2, 4, 12. *Rom.* 2 : 16.

It's vain, moreover, for Men to cover the least iniquity:
The Judge hath seen, and privy been to all their villany.
He unto light, and open sight the works of darkness brings:
He doth unfold both new and old, both known and hidden things.

(58)

All filthy facts, and secret acts, however closly done, — *Eccles.* 12 : 14.
And long conceal'd, are there reveal'd before the mid-day Sun.
Deeds of the night shunning the light, which darkest corners sought,
To fearful blame, and endless shame, are there most justly brought.

(59)

And as all facts and grosser acts, so every word and thought, — *Mat.* 12 : 36. *Rom.* 7 : 7.
Erroneous notion, and lustful motion, are unto judgment brought.
No sin so small and trivial but hither it must come:
Nor so long past, but now at last it must receive a doom.

. . .

(188)

The Judge is strong, doers of wrong cannot his power withstand: — *Mat.* 28 : 18. *Psal.* 139 : 7.
None can by flight run out of sight, nor scape out of his hand.
Sad is their state: for Advocate to plead their Cause there's none:
None to prevent their punishment, or misery bemone.

(189)

O dismal day! whither shall they for help and succour flee?
To God above, with hopes to move their greatest Enemee:
His wrath is great, whose burning heat no floods of tears can slake: — *Isa.* 33 : 14. *Psal.* 11 : 6.
His word stands fast, that they be cast into the burning Lake. — *Numb.* 23 : 19.

(190)

To Christ their Judge, he doth adjudge them to the Pit of Sorrow; — *Matt.* 25 : 41.
Nor will he hear, or cry, or tear, nor respite them one morrow.
To Heav'n alas, they cannot pass, it is against them shut; — *Matt.* 25 : 10, 11, 12.
To enter there (O heavy cheer) they out of hopes are put.

(191)

Luk. 12 : 20. *Psal.* 49 : 7, 17.
Unto their Treasures, or to their Pleasures, all these have them forsaken:
Had they full Coffers to make large offers, their Gold would not be taken
Deut. 32 : 22.
Unto the place where whilome was their Birth and Education?
Lo! Christ begins for their great sins to fire the Earths Foundation:

(192)

2 Pet. 3 : 10.
And by and by the flaming Sky shall drop like molten Lead
About their ears, t'increase their fears, and aggravate their dread.
To Angels good that ever stood in their integrity,
Should they betake themselves, and make their sute incessantly?

(193)

Matt. 13 : 41, 42.
They neither skill,[8] nor do they will to work them any ease:
They will not mourn to see them burn, nor beg for their release.
To wicked men, their bretheren, in sin and wickedness,
Rev. 20 : 13, 15.
Should they make mone? their case is one, they're in the same distress.

(194)

Ah, cold comfort, and mean support from such like Comforters!
Ah, little joy of Company, and fellow-sufferers!
Luk. 16 : 28.
Such shall increase their hearts disease, and add unto their woe,
Because that they brought to decay themselves and many moe.[9]

(195)

Unto the Saints with sad complaints should they themselves apply?
Rev. 21 : 4.
They're not dejected, nor ought affected with all their misery.
Psal. 58 : 10.
Friends stand aloof, and make no proof what Prayers or Tears can do:
Your godly friends are now more friends to Christ than unto you.

(196)

Where tender love mens hearts did move unto a sympathy,
And bearing part of others smart in their anxiety;
Now such compassion is out of fashion, and wholly laid aside: *1 Cor.* 6 : 2.
No Friends so near, but Saints to hear their Sentence can abide.

(197)

One natural Brother beholds another in this astonied fit,
Yet sorrows not thereat a jot, nor pitties him a whit.
The godly wife conceives no grief, nor can she shed a tear
For the sad state of her dear Mate, when she his doom doth hear.

Compare Prov 1 : 26. *with* 1 *Joh.* 3 : 2. & 2 *Cor.* 5 : 16.

(198)

He that was erst a Husband pierc't with sense of Wives distress,
Whose tender heart did bear a part of all her grievances,
Shall mourn no more as heretofore because of her ill plight;
Although he see her now to be a damn'd forsaken wight.

(199)

The tender Mother will own no other of all her numerous brood,
But such as stand at Christ's right hand acquitted through his Blood.
The pious Father had now much rather his graceless Son should ly *Luk.* 16 : 25.
In Hell with Devils, for all his evils burning eternally,

(200)

Then God most high should injury, by sparing him sustain;
And doth rejoyce to hear Christ's voice adjudging him to pain; *Psal.* 58 : 10.
Who having all, both great and small, convinc'd and silenced,
Did then proceed their Doom to read, and thus it uttered:

(201)

The Judge pronounceth the Sentence of condemnation. *Mat.* 25 : 41.

Ye sinful wights, and cursed sprights, that work Iniquity,
Depart together from me for ever to endless Misery;
Your portion take in yonder Lake, where Fire and Brimstone flameth:
Suffer the smart, which your desert as it's due wages claimeth.

(202)

Oh piercing words more sharp than swords! what, to depart from *Thee,*
The terrour of it. Whose face before for evermore the best of Pleasures be!
What? to depart (unto our smart) from thee *Eternally:*
To be for aye banish'd away, with *Devils* company!

(203)

What? to be sent to *Punishment,* and flames of *Burning Fire,*
To be surrounded, and eke confounded with Gods *Revengeful ire.*
What? to abide, not for a tide these Torments, but for *Ever:*
To be released, or to be eased, not after years, but *Never.*

(204)

Oh, *fearful Doom!* now there's no room for hope or help at all:
Sentence is past which aye shall last, Christ will not it recall.
There might you hear them rent and tear the Air with their out-cries:
The hideous noise of their sad voice ascendeth to the Skies.

(205)

Luk. 13 : 28. They wring their hands, their caitiff-hands and gnash their teeth for terrour;
They cry, they roar for anguish sore, and gnaw their tongues for horrour.
But get away without delay, Christ pitties not your cry:
Prov. 1 : 26. Depart to Hell, there may you yell, and roar Eternally.

(206)

It is put in Execution. That word, *Depart,* maugre their heart, drives every wicked one,
With mighty pow'r, the self-same hour, far from the Judge's Throne.

Away they're chased[10] by the strong blast of his Death-threatning mouth: *Mat.* 25 : 46.
They flee full fast, as if in haste, although they be full loath.

(207)

As chaff that's dry, and dust doth fly before the Northern wind:
Right so are they chased away, and can no Refuge find.
They hasten to the Pit of Wo, guarded by Angels stout; *Matt.* 13 : 41,
Who to fulfil Christ's holy will, attend this wicked Rout. 42.

(208)

Whom having brought, as they are taught, unto the brink of Hell *Hell.* *Mat.* 25 : 30.
(That dismal place far from Christ's face, where Death and Darkness dwell: *Mark.* 9 : 43. *Isa.* 30 : 33. *Rev.* 21 : 8.
Where Gods fierce Ire kindleth the fire, and vengeance feeds the flame
With piles of Wood, and Brimstone Flood, that none can quench the same,)

(209)

With Iron bands they bind their hands, and cursed feet together, *Wicked Men and Devils cast into it for ever.*
And cast them all, both great and small, into that Lake for ever.
Where day and night, without respite, they wail, and cry, and howl *Mat.* 22 : 13. & 25 : 46.
For tort'ring pain, which they sustain in Body and in Soul.

(210)

For day and night, in their despight, their torments smoak ascendeth. *Rev.* 14 : 10, 11.
Their pain and grief have no relief, their anguish never endeth.
There must they ly, and never dy, though dying every day:
There must they dying ever ly, and not consume away.

(211)

Dy fain they would, if dy they could, but Death will not be had;
God's direful wrath their bodies hath for ev'r Immortal made.

They live to ly in misery, and bear eternal wo;
And live they must whilst God is just, that he may plague them so.

(212)

The unsufferable torments of the damned. *Luk.* 16 : 24. *Jude* 7.

But who can tell the plagues of Hell, and torments exquisite?
Who can relate their dismal state, and terrours infinite?
Who fare the best, and feel the least, yet feel that punishment
Whereby to nought they should be brought, if God did not prevent.

(213)

Isa. 33 : 14. *Mark* 9 : 43, 44.

The least degree of miserie there felt's incomparable,
The lightest pain they there sustain more than intolerable.
But God's great pow'r from hour to hour upholds them in the fire,
That they shall not consume a jot, nor by it's force expire.

(214)

Luk. 12 : 47.

But ah, the wo they undergo (they more than all besides)
Who had the light, and knew the right, yet would not it abide.
The sev'n-fold smart, which to their part, and portion doth fall,
Who Christ his Grace would not imbrace, nor hearken to his call.

(215)

Mat. 11 : 24.

The *Amorites* and *Sodomites* although their plagues be sore,
Yet find some ease, compar'd to these, who feel a great deal more.
Almighty God, whose Iron Rod, to smite them never lins,[11]
Doth most declare his Justice rare in plaguing these mens sins.

(216)

Luk. 16 : 23, 25. *Luk.* 13 : 28.

The pain of loss their Souls doth toss, and wond'rously distress,
To think what they have cast away by wilful wickedness.
We might have been redeem'd from sin, think they, and liv'd above,
Being possest of heav'nly rest, and joying in God's love.

(217)

But wo, wo, wo our Souls unto! we would not happy be; *Luk.* 13 : 34.
And therefore bear Gods Vengeance here to all Eternitee.
Experience and woful sense must be our painful teachers
Who n'ould [12] believe, nor credit give, unto our faithful Preachers.

(218)

Thus shall they ly, and wail, and cry, tormented, and tormenting *Mark* 9 : 44. *Rom.* 2 : 15.
Their galled hearts with pois'ned darts but now too late repenting.
There let them dwell i'th' Flames of Hell; there leave we them to burn,
And back agen unto the men whom Christ acquits, return.

(219)

The Saints behold with courage bold, and thankful wonderment, *The Saints rejoyce to see Judgment executed upon the wicked World.* *Ps.* 58 : 10. *Rev.* 19 : 1, 2, 3.
To see all those that were their foes thus sent to punishment:
Then do they sing unto their King a Song of endless Praise:
They praise his Name, and do proclaim that just are all his ways.

(220)

Thus with great joy and melody to Heav'n they all ascend, *They ascend with Christ into Heaven triumphing.* *Mat.* 25 : 46. 1 *Joh.* 3 : 2. 1 *Cor.* 13 : 12.
Him there to praise with sweetest layes, and Hymns that never end,
Where with long Rest they shall be blest, and nought shall them annoy:
Where they shall see as seen they be, and whom they love enjoy.

(221)

O glorious Place! where face to face Jehovah may be seen, *Their Eternal happiness and incomparable Glory there.*
By such as were sinners whilere and no dark vail between.
Where the Sun shine, and light Divine, of Gods bright Countenance,
Doth rest upon them every one, with sweetest influence.

(222)

O blessed state of the Renate! O wondrous Happiness,
To which they're brought, beyond what thought can reach, or words express!
Rev. 21 : 4. Griefs water-course, and sorrows sourse, are turn'd to joyful streams.
Their old distress and heaviness are vanished like dreams.

(223)

For God above in arms of love doth dearly them embrace,
Psal. 16 : 11. And fills their sprights with such delights, and pleasures in his grace;
As shall not fail, nor yet grow stale through frequency of use:
Nor do they fear Gods favour there, to forfeit by abuse.

(224)

Heb. 12 : 23. For there the Saints are perfect Saints, and holy ones indeed,
From all the sin that dwelt within their mortal bodies freed:
Rev. 1 : 6. & 22 : 5. Made Kings and Priests to God through Christs dear loves transcendency,
There to remain, and there to reign with him Eternally.

[The End]

A SHORT DISCOURSE ON ETERNITY.

(1)

WHAT mortal man can with his Span mete out Eternity?
Isa. 57 : 15. *Mark* 3 : 29. *Mat.* 25 : 46. Or fathom it by depth of Wit, or strength of Memory?
The lofty Sky is not so high, Hells depth to this is small:
The World so wide is but a stride, compared therewithall.

(2)

It is a main great Ocean, withouten bank or bound:
A deep Abyss, wherein there is no bottom to be found.

This World hath stood now since the Flood, four thousand years well near,
And had before endured more than sixteen hundred year.

. . .

(19)

Then, Ah poor men! what, not till then? No, not an hour before:
For God is just, and therefore must torment them evermore.
Eternity! Eternity! thou mak'st hard hearts to bleed:
The thoughts of thee in misery, do make men wail indeed.

(20)

When they remind what's still behind, and ponder this word Never, *Mark* 9: 43, 44, 45, 46, *&c.*
That they must here be made to bear Gods Vengeance for Ever:
The thought of this more bitter is, then all they feel beside:
Yet what they feel, nor heart of steel, nor Flesh of Brass can bide.

(21)

To lye in wo, and undergo the direful pains of Hell, 2 *Thes.* 1: 8, 9.
And know withall, that there they shall for aye, and ever dwell;
And that they are from rest as far when fifty thousand year, *Mat.* 25: 46. *Rev.* 14: 10, 11.
Twice told, are spent in punishment, as when they first came there.

(22)

This, Oh! this makes Hells fiery flakes much more intolerable;
This makes frail wights and damned sprights, to bear their plagues unable.
This makes men bite, for fell despite, their very tongues in twain:
This makes them rore for great horror, and trebleth all their pain.

[The End]

A SONG OF EMPTINESS,

To fill up the Empty Pages following.

Vanity of Vanities.

Vain, frail, short liv'd, and miserable Man,
Learn what thou art when thine estate is best:
A restless Wave o'th' troubled Ocean,
A Dream, a lifeless Picture finely drest:

A Wind, a Flower, a Vapour, and a Bubble,
A Wheel that stands not still, a trembling Reed,
A rolling Stone, dry Dust, light Chaff, and Stubble,
A Shadow of Something, but nought indeed.

Learn what deceitful Toyes, and empty things,
This World, and all its best Enjoyments bee:
Out of the Earth no true Contentment springs,
But all things here are vexing Vanitee.

For what is *Beauty*, but a fading Flower?
Or what is *Pleasure*, but the Devils bait,
Whereby he catcheth whom he would devour,
And multitudes of Souls doth ruinate?

And what are *Friends* but mortal men, as we?
Whom Death from us may quickly separate;
Or else their hearts may quite estranged be,
And all their love be turned into hate.

And what are *Riches* to be doted on?
Uncertain, fickle, and ensnaring things;
They draw Mens Souls into Perdition,
And when most needed, take them to their wings.

Ah foolish Man! that sets his heart upon
Such empty Shadows, such wild Fowl as these,
That being gotten will be quickly gone,
And whilst they stay increase but his disease.

As in a Dropsie, drinking draughts begets,
The more he drinks, the more he still requires:
So on this World whoso affection sets,
His Wealths encrease encreaseth his desires.

O happy Man, whose portion is above,
Where Floods, where Flames, where Foes cannot
  bereave him,
Most wretched man, that fixed hath his love
Upon this World, that surely will deceive him!

For, what is *Honour?* What is *Sov'raignty*,
Whereto mens hearts so restlesly aspire?
Whom have they Crowned with Felicity?
When did they ever satisfie desire?

The Ear of Man with hearing is not fill'd:
To see new sights still coveteth the Eye:
The craving Stomack though it may be still'd,
Yet craves again without a new supply.

All Earthly things, man's Cravings answer not,
Whose little heart would all the World contain,
(If all the World should fall to one man's Lot)
And notwithstanding empty still remain.

The *Eastern Conquerour* was said to weep,
When he the *Indian* Ocean did view,
To see his Conquest bounded by the Deep,
And no more Worlds remaining to subdue.

Who would that man in his Enjoyments bless,
Or envy him, or covet his estate,
Whose gettings do augment his greediness,
And make his wishes more intemperate?

Such is the wonted and the common guise
Of those on Earth that bear the greatest Sway:
If with a few the case be otherwise
They seek a Kingdom that abides for ay.

Moreover they, of all the Sons of men,
That Rule, and are in highest places set,
Are most inclin'd to scorn their Bretheren
And God himself (without great grace) forget.

For as the Sun doth blind the gazer's eyes,
That for a time they nought discern aright:
So Honour doth befool and blind the Wise,
And their own Lustre 'reaves them of their sight.

Great are their Dangers, manifold their Cares;
Thro' which, whilst others Sleep, they scarcely Nap:
And yet are oft surprized unawares,
And fall unweeting into Envies Trap!

The mean Mechanick finds his kindly rest,
All void of fear Sleepeth the Country-Clown,
When greatest Princes often are distrest,
And cannot Sleep upon their Beds of Down.

Could *Strength* or *Valour* men Immortalize,
Could *Wealth* or *Honour* keep them from decay,
There were some cause the same to Idolize,
And give the lye to that which I do say.

But neither can such things themselves endure
Without the hazard of a Change one hour,
Nor such as trust in them can they secure
From dismal dayes, or Deaths prevailing pow'r.

If *Beauty* could the beautiful defend
From Death's dominion, than fair *Absalom*
Had not been brought to such a shameful end:
But fair and foul unto the Grave must come.

If *Wealth* or *Scepters* could Immortal make,
Then wealthy *Crœsus*, wherefore art thou dead?
If *Warlike force*, which makes the World to quake,
Then why is *Julius Cæsar* perished?

Where are the *Scipio's* Thunder-bolts of War?
Renowned *Pompey*, *Cæsars* Enemie?
Stout *Hannibal*, *Romes* Terror known so far?
Great *Alexander*, what's become of thee?

If *Gifts* and *Bribes* Death's favour might but win,
If *Power*, if force, or *Threatnings* might it fray,
All these, and more, had still surviving been:
But all are gone, for Death will have no Nay.

Such is this World with all her Pomp and Glory,
Such are the men whom worldly eyes admire:
Cut down by Time, and now become a Story,
That we might after better things aspire.

Go boast thy self of what thy heart enjoyes,
Vain Man! triumph in all thy worldly Bliss:
Thy best enjoyments are but Trash and Toyes:
Delight thy self in that which worthless is.

Omnia praetereunt praeter amare Deum.[13]

GOD'S CONTROVERSY WITH NEW-ENGLAND

Written in the time of the great drought Anno 1662.

[God speaks against the languishing state of New-England]

. . .

Are these the men that erst at my command
  Forsook their ancient seats and native soile,
To follow me into a desart land,
  Contemning all the travell and the toile,
Whose love was such to purest ordinances
  As made them set at nought their fair inheritances?

Are these the men that prized libertee
  To walk with God according to their light,
To be as good as he would have them bee,
  To serve and worship him with all their might,
Before the pleasures which a fruitfull field,
  And country flowing-full of all good things, could yield,

Are these the fold whom from the brittish Iles,
  Through the stern billows of the watry main,
I safely led so many thousand miles,
  As if their journey had been through a plain?
Whom having from all enemies protected,
  And through so many deaths and dangers well directed,

I brought and planted on the western shore,
  Where nought but bruits and salvage wights did swarm
(Untaught, untrain'd, untam'd by vertue's lore)
  That sought their blood, yet could not do them harm?
My fury's flaile them thresht, my fatall broom
  Did sweep them hence, to make my people elbow-room.

Are these the men whose gates with peace I crown'd,
   To whom for bulwarks I salvation gave,
Whilst all things else with rattling tumults sound,
   And mortall frayes send thousands to the grave?
Whilest their own brethren bloody hands embrewed
   In brothers blood, and fields with carcases bestrewed?

Is this the people blest with bounteous store,
   By land and sea full richly clad and fed,
Whom plenty's self stands waiting still before,
   And powreth out their cups well tempered?
For whose dear sake an howling wildernes
   I lately turned into a fruitfull paradeis?

Are these the people in whose hemisphere
   Such bright-beam'd, glist'ring, sun-like starrs I placed,
As by their influence did all things cheere,
   As by their light blind ignorance defaced,
As errours into lurking holes did fray,
   As turn'd the late dark night into a lightsome day?

Are these the folk to whom I milked out
   And sweetnes stream'd from consolations brest;
Whose soules I fed and strengthened throughout
   With finest spirituall food most finely drest?
On whom I rained living bread from Heaven,
   Withouten Errour's bane, or Superstition's leaven?

With whom I made a Covenant of peace,
   And unto whom I did most firmly plight
My faithfulness, If whilst I live I cease
   To be their Guide, their God, their full delight;
Since them with cords of love to me I drew,
   Enwrapping in my grace such as should them ensew.

Are these the men, that now mine eyes behold,
   Concerning whom I thought, and whilome spake,
First Heaven shall pass away together scrold,
   Ere they my lawes and righteous wayes forsake,
Or that they slack to runn their heavenly race?
   Are these the same? or are some others come in place?

If these be they, how is it that I find
   In stead of holiness Carnality,

In stead of heavenly frames an Earthly mind,
  For burning zeal luke-warm Indifferency,
For flaming love, key-cold Dead-heartedness,
  For temperance (in meat, and drinke, and cloaths) excess?

Whence cometh it, that Pride, and Luxurie
  Debate, Deceit, Contention, and Strife,
False-dealing, Covetousness, Hypocrisie
  (With such like Crimes) amongst them are so rife,
That one of them doth over-reach another?
  And that an honest man can hardly trust his Brother?

How is it, that Security, and Sloth,
  Amongst the best are Common to be found?
That grosser sins, in stead of Graces growth,
  Amongst the many more and more abound?
I hate dissembling shews of Holiness.
  Or practise as you talk, or never more profess.

Judge not, vain world, that all are hypocrites
  That do profess more holiness then thou:
All foster not dissembling, guilefull sprites,
  Nor love their lusts, though very many do.
Some sin through want of care and constant watch,
  Some with the sick converse, till they the sickness catch.

Some, that maintain a reall root of grace,
  Are overgrown with many noysome weeds,
Whose heart, that those no longer may take place,
  The benefit of due correction needs.
And such as these however gone astray
  I shall by stripes reduce into a better way.

Moreover some there be that still retain
  Their ancient vigour and sincerity;
Whom both their own, and others sins, constrain
  To sigh, and mourn, and weep, and wail, & cry:
And for their sakes I have forborn to powre
  My wrath upon Revolters to this present houre.

To praying Saints I always have respect,
  And tender love, and pittifull regard:
Nor will I now in any wise neglect
  Their love and faithfull service to reward;

Although I deal with others for their folly,
  And turn their mirth to tears that have been too jolly.

For thinke not, O Backsliders, in your heart,
  That I shall still your evill manners beare:
Your sinns me press as sheaves do load a cart,
  And therefore I will plague you for this geare
Except you seriously, and soon, repent,
  Ile not delay your pain and heavy punishment.

And who be those themselves that yonder shew?
  The seed of such as name my dreadfull Name!
On whom whilere compassions skirt I threw
  Whilest in their blood they were, to hide their shame!
Whom my preventing love did neer me take!
  Whom for mine own I mark't, lest they should me forsake!

I look't that such as these to vertue's Lore
  (Though none but they) would have Enclin'd their ear:
That they at least mine image should have bore,
  And sanctify'd my name with awfull fear.
Let pagan's Bratts pursue their lusts, whose meed
  Is Death: For christians children are an holy seed.

But hear O Heavens! Let Earth amazed stand;
  Ye Mountaines melt, and Hills come flowing down:
Let horro[r] seize upon both Sea and Land;
  Let Natures self be cast into a stown.
I children nourisht, nurtur'd and upheld:
  But they against a tender father have rebell'd.

What could have been by me performed more?
  Or wherein fell I short of your desire?
Had you but askt, I would have op't my store,
  And given what lawfull wishes could require.
For all this bounteous cost I lookt to see
  Heaven-reaching-hearts, & thoughts, Meekness, Humility. . . .

One wave another followeth,
  And one disease begins
Before another cease, becaus
  We turn not from our sins.
We stopp our ear against reproof,
  And hearken not to God:
God stops his ear against o[r] prayer,
  And takes not off his rod.

Our fruitful seasons have been turnd
  Of late to barrenness,
Sometimes through great & parching drought,
  Sometimes through rain's excess.
Yea now the pastures & corn fields
  For want of rain do languish:
The cattell mourn, & hearts of men
  Are fill'd with fear & anguish.

The clouds are often gathered,
  As if we should have rain:
But for o[r] great unworthiness
  Are scattered again.
We pray & fast, & make fair shewes,
  As if we meant to turn:
But whilst we turn not, God goes on
  Our field, & fruits to burn.

And burnt are all things in such sort,
  That nothing now appears,
But what may wound our hearts with grief,
  And draw foorth floods of teares.
All things a famine do presage
  In that extremity,
As if both men, and also beasts,
  Should soon be done to dy.

This O New-England hast thou got
  By riot, & excess:
This hast thou brought upon thy self
  By pride & wantonness.
Thus must thy worldlyness be whipt.
  They, that too much do crave,
Provoke the Lord to take away
  Such blessings as they have.

We have been also threatened
  With worser things then these:
And God can bring them on us still,
  To morrow if he please.
For if his mercy be abus'd,
  Which holpe us at our need
And mov'd his heart to pitty us,
  We shall be plagu'd indeed.

Beware, O sinful Land, beware;
  And do not think it strange
That sorer judgements are at hand,
  Unless thou quickly change.
Or God, or thou, must quickly change;
  Or else thou art undon:
Wrath cannot cease, if sin remain,
  Where judgement is begun.

Ah dear New England! dearest land to me;
  Which unto God hast hitherto been dear,
And mayst be still more dear than formerlie,
  If to his voice thou wilt incline thine ear.

Consider wel & wisely what the rod,
  Wherewith thou art from yeer to yeer chastized,
Instructeth thee. Repent, & turn to God,
  Who wil not have his nurture be despized.

Thou still hast in thee many praying saints,
  Of great account, and precious with the Lord,
Who dayly powre out unto him their plaints,
  And strive to please him both in deed & word.

Cheer on, sweet souls, my heart is with you all,
  And shall be with you, maugre Sathan's might:
And whereso'ere this body be a Thrall,
  Still in New-England shall be my delight.

[The End]

MEAT OUT OF THE EATER[14]

Meditation V.

The fifth perswades to Patience,
From that Rich future Recompense;
Minding us of our Heavenly Rest,
Which should revive vs when distrest.

[1]

Meekly to bear Christ's yoke it is an Honour high:
  Thou Christ wilt surely them reward who bear it patiently.
2 *Cor.* 4 : 17. For this short Grief of ours, and our Affliction light
Shall work of glorious Happiness a far more lasting weight.

[2]

For just men light is sown (reward laid up in store) *Psal.* 97 : 11.
Who sow in tears shall reap in joy, and after mourn no more. *Psal.* 126 : 5.
They'll one day wear a Crown, who now the Cross sustain:
In Christ our Lord no suffering, nor labour shall be vain. 1 *Cor.* 15 : 58.

[4]

Reign with him long shall they, with him that suffer do: 1 *Tim.* 2 : 12.
Who follow him in's Death, partake shall of his Glory too.
Not that our services, deserve such Recompence: *Isa.* 64 : 6.
But he resolveth to set forth his own Munificence. 2 *Thess.* 1 : 10.

[4]

Who can expect a Crop or Harvest to obtain,
That breaks no ground, that sows no feed, that undergoes no pain?
To triumph who can hope that doth the Battel shun?
Eternal Glory whoso findes, must first through rough ways run.

[5]

Thou art a Pilgrim here; this world is not thy home: *Psal.* 39 : 12.
Then be content with Pilgrims fare, till thou to Heaven come.
What if thou tossed art with boisterous winds and seas?
Behold the Haven where thou shalt enjoy long rest and ease. *Heb.* 4 : 9.

[6]

What if thy conflict with the roaring Lion be?
If thou be call'd to fight against World, Flesh, and Devil, all three.
Stronger is Christ in thee then strongest Enemy, *Joh.* 4 : 4.
Who Satan under thy Souls feet shall tread down speedily. *Rom.* 16 : 20.

[7]

Heb. 2 : 10. Souldier be strong, who fightest under a Captain Stout:
Dishonour not thy conquering Head by basely giving out.
Endure a while, Bear up, and hope for better things:
War ends in peace; and Morning light mounts up on Midnights wing.

[8]

Through Changes manifold, and Dangers perilous,
Isa. 43 : 2. *Heb.* 11 : 14, 16. Through fiery flames, and water-floods, through ways calamitous.
Mat. 25 : 34. We travel towards Heaven a quiet Habitation:
Christ shews a Kingdom there prepar'd ev'n from the worlds foundation.

[9]

2 *Cor.* 2 : 4, 8. O Heaven, most holy place, which art our country dear!
What cause have I to long for thee, and Beg with many a tear.
Earth is to me a Prison; this Body an useless wight:
And all things else vile, vain, and nought, to one in such ill plight.

[10]

O Christ make haste, from bands, of Sin and Death me free;
And to those Heavenly Mansions, be pleas'd to carry me.
1 *Thes.* 4 : 17. Where glorified Saints for ever are possest,
Of God in Christ their chiefest Good. And from all troubles Rest.

Meditation VIII.

Saints happier be when most distrest,
Then wicked men are at the best.

[1]

We have the wicked view'd, and seen his best estate
And who would chuse with him to share, except a Reprobate?
Prov. 1 : 32. For sure the Simple's ease shall turn to his decay:
And the Prosperity of Fools shall utterly them slay.

[2]

When wicked men like Grass do springing up arise, *Psal.* 92 : 7.
When they are in a flourishing case that work iniquities:
'Tis for their cutting down to perpetuity;
It's but to ripen them for woe, and endless Misery.

[3]

The less Affliction here they feel, the more's to come: *Luk.* 16 :
The greater Blessings they abuse, the heavier is their Doom. 23, 24, 25.
Now let us take a Saint whom men account accurst,
Because they judge him plagu'd of God, and view him at his worst.

[4]

Suppose his case as bad, as bad it well can be:
And his Calamity more sad then commonly we see.
Dispose him where you will, do with him what you can:
Yet God is present with him still; he is a happy man.

[5)

Let Sickness come upon him, or great Tormenting Pain: *Jam.* 5 : 11. *Act.* 23 : 11.
God will not lose him, but a Saint a Saint shall still remain.
In Prison him immure, all comforts from him take:
You cannot rob him of his God, nor him unhappy make.

[6]

Plunge him into the mire, or water; God is near: *Isa.* 43 : 2.
Cast him into the burning Fire; God will be with him there. *Psal.* 42 : 7, 8.
If many roaring waves of great Affliction roll
Over his head: God so supports they cannot sink his Soul.

[7]

(*Jacob* in servitude. *Joseph* in Prison Chains,
Moses in his long Banishment Heaven's Favourite still remains.
Three Children in the Fire *Daniel* i'th' Lions Den
Have God to guard them: so had *Paul* when Shipwrack'd. Happy Men!)

[8]

Deut. 33 : 27.

The Everlasting Arms are underneath his head
To bear him up; and hence it comes he is not swallowed,

Psal. 44 : 17, 18, 22.

Nor suffered wickedly from God to turn aside:
As by his carriage will appear when troubles him betide.

Meditation IX.

The Carriage of a Child of God
Under his Fathers smarting Rod,

(1)

Job 1 : 21. & 2 : 20. 2 *Sam.* 16 : 11.

He sees a hand of God in his Afflictions all,
And owns it for to be his Rod, Whatever Cross befall.
For whosoever be th'immediate instrument,
He knows right well that God himself was the Efficient.

(2)

Job 5 : 6. 1 *Kings* 22 : 48, 49.

And that Afflictions rise not out of the Dust:
Nor are they order'd by the will of Man, or Devils lust.
If that the Grief be small or the Chastisement light:
Yet since God finds it not in vain, light strokes he dare not slight.

(3)

Heb. 12 : 6. *Joel* 2 : 12. *Amos* 4 : 12.

If greater be the Blow, it doth not him dismay:
Because he knows a Fathers hand such stripes may on him lay,
But he prepares himself betimes to meet the Lord
By true Repentance, as he hath commanded in his Word.

(4)

Lam. 3 : 40. *Job* 10 : 2. *Job* 34 : 31, 32. *Job* 42 : 6.

To search and try his wayes to find out what's amiss,
To leave his sins, to loath himself his first great Business is.
And having once found out what sin hath God offended;
He seriously bewails it, and endeavours to amend it.

(5)

Unto the cleansing Blood of Jesus Christ he flies;
And to his wounded Conscience that Soveraign Balm applies:
Which can both cleanse and heal; both pacifie God's wrath,
And cure a guilty sin-sick Soul, when 'tis improv'd by Faith.

Heb. 6 : 18. *Psal.* 51 : 7. *Job.* 2 : 2. *Heb.* 9 : 14. *Rev.* 1 : 5.

(6)

And though he be unworthy to look God in the face;
Yet through the Merits of his Son he begs and hopes for Grace:
Being right well assur'd that though the Lord chastise him;
Yet will he not cast off his Soul, nor utterly despise him.

Heb. 4: 15, 16. *Job* 19: 25, 26, 27. *Lam.* 3 : 31, 32.

[7]

But if by all his search he cannot find the cause
For which the Lord afflicteth him, or from his Soul withdraws:
Yet he believeth, that for just and holy ends,
To humble, purge, and better him the Lord Affliction sends.

[8]

And though he cannot say, I have at random run,
Or wickedly by some known sin away from God have gon:
Yet so much sin he sees both in his heart and wayes,
As God may judge it meet therefore to scourge him all his dayes.

Job 10 : 2, 7. *Job* 7 : 2. *Job* 9 : 3.

[9]

Himself he humbleth under the mighty hand of God:
And for the sake of that sweet hand doth kiss the sharpest Rod.
He taketh up his Cross, denieth his own will,
Advanceth God's above his own, and yieldeth to him still.

1 *Pet.* 5. 1 *Sam.* 3 : 18. *Job* 2: 10.

[10]

Unto the yoke of Christ he doth his neck submit:
He turns his cheek to him that smites, and meekly taketh it.
Yea when his grief is most, and sorest is his pain:
He still endeavoureth good thoughts of God for to retain.

Lam. 3 : 29, 30. *Lam.* 3 : 22, 23, 25.

[11]

His earnest care and prayer when greatest is his smart,
Is that he never may blaspheme God with his mouth or heart.
He beggeth Patience in his extremities
To bear Gods hand, that so his heart may not against him rise.

[12]

Psal. 73: 13, 14, 15, 22. If murmuring thoughts do rise (or hearts begin to swell)
He strives to beat them down again; he hates such thoughts like Hell.
God he resolves to love, deal with him as he will:
Job 13: 15. And in his mercy to confide although he should him kill.

[13]

To God that smiteth him he strives to get more near
He will not cease to pray, although God seem to stop his ear.
Psal. 88: 1, 2, 9, 13. *Psal.* 42: 7, 8, 9. Though God hath long delay'd to answer his request,
Yet will he seek, and never cease, whilst life is in his brest.

[14]

Psal. 40: 1, 2, 4. *Isa.* 28: 16. He waiteth patiently untill deliverance come,
And will not use dishonest means to shun what's troublesome.
Psal. 116: 16. He hates all sinful sleights to get his Cross from under:
And will not break his Bonds, but stay till God them cut asunder.

[15]

Gen. 8: 13, 14, 16. *Noah* would not leave his Ark, nor out of Prison break,
Although he saw the Ground was dry, till God did to him speak.
1 *Samuel* 26: 9, 11. *David* refus'd to kill, King *Saul* his mortal Foe,
That persecuted him to Death, and wrought him so much woe.

[16]

He rather chose to wait, till God should plead his Cause,
And of his Enemy him avenge, then for to break God's Laws.

Thus every Saint will rather, chuse Suffering, then to Sin, *Job* 36 : 21.
He will not God offend Self-ease, or safety for to win.

[17]

But if through Humane frailty, and over-bearing power, *Mat.* 26 : 70, 75.
Of Strong Temptation, he do swerve, and fall i'th evil hour:
(As sometimes *Peter* did,) it grieveth him full sore, *Luke* 22 : 32.
He weeps and mourns, repents, returns, grows stronger then before,

[18]

The longer God afflicts him, the better he is for it, *Psal.* 119 : 67, 71.
Love's Holiness the more, loath's sin and learneth to abhor it. *Eccles.* 7 : 3.
The more he is bereft, and stript of outward things:
The less he dotes on these wild Fowl, that take them to their wings.

[19]

When creature comforts fail, when sorrows him surround,
He takes the faster hold of God, in whom true Comfort's found.
When Conduit-pipes are stopt, when Streams are vanished,
The more he to the Fountain hastes, and lives at the well-head.

[20]

Thus *David* comforted and cheer'd himself in God, 1 *Sam.* 30 : 6.
When all was gone, although he felt the anguish of the Rod. *Gen.* 32 : 26, 28.
Thus *Jacob* took fast hold, and wrestled with the Lord,
When as he was distrest for fear of cruel *Esau*'s sword.

[21]

Prince-like he wrestled and would not let him go,
Until he had a Blessing got to shield him from his Foe.
Thus every suffering Saint by wrestling shall prevail,
And having overcome at last be styled *Israel*.

LIGHT IN DARKNESS[15]

Song V.

A Dialogue between the Flesh *and* Spirit.

Flesh. [1]

But oh methinks the Lord is angry with my Prayers,
The more I cry to him for help the worse it with me fares.
The more I sue for grace and beg for some relief:
The more he lets me be distrest, and doubled is my grief.

[2]

I fear he reckoneth my Prayers to me for sin,
And rather is displeas'd therewith then takes delight therein.
If God reject my Prayer, I fear he me rejects.
For how can he despise their Prayer whose persons he respects?

Spirit. [3]

Psal. 80 : 4. *Psal.* 66 : 18. Against his People's Prayers the Lord sometimes may smoke,
When some sin unrepented of his anger doth provoke.
Lam. 3 : 40. If *David* sin regard God will not hear his Prayer:
To search for, find out, mourn for sin, my Soul make this thy care.

[4]

Josh. 7 : God puts thee upon search, would have thee diligent
13, 14. To find out what offensive is and to be Penitent.
Jer. 3. Be thou displeas'd with sin, and he'll be pleas'd with
4 : 13, 14, 17. thee:
Chap. 3 : 19, 20. He'll turn to thee his face, if thou turn from iniquitie.

[5]

Mat. 15 : Some-Times the Lord delayes, and makes us long to
23, 24, 29. wait,
For other ends; as for to make us more importunate;
To try our Self-denial, our Faith, Love, Patience.
Sometimes to make his Power shine forth in our deliverance.

[6]

He lets our troubles grow unto the greater height, *Exod.* 14 & 15 *chapters*
That his Salvation might appear more glorious in our sight.
For these, and other more, such great and gracious Ends
The Lord defers to hear our prayer, for he no hurt intends.

[7]

Our Prayers are sometimes heard, not just unto our mind, *Gen.* 18:19.
Yet heard they are, and answered in some far better kind.
God may deny to grant that thing that we request, 2 *Cor.* 12:8, 9.
Yet answer in a better thing, for he knows what is best.

[8]

Be silent then frail Flesh, thou favourest not these things:
Thy wisdom doth but vex my Soul; leave off thy Reasonings.
Satan by Serpents mouth mankind did undermine: *Gen.* 3.
And I perceive he now assayes to ruine me by thine.

Song VI.

Another Combate between the Flesh *and* Spirit.

Flesh. [1]

Soul thou hast cause to fear thy Faith will not hold out:
And that it is but counterfeit thou do'st so often doubt.
See what a mighty power of Unbelief prevails
From time to time! and how thine heart and Faith thee often fails!

Spirit. [2]

Oh sly and sinful flesh! Thou art a treacherous Thief,
That robs me of my Faith, and then condemns for Unbelief.
They're thy suggestions vile (that do'st with Hell comply)
That make me doubt, who otherwise on Christ alone rely.

[3]

Joh. 1: Whole Christ with all my heart I earnestly Embrace;
12. And for my whole Salvation I relie upon his grace:
Act. 8: 37. Renouncing all my own both Righteousness, and Sin;
1 *Cor.* 1: 30. *Phil.* 3: 9, 10. *Heb.* 12: 14. Endeav'ring Holiness, as well as Happiness to win.

[4]

And blessed be the Lord, who will compleat my Faith,
Phil. 1: 6. Weak though it be, as he the same at first begotten hath:
1 *Pet.* 1: 5. Mean while he it supports; and as himself doth tell,
Mat. 16: 18. It never shall be vanquished by all the force of Hell.

STRENGTH IN WEAKNESS

Song IV

[1]

Isai. 40: WHY SAY'ST thou *Jacob*, and, O *Israel* spoken hast,
27, My way is hidden from the Lord, my judgment from him past?
28, Hast thou not known nor heard, th'Eternal God, the Lord
Who hath the Ends of all the Earth created by his Word.

[2]

He never waxeth faint, nor wearied is he:
His understanding is so deep it cannot searched be.
29, He giveth strength unto the faint and feeble wight:
And he bestows increase of strength on such as have no might.

[3]

30, The youth shall faint and tire, and young men wholly fall:
31. But those that wait upon the Lord their strength recover shall.
They shall mount up with wings like Eagles; run shall they
And not be weary: they shall walk and shall not faint away.

POOR MENS WEALTH

TO TALK of Poor mens Wealth, or Rich mens Poverty,
Seems to the World an Old Wives Tale, or idle foolery:
But whoso reads our Lines, if God but give him eyes,
Shall see that these things are no Tales, but Spiritual Mysteries.

MEDITATION I.

[1]

What means this Paradox? How can the Rich be poor?
Or Poor men Rich? What is their Wealth? Or where is
all their store?
I know thy Poverty, saith Christ, yet thou art Rich, *Rev.* 2.
To *Smyrna*'s undefiled Church: thou seest there may be
such.

[2]

But to *Laodicea;* thou say'st that I am rich,
But thou art naked, blind and poor, a miserable wretch. *Rev.* 3 : 17, 18.
I counsel thee to buy Eye-salve that thou may'st see,
Of me; try'd Gold to make thee rich, white Robes to
cover thee.

[3]

The Beggar *Lazarus* laid at the Rich man's doores *Luk.* 16 :
To beg relief, all Ulcerous, and full of running sores; 20, 22,
When once his Body dies with many griefs opprest:
His Soul by Angels carried is unto that Heavenly Rest.

[4]

The Riotous Epicure, that feasted every day,
That cloath'd himself with Purple, and most gorgeous
array:
He dy'd and went to Hell, suff'ring Eternal Pain. 23.
What thinkest thou my Soul? which was the richer of
these twain?

[5]

He was a Rich Poor man, whose Poverty prepar'd
him
For Heav'n: But he a Poor Rich man whose Worldly
Wealth ensnar'd him.
That man is Poor indeed both when he lives and dies,
That hath some Treasure here on Earth, but none above
the Skies.

[6]

He that enlarg'd his Barns to treasure up his store, *Luk.* 12 :
Was fetch'd away to Hell that night, and died worse 18, 20, 21.
then poor.
And so is every man, that being worldly-wise
Provides for th' outward man, but doth the Heavenly
wealth despise.

[7]

All Poor men are not Rich ('twere happy if they were)
But such as Christ enriched hath, and unto God brought near.
All Rich men are not Poor (that were a woful case)
But such as have no part in Christ, nor any saving grace.

[8]

Let not the poorest Saint despond; for thou art rich:
Mat. 9 : 33. *Luk.* 16 : 9. *Luk.* 12 : 33. Nor richest Worldling bless himself; for thou may'st be a wretch.
But let both Rich and Poor endeavour to make sure
Of Heavenly Treasure, Spiritual Wealth. This only will endure.

[9]

If others will be fools and no true wisdom learn:
Yet what belongs unto my peace, Lord, help me to discern.
To have my portion here Oh never let me chuse,
Psal. 17 : 4. Not for the sake of trifling Toyes eternal Joyes refuse.

[10]

My Soul craves better things then this World can afford:
Psal. 73 : 25, 26. Thou art the Portion that I chuse, give me thy self, O Lord.
I shall be richer then, then if I were possest
Of all the Riches, that are found both in the East and West.

HEAVENLY CROWNS FOR THORNY WREATHS.

Song I.

[1]

Mat. 27 : 29, 30. When Christ was crown'd with Thorns, and smitten with a Reed
Upon the Thorns, to wound his Head and for to make him bleed;
The world did little think this was the King of Glory:
So when we speak of Crowns for Thorns, they think it's but a story.

[2]

But as our Lord doth now his Crown of Glory wear;
Who for our sake did wear those Thorns, and such Abuses bear:
So shall th' Afflicted Saints that suffer for his sake
E're long be Crowned like their Head, and of his Joyes partake.

[3]

Those that for doing well, for keeping Christ's Commands,
For bearing witness to his Truth suffer Reproach or Bands,
Or any other Pain to keep their Conscience pure; *Rev.* 7 : 14, 15,
Such of a glorious Recompence and rich Reward are sure. 16, 17.

[4]

Those that are persecuted because of Righteousness,
Are Blessed ones, saith Christ, for they Heav'ns Kingdom shall possess. *Mat.* 5 : 10, 11, 12.
And Blest are ye whom men revile and persecute,
To whom for my sake heinous Crimes they wrongfully impute.

[5]

Rejoyce and be ye glad hereat exceedingly;
Because there is a great Reward laid up for you on high.
For thus they persecuted the Prophets that of old
Reprov'd their sins, and faithfully God's Counsel to them told.

[6]

Who Father, Mother Wife, for love of Christ forsakes *Mark* 10:
Or of his houses, Lands Estate for him small reckoning makes. 29, 30.
Shall here an hundred fold with persecutions gain;
And in the world that is to come eternal Life obtain.

[7]

If in a suff'ring state of Christ we followers be, 2. *Tim.* 2:
We shall be unto him conform'd in Royal dignitie. 11, 12.
Those that have stuck to Christ in Tribulations great *Mat.* 19 : 28.
Shall reign with Christ, and sit with him, upon his Judgment seat.

[8]

But those that suffer pain foul Errours to defend,
That for vile Fancies of their own dread not their lives
to spend
Such do in vain suppose they suffer for Christ's sake.
'Tis not the Suff'ring but the cause that doth a Martyr
make.

EDWARD JOHNSON

[The narrative of Edward Johnson's *Wonder-working Providence* (1654) (see p. 143) is interspersed with many short verse tributes celebrating men and events. One of the best is the epitaph for Roger Harlackenden (1611–1638), the young assistant who emigrated with his eighteen-year-old wife in the company of his close friend Thomas Shepard. His early death deprived the Bay Colony of one of its sturdiest leaders. The lines praising the new churches established in 1648 at Haverhill (Andover), Malden, and Boston are picturesque and touching in their sincerity.

The text is from the edition of J. Franklin Jameson (New York, 1910), pp. 103, 249, 250. The lines on Harlackenden have been refashioned to conform to the original stanzaic arrangement. The meter throughout is thoroughly correct by Johnson's standards.]

TWO EPITAPHS FROM WONDER-WORKING PROVIDENCE

[Roger Harlackenden]

Harlackenden,
Among these men
Of note Christ hath thee seated:
In warlike way
Christ thee aray
With zeal, and love well heated.
As generall
Belov'd of all,
Christ Souldiers honour thee:
In thy young yeares,
Courage appeares,
And kinde benignity.
Short are thy days
Spent in his praise,

Whose Church work thou must aid,
His work shall bide,
Silver tride,
But thine by death is staid.

[To the New Churches]

Thou Sister young, Christ is to thee a wall
Of flaming fire, to hurt thee none may come,
In slipp'ry paths and dark wayes shall they fall,
His Angels might shall chase their countless sum.
Thy Shepheard with full cups and table spread,
Before thy foes in Wilderness thee feeds,
Increasing thy young lambs in bosom bred,
Of Churches by his wonder-working deeds:
To countless number must Christ's Churches reach,
The day's at hand, both Jew and Gentile shall
Come crowding in his Churches, Christ to preach,
And last for aye, none can cause them to fall.

SAMUEL BRADSTREET and DANIEL RUSSELL

[*An Almanack for The Year of Our Lord 1657* was issued in Cambridge by Samuel Bradstreet (1633?–1682), eldest son of Governor Simon and Anne Bradstreet, a graduate of Harvard in 1653, and a Fellow of the college. He appropriated the second page of the Almanac for a six-stanza account of Apollo's wooing of the earth-goddess Tellus. Bradstreet later spent four years abroad, and upon his return in 1661 practiced medicine in Boston. In 1670 he removed to Jamaica in the West Indies, where he died. See Sibley, *Biographical Sketches*, I, 360–361.

To Daniel Russell (1642–1679), son of the Hon. Richard Russell of Charlestown, was given the opportunity of preparing *An Almanack of Coelestiall Motions for the year of the Christian Aera, 1671*. At the foot of each page he placed an eight-line eclogue on the Tellurian theme appropriate to the calendar month. Florid in style, the verses nevertheless are in the Vergilian tradition, and it was the first almanac poetry after 1664 to draw upon the classics. Russell was elected a Fellow of the college in 1675. Two years later he was called to the Charlestown church, but he died before his installation. See Sibley, *ibid.*, II, 284–287.]

TWO ALMANAC POEMS

An Almanack for The Year of Our Lord, 1657

Aspice venturo latentur ut omnia Seclo.[1]

IT WAS, when scarce had rang the morning bells
That call the dead to rise from silent tombes,
Whilst yet they were lockt up in darker Cells,
Ne had the light posses'd their shady roomes,
That slumbring Tellus [2] in a dream did see
Apollo [3] come to cure her Lethargee.

Strait shee awoke, and lifting up her eyes
To top of tall Mount-Æthers [4] burning brow;
From flaming Globes, the Titans Herauld spies
Herward approach; Then 'fore her shrine to bow;
Who bids her in great Phæbus name to cheer,
For he was coming, and would soon be heer.

Now rapt with joy, she takes her mantle soft,
On colder Couch ne longer will shee lie;
But decks her self by christall glass aloft
That hangs above her spangled Canopie,
With pearly drops that fall from Limpid stilles
She dights her too, and then with pleasance smiles.

Whilst fleet-fire-foming-steeds from farre appear
In speedy race the lofty hills to stride:
They Scout the smoaking Plaines, and then draw near
With burning Carre, that none but he can guide
Who baulks their course with curb & gars [5] them bound
Whilst he steps down to Sublunary-round:

To greet his Tellus then he hies apace,
Whom sprusely deckt he findes i'th verdant gown
He whilom sent. Each other doth embrace
In loving armes, and then they sitten down
Whilst high-born states, and low Tellurean bands
Rejoyce to see sage Hymen joyn their hands.

Eftsoones Apollo gives a Girlond rare
With flowers deckt (for Tellus front alone)
To her: and sayes in mind of me this weare
And Babyes deft will thence arise anon.
She dons it strait: And buds that erst were green
Now sucklings at her milkey papps they been.

Samuel Bradstreet

AN ALMANACK OF COELESTIALL MOTIONS FOR THE YEAR OF THE CHRISTIAN AERA, 1671.

By D. R. Philomathemat.

March:[6]

The Starry Monarch now to's full careere,
Comes marching up to our North Hemisphere,
And by his burning Beams, our Frigid Zone
Doth Metamorphize to a temperate one;
Re-animating with Celestial Fire,
Those liveless Natures *Hyem*'s [7] caus'd t'expire:
And causing *Tellus* t'doff her Winter Yest,
For joy of th'Spring; her new-come, welcome guest.

April:

The Airy Choristers, they now begin
To warble forth their Native Musick in
The new-leaf'd Boughs; and in each pleasant Field,
By Natures Art their curious Nests do build.
Now big with hopes, the toyling Country Swain
Buries in th'Earth his multiplying Grain,
On which the Heavens do fertile Showers distill,
Which th'Earth with fruits, the Swain with joy doth fill.

May:

Dame *Tellus* cloathed in a grass-green Coat,
By *Flora*'s curious Needle-work well wrought,
'Gins to appear; for now the Meads abound
With fragrant Roses, and with Lillies Crown'd.
The Proverb's verified, that *April* Showers
On *Maia*'s Fields do rain down glittering Flowers;
And now the croaking Crew, late *All a-Mort*,
By their Night-chantings, their new life report.

June:

The smiling Fields, attired in their Suits
Of Taste-delighting, and Eye-pleasing Fruits;
Their Strawb'ry Mantles now begin to wear,
And many Orchards Cherry-cheekt appear.
Now *Sol* in's Crabbed Throne doth take his place,
Where he performs his Longest daily Race:
Soon after which, the dayes length 'gins to fade,
And *Phoebus*, *Cancer*-like turns Retrograde.[8]

July:

Now *Ceres* Offspring's numerous every where,
And mighty Armies of Tall Blades appear
In many Fields, all Rank'd and Fil'd they stand
Ready for Battel: With whom hand to hand
Fierce Husbandmen with crooked Cutlash meet,
And being Victors lay them at their feet.
This don't suffice; together th'Blades are bound,
Transported home, and soundly thresh'd on th'ground.

August:

Now *Sol* and *Mercury* near th'*Virgin* [9] meet,
Where in Conjunction they each other greet,
The best of Aspects; which doth signify,
Advancement to the Sons of *Mercury*.
And now the verdant Meads begin to feel
The sharp encounter of the Mowers Steel:
The Noble Vines with Grapes, the Grapes begin
To swell with *Bacchus*, which is Barell'd in.

September:

The *Indian* Stalks, now richly fraught with store
Of golden-colour'd Ears, seem to implore
By humble bowing of their lofty Head,
From this their load to be delivered.
Pomona's Daughters now at age, and dight
With pleasing Beauty, Lovers do invite
In multitudes: it's well if they escape
From each of these, without a cruel Rape.

October:

Now the *Aeolian* Lords and Commons meet
In Parliament, where it is Voted fit,
Yea and Resolv'd upon, what-ere it cost,
They'll King it over all, and rule the Rost.
Which to effect, it is Agreed by all,
That blustring *Boreas* shall be Generall
Of their great Forces; and then to't they go,
And *Tellus* Kingdom first they'll overthrow.

November:

Where thundring *Boreas*, with his Troops, doth shake
The trembling Woods, and makes the Trees to quake:
The Leaves for very fear the Trees have left,
Which of their July garb, now're quite bereft:

The Fruits, those pleasant Fruits, the painted Flowers,
The Flow'ry Meads, gay Fields, and shady Bowers,
Are now destroy'd; and th'Earths depriv'd of all
Her Summer glory by this Wasting FALL.

December:
Exit Autumnus: Winter now draws neare,
Armed with Frost i'th'Van, with Snow i'th'Rere;
Whose freezing Forces cause men to retire,
For help to th'Fortress of a well-made Fire.
Phoebus himself, as if with pannick fear
Hereat affrighted, now in's full Careere
Doth poste away, and speeds him from our sight
In greatest haste, bidding the World good-night.

January:
The Northern Captains Siege still fiercely lasts,
And still the Roaring Canons of his Blasts
Are fired off; which brings both Land and Sea
His Chained Captives quickly for to be:
And lest they should rebell, if load they lack,
Mountains of Snow are heap'd on *Tellus* back;
The lofty swelling Waves, stout *Neptunes* pride,
Are made a packhorse on which men may ride.

February:
And now the Worlds bright Torch, whose radiant Light
Dispels the gloomy Mists of black-fac'd Night:
The Twelve *Herculean* Labours of his *Sphere*,
Compleated hath, and Periodiz'd the Year,
But not his Motion: Natures Law commands
That fiery *Phoebus* Charriot never stands,
Without a Miracle; but that it be,
Still termed *Certus: semper Mobile.*[10]

Daniel Russell

BENJAMIN TOMPSON, 1642–1714

[Benjamin Tompson, first native-born colonial poet,was the youngest son of the Reverend Mr. William Tompson of Braintree, Massachusetts. After graduation from college in 1662, he taught school and studied medicine; in 1670 he was chosen assistant to Ezekiel Cheever, headmaster of the "Free Schoole" in Boston, (known since 1690 as the Boston Latin School), but he left shortly to teach and practice medicine in Charlestown. In 1674 he removed to Braintree, and in 1700 he took up residence in Roxbury, where his tombstone records him as "Learned Schoolmaster & Physician & ye Renouned Poet of N: Engl:."

His most ambitious poetic flight, a narrative of King Philip's War, appeared in Boston and London in 1676: *New Englands Crisis. Or a Brief Narrative, Of New-Englands Lamentable Estate at present, compar'd with the former (but few) years of Prosperity . . . Poetically Described. By a Well wisher to his Countrey.* Much of the contents he repeated in *New-Englands Tears for her Present Miseries,* issued in the same year, written probably as an afterthought.

The best edition of his works is that of Howard J. Hall, *Benjamin Tompson . . . His Poems Collected with an Introduction* (Boston, 1924). Kenneth B. Murdock, *Handkerchiefs from Paul* (Cambridge, 1927), offers minor corrections and two additions. See also Tyler, *A History of American Literature,* II, 21–23; Sibley, *Biographical Sketches,* II, 103–111; and *Dictionary of American Biography.* The text is from the 1676 Boston edition.]

NEW ENGLANDS CRISIS

Marlburyes Fate [1]

When *Londons* fatal bills [2] were blown abroad
And few but Specters travel'd on the road,
Not towns but men in the black bill enrol'd
Were in *Gazetts* by *Typographers* sold:
But our *Gazetts* without *Erratæs* must
Report the plague of towns reduct to dust:
And feavers formerly to tenants sent
Arrest the timbers of the tenement.
Ere the late ruins of old *Groton*'s cold,
Of *Marlbury*'s peracute disease we're told.
The feet of such who neighbouring dwellings urnd
Unto her ashes, not her doors return'd.
And what remaind of tears as yet unspent
Are to its final gasps a tribute lent.
If painter overtrack my pen let him
An olive colour mix these elves to trim;
Of such an hue let many thousand thieves
Be drawn like Scare-crows clad with oaken leaves,
Exhausted of their verdant life and blown
From place to place without an home to own.
Draw Devils like themselves, upon their cheeks
The banks for grease and mud, a place for leeks.

Whose locks *Medusaes* snakes, do ropes resemble,
And ghostly looks would make *Achilles* tremble.
Limm them besmear'd with Christian Bloud & oild
With fat out of white humane bodyes boil'd,
Draw them with clubs like maules & full of stains,
Like *Vulcans* anvilling *New-Englands* brains.
Let round be gloomy forrests with crag'd rocks
Where like to castles they may hide their flocks,
Till oppertunity their cautious friend
Shall jogge them fiery worship to attend.
Shew them like serpents in an avious path
Seeking to sow the fire-brands of their wrath.
Most like Æneas in his cloak of mist,
Who undiscover'd move where ere they list
Cupid they tell us hath too sorts of darts.
One sharp and one obtuse, one causing wounds,
One piercing deep the other dull rebounds,
But we feel none but such as drill our hearts.
From Indian sheaves which to their shoulders cling,
Upon the word they quickly feel the string.
Let earth be made a screen to hide our woe
From Heavens Monarch and his Ladyes too;
And least our Jealousie think they partake,
For the red stage with clouds a curtain make.
Let dogs be gag'd and every quickning sound
Be charm'd to silence, here and there all round
The town to suffer, from a thousand holes
Let crawle these fiends with brands and fired poles,
Paint here the house & there there the barn on fire,
With holocausts ascending in a spire.
Here granaries, yonder the Churches smoak
Which vengeance on the actors doth invoke.
Let *Morpheus* with his leaden keyes have bound
In feather-beds some, some upon the ground,
That none may burst his drowsie shackles till
The bruitish pagans have obtain'd their will,
And *Vulcan* files them off then *Zeuxis* paint
The phrenzy glances of of the sinking saint.
Draw there the Pastor for his bible crying,
The souldier for his sword, The Glutton frying
With streams of glory-fat,[3] the thin-jaw'd Miser
Oh had I given this I had been wiser.
Let here the Mother seem a statue turn'd
At the sad object of her bowels burn'd.
Let the unstable weakling in belief

Be mounting *Ashurs*[4] horses for relief.
Let the half Convert seem suspended twixt
The dens of darkness, and the Plantes fixt,
Ready to quit his hold, and yet hold fast
By the great *Atlas* of the Heavens vast.
Paint Papists mutterring ore their apish beads
Whome the blind follow while the blind man leads.
Let *Ataxy* be mounted on a throne
Imposing her Commands on every one,
A many-headed monster without eyes
To see the wayes which wont to make men wise.
Give her a thousands tongues with wings and hands
To be ubiquitary in Commands,
But let the concave of her skull appear
Clean washt and empty quite of all but fear,
One she bids flee, another stay, a third
She bids betake him to his rusty sword,
This to his treasure, th'other to his knees,
Some counsels she to fry and some to freeze,
These to the garison, those to the road,
Some to run empty, some to take their load:
Thus while confusion most mens hearts divide
Fire doth their small exchecquer soon decide.
Thus all things seeming ope or secret foes,
An Infant may grow old before a close,
But yet my hopes abide in perfect strength.

The Town called *Providence*
Its Fate.

Why muse wee thus to see the wheeles run cross
Since *Providence* it self sustaines a loss:
And yet should *Providence* forget to watch
I fear the enemy would all dispatch;
Celestial lights would soon forget their line,
The wandering planets would forget to shine,
The stars run all out of their common spheres,
And quickly fall together by the eares:
Kingdoms would jostles out their Kings and set
The poor Mechanick up whome next they met,
Or rather would whole kingdoms with the world
Into a *Chaos* their first egge be hurl'd.
Ther's none this Providence of the Most High
Who can survive and write its Elegie:
But of a solitary town I write,
A place of darkness yet receiving light

From pagan hands, a miscellanious nest
Of errors Hectors, where they sought a rest.
Out of the reach of Lawes but not of God,
Since they have felt the smart of common rod.
Twas much I thought they did escape so long,
Who Gospel truth so manifestly wronge:
For one *Lots* sake perhaps, or else I think
Justice did at greatest offenders wink
But now the shott is paid, I hope the dross
Will be cashiered in this common loss.
Houses with substance feel uplifting wings,
The earth remains, the last of humane things:
But know the dismal day draws neer wherein
The fire shall earth it self dissolve and sin.

Seaconk Plain Engagement.

On our *Pharsalian Plaines*, comprizing space
For *Cæsars* host brave *Pompey* to outface,
An handfull of our men are walled round
With Indian swarmes; anon their pieces sound
A *Madrigal* like heav'ns artilery
Lightning and thunderbolts their bullets fly.
Her's hosts to handfulls, of a fevv they leave
Fewer to tell how many they bereave.
Fool-hardy fortitude it had been sure
Fierce storms of shot and arrows to endure
Without all hopes of some requital to
So numerous and pestilent a foe.
Some musing a retreat and thence to run,
Have in an instant all their business done,
They sink and all their sorrows ponderous weight
Down at their feet they cast and tumble straight.
Such who outliv'd the fate of others fly
Into the Irish bogs of misery.
Such who might dye like men like beasts do range
Uncertain whither for a better change,
These Natives hunt and chase with currish mind,
And plague with crueltyes such as they find.
When shall this shower of Bloud be over? When?
Quickly we pray oh Lord! say thou Amen.

Seaconk or *Rehoboths* Fate.

I once conjectur'd that those tygers hard
To reverend *Newmans* [5] bones would have regard,
But were all *SAINTS* they met twere all one case,

They have no rev'rence to an Angels face:
But where they fix their griping lions paws
They rend without remorse or heed to laws.
Rehoboth here in common english, Rest
They ransack, *Newmans* Relicts to molest.
Here all the town is made a publick stage
Whereon these *Nimrods* act their monstrous rage.
All crueltyes which paper stain'd before
Are acted to the life here ore and ore.

Chelmsfords Fate.

Ere famous *Winthrops* bones are laid to rest
The pagans *Chelmsford* with sad flames arrest,
Making an artificial day of night
By that plantations formidable light.
Here's midnight shrieks and Soul-amazing moanes,
Enough to melt the very marble stones:
Fire-brands and bullets, darts and deaths and wounds
Confusive outcryes every where resounds:
The natives shooting with the mixed cryes,
With all the crueltyes the foes devise
Might fill a volume, but I leave a space
For mercyes still successive in there place
Not doubting but the foes have done their worst,
And shall by heaven suddenly be curst.

Let this dear Lord the sad conclusion be
Of poor New-Englands *dismal tragedy.*
Let not the glory of thy former work
Blasphemed be by pagan Jew or Turk:
But in its funeral ashes write thy Name
So fair all Nations may expound the same:
Out of her ashes let a Phœnix rise
That may outshine the first and be more wise.

B. Tompson.

URIAN OAKES

[Most of the funeral verses and elegies which Puritan poets wrote so facilely are better forgotten, but Urian Oakes's *An Elegy upon the Death of the Reverend Mr. Thomas Shepard* (Cambridge, 1677), deserves to survive on its own merits. Thomas Shepard (1635–1677) of Charlestown was a son of the famous Cambridge pastor of the same name.

He prepared the Almanac for 1656, and his election sermon for 1672, *Eye-Salve, Or A Watch-Word From our Lord Jesus Christ unto his Churches,* enunciated important views on toleration. For an account of Oakes, see p. 350. The text is from the original in the library of the Massachusetts Historical Society.]

AN ELEGY UPON THE DEATH OF THE REVEREND MR. THOMAS SHEPARD

(1)

OH! THAT I were a Poet now in grain!
How would I invocate the Muses all
To deign their presence, lend their flowing Vein,
And help to grace dear *Shepard's* Funeral!
How would I paint our griefs, and succours borrow
From Art and Fancy, to limn out our sorrow!

(2)

Now could I wish (if wishing would obtain)
The sprightli'est Efforts of Poetick Rage,
To vent my Griefs, make others feel my pain,
For this loss of the Glory of our Age.
Here is a subject for the loftiest Verse
That ever waited on the bravest Hearse.

[3]

And could my Pen ingeniously distill
The purest Spirits of a sparkling wit
In rare conceits, the quintessence of skill
In *Elegiack Strains;* none like to it:
I should think all too little to condole
The fatal loss (to us) of such a Soul.

[4]

Could I take highest Flights of Fancy, soar
Aloft; If Wits Monopoly were mine:
All would be much too low, too light, too poor,
To pay due tribute to this great Divine.
Ah! Wit avails not, when th'Heart's like to break,
Great griefs are Tongue-ti'ed, when the lesser speak.

[5]

Away loose rein'd Careers of Poetry,
The celebrated Sisters may be gone;
We need no *Mourning Womens* Elegy,
No forc'd, affected, artificial Tone.
  Great and good *Shepard*'s Dead! Ah! this alone
  Will set our eyes abroach, dissolve a stone.

[6]

Poetick Raptures are of no esteem,
Daring *Hyperboles* have here no place,
Luxuriant Wits on such a copious Theme,
Would shame themselves, and blush to shew their face
  Here's worth enough to overmatch the skill
  Of the most stately Poet *Laureat's Quill*.

[7]

Exube'rant Fancies useless here I deem,
Transcendent vertue scorns feign'd Elogies:
He that gives *Shepard* half his due, may seem,
If Strangers hear it, to Hyperbolize.
  Let him that can, tell what his vertues were,
  And say, this Star mov'd in no common Sphere.

[8]

Here need no Spices, Odours, curious Arts,
No skill of *Egypt*, to embalm the Name
Of such a Worthy: let men speak their hearts,
They'l say, He merits an Immortal Fame.
  When *Shepard* is forgot, all must conclude,
  This is prodigious ingratitude.

[9]

But live he shall in many a gratefull Breast,
VVhere he hath rear'd himself a Monument,
A Monument more stately than the best,
On which Immensest Treasures have been spent.
  Could you but into th'Hearts of thousands peep,
  There would you read his Name engraven deep.

[10]

Oh! that my head were Waters, and mine Eyes
A flowing Spring of Tears, still issuing forth

In streams of bitterness, to solemnize
The *Obits* of this Man of matchless worth!
  Next to the Tears our sins do need and crave,
  I would bestow my Tears on *Shepards* Grave.

(11)

Not that he needs our Tears: for he hath dropt
His measure full; not one Tear more shall fall
Into God's Bottle from his eyes; *Death* stopt
That water-course, his sorrows ending all.
  He Fears, he Cares, he Sighs, he Weeps no more:
  Hee's past all storms, Arriv'd at th'wished Shoar.

[12]

Dear *Shepard* could we reach so high a strain
Of pure Seraphick love, as to devest
Our selves, and love, of self-respects, thy gain
Would joy us, though it cross our interest.
  Then would we silence all compaints with this,
  Our Dearest Friend is doubtless gone to Bliss.

(13)

Ah! but the Lesson's hard, thus to deny
Our own dear selves, to part with such a Loan
Of Heaven (in time of such necessity)
And love thy comforts better than our own.
  Then let us moan our loss, adjourn our glee,
  Till we come thither to rejoice with thee.

[14]

As when some formidable Comets blaze,
As when Portentous Prodigies appear,
Poor Mortals with amazement stand and gaze,
With hearts affrighted, and with trembling fear:
  So are we all amazed at this blow,
  Sadly portending some approaching woe.

[15]

We shall not summon bold Astrologers,
To tell us what the Stars say in the case,
(Those Cousin-Germans to black Conjurers)
We have a sacred Oracle that says,
  When th'Righteous perish, men of mercy go,
  It is a sure presage of coming wo.

[16]

He was (ah woful word! to say he was)
Our wrestling *Israel*, second unto none,
The man that stood i'th'gap, to keep the pass,
To stop the Troops of Judgments rushing on.
  This Man the honour had to hold the hand
  Of an incensed God against our Land.

[17]

When such a Pillar's faln (Oh such an one!)
When such a glorious, shining Light's put out,
When Chariot and Horsemen thus are gone;
Well may we fear some Downfal, Darkness, Rout.
  When such a Bank's broke down, there's sad occasion
  To wail, and dread some grievous Inundation.

[18]

What! must we with our God, and Glory part?
Lord! Is thy Treaty with *New-England* come
Thus to an end? And is War in thy Heart?
That this Ambassadour is called home.
  So Earthly Gods (Kings) when they War intend,
  Call home their Ministers, and Treaties end.

[19]

Oh for the Raptures, Transports, Inspirations
Of *Israel's Singers* when his *Jon'athan's* Fall
So tun'd his mourning Harp! what Lamentations
Then would I make for *Shepards* Funerall
  How truly can I say, as well as He?
  My *Dearest Brother I'am distress'd for thee.*

[20]

How Lovely, Worthy, Peerless, in my view?
How Precious, Pleasant hast thou been to me?
How Learned, Prudent, Pious, Grave, and True?
And what a Faithful Friend? who like to thee?
  Mine Eye's desire is vanish'd: who can tell
  Where lives my dearest *Shepard's* Parallel?

[21]

'Tis strange to think: but we may well believe,
That not a few of different Perswasions

From this great Worthy, do now truly grieve
I'th'Mourning croud, and joyn their Lamentations.
  Such Powers Magnetick had He to draw to Him
  The very Hearts, and Souls, of all that knew Him!

[22]

Art, Nature, Grace, in Him were all combin'd
To shew the World a matchless *Paragon:*
In whom of Radiant Virtues no less shin'd,
Than a whole Constellation: but hee's gone!
  Hee's gone alas! Down in the Dust must ly
  As much of this rare Person as could dy.

[23]

If to have solid Judgement, Pregnant Parts,
A piercing Wit, and comprehensive Brain;
If to have gone the *Round* of all the Arts,
Immunity from Deaths Arrest would gain,
  Shepard would have been Death-proof, and secure
  From that All conquering Hand, I'm very sure.

[24]

If Holy Life, and Deeds of Charity,
If Grace illustrious, and Virtue tri'ed,
If modest Carriage, rare Humility,
Could have brib'd Death, good *Shepard* had not di'ed.
  Oh! but inexorable Death attacks
  The best Men, and promiscu'ous havock makes.

[25]

Come tell me, Criticks, have you ever known
Such Zeal, so temper'd well with moderation?
Such Prudence, and such Inno'cence met in one?
Such Parts, so little Pride and Ostentation?
  Let *Momus* carp, and *Envy* do her worst,
  And swell with *Spleen* and *Rancour* till she burst.

[26]

To be descended well, doth *that* commend?
Can Sons their Fathers Glory call their own?
Our *Shepard* justly might to this pretend,
(His Blessed Father was of high Renown,
  Both *Englands* speak him great, admire his Name)
  But his own pers'onal worth's a better claim.

[27]

Great was the Father, once a glorious Light
Among us, Famous to an high Degree:
Great was this Son: indeed (to do him right)
As Great and Good (to say no more) as He.
  A double portion of his Fathers Spirit
  Did this (his Eldest) Son, through Grace, inherit.

[28]

His Look commanded Reverence and Awe,
Though Mild and Amiable, not Austere:
Well Humour'd was He (as I ever saw)
And rul'd by Love and Wisdome, more than Fear.
  The Muses, and the Graces too, conspir'd
  To set forth this Rare Piece, to be admir'd.

[29]

He govern'd well the Tongue (that busie thing,
Unruly, Lawless and Pragmatical)
Gravely Reserv'd, in Speech not lavishing,
Neither too sparing, nor too liberal.
  His Words were few, well season'd, wisely weigh'd,
  And in his Tongue the Law of kindness sway'd.

[30]

Learned he was beyond the common Size,
Befriended much by Nature in his Wit,
And Temper, (Sweet, Sedate, Ingenious, Wise)
And (which crown'd all) he was Heav'ens Favourite:
  On whom the God of all Grace did command,
  And show'r down Blessings with a lib'eral hand.

[31]

Wise He, not wily, was; Grave, not Morose;
Not stiffe, but steady; Seri'ous, but not Sowre;
Concern'd for all, as if he had no Foes;
(Strange if he had!) and would not wast an Hour.
  Thoughtful and Active for the common good:
  And yet his own place wisely understood.

[32]

Nothing could make him stray from Duty; Death
Was not so frightful to him, as Omission

Of Ministerial work; he fear'd no breath
Infecti'ous, i'th'discharge of his Commission.
  Rather than run from's work, he chose to dy,
  Boldly to run on Death, than duty fly.

[33]

(Cruel Disease! that didst (like *High-way-men*)
Assault the honest Trav'eller in his way,
And rob dear *Shepard* of his life (Ah!) then,
When he was on the Road, where Duty lay.
  Forbear, bold Pen! 'twas God that took him thus,
  To give him great Reward, and punish us.)

[34]

Zealous in God's cause, but meek in his own;
Modest of Nature, bold as any Lion,
Where Consc'ience was concern'd: and there were none
More constant Mourners for afflicted Sion:
  So gene'ral was his care for th'Churches all,
  His Spirit seemed Apostolical.

[35]

Large was his Heart, to spend without regret,
Rejoycing to do good: not like those *Moles*
That root i'th'Earth, or roam abroad, to get
All for themselves (those sorry, narrow Souls!)
  But He, like th'Sun (i'th'Center, as some say)
  Diffus'd his Rayes of Goodness every way.

[36]

He breath'd Love, and pursu'd Peace in his day,
As if his Soul were made of Harmony:
Scarce ever more of Goodness crouded lay
In such a piece of frail Mortality.
  Sure Father *Wilsons* genuine Son was he,
  New-England's Paul had such a *Timothy*.

[37]

No slave to th' Worlds grand *Idols;* but he flew
At *Fairer Quarries*, without stooping down
To Sublunary prey: his great Soul knew
Ambition none, but of the Heave'nly Crown.
  Now he hath won it, and shall wear't with Honour,
  Adoring Grace, and God in Christ, the Donour.

[38]

A Friend to Truth, a constant Foe to Errour,
Pow'erful i'th'*Pulpit*, and sweet in converse,
To weak ones gentle, to th'Profane a Terrour.
Who can his vertues, and good works rehearse?
  The Scripture-Bishops-Character read o'er,
  Say this was *Shepards:* what need I say more?

[39]

I say no more: let them that can declare
His rich and rare endowments, paint this Sun,
With all its dazling Rayes: But I despair,
Hopeless by any hand to see it done.
  They that can *Shepards* goodness well display,
  Must be as good as he: But who are they?

[40]

See where our Sister *Charlstown* sits and Moans!
Poor Widowed *Charlstown!* all in Dust, in Tears!
Mark how she wrings her hands! hear how she groans!
See how she weeps! what sorrow like to hers!
  Charlstown, that might for joy compare of late
  With all about her, now looks desolate.

[41]

As you have seen some Pale, Wan, Ghastly look,
When grisly Death, that will not be said nay,
Hath seiz'd all for it self, Possession took,
And turn'd the Soul out of its house of Clay:
  So Visag'd is poor *Charlstown* at this day;
  Shepard, her very Soul, is torn away.

[42]

Cambridge groans under this so heavy cross,
And Sympathizes with her Sister dear;
Renews her Griefs afresh for her old loss
Of her own *Shepard*, and drops many a Tear.
  Cambridge and *Charlstown* now joint Mourners are,
  And this tremendous loss between them share.

[43]

Must Learnings Friend (Ah! worth us all) go thus?
That Great Support to *Harvards* Nursery!

Our *Fellow* (that no Fellow had with us)
Is gone to Heave'ns great University.
Our's now indeed's a lifeless *Corporation*,
The Soul is fled, that gave it *Animation!*

[44]

Poor *Harvard's* Sons are in their Mourning Dress:
Their sure Friend's gone! their Hearts have *put on Mourning;*
Within their Walls are Sighs, Tears, Pensiveness;
Their new Foundations dread an overturning.
Harvard! where's such a fast Friend left to thee!
Unless thy great Friend, *LEVERET*, it be.[1]

[45]

We must not with our greatest Soveraign strive,
Who dare find fault with him that is most High?
That hath an absolute Prerogative,
And doth his pleasure: none may ask him, why?
We're Clay-lumps, Dust-heaps, nothings in his sight:
The Judge of all the Earth doth always right.

[46]

Ah! could not Prayers and Tears prevail with God!
Was there no warding off that dreadful Blow!
And was there no averting of that Rod!
Must *Shepard* dy! and that good Angel go!
Alas! Our heinous sins (more than our haits)
It seems, were louder, and out-crie'd our Prayers.

[47]

See what our sins have done! what Ruines wrought
And how they have pluck'd out our very eyes!
Our sins have slain our *Shepard!* we have bought,
And dearly paid for, our Enormities.
Ah Cursed sins! that strike at God, and kill
His *Servants*, and the Blood of *Prophets* spill.

[48]

As you would loath the Sword that's warm and red,
As you would hate the hands that are embru'd
I'th'Hearts-blood of your dearest Friends: so dread,
And hate your sins; Oh! let them be pursu'd:
Revenges take on bloody sins: for there's
No Refuge-City for these Murtherers.

[49]

In vain we build the Prophets Sepulchers,
In vain bedew their Tombs with Tears, when Dead;
In vain bewail the Deaths of Ministers,
Whilst Prophet-killing sins are harboured.
  Those that these Murth'erous Traitors favour, hide;
  Are with the blood of Prophets deeply di'ed.

[50]

New-England! know thy Heart-plague: feel this blow;
A blow that sorely wounds both Head and Heart,
A blow that reaches All, both high and low,
A blow that may be felt in every part.
  Mourn that this *Great Man's* faln in *Israel:*
  Lest it be said, *with him New-England fell!*

[51]

Farewel, Dear *Shepard!* Thou art gone before,
Made free of *Heaven*, where thou shalt sing loud *Hymns*
Of *High triumphant Praises* evermore,
In the sweet Quire of *Saints* and *Seraphims.*
  Lord! look on us here, clogg'd with sin and clay,
  And we, through Grace, shall be as happy as they.

[52]

My Dearest, Inmost, Bosome-Friend, is Gone!
Gone is my sweet Companion, Soul's delight!
Now in an Huddling Croud I'm all alone,
And almost could bid all the World *Goodnight:*
  Blest be my Rock! God lives: Oh let him be,
  As He is, so All in All to me.

The Bereaved, Sorrowful
Urian Oakes.

EDWARD TAYLOR (*ca.* 1645–1729)

In this 1963 reissue of *The Puritans*, the section on Edward Taylor has been recast, a change made necessary by the fact that since the discovery of Taylor's poetry twenty-five years ago, Taylor has taken rank as a major American poet. Significantly, the first critical examination of the manuscript "Poetical Works" (a gift to the Yale University Library by a Taylor descendant in 1883) was made during the course of preparing the 1936 edition of *The Puritans*. The text of all but one of the selections here added is from *The Poetical Works of Edward Taylor* (1939); that of "Upon a Sweeping Flood" is from *New England Quarterly*, XVI (1943), 284.

After the Restoration, Parliament by an Act of Uniformity (1662) required clergymen, college fellows, and schoolmasters to accept everything in the Book of Common Prayers. The Taylor family were Nonconformists, living in Leicestershire near Coventry, and Edward Taylor was a staunch Congregationalist evidently determined to enter the ministry. He therefore migrated to the Bay Colony, was immediately admitted to Harvard, and after graduation (1671) accepted a call to organize a church in the frontier village of Westfield, Massachusetts, where he remained as pastor and physician throughout his long life. He was twice married and the father of thirteen children, and by will he left an impressive library of some two hundred volumes (including his 400-page "Poetical Works") to his grandson Ezra Stiles, later president of Yale.

Except for a few short lyrics (of which the "Three Poems" here included are a part) and some topical verses, the "Poetical Works" divide into two major groups: "Gods Determinations Touching His Elect," and "Preparatory Meditations before my Approach to the Lords Supper." "Gods Determinations," written before 1690, is an extended verse sequence, medieval in structure, and thus it probably reflects Taylor's grammar schooling. In idiom it is a semi-dramatic dialogue about sin and redemption, and ends with Christ's limitless power to defeat Satan. Its lyrical ardor, couched in homely language, can be felt in the six concluding poems, here presented as a unit. The joy of the Soul's achievement is refracted through the illuminated faith of the poet, and displayed with metaphoric skill.

Taylor's "Preparatory Meditations" were written, approximately once every two months, over a period of forty-three years, from 1682 to 1725. They are dated and numbered in two series (respectively 49 and 165), and composed in six-line stanzas, each preceded by a text from scriptures. A belated metaphysical poet writing in the manner of Donne and Herbert, Taylor links incongruities by stressing a paradox: balancing the concrete and the abstract, the minute and the transcendent, the comic and the serious, the commonplace and the shocking. Thus in Meditation Eight the soul, a bird of paradise, tweedles praise to God from its wicker cage; and God grinds the bread of life, his Son, to serve as "Heavens Sugar Cake," a food too fine for angels. These associations produce, as they are intended to do, almost unbearable tensions.

In addition to metaphors and other tropes, Taylor employs the "type" to create images. Types in theology are foreshadowings of things to come (the antitype). Typographical exegesis fascinated Puritan preachers, who used it as a way to link the historical events of the Bible. They intended thereby to present the solid core of facts, and not to bemuse their hearers by tropes, mere figures of speech which could mean to each listener what his imagination conjured. Thus Joseph, envied by his brothers (in Meditation Seven, second series) is said to foreshadow the treatment of Christ by the Pharisees. What gives vitality to such poems by Taylor is not the device he used, but the intensity of his love for the world God made and for the God who made it.

Indeed, this quality of intensity involved something of a dilemma for a colonial Puritan who happened to be a poet. The book of the Bible to which Taylor turned most often for inspiration was Canticles, the Song of Songs, for which the poet seems to have felt a humanly vigorous fascination. The fact that Taylor's ecstatic moods, quite literally redolent of altar incense, overleaped the limits of the doctrines he professed, must account in large part for his injunction that his heirs should never publish his verses. In Taylor's love of language for itself, he commands an eminence unique among Puritan writers in America, and today critical assessment gives him first rank among American poets before the nineteenth century.

From *GODS DETERMINATIONS . . .*

The Preface

Infinity, when all things it beheld,
In Nothing, and of Nothing all did build,
Upon what Base was fixt the Lath[e] wherein
He turn'd this Globe, and riggalld[1] it so trim?
Who blew the Bellows of his Furnace Vast?
Or held the Mould wherein the world was Cast?
Who laid its Corner Stone? Or whose Command?
Where stand the Pillars upon which it stands?
Who Lac'de and Fillitted the earth so fine,
With Rivers like green Ribbons Smaragdine?[2]
Who made the Sea's its Selvedge, and it locks
Like a Quilt Ball within a Silver Box?
Who Spread its Canopy? Or Curtains Spun?
Who in this Bowling Alley bowld the Sun?
Who made it always when it rises set:
To go at once both down, and up to get?

Who th'Curtain rods made for this Tapistry?
Who hung the twinckling Lanthorns in the Sky?
Who? who did this? or who is he? Why, know
It's Onely Might Almighty this did doe.
His hand hath made this noble worke which Stands
His Glorious Handywork not made by hands.
Who spake all things from nothing; and with ease
Can speake all things to nothing, if he please.
Whose Little finger at his pleasure Can
Out mete ten thousand worlds with halfe a Span:
Whose Might Almighty can by half a looks
Root up the rocks and rock the hills by th'roots.
Can take this mighty World up in his hande,
And shake it like a Squitchen[3] or a Wand.
Whose single Frown will make the Heavens shake
Like as an aspen leafe the Winde makes quake.
Oh! what a might is this! Whose single frown
Doth shake the world as it would shake it down?
Which All from Nothing fet, from Nothing, All:
Hath All on Nothing set, lets Nothing fall.
Gave All to nothing Man indeed, whereby
Through nothing man all might him Glorify.
In Nothing is imbosst the brightest Gem
More pretious than all pretiousness in them.
But Nothing man did throw down all by sin:
And darkened that lightsom Gem in him,
  That now his Brightest Diamond is grown
  Darker by far than any Coalpit Stone.

Our Insufficiency to Praise God suitably for his Mercy

Should all the World so wide to atoms fall,
  Should th'Aire be shred to motes; should we
  Se[e] all the Earth hackt here so small
    That none Could smaller bee?
Should Heaven and Earth be Atomizd, we guess
The Number of these Motes were numberless.

But should we then a World each Atom deem,
  Where dwell as many pious men
  As all these Motes the world Could teem,
    Were it shred into them?
Each Atom would the World surmount, wee guess,
Whose men in number would be numberless.

But had each pious man as many Tongues
   At singing all together then
   The Praise that to the Lord belongs,
      As all these Atoms men?
Each man would sing a World of Praise, we guess,
Whose Tongues in number would be numberless.

And had each Tongue, as many Songs of Praise
   To sing to the Almighty ALL;
   As all these men have Tongues to raise
      To him their Holy Call?
Each Tongue would tune a World of Praise, we guess,
Whose songs in number would be numberless.

Nay, had each song as many Tunes most sweet,
   Or one intwisting in't as many,
   As all these Tongues have songs most meet
      Unparallelld by any?
Each song a world of Musick makes, we guess,
Whose Tunes in number would be numberless.

Now should all these Conspire in us, that we
   Could breath such Praise to thee, Most High:
   Should we thy Sounding Organs be
      To ring such Melody?
Our Musick would the World of Worlds outring,
Yet be unfit within thine Ears to ting.

Thou didst us mould, and us new mould when wee
   Were worse than mould we tread upon.
   Nay, Nettles made by Sin wee bee:
      Yet hadst Compassion.
Thou hast pluckt out our Stings; and by degrees
Hast of us, lately Wasps, made Lady-Bees.

Though e're our Tongues thy Praises due can fan,
   A Weevle with the World may fly,
   Yea fly away: and with a span
      We may out mete the sky.
Though what we can is but a Lisp, we pray
Accept thereof. We have no better pay.

The Soule Seeking Church-Fellowship

The Soul refresht with gracious Steams, behold,
  Christs royall Spirit richly tended
With all the guard of Graces manifold
  Throngs in to solace it amended
  And by the Trinity befriended.

Befriended thus! It lives a Life indeed.
  A Life! as if it Liv'd for Life,
For Life Eternall: wherefore with all heed,
  It trims the same with Graces rife
  To be the Lambs espoused Wife.

Yea like a Bride all Gloriously arraide
  It is arrai'de, Whose dayly ware
Is an Imbrodery with Grace inlaide,
  Of Sanctuary White most Faire:
  Its drest in Heavens fashion rare.

Each Ordinance and Instrument of Grace
  Grace doth instruct are Usefull here;
They're Golden Pipes where Holy Waters trace
  Into the spirits spicebed Deare,
  To vivify what withering were.

Hence do their Hearts like Civit-Boxes sweet
  Evaporate their Love full pure,
Which through the Chincks of their Affection reech
  To God, Christ, Christians all, though more:
  To such whose Counsills made their Cure.

Hence now Christ[s] Curious Garden fenced in
  With Solid Walls of Discipline
Well wed, and watered, and made full trim:
  The Allies all Laid out by line:
  Walks for the Spirit all Divine.

Whereby Corruptions are kept out, whereby
  Corrupters also get not in,
Unless the Lyons Carkass secretly
  Lies lapt up in a Lamblike skin,
  Which Holy seems, yet's full of sin.

For on the Towers of these Walls there stand
  Just Watchmen Watching day and night,
And Porter[s] at each Gate, who have Command
  To open onely to the right.
  And all within may have a sight.

Whose Zeale, should it along a Channell slide
  Not banckt with Knowledg right and Good,
Nor Bottomed with Love: nor wiers ti'de
  To hinder prejudiciall Blood,
  The Currant will be full of mud.

But yet this Curious Garden richly set,
  The Soul accounts Christs Paradise
Set with Choice slips and flowers, and longs to get
  Itself set here: and by advice
  To grow herein and so rejoyce.

The Soul admiring the Grace of the Church Enters into Church-Fellowship

How is this City, Lord, of thine bespangled
  With Graces shine?
With Ordinances alli'de and inam'led
  Which are Divine?
Wall'd in with Discipline her Gates obtaine
Just Centinalls with Love Imbellisht plain.

Hence glorious and terrible she stands;
  That Converts new
Seeing her Centinalls, of all demand
  The Word to shew;
Stand gazing much between two Passions Crusht:
Desire and Feare at once, which both wayes thrust.

Thus are they wrackt. Desire doth forward screw
  To get them in,
But Feare doth backward thrust, that lies purdue,
  And slicks that Pin.
You cannot give the word, Quoth she, which though
You stumble on't, its more than yet you know.

But yet Desires Screw Pin doth not slack:
  It still holds fast.
But Fears Screw Pin thrusts back, or Screw doth Crack,
  And breaks at last.
Hence on they go, and in they enter: where
Desire Converts to joy, joy Conquours Fear.

They now encovenant with God, and His;
  They thus indent
The Charters Seals belonging unto this,
  The Sacrament.
So God is theirs avoucht, they his in Christ,
In whom all things they have, with Grace are splic'te.

Thus in the usuall Coach of Gods Decree
  They bowle and swim
To Glory bright, if no Hypocrisie
  Handed them in.
For such must shake their handmaid off, lest they
Be shakt out of this Coach, or dy in th'way.

The Glory of and Grace in the Church set out

    Come now behold
  Within this Knot what Flowers do grow:
    Spanglde like gold:
  Whence Wreaths of all Perfumes do flow.
Most Curious Colours of all sorts you shall
With all Sweet Spirits s[c]ent. Yet thats not all.

    Oh! Look, and finde
  These Choicest Flowers most richly sweet
    Are Disciplinde
  With Artificiall Angells meet.
An heap of Pearls is precious: but they shall
When set by Art Excell. Yet that's not all.

    Christ's Spirit showers
  Down in his Word and Sacraments
    Upon these Flowers,
  The Clouds of Grace Divine Contents.
Such things of Wealthy Blessings on them fall
As make them sweetly thrive. Yet that's not all.

Yet still behold!
All flourish not at once. We see
While some Unfold
Their blushing Leaves, some buds there bee:
Here's Faith, Hope, Charity in flower, which call
On yonders in the Bud. Yet that's not all.

But as they stand
Like Beauties reeching in perfume
A Divine Hand
Doth hand them up to Glories room:
Where Each in sweet'ned Songs of Praises shall
Sing all ore heaven for aye. And that's but all.

The Souls Admiration hereupon

What! I such Praises sing? How can it bee?
Shall I in Heaven sing?
What! I that scarce durst hope to see,
Lord, such a thing?
Though nothing is too hard for thee,
One Hope hereof seems hard to mee.

What! Can I ever tune those Melodies,
Who have no tune at all?
Not knowing where to stop nor Rise,
Nor when to Fall.
To sing thy Praise I am unfit:
I have not learn'd my Gam-ut yet.

But should these Praises on string'd Instruments
Be sweetly tun'de? I finde
I nonplust am, for no Consents
I ever minde.
My Tongue is neither Quill nor Bow:
Nor Can my Fingers Quavers show.

But was it otherwise, I have no Kit:
Which though I had, I could
Not tune the strings, which soon would slip,
Though others should.
But should they not, I cannot play,
But for an F should strike an A.

And should thy Praise upon Winde Instruments
Sound all o're Heaven Shrill?
My Breath will hardly through such Vents
A Whistle fill:
Which though it should, its past my spell
By Stops and Falls to sound it Well.

How should I then, joyn in such Exercise?
One Sight of thee'l intice
Mine Eyes to heft: whose Extasies
Will stob my Voice.
Hereby mine Eyes will bind my Tongue,
Unless thou, Lord, do Cut the thong.

What use of Uselesse mee then there, poore snake?
There Saints and Angels sing
Thy Praise in full Cariere, which make
The Heavens to ring.
Yet if thou wilt, thou Can'st me raise
With Angels bright to sing thy Praise.

The Joy of Church Fellowship rightly attended

In Heaven soaring up, I dropt an Eare
On Earth: and oh! sweet Melody!
And listening, found it was the Saints who were
Encoacht for Heaven that sang for Joy.
For in Christs Coach they sweetly sing,
As they to Glory ride therein.

Oh! joyous hearts! Enfir'de with holy Flame!
Is speech thus tasseled with praise?
Will not your inward fire of Joy contain,
That it in open flames doth blaze?
For in Christ[s] Coach Saints sweetly sing,
As they to Glory ride therein.

And if a string do slip by Chance, they soon
Do screw it up again: whereby
They set it in a more melodious Tune
And a Diviner Harmony.
For in Christs Coach they sweetly sing,
As they to Glory ride therein.

In all their Acts, publick and private, nay,
  And secret too, they praise impart.
But in their Acts Divine, and Worship, they
  With Hymns do offer up their Heart.
  Thus in Christs Coach they sweetly sing,
  As they to Glory ride therein.

Some few not in; and some whose Time and Place
  Block up this Coaches way, do goe
As Travellers afoot: and so do trace
  The Road that gives them right thereto;
  While in this Coach these sweetly sing
  As they to Glory ride therein.

THREE POEMS

Huswifery

Make me, O Lord, thy Spin[n]ing Wheele compleat;
  Thy Holy Worde my Distaff make for mee.
Make mine Affections thy Swift Flyers neate,
  And make my Soule thy holy Spoole to bee.
  My Conversation make to be thy Reele,
  And reele the yarn thereon spun of thy Wheele.

Make me thy Loome then, knit therein this Twine:
  And make thy Holy Spirit, Lord, winde quills:
Then weave the Web thyselfe. The yarn is fine.
  Thine Ordinances make my Fulling Mills,
  Then dy the same in Heavenly Colours Choice,
  All pinkt with Varnish't Flowers of Paradise.

Then cloath therewith mine Understanding, Will,
  Affections, Judgment, Conscience, Memory;
My Words and Actions, that their shine may fill
  My wayes with glory and thee glorify,
  Then mine apparell shall display before yee
  That I am Cloathd in Holy robes for glory.

The Ebb and Flow

When first thou on me, Lord, wrought'st thy Sweet Print,
  My heart was made thy tinder box.
  My 'ffections were thy tinder in't:
    Where fell thy Sparkes by drops.
Those holy Sparks of Heavenly fire that came
Did ever catch and often out would flame.

But now my Heart is made thy Censar trim,
Full of thy golden Altars fire,
To offer up Sweet Incense in
Unto thyselfe intire:
I finde my tinder scarce thy sparks can feel
That drop out from thy Holy flint and Steel.

Hence doubts out bud for feare thy fire in mee
'S a mocking Ignis Fatuus,
Or lest thine Altars fire out bee,
It's hid in ashes thus.
Yet when the bellows of thy Spirit blow
Away mine ashes, then thy fire doth glow.

Upon the Sweeping Flood[4]

O! that I'd had a tear to've quencht that flame
Which did dissolve the Heavens above
Into those liquid drops that Came
To drown our Carnal love.
Our cheeks were dry and eyes refusde to weep.
Tears bursting out ran down the skies darke Cheek.

Were th'Heavens sick? must wee their Doctors bee
And Physick them with pills, our sin?
To make them purge and vomit; see:
And Excrements out fling?
We've griev'd them by such Physick that they shed
Their Excrements upon our lofty heads.

From *PREPARATORY MEDITATIONS*

Meditation One

What love is this of thine, that Cannot bee
In thine Infinity, O Lord, Confinde,
Unless it in thy very Person see
Infinity and Finity Conjoyn'd?
What! hath thy Godhead, as not satisfi'de,
Marri'de our Manhood, making it its Bride?

Oh, Matchless Love! Filling Heaven to the brim!
O'rerunning it: all running o're beside
This World! Nay, Overflowing Hell, wherein
For thine Elect, there rose a mighty Tide!
That there our Veans might through thy Person bleed,
To quench those flames, that else would on us feed.

Oh! that thy love might overflow my Heart!
  To fire the same with Love: for Love I would.
But oh! my streight'ned Breast! my Lifeless Sparke!
  My Fireless Flame! What Chilly Love, and Cold?
  In measure small! In Manner Chilly! See!
  Lord, blow the Coal: Thy Love Enflame in mee.

The Experience

Canticles I:3: . . . thy name is as ointment poured forth.

Oh, that I alwayes breath'd in such an aire
  As I suck't in, feeding on sweet Content!
Disht up unto my Soul ev'n in that pray're
  Pour'de out to God over last Sacrament.
  What Beam of Light wrapt up my sight to finde
  Me neerer God than ere Came in my minde?

Most strange it was! But yet more strange that shine
  Which fill'd my Soul then to the brim to spy
My nature with thy Nature all Divine
  Together joyn'd in Him that's Thou, and I.
  Flesh of my Flesh, Bone of my Bone: there's run
  Thy Godhead and my Manhood in thy Son.

Oh! that that Flame which thou didst on me Cast
  Might me enflame, and Lighten ery where.
Then Heaven to me would be less at last,
  So much of heaven I should have while here.
  Oh! Sweet though Short! I'le not forget the same.
  My neerness, Lord, to thee did me Enflame.

I'le Claim my Right: Give place ye Angells Bright.
  Ye further from the Godhead stande than I.
My Nature is your Lord; and doth Unite
  Better than Yours unto the Deity.
  Gods Throne is first and mine is next: to you
  Onely the place of Waiting-men is due.

Oh! that my Heart, thy Golden Harp might bee
  Well tun'd by Glorious Grace, that e'ry string
Screw'd to the highest pitch, might unto thee
  All Praises wrapt in sweetest Musick bring.
  I praise thee, Lord, and better praise thee would,
  If what I had, my heart might ever hold.

The Reflexion

Canticles II:1: I am the rose of Sharon.

Lord, art thou at the Table Head above
  Meat, Med'cine, Sweetness, sparkling Beautys, to
Enamour Souls with Flaming Flakes of Love,
  And not my Trencher, nor my Cup o'reflow?
  Ben't I a bidden guest? Oh! sweat mine Eye:
  O'reflow with Teares: Oh! draw thy fountains dry.

Shall I not smell thy sweet, oh! Sharons Rose?
  Shall not mine Eye salute thy Beauty? Why?
Shall thy sweet leaves their Beautious sweets upclose?
  As halfe ashamde my sight should on them ly?
  Woe's me! For this my sighs shall be in grain,
  Offer'd on Sorrows Altar for the same.

Had not my Soule's, thy Conduit, Pipes stopt bin
  With mud, what Ravishment would'st thou Convay?
Let Graces Golden Spade dig till the Spring
  Of tears arise, and cleare this filth away.
  Lord, let thy Spirit raise my sighings till
  These Pipes my soule do with thy sweetness fill.

Earth once was Paradise of Heaven below,
  Till inkefac'd sin had it with poyson stockt;
And Chast this Paradise away into
  Heav'ns upmost Loft, and it in Glory Lockt.
  But thou, sweet Lord, hast with thy golden Key
  Unlock[t] the Doore, and made a golden day.

Once at thy Feast, I saw thee Pearle-like stand
  'Tween Heaven and Earth, where Heavens Bright glory all
In streams fell on thee, as a floodgate and,
  Like Sun Beams through thee on the World to Fall.
  Oh! Sugar sweet then! My Deare sweet Lord, I see
  Saints Heaven-lost Happiness restor'd by thee.

Shall Heaven and Earth's bright Glory all up lie,
  Like Sun Beams bundled in the sun in thee?
Dost thou sit Rose at Table Head, where I
  Do sit, and Carv'st no morsell sweet for mee?
  So much before, so little now! Sprindge,[5] Lord,
  Thy Rosie Leaves, and me their Glee afford.

Shall not thy Rose my Garden fresh perfume?
  Shall not thy Beauty my dull Heart assaile?
Shall not thy golden gleams run through this gloom?
  Shall my black Velvet Mask thy fair Face Vaile?
  Pass o're my Faults; shine forth, bright sun; arise!
  Enthrone thy Rosy-selfe within mine Eyes.

Meditation Eight

John VI:51: I am the living bread.

I ken[n]ing through Astronomy Divine
  The Worlds bright Battlement, wherein I spy
A Golden Path my Pencill cannot line
  From that bright Throne unto my Threshold ly.
  And while my puzzled thoughts about it pore,
  I find the Bread of Life in't at my doore.

When that this Bird of Paradise put in
  This Wicker Cage (my Corps) to tweedle praise
Had peckt the Fruite forbid: and so did fling
  Away its Food, and lost its golden dayes,
  It fell into Celestiall Famine sore,
  And never could attain a morsell more.

Alas! alas! Poore Bird, what wilt thou doe?
  The Creatures field no food for Souls e're gave:
And if thou knock at Angells dores, they show
  An Empty Barrell: they no soul bread have.
  Alas! Poore Bird, the Worlds White Loafe is done,
  And cannot yield thee here the smallest Crumb.

In this sad state, Gods Tender Bowells run
  Out streams of Grace: And he to end all strife,
The Purest Wheate in Heaven, his deare-dear Son
  Grinds, and kneads up into this Bread of Life:
  Which Bread of Life from Heaven down came and stands
  Disht on thy Table up by Angells Hands.

Did God mould up this Bread in Heaven, and bake,
  Which from his Table came, and to thine goeth?
Doth he bespeake thee thus: This Soule Bread take;
  Come, Eate thy fill of this, thy Gods White Loafe?
  Its Food too fine for Angells; yet come, take
  And Eate thy fill! Its Heavens Sugar Cake.

What Grace is this knead in this Loafe? This thing
Souls are but petty things it to admire.
Yee Angells, help: This fill would to the brim
Heav'ns whelm'd-down Chrystall meele Bowle, yea and higher.
This Bread of Life dropt in thy mouth doth Cry:
Eate, Eate me, Soul, and thou shalt never dy.

Meditation Thirty-Eight

I John II: 1: And if any man sin, we have an advocate with the Father.

Oh! What a thing is Man? Lord, Who am I?
That thou shouldst give him Law (Oh! golden Line)
To regulate his Thoughts, Words, Life thereby:
And judge him wilt thereby too in thy time.
A Court of Justice thou in heaven holdst,
To try his Case while he's here housd on mould.

How do thy Angells lay before thine eye
My Deeds both White and Black I dayly doe?
How doth thy Court thou Pannellst there them try?
But flesh complains. What right for this? let's know!
For right or wrong, I can't appeare unto't.
And shall a sentence Pass on such a suite?

Soft; blemish not this golden Bench, or place.
Here is no Bribe, nor Colourings to hide,
Nor Pettifogger to befog the Case;
But Justice hath her Glory here well tri'de:
Her spotless Law all spotted Cases tends;
Without Respect or Disrespect them ends.

God's Judge himselfe, and Christ Atturny is;
The Holy Ghost Regesterer is founde.
Angells the sergeants are, all Creatures kiss
The booke, and doe as Evidence abounde.
All Cases pass according to pure Law,
And in the sentence is no Fret nor flaw.

What saith, my soule? Here all thy Deeds are tri'de.
Is Christ thy Advocate to pleade thy Cause?
Art thou his Client? Such shall never slide.
He never lost his Case: he pleads such Laws
As Carry do the same, nor doth refuse
The Vilest sinners Case that doth him Choose.

This is his Honour, not Dishonour: nay,
  No Habeas-Corpus 'gainst his Clients came;
For all their Fines his Purse doth make down pay.
  He Non-Suites Satan's suite or Casts the same.
  He'l plead thy Case, and not accept a Fee.
  He'l plead Sub Forma Pauperis for thee.

My Case is bad. Lord, be my Advocate.
  My sin is red: I'me under Gods Arrest.
Thou hast the Hit of Pleading; plead my state.
  Although it's bad, thy Plea will make it best.
  If thou wilt plead my Case before the King,
  I'le Waggon Loads of Love and Glory bring.

Meditation Forty-Nine

Matthew XXV: 21: Enter thou into the joy of thy lord.

Lord, do away my Motes and Mountains great.
  My nut is vitiate. Its kirnell rots:
Come, kill the Worm that doth its kirnell eate,
  And strike thy sparkes within my tinderbox.
  Drill through my metall heart an hole, wherein
  With graces Cotters to thyselfe it pin.

A Lock of Steel upon my Soule, whose key
  The serpent keeps, I feare, doth lock my doore:
O pick 't: and through the key-hole make thy way,
  And enter in, and let thy joyes run o're.
  My Wards are rusty. Oyle them till they trig
  Before thy golden key: thy Oyle makes glib.

Take out the Splinters of the World that stick
  Do in my heart. Friends, Honours, Riches, and
The Shivers in't of Hell whose venoms quick
  And firy, make it swoln and ranckling stand.
  These wound and kill: those shackle strongly to
  Poore knobs of Clay, my heart; hence sorrows grow.

Cleanse and enlarge my kask: it is too small:
  And tartariz'd with worldly dregs dri'de in't.
It's bad mouth'd too: and though thy joyes do Call
  That boundless are, it ever doth them stint.
  Make me thy Chrystall Caske: those wines in't tun
  That in the Rivers of thy joyes do run.

Lord, make me, though suck't through a straw or Quill,
  Tast of the Rivers of thy joyes, some drop.
  'Twill sweeten me: and all my Love distill
  Into thy glass; and me for joy make hop.
  'Twill turn my water into wine, and fill
  My harp with Songs my Masters joyes distill.

Meditation Three

(Second series)

Romans V:14: [Adam:] who is the figure of him that was to come.

Like to the Marigold, I blushing close
  My golden blossoms when thy sun goes down:
Moist'ning my leaves with Dewy Sighs, half frose
  By the nocturnall Cold, that hoares my Crown.
  Mine Apples ashes are in apple shells
  And dirty too: strange and bewitching spells!

When Lord, mine Eye doth spie thy Grace to beame
  Thy Mediatoriall glory in the shine
Out Sprouted so from Adams typick streame
  And Emblemiz'd in Noahs pollisht shrine
  Thine theirs outshines so far it makes their glory
  In brightest Colours, seem a smoaky story.

But when mine Eye full of these beams, doth cast
  Its rayes upon my dusty essence thin
Impregnate with a Sparke Divine, defacde,
  All candi[e]d o're with Leprosie of Sin,
  Such Influences on my Spirits light,
  Which them as bitter gall, or Cold ice smite.

My brissled sins hence do so horrid peare,
  None but thyselfe, (and thou deckt up must bee
In thy Transcendent glory sparkling cleare)
  A Mediator unto God for mee.
  So high they rise, Faith scarce can toss a Sight
  Over their heads upon thyselfe to light.

Is't possible such glory, Lord, ere should
  Center its Love on me Sins Dunghill else?
My Case up take? make it its own? Who would
  Wash with his blood my blots out? Crown his shelfe
  Or Dress his golden Cupboard with such ware?
  This makes my pale facde Hope almost despare.

Yet let my Titmouses Quill suck in
  Thy Graces milk Pails some small drop: or Cart
A Bit, or Splinter of some Ray, the wing
  Of Grace's sun sprindgd out, into my heart:
  To build there Wonders Chappell where thy Praise
  Shall be the Psalms sung forth in gracious layes.

Meditation Seven

(Second series)

Psalms CV: 17: He sent a man before them, even Joseph, who was sold for a servant.

All Dull, my Lord, my Spirits, flat and dead;
  All water sockt and sapless to the skin.
Oh! Screw mee up, and make my Spirits bed
  Thy quickening vertue, for my inke is dim;
  My pencill blunt. Doth Joseph type out thee?
  Harraulds of Angells sing out, Bow the Knee.

Is Josephs glorious shine a Type of thee?
  How bright art thou? He envi'de was as well.
And so wast thou. He's stript and pick't, poore hee,
  Into the pit. And so was thou. They shell
  Thee of thy kirnell. He by Judah's sold
  For twenty bits: thirty for thee [we're] told.

Joseph was tempted by his Mistress vile;
  Thou by the Divell, but both shame the foe.
Joseph was cast into the jayle awhile,
  And so was thou. Sweet apples mellow so.
  Joseph did from his jayle to glory run:
  Thou from Death's pallot rose like morning sun.

Joseph layes in against the Famine, and
  Thou dost prepare the Bread of Life for thine;
He bought with Corn for Pharaoh men and Land;
  Thou with thy Bread mak'st such themselves Consign
  Over to thee, that eate it. Joseph makes
  His brethren bow before him. Thine too quake.

Joseph constrains his Brethren till their sins
  Do gall their Souls. Repentence babbles fresh.
Thou treatest sinners till Repentance springs.
  Then with him sendst a Benjamin-like messe.
  Joseph doth Cheare his humble brethren. Thou
  Dost stud with joy the mourning Saints that bow.

Josephs bright shine th'Eleven Tribes must preach,
And thine Apostles now Eleven, thine.
They beare his presents to his Friends: thine reach
Thine unto thine, thus now behold a shine.
How hast thou pensild out, my Lord, most bright
Thy glorious Image here, on Josephs Light.

This I bewaile, in me under this shine,
To see so dull a Colour in my Skin.
Lord, lay thy brightsome Colours on me: thine;
Scoure thou my pipes, then play thy tunes therein.
I will not hang my Harp in Willows by,
While thy sweet praise, my Tunes doth glorify.

Meditation One Hundred Ten

(Second series)

Matthew XXVI: 30: And when they had sung an hymn,
they went out into the mount of Olives.

The Angells sung a Carole at thy Birth,
My Lord, and thou thyselfe didst sweetly sing
An Epinicioum[6] at thy Death on Earth.
And order'st thine, in memory of this thing,
Thy Holy Supper, closing it at last
Up with an Hymn, and Choakst the foe thou hast.

This Feast thou madst in memory of thy death:
Which is disht up most graciously: and towers
Of reeching vapours from thy Grave (Sweet breath)
Aromatize the Skies: That sweetest Showers,
Richly perfumed by the Holy Ghost,
Are rained thence upon the Churches Coast.

Thy Grave beares flowers to dress thy Church withall,
In which thou dost thy Table dress for thine.
With Gospell Carpet, Chargers, Festivall
And Spirituall Venison, White Bread and Wine:
Being the Fruits thy Grave brings forth and hands
Upon thy Table where thou waiting standst.

Dainties most rich, all spiced o're with Grace,
That grow out of thy Grave do deck thy Table.
To entertain thy Guests, thou callst, and place
Allowst, with welcome: (and this is no Fable)
And with these Guests I am invited to't
And this rich banquet makes me thus a Poet.

Thy Cross planted within thy Coffin beares
  Sweet Blossoms and rich Fruits, Whose steams do rise
Out of thy Sepulcher and purge the aire
  Of all Sins damps and fogs that Choake the Skies.
  This Fume perfumes Saints hearts as it out peeps
  Ascending up to bury thee in th'reechs.

Joy stands on tiptoes all the while thy Guests
  Sit at thy Table, ready forth to sing
Its Hallilujahs in sweet musicks dress,
  Waiting for Organs to imploy herein.
  Here matter is allowd to all, rich, high,
  My Lord, to tune thee Hymns melodiously.

Oh! make my heart thy Pipe: the Holy Ghost
  The Breath that fills the same and Spiritually.
Then play on mee thy pipe that is almost
  Worn out with piping tunes of Vanity.
  Winde musick is the best if thou delight
  To play the same thyselfe, upon my pipe.

Hence make me, Lord, thy Golden Trumpet Choice,
  And trumpet thou thyselfe upon the same
Thy heart enravishing Hymns with Sweetest Voice.
  When thou thy Trumpet soundst, thy tunes will flame.
  My heart shall then sing forth thy praises sweet
  When sounded thus with thy Sepulcher reech.

Make too my Soul thy Cittern, and its wyers
  Make my affections: and rub off their rust
With thy bright Grace: and screw my Strings up higher,
  And tune the same to tune thy praise most Just.
  Ile close thy Supper then with Hymns most sweet,
  Burr'ing thy Grave in thy Sepulcher's reech.

ROGER WOLCOTT, 1679–1767

[*Poetical Meditations, being the Improvement of some Vacant Hours* was published in New London in 1725 by Roger Wolcott of Windsor, Connecticut. Apprenticed to a weaver at twelve, Wolcott, without formal schooling, by industry and thrift acquired a competent fortune and distinguished himself in public affairs: as Major General he was second in command at the capture of Louisburg; successively he became legislator, county judge, chief-justice of the Supreme Court, and governor (1751–1754) of Connecticut. Though his verse is not intrinsically important, in one poem, "A Brief Account of the Agency Of the Honourable John Winthrop, Esq; in the Court of King Charles the Second, Anno Dom. 1662. When he Obtained for the Colony of Connecticut His Majesty's Gracious Charter," Wolcott attempted an epic in celebration of his native land. See his "Journal at the Siege of Louisburg," *Collections of the Connecticut Historical Society*, I (1860), 131–161; "Wolcott Papers, 1750–1754," 2 vols.; *ibid.*, XV, XVI. *Poetical Meditations* was reprinted in *Collections of the Massachusetts Historical Society*, first series, IV (1795), 262–298; also by the Club of Odd Volumes (Boston, 1898). The text is from the first edition, pp. 11–35, with omissions indicated.]

POETICAL MEDITATION

Proverbs XXXI. 10.

Who can find a Vertuous Woman, for her Price is far above Rubies.

Vertue's a Babe, first born in Paradice,
And hath by birth priority of Vice.
Vertue is all that's good we brought from thence
The dear remains of our first Innocence.
Vertue still makes the Vertuous to shine,
Like those that Liv'd in the first week of time.
Vertue hath force the vile to cleanse again,
So being like clear shining after Rain.
A Kind and Constant, Chearful Vertuous Life,
Becomes each Man, and most Adorns a Wife.
But such a Vertue, ah, where shall we find,
That's Bright, especially in Woman Kind?
If such an one had been on Earth, no doubt
Searching King *Solomon* had found her out.
But stay my Muse, nor may we thence Conclude,
There is not One in all their Multitude:
For tho' it be too True, that *Solomon*
Amongst a Thousand found not such an one;
It follows not at all but such an one
Amongst an Hundred Thousand may be shown;
Which if she may, her Price beyond Compare,
Excels the Price of Rubies very fair.

Psalm LXIV. 6.

The Heart is Deep.

He that can trace a Ship making her way,
Amidst the threatening Surges on the Sea;
Or track a Towering Eagle in the Air,
Or on a Rock find the Impressions there
Made by a Serpents Footsteps. Who Surveys
The Subtile Intreagues that a Young Man lays,

In his Sly Courtship of an harmless Maid,
Whereby his Wanton Amours are Convey'd
Into her Breast; Tis he alone that can
Find out the Cursed Policies of Man.

A BRIEF ACCOUNT OF . . . WINTHROP [1]

The King is Restored to the Throne

These happy Tidings soon found out their way,
Unto the *English* in *America;*
Who join with *Britain* in the Celebration,
Of their just Princes happy Restauration.
The Sages of *Connecticut* do meet,
To pay their Homage at their Princes Feet;
To whom they seek to hasten an Address,
To shew their Duty and their Joys Excess.
Learned *Winthrop* then by general Consent,
Sat at the Helm to sway the Government;
Who prudently the People doth Advise,
To ask the King for Charter Liberties.

All like his Counsel well; and all reply,
Sir, You must undertake our Agency;
For there is none but You we may expect,
Can make the thing you Counsel take Effect:
Your Serving us in this Important Thing,
And Personating Us before the King,
Will sure Endear a *Winthrop*'s Memory
To Us, and to our Last Posterity.

His Mind, vast as the Heavenly Spheres above,
Was all bespangled with the Stars of Love;

And Zealous Care for their Posterity,
Of all his Acts the *Primum Mobile;*
Led on by these bright Stars kind Influence,
He hastens to the Palace of his Prince;
There waiting for an Opportunity,——

E're long, Great CHARLES was in his Council sat
With some Choice Nobles of his Cabinet:
His Royal Mind Intent on his Affairs,
He thus Unbosoms to his Counsellers;

What News, My Lords? *How go Affairs Abroad?*
What more Remains to do for Englands *Good?*
Do distant Parts of our Dominion
Want farther Help or Favour from the Throne?

At this arose one of the Lords of Trade,
And to his Majesty this Answer made,
An Agent from *Connecticut* doth wait,
With an Address before your Palace Gate.

Let him come in, says CHARLES, *and let us Hear,*
What has been done, and what's a doing there?

Winthrop brought in before his Princes Feet,
Prostrates himself with Reverence, the *King* to *Greet;*
And thanks His Majesty for his Access:
Then for his People offers this Address;

"*GREAT SIR*, Since Reconciled Heaven Restores
You to the Throne of Your High Ancestors,
See how each Subject Emulating tries,
To Express our National Felicities:
The Joy of Your Accession to the Throne,
Is like the Lustre of the Morning Sun;
Which from the East Salutes the Western Shores,
Still trampling under foot Nights horrid Powers:
So the loud Accents of this boundless Joy,
Ecchoing in our Ears from *Britanny*,
Gave Light & Gladness where-so'ere it came,
And fill'd our joyful Hearts with equal Flame.
The sad Remembrance of those days of Wo,
Which in Your Absence we did undergo,
Transports our present Joys to that Excess,
As passeth all Expressions to express.

May Heaven preserve Your Majesty, and Bless
Your Reign with Honour, & with Length of Days;
And in Your Line the Regal Power extend,
Until the Suns last Revolution end.

"And since we are at mighty *Cæsar*'s Feet,
O may He Pardon us, while we Entreat,
Your Royal Favour in the thing we want;
T' Incorporate us by Your CHARTER-Grant.
The Land we've Purchas'd, or Subdu'd by Fight,
And Bought of *Fenwick* what was *Warwick*'s Right,
And all at the Endeavour of our Own,
Without the least Dis-bursement from the Throne."

Rise up, Quoth *Charles; My Liberal Hand Supplies,*
All needful Help to every One that Cries;
Nor shall I be Illiberal to You:
But, Prithee, Winthrop, *Please to let me Know,*
By whom it was your Place did first Commence,
Your Patriarchs that Led your Tribes from Hence? . . .

[After an account of the trials of the early settlers, Winthrop thus describes the Connecticut Valley:]

"After the *Meadows* thus have took their Place,
The Champion Plains draw up to fill the space.
Fair in their Prospect, Pleasant, Fruitful, Wide,
Here *Tellus* may be seen in all his Pride.
Cloud kissing Pines in stately Man groves stand,
Firm *Oaks* fair *Branches* wide and large extend.
The *Fir*, the *Box*, the *Balm-Tree* here stand mute,
So do the *Nut-Trees* Laden down with Fruit.
In shady Vales the Fruitful *Vine* o're whelms,
The Weaving Branches of the bending *Elms*.

"Within the Covert of these shady Boughs,
The Loving *Turtle* and his Lovely Spouse
From Bough to Bough in deep Affection move,
And with Chast Joy reciprocate their Love.
At the Cool Brooks, the *Beavers* and the *Minks*
Keep House, and here the *Hart* & *Panther* Drinks.
And *Partridges* here keep in Memory,
How to their Loss they soared once too high.

"Within these Spacious Forests, Fresh & Green,

No Monsters of Burn *Africk* may be seen.
No hissing *Bassalisk* stands to affright.
Nor *Seps*, nor *Hemorhus* with Mortal bite,
The Lybian *Lyon* ne'er set Footing here,
Nor *Tygers* of *Numedia* do appear.
But here the *Moose* his spreading *Antlers* sways,
And bears down Stubborn standels with their *sprays*,
These sport themselves within these *Woods*, & here
The Fatted *Roe-Buck* and the *Fallow Deer*,
Yield Venison as good as that which won
The Partriarchial Benediction.
"Each Plain is bounded at its utmost Edge
With a long Chain of Mountains in a ridge,
Whose Azure tops advance themselves so high
They seem like Pendants hanging in the Skie.
Twenty Four Miles, Surveyers do account
Between the *Eastern* and the *Western* Mount;
In which vast Interspace, Pleasant and Fair,
Zephirus Whispers a Delightful Air.
These Mountains stand at Equi-distant space,
From the fair Flood in such Majestick Grace.
Their looks alone are able to Inspire
An Active Brain with a Mercurial Fire.
The Muses hence their ample Dews Distil,
More than was Feigned from the [tree] topt Hill.
And if those Witty Men that have us told
Strange Tales of Mountains in the Days of Old,
Had they but seen how these are Elevated,
We should have found them far more Celebrated,
In the Fine Works that they have left to us,
Than high *Olimpus* or long *Caucassus;*
Or *Latmos* which *Diana* stops upon,
There to Salute her dear *Endimion.*"

MATHER BYLES, 1706/7–1788

[Were it not that in background, training, and subsequent influence the Reverend Mr. Mather Byles of Boston was an orthodox Calvinist, he would hardly be considered among the Puritans. He is remembered today as a wit, a Tory, and a lover of good society and polite letters. But as a grandson of Increase Mather, trained up by his uncle Cotton Mather, and as first pastor of the Hollis Street Congregational Church from 1732 till the Revolution, he is perhaps the last link with the Puritan tradition in letters. The discomforts he suffered because of his Loyalist sympathies were mitigated somewhat by the fame he won as writer, preacher, and scholar. Much of his poetry was issued in the *New England Weekly Journal*. For the rest, *Poems on Several Occasions* (Boston, 1744) and *The Conflagration* (1755) contain most of his verses.

His poems, modeled upon the verses of Pope, Thomson, and Watts, reflect current literary fashions. "An Hymn to Christ" is written in the manner of the last named, and is taken from the last page of *Mr. Byle's Two Sermons at Dorchester* (Boston, 1732). See Tyler, *A History of American Literature*, II, 55–57, 192–198; and Arthur W. H. Eaton, *The Famous Mather Byles* (Boston, 1914). See also *Dictionary of American Biography* for a good biographical account and for further bibliographical material.]

AN HYMN *TO* CHRIST *FOR OUR* REGENERATION *AND* RESURRECTION.

I.

TO THEE, my LORD, I lift the Song,
Awake, my tuneful Pow'rs:
In constant Praise my grateful Tongue
Shall fill my foll'wing Hours.

II.

Guilty, condemn'd, undone I stood;
I bid my GOD depart:
He took my Sins, and paid his Blood,
And *turn'd* this wand'ring Heart.

III.

Death, the grim Tyrant, seiz'd my Fame,
Vile, loathsome and accurst:
His Breath renews the vital Flame,
And Glories *change* the Dust.

IV.

Now, SAVIOUR, shall thy Praise commence;
My Soul by Thee brought Home,
And ev'ry Member, ev'ry Sense,
Recover'd from the Tomb.

V.

To Thee my Reason I submit,
My Love, my Mem'ry, Lord,
My Eyes to read, my Hands to write,
My Lips to preach thy Word.

46.

The Glory of & Grace in the Church set out.

Come now behold
Within this Knot what Flowers do grow
Spangld like gold:
Whence Wreaths of all Perfumes do flow.
Most Curious Colours of all Sorts you shall
With all Sweete Spirits Sent. Yet thats not all.

Oh! Look, & finde
These Choicest Flowers most richly sweet
Are Disciplinde
With Artificiall Angels meet.
An heap of Pearls is precious: but they shall
When set by Art Excell. Yet that's not all.

Christ's Spirit Showers
Down in his Word, & Sacraments
Upon these Flowers
The Clouds of Grace Divine Contents.
Such things of Wealthy Blessings on them fall
As make them sweetly thrive: Yet that's not all.

Yet still behold!
All flourish not at once. We see
While some Unfold
Their blushing Leaves, some buds there bee.
Here's Faith, Hope, Charity in flower, which call
On yonders in the Bud. Yet that's not all.

But as they stand
Like Beauties reeching in perfume
A Divine Hand
Doth hand them up to Glories room:
Where Each in sweet'ned Songs all Praises shall
Sing all ore Heaven for aye. And that's but all.

The Souls Admiration hereupon.

What I such Praises sing! How can it bee?
Shall I in Heaven sing?
What I, that fear'd I'd ne'er come to the
Lord, such a thing?
Tho nothing is too hard for thee:
One Hope hereof seems hard to mee.

What, Can I ever tune those Melodies
Who have no tune at all?

Page of Edward Taylor's Manuscript. (For text, see p. 653.)

Chapter VII

LITERARY THEORY

THOUGH it is evident that the Puritans as a group never developed a lively aesthetic sense in their appreciation of music, painting, and sculpture, yet they left on record a great number of brief comments upon the art of writing, as well as a few extended essays. In each instance the writer is concerned with the question: How can prose or verse be made more useful to the preacher, historian, poet, or controversialist? Usually the remarks are incidental to some broader aim. The motive behind Puritan writing was utilitarian: the author might chronicle the story of his times, attack unwelcome schools of thought, discourse upon man's duties, narrate the lives of famous men, or hymn praises to God, but the end he purposed was never merely an enjoyment of belles-lettres or of literature for its own sake. This is not to say that he was devoid of literary sensibilities. On the contrary, Michael Wigglesworth's college declamation praises eloquence because it is an art which "gives new luster and bewty, new strength new vigour, new life unto trueth" (see p. 674). The interest is utilitarian in the finest sense, for it does not limit eloquence to the service of one type or class of men; it is conceived rather as the art behind which other arts are hidden.

The early Puritan authors in this country were almost without exception college graduates who could look back upon a classical training acquired by seven years of grammar school study, concluded by four college years wherein the students were intensively drilled in rhetoric. They were, to begin with, inheritors of such Elizabethan training and rhetorical theory as had been in vogue at the English universities; they knew what Erasmus, Peacham, and Florio had to say on the art of writing well,—they further studied apophthegms culled from the rhetoric texts of Farnaby, Dugard, Draxe, and Buchler. Rapin's works, especially his *Reflections upon the Eloquence of these Times; particularly of the Barr and Pulpit* (London, 1672), and the usual *artes concionandi* [1] of Keckermann, Chappell, and others were the standard texts for divinity students. The consciousness of literary style was clearly a matter not left to chance; the gentlemen who came to establish a "*Plantation Religious*" were steeped in the humanistic tradition, and believed that the key to "truth" lay in advancement of learning. They believed therefore that such art was reckoned best which was clearest, most convincing, ingratiating, and appropriate.

[1] Manuals designed to teach the art of stirring the emotions.

Pulpit eloquence, especially the florid oratory, the figured, harmonious, "Ciceronian" periods of Hooker, Andrewes, and Donne had won high favor during the first quarter of the seventeenth century; and some few Puritans there were who defended the older tradition. "And where are there such high straines of all sorts of *Rhetoricall Tropes, & figures*, to be found in any Author," asks Charles Chauncy in 1655, "as there are in the writings of the *Prophets & Apostles?*" [1] Chauncy's apology for the fashions of an earlier day is the more striking since his voice was raised too late to win a hearing. After Perkins's *The Art of Prophesying* (1631), with its emphasis upon plainness, achieved wide currency, "high style" fell into disrepute. In 1642 John Cotton disparaged "affecting carnall eloquence" in the pulpit, on the grounds that "swelling words of humane wisedome make mens preaching seeme to Christ (as it were) a blubber-lipt Ministry." [2] It is a point of view even more elaborately stated by Thomas Hooker (see p. 672). The view held by Puritans that Holy Writ needed not the profane intermingling of human embellishment is echoed in the preface to the Bay Psalm Book (see p. 670), and Roger Williams, whose literary art was really not so uninspired as he would have his readers believe, asks: "And yet, is the *Language* plaine? it is the liker *Christs:* Is the composure rude? such was his outward *Beauty*." [3]

Plain style was not confined to pulpit eloquence or to theological treatises alone. Historians like Daniel Gookin and William Bradford take pains to see that their narratives were adapted to their audience. Gookin remarks that his stories are "not clothed in elegancy of words and accurate sentences," but rather that he has "endeavoured all plainness . . . that the most vulgar capacity might understand; [4] Governor Bradford commends "Of Plimmoth Plantation" by saying in

[1] *Gods Mercy, shewed to his people in giving them a faithful Ministry*, p. 37. The example of the court and university preachers is cited by W. Fraser Mitchell, *English Pulpit Oratory*, p. 106, as the reason for the ornate fashion in rhetoric. Richard F. Jones, "The Attack on Pulpit Eloquence in the Restoration: An Episode in the Development of the Neo-Classical Standards for Prose," *Journal of English and Germanic Philology*, XXX (1931), 188–217, notes the turn to plainness after 1660, and in "Science and Language in England in the Midseventeenth Century," *ibid.*, XXXI (1932), 315–331, he remarks on the great influence of Bacon and Boyle in bringing about a simpler prose style. See also his "Science and English Prose Style in the Third Quarter of the Seventeenth Century," *Publications of the Modern Language Association*, XLV (1930), 977–1009.

[2] *A Brief Exposition Of the whole Book Of Canticles* (London, 1642), p. 112.

[3] *Experiments of Spiritual Life & Health* (London, 1652). Dedicatory address to Lady Vane the Younger.

[4] Preface to *Historical Collections of the Indians in New-England, Collections of the Massachusetts Historical Society*, first series, I (1792), 141–226. Preface dated November, 1674.

his brief preface that he is about to narrate events "in a plaine stile; with singuler regard unto ye simple trueth in all things."[1] Indeed, the belief that truth was integral with well-written history was so firmly established by the second quarter of the seventeenth century that Hobbes assumed its acceptance in his preface to *Homer's Odysses* (1675): "For both the Poet and the Historian writeth only (or should do) matter of Fact."[2]

As we have already seen,[3] the Puritan held to a belief in the poet's high calling, but thought that the danger of poetry lay in its magic spell,—that it tempted men away from truth to fable; Sprat and other members of the Royal Society expressed the view that too much fictional nonsense achieved the dignity of poetic treatment. Yet the fact that danger lurked within the form in no way meant that men should shun it, providing they exhibited skill and high seriousness in handling their theme. The gentlemen who compiled *The Whole Booke of Psalmes*, saying that "Gods Altar needs not our pollishings," were employing poetry the better to honor God, while at the same time modestly deprecating their ability to write verse,—assuming God's gracious acceptance of their poor offering. Edward Taylor throughout his life chose verse to express his ardent love of Christ (see p. 650); Wigglesworth told the story of judgment day in monotonous fourteeners, though he "attended Conscience rather than Elegance, fidelity rather than poetry,"[4] thus sensibly acknowledging his inadequacy as a poet, for "every good minister hath not a gift of spiritual poetry";[5] and Jonathan Mitchell stated the case very clearly by saying: "Great Truths to dress in Meeter; Becomes a Preacher," adding,

> No Cost too great, no Care too curious is
> To set forth Truth, and win mens Souls to bliss.[6]

Along with the conception of the poet's high calling a further view obtained. Puritan schoolboys, like their Anglican cousins, were set the task of composing verse merely as rhetorical exercises. John Wilson's *Song of Deliverance* had been written in doggerel staves that children might more easily memorize history. Richard Steere's *Monumental Memorial* is recommended to the reader as a narrative which "in the Attire of *Measure* and *Cadency*, whose even and easie Pace being more

[1] MS (*ca.* 1650) in Massachusetts State Library, Boston. See Facsimile, ed. John A. Doyle (London, 1896).

[2] Ed. J. E. Spingarn, *Critical Essays of the Seventeenth Century*, II, 70.

[3] See p. 547.

[4] Preface, *The Day of Doom* (1662), sig. xx3v.

[5] *Ibid.*, sig. x3v.

[6] *Ibid.*, sig. B1.

Alluring and Captivating (Especially with youth, or the Crittically Ingenious of this Age) than the Elaborate *Volumes* of *Prose* left to us by our Worthy Ancestors, may probably the sooner *Decoy* or Invite thy Perusal."[1] Though the emphasis is still upon the matter, we are given to believe that a pleasing manner will do no harm. To none of the earlier generation, however, would Addison's conception of poetry as a mental relaxation, an indulgence of the imagination, have been adequate. Not until the eighteenth century did the urbane appreciation of poetry as a social accomplishment supersede an enthusiasm for verse as a means of expressing great truths in exalted moods.

The more critical dissection of "polite letters" gained no headway among Puritans until after Dryden's famous prefaces had appeared; nor indeed until Blackmore, Addison, and Pope, by calling attention to the neglected beauties in classic literature and by their example and analysis of epic poetry, had awakened a literary consciousness. The eighteenth century was well advanced in its first quarter before Cotton Mather in his preface to *Psalterium Americanum* attempted to defend the new idiom of blank verse by translating the Psalms (see p. 678). It is clear that Mather did not grasp the meaning of "blank verse," for each Bible stave is fashioned into an unrimed septinary couplet, lacking even the naïve charm of the Bay Psalm versions. Here, for example, is one stanza:

> Smooth were his Mouth's fine butter'd Words;
> but war was in his heart;
> much softer were his words than oil;
> and yet drawn Swords they were.[2]

But whether he understood the character of blank verse or not, his defense of it and of a good English idiom in the preface is a very conscious attempt to explore the possibilities of language, as well as to liberate colonial writers from the charge of provincialism. It is all the more significant in view of the fact that even in England blank verse was by no means established as a poetic form in 1718. Between *Paradise Lost* (1667) and Thomson's *Winter* (1726), few poets had used it and fewer still had discussed it; indeed, Addison's famous Spectator essays on the great Puritan epic barely touch upon blank verse.[3] By the time

[1] Address "To the Reader," *A Monumental Memorial of Marine Mercy Being an Acknowledgement of an High Hand of Divine Deliverance on the Deep in the Time of distress* (Boston, 1684).

[2] Psalm LV, verse 21 (Boston, 1718), p. 135.

[3] Cf. *Spectator* 285: ". . . Where the verse is not built upon rhymes, there pomp of sound and energy of expression are indispensably necessary to support the style.

John Bulkley came to write his preface to Wolcott's *Poetical Meditations* (see p. 680) the Puritan era was at its close. Bulkley's definition of wit, his discrimination between "the *Accomplish'd Poet* and the *Great Man*," and his apology for the poet as one who, by choosing a verse medium, has "Diverted some of his Leisure Hours" were the commonplaces that might be uttered by any eighteenth-century gentleman. In the same year Cotton Mather was preparing his handbook for divinity students, *Manuductio ad Ministerium*, with its essay "Of Poetry and Style" (see p. 684), which in its catholicity of taste and urbanity suggests the spirit of current periodical essays rather than the utilitarian aim of a preaching manual. It was not until 1745 that a literary essay, written solely for entertainment, was published in the colonies. The satire on style which Mather Byles printed in *The American Magazine* "to cultivate *polite* Writing" (see p. 689) really ushers in a new era of conscious literary feeling; here is an essay wherein the art of writing is conceived as an end in itself, one in which the utilitarian motive for presentation is forgotten and the artfulness of a cultivated style is extolled. Though serviceability still remained the criterion of good writing for mid-eighteenth-century colonial writers, there was often bound with it too great a literary self-consciousness to be characteristically Puritan. The idea of "taste" that Byles implies is one far removed from that expressed by Richard Mather a century before in his preface to the Bay Psalm Book. The eighteenth-century minister, witty and urbane, was guided by very different literary standards from those in fashion during his great-grandfather's day, for Byles's writing indicate that God's altar received from his hands very solicitous "pollishings."

PREFACE TO THE BAY PSALM BOOK

[The original draft of the preface to the Bay Psalm Book, written by Richard Mather (1596–1669), has been recently discovered among the papers of the Prince Collection in the Boston Public Library. See

---

and keep it from falling into the flatness of prose," ed. Chalmers (Boston, 1854), p. 275. It is worth notice that a Richard Steere published at Boston in 1713 a poem, *The Daniel Catcher*, "To which is Added, Earth's Felicities, Heaven's Allowances, A Blank Poem." It opens thus:

> Upon the Earth there are so many Treasures
> Various Abounding objects of Delight,
> That to Enumerate, would be a Task
> Too ponderous for my Imperfect Skill,
> Or Pen, to Charactise Effect'ally.

"The Preface to *The Bay Psalm Book*," *More Books*, IV (1929), 223–229. See the introduction to selections from the Bay Psalm Book, p. 555.]

THE PREFACE.

THE singing of Psalmes, though it breath forth nothing but holy harmony, and melody: yet such is the subtilty of the enemie, and the enmity of our nature against the Lord, & his wayes, that our hearts can finde matter of discord in this harmony, and crotchets of division in this holy melody.-for- There have been three questions especially stirring concerning singing. First. what psalmes are to be sung in churches? whether Davids and other scripture psalmes, or the psalmes invented by the gifts of godly men in every age of the church. Secondly, if scripture psalmes, whether in their owne words, or in such meter as english poetry is wont to run in? Thirdly. by whom are they to be sung? whether by the whole churches together with their voices? or by one man singing alone and the rest joyning in silence, & in the close saying amen.

Touching the first, certainly the singing of Davids psalmes was an acceptable worship of God, not only in his owne, but in succeeding times. . . .

As for the scruple that some take at the translation of the book of psalmes into meeter, because Davids psalmes were sung in his owne words without meeter: wee answer- First. There are many verses together in several psalmes of David which run in rithmes (as those that know the hebrew and as Buxtorf shews [1] *Thesau.* pa. 629.) which shews at least the lawfullnes of singing psalmes in english rithmes.

Secondly. The psalmes are penned in such verses as are sutable to the poetry of the hebrew language, and not in the common style of such other bookes of the old Testament as are not poeticall; now no protestant doubteth but that all the bookes of the scripture should by Gods ordinance be extant in the mother tongue of each nation, that they may be understood of all, hence the psalmes are to be translated into our english tongue; and is in our english tongue wee are to sing them, then as all our english songs (according to the course of our english poetry) do run in metre, soe ought Davids psalmes to be translated into meeter, that soe wee may sing the Lords songs, as in our english tongue soe in such verses as are familar to an english eare which are commonly metricall: and as it can be no just offence to any good conscience, to sing Davids hebrew songs in english words, soe neither to sing his poeticall verses in english poeticall metre: men might as well stumble at singing the hebrew psalmes in our english tunes (and not in the hebrew tunes) as at singing them in english meeter, (which are our verses) and not in such verses as are generally used by David according to the poetry of the hebrew language: but the truth is, as the Lord hath hid from us the hebrew tunes, lest wee should think our selves bound to imitate them; soe also the course and frame (for the most part) of their hebrew poetry, that wee might not think our selves bound to imitate that, but that every nation without scruple might follow as the grave sort of tunes of their owne country songs, soe the graver sort of verses of their owne country poetry.

Neither let any think, that for the meetre sake wee have taken liberty or poeticall licence to depart from the true and proper sence of Davids words in the hebrew verses, noe; but it hath beene one part of our religious care and faithfull indeavour, to keepe close to the originall text. . . .

For although wee have cause to bless God in many respects for the religious indeavours of the translaters of the psalmes into meetre usually annexed to our Bibles, yet it is not unknowne to the godly learned that they have rather presented a paraphrase then the words of David translated according to the rule 2 *chron.* 29. 30. and that their addition to the words, detractions from the words are not seldome and rare, but very frequent and many times needles, (which we suppose would not be approved of if the psalmes were so translated into prose) and that their variations of the sense, and alterations of the sacred text too frequently, may iustly minister matter of offence to them that are able to compare the translation with the text; of which failings, some iudicious have oft complained, others have been grieved, wherupon it hath bin generally desired, that as wee doe inioye other, soe (if it were the Lords will) wee might inioye this ordinance also in its native purity: wee have therefore done our indeavour to make a plaine and familiar translation of the psalmes and words of David into english metre, and have not soe much as presumed to paraphrase to give the sense of his meaning in other words; we have therefore attended heerin as our chief guide the originall, shunning all additions, except such as even the best translators of them in prose supply, avoiding all materiall detractions from words or sence. . . .

As for our translations, wee have with our english Bibles (to which next to the Originall wee have had respect) used the Idioms of our owne tongue in stead of Hebraismes, lest they might seeme english barbarismes.

Synonimaes wee use indifferently: as *folk* for *people*, and *Lord* for

Iehovah, and sometime (though seldome) *God* for *Iehovah;* for which (as for some other interpretations of places cited in the new Testament) we have the scriptures authority ps. 14. with 53. Heb. 1. 6. with psalme 97. 7. Where a phrase is doubtfull wee have followed that which (in our owne apprehension) is most genuine & edifying:

Somtime wee have contracted, somtime dilated the same hebrew word, both for the sence and the verse sake: which dilatation wee conceive to be no paraphrasticall addition no more then the contraction of a true and full translation to be any unfaithfull detraction or diminution: as when wee dilate *who healeth* and say *he it is who healeth;* soe when wee contract, *those that stand in awe of God* and say *Gods fearers.*

Lastly. Because some hebrew words have a more full and emphaticall signification then any one english word can or doth somtime expresse, hence wee have done that somtime which faithfull translators may doe, *viz.* not only to translate the word but the emphasis of it. . . .

As for all other changes of numbers, tenses, and characters of speech, they are such as either the hebrew will unforcedly beare, or our english forceably calls for, or they no way change the sence; and such are printed usually in an other character.

If therefore the verses are not alwayes so smooth and elegant as some may desire or expect; let them consider that Gods Altar needs not our pollishings: Ex. 20. for wee have respected rather a plaine translation, then to smooth our verses with the sweetnes of any paraphrase, and soe have attended Conscience rather then Elegance, fidelity rather then poetry, in translating the hebrew words into english language, and Davids poetry into english meetre; that soe wee may sing in Sion the Lords songs of prayse according to his owne will; untill hee take us from hence, and wipe away all our teares, & bid us enter into our masters ioye to sing eternall Halleluiahs.

THOMAS HOOKER

[For a discussion of Thomas Hooker, see p. 290. The text is from the original edition (London, 1648).]

FROM PREFACE TO A SURVEY OF THE SUMME OF CHURCH-DISCIPLINE

THAT the discourse comes forth in such a homely dresse and course habit, the Reader must be desired to consider, It comes *out of the wildernesse*, where curiosity is not studied. Planters if they can provide cloth to go warm, they leave the cutts and lace to those that study to go fine.

As it is beyond my skill, so I professe it is beyond my care to please the nicenesse of mens palates, with any quaintnesse of language. They who covet more sauce then meat, they must provide cooks to their minde. It was a cavill cast upon *Hierom*,[1] that in his writings he was *Ciceronianus non Christianus:* My rudenesse frees me wholly from this exception, for being Λόγῳ Ι'διώτης,[2] as the Apostle hath it, if I would, I could not lavish out in the loosenesse of language, and as the case stands, if I could answer any mans desire in that daintinesse of speech, I would not do the matter that Injury which is now under my hand: *Ornari res ipsa negat.*[3] The substance and solidity of the frame is that, which pleaseth the builder, its the painters work to provide varnish.

Erasmus in vita Hier.

If the manner of the discourse should occasion any disrellish in the apprehension of the weaker Reader, because it may seem too *Logicall, or Scholasticall,* in regard of the *terms* I use, or the way of dispute that I proceed in, in some places: I have these two things to professe,

1. That plainesse and perspicuity, both for matter and manner of expression, are the things, that I have conscientiously indeavoured in the whole debate: for I have ever thought writings that come abroad, they are not to dazle, but direct the apprehension of the meanest, and I have accounted it the chiefest part of Iudicious learning, to make a hard point easy and familiar in explication. *Qui non vult intelligi, debet negligi.*[4]

MICHAEL WIGGLESWORTH

[College undergraduates were required to deliver orations as part of their training in rhetoric. Michael Wigglesworth's declamation, "The prayse of Eloquence," was delivered in 1650, early in his senior bachelor year. Though it nowhere mentions pulpit oratory as the chief end of eloquence, we must keep in mind that Wigglesworth would assume, as well as his listeners, that sermonizing was indeed the chiefest part of oratory. The passage expounds the Protestant theory that oratory is the "means" of conviction; that the principal use of public speaking as a "means" was for working conversion by the sermon. For an account of Wigglesworth, see p. 548. The selection is from Samuel E. Morison, *Harvard College in the Seventeenth Century*, pp. 180–183, passages transcribed from the manuscript original in the library of the New England Historical Genealogical Society, and used by permission.]

THE PRAYSE OF ELOQUENCE

How sweetly doth eloquence even inforce trueth upon the understanding, and subtly convay knowledge into the minde be it never so dull of conceiving, and sluggish in yeelding its assente. So that let a good Oratour put forth the utmost of his skill, and you shall hear him so lay open and unfould, so evidence and demonstrate from point to point what he hath in hand, that he wil make a very block understand his discourse. Let him be to giue a description of something absent or unknown; how strangely doth he realize and make it present to his hearers apprehensions, framing in their mindes as exact an idea of that which they never saw, as they can possibly have of any thing that they have bin longest and best acquainted with. Or doth he take upon him to personate some others in word or deedes why he presents his hearers not with a lifeless picture, but with the living persons of those concerning whom he speaks. They see, they hear, they handle them, they walk they talk with them, and what not? Or is he to speak about such things as are already known? Why should he here discourse after the vulgar manner, and deliver his mind as a cobler would doe: his hearers might then have some ground to say they knew as much as their oratour could teach them. But by the power of eloquence ould truth receivs a new habit. though its essence be the same yet its visage is so altered that it may currently pass and be accepted as a novelty. The same verity is again and again perhaps set before the same guests but drest and disht up after a new manner, and every manner season'd so well that the intellectuall parts may both without nauseating receiv, and so oft as it doth receiv it still draw some fresh nourishing virtue from it. So that Eloquence giues new luster and bewty, new strength new vigour, new life unto trueth; presenting it with such variety as refresheth, actuating it with such hidden powerful energy, that a few languid sparks are blown up to a shining flame.

And which is yet more: Eloquence doth not onely reviue the things known but secretly convay life into the hearers understanding rousing it out of its former slumber, quickning it beyond its naturall vigour, elevating it aboue its ordinary conception. There are not onely objects set before it, but ey's (after a sort) giuen it to see these objects in such wise as it never saw. Yea it is strengthened as to apprehend that which is taught it, so of it self with enlargment to comprehend many things which are not made known unto it. Hence it comes to pass that after the hearing of a wel-composed speech livelily exprest the understanding of the Auditor is so framed into the mould of Eloquence, that he could almost goe away and compose the like himself either upon the same or another subject. And whats the reason of this? why his mind is transported with a kind of rapture, and inspired with a certain oratoric fury, as if the oratour together with his words had breathed his soul and spirit into those that hear him.

These and the like effects hath Eloquence upon the understanding. But furthermore 'tis a fit bait to catch the will and affections. For hereby they are not onely layd in wait for, but surprized: nor onely surprized, but subdued; nor onely subdued, but triumphed over. Yet Eloquence beguil's with such honesty, subdues with such mildness, triumphs with such sweetness: that here to be surprized is nothing dangerous, here to be subject is the best freedom, this kind of servitude is more desireable then liberty. For whereas our untractable nature refuseth to be drawn, and a stiff will scorn's to be compel'd: yet by the power of wel-composed speech nature is drawn against the stream with delight, and the will after a sort compelled with its owne consent. Altho: for a time it struggle and make resistance, yet at length it suffer's it self to be vanquish't, and takes a secret contentment in being overcome.

In like manner, for the affections. Look as a mighty river augmented with excessiue rains or winter snows swelling above its wonted channel bear's down banks and bridges, overflows feilds and hedges, sweeps away all before it, that might obstruct its passage: so Eloquence overturn's, overturn's all things that stand in its way, and carrys them down with the irresistible stream of its all controuling power. Wonderful it were to speak of the severall discoverys of the power in severall affections: wonderfull but to think in generall, how like a blustering tempest it one while driues before it the raging billow's of this troubled Ocean: how other whiles (as though it had them in fetters it curb's and calm's the fury at a word. And all this without offering violence to the party's so affected; nay with a secret pleasure and delight it stirs men up to the greatest displeasure and distast. Doth it affect with grief? why to be so grieved is no grievance. doth it kindle coales, nay flames of fiery indignation? why those flames burn not, but rather cherish. doth it draw tears from the eys? why even tears flow with pleasure. For as is wel sayd by one upon this point In omni animi motu etiam in dolore est quaedam jucunditas.[1] So potently, so sweetly doth Eloquence command. and of a skilfull orator in point of the affections that may be spoken really, which the Poet affirmeth fabulously of Æolus god of the winds. . . .

But I need instance no more. some of you I hope will by this time assent unto what has bin hitherto prov'd that Eloquence is of such useful concernment and powerfull operation. But methinks I hear some still objecting. 'Tis very true Eloquence is a desirable thing, but what are we the better for knowing its worth unless we could hope our selues to attain it? It is indeed a right excellent indowment but 'tis not every capacity, nay scarce one of a hundreth that can reach it. How many men of good parts do we find that yet excel not here? Cicero indeed, a man in whom vast understanding and naturall fluent facility of speech conspire together; no marvail if he make judges weep and princes tremble. But to what purpose is it for a man of weak parts and mean abilitys to labour after that which he is never like to compass? Had we not as good toss our caps against the wind as weary out our selves in the pursuit of that which so few can reach to?

An. To these I would answer first, the reason why so few attain it is because there [are] few that indeed desire it. hence they run not as if they ment to win, they pursue not as if they hop't to overtake. But 2ly let me answer them with Turner's [2] words upon this very argument Negligentiam nostram arguit, qui cum non possimus. quod debemus, optimus, nolumus quod possimus, benè. we cannot do what we would therefore will not doe what we may. This savours of a slouthfull sistem. Because we cannot keep pace with the horsemen, shall we refuse to accompany the footmen? Because we cannot run, shall we sit down and refuse to goe? we cannot reach so far as our selues desire and as some others it may be attain, shall we not therefore reach as far as our endeavours may carry us? Because we cannot be Oratores optimi, do we content our selues to be Oratores Pessimi?

And as for those that have most excell'd in this kind, whence had they their excellency? they did not come declaming into the world: they were not born with orations in their mouths: eloquence did not sit upon their lips whilest they lay in their cradles: neither did they suck it in from their mothers brests. But if you examine the matter you shall find that by incredible paines and daly exercise, they even turn'd the cours of nature into another channel, and cut out a way for the gentle stream of Eloquence, where naturall impediments seem'd altogether to deny it passage: thereby effecting as much as another could bragg, viam aut inveniam aut faciam: [3] Eminent in this respect is the example of the two best oratours that fame has brought to our ears. Of Cicero, who when he had naturally a shrill, screaming, ill-tun'd voyce rising to such a note that it indanger'd his very life: yet by art and industry he acquired such a commendable habit, as none with ease could speak more sweetly than he. And Demosthenes, though he were naturally of a stammering tongue crasy-body'd and broken-winded, and withall had accustom'd himself to a jetting uncomely deportment of his body, or some part of it at least: when to conclude he had scarce any part of an oratour, saue onely an ardent desire to be an oratour: yet by his indefatigable paines he so overcame these naturall defects, as that he came to be reputed prince of the Græcian Eloquence. Though this was not gotten without some further difficulty and seeming vain attempts. Insomuch as he was severall times quite discouraged, and once threw all aside, dispairing ever to become an oratour because the people laught at his orations. yet notwithstanding being heartned to it again by some of his welwillers, he never left striving till he had won the prize.

Go too therefore my fellow-students (for to you I address my speech, my superiours I attempt not to speak to, desiring rather to learn of them more of this nature, but) to you giue me leav to say: Let no man hereafter tel me I despair of excelling in the oratoricall faculty, therefore 'tis bootless to endeavour. Who more unlike to make an oratour than Demosthenes except it were one who had no tongue in his head? yet Demosthenes became orator optimus. Tell me not "I have made trial once and again, but find my labour fruitless." Thou art not the first that hast made an onset, and bin repelled; neither canst thou presage what renew'd endeavors may produce. Would you then obtain this skill? take Demosthenes his course; gird up your loines, put to your shoulders, and to it again, and again, and agen, let nothing discourage you. Know that to be a dunce, to be a stammerer, unable to bring forth three or four sentences hanging well together, this is an easy matter: but to become an able speaker, hic labor, hoc opus est.[4] Would you haue your orations pleas, such as need not be laughts at? why follow him in that also. Let them be such as smell of the lamp, as was sayd of his. Not slovenly I mean, but elaborate, diurnam industriam et nocturnis lucubrationibus elaboratæ,[5] such as savour, of some paines taken with them. A good oration is not made at the first thought, nor scarce at the first writing over. Nor is true Eloquence wont to hurry it out thick and threefould, as if each word: were running for a wadger: nor yet to mutter or whisper it out of a book after a dreaming manner, with such a voyce as the oratour can scantly heare himself speak; but to utter it with lively affection, to pronounce it distinctly with audible voyce.

But I shall burden your patience no further at the present. Those and the like vices in declaming that are contrary to Eloquence, were the chief motives that drew me first into thoughts of this discourse. But I see I cannot reach at this season to speak of them particularly. wherefore with your good leav and gods assistance I shall rather treat of them at another opportunity. . . .

COTTON MATHER

[Cotton Mather published his translations of the Psalms, *Psalterium Americanum* (Boston, 1718), because, as the selection from his preface states, he felt all previous renderings had not kept faithfully enough to the Hebrew original. His attempt to use what he calls "blank verse" sets the translation apart and gives special interest to the introduction (see p. 668). The text is from the preface, pp. vii–xiii, with omissions indicated. For Mather, see p. 162.]

PREFACE TO PSALTERIUM AMERICANUM

§. 3. Our Poetry has attempted many Versions of the Psalms, in such *Numbers* and *Measures*, as might render them capable of being *Sung*, in those grave *Tunes*, which have been prepared and received for our *Christian Psalmody*. But of all the more than twice Seven Versions which I have seen, it must be affirmed, That they *leave out* a vast heap of those rich things, which the Holy Spirit of God speaks in the Original Hebrew; and that they *put in* as large an Heap of poor Things, which are intirely *their own*. All this has been meerly for the sake of preserving the *Clink* of the *Rhime:* Which after all, is of small consequence unto a Generous *Poem;* and of none at all unto the Melody of *Singing;* But of how little then, in *Singing unto the Lord!* Some famous pieces of Poetry, which this Refining Age has been treated withal, have been offered us in **Blank Verse**. And in **Blank Verse** we now have the Glorious Book of Psalms presented unto us: The Psalms fitted unto the *Tunes* commonly used in the Assembles of our *Zion:* But so fitted, that the *Christian Singer* has his Devotions now supplied, with All that the Holy Spirit of God has dictated, in this Illustrious and Cælestial Bestowment upon His Church in the World; and there is Nothing Besides the pure Dictates of that Holy Spirit imposed on him. Now, True Piety, Thou shalt be Judge, whether such a *Divine matter* for thy *Songs* thus disencumbred from every thing that may give them any *Humane Debasements*, be not really to be preferred before any Compositions thou hast ever yet been entertain'd withal. Doubtless, the more that any are desirous to offer unto the Glorious God what is purely *His Own*, and the more concerned that any are to have their *Worship* entirely Regulated and Animated, by the Spirit of God, the more agreeable to them, will be such an *Instrument of Devotion*, as is here prepared. Tho' the *Hymns* have not the Trifle of *Rhime*, as a Lace to set them off, yet they are *all Glorious within*, which is the thing that *Manly Christianity* has its eye most upon; and in the *Spiritual Songs* thus enjoyed and improved, thou mayst most hope to have the Holy Spirit of God, who indited them, *speaking* unto thee, even such Things as *cannot be uttered*.

But that our **Cantional** [1] may be furnished with a superabundance, and the Faithful be plentifully feasted with *Angels Food*, Behold, an Addition of Passages Collected in Metre, (but still as exactly translated) from some *other parts* of the Sacred Scriptures, to answer the various occasions of Christianity.

§. 4. For the *New Translation* of the Psalms, which is here endeavoured, an *Appeal* may be with much Assurance made, unto all that are Masters of the **Hebrew Tongue**, whether it be not much more agreeable to the *Original*, than the *Old* one, or than any that has yet been offered unto the World. Perhaps there is more Liberty taken here in Translating the *First Verse* of the *Psalter*, than almost any Verse in the whole Book beside. It keeps close to the *Original;* and even when a *word of supply* is introduced, it is usually a needless Complement unto the *care of exactness*, to distinguish it at all, as we have done, with an *Italica-Character;* for it is really in the Intention and Emphasis of the *Original*. Yea, the just *Laws of Translation* had not been at all violated, if a much greater Liberty had been taken, for the beating out of the Golden and Massy *Hebrew* into a more *Extended English*. For, it may be observed, if you Translate a *French Book*, suppose, into *English*, you turn it into *English Phrase*, and make not a *French English* of it; For, *Il fait froid*, for instance, you do not say, *It makes Cold*, but, *It is Cold*. We have tied our selves to *Hebraisms*, more scrupulously, than there is real occasion for. . . .

§. 5. Most certainly, our Translation of the Psalms, without the Fetters of *Rhime* upon it, can be justly esteemed no prejudice to the Character of *Poetry* in the performance. For indeed, however it is now appropriated, according to the true sense of the Term, to *Rhythme* it self a *Similis Desinentia*, or, a *likeness of sound* in the last Syllables of the Verse, is not essential. Old *Bede* will give you such a Definition of *Rhythme*, and bring other Authorities besides *Austins* for it, that *Scaliger* thereupon holds, all *Verses* wherein Regard is had unto the *Number of Syllables*, to have a claim unto it. Be that as the Criticks on the Term shall please, our *Translation* is all in *Metre;* and really more tied unto *Measure*, than the *Original* appears to have been, by all the Examinations that have as yet been employ'd upon it. . . .

I am therefore strongly of the Opinion, That the *Poesie* of the Ancient *Hebrews*, knew no *Measure*, but that of the unknown *Music*, wherein it was to be accommodated. Our PSALMS in the *Hebrew*, are not so much *Metrical* as *Musical;* And hence, the very Inscriptions of them sometimes intimate, that there was a sort of *Melody*, unto which they were adapted. It is true, the *Oriental Nations* at this day, have their *Metred Poetry;* But it is of a late Original. However, 'tis very certain, that all the skill in the World, will hardly find the Rules of that *Metred Poetry* observed with any exactness in the Songs of the Sacred Scriptures. There is little value to be set on the Authority, of either *Philo*, or *Josephus*, and and after them, of *Jerom*, who quotes *Origen* and *Eusebius* for it, when they go to resolve the *Hebrew Poesie*, into I know not what, *Lyricks* and *Hexameters*. And therefore it may be hoped, that our Version may be released from the *Chime* of a, *Similis Desinentia*, without being censured for *Unpoetical*. The *Sublime Thought*, and the *Divine Flame*, alone is enough, to challenge the Character of *Poetry* for these Holy Composures. And if any *Beauties* be wanting, 'tis owing to the lowness of the *Language*, whereinto a strict and close *Translation*, is what we are here tied unto.

JOHN BULKLEY, 1679–1731

[The Reverend Mr. John Bulkley of Colchester, Connecticut, was the brilliant son of the Reverend Mr. Gershom Bulkley. He was graduated from Harvard College in 1699, and like his more famous father devoted his life to medicine as well as to the service of Christ. Isolation only whetted the curiosity of this orthodox Calvinist, in philosophy, politics, and polite letters. He was reckoned by Charles Chauncy (1705–1787) one of "the three first for extent and strength of genius and powers New-England has ever yet produced" (*Collections of the Massachusetts Historical Society*, first series, X, 155).

Bulkley's preface to the *Poetical Meditations* (1725) of Roger Wolcott (see p. 657) is both an essay upon poetry and upon the rights of man. It was reprinted in part as "An Inquiry into the Right of the Aboriginal Natives to the Lands in America," in *Collections of the Massachusetts Historical Society*, first series, IV (1795), 159–181. For biographical data, see Sibley, *Biographical Sketches*, IV, 450–454. The text following is from the 1725 edition, pp. i–x, with omissions indicated.]

PREFACE TO WOLCOTT'S POETICAL MEDITATIONS

§ 1. The buisy and restless Soul of Man which in all Ages has been Fruitful in *Many Inventions*, as it has been greatly Disserviceable to the Good and Comfort of Humane Life by the Discovery of things Prejudicial to it; so at the same time may we not say, has made some Compensation by the Invention of others of a Proportionable Advantage and Benefit. It were easy by a detail of some of the many Useful Arts found out by Man to give Evidence of this, but it must Suffice at Present, to Instance in one only, *viz.* That *Art of Writing* or Expressing all Sounds, and Consequently the Conceptions of our Minds, by a *Few Letters Variously Disposed or Plac'd*, the Commodity or Profit of which to Mankin'd is so Various & Extensive as not to be easily accounted for. This Art is stiled by One **Admirandarum Omnium inventionum humanarum Signaculum. i. e.* The Wonder or Master-piece of all Humane Inventions: And how deservedly is it so, whether we Speak with Reference to the *Strangeness* or the *Benefit* of it? How Strange is it that by the Various Disposition of so *Few Letters* as Our *Alphabet* contains, *all Sounds* should be express'd, and thereby all the Conceptions or Ideals of our Minds! And as for the *Commodity* of it; not to mention others, from hence it comes to pass that we are Furnish'd with so much Useful History, which bringing into our View both Persons and Things most distant from us in time and place, does greatly delight and entertain us, and at the same time Instruct or Teach and Furnish us with a main part of our most useful Knowledge.

§ 2 In the Early Ages of the World, before this most certain way of Communicating the Knowledge of things was found out; other *Mediums* were made use of for that end, the Principal of which seems to have been Representative *Symbols* or *Hieroglyphicks*, which way or Method of Communication every one knows still Obtains among many *Unletter'd Nations* in the World. But this as its very uncertain on the Account of that great Variety of *Interpretations* such *Symbols* are liable to, and as the Misconstruction of them, its reasonable to think, has been none of the least Prolifick Fountains of the *Heathen Mythology*, by which the Antient & True Tradition of the First Ages of the World has been so much Corrupted and Alter'd, so is now out of use with such Nations, as among whom the *Use of Letters* has been Introduced. I said above that to this we are Debtors for the useful History we are Furnish'd with: and I must observe on this Occasion that there are two ways in which those who have Oblig'd us with it, according to

*Galileo. [*Wolcott's note.*]

their different Genius and Humours, have Improv'd this Noble Invention in Composing the Historys they have put into our Hands; that some therein have Confin'd themselves to *Poetical Numbers* and *Measures*, others not so restricting themselves, have Written in *Prose*, which last in latter Ages has been the more common way. That a considerable part, especially of our more *Ancient History*, is delivered to us in the former of these ways, is known to most that are not Strangers to Books, a considerable part of the Writings both of the *Latin* and *Greek* Poets what are they but *Poemata Historica?* Among the former, *Ovid* assures us his Book *Metamorphoseon*, in part, at least is no other; when in the beginning of it he Invokes the Gods in these Words, *viz.*

——Dij Cœptis (——)
Adspirate meis, Primaque ab Origine Mundi
Ad mea Perpetuum deducite Tempora carmen,

In English thus rendred by one,[1]

Ye Gods Vouchsafe (——————
——————————)
To further this mine Enterprise;
  and from the World begun,
Grant that my Verse may to my time
  his Course directly run.

And whoever has read it with understanding can't but see its so. . . .

. . . Its true he Writes in the Strain and Manner of others of his Tribe, who are wont generally to mingle a great deal of *Mythology* with the Truth; yet notwithstanding how easy is it for every Intelligent Reader to trace in him the Footsteps of the Sacred History, particularly in its accounts of the most Early Times?

§ 4. And may we not with equal Truth say the same of *Virgils* Æneids? which seem to be no other than a *Mythological* History of the Affairs of *Æneas*, or the Various Occurrences of his Life; to which *Homer* his *Iliads* with others from the *Greeks* might be added. Its Observed by some Learned Men, that this was the most Antient way of Writing, and that *Prose* is only an Imitation of *Poetry*, and that the *Grecians* in particular at their first delivery from *Barbarism*, had all their Phylosophy and Instruction from the *Poets*, such as *Orpheus*, *Hesiod*, *Parmenides*, *Xenophanes*, &c.—which seems to have Occasion'd those Lines of *Horace*, *Cap. de Arte Poetica*

——Fuit hæc sapientia quondam
Publica privatis Sacernere, sacra Profanis:
Concubitu Prohibere Vago; dare jura Maritis:
Oppida moliri: leges incidere ligno.
Sic honor & nomen Divinis Vatibus atque
Carminibus venit.

The sum of which is this, *viz.*

That in Old Time *Poets* were the Lights and Instructors of the World, and gave Laws to Men for their Conduct in their several Relations and Affairs of Life.

And Finally, To this seems to agree that of *Cato* in his Distichs,

Si Deus est Animus nobis ut carmina dicunt,

If God a Spirit be as Poets Teach, *&c.*

§ 5. I have premis'd this in way of *Apology* for the manner in which this *Worthy Person* has given us the *Ensuing History*, in Composing which he has Diverted some of his *Leisure Hours*. And from hence tis evident he has for a Precedent some of the most *Antient History*, and has trod in the steps of many of the most Eminent *Sages*, and earliest *Writers* History gives us any Knowledge of, who have taken that same way to raise up Monuments to, and eternize the Names and Actions of their Admired *Heroes*.

§ 6. Its undoubtedly true that as the Minds of Men have a very different *Cast*, *Disposition* or *Genius* leading to & accomplishing for very differing Improvements, so generally speaking, those are the most Accomplished to make a Judgment on any Performance that have by Nature a Genius Leading to and Accomplishing for the same: And it being so, and withal there being none among the *whole number of Mortals* less furnish'd for a Performance of this Nature *than my self*, I may well be excus'd in Omitting the part of a *Censor* or *Judge* upon it, further than to say that the Intelligent Reader will herein discern an uncommon *Vigour* of *Mind*, considerable *Reading*, and see reason to say, that herein we have a *Specimen* what good parts cultivated with a laudable Ambition to Improve in Knowledge will do, tho' not Assisted with those Advantages of *Education* which some are favoured withal.

§ 7. Some there are that have remark't, That the *Accomplish'd Poet* and the *Great Man* are things seldom meeting together *in one Person*, Or that its rare those Powers of Mind that *make* the one, are found *United* with those that Constitute the other. And perhaps it may be a Truth which for the main holds true. For whereas what is properly call'd *Wit*, (which is no other than a ready Assemblage of Ideas, or a putting those together with quickness & variety wherein there can be found any *Congruity* or *Resemblance;* or to speak more plain, an aptness at Metaphor and Allusion) is what, as I take it, makes the *Accomplish'd Poet;* exactness of Judgment, or Clearness of reason (which we commonly and truly say makes *the Great Man*) on the other hand lies in an Ability of Mind nicely to distinguish its Ideas the one from the other, where there is but the least difference thereby avoiding being misled by Similitude, and by Affinity to take one thing from another. And the process of the Mind in these two things being so *contrary* the one to the other, tis not strange if they are Powers not ever *United* in the same Subject, yet this notwithstanding, all must say, this is not a Remark that universally and without exception will hold true; but that how contrary and inconsistent soever the process of the mind in the exercise of these two Powers may seem to be, yet there are *Instances* wherein they are United in a Wonderful Measure: And many Men in whom we find a great deal of *Pleasantry* or *Wit*, are notwithstanding very *Judicious* and *Rational*. And tho' Modesty forbids me to say this of the *Author*, yet this I shall venture to say, *viz.* That whatever may be said in Commendation of this Performance by the Accomplished for a Judgment upon it; yet that there will not that Honour be done him thereby, as I conceive may with a great deal of Truth and Justice otherwise.

COTTON MATHER

[Undoubtedly the best essay "of poetry and style" written in the American colonies came from the pen of Cotton Mather (*q.v.*, p. 162). In 1726 he published at Boston a handbook for divinity students, *Manuductio ad Ministerium*, wherein he discusses science, experimental philosophy, the classics, modern languages, and polite letters with remarkable acumen. It was reprinted in London in 1781, and again in 1789 under the title *Dr. Cotton Mather's Student and Preacher*. The text of the chapter following is from the 1789 edition, pp. 110–120.]

OF POETRY AND STYLE.

POETRY, whereof we have now even an *Antediluvian* piece in our hands, has from the beginning been in such request, that I must needs recommend unto you some acquaintance with it. Though some have had a soul so unmusical, that they have decried all verse as being but a meer playing and fiddling upon words; all versifying, as if it were more unnatural than if we should chuse dancing instead of walking;

and rhyme, as if it were but a sort of morisce-dancing with bells: yet I cannot wish you a soul that shall be wholly unpoetical. An old Horace has left us an art of poetry, which you may do well to bestow a perusal on. And besides your lyric hours, I wish you may so far understand an epic poem, that the beauties of an Homer and a Virgil may be discerned with you. As to the moral part of Homer, it is true, and let me not be counted a Zoilus [1] for saying so, that by first exhibiting their gods as no better than rogues, he set open the flood-gates for a prodigious inundation of wickedness to break in upon the nations, and was one of the greatest apostles the devil ever had in the world. Among the rest that felt the ill impressions of this universal corrupter, (as men of the best sentiments have called him,) one was that overgrown robber, of execrable memory, whom we celebrate under the name of Alexander the Great; who by his continual admiring and studying of his Iliad, and by following that false model of heroic virtue set before him in his Achilles, became one of the worst of men, and at length inflated with the ridiculous pride of being himself a deity, exposed himself to all the scorn that could belong to a lunatic. And hence, notwithstanding the veneration which this idol has had, yet Plato banishes him out of a common-wealth, the welfare whereof he was concerned for. Nevertheless, custom or conscience obliges him to bear testimonies unto many points of morality. And it is especially observable, that he commonly propounds prayer to heaven as a most necessary preface unto all important enterprizes; and when the action comes on too suddenly for a more extended supplication, he yet will not let it come on without an ejaculation; and he never speaks of any supplication but he brings in a gracious answer to it. I have seen a travesteering high-flier, not much to our dishonour, scoff at Homer for this; as making his actors to be like those whom the English call dissenters. . . .

. . . Nevertheless, it is observed, that the Pagans had no rules of manners that were more laudable and regular than what are to be found in him. And some have said, it is hardly possible seriously to read his works without being more disposed unto goodness, as well as being greatly entertained. To be sure, had Virgil writ before Plato, his works had not been any of the books prohibited. But then, this poet also has abundance of rare antiquities for us: and such things, as others besides a Servius, have imagined that they have instructed and obliged mankind, by employing all their days upon. Wherefore if his Æneid, (which though it were once near twenty times as big as he has left it, yet he has left it unfinished,) may not appear so valuable to you, that you may think twenty-seven verses of the part that is the most finished in it, worth one and twenty hundred pounds and odd money, yet his Georgics, which he put his last hand to, will furnish you with many things far from despicable. But after all, when I said, I was willing that the beauties of these two poets might become visible to your visive faculty in poetry, I did not mean that you should judge nothing to be admittable into an epic poem, which is not authorized by their example; but I perfectly concur with one who is inexpressibly more capable to be a judge of such a matter than I can be; that it is a false critic who, with a petulant air, will insult reason itself, if it presumes to oppose such authority.

I proceed now to say, that if (under the guidance of a Vida [2]) you try your young wings now and then to see what flights you can make, at least for an epigram, it may a little sharpen your sense, and polish your style for more important performances; for this purpose you are now even overstocked with patterns, and——*Poemata passim,*[3] you may, like Nazianzen,[4] all your days make a little recreation of poetry in the midst of your painful studies. Nevertheless, I cannot but advise you. Withhold thy throat from thirst. Be not so set upon poetry, as to be always poring on the passionate and measured pages. Let not what should be sauce, rather than food for you, engross all your application. Beware of a boundless and sickly appetite for the reading of the poems which now the rickety nation swarms withal; and let not the Circæan cup intoxicate you. But especially preserve the chastity of your soul from the dangers you may incur, by a conversation with muses that are no better than harlots: among which are others besides Ovid's Epistles, which for their tendency to excite and foment impure flames, and cast coals into your bosom, deserve rather to be thrown into the fire, than to be laid before the eye which a covenant should be made withal. Indeed, not merely for the impurities which they convey, but also on some other accounts; the powers of darkness have a library among us, whereof the poets have been the most numerous as well as the most venemous authors. Most of the modern plays, as well as the romances, and novels and fictions, which are a sort of poems, do belong to the catalogue of this cursed library. The plays, I say, in which there are so many passages that have a tendency to overthrow all piety, that one, whose name is Bedford,[5] has extracted near seven thousand instances of them, from the plays chiefly of but five years preceding; and says awfully upon them, They are national sins, and therefore call for national plagues; and if God should enter into judgment, all the blood in the nation would not be able to atone for them. How much do I wish that such pestilences, and indeed all those worse than

Egyptian toads, (the spawns of a Butler, a Brown, and a Ward,[6] and a company whose name is legion!) might never crawl into your chamber! The unclean spirits that come like frogs out of the mouth of the dragon, and of the beast; which go forth unto the young people of the earth, and expose them to be dealt withal as the enemies of God, in the battle of the great day of the Almighty. As for those wretched scribbles of madmen, my son, touch them not, taste them not, handle them not: thou wilt perish in the using of them. They are the dragons, whose contagious breath peoples the dark retreats of death. To much better purpose will an excellent but an envied Blackmore[7] feast you, than those vile rhapsodies (of that *Vinum dæmonum*)[8] which you will find always leave a taint upon your mind, and among other ill effects, will sensibly indispose you to converse with the holy oracles of God your Saviour.

But there is, what I may rather call a parenthesis than a digression, which this may be not altogether an improper place for the introducing of.

There has been a deal of a-do about a style; so much, that I must offer you my sentiments upon it. There is a way of writing, wherein the author endeavours that the reader may have something to the purpose in every paragraph. There is not only a vigour sensible in every sentence, but the paragraph is embellished with profitable references, even to something beyond what is directly spoken. Formal and painful quotations are not studied; yet all that could be learnt from them is insinuated. The writer pretends not unto reading, yet he could not have writ as he does if he had not read very much in his time; and his composures are not only a cloth of gold, but also stuck with as many jewels as the gown of a Russian ambassador. This way of writing has been decried by many, and is at this day more than ever so, for the same reason that, in the old story, the grapes were decried, that they were not ripe. A lazy, ignorant, conceited set of authors, would persuade the whole tribe to lay aside that way of writing, for the same reason that one would have persuaded his brethren to part with the incumbrance of their bushy tails. But however fashion and humour may prevail, they must not think that the club at their coffee-house is all the world; but there will always be those, who will in this case be governed by indisputable reason: and who will think that the real excellency of a book will never lie in saying of little; that the less one has for his money in a book, it is really the more valuable for it: and the less one is instructed in a book, and the more superfluous margin and superficial harangue, and the less of substantial matter one has in it, the more it is to be accounted of. And if a more massy way of writing be ever so much disgusted at this day, a better gust will come on, as will some other thing, *quæ jam cecidere.*[9] In the mean time, nothing appears to me more impertinent and ridiculous than the modern way (I cannot say, rule; for they have none!) of criticising. The blades that set up for critics, I know not who constituted or commissioned them!—they appear to me, for the most part, as contemptible as they are a supercilious generation. For indeed no two of them have the same stile; and they are as intolerably cross-grained, and severe in their censures upon one another, as they are upon the rest of mankind. But while each of them, conceitedly enough, sets up for the standard of perfection, we are entirely at a loss which fire to follow. Nor can you easily find any one thing wherein they agree for their stile, except perhaps a perpetual care to give us jejune and empty pages, without such touches of erudition (to speak in the stile of an ingenious traveller) as may make the discourses less tedious, and more enriching to the mind of him that peruses them. There is much talk of a florid stile obtaining among the pens that are most in vogue; but how often would it puzzle one, even with the best glasses, to find the flowers! And if they were to be chastised for it, it would be with much the same kind of justice as Jerom was, for being a Ciceronian.[10] After all, every man will have his own stile, which will distinguish him as much as his gait: and if you can attain to that which I have newly described, but always writing so as to give an easy conveyance unto your ideas, I would not have you by any scourging be driven out of your gait; but if you must confess a fault in it, make a confession like that of the lad unto his father while he was beating him for his versifying.

However, since every man will have his own stile, I would pray that we may learn to treat one another with mutual civilities and condescensions, and handsomely indulge one another in this as gentlemen do in other matters.

I wonder what ails people that they cannot let Cicero write in the stile of Cicero, and Seneca write in the (much other!) stile of Seneca; and own that both may please in their several ways.—But I will freely tell you, what has made me consider the humourists that set up for critics upon stile as the most unregardable set of mortals in the world, is this! Far more illustrious critics than any of those to whom I am now bidding defiance, and no less men than your Erasmus's and your Grotius's, have taxed the Greek stile of the New Testament with I know not what solecisms and barbarisms; and how many learned folks have obsequiously run away with the notion! whereas it is an ignorant and an insolent whimsey which they have been guilty of. It may be (and particularly by an ingenious Blackwall,[11] it has been) demonstrated, that the gentlemen are mistaken in every one of their pretended instances; all the unquestionable classics may be brought in to convince them of their mistakes. Those glorious oracles are as pure Greek as ever was written in the world; and so correct, so noble, so sublime is their stile, that never any thing under the cope of Heaven, but the Old Testament, has equalled it.

MATHER BYLES

[By 1745 the literary essay was a commonplace. A variety of English periodicals had found an increasingly large circle of readers ever since *The Tatler* had appeared thirty-six years before. English literary magazines had circulated in the colonies for many years, but not until 1741 did American publishers themselves initiate such productions. In that year Benjamin Franklin and Andrew Bradford each ventured periodicals in Philadelphia, largely extracts from British counterparts, or from newspapers and recent books. Both attempts proved short-lived. In 1743 Joshua Gridley (1702–1767) published *The American Magazine and Historical Chronicle* in Boston. It appeared monthly for three years. Though most of its essays were extracted from English periodicals, it occasionally gave a place to local productions. In January 1745 (pp. 1–4) appeared an essay in light vein on "the *Bombastick* and the *Grubstreet*" style. It is signed "L," and is identified by Lyon N. Richardson (*A History of Early American Magazines, 1741–1789*, New York, 1931, p. 54, note) as the work of Mather Byles (*q.v.*, p. 662).]

BOMBASTIC AND GRUBSTREET STYLE: A SATIRE.

As one great Design of many of the Entertainments in our *Magazine*, is to cultivate *polite* Writing, and form and embellish the Style of our ingenious Countrymen: So, Instead of a Preface to this Volume, we ask Leave to give the following Piece of *Criticism*.

Clamorem immensum tollit, quo pontus et omnes
Intremuere undæ, penitusque exterrita tellus
Italiæ, curvisque immugiit Ætna cavernis. Virg. Æneid.[1]

THERE have been innumerable Authors, from *Aristotle's Rhetorick* to *Longinus's Treatise of the Sublime*, and from thence down to the Compiler of our modern *Horn-book*, who have written Introductions to the Art of Polite Writing. Every one that can just distinguish his

Twenty Four Letters sets up for a Judge of it; as all who are able to flourish a Goose's Quill, pretend to be Masters of that Secret. The noblest Productions have given Birth to many a supercillious Caveller; Criticks of all Sizes and Dimensions have nibled round the divinest Pages; and Ignorance and Conceit have endeavoured to shake down the most beautiful Structures, in order to build themselves a Reputation out of the Ruins. A superiour Genius, though he seems to kindle a wide Horizon of Light all about him, and is admired by the understanding Part of Mankind, yet he must expect to be the Occasion of a great many Absurdities, with which the unknowing and envious will strive to satyrize him: As the Sun scatters Day through a whole Frame of Worlds, but yet may, in some particular Spots, raise a Fog, or hatch a Nest of Vermin. To conclude, the Science of correct Writing having been a Subject exhausted by so many able Hands, and seeing all the Rabble of Scriblers are such indisputable Proficients in it; not to mention my own Incapacity for such an Undertaking; I shall not be so vain as to offer my Thoughts upon it: But I shall apply my Labours at this Time, to an Ornament of a contrary Nature, which is a Theme intirely New, Namely, *The Art of writing Incorrectly.*

This, I take it, is a Work that I am excellently well qualified for, and I doubt not but to convince the World that I am a perfect Master of my Subject. In the Prosecution of this useful Design, I shall show the Excellency of Incorrect Writing in general; I shall lay open the several Artifices, by which a Man of competent Abilities, may, with proper Application, attain to a tolerable Degree of Perfection in it; I shall produce pertinent Examples from Writers of undoubted Eminence in that improving Science: And in the last place, I may possibly address the World with a very pathetick Exhortation, to follow the Instructions which I shall give them, in order to accomplish themselves in the Art of Incorrect Writing. In short, I intend to entertain the Publick, with a regular Criticism upon Nonsense.

Authors of this Kind may be divided into two Classes, generally known under the Denomination of the *Bombastick* and the *Grubstreet.* The latter of these Characters is easily attained, provided a Man can but keep himself from thinking, and yet so contrive Matters, as to let his Pen run along unmolested over a Sheet of White Paper, and drop a convenient Quantity of Words, at proper Intervals on it. A Person who is acquainted with this Secret, may, with great Facility and Composure of Mind, furnish himself with a comfortable Stock of Reputation, as often as he finds it requisite. This he might do, as without any Ruffle to his own Tranquility, so neither would it prove the least Disturbance to his Readers: For while he flow'd along with that unmeaning Softness, every one within the Warble of his Accents would undoubtedly dissolve away in a supine Indolence, and, (as a late Musical Author of this Species has very tenderly expressed it) be *hush'd into lulling Dreams.*

I shall, perhaps, dedicate some future Essay to the Incouragement of these worthy Gentlemen, but at this Time I intend to consider those my ingenious Fellow-Labourers, who deviate into the contrary Extream; I mean the Admirers of Bombast and Fustian.

These Writers, to avoid the Imputation of low and flat, blow up every Subject they take in Hand beyond its natural Dimensions; and nothing will please them that is not big and boisterous, wild and irregular. They wonderfully delight in Noise and Clamour; a Rattle of Words, and an Extravagance of Imagination, they look upon as the Perfection of Rhetorick; and are Transported beyond themselves, at the Tumult and Confusion that bellows through a Hurricane of Nonsense. In short, that which Men of this Turn applaud as the Masterpiece of good Writing, differs from the *true Sublime*, as a Boy's artificial Kite, wadling among the Clouds at the End of a Skein of Pack-thread, does from the natural Flight of an Eagle, towering with steddy Pinions up the Sky, and bearing full upon the Sun.

If this false Taste prevails amongst us, we shall quickly prove such a Generation of Blusterers, that our Country will resemble the Cave of *Æolus*, where the Winds make their general Rendezvous, and battel and clash together in an eternal Din and Uproar. For my own Part, I look upon it to be the Duty of every one, as far as in him lies, to lend his Assistance in banking out this Inundation of Sound, which, if it finds a clear Passage, will not fail to overwhelm us in a Deluge of Folly and Absurdity.

A Friend of mine who writes in this exorbitant Style, Mr. *Richard Stentor* by Name, shall be the Hero of the present Essay. Mr. *Stentor* as to his exterior Figure, is one of the portliest Mortals that have flourished in our World, since *Goliah* over-top'd the *Philistian* Army. He is moderately speaking, Nine Foot high, and Four in Diameter. His Voice is not unlike the Roar and Rapidity of a Torrent foaming down a Mountain, and reverberated amongst the neighbouring Rocks. The Hurry of Vociferation with which he drives along in the Heat of an Argument, imitates the Thunder of a Cart-load of Stones poured out upon a Pavement. He was educated in a Ship of War, and one would imagine he learnt the Notes of his Gamut, from the various Whistlings of a Tempest thro' the Rigging of his Vessel. I was once so unadvised as to offer my Dissent from one of his Opinions; but I had better have held my Tongue: He turned upon me, and rung me such a Peal of Eloquence, that had I not made off with the greatest Precipitation, would have gone near to have stun'd, and made me deaf all my Days. Nay, I have cause to think my Hearing has been never the better for it to this Moment.

This is a short Description of his external Accomplishments; as to the Qualifications of his Mind, they will be best perceived, by a Transcript I shall here make, from an Oration he formerly composed in *Praise* of *Beacon Hill.* I must inform my Readers, that it was conceived as he stood upon the Summit of that little Mount, one Training-Day, when, as he has since owned to me, the Drums and Musquets assisted his Inspiration, and augmented and deepend the Rumbling of his Periods. It begins in the following Manner—

THE gloriously-transcendent, and highly-exalted Precipice, from which the sonorous Accents of my Lungs resound with repeated Echoes, is so pompous, magnificent, illustrious, and loftily-towering, that, as I twirle around my Arm with the artful Flourish of an Orator, I seem to feel my Knucles rebound from the blew Vault of Heaven, which just arches over my Head. I stand upon an amazing Eminence that heaves itself up, on both sides steep and stupendous! high and horrendous! The spiry Teneriffe, *the unshaken* Atlas, *or* Olympus *divine and celestial, when compared to this prodigious Mountain, sink to Sands, and dwindle to Atoms. It is deep-rooted in its ever-during Foundations, firm as the Earth, lasting as the Sun, immoveable as the Pillars of Nature! I behold from this awful and astonishing Scituation, the concave Expanse of uncreated Space, stretch itself above: and the Land and Ocean below, spreading an Infinitude of Extension all about me. But what daring Tropes and flaming Metaphores shall I select, O aspiring Beacon! to celebrate Thee with a suitable Grandeur, or exalt thee to a becoming Dignity? How does it shoot up its inconceivable Pinnacle into the superior Regions, and blend itself with the cerulian circum-ambient Æther! It mocks the fiercest Efforts of the most piercing Sight, to reach to its impenetrable Sublimities. It looks down upon the diminish'd Spheres; the fixt Stars twinkle at an immeasurable Distance beneath it; while the Planets roll away, unperceived, in a vast, a fathomless Profound!* *****

By this little Quotation from Mr. *Stentor's* Panegyrick on Beacon Hill, my Reader will in some Measure be able to judge of his Manner of thinking, and expressing himself. It appears plainly that he heaps his Subject with improper and foreign Thoughts; that he strains those Thoughts into the most unnatural and ridiculous Distortions; and, last of all, that he clouds them with so many needless supernumerary Epithets, as to fling the whole Piece into this unaccountable Huddle of Impertinence and Inconsistency. *Richard* is mighty fond of great sounding Words, and, let his Topick be what it will, he has perpetual Recourse to them upon all Emergencies. He once took it in his Head to be in Love, and wrote a Poem to his Mistress on that delicate Passion: But instead of the gentle Flow of Harmony which any one would reasonably have expected, and which is indeed essential to Compositions of that Kind, his Numbers stalked along as sturdy and outragious as in any other of his Performances. I my self counted in Fifty Six Lines of it, three *Celestials*, eight *Immortals*, eleven *Unboundeds*, six *Everlastings*, four *Eternities*, and thirteen *Infinites;* Besides *Bellowings*, *Ravings*, *Yellings*, *Horrors*, *Terribles*, *Rackets*, *Hubbubs*, and *Clutterings*, without Number. But what pleased me the most of any of my Friend's Compositions, was, *A Poetical Description of a Game at Push-pin*. Sure, thought I, when I read the Title, there can be nothing very loud and impetuous upon so trivial a Matter as This. How I was surprized out of my mistake, my Reader will in some Measure conceive, when he understands that the first Distich of the Poem runs thus,

Rage, fire, and fury in my bosom roll,
And all the gods rush headlong on my soul.

He then proceeded to compare the Pins to two Comets, whose Heads, as he expressed it, enlightned the boundless Desarts of the Skies with a bloody Glare, and threw behind them the ruddy Volumes of their tremendous Trains, into the tractless Wastes of Immensity. When the Pins met in the Progress of the Game, for a Similitude, he supposed the two Continents to be tossed from their Foundations, and encounter, with a direful Concussion, in the midst of the briny *Atlantick:* or rather, *says he*, as if two Systems of Worlds, Suns, Planets and all, should be hurled resistless one against another, and dash a horrible *Chaos*, from the general Ruins of Matter, and Wrecks of a whole Universe. He concluded the Poem with the following Lines, which I look upon to be the most finished Pattern of this Sort of Productions, that I have any where met with; whether I consider, the Uncouthness of the Language, the Ruggedness of the Style, or the Disproportion and Extravagance of the Images. Speaking of the Pins he says,

The Bars of Brass, harsh-crashing, loud resound,
And jarring discords rend th' astonish'd ground.
So when aloft dire hurricanes arise,
And with horrendous shatterings burst the skies,
Dread ghastly terrors drive along in crowds,
And hideous thunder howls amongst the clouds;
Eternal whirlwinds on the ocean roar,
Infinite earth-quakes rock the bounding shore.

I shall conclude these Remarks upon Bombast, with an Observation which I ought in Justice to make, in favour of those who fall into it; *viz. That no Person can be a considerable Proficient this way, who has not a good Share of natural Powers and Abilities*. Hence, when we see a Young Man delivering himself in this warm Manner, he is to be regarded as a good *Genius* run wild, for want of Cultivation from Study, and the Rules of Art: And it follows, that should such a juvenile Writer, take proper Methods to improve his Mind, in innuring himself to a close Way of Reasoning, and by conversing with the best Authors, however defective he might be in this Particular at first, he would in the End make a chaste and excellent Writer. Thus it happened to the immortal *Virgil*, whose divine *Æneid* once shot itself into so great a Luxuriance, as to be near twenty Times as Large as it appears at this Day. As his Imagination cooled by Years, and his Judgment ripened, and hasted on to Maturity, his Style dropped the false Glare of Ornaments, and shone with an equal Purity and Elegance; His Thoughts learned to proportion themselves to his Subject, and cast themselves into that exact Symmetry of Arrangement and Disposition, in which they now charm us; And, in a word, a new Beauty began to dawn in every Line of that exquisite Work which consecrates his deathless Fame to the Admiration of all Posterity.

L.

Chapter VIII

EDUCATION[1]

EVEN as the Puritans, "dreading to leave an illiterate Ministry to the Churches,"[2] demanded that their clergy be well trained, so they expected the laity should receive at least enough instruction to understand the ministers' exposition of doctrine. To that end Massachusetts passed an Act in 1647, which was adopted by Connecticut three years later, requiring that every town of one hundred families or more should provide free common and grammar school instruction. The provision was designed to give children enough training to enable them to read, whether the teaching were conducted privately or in public school, and the cost was met by funds taken from the taxes or raised by tuition. The Puritans preserved in secondary education a humanistic standard—a classical training—which in England was being supplanted by courses with a more utilitarian end in view; and it is noteworthy that they required a longer elementary schooling than the Anglicans. The higher education of the Puritans was erected on the splendid foundation of learning that had obtained in the Church since the Middle Ages,—one to which Renaissance and Reformation traditions had brought renewed vitality. It is well, nevertheless, to make two points clear at the start. One is that in no sense did the Puritans foster church schools; the other is that of all English peoples those with Puritan leanings were most concerned for proper education.

No phase of Puritan manners is more difficult to reconstruct than that which traces the method, aims, discipline, curriculum, and support of the elementary schools. From the very first, we may be sure, something was done to provide common schools, though the records are meager. Until a formal provision was made, we imagine that the child was taught at home by his parents or by the older children. Cotton Mather's "Special Points" relating to the education of his children were probably not substantially different from those of all intelligent parents (see p. 724). The child was first introduced to his studies by way of the "reading-schools"—later known as dame schools, since they were conducted by women. Here boys and girls together as a

[1] This account is frequently indebted to Robert F. Seybolt, *The Public Schools of Colonial Boston* (Cambridge, 1935); *idem*, "The Private Schools of Seventeenth-Century Boston," *New England Quarterly*, VIII (1935), 418–424; and chapters II–IV of Samuel E. Morison, *The Puritan Pronaos* (New York, 1936), wherein is briefly digested much that the author's Harvard History has already presented in detail.

[2] *New Englands First Fruits*, p. 12.

group were taught spelling, reading, writing, and ciphering. At this stage also—that is, while they were not over five years old—girls were started in needlework. If the child were moderately apt, he was advanced to the "writing-schools," kept by a man, where he was prepared for the grammar schools at the age of seven or eight. Such advancement depended, however, upon his capacity to wrestle with Latin and Greek, the only subjects taught in the secondary schools; if he lacked the ability, his formal education was over. The reading-schools, as the name indicates, barely carried children beyond the most rudimentary disciplines:—writing and ciphering came later. It is quite possible that many who learned to read were never taught to write, and that therefore such literacy data as are based upon writing ability do not tell the whole story.

The child began his reading with that time-honored device, the hornbook—a printed alphabet list of one syllable words, together with the Lord's Prayer, held in a wooded frame, the whole covered by a sheet of horn. He was advanced next to a spelling book, and thence to a primer and a catechism. "In Adam's Fall/ We sinned all" begins that most famous of American readers, *The New England Primer or Milk for Babes,* of which it is estimated that seven million copies were printed before 1840. If the first issue was printed, as we have reason to think, in 1683, we can readily understand the hard usage to which the primers were put, when we consider that the earliest known copy dates only from 1727, and that the total number surviving is very small.

All available records yield but scant information regarding the number of private schools or their curriculum before 1700. Boys' education could be continued in the free grammar schools, but the training of girls must either stop after their reading-school days were over, or be conducted privately. During the eighteenth century, records show that such private school instruction included for girls not only the rudiments, but instruction in English diction and grammar, and in "polite accomplishments"—French, vocal and instrumental music, dancing, needlework, painting, and drawing. For boys, there was also training in bookkeeping, shorthand, history, dancing, music and horsemanship; and those who could not spare time during the day might attend evening schools. Whether such instruction was offered in or about Boston during the seventeenth century cannot be definitely stated, though the subjects listed are such that it would not be reasonable to think they were introduced only after the turn of the century.

One of the oldest secondary or grammar schools in the country, and the only one in Boston until 1713, was the "Free Grammar School," better known as the Boston Latin School, opened in 1635. Here innumerable generations have been prepared for college, and here, after 1709, they were annually exhibited on a certain day before the clergy and other notables:—a group of sixty who attended school exercises in a body to pronounce upon the excellence of the year's accomplishments. The schoolmaster in Boston and elsewhere was a man of some standing. He was at times exempt from poll and estate taxes, his house was furnished him by the town, his salary was higher than most of the local officials, and upon retirement he might be granted a pension or allowance. But such provisions were not always forthcoming, and a master's tenure was usually brief; he remained as schoolmaster in a town only while he awaited a more lucrative call to some near-by pulpit. The most famous colonial schoolmaster was Ezekiel Cheever, who taught continuously in and about Boston for seventy years. The veneration in which he was held is charmingly told by Cotton Mather in *Corderius Americanus*, and the picture therein sketched of master and pupils is one that deserves to be remembered (see p. 722).

As we suggested earlier, grammar schools were designed only for the training of boys, and such of them as could handle Latin and Greek. To enter, a student must be at least seven years of age and be able to read. The requirements satisfied, the student faced a seven-years' curriculum which, like that of the Elizabethan grammar schools, was exclusively devoted to a study of the classics, with no place for modern language, history, or science. The purpose was humanistic: to achieve a mastery of the classics and a wide knowledge of the best authors in those tongues. Thus the student was provided with a general education and incidentally fitted for college, though probably less than half of any one graduating class went further with his education. It is noticeable that the religious element was relatively small. The student doubtless went to church on Sunday and attended the Thursday "lecture," even as his Anglican cousin was expected to do, but there was no law whereby the ministers' approval of teachers or curriculum was required until 1701, and evidently then simply to assure the town of sufficiently high teaching standards.

The only seventeenth-century grammar school curriculum which has come down to us is that of the Boston Latin School, which may perhaps serve as typical. The entering students were taught their Latin accidence and grammar. When their vocabulary was sufficient and the rudiments mastered, they passed on to Aesop's Fables. By their fourth year they were reading Erasmus's Colloquies and undertaking Greek. At the same time they were supposed to be ready for Ovid's *de Tristibus* and

Metamorphosis, and Cicero's Letters. By the end of the sixth year they would have completed Cicero's *de Officiis*, and the *Aeneid*. In their seventh and final year, with the language difficulties fairly mastered, they could approach classic literature with some ease: more Cicero, and Vergil, then Horace, Juvenal, Persius, Isocrates, Hesiod, and the New Testament. They composed Latin verse, and studied rhetoric and Roman history and antiquities. It is possible that some especially capable may have begun a study of Hebrew. Thus we see that the grammar-school boy was subjected to a stiff but none the less broadening course in the classics, and that he was well prepared to enter college if he satisfactorily concluded his seven years of preparation.

It is clear that religious training in the Puritan colonies was vastly important in the educational scheme, even though the curriculum and administration of the schools were completely free from church interference. All knowledge was, of course, from God, and all training pursued that His ways might be more clearly manifested:—it was a point of view common to educational systems of Europe, and in no way peculiar to Puritanism. Such an approach continued to be true for the boy who went on to college. Actually no more than half of all Harvard graduates during the seventeenth century became ministers.[1] Those intent upon professional theology remained in residence after they had been granted their Bachelor of Arts degree to study further, and thereby obtain such specialized learning as would qualify them for the pulpit; only by such application could they secure the degree of Master of Arts.

Provision was made for higher education almost as soon as grammar schools were established. Harvard College was founded by the Massachusetts Legislature—the General Court—in October, 1636, and the purpose expressed in the Charter of 1650 was "The aduancement and education of youth in all manner of good literature Artes and Sciences" —that is, in "polite letters" and the seven arts and the three philosophies of the Middle Ages: Grammar, Logic, Rhetoric, Arithmetic, Geometry, Astronomy; Metaphysics, Ethics, and Natural Science. It was actually a course in the mediaeval *trivium* and *quadrivium* with music omitted, geometry slighted, the philosophies stressed, with the Renaissance subjects, history, Greek, and Hebrew added. Not only was Hebrew considered the foundation for an exact understanding of the Old Testament, but it was then as later thought to be the mother of languages; a knowledge of it therefore was believed to advance learning in the best sense.

[1] See Samuel E. Morison, *Harvard College in the Seventeenth Century*, p. 562.

Students entered as freshmen and remained four years, living much as students do today, in a dormitory with a roommate, under the supervision of tutors who shared their commons and gave them instruction. For admission to the freshman class the student must be interviewed by the President or by a tutor under the President's eye. If the interview, conducted in Latin, terminated satisfactorily, the boy was then assigned a subject for a theme; if the composition won presidential approval, the boy was entered as a member of the freshman class. The pursuit of higher education then as now often depended upon the ability of a family to raise money enough to pay for it. Tuition and board, which totaled in mid-seventeenth century about £50 to £75 for the four years, might be paid in produce, for the college ran the commons. His financial obligations discharged, the student, with his classmates, was put in charge of one of the two or three tutors, who acted as instructor in all subjects and as "class officer" for that group throughout their four years.

The curriculum at some points was a continuation of the work undertaken in grammar school, although broadened and deepened. Hesiod was read, as well as Sophocles, Euripides, Homer, and Theocritus. The boy was expected to dispute syllogistically at stated intervals, and at the end of his senior year he must demonstrate his ability to defend a thesis: some philosophical problem which would bring to bear all the arts of persuasion, logic, and rhetoric which he had studied. This final exercise took place at Commencement, and like all other elements of college life—recitations, reports, and even informal conversations—must be delivered in Latin. The training that the colonial college offered, both formally in the classroom and informally in close association with the tutors, was liberal in the true sense of the term—the education of gentlemen. Whoever fears that the Puritan boy had no time to play or lacked red blood must look more closely at the record, for in his free moments we find him copying or imitating the amorous verses of Spenser, Sidney, or Herrick; we see him too consuming much beef, bread, and beer; and we wonder how many fathers must have taken their sons into conference to inquire why the bill for broken window-glass mounted so high.

In its own day President Chauncy's commencement address in 1655 (see p. 705) was no doubt considered sufficient answer to those who thought that the provincial college should serve only the church by training men for the ministry; and the letter of Leonard Hoar to his freshman nephew (see p. 708), written six years later, is warrant enough that a study of the cultural past alone was not thought to advance learning—that a study of the sciences must be cultivated. When at the end of the century President Mather addressed the undergraduates, urging them to search for truth even though the way led through new and disturbing fields of thought (see p. 721), he was enunciating the central theme of Puritan scholarship. Such statements justify the conclusion that in matters of education the Puritans were leaders not reactionaries, as resolute as they were sincere.

NEW ENGLANDS FIRST FRUITS

[No other colonizers in the English-speaking world have provided for higher education so soon upon their arrival as those in Massachusetts Bay. In October, 1636, the General Court voted £400 "towards a schoale or colledge," and by 1642 the first class of nine members was graduated from Harvard College. In the following year a twenty-six-page tract was published in London: *New Englands First Fruits.* It pictured attractively the natural resources, the benefits of climate, the opportunities for converting the heathen, and it made a special point of describing the thriving young college. The promoters of New England took this way to ask for money, and at the same time spread propaganda abroad to counter that which was "selling" the West Indies.

The material for the part "In respect of the Colledge, and the proceedings of *Learning* therein" was very likely supplied by Henry Dunster (1609–1659), the young minister who, emigrating in 1640, served the college as President for fourteen years. Its list of rules by which the students lived and its outline of curriculum furnishes important data about the Puritan educational ideal.

See Worthington C. Ford, "The Authorship of 'New Englands First Fruits,'" *Publications of the Massachusetts Historical Society*, XLII (1909), 259–266. The tract has twice been reprinted in full: Sabin Reprints, Quarto series, No. vii (New York, 1865); Samuel E. Morison, *The Founding of Harvard College* (Cambridge, 1935), Appendix D (where it is given an accurate line-for-line and word-for-word transcription). See further, *ibid.*, pp. 304, 305. The best brief summary of "The Beginnings of Higher Education" in America is in Samuel E. Morison, *The Puritan Pronaos* (New York, 1936), chapter II.

The text which follows is from a copy of the 1643 edition in the New York Public Library, pp. 12–16.]

NEW ENGLANDS FIRST FRUITS:

2. In Respect of the Colledge, and the proceedings of *Learning* therein.

1. After God had carried us safe to *New-England*, and wee had builded our houses, provided necessaries for our liveli-hood, rear'd convenient places for Gods worship, and setled the Civill Government: One of the next things we longed for, and looked after was to advance *Learning* and perpetuate it to Posterity; dreading to leave an illiterate Ministery to the Churches, when our present Ministers shall lie in the Dust. And as wee were thinking and consulting how to effect this great Work; it pleased God to stir up the heart of one Mr. *Harvard* (a godly Gentleman, and a lover of Learning, there living amongst us) to give the one halfe of his Estate (it being in all about 1700. l.) towards the erecting of a Colledge, and all his Library: after him another gave 300. l. others after them cast in more, and the publique hand of the State added the rest: the Colledge was, by common consent, appointed to be at *Cambridge*, (a place very pleasant and accommodate) and is called (according to the name of the first founder) *Harvard Colledge*.

The Edifice is very faire and comely within and without, having in it a spacious Hall; (where they daily meet at Common Lectures) Exercises, and a large Library with some Bookes to it, the gifts of diverse of our friends, their Chambers and studies also fitted for, and possessed by the Students, and all other roomes of Office necessary and convenient, with all needfull Offices thereto belonging: And by the side of the Colledge a faire *Grammar* Schoole, for the training up of young Schollars, and fitting of them for *Academicall Learning*, that still as they are judged ripe, they may be received into the Colledge of this Schoole: Master *Corlet* is the Mr., who hath very well approved himselfe for his abilities, dexterity and painfulnesse, in teaching and education of the youth under him.[1]

Over the Colledge is master *Dunster* placed, as President, a learned conscionable and industrious man, who hath so trained up, his Pupills in the tongues and Arts, and so seasoned them with the principles of Divinity and Christianity, that we have to our great comfort, (and in truth) beyond our hopes, beheld their progresse in Learning and godlinesse also; the former of these hath appeared in their publique declamations in *Latine* and *Greeke*, and Disputations Logicall and Philosophicall, which they have beene wonted (besides their ordinary Exercises in the Colledge-Hall) in the audience of the Magistrates, Ministers, and other Schollars, for the probation of their growth in Learning, upon set dayes, constantly once every moneth to make and uphold: The latter hath been manifested in sundry of them by the savoury breathings of their Spirits in their godly conversation. Insomuch that we are confident, if these early blossomes may be cherished and warmed with the influence of the friends of Learning and lovers of this pious worke, they will by the help of God, come to happy maturity in a short time.

Over the Colledge are twelve Overseers chosen by the generall Court, six of them are of the Magistrates, the other six of the Ministers, who are to promote the best good of it, and (having a power of influence into all persons in it) are to see that every one be diligent and proficient in his proper place.

2. *Rules, and Precepts that are observed in the Colledge.*

1. When any Schollar is able to understand *Tully*,[2] or such like classical Latine Author *extempore*, and make and speake true Latine in Verse and Prose, *suo ut aiunt Marte;* [3] And decline perfectly the Paradigm's of *Nounes* and *Verbes* in the *Greek* tongue: Let him then and not before be capable of admission into the Colledge.

2. Let every Student be plainly instructed, and earnestly pressed to consider well, the maine end of his life and studies is, *to know God and Iesus Christ which is eternall life*, Joh. 17. 3. and therefore to lay *Christ* in the bottome, as the only foundation of all sound knowledge and Learning.

And seeing the Lord only giveth wisedome, Let every one seriously set himselfe by prayer in secret to seeke it of him *Prov* 2, 3.

3. Every one shall so exercise himselfe in reading the Scriptures twice a day, that he shall be ready to give such an account of his proficiency therein, both in *Theoretticall* observations of the Language, and *Logick*, and in *Practicall* and spirituall truths, as his Tutor shall require, according to his ability; seeing *the entrance of the word giveth light, it giveth understanding to the simple*, Psalm. 119. 130.

4. That they eshewing all profanation of Gods Name, Attributes, Word, Ordinances and times of Worship, doe studie with good conscience, carefully to retaine God, and the love of his truth in their mindes, else let them know, that (notwithstanding their Learning) God may give them up *to strong delusions*, and in the end *to a reprobate minde*, 2 Thes. 2. 11, 12. Rom. 1. 28.

5. That they studiously redeeme the time; observe the generall houres appointed for all the Students, and the speciall houres for their owne *Classes:* and then diligently attend the Lectures, without any

disturbance by word or gesture. And if in anything they doubt, they shall enquire, as of their fellowes, so, (in case of *Non satisfaction*) modestly of their Tutors.

6. None shall under any pretence whatsoever, frequent the company and society of such men as lead an unfit, and dissolute life.

Nor shall any without his Tutors leave, or (in his absence) the call of Parents or Guardians, goe abroad to other Townes.

7. Every Schollar shall be present in his Tutors chamber at the 7th. houre in the morning, immediately after the sound of the Bell, at his opening the Scripture and prayer, so also at the 5th. houre at night, and then give account of his owne private reading, as aforesaid in Particular the third, and constantly attend Lectures in the Hall at the houres appointed? But if any (without necessary impediment) shall absent himself from prayer or Lectures, he shall bee lyable to Admonition, if he offend above once a weeke.

8. If any Schollar shall be found to transgresse any of the Lawes of God, or the Schoole, after twice Admonition, he shall be lyable, if not *adultus*, to correction, if *adultus*, his name shall be given up to the Overseers of the Colledge, that he may bee admonished at the publick monethly Act.

3. *The times and order of their Studies, unlesse experience shall shew cause to alter.*

The second and third day of the weeke, read Lectures, as followeth.

To the first yeare at 8th. of the clock in the morning *Logick*, the first three quarters, *Physicks* the last quarter.

To the second yeare, at the 9th. houre, *Ethicks* and *Politicks*, at convenient distances of time.

To the third yeare at the 10th. *Arithmetick* and *Geometry*, the three first quarters, *Astronomy* the last.

Afternoone.

The first yeare disputes at the second houre.

The 2d. yeare at the 3d. houre.

The 3d. yeare at the 4th. every one in his Art.

The 4th. day reads Greeke.

To the first yeare the *Etymologie* and *Syntax* at the eighth houre.

To the 2d. at the 9th. houre, *Prosodia* and *Dialects.*

Afternoone.

The first yeare at 2d. houre practice the precepts of *Grammar* in such Authors as have variety of words.

The 2d. yeare at 3d. houre practice in *Poësy*, [with] *Nonnus*, *Duport*,[4] or the like.

The 3d. yeare perfect their *Theory* before noone, and exercise *Style*, *Composition*, *Imitation*, *Epitome*, both in Prose and Verse, afternoone.

The fift[*h*] *day reads Hebrew, and the Easterne Tongues.*

Grammar to the first yeare houre the 8th.

To the 2d. *Chaldee* [*i.e.* Aramaic] at the 9th. houre.

To the 3d. *Syriack* at the 10th. houre.

Afternoone.

The first yeare practice in the Bible at the 2d. houre.

The 2d. in *Ezra* and *Dan*[*i*]*el* at the 3d. houre.

The 3d. at the 4th. houre in *Trostius*[5] New Testament.

The 6th. day reads Rhetorick to all at the 8th houre.

Declamations at the 9th. So ordered that every Scholler may declaime once a moneth. The rest of the day *vacat Rhetoricis studiis.*[6] *The 7th. day reads Divinity Catecheticall at the 8th. houre, Common places at the 9th. houre.*

Afternoone.

The first houre reads history in the Winter,

The nature of plants in the Summer

The summe of every Lecture shall be examined, before the new Lecture be read.

Every Schollar, that on proofe is found able to read the Originalls of the *Old* and *New Testament* into the Latine tongue, and to resolve them *Logically;* withall being of godly life and conversation; And at any publick Act hath the Approbation of the Overseers and Master of the Colledge, is fit to be dignified with his first Degree.

Every Schollar that giveth up in writing a *System*, or *Synopsis*, or summe of *Logick*, Naturall and Morall *Phylosophy*, *Arithmetick*, *Geometry* and *Astronomy:* and is ready to defend his *Theses* or positions: withall skilled in the Originalls as abovesaid: and of godly life & conversation: and so approved by the Overseers and Master of the Colledge, at any publique *Act*, is fit to be dignified with his 2d. Degree.

CHARLES CHAUNCY, 1591–1671/2

[With Cotton and Hooker, Charles Chauncy was reckoned one of the most learned men of his day. Silenced in England, he emigrated to New England in 1638, and was settled as pastor first at Plymouth and later at Scituate; but his somewhat truculent casuistry—principally his defense of "total immersion"—made him unwelcome to orthodox Puritans. He was on his way through Boston to return to England in 1654, when he was offered the presidency of Harvard College. He accepted the post, promising to keep his unorthodox ideas to himself, and continued in office till his death.

Gods Mercy, shewed to his people in giving them a faithful Ministry and schooles of Learning for the continual supplyes thereof (Cambridge, 1655), delivered as a Commencement sermon, is a defense of liberal education for ministers. Coming from the pen of the leading colonial educator, it significantly answers the tracts which were advocating a purely Christian and Scriptural curriculum for divinity students. See *Dictionary of American Biography*, and Samuel E. Morison, *Harvard College in the Seventeenth Century*, chap. XVI. The text is from a copy in the New York Public Library, pp. 32–38, with omissions indicated.]

A COMMENCEMENT SERMON

. . . But now it is not a verball thankfulness that will serve our turn, (that would be gross hypocrisie) but it must be really expressed, towards the education of youth, & the incouragement of the ministry, and the propagation of the Gospel.

The reality of your thankfulness let it be expressed in your future care,

1. To do (if it be in your power) as *Hezekiah did* 2 Chron: 30. 22. *that spake to the heart of all the Levites, that taught the good knowledg of the Lord* Yea do as *Nehemiah* did *chap:* 13. 11. *See that sufficient portions be allotted & contributed unto them.*

2. Do as *Jehoshaphat* did 2 *Chron:* 19. 8. *reach forth thine hand to send Levites* into the blind and dark places of the country.

3. Be at the cost *to trayn up thy towardly children in good literature:* parents are commanded to *trayn up their children Ephes.* 6. 4. *in putting understanding & instruction* into them: as if children were like bruit beasts without it.

4. In *relieving the sons of the Prophets*, and the *Colledg*, as *Elishah did* 1 Kings 4. 34. In setting up of free schools, as the Lord inables you.

5. If ye be poor, yet *pray for posterity* and means of education, and *pray for the peace of Jerusalem;* and that *Bethel*, the house of God may not be turned into *Bethaven* the house of iniquity, that schools of learning be not poysoned, or the fountains corrupted.

Vse 4. This point may serve for Information, To teach us, that Schools of learning are approved and appointed of God, and of great importance for the benefit of Gods people: Seeing that the Lord works with, & blesseth this means, for the laying up of provision, & making of supplys for the work of the ministry; and the Lord here reckons it up as the chiefest of all the blessings mentioned: and this was always one way (even when there were extraordinary Prophets) of raising up of Prophets &c: And there is much more need of schools now, when those extrardinary Prophets are wanting. . . .

. . . I do much desire that the opposers of schools & universityes would speak plainly what they mean by humane learning, then wee should easily come to some conclusion. Therfore let this distinction be premised, that humane learning may either be taken for all that learning that the heathen Authours or philosophers have delivered in their writings: or else all other Arts besides Theology, as they call *physicks*, *ethicks*, *politicks* &c: take in also the grounds of languages, *Latine Greek & Hebrew*. Now in the former sense, if *Mr. D.*[1] do mean by humane learning, all that learning that the heathen men have uttered out of the light of nature: It will be a great oversight to pass such a sentence upon it. 1. Because we find in Scriptures, some testimonies out of humane writers, as *Tit:* 1. 12. *Acts* 17. 28. 1 *Cor:* 15. 33. &c: which the Spirit of God would not have alledged, if their writings had been utterly unlawfull to read. 2. There are certain principles of trueth written, even in corrupt nature, which heathen authors have delivered unto us, that doe not cross the holy writ, 1 *Cor:* 11. 14. *doth not nature it self teach you &c:* and it cannot be denyed that all trueth, whosoever it be that speakes it, comes from the God of truth. as he is called several times And who can deny but that there are found many excellent & divine morall truths in *Plato*, *Aristotle*, *Plutarch*, *Seneca &c:* and to condemn all pel-mel, will be an hard censure, especially to call universities Antichrists for reading of them. Besides they have treated of the works of God, most excellently in many places, and the works of God ought to be *declared by parents to their children*, Psal. 78. 2–6. Besides they have delivered many excellent sayings of God, and have attested many Scripture historyes, as might be shewed by severall instances, out of *Justine*, *Tacitus &c:* and *Mr. D.* is not ignorant of them, shall all these be thrown away as antichristian, or as lyes?

Object. But they have much profaness and filthiness in them, and besides they are made idolls of in our universities, when as *ipse dixit*, and their authority goeth for currant, as Scripture it self amongst them.

Answ. But 1. All heathenish writers, have not such profaness in them. 2. Those that have, let them be condemned & abhored, & let not youth be poysoned by them. 3. Let God be true & every man a lyer, and let not man, especially any heathen be deified, or his authority be accounted on, or go cheek by jowle with the speaking in the Scriptures: this is indeed to be abhored whersoever it is received, but *abusus non tollit usum.*[2]

II. But now if humane learning be taken in the second sense, for all those Arts that are commonly taught in Universities, as *Physicks, Ethicks, Politicks Oeconomicks, Rhetorick, Astronomy &c:* or also for learned tongues of *Latine, Greek, and Hebrew &c:*

1. I will be bold to affirm, that these in the true sense and right meaning therof are Theologicall & Scripture learning, and are not to be accounted of as humane learning. For who can deny, that the first & second chapters of *Genesis*, and many chapters in *Job*, and the *Psalms*, and diverse other places of holy Scripture, do afford excellent and sure grounds for natural Philosophy, and a just systeme thereof: which *Mr. Zanchy,*[3] *Daneus*, and diverse other eminent Divines have opened & declared unto us? And where are there to be found such *Ethicall, Politicall*, or *Morall* precepts, as are to be found in holy Scriptures? or such principles for the ordering of our lifes, families, or common weals? let any man declare it unto us. And where are there such high straines of all sorts of *Rhetoricall Tropes, & figures*, to be found in any Author, as there are in the writings of the *Prophets & Apostles?* and who can imagine, but that the best & surest Chronology in the world, is to bee found in holy Scriptures, upon which all the computation of times in all ages in the world depends?

LEONARD HOAR, *ca.* 1630–1675

[Born in England, Leonard Hoar was brought by his widowed mother to Braintree, Massachusetts. Soon after graduation from college in 1650, he returned to England to preach, but he was silenced in 1660. During the next ten years he cultivated the friendship of scholars, studied botany, and was created "Doctor of Physick" by the University of Cambridge. He returned to New England in 1672 on invitation from the Third Church in Boston (the Old South), but was never ordained, for he accepted an offer of the presidency of his alma mater to succeed Charles Chauncy. Within three years he was forced to resign for reasons still obscure, but certainly not to his discredit. He died within the year.

The letter to Josiah Flynt was written during his stay abroad, and emphasizes Hoar's conviction that higher education should not merely preserve the cultural past, but should advance learning as well, especially by developing the sciences.

See *Dictionary of American Biography*, and Sibley, *Biographical Sketches*, I, 228–252. See especially Samuel E. Morison, *Harvard College in the Seventeenth Century*, pp. 392–414, and 639–644, from which the text, along with the accompanying notes, has been taken by generous permission.]

LETTER OF LEONARD HOAR

To his Freshman Nephew, Josiah Flynt [1]

[London] March 27, 1661

Cozen Josiah Flint,

Your first second and 3d are before me in answer to one of mine to you the last year: the which you esteemed somewhat sharp but I thought and still doe fear that it was scarce so much as was needfull: and I am sure yourself would be of the same mind if with me you knew the unutterable misery and irreparable mischeif that follows upon the mispense of those Halcyon dayes which you do yet enjoy. The which letter, whilst you fence withall in your first by those seven or eight thin-sculd-paper-put-byes And as many empty excuses; you did but lay more open your own blame-worthinesse and augment my greif insted of giving me satisfaction.

But your two latter epistles are better Containing some acknowledgment of those grand defects, discerned in you, and those errors committed by you: together with your promises of reparation and amendment by redoubling your diligence in your studyes for the time to come. Only remember to doe what you have promised, and I thereupon have believed; that I may see some testimonyes of it in all your succeeding letters; And also hear it testyfyed by others, that shall write to me concerning you. By all things that you can either revere or desire I adjure you that you doe not æmulate those unhappy youths that reckon it a high point of their wisdom to elude the expectations of their friends for a little while; whereby they indeed not only delude, but destroy themselves for ever.

Your account of the course of your studyes, as now ordered, under the worthy Mr. Chancey, is far short of my desire; for its only of what you were then about; Wheras it should have bin a delineation of your whole method and authors, from your matriculation till commencement. Therfore I can still touch but upon a few generalls for your direction.

The first is this that you would not content yourself with the doing that only which you are tasked to; Nor to doe that, meerly as much as needs must, and is expected of you: But dayly somthing more than your task: and that task also somthing better than ordinary. Thus when the classis study only Logick or Nature you may spend some one or two spare houres in Languages Rhetorique History or Mathematiques or the like, And when they recite only the text of an author read you some other of the same subject or some commentator upon it at the same time. Also in your accustomed disputations doe not satisfy yourself only to theiv an argument but study the question before hand and if possible draw in a book on purpose a summary of the arguments and answers on all hands: unto which you may briefly subjoyn any thing choice and accurate which you have heard in the hall upon the debate of it in publick.

Nextly as you must read much that your head may be stored with notion so you must be free and much in all kinds of discourse of what you read: that your tongue may be apt to a good expression of what you doe understand. And further; of most things you must wr[ite] to; wherby you may render yourself exact in judging of what you hear or read and faithfull in remembering of what you once have known. Touching your writing take a few hints of many which I had thought to have given you. 1. let it not be in loose papers for it will prove for the most part lost labour. Secondly, nor in a fortuitous vagrant way But in distinct bookes designed for every severall purpose And the heads of all, wrote aforehand in every page with intermediate spaces left (as well as you can guesse) proportionable to the matter they are like to contain.

3. Let all those heads be in the method of the incomparable P. Ramus, as to every art which he hath wrot upon. Get his definitions and distributions into your mind and memory. Let thesse be the titles of your severall pages and repositoryes in the books aforesaid. He that is ready in these of P. Ramus, may refer all things to them And he may know where again to fetch any thing that he hath judiciously referred; for there is not one axiom of truth ever uttered, that doth not fall under some speciall rule of art.

The Genus on any page, you may (having paged your book before hand) by a figure set before it direct from what page it came: And the species thereof, one or more which, for method and understanding sake shall be set down under it, but not handled there: you may by figures after them direct to the severall pages that are made the repositoryes for the matters referrible to each of them And so need no childish confused Alphabetical indices.

Mr Alexander Richardson's Tables would be as an Ariadne's thred to you in this labyrinth. Which with other his Manuscripts in Logick Physick and Theology, by transcribing, have bin continued in your colledg ever since the foundation thereof among most that were reckoned students indeed. And if you have now lost them I know no way to recover them but of some that were of that society in former times. I suppose Mr Danforth Mr Mitchell and others have them.[2] Mr Hancock a quondam pupil of Mr. Chaunceyes hath his Divinity. But in the utter defect of this, you may make use of the grand Mr Ramus in Grammar Rhetorique Logick (the Mathematiques must be left to your industry and memory unlesse it should be some practicall branches of it, of which you may take short notes) and then for Theology (which you may yet let alone) you have Dr Ames Medulla: Of this Theme I shall be larger: when you shall give me encouragement thereunto by attending to what I have written on the rest fore going.

4ly. As to the authors you should distill into your paper bookes in generall let them not be such as are already methodicall concise and pithy as possible: for it would be but to transcribe them: which is very tedious and uncouth. Rather keep such bookes by you for immediate perusall. But let them be such as are voluminous; intricate and more jejune: Or else those tractabuli that touch only on some smaller tendrells of any science. Especially if they be bookes that you doe only borrow, or hire to read. By this mean I have kept my library in a little compasse: (scarce yet having more bookes then my self can carry in my arms at once my paper bookes only excepted) and yet I have not quite lost any thing that did occur in my multifarious wandring readings. Were a man sure of a stable abode in a place for the whole time of his life, and had an estate also to expend; then indeed the bookes themselves in specie were the better way and only an index to be made of them all. But this was not like to be nor hath bin my condition: and it may be may not be yours. Wherefore, though it be somewhat laborious yet be not discouraged in prosecuting it. It is the surest way and most ready for use in all places and times, yielding the greatest evidences of your growth in knowledge and therefore also the greatest delight. It comprehends the other way of an index to: If for the bookes you read you keep a catalogue of their names authors scope and manner of handling and edition. And so for every severall tract you devise a certain mark, by which you may breifly quote the author from whence you had those collected notes and refer to him for more ample satisfaction in any article when as it shall be to[o] tedious to transcribe him word for word.

5t. For bookes into which you should thus hoard your store Take at present only some quires of paper stitct together, which you may encrease or substract from, as you shall see occasion upon experience. Only let them that concern one thing be all ruld after one fashion; and let them be sewed and written so as that afterwards they may be bound into one volume, in case that you should never have time to digest them again into more handsome order. At least no further then a succinct epitome: or Synopsis.

6. One paper book more adde of the names of all philosophicall authors and divines of ordinary note: of all the severall sects in the schooles and in the Church. Of all the nations famed in the world; of all and singular the most misterious arts and sciences: And of them all write a Latine Alphabeticall Index which by figures shall direct to the severall pages in a book where you have noted or will note the characters commendations and censures which any of them doe give of other and some of the charriteristick differences by which they were known, the time of their rise their progresse subdivisions and several ends. I mean such fragments as shall occur of these things, to you by the by in your reading: and would for most part be lost, if not thus laid up. As for the full history of them wherever that is found, transcribe nothing out of it, for its to laborious and endlesse: but only refer to it. Much lesse doe you doe offer to gather any thing out of the workes of authors who have written volumes to this very purpose, such as are Possewine,[3] Sextus Senensis,[4] Gesner,[5] Draudius,[6] and the like. The great use of this is to preserve these fragments that yourself shall find in your studyes, and could not be otherwise referred. Likewise, that you may know and compare their thoughts of each other especially the moderns; and that accordingly you may be directed and cautioned in the perusal of any of them. Finally that you may have of your own store those characters and lineaments by which you may presently pencill any of them at pleasure: And this not as usually upon prejudice and peradventures; but the testimonyes of some or other that you may also produce. for alway be sure in this, that you note down the author whence you excepted any thing of this nature. But this you will judg so vast as never to be accomplished, and therefore vain to be attempted, you never having heard the names of $\frac{1}{10}$ of those things and persons that I have proposed so that you know not how so much as to begin this platform. I answer that for the progresse or compleating of this work you need not take care: Let it but grow as you studyes grow; you never need seek any thing on purpose to put into this book. And for the entrance I shall shew

it easy. For if you take but one quire of paper and divide the first 2 sheets into 24 narrow columnes, and every page of the rest into two: which also must be paged. Then mark the narrow columnes each with one letter of the Alphabet. And it is ready for use: for tis but to write the name of seid place or person that next occurs into your index with the figure J at it: and again that name, with what is there said of it in your first page of the quire, with the author whence you had it, and its done. And the like of the second in the second. When the index shall grow full tis but write it over again leaving larger spaces where needed. And when that quire shall grow full tis but to take up another and carry on the same columns and numbers. And when they grow to be five or 6 quires to this one index, why then, if that on any name swell to big for its column, tis but to refer it to some other column further forwards. On the contrary if any others have not nor are not like to yeild any thing much upon them, when more titles occur tis but croud those into them, referring them also, as the former, by the index and its figures. Thus I think I have made it facile and plain enough And beleiv me you will find it beyond your estimation, both pleasant and profitable.

7. One more Quire you may take and rule each leaf into 4 columnes And therin also note Alphabetically all those curious criticismes Etymologyes and derivations that you shall meet withall in the English Latin Greek and Hebrew tongues. I still mean by the by: while you are seeking other matters. Not which you may gather out of vocabularyes and Criticks that have purposely written on such subjects. for that were but actum agere.

8. Be forward and frequent in the use of all those things which you have read, and which you have collected: judiciously molding them up with others of your own fancy and memory according to the proposed occasions. Whether it be in the penning of epistles orations Theses or Antitheses, or determinations upon a question. Analyses of any part of an author, or imitations of him, *per modum genésews*.[7] For so much only have you profited in your studyes as you are able to doe these. And all the contemplations and collection in the world, will but only fit you for thesse: tis practise and only your own practise that will be able to perfect you.

My charg of your choyce of company I need not inculcate: nor I hope that for your constant use of the Latine tongue in all your converse together: and that in the purest phrase of Terence and Erasmus etc Musick I had almost forgot I suspect you seek it both to soon, and to much. This be assured of that if you be not excellent at it Its worth nothing at all. And if you be excellent it will take up so much of your mind and time that you will be worth little else: And when all that excellence is attained your acquest will prove little or nothing of real profit to you unlesse you intend to take upon you the trade of fidling. Howbeit hearing your mother's desires were for it for your sisters for whom tis more proper and they also have more leisure to looke after it: For them I say I had provided the Instruments desired, But I cannot now attend the sending them being hurrying away from London by this unexpected providence of your unkle Daniells sicknesse: which with some other circumst: with which its acc[ompanied] dt. nt. a ltl dist. me.[8]

My deservedly honoured friend and colleague Mr Stoughton is coming over. he hath promised me to doe you any civill courtesy either for advice or loan of a book or the like. Therfore to him I wish you modestly to apply your self and hearken to: whom as I am sure you will find able, so I am perswaded that you will find both free and faithfull, to assist you as is meet.

I shall adde but one thing more for a conclusion: But that the crown and perfection of all the rest: which only can make your endeavours succesfull and your end blessed: And that is som thing of the dayly practice of piety and the study of the true and highest wisdome And for gods sake, and your own both present and æternall welfares sake, let me not only entereat, but enjoyn, and obtain of you, that you doe not neglect it: No not a day. For it must be constancy, constancy, as well as labour, that compleats any such work. And if you will take me for an admonitor doe it thus. Read every morning a chapter in the old Test: and every evning one in the new: using your self alwayes as much as you can to one edition of the bible. And as you read, note lightly with your pen in the margent the severall places of remarque, with severall marks. Those I use are: for such as have any thing in them new to me, notable and evident, this sign ·′ for those that are obscure and worthy to consult an interpreter upon: this ‵ For those that are seemingly contradictory to some others, this + For those that must be compared with others this > For those golden sayings that are full of the soul and power of the Gospell; worthy of highest consideration and admiration, thus ∽. And if any 3 or 4 or 10 verses together be of like import I upon the first of them set down the proper mark and double it as ″ ‶ ≫.

2. Out of these latter most eminent sentences cull one or two for to expatiate upon in your own thoughts, half a quarter of an houre by way of meditation. There use your Rhetoricque, your utmost ra-

tionation, or rather indeed your sanctifyed affections: Love faith fear hope joy etc: For your direction and encouragement in this exercise, you may read the practique of Augustine Bernard or Gerard. Or our more modern worthyes I Ambrose, R Baxter, B[isho]p Hall or mr Watson,[9] as to the Theoreticall part.

3ly and lastly, those 2 being premised, close with Prayer. for this I præscribe not whether it should be linguall or mentall longer or breifer: Only let it as wel as its two preparatives, be most solemn and secret: and as tis said of Hannah, the speech of your heart. The barrenest ground, and with but mean tillage, being thus watered with these dews of heaven, will bring forth abundantly: and that, the most excellent fruites. Doe but seriously try these 3 last things, for some good while: and reckon me a Lyar in all the rest, if you find not their most sensible sweet effects. yea (as that Christian Seneca, B[isho]p Hall, said before me so I boldly say again) Doe you curse me from your death-bed, if you doe not reckon these amongst your best spent houres.

Touching the other items about your studyes, either mind them or mend them and follow better. So we shall be freinds and rejoyce in each other. But if you will neither: then (tho I am no prophet, yet) I will fortell you the certain issue of all: viz: that ere a very few years be over, with inconceivable indignation that you will call your self fool and caitif: And then, (then when it is to no purpose) [call] me what I now subscribe my self

Your faithfull freind, and loving unkle

LEON HOAR.

THOMAS SHEPARD, JR. (1635–1677)

[The advice which Leonard Hoar offered his nephew, Josiah Flynt, primarily concerned matters of curriculum. Thomas Shepard, Jr., son of the first minister at Cambridge, emphasized quite different points in the letter to his son Thomas (1658–1685). Shepard had served the College as Tutor shortly after his graduation in 1653, hence his advice was especially apt. Son Thomas was graduated in 1676, and four years later he was ordained pastor of the same church in Charlestown, Massachusetts, which his father served as teacher.

For an account of Thomas Shepard, Jr., see Sibley, *Biographical Sketches*, I, 327–335; for the son, see Sibley, *ibid.*, II, 482–488. The letter was inaccurately printed in Cotton Mather, *Magnalia* (1702), IV, 202–203; also in *American Quarterly Register*, IX (1836), 116–117. The text, together with the notes, is from *Publications of the Colonial Society of Massachusetts*, XIV (1913), 192–198.]

A LETTER FROM THE REV^D M^R THO^S SHEPHARD

To His Son att His Admission into the College.

DEAR Son, I think meet (partly from the advice of your renowned Grandfather to myself att my admission into the College, and partly from some other observations I have had respecting studies in that society) to leave the Remembrances and advice following with you, in this great Change of your life, rather in writing, than viva voce only; that so they may be the better considered and improved by you, and may abide upon your heart when I shall be (and that may be sooner than you are aware) taken from thee, and speak no more: requiring you frequently to read over, and seriously to ponder, and digest, as also conscientiously to putt in practice the same through the Lords assistance.

I. Remember the end of your life, which is acoming back again to God, and fellowship with God; for as your great misery is your separation, and estrangement from him, so your happiness, or last end, is your Return again to him; and because there is no coming to God but by Christs Righteousness, and no Christ to be had but by faith, and no Faith without humiliation or sense of your misery, hence therefore let all your Prayers, and tears be, that God would first humble you, that so you may fly by faith to Christ, and come by Christ to God.

II. Remember the End of this turn of your life, vizt your coming into the College, it is to fitt you for the most Glorious work, which God can call you to, vizt the Holy Ministry; that you may declare the Name of God to the Conversion and salvation of souls; for this End, your Father has sett you apart with many Tears, and hath given you up unto God, that he may accept of you; and that he would delight in you.

III. Remember therefore that God looks for and calls for much holiness from you: I had rather see you buried in your Grave, than grow light, loose, wanton, or prophane. God's secretts in the holy scriptures, which are left to instruct Ministers, are never made known to common and prophane Spirits: and therefore be sure you begin, and end every Day wherein you study with Earnest prayer to God, lamenting after the favour of God; reading some part of the Scriptures daily; and setting apart some time every Day (tho' but one Quarter of an hour) for meditation of the things of God.

IV. Remember therefore, that tho' you have spent your time in the vanity of Childhood; sports and mirth, little minding better things, yet that now, when come to this ripeness of Admission to the College, that now God and man expects you should putt away Childish things: now is the time come, wherein you are to be serious, and to learn sobriety, and wisdom in all your ways which concern God and man.

V. Remember that these are times and Days of much Light and Knowledge and that therefore you had as good be no Scholar as not excell in Knowledge and Learning. Abhorr therefore one hour of idleness as you would be ashamed of one hour of Drunkenness: Look that you loose not your precious time by falling in with Idle Companions, or by growing weary of your Studies, or by Love of any filthy lust; or by discouragement of heart that you shall never attain to any excellency of Knowledge, or by thinking too well of your self, that you have gott as much as is needfull for you, when you have gott as much as your Equals in the same year; no verily, the Spirit of God will not communicate much to you in a way of Idleness, but will curse your Soul, while this sin is nourished, which hath spoiled so many hopefull youths in their first blossoming in the College: And therefore tho' I would not have you neglect seasons of recreation a little before and after meals (and altho' I would not have you Study late in the night usually, yet look that you rise early and loose not your morning thoughts, when your mind is most fresh, and fitt for Study) but be no wicked example all the Day to any of your Fellows in spending your time Idly: And do not content yourself to do as much as your Tutor setts you about, but know that you will never excell in Learning, unless you do Somewhat else in private Hours, wherein his Care cannot reach you: and do not think that Idling away your time is no great Sin, if so be you think you can hide it from the Eyes of others: but Consider that God, who always sees you, and observes how you Spend your time, will be provoked for every hour of that precious time you now mispend, which you are like never to find the like to this in the College, all your Life after.

VI. Remember that in ordering your Studies you make them as pleasant as may be, and as fruitfull as possibly you are able, that so you may not be weary in the work God setts you about: and for this End remember these Rules, viz[t]

1, Single out two or three scholars most Godly, Learned and studious, and whom you can most love, and who love you best, to be helps to you in your Studies; Gett therefore into the acquaintance of some of your Equalls, to spend some time with them often in discoursing and disputing about the things you hear and read and learn; as also grow acquainted with some that are your Superiours, of whom you may often ask questions and from whom you may learn more than by your Equals only.

2, Mark every mans Disputations and Conferences, and study to gett some Good by every thing: and if your memory be not very strong, committ every notion this way gained unto Paper as soon as you gett into your Study.

3, Lett your studies be so ordered as to have variety of Studies before you, that when you are weary of one book, you may take pleasure (through this variety) in another: and for this End read some Histories often, which (they Say) make men wise, as Poets make witty;[1] both which are pleasant things in the midst of more difficult studies.

4, Lett not your Studies be prosecuted in an immethodicall or Disorderly way; but (for the Generality) keep a fixed order of Studies Suited to your own Genius, and Circumstances of things, which in each year, att least, notwithstanding, there will be occasion of some variation of: Fix your Course, and the season for each kind of Study, and suffer no other matters, or Persons needlessly to interrupt you, or take you off therefrom.

5, Lett difficult studies have the strength and flower of your time and thoughts: and therein suffer no difficulty to pass unresolved, but either by your own labour, or by enquiry of others, or by both, master it before you pass from it; pass not cursorily or heedlessly over such things (rivet the knottyest place you meet with) 'tis not so much *multa Lectio sed sedula et attenta*[2] that makes a scholar, as our Phrase speaks.

6, Come to your Studies with an Appetite, and weary not your body, mind, or Eyes with long poreing on your book, but break off & meditate on what you have read, and then to it again; or (if it be in fitt season) recreate your Self a little, and so to your work afresh; let your recreation be such as may stir the Body chiefly, yet not violent, and whether such or sedentry, let it be never more than may Serve to make your Spirit the more free and lively in your Studies.

7, Such books, as it is proper to read over, if they are very choice and not overlarge, read them over oftener than once: if it be not your own and that you are not like to procure it, then collect out of such book what is worthy to be noted therein: in which Collections take these Directions, (1) Write not in loose Papers, but in a fair Paper-book paged thro'out. (2) Write faithfully the words of your Author. (3) Sett down in your Paper-book the name of your Author, with the title of his book, and the page, where you find the Collection. (4) Allow a margin to your paper-book no broader than wherein you may write the letters. a. b. c. d. e. f &c. viz[t] att the beginning of each observable Collection, if you have more Collections than two or three in a side. (5) When you have written out such a book being marked with some distinguishing character (as 1. 2. 3. 4. &c. or α, β, γ, δ, &c.) prepare another of the same dimensions as near as you can, and improve that as the former, and so onwards: which book may be (as the Merchants Journal is to his principal Ledger) preparatory for your Common-place book, as your reason and fancy will easily Suggest how, by Short reference of any subject to be handled, found in, (suppose) the paper book, β. page 10. margine f. Suppose the subject be [Faith] you need only write in your Common place book [Faith] vide β. 10, f: if the Subject be [hope] write [hope, γ 10 d.] which signifies that there is some Description of that Subject [hope] or some sentence about hope that is observable, or some story concerning that Vertue, & y[e] like; In the third paper book marked with [γ] and in the tenth page of that book, begun in the margin at the letter [d] [b] as you have leisure, read over your paper books, wherein you have writen your Collections at large, the frequent perusal thereof will many ways be useful to you as your Experience will in time witness.

8, Choose rather to confess your Ignorance in any matter of Learning, that you may [be] instructed by your Tutor, or another, as there may be occasion for it, than to pass from it, and so continue in your Ignorance thereof, or in any Errour about it; malo te doctum esse quam haberi.[3]

9, Suffer not too much to be spent, and break away in visits (visiting, or being visited) let them be Such as may be a whett to you in your studies, and for your profitt in Learning some way of other, so that you be imparting to others or imparted to from them, or both, in some notion of other, upon all Such occasions.

10, Study the art of reducing all you read to practice in your orations &c: turning and improving elegantly to words and notions, and fancy of your authour to Sett of quite another subject; a delicate example whereof you have in your Chrystiados, whereof Ross is the author, causing Virgil to Evangelize: [4] and as in your orations, so in all you do, labour for exactness, and acurateness, let not crude, lame, bungling Stuff come out of your Study: and for that end, see that you neither play nor sleep, nor idle away a moments time within your Study door, but remember your Study is your work-house only, and place of prayer.

11, So frame an order your Studies, that the one may be a furtherance to the other (the Tongues to the arts and the arts to the Tongues) and endeavour that your first years Studies may become a Clue to lead you on the more clearly, strongly, profitably, & chearfully to the Studies of the years following, making all still usefull, and subservient to Divinity, and so will your profiting in all be the more Perspicuous and methodicall.

12, Be sparing in your Diet, as to meat and drink, that so after any repast your body may be a servant to your mind, and not a Clogg and Burden.

13, Take pains in, and time for preparing in private for your recitations, declamations, disputations, and such other exercises as you are called to attend before your Tutor or others; do not hurry them off indigestly, no not under pretence of Studying some other matter first: but first (I Say in the first place) attend those (straiten not your self in time for the thorough dispatch thereof) and then afterwards you may apply yourself as aforesaid to your private and more proper Studies; In all which, mind that reading without meditation will be in a great measure unprofitable, and rawness and forgetfulness will be the Event: but meditation without reading will be barren soon; therefore read much that so you may have plenty of matter for meditation to work upon; and here I would not have you forgett a speech of your precious Grandfather to a Scholar that complained to him of a bad memory, which did discourage him from reading much in History, or other books, his answer was, [Lege! lege! aliquid haerebit] So I say to you read! read! something will stick in the mind, be diligent and good will come of it: and that Sentence in Prov. 14. 23. deserves to be written in letters of Gold upon your study-table [in all labour there is profitt &c] yet also know that reading, and meditation without prayer, will in the End be both blasted by the holy God, and therefore,

VII. Remember that not only heavenly and spiritual and Supernatural knowledge descends from God, but also all naturall, and humane learning, and abilities; and therefore pray much, not only for the one but also for the other from the Father of Lights, and mercies; and remember that prayer att Christs feet for all the learning you want, shall fetch you in more in an hour, than possibly you may gett by all the books, and helps you have otherwise in many years.

VIII. Remember to be Grave (not Childish) and amiable and loving toward all the Scholars, that you may win their hearts and Honour.

IX. Remember now to be watchful against the two great Sins of many Scholars; the first is youthful Lusts, speculative wantoness, and secret filthiness, which God sees in the Dark, and for which God hardens and blinds young mens hearts, his holy Spirit departing from such, unclean Styes. The second is malignancy and secret distaste of Holiness and the Power of Godliness, and the Professors of it, both these sins you will quickly fall into, unto your own perdition, if you be not carefull of your Company, for there are and will be such in every Scholasticall Society for the most part, as will teach you how to be filthy and how to jest, and Scorn at Godliness, and the professors thereof, whose Company I charge you to fly from as from the Devil, and abhor: and that you may be kept from these, read often that Scripture Prov. 2. 10. 11. 12, 16.

X. Remember to intreat God with Tears before you come to hear any Sermon, that thereby God would powerfully speak to your heart, and make his truth precious to you: neglect not to write after the preacher always, and write not in loose sheets but in handsome Paper-books; and be carefull to preserve and peruse the Same. And upon the Sabbath days make exceeding Conscience of Sanctification; mix not your other Studies, much less Idleness, or vain and casual discourses with the Duties of that holy Day; but remember that Command Lev. 19. 30. Ye shall keep my Sabbaths and reverence my Sanctuary, I am the Lord.

XI. Remember that whensoever you read, hear or conceive of any Divine truth, you Study to affect your heart with it and the Goodness of it. Take heed of receiving Truth into your head without the Love of it in your heart, lest God give you up to strong Delusions to believe lyes, and that in the Conclusion all your learning shall make you more fitt to decieve your Self and others. Take heed lest by seing things with a form of Knowledge, the Lord do not bind you by that Knowledge the more, that in seing you shall not see: If therefore God revealeth any truth to you att any time, be sure you be humbly and deeply thankfull: and when he hides any truth from you, be sure you lie down, and loath yourself, and be humble: the first degree of wisdom is to know and feel your own folly.

2 Tim. 2. 7. Consider what I say and the Lord give thee understanding in all things.

Prov. 23. 15. My Son, if thine heart be wise, my heart shall rejoice, even mine.

Pater tuus

T. Shepard

INCREASE MATHER

[One popular misconception too often repeated has been the belief that Puritan educators were interested in higher learning only as it prepared students by means of a curriculum preponderantly theological. The presidential address delivered in Latin by Increase Mather sometime before 1697, counseling the pupils to search for Truth with evidence derived from the new and disturbing scientific discoveries, is in the finest tradition of humane learning.

For Increase Mather, see p. 334. The English text is from Samuel E. Morison, *Harvard College in the Seventeenth Century*, p. 167, by generous permission.]

A PRESIDENTIAL ADDRESS

IT PLEASETH me greatly that you, who have been initiated in the Liberal Arts, seem to savour a liberal mode of philosophizing, rather than the Peripatetic. I doubt not that the *Exercitationes* of Gassendi [1] are familiar to you; in which he sheweth with many proofs that there are many deficiencies in Aristotle, many excesses, and many errors. It is a trite saying, *He who desireth not to be intelligible, should be negligible;* moreover there are some matters in the books of Aristotle which no mortal can comprehend. Wherefore it is alleged of Hermolaus Barbarus,[2] that he raised a demon from hell, to explain what Aristotle meant by ἐντελέχεια.[3] A right proper interpreter of Aristotle, forsooth! How much in his writings are redolent of their author's paganism! He would have the world uncreated; he denieth a possible resurrection of the dead, he declareth the soul mortal. To Aristotle some prefer Pyrrho, father of the Sceptics; others, Zeno, father of the Stoics; many prefer Plato, father of the Academics. You who are wont to philosophize in a liberal spirit, are pledged to the words of no particular master, yet I would have you hold fast to that one truly golden saying of Aristotle: *Find a friend in Plato, a friend in Socrates* (and I say a friend in Aristotle), *but above all find a friend in TRUTH.*

COTTON MATHER

[Upon the death of Ezekiel Cheever (1615/16–1708), Cotton Mather wrote a biographical sketch of that beloved teacher: *Corderius Americanus. An Essay upon the Good Education of Children.* The tribute to the most famous schoolmaster of the period, with its accompanying verse elegy, bespeaks the esteem in which the venerable master was held. It indicates as well the training which boys received for seven years in Latin and Greek—the only subjects studied in grammar school.

Cheever, a graduate of Emmanuel College, Cambridge, emigrated in 1637. He taught continuously for seventy years, at New Haven, Ipswich, Charlestown, and finally for the last thirty-eight years of his life as master of the Boston Latin School. His Latin Accidence was used as a text for two centuries. Hawthorne's *Grandfather's Chair* pictures him vividly. See also Elizabeth P. Gould, *Ezekiel Cheever, Schoolmaster* (Boston, 1904); and *Dictionary of American Biography.*

Elijah Corlet (1610?–1687/8) was likewise a distinguished schoolmaster. He received his A.B. degree at Oxford in 1631, and emigrated to Cambridge, Massachusetts, where he was master of the Grammar School from 1642 till his death. See William C. Lane, "Nehemiah Walter's Elegy on Elijah Corlet," *Proceedings of the Cambridge Historical Society*, II (1906), 13–20; George E. Littlefield, "Elijah Corlet and the 'Faire Grammar Schoole' at Cambridge," *Publications of the Colonial Society of Massachusetts*, XVII (1915), 131–140. The Elegy is reprinted in *Early American Poetry*, ed. James F. Hunnewell, Boston, 1896. For account of Cotton Mather, see p. 162.

We cannot know how Mather's children reacted to the sententiousness of the "Special Points" relating to their education. The plan was well enough, and doubtless one which all good Puritans strove to execute in some degree. Had Mather been mindful of the principle enunciated by Jonathan Swift in his "Resolutions"—not to apply them all for fear of observing none—he might have been spared the shame brought upon him by his unfilial scapegrace "Cressy."

The text of *An Elegy on Ezekiel Cheever* is from *Corderius Americanus;* that of "Some Special Points" is from *The Diary of Cotton Mather*, ed. by Worthington C. Ford in *Massachusetts Historical Society Collections*, series 7, VII (1911), 534–537, dated February, 1705/6.]

AN ELEGY ON EZEKIEL CHEEVER

YOU THAT are *Men*, & Thoughts of *Manhood* know,
Be Just now to the *Man* that made you so.
Martyr'd by *Scholars* the stabb'd *Cassian* dies,
And falls to cursed Lads a Sacrifice.
Not so my CHEEVER; Not by *Scholars* slain,
But Prais'd, and Lov'd, and wish'd to *Life* again.
A mighty *Tribe* of Well-instructed Youth
Tell what they owe to him, and Tell with Truth.
All the *Eight parts of Speech* he taught to them
They now Employ to *Trumpet* his Esteem.
They fill *Fames Trumpet*, and they spread a Fame
To last till the *Last Trumpet* drown the same. . . .

A Learned Master of the *Languages*
Which to Rich *Stores* of Learning are the *Keyes*
He taught us first *Good Sense* to understand
And put the *Golden Keyes* into our Hand,
We but for him had been for Learning *Dumb*,
And had a sort of *Turkish Mutes* become.
Were *Grammar* quite Extinct, yet at his Brain
The *Candle* might have well been lit again.
If *Rhet'rick* had been stript of all her *Pride*
She from his *Wardrobe* might have been Supply'd,
Do but Name CHEEVER, and the *Echo* straight
Upon that Name, *Good Latin*, will Repeat.
A *Christian Terence*, Master of the *File*
That arms the Curious to Reform their *Style*.
Now *Rome* and *Athens* from their Ashes rise;
See their *Platonick Year* with vast surprize:
And in our *School* a *Miracle* is wrought;
For the *Dead Languages* to *Life* are brought.
His *Work* he Lov'd: Oh! had we done the same:
Our *Play-dayes* still to him ungrateful came.
And yet so well our *Work* adjusted Lay,
We came to *Work*, as if we came to *Play*.
Our *Lads* had been, but for his wondrous Cares,
Boyes of my Lady *Mores* [1] unquiet Pray'rs.
Sure were it not for such informing *Schools*,
Our *Lat'ran* too would soon be fill'd with *Owles*.
Tis CORLET's pains, & CHEEVER's, we must own,
That thou, *New-England*, art not *Scythia* grown.
The *Isles* of *Silly* [2] had o're-run this Day
The *Continent* of our *America*.
Grammar he taught, which 'twas his work to do:
But he would *Hagar* [3] have her place to know.
The *Bible* is the Sacred *Grammar*, where
The *Rules of speaking well*, contained are.
He taught us *Lilly*,[4] and he *Gospel* taught;
And us poor Children to our *Saviour* brought.
Master of Sentences, he gave us more
The [5] we in our *Sententia* had before.
We Learn't Good Things in *Tullies Offices;*
But we from *him* Learn't Better things than these,
With *Cato's* he to us the *Higher* gave
Lessons of JESUS, that our Souls do save.
We Constru'd *Ovid's Metamorphosis*,
But on our selves charg'd, not a *Change* to miss.
Young *Austin* wept,[6] when he saw *Dido* dead,

Tho' not a Tear for a *Lost Soul* he had:
Our Master would not let us be so vain,
But us from *Virgil* did to *David* train,
Textors Epistles [7] would not *Cloathe* our Souls;
Pauls too we heard; we *went to School at Pauls*. . . .
Death gently cut the *Stalk*, and kindly laid
Him, where our God His *Granary* has made.
  Who at *New-Haven* first began to Teach,
Dying *Unshipwreck'd*, does *White-Haven* reach.
At that *Fair Haven* they all Storms forget;
He there his DAVENPORT [8] with Love does meet.
  The *Luminons Robe*, the *Less* whereof with *Shame*
Our Parents wept, when *Naked* they became;
Those Lovely *Spirits* wear it, and therein
Serve God with *Priestly Glory*, free from Sin.
  But in his *Paradisian Rest* above,
To *Us* does the Blest Shade retain his Love.
With *Rip'ned Thoughts* Above concern'd for Us,
We can't but hear him dart his Wishes, thus.
  "TUTORS, Be *Strict;* But yet be *Gentle* too:
  Don't by fierce *Cruelties* fair *Hopes* undo.
  Dream not, that they who are to Learning slow,
  Will mend by Arguments in *Ferio*.
  Who keeps the *Golden Fleece*, Oh, let him not
  A *Dragon* be, tho' he *Three Tongues* have got.
  Why can you not to Learning find the way,
  But thro' the Province of *Severia?*
  Twas *Moderatus*, who taught *Origen;* [9]
  A *Youth* which prov'd one of the Best of men.
  The Lads with *Honour* first, and *Reason* Rule;
  Blowes are but for the *Refractory Fool*.

SOME SPECIAL POINTS, RELATING TO THE EDUCATION OF MY CHILDREN.

I. I pour out continual Prayers and Cries to the God of all Grace for them, that He will be a Father to my Children, and bestow His Christ and His Grace upon them, and guide them with His Councils, and bring them to His Glory.

And in this Action, I mention them distinctly, every one by Name unto the Lord.

II. I begin betimes to entertain them with delightful Stories, especially *scriptural* ones. And still conclude with some *Lesson* of Piety; bidding them to learn that *Lesson* from the *Story*.

And thus, every Day at the ***Table***, I have used myself to tell a *Story* before I rise; and make the *Story* useful to the *Olive Plants about the Table*.

III. When the Children at any time accidentally come in my way, it is my custome to lett fall some *Sentence* or other, that may be monitory and profitable to them.

This Matter proves to me, a Matter of some Study, and Labour, and Contrivance. But who can tell, what may be the Effect of a *continual Dropping?*

IV. I essay betimes, to engage the Children, in Exercises of Piety; and especially *secret Prayer*, for which I give them very plain and brief *Directions*, and suggest unto them the *Petitions*, which I would have them to make before the Lord, and which I therefore explain to their Apprehension and Capacity. And I often call upon them; *Child, Don't you forgett every Day, to go alone, and pray as I have directed you!*

V. Betimes I try to form in the Children a Temper of *Benignity*. I putt them upon doing of Services and Kindnesses for one another, and for other Children. I applaud them, when I see them Delight in it. I upbraid all Aversion to it. I caution them exquisitely against all Revenges of Injuries. I instruct them, to return good Offices for evil Ones. I show them, how they will by this *Goodness* become like to the Good God, and His Glorious Christ. I lett them discern, that I am not satisfied, except when they have a Sweetness of Temper shining in them.

VI. As soon as tis possible, I make the Children learn to *write*. And when they can *write*, I employ them in Writing out the most agreeable and profitable Things, that I can invent for them. In this way, I propose to fraight their minds with *excellent Things*, and have a deep Impression made upon their Minds by such Things.

VII. I mightily endeavour it, that the Children may betimes, be acted by Principles of *Reason* and *Honour*.

I first begett in them an high Opinion of their Father's Love to them, and of his being best able to judge, what shall be good for them.

Then I make them sensible, tis a Folly for them to pretend unto any Witt and Will of their own; they must resign all to me, who will be sure to do what is best; my word must be their Law.

I cause them to understand, that it is an *hurtful* and a *shameful* thing to do amiss. I aggravate this, on all Occasions; and lett them see how *amiable* they will render themselves by well doing.

The *first Chastisement*, which I inflict for an ordinary Fault, is, to lett the Child see and hear me in an Astonishment, and hardly able to beleeve that the Child could do so *base* a Thing, but beleeving that they will never do it again.

I would never come, to give a child a *Blow;* except in Case of *Obstinacy:* or some gross Enormity.

To be chased for a while out of *my Presence,* I would make to be look'd upon, as the sorest Punishment in the Family.

I would by all possible Insinuations gain this Point upon them, that for them to learn all the brave Things in the world, is the bravest Thing in the world. I am not fond of proposing *Play* to them, as a Reward of any diligent Application to learn what is good; lest they should think *Diversion* to be a better and a nobler Thing than *Diligence.*

I would have them come to propound and expect, at this rate, *I have done well, and now I will go to my Father; He will teach me some curious Thing for it.* I must have them count it a *Priviledge,* to be taught; and I sometimes manage the Matter so, that my Refusing to teach them Something, is their *Punishment.*

The *slavish* way of *Education,* carried on with raving and kicking and scourging (in *Schools* as well as *Families,*) tis abominable; and a dreadful Judgment of God upon the World.

VIII. Tho' I find it a marvellous Advantage to have the Children strongly biased by Principles of *Reason* and *Honour,* (which, I find, Children will feel sooner than is commonly thought for:) yett I would neglect no Endeavours, to have *higher Principles* infused into them.

I therefore betimes awe them with the *Eye* of God upon them.

I show them, how they must love JESUS CHRIST; and show it, by doing what their Parents require of them.

I often tell them of the *good Angels,* who love them, and help them, and guard them; and who take Notice of them: and therefore must not be disobliged.

Heaven and *Hell,* I sett before them, as the Consequences of their Behaviour here.

IX. When the Children are capable of it, I take them *alone,* one by one; and after my Charges unto them, to fear God, and serve Christ, and shun Sin, *I pray with them* in my Study and make them the Witnesses of the Agonies, with which I address the Throne of Grace on their behalf.

X. I find much Benefit, by a particular Method, as of *Catechising* the Children, so of carrying the *Repetition* of the public Sermons unto them.

The Answers of the *Catechism* I still explain with abundance of brief

Quaestions, which make them to take in the Meaning of it, and I see, that they do so.

And when the Sermons are to be *Repeated*, I chuse to putt every *Truth*, into a *Quæstion*, to be answered still, with, *Yes*, or, *No*. In this way I awaken their *Attention*, as well as enlighten their *Understanding*. And in this way I have an Opportunity, to ask, *Do you desire such, or such a Grace of God?* and the like. Yea, I have an Opportunity to demand, and perhaps, to obtain their *Consent* unto the glorious Articles of the *New Covenant*. The Spirit of Grace may fall upon them in this Action; and they may be siez'd by Him, and Held as His *Temples*, thro' eternal Ages.

ILLUSTRISSIMIS VIRIS

Tam Pietate, quam Prudentia atque Auctoritate spectatissimis;

Ornatissimis { D. JOHANNI LEVERETTO. / D. JOSIAE WINSLOWAEO. / D. GUILIELMO LEETTO. } Foederatarum Nov-Angliae Coloniarum { Massachusets / Plimouth / Connecticut } Gubernatoribus Honoratissimis;

Caeterisque in Magistratus Onere et Honore Conjunctis, ad Reipublicae clavum jugiter excubantibus, incolumitatis publicae apprime studiosis; Nec non Reverendissimis tum Academiae, tum Ecclesiarum Curatoribus, Theologis Doctissimis et Gravissimis; Omnibus denuo et singulis bonarum Literarum [illegible], benevolis Academiae [illegible]

Theses hasce, quas ([illegible]) Sub Rev: URIANO OAKES, Ecclesiae Cantabrigiensis Pastore, Collegii Harvardini Praeside pro tempore, [illegible] discutiendas, proponunt juvenes [illegible]

Johannes Cottonus.
Cottonus Matherus.
Grindallus Rawsonus.
Urianus Oakes.

D. D. D. Q.

THESES TECHNOLOGICAE:

Ars est ordinata Intelligentiae, Scientiae, Sapientiae, & Prudentiae colligatio & concursus.

2. *Ars praecipuè consistit in Theoria Regulae, & Praxi secundum Regulam.*
3. *Utrumque perficitur per Analysin & Genesin.*
4. *Libri Scripturae & Creaturae sunt mineralia ex quibus haec Regula est effodienda.*
5. *Author enim est Author Artium.*
6. *Praecepta Artis id agunt, ut veteri querelae, Ars longa, vita brevis, medeantur.*
7. [illegible] *est objectum & finis artis.*
8. *Praxis est Theoriae finis, medium finis ultimi.*
9. *Usu confunduntur, speculatione separantur praecognita.*
10. *Genesis & Analysis eadem vestigia premunt.*
11. *In compositione mundi Genesis fuit, in ejusdemque resolutione Analysis erit maximè conspicua.*
12. [illegible]
13. *Non ab artifice Ars, sed ab arte artifex creatur.*
14. *Aliquis in omnibus, nullus in singulis, non est* [illegible]

Non datur Metaphysica ab aliis Disciplinis distincta.

16. *In artium orbe adhuc restat multa Terra incognita.*

LOGICAE.

Dialectica est Ars ratiocinandi.

2. *Logicae munus totum est discernere & disponere.*
3. *Affectio est forma Argumenti.*
4. *Causa cognoscitur per effectum tanquam per aliquid notius nobis, effectus vero per causam, tanquam per aliquid notius naturâ.*
5. *Fortuna (quae dicitur) est particula* [illegible]
6. *Materia est omnium entium a primo communis.*
7. *Forma est principium distinctionis.*
8. *Posita forma, ponuntur esse, distinctio, & operatio.*
9. *Finis rei nihil aliud est quam rei bonitas, movens efficientem, perficiens effectum.*
10. *Finis in intentione est finis conceptus, finis in executione est finis natus.*
11. *Existentia est Essentia actualis.*
12. *Locus & Tempus sunt entia merè Logica*
13. *Diversa & Opposita aequè conveniunt dissentire, sed non conveniunt aequè dissentire.*
14. *Sola opposita realiter distinguuntur.*
15. *Comparatio id agit, ut comparata aeque nota evadant.*
16. *Distributio maximè accurata est dichotomia.*
17. *Totum in distributione, est pars in definitione.*
18. *Pars in distributione est totum in definitione.*
19. *Genus habet naturam distinctam à speciebus, non separatam.*
20. *Testimonium divinum est firmissimum.*
21. *Omnis veritas est certa, licet non necessaria.*
22. *Discreta Axiomata non concludunt, sed distinguunt.*
23. *De axiomate immediatè, de syllogismo mediatè fit judicium.*
24. *Nulla datur syllogismi contingentia.*
25. *Tertium Argumentum est syllogismi Arbiter.*
26. *Explicatus primus est syllogismus refutationis.*

GRAMMATICAE.

Grammatica est Antidotus contrà confusarum linguarum maledictionem.

2. *Suum Idioma servare est omni lingua privilegium necessarium.*
3. *Prima sermonis gratia est purè loqui.*
4. *Notae rerum aliae possunt cudi praeter verba et literas.*
5. *Aliquid de populorum moribus potest colligi ex ipsorum linguis.*
6. *Distinctio inter verba Homonyma est praecipuus Orthographiae usus.*
7. *Quantitas & accentus sunt syllabarum condimenta.*
8. *Syntaxis est agnatura quae Idiotam dirigit in sensum sententiarum.*

RHETORICAE.

Rhetoricae munus est dictamina Rationis Phantasiae applicare.

2. *Rhetorica facit bonum apparens.*
3. *Copia Troporum fluxit ex inopiâ verborum.*
4. *Omnis tropus in axiomatibus si non aptè adhibitus, est Catachresis.*
5. *Hyperbole vel suprà vel infra metam semper volat.*
6. *Hyperbole quamvis ultra fidem, non tamen ultra modum esse debet.*
7. [illegible]
8. *Tropus doctis, figura Idiotis est elocutionis pars mellitissima.*
9. *Apostrophe est orationis circumactio, ut auditores commodius, inopinato opprimat.*

MATHEMATICAE

Unitas est numeri forma.

2. *Extractio radicum est arithmeticae pars longè dignissima.*
3. *Lineae Geometricae sunt reales, quamvis non sensibus perceptibiles.*
4. *Linea non constat è punctis.*
5. *Linea solida oritur è corporis sectione.*
6. *Aequalitas est mensura inaequalitatis.*
7. *Recto non datur rectius.*
8. *Ubi Anguli sunt aequicruri Basis tantummodo constituit differentiam.*
9. *Pyramis est solidorum prima.*
10. *Aequator est praecipua temporis mensura.*
11. *Astronomiae pars utilissima non adhuc ex hypothesibus colligenda exhibetur.*
12. *Astrologia, quae dicitur judiciaria est sani judicii expers.*

PHYSICAE.

Physica est ars benè naturandi.

2. *Physicam tractandi ordo perfectissimus exhibetur in primo Geneseos Capite:*
3. *Adaequatum Physicae subjectum est Natura:*
4. *Non in tempore, sed cum tempore mundus creabatur:*
5. *Infinita non possunt esse principia:*
6. *Natura non agit nisi virtute primae causae:*
7. *Angeli sunt quanti quamvis non corporei:*
8. *Omnis inconstans natura est prava:*
9. *Elementa non agunt et patiuntur nisi per qualitates:*
10. *Monstra sunt* [illegible] *naturae impedimenta:*
11. *Generatio et Corruptio non sunt propriè motus sed termini motus:*
12. *Qualitatum Perceptio non fit* [illegible] *in subjecto sed* [illegible]
13. *Sonus non est mera collisio aeris:*

Dantur tres Animae in eodem homine.

15. *Res intelligitur Intellectione rectâ & Veritas Intellectione reflexâ.*

Voluntas semper determinatur ab ultimo Intellectus practici Judicio.

Ethica non datur specie distincta a Theologia.

Cantabrigiae Nov-Anglorum Idibus Sextilibus: MDCLXXVIII.

Broadside of Theses for a Harvard Commencement, 1678.

Chapter IX

SCIENCE

SUBSEQUENT generations have generally assumed that the Puritans in their day were hostile to experimental philosophy. "Science," as we have understood it, portrays a world subject to immutable natural laws, and at first sight there would seem to be nothing in common between it and the Puritan conception of a universe in the control of an unpredictable deity. Yet the fact is that the Puritans were no more negligent in fostering scientific inquiry than any other group, and were as ready as others to accept the implications of the great scientific discoveries of the century. Even as late as 1650, it was the "absence of mathematical training in Oxford and Cambridge, not any imaginary hostility of Puritanism to mathematics," [1] that prevented students of science from establishing a firm basis for research. Both in the English universities and at Harvard algebra was not studied, geometry was slighted, and physics taught by way of commentaries on Aristotle. Free inquiry into natural phenomena was hindered much more by lack of adequate equipment than by theological opposition.

There was indeed a religious reason for not giving the study of nature too exalted an importance in the Puritan scale of values. The principal business of man in this life, as the Puritans saw it, was the salvation of his soul, not the investigation of curious phenomena or the accumulation of irrelevant data. We must remember that in the seventeenth century natural science had not yet demonstrated its utility by the invention of time- and labor-saving devices, and that the best body of scientific theory available to educated persons still explained very little and provided no indubitable certainty. Consequently John Cotton warned his hearers that the pursuit of scientific knowledge was a very unsatisfying occupation:

> . . . the study of these natural things, is not available to the attainment of true happinesse; For how should that which is restlesse . . . procure us setled rest and tranquillity, which accompanieth true happinesse? . . . In particular, the Study and Knowledge of the passing away of one Generation after another, sheweth us our mortality and misery, and thereby yeildeth us grief and vexation, but no reliefe if we rest there.[2]

[1] Samuel E. Morison, *The Puritan Pronaos*, p. 236.
[2] *A Briefe Exposition . . . upon . . . Ecclesiastes* (London, 1654), p. 13.

However, in such a passage Cotton was not speaking merely as a Puritan, he was voicing the traditional sense of Christian culture. He was actually far from condemning scientific inquiry altogether. Indeed, it is demonstrable that the very tenets of Puritanism favored such inquiry, and that the Puritans therefore welcomed phenomenal proof of natural law in the universe.

The key to the Puritan conception of nature was the doctrine of providence, of which Urian Oakes's sermon is an excellent exposition (pp. 350–367). The natural world was God's providence in operation. Man was free to study nature and arrive at such conclusions as his observations warranted, but the facts should not interest him as facts merely. The Puritan felt that unless he could see the divine purpose in the phenomenal world he had failed to interpret his facts correctly. For him nature was a revelation of the divine order which had preexisted in the mind of God before it was incarnated in matter, and its highest value was symbolic. "The stately theater of heaven and earth," said Thomas Shepard, is a visible manifestation of the invisible wisdom:

> Every creature in Heaven and Earth is a loud preacher of this truth: Who set those candles, those torches of heaven on the table? Who hung out those lanthorns in heaven to enlighten a dark world? . . . Who taught the Birds to build their nests, and the Bees to set up and order their commonwealth?[1]

John Cotton expounded the Puritan attitude in a sermon upon Christ's rebuke to the Pharisees, wherein he censured those who were versed in the signs of the weather, but not in the evidences of their salvation. A red sky at sunset generally does foretell a fine day, Cotton explained; there is some possibility of ascertaining a few natural sequences, and erecting the facts into a "law." For this particular law Cotton offered his congregation the best scientific account he had been able to discover. A red cloud, he said, is a thin one into which the rays of the sun can penetrate, thereby dissipating "the matter or cause of foule weather." But in all explanations of this sort, "every man that observes them to bee evident, yet findes them not alwaies certain"; the best of philosophers "are not able to say that the event hath and will alwayes follow." [2] Furthermore, to what end is this knowledge? Only the lowest practical

[1] *The Sincere Convert* (London, 1652), p. 4.

[2] It is interesting to note that even when declaring that natural causes are unreliable, Cotton suggests a natural explanation for this one failing to create its effect: "yet who can tell, but that the Sunne may gather up new clouds, from the other side of the Heaven, before it rise to us in the next morning."

interest is served. It affects what business a man intends to do the next day, and "if he be crossed, it is not greatly material with him," whereas the signs of his own spiritual condition involve his eternal welfare. Hence he who seeks scientific knowledge for its own sake alone, who is "very quick sighted in points of nature, but very dull and heavy in matters of Religion and grace," endangers his soul. Yet a man who is not heavy and dull in matters of grace, who studies laws of the weather not to rest content with mechanistic solutions but to behold the workings of God within them, will secure true knowledge, "God having usually made this world to be a mappe and shadow of the spiritual estate of the soules of men." It is not the study of nature that is dangerous, it is the study of nature in the wrong spirit; if the visible world is seen correctly, as the map and shadow of the spiritual estate of the beholder, as a means of divine communication with the devout worshiper, then the understanding of its laws and workings becomes an essential part of Christian knowledge:

> This serves to shew you, that it is not utterly unlawfull for men to make observation of the estate of the weather, and face of the sky; our Saviour doth not reproove it in them, but onely reprooves this, in that they were better skilled in the face of the sky, and signes of the weather, then in the signes of the times . . . hee rejects not such kind of conjectures, there is a workemanship of God in them, nor doth hee mislike the study of nature.[1]

Indeed, not only did Cotton say that the investigation of nature was lawful, but in another connection he actually declared it to be the positive duty of all men:

> To study the nature and course, and use of all Gods works, is a duty imposed by God upon all sorts of men; from the King that sitteth upon the Throne to the Artificer.[2]

Since nature was under God's direction, God was responsible for the order, and it was the duty of the philosopher and theologian alike to formulate this order into "laws" of nature.

Puritans did not forbid the teachings of the "new science" during the seventeenth century, and often they were enthusiastic exponents of it; but the student of today must keep in mind that they never abandoned the assumption that God was sovereign and therefore reserved to himself the right to reverse or interrupt the laws of nature, which though usual, customary, and ordinary, were not inevitable. God

[1] *Gods Mercie Mixed with His Iustice* (London, 1641), pp. 113–134.

[2] *A Briefe Exposition . . . upon . . . Ecclesiastes*, p. 23.

could and sometimes did warn men by fire, flood, earthquake, and "blazing star," by apparition and providential intervention, in order that He might chasten whom He wished, condemn or save at will. Yet from the first, Puritans were disposed to place more emphasis upon the rules than upon the exceptions. John Cotton said that miracles were not to be multiplied without necessity.[1] Almost all the "special providences" by which men were saved from drowning or punished by plagues or conflagrations were viewed not as miracles, rending the appointed order, but as instances of God's skillful management of causes to produce the proper effects in accordance with the laws of nature. "God can work miracles, but when ordinary means may be had, he will not work miracles." [2] God will still deliver his faithful children out of Egypt, but not often by such a defiance of His own order as the division of the Red Sea: "we in these days have no promise of such a miraculous & immediate assistance; God works now by men and meanes, not by miracles." [3] As the seventeenth century progressed, the conviction grew that God abided by His laws. Though all phenomena were still investigated for their spiritual meaning, still the Puritan became more and more assured that God almost without exception works within the frame of nature and not by doing violence to it. When Samuel Danforth points out to the general public in the 1665 almanac—the only periodical literature that circulated at the time—that the comet of 1664 is a divine portent of disaster, he is stating a traditional theory of honorable antiquity. When at the same time he holds it to be subject to natural law (see p. 738), he is expressing belief in the Copernican system,[4] whereas European

[1] *Way of the Congregational Churches Cleared* (London, 1648), Pt. I, 42

[2] Samuel Nowell, *Abraham in Arms* (Boston, 1678), p. 11.

[3] John Richardson, *The Necessity of a Well Experienced Souldiery* (Cambridge, 1679), p. 6. The interdependence of the religious beliefs and the scientific can be further illustrated from the fact that once Mrs. Hutchinson started on the road to theological heresy she was compelled to make rash assertions about the unimportance of secondary causes. She horrified the Court by declaring that she had immediate revelations from God, and she sealed her doom in their opinion by asserting that God Himself had promised her He would deliver her from their persecution. They immediately asked her if she expected this deliverance by a miracle, "a work above nature," or "from the hand of God by his providence." John Cotton labored heroically to force her to confine herself to the second sort of expectation, and said before all the assembled people that if she believed she would be saved by a miracle, "I do not assent to, but look at it as a delusion." She would not accept Cotton's distinction, and was banished, among other reasons, for attributing to the deity too free a disposition to work miracles in opposition to the laws of nature and of probability (Hutchinson, *History*, ed. Mayo, II, 384–391).

[4] Zechariah Brigden, a graduate of Harvard in 1657, brought out the almanac for 1659, wherein he eagerly displayed his acquaintance with Vincent Wing's *As-*

astronomers were usually forbidden to teach such doctrine until the end of the century:—here is the "new science" which the young college graduates were so excitedly disseminating into every household through the medium of the yearly almanac (see p. 744). They had gleaned their information from their college textbooks: Robert Boyle's *Usefulness of Experimental Natural Philosophy* (1663); Charles Morton's *Compendium Physicae*—a manuscript text in use at Harvard till 1725; and especially from the popular Copernican expositions of Vincent Wing and Adrian Heereboord, whose works had acquainted the students with Galileo, Kepler, and Gassendi, even before the epochal discoveries of Halley and Newton.

The Newtonian triumph established the concept of a necessary and inviolable system of law which God Himself cannot break even though he created it. All deists were followers of Newton, and there are deistic tendencies perceptible in Puritan writings, though the more central orthodoxy strove to reconcile God's sovereign freedom and the reign of law. Perhaps the New England orthodox rationalism is most clearly seen in Cotton Mather's *The Christian Philosopher* (see p. 750). Mather therein attempts to show how divine order manifests itself throughout the phenomenal universe; he sees God as a creating force in the world of nature as well as a Divine Original for man's spirit and mind. A pedant rather than a learned scholar, Mather depended upon a few intermediary works for his array of data; he quoted erudite sources at second hand, but the resulting compendium is enriched by observations of his own which enunciate the deistic principle that God's benevolence is manifested in the well-ordered beauty of Nature, apparent to man through his Reason. Such a point of view marks the beginning in America of the "enlightenment" which, first expounded by Franklin, Paine, and Jefferson, later flowered in Emerson and Thoreau. But Mather did not abandon his essentially Puritan view that Jehovah is a jealous God who can set all law aside to intervene directly in man's affairs. If he realized the antinomy, he took no step to resolve it.[1]

The colonists were as alert to the new discoveries in science as their English contemporaries who, under the aegis of Boyle, Pepys, Evelyn,

---

tronomia instaurata (1656), the first work in English to popularize Copernicus, and a book already adopted as a text at Harvard.

[1] Evidently Mather was considered by the older generation somewhat "advanced," for on December 23, 1714, Sewall notes: "Dr. C. Mather preaches excellently from Ps. 37. Trust in the Lord &c. only spake of the Sun in the centre of our System. I think it inconvenient to assert such Problems" (*Diary*, III, 31).

and Sprat were stimulating scientific inquiry by founding the Royal Society of London, membership in which body was conferred only for substantial scientific achievement. Governor John Winthrop, Jr., of Connecticut, was chosen fellow at the first regular election of the Society in 1663. He had brought with him to the colonies in the same year a three-and-one-half-foot telescope which he presented to Harvard College in 1672; Newton was assisted by observations made with it in arriving at his laws of gravitation. Winthrop's further active scientific inquiries and his communications of them to the Society (see p. 740), establish for him an important role in the history of American science. No other New Englanders were chosen members of the Society during the seventeenth century, though in 1683 a Philosophical Society was formed in Boston, modeled on the English counterpart; it met fortnightly for about ten years—the first of many scientific clubs in the English-speaking world founded on the plans of the "Illustrious Body" in London. Cotton Mather was elected to the Royal Society probably in 1713, though as he never went to London to sign the constitution, he could never qualify as member in full standing. At the time of Thomas Brattle's death in 1713 the Royal Society desired "his mss. relating to Astronomy, Musick and other parts of ye Mathematicks" so eagerly that they elected his brother William a member in the following year the more gracefully to procure them,[1] but William Brattle declined in modest deprecation of his own talents. The contributions of Winthrop and Thomas Brattle to pure science (see p. 739) were more substantial than those made by any other Americans of their day (see p. 758), though Paul Dudley, elected in 1721, was a frequent correspondent of the London body (see p. 747). John Leverett, elected in 1714, and Thomas Brattle are spoken of as having "many years since perus'd with delight their Transactions & recommended 'em to their Pupils as the best standards of Natural Philosophy now extant";[2] and in truth, there were no higher scientific standards at that time.

A discussion of the Puritan's concern in science must inevitably touch upon the tragic witchcraft trials of 1692. One point must be clearly understood at the start: witches were creatures whose existence was questioned by no one in his right senses, and even as late as the

[1] Letter of Henry Newman to John Chamberlayne, *Publications of the Colonial Society of Massachusetts*, XXVIII (1935), 223.

[2] *Ibid.* Of the nine members from the American colonies elected before 1740, only William Byrd of Virginia was not a New Englander; Thomas Robie was elected in 1725; Zabdiel Boylston, 1726; Fitz-John Winthrop, 1734. The list of eighteen, carried to 1795, is in Samuel E. Morison, *The Puritan Pronaos*, p. 266.

close of the seventeenth century hardly a scientist of repute in England but accepted certain phenomena as due to witchcraft. Three factors conjoined to start the trouble in New England,—where after all it played but a small role in the drama of a great delusion. First, since God could intervene directly in the natural order of events, He therefore could manifest His power against His adversaries in the invisible world; in the second place, no class of literature at the time more deeply impressed all classes of men than chronicles and narratives written to demonstrate remarkable providences wherein God interposed Himself in man's affairs; finally, it was not only the privilege but the duty of ministers to record such providences, for by their scholarly training and priestly office they were peculiarly fitted to perceive, interpret, and justify God's way to man. Now to observe the fatal conjunction of these separately reasonable views.[1]

Four children in Boston were seized by convulsions, and accused an old woman of bewitching them; the woman confessed her guilt, was tried, condemned, and executed by a most orderly procedure of law. The children still being "sadly molested with Evil Spirits," their minister Cotton Mather gave them spiritual consolation—psychiatric ministrations perhaps—to such good effect that they recovered. Elated by his success, Mather immediately published *Memorable Providences, Relating to Witchcrafts and Possessions* (1689), but his book, with its lurid details, instead of leading readers to see that God's power once again had triumphed over Satan, was seized upon by some of the more emotionally unstable as an exciting manual for the practice of witchcraft. Undue prominence was therefore given to abnormal states of mind. The situation was badly out of hand by 1692, when an outburst of accusations against witches gained headway in Salem Village (Danvers)—a parish that evidently had more than its share of neurotic women and hysterical children, and less than it needed of understanding leaders. By September, twenty people and two dogs had been executed as witches, one hundred and fifty were in prison awaiting trial, and two hundred more stood accused. Yet the Court, chosen by Governor Phips, and composed of distinguished citizens, had reviewed

[1] Two books especially should be noted among the great number that deal with the history of witchcraft in New England: George L. Burr, ed., *Narratives of the Witchcraft Cases* (New York, 1914), a reprint of essential documents with an introduction that discusses many details; and George L. Kittredge, *Witchcraft in Old and New England* (Cambridge, 1929), a work that treats the history of the subject in its wider implications. A brief summary of "Witchcraft" is included in Samuel E. Morison, *The Puritan Pronaos*, pp. 248–257, to which this summary is at a few points indebted.

the cases according to established law and had proceeded against the accused only after deliberation among themselves and upon the advice of leading ministers.

The point at issue was this: alleged victims claimed they were attacked by spirits in the likeness of some resident whom they identified. Was the evidence of mere allegation sufficient to convict the accused? If it was, who could escape hanging once the accusation were made? In Europe the best legal opinion, available to the New England court, advised that such "spectral evidence" was not adequate by itself to convict, yet those sitting in judgment at Salem continued to admit it as sole basis for conviction. The position in which even the most conservative and clear-headed gentlemen found themselves is well expressed by Thomas Brattle in "A Full and Candid Account of the Delusion called Witchcraft" (see p. 758). The tragedy is not difficult to comprehend when we recognize the frenzy and mass madness which confused even the wisest. As soon as the enormity of the panic became evident, the ministers gathered to find a way to stop it. That way seemed clearly to attack "spectral evidence"—the one real flaw in the legal machinery. Increase Mather therefore wrote a pamphlet, *Cases of Conscience concerning Evil Spirits* (1693), at first circulated in manuscript, in which he affirms his belief that witches exist, prays that none will think him unfair to the judges, who "are wise and good men, and have acted with all Fidelity according to their Light";[1] but he states positively, "This notwithstanding, I will add; It were better that Ten Suspected Witches should escape, than that one Innocent Person should be Condemned."[2] The Governor harkened especially to the opinion presented by twelve ministers therein added as a Postscript, which condemned the uses that the Court had made of spectral evidence; he ruled such evidence out, and without it the cases fell through; accusations were dropped, and the condemned—if they recanted—were free. But a great blot remained, even though indemnities were granted bereaved families. Five years later the noblest among the deliberative body, Samuel Sewall, rose in church to make public confession and ask humble forgiveness for the part he had taken in supporting a procedure which he had good reason to know was not sound.[3]

In the dispassion of a long-range view of the facts we do not entirely credit Robert Calef's prejudiced tirade directed against the part which the ministers played in the affair, headed by Increase Mather, —who, mistaken, yet was honest. We can only realize that eminently

[1] Page 70. [2] Page 66. [3] *Diary*, I, 445.

sane leaders of church and state, acting in accordance with the accepted scientific beliefs of their day, became momentarily victims of mass frenzy; they soon came to their senses and revised their legal and sociological viewpoint toward the wonders of the invisible world. Witches were never again brought to trial in New England, even though witchcraft trial continued in England till well into the eighteenth century.

It is pleasant to turn from the misty mid-regions of demonology to relate in a few words the story of the role played by Puritans in the development of preventive medicine. The place of medicine in the New England colonies is elsewhere briefly discussed (see p. 386), but one phase of it, the introduction of smallpox inoculation, deserves special record. In April, 1721, an epidemic of smallpox spread through Boston and vicinity, and by June had struck down nearly fifty-nine hundred persons; eight hundred and forty-four died. Cotton Mather, whose essays to do good were never more productive of beneficial results, recalled that he had not only read about the favorable outcome of inoculation as reported in the Transactions of the Royal Society,[1] but that his slave Onesimus claimed to have recovered from the dread disease after some such treatment in Africa. Mather suggested to the Boston physicians that they might profitably give inoculation a trial, but only Zabdiel Boylston among them agreed with him. To be sure, it was a risky undertaking, for the method in use was still untested. Boylston had been attacked by the disease some years before, hence it was useless to experiment on himself. He therefore tried out the method on his willing children and servants. The town was horrified and ready to cry murder if any of them died. A pamphlet war started between the proponents of inoculation, led by Increase and Cotton Mather, Boylston, and Benjamin Colman on the one side, and on the other a very much aroused opposition headed by the physician William Douglass. Feeling rose to such a pitch that the lives of Boylston and Cotton Mather were actually endangered by mob violence. But the good effects of inoculation became apparent —of two hundred and forty-one persons treated, only six died—and a bill introduced in the legislature aiming to forbid inoculation by law failed to pass. In November, 1721, a report of the treatment of cases—the first clinical treatise ever written on the subject—was communicated to the Royal Society and published in their Transactions [2] (see p. 763). It is a document of prime importance in medical history,

[1] See Vol. XXIX (1714–1716).
[2] Vol. XXXII (1721), 33–35, No. 370.

and one which appropriately closes the first period of scientific inquiry in this country.[1]

SAMUEL DANFORTH, 1626–1674

[The significance of *An Astronomical Description of the Late Comet or Blazing Star* . . . (Cambridge, 1665), by Samuel Danforth, lies in the fact that though it holds comets to be divine portents of disaster, it recognizes that they are not "Exhalations," but stellar phenomena, subject to natural law.

Danforth was born in Cambridge and graduated from Harvard in 1643. For some years he devoted his time to astronomical studies, and prepared the yearly Almanacs from 1645 to 1649. In them he presented descriptions of heavenly bodies as well as specimens of his poetry. He was ordained at Roxbury as assistant to John Eliot in 1650, and remained there as pastor for twenty-four years—until he "passed from *Natural Health*, to *Eternal Peace*."

See Cotton Mather, *Magnalia*, IV, 153 (whence the quotation); Sibley, *Biographical Sketches*, I, 88–92. For an account of astronomy in early New England, see Samuel E. Morison, *Harvard College in the Seventeenth Century*, chap. X.]

AN ASTRONOMICAL DESCRIPTION

I. *This Comet is no sublunary Meteor or sulphureous Exhalation, but a Celestial Luminary, moving in the starry Heavens.*

The Truth hereof may be demonstrated, 1. *By the vast Dimensions of it's body.* Some Comets have been observed by Astronomers to be halfe as big as the *Moon*, some bigger then the *Moon*, yea some bigger then the *Earth*. The exact Dimensions of this Comet, I may not presume to determine, but it seemeth not to be of the smallest size. Now 'tis not easy to imagine how the *Earth* should afford matter for a *Meteor* of such a huge magnitude, except we grant the greater part of the lower World, to be turned into an exhalation. 2. *By the smalness of it's Parallax.* The Parallax is the Distance between the *true* place of a

[1] An interest in natural history and botany was very slow to develop in New England, and the fact is surprising in view of the alertness of Puritans to physical science. Fitz-John Winthrop, F.R.S., was the only New Englander to win a place for himself as a naturalist before 1750. The greatest colonial naturalist was John Bartram of Pennsylvania, called by Linnaeus the greatest botanist in the world. Others who made contributions of value on the fauna and flora of the country were John Banister, William Byrd, Mark Catesby, John Clayton, and John Mitchell—all of Virginia.

Planet and the *apparent*. The lower and neerer any *Planet* is to the Earth, it hath the greater *Parallax*. . . .

IV. *This Comet is not a new fixed Star, but a Planetick or Erratick Body, wandring up & down in the etherial firmament under the fixed stars.*

Some learned Astronomers distinguish these more noble and celestial *Phænomena* or *Appearances* into *Fixed* and *Erratick*. Several new Stars have appeared which are fixed, *i.e.* they keep the same place in the *Heavens*, and the same distance from the *fixed Stars*. One in *Cassiopeia* Anno 1572. which continued a year and four months. . . .

Iuly 20 1663. That bright and radiant Star, a Star of the first magnitude, Mr. *Samuel Stone*,[1] the strength and glory of *Connecticut*, rested from his labours and sorrows, and fell a sleep sweetly and placidly in the Lord. A little before Him, Mr *Iohn Miller* [2] and Mr. *Samuel Newman*,[3] faithful, painful and affectionate Preachers of the Gospel, were also taken from us by death. Thus our Pillars are cut down, our strongest Stakes pluck't up, and our breaches not repaired. Is it a small thing in our eyes, our principal Congregations & Head-townes, should be so badly bereaved, as they are at this day?

3. The sad *Mildew* and *Blasting*, whereby we have been greatly afflicted the last Summer, and some of us the Summer before: our principal grain being turned into an husk & rotteness.

4. Severe *Drought* this last Summer, which burnt up the Pastures and the latter growth.

5. Early *Frosts*, which smote our *Indian Corn*, and greatly impoverished our latter Harvest.

Unto these and some other no less threatning Visitations, is superadded this strange and fearful Appearance in the Heavens, which is now seconded by a new Appearance this Spring, concomitant to the translation of our Honoured and Aged Governour, Mr. *John Endicot*,[4] from hence to a better World: By all which doubtless the Lord calls upon *New-England* to awake and to repent.

To this End Consider.

1. What a jealous eye the Lord hath upon us, observing how we carry and behave our selves at such a time as this.

JOHN WINTHROP, JR., 1605/6–1676

[John Winthrop, Jr., eldest son of Governor Winthrop, was probably the most versatile colonial figure in the seventeenth century. After attending Trinity College, Dublin, for two years, he was admitted to the Inner Temple, London, in 1624. He traveled widely before emigrating to New England in 1631, where he founded Ipswich and New London. As governor of Connecticut he secured exceptional privileges for the Colony. His business acumen and public benefactions in both colonies earned for him the respect and affection of all men. Even though far removed from England, he remained in terms of warm intimacy with Wren, Boyle, Stirk, Digby, and Newton. Indeed, he may rightly be claimed as the first American scientist. As physician he explored the composition of plants and minerals, took notes on his investigations, and communicated the results to the Royal Society of London. In 1663 he was elected a Fellow of that body, the first colonial so honored. The remains of his library, rich in scientific lore, are now in the New York Society Library.

The letter here quoted from the *Philosophical Transactions* of the Royal Society of London was published in 1670 (V, 1151–1153), and is a fair sample of the scientific observations then being gathered. See *Dictionary of American Biography;* Tyler, *A History of American Literature*, I, 99–103; II, 311–312. See especially Samuel E. Morison, *Builders of the Bay Colony*, chap. IX.]

AN EXTRACT OF A LETTER,

WRITTEN BY JOHN WINTHROP ESQ; GOVERNOUR OF CONNECTICUT IN NEW ENGLAND, TO THE PUBLISHER, CONCERNING SOME NATURAL CURIOSITIES OF THOSE PARTS, ESPECIALLY A VERY STRANGE AND VERY CURIOUSLY CONTRIVED FISH, SENT FOR THE REPOSITORY OF THE R. SOCIETY.

I KNOW not, whether I may recommend some of the productions of this Wilderness as rarities or novelties, but they are such as the place affords. There are, amongst the rest, 2. or 3. smal Oaks, which though so slender and low (as you may see, if they come safe) have yet Acorns and cups upon them, so that it may be truly said, that there is a Country, where Hoggs are so tall, that they eat acorns upon the standing growing Oakes. This is every year visible in many parts here, there being of this sort of dwarf-Oak whole Forrests in the Inland Country; too many for the Husband-man, who finds that sort of land most difficult to break up at first with his plough, in regard that the whole surface is fill'd with spreading strong roots of this sort of Oak. Neither must it be thought, that they are small shoots, which in time would grow big trees; for, where these grow, there are no great Oaks, or very few amongst them. But whether it be a novelty to see such kind of dwarf-trees bearing acorns, I know not: It was to me, having not seen the like (as far as I remember,) in *England* or *France*, or other parts. Mean time I have observed, that in some Plains, full of these shrubs, there have been no acorns on most of them; but whether in other years they were not fruitful, I know not. Some years, we know, even the great Oaks bear no fruit, which are very full at other times; but this year throughout the whole Country there is plenty of acorns; and I should be glad to be informed, whether this year they have been also abounding in *England*, or other parts of Europe; and if so, or not so, possibly something not altogether inconsiderable may be thence inferr'd. Besides, if such dwarfish Oakes, as these, should be found in other parts of the World, it were not amiss, me thinks, to inquire, Whether it be not some Mineral ground, where these grow; and if so, what sorts of Minerals those places afford?

There are also sent you some pieces of the Bark of a Tree, which grows in *Nova-Scotia*, and (as I hear) in the more Easterly parts of N. *England*. Upon this bark there are little knobs, within which there is a liquid matter like Turpentine (which will run out, the knob being cut open) of a very sanative nature, as I am informed by those, who affirm, that they have often tryed it.

In the same Box are Pods of a Vegetable, we call *Silk-grass*, which are full of a kind of most fine down-like Cotton-wool, many such flocks in one and the same pod ending in a flat Seed. 'Tis used to stuff up Pillows and Cushions; being tryed to spin, it proves not strong enough. The Seeds 'tis like may grow with you, if set in some Garden; whereby the whole Plant may be seen.

You'l find also a Branch of the Tree, call'd the Cotton-tree, bearing a kind of Down which also is not fit to spin. The Trees grow high and big. At the bottom of some of the Leaves, next to the stalk of them, is a knob, which is hollow, and a certain fly, some-what like a pis-mire-fly, is bred therein.

More-over, there are some of the *Matrices*, in which those Shels are bred, of which the *Indians* make the white *Wampanpeage*, one sort of their mony: They grow on the bottom of Sea-bays, and the shels are like Periwinkles, but greater. Whilst they are very smal, and first growing, many of them are within one of the concave receptacles of these *Matrices*, which are very tough, and strong, so contrived, that they are separate from one another, yet so, that each of them is fastned to a kind of skin, subtended all along to all these cases or baggs.

There is, besides, in a large round Box, a strange kind of *Fish*, which was taken by a Fisherman, when he was fishing for Codfish in that

Sea, which is without *Massachuset* Bay in N. *England.* It was living, when it was taken, which was done, I think, by an hook. The name of it I know not, nor can I write more particularly of it, because I could not yet speak with the Fisherman, who brough it from Sea. I have not seen the like. The Mouth is in the middle; and they say, that all the Arms, you see round about, were in motion, when it was first taken. . . .

LEONARD HOAR

[Though Leonard Hoar is remembered primarily as an educator (see p. 707), he had the born scientist's love for investigating natural phenomena at first hand. The letter here reproduced is from Boyle, *Works* (1744), V, 642, 643. Robert Boyle (1627–1691), natural philosopher and chemist, was a founder of the Royal Society of London, a voluminous writer, and one of the greatest scientists of his day. He was deeply interested in theology, and a student of Hebrew, Greek, Chaldee, and Syriac. The letter has been reprinted in Sibley, *Biographical Sketches*, I, 588–590; and in Samuel E. Morison, *Harvard College in the Seventeenth Century*, 644–646.]

MR. *LEONARD HOAR* TO MR. *ROBERT BOYLE.*

Cambridge, New-England, December the 13th, 1672.

RIGHT honourable,

Your freedom and courteous treating me, when hither coming, giveth me the hardiness to present you with my acknowledgments, although it be but your interpellation; judging it better, that I were censured for troublesomness, than for ingratitude. Yea the chiefest of this colony, a poor, but yet pious and industrious people, know and acknowledge your kindness often and on considerable occasions expressed towards them, in their just defences, *&c.* although they know not where or how to publish their tabula votiva, or memorials of it unto your acceptation, but still do gratefully recommend you and your well-devoted labours in their prayers to God; and any publick affair them concerning, that shall unexpectedly, emerge unto your prudence, love and candor, hoping, that nothing shall ever be believed or concluded against them before that they be heard.

Noble Sir, I am not unmindful of your desires to see what rarities the country might yield; and have taken course, that now be presented to you, first, a sort of berries, that grow closely conglomerated unto the stalk of a shrub, in its leaf, smell and taste, like the broadest leaved myrtle, or to a dwarf-bay; which, by plain distillation, yields an almost unctuous matter; and by decoction, not a resina, nor oil, but a kind of serum, such as I have not known ordinarily for any vegetables. I believe it excels for the wind-colick.

Though I thought myself an indifferent botanist for any thing could grow in *England*, yet here in our wild plants I am presently [at a loss] but I hope I shall in season search out their pedigrees; and would be free to gratify any person valuing them with their seeds, or bodies dried. Mr. *Alexander Balaam*,[1] my master in those studies, and a person well known to Mr. *Charles Howard* and Dr. *Morrison*,[2] are now in your land.

Also (pardon, I beseech you, the confidence) I make bold to present your honour with a model of our natives ships. With one of them twenty foot long they will carry six or eight persons, their house and furniture and provisions, by one padling her forwards in the stern, swifter than any sculler. And when they come to falls, or would go over the land, [the passengers] load themselves away with the ship and her freight too.

I doubt they are not for the wars; for if you but stamp hard, you may strike out the bottom; and if you lay your tongue on one side of your mouth, it may over-set.

Also Sir, a piece of their plate, a fish I call the sea-spider, and some stones, I doubt more ponderous than precious; but that your honour will prove.

It hath pleased even all to assign the college for my Sparta. I desire I may adorn it; and thereby encourage the country in its utmost throws for its resuscitation from its ruins. And we still hope some helpers from our native land; of which your honoured self, Mr. *A.*[3] and some others have given a pledge.

A large well-sheltered garden and orchard for students addicted to planting; an ergasterium for mechanick fancies; and a laboratory chemical for those philosophers, that by their senses would culture their understandings, are in our design, for the students to spend their times of recreation in them; for readings or notions only are but husky provender.

And, Sir, if you will please of your mature judgment and great experience to deign us any other advice or device, by which we may become not only nominal, but real scholars, it shall, I hope, be as precious seed, of which both you and me and many by us shall have uberous provent at the great day of reckoning, which I know you do respect above all.

If I durst, I would beg one of a sort of all your printed monuments, to enrich our library, and encourage our attempts this way.

I know nothing so stunting our hopes and labours in this way, as that we want one of a sort of the books of the learned, that come forth daily in *Europe*, of whose very names we are therefore ignorant.

To Mr. *Ashhurst* I have written more. Let not, I beseech you, my prolixity tire or deter your acception of things hinted, or your honour's condonation of

Your devoted humble servant,
Leonard Hoar.

NOADIAH RUSSELL AND WILLIAM WILLIAMS

[The *Cambridge Ephemeris* for 1684 was brought out by Noadiah Russell (1659–1713), a graduate of Harvard in 1681, who after teaching at Ipswich for three and one-half years, returned in 1688 to his birthplace, Middletown, Connecticut, as minister where he thenceforth remained. He was a founder and trustee of Yale College, and among the framers of the Saybrook Platform. (See Sibley, *Biographical Sketches*, III, 216–222.)

William Williams (1665–1741) prepared the Cambridge almanac for 1685. Born in Newton, he was graduated from Harvard in 1683, and was later settled as pastor in Hatfield, where he died. Among his published discourses is the Massachusetts Election Sermon for 1719. (See Sibley, *ibid.*, III, 263–269.)

The almanac science of 1684 and 1685 is quaint only in relation to present-day knowledge. It was alert to the latest advancements and free from religious cant. For a summary of developments of astronomy, see Samuel E. Morison, *Harvard College in the Seventeenth Century*, 216–222. The text for both selections is from photostat copies of the unique originals in possession of the Massachusetts Historical Society.]

FROM THE ALMANAC FOR 1684.

Concerning Lightning, and Thunder, with some Observations and Cautions touching the same.

Lightning is an exhalation hot and dry, as also hot and moist; which being Elevated by the Sun to the middle Region of the Air, is there included or shut up within a cloud and cannot ascend; but by an Antiperistasis grows hotter and is enkindled, attenuated, and so seeks for more room, which it not finding in the cloud, violently rends the same, breaks out of it, and continues burning so long that it comes to the very ground.—By its rending of the cloud, there is caused a most dreadful noise or rumbling, and this we call Thunder: So that Thunder is improperly reckoned among the kinds or *species* of *Meteors*.

Of Lightning, [*fulmen*] there are three sorts, *viz.* piercing, [*Terebrans*], dashing in pieces [*disentiens*] and burning [*urens*] Piercing Lightning (which is also called white Lightning,) does consist of a most Subtile and thin exhalation and is very penetrating.

Observ. By reason of its subtile nature, many strange effects are produced thereby; A sword blade will be melted in its scabbard, and the scabbard not hurt at all: The pores in the scabbard are so great, that this Lightning passeth through them without any hurt, but coming to a more solid body (as the sword blade is) it meets with opposition there, and so through its heat melts it.

The *Second* sort of Lightning, is such as consists of a more fat and thick exhalation, which meeting with things, burnes not to ashes, but blasts and scorcheth them.

Observ. With this Lightning, there happens to be (yet seldome) a Stone, that is called a Thunderbolt, which breaketh forth with the exhalation, (as a bullet out of a gun) and breaks into pieces whatever it meets. When it strikes the earth it is reported to go not above five foot deep.

The *Third* sort of Lightning is fulmen urens [*burning Lightning*] and is more fiery then flamy; of a more grosse and earthy substance then the preceding sorts.

Observ. If Lightning kill one in his sleep, he dyes with his eyes opened, the Reason is because it just wakes him and kills him before he can shut his eyes again: If it kills one waking his eyes will be found to be shut, because it so amaseth him, that he winketh and dyes before he can open his eyes again.

Caution. It is not good to stand looking on the lightning at any time, for if it hurts no otherway, yet it may dry up or so waste the Chrystalline Humour of the eyes that it may cause the sight to perish, or it may swell the face, making it to break out with scabs, caused by a kind of poyson in the exhalation which the pores of the face and eyes do admit.

FINIS.

FROM THE ALMANAC FOR 1685.

CONCERNING THE NATURE OF *COMETS*, &c.

COMETS are judged by many excellent Philosophers to be *Meteors*, whose matter is an Exhalation, hot and dry, fat and clammy; drawn by vertue of the heavenly bodies into the highest part of the

Air, (and sometimes into the Starry region) where it is closely conglutinated into a great Lump, by reason of supply that it hath from below, so long as there is a working to exhale: and being thus compacted, it is set on fire in convenient time by the excessive heat of the place where it resteth: Sometimes they continue burning long, sometimes but a little time, seven dayes is reckoned to be the least, whereas some have continued 6 months and more, all which commeth to pass by reason of the paucity or plenty of the matter whereof it consisteth.

There are 2 things observable in Comets. The colour and the form or Fashion, both which proceed from the diverse disposing of the matter.

Their colours are principally 3. White, which comes to pass when the matter is thin 2. Ruddy, looking like fire when the matter is meanly thick. 3 Of a blew colour when the matter is very thick.

Their forms or Fashions are principally. 2. 1 Roundish, having beams round about them, which happens when the matter is thin on the edges and thick every there else 2 They appear with a beard or tail, which happens when the matter is but meanly thick towards some one side or other and rather long then round.

Thus are Comets made to be meteors, and certain it is that there are difficulties which will arise from the other notion which some have of them, which may be as difficult yea far more difficult to a rational head then any that will proceed from this notion we have here presented you with.

The cheifest objections against this opinion seem to me to be two. The one is the greatness and duration or long continuance of Comets sometimes. The other objection is grounded upon the place of the Comets existence sometimes, it being found to be above the Moon.

As for the first objection (which might have been made two) Certain it is that a spoonfull of water will yield a vapor an 100 times as big as to its dilation, and since so why may not the like be rationally asserted of fumes or earthy exhalations, that tho' in themselves they may be very large yet originally very small: and if this is considered we need not wonder that the earth yields so much of exhalations as to cause such vast beings as Comets are and yet to the eye loose nothing of its bigness.

As for the other objection; all the answer, I shall give to it, may be seen in tendring to consideration these two things.

1 That after Comets are above the highest region of the air, or the Moon yet they are under the starry heaven which hath an at-

tractive power 2 That the nature of the place aboue the Moon is falsly concieved of, if imagined to be really different from [the] place below the Moon, Now if thus why may not Comets ascend above the Moon as well as up to the Moon.

FINIS.

PAUL DUDLEY, 1675–1750/51

[Paul Dudley, son of Governor Joseph Dudley of Massachusetts, began life after graduation from Harvard College in 1690 as a lawyer. Soon appointed attorney-general, he later became Chief Justice of Massachusetts. Intellectually curious, he was alive to every cultural development, especially in natural philosophy. His unbending mannerisms, aristocratic background, wealth, and religious bigotry lent easy target during his lifetime and after for the opprobrious detractions which his high office made inevitable. The dispassionate judgment of time, however, reveals him as a jurist of probity and courage. By his will Harvard received the endowment of what were soon known as the Dudleian Lectures, for which incumbents are still annually chosen.

After contributing his account of maple-sugar making in New England to the Royal Society of London in 1720, Dudley was elected a Fellow of that learned body. During the course of the next fifteen years he submitted eleven more papers—all published in due course—ranging from accounts of the rattlesnake and of Niagara Falls to "An Essay upon the Natural History of Whales."

See *Dictionary of American Biography;* and especially Sibley, *Biographical Sketches*, IV, 42–54. The text of the essay on sugar making is from *Philosophical Transactions* of the Royal Society of London, XXXI (1720), No. 364 (pp. 27, 28); that of the essay on hiving of bees, *ibid.*, No. 367 (pp. 148–150).]

VII. *AN ACCOUNT OF THE METHOD OF MAKING SUGAR FROM THE JUICE OF THE* MAPLE TREE *IN* NEW ENGLAND.

BY PAUL DUDLEY, ESQ; F.R.S.

MAPLE Sugar is made of the Juice of Upland Maple, or Maple Trees that grow upon the Highlands. You box the Tree, as we call it, *i.e.* make a hole with an Axe, or Chizzel, into the Side of the Tree, within a Foot of the Ground; the Box you make may hold about a Pint, and therefore it must shelve inwards, or towards the bottom of the Tree; you must also bark the Tree above the Box, to steer or direct the Juice to the Box.

You must also Tap the Tree with a small Gimblet below your Box, so as to draw the Liquor off. When you have pierced or tapp'd your Tree, or Box, you put in a Reed, or Pipe, or a bit of Cedar scored with a Channel, and put a Bowl, Tray, or small Cask at the Foot of the Tree, to receive your Liquor, and so tend the Vessels as they are full.

After you have got your Liquor, you boil it in a Pot, Kettle, or Copper. Ten Gallons will make somewhat better than a pound of Sugar.

It becomes Sugar by the thin part evaporating in the boiling, for you must boil it till it is as thick as Treacle. Ten Gallons must boil till it comes to a pint and half.

A Kettle of twenty Gallons will be near 16 Hours in boiling, before you can reduce it to three Pints; a good Fire may do it sooner.

When you take it off, you must keep almost continually stirring it, in order to make it Sugar: otherwise it will candy as hard as a Rock.

Some put in a little Beef Sewet, as big as a Walnut, when they take it off the Fire, to make it turn the better to Sugar, and to prevent its candying, but it will do without. A good large Tree will yield twenty Gallons. The Season of the Year is from the beginning of *February* to the beginning of *April*.

Mr. Dudley *in a following Letter adds this Note.*

I have nothing to add to my Chapter of Maple Sugar, but that our Physicians look upon it not only to be as good for common use as the *West India* Sugar, but to exceed all other for its Medicinal Virtue.

VII. *AN ACCOUNT OF A METHOD LATELY FOUND OUT IN* NEW-ENGLAND, *FOR DISCOVERING WHERE THE BEES HIVE IN THE WOODS, IN ORDER TO GET THEIR HONEY.*

BY THE SAME MR. DUDLEY.

THE HUNTER in a clear Sun-shiny day, takes a Plate or Trencher, with a little Sugar, Honey or Molosses spread on it, and when got into the Woods, sets it down on a Rock or Stump in the Woods: this the Bees soon scent and find out; for 'tis generally supposed a Bee will scent Honey or Wax above a Mile's distance. The Hunter secures in a Box or other Conveniency, one or more of the Bees as they fill themselves, and after a little time, lets one of them go, observing very carefully the Course the Bee steers; for after he rises in the Air, he flies directly, or upon a streight Course to the Tree where the Hive is.

In order to this, the Hunter carries with him his Pocket Compass, his Rule, and other Implements, with a Sheet of Paper, and sets down the Course, suppose it be West; by this he is sure the Tree must be somewhere in a West Line from where he is, but wants to know the exact Distance from his Station; in order to determine that, he makes an off-set either South or North (we'll suppose North) an hundred Perch or Rod, (if it be more, it will still be more exact, because the Angle will not be so acute) then he takes out another Bee and lets him go, observing his Course also very carefully, for he being loaded will, as the first, (after he is mounted a convenient height) fly directly to the Hive; this second Course, (as I must call it) the Hunter finds to be South, 54 Degrees West; then there remains nothing but to find out where the two Courses intersect, or, which is the same thing, the Distance from *B* to *A*, or from *C* to *A*, as in the Figure, Tab. 3d. for there the Honey-Tree is.

For which Reason, if the Course of the second Bee from *C* had been South-west, and by South, *viz.* to *D*, then the Hive-Tree must have been there, for there the Lines are found to intersect.

The Foundation of all this is the streight or direct motion of Bees, when bound home with their Honey, and this is found to be certain by the Observation and Experience of our Hunters every Year, and especially of late Years, since this Mathematical way of finding Honey in the Woods has been used with such Success.

An ingenious Man of my Acquaintance the last Year took two or three of his Neighbours that knew nothing of the matter, and after he had taken his Bees, set the Courses the first and second Bee steered, made the off-set, and taken the Distance from the two Stations to the Intersection, he have orders to cut down such a Tree, pointing to it; the Labourers smiled, and were confident there was no Honey there, for they could not perceive the Tree to be hollow, or to have any hole for the Bees to enter by, and would have disswaded the Gentleman from felling the Tree, but he insisted on it, and offered to lay them any Wager that the Hive was there, and so it proved to the great surprize of the Country-men.

I cannot dismiss this Subject, without acquainting you, that all the Bees we have in our Gardens, or in our Woods, and which now are in great numbers, are the produce of such as were brought in Hives from *England* near a hundred Years ago, and not the natural produce of this part of *America;* for the first Planters of *New England* never observed a Bee in the Woods, until many Years after the Country was settled; but that which proves it beyond question is, that the *Aborigines* (the *Indians*) have no word in their Language for a Bee, as they have for all Animals whatsoever proper to, or aboriginally of the Country, and therefore for many Years called a Bee by the name of *English Man's Fly.*

Our People formerly used to find out Honey in the Woods, by surprizing and following one Bee after another by the Eye, till at length they found out where the Bees hived.

I will mention another thing with respect to Bees, tho' I don't know but it may have been commonly observed; and that is, when they Swarm they never go to the Northward, but move Southward, or inclining that way.

I should have taken notice in the proper place, that when one Bee goes home from the Sugar-plate, he returns with a considerable number from the Hive.

COTTON MATHER

[No Puritan more clearly represents the temper of seventeenth-century curiosity in the phenomenal universe than Cotton Mather (see p. 162). One encounters his ubiquitous mind at every turn, sometimes trivial and credulous, often pedantic, but never unresponsive to intellectual stimuli. He planned *The Christian Philosopher: A Collection of the Best Discoveries in Nature, with Religious Improvements* (London, 1721) to reconcile science and religion. One should not overlook Mather's skill throughout as a literary craftsman.

The text here reproduced is from the original edition: "Of the Vegetables," pp. 122–127, 130, 131, 134–139; "Of Man," pp. 301, 303, 304. These and further selected essays may be found in *Selections from Cotton Mather*, ed. Murdock (New York, 1926). The notes for this text correspond, with some additions and variations, to those in the *Selections*. See especially the introduction to *Selections*, pp. xlviii–liv.]

FROM *THE CHRISTIAN PHILOSOPHER*

Essay XXVI. Of the Vegetables.

The contrivance of our most Glorious Creator, in the Vegetables growing upon this Globe, cannot be wisely observed without Admiration and Astonishment.

We will single out some Remarkables, and glorify our God!

First, In *what manner* is *Vegetation* performed? And how is the Growth of *Plants* and the Increase of their *Parts* carried on? The excellent and ingenious Dr. *John Woodward*[1] has, in the way of nice Experiment, brought this thing under a close Examination. It is evident that *Water* is necessary to *Vegetation;* there is a *Water* which ascends the Vessels of the *Plants,* much after the way of a *Filtration;* and the Plants take up a larger or lesser Quantity of this Fluid, according to their Dimensions. The much greater part of that *fluid Mass* which is conveyed to the Plants, does not abide there, but exhale thro them up into the *Atmosphere.* Hence Countries that abound with *bigger Plants* are obnoxious to greater Damps, and Rains, and inconvenient Humidities. But there is also a *terrestrial Matter* which is mixed with this *Water,* and ascends up into the *Plants* with the *Water:* Something of this Matter will attend *Water* in all it motions, and stick by it after all its Percolations. Indeed the Quantity of this *terrestrial Matter,* which the Vapours carry up into the *Atmosphere,* is very *fine,* and not very *much,* but it is the truest and the best prepared *vegetable Matter;* for which cause it is that *Rain-Water* is of such a singular Fertility. 'Tis true there is in *Water* a *mineral Matter* also, which is usually too scabrous, and ponderous, and inflexible, to enter the Pores of the *Roots.* Be the *Earth* ever so rich, 'tis observed little good will come of it, unless the Parts of it be loosened a little, and separated. And this probably is all the use of *Nitre* and other *Salts* to Plants, to loosen the Earth, and separate the Parts of it. It is this *terrestrial Matter* which fills the *Plants;* they are more or less nourished and augmented in proportion, as their *Water* conveys a greater or lesser quantity of proper *terrestrial Matter* to them. Nevertheless 'tis also probable that in this there is a variety; and all Plants are not formed and filled from the same sort of *Corpuscles.* Every *Vegetable* seems to require a *peculiar and specifick Matter* for its Formation and Nourishment. If the Soil wherein a Seed is planted, have not all or most of the Ingredients necessary for the *Vegetable* to subsist upon, it will suffer accordingly. Thus *Wheat* sown upon a Tract of Land well furnish'd for the Supply of that *Grain,* will succeed very well, perhaps for divers Years, or, as the Husbandman expresses it, *as long as the Ground is in heart;* but anon it will produce no more of that *Corn;* it will of some other, perhaps of *Barley:* and when it will subsist this no more, still *Oats* will thrive there; and perhaps *Pease* after these. When the Ground has lain fallow some time, the *Rain* will pour down a fresh Stock upon it; and the care of the *Tiller* in manuring of it, lays upon it such things as are most impregnated with a Supply for *Vegetation.* It is observ'd that *Spring-*

water and *Rain-water* contain pretty near an equal charge of the *vegetable Matter*, but *River-water* much more than either of them; and hence the Inundations of *Rivers* leave upon their Banks the fairest Crops in the World. It is now plain that *Water* is not the *Matter* that composes *Vegetables*, but the *Agent* that conveys that *Matter* to them, and introduces it into the several parts of them. Wherefore the plentiful provision of this Fluid supplied to all Parts of the Earth, is by our *Woodward* justly celebrated with a pious Acknowledgment of that *natural Providence* that superintends over the Globe which we inhabit. The Parts of *Water* being exactly spherical, and subtile beyond all expression, the Surfaces perfectly polite, and the Intervals being therefore the largest, and so the most fitting to receive a *foreign Matter* into them, it is the most proper Instrument imaginable for the Service now assign'd to it. And yet *Water* would not perform this Office and Service to the *Plants*, if it be not assisted with a due quantity of *Heat; Heat* must concur, or *Vegetation* will not succeed. Hence as the *Heat* of several *Seasons* affords a different face of things, the same does the *Heat* of several *Climates*. The *hotter* Countries usually yield the *larger Trees*, and in a greater variety. And in *warmer* Countries, if there be a remission of the *usual Heat*, the Production will in proportion be diminish'd.

That I may a little contribute my *two Mites* to the illustration of the way wherein *Vegetation* is carried on, I will here communicate a couple of Experiments lately made in my Neighbourhood.

My Neighbour planted a Row of Hills in his Field with our *Indian Corn*, but such a Grain as was colour'd *red* and *blue;* the rest of the Field he planted with Corn of the most usual Colour, which is *yellow*. To the most *Windward-side* this Row infected *four* of the next neighbouring Rows, and part of the fifth, and some of the sixth, to render them colour'd like what grew on itself. But on the *Leeward-side* no less than seven or eight Rows were so colour'd, and some smaller impressions were made on those that were yet further distant.

The same Neighbour having his Garden often robb'd of the *Squashes* growing in it, planted some *Gourds* among them, which are to appearance very like them, and which he distinguish'd by certain adjacent marks, that he might not be himself imposed upon; by this means the Thieves 'tis true found a very *bitter Sauce*, but then all the *Squashes* were so infected and embitter'd, that he was not himself able to eat what the Thieves had left of them.

That most accurate and experienc'd Botanist Mr. *Ray* [2] has given us the *Plants* that are more commonly met withal, with certain characteristick Notes, wherein he establishes *twenty-five Genders* of them. These *Plants* are to be rather stiled *Herbs*.

But then of the *Trees* and *Shrubs*, he distinguishes *five Classes* that have their *Flower* disjoined and remote from the *Fruit*, and as many that have their *Fruit* and *Flower* contiguous.

How unaccountably is the *Figure* of *Plants* preserved? And how unaccountably their *Growth* determined? Our excellent *Ray* flies to an intelligent *plastick Nature*, which must understand and regulate the whole Oeconomy.

Every particular *part* of the *Plant* has its astonishing Uses. The *Roots* give it a Stability, and fetch the Nourishment into it, which lies in the Earth ready for it. The *Fibres* contain and convey the Sap which carries up that Nourishment. The *Plant* has also larger Vessels, which entertain the proper and specifick Juice of it; and others to carry the Air for its necessary respiration. The outer and inner *Bark* defend it from Annoyances, and contribute to its Augmentation. The *Leaves* embrace and preserve the *Flower* and *Fruit* as they come to their explication. But the principal use of them, as *Malpighi*, and *Perault*, and *Mariotte*,[3] have observed, is, to concoct and prepare the *Sap* for the Nourishment of the *Fruit*, and of the whole *Plant;* not only that which ascends from the Root, but also what they take in from without, from the Dew, and from the Rain. For there is a *regress* of the *Sap* in Plants from above downwards; and this descendent Juice is that which principally nourishes both Fruit and Plant, as has been clearly proved by the Experiments of Signior *Malpighi* and Mr. *Brotherton*.

How agreeable the *Shade* of *Plants*, let every Man say that *sits under his own Vine, and under his own Fig-tree!*

How charming the Proportion and Pulchritude of the *Leaves*, the *Flowers*, the *Fruits*, he who confesses not, must be, as Dr. *More* says, *one sunk into a forlorn pitch of Degeneracy, and stupid as a Beast*.

Our Saviour says of the *Lillies* (which some, not without reason, suppose to be *Tulips*) *that* Solomon *in all his Glory was not arrayed like one of these*. And it is observed by *Spigelius*, that the Art of the most skilful Painter cannot so mingle and temper his *Colours*, as exactly to imitate or counterfeit the *native* ones of the *Flowers* or *Vegetables*.

Mr. *Ray* thinks it worthy a very particular Observation, that *Wheat*, which is the best sort of Grain, and affords the wholesomest Bread, is in a singular manner patient of both Extremes, both Heat and Cold, and will grow to maturity as well in *Scotland*, and in *Denmark*, as in *Egypt*, and *Guiney*, and *Madagascar*. It scarce refuses any Climate. And the exceeding *Fertility* of it is by a Pagan *Pliny* acknowledged as an

Instance of the Divine Bounty to Man, *Quod eo maxime Hominem alat;*[4] one Bushel in a fit Soil, he says, yielding one hundred and fifty. A *German* Divine so far plays the Philosopher on this Occasion, as to propose it for a Singularity in *Bread*, that *totum Corpus sustentat, adeo, ut in unicâ Bucellâ, omnium Membrorum totius externi Corporis, nutrimentum contineatur, illiusque Vis per totum Corpus sese diffundat.*[5] A Friend of mine had *thirty-six Ears* of Rye growing from *one Grain*, and on *one Stalk*.

But of our *Indian Corn*, one Grain of *Corn* will produce above a *thousand*. And of *Guiney Corn*, one Grain has been known to produce *ten thousand*.

The *Anatomy of Plants*, as it has been exhibited by the incomparable Curiosity of Dr. *Grew*, what a vast *Field of Wonders* does it lead us into!

The most inimitable *Structure* of the Parts!

The particular *Canals*, and most adapted ones, for the conveyance of the lymphatick and essential Juices!

The *Air-Vessels* in all their curious Coylings!

The *Coverings* which befriend them, a Work unspeakably more curious in reality than in appearance!

The strange Texture of the *Leaves*, the angular or circular, but always most orderly Position of their *Fibres;* the various *Foldings*, with a *Duplicature*, a *Multiplicature*, the *Fore-rowl*, the *Back-rowl*, the *Tre-rowl;* the noble Guard of the *Films* interposed!

The *Flowers*, their Gaiety and Fragrancy; the *Perianthium* or *Empalement* of them; their curious Foldings in the *Calyx* before their Expansion, with a *close Couch* or a *concave Couch*, a *single Plait* or a *double Plait*, or a *Plait* and *Couch* together, or a *Rowl*, or a *Spire*, or *Plait* and *Spire* together; and their luxuriant Colours after their *Foliation*, and the expanding of their *Petala!*

The *Staminà*, with their *Apices;* and the *Stylus* (called the *Attire* by Dr. *Grew*) which is found a sort of *Male Sperm*, to impregnate and fructify the Seed!

At last the whole Rudiments and Lineaments of the *Parent-Vegetable*, surprizingly lock'd up in the little compass of the *Fruit* or *Seed!*[6]

Gentlemen of Leisure, consult my illustrious Doctor, peruse his *Anatomy of Plants*, ponder his numberless Discoveries; but all the while consider that rare Person as inviting you to join with him in adoring the *God of his Father*, and the God who has *done these excellent things*, which ought to be *known in all the Earth*. . . .

The peculiar Care which the great God of Nature has taken for the Safety of the *Seed* and *Fruit*, and so for the Conservation of the *Plant*, is by my ingenious *Derham* considered as a loud Invitation to His Praises.

They which dare shew their Heads all the Year, how securely is their *Seed* or *Fruit* lock'd up in the Winter in their *Gems*,[7] and well cover'd with neat and close *Tunicks* there!

Such as dare not expose themselves, how are they preserved under the Coverture of the *Earth*, till invited out by the kindly Warmth of the Spring!

When the *Vegetable Race* comes abroad, what strange Methods of Nature are there to *guard* them from Inconveniences, by making some to lie down prostrate, by making others, which were by the Antients called *Æschynomenæ*, to close themselves up at the Touch of Animals, and by making the most of them to shut up under their guard in the cool of the Evening, especially if there be foul Weather approaching; which is by *Gerhard*[8] therefore called, *The Countryman's Weather-wiser!*

What various ways has Nature for the *scattering* and the *sowing* of the *Seed!* Some are for this end winged with a light sort of a *Down*, to be carried about with the *Seed* by the Wind. Some are laid in springy cases, which when they burst and crack, dart their Seed to a distance, performing therein the part of an Husbandman. Others by their good Qualities invite themselves to be swallowed by the Birds, and being fertiliz'd by passing thro their Bodies, they are by them transferred to places where they fructify. *Theophrastus* affirms this of the *Misletoe;* and *Tavernier* of the *Nutmeg*. Others not thus taken care for, do, by their Usefulness to *us*, oblige us to look after them.

It is a little surprizing, that *Seeds* found in the *Gizzards* of *Wild-fowl*, have afterwards sprouted in the Earth; and *Seeds* left in the *Dung* of the *Cattel*. The Seeds of *Marjoram* and *Strammonium*, carelesly kept, have grown after seven Years.

How nice the provision of Nature for their Support in *standing* and *growing*, that they may keep their Heads above ground, and administer to our Intentions! There are some who stand by their own Strength; and the ligneous parts of these, tho' like our Bones, yet are not, like them, inflexible, but of an elastick nature, that they may dodge the Violence of the Winds: and their Branches at the top very commodiously have a tendency to an hemispherical Dilatation, but within such an Angle as makes an Æquilibration there. An ingenious Observer upon this one Circumstance, cannot forbear this just Reflection: *A visible Argument that the plastick Capacities of Matter are govern'd by an all-wise and infinite Agent, the native Strictnesses and Regularities of them plainly shewing from whose Hand they come.* And then such as are too weak to stand of *themselves*, 'tis wonderful to see how they use the

Help of their *Neighbours*, address them, embrace them, climb up about them, some twisting themselves with a strange *convolving* Faculty, some catching hold with *Claspers* and *Tendrels*, which are like Hands to them; some striking in rooty *Feet*, and some emitting a natural *Glue*, by which they adhere to their Supporters.

But, Oh! the glorious *Goodness* of our God in all these things! . . .

The Persuasion which Mankind has imbib'd of *Tobacco* being good for us, has in a surprizing manner prevail'd! What incredible Millions have *suck'd in* an Opinion, that it is an *useful* as well as a *pleasant* thing, for them to spend much of their Time in drawing thro a Pipe the *Smoke* of that lighted Weed! It was in the Year 1585, that one Mr. *Lane* [9] carried over from *Virginia* some *Tobacco*, which was the first that had ever been seen in *Europe;* and within an hundred Years the *smoking* of it grew so much into fashion, that the very Customs of it brought *four hundred thousand Pounds a Year* into the *English* Treasury.

It is doubtless a *Plant* of many Virtues. The *Ointment* made of it is one of the best in the Dispensatory. The Practice of *smoking* it, tho a great part of them that use it might very truly say, *they find neither Good nor Hurt by it;* yet it may be fear'd it rather does more *Hurt* than *Good*.

"May God preserve me from the indecent, ignoble, criminal *Slavery*, to the mean Delight of *smoking a Weed*, which I see so many carried away with. And if ever I should *smoke* it, let me be so wise as to do it, not only with *Moderation*, but also with such Employments of my Mind, as I may make that Action afford me a Leisure for!"

Methinks *Tobacco* is but a poor *Nepenthe*, tho the Takers thereof take it for such an one. It is to be feared the *caustick Salt* in the *Smoke* of this Plant, convey'd by the *Salival Juice* into the Blood, and also the *Vellication* [10] which the continual use of it in *Snuff* gives to the *Nerves*, may lay Foundations for Diseases in Millions of unadvised People, which may be commonly and erroneously ascribed to some other Original. . . .

But then we have one *far-fetch'd* and *dear-bought* Plant, on which we have so many Volumes written, that they alone almost threaten to become a *Library*. Tea is that charming Plant. Read *Pecklinus*'s [11] Book *de Potu Theæ*, and believe the medicinal and balsamick Virtues of it; it strengthens the *Stomach*, it sweetens the *Blood*, it revives the *Heart*, and it refreshes the *Spirits*, and is a Remedy against a World of Distempers. Then go to *Waldschmidt*,[12] and you'll find it also to brighten the *Intellectuals*. When *Prose* has done its part, our *Tate* [13] will bring in *Verse* to celebrate the sovereign Virtues of it. . . .

Essay XXXII. Of Man

. . . Nor may we lay aside a grateful Sense of this, that as the *Son* of God is *the Upholder of all Things in all Worlds*, thus, that it is owing to his potent *Intercession* that the *Sin of Man* has made no more havock on this *our World.* This *our World* has been by the *Sin of Man* so perverted from the *true Ends* of it, and rendred full of such loathsome and hateful Regions, and such *Scelerata Castra,*[14] that the Revenges of God would have long since rendred it as a *fiery Oven*, if our blessed Jesus had not *interceded* for it: *O my Saviour, what would have become of me, and of all that comforts me, if thy Interposition had not preserved us!* . . .

I will finish with a Speculation, which my most valuable Dr. *Cheyne*[15] has a little more largely prosecuted and cultivated.

All *intelligent compound Beings* have their whole Entertainment in these three Principles, the Desire, the Object, and the Sensation arising from the *Congruity* between them; this *Analogy* is preserved full and clear thro the *Spiritual World*, yea, and thro the *material* also; so *universal* and *perpetual* an *Analogy* can arise from nothing but its *Pattern* and *Archetype* in the infinite God or Maker; and could we carry it up to the Source of it, we should find the Trinity of Persons in the eternal Godhead admirably exhibited to us. In the Godhead we may first apprehend a *Desire*, an infinitely active, ardent, powerful *Thought*, proposing of *Satisfaction;* let this represent God the Father: but it is not possible for any Object but God Himself, to *satisfy Himself*, and fill His *Desire* of Happiness; therefore He Himself *reflected* in upon Himself and contemplating His own infinite Perfections, even the *Brightness of His Glory*, and the *express Image of His Person*, must answer this glorious Intention; and this may represent to us God the Son. Upon this Contemplation, wherein God Himself does behold, and possess, and enjoy Himself, there cannot but arise a *Love*, a *Joy*, an *Acquiescence* of God Himself within Himself, and worthy of a God; this may shadow out to us the third and the last of the Principles in this *mysterious Ternary*, that is to say, the Holy Spirit. Tho these *three Relations* of the Godhead in itself, when derived analogically down to Creatures, may appear but *Modifications* of a *real Subsistence*, yet in the supreme Infinitude of the Divine Nature, they must be infinitely *real* and *living* Principles. Those which are but *Relations*, when transferred to *created Beings*, are glorious *Relatives* in the infinite God. And in this View of the Holy Trinity, low as it is, it is impossible the Son should be without the Father, or the Father without the Son, or both without the Holy Spirit; it is impossible the Son should not be necessarily and eternally begotten of the FATHER, or that the Holy SPIRIT should not necessarily and eternally proceed both from Him and from the SON. Thus from what occurs throughout the whole Creation, *Reason* forms an imperfect Idea of this incomprehensible Mystery.

But it is time to stop here, and indeed how can we go any further!

THOMAS BRATTLE, 1658–1713

[Thomas Brattle of Boston was a scion of the wealthiest family in New England. In 1676 he was graduated from Harvard College where he had developed a marked skill in mathematical sciences. After travel abroad he settled in Boston, and served the College as treasurer for twenty years. He never married. In 1698 he was the chief organizer of the Brattle Street Church where the liberal principles of its members under the Reverend Benjamin Colman brought down the outspoken scorn of Increase Mather and his son Cotton. Brattle declined a judgeship in 1712. By will he left his organ—the first in New England—to the church he had founded, provided the institution should "procure a Sober person [to] play skilfully thereon with a loud noise" (Sibley, II, 496). The instrument was declined for reasons of church polity.

Brattle wrote out "A Full and Candid Account of the Delusion called Witchcraft, which prevailed in New England; and of the Judicial Trials and Executions at Salem, in the County of Essex, of that Pretended Crime, in 1692" in October of the same year. It was circulated as a private letter, and remained in manuscript for over a century. The criticisms directed against it in recent years blame the author, together with such other disapproving leaders as Saltonstall, Willard, Bradstreet, and Increase Mather, for not speaking out against the judges. But the modern reader must bear in mind that while the rage was at its height, any outspoken critic of the court would have been answered with an accusation of complicity in the crime.

See *Dictionary of American Biography;* and Sibley, *Biographical Sketches*, II, 489–498. For thoughtful discussion of "Dolefull Witchcraft," see Kenneth B. Murdock, *Increase Mather, Foremost American Puritan* (Cambridge, 1926), chap. XVII. The text here is from *Collections of the Massachusetts Historical Society*, series I, V (1798), 61–80, with omissions indicated.]

THE WITCHCRAFT DELUSION

. . . This Salem philosophy, some men may call the new philosophy; but I think it rather deserves the name of Salem superstition and sorcery, and it is not fit to be named in a land of such light as New-England is. I think the matter might be better solved another way; but I shall not make any attempt that way, further than to say, that these afflicted children, as they are called, do hold correspondence with the devil even in the esteem and account of the S[alem] G[entlemen]; for when the black man, i.e. say these gentlemen, the devil, does appear to them, they ask him many questions, and accordingly give information to the inquirer; and if this is not holding correspondence with the devil, and something worse, I know not what is.

But furthermore, I would fain know of these Salem justices what need there is of further proof and evidence to convict and condemn these apprehended persons, than this look and touch, if so be they are so certain that this falling down and arising up, when there is a look and a touch, are natural effects of the said look and touch, and so a perfect demonstration and proof of witchcraft in those persons. What can the jury or judges desire more, to convict any man of witchcraft, than a plain demonstration, that the said man is a witch? Now if this look and touch, circumstanced as before, be a plain demonstration, as their philosophy teaches, what need they seek for further evidences, when, after all, it can be but a demonstration? But let this pass with the S. G. for never so plain and natural a demonstration; yet certain is it, that the reasonable part of the world, when acquainted herewith, will laugh at the demonstration, and conclude that the said S. G. are actually possessed, at least, with ignorance and folly.

I most admire that Mr. N[icholas] N[oyes] the Reverend Teacher at Salem, who was educated at the school of knowledge, and is certainly a learned, a charitable, and a good man, though all the devils in Hell, and all the possessed girls in Salem, should say to the contrary; at him, I say, I do most admire; that he should cry up the above mentioned philosophy after the manner that he does. I can assure you, that I can bring you more than two, or twice two, (very credible persons), that will affirm, that they have heard him vindicate the above mentioned demonstration as very reasonable.

Secondly, with respect to the confessors, as they are improperly called, or such as confess themselves to be witches, (the second thing you inquire into in your letter), there are now about fifty of them in prison; many of which I have again and again seen and heard; and I cannot but tell you, that my faith is strong concerning them, that they are deluded, imposed upon, and under the influence of some evil spirit; and therefore unfit to be evidences either against themselves, or any one else. . . .

The great cry of many of our neighbours now is, What, will you not believe the confessors? Will you not believe men and women who confess that they have signed to the devil's book? that they were baptized by the devil; and that they were at the mock-sacrament once and again? What! will you not believe that this is witchcraft, and that such and such men are witches, although the confessors do own and assert it?

Thus, I say, many of our good neighbours do argue; but methinks they might soon be convinced that there is nothing at all in all these their arguings, if they would but duly consider of the premises. . . .

Now for the proof of the said sorcery and witchcraft, the prisoner at the bar pleading not guilty.

1. The afflicted persons are brought into court; and after much patience and pains taken with them, do take their oaths, that the prisoner at the bar did afflict them: And here I think it very observable, that often, when the afflicted do mean and intend only the appearance and shape of such an one, (say G. Proctor), yet they positively swear that G. Proctor did afflict them; and they have been allowed so to do; as though there was no real difference between G. Proctor and the shape of G. Proctor. This, methinks, may readily prove a stumbling block to the jury, lead them into a very fundamental error, and occasion innocent blood, yea the innocentest blood imaginable, to be in great danger. Whom it belongs unto, to be eyes unto the blind, and to remove such stumbling blocks, I know full well; and yet you, and every one else, do know as well as I who do not.

2. The confessors do declare what they know of the said prisoner; and some of the confessors are allowed to give their oaths; a thing which I believe was never heard of in this world; that such as confess themselves to be witches, to have renounced God and Christ, and all that is sacred, should yet be allowed and ordered to swear by the name of the great God! This indeed seemeth to me to be a gross taking of God's name in vain. I know the S. G. do say, that there is hope that the said confessors have repented: I shall only say, that if they have repented, it is well for themselves; but if they have not, it is very ill for you know who. But then,

3. Whoever can be an evidence against the prisoner at the bar is ordered to come into court; and here it scarce ever fails but that evidences, of one nature and another, are brought in, though, I think, all of them altogether alien to the matter of indictment; for they none of them do respect witchcraft upon the bodies of the afflicted, which is the alone matter of charge in the indictment.

4. They are searched by a jury; and as to some of them, the jury brought in, that on such or such a place there was a preternatural excrescence. And I wonder what person there is, whether man or woman, of whom it cannot be said but that, in some part of their body or other, there is a preternatural excrescence. The term is a very general and inclusive term.

Some of the S. G. are very forward to censure and condemn the poor prisoner at the bar, because he sheds no tears: but such betray great ignorance in the nature of passion, and as great heedlessness as to common passages of a man's life. Some there are who never shed tears; others there are that ordinarily shed tears upon light occasions, and yet for their lives cannot shed a tear when the deepest sorrow is upon their hearts; and who is there that knows not these things? Who knows not that an ecstacy of joy will sometimes fetch tears, when as the quite contrary passion will shut them close up? Why then should any be so silly and foolish as to take an argument from this appearance? But this is by the by. In short, the prisoner at the bar is indicted for sorcery and witchcraft acted upon the bodies of the afflicted. Now, for the proof of this, I reckon that the only pertinent evidences brought in are the evidences of the said afflicted.

. . . I cannot but admire that the justices, whom I think to be well-meaning men, should so far give ear to the devil, as merely upon his authority to issue out their warrants, and apprehend people. Liberty was evermore accounted the great privilege of an Englishman; but certainly, if the devil will be heard against us, and his testimony taken, to the seizing and apprehending of us, our liberty vanishes, and we are fools if we boast of our liberty. Now, that the justices have thus far given ear to the devil, I think may be mathematically demonstrated to any man of common sense: And for the demonstration and proof hereof, I desire, only, that these two things may be duly considered, viz.

1. That several persons have been apprehended purely upon the complaints of these afflicted, to whom the afflicted were perfect strangers, and had not the least knowledge of imaginable, before they were apprehended.

2. That the afflicted do own and assert, and the justices do grant, that the devil does inform and tell the afflicted the names of those persons that are thus unknown unto them. Now these two things being duly considered, I think it will appear evident to any one, that the devil's information is the fundamental testimony that is gone upon in the apprehending of the aforesaid people.

If I believe such or such an assertion as comes immediately from the minister of God in the pulpit, because it is the word of the ever-living God, I build my faith on God's testimony: and if I practise upon it, this my practice is properly built on the word of God: even so in the case before us.

If I believe the afflicted persons as informed by the devil, and act thereupon, this my act may properly be said to be grounded upon the testimony or information of the devil. And now, if things are thus, I think it ought to be for a lamentation to you and me, and all such as would be accounted good christians. . . .

What will be the issue of these troubles, God only knows; I am afraid that ages will not wear off that reproach and those stains which these things will leave behind them upon our land. I pray God pity us, humble us, forgive us, and appear mercifully for us in this our mount of distress: herewith I conclude, and subscribe myself,

Reverend sir, your real friend and humble servant,

T. B.

[N. B. *As there is no superscription on the copy of this letter, it is not known to whom it was addressed.*]

ZABDIEL BOYLSTON, 1680–1766

[Cotton Mather very possibly wrote up the anonymous account here presented from information gathered by Boylston. See George L. Kittredge, "Some Lost Works of Cotton Mather," *Proceedings of the Massachusetts Historical Society*, XLV (1912), 418–479. Zabdiel Boylston, great-uncle of President Adams, never procured a medical degree, though he enjoyed an enviable reputation as a physician. His work during the smallpox epidemic of 1721 was recognized five years later by a Fellowship in the Royal Society. See account of him in *Dictionary of American Biography;* see also Reginald H. Fitz, "Zabdiel Boylston, Inoculator, and the Epidemic of Smallpox in Boston in 1721," *Johns Hopkins Hospital Bulletin*, XXII (1911), 315–327.

Henry Newman (1670–*ca.* 1750) of Rehoboth, Massachusetts, was graduated from Harvard in 1687. He published the Cambridge almanac for 1691 and served as college librarian from 1690 to 1693. Before 1700 he went to England, where he resided till his death. Though he conformed to the Established Church, he remained on intimate terms with several New Englanders, acting as agent in England for the Corporation of Harvard College, agent for New Hampshire, and secretary for the Society for Promotion of Christian Knowledge. See Sibley, *Biographical Sketches*, III, 389–394; see also George L.

Kittredge, introduction to the Cleveland 1921 reprint of Increase Mather, *Severall Reasons Proving that Inoculation . . . is a Lawful Practice* (Boston, 1721). The text is from the *Philosophical Transactions* of the Royal Society of London, XXXII (1721), 33–35.]

THE WAY OF PROCEEDING IN THE SMALL POX INOCULATED IN NEW ENGLAND.

COMMUNICATED BY HENRY NEWMAN, ESQ; OF THE MIDDLE TEMPLE.

1. We make usually a Couple of *Incisions* in the *Arms* where we make our *Issues*, but somewhat larger than for them, some times in one *Arm*, and one *Leg*.

2. Into these we put bits of *Lint*, (the patient at the same time turning his Face another way, and guarding his Nostrils) which have been dipt in some of the *Variolus Matter* [1] taken in a Vial, from the Pustules of one that has the *Small Pox* of the more laudable Sort, now turning upon him, and so we cover them with a Plaister of *Diachylon.*[2]

3. Yet we find the *Variolous Matter* fetched from those, that have the *inoculated Small Pox*, altogether as agreeable and effectual as any other. And so we do what is taken from them that have the *Confluent Sort*.

4. Within Four and Twenty Hours, we throw away the *Lint*, and the *Sores* are dressed once or twice every Four and Twenty Hours, with warmed *Cabbage Leaves*.

5. The Patient continues to do all Things, *as at other times*, only he exposes not himself unto the Injuries of the *Weather*, if that be at all Tempestuous.

6. About the Seventh Day the Patient feels the usual Symptoms of the *Small Pox* coming upon him; and he is now managed as in an ordinary *Putrid Fever*. If he cannot hold up, he goes to *Bed;* If his *Head ach* too much, we put the common *Poultice* to his *Feet*, if he be very Sick at the *Stomach*, we give him a *gentle Vomit*, yea, we commonly do these Things *almost of Course*, whether we find the Patient want them or no. And we reckon the *sooner* we do these Things, the *better*. If the *Fever* be too high, in some Constitutions, we *Bleed* a little: And finally, to hasten the Eruption, we put on a Couple of *Blisters*.

7. On or about the Third Day from the Decumbiture the *Eruption* begins. The Number of the *Pustules* is not alike in all, in some they are a *very few*, in others they amount to an *Hundred* yea, in many they

amount unto *several Hundreds;* frequently unto more than what the Accounts from the *Levant* say is usual there.

8. The *Eruption* being made, *all Illness* vanishes; except perhaps a little of the *Vapours* in those that are troubled with them; there is nothing more to do, but to *keep Warm,* drink proper Teas, eat Gruel, Milk Pottage, Panada, Bread, Butter, and almost any thing equally Simple and Innocent.

9. Ordinarily the Patient *sits* up every Day, and entertains his Friends yea, ventures upon a *Glass of Wine* with them. If he be too Intent upon hard *Reading* and *Study* we take him off.

10. Sometimes, tho' the Patient be on other Accounts easy enough, yet he *can't Sleep* for divers Nights together. In this Case we do not give him *Anodynes* or *Opiates,* because we find, That they who have taken these Things in the *Small Pox* are generally pestered with miserable *Biles* after their being recovered. So we *let them alone;* their *Sleep* will come of it self, as their *Strength* is coming on.

11. On the Seventh Day the *Pustules* usually come to their Maturity; *and soon after* this they go away, as those of the *Small Pox* in the *Distinct Sort* use to do.

12. The Patient gets abroad quickly, and is most sensibly *Stronger,* and in *better* Health than he was before. The Transplantation has been given to *Women in Child-bed,* Eight or Nine Days after their Delivery; and they have got earlier out of their Child-bed, and in better Circumstances, than ever in their Lives. Those that have had ugly *Ulcers* long running upon them, have had them healed on, and by this *Transplantation.* Some very feeble, crazy, *Consumptive* People, have upon this *Transplantation,* grown hearty and got rid of their former Maladies.

13. The *Sores* of the *Incision* do seem to dry a little in Three or Four Days of the Feverish Preparation for *Eruption.* After this there is a *plentiful Discharge* at them. The discharge may continue a little while after the Patient is quite well on other Accounts; But the *Sores* will soon enough dry up of themselves; but the *later,* the *better,* as we think. If they happen to be *inflamed,* or otherwise Troublesome, we presently help them in the ways we do any *Ordinary Sores.*

NOTES

Volume II

Chapter IV—Manners, Customs, and Behavior

JOHN SMITH

1. *neare* = nearer. Obsolete comparative of "nigh."

2. *secure* = careless.

3. Son of Sir Humphrey Mildmay (*d.* 1613), and grandson of Sir Walter Mildmay, chancellor of the exchequer under Elizabeth and founder of Emmanuel College, Cambridge.

4. For an account of Winthrop, see p. 125.

THOMAS LECHFORD

1. A perennial herb growing in the northern part of both Europe and America. Powerfully astringent, its root was often employed medicinally.

2. This may refer to the land about Providence, Rhode Island, though there seems to be no record of any "Lords Isle."

JASPER DANCKAERTS

These notes on Danckaerts's *Journal* are from the James and Jameson edition of 1913 (see p. 404).

1. This seems to mean the creek which made in from the cove at the foot of Milk Street.

2. Simon Bradstreet, elected in May, 1679, was governor of Massachusetts till 1686—the last governor under the old charter. He had come out in 1630, and was now seventy years old.

3. Original, "Jan Tayller of [Dutch for *or*] Marchand Tayller." No John Taylor of Boston answering to the description has been identified.

4. Sluyter was from Wesel, on the Rhine. Though it was a German town, many of its inhabitants were Dutch (like Peter Minuit) and Walloon.

5. Captain John Foy appears in the records of the court of assistants, as still master of the *Dolphin,* in 1691.

6. A Dutch settlement in Guiana, owned at the time by the province of Zeeland; the present Dutch Guiana.

7. In the Azores.

8. The Thursday Lecture.

9. This fast is not noted in the elaborate list in Mr. Love's *Fast and Thanksgiving Days of New England.* The Old South Church had a fast on June 29, O.S., but this was June 28, N.S.

10. Rev. John Eliot (1604–1690), the Apostle to the Indians, came over to Massachusetts in 1631, and in 1632 was ordained as "teacher" of the church of Roxbury. He soon engaged in efforts to Christianize the Indians, and in 1646 began to preach to them in their own tongue. He formed a community and church of "praying Indians" at Natick, and others elsewhere. His translation of the Bible into the dialect of the Massachusetts Indians was completed in 1658. The first edition of the New Testament, printed at Cambridge, was issued in 1661, the whole Bible (Old Testament of 1663, New Testament of 1661 imprint, and metrical version of the Psalms) in 1663.

11. Eliot was not quite seventy-six.

12. The first edition of the whole Bible seems to have been 1040 copies; of the separate New Testament, 500. Many copies were lost or destroyed in the Indian war of 1675–1676; but 16 copies now existing of the New Testament, and 39 of the Bible, in this first edition, are listed in Mr. Wilberforce Eames's bibliography. In 1677 Eliot began to prepare a revised edition of the whole work. It was published in 1685. The printing of the New Testament portion was begun in 1680 and finished in the autumn or winter of 1681; the printing of the Old Testament was not begun until 1682.

Wonderful to relate, the identical copy of the Old Testament (edition of 1663, and metrical Psalms) which Eliot presented to Danckaerts and Sluyter is still in existence, in the library of the Zeeland Academy of Sciences at Middelburg in the Netherlands. It lacks the title-page, but in its place contains the following manuscript note. See the *Proceedings* of the Massachusetts Historical Society, XIII, 307–310, and the Dutch pamphlet there named.

"All Bibles of the Christian Indians were burned or destroyed by these heathen savages. This one alone was saved; and from it a new edition, with improvements, and an entirely new translation of the New Testament, was undertaken. I saw at Roccsberri, about an hour's ride from Boston, this Old Testament printed, and some sheets of the New. The printing-office was at Cambridge, three hours' ride from Boston, where also there was a college of students, whether of savages or of other nations. The Psalms of David are added in the same metre.

"At Roccsberri dwelt Mr. Hailot, a very godly preacher there. He was at this time about seventy years old. His son was a preacher at Boston. This good old man was one of the first Independent preachers to settle in these parts, seeking freedom. He was the principal translator and director of the printing of both the first and second editions of this Indian Bible. Out of special zeal and love he gave me this copy of the first edition, for which I was, and shall continue, grateful to him. This was in June, 1680.

"Jasper Danckaerts."

13. The first building of Harvard College, the building "thought by some to be too gorgeous for a Wilderness, and yet too mean in others apprehensions for a Colledg" (Johnson, *Wonder-working Providence*, p. 201), had partly tumbled down in 1677. The building now visited was the "New College," the second Harvard Hall, built with difficulty 1672–1682 and destroyed by fire in 1764. Edward Randolph, in a report of October 12, 1676, writes: "New-colledge, built at the publick charge, is a fair pile of brick building covered with tiles, by reason of the late Indian warre not yet finished. It contains 20 chambers for students, two in a chamber; a large hall which serves for a chappel; over that a convenient library." A picture of the building may be seen in the *Proceedings* of the Massachusetts Historical Society, XVIII, 318.

14. Rev. Urian Oakes, minister of Cambridge, was at this time acting president, and was installed as president in the next month. There were apparently seventeen students in the college at this time who subsequently graduated, and perhaps a few others. The library no doubt contained more than a thousand, perhaps more than fifteen hundred books.

15. The allusion is to the printing-office at Wieuwerd, which Dittelbach, *Verval en Val der Labadisten* (Amsterdam, 1692), p. 50, says was a very costly one. The Labadists had everywhere maintained their own printer, Louriens Autein going with them in that capacity from Amsterdam to Herford. As to the building occupied by the famous Cambridge press, Randolph mentions "a small brick building called the Indian colledge, where some few Indians did study, but now it is a printing house." Printing here was this year at a low ebb; nothing is known to have been printed but the second edition of Eliot's Indian New Testament.

16. This is to ignore the voyages of Gosnold, Pring, Weymouth, etc., and the settlement at Fort St. George in 1607.

17. The Connecticut.

18. The reading is *eer*, but *heer* was of course intended. The control by the English king was much more real than is here indicated. The next sentence alludes to the Navigation Acts and their evasion. As to customs, Edward Randolph had in 1678 been appointed collector for New England, and had begun his conflict with the Massachusetts authorities, but with little success thus far. Land-taxes did in fact exist.

19. On Endicott's [*sic*] cutting of the cross from the flag, in 1634, see Winthrop's *Journal*, in this series, I, 137, 174, 182. Since the decision then reached (1636), the cross had been left out of all ensigns in Massachusetts bay except that on Castle Island.

JOHN DUNTON

1. Now Court Street, Boston.
2. Increase Mather, *A Sermon . . . of Murder* (Boston, 1687).
   Cotton Mather, *The Call of the Gospel* (Boston, 1687).

Joshua Moody, *An Exhortation to a Condemned Malefactor* (Boston, 1687).

See also Cotton Mather, *Magnalia* (1702), for Morgan's edifying speeches.

3. Samuel Willard was teacher of the Third (Old South) Church in Boston. The "New Church" probably refers to the Second (Old North) Church, of which the Mathers were co-ministers. It had been rebuilt after the Boston conflagration of 1676. These were the two largest auditoriums in Boston.

4. About 1690, Major Jonathan Wade built a tavern in Medford, which was kept by Nathaniel Pierce.

5. John Cotton (1658–1710), eldest son of Seaborn, and grandson of the first John Cotton, was graduated from Harvard College, along with his cousin Cotton Mather, in 1678. Three years later he was chosen a Fellow and Librarian of the College. In 1696 he was ordained as pastor of Hampton, New Hampshire.

6. John Eliot, who was eighty-two at the time, lived until 1690.

SARAH KEMBLE KNIGHT

1. The Reverend Joseph Belcher (1669–1723).

2. I.e., Madam Belcher, wife of the pastor. She was a daughter of the poet Benjamin Tompson, *q.v.* p. 635.

3. The works of the Elizabethan romancer, Emmanuel Ford. *The most Famous, Delectable, and pleasant, History of Parismus, the most renowned Prince of Bohemia* . . . (1598) went through twenty-six printings before the middle of the eighteenth century. It is listed by Francis Meres, *Palladis Tamia* (1598) as one of the books that should be forbid youth, as tending to corrupt morals. *The Famous History of Montelion, Knight of the Oracle* (earliest extant edition, 1633) is less known today. It is worth noting that Madam Knight speaks of both romances as if they were well known in her day.

4. That the word clearly means a pipe for smoking is evident from its use on p. 433; see below, note 9. Such a meaning for *junk* is not recorded in the *New English Dictionary.*

5. Prov. Eng.: ringed; having a ring through the snout.

6. A lean-to room; that is, one having a low, slanting roof.

7. Lieutenant. Sometimes still pronounced, and formerly spelled, *leftenant.*

8. English proverb: "Bare walls make gadding housewives."

9. See above, note 4.

10. Gurdon Saltonstall (1666–1724), minister at New London, was a celebrated preacher. He sat at one time as Chief Justice of the Supreme Court of the Connecticut Colony.

11. Pumpkins.

12. The regular midweek religious lecture was held on Thursdays. Training days were those appointed for militia drill.

13. "The law of merchants": the system of usages of commerce in force and recognized by law.

14. Spanish saddlebags. Here facetiously used of cheeks.

15. Genteel.

16. I.e., election days are ceremoniously observed.

17. Fitz-John Winthrop (1638–1707), eldest son of Governor John Winthrop, Jr. of Connecticut. He was educated at Harvard, but took no degree. After some time spent in the army in England, he returned to New England and served as a major-general in the expedition against Canada, 1690. He was the Connecticut agent in London, 1693–1697. He filled the office of governor of Connecticut from 1698 till his death.

18. That is, "paid our tavern reckoning."

19. Place of public sale or auction.

20. Beams and joints.

21. Edward Hyde, Lord Cornbury, governor of New York, 1702–1708. He was the disreputable son of the famous Earl of Clarendon.

22. A beverage, usually fermented, of honey and water.

23. Spuyten Duyvil Creek, at Kingsbridge. The creek divides Manhattan Island from the mainland, and connects the Harlem River with the Hudson.

24. Joseph Webb (1666–1732), pastor in Fairfield from 1694 till his death. He was one of the first Fellows of Yale College.

25. James Pierpont (1660–1714), father-in-law of Jonathan Edwards, was an original trustee of Yale College and a Professor of Moral Philosophy.

JOSEPH GREEN

1. A small island near the tip of Long Island, settled by Lion Gardiner in 1639, and owned by direct descent until it was sold out of the family in 1936. It was originally in the township of East Hampton.

2. East Hampton was originally bought from the Indians in 1648, and settled by residents from Lynn, Massachusetts.

3. Probably the Reverend Mr. Ebenezer White (1672–1756), pastor of Sagg. Sag Harbor was a New England settlement with as many Indians and negroes as whites; largely a whaling village.

4. The Reverend Mr. Joseph Whiting (1641–1723), called by Cotton Mather "a Worthy and Painful Minister of the Gospel" (*Magnalia,* III, 157).

5. Joseph Coit, shipbuilder and deacon of the church at New London. His son Joseph had graduated from college two years later than Green.

6. Thomas Blowers (1677–1729), classmate of Green and pastor at Beverly.

7. Samuel Gerrish of Boston, bookseller and Town Clerk, was Green's brother-in-law.

8. Probably Increase Mather.

9. The Reverend Mr. Benjamin Wadsworth (1670–1737) was later president of Harvard College. He was an influential Boston preacher. In his youth, as a college tutor, he had been one of three who contributed money to help pay for Green's education.

10. The Reverend Mr. John Rogers (1666–1745), pastor at Ipswich, the eldest son of President Rogers of Harvard.

11. The Reverend Mr. Nicholas Noyes (1647–1717), pastor at Salem.

COTTON MATHER

1. The metrical version of the Psalms, published in 1562, that remained in use into the eighteenth century, though generally supplanted in New England by the *Bay Psalm Book*, *q.v.* p. 555.

2. Abenezra or Ibn Ezra (1092–1167), distinguished Spanish Jew whose Old Testament commentaries were notable.

SOLOMON STODDARD

1. Thomas Fuller (1608–1661).

2. Henry Hammond (1605–1660), English scholar and divine, a writer of controversial tracts.

3. "The long-haired Greeks."

4. "An empty habitation."

Chapter V—Biographies and Letters

JOHN WINTHROP

1. The first hint of a possible emigration in Winthrop's correspondence.

THOMAS SHEPARD

1. Lawrence Chadderton (1536–1640), Master of Emmanuel College, a majestic figure, who exerted a great influence on all Puritans of the early seventeenth century through his teaching and preaching, his splendid personality, and his amazing longevity.

2. The Pequot War.

ROGER WILLIAMS

1. *Experiments of Spiritual Life & Health* (London, 1652).

2. Cromwell.

3. "The King's Book" is the *Eikon Basilike.* The sermons of Bishop Launcelot Andrewes were the arch-embodiment of the High Church ideal of pulpit style and doctrine, as opposed to plain sermon and the Calvinist doctrine of the Puritan variety. Jackson and Taylor were Anglican authors, but Jeremy Taylor had recently advocated toleration in *The Liberty of Prophesying*, so that in citing him Mrs. Sadleir gave Williams an opening, of which he did not hesitate to avail himself.

4. *Eikonoklastes*, 1649.

5. Andrew Marvell (1621–1678), the poet, a friend of Milton, whom Milton recommended for assistant secretary in 1653, though he was not appointed to the post until 1657; he was identified with Milton's group, but that he helped Milton write *Eikonoklastes* is not true.

6. John Winthrop, Jr., married a

daugher of Hugh Peter.

7. Edward Winslow (1595–1655), a leader among the Plymouth settlers, agent for the colony in England, governor in 1633, 1636, and 1644, to relieve Bradford. It is probably a commentary upon the personality of Williams that both Winthrop and Bradford should think him a true saint even when they condemned his opinions, and that both Winthrop and Winslow, men of broad, statesmanlike qualities, should take pains to give him secret advices and even encouragements, but would not have him within their own jurisdictions.

INCREASE MATHER

1. Puritans objected to stated holy days and fixed days for celebrations because they believed them pagan in origin, because they almost always became occasions for dissipation and profanity among the people, and because they believed that God desired men to observe days of thanksgiving or of humiliation as events seemed to indicate from time to time, or as the spirit seemed to dictate.

2. "Hence the custom of praising the dead, to which we are enslaved."

3. "No one can acquire a great fame and a great quiet at the same time," Quintillian.

4. Thomas Cartwright (1535–1603) was the foremost spokesman for the Puritan cause in Elizabeth's reign. Robert Parker (1564–1614), Paul Baynes (d. 1617), and William Ames (1576–1633) were Puritan theologians and writers who worked out in common the draft of the non-separating Congregational church polity and were the true fathers of the New England ecclesiastical order.

5. William Prynne (1600–1669), Puritan agitator and pamphleteer, pilloried and his ears cut off by sentence of Laud for his attack upon the Queen's theatricals and upon the Laudian bishops.

6. "A wise man foresees."

7. Thus Increase Mather married his father's step-daughter.

8. Girolamo Zanchius, Italian Protestant theologian, whose works were textbooks in New England.

9. "Good diet is better than any Hippocrates," i.e., than any physician.

10. "The flail of the studious."

11. A quarrel in the First Church of Boston over the introduction of the Half-Way Covenant and the calling of the aged John Davenport from New Haven; the issue became a political one and resulted in the secession of half the congregation from the First Church to form the Third, or Old South.

12. "We have prospered in Synods, and now we die in this one."

13. Richard Mather was pleading on his deathbed with his son to embrace the decision of the Synod of 1662 setting up the Half-Way Covenant, the device by which it was determined that the children of persons who had been baptized but had never yet had an experience that could be ascertainably recognized as regeneration could be baptized on the strength of their parents' being "Half-Way" members of the churches. Increase had publicly opposed his father on this question, and that he should print his father's dying injunction to maintain the Half-Way Covenant was a handsome and pious manner of serving notice of his own conversion.

14. "Strange things familiarly and familiar things unusually."

15. "The art is to conceal the art."

16. Arthur Hildersham (1563–1632), Puritan divine and controversialist.

COTTON MATHER

1. "I scarcely call them mine," Ovid, *Metamor.*, 13, 141.

2. Thomas Wilson (1525–1581), author of *The Arte of Rhetorique;* quotation from Clark's *Lives*, ed. 1683, p. 19.

3. "A dusty and most troublesome vocation, but by far the most favoured of God."

4. "Grotian" means of the opinion of Grotius, the great lawyer and theologian of the Arminian party in Holland; Grotius was read widely in New England, though his theories of the freedom of the will and of the atonement were considered heretical.

5. "Impart no life, because they have none," reference to a knotty and threadbare dispute in scholastic philosophy.

6. Published Boston, 1678.

7. Edward Winslow, in *The Glorious Progress of the Gospel amongst the Indians of New England*, 1649 (*Collections of the Massachusetts Historical Society*, Series 3, IV, 89).

8. Cf. Cambden's *Remains* (1637), p. 357: "His conceit was obscure to me which painted a savadge of America pointing toward the sun, with Tibi accessu, Mihi Recessu." Mather either deliberately or unwittingly transposes the motto to read "As I approach, you recede"; he means that though Cambden could not understand this "device," it might well serve as the emblem for the life of Eliot.

9. "Interminable words."

10. "Soldier emeritus."

11. "When the luminaries undergo an eclipse, it is a bad sign for the world."

12. "Two fortresses stand against the visage of the foe."

SAMUEL SEWALL

1. "We have come even to Cambridge to stabilize and correct manners."

EBENEZER TURELL

1. William Whiston (1667–1752), theologian, divine, professor and free-lance popularizer of knowledge, friend of Newton, in trouble for supposedly being an Arian, a brilliant but eccentric mind, ranging over the fields of theology, church history, astronomy, physics, and chemistry.

2. "Long nocturnal studies are most dangerous."

3. "No day without letters."

Chapter VI—Poetry

JOHN WILSON

1. In 1625 occurred the great London plague during which in the capital alone 35,417 souls perished. Wilson's figures are exaggerated. The "Bills of Mortality" issued in London, on which his figures are based, were compiled on the evidence of ignorant people. The first great plague in 1603 destroyed as great a number as that of 1625; that of 1609 about half as many.

2. Surrounding districts over which London exercised jurisdiction.

3. Obsolete form of "more" (O.E. adverb *ma*), used of number rather than size.

ANNE BRADSTREET

1. The glede is the common European kite.

2. Small wooden casks for butter, lard, etc.

3. Hebrew *fleeing*. The land into which Cain fled, Genesis 4 : 16.

4. The ocean. Thetis was one of the Nereids.

5. The nightingale. Here Mistress Bradstreet is following poetic convention, for nightingales have never been native to America.

6. Precede; anticipate (L. *praevenire*). The original meaning, but now obsolete.

7. Revelation 2 : 17: He that hath an ear let him hear what the Spirit saith unto the churches; To him that overcometh will I give to eat of the hidden manna, and will give him a white stone, and in the stone a new name written, which no man knoweth saving he that receiveth it.

8. The poem seems to be based upon the idea of St. Paul (Romans 8), of the strife between the Flesh and the Spirit, or the law of the members and the law of the mind.

9. Revelation 21 : 10–27; 22 : 1–5.

10. I.e., winter. The tenth sign of the Zodiac, which the sun enters about December 21.

11. I.e., summer. The fourth sign of the Zodiac, which the sun enters about June 21.

NATHANIEL WARD, JOHN ROGERS, AND JOHN NORTON

1. Joshua Sylvester (1563–1618) translated Du Bartas's *Divine Weeks and Works* (collected ed., 1605).

2. "for weariness."

3. "marvel."

4. "shod by."

5. I.e., lying in the shelter.

6. Pertaining to a town in Samnium (Maronea), famous for its wines.

7. Mount Hybla in Sicily, famed for its honey.
8. Dreary(?).
9. Affrays.
10. Site.
11. Leave-takings; congés.
12. Peneus, the chief river in Sicily. Also the name of the river god.
13. Greek: "all-virtuous."
14. Perhaps a reference to Ormazd, the supreme deity of Zoroastrianism.
15. Publius Vergilius Maro.
16. Marcus Tullius Cicero.
17. Cf. Francis Beaumont *Ad Comitissam Rutlandiae:*

"Although I know whate'er my verses be,
They will like the most servile flattery show,
If I write truth, and make the subject you."

18. "Let all the people of Rome be silent before this marvel."

MICHAEL WIGGLESWORTH

1. Careless. (Obsolete.)
2. Practice or condition. (Obsolete.)
3. The text reads "Gold."
4. As the 1715 edition and later. The text here reads "cush."
5. The spiritually reborn; regenerate.
6. As the 1715 edition and later. The text here reads "where."
7. Assistant or helper. (Obsolete.)
8. Know how to.
9. Obsolete form of "more."
10. As the 1715 edition and later. The text here reads "chaste."
11. Ceases.
12. Would not.
13. "All things pass except the love of God."
14. Judges 14 : 14: And he said unto them, Out of the eater came forth meat, and out of the strong came forth sweetness. And they could not in three days expound the riddle.
15. Cf. with Anne Bradstreet's poem "The Flesh and the Spirit." This and all the following selections of Wigglesworth's verse are from a group of poems printed with the 1689 edition of *Meat out of the Eater* (pp. [51]–208), but bearing a separate title-page: *Riddles unriddled, or Christian Paradoxes Broke open, smelling like sweet Spice New taken out of Boxes.*

SAMUEL BRADSTREET AND DANIEL RUSSELL

1. "Everything that lies concealed will be manifest in due time."
2. *Tellus mater* was the ancient Italian earth deity of marriage and fertility.
3. Apollo is invoked as sun-god.
4. Personifying Heaven.
5. Archaic: "holds perforce."
6. Until 1752 in the British colonies in America the new year was reckoned as beginning in March.
7. Lat. *Hiems:* "stormy weather."
8. Cancer, the fourth sign of the Zodiac, which ushers in summer.
9. The sun enters Virgo, the sixth sign of the Zodiac, about August 22.
10. "Stable, yet always in motion."

BENJAMIN TOMPSON

1. During King Philip's Narraganset war the Indians attacked Marlborough, Groton, Rehoboth, and Chelmsford, Massachusetts, and Providence, Rhode Island, in February and March, 1676, burning houses and barns, destroying cattle, and slaying the inhabitants.
2. Official statistics recording the number of deaths.
3. Glory-fat or gloar-fat: especially dirty or unrefined fat.
4. Asshur was the chief god of the Assyrians, usually depicted as a war deity.
5. Samuel Newman (1600–1663), first minister of Rehoboth. His concordance of the Bible (London, 1643) was one of the best known prior to Cruden's.

URIAN OAKES

1. John Leverett (1662–1724), president of Harvard College, 1707–1724.

EDWARD TAYLOR

1. *riggal:* to make a groove for (archaic).
2. *smaragdine:* L. *smaragdus*, emerald.
3. *squitchen:* possibly a switch or stick.

4. Taylor dated this poem "Aug. 13. 14. 1683."

5. *sprindge:* to spread out.

6. An *epiniciowm* is a song of triumph.

ROGER WOLCOTT

1. For a sketch of John Winthrop, Jr., see p. 739. In 1661, while Winthrop was governor of Connecticut, he was appointed agent to go to England to procure a charter from the King. By astute diplomacy Winthrop secured a charter so liberal that it served the colony and state until 1818.

The selection opens with the arrival of news that the monarchy has been reestablished under King Charles, 1660.

Chapter VII—Literary Theory

PREFACE TO THE BAY PSALM BOOK

1. Johannes Buxtorf (1564–1629), German Hebrew and Rabbinic scholar; author of *Thesaurus Grammaticus Linguae Sanctae Hebraeae* (1629).

THOMAS HOOKER

1. St. Jerome. His Life is included in Erasmus's Complete Works (9 vols., Basel, 1516–1520).

2. "Ignorant of the Word."

3. "That a work needs decoration argues weakness of structure."

4. "He who does not wish to be understood (clearly) ought to be passed over."

MICHAEL WIGGLESWORTH

1. "In every activity of the spirit, yea even in sorrow, there is a certain pleasure."

2. Robert Turner, *Orationes Septemdecim* (1602). "It is proof of our slothfulness that since we are not able at best to do that which we ought, we are unwilling to do well that which we could."

3. "I shall either find a way or make one."

4. "This is the task, this is the work."

5. "By day hard work, by night unending toil, such as savor of some pains."

COTTON MATHER

1. Pertaining to song (obsolete).

JOHN BULKLEY

1. Arthur Golding (*ca.* 1536–*ca.* 1605). His chief work was his translation of Ovid. A man of strong Puritan sympathies, he also translated many of the works of Calvin.

COTTON MATHER: "OF POETRY AND STYLE"

1. I.e., a spiteful critic. Zoïlus (*ca.* 400–320 B.C.) was a Greek grammarian, remembered chiefly for splenetic attacks on Homeric mythology.

2. Marco Girolamo Vida (1490–1566), Italian epic poet and critic.

3. "(writing) poetry now and then."

4. St. Gregory Nazianzen (329–389), a father of the Eastern church, bishop of Sasima. He devoted his later life to literary pursuits.

5. Arthur Bedford, *The Evil and Danger of Stage Plays* (1706).

6. Samuel Butler (1612–1680), author of *Hudibras* (1663–1668), a satire on Puritans.

Thomas Brown (1663–1704), schoolmaster near London whose satires were witty, coarse, and abusive.

Edward ("Ned") Ward (1667–1731), humorist who wrote coarse satires upon the Whigs and Low Church. He was pilloried for his *Hudibras Redivivus* (1705).

7. Sir Richard Blackmore (1650–1729), physician and author of voluminous and turgid epics that were immensely popular with the Puritans.

8. "Heady wine."

9. "Which (discourse) now to cut short."

10. See Hooker's comment on St. Jerome, p. 673.

11. Anthony Blackwall (1674–1730), classical scholar. Among his writings were *The Sacred Classics* (1725) and *Introduction to the Classics* (1718), a scholarly description of the beauties of ancient writers.

MATHER BYLES

1. "He raises a mighty roar, whereat

the sea and all its waves shuddered and the land of Italy was affrighted far within, and Aetna bellowed in its winding caverns" (Aeneid, III, 672–674).

Chapter VIII—Education

NEW ENGLANDS FIRST FRUITS

1. Elijah Corlet (1610–1688), master of the Grammar School at Cambridge from 1642 until his death. See p. 722.

2. Marcus Tullius Cicero.

3. "To stand, as they say, on his own feet."

4. Both are little known today and not used long at Harvard. Nonnus, an Alexandrian Christian of the fifth century, was author of *Paraphrase of St. John.* James Duport, colleague of Charles Chauncy at Trinity College, Cambridge. The reference is either to his paraphrase in Homeric verse of the Bible poetry, or to his *Homeri Gnomologia*, aphorisms collected from Homer.

5. Martin Trost, Professor of Theology at Wittenberg, was the editor (1621–1622) of the Syriac New Testament.

6. ". . . is given over to the study of rhetoric."

CHARLES CHAUNCY

1. William Dell, *The tryal of spirits* (London, 1653).

2. "The evil use of a thing does not destroy its good."

3. Girolamo Zanchi (Zanchius), *Opera Theologica* (Geneva, 1605).

LEONARD HOAR

1. M.H.S., "Papers 1636–75," fol. 4. Printed inaccurately in 1 *Coll. M.H.S.*, VI, 100–108. The then (1799) editor of the Society touched up the original letter in ink, and used it for printer's copy, thus making the establishment of the original text somewhat difficult. For a discussion of Peter Ramus, see pp. 28–41.

2. Evidence that Jonathan Mitchell (A.B. 1647) had the Theses Logicae at least, is found in his MS theses, Mass. Archives, CCXL, 141. 5a. Richardson was the author of *The Logicians School-Master* (1657).

3. Antonio Possevino, *Bibliotheca de Ratione Studiorum* (1607).

4. The *Bibliotheca Sancta* (Venice, 1566; and later editions to 1626), by Sixtus of Siena (1520–1569), a converted Jew and Dominican. See article "Sixtus von Siena" in Wetzer and Welte, *Kirchenlexikon.*

5. Conrad Gesner (1516–1565), the Swiss botanist, physician, universal savant, and pioneer Alpinist (cf. Arnold Lunn, *The Alps*, pp. 33–39). Hoar doubtless refers to his remarkable, though incompleted, *Bibliotheca Universalis* (Zürich, 1545–1549, and later editions and epitomes), a catalogue in the three learned tongues of all known writers and books.

6. Georg Draud (1573–1635?), *Bibliotheca Classica* (Frankfort-am-Main, 1611 and 1625), a catalogue of books and authors that was superseded by Bayle's *Dictionnaire* in 1697.

7. "by way of birth."

8. "doth not a little distress me."

9. Isaac Ambrose, nonconformist, writer of *Looking unto Jesus* (1658) and other devotional works; Richard Baxter, author of *The Saints Everlasting Rest* (1650); Bishop Joseph Hall of *Epistles* fame, author of *Christian Moderation* (1640); and, probably, Thomas Watson (d. 1686), Rector of St. Stephen's, Walbrook, whose *Three Treatises* reached a sixth edition in 1660.

THOMAS SHEPARD, JR.

1. "*Histories* make Men Wise; *Poets* Witty; The *Mathematicks* Subtill; *Naturall Philosophy* deepe; *Morall* Graue; *Logick* and *Rhetorick* Able to Contend" (Bacon, "Of Studies," in *Essayes*, 1625, p. 294).

2. "Frequent perusal, but rather diligence and industry."

3. "I prefer that you *be* educated rather than be so esteemed."

4. *Virgilii Evangelisantis Christiados Libri XIII. . . . Instante Alexandro Rosæo Aberdonese.* Londini, 1638. There is a copy of this edition in the Boston Athenaeum. A notice of the Rev. Alexander Ross (1591–1654) will be found in the *Dictionary of National Biography.*

INCREASE MATHER

1. Pierre Gassendi (1592–1655), French

philosopher, scientist, and mathematician, whose texts were widely used by students. Mather probably refers to *Exerciattiones Paradoxicae adversus Aristoteles* (Grenoble, 1624).

2. Ermolao Barbaro (1454–1495), Italian scholar and diplomat. He translated the paraphrase of Themistius on Aristotle at the age of nineteen.

3. "Complete reality."

COTTON MATHER: ELEGY ON CHEEVER

1. Gr. folly.

2. A group of wild and picturesque islands 25 miles southwest of Cornwall, England.

3. Abraham's concubine; mother of Ishmael. A type of bondservant.

4. William Lily (*ca.* 1460–1522). His *Eton Latin Grammar* was a common text for generations of school boys.

5. Then (than).

6. St. Augustine in his youth studied at Carthage, devoting his time to Latin poets. See *Confessio*, xiii, 21.

7. Jean Tixier de Ravisi (*ca.* 1480–1524), French humanist, whose works were widely used throughout Europe as texts for a century and a half.

8. John Davenport (1597–1670), founder of the New Haven Colony.

9. Probably the most famous and influential of all theologians of the ancient Christians.

Chapter IX—Science

SAMUEL DANFORTH

1. Samuel Stone (1602–1663), a founder of Connecticut, and teacher of the church at Hartford.

2. John Miller (1604–1663), pastor of Yarmouth and later of Groton.

3. Samuel Newman (1600–1663), first minister of Rehoboth. He is said to have predicted the exact moment of his death.

4. John Endecott (1589–1665), bigoted and fanatical persecutor of the Quakers. He was many times elected governor of the Massachusetts Bay Colony.

LEONARD HOAR

1. Alexander Balaam (*fl.* 1656–1680), English merchant, traveler, and amateur botanist.

2. Dr. Robert Morison (1620–1683), senior physician to Charles II, and first Professor of Botany at Oxford University.

3. Henry Ashurst, merchant of London, treasurer of the New England Company; not to be confused with his son Sir Henry Ashurst, friend of Increase Mather.

COTTON MATHER: THE CHRISTIAN PHILOSOPHER

1. John Woodward (1665–1728), English naturalist and geologist. See his contribution "Some Thoughts and Experiments concerning Vegetation," *Philosophical Transactions*, XXI.

2. John Ray (or Wray) (1628–1705) was a pioneer in English natural history.

3. Mather is drawing from John Ray's sermon *Wisdom of God in the Creation*, Pt. I, for his references to other botanists.

4. "Because he feeds man chiefly with it"; quoted from Ray.

5. "It sustains all the body, to such a degree that in one bushel is contained nutriment for all the members of the whole body, and its strength is spread through all the body." Mather adds this quotation to what he has read in Ray.

6. The nine preceding paragraphs are taken directly from William Derham's *Physico-Theology* (1713), wherein Mather found references to Grew. The work is a teleological argument for God, used by Paley a hundred years later.

7. Buds.

8. John Gerard (1545–1612), English herbalist. Quoted from Derham.

9. Ralph Lane was the first governor of Virginia. Said to be the first smoker in England, he brought from Virginia tobacco and pipes which he gave to Sir Walter Raleigh.

10. Irritation.

11. Johannes Pechlin (1646–1706), Dutch physician.

12. Probably Johann Jacob Waldschmidt (1644–1689), German physician and medical writer.

13. Nahum Tate (1652–1715).

14. "Wicked settlements."

15. Mather refers to Dr. George Cheyne, *Philosophical Principles of Religion, Natural and Revealed* (London, 1715).

ZABDIEL BOYLSTON

1. Pertaining to pits caused by small-pox.

2. A plaster containing lead salts of the fatty acids, used for wounds.

◆ BIBLIOGRAPHIES

Volume II

IV. MANNERS

This section is designed to list items that shed light upon the diversions and vocations of Puritans, their daily lives and behavior. The student will find further essential material listed under Section V (Biography), especially in the part dealing with diaries, journals, and personal papers. See also Section I A.

A. Primary Sources

The bibliography could be indefinitely extended, for good pastors never wearied of advising their flocks in matters of conduct.

Allin, James, *Serious Advice to Delivered Ones From Sickness*, Boston, 1679.

Belcher, Joseph, *Duty of Parents*, Boston, 1710.

Bridge, William, *Word to the Aged*, Boston, 1679.

Colman, Benjamin, *The Government & Improvement of Mirth*, Boston, 1707.

—— *The Hainous Nature of the Sin of Murder*, Boston, 1713.

—— "Letter to Mrs. John George" (1701), *Publications of the Colonial Society of Massachusetts*, VIII (1906), 246–250. (Advice on women's apparel.)

Constables Pocket-Book, The, 2nd ed., Boston, 1727.

Danckaerts, Jasper, *Journal of Jasper Danckaerts [and Peter Sluyter], 1679–1680*, printed from manuscript by the Long Island Historical Society, 1867; also in Original Narratives Series, ed. B. B. James and J. F. Jameson, New York, 1913. (Contains notes on a visit to Cambridge and Boston, together with sketches of some of the residents.)

Danforth, Samuel, *The Woful Effects of Drunkenness*, Boston, 1710.

Dunton, John, *John Dunton's Letters from New-England* [*ca.* 1686], ed. W. H. Whitmore, Boston, Prince Society, 1867. (Agreeable but unreliable; see C. N. Greenough, "John Dunton's Letters," *Publications of the Colonial Society of Massachusetts*, XIV (1913), 213–257.)

Gay, Ebenezer, *Ministers are Men of Like Passions with Others*, Boston, 1725.

Hubbard, William, *The Benefit of a Well-Ordered Conversation*, Boston, 1684.

Mather, Cotton, *The Accomplished Singer* Boston, 1721.

—— *Agricola; Or, the Religious Husbandman*, Boston, 1727.

—— *Bonifacius*, Boston, 1710; reprinted as *Essays to do Good* in many subsequent eighteenth- and nineteenth-century editions published in Boston and London.

—— *A Family Well-Ordered*, Boston, 1699.

—— *Gospel for the Poor*, Boston, 1697.

—— *Lex Mercatoria; Or, The Just Rules of Commerce Declared*, Boston, 1704.

—— *Ornaments for the Daughters of Zion*, Boston, 1692. (The position of women in society and the code of feminine deportment.)

—— *The Religious Marriner*, Boston, 1700.

—— *Sober Considerations, on a growing Flood of Iniquity: . . . the Woful Consequences [of] the Prevailing Abuse of Rum*, Boston, 1708.

—— *The Way to Prosperity*, Boston, 1690.

Mather, Increase, *An Arrow against Profane and Promiscuous Dancing. Drawn out of the Quiver of the Scriptures*, Boston, 1684; 1686.

—— *Meditations on the Glory of the Heavenly World*, Boston, 1711.

—— *The Original Rights of Mankind Freely to Subdue and Improve the Earth*, Boston, 1722.

—— *Seasonable Meditations Both for Winter & Summer*, Boston, 1712. (Orthodox views on Sabbath-keeping.)

—— *A Testimony against several Prophane*

and Superstitious Customs, Now practised by some in New-England, London, 1687; ed. with critical comment by William Peden, Charlottesville, 1953.

Mather, Samuel, *An Essay Concerning Gratitude,* Boston, 1732.

Moody, Samuel, *The Debtor's Monitor,* Boston, 1715.

New Husbandry to New-England, Philadelphia, 1692.

Pemberton, Ebenezer, *Advice to a Son: A Sermon Preached at the Request of a Gentleman . . . Upon his Son's going to Europe,* Boston, 1705.

Prince, Thomas, *The Vade Mecum for America; Or, A Companion for Traders and Travellers,* Boston, 1732. (A manual for travel, with tables of weights, charts of distance, etc., prepared by the learned Boston minister.)

Salva Conducta; Or, A Safe Conduct for the Increase of Trade in New-England, Boston, 1699. (Issued 13 times before 1700.)

School of Good Manners, The, New London, 1715.

Sewall, Samuel, *The Selling of Joseph,* Boston, 1700. (The earliest antislavery pamphlet in America.)

Shepard, Thomas, Jr., *Wine for Gospel Wantons,* Cambridge, 1668.

Stoddard, Solomon, *An Answer to Some Cases of Conscience Respecting the Country,* Boston, 1722.

Symmes, Thomas, *The Reasonableness of Regular Singing,* Boston, 1720.

Twichell, Joseph H., ed., *Some Old Puritan Love-Letters, John and Margaret Winthrop, 1618–1638,* New York, 1893.

Wadsworth, Benjamin, *The Well-Ordered Family,* Boston, 1712.

Walter, Thomas, *The Grounds and Rules of Musick Explained,* Boston, 1721.

—— *The Sweet Psalmist of Israel,* Boston, 1722.

Whitman, Samuel, *Practical Godliness the Way to Prosperity,* New London, 1714.

Wise, John, *A Word of Comfort to a Melancholy Country,* Boston, 1721. (A plea for paper money and "inflation" against the "sound money" merchants of Boston.)

B. Secondary Works

The customs and behavior of Puritans have long been a subject for discussion and comment, all too often misleadingly presented.

1. Almanacs

The most widely distributed item to be issued from the colonial press, the almanac today is also the scarcest; it took the place of a newspaper during the seventeenth century, and like a newspaper was discarded when out of date. See Section IX-B for a chronological checklist dealing with "Popular Science in the Almanacs."

Bates, Albert C., "Check List of Connecticut Almanacs, 1709–1850, with Introduction and Notes," *Proceedings of the American Antiquarian Society,* N.S. XXIV (1914), 93–215.

—— "Part of an Almanack," *Proceedings of the American Antiquarian Society,* LII (1942), 38–44.

Briggs, Samuel, *The Essays, Humor, and Poems of Nathaniel Ames, Father and Son . . . from their Almanacks, 1726–1775,* Cleveland, 1891.

—— "The Origin and Development of the Almanack," Western Reserve and Northern Ohio Historical Society, *Tract No. 69* (1887), 435–477.

Brigham, Clarence S., "An Account of American Almanacs and their Value for Historical Study," *Proceedings of the American Antiquarian Society,* N.S. XXXV (1925), 1–25, 194–209.

Chapin, Howard M., "Check List of Rhode Island Almanacs, 1643–1850, with Introduction and Notes," *Proceedings of the American Antiquarian Society,* N.S. XXV (1915), 19–54.

Denker, David D., "American Almanacs in the Eighteenth Century," *Journal of the Rutgers University Library,* XVIII No. 2 (June, 1955), 12–55.

Eisenger, Chester E., "The Farmer in the Eighteenth Century Almanac," *Agricultural History,* July, 1954.

Gummere, Richard M., "The Classical

Element in Early New England Almanacs," *Harvard Library Bulletin*, IX (1955), 181–196. (Allusions to the classics were second only to those to Scripture.)

Kittredge, George L., *The Old Farmer and his Almanack*, Boston, 1904.

Littlefield, George E., "Notes on the Calendar and the Almanac," *Proceedings of the American Antiquarian Society*, N.S. XXIV (1914), 11–64.

Lovely, Napoleon W., "Notes on New England Almanacs," *New England Quarterly*, VIII (1935), 264–277.

Morrison, Hugh A., *Preliminary Check List of American Almanacs, 1639–1800*, Washington, 1907.

Nichols, Charles L., "Checklist of Maine, New Hampshire and Vermont Almanacs," *Proceedings of the American Antiquarian Society*, N.S. XXXVIII (1928) 63–163.

—— "Notes on the Almanacs of Massachusetts," *Proceedings of the American Antiquarian Society*, N.S. XXII (1912), 15–134.

Perry, Amos, "New England Almanacs, with Special Mention of Those Published in Rhode Island," *Narragansett Historical Register*, IV (1885), 27–39.

Stickney, Matthew A., "Almanacs and their Authors," *Essex Institute Historical Collections*, VIII (1866), 28–32, 75, 101–104, 158–164, 193–205; XIV (1877), 81–93, 212–223, 242–248.

2. Daily Life and Behavior

In addition to the items listed below, the student should consult town histories and family genealogies.

Adams, Charles F., "Some Phases of Sexual Morality and Church Discipline in Colonial New England," *Proceedings of the Massachusetts Historical Society*, XXVI (1891), 477–516. (For a counter-statement, see H. B. Parker, *New England Quarterly*, III (1930), 133–135.

Adams, James Truslow, *Provincial Society, 1690–1763*, New York, 1927. (Volume III of *A History of American Life*, ed. Arthur M. Schlesinger and Dixon R. Fox. A substantial description of general culture and social and economic life in the colonies. The "Critical Essay on Authorities," pp. 324–356, is of great value.)

——, and others, eds., *Album of American History: Colonial Period*, New York, 1944. (A good pictorial miscellany, but disregard the text.)

Albertson, Dean, "Puritan Liquor in the Planting of New England," *New England Quarterly*, XXIII (1950), 477–490. (Drinking habits of Puritans and the attempt to regulate them. No taint of immorality was attached to drinking, and prodigious amounts were consumed in comparative sobriety.)

Andrews, Charles McL., *Colonial Folkways: A Chronicle of American Life in the Reign of the Georges*, New Haven, 1919. (*The Chronicle of America*, Vol. IX. Excellent, readable survey.)

Bardsley, Charles W., *Curiosities of Puritan Nomenclature*, London, 1880.

Benton, Josiah H., *Warning out in New England, 1656–1817*, Boston, 1911. (A history of poor-relief.)

Bliss, William R., *Side Glimpses from the Colonial Meeting-House*, Boston, 1894. (Chatty and informative.)

Bridenbaugh, Carl, *Cities in Revolt: Urban Life in America 1743–1776*, New York, 1955. (A continuation of *Cities in the Wilderness*, documenting the rise of urban culture.)

—— *Cities in the Wilderness: The First Century of Urban Life in America 1625–1742*, New York, 1938; 1955. (Contains, among others, intensive studies of Boston and Newport, and shows them to be mature cities by the European standards of the day.)

—— "The New England Town: A Way of Life," *Proceedings of the American Antiquarian Society*, LVI (1946), 19–48.

Buffinton, Arthur H., "Sir Thomas Temple in Boston, a Case of Benevolent Assimilation," *Publications of the Colonial Society of Massachusetts*, XXVII (1932), 308–319.

Bushnell, David, "The Treatment of the Indians in Plymouth Colony," *New England Quarterly*, XXVI (1953), 193–218.

Calhoun, Arthur W., *A Social History of the American Family from Colonial Times to the Present*, Cleveland, 1917–1919, 3 vols. (The first seven chapters of Vol. I, "Colonial Period," relate to New England. Stimulating.)

Caulfield, Ernest, "Pediatric Aspects of the Salem Witchcraft Tragedy: A Lesson in Mental Health," *American Journal of Diseases of Children*, LXV (1943), 788–802. (Argues that the child-accusers were hysterics, not frauds, and that their hysteria was a by-product of Puritan piety and theology.)

—— "The Pursuit of a Pestilence," *Proceedings of the American Antiquarian Society*, LX (1950), 21–52. (Influenza in the colonies.)

—— "Some Common Diseases of Colonial Children," *Publications of the Colonial Society of Massachusetts*, XXXV (1942–1946), 1951, 4–65.

Chapman, Clayton Harding, "Benjamin Colman's Daughters (1708–1745)," *New England Quarterly*, XXVI (1953), 162–192. (Family life in early New England.)

Chase, Gilbert, *America's Music: From the Pilgrims to the Present*, New York, 1955; 1960. (The most scholarly general history of music in the United States.)

Child, Frank S., *The Colonial Parson of New England*, New York, 1896.

"Colonial Scene 1602–1800, The," *Proceedings of the American Antiquarian Society*, LX (1950), 53–160. (An invaluable annotated list of books, broadsides, prints and maps revealing daily life and occupations of the colonists, compiled by the staffs of the A. A. S. and of the John Carter Brown Library.)

Covey, Cyclone, "Puritanism and Music in Colonial America," *William and Mary Quarterly*, VIII (1951), 378–388.

Cowell, Henry J., *John Winthrop: A Seventeenth Century Puritan Romance*, Colchester, Eng., 1949. (A brief pamphlet on John and Margaret Winthrop, containing a collection of their love letters.)

Crawford, Mary C., *In the Days of the Pilgrim Fathers*, Boston, 1920.

—— *Little Pilgrimages among Old New England Inns*, Boston, 1907.

—— *The Romance of Old New England Churches*, Boston, 1904.

—— *Social Life in Old New England*, Boston, 1914.

Cutler, U. Waldo, "Tools, Trades and an Honest Living in Early New England," *Publications of the Worcester Historical Society*, N.S. I (1935), 479–486.

Davis, Andrew McF., "Hints of Contemporary Life in the Writings of Thomas Shepard," *Publications of the Colonial Society of Massachusetts*, XII (1911), 136–163.

—— "John Harvard's Life in America," *Publications of the Colonial Society of Massachusetts*, XII (1911), 4–45. (Life and manners in the first decades.)

Dawes, Norman H., "Titles as Symbols of Prestige in Seventeenth-Century New England," *William and Mary Quarterly*, VI (1949), 69–83.

Day, Clive H., "Capitalistic Tendencies in the Puritan Colonies," *Annual Report of the American Historical Association*, Washington, 1925, 225–235.

Deutch, Albert, "The Sick Poor in Colonial Times," *American Historical Review*, XLVI (1941), 560–579.

Dexter, Elizabeth A., *Colonial Women of Affairs: Women in Business and the Professions in America before 1776*, 2nd ed., Boston, 1931.

Dodge, Daniel K., "Puritan Names," *New England Quarterly*, I (1928), 467–475.

Dow, George F., *Domestic Life in New England in the Seventeenth Century*, Topsfield, Mass., 1925.

—— *Every Day Life in the Massachusetts Bay Colony*, Boston, 1935.

Drake, Samuel A., *A Book of New England Legends and Folk Lore*, Boston, 1884.

—— *Old Boston Taverns and Tavern Clubs*, Boston, 1917.

Duffy, John, *Epidemics in Colonial America*, Baton Rouge, 1953.

Dulles, Foster Rhea, *America Learns to Play: A History of Popular Recreation, 1607–1940*, New York, 1940.

Earle, Alice M., *Child Life in Colonial Days*, 2nd ed., New York, 1927.

—— *Colonial Dames and Good Wives*, New York, 1895.

—— *Costume of Colonial Times*, New York, 1894.

—— *Customs and Fashions in Old New England*, New York, 1894.

—— *Home Life in Colonial Days*, New York, 1898.

—— *The Sabbath in Puritan New England*, New York, 1891.

—— *Stage-Coach and Tavern Days*, New York, 1900.

—— *Two Centuries of Costume in America*, New York, 1903.

Eggleston, Edward, *The Beginners of a Nation*, New York, 1896.

—— *The Transit of Civilization from England to America*, New York, 1901.

Englishmen at Rest and Play, 1558–1714, by members of Wadham College, Oxford, 1931. (Important for background of New England society.)

Ezell, John Samuel, *Fortune's Merry Wheel: The Lottery in America*, Cambridge, 1960.

Felt, Joseph B., *The Customs of New England*, Boston, 1853.

Ferguson, J. DeLancey, "The Roots of American Humor," *American Scholar*, IV (1935), 41–48.

Field, Edward, *The Colonial Tavern: A Glimpse of New England Town Life in the Seventeenth and Eighteenth Centuries*, Providence, 1897.

Fisher, Sydney G., *Men, Women and Manners in Colonial Times*, Philadelphia, 1898, 2 vols.

Fitzpatrick, Kathleen, "The Puritans and the Theatre," *Historical Studies of Australia and New Zealand*, III (1944–1949), 253–276.

Fleming, Sandford, *Children & Puritanism: The Place of Children in the Life and Thought of the New England Churches, 1620–1847*, New Haven, 1933.

Foote, Henry Wilder, *Three Centuries of American Hymnody*, Cambridge, 1940; Hamden, 1961. (Important and authoritative. Contains, for example, the best brief account of the Bay Psalm Book.)

Forbes, Esther, *Paradise*, New York, 1937. (A brilliant novel of seventeenth century Boston and vicinity. The manners of the Bay Colony settlers, especially of those living in the countryside, are portrayed with authentic vigor.)

Ford, Edwin H., "Colonial Pamphleteers," *Journalism Quarterly*, XIII (1936), 24–36.

Ford, Worthington C., "Samuel Sewall and Nicholas Noyes on Wigs," *Publications of the Colonial Society of Massachusetts*, XX (1920), 109–128.

Gabriel, Ralph H., ed., *The Pageant of America*, New Haven, 1925–1929, 15 vols. (A useful collection of social and cultural remains.)

Gretton, Richard H., *The English Middle Class*, London, 1917. (Important backgrounds.)

Griswold, A. Whitney, "Three Puritans on Prosperity, *New England Quarterly*, VII (1934), 475–493.

Haller, William and Malleville Haller, "The Puritan Art of Love," *Huntington Library Quarterly*, V (1942), 235–272. (An account of the teachings of the Puritan pulpit concerning love and marriage.)

Hanscom, Elizabeth D., ed., *The Heart of the Puritan; Selections from Letters and Journals*, New York, 1917.

Haynes, Henry W., "Cotton Mather and His Slaves," *Proceedings of the American Antiquarian Society*, N.S. VI (1889–1890), 191–195.

Holliday, Carl, *Woman's Life in Colonial Days*, Boston, 1922.

—— *The Wit and Humor of Colonial Days (1607–1800)*, Philadelphia, 1912.

Hooker, Roland M., *The Colonial Trade of Connecticut, Publications of the Tercentenary Commission of the State of Connecticut*, New Haven, 1936.

Howard, John T., *Our American Music: Three Hundred Years of It*, 4th ed. rev., New York, 1955.

Jameson, John F., ed., *Privateering and Piracy in the Colonial Period; Illustrative Documents*, New York, 1923.

Jewett, Amos E., "Deacon John Pearson and his Fulling Mill at Rowley," *Publications of the Rowley Historical Society*, 1948, 24–26.

—— "A New England Shoemaker's Shop," *Ibid.*, 27–29.

—— "The Tidal Marshes of Rowley and Vicinity with an Account of the Old-Time Methods of Marshing," *Essex Institute Historical Collections*, LXXXV (1949), 272–291.

Jones, Matt B., 'Some Bibliographical Notes on Cotton Mather's 'The Accomplished Singer,'" *Publications of the Colonial Society of Massachusetts*, XXVIII (1935), 186–193.

—— "Bibliographical Notes on Thomas Walter's 'Grounds and Rules of Musick Explained,'" *Proceedings of the*

American Antiquarian Society, N.S. XLII (1932), 235–246.

Kelly, J. Frederick, "Raising Connecticut Meeting-Houses," *Old-Time New England*, XXVII (1936), 3–9.

Kelso, Robert W., *The History of Public Poor Relief in Massachusetts, 1620–1920*, Boston, 1922.

Kouwenhoven, John A., "Some Unfamiliar Aspects of Singing in New England, 1620–1810," *New England Quarterly*, VI (1933), 567–588.

Langdon, William Chauncy, *Everyday Things in American Life, 1607–1776*, New York, 1937.

Lawrence, Henry W., *The Not-Quite Puritans*, Boston, 1928. (A labored striving to present the peccadilloes of Puritans with humor.)

—— "Puritan Scandals—Courtship, Marriage and Divorce Three Centuries Ago," *Yankee*, III (1937), 7–9, 29.

Lawrence, Robert M., *New England Colonial Life*, Cambridge, 1927.

Love, William de L., *The Fast and Thanksgiving Days of New England*, Boston, 1895.

Lovell, John, Jr., "The Beginnings of the American Theatre," *Theatre Annual*, X (1952), 7–19. (Finds the beginnings of the American theatre in the colonial meetinghouse.)

McClusker, Honor, "Scholars, Rogues, and Puritans," *More Books*, XIII (1938), 1–8.

Mangler, Joyce Ellen, and William Dinneen, "Early Music in Rhode Island Churches," *Rhode Island History*, XVII (1958), 1–9, 33–44, 73–84, 108–118.

Morgan, Edmund S., *The Puritan Family: Essays on Religion and Domestic Relations in Seventeenth Century New England*, Boston, 1944. (A valuable collection of literate scholarly essays, most of which originally appeared in *More Books*, published by the Boston Public Library.)

Muzzey, David S., "The Heritage of the Puritans," *Annual Report of the American Historical Association*, 1925, 239–249. (Stresses the point that they educated for responsibility.)

Myers, Gustavus, *Ye Olden Blue Laws*, New York, 1921.

Nordell, Philip G., "Cotton Mather in Love," *Harper's Magazine*, CLIII (1926), 556–572.

Oberholzer, Emil, Jr., "The Church in New England Society," *Seventeenth Century America: Studies in Colonial History*, ed. James Morton Smith, Chapel Hill, 1959, 143–165. (A study in the ecclesiastical regulation of social behavior.)

—— *Delinquent Saints: Disciplinary Action in the Early Congregational Churches of Massachusetts*, New York, 1950.

Parkes, Henry B., "Morals and Law Enforcement in Colonial New England," *New England Quarterly*, V (1932), 431–452.

—— "New England in the Seventeen-Thirties," *New England Quarterly*, III (1930), 397–419. (A picture of affairs, books, reading, and trends.)

—— "Sexual Morals and the Great Awakening," *New England Quarterly*, III (1930), 133–135.

Porter, Katherine A., "Affection of Praehiminincies," *Accent*, II (1942), 131–138, 226–232. (A fragment of a domestic biography of Cotton Mather.)

—— "A Bright Particular Faith, A.D. 1700. A Portrait of Cotton Mather," *Perspectives USA*, No. 7 (Spring 1954), 83–92. (An imaginative study of Mather's conflicting emotions during the long illness of his wife, Abigail, and after her death.)

Powell, Chilton L., "Marriage in Early New England," *New England Quarterly*, I (1928), 323–334.

Schafer, Joseph, *The Social History of American Agriculture*, New York, 1936.

Schlesinger, Elizabeth Bancroft, "Cotton Mather and His Children," *William and Mary Quarterly*, X (1953), 181–189.

Scholes, Percy A., *The Puritans and Music in England and New England*, London, 1934. (An authoritative work, even though prone to special pleading.)

—— "The Truth about the New England Puritans and Music," *Musical Quarterly*, XIX (1933), 1–17.

Sonneck, Oscar G., *Early Concert Life in America, 1731–1800*, Leipzig, 1907.

Sprott, S. E., "The Puritan Problem of Suicide," *Dalhousie Review*, XXXVIII (1958), 222–233.

Stetson, Sarah Pattee, "American Garden Books Transplanted and Native Before 1807," *William and Mary Quarterly*, III (1946), 343–369.

Stevenson, Noel C., "Marital Rights in

the Colonial Period," *New England Historical and Genealogical Register*, CIX (1955), 84–91.

Stewart, George R., "Men's Names in Plymouth and Massachusetts in the Seventeenth Century," *University of California Publications in English*, Vol. VII, No. 2, 109–137.

Stiles, Henry R., *Bundling; its Origin, Progress and Decline in America*, Albany, 1871; Harrisburg, Pa., 1928.

Thwing, Leroy L., "Lighting in Early Colonial Massachusetts," *New England Quarterly*, XI (1938), 166–170.

Trewartha, Glenn T., "Types of Rural Settlement in Colonial America," *Geographical Review*, XXXVI (1946), 568–596. (Social desiderata determined the settlement pattern in New England.)

Walcott, Robert R., "Husbandry in Colonial New England," *New England Quarterly*, IX (1936), 218–252.

Weeden, William B., *Early Rhode Island, A Social History of the People*, New York, 1910.

—— "Ideal Newport in the 18th Century," *Proceedings of the American Antiquarian Society*, N.S. XVIII (1906), 106–117.

Weld, Ralph F., *Slavery in Connecticut*, Hartford, 1935.

Wendell, Barrett, "Some Neglected Characteristics of the New England Puritans," *Annual Report of the American Historical Association*, 1891, 245–253.

Wertenbaker, Thomas J., *The First Americans, 1607–1690*, New York, 1927. Volume II of *A History of American Life*.

—— *The Golden Age of Colonial Culture*, New York, 1942. (Eighteenth-century cultural interests in Boston, New York, Philadelphia, Annapolis, Williamsburg, and Charleston.)

Wharton, Anne H., *Colonial Days and Dames*, Philadelphia, 1895.

Woodhouse, Julia, "Judge Sewall and Antislavery Sentiment in Colonial New England," *Negro Historical Bulletin*, VI (1943), 125, 143.

Wright, Harry A., "Those Human Puritans," *Proceedings of the American Antiquarian Society*, L (1940), 80–90.

Wright, Louis B., "The Colonial Struggle Against Barbarism," *Culture on the Moving Frontier*, Bloomington, 1955; Harper Torchbook edition, 1961, 11–45.

—— *The Cultural Life of the American Colonies*, New York, 1957; Harper Torchbook edition, 1962. (This admirably concise, immensely valuable little book has chapters on "Zeal for Education," "Books, Libraries and Learning," "Literary Production," "Drama, Music and Other Diversions," etc., and could well be listed under a half dozen rubrics of this bibliography.)

V. BIOGRAPHY

Only a few "Lives" were published as such during the first century of the settlements. Eventually, when the funeral sermons, historical essays, diaries, journals, and the large collections of personal papers (usually in manuscript) have been consulted, the amount of biographical material covering the period will prove enormous. This bibliography is confined to printed sources only. Such libraries as those of the New England Historical Genealogical Society, Congregational Library, and Massachusetts Historical Society in Boston; as well as those of Harvard and Yale Universities, and of the American Antiquarian Society in Worcester, are especially rich in manuscript material.

A. Puritan Biographies

Certain items, often biographical in nature, are more properly classified elsewhere. Such historical narratives, for instance, as John Williams's *The Redeemed Captive*, Cotton Mather's *Magnalia*, John Winthrop's *Journal*, will be found in section I A. See also section IV A.

Barnard, John, *Ashton's Memorial. An History of the Strange Adventures, and Signal Deliverances, of Mr. Philip Ashton*, Boston, 1725.

Colman, Benjamin, *Reliquiae Turellae, et Lachrymae Paternae*, Boston, 1735; London, 1741.

—— *The Prophet's Death Lamented and*

Improved, Boston, 1723. (Funeral sermon on Increase Mather.)

Mather, Cotton, *Chrysostomus Nov-Anglorum*, Boston, 1695. (Life of John Davenport.)

—— *Ecclesiastes*, Boston, 1697. (Life of Jonathan Mitchell.)

—— *Johannes in Eremo. Memoirs, Relating to The Lives, Of . . . John Cotton, . . . John Norton*, Boston, 1695.

—— *The Life of Mr. Thomas Dudley*, ed. Charles Deane, Cambridge, 1870.

—— *Memoria Wilsonia*, Boston, 1695. (Life of John Wilson.)

Mather, Samuel, *The Life of . . . Cotton Mather*, Boston, 1729.

Mather, Samuel (of Witney), *Memoirs of the Life of the Late Reverend Increase Mather*, London, 1725.

Norton, John, *Abel being dead yet speaketh*, Cambridge, 1657; London, 1658; ed. E. Pond, 1842. (Life of John Cotton; see Dana K. Merrill, in part D of this section.)

Turell, Ebenezer, *The Life and Character of the Reverend Benjamin Colman*, Boston, 1749.

—— *Memoirs of the Life and Death Of the Pious and Ingenious Mrs. Jane Turell*, Boston, 1735; London, 1741. (Jane Turell was a daughter of Benjamin Colman.)

—— *Observanda*, Boston, 1695. (Life of Queen Mary.)

—— *Parentator*, Boston, 1724. (Life of Increase Mather.)

—— *Pietas in Patriam*, Boston, 1697. (Life of Sir William Phips.)

—— *Piscator Evangelicus. Or, The Life of Mr. Thomas Hooker*, Boston, 1695.

—— *The Triumphs of the Reformed Religion, in America*, Boston, 1691. Subsequently published as *The Life and Death Of The Renown'd Mr. John Eliot*, London, 1691, 1694, 1820.

Mather, Increase, *The Life and Death Of That Reverend Man of God, Mr. Richard Mather*, Cambridge, 1670; reprinted in *Collections of the Dorchester Antiquarian and Historical Society*, No. 3, Boston, 1850.

B. Diaries, Journals, and Collections of Personal Papers

Thousands of Puritans kept diaries, and many also preserved their correspondence and papers. For a bibliography of diaries, see Harriette M. Forbes, *New England Diaries, 1602–1800*, Topsfield, Mass., 1923.

Aspinwall Papers, The, Collections of the Massachusetts Historical Society, fourth series, Vols. IX and X (1871).

Barnard, John, "Autobiography," *Collections of the Massachusetts Historical Society*, third series, V (1836), 177–243.

—— "Memoranda Quotidiana, 1715–1735," *Congregational Quarterly*, IV (1862), 376 ff.

Belcher Papers, The, Collections of the Massachusetts Historical Society, sixth series, Vols. VI and VII (1893–1894).

Bradford, William, "Letter Book," *Collections of the Massachusetts Historical Society*, first series, III (1794), 27–76.

Brainerd, David, *An Account of the Life of the Late Reverend Mr. Brainerd*, ed. by Jonathan Edwards, Boston, 1749; numerous editions, the latest *The Life and Diary of David Brainerd with a Biographical Sketch of President Edwards* by Philip E. Howard, Jr., Chicago, 1949.

Brock, John, "The Autobiographical Memoranda of John Brock, 1636–1659," ed. by Clifford K. Shipton, *Proceedings of the American Antiquarian Society*, LIII (1943), 96–105.

Burr, Esther, "Journal," ed. Josephine Fisher, *New England Quarterly*, III (1930), 297–315.

Calder, Isabel M., ed., *Letters of John Davenport, Puritan Divine*, New Haven, 1937.

Dow, George F., ed., *The Holyoke Diaries, 1709–1856*, Salem, Mass., 1911.

Green, Joseph, "The Commonplace Book of Joseph Green (1675–1715)," ed. by Samuel E. Morison, *Publications of the Colonial Society of Massachusetts*, XXXIV (1943), 191–253.

—— "Diary," (together with a biographical sketch of Green by Samuel P. Fowler), *Essex Institute Historical Collections*, VIII (1868), 91–96, 105–174, 215–224; X (1870), pt. I, 73–104; XXXVI (1900), 325–330.

Hinckley Papers, The, Collections of the Massachusetts Historical Society, fourth series, Vol. V (1861).

Homes, William, "Diary of Rev. William Homes of Chilmark, Martha's Vineyard, 1689–1746." *New England Historical and Genealogical Register*, XLVIII (1894), 446–453; XLIX (1895), 413–416; L (1896), 155–166.

Hull, John, "The Diaries of John Hull," *Transactions and Collections of the American Antiquarian Society*, III (1857), 109–316.

Jones, Matt B., "Thomas Maule, the Salem Quaker, and Free Speech in Massachusetts Bay," *Essex Institute Historical Collections*, LXXII (1936), 1–42.

Knight, Sarah Kemble, *The Journals of Madam Knight, and Rev. Mr. Buckingham*, New York, 1825; *The Journal of Madam Knight*, ed. George P. Winship, Boston, 1920.

Lynde, Benjamin, *The Dairies of Benjamin Lynde and Benjamin Lynde, Jr.*, [*1690–1780*], Boston, 1880.

Mather, Cotton, *Diary of Cotton Mather*, [*1681–1724*], *Collections of the Massachusetts Historical Society*, seventh series, Vols. VII and VIII (1911, 1912); New York, 1957, 2 vols.

Mather, Increase, *Diary*, with Introduction by Samuel A. Green, Cambridge, 1900. (Brief extracts.)

Mather, Richard, *Journal, Collections of the Dorchester Antiquarian and Historical Society*, No. 3 (1850).

Mather Papers, The, Collections of the Massachusetts Historical Society, fourth series, Vol. VIII (1868).

[Sewall, Joseph], "Sins and Mercies of a Harvard Student," *More Books*, XI (1936), 277–285. (Sewall's Diary *ca.* 1707).

Sewall, Samuel, *Diary of Samuel Sewall, 1674–1729, Collections of the Massachusetts Historical Society*, fifth series, Vols. V–VII (1878–1882). Selections from the Diary in convenient form in *Samuel Sewall's Diary*, ed. Mark Van Doren, New York, 1927.

—— *Letter-Book of Samuel Sewall, Collections of the Massachusetts Historical Society*, sixth series, Vols. I–II (1886–1888).

Shepard, Thomas, "The Autobiography of Thomas Shepard," *Publications of the Colonial Society of Massachusetts*, XXVII (1932), 345–400. (Prefaced by a complete bibliography.)

Stearns, Raymond P., ed., "Letters and Documents by or Relating to Hugh Peter," *Essex Institute Historical Collections*, LXXI (1935), 303–318; LXXII (1936), 43–72, 117–134, 208–232, 303–349; LXXIII (1937), 130–157.

Thacher, Peter, "The Diary of a Colonial Clergyman: Peter Thacher of Milton," ed. by Edward Pierce Hamilton, *Proceedings of the Massachusetts Historical Society*, LXXI (1953–1957), 1959, 50–63. (A revealing account of day to day life of a well-to-do clergyman.)

Trumbull Papers, The, Collections of the Massachusetts Historical Society, fifth series, Vols. IX and X (1885, 1888); seventh series, Vols. II and III (1902).

Wigglesworth, Michael, "The Diary of Michael Wigglesworth (1653–1657)," ed. by Edmund S. Morgan, *Publications of the Colonial Society of Massachusetts*, XXXV (1942–1946), 1951, 311–444.

Williams, Roger, *Letters of Roger Williams, 1632–1682*, ed. John R. Bartlett, Providence, 1874.

—— *Letters and Papers of Roger Williams, 1629–1682*, Boston, 1924.

Winthrop Papers, The, Collections of the Massachusetts Historical Society, fourth series, Vols. VI and VII (1863, 1865); fifth series, Vols. I and VIII (1871, 1882); sixth series, Vols. III and V (1889, 1892). The "Papers" are now being re-edited, with copious notes, by the Society (Vols. III, IV and V, ed. by Allyn Bailey Forbes): Vol. I, 1929; Vol. II, 1931; Vol. III, 1943; Vol. IV, 1944; Vol. V, 1947. (Rich in details of everyday life for Puritans in England and Massachusetts Bay.)

"Winthrop-Davenport Papers," *Bulletin of the New York Public Library*, III (1899), 393–408.

C. Collections

First of all, the student should consult the *Dictionary of American Biography* (containing bibliographies), and the *Dictionary of National Biography;* secondly, such repositories of genealogical information as James Savage, *Genealogical Dictionary of the First Settlers of New England*, Boston, 1860–1862, 4 vols., or the pages of *The New England Historical and Genealogical Register*, Boston, 1847—current. In addition the following are useful:

Brook, Benjamin, *Lives of the Puritans*, London, 1813, 3 vols.

Calamy, Edmund, *Calamy Revised*, ed. A. G. Matthews, Oxford, 1934; London, 1959, with a revision of the original introduction. (Revision of Calamy's *Account of the Ministers and Others Ejected and Silenced, 1660–1662*. Biographies of the English Puritans, some of them New England figures.)

Chauncy, Charles, "A Sketch of Eminent Men in New England," *Collections of the Massachusetts Historical Society*, first series, X (1809), 154–165. (A letter to Ezra Stiles, written in 1768, giving sketches of twenty-two Puritan divines.)

Dexter, Franklin B., *Biographical Sketches of the Graduates of Yale College with Annals of the College History*, New York, 1885–1912, 6 vols.

Foster, Joseph, *Alumni Oxonienses, 1500–1714*, Oxford, 1891–1892, 4 vols.

Lives of the Chief Fathers of New England, Boston, 1846–1849, 6 vols. (Cotton, Wilson, Norton, Davenport, Eliot, Shepard, I. Mather, Hooker.)

Peel, Albert, *The Congregational Two Hundred*, London, 1948. (A short biographical guide to two hundred leaders of Congregational thought and polity, with emphasis on the earlier leaders.)

Sibley, John L., *Biographical Sketches of Graduates of Harvard University in Cambridge, Massachusetts*, Cambridge, 1873–1885, 3 vols. (Includes Harvard classes 1642–1689.) Vol. IV, Cambridge, 1933, and Vols. V–XI, Boston, 1937–1960 (Harvard classes 1699–1745), ed. Clifford K. Shipton. (The series is a joy to read and an indispensable biographical and bibliographical guide for the period and subjects covered.)

Sprague, William B., *Annals of the American Pulpit*, New York, 1857–1869, 9 vols.

Venn, John, and J. A. Venn, *Alumni Cantabrigienses*, Cambridge, Eng., 1922–1927, 4 vols.

Walker, Williston, *Ten New England Leaders*, New York, 1901. (Bradford, Cotton, R. Mather, Eliot, I. Mather, Edwards, Chauncy.)

Wendell, Barrett, *Stelligeri, and Other Essays Concerning America*, New York, 1893.

Wood, Anthony, *Athenae Oxonienses*, ed. Philip Bliss, 1813–1820, 4 vols. (The best edition.)

D. Secondary Works

This list is far from complete. The student should consult the bibliography appended to the articles in *Dictionary of American Biography*. Further biographical material will be found listed throughout the text of this book in the brief notices which introduce the selections.

Allen, Alexander V. G., *Jonathan Edwards*, Boston, 1889. (An able analysis of Edwards' position as a theologian.)

Augur, Helen, *An American Jezebel: The Life of Anne Hutchinson*, New York, 1930. (Novelized invective.)

Bingham, Hiram, "Elihu Yale, Governor, Collector and Benefactor," *Proceedings of the American Antiquarian Society*, XLVII (1937), 93–144.

Boas, Ralph P., and Louise Boas, *Cotton Mather: Keeper of the Puritan Conscience*, New York, 1928. (Somewhat journalistic.)

Bradford, Alden, *Memoir of the Life and Writings of Rev. Jonathan Mayhew*, Boston, 1838.

Burgess, Walter H., *John Robinson, Pastor of the Pilgrim Fathers*, London, 1920.

Campbell, Helen S., *Anne Bradstreet and Her Time*, Boston, 1891.

Carpenter, Edmund J., *Roger Williams;*

A Study of the Life, Times and Character of a Political Pioneer, New York, 1909.

Chamberlain, Nathan H., *Samuel Sewall and the World He Lived In*, Boston, 1897.

Clarke, Hermann Frederick, *John Hull: A Builder of the Bay Colony*, Portland, 1940.

Curtis, Edith, *Anne Hutchinson: A Biography*, Cambridge, 1930.

Cavis, Richard B., *George Sandys, Poet Adventurer: A Study in Anglo-American Culture in the Seventeenth Century*, New York, 1955.

Dean, John W., *A Memoir of the Rev. Nathaniel Ward*, Albany, 1868.

—— *Memoir of Rev. Michael Wigglesworth*, Albany, 1871.

De Levie, Dagobert, "Cotton Mather, Theologian and Scientist," *American Quarterly*, III (1951), 362–365.

Earle, Alice M., *Margaret Winthrop*, New York, 1895.

Easton, Emily, *Roger Williams, Prophet and Pioneer*, New York, 1930. (A popular work, stressing the early and little-known years.)

Eaton, Arthur W. H., *The Famous Mather Byles*, Boston, 1914.

Ernst, James E., *Roger Williams: New England Firebrand*, New York, 1932. (Over-enthusiastic and inaccurate.)

—— "Roger Williams and the English Revolution," *Collections of the Rhode Island Historical Society*, XXIV (1931), 1–58, 118–128.

—— "New Light on Roger Williams' Life in England," *Collections of the Rhode Island Historical Society*, XXII (1929), 97–103.

Foote, Henry W., "George Phillips, First Minister of Watertown," *Proceedings of the Massachusetts Historical Society*, LXIII (1931), 193–227.

Freiberg, Malcolm, "Thomas Hutchinson: The First Fifty Years (1711–1761)," *William and Mary Quarterly*, XV (1958), 35–55.

—— "William Bollan, Agent of Massachusetts," *More Books*, XXIII (1948), 43–53, 90–100, 135–146, 168–182, 212–220.

Gookin, Frederick W., *Daniel Gookin, 1612–1687*, Chicago, 1912.

Gorton, Adelos, *The Life and Times of Samuel Gorton*, Philadelphia, 1907.

Gould Elizabeth P., *Ezekiel Cheever, Schoolmaster*, Boston, 1904.

Green, Samuel A., *Benjamin Tompson*, Boston, 1895.

Gummere, Richard, "John Wise, A Classical Controversialist," *Essex Institute Historical Collections*, XCII (1956), 265–278.

Hare, Lloyd C. M., *Thomas Mayhew, Patriarch to the Indians, 1593–1682*, New York, 1932.

Harkness, Reuben E. E., "Roger Williams—Prophet of Tomorrow," *Journal of Religion*, XV (1935), 400–425.

Holmes, Thomas J., "Samuel Mather of Witney, 1674–1733," *Publications of the Colonial Society of Massachusetts*, XXVI (1927), 312–322.

Hornberger, Theodore, "Samuel Lee (1625–1691), A Clerical Channel for the Flow of New Ideas to Seventeenth-Century New England," *Osiris*, I (1936), 341–355.

Hosmer, James K., *The Life of Young Sir Henry Vane*, Boston, 1888.

Kimball, Everett, *The Public Life of Joseph Dudley*, New York, 1911.

Kittredge, George L., *Doctor Robert Child the Remonstrant*, Cambridge, 1919. (Reprinted from *Publications of the Colonial Society of Massachusetts*, XXI (1920), 1–146.

Marvin, Abijah P., *The Life and Times of Cotton Mather*, Boston, 1892.

Mason, Louis B., *The Life and Times of Major John Mason of Connecticut: 1600–1672*, New York, 1935.

Matthews, Albert, "Samuel Mather," *Publications of the Colonial Society of Massachusetts*, XVIII (1917), 206–228.

Mayo, Lawrence S., *John Endecott*, Cambridge, 1936.

—— *The Winthrop Family in America*, Boston, 1948.

Merrill, Dana K., "The First American Biography," *New England Quarterly*, XI (1938), 152–154. (A sketchy account of John Norton's life of John Cotton.)

Miller, Perry, *Jonathan Edwards*, New York, 1948; Meridian paperback. (A full-bodied presentation of Edwards as a great theologian, philosopher and intellect.)

—— "Jonathan Edwards and the Great Awakening," *America in Crisis*, ed. Daniel Aaron, New York, 1952. Reprinted in Perry Miller, *Errand into the Wilderness*, Cambridge, 1956, 153–166.

—— *Roger Williams: His Contribution to the American Tradition*, Indianapolis, 1953. (Combines selections and comment.)

Mood, Fulmer, "Notes on John Josselyn, Gent.," *Publications of the Colonial Society of Massachusetts*, XXVIII (1935), 24–36.

Morgan, Edmund S., *The Puritan Dilemma: The Story of John Winthrop*, Boston, 1958. (The Reconciliation of the Puritan ethic to political life.)

Morison, Samuel E., "William Pynchon, The Founder of Springfield," *Proceedings of the Massachusetts Historical Society*, LXIV (1932), 67–107.

Morris, Maxwell H., "Roger Williams and the Jews," *American Jewish Archives*, III (1951), 24–27.

Murdock, Kenneth B., *Increase Mather, the Foremost American Puritan*, Cambridge, 1925. (A definitive biography and an authoritative study of the period.)

Nickerson, Philip Tillinghast, "More about Reverend John Mayo of Cape Cod and Boston," *New England Historical and Genealogical Register*, CIII (1949), 32–42.

—— "Rev. John Mayo, First Minister of the Second Church in Boston, Massachusetts," *New England Historical and Genealogical Register*, XCV (1941), 39–49, 100–108.

Patrick, J. Max, "The Arrest of Hugh Peters," *Huntington Library Quarterly*, XIX (1955–1956), 343–351.

—— *Hugh Peters, A Study in Puritanism, The University of Buffalo Studies*, XVII, 4, Buffalo, 1946.

Porter, Kenneth W., "Samuel Gorton, New England Firebrand," *New England Quarterly*, VII (1934), 405–444.

Powicke, Frederick J., *John Robinson*, London, 1920.

Preston, Richard Arthur, *Gorges of Plymouth Fort: A Life of Sir Fernando Gorges, Captain of Plymouth Fort, Governor of New England, and Lord of the Province of Maine*, Toronto, 1953.

Reuter, Karl, *Wilhelm Amesius*, Neukirchen, 1940. (The only full-scale study of Ames.)

Rice, Howard C., "Cotton Mather Speaks to France," *New England Quarterly*, XVI (1943), 198–233. (Mather's *Une Grande Voix du Ciel a la France* 1725, a plea for French Protestants, reveals his energy as a propagandist.)

Rose-Troupe, Frances, *John White, the Patriarch of Dorchester and the Founder of Massachusetts, 1575–1648*, New York, 1930. (Detailed but injudicious.)

Rugg, Winifred K., *Unafraid: A Life of Anne Hutchinson*, Boston, 1930. (Somewhat sentimentalized, but careful and fair-minded.)

Shipton, Clifford K., *Roger Conant: A Founder of Massachusetts*, Cambridge, 1944.

Stearns, Raymond P., "Hugh Peter and his Biographers," *Proceedings of the Bostonian Society* (1935), 27–50.

—— *The Strenuous Puritan: Hugh Peters, 1598–1660*, Urbana, 1954.

Straus, Oscar S., *Roger Williams: The Pioneer of Religious Liberty*, New York, 1894.

Swan, Bradford F., *Gregory Dexter of London and New England, 1610–1700*, Rochester, N.Y., 1949.

Titus, Anson, "Madam Sarah Knight, Her Diary and Her Times," *Bostonian Society Publications*, IX (1912), 99–126.

Turnbull, G. H., "George Stirk, Philosopher by Fire (1628?–1665)," *Publications of the Colonial Society of Massachusetts*, XXXVIII (1947–1951), 1959, 219–251. (A fascinating account of a New England doctor and alchemist.)

—— "Robert Child," Publications of the Colonial Society of Massachusetts, XXXVIII (1947–1951), 1959, 21–53. (Supplements Kittredge's article *supra* with new information based on Hartlib's papers.)

Tuttle, Charles W., *Captain John Mason*, Boston, 1887.

Updike, Daniel, *Richard Smith, First English Settler of Narragansett Country, Rhode Island, With a Series of Letters written by his son Richard Smith to members of the Winthrop Family* . . . , Boston, 1937. (The letters are of interest for the light they shed on the politics of speculation in the Narragansett lands.)

Walker, George L., *Thomas Hooker*, New York, 1891.

Wendell, Barrett, *Cotton Mather, the Puritan Priest*, New York, 1891.

Wiener, Frederick B., "Roger Williams' Contribution to Modern Thought," *Collections of the Rhode Island Historical Society*, XXVIII (1935), 1–20.

Willcock, John, *Life of Sir Henry Vane the Younger*, London, 1913.

Winslow, Ola E., *Jonathan Edwards, 1703–1758*, New York, 1940. (A straightforward, reliable biography.)

—— *Master Roger Williams: A Biography*, New York, 1957.

Winthrop, Robert C., *Life and Letters of John Winthrop*, Boston, 1864–1867, 2 vols. (Contains many important original papers.)

Wolkins, George C., "Edward Winslow (O. V. 1606–1611), King's Scholar and Printer," *Proceedings of the American Antiquarian Society*, LX (1950), 237–266.

VI. LITERARY THEORY

Literature as a separate and self-sufficient art did not exist for Puritans. The art of writing, either in prose or verse, was first and foremost a means to the end of expressing some truth, theological, historical, or philosophical. Yet Puritans wrote voluminously, and no study of their ideology would be complete without a careful presentation of such theory as they expressed, or some attempt at an evaluation of their artistry in prose and verse.

A. Primary Sources

Puritans almost never discussed literature as *belles lettres*, and very seldom devoted a whole discussion to theories of rhetoric and composition. Consequently, a list of passages in which the Puritan standards of composition, vocabulary, and style are proclaimed almost always will be found as incidental remarks in passing, or in prefaces of commendation. The following list cannot have exhausted all such passages, but it gives at least a representative selection. No list of secondary works has been added to this section, since so few studies of the literary theories of Puritans have been made. All appropriate items have been assembled in Section VII B, under the general heading: "Puritan Literature—Secondary Works."

Adams, Eliphalet, *A Funeral Discourse*, New London, 1724, Sig. K3 verso.

—— Preface to Nehemiah Hobart, *The Absence of the Comforter Described and Lamented*, New London, 1717.

Adams, John, *Poems on Several Occasions*, Boston, 1745, "The Publisher to the Reader."

Allen, James, *New-Englands choicest Blessing*, Boston, 1679, "To the Reader."

—— *Serious Advice to delivered Ones from Sickness*, Boston, 1679, "To the Reader."

Allen, Thomas, Preface to John Cotton, *An Exposition upon . . . Revelation*, London, 1656.

Ames, William, *The Marrow of Sacred Divinity*, London, 1643, Sig. A4 verso; pp. 157–162.

Appleton, Nathaniel, *The Great Apostle Paul exhibited, and recommended as a Pattern of true Gospel Preaching*, Boston, 1751, pp. 26–30.

—— *Faithful Ministers of Christ*, Boston, 1743, p. 25.

—— *Superior Skill and Wisdom necessary for Winning Souls*, Boston, 1737, pp. 26, 32.

Barnard, John, *Elijah's Mantle*, Boston, 1724, p. 36.

—— *Sermons on Several Subjects*, London, 1727, Dedication; and pp. 11, 38.

[*Bay Psalm Book*,] *The Whole Book of Psalmes*, Cambridge, 1640, preface.

Belcher, Jonathan, Manuscript commonplace book, Harvard College Library *ca.* 1725–1728.

Bradford, William, "Of Plimmoth Plantation," Manuscript in Massachussetts State Library; Facsimile, London, 1896, p. 19.

Brocklesby, Richard [?], *Private Vertue and Public Spirit display'd. In a Succinct Essay on the Character of Captain Thomas Coram*, Boston, 1751, p. 15. (Reprinted in *Proceedings of the Massachusetts Historical Society*, LVI (1922), 15.

Bulkley, John, Preface to Roger Wolcott, *Poetical Meditations*, New London, 1725.

Byles, Mather, *A Discourse on the Present Vileness of the Body*, Boston, 1732, preface.

—— An essay on style in *The American Magazine and Historical Chronicle*, Boston,

January, 1745, pp. 1–4. (Signed "L," and identified as Byles's by Lyon N. Richardson, *A History of Early American Magazines, 1741–1789*, p. 54 note.)

—— Letter to Alexander Pope, October 7, 1727. Manuscript in New England Historical Genealogical Society, Boston. (Printed in Arthur W. H. Eaton, *The Famous Mather Byles*, Boston, 1914, p. 233.)

Chappell, William, *Methodus Concionandi*, London, 1648; translated as *The Preacher, or The Art and Method of Preaching*, London, 1656. (One of the best manuals of sermon style and practice.)

Chauncy, Charles (1592–1672), *Gods Mercy*, Cambridge, 1655, p. 37.

Chauncy, Charles (1705–1787), *Ministers cautioned against the Occasions of Contempt*, Boston, 1744, pp. 29, 35.

A Collection of Poems. By Several Hands, Boston, 1744. (Incidental critical phrases throughout, in poems by Mather Byles, John Adams, John Perkins, Matthew Adams, and Jonathan Belcher.)

Colman, Benjamin, Preface to Josiah Smith, *A Discourse*, Boston, 1726.

—— *The Government & Improvement of Mirth*, Boston, 1707, p. 45.

—— *Practical Discourses*, London, 1707, p. 57.

—— *The Prophet's Death Lamented*, Boston, 1723, p. 32.

—— *Reliquiae Turellae*, London, 1741, p. 153.

Cooke, William, *The Great Duty of Ministers*, Boston, 1742, p. 7.

Cotton, John, *A brief exposition with practical observations upon the whole book of Canticles*, London, 1655, p. 92.

—— *A Brief Exposition Of the whole Book of Canticles*, London, 1642, pp. 7–9, 112.

—— *A Briefe Exposition with Practicall Observations upon the Whole Book of Ecclesiastes*, London, 1654, pp. 265–266, 269, 272.

Douglass, William, *A Summary, Historical and Political, Of the first Planting*, Boston, 1749–1752, 2 vols. Vol. I, p. 1; Vol. II, title-page and p. 1.

Edwards, Jonathan, Rules on the cover of "Notes on Natural Science," *ca.* 1719. (Manuscript in Yale University Library; see C. H. Faust and T. H. Johnson, *Jonathan Edwards, Representative Selections*, New York, 1935.

—— *Five Discourses*, Boston, 1738, preface.

—— *An Humble Inquiry*, Boston, 1749, conclusion.

—— *The Life of President Edwards*, by Sereno E. Dwight, New York, 1829, p. 601.

Eliot, Andrew, *A burning and shining Light*, Boston, 1750, p. 31.

Eliot, Jared, *Essays upon Field-Husbandry*, New York, 1748, preface.

Fitch, James, *Peace The End of the Perfect and Upright*, Cambridge, 1672, preface.

Foxcroft, Thomas, *The day of a godly Man's Death*, Boston, 1722, preface.

—— *A practical Discourse*, Boston, 1718, pp. 24–40. (One of the best discussions of style, delivered in a sermon at his own ordination by a minister who throughout his career was preoccupied with the problem of style and form.)

—— *Some seasonable Thoughts on Evangelic Preaching*, Boston, 1740, pp. 4, 5.

—— Preface to Jonathan Dickinson, *The True Scripture-Doctrine*, Boston, 1741.

Gookin, Daniel, *Historical Collections of the Indians in New-England, ca.* 1675, first printed in *Collections of the Massachusetts Historical Society*, first series, I (1792), p. 143.

Hobby, William, *An Inquiry*, Boston, 1745, pp. 19, 24.

Hooker, Thomas, *The Soules Exaltation*, London, 1638, pp. 26, 110.

—— *The Soules Preparation*, London, 1632, p. 66.

—— *A Survey of the Summe*, London, 1648, preface.

Hubbard, William, *The Happiness of a People*, Boston, 1676, pp. 8–15, 36–38.

Knapp, Francis, *Gloria Britannorum*, Boston, 1723, p. 11.

Lawson, Deodat, *The Duty & Property of a Religious Hous[e]holder Opened*, Boston, 1693, Sig. A4.

Mather, Cotton, *The A. B. C. of Religion*, Boston, 1713, p. 4.

—— *Bonifacius*, Boston, 1710, preface.

—— *Brethren*, Boston, 1718, pp. 21, 23.

—— *Corderius Americanus*, Boston, 1708, Introduction, and pp. 28, 29.

—— *Duodecennium Luctuosum*, Boston, 1714, Introduction, and p. 12.

—— *Just Commemorations*, Boston, 1715, preface and p. 34.

—— *Magnalia*, London, 1702. (See *Selections from Cotton Mather*, ed. K. B. Murdock, New York, 1926, pp. 1, 6, 13, 14, 18, 19, 26, 27.)

—— *Malachi*, Boston, 1717, pp. 27, 73.

—— *Manuductio*, Boston, 1726, pp. 28–35, 42, 44–50. (The section "Of Poetry and Style" is the only essay on the subject in America before Mather Byles's essay on style in *The American Magazine* for January, 1745, and it is the best treatment of the subject before Franklin's *Autobiography*.)

—— *Parentator*, Boston, 1724, Introduction, and p. 215.

—— *Psalterium Americanum*, Boston, 1718, Introduction. (Very important for the statement of his theories of translation and his conception of blank verse.)

Mather, Increase, *A Call from Heaven*, Boston, 1679, "To the Reader."

—— *Some Important Truths*, London, 1674, "To the Reader."

Mather, Richard, in Increase Mather, *The Life . . . of Richard Mather*, Cambridge, 1670, p. 85.

Mather, Samuel, *The Life of . . . Cotton Mather*, Boston, 1729, pp. 33, 68, 69, 72.

Mayhew, Experience, *Indian Converts*, Boston, 1727, Introduction.

Mitchell, Jonathan, Poem prefacing Michael Wigglesworth, *The Day of Doom*, Cambridge, 1662.

Morgan, Joseph, *Sin its own Punishment*, Boston, 1728, "To the Reader."

Morrell, William, *New-England*, London, 1625, "To the Reader."

Morton, William, preface to John Cotton, *The way of Life*, London, 1641.

Norton, John, *The Heart of N-England rent*, Cambridge, 1659, pp. 6, 58.

Noyes, Nicholas, Prefatory poem to Cotton Mather, *Magnalia*, London, 1702.

Oakes, Urian, *An Elegie upon . . . Shepard*, Cambridge, 1677, "To the Reader."

Penhallow, Samuel, *The History of the Wars of New-England*, Boston, 1726, preface.

Perkins, William, *The Art of Prophecying* (1592), *Works*, London, 1631, II, 670 ff. (A work regarded as the authoritative manual of sermon style and practice in New England.)

Pigot, George, *A Vindication*, Boston, 1731, preface.

Prince, Thomas, *A Chronological History of New-England*, Boston, 1736, preface.

—— Preface to Thomas Hooker, *The Poor Doubting Christian*, Boston, 1743.

—— Introduction to *Meditations and Spiritual Experiences of Mr. Thomas Shepard*, Boston, 1749.

Prince, Thomas, and Joseph Sewall, Preface to Samuel Willard, *A Compleat Body of Divinity*, Boston, 1726.

Saffin, John, Dedicatory poem in William Hubbard, *A Narrative of the Troubles with the Indians*, Boston, 1677.

—— *John Saffin His Book*, ed., with introduction by Caroline Hazard, New York, 1928, pp. 2, 47, 60.

Seccomb, Joseph, *On the Death Of the Reverend Benjamin Colman*, Boston 1747, p. 8.

Select Essays, With some few Miscellaneous Copies of Verses, Boston [?]. 1714, pp. 10, 11. (Unique copy in library of Massachusetts Historical Society.)

Shepard, Thomas, "Subjection to Christ," *Works*, ed. Albro, 1853, III, 278. (Preface by William Greenhill and Samuel Mather.)

Steere, Richard, *A Monumental Memorial of Marine Mercy*, Boston, 1684, "To the Reader," and p. 1.

Symmes, Thomas, *Lovewell Lamented*, Boston, 1725, pp. 5, 6.

"To Mr. B[yles] occasioned by his verses to Mr. Smibert on seeing his Pictures," *Proceedings of the Massachusetts Historical Society*, LIII (1920), 59.

Turell, Ebenezer, *The Life and Character of the Reverend Benjamin Colman*, Boston, 1749, pp. 167–169.

—— *Memoir of . . . Mrs. Jane Turell*, London, 1741, pp. 15, 25–31.

—— *Ministers should carefully avoid giving Offence*, Boston, 1740, pp. 14, 15.

Walter, Thomas, *The Sweet Psalmist of Israel*, Boston, 1722, Dedication and pp. 1–15.

Webb, John, *The Duty of Survivers*, Boston, 1739, p. 27.

White, John, *The Planters Plea*, London, 1630, "To the Reader."

Wigglesworth, Michael, *The Day of Doom*, Boston, 1701, Invocation.

—— "The prayse of Eloquence," in Samuel E. Morison, *Harvard College in the Seventeenth Century*, Cambridge, 1936, pp. 180–183. (From manuscript notebook in possession of the New England Historical Genealogical Society.)

Wilkins, John, *Ecclesiastes, or A Discourse concerning the Gift of Preaching*, London, 1646.

Willard, Samuel, *Ne Sutor*, Boston, 1681, p. 2.

—— "Particular Application, the best way of teaching," *The Truly Blessed Man*, Boston, 1700, pp. 423–434.

Wise, John, and Jonathan Mitchell, Preface to Samuel Whiting, *A Discourse of the Last Judgment*, Cambridge, 1664.

VII. PURITAN POETRY

Though the Puritans remained relatively indifferent to poetry as an art, there were many among them who chose it as a vehicle to express their deepest feelings, and a few who achieved in it some measure of excellence. Elegies, memorial odes, satires and hymns (or stanzas designed for congregational singing) make up the largest portion of the Puritan verses.

A. Primary Sources

No attempt is made to list the great number of elegies which were written, and all too often printed, during the first century of the New England settlements. Such items are usually found in broadsides. Occasionally they were appended to funeral sermons, or scattered through such histories as Johnson's *Wonder-working Providence*, Morton's *New-Englands Memoriall*, or Mather's *Magnalia*. (See Ford and Winslow below.)

Adams, John, *Poems on Several Occasions, Original and Translated*, Boston, 1745.

[*The Bay Psalm Book.*] *The White Booke of Psalmes Faithfully Translated into English Metre*, Cambridge, 1640. Many editions; the latest, a facsimile reprint, Chicago, 1956.

Bradstreet, Anne, *The Tenth Muse Lately sprung up in America*, London, 1650. Second edition published with title *Several Poems Compiled with great variety of Wit and Learning, full of delight*, Boston, 1678; 1758. *Works*, ed. John H. Ellis, Charlestown, Mass., 1867; ed. Charles E. Norton, New York, 1897.

Bradstreet, Samuel, *An Almanack for . . . 1657*, Cambridge, 1657.

Byles, Mather, *The Comet*, Boston, 1744.

—— *On the Death of the Queen: A Poem*, Boston, 1738.

—— *A Poem on the Death of His Late Majesty, King George*, Boston, 1727.

—— *Poems. The Conflagration*, Boston, 1755.

—— *Poems on Several Occasions*, Boston, 1736; 1744.

—— *To His Excellency Governor Belcher on the Death of his Lady*, Boston, 1736.

Byles, Mather, Joseph Green, John Adams, and others, *A Collection of Poems. By Several Hands*, Boston, 1744.

Colman, Benjamin, *A Poem on Elijah's Translation*, Boston, 1707.

Folger, Peter, *A Looking Glass For the Times*, Cambridge, 1676; 1763. (No Puritan, Folger was a Nantucket Quaker, grandfather of Benjamin Franklin.)

Ford, Worthington C., ed., "Epitaphs on Nowell, Endicott, Withington and Pole," *Publications of the Colonial Society of Massachusetts*, VIII (1906), 224–233.

Green, Joseph, *Entertainment for a Winter's Evening*, Boston, 1750.

—— *The Grand Arcanum Debated*, Boston, 1755.

—— *A Mournfull Lamentation for the Death of Mr. Old Tenor*, Boston, 1750.

Handkerchiefs from Paul, ed. K. B. Murdock, Cambridge, 1927. (Poems from six seventeenth-century Puritans. This well-edited volume contains the best introduction on Puritan poetry to be found.)

Harvard Heroics: A Collection of Eighteenth Century Verse Descriptions of Harvard College, ed. Robert A. Aubin, Cambridge, 1934. (Contains Mather Byles's Hogarthian sketch of a public Commencement.)

Hubbard, John, *A Monumental Gratitude Attempted, In a Poëtical Relation of the Danger and Deliverance of Several of the Members of Yale-College in Passing the Sound, from Southhold to New-Haven*, New London, 1727.

Johnson, Edward, *Wonder-working Providence*. [See section II A.] (Johnson's history is interspersed with many epitaphs and poetic memorials.)

Oakes, Urian, *An Elegy upon The Death of the Reverend Mr. Thomas Shepard*, Cambridge, 1677. Reprinted Boston, 1896. (Perhaps the best elegy written by a colonial Puritan.)

Pain, Philip, *Daily Meditations; or, Quotidian Preparations for and Considerations of Death and Eternity*, Cambridge, 1670. Reprinted with an Introduction by Leon Howard, San Marino, Calif., 1936.

Russell, Daniel, *An Almanack*, Cambridge, 1671.

Seccombe, John, "Father Abbey's Will," Cambridge, 1730; ed. John L. Sibley, 1854. (Verses on the college bedmaker.)

Select Essays, Boston, 1714. (A collection of poems and prose essays, written perhaps by young Harvard graduates.)

Steere, Richard, *The Daniel Catcher. The Life Of the Prophet Daniel: in a Poem. To which is Added, Earth's Felicities, Heaven's Allowances, A Blank Poem. With several other Poems*, Boston, 1713. (The earliest attempt in America to write black verse.)

—— *A Monumental Memorial of Marine Mercy Being An Acknowledgment of an High Hand of Divine Deliverance on the Deep in the Time of distress, in A Late Voyage from Boston in New-England To London*, Boston, 1684.

Taylor, Edward, "The Earliest Poems of Edward Taylor," ed. Donald E. Stanford, *New England Quarterly*, XXXIII (1960), 136–151. (Early poems not included in Stanford's *Poems of Edward Taylor*, 1960.

—— "Nineteen Unpublished Poems by Edward Taylor," ed. Donald E. Stanford, *American Literature*, XXIX (1957), 18–46. (The essential Calvinism of Taylor's thought appears in these selections from "Sacramental Meditations.")

—— *The Poems of Edward Taylor*, ed. Donald E. Stanford, New Haven, 1960. (A full edition.)

—— "Poetical Works," Manuscript in Yale University Library. Selections ed. Thomas H. Johnson, *New England Quarterly*, X (1937), 290–322.

—— *The Poetical Works of Edward Taylor*, ed. Thomas H. Johnson with Introd. and Notes, New York, 1939. (Johnson's article in the *New England Quarterly* [above] and the publication of Taylor's collected works brought about a re-evaluation of the literature of the Puritans.)

—— "Some Edward Taylor Gleanings," *New England Quarterly*, XVI (1943), 280–295.

Tompson, Benjamin, *Works*, ed. Howard J. Hall, Boston, 1924.

Wigglesworth, Michael, "Gods Controversy with New England" (1662), *Proceedings of the Massachusetts Historical Society*, XII (1873), 83–93.

—— *Meat out of the Eater*, Cambridge, 1670[?]; 6th ed., New London, 1770. (See *Yale University Gazette*, V (1931), 45–47.)

—— *The Day of Doom*, Cambridge, 1662; ed. Kenneth B. Murdock, New York, 1929.

Wilson, John, *A Song or, Story, For the Lasting Remembrance of divers famous works*, London, 1626. (The same, Boston, 1680, *A Song of Deliverance*.)

Winslow, Ola E., ed., *American Broadside Verse from Imprints of the 17th and 18th Centuries*, New Haven, 1930.

Wolcott, Roger, *Poetical Meditations, being the Improvement of Some Vacant Hours*, New London, 1725; reprinted Boston, 1898.

B. Puritan Literature—Secondary Works

No general history of colonial literature has yet superseded Tyler's account, undertaken in the last quarter of the nineteenth century. The two-volume Duyckinck *Cyclopædia*, issued over a century ago, contains a large gathering of prose and verse; Stedman and Hutchinson's *Library* devotes three volumes to literature in the American colonial period, and remains the most extensive anthology.

Adams, Charles, F., "Milton's Impress on the Provincial Literature of New England," *Proceedings of the Massachusetts Historical Society*, XLII (1909), 154–170.

Barbeau, Marius, "Indian Captivities," *Proceedings of the American Philosophical Society*, XCIV (1950), 522–548.

Black, Mindele, "Edward Taylor: Heaven's Sugar Cake," *New England Quarterly*, XXIX (1956), 159–181.

Blau, Herbert, "Heaven's Sugar Cake: Theology and Imagery in the Poetry of Edward Taylor," *New England Quarterly*, XXVI (1953), 337–360.

Bleyer, Willard G., *Main Currents in the History of American Journalism*, Boston, 1927.

Bowden, Edwin T., "Benjamin Church's *Choice* and American Colonial Poetry," *New England Quarterly*, XXXII (1959), 170–184.

Boys, Richard C., "The Beginnings of the American Poetical Miscellany, 1714–1800," *American Literature*, XVII (1945), 127–139.

—— "The English Poetical Miscellany in Colonial America," *Studies in Philology*, XLII (1945), 114–130. (An annotated list of English miscellanies in American libraries, together with critical notes on the reception of poetic miscellanies in the American colonies.)

Bradford, Eugene F., "Conscious Art in Bradford's *History of Plymouth Plantation*," *New England Quarterly*, I (1928), 133–157.

Brown, Wallace C., "Edward Taylor, American Metaphysical," *American Literature*, XVI (1944), 186–197.

Cady, Edwin H., "The Artistry of Jonathan Edwards," *New England Quarterly*, XXII (1949), 61–72.

Cambridge History of American Literature, The, ed. William P. Trent and others, New York, 1917–1921, 4 vols.; 1933, 3 vols.; 1954, 3 vols. in one without the useful bibliographies of the earlier editions. (Vol. I covers the colonial period.)

Carleton, Phillips D., "The Indian Captivity," *American Literature*, XV (1943), 169–180. (Revaluation of the place of "captivity literature" in the social and literary history of America.)

Cook, Elizabeth C., *Literary Influences in Colonial Newspapers, 1704–1750*, New York, 1912.

Duyckinck, Evert A., and George L., eds., *Cyclopædia of American Literature*, New York, 1855, 2 vols. (Still useful.)

Dykema, Karl W., "Samuel Sewall Reads John Dryden," *American Literature*, XIV (1942), 157–161.

Fisch, Harold, "The Puritans and the Reform of Prose Style," *Journal of English Literary History*, XIX (1952), 229–248. (Influences of sermons and other writings of the Puritans in shaping plain prose.)

Fussell, Edwin S., "Benjamin Tompson, Public Poet," *New England Quarterly*, XXVI (1953), 494–511.

Galinsky, Hans, "Anne Bradstreet, Du Bartas, und Shakespeare in Zusammenhang kolonial Verpflanzung und Umformung europäischer Literatur: Ein forschungsbericht und eine Hypothese," *Festschrift fur Walther Fischer*, ed. Carl Winter, Heidelberg, 1959.

Goodman, William B., "Edward Taylor Writes His Love," *New England Quarterly*, XXVII (1954), 510–515.

Grabo, Norman S., "Catholic Tradition, Puritan Literature, and Edward Taylor," *Papers in Michigan Academy of Science, Arts, and Letters*, XLV (1959), 395–402.

—— "Edward Taylor on the Lord's Supper," *Boston Public Library Quarterly*, XII (1960), 22–36.

Greenough, Chester N., "The Publication of Cotton Mather's *Magnalia*," *Publications of the Colonial Society of Massachusetts*, XXVI (1927), 296–312.

Grierson, Herbert J. C., *Cross Currents in English Literature of the Seventeenth Century*, London, 1929.

Gummere, Richard M., "The Classics in a Brave New World," *Harvard Studies in Classical Philology*, LXII (1957), 118–139.

—— "The Heritage of the Classics in Colonial North America, an Essay in the Greco-Roman Tradition," *Proceedings of the American Philosophical Society*, XCIX (15 April, 1955), 68–78.

Haraszti, Zoltàn, *The Enigma of the Bay Psalm Book*, Chicago, 1956. (Attributes preface and a large part of the translations to John Cotton.)

Hart, James D., *The Oxford Companion to American Literature*, New York, 1956, 3rd edn. (A standard handbook.)

—— "A Puritan Bookshelf," *New Colophon*, I (1948), 13–26. (Reading and love of books among the New England colonists.)

Henson, Robert, "Form and Content of the Puritan Funeral Elegy," *American Literature*, XXXII (1960), 11–27.

Holden, William P., *Anti-Puritan Satire, 1572–1642*, New Haven, 1954.

Hornberger, Theodore, "A Note on Eighteenth-Century American Prose Style," *American Literature*, X (1938), 77–78. (Cites an early example (1708) of an American author being charged with provinciality in style.)

Howell, W. S., *Logic and Rhetorics in England, 1500–1700*, Princeton, 1956.

Jantz, Harold S., "The First Century of New England Verse," *Proceedings of the American Antiquarian Society*, LIII (1943), 219–258; reprinted Worcester, Mass., 1945. (Contains a critical and descriptive survey, selections, and an annotated, inclusive bibliography of early New England verse.)

—— "A Funeral Elegy for Thomas Danforth, Treasurer of Harvard," *Harvard Library Bulletin*, I (1947), 113–115.

Johnson, Thomas H., "The Discovery of Edward Taylor's Poetry," *Colophon, New Graphic Series* I, No. 2 (1939).

—— "A Seventeenth Century Printing of Some Verses of Edward Taylor," *New England Quarterly*, XIV (1941), 139–141. (Taylor exercised true poetic craftsmanship in giving his verses form.)

Jones, Howard M., "American Prose Style: 1700–1770," *Huntington Library Bulletin*, No. 6, 1934, 115–151.

—— "Desiderata in Colonial Literary History," *Publications of the Colonial Society of Massachusetts*, XXXII (1938), 428–439.

Jones, Richard F., "The Attack on Pulpit Eloquence in the Restoration: An Episode in the Development of the Neo-classical Standards for Prose," *Journal of English and Germanic Philology*, XXX (1931), 188–217. (A much neglected essay; essential reading for anyone with ideas about "Puritan Plain Style.")

—— "Science and English Prose Style in the Third Quarter of the Seventeenth Century," *Publications of the Modern Language Association*, XLV (1930), 977–1009.

—— "Science and Language in England of the Mid-seventeenth Century," *Journal of English and Germanic Philology*, XXXI (1932), 315–331. (The preceding three essays were republished in *The Seventeenth Century: Studies in the History of English Thought*, Stanford, 1948.)

—— *The Triumph of the English Language*, Stanford, 1953. (For Puritan views on Language, see especially Chapter X, "The Useful Language.")

Jordan, Philip D., "The Funeral Sermon; A Phase of American Journalism," *American Book Collector*, IV (1933), 177–188.

Koller, Kathrine, "The Puritan Preacher's Contribution to Fiction," *Huntington Library Quarterly*, XI (1948), 321–340.

Lee, James M., *History of American Journalism*, rev. ed., Boston, 1923.

Lind, S. E., "Edward Taylor, A Re-valuation," *New England Quarterly*, XXI (1948), 518–530.

MacDougall, Hamilton C., *Early New England Psalmody: An Historical Appreciation, 1620–1820*, Brattleboro, 1940.

Manierre, William Reid, "Some Characteristic Mather Redactions," New England Quarterly, XXXI (1958), 496–505. (Mather's use of sources in the *Magnalia Christi Americana*.)

Matthiessen, Francis O., "Michael Wigglesworth, A Puritan Artist," *New England Quarterly*, I (1928), 491–504.

Miller, Perry, "The Rhetoric of Sensation," *Perspectives of Criticism*, ed. H. Levin, Cambridge, 1950; reprinted in P. Miller, *Errand into the Wilderness*, Cambridge, 1956, 167–183. (Edward's rhetoric of the naked idea.)

Mitchell, W. Fraser, *English Pulpit Oratory from Andrewes to Tillotson: A Study of its Literary Aspects*, London, 1932. (Indispensable for literary forms and values of sermons; excellent bibliography.)

Morison, Samuel E., "The Reverend Seaborn Cotton's Commonplace Book," *Publications of the Colonial Society of Massachusetts*, XXXII (1938), 320–352. (Family and church records interspersed with extracts from Sidney's *Arcadia*, and verses from ballads and amorous poetry.)

Murdock, Kenneth B., "The Colonial Experience in the Literature of the United States," *Papers of the American Philosophical Society*, C (1956), 129–132.

—— *Literature and Theology in Colonial*

New England, Cambridge, 1949; Harper Torchbook edition, 1962.

Nichols, Charles L., "The Holy Bible in Verse," *Proceedings of the American Antiquarian Society*, N.S. XXXVI (1926), 71–82. (Earliest written, 1699; earliest extant, 1717.)

Owst, Gerald R., *Literature and Pulpit in Medieval England*, Cambridge, Eng., 1933. (Important background.)

Pearce, Roy Harvey, "Edward Taylor: The Poet as Puritan," *New England Quarterly*, XXIII (1950), 31–46.

—— "The Significance of the Captivity Narrative," *American Literature*, XIX (1947), 1–20.

Peckham, Howard H., ed., *Captured by Indians: True Tales of Pioneer Survivors*, New Brunswick, N. J., 1954. (A popular retelling of fourteen "captivity" stories.)

Piercy, Josephine K., "The Character in the Literature of Early New England," *New England Quarterly*, XII (1939), 470–476.

—— *Studies in Literary Types in Seventeenth-Century America (1607–1710)*, New Haven, 1939.

Putnam, Michael C. J., ed., "The Story of the Storm," *New England Quarterly*, XXXIII (1960), 489–501. (Latin verse, c. 1706–1707; perhaps Sewall's.)

Quinn, Arthur Hobson, *et al.*, *The Literature of the American People: An Historical and Critical Survey*, New York, 1951. ("The Colonial and Revolutionary Period" by Kenneth B. Murdock is a valuable survey, but does not supplant *Literature and Theology in Colonial New England*. A useful bibliography with critical comments.)

Richardson, Caroline F., *English Preachers and Preaching, 1640–1670. A Secular Study*, New York, 1928. (Very useful for understanding the character of sermon literature.)

Richardson, Lyon N., *A History of Early American Magazines, 1741–1789*, New York, 1931. (Best history of the subject; immense bibliography.)

Rosenbach, Abraham S. W., *Early American Children's Books*, Portland, Me., 1933.

Russell, Jason A., "The Narratives of the Indian Captivities," *Education*, LI (1930), 84–88.

Shaaber, Matthias A., "Forerunners of the Newspaper in the United States," *Journalism Quarterly*, XI (1934), 339–347.

Shipton, Clifford K., "Literary Leaven in Provincial New England," *New England Quarterly*, IX (1936), 203–217.

Spiller, Robert E., *et al.*, *Literary History of the United States*, New York, 1948; 2 vols., with 3rd vol. of bibliographies, comp. by Thomas H. Johnson; revised one vol. edn., New York, 1953. (The best work of its kind.) *Bibliographical Supplement*, ed. Richard M. Ludwig, New York, 1959. (Earlier bibliographical vol. by Thomas H. Johnson continued through 1957 with some listings for 1958, and supplementary entries throughout.)

Stanford, Donald E., "Edward Taylor and the Lord's Supper," *American Literature*, XXVII (1955), 172–178. (Asserts Taylor's orthodoxy in this sacrament.)

—— "The Puritan Poet as Preacher, an Edward Taylor Sermon," *Studies in American Literature*, ed. Waldo McNeir and Leo B. Levy, Baton Rouge, 1960, 1–10.

Stedman, Edmund C., and Ellen M. Hutchinson, eds., *A Library of American Literature from the Earliest Settlement to the Present Time*, New York, 1888–1890, 11 vols. (Vols. I, II, and III cover the colonial period; the most extensive anthology.)

Stewart, Randall, "Puritan Literature and the Flowering of New England," *William and Mary Quarterly*, III (1946), 319–342.

Strange, Arthur, "Michael Wigglesworth Reads the Poets," *American Literature*, XXXI (1959), 325–326.

Svendsen, J. Kester, "Anne Bradstreet in England: A Bibliographical Note," *American Literature*, XIII (1941), 63–65. (Evidence of Anne's popularity in England during her lifetime.)

Swan, Bradford F., "Some Thoughts on the Bay Psalm Book of 1640, with a Census of Copies," *Yale University Library Gazette*, XXII (1948), 56–76.

Thayer, William R., "Pen Portraiture in Seventeenth Century Colonial Historians," *Proceedings of the American Antiquarian Society*, N.S., XXXI (1921), 61–69.

Thompson, W. Lawrence, "Classical Echoes in Sewall's Diaries (1674–1729),"

New England Quarterly, XXIV (1951), 374–377. (A temporary decline in the classical tradition revealed by "primitive" specimens of colonial Latin verse.)

Titus, Anson, "Madam Sarah Knight, Her Diary and Her Times," *Bostonian Society Publications*, IX (1912), 99–126.

Tyler, Moses C., *A History of American Literature during the Colonial Period, 1607–1765*, New York, 1878, 2 vols.; rev. ed., 1897; Ithaca, New York, 1949. (Still the best discussion of colonial American literature. Should be consulted in the 1949 edn., a reprint of the 1878 edn. with the changes made in the three later edns. indicated in footnotes containing Tyler's own marginal notes to the first edn. Introduction by Howard Mumford Jones.)

Vail, Robert W. G., "Certain Indian Captives of New England," *Proceedings of the Massachusetts Historical Society*, LXVIII (1944–1947), 1952, 113–131.

Warren, Austin, "Edward Taylor's Poetry: Colonial Baroque," *Kenyon Review*, III (1941), 355–371. Reprinted in Warren's *Rage for Order*, Chicago, 1947, 1–18.

Watters, Reginald E., "Biographical Technique in Cotton Mather's *Magnalia*," *William and Mary Quarterly*, II (1945), 154–163.

Weathers, Willie T., "Edward Taylor, Hellenistic Puritan," *American Literature*, XVIII (1946), 18–26.

—— "Edward Taylor and the Cambridge Platonists," *American Literature*, XXVI (1954), 1–31. (His large debt to the Southern Renaissance and the Platonists explains why he could be both a good New England Puritan and a good poet.)

Wendell, Barrett, *A Literary History of America*, 6th ed., New York, 1911. (Heavily biased in favor of the Puritan tradition, but written on the basis of deep knowledge of the seventeenth century.)

—— *The Temper of the Seventeenth Century in English Literature*, New York, 1904.

White, Elizabeth Wade, "The Tenth Muse—A Tercentenary Appraisal of Anne Bradstreet," *William and Mary Quarterly*, VIII (July, 1951), 355–377.

White, Helen C., *English Devotional Literature, 1600–1640*, Madison, Wis., 1931. (Valuable study of religious prose.)

White, Trentwell M., and Paul W. Lehmann, *Writers of Colonial New England*, Boston, 1929.

Winship, George Parker, *The Cambridge Press, 1638–1692. A Reexamination of the Evidence Concerning the Bay Psalm Book and the Eliot Indian Bible as well as other Contemporary Books and People*, Philadelphia, 1945.

Wright, Nathalia, "The Morality Tradition in the Poetry of Edward Taylor," *American Literature*, XVIII (1946), 1–17.

Wroth, Lawrence C., "John Maylem: Poet and Warrior," *Publications of the Colonial Society of Massachusetts*, XXXII (1938), 87–120.

VIII. EDUCATION

No colonizing Puritan wrote formal discourses on education; his theories for the training of youth are expressed in funeral sermons, diaries, letters, and public addresses. Further bibliographical data is supplied in the headings throughout the chapter on Education.

A. Primary Sources

Puritans, like other cultivated Englishmen of the time, were deeply concerned in acquiring an education, as their incidental remarks make sufficiently clear.

Chauncy, Charles, *Gods Mercy, shewed to his people in giving them a faithful Ministry and schooles of Learning for the continual supplyes thereof*, Cambridge, 1655.

Colman, Benjamin, *The Master Taken up from the Sons of the Prophets*, Boston, 1724. (Funeral sermon on President Leverett.)

Hancock, John, *The Danger of an Unqualified Ministry*, Boston, 1743. (A sermon directed against itinerant preachers and an illiterate clergy.)

Harvard College Records, Publications of the Colonial Society of Massachusetts, Vols. XV, XVI, XXXI (1925–1935).

Hoar, Leonard, "[Letter] To his

Freshman Nephew, Josiah Flynt," 1661, in Samuel E. Morison, *Harvard College in the Seventeenth Century*, Cambridge, 1936, 639–644.

Keach, Benjamin, *The Protestant Tutor for Children*, Boston, 1685.

Mather, Cotton, *Corderius Americanus. An Essay upon the Good Education of Children*, Boston, 1708. (A funeral sermon upon Ezekiel Cheever.)

—— "Special Points," *The Diary of Cotton Mather*, ed. Worthington C. Ford, *Collections of the Massachusetts Historical Society*, seventh series, VII (1911), 534–537. (An outline, dated February 1705/06, relating to the education of his children.)

Mather, Increase, "Presidential Address," *ca.* 1696, in Samuel E. Morison, *Harvard College in the Seventeenth Century*, Cambridge, 1936, p. 167.

New Englands First Fruits, London, 1643. Reprinted various times: most recently in a line-for-line and word-for-word reprint in Samuel E. Morison, *The Founding of Harvard College*, Cambridge, 1935, 419–447. (An account of the first commencement at Harvard in 1642; classic statement of the Puritan educational ideal.)

Shepard, Thomas, Jr., "A Letter . . . to his Son at his Admission into the College," *Publications of the Colonial Society of Massachusetts*, XIV (1913), 192–198.

B. Secondary Works

Detailed and accurate studies of Puritan education, necessarily slow in appearing, are still in progress. The works in this field by Morison and Seybolt are especially noteworthy.

Adamson, John W., *Pioneers of Modern Education, 1600–1700*, Cambridge, Eng., 1905.

Allen, Phyllis, "Medical Education in Seventeenth Century England," *Journal of the History of Medicine and Allied Sciences*, I (1946), 115–143.

—— "Scientific Studies in Seventeenth Century English Universities," *Journal of the History of Ideas*, X (1949), 219–253.

Bainton, Roland H., *Yale and the Ministry: A History of Education for the Christian Ministry at Yale from the Founding in 1701*, New York, 1957.

Cairns, Earle E., "The Puritan Philosophy of Education," *Biblioteca Sacra*, CIV (1947), 326–336.

Chamberlain, Joshua L., and others, *Yale University*, Boston, 1900.

Chaplin, Jeremiah, *Life of Henry Dunster*, Boston, 1872. (Contains many important documents.)

Clapp, Clifford B., "Christo et Ecclesiae," *Publications of the Colonial Society of Massachusetts*, XXV (1924), 59–83.

Costello, William T., *The Scholastic Curriculum of Early Seventeenth-Century Cambridge*, Cambridge, 1958.

Cubberley, E. P., *Public Education in the United States*, Boston, 1919. (Convenient bibliographies.)

Dexter, Franklin B., *Documentary History of Yale University, 1701–1745*, New Haven, 1916.

Ford, Paul L., *The New-England Primer*, New York, 1897.

Gambrell, Mary L., *Ministerial Training in Eighteenth-Century New England*, New York, 1937.

Hale, Richard Walden, "The First Independent School in America," *Publications of the Colonial Society of Massachusetts*, XXXV (1942–1946), 1951, 225–297. (Early history of Roxbury Latin School, and some records of the Ipswich Grammar School.)

—— *History of the Roxbury Latin School*, Cambridge, 1946.

Hansen, Allen O., *Liberalism and American Education in the Eighteenth Century*, New York, 1926. (The emphasis is mainly on the latter half of the century; well documented, with a good bibliography of primary sources.)

Hazlitt, William C., *Schools, School-books and Schoolmasters*, London, 1888.

Holmes, Pauline, *A Tercentenary History of the Boston Public Latin School*, 1635–1935, Cambridge, 1935.

Hudson, Winthrop S., "The Morison Myth Concerning the Founding of Harvard College," *Church History*, VIII (1939), 148–159. (Morison "represents the establishment of Harvard College as a great adventure in secular education," rather than as an effort to provide for the training of ministers.)

Johnson, Clifton, *Old-Time Schools and School-Books*, New York, 1904.

Klain, Zora, *Educational Activities of New England Quakers*, Philadelphia, 1928.

Lane, William C., "Early Harvard Broadsides," *Proceedings of the American Antiquarian Society*, N.S. XXIV (1914), 264–304.

Latimer, John F. and Kenneth B. Murdock, "The 'Author' of Cheever's Accidence," *Classical Journal*, XLVI (1951), 391–397. (Establishes that Nathaniel Williams was "Author" or editor of the first five editions of the first Latin text written and published in America.)

Littlefield, George E., *Early Schools and School-Books of New England*, Boston, 1904.

—— "Elijah Corlet and the 'Faire Grammar Schoole' at Cambridge," *Publications of the Colonial Society of Massachusetts*, XVII (1915), 131–140.

McAnear, Beverly, "The Raising of Funds by the Colonial Colleges," *Mississippi Valley Historical Review*, XXXVIII (1951–1952), 591–612.

Matthews, Albert, "A Proposal for the Enlargement of University Learning in New England, 1658–1660," *Proceedings of the Massachusetts Historical Society*, XLI (1908), 301–308.

Meriwether, Colyer, *Our Colonial Curriculum, 1607–1776*, Washington, 1907.

Meyer, Isidore S., "Hebrew at Harvard, 1636–1760," *Publications of the American Jewish Historical Society*, No. 35, 145–170.

Middlekauff, Robert, "The Classical Curriculum in Eighteenth Century New England," *William and Mary Quarterly*, XVIII (1961), 54–67.

Morgan, Edmund S., "Ezra Stiles: The Education of a Yale Man, 1742–1746," *Huntington Library Quarterly*, XVII (1953–1954), 251–268.

Morison, Samuel E., *The Founding of Harvard College*, Cambridge, 1935. (A history of intellectual backgrounds and movements as well as of Harvard, the volume presents the college as a school of culture, not simply as a theological seminary.)

—— *Harvard College in the Seventeenth Century*, Cambridge, 1936, 2 vols.

—— "Precedence at Harvard College in the Seventeenth Century," *Proceedings of the American Antiquarian Society*, N.S. XLII (1932), 371–431.

Murdock, Kenneth B., "The Teaching of Latin and Greek at the Boston Latin School in 1712," *Publications of the Colonial Society of Massachusetts*, XXVII (1932), 21–29.

—— "Cotton Mather and the Rectorship of Yale College," *Publications of the Colonial Society of Massachusetts*, XXVI (1927), 388–401.

Nash, Roy, "Abiah Holbrook and His 'Writing-Master's Amusement'," *Harvard Library Bulletin*, VII (1953), 88–104.

—— "A Colonial Writing Master's Collection of English Copybooks," *Harvard Library Bulletin*, XIV (1960), 12–19.

Oviatt, Edwin, *The Beginnings of Yale, 1701–1726*, New Haven, 1916.

Parker, Irene, *Dissenting Academies in England*, Cambridge, Eng., 1914.

Pears, Thomas Clinton, Jr., "Colonial Education among Presbyterians," *Journal of Presbyterian History*, XXX (1952), 115–126, 165–174.

Perrin, Porter G., "Possible Sources of *Technologia* at Early Harvard," *New England Quarterly*, VII (1934), 718–724.

—— "The Teaching of Rhetoric in American Colleges before 1750," Manuscript dissertation, University of Chicago, 1936.

Pfeiffer, Robert H., "The Teaching of Hebrew in Colonial America," *Jewish Quarterly Review*, XLV (1955), 363–373.

Plimpton, George A., "The Hornbook and Its Use in America," *Proceedings of the American Antiquarian Society*, N.S. XXVI (1916), 264–272.

Pool, David de S., "Hebrew Learning Among the Puritans of New England Prior to 1700," *Publications of the American Jewish Historical Society*, XX (1911), 31–83.

Potter, David, *Debating in the Colonial Chartered Colleges: 1642–1900*, New York, 1944.

Rand, Benjamin, "Philosophical Instruction in Harvard University from 1636 to 1906," *Harvard Graduates' Magazine*, XXXVII (1928), 29–47, 188–200, 296–311.

Rand, Edward K., "Liberal Education in Seventeenth-Century Harvard," *New England Quarterly*, VI (1933), 525–551.

Rashdall, Hastings, *The Universities of Europe in the Middle Ages*, revised by F. M. Powicke and A. B. Emden, Oxford, 1936. (Essential for backgrounds of Puritan education and culture.)

Robbins, Fred G., "Salaries of Schoolteachers in Colonial America," *Monthly Labor Review*, XXVIII (1929), 27–31.

Seybolt, Robert F., *Apprenticeship & Apprenticeship Education in Colonial New England & New York*, New York, 1917.

—— *The Evening School in Colonial America*, Urbana, Ill., 1925.

—— *The Private Schools of Colonial Boston*, Cambridge, 1935.

—— "The Private Schools of Seventeenth-Century Boston," *New England Quarterly*, VIII (1935), 418–424.

—— *The Public Schools of Colonial Boston, 1635–1775*, Cambridge, 1935.

—— "Schoolmasters of Colonial Boston," *Publications of the Colonial Society of Massachusetts*, XXVII (1932), 130–156.

Shipton, Clifford K., "Secondary Education in the Puritan Colonies," *New England Quarterly*, VII (1934), 646–661. (During the eighteenth century public schools improved in quality.)

Small, Walter H., *Early New England Schools*, Boston, 1914.

Steiner, Bernard C., *The History of Education in Connecticut*, Washington, 1893.

Tucker, Louis Leonard, "President Thomas Clap and the Rise of Yale College, 1740–1766," *The Historian*, XIX (1956–1957), 66–81.

Tuer, Andrew W., *The History of the Horn-Book*, London, 1896.

Updegraff, Harlan, *The Origin of the Moving School in Massachusetts*, New York, 1907.

Vincent, W. A. L., *The State and School Education 1640–1660 in England and Wales*, London, 1950.

Walsh, James J., "Scholasticism in the Colonial Colleges," *New England Quarterly*, V (1932), 483–532.

Williams, George H., *Wilderness and Paradise in Christian Thought*, New York, 1961. (Part Two, a revision of "Excursus" from *Harvard Divinity School*, Boston, 1954, traces the Christian tradition in the Puritan idea of education.)

Wood, Norman, *The Reformation and English Education*, London, 1931.

IX. SCIENCE

The speculative nature of the Puritan made him keenly alert to developments in the scientific field. As long as he saw the shaping hand of God in the phenomenal universe, he not only accepted scientific inquiry but sought to advance it. He gathered data on earthquakes, thunderstorms, comets; on farming and the natural history of New England; on medical prodigies and physical disease. Most notably of all, he advanced the cause of inoculation for smallpox.

A. Primary Sources

The student should note particularly the number of contributions made by Puritans to the *Philosophical Transactions* of the Royal Society of London.

Boylston, Zabdiel, "The way of proceeding in the Small Pox inoculated in New England," *Philosophical Transactions*, Royal Society of London, XXXII (1721), No. 370, pp. 33–35. (Written in collaboration with Cotton Mather.)

Brattle, William, *Sundry Rules and Regulations for Drawing up a Regiment*, Boston, 1733.

A Brief Rule To guide the Common-People of New-England How to order themselves and theirs in the Small Pocks, or Measles, Boston, 1677. (A broadside; the earliest medical treatise printed in the colonies.)

Colman, Benjamin, *Some Observations on the New Method of Receiving the Small-Pox, by ingrafting or inoculating*, Boston, 1721.

Cooper, William, *A Letter . . . Attempting a Solution of the Objections . . . Against the New Way of Receiving the Small-Pox*, Boston, 1721.

Danforth, Samuel, *An Astronomical Description of the Late Comet or Blazing Star, As it appeared in New-England in the 9th,*

10th, 11th and in the beginning of the 12th Moneth, 1664. Together With a brief Theological Application thereof, Cambridge, 1665.

Doolittle, Thomas, *Earthquakes Explained and practically Improved*, London, 1693.

Dudley, Paul, "An Account of the Method of Making Sugar from the Juice of the Maple Tree in New England," *Philosophical Transactions*, Royal Society of London, XXXI (1720), No. 364, pp. 27, 28. (Dudley contributed in all, twelve scientific essays to the *Philosophical Transactions*. For a bibliography, see Sibley's *Biographical Sketches*, IV, 54.)

Edwards, Jonathan, "Some Early Writings of Jonathan Edwards," ed. Egbert C. Smyth, *Proceedings of the American Antiquarian Society*, N.S. X (1895), 212–247; XI (1896), 251–252.

—— "Of Insects," ed. Egbert C. Smyth, *Andover Review*, XIII (1890), 1–19.

Greenwood, Isaac, *An Experimental Course on Mechanical Philosophy*, Boston, 1726.

—— *A Friendly Debate; or, A Dialogue Between Academicus; and Sawny & Mundungus, Two Eminent Physicians, About some of their Late Performances*, Boston, 1722. (A satire.)

—— *A Philosophical Discourse concerning the Mutability and Changes of the Material World*, Boston, 1731.

Hoar, Leonard, "Letter to Mr. Robert Boyle," in Boyle's *Works* (London, 1744, 6 vols.), V, 642, 643; reprinted in S. E. Morison, *Harvard College in the Seventeenth Century*, Cambridge, 1936, pp. 644–646.

Lee, Samuel, 'Ελεοριαμβος. *Or the Triumph of Mercy in the Chariot of Praise. A Treatise Of Preventing secret & unexpected Mercies*, Boston, 1718.

A Letter from One in the Country, to His Friend in the City; in Relation to the Distress Occasioned by . . . Inoculation, Boston, 1721.

Mather, Cotton, "Account of a great storm, 1723," *Collections of the Massachusetts Historical Society*, first series, II, (1810), 11.

—— *A Letter to a Friend in the Country, Attempting a Solution of the Scruples . . . against the New Way of receiving the Small-Pox*, Boston, 1721.

—— *The Christian Philosopher: A Collection of the Best Discoveries in Nature, with Religious Improvements*, London, 1721. (The most important indication of New England's familiarity with the scientific advance.)

—— *Ignorantia Scientifica*, Boston, 1727.

Mather, Increase, *A Discourse Concerning Earthquakes*, Boston, 1706.

—— *An Essay for the Recording of Illustrious Providences*, Boston, 1684. Reprinted with introduction by George Offor, under the title *Remarkable Providences*, London, 1856; 1890.

—— ΚΟΜΗΤΟΓΡΑΦΙΑ. *Or A Discourse Concerning Comets*, Boston, 1683; London, 1811.

—— *The Latter-Sign Discoursed of*. Paged separately in the second edition of *Heavens Alarm to the World*, Boston, 1682.

—— *Severall Reasons Proving that Inoculation . . . is a Lawful Practice*, Boston, 1721; ed. with introduction by George L. Kittredge, Cleveland, 1921.

—— *The Voice of God, in Stormy Winds*, Boston, 1704.

Mather, Samuel, *A Letter to Doctor Zabdiel Boylston; Occasion'd by a late Dissertation concerning Inoculation*, Boston, 1730.

Morton, Charles, *Compendium Physicae*, ed. Theodore Hornberger with introd. by Samuel Eliot Morison. Publications, Colonial Society of Massachusetts, XXXIII (*Collections*), Boston, 1940. (In manuscript, this was the standard textbook of natural science at Harvard College at the end of the seventeenth century.)

Paine, Thomas, *The Doctrine of Earthquakes*, Boston, 1728.

Prince, Thomas, "Account of the Northern Lights, when first seen in England, 1716," *Collections of the Massachusetts Historical Society*, first series, II (1793), 14–20.

—— *Earthquakes the Works of God*, Boston, 1727.

Robie, Thomas, *A Letter to a Certain Gentleman desiring a particular Account may be given of a wonderful meteor*, Boston, 1719.

Thatcher, Thomas, *A Brief Rule to Guide the Common-people of New-England how to Order Themselves and Theirs in the Small Pocks, or Measles*, Boston, 1677; reprinted with a valuable introd. by Henry R. Viets, Baltimore, 1937.

Williams, John, *Several Arguments Proving that the Inoculating of the Small-Pox is not Contained in the Law of Physick, Either Natural or Divine, and therefore Unlawful,* Boston, 1721.

—— *An Answer to a Late Pamphlet, intitled, A Letter to a Friend in the Country,* Boston, 1722.

Winthrop, John, Jr., "Correspondence with Members of the Royal Society," *Proceedings of the Massachusetts Historical Society,* XVI (1878), 206–251.

—— "An Extract of a Letter . . . concerning some Natural Curiosities," *Philosophical Transactions,* Royal Society of London, V (1670), 1151–1153.

Winthrop, John (1681–1747), "Account of the Winter, 1717," *Collections of the Massachusetts Historical Society,* first series, II (1793), 11, 12. (This John Winthrop of Boston, as well as his uncle, John Winthrop, Jr., governor of Connecticut, was a member of the Royal Society of London.)

B. Popular Science in the Almanacs

The almanacs of New England, edited by a series of young Harvard graduates, often contain a page or two of scientific information especially designed for popular instruction. Even though brief, the articles indicate on the one hand the knowledge of the authors, and on the other the interest of the people. See Samuel E. Morison, *Harvard College in the Seventeenth Century,* pp. 216–219; see also in this bibliography Section IV B 1. The arrangement here is chronological.

T. S. [Thomas Shepard, Jr.?], "A Brief Explication of the most observable Circles in the Heavens," *Almanack,* Cambridge, 1656.

Brigden, Zechariah, "A breif Explication and proof of the Philolaick Systeme," *Almanack,* Cambridge, 1659; reprinted in *New England Quarterly,* VII (1934), 9–12. (The first recorded exposition of the Copernican system in New England.)

Cheever, Samuel, "A breif discourse concerning the various Periods of time," *Almanack,* Cambridge, 1660.

—— "A breif Discourse of the Rise and Progress of Astronomy," *Almanack,* Cambridge, 1661.

Chauncy, Nathaniel, "The primum mobile," *Almanack,* Cambridge, 1662.

Chauncy, Israel, "The Theory of Planetary Orbs," *Almanack,* Cambridge, 1663.

Nowell, Alexander, "The Suns Prerogative Vindicated," *Almanack,* Cambridge, 1665.

J. S. [John Sherman or Jeremiah Shepard?], "A Postscript to the preceding Kalender," *Almanack,* Cambridge, 1674.

Foster, J[ohn], "A brief Description of the Coelestial Orbs according to the Opinion of that Ancient Philosopher Pythagoras, and of all later Astronomers," *Almanack,* Boston, 1675. (Foster was the first printer in Boston.)

Sherman, John, "Of Eclipses of the Sun and Moon," *Almanack,* Cambridge, 1676.

J. F. [John Foster], "The Course of the Spring-tides this year," *Almanack,* Boston, 1678.

J. D. [John Danforth], "A Brief Memorial of some few Remarkable Occurrences in the 6 preceding yeares," *Almanack,* Cambridge, 1679.

Foster, John, "Postscript," *Almanack,* Boston, 1679. (An explanation of leap-year.)

—— "The Natures and Operations of the seven Planets," *Almanack,* Boston, 1680.

—— "Of Comets, Their Motion, Distance & Magnitude," followed by "Observations of a Comet seen this last Winter 1680, and how it appeared at Boston," *Almanack,* Boston, 1681.

Brattle, William, "An Explanation of the Preceding *Ephemeris,*" *Ephemeris,* Cambridge, 1682. (A series of philosophical and scientific observations on Reason, the calendar, eclipses, and the planets.)

Mather, Cotton, "A Description of the Last Years Comet," *Ephemeris,* Boston, 1683.

Russell, N[oadiah], "Concerning Lightning, and Thunder," *Ephemeris,* Cambridge, 1684.

Williams, W[illiam], "Concerning a Rainbow"; "Concerning the nature of Comets," *Ephemeris,* Cambridge, 1685.

Mather, Nathaniel, "A short view of the Discoveries that have been made in the Heavens with, and since the invention of the Telescope," *Ephemeris*, Boston, 1685.

—— "Concerning some late discoveries respecting the fixed Stars"; "Concerning late marvellous Astronomical Discoveries in the Planets," *Ephemeris*, Boston, 1686.

Danforth, Samuel, "Ad Librum," *New-England Almanack*, Cambridge, 1686. (Dedicatory poem, with defence of astronomy.)

Tulley, John, "Of the Rain-bow: Whence it is, and what it signifieth"; "Of Thunder and Lightning," *Almanack*, Boston, 1690.

Newman, Henry, "A Postscript Exhibiting somewhat Touching the Earth's Motion," *Harvard's Ephemeris, or Almanack*, Cambridge, 1690.

—— "Of Telescopes," *News from the Stars, An Almanack*, Boston, 1691.

Tulley, John, "Astronomicall Observations of the Weather & Winds from the Planets & their Aspects," *Almanack*, Cambridge, 1692.

Brattle, William, "A Postscript concerning the Tides, Weather, etc.," *Almanack*, Boston, 1694.

Lodowick, C[hristian], Concerning "certain Impieties and Absurdities" in the "Astrological Predictions" of Tulley: "As for Meteorology, it is meerly conjectural," *New-England Almanack*, Boston, 1695.

Tulley, John, "Concerning Astrology & Meteorology," *Almanack*, Boston, 1696. (An answer to the attack of Lodowick.)

C. Witchcraft

Material concerning witchcraft is also to be found in the *Diary* of Cotton Mather and the *Diary* of Samuel Sewall. See also Justin Winsor, *The Memorial History of Boston*, Vol. II; John G. Palfrey, *A Compendious History of New England*, IV, 96 ff; John Fiske, *New France and New England* (New York, 1902).

1. Primary Sources

The number of items here listed is limited to such as are historically important; the list is by no means exhaustive.

Brattle, Thomas, "A Full and Candid Account of the Delusion called Witchcraft which prevailed in New England," (MS. *ca.* 1692), *Collections of the Massachusetts Historical Society*, first series, V (1798), 61–80.

Burr, George L., ed., *Narratives of the Witchcraft Cases, 1648–1706*, New York, 1914; 1959. (The volume includes the essential portions of works concerned with Salem witchcraft: Cotton Mather, *Late Memorable Providences*, 1691; Deodat Lawson, *Brief and True Narrative*, 1692; Thomas Brattle, *A Full and Candid Account of the Delusions*, 1692; Cotton Mather, *Wonders of the Invisible World*, 1693; Cotton Mather, *A Brand Pluck'd out of the Burning*, 1693; Robert Calef, *More Wonders*, 1700.)

Hale, John, *A Modest Enquiry into the Nature of Witchcraft*, Boston, 1702.

Hutchinson, Francis, *An Historical Essay concerning Witchcraft*, London, 1718.

Hutchinson, Thomas, *The Witchcraft Delusion of 1692*, ed. W. F. Poole, Boston, 1870.

Lawson, Deodat, *Christs Fidelity the Only Shield Against Satans Malignity*, Boston, 1693. (A terrifying sermon, delivered at Danvers (Salem Village), March 24, 1692, at the height of the panic; an explicit statement of the Puritan conception of the character and role of the devil.)

Mather, Increase, *Cases of Conscience Concerning Evil Spirits Personating Men; Witchcrafts, Infallible Proofs of Guilt in such as are Accused with that Crime*, Boston, 1693; London, 1693; 1862. (The statement of rules and procedure in the examination of witches which, had it been followed by the Court at Salem, would have prevented the craze and the executions. See Kenneth B. Murdock, *Increase Mather*, pp. 287–316.)

—— *A Disquisition Concerning Angelical-Apparitions*, Boston, 1696.

Turell, Ebenezer, "Detection of Witchcraft," *Collections of the Massachusetts Historical Society*, second series, X (1823), 6–22.

Woodward, William E., ed., *Records of Salem Witchcraft*, Roxbury, Mass., 1864, 2 vols.

2. Secondary Works (Witchcraft)

Because of the fierceness of the controversy, the witchcraft delusion has often been disproportionately emphasized in Puritan history. Actually it played but a small part in affairs and was soon over.

Coffin, Joshua, *A Sketch of the History of Newbury*, [*Massachusetts*], . . . *from 1635 to 1845*, Boston, 1845.

Drake, Samuel G., *Annals of Witchcraft in New England, and Elsewhere in the United States*, Boston, 1869.

—— *The Witchcraft Delusion in New England*, Roxbury, Mass., 1866, 3 vols. (Contains original records and depositions.)

Fowler, Samuel P., *An Account of the Life . . . of the Rev. Samuel Parris*, Salem, 1857.

Fuess, Claude Moore, "Witches at Andover," *Proceedings of the Massachusetts Historical Society*, LXX (1950–1953), 1957, 8–20.

Greene, Samuel A., *Groton in Witchcraft Times*, Groton, Mass., 1883.

Gummere, Amelia M., *Witchcraft and Quakerism*, Philadelphia, 1908.

Haraszti, Zoltán, "Cotton Mather and the Witchcraft Trials," *More Books*, XV (1940), 179–184. (In a letter of Cotton Mather to John Cotton, Mather betrays sensitiveness to criticism of the judges of the witchcraft cases.)

Haven, Samuel F., *The Mathers and the Witchcraft Delusions*, Worcester, 1874.

Holmes, Thomas J., "Cotton Mather and His Writings on Witchcraft," *Papers of the Bibliographical Society of America*, XVIII (1925), 30–59.

Kittredge, George L., *Witchcraft in Old and New England*, Cambridge, 1929. (The chapter on witchcraft in New England is the definitive analysis, based upon exhaustive knowledge of the whole history of witchcraft in Europe.)

Lea, Henry Charles, *Materials toward a History of Witchcraft, collected by Henry Charles Lea*, **arranged and edited by Arthur C. Howland, Philadelphia, 1939. (Provides a background for the American student with its exposition of the logical system that directed popular opinion and guided the actions of ecclesiastical and secular authorities in witchcraft cases. Describes methods of trial and court procedures.)**

Levermore, Charles H., "Witchcraft in Connecticut," *New England Magazine*, N.S. VI (1892), 636–644.

Nevins, Winfield S., *Witchcraft in Salem Village in 1692*, Salem, 1916.

Notestein, Wallace, *A History of Witchcraft in England from 1558 to 1718*, Washington, 1911.

Poole, William F., "Cotton Mather and Salem Witchcraft," *North American Review*, CVIII (1869), 337–397. (Defense of Mather against C. W. Upham.)

Starkey, Marion L., *The Devil in Massachusetts: A Modern Inquiry Into the Salem Witch Trials*, New York, 1949. (A triumph of historical reconstruction; makes the trials, confessions, hysteria, and repentances credible.)

Summers, Montague, *The Geography of Witchcraft*, New York, 1927.

—— *The History of Witchcraft and Demonology*, New York, 1926.

Tapley, Charles S., *Rebecca Nurse, Saint but Witch Victim*, Boston, 1930.

Taylor, John M., *The Witchcraft Delusion in Colonial Connecticut, 1647–1697*, New York, 1908.

Upham, Charles W., *Salem Witchcraft and Cotton Mather*, Morrisania, N.Y., 1869. (Reply to Poole's defense.)

—— *Salem Witchcraft; with an Account of Salem Village, and a History of Opinions on Witchcraft and Kindred Subjects*, Boston, 1867, 2 vols.

Williams, Charles, *Witchcraft*, London, 1941; Forest Hills, 1944. (A history of witchcraft in Christendom.)

Winsor, Justin, "The Literature of Witchcraft in New England," *Proceedings of the American Antiquarian Society*, N.S. X (1895), 351–373.

D. Secondary Works

In addition to the items here listed, the student should consult Samuel E. Morison, *Harvard College in the Seventeenth Century*, chapters X, XI, and XIII, dealing with the teaching of mathematics, astronomy, physics, and medicine.

Bates, Ralph S., *Scientific Societies in the United States*, New York, 1945.

Beall, Otho T., Jr., "Cotton Mather's Early 'Curiosa Americana' and the Boston Philosophical Society of 1683," *William and Mary Quarterly*, XVIII (1961), 360–372. (Reports of a short-lived scientific society, the earliest in America.)

——, and Richard H. Shryock, *Cotton Mather: First Significant Figure in American Medicine*, Baltimore, 1954. (An important contribution to our understanding of colonial medical thought; contains generous selections from Cotton Mather's *Angel of Bethesda*.)

Bedinfeld, Malcolm S., "The Early New England Doctor: An Adaptation to a Provincial Environment," *Yale Journal of Biology and Medicine*, XV (1942–1943), 99–132, 271–288. (A Senior Thesis in History, Yale University, based on printed records and other literature.)

Bell, Whitfield J., "Medical Practice in Colonial America," *Bulletin of the History of Medicine*, XXXI (1957), 442–453.

Bernstein, Solon S., "Smallpox: Its Historical Significance in American Colonies," *Autograph Collectors' Journal*, V (1953), 14–23.

Blake, John R., *Public Health in the Town of Boston, 1630–1822*, Cambridge, 1959. (Illustrates and illuminates the attitudes of the time not only toward disease and death but also toward other basic social and political questions.)

Brasch, Frederick E., *John Winthrop (1714–1779), America's First Astronomer, and the Science of His Period*, San Francisco, 1916.

—— "The Newtonian Epoch in the American Colonies [1680–1783]," *Proceedings of the American Antiquarian Society*, XLIX (1939), 314–332.

—— "Newton's First Critical Disciple in the American Colonies—John Winthrop [Jr.]," in *Sir Isaac Newton*, 1727–1927, Baltimore, 1928, 301–338.

—— "The Royal Society of London and Its Influence upon Scientific Thought in the American Colonies," *Scientific Monthly*, XXXIII (1931), 336–355, 448–469.

Bronfenbrenner, Martha (Ornstein), *The Role of the Scientific Societies in the Seventeenth Century*, New York, 1913. (A key book for the study of the influence of science on general thought.)

Brown, Francis H., "The Practice of Medicine in New England Before the Year 1700," *Bostonian Society Publications*, VIII (1911), 93–120.

Browne, Charles A., "Scientific notes from the books and letters of John Winthrop, Jr.," *Isis*, XI (1928), 325–342.

Buck, Albert H., *The Growth of Medicine from the Earliest Times to about 1800*, New Haven, 1917.

Bush, Douglas, "Two Roads to Truth: Science and Religion in the Early Seventeenth Century," *Journal of English Literary History*, VIII (1941), 81–102.

Butterfield, Herbert, *The Origins of Modern Science 1300–1800*, London and New York, 1949.

Cohen, I. Bernard, *Some Early Tools of American Science: An Account of Early Scientific Instruments and Mineralogical and Biological Collections in Harvard College*, Cambridge, 1950.

Farmer, Laurence, "When Cotton Mather Fought the Smallpox," *American Heritage*, VIII (1957), 40–43, 109.

Fitz, Reginald H., "Zabdiel Boylston, Inoculator, and the Epidemic of Smallpox in Boston in 1721," *John Hopkins Hospital Bulletin*, XXII (1911), 315–327.

Forbes, Allyn B., "William Brattle and John Leverett, F.R.S.," *Publications of the Colonial Society of Massachusetts*, XXVIII (1935), 222–224.

Gordon, Maurice Bear, *Aesculapius Comes to the Colonies: The Story of the Early Days of Medicine in the Thirteen Original Colonies*, Ventnor, N. J., 1949. (Little original research, occasionally inaccurate.)

Green, Samuel A., *History of Medicine in Massachusetts*, Boston, 1881.

Guerra, F., "Harvey and the Circulation of Blood in America during the Colonial Period," *Bulletin of the History of Medicine*, XXXIII (1959), 212–229.

Hornberger, Theodore, "American Puritanism and the Rise of the Scientific Mind," unpublished dissertation, University of Michigan, 1934.

—— "Cotton Mather's Annotations on the First Chapter of Genesis," *University of Texas Publications*, 3826 (July 8, 1938), *Studies in English*, 112–122. (The annotations reveal Cotton Mather's reading and his interest in Newtonian science.)

—— "The Date, the Source, and the Significance of Cotton Mather's Interest in Science," *American Literature*, VI (1935), 413–420.

—— "The Effect of the New Science upon the Thought of Jonathan Edwards," *American Literature*, IX (1937), 196–207.

—— "Puritanism and Science: The Relationship Revealed in the Writings of John Cotton," *New England Quarterly*, X (1937), 503–515.

—— "Samuel Johnson of Yale and King's College. A Note on the Relation of Science and Religion in Provincial America," *New England Quarterly*, VIII (1935), 378–397.

—— "Science and the New World," *Catalogue of the Huntington Library* (1937), 3–18. (Refers especially to the Mathers and Winthrops.)

—— "The Science of Thomas Prince," *New England Quarterly*, IX (1936), 26–42.

—— *Scientific Thought in the American Colleges, 1638–1800*, Austin, 1945.

Jones, Richard F., *Ancients and Moderns: A Study of the Background of the Battle of the Books*, St. Louis, 1936; reprinted with some revisions in *The Seventeenth Century Studies in the History of English Thought and Literature from Bacon to Pope*, R. F. Jones and others, Stanford, 1951. (A discussion of the rise and progress of experimental philosophy during the seventeenth century in England. See also bibliography section V, C above.)

Jorgenson, Chester E., "The New Science in the Almanacs of Ames and Franklin," *New England Quarterly*, VIII (1935), 555–561.

Kincheloe, Isabel, "Nature and the New England Puritan," *Americana*, XXXI (1937), 569–588.

Kittredge, George L., "Some Lost Works of Cotton Mather," *Proceedings of the Massachusetts Historical Society*, XLV (1912), 418–479. (Important for the innoculation controversy.)

—— "Cotton Mather's Election into the Royal Society," *Publications of the Colonial Society of Massachusetts*, XIV (1913), 81–114, 281–292.

—— "Cotton Mather's Scientific Communications to the Royal Society," *Proceedings of the American Antiquarian Society*, N.S. XXVI (1916), 18–57.

Mason, S. F., "Science and Religion in 17th Century England," *Past and Present*, 3 (Feb. 1953), 28–44. (The contribution of Calvinism to the development of seventeenth century science.)

Matthews, Albert, "Notes on Early Autopsies and Anatomical Lectures," *Publications of the Colonial Society of Massachusetts*, XIX (1918), 273–290.

Mood, Fulmer, "John Winthrop, Jr., on Indian Corn," *New England Quarterly*, X (1937), 121–133.

Morison, Samuel E., "The Harvard School of Astronomy in the Seventeenth Century," *New England Quarterly*, VII (1934), 3–24.

Packard, Francis R., *The History of Medicine in the United States before 1800*, Philadelphia, 1901.

"Thomas Prince, Scientist and Historian," *Publications of the Colonial Society of Massachusetts*, XXVIII (1935), 100–104.

Russell, Gurdon W., *Early Medicine and Early Medical Men in Connecticut*, Hartford, 1892.

Shryock, Richard Harrison, *Medicine and Society in America, 1660–1860*, New York, 1960. (An analysis of concepts and movements in medical history.)

Stahlman, William D., "Astrology in Colonial America: An Extended Query," *William and Mary Quarterly*, XIII (1956), 551–563.

Stearns, Raymond P., "Colonial Fellows of the Royal Society of London, 1661–1788," *William and Mary Quarterly*, III (1946), 208–268.

Steiner, Walter R., "Governor John Winthrop, Jr., of Connecticut as a

Physician," *Johns Hopkins Hospital Bulletin*, XIV (1903), 294–302.

—— "The Reverend Gershom Bulkeley, of Connecticut, an Eminent Clerical Physician," *Johns Hopkins Hospital Bulletin*, XVII (1906), 48–53.

Stimson, Dorothy, "Puritanism and the New Philosophy in Seventeenth Century England," *Bulletin of the Institute of the History of Medicine*, III (1935), 321–334.

Streeter, John W., "John Winthrop, Junior, and the Fifth Satellite of Jupiter," *Isis*, XXXIX (1948), 159–163.

Thoms, Herbert, "The Beginnings of Obstetrics in America," *Yale Journal of Biology and Medicine*, IV (1932), 665–675.

Thorndike, Lynn, "Medieval Magic and Science in the Seventeenth Century," *Speculum*, XXVIII (1953), 692–704.

Viets, Henry R., *A Brief History of Medicine in Massachusetts*, Boston, 1930.

—— "Some Features of the History of Medicine in Massachusetts during the Colonial Period, 1620–1770," *Isis*, XXIII (1935), 389–405.

Westfall, Richard S., *Science and Religion in Seventeenth Century England*, New Haven, 1958.

White, Andrew D., *A History of the Warfare of Science with Theology in Christendom*, New York, 1896, 2 vols. (Interesting but not too trustworthy.)

Wilson, William J. and C. A. Browne, "Robert Child's Chemical Book List of 1641," *Journal of Chemical Education*, XX, 123–129.

Zirkle, Conway, "The Theory of Concentric Spheres: Edmund Halley, Cotton Mather, and John Cleves Symmes," *Isis*, XXXVII (1947), 155–157.

X. PURITAN LIBRARIES, BOOKS, AND READING

Omnivorous readers, the cultivated Puritans collected libraries whenever their means allowed. Students of colonial history are now undertaking to examine inventories of libraries and estates, and are culling diaries and other source material in order to present a picture of colonial books and reading.

[Adams, William,] "Acc^{t} of Books y^{t} William Adams put up to carry to College, Nov. 5, 1726," *Collections of the Massachusetts Historical Society*, fourth series, I (1852), 43, 44.

Bacon, Edwin M., and Lyman H. Weeks, *An Historical Digest of the Provincial Press [1689–1707]*, Boston, 1908.

Bates, Albert C., "Some Notes on Early Connecticut Printing," *Papers of the Bibliographical Society of America*, XXVII (1933), pt. I.

Baxter, Joseph, "Catalogue of Books in his library," Congregational Library, Boston (*ca.* 1745.)

Baxter, William T., "Daniel Henchman [1689–1761], A Colonial Bookseller," *Essex Institute Historical Collections*, LXX (1934), 1–30.

Belcher, Jonathan (1710–1776), Manuscript Commonplace Book in Harvard College Library. (Extracts from his reading during his college years.)

Bowman, George E., "Governor Thomas Prence's [*sic*] Will and Inventory, and the Records of His Death," *Mayflower Descendents*, III (1901), 203–216. (A list of books is itemized to a value of more than £13.)

Boynton, Henry W., *Annals of American Bookselling, 1638–1850*, London, 1932.

Brayton, Susan S., "The Library of an Eighteenth-Century Gentleman of Rhode Island," *New England Quarterly*, VIII (1935), 277–283.

Brigham, Clarence S., "Harvard College Library Duplicates, 1682," *Publications of the Colonial Society of Massachusetts*, XVIII (1917), 407–417.

—— *History and Bibliography of American Newspapers, 1690–1820*, 1947, 2 vols. First installment appeared in *Proceedings of the American Antiquarian Society*, XXIII (1913), 207–403.

—— "History of Book Auctions in America," *Bulletin of the New York Public Library*, XXXIX (1935), 55–90.

—— *Journals and Journeymen: A Contribution to the History of Early American Newspapers*, Philadelphia, 1950.

Cadbury, Henry J., "Bishop Berkeley's Gifts to Harvard Library," *Harvard*

Library Bulletin, VII (1953), 75–87; 196–207.

—— "Harvard College Library and the Libraries of the Mathers," *Proceedings of the American Antiquarian Society*, L (1940), 20–48.

—— "John Harvard's Library," *Publications of the Colonial Society of Massachusetts*, XXXIV (1937–1942), 353–377. (An identifying list, supplementing the list of Alfred C. Potter, listed below.)

Cannon, Carl L., *American Book Collectors and Collecting from Colonial Times to the Present*, New York, 1941. (See chapter on Thomas Prince.)

Clapp, Thomas, *Manuscript catalogue of books in the Yale Library*, Yale College Library. (A list of over 700 books given by Jeremiah Dummer in 1714; over 400 given by Elihu Yale in 1718.)

Cotton, Rowland, and Nathaniel Rogers, *A Catalogue of Curious and Valueable Books, Being the greatest part of the Libraries of the Reverend and Learned Mr. Rowland Cotton, . . . and Mr. Nathaniel Rogers . . . To be Sold by Auction*, Boston, 1725. (Six hundred and ninety-five titles; unique copy in the Boston Public Library.)

Curwin, George, *Catalogue of the Greatest Part of the Library of the Reverend Mr. George Curwen* [*sic*], *Late of Salem . . . to be sold by auction*, Boston, 1718. (Nearly 600 titles; unique copy in Harvard College Library.)

Dexter, Franklin B., "Early Private Libraries in New England," *Proceedings of the American Antiquarian Society*, N.S. XVIII (1907), 135–147.

—— "The First Public Library in New Haven," *Papers of the New Haven Colony Historical Society*, VI (1900), 301–313. (Library of Samuel Eaton, 1658.)

Dexter, Henry M., "Elder Brewster's Library," *Proceedings of the Massachusetts Historical Society*, XXV (1890), 37–85.

Duniway, Clyde A., *The Development of Freedom of the Press in Massachusetts*, New York, 1906.

Ernle, Rowland E., *The Light Reading of our Ancestors*, London, 1921. (Popular in treatment.)

Evans, Evan A., Jr., *Literary References in New England Diaries, 1700–1730*, unpublished thesis in Harvard College Library.

Ford, Worthington C., *The Boston Book Market, 1679–1700*, Boston, 1917.

—— *Broadsides, Ballads, &c. Printed in Massachusetts, 1639–1800*, Boston, 1922. (Check list, with short introduction.)

Gilman, D. C., "Bishop Berkeley's Gifts to Yale College," *New Haven Colony Historical Society Papers*, I (1865), 146–170.

Green, Samuel A., *John Foster, the Earliest American Engraver and the First Boston Printer*, Boston, 1909.

—— *Ten Fac-simile Reproductions Relating to Old Boston and Neighborhood*, Boston, 1901.

—— *Ten Fac-simile Reproductions Relating to New England*, Boston, 1902.

—— *Ten Fac-simile Reproductions Relating to Various Subjects*, Boston, 1903.

Greenberg, Herbert, "The Authenticity of the Library of John Winthrop the Younger," *American Literature*, VIII (1937), 449–452.

Hall, Howard J., "Two Book-Lists: 1668 and 1728," *Publications of the Colonial Society of Massachusetts*, XXIV (1923), 64–71.

Harris, J. Rendel, and S. K. Jones, *The Pilgrim Press*, Cambridge, Eng., 1922.

Harvard University, *Catalogus Librorum Bibliothecae Collegii Harvardiani*, Boston, 1723. (Two *Continuatio* published before 1730.)

Harvard University, Library of, "Books given to the Library by John Harvard, Peter Bulkley, Sir Kenelme Digby, and Governor Bellingham," *Bibliographical Contributions*, No. 27 (1888), 5–14.

Herrick, C. A., "The Early New-Englanders: What Did They Read?" *Library*, third series, IX (1918), 1–17.

Howard, Leon, "Early American Copies of Milton," *Huntington Library Bulletin*, No. 7, 1935, 169–179.

—— "The Influence of Milton on Colonial American Poetry," *Huntington Library Bulletin*, No. 9, 1936, 63–89.

"Hubbard's Narrative, 1677," *Colophon*, I (1936), 456–457.

Jantz, Harold S., "German Thought and Literature in New England, 1620–1820," *Journal of English and German Philology*, XLI (1942), 1–45. (Contains important material on early colonial libraries.)

—— "Unrecorded Verse Broadsides of

Seventeenth-Century New England," *Papers of the Bibliographical Society of America*, XXXIX (1945), 1–19. (Adds sixteen broadsides to the list of those already known.)

Johnson, Thomas H., "Jonathan Edwards' Background of Reading," *Publications of the Colonial Society of Massachusetts*, XXVIII (1935), 193–222.

Kimber, Sydney A., *Cambridge Press Title-pages, 1640–1665*, Takoma Park, Md., 1954. (A pictorial representation of the work done in the first printing office in British North America.)

Kittredge, George L., "A Harvard Salutatory Oration of 1662," *Publications of the Colonial Society of Massachusetts*, XXVIII (1935), 1–24. (Analysis of the commonplace book of Elnathan Chauncy, Harvard A.B. 1661; a record of taste in reading and poetry.)

Kobre, Sidney, *The Development of the Colonial Newspaper*, Pittsburgh, 1944.

Lee, Samuel, *The Library of . . . Mr. Samuel Lee . . . Exposed . . . to Sale*, Boston, 1693. (Unique copy in Boston Public Library. See also chapter VI, "The Earliest Book-Catalogue Printed in this Country, 1693," in Samuel A. Green, *Ten Fac-simile Reproductions Relating to Old Boston and Neighborhood*, Boston, 1901.)

Lehmann-Haupt, Helmut, and others, *The Book in America: A History of the Making, the Selling, and the Collecting of Books in the United States*, New York, 1939; revised edn. 1951. (A primer first published in Germany, 1937, this is primarily a book of facts. Laurence Wroth has contributed for the period 1638–1860.)

Littlefield, George E., *Early Boston Booksellers, 1642–1711*, Boston, 1900. (Superseded by Worthington C. Ford, *The Boston Book Market, q.v.*)

—— *The Early Massachusetts Press, 1638–1711*, Boston, 1907, 2 vols. (To be used with care; very inaccurate.)

McKay, George L., comp., "American Book Auction Catalogues, 1713–1934," *Bulletin of the New York Public Library*, XXXIX (1935), 141–166. (Part I lists catalogues to 1800.)

Matthews, Albert, "Knowledge of Milton in Early New England," *Nation* (New York), LXXXVII (1908), 624, 625, 650.

Mayflower Descendant, The: A Quarterly Magazine of Pilgrim Genealogy and History, Boston, 1899—1940. (Often lists inventories of private libraries, or brief diary comments on reading.)

Moody, Joshua, and Daniel Gookin, *A Catalogue of Rare and Valuable Books . . . of . . . Moodey, and . . . Gookin . . .*, Boston, 1718. (A list of 780 items put up for auction sale; unique copy in the library of the American Antiquarian Society, Worcester, Mass.)

Morgan, Edmund S., "The Colonial Scene, 1602–1800," *Proceedings of the American Antiquarian Society*, LX (1950), 53–160. (An annotated list of books, broadsides, prints and maps.)

Morison, Samuel E., "The Library of George Alcock, Medical Student, 1676," *Publications of the Colonial Society of Massachusetts*, XXVIII (1935), 350–357.

Morris, Edward P., "A Library of 1742," *Yale University Library Gazette*, IX (1935), 1–11. (Notes on a Yale Library Catalogue of 1742.)

Mott, Frank Luther, *American Journalism: A History of Newspapers in the United States Through 260 Years: 1690–1950*, revised ed., New York, 1950.

Murdock, Kenneth B., "The Puritans and the New Testament," *Publications of the Colonial Society of Massachusetts*, XXV (1924), 239–243. (A denial that the Puritans used the Old Testament rather than the New.)

Myres, J. N. L., "Oxford Libraries in the Seventeenth and Eighteenth Centuries," *The English Library before 1700: Studies in its History*, ed. Francis Wormald and C. E. Wright, London, Toronto, New York; 1958; 236–255.

Norton, Arthur O., "Harvard Textbooks and Reference Books of the Seventeenth Century," *Publications of the Colonial Society of Massachusetts*, XXVIII (1935), 361–438.

Oates, J. C. T., "The Libraries of Cambridge, 1570–1700," *The English Library Before 1700: Studies in its History*, London, Toronto, New York; 1958; 213–235.

Paltsits, Victor Hugo, "New Light on *Publick Occurences*: America's First Newspaper," *Proceedings of the Massachusetts Historical Society*, LIX (1949), 75–88.

(Cotton Mather's letter of October 17, 1690, here for the first time printed, calls the paper noble, useful, laudable.)

Pemberton, Ebenezer, *A Catalogue Of Curious and Valuable Books*, Boston, 1717. (A list of about a thousand items put up for auction sale, principally Pemberton's library; unique copy in the New York Public Library.)

Perry, Michael, "Inventory of the estate of Michael Perry, a Boston bookseller, taken A.D. 1700," *John Dunton's Letters*, Boston, 1867, Appendix B, 314–319.

Potter, Alfred C., "Catalogue of John Harvard's Library," *Publications of the Colonial Society of Massachusetts*, XXI (1920), 190–230. (See supplementary list of H. J. Cadbury, above.)

—— "The Harvard College Library, 1723–1735," *Publications of the Colonial Society of Massachusetts*, XXV (1924), 1–14.

Powell, William S., "Books in the Virginia Colony Before 1624," *William and Mary Quarterly*, 3rd series, V (1948), 177–184. (Interesting for inclusion of works by H. Smith, Perkins, and other Puritan favorites.)

Pratt, Ann Stokely, *Isaac Watts and His Gift of Books to Yale College*, New Haven, 1938.

Prince, Thomas, *Catalogue of The American Portion of the Library of the Rev. Thomas Prince*, ed. W. W. Whitmore, Boston, 1868.

Robbins, Caroline, "Library of Liberty—Assembled for Thomas Hollis of Lincoln's Inn," *Harvard Library Bulletin*, V (1951), 5–23, 181–196. (A valuable study of the significant contribution of books made by Hollis to Harvard College and eighteenth-century New England.)

Robinson, Charles F., and Robin Robinson, "Three Early Massachusetts Libraries," *Publications of the Colonial Society of Massachusetts*, XXVIII (1935), 107–175. (A list of 565 items from three seventeenth-century libraries.)

Roden, Robert F., *The Cambridge Press, 1638–1692*, New York, 1905.

Salisbury, Stephen, "Early Books and Libraries," *Proceedings of the American Antiquarian Society*, N.S. V (1887–1888), 183–215.

Seybolt, Robert F., "Student Libraries at Harvard, 1763–1764," *Publications of the Colonial Society of Massachusetts*, XXVIII (1935), 449–461.

Shera, Jesse H., "The Beginnings of Systematic Bibliography in America, 1642–1799," *Essays Honoring Lawrence C. Wroth*, Portland, Me., 1951.

Silver, Rollo G., "Government Printing in Massachusetts-Bay, 1700–1750," *Proceedings of the American Antiquarian Society*, LXVIII (1958), 135–162.

—— "Publishing in Boston, 1726–1757: The Accounts of Daniel Henchman," *Proceedings of the American Antiquarian Society*, LXVI (1956), 17–36.

Sloane, William, *Children's Books in England and America in the Seventeenth Century: A History and Checklist*, New York, 1955.

Thomas, Isaiah, *The History of Printing in America*, Worcester, Mass., 1810, 2 vols.

Thompson, Lawrence, "Notes on Some Collectors in Colonial Massachusetts," *Colophon*, N.S. II (1936), 82–100.

Tuttle, Julius H., "The Library of Dr. William Ames," *Publications of the Colonial Society of Massachusetts*, XIV (1913), 63–66.

—— "Early New England Libraries": Manuscript card catalogue in the library of the Massachusetts Historical Society, Boston. See "Early Libraries in New England," *Publications of the Colonial Society of Massachusetts*, XIII (1912), 288–292.

—— "The Libraries of the Mathers," *Proceedings of the American Antiquarian Society*, N.S. XX (1910), 269–356.

Vail, Robert W. G., "Seventeenth Century American Book Labels," *American Book Collector*, IV (1933), 164–176.

Whitehill, Walter Muir, "The King's Chapel Library, 1698–1948," *Athenaeum Items*, June, 1948, 1–2.

Wigglesworth, Michael, "Catalogue of Mr. Wigglesworth's Books Taken Oct. 22, 1705," in John W. Dean, *Memoir of Rev. Michael Wigglesworth*, 2nd ed., Albany, 1871, Appendix III (pp. 151–152); reprinted from *New England Historical and Genealogical Register*, XVII (1863), 129ff.

Winship, George Parker, *The Cambridge Press*. (See VII, B.)

—— *The Literature of the History of Printing in the United States*, London, 1923.

—— "Old Auction Catalogues," *American Collector*, IV (1927), 188–193.

Winterich, John T., *Early American Books and Printing*, Boston, 1933.

Winthrop, John, Jr., "Library of John Winthrop, Jr.," *Catalogue of the New York Society Library*, New York, 1850, 491–505.

Wright, Louis B., "Pious Reading in Colonial Virginia," *Journal of Southern History*, VI (1940), 383–392.

—— "The Purposeful Reading of Our Colonial Ancestors," *English Literary History*, IV (1937), 85–111. (Emphasizes the general culture of Puritans as demonstrated in their reading.)

Wright, Thomas G., *Literary Culture in Early New England, 1620–1730*, New Haven, 1920. (The best comprehensive survey of Puritan reading and book business; needs to be supplemented by subsequent work done on the subject.)

Wroth, Lawrence C., *An American Bookshelf, 1755*, Philadelphia, 1934. (An examination of the books that might be found in the library of a cultivated gentleman in the mid-eighteenth century.)

—— *The Colonial Printer*, New York, 1931; Portland, 1938. (The best book on the subject.)

—— "The First Press in Providence: A Study in Social Development," *Proceedings of the American Antiquarian Society*, LI (1941), 351–383. (A study of the printer in colonial America.)

—— *The Oath of a Free-Man*, with a Historical Study by Lawrence C. Wroth and a Note on the Stephen Daye Press by Melbert B. Cary, New York, 1939. (A reprinting of the first work done in confines of what is now the United States.)

XI. ARTS AND CRAFTS

The Puritans were little concerned with aesthetic problems. They produced no sculpture or statuary; painting was confined to portrait likenesses. For many decades after the founding of New England, artistic creations—household necessities, textiles, and decorations—were generally imported. The craftsmanship of the architects, cabinetmakers, and silversmiths became evident in larger centers as soon as money was plentiful enough to commission their services. The Puritans were by no means constitutionally incapable of displaying good taste, but because of their relative indifference to the arts they did not write critiques upon the subject. In recent years the *Magazine of Antiques* has shown an increasing interest in early American arts and crafts. For further items that might have been listed here, see Section IV, B-2.

American Church Silver of the Seventeenth and Eighteenth Centuries . . . Exhibited at the [Boston] Museum of Fine Arts, Introduction by George N. Curtis, Boston, 1911.

American Silver . . . Exhibited at the [Boston] Museum of Fine Arts, Introduction by Richard T. H. Halsey, Boston, 1906.

Ayars, Christine M., *Contributions to the Art of Music in America by the Music Industries of Boston, 1640–1936*, New York, 1936.

Bach, Richard F., "Early American Architecture and the Allied Arts: a Bibliography," *Architectural Record*, LIX (1926), 265–273, 328–334, 483–488, 525–532; LX (1926), 65–70; LXIII (1928), 577–580; LXIV (1928), 70–72, 150–152, 190–192.

Bagg, Ernest N., "The Psalms, Tune Books and Music of the Forefathers," *Proceedings of the Bostonian Society*, V (Jan., 1904), 38–57.

Baker, C. H. Collins, "Notes on Joseph Blackburn and Nathaniel Dance," *Huntington Library Quarterly*, IX (1945–1946), 33–47. (Early American portrait painters.)

Barker, Virgil, *American Painting: History and Interpretation*, New York, 1950.

Bayley, Frank W., *Five Colonial Artists of New England*, Boston, 1929. (Reproductions of portraits of many colonial leaders.)

—— *Little Known Early American Portrait Painters*, Boston, n.d.

Belknap, Henry W., *Artists and Craftsmen of Essex County, Massachusetts*, Salem, 1927.

Belknap, Waldron P., *American Colonial*

Painting; Materials for a History, Cambridge, 1955. (See especially "The Identity of Robert Feke," pp. 3–34, and "English Mezzotint as Prototype of American Colonial Portraiture," pp. 273–322.)

Bigelow, Francis H., *Historic Silver of the Colonies and Its Makers*, New York, 1917.

Bolton, Charles K., *The Founders; Portraits of Persons born abroad who came to the Colonies . . . [to] 1701*, Boston, 1919–1926, 3 vols.

Bolton, Ethel S., and Eva J. Coe, *American Samplers*, Boston, 1921.

Bridenbaugh, Carl, *The Colonial Craftsman*, New York, 1950. (Social and economic history.)

—— *Peter Harrison, First American Architect*, Chapel Hill, 1949.

Briggs, Martin S., *The Homes of the Pilgrim Fathers in England and America, 1620–1685*, London, 1932. (Illustrated in detail.)

Brown, Madelaine R., "Rhode Island Pewterers," *Collections of the Rhode Island Historical Society*, XXXI (1938), 1–8.

Burroughs, Alan, *Limners and Likenesses; Three Centuries of American Painting*, Cambridge, 1936.

Caffin, C. H., *The Story of American Painting; the Evolution of Painting in America from Colonial Times to the Present*, London, 1907.

Casey, Dorothy N., "Rhode Island Silversmiths," *Collections of the Rhode Island Historical Society*, XXXIII (1940), 49–64.

Chandler, Joseph E., *The Colonial House*, New York, 1916.

Christensen, Erwin O., *Early American Wood Carving*, Cleveland, 1952.

Clarke, Herman Frederick, "The Craft of Silversmith in Early New England," *New England Quarterly*, XII (1939), 68–79.

Coburn, Frederick W., "Artistic Puritans," *American Magazine of Art*, XXI (1930), 481–496. (A description of portraits of the Puritan era.)

Colonial Dames of America, National Society of the, *Old Houses in the South County of Rhode Island*, Providence, 1933.

Crouch, Joseph, *Puritanism and Art, An Inquiry into a Popular Fallacy*, London, 1910.

Dorsey, Stephen, *Early English Churches in America, 1607–1807*, New York, 1952.

Dow, George F., *The Arts and Crafts in New England, 1704–1775*, Topsfield, Mass., 1927.

Downs, Joseph, *American Furniture: Queen Anne and Chippendale Periods in the Henry Francis Du Pont Winterthur Museum*, New York, 1952.

—— "Three Early New England Rooms," *The New York Historical Society*, XXXV (1951), 141–155. (Late seventeenth and early eighteenth-century rooms of *The New York Historical Society*.)

Dresser, Louisa, *Likeness of America, 1680–1820; Catalogue*, Colorado Springs [1949].

Dunlap, William, *History of the Rise and Progress of the Arts of Design in the United States*, New York, 1834, 2 vols.; reprinted Boston, 1918, 3 vols.

Eberlein, Harold D., *The Architecture of Colonial America*, Boston, 1915; 1927.

——, and Abbot McClure, *The Practical Book of Early American Arts and Crafts*, Philadelphia, 1916.

Ensko, Stephen G. C., *American Silversmiths and Their Marks*, New York, 1927.

"Fabrics, Clothing and Tools Purchased in England, in 1639–1642, for Governor George Wyllys of Hartford, Connecticut," *Old Time New England*, XXVI (1936), 142–145.

Flexner, James Thomas, *American Painting: First Flowers of our Wilderness*, Boston, 1947. (A good general work in the subject, but marred by broad, unsubstantiated generalizations.)

Foote, Henry Wilder, "Benjamin Blyth of Salem: Eighteenth Century Artist," *Proceedings of the Massachusetts Historical Society*, LXXI (1953–1957), 1959, 64–107.

—— *John Smibert, Painter*, Cambridge, 1950.

—— "Mr. Smibert Shows His Pictures, March, 1730," *New England Quarterly*, VIII (1935), 14–28. ("John Smibert was the first professional portrait-painter to settle in Boston.")

Forbes, Hariette M., *Gravestones of Early New England and the Men Who Made Them, 1653–1800*, Boston, 1927.

French, Hollis, *A List of Early American Silversmiths and their Marks*, New York, 1917.

Garvan, Anthony, *Architecture and Town Planning in Colonial Connecticut*, New Haven,

1951. (A broad and scholarly view of the work involved in planning domains, and designing settlements, towns, dwelling houses and meeting-houses.)

Grace, George C., and David H. Wallace, *The New York Historical Society Dictionary of Artists in America*, New Haven, 1957. (A biographical dictionary of American artists.)

Griffin, Gillett, "John Foster's Woodcut of Richard Mather," *Printing and Graphic Arts*, (Lunenberg, Va.), VII (1959), 1–19. (Technical but also critical.)

Guyol, Philip N., "The Prentis Collection," *Historical New Hampshire*, XIV (Dec., 1958), 9–17. (Description of the furnishings of a suite of early New England rooms of the New Hampshire Historical Society. Excellent photographs.)

Haddon, Rawson, *A Tourist's Guide to Connecticut*, Waterbury, 1923.

Hamilton, Sinclair, "Portrait of a Puritan: John Foster's Woodcut of Richard Mather," *Princeton University Library Catalogue*, XVIII (1957), 43–48.

Hipkiss, Edwin J., "Boston's Earliest Silversmiths: The Philip Leffingwell Spalding Collection," *Bulletin of the Museum of Fine Arts*, XL (1942), 82–86.

—— *Eighteenth-Century American Arts: The M. & M. Karolik Collection of Paintings, Drawings, Engravings, Furniture, Silver, Needlework, and Incidental Objects . . . , 1720 to 1820*, Cambridge, 1941.

Isham, Norman M., *Early American Houses*, Boston, 1928.

——, and Albert F. Brown, *Early Connecticut Houses*, Providence, 1900.

——, and Albert F. Brown, *Early Rhode Island Houses*, Providence, 1895.

Jackson, Russell Leigh, "Essex Institute Museum Collections, Silver," *Essex Institute Historical Collections*, LXXXI (1945), 97–104.

Jones, Edward Alfred, *The Old Silver of American Churches*, Letchworth, Eng., 1913.

Kelly, John Frederick, *Early Connecticut Meetinghouses*, New York, 1948; 2 vols. (A scholarly study; invaluable for the history of architecture, state and religion, of early America.)

—— *The Early Domestic Architecture of Connecticut*, New Haven, 1924.

—— *Architectural Guide for Connecticut*, Hartford, 1936.

Kettell, Russell H., ed., *Early American Rooms, 1650–1858: A Consideration of the Changes in Style Between the Arrival of the Mayflower and the Civil War in the Regions Originally Settled by the English and the Dutch*, Portland, Me., 1936.

—— *The Pine Furniture of Early New England*, New York, 1949.

Kimball, Sidney F., *Domestic Architecture of the American Colonies and of the Early Republic*, New York, 1922; 1927. (Authoritative and standard.)

Knittle, Rhea M., *Early American Glass*, New York, 1927.

Langdon, William C., *Everyday Things in American Life, 1607–1776*, New York, 1937.

Larkin, Oliver W., *Art and Life in America*, New York, 1949. (The best one volume historical survey; contains useful illustrations and bibliographies.)

Lee, Cuthbert, *Early American Portrait Painters*, New Haven, 1929.

Lockwood, Luke V., *Colonial Furniture in America*, New York, 1921, 2 vols.

Lyon, Irving W., *The Colonial Furniture of New England*, Boston, 1891.

McCausland, Elizabeth, "A Selected Bibliography of American Painting and Sculpture from Colonial Times to the Present," *Magazine of Art*, XXXIX (1946), 329–349.

McClellan, Elizabeth, *Historic Dress in America, 1607–1800*, Philadelphia, 1904. New ed., New York, 1937, with title *History of American Costume, 1607–1870*.

Mendelowitz, Daniel M., *A History of American Art*, New York, 1960. (A popular general introduction.)

Mixer, Knowlton, *Old Houses of New England*, New York, 1927. (Pleasant, but unreliable in details.)

Monograph Series Recording the Architecture of the American Colonies and Early Republic, The, ed. Russell V. Whitehead. Vols. 15–18 (1929–1932), N. Y. Vols. 1–14 (1915–1928) called *White Pine Series of Architectural Monographs*. Vols. 19–26 (1933–1940) published in *Pencil Points*. (A valuable series which presents classified illustrations of the more beautiful and suggestive examples of early American architecture together with a critical description by modern architects.)

Morgan, John H., *Early American Painters*, New York, 1921.

Morrison, Hugh, *Early American Architecture, from the First Colonial Settlements to the National Period*, New York, 1952. (The best of its kind; a judicious compilation largely from secondary sources. Contains five chapters on seventeenth-century buildings.)

Northend, Mary H., *Historic Homes of New England*, Boston, 1914.

Nutting, Wallace, *Furniture of the Pilgrim Century, 1620–1720*, Boston, 1921.

Old Time New England, Boston, 1910-current. Published by the Society for the Preservation of New England Antiquities. (Repository for articles on New England antiquities and monuments; the student of Puritan culture should search its pages carefully.)

Phillips, John Marshall, "Gold and Silver in the Prentis Collection (New York)", *The New York Historical Society Quarterly*, XXXV (1951), 165–169.

—— "Portraits in the Prentis Collection, (New York)," *The New York Historical Society Quarterly*, XXXV (1951), 157–164. (Seventeenth-century portraits.)

Poor, Alfred E., *Colonial Architecture of Cape Cod, Nantucket and Martha's Vineyard*, New York, 1932.

Rawson, Marion N., *Candleday Art*, New York, 1938. (A broadly informal and sketchy survey of American fold art.)

—— *Handwrought Ancestors: The Story of Early American Shops and Those Who Worked Therein*, New York, 1936.

Robinson, A. G., *Old New England Doorways*, New York, 1920.

—— *Old New England Houses*, New York, 1920.

Scott, Kenneth, "Daniel Greenough, Colonial Silversmith of Portsmouth," *Historical New Hampshire*, XV (Nov., 1960), 26–31.

Seventeenth-Century Painting in New England. A Catalogue of an Exhibition held at the Worcester Art Museum in Collaboration with the American Antiquarian Society, July and August, 1934, ed. Louisa Dresser and Alan Burroughs, Worcester, 1935.

Shurtleff, Harold R., *The Log Cabin Myth: A Study of the Early Dwellings of the English Colonies in North America*, ed. with an Introduction by Samuel Eliot Morison, Cambridge, 1939.

Singleton, Esther, *The Furniture of Our Forefathers*, New York, 1901, 2 vols.

Starkey, Laurence G., "Benefactors of the Cambridge Press: A Reconsideration," *Studies in Bibliography*, III (1950), 267–269.

—— A Descriptive and Analytical Bibliography of the Cambridge, Massachusetts, Press from its Beginnings to the Publication of Eliot's Indian Bible in 1663, Lexington, Ky., 1955. (Ten micro-cards.)

—— "The Last Broadside on the Quakers from the Cambridge Press in Massachusetts," *English Studies in Honor of James Southall Wilson*, Charlottesville, 1951.

Stow, Charles M., *Seventeenth and Eighteenth Century American Silver*, New York, 1934.

Sweet, Frederick A., Hans Huth and others, eds., *From Colony to Nation: An Exhibition of American Painting, Silver, and Architecture from 1650 to the War of 1812*, Chicago Art Institute, 1949.

Vanderpoel, Emily N., *American Lace and Lace-Makers*, New Haven, 1924.

Waterman, Thomas T., *The Dwellings of Colonial America*, Chapel Hill, 1950.

Watkins, Lura Woodside, *Early New England Potters and Their Wares*, Cambridge, 1950. (A definitive study.)

Whitmore, William H., "The Early Painters and Engravers of New England," *Proceedings of the Massachusetts Historical Society*, IX (1867), 197–216.

Yale University Portrait Index, 1701–1951, New Haven, 1951.

XII. BIBLIOGRAPHY

Current publications on the Puritan period are listed in the issues of *Isis*, in the quarterly bibliographies in *American Literature*, and the annual bibliographies in *Publications of the Modern Language Association* and the *New England Quarterly*, in the bulletins of the Modern Humanities Research Association, and in the *Writings on American History*, 1902—. (Vols. for the years 1904–1905, 1941–1947, have not been published; latest vol., 1953, appeared in 1960.)

The following list contains the principal bibliographies of source material for the period. Several secondary works listed contain further bibliographical material.

Adams, James Truslow, ed., *Atlas of American History*, New York, 1943. (A companion volume to the *Dictionary of American History*, below.)

——, and others, eds., *Dictionary of American History*, 6 vols., New York, 1940.

Allison, William H., *Inventory of Unpublished Material for American Religious History in Protestant Church Archives and Other Repositories*, Washington, 1910.

American Literary Manuscripts: A Checklist of Holdings in Academic, Historical, and Public Libraries in the United States, Compiled and Published under the Auspices of the American Literature Group, Modern Language Association of America, Committee on Manuscripts, Austin, 1961.

Ayer, Mary F., *Check-List of Boston Newspapers, 1704–1780*, Boston, 1907. (Bibliographical notes by Albert Matthews.)

Baginsky, Paul, *German Works Relating to America, 1493–1800: A List Compiled from the Collections of the New York Public Library*, New York, 1942.

Basler, Roy D., and others, *A Guide to the Study of the United States of America*, Washington, 1960.

Beers, Henry P., *Bibliographies in American History: Guide to Materials for Research*, 2nd ed., New York, 1942.

Bibliotheca Americana: Catalogue of the John Carter Brown Library in Brown University, 3 vols., Providence, 1919–1931. (Lists by year of publication *Americana* published before 1675, and acquired by the Library before 1931.)

Billington, Roy Allen, "Guide to American Historical Manuscript Collections in Libraries of the United States," New York, 1952; reprinted from *Mississippi Valley Historical Review*, XXXVIII (1951–1952), 467–496.

Blanck, Jacob, *Bibliography of American Literature*, New Haven; Vol. I, 1955; Vol. II, 1957; Vol. III, 1959. (Full bibliographies of American authors whose work, primarily belles-lettres, was at one time read and considered significant. To date three volumes have been published.

Bowen, Richard Le Baron, *Massachusetts Records. A Handbook for Genealogists, Historians, and Other Researchers*, Rehoboth, Mass., 1957.

Bradford, Thomas L., and Stanley V. Henkels, *The Bibliographer's Manual of American History*, Philadelphia, 1907–1910, 5 vols. (For state and county histories.)

Brigham, Clarence S., "Bibliography of American Newspapers: Massachusetts," *Proceedings of the American Antiquarian Society*, XXV (1915), 193–293, 398–501. (The definitive check list; for other states consult Vols. XXIII–XXX, XXXII, XXXIV, XXXV, XXXVII.)

Cambridge History of American Literature, The. (See in section VII, B. Bibliographies covering Puritan New England, I, 363–442, 452–467.)

Channing, Edward, Albert B. Hart, and Frederick J. Turner, *Guide to the Study and Reading of American History*, Boston, revised edition, 1912.

Child, Sargent B., and others, *Check List of Historical Records Survey Publications; W. P. A. Technical Series, Research and Records. Bibliography No. 7*, Washington, 1943.

Cuthbert, Norma B., *American Manuscripts Collections in the Huntington Library for the History of the Seventeenth and Eighteenth Centuries*, San Marino, 1941.

Dissertation Abstracts; A Guide to Dissertations and Monographs Available in Microfilm, Ann Arbor, 1938—. (Beginning with vol. 16 the last number of each volume contains an "Index to American Doctoral Dissertations.)

Dorgan, Marion, *Guide to American Biography. Part I: 1607–1815*, Albuquerque, 1949. (A working bibliography more extensive than exhaustive.)

Early Catholic Americana 1729–1830, comp. Wilfred Parsons, New York, 1939.

—— *Additions and Corrections to*, comp. Forrest Bowe, New York, 1952.

Emerson, Everett H., "Notes on the Thomas Hooker Canon," *American Literature*, XXVII (1956), 554–555. (Some false ascriptions and some overlooked titles.)

Evans, Charles, *American Bibliography, 1639–1820*, Chicago, 1903–1934, 12 vols.; New York, 1942. (The most exhaustive; compiled by years, well indexed.) Vol. 13, *Index*, comp. by Roger Pattrell Bristol, Worcester, 1959.

—— "American Imprints before 1801 in the University of Pennsylvania Library and not in Evans," comp. Thomas R. Adams, *Library Chronicle of the University of Pennsylvania*, XXII (1956), 41–57.

Flagg, Charles A., *A Guide to Massachusetts Local History*, Salem, 1907.

—— "Reference List on Connecticut Local History," *New York State Library Bulletin*, No. 53, Albany, 1900.

Gohdes, Clarence, *Bibliographical Guide to the Study of the Literature of the United States of America*, Durham, 1959.

Haller, William, *The Rise of Puritanism*. (See Section III, B. Contains a useful bibliography of sermons and other works of English Puritan preachers.)

Hamer, Philip M., *A Guide to Archives and Manuscripts in the United States*, New Haven, 1961. (Compiled for the National Historical Publications Commission; it lists manuscript and archival holdings of 1300 depositories.)

Handbook of the Massachusetts Historical Society, 1791–1948, Foreword and Historical Sketch by Stewart Mitchell, Boston, 1949. (Contains a check-list of publications and another of the major manuscript collections in the Society's library.)

Harvard Guide to American History, ed. Oscar Handlin and others, Cambridge, 1954.

Hill, Robert W., "Resources on Colonial History in the New York Public Library," *New York History*, XL (1959), 387–413.

Holmes, Thomas J., *Cotton Mather: A Bibliography of His Works*, 3 vols., Cambridge, 1940. (A landmark in American bibliographical scholarship.)

—— *Increase Mather: A Bibliography of His Works*, Cleveland, 1931, 2 vols. (A superlative work; contains summaries and extracts from the volumes.)

—— *The Minor Mathers: A List of Their Works*, Cambridge, 1940.

Henry E. Huntington Library and Art Gallery, *American Imprints, 1648–1797, in the Huntington Library*, Cambridge, 1933.

Jefferey, William, and Zechariah Chaffee, Jr., "Early New England Court Records: A Bibliography of Published Materials," *Boston Public Library Quarterly*, VI (1954), 160–184.

Jensen, Merrill, *English Historical Documents*, Vol. IX. See Section I, A.

Johnson, Thomas H., ed., *Literary History of the United States*, Vol. 3, New York, 1948; 1953. (The most extensive bibliography of the subject. See also *Literary History of the United States. Bibliography Supplement*, comp. Richard M. Ludwig, New York, 1959, which adds materials published since 1948.)

—— *The Printed Works of Jonathan Edwards*, Princeton, 1940.

Lancour, A. Harold, *Passenger Lists of Ships Coming to North America 1607–1825; A Bibliography*, New York, 1937.

Larned, Josephus N., *The Literature of American History, A Bibliography*, Boston, 1902.

Leary, Lewis, *Articles on American Literature Appearing in Current Periodicals, 1920–1945*, Durham, 1947. (Edited from materials supplied by the Committee on Bibliography of the American Literature group of the Modern Language Association and the University of Pennsylvania Library. Bibliography of current articles in American literature appear quarterly in *American Literature*.)

List of Doctoral Dissertations in History Completed or in Progress at Colleges and Universities in the United States since 1955, Washington, 1958. (Published triennially by the American Historical Association.)

Lord, Clifford, and Elizabeth H. Lord, *Historical Atlas of the United States*, New

York, 1944. (Section II, "Colonial Period.")

Matteson, D. M., and others, *Index to Writings on American History, 1902–1940*, Washington, 1956.

Matthews, William, *British Diaries: An Annotated Bibliography of British Diaries Written Between 1442 and 1942*, Berkeley, 1950.

——, and Roy Harvey Pearce, *American Diaries: An Annotated Bibliography of American Diaries Written Prior to 1861*, Berkeley and Los Angeles, 1945. (List restricted to published diaries; arranged chronologically by date of first entries published.)

Mode, Peter G., *Source Book and Bibliographical Guide for American Church History*, Menasha, Wisconsin, 1921.

Morey, Verne D., "American Congregationalism: A Critical Bibliography 1900–1952," *Church History*, XXI (1952), 323–329.

Morris, Richard B., *Encyclopædia of American History*, New York, 1953.

Morse, Jarvis M., *American Beginnings*, Washington, 1952. (A critical commentary on writings on British America published before 1775.)

Otis, William B., *American Verse, 1625–1807*, New York, 1909. (Valuable bibliography.)

Pauldin, Charles Oscar, *Atlas of the Historical Geography of the United States*, ed. John K. Wright, Baltimore, 1932. (The standard work; a monumental achievement.)

Prager, Herta, and William W. Price, "A Bibliography on the History of the Courts of the Thirteen Original Colonies, Maine, Ohio, and Vermont," *American Journal of Legal History*, I (1957), 336–362; II (1958), 35–52, 148–154.

Quinn, Arthur H., ed., *The Literature of the American People*. See VII, B. (Has a useful bibliography of colonial literature with critical comments.)

Riley, Stephen T., "The Manuscript Collections of the Massachusetts Historical Society: A Brief Listing," *Massachusetts Historical Society Miscellany*, No. 5, December, 1958, 1–15.

Ring, Elizabeth. and others, *A Reference List of Manuscripts Relating to the History of Maine*. Part I, Orono, 1938; Part II, 1939 (with an introduction and Maine maps by Fannie Hardy Eckstrom); Part III, 1941.

Sabin, Joseph, *Bibliotheca Americana: A Dictionary of Books Relating to America, from its Discovery to the Present Time*, New York, 1867–1936. 29 vols. (Trustworthy and exhaustive; later volumes continued by Wilberforce Eames.)

Starr, Edward C., *A Baptist Bibliography; Being a Register of Printed Materials By and About Baptists, Including Works Written Against the Baptists*. Vol. I, Philadelphia, 1947; Vols. II, III, IV, Chester, 1952–1954; Vol. V, Rochester, 1955. (An author and title index; present volumes, A–Cz.)

Stillwell, Margaret B., *Incunabula and Americana, 1450–1800: A Key to Bibliographical Study*, New York, 1931. (Important check lists.)

Trumbull, James H., *List of Books Printed in Connecticut, 1709–1800*, Hartford, 1904.

Vail, R. W. G., *The Voice of the Old Frontier*, Philadelphia, 1949. (Valuable for its bibliography of works "written before 1800 by those living on the frontier . . . principally stories of Indian captivity, and promotion tracts by agents for the sale of frontier lands . . .".)

Waldman, Milton, *Americana; the Literature of American History*, New York, 1925.

Walker, Williston, *The Creeds and Platforms of Congregationalism*, New York, 1893. (The principal documents in New England ecclesiastical disputes, with full bibliographies for the background of each episode.)

Watkins, George T., *American Typographical Bibliography, being a list of brief titles of books and pamphlets relating to the history of Printing in America*, Indianapolis, 1898.

—— *Bibliography of Printing in the United States*, Boston, 1906.

Watt, Robert, *Bibliotheca Britannica*, Edinburgh, 1824, 4 vols. (Often extremely useful, particularly the subject index of the last two volumes.)

Wegelin, Oscar, *Early American Poetry*, second edition revised and enlarged, New York, 1930, 2 vols. (Vol. I, 1650–1799.)

Weimer, David R., ed., *Bibliography of*

American Culture, 1493–1875, Ann Arbor. University micro-films.

Whitley, W. T., *A Baptist Bibliography; Being a Register of the chief materials for Baptist history, whether in manuscript or in print, preserved in Great Britain, Ireland and the Colonies*, London, 1916. Vol. I, 1526–1776. (Chronologically arranged.)

Wing, Donald, *Short-title Catalogue of Books Printed in England, Scotland, Ireland, Wales, and British America and of English Books Printed in Other Countries, 1641–1700*, 3 vols., New York, 1945–1951.

Woodress, James; *Dissertations in American Literature, 1891–1955*, Durham, N.C., 1957. (Subsequent lists of dissertations completed or in progress appear annually in *American Literature*.)

INDEX TO BOTH VOLUMES

A CATALOG OF SELECTED

DOVER BOOKS

IN ALL FIELDS OF INTEREST

STICKLEY CRAFTSMAN FURNITURE CATALOGS, Gustav Stickley and L. & J. G. Stickley. Beautiful, functional furniture in two authentic catalogs from 1910. 594 illustrations, including 277 photos, show settles, rockers, armchairs, reclining chairs, bookcases, desks, tables. 183pp. 6½ x 9¼. 23838-5 Pa. $11.95

AMERICAN LOCOMOTIVES IN HISTORIC PHOTOGRAPHS: 1858 to 1949, Ron Ziel (ed.). A rare collection of 126 meticulously detailed official photographs, called "builder portraits," of American locomotives that majestically chronicle the rise of steam locomotive power in America. Introduction. Detailed captions. xi+ 129pp. 9 x 12. 27393-8 Pa. $13.95

AMERICA'S LIGHTHOUSES: An Illustrated History, Francis Ross Holland, Jr. Delightfully written, profusely illustrated fact-filled survey of over 200 American lighthouses since 1716. History, anecdotes, technological advances, more. 240pp. 8 x 10¾. 25576-X Pa. $12.95

TOWARDS A NEW ARCHITECTURE, Le Corbusier. Pioneering manifesto by founder of "International School." Technical and aesthetic theories, views of industry, economics, relation of form to function, "mass-production split" and much more. Profusely illustrated. 320pp. 6⅛ x 9¼. (Available in U.S. only.) 25023-7 Pa. $10.95

HOW THE OTHER HALF LIVES, Jacob Riis. Famous journalistic record, exposing poverty and degradation of New York slums around 1900, by major social reformer. 100 striking and influential photographs. 233pp. 10 x 7⅞. 22012-5 Pa. $11.95

FRUIT KEY AND TWIG KEY TO TREES AND SHRUBS, William M. Harlow. One of the handiest and most widely used identification aids. Fruit key covers 120 deciduous and evergreen species; twig key 160 deciduous species. Easily used. Over 300 photographs. 126pp. 5⅜ x 8½. 20511-8 Pa. $3.95

COMMON BIRD SONGS, Dr. Donald J. Borror. Songs of 60 most common U.S. birds: robins, sparrows, cardinals, bluejays, finches, more–arranged in order of increasing complexity. Up to 9 variations of songs of each species. Cassette and manual 99911-4 $8.95

ORCHIDS AS HOUSE PLANTS, Rebecca Tyson Northen. Grow cattleyas and many other kinds of orchids–in a window, in a case, or under artificial light. 63 illustrations. 148pp. 5⅜ x 8½. 23261-1 Pa. $7.95

MONSTER MAZES, Dave Phillips. Masterful mazes at four levels of difficulty. Avoid deadly perils and evil creatures to find magical treasures. Solutions for all 32 exciting illustrated puzzles. 48pp. 8¼ x 11. 26005-4 Pa. $2.95

MOZART'S DON GIOVANNI (DOVER OPERA LIBRETTO SERIES), Wolfgang Amadeus Mozart. Introduced and translated by Ellen H. Bleiler. Standard Italian libretto, with complete English translation. Convenient and thoroughly portable–an ideal companion for reading along with a recording or the performance itself. Introduction. List of characters. Plot summary. 121pp. 5¼ x 8½. 24944-1 Pa. $3.95

TECHNICAL MANUAL AND DICTIONARY OF CLASSICAL BALLET, Gail Grant. Defines, explains, comments on steps, movements, poses and concepts. 15-page pictorial section. Basic book for student, viewer. 127pp. 5⅜ x 8½. 21843-0 Pa. $4.95

FRANK LLOYD WRIGHT'S DANA HOUSE, Donald Hoffmann. Pictorial essay of residential masterpiece with over 160 interior and exterior photos, plans, elevations, sketches and studies. 128pp. 9¼ x 10¾. 29120-0 Pa. $14.95

THE MALE AND FEMALE FIGURE IN MOTION: 60 Classic Photographic Sequences, Eadweard Muybridge. 60 true-action photographs of men and women walking, running, climbing, bending, turning, etc., reproduced from rare 19th-century masterpiece. vi + 121pp. 9 x 12. 24745-7 Pa. $12.95

1001 QUESTIONS ANSWERED ABOUT THE SEASHORE, N. J. Berrill and Jacquelyn Berrill. Queries answered about dolphins, sea snails, sponges, starfish, fishes, shore birds, many others. Covers appearance, breeding, growth, feeding, much more. 305pp. 5¼ x 8¼. 23366-9 Pa. $9.95

ATTRACTING BIRDS TO YOUR YARD, William J. Weber. Easy-to-follow guide offers advice on how to attract the greatest diversity of birds: birdhouses, feeders, water and waterers, much more. 96pp. 5³⁄₁₆ x 8¼. 28927-3 Pa. $2.50

MEDICINAL AND OTHER USES OF NORTH AMERICAN PLANTS: A Historical Survey with Special Reference to the Eastern Indian Tribes, Charlotte Erichsen-Brown. Chronological historical citations document 500 years of usage of plants, trees, shrubs native to eastern Canada, northeastern U.S. Also complete identifying information. 343 illustrations. 544pp. 6½ x 9¼. 25951-X Pa. $12.95

STORYBOOK MAZES, Dave Phillips. 23 stories and mazes on two-page spreads: Wizard of Oz, Treasure Island, Robin Hood, etc. Solutions. 64pp. 8¼ x 11. 23628-5 Pa. $2.95

AMERICAN NEGRO SONGS: 230 Folk Songs and Spirituals, Religious and Secular, John W. Work. This authoritative study traces the African influences of songs sung and played by black Americans at work, in church, and as entertainment. The author discusses the lyric significance of such songs as "Swing Low, Sweet Chariot," "John Henry," and others and offers the words and music for 230 songs. Bibliography. Index of Song Titles. 272pp. 6½ x 9¼. 40271-1 Pa. $10.95

MOVIE-STAR PORTRAITS OF THE FORTIES, John Kobal (ed.). 163 glamor, studio photos of 106 stars of the 1940s: Rita Hayworth, Ava Gardner, Marlon Brando, Clark Gable, many more. 176pp. 8⅜ x 11¼. 23546-7 Pa. $14.95

BENCHLEY LOST AND FOUND, Robert Benchley. Finest humor from early 30s, about pet peeves, child psychologists, post office and others. Mostly unavailable elsewhere. 73 illustrations by Peter Arno and others. 183pp. 5⅜ x 8½. 22410-4 Pa. $6.95

YEKL and THE IMPORTED BRIDEGROOM AND OTHER STORIES OF YIDDISH NEW YORK, Abraham Cahan. Film Hester Street based on *Yekl* (1896). Novel, other stories among first about Jewish immigrants on N.Y.'s East Side. 240pp. 5⅜ x 8½. 22427-9 Pa. $7.95

SELECTED POEMS, Walt Whitman. Generous sampling from *Leaves of Grass*. Twenty-four poems include "I Hear America Singing," "Song of the Open Road," "I Sing the Body Electric," "When Lilacs Last in the Dooryard Bloom'd," "O Captain! My Captain!"–all reprinted from an authoritative edition. Lists of titles and first lines. 128pp. 5³⁄₁₆ x 8¼. 26878-0 Pa. $1.00

THE BEST TALES OF HOFFMANN, E. T. A. Hoffmann. 10 of Hoffmann's most important stories: "Nutcracker and the King of Mice," "The Golden Flowerpot," etc. 458pp. 5⅜ x 8½. 21793-0 Pa. $9.95

FROM FETISH TO GOD IN ANCIENT EGYPT, E. A. Wallis Budge. Rich detailed survey of Egyptian conception of "God" and gods, magic, cult of animals, Osiris, more. Also, superb English translations of hymns and legends. 240 illustrations. 545pp. 5⅜ x 8½. 25803-3 Pa. $13.95

FRENCH STORIES/CONTES FRANÇAIS: A Dual-Language Book, Wallace Fowlie. Ten stories by French masters, Voltaire to Camus: "Micromegas" by Voltaire; "The Atheist's Mass" by Balzac; "Minuet" by de Maupassant; "The Guest" by Camus, six more. Excellent English translations on facing pages. Also French-English vocabulary list, exercises, more. 352pp. 5⅜ x 8½. 26443-2 Pa. $9.95

CHICAGO AT THE TURN OF THE CENTURY IN PHOTOGRAPHS: 122 Historic Views from the Collections of the Chicago Historical Society, Larry A. Viskochil. Rare large-format prints offer detailed views of City Hall, State Street, the Loop, Hull House, Union Station, many other landmarks, circa 1904-1913. Introduction. Captions. Maps. 144pp. 9⅜ x 12¼. 24656-6 Pa. $12.95

OLD BROOKLYN IN EARLY PHOTOGRAPHS, 1865-1929, William Lee Younger. Luna Park, Gravesend race track, construction of Grand Army Plaza, moving of Hotel Brighton, etc. 157 previously unpublished photographs. 165pp. 8⅞ x 11¾. 23587-4 Pa. $13.95

THE MYTHS OF THE NORTH AMERICAN INDIANS, Lewis Spence. Rich anthology of the myths and legends of the Algonquins, Iroquois, Pawnees and Sioux, prefaced by an extensive historical and ethnological commentary. 36 illustrations. 480pp. 5⅜ x 8½. 25967-6 Pa. $10.95

AN ENCYCLOPEDIA OF BATTLES: Accounts of Over 1,560 Battles from 1479 B.C. to the Present, David Eggenberger. Essential details of every major battle in recorded history from the first battle of Megiddo in 1479 B.C. to Grenada in 1984. List of Battle Maps. New Appendix covering the years 1967-1984. Index. 99 illustrations. 544pp. 6½ x 9¼. 24913-1 Pa. $16.95

SAILING ALONE AROUND THE WORLD, Captain Joshua Slocum. First man to sail around the world, alone, in small boat. One of great feats of seamanship told in delightful manner. 67 illustrations. 294pp. 5⅜ x 8½. 20326-3 Pa. $6.95

ANARCHISM AND OTHER ESSAYS, Emma Goldman. Powerful, penetrating, prophetic essays on direct action, role of minorities, prison reform, puritan hypocrisy, violence, etc. 271pp. 5⅜ x 8½. 22484-8 Pa. $8.95

MYTHS OF THE HINDUS AND BUDDHISTS, Ananda K. Coomaraswamy and Sister Nivedita. Great stories of the epics; deeds of Krishna, Shiva, taken from puranas, Vedas, folk tales; etc. 32 illustrations. 400pp. 5⅜ x 8½. 21759-0 Pa. $12.95

THE TRAUMA OF BIRTH, Otto Rank. Rank's controversial thesis that anxiety neurosis is caused by profound psychological trauma which occurs at birth. 256pp. 5⅜ x 8½. 27974-X Pa. $7.95

A THEOLOGICO-POLITICAL TREATISE, Benedict Spinoza. Also contains unfinished Political Treatise. Great classic on religious liberty, theory of government on common consent. R. Elwes translation. Total of 421pp. 5⅜ x 8½. 20249-6 Pa. $10.95

PERSPECTIVE FOR ARTISTS, Rex Vicat Cole. Depth, perspective of sky and sea, shadows, much more, not usually covered. 391 diagrams, 81 reproductions of drawings and paintings. 279pp. 5⅜ x 8½. 22487-2 Pa. $9.95

DRAWING THE LIVING FIGURE, Joseph Sheppard. Innovative approach to artistic anatomy focuses on specifics of surface anatomy, rather than muscles and bones. Over 170 drawings of live models in front, back and side views, and in widely varying poses. Accompanying diagrams. 177 illustrations. Introduction. Index. 144pp. 8⅜ x11¼. 26723-7 Pa. $9.95

GOTHIC AND OLD ENGLISH ALPHABETS: 100 Complete Fonts, Dan X. Solo. Add power, elegance to posters, signs, other graphics with 100 stunning copyright-free alphabets: Blackstone, Dolbey, Germania, 97 more–including many lower-case, numerals, punctuation marks. 104pp. 8⅛ x 11. 24695-7 Pa. $9.95

HOW TO DO BEADWORK, Mary White. Fundamental book on craft from simple projects to five-bead chains and woven works. 106 illustrations. 142pp. 5⅜ x 8. 20697-1 Pa. $5.95

THE BOOK OF WOOD CARVING, Charles Marshall Sayers. Finest book for beginners discusses fundamentals and offers 34 designs. "Absolutely first rate . . . well thought out and well executed."–E. J. Tangerman. 118pp. 7¾ x 10⅝. 23654-4 Pa. $7.95

ILLUSTRATED CATALOG OF CIVIL WAR MILITARY GOODS: Union Army Weapons, Insignia, Uniform Accessories, and Other Equipment, Schuyler, Hartley, and Graham. Rare, profusely illustrated 1846 catalog includes Union Army uniform and dress regulations, arms and ammunition, coats, insignia, flags, swords, rifles, etc. 226 illustrations. 160pp. 9 x 12. 24939-5 Pa. $12.95

WOMEN'S FASHIONS OF THE EARLY 1900s: An Unabridged Republication of "New York Fashions, 1909," National Cloak & Suit Co. Rare catalog of mail-order fashions documents women's and children's clothing styles shortly after the turn of the century. Captions offer full descriptions, prices. Invaluable resource for fashion, costume historians. Approximately 725 illustrations. 128pp. 8⅜ x 11¼. 27276-1 Pa. $12.95

THE 1912 AND 1915 GUSTAV STICKLEY FURNITURE CATALOGS, Gustav Stickley. With over 200 detailed illustrations and descriptions, these two catalogs are essential reading and reference materials and identification guides for Stickley furniture. Captions cite materials, dimensions and prices. 112pp. 6½ x 9¼. 26676-1 Pa. $9.95

EARLY AMERICAN LOCOMOTIVES, John H. White, Jr. Finest locomotive engravings from early 19th century: historical (1804–74), main-line (after 1870), special, foreign, etc. 147 plates. 142pp. 11⅜ x 8¼. 22772-3 Pa. $12.95

THE TALL SHIPS OF TODAY IN PHOTOGRAPHS, Frank O. Braynard. Lavishly illustrated tribute to nearly 100 majestic contemporary sailing vessels: Amerigo Vespucci, Clearwater, Constitution, Eagle, Mayflower, Sea Cloud, Victory, many more. Authoritative captions provide statistics, background on each ship. 190 black-and-white photographs and illustrations. Introduction. 128pp. 8⅞ x 11¾. 27163-3 Pa. $14.95

LITTLE BOOK OF EARLY AMERICAN CRAFTS AND TRADES, Peter Stockham (ed.). 1807 children's book explains crafts and trades: baker, hatter, cooper, potter, and many others. 23 copperplate illustrations. 140pp. 4⅝ x 6.
23336-7 Pa. $4.95

VICTORIAN FASHIONS AND COSTUMES FROM HARPER'S BAZAR, 1867–1898, Stella Blum (ed.). Day costumes, evening wear, sports clothes, shoes, hats, other accessories in over 1,000 detailed engravings. 320pp. 9⅜ x 12¼.
22990-4 Pa. $16.95

GUSTAV STICKLEY, THE CRAFTSMAN, Mary Ann Smith. Superb study surveys broad scope of Stickley's achievement, especially in architecture. Design philosophy, rise and fall of the Craftsman empire, descriptions and floor plans for many Craftsman houses, more. 86 black-and-white halftones. 31 line illustrations. Introduction 208pp. 6½ x 9¼. 27210-9 Pa. $9.95

THE LONG ISLAND RAIL ROAD IN EARLY PHOTOGRAPHS, Ron Ziel. Over 220 rare photos, informative text document origin (1844) and development of rail service on Long Island. Vintage views of early trains, locomotives, stations, passengers, crews, much more. Captions. 8⅞ x 11¾. 26301-0 Pa. $14.95

VOYAGE OF THE LIBERDADE, Joshua Slocum. Great 19th-century mariner's thrilling, first-hand account of the wreck of his ship off South America, the 35-foot boat he built from the wreckage, and its remarkable voyage home. 128pp. 5⅜ x 8½.
40022-0 Pa. $5.95

TEN BOOKS ON ARCHITECTURE, Vitruvius. The most important book ever written on architecture. Early Roman aesthetics, technology, classical orders, site selection, all other aspects. Morgan translation. 331pp. 5⅜ x 8½. 20645-9 Pa. $9.95

THE HUMAN FIGURE IN MOTION, Eadweard Muybridge. More than 4,500 stopped-action photos, in action series, showing undraped men, women, children jumping, lying down, throwing, sitting, wrestling, carrying, etc. 390pp. 7⅞ x 10⅝.
20204-6 Clothbd. $29.95

TREES OF THE EASTERN AND CENTRAL UNITED STATES AND CANADA, William M. Harlow. Best one-volume guide to 140 trees. Full descriptions, woodlore, range, etc. Over 600 illustrations. Handy size. 288pp. 4½ x 6⅜.
20395-6 Pa. $6.95

SONGS OF WESTERN BIRDS, Dr. Donald J. Borror. Complete song and call repertoire of 60 western species, including flycatchers, juncoes, cactus wrens, many more–includes fully illustrated booklet. Cassette and manual 99913-0 $8.95

GROWING AND USING HERBS AND SPICES, Milo Miloradovich. Versatile handbook provides all the information needed for cultivation and use of all the herbs and spices available in North America. 4 illustrations. Index. Glossary. 236pp. 5⅜ x 8½.
25058-X Pa. $7.95

BIG BOOK OF MAZES AND LABYRINTHS, Walter Shepherd. 50 mazes and labyrinths in all–classical, solid, ripple, and more–in one great volume. Perfect inexpensive puzzler for clever youngsters. Full solutions. 112pp. 8⅛ x 11.
22951-3 Pa. $5.95

PIANO TUNING, J. Cree Fischer. Clearest, best book for beginner, amateur. Simple repairs, raising dropped notes, tuning by easy method of flattened fifths. No previous skills needed. 4 illustrations. 201pp. 5⅜ x 8½. 23267-0 Pa. $6.95

HINTS TO SINGERS, Lillian Nordica. Selecting the right teacher, developing confidence, overcoming stage fright, and many other important skills receive thoughtful discussion in this indispensible guide, written by a world-famous diva of four decades' experience. 96pp. 5⅜ x 8½. 40094-8 Pa. $4.95

THE COMPLETE NONSENSE OF EDWARD LEAR, Edward Lear. All nonsense limericks, zany alphabets, Owl and Pussycat, songs, nonsense botany, etc., illustrated by Lear. Total of 320pp. 5⅜ x 8½. (Available in U.S. only.) 20167-8 Pa. $7.95

VICTORIAN PARLOUR POETRY: An Annotated Anthology, Michael R. Turner. 117 gems by Longfellow, Tennyson, Browning, many lesser-known poets. "The Village Blacksmith," "Curfew Must Not Ring Tonight," "Only a Baby Small," dozens more, often difficult to find elsewhere. Index of poets, titles, first lines. xxiii + 325pp. 5⅝ x 8¼. 27044-0 Pa. $12.95

DUBLINERS, James Joyce. Fifteen stories offer vivid, tightly focused observations of the lives of Dublin's poorer classes. At least one, "The Dead," is considered a masterpiece. Reprinted complete and unabridged from standard edition. 160pp. 5³⁄₁₆ x 8¼. 26870-5 Pa. $1.50

GREAT WEIRD TALES: 14 Stories by Lovecraft, Blackwood, Machen and Others, S. T. Joshi (ed.). 14 spellbinding tales, including "The Sin Eater," by Fiona McLeod, "The Eye Above the Mantel," by Frank Belknap Long, as well as renowned works by R. H. Barlow, Lord Dunsany, Arthur Machen, W. C. Morrow and eight other masters of the genre. 256pp. 5⅜ x 8½. (Available in U.S. only.) 40436-6 Pa. $8.95

THE BOOK OF THE SACRED MAGIC OF ABRAMELIN THE MAGE, translated by S. MacGregor Mathers. Medieval manuscript of ceremonial magic. Basic document in Aleister Crowley, Golden Dawn groups. 268pp. 5⅜ x 8½. 23211-5 Pa. $9.95

NEW RUSSIAN-ENGLISH AND ENGLISH-RUSSIAN DICTIONARY, M. A. O'Brien. This is a remarkably handy Russian dictionary, containing a surprising amount of information, including over 70,000 entries. 366pp. 4½ x 6⅛. 20208-9 Pa. $10.95

HISTORIC HOMES OF THE AMERICAN PRESIDENTS, Second, Revised Edition, Irvin Haas. A traveler's guide to American Presidential homes, most open to the public, depicting and describing homes occupied by every American President from George Washington to George Bush. With visiting hours, admission charges, travel routes. 175 photographs. Index. 160pp. 8¼ x 11. 26751-2 Pa. $13.95

NEW YORK IN THE FORTIES, Andreas Feininger. 162 brilliant photographs by the well-known photographer, formerly with *Life* magazine. Commuters, shoppers, Times Square at night, much else from city at its peak. Captions by John von Hartz. 181pp. 9¼ x 10¾. 23585-8 Pa. $13.95

INDIAN SIGN LANGUAGE, William Tomkins. Over 525 signs developed by Sioux and other tribes. Written instructions and diagrams. Also 290 pictographs. 111pp. 6⅛ x 9¼. 22029-X Pa. $3.95

ANATOMY: A Complete Guide for Artists, Joseph Sheppard. A master of figure drawing shows artists how to render human anatomy convincingly. Over 460 illustrations. 224pp. 8⅜ x 11¼. 27279-6 Pa. $11.95

MEDIEVAL CALLIGRAPHY: Its History and Technique, Marc Drogin. Spirited history, comprehensive instruction manual covers 13 styles (ca. 4th century through 15th). Excellent photographs; directions for duplicating medieval techniques with modern tools. 224pp. 8⅜ x 11¼. 26142-5 Pa. $12.95

DRIED FLOWERS: How to Prepare Them, Sarah Whitlock and Martha Rankin. Complete instructions on how to use silica gel, meal and borax, perlite aggregate, sand and borax, glycerine and water to create attractive permanent flower arrangements. 12 illustrations. 32pp. 5⅜ x 8½. 21802-3 Pa. $1.00

EASY-TO-MAKE BIRD FEEDERS FOR WOODWORKERS, Scott D. Campbell. Detailed, simple-to-use guide for designing, constructing, caring for and using feeders. Text, illustrations for 12 classic and contemporary designs. 96pp. 5⅜ x 8½. 25847-5 Pa. $3.95

SCOTTISH WONDER TALES FROM MYTH AND LEGEND, Donald A. Mackenzie. 16 lively tales tell of giants rumbling down mountainsides, of a magic wand that turns stone pillars into warriors, of gods and goddesses, evil hags, powerful forces and more. 240pp. 5⅜ x 8½. 29677-6 Pa. $6.95

THE HISTORY OF UNDERCLOTHES, C. Willett Cunnington and Phyllis Cunnington. Fascinating, well-documented survey covering six centuries of English undergarments, enhanced with over 100 illustrations: 12th-century laced-up bodice, footed long drawers (1795), 19th-century bustles, 19th-century corsets for men, Victorian "bust improvers," much more. 272pp. 5⅝ x 8¼. 27124-2 Pa. $9.95

ARTS AND CRAFTS FURNITURE: The Complete Brooks Catalog of 1912, Brooks Manufacturing Co. Photos and detailed descriptions of more than 150 now very collectible furniture designs from the Arts and Crafts movement depict davenports, settees, buffets, desks, tables, chairs, bedsteads, dressers and more, all built of solid, quarter-sawed oak. Invaluable for students and enthusiasts of antiques, Americana and the decorative arts. 80pp. 6½ x 9¼. 27471-3 Pa. $8.95

WILBUR AND ORVILLE: A Biography of the Wright Brothers, Fred Howard. Definitive, crisply written study tells the full story of the brothers' lives and work. A vividly written biography, unparalleled in scope and color, that also captures the spirit of an extraordinary era. 560pp. 6⅛ x 9¼. 40297-5 Pa. $17.95

THE ARTS OF THE SAILOR: Knotting, Splicing and Ropework, Hervey Garrett Smith. Indispensable shipboard reference covers tools, basic knots and useful hitches; handsewing and canvas work, more. Over 100 illustrations. Delightful reading for sea lovers. 256pp. 5⅜ x 8½. 26440-8 Pa. $8.95

FRANK LLOYD WRIGHT'S FALLINGWATER: The House and Its History, Second, Revised Edition, Donald Hoffmann. A total revision–both in text and illustrations–of the standard document on Fallingwater, the boldest, most personal architectural statement of Wright's mature years, updated with valuable new material from the recently opened Frank Lloyd Wright Archives. "Fascinating"–*The New York Times*. 116 illustrations. 128pp. 9¼ x 10¾. 27430-6 Pa. $12.95

PHOTOGRAPHIC SKETCHBOOK OF THE CIVIL WAR, Alexander Gardner. 100 photos taken on field during the Civil War. Famous shots of Manassas Harper's Ferry, Lincoln, Richmond, slave pens, etc. 244pp. 10⅝ x 8¼. 22731-6 Pa. $10.95

FIVE ACRES AND INDEPENDENCE, Maurice G. Kains. Great back-to-the-land classic explains basics of self-sufficient farming. The one book to get. 95 illustrations. 397pp. 5⅜ x 8½. 20974-1 Pa. $7.95

SONGS OF EASTERN BIRDS, Dr. Donald J. Borror. Songs and calls of 60 species most common to eastern U.S.: warblers, woodpeckers, flycatchers, thrushes, larks, many more in high-quality recording. Cassette and manual 99912-2 $9.95

A MODERN HERBAL, Margaret Grieve. Much the fullest, most exact, most useful compilation of herbal material. Gigantic alphabetical encyclopedia, from aconite to zedoary, gives botanical information, medical properties, folklore, economic uses, much else. Indispensable to serious reader. 161 illustrations. 888pp. 6½ x 9¼. 2-vol. set. (Available in U.S. only.) Vol. I: 22798-7 Pa. $10.95
Vol. II: 22799-5 Pa. $10.95

HIDDEN TREASURE MAZE BOOK, Dave Phillips. Solve 34 challenging mazes accompanied by heroic tales of adventure. Evil dragons, people-eating plants, blood-thirsty giants, many more dangerous adversaries lurk at every twist and turn. 34 mazes, stories, solutions. 48pp. 8¼ x 11. 24566-7 Pa. $2.95

LETTERS OF W. A. MOZART, Wolfgang A. Mozart. Remarkable letters show bawdy wit, humor, imagination, musical insights, contemporary musical world; includes some letters from Leopold Mozart. 276pp. 5⅜ x 8½. 22859-2 Pa. $9.95

BASIC PRINCIPLES OF CLASSICAL BALLET, Agrippina Vaganova. Great Russian theoretician, teacher explains methods for teaching classical ballet. 118 illustrations. 175pp. 5⅜ x 8½. 22036-2 Pa. $6.95

THE JUMPING FROG, Mark Twain. Revenge edition. The original story of The Celebrated Jumping Frog of Calaveras County, a hapless French translation, and Twain's hilarious "retranslation" from the French. 12 illustrations. 66pp. 5⅜ x 8½. 22686-7 Pa. $4.95

BEST REMEMBERED POEMS, Martin Gardner (ed.). The 126 poems in this superb collection of 19th- and 20th-century British and American verse range from Shelley's "To a Skylark" to the impassioned "Renascence" of Edna St. Vincent Millay and to Edward Lear's whimsical "The Owl and the Pussycat." 224pp. 5⅜ x 8½. 27165-X Pa. $5.95

COMPLETE SONNETS, William Shakespeare. Over 150 exquisite poems deal with love, friendship, the tyranny of time, beauty's evanescence, death and other themes in language of remarkable power, precision and beauty. Glossary of archaic terms. 80pp. 5$\frac{3}{16}$ x 8¼. 26686-9 Pa. $1.00

THE BATTLES THAT CHANGED HISTORY, Fletcher Pratt. Eminent historian profiles 16 crucial conflicts, ancient to modern, that changed the course of civilization. 352pp. 5⅜ x 8½. 41129-X Pa. $9.95

THE WIT AND HUMOR OF OSCAR WILDE, Alvin Redman (ed.). More than 1,000 ripostes, paradoxes, wisecracks: Work is the curse of the drinking classes; I can resist everything except temptation; etc. 258pp. 5⅜ x 8½. 20602-5 Pa. $6.95

SHAKESPEARE LEXICON AND QUOTATION DICTIONARY, Alexander Schmidt. Full definitions, locations, shades of meaning in every word in plays and poems. More than 50,000 exact quotations. 1,485pp. 6½ x 9¼. 2-vol. set.
Vol. 1: 22726-X Pa. $17.95
Vol. 2: 22727-8 Pa. $17.95

SELECTED POEMS, Emily Dickinson. Over 100 best-known, best-loved poems by one of America's foremost poets, reprinted from authoritative early editions. No comparable edition at this price. Index of first lines. 64pp. 5$\frac{3}{16}$ x 8¼.
26466-1 Pa. $1.00

THE INSIDIOUS DR. FU-MANCHU, Sax Rohmer. The first of the popular mystery series introduces a pair of English detectives to their archnemesis, the diabolical Dr. Fu-Manchu. Flavorful atmosphere, fast-paced action, and colorful characters enliven this classic of the genre. 208pp. 5$\frac{3}{16}$ x 8¼. 29898-1 Pa. $2.00

THE MALLEUS MALEFICARUM OF KRAMER AND SPRENGER, translated by Montague Summers. Full text of most important witchhunter's "bible," used by both Catholics and Protestants. 278pp. 6⅝ x 10. 22802-9 Pa. $12.95

SPANISH STORIES/CUENTOS ESPAÑOLES: A Dual-Language Book, Angel Flores (ed.). Unique format offers 13 great stories in Spanish by Cervantes, Borges, others. Faithful English translations on facing pages. 352pp. 5⅜ x 8½.
25399-6 Pa. $9.95

GARDEN CITY, LONG ISLAND, IN EARLY PHOTOGRAPHS, 1869–1919, Mildred H. Smith. Handsome treasury of 118 vintage pictures, accompanied by carefully researched captions, document the Garden City Hotel fire (1899), the Vanderbilt Cup Race (1908), the first airmail flight departing from the Nassau Boulevard Aerodrome (1911), and much more. 96pp. 8⅞ x 11¾. 40669-5 Pa. $12.95

OLD QUEENS, N.Y., IN EARLY PHOTOGRAPHS, Vincent F. Seyfried and William Asadorian. Over 160 rare photographs of Maspeth, Jamaica, Jackson Heights, and other areas. Vintage views of DeWitt Clinton mansion, 1939 World's Fair and more. Captions. 192pp. 8⅞ x 11. 26358-4 Pa. $14.95

CAPTURED BY THE INDIANS: 15 Firsthand Accounts, 1750-1870, Frederick Drimmer. Astounding true historical accounts of grisly torture, bloody conflicts, relentless pursuits, miraculous escapes and more, by people who lived to tell the tale. 384pp. 5⅜ x 8½. 24901-8 Pa. $9.95

THE WORLD'S GREAT SPEECHES (Fourth Enlarged Edition), Lewis Copeland, Lawrence W. Lamm, and Stephen J. McKenna. Nearly 300 speeches provide public speakers with a wealth of updated quotes and inspiration–from Pericles' funeral oration and William Jennings Bryan's "Cross of Gold Speech" to Malcolm X's powerful words on the Black Revolution and Earl of Spenser's tribute to his sister, Diana, Princess of Wales. 944pp. 5⅜ x 8⅜. 40903-1 Pa. $15.95

THE BOOK OF THE SWORD, Sir Richard F. Burton. Great Victorian scholar/adventurer's eloquent, erudite history of the "queen of weapons"–from prehistory to early Roman Empire. Evolution and development of early swords, variations (sabre, broadsword, cutlass, scimitar, etc.), much more. 336pp. 6⅛ x 9¼.
25434-8 Pa. $9.95

THE INFLUENCE OF SEA POWER UPON HISTORY, 1660–1783, A. T. Mahan. Influential classic of naval history and tactics still used as text in war colleges. First paperback edition. 4 maps. 24 battle plans. 640pp. 5⅜ x 8½. 25509-3 Pa. $14.95

THE STORY OF THE TITANIC AS TOLD BY ITS SURVIVORS, Jack Winocour (ed.). What it was really like. Panic, despair, shocking inefficiency, and a little heroism. More thrilling than any fictional account. 26 illustrations. 320pp. 5⅜ x 8½. 20610-6 Pa. $8.95

FAIRY AND FOLK TALES OF THE IRISH PEASANTRY, William Butler Yeats (ed.). Treasury of 64 tales from the twilight world of Celtic myth and legend: "The Soul Cages," "The Kildare Pooka," "King O'Toole and his Goose," many more. Introduction and Notes by W. B. Yeats. 352pp. 5⅜ x 8½. 26941-8 Pa. $8.95

BUDDHIST MAHAYANA TEXTS, E. B. Cowell and others (eds.). Superb, accurate translations of basic documents in Mahayana Buddhism, highly important in history of religions. The Buddha-karita of Asvaghosha, Larger Sukhavativyuha, more. 448pp. 5⅜ x 8½. 25552-2 Pa. $12.95

ONE TWO THREE . . . INFINITY: Facts and Speculations of Science, George Gamow. Great physicist's fascinating, readable overview of contemporary science: number theory, relativity, fourth dimension, entropy, genes, atomic structure, much more. 128 illustrations. Index. 352pp. 5⅜ x 8½. 25664-2 Pa. $9.95

EXPERIMENTATION AND MEASUREMENT, W. J. Youden. Introductory manual explains laws of measurement in simple terms and offers tips for achieving accuracy and minimizing errors. Mathematics of measurement, use of instruments, experimenting with machines. 1994 edition. Foreword. Preface. Introduction. Epilogue. Selected Readings. Glossary. Index. Tables and figures. 128pp. 5³/₈ x 8¹/₂. 40451-X Pa. $6.95

DALÍ ON MODERN ART: The Cuckolds of Antiquated Modern Art, Salvador Dalí. Influential painter skewers modern art and its practitioners. Outrageous evaluations of Picasso, Cézanne, Turner, more. 15 renderings of paintings discussed. 44 calligraphic decorations by Dalí. 96pp. 5⅜ x 8½. (Available in U.S. only.) 29220-7 Pa. $5.95

ANTIQUE PLAYING CARDS: A Pictorial History, Henry René D'Allemagne. Over 900 elaborate, decorative images from rare playing cards (14th–20th centuries): Bacchus, death, dancing dogs, hunting scenes, royal coats of arms, players cheating, much more. 96pp. 9¼ x 12¼. 29265-7 Pa. $12.95

MAKING FURNITURE MASTERPIECES: 30 Projects with Measured Drawings, Franklin H. Gottshall. Step-by-step instructions, illustrations for constructing handsome, useful pieces, among them a Sheraton desk, Chippendale chair, Spanish desk, Queen Anne table and a William and Mary dressing mirror. 224pp. 8⅛ x 11¼. 29338-6 Pa. $16.95

THE FOSSIL BOOK: A Record of Prehistoric Life, Patricia V. Rich et al. Profusely illustrated definitive guide covers everything from single-celled organisms and dinosaurs to birds and mammals and the interplay between climate and man. Over 1,500 illustrations. 760pp. 7½ x 10⅛. 29371-8 Pa. $29.95

Prices subject to change without notice.

Available at your book dealer or write for free catalog to Dept. GI, Dover Publications, Inc., 31 East 2nd St., Mineola, N.Y. 11501. Dover publishes more than 500 books each year on science, elementary and advanced mathematics, biology, music, art, literary history, social sciences and other areas.